A NEW LITERARY HISTORY OF AMERICA

A NEW LITERARY HISTORY
OF AMERICA

EDITED BY

GREIL MARCUS AND WERNER SOLLORS

THE BELKNAP PRESS OF
HARVARD UNIVERSITY PRESS

Cambridge, Massachusetts
London, England 2009

Library of Congress Cataloging-in-Publication Data

A new literary history of America / edited by Greil Marcus and Werner Sollors.
    p.   cm. — (Harvard University Press reference library)
  Includes bibliographical references and index.
  ISBN 978-0-674-03594-2 (alk. paper)
  1. American literature — History and criticism.
2. United States — Civilization.
I. Marcus, Greil.   II. Sollors, Werner.
  PS92.N39   2009
  810.9 — dc22   2009014255

CONTENTS

INTRODUCTION

A literary history of America? Leafing through these pages, a reader will find entries on Anne Bradstreet, Phillis Wheatley, Nathaniel Hawthorne, Herman Melville, Emily Dickinson, Edith Wharton, W. E. B. Du Bois, Gertrude Stein, Ernest Hemingway, Eugene O'Neill, Jean Toomer, William Faulkner, Saul Bellow, Robert Lowell, Flannery O'Connor, Philip Roth, and Toni Morrison, but also on Stephen Foster, the invention of the telephone, the Winchester rifle, *Steamboat Willie,* Alcoholics Anonymous, *Porgy and Bess,* the first issue of *Life,* the atomic bomb, Jackson Pollock's drip paintings, Chuck Berry's "Roll Over Beethoven," Alfred Hitchcock's *Psycho,* and Ronald Reagan's 1964 campaign speech for Barry Goldwater.

> "All of you know the Doom Story, handed down . . . How just after this world began, the tall forefathers, white as snow, knew a magic to build all kinds of great things. And how the shadow people came from another place. So black that nobody ever saw their faces. Then the fearsome fighting when the shadows tried to keep the sun from rising and make it always night.
>
> "You know the story as well as I do—how all the forefather things were ruined even though the shadows died. Then the long sickness and starving time when just a few of the forefather children lived in the woods. That's the old story."

So says a woman in Robie Macauley's novel *A Secret History of Time to Come,* published in 1979. The woman is offering an after-the-flood myth of origins, and like most such myths, this one has its core of truth: what she is describing, perhaps two hundred years after the fact, is a full-scale race war that broke out in the United States near the end of the twentieth century. Before all black people were exterminated, the struggle paralyzed the country and disrupted the international balance of power, leading the Soviet Union to launch an attack on China—this being, in Macauley's telling, history, not myth, entries from the journal of a black revolutionary that Macauley scatters through the first pages of his book. "The white ones left went to sleep," says another handed-down-tale teller, "and then, waking up the next morning, had forgotten all they had ever known."

Macauley was an editor at the *Kenyon Review, Playboy,* and Houghton Mifflin; he died in 1995. This was his only novel. In his secret history, America is again a wilderness: there are scattered settlements, recalling the backward frontier clearings of the eighteenth and nineteenth centuries. In some places, people can read and write; in others they have regressed almost beyond speech. Artifacts—ruined buildings, roads, random books treated as the iconic library of the forgotten country (the treasured shelf of one settlement: *Home Radio Repair, Lawrence Welk:*

*The Man and His Music, Ben-Hur, Practical Accounting, Learn to Invest Wisely, Short-
hand Made Easy: The Gregg System, Caring for Your Parakeet, The Songs of Stephen
Foster)* — survive, but the connections between them are all gone.

"We used to sit around and the old folks would tell us the story of how we
came here" — like the story of the Lost White Boy, encountered in the forest by a
band of freed slaves journeying north in 1867 to found a town, and how one leader,
who only saw the light in others' eyes, wanted the boy guided back to his people,
while another, who only saw the dark, wanted the group to point the boy in the
right direction, pick up stakes, and run. As Colson Whitehead, born in 1969, tells
the tale in *Apex Hides the Hurt,* his third novel, published in 2006, the first course
was followed: "The Niggers found me," the boy says when he's safe at home. His
guide flees, the rest of the company as soon as they see him coming, and, as the
story has been passed down the generations, always in the voice of a woman who
was there, "When we looked back, all the horizon was lit up as if by a giant bon-
fire. We knew they had set fire to what remained at our camp, and had we tarried,
we would have been ash." "There was always that kindling problem of being black
in America," Whitehead's unnamed hero, a young nomenclature consultant,
brought in to rename the town, says, " — namely, how to avoid becoming it."

Abraham Goode, a patriarch who was one of the leaders of the original fourteen black families, and William Field, who had lost his own family in slavery,
were the Light and the Dark: "My favorite dynamic duo founding fathers," says
the name man. "He recognized them as a common business pair: a marketing, vision guy teamed up with a bottom-line, numbers guy." In a diary kept by Goode's
daughter, the consultant finds, Goode was "the optimist-prophet type, quick on
the draw with a pick-me-up from the Bible and a reminder of their rights as American citizens"; Field "turned out to be the downer-realist figure, handy with a 'this
stretch of the river is too treacherous to cross' and 'it is best we not tarry here
past sundown.' His perspective may have been overcast, but from the diary, it
seemed that Field had a knack for being right. The Lost White Boy Incident was
a good example."

The town they made was called Freedom — Goode's choice (That'll bring 'em
in!), winning out over Field's Struggle (Hey, Bill, why not go all the way and call it
Suffering?) — until the white barbed-wire manufacturer Sterling Winthrop showed
up, and, with Goode's vote against Field's (Jobs! New schools! And I won't drive
you off your land!), had the settlement renamed for himself, not to mention another of America's founding fathers. Over time, the city divided itself by race; the
consultant finds himself "in the Winthrop Suite of the Hotel Winthrop on Winthrop Street in Winthrop Square in the Town of Winthrop in Winthrop County,"
and the fact that the town was found, made up, made by black people is a whisper
in the night.

But the century has turned: Lucky Aberdeen, a software millionaire back in
his hometown, wants to remake the place in his own image as New Prospera. The
mayor, Regina Goode, descendant of Abraham, wants to go back to Freedom. Al-
bie Winthrop, the last of his line, is holding on to Winthrop as if it's the only
proof of his existence. So the pro from New York arrives to settle the matter:

"His contract called for his clients to keep the name he gave them for one year. Who knew? They might even come to like it. Recognize it as their own. Grow as comfortable with it as if it were their very skin."

For him, the act of naming is the act of founding, of making, even of discovery. Names are where his mind goes; anything he sees or hears takes him in an instant to a new brand, a different spin, a whole world changed by an adjective. "He'd always had a soft spot for Amerigo Vespucci, who got lost while looking for the Indies and hit nomenclature's Big Kahuna instead . . . He couldn't argue with America. It was one of those balloon names. It kept stretching as it filled up, getting bigger and bigger and thinner and thinner. What kind of gas it was, stretching the thing to its limits, who could say. Whatever we dreamed. And of course one day it would pop. But for now, it served its purpose. For now, it was holding together."

There, then, are two literary histories of America: made-up histories, as America was made up, as its historical story has always stood, from its first steps, as a temptation to the imagination. As America is made up out of nothing, it can vanish in an instant. "The story of Rip Van Winkle has never been finished," Constance Rourke wrote in 1931, but Robie Macauley's America is Rip Van Winkle in reverse: when they woke up, they had forgotten that the country had ever been. As America is a story of discovery and founding, it can be rediscovered and refounded at any time: "As he fell asleep," Whitehead writes of his consultant after he makes his decision, "he heard the conversations they will have. Ones that will get to the heart of this mess. The sick swollen heart of this land. They will say: I was born in Struggle. I live in Struggle and come from Struggle." And yet, as both fables make as plain as the line that divides day from night—that is, as the one fades into the other—America was made up out of crime, sin, and, as the country found the words to name its mission, violation, a rebuke to its own professed ideals. As America was made, it can be unmade; with slavery, it was unmade as it was made. Macauley's and Whitehead's literary histories share two questions: Does America even exist? Should it? All the names that appear above, fictional and real, Dickinson and Steamboat Willie, Porgy and Bess and Philip Roth, the Light and the Dark, push this drama forward.

In 1989 Harvard published *A New History of French Literature,* edited by Denis Hollier, and in 2004 *A New History of German Literature,* edited by David Wellbery; this book represents an entirely different sort of challenge. The earlier projects began in the eighth century and moved forward to trace the organic literatures of organic societies that long preceded the emergence of the modern French and German nations. *A New Literary History of America* begins early in the sixteenth century; the nineteenth and twentieth centuries dominate the story it tells, and this is the story of a made-up nation that in many ways preceded its society. Its literature was not inherited but invented, as if it were a tool or a machine, and discovered, as if it were a gold strike or the next wonder of the Louisiana Purchase. No tradition has ever ruled; no form has ever been fixed; American history, literary, social, political, religious, cultural, and technological, has been a matter of what one could make of it, and of how one got across what he or she meant to say to his or her fellow citizens, as they no less than the speaker struggled to define themselves as individuals, and as part of a whole.

This book is a reexamination of the American experience as seen through a literary glass, where what is at issue is speech, in many forms. Throughout, the search has been for points in time and imagination where something changed: when a new idea or a new form came into being, when new questions were raised, when what before seemed impossible came to seem necessary or inevitable. The goal of the book is not to smash a canon or create a new one, but to set many forms of American speech in motion, so that different forms, and people speaking at different times in sometimes radically different ways, can be heard speaking to each other. Thus this broadly cultural history—a history of America in which literary means not only what is written but also what is voiced, what is expressed, what is invented, in whatever form. The focus is on the whole range of all those things that have been created in America, or for it, or because of it: poems, novels, plays, and essays, but also maps, histories, and travel diaries, sermons and religious tracts, public speeches and private letters, political polemics, addresses, and debates, Supreme Court decisions, literary histories and criticism, folk songs, magazines, dramatic performances, the blues, philosophy, paintings and monuments, jazz, war memorials, museums, book clubs, photographs, comic strips and comic books, country music, films, radio, rock and roll, cartoons, musicals, and hip-hop: "Made in America."

"Made in America"—America, made. In many ways, the story that comes together in the pieces of this book is that of people taking up the two elemental American fables—the fable of discovery and the fable of founding—and making their own versions: their own versions of the fables, which is to say their own versions of America itself. Who knows if it is John F. Kennedy delivering his Inaugural Address or Jay Gatsby throwing one more party who is more truly invoking John Winthrop's "A Model of Christian Charity" from three centuries before? Is it Frederick Douglass or Hank Williams who has the most to tell us, not to mention Jefferson's ghost, about the real meaning of the Declaration of Independence? Doesn't Emily Dickinson, within her own Amherst walls, invent as complete a nation—loose in the wilderness in flight from all forms of restraint, be they those of God or man—as Ahab on the quarterdeck or Lincoln at the East Face of the Capitol?

Deep cultural obsessions and passing fads rooted in deep cultural obsessions— or resulting in them—creations that have traveled around the world and those that have remained local—only to be sought to their roots by people from all over the world—are taken up in more than two hundred essays commissioned and newly written for this book. The contributors were asked for their own arguments, their own points of view, their own embraces and dissents: to surprise not only their editors, or their readers, but themselves. The essays map their own territory and stake out their own ground, generating unexpected threads of information and startling claims that move the story on—forward, and doubling back, the twentieth century longing for the ideals of the seventeenth, the past plotting its revenge on the corruptions of the future.

From the first appearance of the word "America" on a map to Jimi Hendrix's rewrite of the national anthem, from Anne Bradstreet to Maya Lin, from Samuel Sewall to Saul Bellow, from Father Marquette to Jelly Roll Morton, from Sequoyah to Susan B. Anthony, from Margaret Fuller to Charlie Parker, from "Yankee Doodle" to Yusef Komunyakaa, *A New Literary History of America* takes the reader through the matrix of American culture. Asking if Linda Lovelace belongs in this book alongside Louisa May Alcott is taking a chance; sitting around the table, the editors rolled the dice, and, months later, when the writer asked to make good on the bet delivered her work, the dice came up sevens.

In the pages of this book readers may encounter such means of transportation as the ships *Arbella* and *Phillis* as well as the train that took Carrie Meeber from Wisconsin to Chicago, contemplate images from Virginia watercolors and Audubon's birds to *Little Nemo in Slumberland* and conceptual art, or find themselves in places as different from each other as the Cherokee Nation and Corinthian Hall, Crèvecoeur's farm and the Nuyorican Poets Café, John Muir's Alaska and Norman Bates's motel. Some technological inventions had deep cultural roots and others had long-lasting cultural consequences, and this book moves from industrial beauty to skyscrapers to cybernetics.

There is a certain balance between old and new, and the reader will find Washington Irving as well as Charlie Chaplin, Henry Wadsworth Longfellow as well as Walt Whitman, Uncle Tom as well as Ursa Corregidora, Nate Shaw as well as Malcolm X, Henry Adams as well as Queen Lili'uokalani, Mark Twain as well as Chief Simon Pokagon, Carl Sandburg as well as Wallace Stevens, John Steinbeck as well as Zora Neale Hurston. The most accomplished writers share these pages with popular authors they hardly would have admired. Between the covers of this book, Henry James finds himself in bed with Edgar Rice Burroughs; Faulkner's *Absalom, Absalom!* must share not only the book's pages but its own entry with Margaret Mitchell's *Gone with the Wind*. Read in pairs, various essays bridge what were once considered unbridgeable cultural gulfs (T. S. Eliot and Mickey Mouse) and present contrary political and aesthetic options in peaceful coexistence (William F. Buckley and Seymour Hersh, or Harry S. Truman and Vladimir Nabokov); single entries may combine a historical moment with a specific writer (Jack London and the San Francisco earthquake), a book and a visual artist (*The Grapes of Wrath* as illustrated by Thomas Hart Benton), or a car manufacturer and a muralist (Henry Ford and Diego Rivera).

Some writers for this book were inspired by D. H. Lawrence, William Carlos Williams, Constance Rourke, Edmund Wilson, Perry Miller, F. O. Matthiessen, John Kouwenhoven, C. L. R. James, and Leslie Fiedler (and some of these pioneering and persistent examiners of American culture are also subjects of entries), or by the Minnesota Writers Pamphlets, and it is hoped that the reader will find *A New Literary History of America* entertaining as well as informative. There are numerous novelists, poets, playwrights, and screenwriters among the contributors, including Elizabeth Alexander (on Jean Toomer), Clark Blaise (on Hawthorne and Melville), David Bradley (on Malcolm X), Sarah Shun-lien Bynum (on Edmund White), Norma Cantú (on the siege of the Alamo), Robert Clark (on Edgar Allan Poe), Joshua Clover (on Bob Dylan), Andrei Codrescu (on New Orleans), Steve Erickson (on Stephen Foster), Mark Ford (on Frank O'Hara), Mary Gaitskill (on Norman Mailer), Gish Jen (on *The Catcher in the Rye*), Jonathan Lethem (on Thomas Edison), Douglas McGrath (on Preston Sturges), Maureen McLane (on Adrienne Rich), Walter Mosley (on detective fiction), Bharati Mukherjee (on *The Scarlet Letter*), Paul Muldoon (on Carl Sandburg), Richard Powers (on the Shaw Memorial), Ishmael Reed (on *Huckleberry Finn*), Peter Sacks (on Robert Lowell), Stephen Schiff (on *Lolita*), Susan Stewart (on Emily Dickinson), Michael Tolkin (on Alcoholics Anonymous), Lan Tran (on *The Great Gatsby*), John Wideman (on Charles Chesnutt), Rob Wilson (on Queen Liliʻuokalani), Christian Wiman (on Robert Frost), and Elizabeth Winthrop (on John Winthrop). The participation of artists—including Kara Walker, on the election of Barack Obama—sets a tone that distinguishes this book from many others devoted to American culture. Numerous essays were contributed by academics and unaffiliated writers in the United States as well as other countries, from a great variety of fields, typically from the vantage point not of a specialist but of an enthusiast, a skeptic, a digger, a reader, a listener, a viewer: from the vantage point of a cultural citizen, where, as writers accepted their assignments, the work of African Americans is the heritage of Jewish Americans, and speaking for Edith Wharton may be someone who would never have spoken in her pages. In all cases the wish was to arouse the reader's curiosity, to open questions, not to close cases: to examine the first post-Columbian Americans as if for the first time, to take on more proximate ancestors as if they were still present and able to answer back.

The essays are arranged in a chronological order, for it is history that has given shape to these cultural creations, and the chronology also provides a first orientation to the reader, anchoring the many examples of creativity in time over the span of five centuries—and there are leaps across time and territory where it may not be obvious just where a particular anchor has been thrown. If the great majority of the entries date from 1865 and after, it is not only because, as a matter of numbers, the American population has increased so dramatically from that time; beginning with the second wave of Irish immigration in the mid-nineteenth century, the story of the United States becomes a story of previously disenfranchised, despised, degraded, excluded, enslaved, brutalized, and even unspeakable Americans claiming their place as full citizens, demanding not only the right to speak but the right to be heard, remaking the country as surely as any before them, and, in novels, poems, paintings, speeches, and acts, judging it as it had never been judged before. And it was only in the nineteenth and twentieth centuries that the world took notice of American literature, voices, expression.

A New Literary History of America can be read in many other ways than in its chronological order: the reader might select entries from the table of contents or from the headlines that appear in front of each essay, or read all those entries together first that the index tells us mention, say, Lincoln or Whitman. Even though there is no party line in this book, and different, at times truly contradictory perspectives emerge, we hope that reading more and more essays will generate a new and fresh sense of America. Together these essays illuminate the religious and heretical impulses in the culture, its gothic and paranoid scenarios, its democratic promise, its slave narrative and persistent, though ever-changing issue of race, its Western and captivity narrative, its children's literature, the power of its sentimentalism, its love for the success story and its faith in self-improvement, its hardboiled speech, its immigrant autobiography, its science fiction, its investigative reporting, and its tension between bursts of freewheeling creativity and repression, between experimentation and orthodoxy, between censorship and the broad laughter at any restraint. Gun culture and reform movements, hopes for regeneration and doomsday fears, loud exaggeration and quiet inwardness have been equally at home in America. It is the task of this book to remind the reader of what is most familiar and to raise the specter of what remains out of sight—forgotten, suppressed, or biding its time.

There is no attempt to give every name its due, to visit every state or the era of every presidency, only the hope that the essays gathered here might be so suggestive as to invite the reader to think of countless other moments in the American story that could be addressed as this book tries to speak to its subjects.

The imaginative energy and activist editorial participation of Lindsay Waters, the perpetuum mobile of Harvard University Press, were the true engines of this book. When Stephen Burt, Gerald Early, Farah Jasmine Griffin, Kirsten Silva Gruesz, Hua Hsu, Michael Leja, David Mindell, Yael Schacher, David Thomson, David Treuer, Ted Widmer, and Sean Wilentz, the members of the editorial board of *A New Literary History of America,* proposed more than four hundred entries and then helped whittle the list down to those that appear here, they gave the book its shape; when they not only commissioned authors, reviewed and edited incoming essays, but also wrote essays of their own, they gave it their own imprint. Drew Faust and Phyllis Strimling at the Radcliffe Institute for Advanced Study generously supported the project early on with an Exploratory Seminar that served as a series of brainstorming sessions among scholars and writers, many of whom later joined the editorial board, and with an Advanced Seminar that brought members of the board together again at a time when about half the entries had come in. William Sisler, the director of Harvard University Press, supported the venture from its inception and made possible another editorial board meeting at the Press offices. Phoebe Kosman, whose probing and energetic editorial oversight kept the endeavor on its course, also contributed an essay; Seo-Young Chu jumped into the editing fray at the halfway mark, provided much editorial help, and also contributed her own entry; Thomas Dichter and Kelsey LeBuffe provided research assistance; Jack Hamilton helped with proofreading; the indefatigable Julie Hagen copyedited the manuscript from first to last; Jennifer Snodgrass brought the ship into port. We could not have asked for better colleagues.

GREIL MARCUS and WERNER SOLLORS

A NEW LITERARY HISTORY OF AMERICA

A New Geography

On March 4, 1493, seeking refuge from heavy seas, a storm-battered caravel flying the Spanish flag limped into Portugal's Tagus River estuary. In command was Cristoforo Colombo, a Genoese sailor soon to become better known to the world by the Latinized version of his name: Christopher Columbus.

After finding a suitable anchorage site, Columbus dispatched a hastily written letter to his royal sponsors, the king and queen of Spain. As promised, he told them, he had sailed across the Atlantic in search of the eastern limits of Asia— and he now had a "great triumph" to report. After a thirty-three-day crossing he had reached the Indies, a realm of "very many islands." Japan and China, he declared, were surely nearby.

The news pleased the Spanish sovereigns immensely. Almost immediately they had Columbus's letter printed, to register their claim on the new islands. Word of the new discovery traveled fast, but it wasn't greeted as revolutionary. European sailors had been discovering and settling ever-more-distant islands in the Atlantic for more than a century—the Canaries, the Madeiras, the Azores, the Cape Verde Islands—and in 1493 they had good reason to assume that still more remained to be found.

Some people hearing Columbus's news thought that he had found nothing more than some new Canary Islands. "The king of Spain discovered many islands again this year," the Siennese chronicler Allegretto Allegretti wrote in his diary on April 25, 1493—"that is, in the Canaries." Likewise, on June 15 the poet Giuliano Dati published a verse adaptation of Columbus's letter designed to be recited aloud in Italy's public piazzas, and titled it "The History of the Discovery of the New Islands of the Indian Canaries." Dati celebrated the discovery in his poem but left out all of Columbus's talk about having opened up a western route to China. About that claim he was clearly skeptical; like almost all Europeans, he knew the world was round, and he had a reasonably good idea of its size. Thirty-three days might be enough time to sail to islands west of the Canaries, but it was *not* enough to sail almost halfway around the world.

Columbus's discovery wasn't considered revolutionary even by those who believed his claims about having reached the Indies. In their view he had done nothing more than pioneer a route to a part of the world already visited and described by European travelers in previous centuries, a feat that confirmed the widely held theory that nothing but the ocean and the islands of the Indies separated Europe from Asia. By confirming this theory and by proving the voyage to be so short, Columbus had narrowed, not expanded, Europe's geographical horizons.

Columbus crossed the Atlantic three more times, in 1493, 1498, and 1502. Each time, as he sailed through a maze of Caribbean islands, he desperately tried to confirm that he had reached Asia. And famously, on his third voyage, just beyond Trinidad, he explored part of the Venezuelan coast, where he came across four great rivers gushing out into the sea. Could it be, he wondered, that he had arrived at "a land of infinite size to the south, of which we have no knowledge as yet"?

It was a prophetic guess. But Columbus soon rejected it in favor of a different idea. He hadn't found a new world, he decided. He had found the oldest one of all—the land of the Terrestrial Paradise and its four great rivers, abandoned at the easternmost limits of Asia ever since Adam and Eve had been expelled from Eden. Human history after the Fall had been a gradual procession from east to west: across Asia to Greece and Rome, then to Jerusalem, then through Western Europe all the way to the sea—and now, finally, Columbus felt, across the Atlantic right back to where everything had begun.

The idea wasn't as crazy as it sounds. The Bible placed the Terrestrial Paradise in the distant east, and most medieval maps placed it at the far-eastern edge of Asia. Humanity's march west through space was also seen as a march west toward the end of time—an apocalyptic notion that medieval theologians had been bandying about for centuries. "The order of space and the order of time seem to be in almost complete correspondence," Hugh of St. Victor had written, for example, at the end of the twelfth century: "Therefore, divine providence's arrangement seems to have been that what was brought about at the beginning of time would also have been brought about in the East—at the beginning, so to speak, of the world as space—and then, as time proceeded towards its end, the center of events would have shifted to the West, so that we may recognize out of this that the world nears its end in time as the course of events has already reached the extremity of the world in space." In his later years, Columbus imagined himself to be playing a starring role in this cosmic drama—a Messianic figure who, by carrying the Christian message across the ocean, was hastening the coming of the End of Days. He was no longer just Colombo or Columbus. He was also Christopher— that is, *Christo-ferens,* or "Christ-bearer."

Such talk, however, was no substitute for gold. Increasingly disappointed by Columbus, who never managed to produce the riches he had promised them in his first letter, the Spanish sovereigns backed away from trumpeting his discoveries, and by the end of the fifteenth century his whole enterprise seemed to be a bust. All anybody could say for sure about Spain's new oceanic venture was this: a boastful Genoese sailor in their service had sailed to the west of the Canaries, where he had located some beautiful but unprofitable islands. Columbus's star fell even further in 1499, when the Portuguese announced to the world that they had managed to sail around Africa to India and back. By sailing east they had found the very thing that Columbus was still unsuccessfully looking for by sailing west: a viable ocean passage to the Indies.

Confirmation that something new and truly remarkable lay out in the western Atlantic didn't reach most Europeans until a few years later—and when it did, the discovery was striking not because it lay far off to the *west* but rather because it

lay so far to the *south*. The news came from Amerigo Vespucci, a Florentine merchant who at about the turn of the century had taken part in at least two voyages across the Atlantic. Upon his return he had written letters home in which he
claimed not just to have visited islands to the west, as Columbus had done, but
also to have sailed south for thousands of miles, all the while hugging the coast of
a strange new land that teemed with people.

Printers in Florence jumped at the chance to publicize this news. In late 1502
or early 1503 they published a doctored version of one of Vespucci's letters and
gave it the title *Mundus Novus*, or *New World*. Editions of the letter proliferated in
the major cities of Europe and it soon became the early version of a best seller—
largely because of what Vespucci had purportedly written in his opening paragraph. "In the past," he told his Florentine patron, Lorenzo di Pierfranceso de'
Medici,

> I have written to you in rather ample detail about my return from those new re-
> gions . . . which can be called a new world, since our ancestors had no knowledge
> of them, and they are entirely new matter to those who hear about them. Indeed,
> it surpasses the opinion of our ancient authorities, since most of them assert that
> there is no continent south of the equator, but merely that sea which they called
> the Atlantic; furthermore, if any of them did affirm that a continent was there,
> they gave many arguments to deny that it was habitable land. But this last voyage
> of mine has demonstrated that this opinion of theirs is false and contradicts all
> truth, since I have discovered a continent in those southern regions that is inhab-
> ited by more numerous peoples and animals than in our Europe, or Asia or Africa.

This passage is often described as a watershed moment in European geographical thought. But "new world" didn't necessarily mean to Vespucci what it
means to us today. In the fifteenth century the Portuguese had used the term to
describe their discoveries in Africa, and before that, in the thirteenth and fourteenth centuries, Christian missionaries returning from Asia had used very similar language to sum up what they had found. A new world often meant nothing
more than a part of the known world not previously visited or described. As several maps produced at the end of the fifteenth century in Florence reveal, geogra-
phers had begun speculating by that time that a giant Asian peninsula extended
down from China far into the Southern Hemisphere—a peninsula that appeared
on no ancient maps and that even Marco Polo had not described. In all likelihood
it was the coast of this hypothetical peninsula that, at least initially, Vespucci
thought he had found. "We concluded," he wrote after his first visit to what today
we know is South America, "that this was continental land, which I esteem to be
bounded by the eastern part of Asia."

In 1504 or so, a copy of the *Mundus Novus* letter fell into the hands of an Alsa-
tian scholar and poet named Matthias Ringmann. In his early twenties, the young
Ringmann was working at the time as a proofreader at a small printing press
in Strasbourg. One of Ringmann's special interests was classical geography—
specifically, the work of the ancient Greek geographer Claudius Ptolemy. In the
second century, in a work known as the *Geography*, Ptolemy had explained how to

map the world in degrees of latitude and longitude, and had then gone on to use this system to pull together a comprehensive picture of the world as it was known in his time. In effect, the *Geography* was a precursor to the modern-day atlas: it contained a world map followed by many smaller regional maps, each drawn appropriately to scale. Ptolemy's maps displayed a three-part known world—Europe, the northern half of Africa, and the western half of Asia—but they didn't extend far enough to the east to show the parts of the Far East visited by Marco Polo in the thirteenth century, or far enough south to show the parts of southern Africa discovered by the Portuguese in the latter half of the fifteenth century.

Ringmann was immersed in a careful study of Ptolemy's *Geography* when he came across the *Mundus Novus* letter. He immediately recognized that Vespucci was claiming to have sailed right off the edge of Ptolemy's map, something Columbus himself never claimed to have done. Thrilled by the idea, Ringmann printed his own version of the letter in 1505—and to emphasize what he felt was most important about it he changed its title from *Mundus Novus* to *De ora antarctica per regem Portugallie pridem inventa* (Concerning the Southern Shore Recently Discovered by the King of Portugal). For those who missed his point, he returned to it in a dedicatory poem. "Beyond the Ethiopians," he wrote, "is a world not known on your maps, O Ptolemy . . . a land far under the Antarctic Pole"—a land, that is, far into the Southern Hemisphere.

Ringmann wasn't studying the *Geography* just for his own edification. Along with the German cartographer Martin Waldseemüller, he would soon begin preparing a new edition of the *Geography* for publication—a job sponsored by René II, the duke of Lorraine. At the invitation of René's private secretary, the two men set up shop in the little town of St. Dié, an easy day's ride up into the mountains northwest of Strasbourg, where a modest printing press had just been established.

Ringmann and Waldseemüller had high hopes for their new *Geography*. They planned to produce a text that would include twenty-seven definitive maps of the ancient world, all cut into woodblocks according to Ptolemy's original specifications. They also planned to produce an equal number of modern maps that would systematically update Ptolemy's picture of the ancient world with new information learned about the world since Ptolemy's time—a historical first. In this latter endeavor Duke René turned out to be particularly helpful: he had friends in Portugal who sent him a new, longer letter by Vespucci and at least one nautical chart depicting the new Atlantic coastlines discovered to date. The letter and the chart confirmed for Ringmann and Waldseemüller what they had read in the *Mundus Novus* letter: a huge unknown southern land had been discovered across the ocean to the south.

Exactly what happened next is a mystery. At some point in 1505 or 1506, for reasons that aren't clear, Ringmann and Waldseemüller came to the conclusion that this land wasn't an extension of Asia, even though all other maps of the period suggested that it had to be. What Vespucci had discovered, they decided, was an entirely new continent: a fourth part of the world. Ringmann therefore revised the poem he had written in 1505. Dropping his earlier reference to "a land far under the Antarctic Pole," which was no longer a bold-enough statement,

Ringmann now addressed Ptolemy in his poem and told him that the new world recently discovered was "a land surrounded by an immense sea."

This is an astonishing statement for him to have made. Europeans are supposed to have learned about the existence of the Pacific only in 1513, when Balboa first caught sight of it, and they are supposed to have begun exploring the west coast of South America only some seven years later, after Magellan had sailed around its tip. If what had been found across the Atlantic was a part of Asia, as Vespucci believed, then it could not be described as surrounded by water. Either Ringmann was making an inspired guess, or he and Waldseemüller had access to information about now-forgotten early voyages of discovery.

Ringmann and Waldseemüller decided to go public with their idea. Temporarily setting aside their work on the *Geography,* they threw themselves into the production of a giant new Ptolemaic map of the world. For months they supervised a crew of woodcutters and artists as they prepared twelve large woodblocks, each containing a portion of the map, which was to be printed on oversized pieces of paper and then assembled as a whole. When the map was finally ready, in April 1507, Ringmann and Waldseemüller printed a thousand copies.

The map, measuring eight feet by four and a half feet, was astonishing to behold—a "cartographic monster," as one modern writer has put it. Its depiction of Europe and North Africa came directly from Ptolemy, its depiction of sub-Saharan Africa came from recent Portuguese explorations, and its depiction of Asia was a mix of Ptolemy and Marco Polo. Europe, Africa, and Asia: these were familiar parts of the world, even if they hadn't yet been fully explored. But on the map's left side, rising out of the formerly uncharted waters of the Atlantic and stretching almost from the map's top to its bottom, warped considerably by its location at the edge of the map's projection, was a strange new continent, long and thin and mostly blank. And there, in the general vicinity of what is known today as Brazil, a strange new name appeared: America.

Ringmann and Waldseemüller published a small companion volume to accompany their map. The work, titled *Cosmographiae Introductio,* or *Introduction to Cosmography,* lays out some basic principles of geometry, describes the geography of the world as it was known at the time, and provides a Latin translation of Vespucci's new letter. And it also records for posterity how the word *America* came into being. "Now truly these parts [Europe, Africa, Asia] have been more widely explored, and another, fourth part has been discovered by Americus Vesputius (as will be heard in what follows), and I do not see why anyone should rightly forbid naming it Amerige, land of Americus, as it were, after its discoverer, Americus, a man of acute genius, or America, inasmuch as both Europe and Asia have received their names from women."

It was a poetic choice, one that would echo down throughout the ages. A New World had been discovered in the south—and it finally had a name.

Bibliography: Felipe Fernández-Armesto, *Amerigo: The Man Who Gave His Name to America* (New York, 2007). Jos. Fischer S. J. and Fr. R. v Wieser, eds., *The Oldest Map with the Name America of the Year 1507 and the Carta Marina of the Year 1516 by M. Waldseemüller (Ilacomilus)* (London,

1903). Luciano Formisano, ed., *Letters from a New World: Amerigo Vespucci's Discovery of America* (New York, 1992). John W. Hessler, trans., *The Naming of America: Martin Waldseemüller's 1507 World Map and the* Cosmographiae introductio (London, 2007). Christine R. Johnson, "Renaissance German Cosmographers and the Naming of America," in *Past and Present* 191, no. 1 (May 2006): 3–43. Franz Laubenberger and Steven Rowan, "The Naming of America," *Sixteenth-Century Journal* 13, no. 4 (Winter 1982): 91–113. Toby Lester, *The Fourth Part of the World* (New York, 2009). Hugonis de S. Victore, "De arca noe morali," 4.9, in *Opera Omnia* (Paris, 1880), English trans. in Alessandro Scafi, *Mapping Paradise* (Chicago, 2006). Seymour I. Schwartz, *Putting "America" on the Map: The Story of the Most Important Graphic Document in the History of the United States* (Amherst, MA, 2007).

TOBY LESTER

1521, August 13
The Aztec empire surrenders Tenochtitlán to the Spanish

MEXICO IN AMERICA

For sheer tragic drama, few chapters from history rival the fall of Tenochtitlán. Even its best-known witness, Bernal Díaz del Castillo, betrays ambivalence about the violent conquest in which he participated. He recalls the Spaniards' first sight of the gleaming city surrounded by canals: "We were astounded. These great towns and buildings made of stone, rising from the water, seemed like an enchanted vision . . . it was all so marvelous that I do not know how to tell it: things never seen, heard of, or even dreamed of before . . . But now all is overthrown and lost; nothing is left standing." Close by the wonder comes recognition of the price of attaining it. The tenor of New World writing is the language of loss.

Díaz's account, written decades later and disseminated all over Europe, established the version of this story that became known to practically every schoolchild: there was once a mighty city, its buildings and marketplaces a testament to order and beauty. Four causeways crossed a man-made lake on which food was raised in floating gardens. Tidy streets radiated inward to the heart of the city, where two temples loomed over an enormous plaza. Díaz draws the key personalities with epic strokes: Hernán Cortés, the ambitious conquistador who had defied his governor's orders to march on Mexico and led his few hundred men into this stronghold of a quarter million; Moctezuma, a gentle and cultured king revered by his people; Marina/Malinche, a Mayan noblewoman sold into slavery who became Cortés's lover as well as translator. The two leaders asserted their brotherhood, and for months the Spaniards lapped up the city's delights. Inevitably, tensions erupted. In Cortés's absence, his men attacked the cream of the Aztec warriors, who had assembled suspiciously at the Templo Mayor. Those who survived rallied to expel the intruders in a night of slaughter called by the Spanish *La noche triste.* Soldiers leaped to their deaths from the flower-covered bridges, drowned by the weight of their armor and plundered gold. Moctezuma, Díaz tells us, was stoned to death by his betrayed followers.

Retreating, Cortés strengthened his alliances with the disgruntled tributaries of the Aztec military empire and with the Aztecs' unconquered rivals, the Tlaxcaltecans. After gathering his forces, he returned and laid siege to the city, by this time starving and decimated by smallpox, for eighty days. Under the leadership of its new teenage emperor, Cuauhtémoc, Tenochtitlán bravely resisted to the end.

Among the many seductions of this story is that it epitomizes the utter shock of two cultures wholly ignorant of each other's existence: one amazed by domesticated animals, the other by perfumed saunas (and, of course, the casually available gold). It is also one of the classic points of historical second-guessing: what was most instrumental in Cortés's astonishing victory—leadership, technology, strategy, or dumb luck? Díaz's version, however influential, is far from the only one, and the multiplicity of interpretive stances is one reason writers keep returning to this world-shifting event. The Mexica—as they called themselves—had their own record-keeping systems, folded bark codices on which they painted their genealogy, theology, history, astronomical calculations. Very few of these records survived the purge by Catholic priests, but soon after the fall a Franciscan, Bernardo de Sahagún, retrained some Mexica scribes to paint what they remembered. Fluent in Nahuatl, Sahagún censored some of their accounts, but in gathering their material so conscientiously he set the precedent for the native informant as authoritative historical source. In the Florentine Codex and five hundred or so other books from this period, as well as in oral traditions, resides some portion of their "vision of the vanquished," as Miguel León-Portilla describes it.

According to the codices, the Mexica had come from the far northwest, guided by their warrior god, Huitzilopochtli. Prophecy played a major role in their cosmology, as it did for the Christians, but the old saw that Moctezuma thought Cortés the reincarnation of Huitzilopochtli was an exculpatory invention of later historians. Building on the cultural forms developed by the many other civilizations of central Mexico, within two centuries the Mexica had come to control an empire spreading from Pacific to Atlantic. Even with the advantages of iron and firearms, horses and dogs, the Spaniards could not have prevailed without exploiting the political fissures in that empire and bringing 150,000 native allies into their ranks. In the Mexica version of the massacre at Huitzilopochtli's temple, the warriors were unarmed, celebrating a religious festival. On *La noche triste,* they say, Cortés himself stabbed Moctezuma in the back.

The fall of Tenochtitlán has become less a fixed event than an emblematic point of origin that generates multiple fables: of betrayal and treachery, hubris and retribution, unthinkable violence and prolonged mourning. The opposing personalities of Cortés and Moctezuma established a template for representing subsequent encounters between Europeans and indigenous Americans, as when Pizarro entered the Incan realm only a decade later. English explorers and colonists knew these stories well, and sought both to match their perceived achievements and to denounce them. Although the Carolina colony existed in uneasy proximity to Spanish outposts in Florida, New Englanders regarded New Spain as a kind of mythic antithesis. In seventeenth-century Boston, Judge Samuel Sewall sipped chocolate with a traveler who told him that Mexico City—which had again become the richest, most spectacular city in the Western Hemisphere—was ripe for Protestant conversion, and Sewall urged Cotton Mather to "bomb" the Spanish Indies with tracts. The fundamental rivalry, both political and religious, between England and Spain in the Atlantic fomented the "Black Legend" of Spanish excess, cruelty, and corruption.

During the Revolutionary period, patriotic poets Joel Barlow and Philip Freneau identified their cause with that of the Aztecs, to demonstrate both the innate historical glory of the New World and the unnaturalness of colonial power itself. Anglo-Americans were not alone in associating the pre-Columbian past with the democratic future: the anonymous Cuban novelist who published *Jicotencal* in Philadelphia in 1826 identified the Tlaxcaltecan government as a proto-democracy, with a senate and elected leaders, thereby offering a native precedent for republican governance in the Americas. Robert Montgomery Bird's immensely popular novels *Calavar* (1834) and *The Infidel* (1835) likewise celebrated Aztec virtue and repudiated the Spanish legacy.

If the new North American nation was to become an "empire for liberty," as Jefferson described it, it would need to establish itself as an ultimate point in the historical succession of civilizational powers. The Spanish had built the imposing cathedral in Mexico City out of the rubble of destroyed temples, but such a visible sign of domination eluded the descendants of the English. From their first sightings of the great ceremonial mounds that dotted the Mississippi and Ohio River Valleys, colonists had sought to attribute them to some fallen civilization on the scale of the Aztec empire, assuming the local tribes incapable of such construction. Romantic poet William Cullen Bryant spun an elaborate story about these mounds in "The Prairies" (1832), imagining them the ruins of Grecian temples built by a peaceful, pastoral culture destroyed by barbarous "red men": analogues for the still-unvanquished Plains Indians, but also for the bloodthirsty Spanish. When John Lloyd Stephens and Frederick Catherwood brought news of the ruined Mayan cities of Copán, Palenque, and Uxmal to readers in *Incidents of Travel in Yucatan* (1843), many devout followers of Joseph Smith took their discoveries as evidence of another kind of sanctified historical succession: the three migrations from ancient Judea to the Americas described in the *Book of Mormon* (1830).

In a perfect accident of timing, William Hickling Prescott's *History of the Conquest of Mexico,* which set the consensus view of Tenochtitlán for the United States, was released in 1843, just three years before the nation's territorial war with Mexico began. Many soldiers reportedly carried Prescott's book on their march toward "the halls of the Montezumas," and General Winfield Scott even halted his army at the great pyramid of Cholula (begun by a civilization a thousand years older than the Aztecs) so that his men could gaze on this wonder of "our Egypt." Scott had landed his army at Veracruz, like Cortés himself. The novelist Bird depicted General Scott as following in the footsteps of the conquistador, to whom Prescott had attributed the particularly "American" traits of independent-mindedness and decisiveness. But once they had occupied Mexico City, Scott's officers formed the "Aztec Club of 1847," aligning themselves romantically with the city's original builders, not its conquerors. Even those Americans who opposed the war generally embraced the declensionist narrative that Prescott put forth about the contemporary Mexicans: they were, he intimated, "mongrels" who had inherited the weakest traits of their two ancestral bloodlines. It would take a ten-year revolution in Mexico to formulate a powerful response to this prevalent racism by celebrating the *mestizo* (mixed) race symbolized by the child that Marina/Malinche had borne Cortés.

The Prescott-addled soldiers at the Cholula pyramid were harbingers of the anthropological tourists who would be drawn during the first half of the twentieth century to Mexico as a source of the timeless, the picturesque, and the primitive. Ambrose Bierce, Hart Crane, Langston Hughes, and Katherine Anne Porter sought refuge in Mexican villages from the relentless forward press of modernity—but with the exception of Hughes, these writers rarely focused on Mexico's daring political experiments or its rapid urbanization and social change. Even early Latina fiction writers like Josefina Niggli and María Cristina Mena, who wrote in English, exploited this moment of romantic Mexicophilia, as did the Mexican tourist industry. The attraction to alterity that the *New York Times* dubbed "the enormous vogue of things Mexican" peaked in the interwar years, although William S. Burroughs, Jack Kerouac, and others continued to make their pilgrimages into Mexico in later years, imagining themselves crossing into the realm of danger and death.

As these conspicuously partial perceptions suggest, U.S. writers have tended to take Mexico's foundational identity narrative as the polar opposite of their own. If one is looking for some fundamental difference between the English and Spanish modes of colonialism—and from there, however tenuously, to present national character—the Zócalo, or central plaza of Mexico City, may best express it. In building the civic and spiritual heart of New Spain over grounds already sanctified by tradition, the Spanish practiced a selective *adaptation* of indigenous institutions rather than their wholesale eradication—which is not to say the process occurred without violence. This syncretism is embodied in the spiritual patroness of the continent's Catholics, the dark-skinned Virgin of Guadalupe. She appeared in 1531, only a decade after the fall of Tenochtitlán, speaking Nahuatl to a humble Indian servant; her shrine was built over a temple to the Mexica mothergoddess, Coatlicue, where it still stands. When an eighteenth-century plumber digging in the Zócalo turned up a statue of Coatlicue, it was quickly reburied so as not to challenge the Guadalupe cult. But in 1978 electrical workers unearthed a carved ceremonial stone from the old Templo Mayor and spurred an ongoing excavation that now defines the plaza as a permanent site of visible memory: one can literally descend into the foundation of Tenochtitlán and see the past while walking down to the subway. There is no ready comparison in the United States to this physical palimpsest, at once sacred and ordinary. Imagine an excavated section of the Mall in Washington, D.C., reverentially revealing a trading village of the Piscataway-Conoy, or a hole in Times Square blocked off to display Lenape

oyster middens. More than one commentator has suggested that the living presence of the past in Mexico is the antithesis of the Anglo-American cult of progress and forward movement.

At the same time, the continued presence in the United States of Mexicans
and their descendants complicates any such distinction. Some Mexican-Americans
were repatriated by the terms of the 1848 treaty; others migrated north to work
on railroads during the Mexican Revolution, in agriculture during the labor short-
ages of the 1940s, in domestic work after the collapse of Mexico's oil wealth in
the 1980s. The Mexican state refers to this diaspora as *México afuera* (Mexico outside): lost ones eventually to be gathered home. The young activists who embraced the once-pejorative label "Chicano" in the 1970s, however, returned to the
traumatic source of the Tenochtitlán story to construct a more positive sense of
themselves. They claimed rights over the ancestral homeland of the Mexica, a
place called "Aztlán" in the Aubin Codex and identified as the U.S. Southwest.
Chicanos in the United States likened themselves to the Mexica under Spanish
rule: a colonized people. Some learned Nahuatl and organized poetry festivals in
homage to aesthetic traditions like *in xochitl in cuicatl*, flower and song. Octavio
Paz's *The Labyrinth of Solitude* (1950) had dismissed the Mexican-American as a
pocho, deracinated and speech deprived; Paz identified "La Malinche" as the original traitor who had sold out indigenous Mexico, and the *pocho* as her latter-day
heir. Chicana feminists responded by reclaiming both of those repudiated figures,
restoring a proper name, Malintzín, to the woman caught in between. By turning
to this third-party translator, Chicana and Chicano writers rejected the duality
inherent in that archetypal story of the encounter between Cortés and Moctezuma. In most U.S. immigrant fictions the clash of radically different worlds ends
in assimilation, but often as not Chicano novelists represent their identity as a
syncretic adaptation, like the Virgin of Guadalupe, to the dominant culture and
language.

In his 1925 inquiry *In the American Grain*, William Carlos Williams anticipated
that American history would need to be retooled to begin with the destruction of
Tenochtitlán, as well as the failed schemes of Red Eric and the errant mysticism
of Columbus. Williams suggested that what was thought "overthrown and lost"
maintains a persistent life under the surface of things; he called for a new language to "re-name the things seen, now lost in the chaos of buried titles . . . under
which their true character lies hid." His point is echoed in Guillermo Bonfil
Batalla's notion of "deep Mexico," which has eclipsed Paz's pessimistic view of
the *mestizo* and the *pocho*. The indigenous cosmovision, Bonfil Batalla says, was
never erased or even effectively covered over; only by recognizing its present vitality can Mexico address its social problems, including those caused by globalization.

The United States has become the fifth-largest Spanish-speaking nation in
the world, raising suggestive questions about whether its literature will continue
to be written predominantly in English. One in ten Americans claims Mexican
descent; one in ten Mexican nationals lives the migrant life among *los gringos*,
sending home more in remittances than the revenues generated by any other in-

dustry in Mexico. Richard Rodriguez observes, "The United States shares with Mexico a two-thousand-mile connection—the skin of two heads." That unnerving metaphor suggests both the history of bodily violence behind all colonialism in the Americas, and the deeply symbiotic relationship between the two nations. A border wall can no more do away with this profound connection than barricading the four causeways leading to Tenochtitlán could defend that city from determined outsiders.

Bibliography: Guillermo Bonfil Batalla, *México Profundo: Reclaiming a Civilization* (Austin, 1996). J. H. Elliott, *Empires of the Atlantic World* (New Haven, CT, 2007). Robert W. Johannsen, *To the Halls of the Montezumas: The Mexican War in the American Imagination* (New York, 1988). Miguel León-Portilla, *The Broken Spears: The Aztec Account of the Conquest of Mexico* (1959; rpt. Boston, 2007). Richard Rodriguez, *Days of Obligation: An Argument with My Mexican Father* (New York, 1993). Eric Wertheimer, *Imagined Empires: Incas, Aztecs, and the New World of American Literature* (New York, 1998).

KIRSTEN SILVA GRUESZ

1536, July 24
Four survivors of a 600-man expedition to Florida reach Mexico City after eight years of wandering

ALVAR NÚÑEZ CABEZA DE VACA, *LA RELACIÓN*

Six years after the survivors of a Spanish expedition ended an amazing North American journey with their arrival in Mexico City, one of the few, Alvar Núñez Cabeza de Vaca, was back in Spain preparing an account of his travels: over sea from Spain to Cuba to Florida, and onward by foot into what is now Texas, New Mexico, Arizona, and northern Mexico. *La relación,* as the chronicle is generally known in Spanish, is the first ethnographic description by a European of large portions of the country that would eventually become the United States, and of the natives who inhabited it. Written with naked honesty, the document abounds in astonishing depictions of life under adverse and transformative circumstances. Cabeza de Vaca offers a self-portrait of the Iberian conquistador—as intrepid trailblazer and magical healer, but also as swindler and penitent sinner.

An average soldier with a limited education, Cabeza de Vaca was born sometime between 1485 and 1492. This was a period of deep social ferment in Spain, as the effort to retake the Iberian Peninsula from the Arabs and homogenize it under a single Catholic faith coincided with the growing efforts of the Inquisition to expel Jews from the land. Reports of the newly found territories across the Atlantic would have reached Cabeza de Vaca's ears when he was a young man. In his midthirties, after fighting abroad in the service of four different dukes and helping to put down a popular rebellion in southern Spain against recent converts from Judaism known as *conversos,* he embarked for the colonies in a flotilla of six ships that sailed from the mouth of the Guadalquivir River. He sailed under the command of Pánfilo de Narváez, the newly named governor, or *adelantado,* of the little-known territory known as La Florida—in North America.

La relación has also circulated under the Spanish title of *Los naufragios,* the shipwrecks, and from the beginning the expedition is described as being dogged by bad luck and worse leadership. A hurricane destroys two ships and scores of men before they even leave Cuba. Upon their arrival in Florida, Narváez, impatient to find gold, makes the foolish decision to leave the ships virtually unguarded and march into the interior, where the Spaniards are repeatedly attacked by Indians because of Narváez's inept diplomacy and heedless pillaging of corn. Lost in the dense interior, their numbers reduced by two-thirds and with nothing to eat but their own horses, the men grow mutinous and build rudimentary boats. When they finally reach the Gulf, Narváez rows off with the healthiest, strongest men, callously telling Cabeza de Vaca that "one should do the best he could to save himself, which is what he intended to do." Cabeza de Vaca's boat is shipwrecked again, this time on Galveston Island, where he and the others beg local Indians to take them in. Forced by "the people of this country" to become medicine men, the remaining Spaniards survive as faith healers, petty traders, and often as slave laborers. Ultimately Cabeza de Vaca decides to pursue his own route west along with the other three men who finally remain of the original six hundred: a Moroccan named Estevanico, once a slave himself, and the Spaniards Andrés Dorantes and Alonso de Castillo Maldonado. Together they traverse approximately a thousand miles on foot.

Consisting of a preface and thirty-eight brief chapters, some only a few paragraphs long, *La relación* is written in the straightforward, unadorned style of the chronicler. The purpose of his narrative, as Cabeza de Vaca writes in the preface, is to highlight his "deeds and services" to the "Holy, Imperial, Catholic Majesty." By detailing Narváez's cowardice, he also intends to absolve himself of any potential charge of insubordination, for rumors about the expedition's mishaps had spread with such viciousness back at home that Cabeza de Vaca felt the need to set the record straight (despite his ordeal, he had hopes of being appointed the new governor of La Florida).

Travelers to the Americas faced an uncommon task in writing about their experiences: to make plausible what to an average European would seem utterly implausible. The New World posed the epistemological problem of how to make the average reader believe in things never before imagined, like parakeets, turkeys, chocolate, and tomatoes. "This account," Cabeza de Vaca states in the preface, "will be counsel of no little use to those who, in your name, may go to conquer those territories, and collectively, bring them knowledge of the true faith and true lord . . . For this I have written with great surety so that even though one will read about many new things that many people will find hard to believe, they should be able to believe them without hesitation." Yet *La relación* is also full of inconsistencies and ellipses, often at the most interesting moments: "I will discontinue telling this story at this point. Anyone can imagine what might be experienced in a land so foreign and evil."

Making frequent rhetorical gestures toward God's great mercy, Cabeza de

Vaca recounts the fates of the other officers and their men as he pieces the story together later, with biblical solemnity. Those who abandoned their men got what they deserved: they were killed, drowned, or dead of hunger and thirst. Some resorted to cannibalism, which (in a reversal of European stereotypes) horrifies the natives. At times Cabeza de Vaca presents himself as a Christ-like figure, feeding the hungry and healing the sick, even resurrecting a man thought to be dead by breathing on him and making the sign of the cross. The narrative is also imbued with the spirit of the novels of chivalry popular in the Iberian Peninsula at the time, in which the gallant hero undergoes a series of challenges yet maintains his sense of morality.

At other points, Cabeza de Vaca's narrative takes on a distinctly ethnographic tone, offering a subjective appraisal of what he sees with a conviction not so different from that of the modern social scientist. He describes marriage customs, funeral rites, and tantalizing bits of languages that vanished before they could be recorded by anyone else. This careful observation does not stop him, however, from moralizing about practices that in his eyes look barbaric, such as the "repulsive" sight of "a man married to another, who did women's work." Not only interested in people—their political organizations, health practices, and religious beliefs—Cabeza de Vaca also includes insightful if limited descriptions of the flora and fauna of the region, allowing naturalists of the future a glimpse of the New World before it was transformed by European contact. His life, like that of the dozen or so different tribes he lives among during his eight-year journey, becomes measured by the seasons for root digging in the swamps, or harvesting prickly pears. He throws himself into the role that had been thrust on him, practicing surgery with a deer-bone needle and sinew thread: "I was the most daring and reckless of all in undertaking cures. We never treated anyone that did not afterward say he was well."

By the time the four survivors reach Arizona—a relative land of plenty, full of squash, corn, and beans—they have gathered a loyal retainer of Indians who willingly follow them southward to New Spain. Cabeza de Vaca tries to explain away his personal following as new converts to the true faith, although the orthodoxy of his own faith-healing practices is a bit hazy at this point. Their triumphant arrival in the village of San Miguel, and then in Mexico City in 1536, might well have been the hook on which the entire narrative hangs. The redemptive return to "civilization" provides closure, as in the captivity narratives that later become so important in the Anglo-American tradition. But interestingly, by this point in his narrative Cabeza de Vaca appears to have lost his trust in the culture from which he came. The period of wandering has been long and, although the chronicle is not a bildungsroman per se, he has been transformed by it. He sees the "Christians" and native people as equally brutish: "We had many and bitter quarrels with the Christians, for they wanted to make slaves of our Indians." For their part, Cabeza de Vaca's followers refuse to believe that their healer belongs to the same race as the Spaniards, because unlike them, he says, "we asked for nothing, but gave away all we were presented with." He struggles to persuade "his" Indians to return to their own lands. Having been a bridge between the two worlds, aboriginal and European, Cabeza de Vaca ultimately refuses to bring them together.

Thus, unlike scores of sixteenth- and seventeenth-century testimonies of the Spanish conquest, *La relación* lacks a triumphant moral, coming across more as a cautionary tale about the brutality and nobility witnessed on both sides.

It is fascinating to imagine the status *La relación* would have in the American psyche had its author been an English-speaking frontiersman. Would his audacity have been better appreciated? Would his cautionary tale have been embraced as a saga of humility in extreme conditions? The Spanish past as a whole has seemed suspect in the traditional narrative of national identity that stresses a teleological vision of exceptional destiny, beginning with the arrival of the *Mayflower* pilgrims in search of their New Canaan. The narrative of new beginning on this side of the ocean has insisted on refuting everything that preceded or coincided with it. Not only does it refuse to acknowledge the legitimacy of the indigenous inhabitants of these lands; it also rejects the Spanish and the French as cruel, even demonic, in their method of conquest.

After the Texas Revolution and the Treaty of Guadalupe Hidalgo transferred two-thirds of Mexico's territory to the United States, those newly acquired lands also needed to be integrated into the nation's narrative, and the existence of a work like Cabeza de Vaca's gave the "West" a history. The first English translation in the United States of his story appeared in 1871. Early interpretations stressed the dissoluteness of *conquistadores* like Narváez, part of a campaign of vilification known as the Black Legend that reached its climax in 1898, during the U.S. war with Spain. (Indeed, by the end of the nineteenth century such chronicles of the conquest were increasingly perceived with embarrassment in the Iberian Peninsula as sordid evidence of the nation's damaging imperial quest, which was thought to have overextended Spain.) Nonetheless, the narrative became well known to regional history buffs, such as the amateur Texas historians who sought in the early twentieth century to trace Cabeza de Vaca's exact route, which is still open to debate.

Having languished as a marginal text for centuries, Cabeza de Vaca's narrative has achieved the status of a classic in our skeptical age of cultural relativism. In Latin America during the second half of the twentieth century, and especially leading up to the Columbus quincentenary in 1992, it was read as proof of the European disorientation that was a prelude to the difficult but necessary birth of a *mestizo,* or mixed, civilization. Half a dozen different English translations are currently available, and they differ widely in their agenda—in the uses they make of the past. The 1999 edition published by University of Nebraska Press seeks to standardize the text and pays meticulous attention to its historical context in Spain and the Americas. The Penguin Classics translation (2002) invites readers to see *La relación* as an embattled account of selfhood that presupposes that our national past is open to contest. And the edition produced in 1993 under the aegis of the Recovering the U.S. Hispanic Literary Heritage Project, as the project name indicates, offers Cabeza de Vaca's work as a statement of origins, as proof that the Spanish-speaking population in the United States has been continuously present in these lands since the colonial period—although the editors see him as somewhat villainous. The explosive growth of the U.S. Latino population in the past few decades has driven this search for roots and origins, and anthologies and

literary histories often name Cabeza de Vaca as the "first Latino writer"—a problematic label, given that most accounts of Latino identity stress *mestizo* origins,
whereas he was a Spaniard with nothing to say on the topic of intermarriage.

While Cabeza de Vaca's eminently readable chronicle continues to be the subject of competing interpretations, his place in the canon seems secure. Anthologies of "American" literature frequently begin with Cabeza de Vaca, as a way
to emphasize that the complicated encounter between indigenous Americans,
Spaniards, English, and French people—a colonial past that can be read as a series of exercises in subjugation—was central to the formation of national identity.
Reading *La relación* against the work of later Protestant authors allows for a consideration of different ways of understanding the bridge between self and other
in the colonial encounter. How does Cabeza de Vaca's semi-integration into multiple tribes compare with the experience of redeemed captives who paint the Indians as demonic, such as Mary Rowlandson, or of those who chose to remain
with their captors, like Sarah Winnemucca? The text can also be viewed in the
context of the later literary tradition of *The Call of the Wild* or *The Old Man and the
Sea,* as the ultimate frontier story, a tale of endurance and personal courage. Or,
following a different tack, Cabeza de Vaca's pilgrimage may be taken as a preview
of Henry Thoreau's civil disobedience and refusal of social mores, or of John
Muir's retreat into the wilderness.

In the end, Cabeza de Vaca, Estevanico, Dorantes, and Maldonado were ordinary figures who, in a stroke of luck and by virtue of their naïveté, redefined the
entire worldview from which they had sprung. In retrospect, they appear to have
defied the natural and human orders by crisscrossing the continent without a
map. Moreover, their story invites readers to ponder the relative merits of spiritual belief systems, to reorient fundamental assumptions about what counts as
civilized.

Bibliography: Alvar Núñez Cabeza de Vaca, *Chronicle of the Narváez Expedition,* trans. Fanny
Bandelier, rev. and annot. Harold Augenbraum, introd. Ilan Stavans (New York, 2002); *Alvar
Núñez Cabeza de Vaca: His Account, His Life, and the Expedition of Pánfilo de Narváez,* ed. Rolena
Adorno and Patrick Charles Pautz, 3 vols. (Lincoln, NE, 1999); *The Account: Alvar Núñez Cabeza
de Vaca's Relación,* trans. and ed. Martin A. Favata and José B. Fernandez (Houston, 1993). J. H.
Elliott, *Empires of the Atlantic World: Britain and Spain in America, 1492–1830* (New Haven, CT,
2006).

ILAN STAVANS

1585
John White paints Virginia

"COUNTERFEITED ACCORDING TO THE TRUTH"

England's first attempt to plant a self-sustaining colony in America was a
short-lived affair. The "Cittie of Raleigh," established in 1587 in the Outer Banks
of what is now North Carolina, fared poorly in its first months and by August the

colonial governor, John White, was forced to return to England for supplies. He never reunited with the members of what has become known as the Lost Colony, and the English would not boast a successful settlement in America until the Jamestown colonists discovered the value of tobacco as a commercial crop in the early 1600s. But if England's early expeditions to Virginia during the 1580s failed to establish a colonial presence in the New World, they were quite successful as a knowledge-making enterprise, thanks in no small part to John White's efforts.

Two years before he assumed the role of governor, White sailed as a member of a military expedition that aimed to fortify and survey the Virginia coast. His role on that voyage was painter, and during the summer of 1585 he produced a remarkable collection of watercolors, now housed in the British Museum, depicting the native peoples and natural history of the region. This collection would have a profound impact on how Europeans imagined nature and society in North America. Particularly after they were popularized as printed engravings, White's images began to play an important part in the European trade in scientific knowledge and remained a crucial bank of visual information about America into the nineteenth century.

The title page of White's original album of watercolors describes the contents as "the pictures of sondry things collected and counterfeited according to the truth," and the surviving pictures are indeed "sondry." They include maps of the eastern coast of North America; bird's-eye views of forts and encampments in the West Indies; coastal profiles; naturalistic studies of fruit and flowers, as well as fish, insects, birds, crabs, turtles, and other New World animals; ethnographic studies of Carolina Algonquians, along with views of their towns and various customs and practices. In making the claim that his pictures of Virginia were "counterfeited," White was drawing on a new language of image making. To "counterfeit" was to engage in a reportorial mode of visual depiction that recorded things and events as they were witnessed by the eye, not as they were composed by the artist. It was not a particular style or subject matter that defined the counterfeit; rather, it was defined by its epistemological status as uninterpreted nature. Through his counterfeits, White helped transport America back to Europe in raw, visible fragments.

A basic characteristic of White's visual rhetoric, a characteristic that one might even say constitutes the *modernity* of his collection, is its decontextualization of America. Whether he is representing a firefly, an Algonquian religious man, or the cooking of fish on a barbecue, White avoids all extraneous information by isolating his subjects and setting them against an empty background. In contrast to the depictions of Florida by his contemporary Jacques Le Moyne, who had traveled to Florida with a Huguenot expedition in the 1560s, White's pictures of Virginia never complicate the observer's own point of view by showing scenes of encounter between Europeans and Americans. Nor does White rely on visual conventions such as that of the "monstrous races," an iconography that had the advantage of making the exotic intelligible within the outlines of a sacred Christian geography. A 1599 German edition of Sir Walter Raleigh's *Discovery of Guiana,* for instance, invokes the tradition of the monstrous races by picturing

turned with them to his family workshop in Frankfurt. De Bry engraved these pictures for his 1590 publication *A Briefe and True Report of the New Found Land of Virginia,* a folio-size book that combined high-quality illustrations with written descriptions of the Algonquians by White's partner in surveying Virginia, Thomas Harriot. This brief volume, published in four languages including English, became the first of thirteen volumes that would ultimately constitute de Bry's extraordinarily popular *America* (1590–1634).

Through de Bry's many editions of the *Report,* and through the many later texts that borrowed directly or indirectly from de Bry's engravings, White's collection continued to serve into the nineteenth century as a visual prototype for images of the North American Indian. De Bry's plates were reproduced and adapted, often creatively and in the service of various agendas, in descriptive accounts of the New World such as William Strachey's *The Historie of Travell into Virginia Britania* (1612), John Smith's *Generall Historie of Virginia* (1624), and Robert Beverley's *History and Present State of Virginia* (1705); they also proved to be indispensable material for some of the most important early anthropological studies of American Indians, such as Bernard Picart's *Cérémonies et coutumes religieuses de tous les peuples du monde* (1723–1743) and Joseph-François Lafitau's *Moeurs des sauvages ameriquains, comparées aux moeurs des premiers temps* (1724). Aside from this recycling of de Bry's plates in later texts, the *Briefe and True Report* itself remained a widely known and authoritative book long after its publication in 1590. When John Adams wrote to Thomas Jefferson in 1812 for suggestions on where to learn about the traditions of the American Indians, one of the texts to which Jefferson directed his friend was de Bry's *America,* the first three volumes of which he proudly held in his own library.

Audiences kept returning to White's Virginia images because they satisfied a need to witness the radical difference of the New World with one's own eyes. To be sure, the idea that one had to *see* America in order to believe it had been expressed regularly since the earliest European accounts of the Americas. But it was not until almost a century after Columbus first landed in the West Indies that New World images actually began to circulate widely throughout Europe. De Bry certainly played an important part in this phenomenon by recognizing and tapping the public's appetite for visual spectacle (later volumes of de Bry's America become increasingly sensational), but those who actually planned and sponsored expeditions to the Americas were also increasingly aware of the importance of commissioning visual accounts. Jacques Le Moyne's pictures of Florida from the 1560s; Francisco Hernández's monumental *History of the Plants and Animals of New Spain* made for Philip II in the 1570s (comprising multiple volumes with thousands of color illustrations, all of them destroyed by fire in 1671); John White's Virginia watercolors from the 1580s; the stunning visual record of Dutch Brazil created by Albert Eckhout and Frans Post between 1637 and 1644: all of these artistic projects exemplify the growing significance of visual documentation within the nexus of political, commercial, and scholarly interests that motivated early modern colonial expeditions in the Americas.

As metropolitan sponsorship of scientific expeditions in the Americas continued through the seventeenth and eighteenth centuries, it stimulated the work of colonial naturalists like William Bartram (1739–1823). Inspired in part by Catesby's illustrated natural history of the southern colonies and the Caribbean (and so indirectly inspired by White), Bartram set out in 1773 on a four-year expedition through the southern colonies, during which he made numerous drawings of flora and fauna for his London patron, Dr. John Fothergill. Culminating in his influential *Travels through North and South Carolina, Georgia, East and West Florida* (1791), Bartram's work signals an intensifying phase of interest in natural science and ethnography in the early national period. Other notable endeavors in the visual documentation of America at this time include the founding in the early 1780s of Charles Willson Peale's natural history museum in Philadelphia, the publication of Alexander Wilson's *American Ornithology* (1807–1814), and the work of Titian Ramsey Peale and Samuel Seymour on the federally sponsored Long expedition to the Rocky Mountains (1819–1820). All of these artists were continuing the work of counterfeiting the New World initiated by White, but in their hands this empirical work became a distinctly national project as well. The visual cataloging of the American landscape and its native inhabitants held the promise of discovering the universal knowledge that a broad public might agree upon, a set of indisputable truths that would provide a common foundation not only for further scientific work but for a project of nation building. While competing ideas could all too easily lead to dispute and faction, the careful observing and cataloging of nature could lead to what the Philadelphia naturalist Benjamin Smith Barton in 1796 called a "democracy of facts."

The scientific community of the early republic was thus strongly invested in seeing nature with Baconian eyes, uncorrupted by preconceptions. As Bartram wrote to Fothergill, "I attempt only to exhibit to your Notice, the outward furniture of Nature, or the productions of the Surface of the earth; without, troubling you with any notions, of their particular causes or design by Providence, such attempts I leave for the amusement of Men of Letters & Superior genius." Jefferson similarly wrote that "the plan of creation is inscrutable to our limited faculties." Extrapolating from experience into the deepest causes of nature was considered the province of European science, and for that very reason a cause for suspicion. Of the three European texts on North American Indians that Jefferson recommended to Adams, he thought that none was fully satisfactory. In his *Moeurs des sauvages ameriquains* the Frenchman Lafitau was far too in love with his own "preconceived theory." The *History of the American Indians* (1775) by the Englishman James Adair was likewise to be approached with care, for despite the fact that this book contained a "great deal of instruction," Adair's science was hampered by his theory that the Indians of America were all descended from the Lost Tribes of Israel. De Bry, on the other hand, could be admired for lacking any "favorite system," but he also lacked proper scientific methods: Jefferson writes that in de Bry's volumes "facts and fable are mingled together."

Witnessing the New World with innocent eyes was difficult, indeed impossible work, and yet the stakes in doing that work were very high. Before the American landscape and its inhabitants could be put into the service of science or politics, they had to be transformed into facts. In the United States, federally sponsored survey expeditions would continue through the nineteenth century and would ultimately replace the artist's brush with the mechanical eye of the camera. On the government surveys that followed the Civil War, photographers made the western landscape available to scientists and policymakers in the East by transforming it into a collection of mobile, visible fragments. These new merchants of light were carrying on the work White had begun in Virginia 300 years before.

Bibliography: Francis Bacon, *A Selection of His Works,* ed. Sidney Warhaft (New York, 1965). William Bartram, *Travels and Other Writings,* ed. Thomas P. Slaughter (New York, 1996). Daniel J. Boorstin, *The Lost World of Thomas Jefferson* (Boston, 1948). Paul Hulton, *America 1585: The Complete Drawings of John White* (Chapel Hill, NC, 1984). Lester J. Cappon, ed., *The Adams-Jefferson Letters* (Chapel Hill, NC, 1959). Susan Scott Parrish, *American Curiosity: Cultures of Natural History in the Colonial British Atlantic World* (Chapel Hill, NC, 2006). David Beers Quinn, ed., *The Roanoke Voyages 1584–1590* (New York, 1991). Kim Sloan, *A New World: England's First View of America* (Chapel Hill, NC, 2007).

MICHAEL GAUDIO

1607

John Smith arrives in Chesapeake Bay

Fear and Love in the Virginia Colony

In May of 1607, a small ship sailed into the mouth of the Chesapeake Bay after a long and tedious voyage. Of the travelers aboard, there was probably only one who did not crowd along the rail to catch a first glimpse of the looming green continent—not for lack of interest, certainly, but because he lay chained below-decks. This prisoner would become the founding author of American literature—and also, at the same time, its first great literary protagonist.

The author-as-hero . . . a creature, as yet, barely known to the faithful readers of old Europe. Who then could have guessed that the New World would prove this prodigy's most fertile literary habitat, its fields and forests and undreamt cities spawning thousands to come? Only this man himself, perhaps. Alone among the settlers of the Virginia Company, John Smith embraced this new place like an exile arriving home. He was not, as many people today wrongly recollect, the leader of the Jamestown expedition; in fact, he had been clapped in irons midway across the Atlantic, accused of plotting, as Smith would later describe it, to "make himselfe king." But more important, he was, in a sense, a natural-born American. His relentless schemes of upward mobility were just one of the telltale signs.

Smith was a natural-born writer. Torn unwillingly from the Chesapeake, he would spend most of the rest of his life disconsolate in England, pining and scheming to return, wielding not a sword but a pen, reliving time and again in his imagination those months he had spent here. This involuntary return probably saved his life, leaving him almost the sole survivor when his former Jamestown comrades had succumbed to Virginia's swamp fevers, her Indian arrows, her starving winters. But the colony somehow endured—the first lasting English settlement in North America—which meant that its story would endure, too.

A lesson worth remembering: first, survive; second, publish. It is because Smith knew this that he still lives in our imagination today, this little man with no parentage, no progeny, and the homeliest of names the English language affords, while so many of his more richly plumaged fellow adventurers (Edward-Maria Wingfield, Sir Christopher Newport, Captain Bartholemew Gosnold) lie more or less irretrievable in the dust. But it is time we started remembering him not as an explorer, not as a fighter, not as a lover—lord knows, not that!—but as a literary man. He was busily inventing American literature before the wordy Puritans ever thought to sail.

As both author and explorer, Smith, like the Jamestown venture itself, stood with one foot in the Middle Ages and the other in modernity. The year before he and his comrades embarked for Virginia, the first edition of Cervantes's *Don Quixote* was published in Madrid. Like Cervantes's protagonist, Smith came from yeoman stock but left home to reinvent himself as a knight-errant. Both men read too much (in Smith's case, Machiavelli and Marcus Aurelius, along with medieval romances), and took it too literally. If Smith didn't actually tilt at windmills, he certainly saw giants and monsters and damsels in distress where more workaday minds would have overlooked them.

Rusty armor figures in his tale, too. When you visit Jamestown today, among the more than a million artifacts excavated over the years by archaeologists you will find a few corroded breastplates and visored helmets. These now hang under spotlights in gleaming display cases, as ancient and out of context as dinosaur bones or moon rocks, foreign emblems of knighthood and chivalry unearthed in the soil of America. The bold foray into a new continent was about adventurers in knightly armor, but it was also about international commerce, corporate greed, investor relations, and maximizing share value. Both strands of Jamestown's identity, the medieval and the modern, the chivalrous and the corporate, would twine themselves inextricably into the American fabric.

In his youth, John Smith must have been one of those boys—like so many immigrants and authors to follow—who lived more in his imagination than in prosaic reality. He was born in 1580 in marshy Lincolnshire, apprenticed at fifteen to a local merchant, and yet never stopped dreaming of adventure across distant seas. As a young man, he headed to the Continent as a mercenary, fighting first for Dutch independence and then joining Austrian forces in Hungary doing battle against the invading Turks. According to Smith's own tale, he fought valiantly against the infidels but was finally wounded in battle, captured, and sent off to Constantinople as a slave, his head shaved and a ring of iron riveted around his neck; he killed his captor with a threshing tool and escaped, finally making his way back to England by way of Russia, Poland, and North Africa.

Whatever the proportion of truth and myth in the details of Smith's early adventures, he had gained hard-won experience that would serve him well in America. As Thomas Jefferson, an earnest student of early Virginia history, would write of Smith, he was "honest, sensible, and well-informed." He had learned to make his way through unmapped territory and among diverse foreign tribes, as both an ally and an enemy. He had leapt skillfully over language barriers. He had dealt resourcefully with sudden and dramatic reversals of fortune. Having set forth to become a picaresque hero, he had learned some very modern lessons about getting by in the world, with either his wits or a threshing tool, as the particular occasion demanded.

In Virginia, Smith quickly put these lessons to use. A runty man, tough as a leather strap, he was one of the few colonists with the mettle to deal with the hostile natives, who were none too happy at having their territory invaded. Like any savvy multinational corporation, the Virginia Company had no desire to antagonize the locals with its overseas operations. "Have great care not to offend the naturals," its written instructions advised. But the colonists' expectations of harmony were as ill founded as their dreams of a Chesapeake El Dorado. One of the leading propagandists for English colonization, Thomas Hariot, who had participated in the Roanoke venture twenty years earlier, wrote: "They in respect of troubling our inhabiting and planting, are not to be feared, but . . . they shall have cause both to fear and love us that shall inhabit with them."

In the event, there was plenty of trouble, to say the least. (Several unfortunate Englishmen who ended up having their flesh scraped off with sharpened shells and roasted as they watched no doubt spent their dying breaths cursing such rosy predictions.) But Hariot was prescient in his forecast that "fear and love" would be the recipe for relations with the Virginia natives. John Smith knew how to play both good cop and bad cop to perfection, cajoling one day and coercing the next—anything to procure the food that the colonists needed to survive. Before long, he had become president of the colony. Along the way, though, Smith managed to make powerful rivals among his own countrymen, and in September 1609, when Smith was injured by an explosion of gunpowder (a suspicious accident), he found himself stripped of power and bundled off aboard the next ship leaving for England.

He would never return to Virginia. After recovering from his wound, he remained entangled in company politics, stymied in all his attempts to gain a new post. At a time when the Chesapeake's atrocious mortality rates were swallowing up settlers by the hundreds, and when the colony's backers were desperate for almost any warm body they could ship over to keep the settlement populated, Smith's seems to have been one of the few they would not take. The precise reasons remain somewhat obscure, but one guesses that this cocksure little upstart simply rubbed too many powerful men the wrong way.

Yet one happier surprise did await Smith in England. During his three-year absence, he had become—apparently without his knowledge—a published author, and a somewhat acclaimed one at that. In 1608, a ship returning from Jamestown had carried with it a letter from Smith to an acquaintance back in the mother country, forty or so pages of close-written foolscap detailing the colonists' adventures and travails in the New World. Within a few weeks it had been entered for publication as *A True Relation of Such Occurrences and Accidents of Noate as Hath Hapned in Virginia Since the First Planting of that Collony, Which is Now Resident in the South Part Thereof, Till the Last Return from Thence.* Despite this unwieldy title, the text itself was—by the prose standards of the time—direct, forthright, and vivid, especially in its portraits of some of the characters Smith had met among the Virginia natives. There was Powhatan, the shrewd emperor-priest of the tidewater, presiding in state with chains of pearls around his neck and naked concubines at his feet. There was the chief's trusted lackey, Rawhunt, "much exceeding in deformitie of person, but of a subtill wit and crafty understanding." And there was Powhatan's memorable daughter, "a child of tenne yeares old, which not only for feature, countenance, and proportion much exceedeth any of the rest of the people, but for wit, and spirit, the only Nonpareil of his Country." (In the margin of the British Library's copy next to this passage, a seventeenth-century hand has inserted the word "Pokahontas.")

It is still anyone's guess whether these descriptions caught the eye of the playwright who would soon invent a romance of a brave new world—the chief inhabitants of which were a shrewd magician-king, his malformed and conniving lackey, and his sprightly daughter. In any case, by the time *The Tempest* was first performed in the fall of 1611, John Smith was at work on another book. This one (known today as *A Map of Virginia*) accompanied a large and astonishingly accurate engraved chart of the Chesapeake region, principally based on explorations that Smith himself had conducted in 1608. The text encompassed not just geography but also natural history and ethnography, with careful descriptions of the flora and fauna of the region, as well as the religion, laws, and family life of the native inhabitants, and even a short phrasebook of the Algonkian language. ("*Kekaten pokahontas patiaquagh ningh tanks manotyens neer mowchick rawrenock audowgh.* Bid Pokahontas bring hither two little Baskets, and I wil give her white beads to make her a chaine.") Smith wrapped up his account with a withering critique of his fellow colonists ("idle contemplatours . . . false informers . . . ingenious verbalists") that cannot have done much to endear him to the Virginia Company's officers.

With an orphan's single-minded yearning he still pined for return, even as new reports from Virginia told of continued misery and failure. "It were more proper for mee," Smith complained, "to be doing what I say, then writing what I knowe." In 1614 he did get back across the Atlantic, on a brief exploring expedition to the coast of what is now Maine, New Hampshire, and Massachusetts—long enough for him to name the region "New England," and to collect material for another book. Yet his fresh attempts at colonization seemed cursed: though he scraped together several fleets, the ships sprang leaks, fell prey to pirates, were driven back by gales, each time stranding Smith again in London. In 1620, he learned of a new group setting sail for North America, and lobbied hard to lead the Pilgrims into their promised land, but lost the job to the less seasoned (and less stiff-necked) Captain Miles Standish.

However, even if the *Mayflower* did not carry Smith himself on the voyage, it did carry the wisdom and knowledge that he had accumulated at such great cost. The Pilgrims—and the English settlers who followed them in the years to come—

succeeded in no small part because they had read Smith's books and learned from his experiences.

And still he wrote and published. Throughout the next decade or so, as Captain Standish and his companions were trying their own hands at "fear and love" with the Indians, more volumes appeared under Captain Smith's name: two guidebooks for young mariners, a practical handbook "for unexperienced planters of New England, or anywhere"—and the two heftier books for which he would be most remembered, the *Generall Historie of Virginia* (1624) and *The True Travels, Adventures, and Observations of Captaine John Smith* (1630).

The *Generall Historie* has enchanted and perplexed its readers for nearly 400 years; Smith himself predicted accurately that it would be "wrested, tossed, and turned as many waies as there is leaves." It was still an intermittent best seller in the 1790s, when an itinerant bookseller named Mason Locke Weems—soon to become famous for transmuting another American hero's life into legend—wrote to his supplier asking for more copies: "I coud sell you many a thousand of that curious work." And just like Weems's *Life of Washington,* Smith's *Generall Historie* is a cornerstone of American myth. To open its pages is, for American readers of the twenty-first century, to be transported into a landscape at once domestic and exotic, familiar and wholly new: a Chesapeake Bay with flocks of green parakeets, shoals of oysters the size of dinner plates, and naked warriors in birchbark canoes—and where, moreover, the fabled passage to India might lurk behind any headland, or a mountain of gold around the next bend of any muddy creek: "Here we found mighty Rocks, growing in some places above the grownd as high as the shrubby trees, and divers other quarries of divers tinctures: and divers places where the waters had falne from the high mountaines they had left a tinctured spangled skurfe that made many bare places seeme as guilded . . ."

To read the *Generall Historie* and the autobiographical *True Travels* is also to be transported into the even more convoluted and fantastic geography of Smith's own personality. Like most of literature's great egotists, Smith did not grow any humbler or more tactful as he grew older. Moreover, by the time he sat down to recount his adventures and accomplishments in full, there were few left to refute them: of the hundred original settlers of Jamestown, only one other man survived. ("And I only am escaped alone to tell thee.") The *Generall Historie* is an unwieldy, episodic text, recounted by multiple narrators, yet all of them speak with Smith as their controlling ventriloquist; the book bursts at its seams with jealousy, politics, ambition, self-aggrandizement. In other words, perhaps more than any other "American" book of its century, certainly more than the dry-mouthed religious tractates of the New England Puritans, it foreshadowed much that would come after it, from Twain and Melville to Barth and Pynchon. It stands at the beginning of American literature much as *Don Quixote* does at the beginning of Spanish.

Not much is known about Smith's life in his final years—imagine the task of a historian trying to trace a John Smith in the documentary record!—but we can imagine some of its details well enough: the furious scratching of a pen, the bachelor's garret, and less and less welcome visits of supplication to the good and the great. His life, and writings, end with two last, failing strokes of the pen: the cross-shaped mark with which he feebly signed his will in 1631. A more fitting epitaph may be found in a curious poem that appears in the front matter of his final book, *Advertisement for Unexperienced Planters,* which lay fresh on the booksellers' stalls as its author lay dying:

> Aloofe, aloofe, and come no near,
>   the dangers doe appeare;
> Which if my ruine had not beene
>   you had not seene:
> I onely lie upon this shelfe
>   to be a marke to all
>   which on the same might fall,
> That none may perish but my selfe.

Bibliography: Philip L. Barbour, ed., *The Complete Works of Captain John Smith (1580–1631) in Three Volumes* (Williamsburg, VA, 1986); *The Three Worlds of Captain John Smith* (Boston, 1964). Karen Ordahl Kupperman, *The Jamestown Project* (Cambridge, MA, 2007). J. A. Leo Lemay, *The American Dream of Captain John Smith* (Charlottesville, VA, 1991). David A. Price, *Love and Hate in Jamestown* (New York, 2003). Captain John Smith, *Writings, with Other Narratives of Roanoke, Jamestown, and the First English Settlement of America* (New York, 2007).

ADAM GOODHEART

1630

John Winthrop explains the bonds of community

The City upon a Hill

In 1630, John Winthrop gave a speech that has continued to reverberate through American history to this day. "For we must consider that we shall be as a city upon a hill; the eyes of all people are upon us," Winthrop said, thereby giving life to the enduring myth of America as a beacon and an example to the rest of the world. His words have been echoed by leaders throughout American history, from John Adams to John F. Kennedy to Ronald Reagan, who lifted the phrase "city upon a hill" wholesale in his farewell address.

At the time Winthrop delivered his sermon, it got little attention beyond the small audience of Puritans for whom it was intended. Historians cannot say with certainty where the speech was given, whether in England before Winthrop embarked with his fleet for the New World, or else aboard the *Arbella,* the flagship that carried him there. Winthrop had been chosen as leader of an expedition of Puritans who sought to create a holy community in the New World of America, far removed from the heresies and moral corruption of England. Nearly 400 years later, Winthrop's speech has an aura more mythical than political, in that it was an attempt to define what sort of community theirs would be before it had even been established; it exhorted the emigrants to embrace their roles in making that community a "model of Christian Charity."

The Puritans of 1630 were a deeply religious group whose theological roots stretched back to the continental Protestant Reformation of the 1500s. Intensely Protestant, they believed that the English Reformation had not gone far enough in divorcing the Church of England from the structure and tenets of Roman Catholicism, and they were particularly disappointed in the hierarchical organization of the Church of England, for they firmly believed that while secular leaders were accountable to God, they were so alongside the church, and not through it.

The Anglican bishops and their allies within the monarchy did not fail to understand that the doctrines the Puritans espoused posed a threat to their power and to the fundamental hierarchy of society. To do away with the traditional network of bishops that controlled the churches locally according to the monarch's commands would be to remove essential scaffolding that reinforced the status quo. Persecution of Puritans therefore grew increasingly harsh during the early 1600s; one layman had his property confiscated, his ear cut off, his nose slit, and his forehead branded with the initials "S. S.," which stood for "sewer of sedition." When in 1629 Charles I dissolved Parliament, its many Puritan members suddenly found themselves without a political voice or any means by which to bring about their desired reforms.

It was under these circumstances that, in the same year, John Winthrop and other wealthy Puritan friends obtained a charter from King Charles I for the Massachusetts Bay Colony. Although it was nominally a commercial venture—the Massachusetts Bay Company—the stockholders viewed the colony as a political and religious refuge in the New World. In August of that year the stockholders signed the Cambridge Agreement, by which the emigrating stockholders bought out the nonemigrating stockholders, thereby ensuring that they could exercise local control unencumbered by ties to a board in London. In this way, they guaranteed that the Massachusetts Bay Company would be a self-governing colony, accountable only to the king. John Winthrop was to be the governor.

Winthrop was born in 1588 to a wealthy landowning family in Groton, Suffolk, England. While in his younger years he professed an interest in entering the clergy—having caught the Puritan fever early in life—ultimately he followed in his father's footsteps to study law at Gray's Inn. He returned to Groton as a justice of the peace, where he presided over the manorial court and busied himself with raising a growing brood of children. His first two wives died quickly and young; in his third wife, Margaret Tyndall, he found a soul mate with whom he could share the uniquely Puritan struggle of being in the world but not of it. He and Margaret, like their Puritan brethren, were convinced that God would bring down his wrath on England for its heresies; they saw evidence of God's displeasure in the poverty and unemployment that resulted from a depression in the textile industry. Indeed, Winthrop's own wealth declined, and he was forced to leave his family and move to London, where he took the more lucrative position of lawyer in the Court of Wards, an archaic institution that did little more than deprive widows and orphans of their rightful inheritance.

In London, Winthrop found his personal faith and integrity increasingly irreconcilable with the worldly corruption he daily encountered, and he badly missed his wife and children. Yet he and other Puritans in London persevered in their hope for reform, struggling, through Parliament, to punish sin and bring about purifying change. With the dissolution of Parliament in 1629, the situation came to a head and the movement for relocation to the New World gained serious momentum. Initially, Winthrop was hesitant to join the venture, let alone lead it; he was, after all, emphatically *not* a separatist, and felt it his duty to reform what was instead of engender what ought to be. He did not want to escape. At the same time, the situation in England had become untenable. Without Parliament, there was no vehicle for change. The economy was weak. Moreover, three of his sons had come of age, and with his gifts to them Winthrop's property holdings had shrunk considerably. Worse, one of his sons was drifting off a moral course, and Winthrop believed that living in a religious community might set him straight. In this context, Winthrop's friends were ultimately able to convince him that he would be more effective in New England than he could possibly be at home. And so he accepted the role of governor of a holy community that would not, in Winthrop's mind, be a refuge as much as an example, a "city on a hill" that could demonstrate to England the great possibilities inherent in a society shaped according to Puritan ideals.

The Winthrop Fleet of 1630, the largest ever assembled to carry Englishmen overseas, consisted of 700 passengers on eleven ships. It was an entirely different population from that of previous expeditions, which had comprised groups of young men seeking economic success in distant markets. Now there were both families and individuals of all ages, and about half of the emigrants were women. While most emigrating were driven by religious zeal, Winthrop was careful to recruit others according to profession; it would be necessary to have carpenters, doctors, blacksmiths, and teachers alike for the success of any new community.

Whether his sermon was given onshore or under sail, Winthrop had important questions to answer and challenges to address in "Model of Christian Charity," and his words truly announced the beginning of a historical and cultural movement; over the next ten years, more than 20,000 English emigrants would follow. The Puritans migrating to the New World believed that they were a part of a pact with God to create a new holy community. Their exodus gave them the opportunity to form a state and society that would evolve according to their own beliefs, freed from the shackles of the tradition and hierarchy they so detested. Yet, as the Anglicans knew, those shackles were also structural supports, and without them, a group of individuals who believed in spiritual freedom and adherence to individual conscience could fall to ruin in their efforts to create a viable community. And while a unified society was of paramount importance to Puritans anywhere, it would be of particular urgency in the rugged wilderness of the New World, where hopeful expeditions had met defeat in the past.

Winthrop did not attempt to define a practical, tangible strategy for success, and for good reason. While the emigrating Puritans were in agreement that religion and society in contemporary England were both heretical and intolerable, they had not achieved a coherent vision of what institutions and statutes should regulate their new society. For Winthrop to impose his own vision on individuals who held their own opinions might have engendered the very divisiveness he was trying to avoid. Instead of presenting a tactical plan for success, then, in "Christian Charity" Winthrop delineated the moral framework within which the Puritans must operate in order not only to succeed but to *survive*—a framework that emphasized the values of community, charity, and love.

Speaking directly to the diverse members of the expedition, Winthrop began his sermon by attempting to explain why God made all men different, and from these reasons, he argued, stemmed important implications for their new community. The first reason, according to Winthrop, was "to hold conformity with the rest of His works, being delighted to show forth the glory of His wisdom in the variety and difference of the creatures." Diversity, then, is inherently superior to uniformity as a reflection of all God's parts.

The second reason for diversity, Winthrop continued, was so that God "might have more occasion to manifest the work of His Spirit: first upon the wicked in moderating and restraining them, so that the rich and mighty should not eat up the poor, nor the poor and despised rise up against their superiors and shake off their yoke." With this reason, Winthrop not only set a moral compass for acceptable behavior but also presented, as God's will, mutual respect among the classes—the respect necessary for an orderly society. He himself would live up to this ideal; later, when a poor man was caught stealing from his woodpile, Winthrop chose not to punish him but to allow him to take what wood he needed so that he wouldn't have to steal—that is, *sin*—again. Here was set a precedent for social responsibility; here, too, though couched in religious terms, was articulated the policy of mutual respect between all people necessary for the survival of any nation.

In the next portion of his sermon Winthrop continues to examine the role of the individual in relation to the community, particularly with regard to wealth and its stewardship. He does so in the classic style of Puritan sermons—via a series of anticipated objections and corresponding answers, leading to his assertion that prosperous Puritans have a responsibility to share their riches with needy members of the community, for the sake of the community as a whole. While excessive wealth can lead one away from God, Winthrop contended, wealth can also help build the religious state. This argument seems to be in part a justification for the creation of wealth—a practical necessity in the New World. If individual wealth is a source of the "Common Good," then prosperity has a rightful place in a religious society. Central to Winthrop's argument, however, is the idea that sharing wealth ought to be done not according to law but according to the all-important ideals of love. A community is made up of parts of a body, Winthrop said; love forms the ligaments that hold the body together.

Thus Winthrop set forth his vision for the Puritan's new holy community in terms of moral duty. If the Puritans worked according to that formulation, he concluded in his sermon, they might form a fruitful holy community, one based on contract and consent, on mutual love and respect among all members. Their community would be the "city upon a hill" that Winthrop took directly from the Gospel, borrowing from Christ's statement in Matthew 5:14: "Ye are the light of the world. A city that is set on an hill cannot be hid."

It is this last metaphor for which Winthrop's sermon is most famous, more so than for his emphasis on the importance of community, charity, and love. This is largely due to its role as forerunner to and justification for American exceptionalism—the belief that the American nation is categorically superior to others in its promise of hope and opportunity, in its balance of public and private interests, and in its constitutionally proclaimed and protected ideals. American exceptionalism, or the vision of the United States as Winthrop's "city on a hill," an example to the world, has been evoked throughout American history: as a fundamental rationale of the Revolution, as justification for Manifest Destiny in the 1840s and again in the 1860s for expansion outside North America. In recent times, American exceptionalism was the moral engine during the Cold War, and it functioned also in the "war against terror." From John F. Kennedy to Walter Mondale to Michael Dukakis to Wesley Clark, leaders have repeatedly paid Winthrop's metaphor the compliment of imitation. Consider George H. W. Bush's "thousand points of light," or Ronald Reagan's "shining city on a hill," which differed from Winthrop's only because it was now "shining."

The further in time from 1630, the less understood Winthrop's context becomes, and the more malleable his ideas grow to be. In "Model of Christian Charity," John Winthrop did not intend to coin a slogan for a nation that did not yet exist, and he explicitly acknowledged something that later leaders have often neglected or ignored in their echoing words—the possibility of failure on the world's stage. With the "eyes of the world upon [them]," he warned, if they failed they would be "made a story and a by-word through the world." The mission of his sermon, wherever it was given, was urgent and immediate: to set the moral guidelines by which a holy community might exist and thrive in an untamed wilderness, far from familiar faces, landscapes, and traditions. In the balance they allow between community and individual, these ethical parameters would be essential, first and foremost, to survival; after that, God willing, they might form the foundations for the "city on a hill."

Bibliography: Marc Aronson, *John Winthrop, Oliver Cromwell, and the Land of Promise* (New York, 2004). Francis J. Bremer, *John Winthrop: America's Forgotten Founding Father* (New York, 2003). Edmund S. Morgan, *The Puritan Dilemma* (New York, 2007). Larry Witham, *A City Upon a Hill: How Sermons Changed the Course of American History* (New York, 2008).

ELIZABETH WINTHROP

1643

Roger Williams finds *A Key into the Language of America*

A NEARER NEIGHBOR TO THE INDIANS

In 1643, Roger Williams published a well-named book, *A Key into the Language of America,* that continues to find new life as readers encounter its subtleties, delights, and irrepressible humanity. At a time of extreme opinions and extreme ignorance about the New World, this refreshingly realistic work may have done more to explain the first years of settlement than any of the denser theological tracts for which New England was famous—and which Williams was also known to write. On the surface, it was a grammar of sorts, explicating familiar phrases spoken by Narragansett Indians. But more than that, it offered a fascinating window into the daily encounters between the very different peoples now living in close proximity in New England. In its quirky way, it can also be seen as a forerunner to the long tradition of works by iconoclasts experiencing nature, from Thoreau to Al Gore. The underlying assumption of the *Key*—that natives mattered—sounded a most unusual note in early American history, and set a distant precedent for the clamorous celebration of diversity that we now take for granted. As Williams discovered, the best way to get at the basic truths of America was to talk with—and more important, listen to—the original Americans themselves.

Only thirty-nine at the time the book was published, Williams had already achieved the two things for which he is most famous, the settlement of Providence in 1636, after his banishment from Massachusetts, and the founding of the first Baptist congregation in America in 1638. Each stemmed from his talent for controversy. He had grown up in London, and had attended Cambridge University, displaying an unusual flair for languages (a facility he shared with his friend John Milton). Despite a well-assured future in England, he shared in the broad Puritan dissent of the moment and emigrated to New England, arriving in Boston in early 1631. Because of his scholarly reputation (few Puritans could speak other languages; Williams spoke at least four), he was offered the ministry of the Boston church shortly after his arrival, but he rejected it because of its insufficient independence from the Church of England. An eternal wanderer, he moved to Salem, then to Plymouth, then back to Salem, where he enraged Massachusetts authorities with a steady drumbeat of criticism, targeting not only their combination of church and civil powers (he felt the two should be separate) but also their way of treating natives. His persistent questions went the to heart of the Puritan errand, by wondering if they were all there for truly spiritual reasons, or because of the usual greed for land and wealth. At the heart of this religious debate was an anthropological one—if the natives were reasoning human beings with souls, then their possessions could not be taken from them and they were to be treated with respect and due process.

An early manuscript he wrote on Anglo-Indian relations no longer exists, but it sufficiently annoyed John Winthrop that Williams was called to account for his multiple heresies and banished from the colony in 1635. Eager to avoid arrest, Williams fled into the wilderness in the dead of winter. He ultimately found his way south to Narragansett Bay, where he quickly established friendly relations with local natives (Narragansetts) and purchased a large tract of land from them, known as the Providence Plantations. The fact that the land was purchased by contract, at a price deemed fair by the Narragansetts, was only one of many ways that Williams managed to continue to irritate the Massachusetts authorities, even from his new home beyond the pale.

Empowered by his new friendships with the natives, Williams soon began offering land to fellow dissenters equally committed to his radical notion of religious toleration, which he called "Liberty of Conscience" or "Soul Liberty." These early experiments in communal living set an important precedent, enshrining the principle that worship cannot be forced upon people, and inaugurating a far purer form of democracy than America had yet seen. His decision to embrace Baptist principles sprang from a similar open-mindedness—he considered that all state-sanctioned baptisms were corrupt and that worshippers needed to start anew, baptizing themselves. Call it what you will—naïveté or arrogance—but Williams was not a man to accept quietly the pieties of the past.

From the time of his arrival in the place he named Providence, Williams pondered the natives deeply, both as a practical necessity (they helped him to survive) and also because they appealed to his natural interest in language and the human condition. He spent more time with them, perhaps, than any other Englishman of the first generation, and certainly more than any other Cambridge alumnus. Like most anthropologists, he reveled in the difficulty of his task: "My souls desire was to do the natives good, and to that end to have their language, which I afterwards printed . . . God was pleased to give me a painful Patient spirit to lodge with them, in their filthy smoke holes (even while I lived at Plymouth and Salem) to gain their tongue." But he seems to have loved those filthy smoke holes at the same time, and he forged genuine, lifelong attachments to the natives, who offered him a literal path out of the wilderness. Throughout his long life he was an honest broker with them—a claim that is difficult to make about most of the original settlers.

A Key into the Language of America was published only seven years after his ordeal of banishment, and in some ways seems to have proceeded from it. If nothing else, it made tangible how much Williams had learned in a short time. In thirty-two chapters and across 205 pages, Williams poured out everything he knew about the Narragansetts. The chapters follow a certain organic logic—the book begins with salutations, then moves to eating, entertainment, and sleep, then covers a wide range of daily topics before ending with sickness, death, and burial. It is as much a study of culture as of language, and he interpolates his observations in between lists of vocabulary words and furtive little poems. Like most first-time authors, he diminished his efforts, saying that he had written the book during his sea voyage to England ("I drew the materials in a rude lumpe at sea"). But it is clear that a great deal of effort went into the *Key,* and many years of hard experience.

Williams opened with an inquiry into the origins of the natives, a matter of debate in Europe, where some savants thought that they might be related to ancient races like the Greeks or the Jews (Williams inclined to the latter belief, because Indian males displayed a trait that seemed Hebraic to him—specifically, they wanted to be as far from their wives as possible during menstruation). As he meditated on where they had come from, he lapsed into the naturalistic language that pervades his entire narrative: "Whence they came into those [parts], it seemes as hard to finde, as to finde the wellhead of some fresh Streame, which running many miles out of the Countrey to the salt Ocean, hath met with many mixing Streames by the way. They say themselves, that they have sprung and growne up in that very place, like the very trees of the wildernesse." From that felicitous starting point, we learn everything we could possibly want to know about the aboriginals—the way they eat, the way they clothe themselves, the way they court, and the way that they interact with the natural world enveloping them—a world just then beginning to recede before the onslaught of civilization, though no one, including Williams, knew that at the time. Still, a faintly elegiac tone pervades the *Key,* as if the act of "discovering" America had somehow ruined it as well. Through Williams, we learn of the natives' extraordinary physical grace and hardihood (they seem not to feel the cold, and can walk hundreds of miles on tiny amounts of food). He observes further that they avoid the extremes of gluttony and drunkenness to which the English often fall victim. We learn that there are many different types of aborigines, just as there are different kinds of English, some "sober and grave," others "Rude and Clownish." There are complicated inter-Indian relationships (the Narragansetts fear the "Tree-Eaters," a neighboring tribe whose members occasionally ate men when they ran out of bark). They love celebrations, and family gatherings, and games (including a form of football). In a word, they are human.

As he wrote about the natives, Williams also inevitably passed judgment on his own kind. Without quite calling attention to the fact, much of the *Key* is a protest against the shabby treatment that the natives had been receiving from the English. Another book from 1643, about Massachusetts, entitled *New Englands First Fruits,* painted the Indians as utterly devoid of "civility" and at an "infinite distance from Christianity." Williams went very far in the opposite direction. He admired all of the aspects of their civilization, including the fact that it *was* a civilization. He praised their religion, an elaborate belief system premised on living in harmony with natural surroundings (native children could name many of the stars). He praised their communitarian government. And he praised their innate sense of ethics, and the kindness to strangers that he had experienced firsthand.

To a striking degree, Williams also found in the Indians the businesslike qualities that Englishmen prided themselves on. The Narragansetts liked to hear the news, they kept their promises, they kept their appointments with him, and they understood very well the concept of property. As Williams wrote, "The Natives are very exact and punctuall, in the bounds of their Lands, belonging to this or that Prince or People." This completely refuted the argument, advanced by John Winthrop and most of the others, that America was a *vacuum domicilium,* a gigantic empty space that all Europeans were free to expand into as they saw fit. This most humanistic argument culminated with a rather profound point, generally at odds with what most of Christendom was saying at the time: "Nature knowes no difference between Europe and Americans in blood, birth, bodies, &c. God having of one blood made all mankind" (Acts 17:26).

Other political arguments are hidden like barbs inside the volume's seemingly innocent grammatical phrases. In subtle ways, the *Key* is a feminist book. In numerous places Williams expresses his admiration for the courage and physical strength of native women, who work as hard or harder than the men and never complain under any circumstances, including childbirth. It also pulses with egalitarianism, as when, in a seemingly innocent meditation on the fur trade, Williams takes a perverse delight in inverting the idea of luxury: "What treasures are hid in some parts of America, and in our New English parts, how have foule hands (in smoakie houses) the first handling of those Furres which are after worne upon the hands of Queens and heads of Princes?"

From a linguist's perspective, the book is infinitely rich as well. Umberto Eco could hardly ask for a more postmodern document than this premodern celebration of the cacophony that ensues when different people talk at each other in the middle of nowhere. There are texts within texts, poems reflecting on what has just been said, winking asides to the reader, and what seem to be encoded suggestions within the vocabulary lists. In other words, it is a reader's delight, offering tantalizing paths through a wilderness that was as linguistic as it was physical.

More than almost any document from seventeenth-century New England, with the possible exceptions of Winthrop's *Model of Christian Charity* and Bradford's history of Plymouth, the *Key* enjoyed a long afterlife. As Williams hoped, it was used in the simple way it was intended, by the missionaries and traders who came after him. Even in the twentieth century, a copy was carried by an explorer of remote Labrador.

Recent research into the *Key* suggests another legacy as well. It is very possible that the state of Rhode Island would not exist if Williams had not written this book. At the time he drove it through the press, in the summer of 1643, Williams was in London fighting desperately for official recognition of the colony he was trying to found—a colony that was in jeopardy because of new encroachments by Massachusetts and Connecticut, each eager to claim the desirable place he had found (and, by so doing, to suppress the free-form experiment he had launched). The *Key*'s appearance delighted the crucial powers in London charged with regulating colonial affairs, and led directly to a patent legitimizing the Providence Plantations once and for all. This patent was a ringing victory for Williams in his fight to keep Massachusetts at bay, but it was even more. The new patent contained no rules for religious worship and set a crucial precedent for toleration, amplified again in 1663 when Rhode Island received a royal charter (again, with help from Williams), and amplified one more time in 1791 when the First Amendment was added to the Constitution by founders who were quite familiar with Williams's example.

The *Key* was printed by a Londoner named Gregory Dexter, who migrated to Providence a year later. All in all, it was very much a Rhode Island production. In fact, one could argue that the book created the place as much as the place created the book. By proclaiming that Indians were as legitimate as Europeans, Williams had ensured that Rhode Island would be as legitimate as Massachusetts—a claim that would have seemed outlandish only a year earlier. Through his words, and those of the Narragansetts, he had given new expression to several new languages at once, including the language of democracy. One of the phrases in the Providence patent still resonates. Explaining why they had granted him his colony, the members of Parliament praised Williams for creating a "neerer neighborhood" with the other people he was living among. To create a nearer neighborhood remains a worthy aspiration.

Williams never expected his little grammar to serve as a final statement, of course. He wrote, "A little key may open a Box, where lies a bunch of keys." But it was a most important beginning, all the same. As he encountered it, the language of America turned out to be the language of Americans—Native Americans. They had voices, and words, and it turned out to be quite possible to hear them. Indeed, we can still hear them, thanks to the excellence of Williams's translations. Perhaps it is fitting to close with his words, and those of the Narragansetts he enjoyed a lifelong conversation with, presented exactly as they appeared in the *Key:*

> Kunnúnni: *Have you seene me?*
>
> Kunnúnnous: *I have seene you.*
>
> Taubot mequaun namêan: *I thank you for your kind remembrance.*

Bibliography: Jonathan Beecher Field, "A Key for the Gate: Roger Williams, Parliament and Providence," *New England Quarterly* 80, no. 3 (September 2007): 353–382. Edwin Gaustad, *Roger Williams* (New York, 2005). *The Correspondence of Roger Williams,* ed. Glenn LaFantasie (Hanover, NH, 1988). Roger Williams, *A Key into the Language of America,* ed. Howard M. Chapin (Providence, 1936).

TED WIDMER

1666, July 10

A poet's house in Andover burns down in the middle of the night

ANNE BRADSTREET

Coming near the end of Anne Bradstreet's life (she would die in 1672), the trauma of losing her house stood as a coda, a grim echo of the trauma of thirty-six years earlier, when she saw the desolate landscape of Massachusetts for the first time. The young Anne, raised in the comfort of an English noble house, had arrived on the *Arbella* in 1630 with her parents and her husband, Simon Bradstreet. We have only a taut account of how she felt upon arrival, the tautness speaking both to her Puritan discipline and to the temptation to break out: "I found a new world and new manners, at which my heart rose. But after I was convinced it was the way of God, I submitted to it and joined to the church of Boston."

Submission was a mental posture that could be summoned with some regularity, though not without some visible effort on Bradstreet's part. After the Andover fire, she would once again call up this commendable state of mind, chiding herself for her attachment to an earthly dwelling, when her true home ought to be somewhere else:

> Thou hast an house on high erect,
> Framed by that mighty Architect . . .
> It's purchased and paid for too
> by Him who hath enough to do.
> A price so vast as is unknown
> Yet by His gift is made thine own.

The heavenly home is not only palatial, it is apparently paid for in full, ready for occupancy. Only the most benighted would fail to see what a great bargain this is, what a real estate bonanza.

There is no awkwardness about the economic language here: it is confident, almost casual, reflexive in its directness. It seems second nature to Bradstreet: she has used it to address her father ("My stock's so small I know not how to pay,/My bond remains in force unto this day; . . ./Such is my debt I may not say forgive,/But as I can, I'll pay it while I live"), and she has used it to address her husband ("Thy love is such I can no way repay,/The heavens reward thee manifold, I pray"). Max Weber needs no better proof for his thesis that there is a deep consonance between two forms of rationality: between the "Protestant ethic" on the one hand, keeping tabs with God's tally sheets, and the "spirit of capitalism" on the other hand, keeping tabs with tally sheets more mundane. The "Puritan outlook" was nothing less than the "cradle of the modern economic man," Weber writes. Anne Bradstreet is modern in just that way as she literally counts her blessings amid her losses.

But she is modern in other ways as well—not least in her vigorous presence among twentieth-century poets. Adrienne Rich, who wrote the foreword to the Belknap edition of Bradstreet's work, clearly sees her as kin, forebear, feminist *avant la lettre.* John Berryman incorporates her seventeenth-century idiom into his *Homage to Mistress Bradstreet.* He is especially struck by the phrase "at which my heart rose," which he repeats several times in his poem. The rising heart, that unruly organ, is indeed a force to reckon with, not to be put down by any cost-benefit analysis. And its rising can take a variety of forms. In "Verses Upon the Burning of Our House," it seems to surge up in a field of vision that continues to hold the past in its gaze, an eye that cannot adjust, cannot shift to the present. In the space where the house no longer is, the house as it once was still stands, kept by that stubborn eye, a counterfactual imagining that flies in the face of any reality principle:

> When by the ruins oft I past
> My sorrowing eyes aside did cast,
> And here and there the places spy
> Where oft I sat and long did lie:
> Here stood that trunk, and there that chest,
> There lay that store I counted best.

The home in heaven might be grand, but the earthly abode was lived-in, and it is lived-in still as the sorrowing eyes are moved to recall it, to linger over its familiar objects, if only in this ghostly form.

Bradstreet's Puritan discipline is perpetually at risk from such ghostly ruptures. And nowhere are they more ghostly than in the poems about her grandchildren, Elizabeth, Anne, and Simon, dead at the respective ages of one year, three
years seven months, and one month and one day. Of Simon's death, Bradstreet
writes:

> No sooner came, but gone, and fall'n asleep,
> Acquaintance short, yet parting caused us weep;
> Three flowers, two scarcely blown, the last i' th' bud,
> Cropt by th' Almighty's hand; yet is He good.
> With dreadful awe before Him, let's be mute,
> Such was His will, but why, let's not dispute,
> With humble hearts and mouths put in the dust,
> Let's say He's merciful as well as just.

The doctrinal belief in God's mercy and justice is indeed dutifully stated, but it
is also qualified (or even ironized) by the thrice-repeated injunction—"let's be
mute," "let's not dispute," and "let's say"—a visible sign of just how *un*self-evident
that belief is, what hard work is needed to keep it going. Mercy and justice seem
awfully far-fetched when the punishing presence of God is so near, so tangible,
and so arbitrary in its executions, when it is an actual hand, caught in the act of
"cropping," swooping down and snipping off the bud.

With God dramatized and physicalized in this way—as a synecdoche, a
hand—bodily demise is a fate one submits to. And, in the early Massachusetts
Bay Colony, bodily demise was in fact on everyone's mind, not just Bradstreet's.
"There is not a house where there is not one dead, and some houses many,"
Thomas Dudley, Bradstreet's father, wrote back to England soon after his arrival.
Bradstreet, walking with a limp, fearful of childbirth, and suffering often from
ill heath, is eloquent on the afflictions of the body and the all-powerful, all-
consuming grip they exert on the mind: "When sorrows had begirt me round, / And
pains within and out, / When in my flesh no part was found." Bodily existence
here is a prison with no respite, no exit. This is a body in the wilderness, in the
colonies, laboring under newly primitive conditions, almost an instance of what
Giorgio Agamben calls "bare life." Bradstreet does take this bodily form in some
of her poems, but she is also something more: an Englishwoman, growing up in a
noble house with a library, and writing in the highly literate culture of the seventeenth century. Her body, for that reason, can be rhetorically full-dressed as well
as physically precarious, not only helplessly ailing but also artfully adorned. In a
poem to her husband—one of three written while he was "absent upon public
employment"—Bradstreet makes a case for marital congress based on the metaphor of the human anatomy: "How stayest thou there, whilst I at Ipswich lie? / So
many steps, head from the heart to sever, / If but a neck, soon should we be together." In another poem she makes the same plea, using an even more elaborate
conceit:

> As loving hind that (hartless) wants her deer,
> Scuds through the woods and fern with hark'ning ear,

> Perplext, in every bush and nook doth pry,
> Her dearest deer, might answer ear or eye;
> So doth my anxious soul, which now doth miss
> A dearer dear (far dearer heart) than this.

The high gloss of this poem—its incessant punning on heart and hart, deer and dear—makes it clear that Bradstreet was writing in the wake of Donne, of Shakespeare, and of the Elizabethan era in general. Her favorite poet, to be sure, was the French Calvinist Guillaume du Bartas (whose *La Sepmaine, ou Creation du monde* was translated by Joshua Sylvester as *Bartas: his devine weekes and workes*). But she was also heir to the English Renaissance, part of the transatlantic print circuit of the long seventeenth century. The first edition of her poems, *The Tenth Muse,* came out in London in 1650, the manuscript brought there by John Wood-bridge, her brother-in-law, and published by Stephen Bowtell, the bookseller who in 1647 had also published *Simple Cobler of Aggawam,* by her Ipswich neighbor, Nathaniel Ward. *The Tenth Muse* was listed in the bookseller's catalogue along with Phineas Fletcher, "Mr. Milton's Poems," Walton's *Compleat Angler,* Sir Thomas Browne's *Religio Medici,* and "Mr. Shaksper's poems."

These—and not just the New England hymnals—were Bradstreet's models and peers. Her prosody (not overly experimental in any case) reflects this dual heritage: it features the pentameter rhymed couplet as well as the four-foot-three-foot hymn-book meter. She is "English," we might say, not in one sense but in two, split between the mother country and her "daughter" in the New World. In "A Dialogue between Old England and New," Bradstreet's allegiance is clearly with the daughter, the Puritan vanguard, issuing this stern warning to her back-sliding parent: "Let's bring Baal's vestments forth to make a fire, . . . / And let their names consume, but let the flash / Light Christendom, and all the world to see / We hate Rome's whore with all her trumpery." This is the voice of the church militant. Bradstreet can speak in its accents, but she also has others, and she can be "English" in ways that are genealogical rather than adversarial, as in her elegy to Sir Philip Sidney, or her poem in honor of Queen Elizabeth. Elizabeth had died in 1603, seven years before Bradstreet was born. But the poet is still determined to pay this tribute:

> Since time was time, and man unmanly man,
> Come show me such a Phoenix if you can . . .
> Was ever people better ruled than hers?
> Was ever land more happy freed from stirs?
> Was ever wealth in England more abound?
> Her victories in foreign coasts resound;
> Ships more invincible than Spain's, her foe,
> She wracked, she sacked, she sunk his Armado . . .

The reign of Elizabeth I was notable for many monumental deeds, notably the Act of Supremacy of 1559, which established the independence of the Church of England, severing its ties to Rome, affirming the queen as its supreme governor. Though vehement elsewhere against "Rome's whore," Bradstreet is silent here on this important sectarian triumph. What she emphasizes instead are the military exploits of this monarch as well as the happiness of her subjects. Elizabeth's shining place is not in Puritan history but in world history, for her reign is, above all, the reign of a capable woman, with large implications for half of humankind: "She hath wiped off th' aspersion of her sex, / That women wisdom lack to play the rex."

When it comes to capable women in world history, though, Elizabeth is not alone. She, in turn, takes her place in a long genealogy, a line of female monarchs, some pagan, in power well before the birth of Christianity. What is the relation between pagan history and Christian history? Bradstreet is surprisingly nonsectarian on this point. In her long historical poem "The Four Monarchies," she pays tribute to one pagan queen, the Assyrian Semiramis, using the same language she had used for Elizabeth: "She like a brave *Virago* played the *Rex* / And was both shame and glory of her Sex." Semiramis had killed her husband Ninus to secure the throne, but Bradstreet does not fuss over this too much, only noting, "She flourishing with *Ninus* long did reign, / Till her Ambition caus'd him to be slain." What others might have considered a heinous crime is passed over lightly, with the act of slaying oddly displaced from Semiramis herself, attributed only to "her ambition," or even more forgivably, to her loyalty to her first husband, Menon, slain by Ninus, and "to seek revenge for Menon's fall." This neutral judgment turns into a decided sense of awe as Bradstreet proceeds to give the exact, numerical dimensions of ancient Babylon, Semiramis's city, located in present-day Iraq:

> With Towers and Bulwarks made of costly stone,
> Quadrangle was the form it stood upon.
> Each square was fifteen thousand paces long,
> An hundred gates it had of mettal strong:
> Three hundred sixty foot the walls in height,
> Almost incredible, they were in breadth
> Some writers say six Chariots might affront
> With great facility, march safe upon't:
> About the Wall a ditch so deep and wide,
> That like a River long it did abide.
> Three hundred thousand men here day by day
> Bestow'd their labour, and receiv'd their pay.

It would be wrong to say that Bradstreet is singing the praises of Semiramis; it would be equally wrong to say that she is censuring her. In this meticulous and respectful invocation of a great Mesopotamian city, Puritan literature is much more capacious than modern readers might think, attentive to ancient cultures, mindful of the long history of the world in a way that has probably become alien, a measure of what has been lost. Much is to be learned from that mindfulness.

Bibliography: Giorgio Agamben, *Homo Sacer: Sovereign Power and Bare Life,* trans. Daniel Heller-Roazen (Stanford, CA, 1998). John Berryman, *Homage to Mistress Bradstreet* (New York, 1956). *The Works of Anne Bradstreet,* ed. Jeannine Hensley, foreword by Adrienne Rich (Cambridge, MA, 1967). J. Kester Svendsen, "Anne Bradstreet in England: A Bibliographical Note," *American Literature* 13 (March 1941): 63–65. Max Weber, *The Protestant Ethic and the Spirit of Capitalism,* trans. Talcott Parsons (New York, 1930).

WAI CHEE DIMOCK

1670

Samuel Danforth invokes the Puritan "errand into the wilderness"

The American Jeremiad

In 1670, during a very turbulent period for the Massachusetts Bay Colony's American Puritans, the Reverend Samuel Danforth preached his Election Day Sermon, "A Brief Recognition of New England's Errand into the Wilderness." Danforth took his text from Matthew 11:7–9, where Jesus asks the people who sought out John the Baptist in the desert, "What went ye out into the wilderness to see?" As John's supporter, Jesus tells them that they went expecting to see a spectacle but they should have gone to listen to John preach the truth. As they, too, seemed to have forgotten their purpose, Danforth asked his listeners what their reasons were for going into the wilderness. He reminded them that for decades they had embraced their spiritual errand—but now they were succumbing to a "radical disease too tremendously growing upon us." He observed that the community was in the grip of a deadly "declension justly calling for so meet an antidote" as he had to offer. In his conclusion Danforth recalled that the first settlers had journeyed "over a vast ocean into this waste and howling wilderness," which they had transformed into God's garden. But now, he said, "the vineyard is all overgrown with thorns, and nettles cover the face thereof, and the stone wall is broken down," and there was a "certain sign of calamity." In the final pages of his sermon, Danforth implored the people to acknowledge the falling away of their faith, confess their sins, and beg for forgiveness. He warned the newly elected leaders that if they did not take religion into consideration in all of their decisions, the people would know whom to blame if the dark days were to continue. If the leaders were to heed his guidance and the people to pray for grace and salvation, Danforth assured them that God would show his favor toward them again.

Fifty years before, in 1620, William Bradford and his small colony of Protestant religious separatists, later known as the Pilgrims, had arrived in New England to found Plymouth Plantation. After facing severe hardships during their first few years, the community of survivors became so successful that, starting in 1630, thirty thousand nonseparating English Congregationalists followed to establish the Massachusetts Bay Colony in Boston. In spite of a brutal war with the Pequot people in 1636 and many internal conflicts over theology and property, the Congregationalists—who were called Puritans by their enemies—built a thriving colony that, in the face of decades of persecution and war in England, attracted thousands more to Massachusetts between 1635 and 1660.

In 1649, the Puritan dissenters in England overthrew the monarchy and executed King Charles I. Oliver Cromwell and the English Presbyterians ruled England until their government collapsed, allowing King Charles II to return from France and restore the monarchy in 1660. Immigration to New England accelerated again after the Puritans lost power in England, but tensions arose when the newcomers could not meet the New England church's strict standards for conversion and church membership and were denied land and voting rights, which were reserved for the converted. Such privileges were also withheld from those adult children and grandchildren of the original settlers who had not had a conversion experience. While the clergy tried to sustain the original Calvinist doctrines and principles, bitter divisions occurred and many of the older members began to demand that their offspring be granted church membership so that they, rather than outsiders, would benefit from the wealth of the colony. A rancorous synod was held in 1662, and the Half-Way Covenant doctrine was devised to allow grandchildren of the founders to be baptized even if their parents were not converted. The 1660s marked a significant transition in New England from corporate assurance and religious fervor to a decline of confidence in the churches and communities.

Throughout the 1670s and 1680s, the New England clergy followed Danforth's model by taking many of their sermon texts from the Book of Jeremiah, in which the Old Testament prophet chastised the Hebrews for their loss of religious zeal and their fall from God's favor. Twentieth-century scholars, such as Perry Miller, have called these sermons "jeremiads." Texts in this genre follow a standard formula: recollection of the community's original joy and fervor; castigation for recent and current sins and backsliding; pleas for the congregation to repent and pray for forgiveness; and assurances that God will forgive his Chosen People and restore harmony. Because the Puritans believed that the Bible and nature should both be closely studied for signs of God's intentions, they were acutely alarmed by a series of terrible events that occurred in these years: earthquakes, plagues, violent storms, explosions and fires in towns and aboard ships, murders and suicides—all providing evidence of God's anger. A few sermon titles from those decades indicate the prevailing themes and tone: "Righteousness Rained from Heaven"; "Days of Humiliation, Times of Affliction"; "The Day of Trouble Is Near"; "Nehemiah on the Wall in Troublesome Times." The most devastating event in these decades was the conflict known as King Philip's War (1674–1676). This war with the Wampanoag people, whose leader, Metacom, was known as Philip to the English, resulted in the loss of 10 percent of the population on each side, making it one of the bloodiest wars ever fought in North America.

While the jeremiads are especially valuable as indicators of the mood and direction of individual churches and communities, many other sermons were devoted to domestic themes—including marriage, the family, the rearing and instruction of children, fairness in business—as well as to a range of theological subjects. Sermons were high points in the week of the congregation. While most church members valued education and were literate, the Puritans were suspicious of all forms of human verbal expression except that found in the Bible, and they considered entertainment sinful (which led them to close the theaters in London during their reign). Thus, sermons and the discussions of them provided the only challenging intellectual stimulation in the society, and it is not surprising that the community was centered around the weekly three-hour sermons preached on Thursdays and Sundays. Members of the congregation took notes, formed study groups for discussions, and debated their minister's interpretations of the scriptures. As scholars and teachers, most ministers possessed the education and rhetorical skills to inspire congregations through their own piety, faith, and learning. Indeed, the Puritans founded Harvard College in 1636 to ensure they would have a well-educated clergy. Because the Puritans believed that people should never presume to compete with the beauty of the Bible, the Puritan clergy practiced a "plain style" designed to convey ideas clearly and without embellishment. They did, however, employ figurative language powerfully and extensively to dramatize their message.

While many Puritan sermons were published in the seventeenth century, few scholars had much interest in those printed texts until the 1930s, when Perry Miller brought his considerable analytical talents to the subject and proposed that Puritan sermons should be studied as literary art, as they offer a "way of conceiving the inconceivable, of making intelligible order out of the transition from European to American experience." For Miller, the sermons were not pedagogical tools; rather, they were dramatic narratives that enabled their audiences to form images and allegories in which they imagined themselves to be part of the unfolding of a sacred history. Miller demonstrated that, through Puritan typology, the clergy and colonial magistrates had produced a myth of America. Through their New Covenant with God, the colonists in the New World became the new Chosen People, members of a new Zion, a new Israel. The center of the Christian world no longer resided in Europe but was now in New England, where it would remain a beacon for those predestined to be converted and saved. For the Puritans, the American continent had been held in reserve by God until this evil time of corruption and persecution had emerged in Europe. God had revealed the New World to enable the exodus of his Chosen People, who would found a Christian utopia there and prepare the way for the new millennium and the return of Christ on the Last Day. The jeremiad always moves from God's wrath to reassurance because, having established a covenant with His Chosen, God would never abandon them.

In his extension and revision of Miller's research on the jeremiad, Sacvan Bercovitch has argued that in time the jeremiad ceased to be a rhetorical tool for frightening congregations into reform and became instead a ritual. From the opening of a jeremiad, listeners knew that the ending would depict a repentant congregation, reassurance of God's love, and the promise of a more zealous and more prosperous future. In Bercovitch's view, the jeremiad ritual was mainly intended to assure them that they would always triumph over sin, Satan, and their enemies. This ritual proved so effective that it did not fade away when the Puritans passed into history.

For many years, in State of the Union addresses and Fourth of July orations, American presidents have offered similar jeremiads. They follow Danforth's familiar formula: we must beware of enemies who plot to destroy us; we must acknowledge the gap between our ideals and current realities; we must reject corruption, greed, selfishness, and other sins; and finally, we must work together to restore our superiority among the world's nations. With God on our side, we shall continue the American mission and fulfill our sacred Manifest Destiny. Bercovitch points out that, as Max Weber argued early in the twentieth century, the Puritan emphasis on working hard in one's earthly calling while seeking spiritual salvation functions well with the spirit of capitalism. From early on, the Puritans had difficulty keeping God's grace and business profits separated. Those who appeared to be genuinely pious seemed to be the same people who grew wealthy. One of the Reverend Samuel Willard's sermons, "Heavenly Merchandize; or the Purchasing of TRUTH Recommended and the Selling of it Diswaded," was written to appeal to the religious pragmatism of his parishioners, who were members of what was known as the merchants' church. The Puritans might have difficulty understanding Weber's or Bercovitch's arguments; their behavior unconsciously reflected a recognition of the ways that the spiritual calling and the material calling, as they understood them, could yield heavenly and earthly rewards at the same time.

The tragic events of the Salem witchcraft trials in the summer of 1692 brought Puritan standards of judgment into question. Community leaders like Samuel Sewall were humbled by their fatal errors and the shattering results, and they began to change their religious and political thinking. By the late 1690s, there were few remnants of the fusion of religion and politics that Perry Miller described as "Federal Theology." Many elements of Puritan thought and practice would endure in American culture in more subtle forms, however—appearing, for example, in Benjamin Franklin's *Autobiography* and other works as a secular version of Puritanism.

In the two years leading up to the American Revolution, the Protestant clergy played a key role in arousing a rather indifferent populace to embrace the spirit of revolt. When the British Parliament passed the Port Bill, several clergymen held a traditional Puritan fast day and preached jeremiads invoking biblical images of the British as tools of "Satan," who had unleashed "the great Whore of Babylon" to ride her "great red dragon" upon America. Of this event, Thomas Jefferson declared: "This day of fasting and humiliation was like a shock of electricity throughout the colonies, placing every man erect." John Adams asked Abigail to urge their local ministers to preach similar jeremiads, and after the war Tories like Peter Oliver and Thomas Hutchinson attributed the success of the Revolution to the "black regiment," the dark-clothed ministers who had encouraged their congregations. During the Civil War, clergymen on both sides again employed the jeremiad to inspire support for their cause.

In the twentieth and twenty-first centuries, the jeremiad has persisted because of its effectiveness in creating mythic imagery that inspires ideals and motivates action. In 1963, in his "Address to the March on Washington for Jobs and Freedom," Reverend Martin Luther King, Jr., depicted the United States as a great country with strong religious traditions that had gone astray. He called for a return to the original ideals of social equality expressed in the Declaration of Independence, and he urged a reassertion of the American dream of freedom and equality for all men and women. Many American writers of the past hundred years adopted the jeremiad pattern to compose their stories; in *The Great Gatsby,* F. Scott Fitzgerald used it to examine the failures of the nation, as symbolized in *Gatsby* by the 1919 Chicago Black Sox scandal. From Melville to Morrison, the list of American novels and plays that follow the jeremiad form would be very long. Since the destruction of the World Trade Center at the start of this century, a host of nonfiction books have appeared that critique the failures in American society that led to that disaster and seek answers for restoring the country to an earlier stability and security. Books on the environment today also follow the formula of failure, blame, reform, and projections of a future that will fulfill original goals and ideals. Every year at Independence Day celebrations, the president and other military and political figures around the country invoke the formula of the jeremiad in remembering the courage and persistence of the Puritans and the revolutionary founders of this nation, lamenting the decline of patriotism and self-sacrifice, and holding up the promise that soon the country will recall the proper direction of its errand into the wilderness.

Bibliography: Sacvan Bercovitch, *The American Jeremiad* (Madison, WI, 1978). Samuel Danforth, "A Brief Recognition of New-Englands Errand into the Wilderness. Made in the Audience of the General Assembly of the Massachusetts Colony, at Boston in N. E. on the 11th of the third Moenth, 1670. Being the Day of Election there," in *American Sermons,* ed. Michael Warner (New York, 1999). David Hall, *The Faithful Servant: A History of New England Ministry in the Seventeenth Century* (Chapel Hill, NC, 1972). Christopher Looby, *Voicing America: Language, Literary Form, and the Origins of the United States* (Chicago, 1995). Perry Miller, *The New England Mind: From Colony to Province* (Cambridge, MA, 1939). Priscilla Wald, *Constituting America: Cultural Anxiety and Narrative Form* (Durham, NC, 1995). Michael P. Winship, *Seers of God: Puritan Providentialism in the Restoration and Early Enlightenment* (Baltimore, 1996).

EMORY ELLIOTT

1670

John Foster prints a woodcut portrait of Richard Mather

THE STAMP OF GOD'S IMAGE

A half-length likeness of Richard Mather floats off-center of a soiled surface in the woodcut portrait reputed to be the first American print. Mather (1596–1669) was a key figure in the first generation of the Puritan settlement in New England. He arrived in Boston in 1635 and soon settled in nearby Dorchester, where he would remain as pastor throughout his life. The print's creator, John Foster (1648–1681), studied at Harvard College (class of 1667) and taught grammar school in Dorchester, also his hometown, before setting up the first

John Foster, woodcut portrait of Richard Mather

printing press in Boston in 1675. Foster also worked as a mathematician and an astronomer.

The woodcut was printed on a small sheet folded in half, with four surfaces; Mather appears on one of the four. The piece of paper bearing the print is, therefore, like a small book in itself. When donated to Harvard in 1908, the sheet was bound at the front of a copy (a false imprint) of Increase Mather's biography of his father, Richard (originally published in Cambridge, Massachusetts, in 1670). The association of the woodcut with the book has led to its dating. The inclusion of small portraits was common in seventeenth-century English biographies, as in the many lives composed by Samuel Clarke, for example. Clarke reprinted Increase's biography in a collection of lives published in London in 1683, albeit without the image.

Foster used two wooden blocks in making the portrait, although the reason for this remains unknown. On the upper block, the head has been somewhat simplified, cut with almond-shaped eyes, but convincingly rendered. Advanced in age, Mather is depicted with a white beard, and he wears a black cap. The image on the lower block, constituting the sitter's torso, has been reduced to a flat, black shape, bowing outward at its top, and obliquely truncated and sharply rectilinear near its bottom. Mather holds spectacles in his right hand and a highly crosshatched small-format Bible in his left, which can be identified as such by the double columns of type on the pages—a format used for few small books besides Bibles in the seventeenth century, as Hugh Amory has noted. The formal combination of Mather's left thumb, lodged in the book, and the conjoined, twin rounds of the undersized spectacles is suggestive of male genitalia. This arrangement posits Richard Mather as patriarch, and it figures his exegetical authority as a male minister, his sanctioned skill being to penetrate and explicate the Word of God. The genital character of this grouping also alludes to the reproductive nature of printing, whether pictorial woodcuts or books.

In the biography, Increase recounts Richard's refusal to wear "the Surpless" while a young minister in England. This refusal inflects the portrait woodcut, in which, in nonconformity, he dons an abstracted black "noncoat." That is, Richard is not so much wearing a scholar's gown as he is *not wearing* the surplice. The Puritans' decision to refrain from wearing this "superstitious" Anglican vestment has been characterized by Ann Kibbey as a "nonviolent act of iconoclasm."

Richard's life is constructed, from the very beginning of the biography, as a model for the reader's imitation. Increase later comments, "He was, especially in his last Sickness, *a Pattern of Patience.*" He notes that at the time of his death Richard was reading Thomas Goodwin's treatise, *Patience and Its Perfect Work.* Thus the book Richard read during his dying hours, on patience as a virtue, reflected mirrorlike upon him. Likewise, he becomes a mirror of patience for readers of his biography—much as his image was printed in mirror reversal from woodblocks to paper. As the biography operates as a textual pattern of Richard for readers, so Richard's woodcut image functions as a pictorial pattern (an "exhibit" or "spectacle") for viewers.

Undergirding the meaning of Foster's portrait and Increase Mather's biography is the Puritan investment in a Protestantized version of the *imitatio Christi*. Although in many ways fervently anti-Catholic, English and American Puritans continued to respect selected Catholic models of thinking and devotion. They read Protestant renditions of several important Catholic devotional manuals. One of the most popular among these was *The Imitation of Christ*, traditionally attributed to Thomas à Kempis. Charles Hambrick-Stowe points out that "more than 60 editions in at least six translations of this work appeared in English before 1640, with 18 more editions before the end of the century." Puritan ministers delivered sermons and composed publications on the imitation of Christ throughout the seventeenth and into the eighteenth century. As authors of biographical literatures, such as funeral sermons, elegies, and epitaphs, they manufactured the lives of the virtuous dead, comparing them with the life of Christ. Exemplary persons "copy" Christ, or they "pattern" themselves after Christ. They "imitate" or "emulate" him. In turn, persons said to be similar to Christ act as suitable examples themselves.

The broader religious context of the Mather woodcut can be drawn by considering the fundamental connotations of both "word" (or "Word") and "image" for English and American Puritanism. Most varieties of Protestantism have been understood as cultures of the word/Word, and Protestantism has been labeled a religion of reading and writing and a religion of the book/Book. Recently scholars have begun to challenge the excesses that may attend this manner of thinking, claiming that problematic assumptions about Protestant logocentrism and iconoclasm have obscured the Protestant investment in material things, including pictures. In reacting to such untenable stereotypes, though, students of Puritan visual and material culture should be wary of overcorrection. New England Puritans often were antimaterialistic or iconoclastic. And if interested in pictures, they were also still very much devoted to texts. The woodcut portrait of Richard Mather is a compelling materialization of a multifaceted interpenetration of word and image and reading and seeing in New England Puritanism.

The scriptural basis for the Puritan understanding of the "image" is Genesis 1:26, which states that human beings were created in God's image. Christian persons, rather than man-made pictures, are described as "true images," with God as the artist to whom this work has been attributed. Randall Zachman has clarified John Calvin's development of the distinction between the "dead images" "contrived" by human hands and God's "living images," who are his people. Zachman argues that seeing living icons is, for Calvin, the equivalent of hearing the Word of God. Whereas the living image is aligned with virtue, self-negation, heavenliness, and Christian devotion, the dead image has associations of sin, selfishness, worldliness, and idolatry.

Much of Puritan theology is based upon the thinking and publications of John Calvin, and one regularly finds references to the distinction between living and dead, good and evil, and "truly" Christian and "falsely" Christian (or non-Christian) images in Puritan writings. In the 1601 tract *A Warning against the Idolatrie of the Last Times,* the English Puritan William Perkins writes, "Man is a liuing image of God, made by the very hand of God: and in this respect a thousand fold more excellent then all Images made by the hand of man." Writing almost one hundred years after Perkins, Cotton Mather (son of Increase and grandson of Richard) remained aligned with Perkins's thinking about the image. In the appendix to his 1698 funeral sermon on John Baily, *A Good Man Making a Good End*, Cotton writes, "The *Images* of the Lord JESUS CHRIST on the Wall, are not Agreeable unto a well instructed *Christian*. But instead of that, the *Christian* would fain have an *Image* of the Lord *Jesus Christ*, in the Dispositions of his own Heart & Life." Pictorial portraiture in Puritan culture, then, constitutes a vexed mixture of the living and dead image. If the Richard Mather woodcut is, in one sense, a dead image of a living image of God, it is, nevertheless, a potent stand-in for Mather and one that would have been understood as capable of reviving the image of God in those who viewed it.

How is the image of God/Christ understood to be "in" or "on" a person? Puritan ministers describe the drawing, painting, and especially printing of the image in/on the human body. The image of God/Christ is "engraven," "impressed," "imprinted," and "stamped" in/on the body (in the heart, soul, or mind). The idea of imprinting the image of God or Christ upon one's heart derives from theological commentaries on the Pauline epistles. Paul typologically redirected the ground of godly writing from tables of stone (as in the Old Testament) to writing upon the fleshy tables of the human heart (in the New Testament). Thomas Hooker, the founder of the Hartford settlement in the Connecticut Colony, published *The Paterne of Perfection* in London in 1640, which expounds on how God's image exists in human beings, before and after the Fall. The image of God remains within postlapsarian man but must be refurbished—Hooker defines salvation in terms of the recovery of the original image of God on Adam: "Looke what is spoken of renovation, the selfe same *Adam* had in creation. Now wee read that the new man is after God, as the print of the wax is after the seale; and a man does his work after a paterne, that is agreeable to it: So the stampe of Gods image was upon *Adam*, that he was agreeable to his will."

Edward Taylor, the minister and poet of Westfield, Massachusetts, employed printing and printmaking terminology to describe the image of God within himself. In one undated meditation, Taylor writes, "Am I new minted by thy Stamp indeed? / Mine eyes are dim; I cannot clearly see. / Be thou my Spectacles that I may read / Thine Image, and Inscription stampt on mee." In a meditation on Hebrews 9:11 dating to February 1696, he writes, "Hath Sin blurd all thy Print / . . . / Lord print me ore again." For Puritans such as Taylor, the image of God is considered susceptible to defacement or erasure—that is, God's "Print" may become "blurd" by sin. Among the techniques that Puritans utilized for curating the image of God in themselves were practices of self-examination and meditation. Such practices included viewing exemplary images and reading exemplary biographies. Enhanced understanding of oneself vis-à-vis God was the aim—Taylor's "Be thou my Spectacles that I may read / Thine Image, and Inscription stampt on mee."

In a section of the biography in which Increase quotes from his father's handwritten account of his own life, Richard expresses his desire that God will "imprint the memory" of one of his mercies (saving Richard and others at sea during a storm) on his and others' hearts. Increase subsequently observes that Richard, together with exemplary Christians ancient and modern, had a foreknowledge of death "imprinted on their Spirits." The reception of other sorts of Puritan objects, most notably funerary monuments, is framed in terms of writing or printing on the body. A tombstone standing in the Ancient Burying Ground in Hartford, Connecticut, explicitly relates the viewing of the object to printing and printmaking. The epitaph upon the David Gardiner tombstone (1689) incorporates the following words:

ENGRAVE THE
REMEMBRANCE OF
DEATH ON THINE
HEART WHEN AS THOV
DOST SEE HOW
SWIFTLY HOVRS
DEPART

Printing is not only the means by which the Richard Mather woodcut portrait was fashioned; cultural ideas about print-related reception structure the way in which the picture was understood. The source of this model of text, image, and memory registration—in which the sensory apparatus is taken to be a receptive, waxy surface—can be located in the writings of Plato and Aristotle. Early modern technologies of printing and printmaking invigorated these ancient notions for the Puritans. As a print registers from an archetypal block onto a piece of paper, so the example should be registered in the heart, soul, or mind of the reader or viewer. Baptized by Richard Mather and a member of his Dorchester congregation, John Foster imitated his ministerial exemplar in making the print. Pressing paper to the pattern, the memory of Mather and his virtues were printed on Foster.

Five additional impressions of the Richard Mather woodcut are known, at least three of which have been printed on paper with a "Pro Patria" watermark, datable to the late seventeenth or early eighteenth century. These later impressions are printed on single sheets, and they are cruder and heavier, lacking the fine, sharp lines and the cleaner contours of the first state. The head and shoulders do not square with the body. While the first-state impression appears to have been pulled on a press, the second-state impressions show evidence of having been "rubbed" or "spooned." Four impressions incorporate a slightly jagged, printed caption below the image, reading "Mr. Richard Mather." Whereas these impressions are not associated with Increase's biography or any other book, a fifth impression is pasted inside the front cover of a 1584 Christopher Plantin polyglot Bible, now at Harvard's Houghton Library, that once belonged to Increase Mather.

In all five second-state impressions, incised lines define the right arm and an opening in Richard's gown, and, as Gillett Griffin has pointed out, the body has been imprinted with various astrological symbols that were used in the production of almanacs. Nothing is known about who made the later impressions—Foster had died by the time they were produced. The constellation-like forms imply that, if Mather is a kind of vacuous no-body, like darkened space (a negation), he is at the same time a site for the projection of heavenly bodies, such as the planets and the stars (a fulfillment). By extension, he is a site for the projection of the images of God and Christ, the most important of all heavenly bodies to New England Puritans. The second-state impressions of the woodcut, though, also show formally the decay that informs the printing of pictures over time from the same woodblocks. Made from altered and perhaps damaged blocks, and less skillfully than the first-state impression, the later impressions portray decomposition and degradation. As such, they are pictures of the Fall. If the first state of John Foster's woodcut portrait of Richard Mather was the first image printed in the English colonies of North America, it is also a work about wanting the restoration of the first printed image of God on man.

Bibliography: Hugh Amory, *Bibliography and the Book Trades: Studies in the Print Culture of Early New England,* ed. David Hall (Philadelphia, 2005). Gillett Griffin, "John Foster's Woodcut of Richard Mather," *Printing and Graphic Arts* 7, no. 1 (February 1959). Charles Hambrick-Stowe, *The Practice of Piety: Puritan Devotional Disciplines in Seventeenth-Century New England* (Chapel Hill, NC, 1982). Ann Kibbey, *The Interpretation of Material Shapes in Puritanism: A Study of Rhetoric, Prejudice, and Violence* (Cambridge, 1986). Lillian Miller, "The Puritan Portrait: Its Function in Old and New England," in *Seventeenth-Century New England,* ed. David Hall and David Grayson Allen (Boston, 1984). Randall Zachman, *Image and Word in the Theology of John Calvin* (Notre Dame, IN, 2007).

JASON D. LaFOUNTAIN

1673

Father Marquette travels down the Mississippi

THE JESUIT RELATIONS

In May 1677 a small party of Native Americans returning from their winter hunting grounds in the Great Lakes paused at a burial site. It was the grave of the French Jesuit priest Father Marquette, who had died of disease two years earlier. According to another Jesuit, Claude Dablon, the members of this group—whom he described "savages named Kiskakons"—had known and loved Marquette, and had "been making public profession of Christianity for about ten years." God, he wrote, "put it into their hearts to remove his bones and bring them to our church at the mission of St. Ignace at missilmakinac, where those savages make their abode."

They "opened the grave, and uncovered the Body, and although the Flesh and Internal organs were all Dried up, they found it entire, so that not even the skin was in any way injured." They then "cleansed the bones and exposed them to the sun to dry; then, carefully laying them in a box of birch-bark, they set out to bring them to our mission," forming a "funeral procession" of thirty canoes. At the mission, Marquette's remains were placed in a vault in the center of the church, and Marquette became the "guardian angel" of the mission. "The savages often come to pray over his tomb," wrote Dablon. A young girl who had been baptized by Marquette fell sick. The priest prescribed, "as sole medicine," that she pray for three days at the tomb of Marquette, and before the third day she was cured. From his grave, it was believed, the priest was performing miracles.

When he died in the midst of the Canadian wilderness, Father Marquette fulfilled his life's dream. "He always entreated God that he might end his life in these laborious missions," wrote Dablon. Marquette had hoped, wrote Dablon, that like St. Francis Xavier, the founder of the Jesuit order, he "might die in the midst of the woods bereft of everything." In his death his prayers had been answered: he had "the happiness to die in a wretched cabin on the shore of lake Illinois, forsaken by all the world." As he was dying, Marquette had consciously celebrated the similarity between his end and that of St. Xavier, between his story and those of the many other saints who had preceded him into martyrdom and sanctity.

Dablon, meanwhile, celebrated Marquette's *life* in the New World, where his "gentleness had rendered him beloved by all, and made him all things to all men — a Frenchman with the French, a Huron with the Hurons, an Algonquin with the Algonquins." What Dablon did not say was that Marquette's life and death had taken place in a landscape that, by the late seventeenth century, was heavy with bones. The diseases brought by the Europeans, and the war and dislocation their presence had triggered, had spread far and wide on the North American continent.

The writings of Dablon, and of Marquette himself, are part of a massive corpus collectively known as the Jesuit Relations, the most voluminous and important written source about the seventeenth- and eighteenth-century world of Native America. There are pages and pages — seventy-three volumes in the classic edition of the texts published in the late nineteenth century — of detailed descriptions of missionary journeys, encounters and ceremonies, debates about the world beyond the living. The accounts are sometimes funny and sometimes tragic, often bizarre in form and content, and also somehow exhausting in their scope. And yet they are also full of silences and absences. If they bear witness to the process of European conquest, they are also relics of the process of representation, and silencing, through which that conquest took place. The texts powerfully embody the paradox of writing about a "New World" that never was. They say a lot about some bones and almost nothing about others.

The Jesuit Relations began as something quite banal. In 1610 the Jesuit missionaries in what was to become Canada began writing letters home to the head of the order, reporting on their deeds, their successes, and their needs. The first collection of these documents was published in France in 1632, and for the next four decades a volume was published each year. At first the Jesuit Relations were essentially collections of long letters, presented seamlessly, page after page, describing the struggles and successes of the Jesuits' missionary work. But within a few years the format began to change significantly and the texts were divided into chapters on behavior, religion, and dress.

One of the ironic miracles of the Jesuit Relations is that the desire to eliminate certain Native American practices led the missionaries to describe them in what might otherwise seem like loving detail, creating an enduring document of the world they sought to destroy. In the process, the Jesuits developed a style that combined travel writing, spiritual reflection, hagiography, and early ethnography. Though the Relations would always retain the form of letters written home to the Jesuit order, the books were in fact meant to educate and entice a more general readership with stories and descriptions of the New World. Many Jesuit missionaries took obvious pleasure in writing their accounts with humor and literary flair. They read the Relations that had come before, referred to them, and inscribed their experiences within the larger epic they felt they were a part of. And their writings became one of the major vehicles through which readers in France learned about the world on the other side of the Atlantic. The Jesuit Relations were read by Enlightenment intellectuals confronting the implications of the cultural diversity of the world, and they therefore informed the theorizing about "natural laws" pursued by Rousseau and others in the eighteenth century. In a curious twist of intellectual history, the writings of Jesuit missionaries devoted to spreading Catholicism helped propel the Enlightenment's humanist theories.

While they described journeys taken, the Jesuit Relations also helped to produce them, for in addition to interesting many French lay readers, the texts served to inspire other Jesuit priests, who pleaded with their superiors to be sent across the Atlantic to take up work in a place that seemed to nearly assure them martyrdom and therefore sanctity. The texts were part of a much longer tradition of Catholic writing about the lives of saints, and they drew directly on the traditions of Jesuit writing about missions in Asia and South America. They were stories that framed and produced new stories of travel, encounter, and martyrdom. Those who volunteered to go to Canada knew that almost no Jesuits ever came back. A few stayed for their whole career, eventually dying of old age, but many others succumbed to sickness or suffered a violent death in one of the wars that shook much of the region during the seventeenth century.

Marquette was among those who was driven precisely by the desire to live out the kinds of stories he had read, both in accounts of the journeys of Francis Xavier to Asia and, most likely, in the Jesuit Relations from the New World. He set out across the Atlantic praying that he would never return, and he did succeed in taking a journey that would become legendary. When Marquette had been in New France for a few years—working among Native communities close to the French settlements, learning their languages, seeking converts—he joined a small party heading west toward the Mississippi. As they traveled through what was still familiar territory, they were warned about the dangers they would encounter: the "Great River," one group told them, "was full of horrible monsters, which devoured men and canoes together; that there was even a demon, who was heard from a great distance, who barred the way, and swallowed up all who ventured to approach him; Finally, that the Heat was so excessive in those countries that it would inevitably cause our death." Later, Marquette wrote, the "Captain" of another group "begged" Marquette's party "not to go farther, on account of the great dangers to which we exposed ourselves." Marquette replied that he "feared not death, and that I regarded no happiness greater than that of losing my life for the glory of Him who has made all." He added for his readers back in France: "This is what these poor people cannot understand."

There were monsters on the Mississippi. "From time to time, we came upon monstrous fish, one of which struck our Canoe with such violence that I thought it was a great tree, about to break the Canoe to pieces." (A footnote by Ruben Thwaites reassures us that this was nothing more than a big catfish—but can we be sure?) And then there were the two "painted monsters" Marquette's group encountered, "which at first made us afraid, and upon which the boldest savages dare not long rest their eyes": "They are as large as a calf; they have Horns on their heads like those of a deer, a horrible look, red eyes, a beard like a tiger's, a face somewhat like a man's, a body covered with scales, and so long a tail that it winds all around the body, passing above the head and going back between the legs, ending in a Fish's tail." Marquette was bothered by how well the images had been painted on their canvas of rock: "These 2 monsters are so well painted that we cannot believe any savage is their author; for good painters in France would find it difficult to paint so well—and besides, they are so high up on the rock that it is difficult to reach that place conveniently to paint them."

As they paddled south, Marquette's party arrived again in an area where Europeans were familiar to those who lived there. When they stopped along the banks of the river, they were invited to have "meat from wild cattle and bear's grease, with white plums" by a group of natives that told them they were just ten days from the sea. The group had traded with Europeans, and they told Marquette, he reported, "that these Europeans had rosaries and pictures; that they played upon Instruments; that some of them looked like me, and had been received by these savages kindly." Marquette saw no sign that any had "received instruction in the faith." He tried to spread the Word among them, and among another group encountered farther downriver—though there he had to speak "by signs, because none of them understood the six languages that I spoke"—but he had no idea whether they understood what he was telling them. "This is a seed cast in the ground," he wrote, "which will bear fruit in its time."

Marquette was right: his journey helped push French exploration, settlement, and conquest farther west, and with the settlement of Louisiana in the early eighteenth century the Mississippi became a major route connecting the two French colonies in North America. Several decades later, in 1727, another Jesuit priest, Father Du Poisson, traveled down a very different Mississippi. Along his journey downriver he encountered various settlements of French and German colonists, and passed the sites of failed settlements as well. Areas along the river were now home to many French settlers, who made their living in trading, farming, or logging, and who were making tracks into the wilderness of the New World, meeting, and sometimes marrying, the indigenous peoples they encountered.

Louisiana and the Mississippi were already legendary, as Du Poisson makes clear in the opening lines to his correspondence for readers in France: "Are you curious, my dear friend, to learn about the least curious thing in the world, which is hardest to learn by experience: the manner of traveling on the Mississippi River, and what this country—praised and despised in the same breath—really is, and what kind of people we find there?"

Du Poisson's narrative was firmly anchored in the long tradition of Jesuit writing about the Americas. And his story also ended exactly as it should. In 1729 the Natchez people, wary of increasing French incursions into their land, attacked French missions and settlements. Among those they killed was Du Poisson—and his bones, like those of Marquette, found their home in the soil of the New World.

Bibliography: Allan Greer, *The Jesuit Relations: Natives and Missionaries in Seventeenth-Century North America* (New York, 2000). Ruben Gold Thwaites, ed., *The Jesuit Relations and Allied Documents: Travels and Explorations of the Jesuit Missionaries in North America 1610–1791,* 73 vols. (Cleveland, 1896–1901); available at *puffin.creighton.edu/jesuit/relations.* Ruben Gold Thwaites and Edna Kenton, eds., *The Jesuit Relations and Allied Documents: Travels and Explorations of the Jesuit Missionaries in North America 1610–1791* (New York, 1925).

LAURENT DUBOIS

1683

The German immigrant ships *America* and *Concord* land in Philadelphia

PASTORIUS, *SICHERE NACHRICHT*

Restrained in a Ship, America by Name,
Into America . . . we came:
A Countrey bitter-sweet & pray! how can't be less,
Consid'ring all the World does lie in Wickedness . . .

In August 1683 Francis Daniel Pastorius arrived in Philadelphia from Germany on the ship *America* after a ten-week voyage from the English port of Deal. Pastorius described the voyage to his family in a letter sent in 1684, known under the title *Sichere Nachricht* (Positive Information), in which he provided a detailed account of the first few months of his life in the Pennsylvania colony, including the challenges he faced, and encouraged other German Pietists to emigrate to Pennsylvania. His own decision to emigrate had been motivated by Pietists in Frankfurt, and Pastorius wrote that he felt "a desire in my soul to continue in their Society, and with them to lead a quiet, godly and honest life in a howling Wilderness." In his letter, Pastorius likens the *America,* which carried about eighty people of varying occupations, ages, and faiths, to Noah's ark. It seemed the ship was repopulating the world.

Like so many others coming to America in the seventeenth century, those aboard the *America* had a difficult journey across the Atlantic. A headwind broke the ship's mast several times; seasickness laid low even some of the hardiest travelers; rations were lousy. A whale repeatedly assaulted the ship. Pastorius spent the months after his arrival preparing for more immigrants. He secured a grant of land near Philadelphia from William Penn. In October 1683, when the ship *Concord* arrived in Philadelphia carrying several families from Crefeld in Germany, Pastorius was there to greet them, and together they began to lay out the township of Germantown and settle the grant.

Much of *Sichere Nachricht* was practical advice: how to negotiate for passage; how to prepare for the trip; where to land; what to expect on arrival. Some of William Penn's promotional literature emphasized the abundant fruits and grains growing in Pennsylvania. In contrast, Pastorius told his readers to expect wilderness: "It is nothing but forest, and very few cleared places are to be found, in which respect as also in some others the hope I had previously formed is deceived, namely, that in these wild orchards no apples or pears are to be found, and this winter (which indeed has been very cold) no deer, turkeys, etc., were to be had. The wild grapes are very small and better suited to make into vinegar than into wine."

There were, however, good points in his description. The colony gave immigrants an opportunity to live a simple life free of the vanity, corruption, scholasticism, and war in Europe. Pastorius wrote favorably of the Native Americans and reminded his readers, "Now, dear friend, let us not hesitate to learn contentment from these people, that they may not hereafter shame us before the judgment-seat of Jesus Christ." The colonization of Pennsylvania was not a project for the weak, but it was one that those hardy enough should undertake without looking back.

Pastorius's mission was to create a godly community in America. That involved participating in the government as a magistrate and judge, as a teacher, as a farmer, as a religious leader, and as a scholar. Pastorius immediately set about becoming both a representative of the Frankfurt Land Company and a part of the colony's government. He served in the Pennsylvania General Assembly (1687–1691) and established laws for Germantown, which he served as mayor and bailiff in the 1690s, and as justice of the peace and judge (in 1686 and 1693–94, respectively).

While serving as a government official, Pastorius continued to teach and write. In the early eighteenth century his father, Melchior Adam Pastorius, collected many of Pastorius's letters home (including *Sichere Nachricht*) and published them together under the title *Umständige Beschreibung der Province Pensylvania* (Frankfurt, 1701). The letters describe life in Pennsylvania and span such diverse topics as the physical environment of the colony, the animals and plants to be found there, descriptions of the European settlers and Native Americans, the prospects for religion, and the colony's economy.

While Pastorius's letters emphasized the opportunity for colonists to live a simple and godly life, he also stressed the spiritual challenges that immigrants faced. One of the key challenges was slavery. In 1688, he joined several others in submitting a petition to the Germantown Quaker Meeting against slaveholding. The argument was straightforward: "Now, tho' they are black, we cannot conceive there is more liberty to have them slaves, as it is to have other white ones." The petition asked readers to recall that Christians were being captured at sea and put into slavery by Turks. Pastorius apparently had dreaded this on his own voyage to Pennsylvania, when the passengers spotted a Turkish ship at a distance and feared they might be captured. "How fearful and fainthearted are many on sea when they see a strange vessel, being afraid it should be a Turck, and they should be taken and sold for slaves into Turckey," he wrote. The heart of the argument was the Golden Rule. "There is a saying, that we shall doe to all men, like as we will be done our selves; making no difference of what generation, descent or colour they are. And those who steal or robb men, and those who buy or purchase them, are they not all alike?" The petition also sought to extend the principle of liberty of conscience to human liberty. "Here is liberty of conscience, which is right and reasonable; here ought to be likewise liberty of ye body, except of evildoers, which is another case." The petition was unsuccessful. The Germantown monthly meeting passed the petition on to the Quakers' quarterly meeting, which passed it on to the Quakers' yearly meeting in Philadelphia, which refused to deal with the issue.

Nevertheless, Pastorius's antislavery ideas continued to gather strength. By the late eighteenth century, Quakers became vocal leaders of the antislavery movement and were central to antislavery advocacy in the nineteenth century. And when they rediscovered Pastorius's petition in the nineteenth century, they celebrated it. In 1872 John Greenleaf Whittier, a Quaker, wrote a poem about Pastorius entitled "The Pennsylvania Pilgrim." It kept alive the memory of Pastorius as a polymath, teacher, jurist, and community leader who was guided by the spirit of simple and pious religious beliefs.

Though he tried to convince his contemporaries to change their ways, Pastorius was pessimistic. He believed there was a cyclical nature to human society, and he identified stages of society "prefigured in a wheel of seven spokes: Poorness, Humility, Peace, Traffik, Wealth, Pride, War." Yet he and the other Pietists and Quakers in early Pennsylvania set about to change that cycle. Besides his petition against slavery, Pastorius tried to remake the world with the ideal of living a simple, humble life in a nonviolent way. He advised James Logan, a justice in Philadelphia: "Do not say that your social rank demands that you do what Christ has forbidden . . . Woe to you eternally, if you seek honors and riches opposed to the meekness of Christ."

As a teacher, Pastorius wrote a *New Primer,* which contained typically moral messages and promotional and religious literature. For instance, students learned that they ought to "obey magistrates, . . . subject themselves to every Ordinance of Man, for the Lord's sake, . . . [be] afraid to spread evil of Dignitaries, . . . not resist the Power, . . . but render unto Caesar the things which are Caesar's, and unto God things that are God's" (see Matthew 22:21). His other writings included criticism of those who used lawsuits and manipulated business relationships for gain, as well as practical treatises on medicine, horticulture, and law.

Despite his efforts to create a peaceful life in Pennsylvania, the colony faced problems springing from some of the same human frailties that Pastorius found everywhere. Tensions grew between Pastorius and some of the more recently arrived Pietists. Pastorius sided with the traditional Quaker community in a dispute that turned on differences regarding Christ's status as the son of God and his resurrection. In the pamphlet war that followed, Henry Bernard Köster published *Advice for All Writers and Professors* (1697) with William Bradford's press in New York. Pastorius responded with *Four Boasting Disputers of this World Briefly Rebuked* (1697), also published by Bradford's press, in which he defended Quakers against the charge that they denied Christ's divinity by saying that Christ was both divine and human.

Some of the new arrivals took office in Germantown. Daniel Falkner was voted a bailiff and Falkner's associates took over other elected positions. Litigation was filed in a dispute involving the Frankfurt Land Company, in part over whether Pastorius or Falkner was the appropriate representative of the company. The dispute, which spilled over to the Philadelphia County Court in 1708, left bitter feelings on all sides and caused Pastorius to write a short essay about the case, "Exemplum sine Exemplo, or the Cheats and the Projectors." In it he explained why he believed that Falkner had lied to people in Germany and then forged documents to obtain control over the Frankfurt Company's property.

Pastorius's largest work is his commonplace book titled the *Bee Hive*. Begun in 1696, it is a collection of thoughts from hundreds of Quaker and non-Quaker books, and includes Pastorius's own original poetry, prose, and an autobiographical sketch. Most of the writing is in English, although at places (particularly in introductory pages) it includes writing in Dutch, Greek, Latin, German, French, and Italian. In hundreds of "honey combs," his name for the entries in the *Bee Hive*, Pastorius recorded the wisdom of other writers, primarily Quakers like George Fox, William Penn, and Isaac Penington, as well as his own thoughts on atheism, usury, judges, piety, debt, justice, magistrates, equity, equality, property, tyranny, nobility, politick, rebellion, and polygamy, among hundreds of other topics. The *Bee Hive* discloses Pastorius's reading habits and his thoughts. Over the course of several hundred poems, Pastorius expounded on the themes of simplicity and humanity. For instance, he asked why humans violate God's law of love:

With his own kind deals bad
neither wolf nor leopard
why then should put Christ the man
Christian against Christian
when he commands constantly
Love and Peace and Unity. John 13:24 etc.

Before the entry for Jeremiah Dykes's *Treatise of Good Conscience,* Pastorius wrote:

Our Duty is to reverence
the good of God in everyman
and Labour too, as much we can,
To get and keep good Conscience.

These themes come together in Pastorius's legal writing—in his work on the laws of Germantown, his work as a magistrate, and his treatise titled *Young Country Clerk's Collection*. The colony's records illustrate the connection of religious beliefs to the organization and practice of government. Pastorius's manuscript copy of the "Laws of Pennsylvania," for instance, had two quotations from the Old Testament on its title page—the Golden Rule and "Love thy neighbor as thyself" (Leviticus 19:18), along with an admonition that the good of the people is the highest law. The *Young Country Clerk's Collection,* which Pastorius may have used to teach basic elements of law to his students, remade English legal treatises to comport with his Pietist beliefs. It included forms for contracts and businesses, as well as forms for criminal prosecutions and for settling disputes by arbitration. However, it eliminated forms for civil lawsuits. Pastorius wanted cooperation, not strife.

Toward the end of his life, Pastorius looked back over what he had wrought. By the late 1710s, Pennsylvania was a thriving colony; the Frankfurt Land Company had facilitated settlement of the colony, despite litigation and fraud; there was now an expanding commercial community. In 1715 he wrote a poem commemorating the thirty-first anniversary of his arrival with Thomas Lloyd aboard the *America.* The poem was given to Lloyd's three daughters, for their father had died several years earlier. Some sense of his reverence for Lloyd appears in the poem, which ran to several hundred lines. Pastorius recalled the difficulty of the voyage and his adjustment to Pennsylvania:

'Twas he that made my Passage short on Sea,
'Twas he & William Penn, that Caused me to stay
In this then uncouth land, & howling Wilderness,
Wherein I saw that I but little should possess,
And if I would Return home to my Father's house,
Perhaps great Riches & Preferments might espouse, &c . . .
And though these Persons, whom I mention with Respect,
(Whom God as Instruments, did graciously elect,
To be His Witnesses unto this faithless Age,)
Are at a distance now from our American Stage,
In which as Actors, or Spectators, we appear,
Their Memory Survives: To me they're very near . . .
In Favour with the Lord, and Unity with Friends:
By three things he excell'd, Faith, Love & Patience . . .
He kindly deal'd with all, to ev'ry one did good,
Endearing chiefly God, and then the Brotherhood.
His Christian Belief was grounded on the Rock,
And so could easily endure the hardest Shock.

The poem illustrates that Pastorius was tempted to abandon his mission to America, but that Lloyd's faith had helped sustain him. Pastorius recalled that friendship and support, and praised Lloyd for his piety, love, and patience, qualities Pastorius esteemed.

After thirty years in America, Pastorius was writing in English instead of German; he had gone from being a lawyer in Germany who had been "making nothing but work for Repentance" (as he recalled in an autobiographical sketch in the *Bee Hive*) to a magistrate, farmer, beekeeper, and schoolteacher in the wilds of Pennsylvania. The task of reconstructing Pastorius's thought and disentangling his world, which stretched from law and Pietism in Germany to Quaker and Pietist thought and business in Pennsylvania, awaits us still. We can see the breadth of the world in his published and manuscript writings. They are testimony to the ways that the Quakers and Pietists sought to remake their worlds wholesale and how they sometimes succeeded.

Bibliography: Alfred L. Brophy, "'Ingenium est Fateri per quos profeceris': Francis Daniel Pastorius' *Young Country Clerk's Collection* and Anglo-American Legal Literature, 1680–1720," *University of Chicago Law School Roundtable* 3 (1996): 637–734; "The Intellectual World of a Seventeenth-Century Jurist: Francis Daniel Pastorius and the Reconstruction of Pietist Thought," in *German? American? Literature? New Directions in German American Studies,* ed. Winfried Fluck and Werner Sollors (New York, 2002), 44–63. Patrick Erben, "'Honey-Combs' and 'Paper-Hives': Positioning Francis Daniel Pastorius's Manuscript Writings in Early Pennsylvania," *American Literature* 37 (2005): 157–194. Marion Dexter Learned, *The Life of Francis Daniel Pastorius, the Founder of Germantown* (Philadelphia, 1908). Francis Daniel Pastorius, "Positive Information from America, concerning the Country of Pennsylvania . . . ," trans. J. Franklin Jamison, in *Narratives of Early Pennsylvania, West New Jersey, and Delaware, 1630–1707,* ed. Albert Cook Myers (New York, 1912), 392–411. John David Weaver, "Francis Daniel Pastorius (1651–1719): Life in Germany with a Glimpse of His Removal to Pennsylvania," PhD diss., University of California, Davis, 1985.

ALFRED L. BROPHY

1692

Four young girls accuse three women of witchcraft

THE SALEM TRIALS

Although the Salem witch trials took place more than three hundred years ago, the most irrational aspects of the American psyche can still be provoked by elements of the story: the hysterical rantings of a group of girls alleging that they are being tormented by unseen demons; the treachery and cupidity of neighbors denouncing neighbors; the readiness to presume the guilt of those accused; the bravery of those refusing to confess to crimes they had not committed; and the deaths of courageous women (and some men) at the hands of the grim, misogynistic Puritans who were their prosecutors.

Seventeenth-century Puritans inhabited a world in which the visible realm of everyday reality mingled with an invisible world inhabited by spirits. In the decade preceding the trials, Increase and Cotton Mather, father and son, had published accounts of demonic possession, malign activities, spectral evidence, and dramatic visions of Satan, said to appear to the unwary as a "black rogue," an Indian, or an animal.

The events leading to the Salem witch trials can be summarized succinctly. According to one source, John Hale, a group of local girls began to experiment with fortune-telling, attempting to discern the future by gazing into an egg and a mirror. One of them was badly frightened by what she saw, "a Spectre in likeness of a Coffin." Soon thereafter, several of them, including Betty Parris, the daughter of the local pastor Samuel Parris, and Abigail Williams, his eleven-year-old niece, began to exhibit strange symptoms, claiming that they were being bitten and pricked by invisible demons. At some juncture, at the instigation of a woman called Mary Sibley, Parris's Carib Indian slave Tituba was asked to prepare a "witch cake," consisting of the girls' urine mixed with rye meal, and feed it to a dog.

Although Parris had the children examined by doctors, their condition continued to worsen. Finally, a local physician, William Griggs, concluded that the girls were "under an Evil Hand." In February 1692 the afflicted children were put under considerable pressure to name those responsible for their suffering, and they named three persons: Sarah Good, Sarah Osborne, and Tituba, the slave. In the interrogations that followed, all three were presumed guilty; indeed, the magistrates did not hesitate to use torture where a presumption of guilt existed. Good and Osborne protested their innocence, but Tituba, possibly out of fear of her master, confessed that she had made the witch cake and that "her Mistress in her own Country was a Witch," but denied being a witch herself. She did, however, go on to give detailed evidence about her encounters with the Devil and the witches' gatherings she had attended in the forest, and alluded to other witches who still had not been identified.

At this point, the witch hunt began in earnest. Local women were denounced, and charges of witchcraft were brought; the local magistrates, John Hathorne and Jonathan Corwin, examined the accused. The accusations spiraled in number, often including relatives of those accused, such as four-year-old Dorcas Good and the farmer John Proctor. More than two hundred persons were accused during the entire episode; of them, three-fourths were women, and half of the men were relatives of accused women. Those who maintained their innocence at trial were executed; unsurprisingly, confessions began to pour forth. Historians have advanced numerous explanations for the outbreak, ranging from class conflict within the Salem congregation to gender issues to the effects of the First and Second Indian Wars. For writers down to our own time, the Salem trials have retained a compelling fascination.

Marion Gibson observes that the representation of witchcraft in accounts of American cultural and literary history is intimately bound up with constructions of national identity. For Nathaniel Hawthorne, a direct descendant of Salem magistrate John Hathorne, Salem's dark legacy provided an opportunity to explore the sinister, shadow side of the Puritan myth of America as an exemplary, God-directed nation. In the story "Young Goodman Brown," Hawthorne's Puritan protagonist leaves his wife, Faith, to embark upon on a mysterious errand in the forest. The wilderness is described as dark, eerie, and full of the unseen hostile presence of Indians. On his way, Goodman Brown meets many eminent local citizens. Finally, he hears a disconcerting murmur of voices and shouts out in despair, "Faith! Faith!" One of his wife's pink ribbons flutters down from a tree, and Goodman Brown reacts in fury and disillusionment, hastening toward what appears to be a witches' Sabbath, where Faith is about to be received into the company of transgressors. On reaching the clearing where the ceremony is taking place, he exhorts his wife to look to heaven and resist Satan. Suddenly the company vanishes, leaving Goodman Brown alone in the night. The following morning he returns to Salem a somber and chastened man.

This is a richly textured story. In it, Hawthorne is evoking the hypocrisy of Puritan society with his picture of external propriety and restraint in Salem alongside an escape to darker passions in the depths of the forest, as well as revealing the ways in which the American landscape and its inhabitants have been demonized by the settlers. The story is also a meditation on the fallibility of spectral evidence—that is, accounts of specters tormenting their victims used as proof against those accused of witchcraft. In "Young Goodman Brown" it is unclear whether the protagonist has witnessed real, unspeakable acts, or whether his visions were nightmares emerging from the depths of his own psyche.

Another Hawthorne short story is "Alice Doane's Appeal," told by a nineteenth-century narrator to two female companions on Gallows Hill. It is the tale of a brother and sister, Alice and Leonard Doane, who are very close. When Alice is attracted to a man called Walter Brome, her brother reacts with extreme jealousy. Leonard is convinced that his sister loves Walter Brome because of the latter's resemblance to himself and kills Brome in a fit of rage, but then he sees that the dead man's face resembles his own father's. Later, it transpires that Alice is Brome's sister, and that Leonard has in effect killed his own twin brother, at the instigation of a mysterious wizard. The narrator describes the emergence of specters from the local cemetery, including Cotton Mather's, "the representative of all the hateful features of his time; the one blood-thirsty man, in whom were concentrated those vices of spirit and errors of opinion, that sufficed to madden the whole surrounding multitude." In this tale, with its dark shadings of incest and fratricide, Hawthorne tells us that the specters haunting New England are not imagined demons but rather the real characters who played a central role in its history.

Hawthorne's 1851 novel *The House of the Seven Gables* is set in his own nineteenth-century milieu. It is the story of Hepzibah and Clifford Pyncheon, two etiolated remnants of Salem's elites: ghostly, faintly absurd presences who find it hard to exist in a world of cent-shops and railroads. Hepzibah laments the fact that she has to go into trade to earn a living; Clifford has just come home after many years in prison for the alleged murder of his uncle. Another phantasm haunting the tale is that of a distant ancestor, one Colonel Pyncheon, who had been engaged in a dispute over land with a neighbor, Matthew Maule. When Maule is condemned as a witch—at, he believes, the instigation of Pyncheon—in words that echo the curse of the condemned Sarah Good of Salem to Reverend Nicholas Noyes in 1692, he curses Pyncheon from the scaffold, saying that God will give him blood to drink, and indeed the curse is fulfilled when Colonel Pyncheon dies in his armchair in the seven-gabled mansion he has built on Maule's land, his beard covered in blood. The curse is repeated when Colonel Pyncheon's descendant, Judge Jaffrey Pyncheon, seeks to dispossess Hepzibah and Clifford in order to seize their land and search for a mysterious document sealing a claim to a vast tract of Indian land in the West. In the end, the evil Jaffrey dies of apoplexy while sitting in his ancestor's chair.

The tale is written in a comic Gothic mode, and yet there are undercurrents of darkness: references to stolen Indian lands, and, once again, to witchcraft (ancestral curses, usurped lands, mesmerism) and a reference to the judge's dark corpse, rotting at the very heart of the mansion. This novel, published at a time when America was expanding westward and undergoing a process of rapid industrialization, reveals not only Hawthorne's uneasiness about his family's witch-hunting past but also his disquietude about the rot at the heart of America, given the direction it had taken in the mid-nineteenth century, when John O'Sullivan had proclaimed that it was America's "Manifest Destiny" to occupy what he saw as the vacant lands to the West.

Other nineteenth-century writers deal with the Salem events from many angles. These include John Neal's exploration of religious bigotry and scapegoating in *Rachel Dyer* (1828), James Kirk Paulding's *A Puritan and His Daughter* (1849), and John William DeForest's *Witching Times* (1856), a mixture of historic, sentimental, and picturesque modes. Plays of the period include Longfellow's *Giles Corey of the Salem Farms* (1868). Decades later, Esther Forbes's novel *A Mirror for Witches* (1928) takes the viewpoint of a Puritan defending the persecution of a witch called Doll Bilby; it is never quite clear whether Doll is merely a young woman who is hounded because of her disturbing eroticism or whether she really does have supernatural powers.

In the 1950s, the Salem witch trials provided a useful template for writers' and dramatists' critiques of the paranoid excesses of the House Un-American Activities Committee (HUAC) and the virulently anticommunist senator Joseph McCarthy's Permanent Subcommittee on Investigations. William Carlos Williams's play *Tituba's Children,* written in 1950, establishes parallels between the Salem events and the HUAC proceedings. Williams had experienced firsthand the consequences of the McCarthyist frenzy when he was deprived in 1948 of the post of consultant in poetry at the Library of Congress because of his leftist affiliations. The first act of *Tituba's Children* is set in Salem, with Tituba bizarrely characterized as an African American mammy figure, despite the fact that in the play's list of characters she is described as "the Parrises' half-Carib, half-Negro slave." The action then shifts to a Washington club on Halloween Eve, where "Mac" MacDee, a State Department official, confides his woes to Stella, a hostess. Mac's wife is expecting twins, and he is the target of vague accusations of subversion. Later, the wonderfully named senators Yokell, Gasser, Pipeline, and Wise come into the club. The staff puts on a Halloween play about the Salem trials, and the tenuous line separating the Puritan past and the McCarthyist present is blurred even further; Williams's stage directions state explicitly that the parts in the Salem and Washington scenes are to be played by the same actors, whom he intended the

audience to recognize as the same persons. The tormented Mac is linked to Giles
Corey, the Puritan farmer in the Salem trials who was executed by "pressing," or
being crushed by stones. Mac acknowledges that he has liberal tendencies but
makes a passionate plea for democratic openness. The play concludes with his arrest. Unsurprisingly, *Tituba's Children* was not published until 1961, and it was first
performed in 1986 by a group of New York high school students, long after the
anticommunist furor had abated.

Probably the best-known twentieth-century dramatization of the Salem
events is Arthur Miller's 1953 play *The Crucible*. In it, the character of Abigail Williams is transformed from an eleven-year-old child into a teenage temptress with
whom the upright John Proctor has lapsed from fidelity to his wife, and the progressive blackening of Tituba is complete, as Miller makes no mention at all of
her Indian blood. A powerful element of the play is Miller's staging of Proctor's
refusal to denounce his fellow citizens to the magistrates, a decision that leads
him to death on the gallows. In 1954 Miller himself was denied a passport, and
in 1956 he was summoned for questioning by the House Un-American Activities
Committee. In an unpleasant instance of life imitating art, he was indicted by a
federal grand jury for contempt of Congress because of his courageous refusal to
betray other writers who were alleged to have leftist leanings. This conviction was
overturned in 1958.

One of the most fascinating portrayals of the Salem events is in Caribbean
writer Maryse Condé's 1986 novel *I, Tituba, Black Witch of Salem*. In it, Condé creates an imagined Barbadian childhood for Tituba, the product of her mother's
rape by an English sailor aboard a slave ship. Years later, when Tituba's mother is
hanged for violence against her owner, the child is taken into the care of Mama
Yaya, who teaches her a benign form of witchcraft in which nature is a living presence and the world of spirits is intermingled with everyday reality as a matter of
course. Later, Tituba is taken to Boston by Samuel Parris, her owner, and there
she encounters religious intolerance, racist abuse, and casual cruelty. When she is
accused of witchcraft, she is aware that if she refuses to confess she will be executed, and so in terror she denounces some of her tormentors. Later, she returns
to Barbados, and the book ends with her participation in a slave revolt and her
death on the gallows.

The Salem witchcraft trials have disquieting resonances in a post-9/11 world
of extraordinary rendition and practices such as waterboarding and other forms
of torture. In our own times, the denial of due process of law and the assumption
of guilt by association are grimly relevant. It remains to be seen whether the
events of Salem will again provide a template for new novels and plays by American writers—a model for describing and denouncing not only external threats to
national security, real or imagined, but also the monsters created by fear in our
own midst.

Bibliography: Paul Boyer and Stephen Nissenbaum, *Salem Possessed: The Social Origins of Witchcraft* (Cambridge, MA, 1974). Marion Gibson, *Witchcraft Myths in American Culture* (New York,
2007). Chadwick Hansen, "The Metamorphosis of Tituba, or Why American Intellectuals Can't

Tell an Indian Witch from a Negro," *New England Quarterly* (March 1974). Carol F. Karlsen, *The Devil in the Shape of a Woman: Witchcraft in Colonial New England* (New York, 1998). Mary Beth Norton, *In the Devil's Snare: The Salem Witchcraft Crisis of 1692* (New York, 2002).

SUSAN CASTILLO

1693–94, March 4
A Puritan divine meditates on the Lord's Supper

EDWARD TAYLOR'S "POETICAL WORKS"

My Trencher, Lord, with thy Roast Mutton dress:
  And my dry Bisket in thy Dripping Sap.
And feed my Soul with thy Choice Angell Mess:
  My heart thy Praise, Will, tweedling Larklike tap.

These lines were among many thousand verses that the English Professor Thomas H. Johnson discovered in a 400-page leatherbound manuscript quarto that he came across in Yale's library. Written by Edward Taylor, an obscure Puritan minister who had lived in Westfield, Massachusetts, these substantial and previously unknown "Poetical Works," samples of which Johnson published in 1939, created a stir of interest, for Taylor had an unmistakable poetic voice.

"The Preface," a poem opening Taylor's several-thousand-lines-long *God's Determinations touching his Elect* (ca. 1682), starts dramatically: "Infinity, when all things it beheld/In Nothing, and of Nothing all did build." Restless anaphoric questions follow, inspired by the Book of Job ("Who blew the Bellows of His Furnace Vast?/Or held the Mould wherein the world was Cast?") and by public life ("Who in this Bowling Alley bowld the Sun?/Who made it always when it rises Set/To go at once both down, and up to get?"). Such questions, punctuated by "Who?" (repeated eighteen times in forty-four lines), create a strong sound effect. The answer, "It's Onely Might Almighty this did doe," leads to an extended contemplation of God's almightiness in contrast to human insignificance, embodied by the word "Nothing," which appears twelve times, intensifying a rhythm independent of rhyme and enhanced by enjambment: "Who Spake all things from nothing; and with ease/Can Speake all things to nothing, if he please." And: "Gave All to nothing Man, indeed whereby/Through nothing man all might him Glorify./In Nothing man imbosst the brightest Gem / More pretious than all pretiousness in them." God's grandeur, rendered in partly abstract yet always vivid language, invites comparison with poetic creation "from nothing," by the employment of such figures as polyptoton ("pretious"/"pretiousness"), chiasmus ("Which All from Nothing fet, from Nothing, All"—"fet" meaning "made"), and a fully developed paradox: How could "Nothing Man" commit original sin when God had created him as the "brightest Gem"? How could a poet, another "Nothing Man," dare to imagine God by mere words like "Infinity"? "The Preface" poeticizes abstractions ("Nothing") and images from everyday life ("Bowling Alley") but questions its own eloquence.

Who was this poet? A nonconformist from Sketchley, Leicestershire, Taylor was educated in England before he sailed for Massachusetts in 1668. He kept a vivid diary of the voyage. For example, on June 16 he wrote: "At length there came a dead butterfly swimming on the water, whereupon we judged we were nigh land, and therefore sounded again, 250 fathoms of cords, for land, but found none." On July 2: "We saw a ship which we took for a New English fishing vessel; and when we came to it, the master of it told us that Bridges in Barbadoes, was burned down about two months and a half [ago?] by a negro's blowing his tobacco-pipe so as it lighted in cotton wool."

Once in Massachusetts, Taylor enrolled at Harvard; he graduated in 1671, a "classmate" of Samuel Sewall (in whose diary the word "classmate" first appeared, according to the *Oxford English Dictionary*). After taking an arduous winter journey westward, crossing the frozen Connecticut River on horseback "though the ice cracked every step," Taylor became the pastor in recently incorporated Westfield (Westfield being the Anglicized version of its Algonquian name, Woromoco), a town of about a hundred inhabitants and one tavern. He composed a whimsical love poem to Elizabeth Fitch and married her in 1674. Five of their eight children died in infancy, and Elizabeth herself passed away in 1689 at age thirty-nine. Death became a strong presence in Taylor's work. Poems like "Upon Wedlock, and Death of Children" and "A Fig for thee Oh! Death" attempted to find solace when "Griefe o're doth flow." Taylor remarried in 1695 and had six more children. His tombstone calls him an "Aged Venerable Learned & Pious Pastor" and gives his age as eighty-seven in 1729, the year he died. The story of a prolific New England poet who lived in a provincial town for more than fifty years and published almost nothing made modern readers think of Emily Dickinson.

Taylor's newly discovered poems soon elicited commentary, whether because of their sustained and striking imagery (the extended analogy of weaving a wedding dress and working toward the soul's salvation in "Huswifery"), their representation of conversion and election ("The Experience"), or their resemblance to work of the English metaphysical poets John Donne and George Herbert ("Upon a Spider Catching a Fly").

A collection titled *Preparatory Meditations before my Approach to the Lords Supper; Chiefly upon the Doctrin preached upon the Day of administration,* the center of Taylor's oeuvre, contains more than 200 poems, in two series, that Taylor composed over the course of forty-two years. The meditations are generally structured in three parts—called "statement," "doctrine," and "prayer" by Ursula Brumm—and written in six-line stanzas with an a-b-a-b-c-c rhyme scheme.

The "statement" part of Meditation II:44, written around Christmas 1701, is a theological critique of rhetorical flourishes:

The Orator from Rhetorick gardens picks
   His Spangled Flowers of Sweet-breathd Eloquence

> Wherewith his Oratory brisk he tricks
>> Whose Spicy Charms Eare jewells do commence.
>> Shall bits of Brains be candid thus for eares?
>> My Theme claims Sugar Candid far more cleare.

Arguing against rhetoric, the poem yet puns on "candid," suggesting "candor" but also candied "bits of Brains"—"Eare jewells." Punning continues with "style" (rhetoric) and "stile" (ladder), as Christ's dual nature is a typological fulfillment of Jacob's ladder: both connect God and man.

> Things styld Transcendent, do transcende the stile
>> Of Reason, reason's stares neere reach so high.
> But Jacob's golden Ladder rounds do foile
>> All reasons Strides, wrought of THEANTHROPIE.
>> Two Natures distance-standing, infinite,
>> Are Onifide, in person, and unite.

There is no nativity scene, merely adoration of "theanthropie," a rare ecclesiastic Greek word ("God-man"). Taylor used "theanthropy" in other poems (I:24, II:33), though it appeared only once in an American imprint before 1800. Another pun with the homophone antonyms "Might" and "Mite" represents Christ's paradoxically united natures.

The central "doctrine" section becomes daring: Christ's "onifying" of God and man elevates humans above the status of angels, though angels never committed original sin:

> You Holy Angell, Morning-Stars, bright-Sparks
>> Give place: and lower your top gallants; shew
> Your top-saile Conjues to our slender barkes:
>> The highest honour to our nature's due.
>> It's neerer Godhead by the Godhead made
>> Than yours in you that never from God stray'd.

Taylor continues with seafaring metaphors (anchor, Cable, bark, tempests), only to shift to printing and cramp-clearing imagery in the "prayer." The concluding couplet is musical:

> If thou wilt blow this Oaten straw of mine,
> The sweetest piped praises shall be thine.

This structure Taylor used again and again. His opening statements are often versions of the topos of modesty or expressions of postlapsarian contrition: "Lord, Can a Crumb of Dust the Earth outweigh" ("Prologue"); "Unclean, Unclean: My Lord, Undone, all vile" (II:26); "A Bond slave in Egyptick Slavery / This Noble Stem, Angellick Bud, this Seed / Of Heavenly Birth, my Soul, doth groaning ly. / When shall its Passo're come? When shall't be Freed?" (II:22). The concluding, hopeful couplets in the "prayers" for God's grace offer praise songs, hosannas: "My Spirit then engrapd and pomegranat'de / Shall sweetly Sing thee o're thy garden gated" (II:64); "This Bread of Life dropt in thy mouth, doth Cry. / Eate,

Eate me, Soul, and thou shalt never dy" (I:8); "My Palmifer'd Hosannah Songs I'le raise / On my Shoshannims blossoming thy praise" (II:24).

At times Taylor develops one metaphor throughout a meditation. Thus in Meditation I:38 the biblical text of "An Advocate with the Father" (1 John 2:1) opens a torrent of legal terms: regulate, Court, judge, Case, Pannelst, Sentence, Atturny, Evidences, Client, Habeas-Corpus, Fines, and Arrest; the prayer asks God, "plead my Case." In II:49 the language of metallurgy (or alchemy) dominates: "Gold in its Ore, must melted be" is followed by "A fining Pot, and Test, and melting fire," Flame, Coale, Embers, and mineral; only the ending shifts from Isaiah's coal to perfume and song. More typically, Taylor switches from one realm to another: thus I:30 moves almost breathlessly from "Pensill"-drawing and Palace Angells, Sun, gold, Scutchons, David's Stock, Chrystall Casements, and the Divell, to "Sill, Plate, Ridge, Rib, and Rafter me with Grace" and the conclusion with its rhythmic reiteration of "new":

> New mould, new make me thus, me new Create
>   Renew in me a spirit right, pure, true.
> Lord make me thy New Creature, then new make
>   All things to thy New Creature here anew,
>   New Heart, New thoughts, New Words, New wayes likewise.
>   New Glory then shall to thyselfe arise.

This is the articulation of Christian rebirth, inspired by 2 Cor. 5:17, "He is a New Creature." Taylor loves repetition: the word "Glory" appears seven times (in I:22), a meaningful number, for Taylor ends the first series with Meditation 49 and explains in II:21, "when Seven years are Seven times turnd about / A Jubilee."

Taylor is self-conscious about "metaphor," a word he uses more than a dozen times. "Thou Glory Darkning Glory, with thy Flame / Should all Quaint Metaphors teem ev'ry Bud / Of Sparkling Eloquence upon the Same / It would appear as dawbing pearls with mud" (I:13). In his college declamation he wrote about rhetorical figures ("Here lies a Metonomy; there doth sculke / An Irony: here underneath this bulke / A Metaphor; Synecdoche doth reare / And open publickly Shopwindows here"). Meditation II:108 ponders the nature of signs. He cares about etymology, uses Greek and Latin phrases, and puns with the Hebrew meaning of words: when he refers to drinking "beere" (II:60[B]), he alludes to the Hebrew word for "fountain," and his "prayer" to Samson (whose name Taylor translates in a sermon as "little Sun") is: "Be thou my Samson, Lord, a Rising Sun, / Of Righteousness unto my soule, I pray" (II:11).

Meditation II:5, devoted to Isaac as a type for Christ ("Christ's Antitype. Isaac his Type up spires"), sets up the typological relationship of Isaac as "Oar" (ore) and Christ as "Metall." They have their sacrifice in common "by typick laws," and Isaac's "leaping from the Altar's bed" foretold Christ's "rising from the Dead." Yet the sacrifice metamorphoses into a New England dinner: "And make my Soul thine Altars Drippen pan / To Catch the Drippen of thy Sacrifice." The prayer for "Roast Mutton" follows.

Taylor's meditations contain folksy English words like "Mullipuff" (I:22), "Snick-Snarls" (I:25), "Washing-Swill" (I:40), and "womble-Crops" (II:30), offsetting Latinate abstractions. Faulty vision is one of Taylor's tropes of inadequacy (see II:21), and one poem sounds like a familiar song: "Mine Eyes are dim; I cannot clearly see./Be thou my Spectacles that I may read/Thine Image" (I:[6]). One prayer section asks the Lord to "soake my Soule in Zions Bucking tub:/With Holy Soap, and Nitre, and rich Lye/From all Defilement mee cleanse, wash and rub" (I:40).

Taylor makes no poetic comment on King Philip's War, which raged in his neighborhood in the 1670s, delaying his ordination, but two meditations allude to indigenous populations with "th'indian broths of Garbagd deer" (II:159) and "Canooes" (II:78), the Arawak word Columbus introduced to European languages.

> And now the Prisoners sent out, do come
>   Padling in their Canooes apace with joyes
> Along this blood red Sea, Where joyes do throng,
>   And sayling in the Arke of Grace that flies
>   Drove sweetly by Gailes of the Holy Ghost
>   Who sweetly briezes all along this Coast.

Like Columbus, he hears "Nighting gaile" (II:67[A]) singing in the New World. His "Hill of Cordilera" (II:56) refers to the American Andes.

Taylor's physical imagery is strong: in I:12 the sweetest flower is deemed "but a Foist to that Perfume beset/In thy Apparell Steaming round about." (A "foist" is a stink.) Meditation I:8 develops the conceit of the Lord's Supper as "Heaven's Sugar Cake," but the baking ingredients are startling, for even if "Bowells" is figuratively the "seat of tender emotions," the metaphors that follow evoke the word's literal meaning: "In this sad state, Gods Tender Bowells run/Out streams of Grace: And he to end all strife/The Purest Wheate in Heaven, his deare-dear Son/Grinds, and kneads up into this Bread of Life."

Taylor writes of "Dunghills reech" (II:63), but "reech" is also a wonderful smell. In I:3 God is sweeter than "reechs of Odours, Gales of Spices, Folds/of Aromaticks," and soon the poet introduces a "Mammulary Catch," referring to the glands in his nostrils that do not let him smell God's sweetness. Yet the "Mammulary" conceit, enhanced by "Mothers Wombs," soon evokes nose *and* nipples: "Oh! let the Clouds of thy sweet Vapours rise,/And both my Mammularies Circumcise./Shall Spirits thus my Mammularies suck?/(As Witches Elves their teats,) and draw from thee/My Dear, Dear Spirit after fumes of muck?"

Are bizarre images not blasphemous in meditations preparatory of the Lord's Supper? Was Taylor a true Puritan or a baroque Anglo-Catholic sympathizer, readers asked? There is no doubt about his orthodoxy—and as for Catholicism and popery, Meditation II:108 declares that the "Pope's a whore," while his *Metrical History of Christianity* makes the popes a central target: "That Peters Chair finds or refines the Bum/That in it sits, and of it makes a Drum."

An orthodox and learned Christian theologian, tinkerer, risk taker, language explorer, multilingual punster, lover of metaphors, and coiner of strange images, a trained rhetorician skeptical of eloquence, a divine with an odd sense of humor, an isolated frontier poet striving for new ways of expressing his meditative search for salvation, fearless of repetition and yet producing a varied, massive body of poetry, Edward Taylor, whose 40,000 lines of poetry and 2,000 manuscript pages of prose were unknown for centuries, has become a new point of origin for American poetry.

Poet Donald Hass, in "What Was Taylor Up To?" (2002), was stunned by Taylor's imagery and found the "Mammularies Circumcise" passage (I:3) "as surreal as it seems": the speaker "wants the foreskin off the nipples of his spiritual sense of smell." Hass puts Taylor in the company not only of Whitman and Dickinson but also of Joyce, Pound, Eliot, and Wallace Stevens. Henry Cowell chose Taylor's "Nothing Man" poem for "—if He Please," one of his *Variations for Orchestra* (1956); liner notes updated the message to the atomic age: if God can undo creation "into Nothing again," that is "a hint of that total annihilation which has become a literal possibility." Joyce Carol Oates adopted the title and general idea of Taylor's poem "Upon the Sweeping Flood" for a 1966 short story. Daniel Pinkham set Taylor's "The Joy of Church Fellowship rightly attended" to a vocal score under the title, "In Heaven soaring up" (1989). Donald Davie's poem "Having No Ear" questions the "preternatural" and is unable to "Tell if Edward Taylor tells/The truth, or no." Davie's poem suggests why Taylor's poetry influences modern writers who are doubtful of religious certainties but attracted to Taylor's search for them: "why should I/Think Paradise by other light than day/Sparkled in Taylor's eye?"

Taylor's prisoners "padling in their Canooes," "Holy Soap" in "Zions Bucking tub," and "Roast Mutton" in a "Drippen pan" may still be awaiting echoes in the arts.

Bibliography: Ursula Brumm, *American Thought and Religious Typology* (New Brunswick, NJ, 1970). Thomas M. Davis and Virginia L. Davis, *Edward Taylor's Minor Poetry* (Boston, 1981). Thomas H. Johnson, ed., *The Poetical Works of Edward Taylor* (New York, 1939). Charles W. Mignon, ed., *Edward Taylor, Upon the Types of the Old Testament* (Lincoln, NE, 1989). Daniel Patterson, ed., *Edward Taylor's* Gods Determinations *and* Preparatory Meditations: *A Critical Edition* (Kent, OH, 2003). Edward Taylor, *Metrical History of Christianity,* online subscription publication (Alexandria, VA: Chadwyck-Healey, 1996).

WERNER SOLLORS

1700

Samuel Sewall writes *The Selling of Joseph*

A Puritan Brief against Slavery

In 1700, Samuel Sewall, a judge, merchant, and diarist in Boston, Massachusetts, was a worried man. His concerns were both personal and social. As the lone judge to repent of his role in condemning accused witches to death in Salem in 1692, as a deeply religious Puritan with a sensitive soul, and as an observer of the vast political-religious turmoil in his insecure colony, Sewall decided to write an unprecedented condemnation of slavery. Predated by Quaker petitions and writings in England and America, *The Selling of Joseph,* a short pamphlet published in June 1700, holds pride of place as the first major abolitionist work by an American colonist.

A group of Pennsylvania Quaker petitioners led by Francis Daniel Pastorius, the founder of Germantown, anticipated some of Sewall's arguments in 1688 when they condemned slave trading as incompatible with the Golden Rule. And in 1693 an English-born Quaker living in the American colonies, George Keith, went even further by condemning his fellow Quakers' slave ownership as "man-stealing," and arguing that all slaves should be freed and then prepared for "Christian education." Condemned by Quaker meetings, the rebellious Keith returned to England where he converted to the Anglican church and eventually worked for proslavery missionaries. Arguments over slavery deeply split the Quakers, as they also would split Sewall from his fellow Puritans. At the turn of the eighteenth century, slavery and the slave trade had few public critics and legions of defenders.

Sewall, born in 1652 in Bishopstoke, Hampshire, England, emigrated across the Atlantic with his parents in 1661. He came of age in the aftermath of the English Civil War, the Glorious Revolution of 1688, and the religious conflict that shaped his life and work. Indeed, Sewall's *The Selling of Joseph* should first be viewed as part of the tremendous wave of religious tensions and schisms that swept through the Anglo-American world from the 1680s well into the eighteenth century. A crisis within Protestant theology generally, and Puritanism specifically, defined the times in which Sewall rose to leadership in Massachusetts as a member of the colony's governing council and a justice on its Superior Court.

The Selling of Joseph is both a lament and an appeal, an altar call to the faithful to save their own souls and those of the slaves as well. It is a work of Christian and social conscience, and it anticipates many arguments to follow over the next century and a half in both antislavery and proslavery thought. Sewall follows the familiar structure of the sermon: he names his texts, elaborates on those texts by citing numerous biblical passages as well as Puritan theological authorities, examines and offers refutations of four possible objections to his argument, and then concludes with Latin quotations from biblical scholars as justification for a case that he surely knew was unpopular. Sewall sought justification in scripture and the reputation of learned authority. But through this structure emerges a remarkable set of arguments for ending slavery based in Christian morality, as well as, perhaps unwittingly, Enlightenment ideals.

Sewall seems to have read widely, if eclectically. Here and there in English Protestant thought over the course of the seventeenth century, a moral distinction grew ever stronger between the almost universally acceptable institution of slavery as the legitimate result of war, crime, or poverty, and the booming business of the slave trade. Capturing, selling, and buying slaves came under increasing scrutiny and attack. Sewall read the early seventeenth-century Puritan writer Paul Baynes, who wrote that though Adam's fall had made all men "Satan's slaves" in their souls, masters of slaves in the everyday world risked special levels of evil because they exercised a dangerous power over the "flesh" and the "will" of other men. Concern for the souls of white masters led some Christians to concern for the souls, indeed the liberties, of African slaves.

Sewall rooted his case against slavery in several famous scriptures, especially Acts 17:26–27 (God "hath made of one blood all nations of men for to dwell on all the face of the earth") and the Golden Rule, Matthew 7:12 ("all things whatsoever ye would that men should do to you, do ye even so unto them"). Moreover, as though suggesting an ancient moral alternative to an ancient system of human exploitation, Sewall cited the Epistle of Paul to the Ephesians to imagine that all humanity might be unified under the "law of love." From such biblical injunctions, Sewall rose occasionally to eloquence and wit. "There is no proportion between twenty pieces of silver and LIBERTY," he wrote, declaring that he who buys another human being risks loss of "his own claim to liberty."

Portions of Sewall's biblical exegesis seem to leave no wiggle room for his opponents. He invoked Exodus 21:16 to condemn the capture and sale of slaves: "He that stealeth a man, and selleth him, or if he be found in his hand, he shall surely be put to death." Using the story of Joseph as his overarching example, Sewall argued that Joseph's brothers "had no more authority to sell him, than they had to slay him." In the tradition of the Puritan jeremiad, Sewall asked: "What louder cry can there be made of that celebrated warning, Caveat Emptor!" Sewall then stressed the daily agonies of the master-slave relationship—the masters' "temptations . . . to connive at the fornication of their slaves," and the breakup of families, white and black.

Many of these arguments would survive for well over a century and reemerge with force in the Christian abolitionism of the 1820s and 1830s. But a parallel characteristic of Sewall's work is its occasional caution, even doubt, about his antislavery pronouncements. The slave trade was "horrible" in its "uncleanness" and "murder." On that score, Sewall did not equivocate. But like virtually all of his fellow Englishmen and American colonists, he had no solution for what to do with freed slaves. He admitted that "white servants" were still much preferred to Africans in New England. And then he worried about the rising numbers of blacks in the Puritan commonwealth. "Few can endure to hear," he admitted, "of a Negro's being made free; and indeed they can seldom use their freedom well; yet their continual aspiring after their forbidden liberty, renders them unwilling servants." Sewall worried about the growing and dangerous lot of free Africans in the midst of his Massachusetts commonwealth.

With the apostles Paul and Matthew at his side, and through Adam's legacy to Joseph and all of humanity, Sewall seemed to have his moral case in order. But then race disrupted and poisoned his thinking, as, throughout the antislavery enterprise for a long time to come, it would disrupt the thinking of so many more. "There is such a disparity in their conditions, colour & hair," he wrote, "that they can never embody with us, and grow up into orderly families, to the peopling of the land." Blacks could only "remain in our body politick," said the judge, "as a kind of extravasat blood" (involuntary resident). Here Sewall remained trapped, as would most Americans for generations, in tragic assumptions about "blood," about physical capacities and characteristics, about conceptions of racial "nature" divorced from history. This passage in *The Selling of Joseph* anticipates the famous lines about black inequalities in Thomas Jefferson's *Notes on the State of Virginia* in 1784 more than it does Frederick Douglass's lonely efforts to refute racial science in *The Claims of the Negro Ethnologically Considered* in 1854. The long historical gestation of antislavery literature and thought has always been packaged in new forms of humanism and old modes of racialism.

Sewall was much more at ease in delivering his moral sermon against "man-stealing." In the second half of the pamphlet he imagined four objections to his case and offered rebuttals. He dismissed the first—that blacks are destined for slavery because of the curse of Ham, the idea that "Ethiopians" bore the mark of the darker, cursed son of Noah—by warning his fellow Christians not to assume the role of "executioner of the vindictive wrath of God." He even asserted the rather modern idea that the curse of Ham may be "long since out of date." Second, he rejected justifications of the slave trade as the redemption of African "pagans" to knowledge of the Gospels. "Evil must not be done, that good may come of it," he declared. Even Joseph's growing faith did not justify his "brethren's sale of him." Sewall dispatched the third possible objection—that Africans were lawful captives taken in war—with the claim that "every war is upon one side unjust." Here the Golden Rule sufficed for Sewall to refute the idea of "just" captives resulting from the "barbarous cruelties" of the slave trade. And fourth, to the claim of slavery's antiquity in Abraham's ownership of slaves, Sewall reminds his reader that even the great patriarch sinned, and that in Leviticus and Jeremiah the "Israelites were strictly forbidden the buying or selling one another for slaves." His biblical legal brief complete, Sewall rested his case in a Latin variation of the Golden Rule from the Puritan scholar William Ames.

As a text, *The Selling of Joseph* compels our literary interest in the Puritan mind, as well as in how the notion of benevolence grew in Anglo-American thought. But immediate and long-term contexts go far to explain why Sewall wrote his pamphlet when he did. Before 1680 African slaves provided only a small portion of the labor and the population of the North American colonies. But between 1680 and the 1720s, as the supply of white indentured laborers dwindled, the importation of African slaves exploded and grew unabated until the American Revolution.

The African population of the Chesapeake region of Maryland and Virginia was 13 percent of the total in 1700 but increased to 30 percent by 1762. The population of South Carolina, founded only in the 1670s, was one-third black slaves by 1700 and one-half by 1708. In the North, Rhode Island counted 9 percent of its people as slaves, and the New York slave population grew to 18 percent by 1700, 25 percent in the port of New York City. In Sewall's Massachusetts, between 1676 and 1708 the number of slaves rose from approximately 200 to 550, 75 percent of whom lived in Boston. When the British Parliament suspended the Royal Africa Company's monopoly on the slave trade, many Boston merchants entered the "Guinea trade," as it was called. Hence, Sewall's opening sentence reflects a reality he saw all around him: "The numerousness of slaves at this day in the province, and the uneasiness of them under their slavery, hath put many upon thinking whether the foundation of it be firmly and well laid."

Along with this immigration crisis, Sewall's entire time as a public official in Massachusetts was defined by devastating wars with New England Indians. An ever-growing problem of piracy on the seas, as well as captives taken in war, caused unprecedented social disorder. Indian, French, African, and English captives, war refugees in custody, forced the formerly homogeneous Massachusetts colony to conceive new definitions of just what criminal enslavement meant. When Sewall wrote *The Selling of Joseph,* fresh in his mind were his personal efforts to help New England fishermen and sailors captured by the Barbary pirates on the coast of Algeria and his guilt-ridden memory of sentencing refugee girls from war-torn Maine to death in the Salem witchcraft crisis.

Also fresh in his mind was the case of a slave named Adam, who belonged to John Saffin, a prosperous merchant and fellow judge on the General Court. In 1694 Saffin had hired Adam out to a tenant farmer with a written promise to free the slave in seven years if he proved a faithful worker. The farmer found Adam unruly and gave him back to his owner, who refused to free him as the end of the seven-year period approached. So Adam went "to Captain Sewall," as he put it, and by 1701 the case came before the court, of which both Sewall and Saffin were sitting members. Amazingly, Saffin refused to disqualify himself. In what became a personal conflict, Sewall accused Saffin of jury tampering, among other ethical lapses, and advised him to free Adam. After long contestation, the Superior Court declared Adam free in 1703.

In the meantime Saffin published a powerful attack on *The Selling of Joseph* in his *A Brief and Candid Answer to a Late Published Sheet, Entitled The Selling of Joseph* . . . (1701). In this first American point-counterpoint over slavery and its future, Saffin answered Sewall's biblical condemnation of manstealing by insisting on a distinction between stealing and buying. Saffin preferred his own injunction from Leviticus 25:44, "Both thy Bond men, and thy Bond maids . . . shall be of the Heathen . . . of them shall you buy Bond men and Bond maids." But this dispute was not merely over biblical interpretation. Saffin accused Sewall of even worse blasphemy—an effort to "invert the Order that God hath set in the world." Anticipating so much to come in proslavery thought in America, Saffin appealed to an organic, hierarchical sense of nature ordained by God with permanent "degrees and orders of men." Distinctions between princes and peasants, kings and slaves, could not be wished away, Saffin insisted.

The Sewall-Saffin exchange exposed many nerves in the Anglo-American and Puritan conscience regarding slavery. But it was the last time Americans would aggressively debate the question for nearly seven decades. In 1706, the most famous New England divine, Cotton Mather, tried to put to rest the vexing question of whether a slave must be freed if converted to Christianity. Mather opposed the slave trade, but in *The Negro Christianized,* he gave slavery a new boost of life by declaring that conversion would make Africans better slaves. Although

Sewall seemed somewhat unresolved on this question himself, his pamphlet had forced Mather, Saffin, and others to refute in print the antislavery tendencies of his arguments. For their generation and the next, Sewall's critics won the day.

Over time, *The Selling of Joseph* fell into obscurity. The reclusive abolitionist Benjamin Lay reprinted it in a publication with other writings in 1737, although it garnered few readers. It was not reprinted again until the Massachusetts Historical Society issued it in 1863, and that repository now holds the only known original edition of the text. No "movement," literary or organizational, consciously traced its roots to Sewall's pamphlet when abolitionism emerged as a political force in the early nineteenth century.

But this text is far more than a curiosity of Puritan and early antislavery thought. It remains a marker in the complex story of how two great traditions—those of the Bible and the Enlightenment—shaped the ultimate crusade to destroy slavery in America. At one point in the document, Sewall asks, "Can an Ethiopian change his skin?" In effect, Sewall answers that it does not matter. Further, in a passage all but neglected in the scholarship on the text, Sewall quotes from the most oft-used verse in the entire tradition of African American Christianity, Psalm 68:31: "Princes shall come out of Egypt and Ethiopia shall soon stretch forth her hands unto God." Well before virtually all his contemporaries, Sewall was absolutely clear on the meaning of at least one part of this great passage. "Under which names [Ethiopia]," writes Sewall, "all Africa may be comprehended; and their Promised Conversion ought to be prayed for." Over the next three centuries black Christians in America would again and again return to Psalm 68 to fashion hope, identity, and a sense of destiny in a hostile world. We can see many aspects of that history anticipated in Sewall's soul-searching attack on slavery in 1700.

Bibliography: N. H. Chamberlain, *Samuel Sewall and the World He Lived In* (1897; repr. New York, 1967). David Brion Davis, *The Problem of Slavery in Western Culture* (Ithaca, NY, 1966). Mark A. Peterson, "*The Selling of Joseph:* Bostonians, Antislavery, and the Protestant International, 1688–1733," *Massachusetts Historical Review* 4 (2002). Samuel Sewall, *The Selling of Joseph: A Memorial* (Boston, 1700), repr. in *The Diary of Samuel Sewall,* ed. M. Halsey Thomas, 2 vols. (New York, 1973). Lawrence Towner, "The Sewall-Saffin Dialogue on Slavery," *William and Mary Quarterly* 21 (1964).

DAVID BLIGHT

1722

Benjamin Franklin submits a pseudonymous satire to his brother's newspaper

THE SILENCE DOGOOD LETTERS

It was a seduction. On a spring evening in 1722, a sly Boston youth slipped the first of fourteen letters to a potential conquest. The letter writer was sixteen-year-old Benjamin Franklin and his target was James Franklin, his brother and master, whom he wished—needed—to impress with his writing. He succeeded beauti-fully. The letters were Benjamin Franklin's first literary triumph, in which he com-bined two powerful American desires, to do good and to be free, into the first of his many aliases, Silence Dogood.

Four years earlier, in 1718, Josiah Franklin had apprenticed his youngest son, Benjamin, to an older, James, a printer. Aged twenty-one, James had just achieved his legal majority; aged twelve, Benjamin signed over nine years of his life as a bonded worker. The printer's trade was a very New England one. Literacy upheld the Bible-reading faith of the region's Puritan founders, who had quickly estab-lished a college, a printing press, and schools to secure their flocks from Satan. Young Benjamin explained himself as a typical product of the place: "I do not re-member when I could not read." By the early eighteenth century, however, New England's culture of the printed word was becoming secular, commercial, and driven by London fashions, a bad outcome for the Puritans but a good one for the development of American literature.

By 1722, James Franklin was twenty-five and still struggling to establish him-self. He decided to launch a newspaper, the *New-England Courant*. Bostonians could already choose between two newspapers, and James knew his would have to make a splash or sink forever. He had one advantage. Unlike the other two pa-pers, his did not need to flatter the authorities because it was not officially li-censed by them. So James solicited writings designed to be noticed, not least be-cause the other newspaper editors would have hesitated to publish them.

The kind of piece James wanted was a satire, an emerging English genre. In Augustan England, most satires were poems—dictionary-maker Samuel Johnson would later define a satire as "a poem in which wickedness or folly is censured." Over the course of the eighteenth century, satire crept from poetry to prose, in-cluding essays, venomous little snaps at any and everyone. Essayists put pseud-onyms to their satires and "sent" them as letters to editors (though it was often the editors themselves who solicited or even wrote the pieces). In this way, the authors of the *Spectator*, a London periodical as short-lived (March 1711 to Decem-ber 1712) as it was influential, published the peevish opinions of "Sir Roger de Coverley." This burlesque or caricature of the dronish country gentry let readers enjoy both de Coverley's complaints and the comic send-up of the complainer. All such satires were evidence of authorial *wit*, the prized quality of the age.

To seem witty, everyone—from Dublin to Dominica—copied the *Spectator*. James Franklin owned a full run of the periodical and Benjamin (with smaller means) bought one treasured volume. "I thought the Writing excellent," he re-called, "and wish'd if possible to imitate it." At night, he painstakingly rendered its essays into verse, then (without consulting the original) back into prose. The results, he said, "encourag'd me to think I might possibly in time come to be a tolerable English Writer, of which I was extreamly ambitious."

He was not alone. Under some rather arch pseudonyms, James Franklin and his fellow satirists, the "Couranteers," were doing their best to affront Boston's powers-that-were. "John Harmony" parodied a fracas over singing in church. "Tom Tram" took a swipe at the local postmaster. Most notoriously, "W. Philanthropos" criticized an emergency program of inoculation that leading minister Cotton Mather spearheaded during a smallpox epidemic that raged from 1721 into 1722. Above all, the Couranteers presented themselves as witty, the clever superiors of the boring worthies whom they mocked. They declared their mission was to *"promote Enquiries after Truth, quicken and rouze the Slothful, animate and inspire the Dull."* They even vied among themselves over whose writing (and opinion) was best. One urged another to keep disgracing himself in print: "Go on, dull Soul, labour in Spite / of Nature, and your Stars to write."

The *Courant* was the first American newspaper to encourage literary effort. While other papers quoted government pronouncements and reprinted month-old news from Europe, the *Courant* did not parrot or reprint—it created. Its essays were read for the first time in Boston, not London; its literature, however imitative, was home-bred. Moreover, James Franklin exploited New England's factionalized politics to make his paper unusually argumentative. He inaugurated a tradition of American journalistic satire that would run through Mark Twain and Ambrose Bierce.

Yet one aspiring author despaired of publishing anything in James Franklin's *Courant*. Benjamin Franklin may have been polishing his prose, but his brother was unlikely to print it. The two Franklins bickered frequently and, when challenged by his sibling, James beat him, as was his legal right. Benjamin took the blows "extreamly amiss" and found his apprenticeship "very tedious." How to escape? A pseudonymous author can also be anonymous, and Benjamin realized that by writing satirical letters he could fool or force his brother into putting him into print.

To do so, Benjamin invented a persona who was a local character, whose name fairly screamed Boston. Puritans often bore hortatory names and "Silence Dogood" carried a double burden. Plus she had a backstory, in contrast to the paper-thin characters the Couranteers gave their personae. In her first letter, Dogood relates the circumstances of her birth while Franklin caricatures her (affectionately) as a censorious know-it-all. Her flawed logic only heightens the comedy of her assured delivery: "My Entrance into this troublesome World was attended with the Death of my Father, a Misfortune, which tho' I was not then capable of knowing, I shall never be able to forget." Dogood's parents had been migrating from London to Boston when her mother gave birth; her father, as he "stood upon the Deck rejoicing at my Birth," was washed overboard. Born midway between old and new worlds, Dogood was the perfect author for provincial satires that imitated metropolitan examples.

She was an instant hit. After Franklin had delivered "her" letter "at Night under the Door of the Printing House," he had "the exquisite Pleasure" the next morning of hearing the assembled Couranteers praise the work and try to guess the author's identity. James Franklin quickly published the letter on the second of April and appended a request that more be delivered either to his office or to the home of Josiah Franklin. His choice of addresses suggests that James had no idea who had created Silence Dogood, as did his subsequent decision to publish her missives in the lead position (upper left corner) on the *Courant*'s front page. Thus vindicated in his maiden effort, Benjamin wrote thirteen more letters from his creation, a meddling country parson's widow. His alter ego's two names, though they seem contradictory (what good is silence?), were actually logical choices and identified Franklin's lifelong goals as a writer.

Dogood's surname announced her main goal. "It is undoubtedly the Duty of all Persons to serve the Country they live in," she lectured, and confessed her "natural Inclination to observe and reprove the Faults of others." She also admitted herself "a mortal Enemy to arbitrary Government and unlimited Power," fair warning to anyone in power that he would be hearing from her.

In quick succession, Dogood scolded the main sources of constituted authority in Massachusetts. Her fourth letter satirizes Harvard College, a supposed center of learning that merely produced young men who were "as great Blockheads as ever, only more proud and self-conceited." Her fifth letter questions the presumed capacity of men to govern women: could men be superior to women if they were "such *Simpletons* as to humble themselves at their Feet" when they courted them? The eighth letter blasts the authorities for their recent censure of the *Courant* by quoting a key London essay on English rights: "*GUILT* only dreads Liberty of Speech." Letters nine and fourteen denounce attempts by both politicians and clerics to mix religion and politics—thus do "hypocritical Pretenders to Religion" and "blind Zealots" damage true faith and piety.

While she advised her readers to mistrust the college-educated, the clergy, government officials, and men, Dogood recommended self-help. She began close to home, with "the lamentable Condition of Widows." Though she herself had thankfully inherited "Contentment and a few Cows," other relicts survived on a humiliating charity. Dogood suggests instead *"An Office of Ensurance for Widows,"* where husbands and wives could invest against disaster. She also promotes temperance by reproducing part of a comically shaming "Drinker's Dictionary"—a drunk person is *"boozey, cogey, tipsey, fox'd, merry, mellow, fuddled,"* and *"Among the Philistines,"* not to mention *"Pretty well enter'd &c."* However amusingly, Dogood echoed serious calls for civic and self-improvement. She cited Daniel Defoe's right-thinking *Essay on Projects* (1697), and her very name brought to mind Cotton Mather's *Essays to Do Good* (1710).

Yet Dogood fulfilled her last name by disobeying her first, *Silence*. Franklin used her paradox to interrogate his society's hierarchy, especially its pervasive contrast between the free and the unfree. Females were less free than males, except when they weren't. In fact, Franklin did not stoop to inhabit a female persona—he reached above himself in order to imagine a state of freedom. An underage apprentice was roughly equivalent to a slave, which was why his master could beat him. A widow, in contrast, was comparatively free; no one beat her. Her husband's death had freed her from his authority, and might have endowed her with power over children, over property, over the community. Thus could Dogood judge Harvard a poor choice for her son, rejoice in the autonomy her few cows provided, and berate her neighbors for their assorted idiocies.

In early America, this really happened. Newspapers routinely printed letters from real women who, accused of misdeeds, wrote to defend themselves and their reputations. Some women had to defend themselves in courts of law, where they were silent at their peril. Others wrote fictions—James Franklin published a satirical letter from a real "Mrs. Staples"—though poetry was the more typical female product. All of this made the ink-stained Dogood a credible character, one through which a boy-apprentice fantasized how a scribbling social inferior might become the talk of the town. Did people think Mrs. Dogood was a real woman? Her washday-wisdom when she appraised drunks ("some shrink in the Wetting, and others swell") was credible, as was her parody of New England's native poetry in the form of funeral elegies. But her extended political discourses were less conventionally feminine. And whereas, after a moonlit stroll on Boston Common, Dogood details the sexual escapades of her fellow "*Night-Walkers*," an actual Puritan matron would have avoided such innuendo.

Perhaps because Dogood's fourteenth letter entered a very hot dispute over religion, Franklin stopped while he was ahead. After that final letter appeared in the *New-England Courant* of October 22, Franklin told his brother that the amusing widow was none other than he.

The revelation led to Benjamin's freedom. In 1723 the authorities finally forbade James Franklin to publish the offending *Courant,* at least under his own name. So he put the paper under the name "Benjamin Franklin" and, while imprisoned for libel, had his brother, now a noted writer, edit it. The subterfuge required James to free his brother from his indentures, but he made Benjamin sign a secret contract to continue his servitude, and even kept beating him. If Benjamin later conceded that he might have been "too saucy and provoking," he also concluded that his brother's violence explained the "Aversion to arbitrary Power that has stuck to me thro' my whole Life." The boy, now seventeen, saw a way to escape. Gambling that his brother would not make public their secret contract, lest that compromise the *Courant,* Benjamin absconded. To save money to buy books, he had given up eating meat; to pay for ship's passage, he sold those books and fled south, eventually to Philadelphia.

Having become free, Franklin continued to do good. As he became a successful printer, author, man of science, and statesman, his many inventions and projects—hospitals and lightning rods, education for women and freedom for slaves—show his conviction that "the noblest question in the world is *What Good may I do in it?*" In his frequent, merciless questioning of authorities who fell short of his ideal, he showed his equally strong belief that there is no power against which one should not kick a little. Thus the famous, instantly recognizable Franklin: the tireless improver and social critic who seized lightning from the sky and the scepter from the tyrants.

That man concealed another, however—a man of silence. Franklin's witty writings invite us to assume he was the life of the party, the best of all possible dinner companions in the best of all possible worlds. But the real Franklin was a reluctant public speaker and, unless huddled with a close friend or two, remarkably taciturn. Many an interlocutor struggled to get more than two words out of him, only to end up carrying the conversation. Their efforts supplied Franklin, shy and sly in equal measure, with more material for the satires that he continued to publish under pseudonyms, each belonging to a chatty character (including several outspoken women) who spoke for him, invariably to defy authority and convention. It is a mark of Franklin's enduring success as an author that these characters seduce us into thinking him someone he was not, just as, in 1722, he had seduced many a Boston reader into thinking him "handsome, and sometimes witty, but always, Sir, Your Friend and Humble Servant, SILENCE DOGOOD."

Bibliography: Joyce E. Chaplin, *The First Scientific American: Benjamin Franklin and the Pursuit of Genius* (New York, 2006). Leonard W. Labaree, ed., *The Papers of Benjamin Franklin*, vol. 1: *January 6, 1706 through December 31, 1734* (New Haven, CT, 1959). Leonard W. Labaree et al., eds., *The Autobiography of Benjamin Franklin* (New Haven, CT, 1964). J. A. Leo Lemay, *The Life of Benjamin Franklin*, vol. 1: *Journalist, 1706–1730* (Philadelphia, 2006).

JOYCE E. CHAPLIN

1740

The itinerant preacher George Whitefield converts
a member of Jonathan Edwards's congregation

THE GREAT AWAKENING

In the autumn of 1740, Samuel Belcher, a saddler in colonial Connecticut, had a sudden conversion experience. For some time, he had been worrying about sin and damnation, observing "what a Dreadfull thing it was to fall into the hands of an angry God," and had enviously regarded his friends and neighbors who visibly felt "the wonderfull workings of the Spirit of God upon the[ir] hearts." Belcher worshipped in the congregation led by Jonathan Edwards, a community that had seen a religious revival five years before, with many surprising conversions and young people reforming their frolicking ways. But Belcher did not convert until the transatlantic celebrity George Whitefield came to town, whose preaching prompted an intensely emotional experience of God's grace. "I was awakened up," writes Belcher, who, by hearing the sermons of both Edwards and Whitefield, stood, unawares, at the heart of what is known as the Great Awakening.

The Great Awakening was a series of religious revivals in the American colonies in which people experienced a "new Birth": described as an acute awareness of sight, sound, and inward feeling, as if just awakened from sleep. This religious fervor, which started in New England before spreading to the Middle Colonies and Virginia in the 1740s and 1750s, manifested itself in scenes of mass conversion, often accompanied by communal weeping and spontaneous singing. Some congregations developed "soul exercises," such as trembling and shaking, to encourage and display the bodily signs of the spirit. Despite concerns about excessive emotionalism, and clerical fears that individual experience would come to rival church authority, the revivals continued unabated. The appeal of the revivals seems to have stemmed from the fact that they supplanted the older schemes of careful intellectual preparation for salvation with an immediate, overpowering experience of conversion.

The only problem is, the Great Awakening may never have happened. The varied and fragmented nature of the revivals and the arguable absence of any long-term consequences belie the idea that a single religious movement swept the colonies. And if such unified fervor did exist, historians argue it was something similar to the European post-Reformation revivals, rather than being a uniquely American phenomenon. However, although scholarly skepticism is certainly warranted, it is still helpful to think of the Great Awakening as an integrated series of events. That way one views the colonies in enlightening ways, by acknowledging transatlantic correspondences, for example, while harnessing great explanatory power for the development of American religious life.

Many regional revivals were sparked or linked by the activities of George Whitefield, an English itinerant preacher who came to America in 1739 and drew crowds of tens of thousands of people to his open-air sermons. Whitefield had cultivated a highly dramatic style of preaching, and his homiletic performances, during which he physically acted out fear and rapture, were widely recognized as sensational. Stomping and cavorting on stage, crawling on his knees, and breaking down in tears, Whitefield exhibited the overpowering effects of divine power on his body, often exclaiming ("Ah! Oh!") as much as speaking. He was accused of exchanging theatrics for substance and, like many celebrity preachers—a persona he arguably pioneered and that remains current in the American context, as seen in the twentieth-century success of Billy Graham—he rarely influenced church attendance or brought about permanent change in religious behavior.

Whitefield's sermons were mainly oral and visual spectacles, and he made his way into American literary history primarily through others' writings: Benjamin Franklin caustically noted Whitefield's "wonderful power over the hearts and purses of his hearers," and the fame of Phillis Wheatley, a black poet from Boston, largely rested on her elegy on Whitefield. Olaudah Equiano, in his abolitionist autobiography, remembers how hard Whitefield worked while preaching, comparing his exertions to slave labor: "He sweat[ed] as much as I ever did while in slavery on Montserrat beach . . . I had never before seen divines exert themselves in this manner." Note that Equiano does not mention anything Whitefield said, only what he looked like, underscoring the preacher's visual and physical appeal. But Whitefield's greatest historical contribution was his mode of itinerant preaching, which continues to be characteristic of revivalist movements in America.

Itinerancy, whereby a preacher travels around, unconnected to a parish or congregation, was widely perceived as a threat to the social order because it situated religious practice and instruction outside the physical structure, and therefore outside the control, of the established church. Itinerants, due to their mobility and capacity to reach large audiences, formed a system of mass communication between settlers in colonial America. Whitefield didn't rely on just word of mouth, however, but also used far-reaching print networks to advertise and promote his appearances. Other itinerants, such as Gilbert Tennent, challenged orthodoxy more directly: preaching against the American Presbyterian church, Tennent famously defined the qualifications of a good minister as personal experience of grace and active faith, rather than credentials. It was, he argued, a good idea not only for ministers to preach in another's territory but also for churchgoers to leave their congregations in search of spiritual growth—a notion that undermined the parish system that was central to colonial religion.

Though some itinerants had no formal training as ministers, most were educated and ordained within a Protestant denomination (usually Anglican, Congregationalist, or Presbyterian). Tennent's radical idea that an immediate knowledge of grace qualified one to preach and teach still subsists in the phenomenon of lay and even child preachers in American evangelicalism today. The translation of spiritual authority into political opinion also has its origins in the eighteenth-century revivals. Whitefield advocated educating and Christianizing slaves; a perspective that, though he never spoke out directly against the institution of slavery, led him to be blamed for "encourag[ing] the negroes" during the New York slave conspiracy of 1741. In 1750s Virginia, Samuel Davies taught slaves to read before he began publicizing his belief that the colony's large black population threatened the security of the whites, causing exasperation and anger among slaveholders. Itinerant preachers fostered an inclusive form of religion, creating communities in open fields rather than church pews, without regard for race, gender, and class. Whitefield (known as the Grand Itinerant), David Brainerd (a missionary to the Indians), and Eleazar Wheelock (the future founder of Dartmouth College) were perceived as proponents of racial equality and social activism: elements that would become more pronounced during the Second Great Awakening in the early nineteenth century.

The cross-cultural and cross-regional appeal of religious revivalism in the mid-eighteenth century is vividly illustrated by the so-called Indian Great Awakening. From the 1740s to the 1760s, Delaware and Mahicans in Pennsylvania experienced a period of religious revitalization consisting of a return to and revival of indigenous practices in combination with sudden conversions to Christianity. Reports from the revival, from Brainerd's *Journal* for example, echo descriptions of Christian congregations: "Most were much affected & many were in much distress; & some could neither go, nor stand; but lay flat on the ground as if stab'd at heart: Crying incessantly for mercy." At the same time, traveling Indian visionaries (itinerants, if you will) counseled separation from the ways of the whites and attributed recent epidemics and famines to divine displeasure. It is important to note that Native American beliefs and Christianity were not mutually exclusive during these episodes: faith in rituals of offering, for example, coexisted with an interest in the Bible and led to the adoption of Christ or "the Lamb" as an accepted sacrificial object. The Indian Awakening is thus neither an instance of all-out Native resistance nor one of wholesale cultural conversion. The ambiguous results of the Indian Awakening are, in a sense, symptomatic of the diffuse workings of the entire Great Awakening.

Connecting the colonial revivals from the 1740s to the 1760s to the religious fervor in Jonathan Edwards's church between 1733 and 1735 requires some historical imagination. Edwards, who was raised and trained in the Puritan tradition, faithfully ministered to one flock in Northampton, Massachusetts, emphasizing the importance of a personally felt conversion experience—a tenet that had been central to the seventeenth-century church in New England. His congregation was already famous for its "spiritual harvests" under the direction of Edwards's grandfather, Solomon Stoddard. Edwards developed a new way of speaking about the sensory experience of grace, linking the beauty of nature and the rapturous joy of salvation in an appeal to the passions of his hearers. Seemingly in response to such stimuli, his parishioners began converting. Edwards described the 1730s events in a letter to Boston preacher Benjamin Colman, who published these observations as a pamphlet called *A Faithful Narrative of the Surprising Work of God* (1738), which provided the blueprint for the later revivals in America and Britain. In Northampton, the spiritual turmoil manifested itself in constant conversations about the requirements for salvation as well as in physical performances of ecstasy and despair: "The assembly in general were . . . in tears . . . some weeping with sorrow and distress, others with joy and love, others with pity and concern for the souls of their neighbors." Though the conversions subsided by 1736, the town's experience is regarded as the beginning of the American revivalist tradition.

In 1740, Edwards invited Whitefield to preach in his parish, which resulted in the conversion of Samuel Belcher. The acquaintance of Edwards and Whitefield is important, as it has historically served to link the earlier isolated events to Whitefield's later success. Though he was not personally involved in the revivals in Pennsylvania and the South, Edwards became the most important philosophical defender of evangelicalism as criticism of the movement mounted. In his *Treatise Concerning Religious Affections* (1746), he tried to distinguish false conversions from real ones and to define the proper place of emotion in religion. Edwards's attachment to New England tradition led him to start requiring conversion narratives—so freely given during the Awakening—from his parishioners, which turned his congregation against him. From 1744 to 1748 not a single churchgoer felt the grace of God, forming an ignominious ending to Edwards's ministerial activities.

Jonathan Edwards's writings, however, became and remained famous in their own right. His sermons include "Sinners in the Hands of an Angry God" (1741), a terrifying evocation of divine punishment, allegedly delivered in monotone, and "Images and Shadows of Divine Things" (compiled from his notebooks), in which he locates divine revelation in nature: a theme that also appears in many of his other works and may have inspired Ralph Waldo Emerson. Copies of Edwards's *Personal Narrative* (ca. 1740), an account of the highs and lows of his personal religious experience, continued to sell in the hundreds of thousands throughout the nineteenth century. In it, he integrates the two strains of thought that also dominate lay conversion narratives from the revivals: joy and bliss at God's goodness and beauty alongside a sense of ingrained sinfulness and self-loathing. This strictly binary approach prompts his prose to swerve from descriptions of apparent corporeal pleasure in the presence of God—"inexpressible purity, brightness, peacefulness and ravishment"—to such a despairing sense of sin that it fractures grammar and meaning: "Infinite upon Infinite. Infinite upon Infinite!" These two extremes are reconciled in Edwards's validation of strict Calvinist doctrine, according to which an all-powerful and just God controls the fate of worthless humans. The most memorable scenes in his narrative, however, are not of abjection but of delight: Edwards's "sweetness and longings and pantings of soul," "burning desire," and "eager thirsting" make spiritual experience sound sensual and seductive.

Edwards's rapturous personal prose also reveals the theological issue at the heart of the Great Awakening: the nature of "saving knowledge." Opponents of the revivals, who came to be known as the "Old Lights" or the "Old Side," argued that true conversion followed an established order and procedure, which operated (in a particularly pre-Enlightenment twist) through reason, rather than through beauty or feeling. Charles Chauncy, a Boston divine, formulated damning indictments of revivalist sentiment, which he disparagingly called enthusiasm: "The cause of this *enthusiasm* is a bad temperament of the blood and spirits; 'tis properly a disease, a sort of madness . . . they are really beside themselves, acting as truly by the blind impetus of a wild fancy, as tho' they had neither reason nor understanding." Chauncy's physiological explanations echo the Awakening's interest in bodily signs, though he of course condemns such corporeal manifestations of religiosity. Yet even in Chauncy's remarks, as in Calvinist philosophy more generally, the revivals caused a shift away from the unknowable nature of God to an assessment of the state of man.

Practically speaking, the effects of the Awakening were limited: aside from schism in the American Presbyterian church, when Gilbert Tennent was ejected from the Synod of Philadelphia and joined the Synod of New York, some churchgoers farther north left their congregations to form separate communities, which would later become the New England Baptist Church. However, the small numbers and marginal status of such breakaway congregations cast real doubt on the concrete influence of the revivals. In light of the few lasting outcomes of the Great Awakening, we might justifiably wonder if the movement existed at all, and why it even matters.

First, the similarities between the Northampton awakening, Edwards's and Whitefield's preaching, and later revivals reveal a change in theological emphasis from doctrine to discourse. These events all stressed personal affect and reconfigured the place of emotion in religious experience in ways that influenced later American philosophers, most notably William James. In the case of Edwards and Whitefield, the combination and intersection of oral delivery and written text established the sermon form and linked commerce and conversion in ways that are characteristic of the eighteenth-century public sphere. The rhetoric of embodiment, which appears far more prominently in preachers' performances than in converts' accounts, also marks the beginnings of the spectacle of religion in America, where some evangelicals still shake and tremble, speak in tongues, and handle snakes.

But the most interesting thing about the Great Awakening is perhaps the inspiration it has provided to generations of American historians. The revivals were at the center of paradigmatic interpretations of American intellectual history and have been variously credited with developing the spirit of Jacksonian democracy (George Bancroft), images and shadows of transcendentalism (Perry Miller), and the origins of the American Revolution (Alan Heimert). The fact that the Awakening has given rise to such widely varying readings proves its versatility and its ultimately enigmatic nature. Though its definitive significance won't ever be established, the Great Awakening exists, one might argue, by virtue of its ability to mean many different things to many different people and its singular capacity to precede or explain distinctively American developments.

Bibliography: Charles Chauncy, *Enthusiasm described and caution'd against. A Sermon Preach'd ... the Lord's Day after the Commencement* (Boston, 1742). Jonathan Edwards, *A Faithful Narrative of the Surprizing Work of God,* 2nd ed. (London, 1738); *Personal Narrative* (1765), *edwards.yale.edu.* Olaudah Equiano, *The Interesting Narrative and Other Writings,* ed. Vincent Carretta (New York, 1995). Frank Lambert, *Inventing the "Great Awakening"* (Princeton, NJ, 1999). J. A. Leo Lemay and P. M. Zall, eds. *The Autobiography of Benjamin Franklin: A Genetic Text* (Knoxville, TN, 1981). Kenneth P. Minkema, "A Great Awakening Conversion: The Relation of Samuel Belcher," *William and Mary Quarterly,* 3rd ser., 44, no. 1 (1987): 121–126. Gilbert Tennent, *The danger of an unconverted ministry, considered in a sermon on Mark VI.34* (Philadelphia, 1740).

JOANNE VAN DER WOUDE

Late 1740s; 1814, September 13–14

"Yankee Doodle" goes to town; Francis Scott Key writes "The Star-Spangled Banner"

Two National Anthems

Like any robust folk tune, "Yankee Doodle" has evolved with the times. The verse about a man who came to town riding on a pony was just one—almost certainly not the first and perhaps not even the most popular—of many set to a melody that, by the Revolutionary War, had already achieved hit status. Throughout the late 1760s and the first half of the 1770s, British soldiers performed "Yankee Doodle" as mock music—a jaunty taunt—in and around Boston. During the occupation of that city, as colonials sought to buy or, better, steal muskets from British soldiers, the occupiers sang:

> Yankee Doodle's come to town
>   For to buy a firelock.
> We will tar and feather him,
>   And so we will John Hancock.

But after Bunker Hill, colonials reclaimed "Yankee Doodle," playing it to surrendering British forces at Saratoga and Yorktown. The British officer Thomas Anburey admitted as much when he wrote in 1777: "*Yankee Doodle* is now their paean, a favorite of favorites, played in their army, esteemed as warlike as the Grenadier's

March—it is the lover's spell, the nurse's lullaby. After our rapid successes, we held the Yankees in great contempt, but it was not a little mortifying to hear them play this tune, when their army marched down to our surrender." Upbeat, comic, "Yankee Doodle" had the quintessential merit of adaptability. Or, as a stanza published in 1799 put it:

> Sing Yankee Doodle, that fine tune
> 　Americans delight in.
> It suits for peace, it suits for fun,
> 　It suits as well for fighting.

In colonial and revolutionary America, one could hear it from fife and fiddle on both sides, for dance as well as song.

While it is generally agreed that the words and music are native to America, the genesis of "Yankee Doodle" remains obscure. The eminent musicologist at the Library of Congress, Oscar Sonneck, in his century-old, as yet unsurpassed investigation of the song's origins, shot such holes in sixteen arguments made by others that he left no single theory intact. Still, there are various points of accord, or at least less discord. Consensus holds that the tune was circulating by the mid-eighteenth century, though its earliest identified printing was in Glasgow, in 1782. The earliest known verses, which reference the 1745 victory of the English and New England colonials over the French at Cape Breton, may have been in oral circulation as long ago as the late 1740s:

> Brother Ephraim sold his Cow
> 　And Bought him a Commission,
> And then he went to Canada
> 　To fight for the Nation.
> But when Ephraim he came home
> 　He prov'd an arrant Coward,
> He wouldn't fight the Frenchmen there,
> 　For fear of being devour'd.

The first known published reference to "Yankee Doodle" appeared in Andrew Barton's *The Disappointment,* a comic opera printed in New York in 1767, which is another indication that the song was popular before the Revolution. But it wasn't until sometime during the last quarter of the eighteenth century, probably around 1775, that the music and words first appeared together, in an undated English broadside published by Thomas Skillern that includes a performance note that is also a jeer at the rustic English roots of many American emigrants: "the Words to be Sung thro' the Nose, & in the West Country drawl & dialect."

We may think of "Yankee Doodle" as a children's song now, with its silly do-little "Yankee," possibly from the Dutch *Janke,* "little John" (originally applied specifically to New Englanders), calling his feathered cap "Macaroni"—not a reference to pasta but to the affected continental fashions of later eighteenth-century foppish Englishmen known as "Macaronies." If "Yankee Doodle" has turned into a nursery rhyme, Skillern's broadside reveals how earthy the original was, or what is as close to an "original" as we are likely to get. Indeed, in its initial forms, noisy, bawdy, and derisive "Yankee Doodle" may in some instances have functioned a bit like earlier rough music had. Sonneck refused to print the broadside's final stanzas in full, finding the lines "too obscene for quotation." For better or, in this case maybe, worse, scholarship too evolves with the times, and so:

> Two and two may go to Bed;
>   Two and two together,
> And if there is not room enough,
>   Lie one a top o'to'ther.

The coarseness of these lines serves to remind us that this tune was, and is, folk music in a bodily sense. Lively "Yankee Doodle" is truly *of* the people. The result was that verses proliferated like limericks: the character Jonathan in Royall Tyler's *The Contrast* (performed in 1787, published in 1790) boasts that he "can't sing but a hundred and ninety-nine verses: Our Tabitha at home can sing it all."

Time and shifting sensibilities have obscured the corporal dimension of "Yankee Doodle," but vestiges remain in the rakish chorus. The chorus is believed to be the work of one Edward Bangs, Harvard sophomore, class of 1777, and Minuteman, who, it has been claimed (on the authority of an assertion by Edward Everett Hale that, as with so much else about this song, has been subsequently questioned), wrote an "official" text for "Yankee Doodle" called "The Yankee's Return from Camp" when Washington took command at Cambridge. This version, which tells of a boy observing the goings-on at the provincial camp, has fifteen stanzas in addition to the chorus, including some adapted from earlier versions. The stanzas are long forgotten, but the familiar chorus survives, alongside the "Macaroni" verse, in what is essentially a composite text, the "Yankee Doodle" we know:

> Yankee Doodle, keep it up,
>   Yankee Doodle dandy,
> Mind the music and the step,
>   And with the girls be handy.

These lyrics, first published in the 1780s, are a call for the dandified everyman not only to keep up his posturing but also to stay light on his feet, alluding on the one hand to Yankee pretension, and on the other to the country dances and military marches that kept colonial bodies in motion. It makes a certain kind of sense that this bit of folk song became so popular that it endures as the remnant from "The Yankee's Return from Camp" in "Yankee Doodle" today. A comic refrain for an aspiring nation, it is an appropriately restless sound track for a people on the move.

If "Yankee Doodle" is a collective production, an American joke set to a jig, "The Star-Spangled Banner" is Francis Scott Key's hymn, an expression of faith in the constancy of his nation as embodied in its most recognizable material handiwork. The story of that fateful night in 1814 when, after obtaining the release of a prisoner of war, Key watched from a sloop offshore as English ships bombarded Fort McHenry in the Battle of Baltimore is well known, in no small part because the poem he drafted at daybreak starts to tell it. "Defence of Fort M'Henry," the title his work bore when it appeared in a broadside on about September 17, has the effect of enlisting readers in his watchful task as Key, all eyes and ears, unfurls his rhetorical questions in meter and rhyme.

As Key on some level likely was aware when writing them, and as was clear upon publication, his words fit perfectly the tune of "Anacreon in Heaven," or, as it became known, "The Anacreontic Song," composed about 1775 with music by John Stafford Smith and lyrics by Ralph Tomlinson. "The Anacreontic" was an import, and was not, as has often been claimed, a rowdy "drinking song" but an English constitutional song initially performed for the London meetings of the Anacreontic Society, a convivial group named for the Greek poet who extolled the virtues of love and wine. The song became a transatlantic success, with at least eighty-five new sets of lyrics appearing in America between 1785 and 1820, including, about a decade before "The Star-Spangled Banner," a version by Key that has several similarities with his later effort. Yet we are left with the undeniable fact that the melody for the future national anthem is a foreign one. In 1814, as he waited through the anxious dawn, did Key choose an English tune to honor American endurance against English attack, as a commentary on what he perceived as a tragically internecine war? Or was it meant as a subversive tweak at the foe? Either explanation risks overreading. In his search for a metric structure to make order out of the chaos and fear he experienced, Key may subconsciously have settled on the musical rhythm that, so widely popular and familiar to him from at least a decade earlier, would have been well lodged in his memory.

In contrast to the folk-song heritage of "Yankee Doodle," "The Star-Spangled Banner" has a closer kinship to parlor music, as Richard Crawford has noted. The unusual—what critics have called unsingable—range of the melody, an octave and a half, hints at the purpose of the original song, as something of a showcase for vocal display. While "Yankee Doodle" evolved orally over decades and shifting contexts, within just months of the publication of Key's poem, "The Star-Spangled Banner" appeared more or less in its familiar form as sheet music. This was a prephonographic type of reproduction that facilitated middle-class domestic consumption, repetition, and patriotic canonization, though official recognition of the song as the national anthem would not come until 1931.

One of the highlights of the 1970 film *Woodstock,* Jimi Hendrix's version of the song still startles because he dispenses with the words and reworks the staid tune into an electric-guitar assault on the Vietnam War, mimicking the sounds of planes and bombs and interpolating the melody of "Taps." The challenge to the common voice presented by the melody parallels the notorious problem of the lyrics. Everyone can remember the words to the modern-day "Yankee Doodle," but who can recite all four verses, let alone, if pop culture is any indication, the first verse of "The Star-Spangled Banner"? As more than one observer has put it, the title might as well be "The Star-Mangled Banner."

Chief among the many ironies surrounding Key's "The Star-Spangled Banner" is that his "land of the free" was also the home of the slave. And, like other Southern landholders of the time, the devoutly religious man who lauded that "land of the free" was a slave owner himself. Key, born in Frederick County, Maryland, and raised on his family's plantation, opposed abolition, helped found the American

Colonization Society, and considered African Americans, in his own words, "a distinct and inferior race of people, which all experience proves to be the greatest evil that afflicts a community." Along with the slave labor that was so essential to and yet unacknowledged in Key's conception of "the land of the free," it is important to remember that the object "whose broad stripes and bright stars" Key strains to see "by the dawn's early light"—the focal point of the entire song—is a product of unsung work, specifically women's work. In 1813, Baltimore flag maker Mary Pickersgill was contracted to make two flags for Fort McHenry: the larger garrison flag, measuring thirty feet by forty-two feet, that is currently in the Smithsonian Institution, and a smaller storm flag, seventeen by twenty-five feet, whereabouts unknown. Assisted by her daughter and likely her mother and nieces, Pickersgill used 400 yards of bunting in the making of the garrison flag alone, which was so large she requested permission from the local brewery to assemble it on the floor of the malt house. After that long night of September 13–14, which flag "was still there"? Eyewitness accounts tell that at dawn the massive garrison flag that inspired Key was raised, to the firing of the morning gun and the playing of (what else?) "Yankee Doodle." However, no one is quite sure which of the two star-spangled banners flew "at the twilight's last gleaming" and "through the night," a stormy one. If contemporary military procedures were followed, it would have been the smaller flag, or possibly both. It turns out that sober Key, in the spirit of Anacreon, may have been seeing double.

Bibliography: Richard Crawford, *America's Musical Life: A History* (New York, 2001). S. Foster Damon, *Yankee Doodle* (Providence, RI, 1959). Edward S. Delaplaine, *Francis Scott Key: Life and Times* (New York, 1937). P. W. Filby and Edward G. Howard, *Star-Spangled Books* (Baltimore, 1972). J. A. Leo Lemay, "The American Origins of 'Yankee Doodle,'" *William and Mary Quarterly*, 3rd ser., 33 (1976): 435–464. Sam Meyer, *Paradoxes of Fame: The Francis Scott Key Story* (Annapolis, MD, 1995). Irvin Molotsky, *The Flag, the Poet and the Song: The Story of the Star-Spangled Banner* (New York, 2001). Oscar George Theodore Sonneck, *Report on "The Star-Spangled Banner," "Hail Columbia," "America," "Yankee Doodle"* (Washington, 1909); *"The Star Spangled Banner"* (Washington, 1914). George J. Svejda, *History of the Star Spangled Banner from 1814 to the Present* (Washington, DC, 1969). Lonn Taylor, *The Star-Spangled Banner: The Flag That Inspired the National Anthem* (New York, 2000). *Filmography: Woodstock,* directed by Michael Wadleigh (1970).

JOHN PICKER

1765, December 23

Michel-Guillaume Jean de Crèvecoeur is naturalized as a citizen of the colony of New York

LETTERS FROM AN AMERICAN FARMER

Despite having left a considerable paper trail and formed friendships with leading figures in America and France, Crèvecoeur remains a quite shadowy figure. Born in 1735 into the minor aristocracy of Normandy, he lived in England for some time in his teens and at twenty became an officer in Montcalm's French forces in what would become Canada, where he distinguished himself as a surveyor and cartographer during the Seven Years' War. However, for unexplained and apparently disreputable reasons, he resigned from the army after the French defeat in the Battle of the Plains of Abraham in 1759. In the following years he traveled extensively in North America, voyaging down the Ohio River clad in bearskin and moccasins.

In 1765 he decided to become a naturalized citizen of the colony of New York, and he gave himself a new name: James Hector St. John. After marrying a pastor's daughter with the fine American name of Mehitable Tippet, he settled down in Orange County, New York, on a 250-acre farm called Pine Hill, where he felled trees, drained swampland, became a successful farmer, sired three children (the first received the symbolic name America-Frances), and began drafting the essays that would form the basis of his literary masterpiece, *Letters from an American Farmer*, which was published in London in 1782.

Crèvecoeur's changes of name—he was also known to the Oneida Indians, who ceremonially adopted him in 1767, as Cahioharra—reflect a chameleonic life story in which his complicated allegiances to France, Britain, and America were constantly shifting, and his book is a fascinating blend of naturalistic detail, romantic fantasy, and nostalgic exaltation of a lost golden age. Crèvecoeur the writer helped to create an abiding myth of America, while Crèvecoeur the man lived through historical complexities that he resolutely elides in his book until just before the end.

The letters in the book, nominally addressed to an Englishman called "F.B.," purport to be the work of an unsophisticated Pennsylvania rustic named James, who doubts that he can be writing anything of interest and whose Quaker wife warns that he will become known contemptuously as "the scribbling farmer." But in an age that glorified the man of feeling, James is proud to be "the farmer of feelings," and he launches into a mellow georgic that is all the more seductive for seeming artlessly sincere, written in an energetic, colloquial style that carries no trace at all of gallicism. James guides the plow while his wife sits knitting in the shade, "praising the straightness of my furrows and the docility of my horses"; he domesticates bees that he traps in the forest; he rescues quail from freezing in the winter; and insofar as the larger political world impinges at all, it is only to confirm the harmony of this peaceable kingdom: "The law is to us precisely what I am in my barnyard, a bridle and check to prevent the strong and greedy from oppressing the timid and weak." The bees play their helpful role precisely because the best government is the one that governs least. "I seldom thwart their inclinations. It is in freedom that they work. Were I to confine them, they would dwindle away and quit their labour." Even a "curious republic of industrious hornets" proves to be benign and is brought indoors to kill flies (snatched improbably from the very faces of the children): "and though they are fierce and vindictive, yet kindness and hospitality have made them useful and harmless."

After setting this auspicious scene, Crèvecoeur the proto-Thoreau becomes a proto-Tocqueville, asking explicitly in the book's third letter, "What is an American?" Even before the separation of the colonies from England, this French immigrant perceives "a new mode of living, a new social system" through which a novel human type has emerged. "The American is a new man, who acts upon new principles," he writes. This letter is pregnant with themes of future promise, from the melting pot to manifest destiny: "Here individuals of all nations are melted into a new race of men, whose labors and posterity will one day cause great changes in the world." Above all it celebrates a Jeffersonian utopia of independent freeholders living in "the intermediate space" between the commercial seaboard and the wild frontier. The original inhabitants, who were hunters with no interest in farming, have withdrawn tactfully into distant forests, and the maternal land "opens her broad lap to receive the perpetual accession of new comers, and to supply them with food." In an antiurban world that has much in common with Jefferson's agrarian ideal, these new Americans are very like the crops they tend and reap. "In Europe they were as so many useless plants, wanting vegetative mould and refreshing showers. They withered, and were mowed down by want, hunger, and war; but now, by the power of transplantation, like all other plants, they have taken root and flourished!" While nature gives her blessing, it is the indefatigable settlers themselves who achieve success through their relentless labors. One immigrant described by James, "Andrew the Hebridean," exemplifies the type, described as thriving in Pennsylvania after leaving barren Scotland, where he had been little better than a serf. Crèvecoeur adds that out of twelve immigrant families, nine Germans would succeed, seven Scots, and only four Irish.

Crèvecoeur's own life as a working farmer was perfectly real. Like James, he built and followed his own plow, and he slaughtered his own pigs. But these opening and best-remembered letters occupy less than half the book. After the accounts of Pennsylvania farm life, the book moves to accounts of life on Nantucket and then in Charleston. Nantucket fascinates Crèvecoeur, with its sandy barrenness—hopeless for farming—out of which its tireless inhabitants have fashioned their own little paradise by hunting the monsters of the deep. They, too, are quintessential Americans, at once soberly practical and irrepressibly adventurous, and also tolerantly Quaker in a style that had been admired by Enlightenment writers ever since Voltaire's *English Letters,* published half a century before. An account of the various types of whales anticipates the "Cetology" chapter in *Moby-Dick,* and Crèvecoeur mentions that some Nantucket whalers even talk of attempting the remote Pacific.

South Carolina, in contrast, represents a cautionary antimodel, "where mankind reap too much, do not toil enough, and are liable to enjoy too fast the benefits of life." Still worse, the self-indulgent luxury of the South is founded on abusive slavery. In a shocking anecdote, Crèvecoeur, writing as James, describes strolling through the woods on his way to a dinner party when he is disturbed by weird inarticulate sounds and encounters a slave, suspended in a cage, who has been left to die because he killed his overseer. Nature itself joins in the torment as swarms of birds pluck at his wounds and insects drink his blood. All James can do is to give the dying man some water and proceed grimly to the dinner, at which he is told matter-of-factly that such barbarism is both justified and necessary. To be sure, although he strongly condemns slavery, it is more for its cruelty than for its institutional status. In Pennsylvania, he comments complacently, "My negroes are tolerably faithful and healthy."

Nature is no longer as benign as she seemed at first. Rattlesnakes and lethal copperheads are described, and even the brilliant hummingbirds turn out to be irascible and belligerent, often fighting each other to the death. By way of relief, however, a new voice, that of a Russian visitor who perhaps stands in for the earlier and more optimistic Crèvecoeur, recounts a visit with the naturalist John Bartram during which he is charmed by the music made by the wind on an aeolian harp, a symbol of man's harmony with nature. But the final letter bids a decisive farewell to any idyllic vision. The Revolutionary War has intervened—though it is never explicitly named—and the continent is deluged in blood, which Crèvecoeur chooses to identify as being the work of Indians in league with the European combatants. Some Indians are still seen as noble savages, however, and James, in despair at the collapsing political situation, resolves to migrate with his family to the deep forest, join a friendly tribe, and live there in the native manner. He explains that he will nevertheless take care to teach his children to farm, lest they regress into primitive hunters, and he will forbid intermarriage with their hosts, "for however I respect the simple, the inoffensive society of these people in their villages, the strongest prejudices would make me abhor any alliance with them in blood, disagreeable no doubt to nature's intentions."

In actuality the trauma of the Revolution was far more complex than this sad but simple story, and Crèvecoeur unexpectedly found himself in a painfully equivocal situation. While he was a citizen of New York, it was British New York, and he believed that British rule was the essential safeguard against factionalism and potential anarchy. Yet by now he also regarded himself as profoundly American, and he hesitated to identify wholeheartedly with the Tory loyalists. Accordingly he resolved to return to France with his eldest son, intending to reclaim his inheritance there. However, when he arrived in New York City ready to sail in 1778, his trunk full of plant specimens was discovered to contain a secret compartment packed with papers. Most of these were drafts of material for the *Letters,* but some writings had political implications and the British authorities suspected that he might be a rebel spy, a man of secrets and duplicity for whom the deceptive trunk was an apt emblem. In an unpublished essay written years afterward, his description of a person under interrogation for disloyalty captures the ambiguity of his position between hostile camps: "My not being a declared enemy made me a passive friend." Penniless and confined to prison for several months, he had a nervous breakdown and contemplated suicide. Crèvecoeur and his son did not reach France until 1780.

Two years after that, *Letters from an American Farmer* was finally published, in English. As Crèvecoeur remarked in a letter in the same year, he wrote in English because he believed it was superior to French in its freedom and its capacity to express novel and daring ideas. The author of *Letters* was given as "J. Hector St. John, a Farmer in Pennsylvania," although by then St. John had metamorphosed once more into Michel-Guillaume de Crèvecoeur and was further than ever from the simple Farmer James. An enthusiastic public hailed the book as a veracious picture of America, as the author encouraged them to do: "Believe me, what I write is all true and real." But in truth *Letters from an American Farmer* was an elegy for a lost paradise; George Washington commented tactfully that it was "embellished with rather too flattering circumstances."

The book's success prompted the French government to send Crèvecoeur back to America in 1783 to serve as consul in New York, where he learned to his grief that Pine Hill farm had burned during the war and his wife had died; his other two children had fortunately been taken to Boston by a well-wisher. After seven years as consul, during which he did his best to conceal his earlier hostility to the Revolution, Crèvecoeur returned to France for good, with his children. His friend Brissot de Warville eloquently captured his habitual mysteriousness during this period: "Crèvecoeur always had a gloomy countenance and unquiet air . . . His conduct before the Revolution wasn't the only thing that Crèvecoeur wanted to hide; he had had domestic sorrows that he enveloped under an impenetrable veil."

Revising and enlarging the *Letters* through successive editions became the main concern of Crèvecoeur's later years, along with completing a three-volume work on his North American travels, and miscellaneous pieces such as a treatise on the culture of the potato. Leaving government service at the time of the French Revolution, he settled into the role of custodian of his own legend, claiming, for example, to have participated in his friend Benjamin Franklin's kite experiments, although he hadn't even met Franklin at that time.

In Crèvecoeur's writings there had always been a sustained lament for the past, even in the earliest version of the *Letters*. With elegiac plangency he had enumerated "those powerful tribes which once dwelt between the rivers Hudson, Connecticut, Piskàtàquà, and Kènnebèck, the Mèhikaudret, Mohiguine, Pèquods, Narragansets, Nianticks, Massachusets, Wampanougs, Nipnets, Tarranteens, etc.—they are gone, and every memorial of them is lost." Even in culturally rich Europe, as the Russian traveler later in the volume tells John Bartram, the pavements of Pompeii "appeared to have been considerably worn by the great number of people which had once traveled over them. But now how distant: neither builder nor proprietors remain; nothing is known!" And Crèvecoeur describes himself, in a prophetic image set down when he was not yet fifty, as resembling "one of the stones of a ruined arch, still retaining that pristine form which anciently fitted the place I occupied, but the center is tumbled down; I can be nothing until I am replaced, either in the former circle, or in some stronger one."

Crèvecoeur died in 1813 at the age of seventy-eight, more than four decades after the experiences that formed the foundation of his fame, brooding, finally, with an unstable mixture of bitterness and sentimentality about prerevolutionary America. The twentieth-century poet John Berryman justly plays on the literal meaning of the name Crèvecoeur in "Dream Song 5" (1964): "Mr. Heartbreak, the New Man, / come to farm a crazy land."

Bibliography: Gay Wilson Allen and Roger Asselineau, *St. John de Crèvecoeur: The Life of an American Farmer* (New York, 1987). J.-P. Brissot de Warville, *Mémoires de Brissot . . . sur ses contemporains, et la Revolution Française* (Paris, 1830). Bernard Chevignard, *Michel Saint-John de Crèvecoeur* (Paris, 2004). Thomas Philbrick, *St. John de Crèvecoeur* (New York, 1970). J. Hector St. John de Crèvecoeur, *Letters from an American Farmer,* ed. Susan Manning (Oxford, 1997); *More Letters from the American Farmer: An Edition of the Works in English Left Unpublished by Crèvecoeur,* ed. Dennis D. Moore (Athens, GA, 1995).

LEO DAMROSCH

1773, September
Phillis Wheatley is manumitted

"Shakespeare's Darker Sister"

More than a century after Phillis Wheatley's death in Boston, Virginia Woolf wrote that it was "unthinkable that any woman in Shakespeare's day should have had Shakespeare's genius. For genius like Shakespeare's is not born among the labouring, uneducated, servile people . . . Intellectual freedom depends upon material things. Poetry depends upon intellectual freedom." Wheatley was born in West Africa nearly a century and a half after the Bard's death and has often been called a genius, but she was also a laborer, if one neither servile nor uneducated.

Born close to what Woolf saw as the nineteenth century's rising swell of published female authors, Wheatley was hobbled by a life of poverty and servitude in America, where she was forced into slavery as a child. Nevertheless she swiftly apprehended her new nation's English language, and Wheatley became a teenage sensation following the 1770 publication of her elegy for the Reverend George Whitefield, a celebrated evangelist. Her trip to England that followed a few years later, in 1773, has been called by Frank Shuffelton the first American author book tour. Wheatley did not, however, become free until later that year, subsequent to the publication of her first and only book, *Poems on Various Subjects, Religious and Moral.*

These two events, the publication of her sole book and her manumission, occurred within months of each other, and constitute the most significant events of her life. In 1773 Wheatley was about twenty years old, and she had already attained what was in the outside world, and perhaps for herself as well, the apogee of her existence: freedom and intellectual recognition. Notwithstanding the singularity of these events, another eleven years of her brief life remained, during which she would marry, have three children, and publish not even a handful of poems. Wheatley's life after manumission, in fact, was marked by a precipitous decline in her published output: four poems only appeared during her years of freedom, years that may have been marked as much or more by hardship as by exhilaration. Once a celebrated slave, Wheatley became after marriage a near-anonymous free black woman. Depending on your allegiance to one aspect of Wheatley's biography or another, her life can be seen as a tragedy or a miracle. She has had plenty of less sanguine readers, dedicated to noting her work as merely a curiosity or as racially self-abasing doggerel. Although long lost in an unmarked grave, Wheatley nonetheless continues to cast a long shadow in literary studies, as a returned, irrepressible, and always significant ancestor.

A little girl when she arrived in colonial Massachusetts—or rather, when she was classified as very small and fragile "cargo" on the merchant ship and slaver *Phillis*—the child who would become Boston's most celebrated domestic servant was judged by her new owners to be about seven or eight years old. As has been iterated for two centuries, Phillis Wheatley's precocity quickly came to the attention of her white owners, who named her after the ship that had brought its cargo of slaves to Boston and gave her their family name. Serendipitously, Susanna Wheatley and her family were so taken with their new servant's intelligence that she was allowed time from her duties to write poetry. How many servants, much less slaves, had so indulgent and encouraging a master?

Wheatley's career as a poet began when she was in her midteens, with her 1767 work "On Mssrs. Hussey and Coffin." The lyrics collected in *Poems,* numbering almost forty, do not encompass all of her work to that date, whether published or in manuscript. Including numerous elegies, occasional poems, and meditations on classical themes, Wheatley's extant verse demonstrates her facility with prevailing poetic forms. Her surviving letters, to varying degrees and depending on to whom the letter is addressed and when it was composed, offer the reader an ironized and sometimes more intimate side of the poet who "pants for deliverance."

To her fellow Methodists, Wheatley's poems brilliantly evoked losses on earth to be rewarded in the afterlife; her abolitionist supporters held her brilliance up as proof of the Negro's intellect, whether achieved or potential. While it is true that that most literary president, Thomas Jefferson, remarked that her works were unworthy of criticism, and that other male critics well into the twentieth century, including African Americans, would set aside her work as irrelevant, stilted, and beholden to the ideology of her captors, Wheatley's work has survived naysayers and simplifiers alike. If the problem of the twenty-first century remains that of the color line, if I may extend W. E. B. Du Bois, then our current apprehension of that divide has led to a greater understanding of Wheatley's nuanced readings of *her* world.

As a slave woman, Wheatley could not have come of age in the sense of gaining her majority; the attainment of adult rights would remain a legal impossibility for African Americans until after the Civil War. She could not even celebrate her birthday, for, as Frederick Douglass would later write, "slaves know as little of their age as horses know of theirs." What she could know, and celebrate, was her legal independence, which she obtained several months "before the death of my dear mistress." Another celebration, five years later in 1778, inaugurated her life as the wife of John Peters, a free black man. In that role, Wheatley's upward trajectory began to stall. Many are the tales that swirl around Peters, from his supposed arrogance to his inability to keep home and hearth together. According to Wheatley's nineteenth-century biographer, Margaretta Odell, Peters "was unsuccessful in business, and failed soon after their marriage; and he is said to have been both too proud and too indolent to apply himself to any occupation below his fancied dignity." That he held numerous positions and that he sold his wife's things after her death to pay his debts may indeed be incontrovertible (her copy of the works of Pope probably began its journey to the Harvard library via such a sale). People continue to point fingers at Peters as the killer of his wife's poetic career. Called self-important or incapable, Peters could have been the love of her life, a bounder, or a man somewhere in between. That Peters was unable to remain employed or keep a business going does not prove that he was an unfit mate for Wheatley; it demonstrates only that he lacked wealth, power, and, perhaps most important, influential patrons, liabilities shared by many whites during the economic hard times of the Revolution and the early national period. And if whites fell by the wayside during this time, how much could have been expected from a black man, especially one without the powerful white patronage that his wife had once possessed? That Peters rejected the helping hand of whites may have made him more admirable to his wife, not less so: Odell admits that the poet was never known to utter a word of reproach against her husband. Peters serves as a lightning rod for the prejudices of those who would admire his wife, then and now. For many, he— rather than the social and racial politics of the early American republic—is the convenient obstacle to his wife's success.

In the years following her marriage, Wheatley struggled to secure her fame. She continued to write, and several times advertised for supporters, to enable her to bring out a second collection of her verse. While some critics have suggested that the reason she found publication more difficult in the Revolutionary era was that she was the protégée of loyalist Bostonians, her inability to command support for a second volume may speak more to the fact that she was a free black without a white sponsor of any political party. Her encomiums to Revolutionary heroes and leaders like Generals Washington and Wooster identified her publicly as a patriot, but patriotism alone could pay neither rent nor the grocery bill. Olaudah Equiano, the former slave, seaman, and author, writing shortly after Wheatley's death, would affirm the vagaries and dangers of life for a free black in the colonies. A wartime economy that could not foster financial independence for free blacks could do little for the arts and letters—no matter which side a poet was on.

The young woman once known for her skill with elegy, for her poetic commiserations on the loss of husbands, wives, and most particularly children, wrote no verses pointing specifically to her own losses—the deaths of two of her children, and the abridgment of her freedom after marriage. We are unlikely to learn much more about Wheatley's last years, even if more letters and poems come to light— and poems by Wheatley do still appear. Julian Mason brought to our attention the manuscript of "Ocean," probably written after her visit to England. Two other poems may provide what little insight we will ever have into the biographical mystery of the last years of Phillis Peters.

Some readers have thought "To Mr. and Mrs. ——, on the Death of Their Infant Son," written before her marriage but published in *Boston Magazine* in the last year of her life, is the poem noted in her 1779 proposals as "To P.N.S. and Lady on the death of their son." While the poem may well have been written before or early in her marriage, I would like to put forward a compatible reading: that is, let us view the poem's *publication* as autobiographical, inspired at least in part by her own experience as a mother. Elegies we know were a favored form of Wheatley's; for proof one need only list the number of such verses in *Poems*. (By the nineteenth century, elegies to dead children constituted a well-known tradition among women poets.) Perhaps, as for many of the parents for whom she had earlier written poems of consolation, the belief in an afterlife provided comfort now to the poet herself, a bereaved black mother. Thus, when Wheatley writes,

> So sweetly blooming once that lovely boy,
> His father's hope, his mother's only joy,
> Nor charms nor innocence hope to save,
> From the grim monarch of the gloomy grave!

we are asked to share the despair of those parents. Any black mother in this era, too, knew such dreadful losses came not only from Death's specter but also from slavery, "the dread terrors of the iron hand." Iron here could as easily refer to metal fetters as to an irrevocable death. Wheatley's children may have been born free, but the specter of slavery still inhabited Massachusetts in the late eighteenth century. (Abolition in Massachusetts followed a judicial decision in 1783, the year before Wheatley died.) "Terrors of the iron hand" may reasonably be compared with lines in her earlier address to the Earl of Dartmouth: "I, young in life, by seeming cruel fate, / Was snatch'd from Afric's fancied happy seat: / What pangs excruciating must molest, / What sorrows labour in my parent's breast?" The poet's use of the first person in that poem has been widely acknowledged to be one of Wheatley's rare instances of overt autobiography, but the first-person pronoun alone does not indicate personal revelation. Wheatley's last published elegy for a lost child could even have been revised after its initial composition in light of the poet's more recent experience: Wheatley's modern editors have shown us cases where revisions signally altered an initial version's meaning. (The most famous example of Wheatley's appreciation of her audience is her encomium to the Reverend Whitefield: the version published in England, a nation in the process of abolishing slavery, refers directly to black freedom, while the colonial version did not.)

If that last published lament to a dead child may be read as biography because of *when* it appeared, an "An Elegy on Leaving——," published in the *Arminian*, a religious magazine, offers more overt clues for the astute reader. Wheatley's contemporary editors and audience could reasonably read her verses as an acknowledgment of the passage of time in this world, and, by the last couplet, as the

Christian's happy expectation of life everlasting. Mukhtar Ali Isani, who rediscovered "An Elegy on Leaving——" in the 1980s, admires Wheatley's use of the pastoral but sees it as mourning her return to a Boston worn with years of war and economic deprivation. However, there is an alternate, gendered view, one less easy to prove but more than possible, given the poet's personal situation and literary sophistication. "On Leaving——," in this view, provides a melancholy tour around the poet's former life, referring to more than literally peaceful geographic spaces. It is to a metaphoric and emotional lost space—the "free footing" to which she once referred in a letter to David Worcester—that "On Leaving" refers. Frank Shuffelton, in fact, has drawn our attention to the scarcely two weeks of genuine freedom for Wheatley: the time between the death of John Wheatley, her white former owner and patron, and her marriage to John Peters.

Wheatley's personal situation was historically specific, yes. But Woolf's observation that insulation from the demands of family and womanhood—a room of one's own—can enable a woman to become a successful author applies as well. When Wheatley sighs,

> Farewel ye friendly bowe'rs
> I leave with sorrow each sequester'd seat . . .
> Where wrapt in thought I pensively have stray'd,

she may refer to a place where no children, however beloved, tug on her clothing for attention. The neat desk captured in the frontispiece of *Poems on Various Subjects* shows that the poet must "crowds and noise, reluctant, . . . forsake." If she and we can imagine the young poet, eyes cast upward in search of inspiration, she can rue that "I [once] pass'd in grateful solitude the day," knowing that "those pleasing hours are ever flown; no more my hand shall wake the warbling lyre." The irony of her life in freedom could scarce escape her: once married, her life as a struggling wife and mother could hobble her in ways that slavery could not. Iron fetters could be replaced by still stronger cords of familial responsibility. Well could she write,

> come sweet hope from thy divine retreat
> come . . . chase my cares away
> bring calm content to gild my gloomy seat
> and cheer my bosom with her heav'nly ray.

Wheatley suffered from the gender-role-bound lot of Shakespeare's imaginary sister, upon whom Virginia Woolf would so famously muse. But Wheatley's female genius would be still more fettered by virtue of her race and "previous condition of servitude." The poet left no living children, a husband who would also soon be lost to history, and an unpublished second manuscript, still sought after today. Her last resting place is unknown. Still, "notwithstanding and in despite of everything around her"—and this is the "difficult miracle of black poetry" that the writer June Jordan invoked about "Phillis Miracle Wheatley"—having survived racially biased critiques, decades of obscurity, the faint praise of literary descendants, and a supposed lack of group consciousness, Wheatley's writings continue into the twenty-first century. And so does she: American, black, woman, poet.

Bibliography: Mukhtar Ali Isani, "'An Elegy on Leaving——': A New Poem by Phillis Wheatley," *American Literature* 58, no. 4 (December 1986): 609–613. June Jordan, "The Difficult Miracle of Black Poetry in America, Or Something Like a Sonnet for Phillis Wheatley," *Massachusetts Review,* Summer 1986, Amherst, MA. Julian Mason, "'Ocean': A New Poem by Phillis Wheatley," *Early American Literature* 34, no. 1 (1999): 1, 78–83. Margaretta Matilda Odell, *Memoir and Poems of Phillis Wheatley, a Native African and a Slave, Dedicated to the Friends of the Africans* (Boston, 1834). Frank Shuffelton, "On Her Own Footing: Phillis Wheatley in Freedom," in *Genius in Bondage,* ed. Vincent Carretta and Philip Gould (Lexington, KY, 2001), 175–189. Phillis Wheatley, *Complete Writings,* ed. Vincent Carretta (New York, 2001).

RAFIA ZAFAR

1776

John Adams disclaims authorship of *Common Sense* but helps declare independence

A Dialectics of Radical Enlightenment

Thousands of political tracts were printed during the British-American taxation crisis of the 1760s and 1770s. One of them turned the dispute between imperial center and colonial provinces into a revolution in the modern sense of the term: *Common Sense,* published anonymously on January 10, 1776. Arguing that England's taxation policy violated the natural rights of the American colonists, rather than their inherited privileges, *Common Sense* effectively replaced a rhetoric of grievance and petition with fierce invective against "the Royal Brute of Britain." The pamphlet also played masterfully on the religious sensibilities of its colonial audience by providing a providential reading of the crisis: even "the distance at which the Almighty hath placed England and America" was cited as proof that the colonies' subjection "was never the design of Heaven." Altogether, *Common Sense* blended traditional themes from English protest rhetoric and Reformation pamphleteering (such as the Norman Yoke and resistance against "low papistical design") with the Enlightenment's confidence in human self-creation, based on a radically new concept of "nature." The result was explosive: "We have it in our power to begin the world over again . . . The birthday of a new world is at hand."

Interestingly, the author of *Common Sense* was a newcomer to the American scene: Thomas Paine had arrived in North America in the winter of 1774. It proved to be the right moment for radical thought in a political environment that was predominantly conservative. After Parliament had frustrated all the colonists' hopes of pursuing their interests *within* the British Empire, the only legitimate position left to them was precisely the one that Parliament had always suspected they secretly favored: independence on the basis of universal human rights. "The cause of America," Thomas Paine explained in *Common Sense,* "is in a great measure the cause of all mankind."

Paine's universalist formula filled a strategic gap by providing a rallying cry for the many competing interest groups within the patriots' ranks. Behind the scenes, however, the struggle over the meaning of the revolution was already well under way. John Adams, for one, read *Common Sense* with mixed feelings. When some of his friends asked him if he was the author of the celebrated pamphlet, he was aghast. An absurd thought, Adams maintained in numerous letters: never, he told his friends, would he have been able to produce such a well-written text. Yet this literary praise contained stringent theoretical criticisms. Although he honored the author of *Common Sense* as a brilliant rhetorician, Adams also dismissed him as a demagogue—a hot-headed populist rather than a sober republican. "Indeed, this writer has a better hand in pulling down than building," Adams wrote to his wife, Abigail, on March 19, 1776. "I should have made a more respectable figure as an architect if I had undertaken such a work." To prove his point he composed *Thoughts on Government* in the spring of 1776.

At first glance, it is hard to see what the debate was all about. *Common Sense* and *Thoughts on Government* agreed on fundamental issues. Both affirmed the sovereignty of the people as the guiding principle of an independent America. Both demanded a written constitution to limit legislative authority. Where Paine stated that, "In America THE LAW IS KING," Adams held: "The very definition of a republic is 'an empire of laws, and not of men.'" Given such consensus, the intensity of Adams's attacks on Paine—whom he called the "Star of Disaster" and the "Disastrous Meteor" of American politics—seems peculiar. No less peculiar, however, was Paine's conclusion, after a conversation with his critic, that "[Adams's] head was as full of kings, queens, and knaves as a pack of cards." The inability of these two founding figures to find common ground anticipated the militant clash of opposing interpretations of the American Revolution that would shake the new United States in the 1790s and that would become a defining mark of American culture throughout the nineteenth and twentieth centuries.

Like those later conflicts, the quarrel between Adams and Paine was based on shared assumptions and values. And yet, each man accused the other of betraying fundamental revolutionary principles. It is tempting to read this early controversy as one that pitted a nascent democratic tradition against an established elitist tradition. Indeed, Adams's distaste for Paine's populist language—a distaste that also guided his aversion to Benjamin Franklin, whom he thought too folksy for his country's good—was riddled with class prejudice. Significantly, however, Adams objected to Paine's demotic rhetoric on pragmatic grounds: it was not the idea of popular government that bothered him but the possible danger of that idea turning into a utopian faith.

Finding more "common-place" than common sense in Paine's pamphlet, Adams disapproved in particular of Paine's "crude, ignorant Notions of Government by one Assembly." According to *Thoughts on Government,* the unicameral system proposed in *Common Sense* (a system also favored by Franklin) would be "liable to all the vices, follies, and frailties of an individual—subject to fits of humor, starts of passion, flights of enthusiasm, partialities, or prejudice—and consequently productive of hasty results and absurd judgments." In other words: if identified with the voice of natural reason, speaking truth "in a language as plain as A, B, C" (as Paine wrote in *The American Crisis* in December 1776), the voice of the people would turn dictatorial. As unanimous as Rousseau's General Will, it would silence all counterspeech as unreasonable.

Adams concluded that enlightened politics needed to take a realistic view both of human psychology and of the nature of political power. One way to do this would be to strike a balance between conflicting interests in a deliberative—rather than expressive—legislature: "[The representative assembly] should be in miniature an exact portrait of the people at large . . . [I]n other words, equal interests among the people should have equal interests in it." This representative assembly would in turn be integrated into a classical system of mixed government, which in Adams's description looked like an early version of what came to be known as the checks and balances among competing branches of government.

The logic of Adams's argument was intricate; it already took account of a dialectics of radical enlightenment. Natural-rights populism may have been what the colonial campaign for self-government needed in 1776, but Adams understood that the principle of home rule and the principle of human rights could be at odds. Enlightened patriotism and enlightened universalism made conflicting claims on the American revolutionaries.

Another document of the same year took a different rhetorical approach—and found Adams's approval. Like *Common Sense,* the Declaration of Independence based its call for self-government on "inalienable rights." But Thomas Jefferson addressed his audience (supposedly "a candid world") in a calm, objective, almost lawyerlike tone, stating with authority: "We hold these truths to be self-evident . . ."

Still, this was a chancy opening, as the nation's history would show. Strictly speaking, self-evident truths require no holders. The "we" of Jefferson's sentence unwittingly called into question the timelessness and placelessness of the propositions that followed. Evidently, the truth that "all men are created equal" was not so self-evident as to prevent dispute over its meaning—neither in 1776 nor later, when this statement's implications for the nation's unity became increasingly contested. The very fact, then, that "these truths" had authors and supporters who signed the document and put a date to it attests to their interestedness. The Declaration of Independence was, among other things, a declaration of war, a propaganda tract, an offer of coalition to France. But it claimed to be all these things in the form of a philosophical treatise, argued in the irrefutable logic of a syllogism, written—as Jefferson put it two years earlier in *A Summary View of the Rights of British America*—in "the language of truth."

By basing colonial resistance against then-existing law on the most forceful legal foundation imaginable—the idea of a law of nature that is valid anywhere and anytime—*Common Sense* and the Declaration of Independence together endowed America with a compelling sense of its own inevitability. As Jefferson explained in 1821 in his *Autobiography,* "The question was not whether, by a declaration of independence, we should make ourselves what we are not; but whether we should declare a fact which already exists." Thus rights were no longer demanded but declared. Subjects no longer negotiated with their rulers but reminded their governors of their obligations. In this sense, the Declaration of Independence, while giving notice of its signers' revolutionary intent, claimed simply to express an empirical state of affairs—as if the revolution was nothing but an opportune instrument to communicate natural facts to the people's consciousness.

In fact, however, the revolutionaries argued in an openly counterfactual manner when they postulated their legal autonomy in 1776. At that time, the claim of de facto independence was self-evidently false: the colonies had not yet constituted themselves as a distinct political entity, nor were the truths of the Declaration of Independence imperative enough to command assent throughout Europe or even throughout British America. America's new language of reason still had a world to convince—or, rather, America's new language of reason still had to bring the world into accord with its propositions.

John Adams was not the only one who was troubled by the utopian cast of this enterprise. Jefferson, too, was acutely aware of the risky novelty of the American position. Thus he composed his radical declarations in the reassuring classicism of syllogistic reasoning and spoke of all men being *created* equal, rather than being born equal. (Natural rights gain nothing in self-evidence, but much in legitimacy, when they appear in the guise of *ius divinum.*) But Thomas Paine, too, knew that his enlightened universalism needed more than a belief in the inevitability of revolution. Exactly because independence could not be avoided, Paine thought it essential that an independent America must not fall victim to a revolutionary demagogue "who laying hold of popular disquietudes, may collect together the desperate and the discontented, and by assuming to themselves the powers of government, may sweep away the liberties of the continent like a deluge." According to Paine, this development could be averted only if Americans decided "to form a constitution of our own in a cool deliberate manner"—a *written* constitution, authoritative and binding upon all lawmakers and all successive governments under that constitution. The most heated controversies in American history, starting with Adams and Paine's 1776 dispute over *Common Sense,* have not been between local interests and universal principles, but almost always centered on the question of how to coordinate universal principles and local realities.

To found a country and to constitute a "people" on the basis of natural rights—rather than to commit an existing country or an existing people to such principles—is an improbable thing to do. It marks that country for utopian overreach or constructive despair. It produces forms of self-obsession that often lead one to forget that there is a world outside one's own country. It produces perennial disputes about the meaning of one's communal existence in the world. To the extent that the United States was founded by force of documents, texts, and clashing forms of rhetoric, the United States is bound to be a nation of competing readers and competing readings. And to the extent that even the most self-evident propositions are invariably confronted with local meanings and interests, the United

States has always been a nation divided in trying to become one nation. There can be, then, no such thing as a nonpartisan American literature—political, historiographical, or otherwise.

While Jefferson, Paine, and Adams were united in their belief that a republic of reason was possible and necessary, this confidence has served as a frame for numerous quarrels of faith and conviction in American history. In all these conflicts, the appeal to a natural order of things—to a universal human longing for freedom, democracy, prosperity—has been a forceful political instrument, both of liberation and coercion. If invoked from a position of substantial power, such liberation offers an absolute choice to its addressees: either participate in the natural course of events or be run over by it. Each reference to a "common sense," each invocation of "self-evident truth" includes the covert assumption that those who see things differently are not competent to use rational speech or to take autonomous action. Rousseau had another way of putting it: the enlightened citizen is asked to act according to his innate freedom—and when he refuses to do this, "one has to force him to be free." This is the lasting dilemma of modern politics, in 1776 and today: its hope to establish a social order that is considered natural but does not arise by itself.

What conclusion can be drawn? Perhaps this: the language of the Declaration of Independence laid the intellectual foundations for a powerful nation and a world-shaping culture, but at its most convincing, this language has been spoken by those who were either maligned in the original document (Jefferson's "merciless Indian savages") or quietly removed from it (when the Continental Congress deleted Jefferson's long paragraph censuring colonial slavery) or not mentioned at all (as Abigail Adams reminded her husband in a letter of March 31, 1776, asking him to "remember the ladies"). Thus, the Declaration of Independence and *Common Sense,* each in its own way, has spawned adaptations, references, and rewritings beyond their authors' wildest dreams: from William Lloyd Garrison's and Frederick Douglass's uncompromising nineteenth-century stem-winders against slavery to Bob Dylan's surreal dropping of Paine's name on his album *John Wesley Harding* (1967, four years after Dylan received the Tom Paine Award from the Emergency Civil Liberties Committee); from the feminist Seneca Falls Declaration (1848), modeled verbatim on Jefferson's document, to a drunken barroom toast to "the pursuit of happiness" in Thomas Pynchon's *Mason & Dixon* (1997).

It is certainly justified to say that American literature starts with political tracts and philosophical treatises. But to read that literature in any meaningful way is to see what those writings about common sense and the self-evident forced into existence: myriad minority reports, many of them collected in the disturbing and disturbed stock of imaginative literature written after 1776. Perhaps the true American literature—true to its nation's wish for local circumscription as well as to its yearning for boundless universality—can be found after the Declaration of Independence, indeed provoked by it: fictions obsessed with their own provenance, mongrel genres, faux classicism, expatriate fantasies and regionalist tales, stories of migration and adventure, visions of deception and passing, raptures and conspiracies. There is almost everything—but no self-evident truth—in these innumerable competing voices.

Bibliography: John Adams, *The Adams Papers: Diary and Autobiography of John Adams,* ed. Lyman H. Butterfield (Cambridge, MA, 1961–1962); *The Political Writings: Representative Selections,* ed. George A. Peek, Jr. (New York, 1954). Thomas Jefferson, *Writings,* ed. Merrill D. Peterson (New York, 1984). Frank Kelleter, *Amerikanische Aufklärung: Sprachen der Rationalität im Zeitalter der Revolution* (Paderborn, 2002). Thomas Paine, *Collected Writings,* ed. Eric Foner (New York, 1995); "To the Citizens of the United States. Letter II," in *The Complete Writings of Thomas Paine,* ed. Philip S. Foner (New York, 1969).

FRANK KELLETER

1784, June

Charles Willson Peale exhibits mastodon bones in his painting gallery

THE ARTIST IN HIS MUSEUM

Like many portrait painters of his day, Charles Willson Peale kept a permanent display of his work on view in a gallery attached to his home and studio in Philadelphia. He did this for the convenience of prospective patrons who wished to assess his skill and his clientele, but also for all citizens of the city who might be interested in seeing the faces of the eminent individuals who had posed for Peale. The leading lights of the period, including signers of the Declaration of Independence, military officers in the subsequent war, and distinguished emissaries from abroad were to be found here, and their likenesses were understood to carry the moral weight of the persons themselves. If new *exempla virtutis* were needed for the democratic republic just taking shape, the place to find them was Peale's gallery, which he installed in a new, skylit addition to his studio just as articles of peace with Britain were being signed in November 1782.

By then Peale had been the leading portraitist in the Baltimore-Annapolis-Philadelphia region for more than a decade. Before the war he had studied painting in London with Benjamin West, a Pennsylvania native who was rising in British art circles en route to becoming court painter to George III and president of the Royal Academy of Arts. Peale was one of West's best students, and he developed a distinctive version of neoclassical portraiture that gave most of his sitters a "family resemblance," recognizable as Peale subjects by their narrow shoulders, sinuously curved bodies, and oval faces wearing genial expressions.

Shortly after opening his new painting gallery, Peale was commissioned to make drawings of some giant animal bones dug out of Big Bone Lick in what is now Kentucky. While working on the drawings, he kept the bones in his painting gallery, where they vied with his portraits for the attention of visitors. The animal whose bones they were had not yet been identified as a mastodon; the mysterious extinct creature was a source of curiosity for naturalists and amateurs of science, who referred to it as the "great American incognitum." Always looking for ways to make extra money, Peale contemplated the idea of uniting works of art and specimens of natural history in his gallery and charging a modest admission fee.

Peale's influential friends were only too happy to help with this project. Benjamin Franklin, who had brought the first Angora cats to America, gave him the cadaver of one and a book on taxidermy—a do-it-yourself kit that started Peale on the road to becoming a master taxidermist. Unfortunately this first effort was a failure, and Franklin's cat had to be buried. George Washington sent Peale two dead Chinese pheasants that had been presented to him, alive, by the Marquis de Lafayette. Later, Thomas Jefferson, who served as president of the museum's advisory board for many years, helped to make Peale's museum an informal depository for national artifacts, almost a half century before the Smithsonian Institution was founded. He arranged for Peale to receive animals and Native American works gathered by Lewis and Clark during their expedition across the continent, and Meriwether Lewis himself became Peale's friend and collaborator. These prominent and powerful supporters—many of whom Peale had first met while serving in the Philadelphia militia during the War of Independence or later as a participant in Philadelphia's political and intellectual circles—also posed for portraits that were featured in the museum. Staring down from their positions above the displays of stuffed birds and animals, their faces affirmed the museum's status as a lofty enterprise endorsed by the preeminent figures of the time.

Gifts were only part of Peale's collection strategy. He and his children, especially Raphaelle and Rembrandt, traveled widely to collect specimens for the museum. By 1790 he had more than 1,000 objects. Once collected and preserved, each item was placed in the gallery in a precise location determined according to the most authoritative scientific classifications of the time: Linnaeus for birds and quadrupeds, Kirwan for minerals and fossils, Buffon and others for everything else. Birds were especially well represented in the collection, each posed "in its natural attitude" and set in a glass-front box painted with appropriate scenery. The scientific accuracy of the arrangement of specimens, together with the quality of the taxidermy and the number of samples, led Peale to claim that his museum "rivaled in value and utility any of a similar nature."

As Peale's collection grew, the pressure on his gallery space and his finances became intense. In 1790 he published the first of several broadsides appealing to the citizens of the United States to nationalize his museum. A second followed in 1792 and a third in 1800. During the decade of the 1790s, while Philadelphia was the temporary capital of the United States, the list of subscribers to Peale's museum and the members of its advisory board included presidents, vice presidents, and all manner of political officeholders. Yet even with so much political support, Peale's drive for nationalization was ultimately unsuccessful. Jefferson seems to have been in favor of the idea, but he did not pursue it, perhaps because he believed that committing government funds to such an institution would provoke insurmountable opposition. Peale was able to win some public support, though, in the form of exhibition space. First, in 1794, the American Philosophical Society, which was committed to the advancement of knowledge in the arts and sci-

Charles Willson Peale, *The Artist in His Museum* (1822). Oil on canvas

Pennsylvania Academy of the Fine Arts, Philadelphia (acc. no. 1878.1.2, gift of Mrs. Sarah Harrison, The Joseph Harrison, Jr. Collection)

ences, invited him to lease its Philosophical Hall, in the very heart of Philadelphia, for his residence and museum. Then in 1802 he was invited to expand his
museum into the upper floors of the State House (now Independence Hall), immediately adjacent to Philosophical Hall. The long gallery in the State House is
the visual image that we have of the museum, thanks to Peale's making it the setting for his painting *The Artist in His Museum* (1822).

In this painting, done when Peale was eighty-one years old, with assistance
from his son Titian, he is shown drawing back a curtain to reveal in the deep space
of the room (which was 100 feet long and 12 high) a neat grid of display boxes containing birds and other creatures. These boxes were stacked to a height of 9 feet
or so, leaving just enough room at the top for two rows of portraits of illustrious
individuals, framed in gold and lined up edge to edge. By this time the number of
specimens in the museum was estimated at 100,000. Part of a mastodon skeleton
is visible beneath the curtain at right, and some stray mastodon bones occupy the
right foreground and lean against the table on which paintbrushes and palette
rest. The mastodon was actually displayed in another gallery off to the left of the
one shown, so its inclusion here is a sign of its centrality to the museum and
Peale's own sense of his achievement. The juxtaposition of loose bones and artist's equipment in the right foreground restages the scene of the museum's founding nearly forty years earlier. In the picture's lower left corner, Peale's taxidermy
toolkit is open in preparation for preserving the dead turkey resting on it. Peale
shows himself dressed in old-fashioned knee breeches, in contrast to the more
fashionable trousers worn by younger men in the gallery behind him. This aligns
him with the older generation of the Enlightenment and its values of order, rationality, and science, which he hoped to instill in museum visitors through his exhibits and his art. His goal was to make visitors and viewers able citizens of the
new republic. Scenes of education, contemplation, and wonder are enacted by
the male and female museum visitors pictured in the painting's background, and
an empty bench, set at an angle to the perspective lines rushing into deep space,
catches viewers as they allow themselves to be drawn in.

The first ticket Peale designed for his museum showed an open book with the
word "nature" inscribed in large letters on its pages; it radiates light as it hovers
above the words "The birds and beasts will teach thee." In Peale's museum, as in
his paintings, nature and art were parallel representations of the harmony and
order of the universe; moreover, they were transparent to each other as mutual
repositories of clarity, reason, and design.

The immaculate order and rationality of the place highlighted in *The Artist in
His Museum* contrasts with another view of Peale's museum, this time seen from
the street. John Lewis Krimmel's watercolor *Election at the State House* (1816, Historical Society of Pennsylvania) shows a chaotic scene of vote trading, drunkenness, and general rowdiness in front of the State House, where the voting took
place. From the windows of Peale's museum on the second floor, just above the
museum's sign, one man leans out behind another who has stepped onto the
ledge, both pursuing an escaped monkey that is on the roof. Far from being
the antithesis of the disorder of daily urban life, Peale's museum is shown here to

be part of it. Krimmel's painting explains the appeal of the rational ideal Peale pursued, and it undermines the claim of *The Artist in His Museum* that he had realized that ideal.

Public education and civic enrichment were fine and good, but Peale depended on income from admission fees to build the museum and support his family. In 1802, the African American Moses Williams no longer appeared as a slave in Peale's tax records but worked as a prolific "profile cutter" in the museum, producing thousands of inexpensive silhouettes of visitors with the help of a newly invented technological gadget, the "physiognotrace." The attraction of having one's shadow profile cut contributed much to the popularity of the museum and drew a significant number of female customers.

Peale was entrepreneur enough to realize that increasing his audience would require tempering the museum's edifying displays with amusement and excitement. The admission fee was always small, roughly equivalent to that of the cheapest seats at a theater or circus, although affluent patrons were encouraged to buy an annual ticket or subscription. Peale took pride in rejecting the low road taken by some of his competitors, who would stoop to anything to "catch the Eye of the gaping multitude." He monitored the activities of institutions such as Gardiner Baker's museum in New York, which displayed a guillotine accompanied by a wax figure with a bloody, severed head. Such showmanship, in Peale's view, compromised a museum's honor and its ability to make deep and lasting impressions on those who came in search of truth and wisdom.

Ideally, the public's appetite for sensations would be satisfied by attractions like the mastodon skeleton, which was scientifically important as well as spectacular. Peale's successful expedition to Newburgh, New York, to purchase a nearly complete skeleton recently excavated there, and to retrieve even more bones from the same bogs, brought considerable publicity to his museum. His own inclination toward showmanship, however, surfaced in the face of a disagreement about how the bones should be assembled. Peale ignored his trusted adviser, a distinguished doctor and professor of anatomy, Caspar Wistar, and inserted spacers between the bones as a substitute for hypothetical cartilage, thereby increasing the size of the skeleton beyond its already impressive dimensions. Moreover, the ballyhoo he organized around the opening of the mastodon exhibit would have been worthy of his successor, P. T. Barnum. Peale later painted for the mastodon gallery a scene of the excavation, which included a massive wheel, powered by children climbing stairs built into its interior, that he had designed for emptying water from the pit while the digging was under way (*Exhumation of the Mastodon*, 1806, Baltimore City Life Museums).

Peale's showmanship manifested itself in other ways as well. Among the wax figures included in his galleries—mostly representations of different races of mankind, and some eminent individuals, such as Meriwether Lewis, who was portrayed wearing Native American clothing and holding a calumet—was an effigy of the artist in the act of painting. According to the testimony of one visitor to the museum in 1787, it was "a perfect likeness" that deceived some visitors. One display titled "A Singular Association" contained a rooster and an eagle living together peacefully in a cage. A later version of the same idea assembled a rattle-snake, a squirrel, and a bird. Among the animal oddities, or *lusus naturae,* on display in Peale's galleries were snakes and pigs with extra heads, and one particularly unfortunate cow with five legs, six feet, and two tails. Human oddities were present only in pictures or samples: a clipping of silvery hair from an albino woman, a portrait of a man alleged to be 134 years old, another portrait of a man named James, "a person born a Negro, or a very dark Mullatoe, who afterwards became white." Also on view was artwork by handicapped women and a painting depicting the sailor John Gallaway with a horn-shaped growth on his chest as the result of a burn wound he suffered during the siege of Cartagena. Most notoriously, Peale exhibited the trigger finger of a murderer, Mr. Bruliman, as a stimulus to courteous behavior. (Bruliman, bent on random violence, had passed over one potential victim because the man greeted him so politely, as Peale's son Rubens explained in the museum accession book of 1810.)

The museum began to disintegrate after Peale's death in 1827. Most of the contents were dispersed at a sheriff's sale in 1848, at which the principal purchasers were the leading figures in the next generation of museum entrepreneurs: P. T. Barnum and Moses Kimball. They remade Peale's museum for the age of commercial amusement, shrewd advertising, and sensational humbug.

Bibliography: David R. Brigham, *Public Culture in the Early Republic: Peale's Museum and Its Audience* (Washington, DC, 1995). Lillian B. Miller et al., eds., *The Selected Papers of Charles Willson Peale and His Family* (New Haven, CT, 1983–2000). Charles Coleman Sellers, *Mr. Peale's Museum* (New York, 1980). Roger Stein, "Charles Willson Peale's Expressive Design: *The Artist in His Museum," Prospects* 6 (1981).

MICHAEL LEJA

1787

James Madison keeps a secret transcript of the Constitutional Convention

A LITERATURE OF SECULAR REVELATIONS

No one came better prepared for the Constitutional Convention of 1787 than James Madison. He arrived in Philadelphia with both a draft proposal for a new plan of government, the product of a prolonged study of constitutions and confederacies of the past, and a commitment to honor the "peculiarity and magnitude of the occasion" by keeping for posterity a detailed account of the Convention's proceedings. Through four sweltering summer months, never leaving his seat at the Convention for "more than a casual fraction of an hour in any day," Madison noted in shorthand every delegate's speech, returning each night to his lodging to write out a complete account of the disciplined, often contentious debates of the day. Though there were a few other sporadic attempts by various delegates to keep an account of the Convention, it is Madison alone who preserved a full day-by-day account of the development of the final Constitution's "bundle of compromises."

The Convention's proceedings took place under a rule of strictest secrecy, shielding the delegates from outside pressures and encouraging uninhibited debate. That such secrecy had, however, still more subtle and profound purposes is evident from the way in which the framers signed the Constitution. By a masterfully evasive formula they claimed to be not authors but witnesses to the ordaining and establishing of a new frame of government, as though the very voice of "We the People" had sounded in the hall and the drafters had served as mere amanuenses. Moreover the ground rules they established for the ratification—permitting neither revision nor qualification, as if forbidding a document so established and ordained to be subject to any ordinary process of negotiated alteration—served to reinforce the tacit assumption of the delegates' active passivity. Most striking of all, especially given the close contest of that ratification, the new Constitution underwent an almost immediate apotheosis, long recognized by historians as without precedent in Western political history. From that moment on, no matter the depth of their disagreements over its interpretation, all Americans adamantly defended the supreme authority of the Constitution.

How remarkable, then, that the Constitution makes no mention whatever of any divine sanction, no prayer for divine assistance. Forced to initiate a political institution in the absence of any kind of deep mythic foundation, the founders turned away from the traditional reliance upon religious sanction and engineered a new paradox, what could be called a secular revelation. They established a supreme authority that managed to evade, without ever altogether abandoning, the secular limits of argument and compromise. What is strictly secular in origin cannot, after all, possess any ultimate, transcendent authority, yet that is precisely what the Constitution achieved. This paradox not only invented the American polity but sustained a new national identity, making the Constitution what its contemporaries called "a roof without walls."

But if for the founding generation the Constitution was a work of heroic national creativity, what about succeeding generations, for whom it would become not an act of self-invention but an inheritance? In 1836 a young Abraham Lincoln addressed this very question. Speaking to the Young Men's Lyceum in Springfield, Illinois, citing the death of all the founders—"the pillars of the temple of liberty . . . have crumbled away"—Lincoln urged a cult of the Constitution, a worship of "the Constitution and its laws," as the only reliable means to preserve the legacy of self-government. "Let it become," he proclaimed, "the political religion of the nation." American political tradition has largely adopted this strategy, rendering explicit opposition to the Constitution almost unheard of.

And yet Americans revere their founding document in a notably paradoxical way, honoring it by relegating it to the professionals: the lawyers and the courts. Madison's *Notes* are a striking case in point. He diligently prepared his notes for posthumous publication, but the Congress required considerable persuasion before it agreed to purchase and publish them, and although the text offers a virtual play script of the day-by-day debates that issued in the nation's defining text, it has never found a large American audience, periodically even going out of print. The legal profession itself has a strong tradition of systematically denying the *Notes* any probative value in Constitutional interpretation, as though Madison's reliable records make the document's all-too-human provenance uncomfortably transparent. The secrecy of the Convention, the evasion of the drafters' authorship, continues to echo in the nation's peculiarly distracted adoration of the Constitution: every American uses the ultimate accusation of "unconstitutional"; few have ever read the brief text. Every year Americans celebrate the nation's independence with greater attention and enthusiasm than they accorded the Constitution's bicentennial, a strikingly underwhelming occasion.

No surprise, then, that the Constitution has remained all but invisible in more general discussions of American culture—on the assumption, it seems, that however central it may be to the nation's history and politics, the Constitution exists in a kind of isolating ether. And yet if we read such a central cultural document as Ralph Waldo Emerson's "The American Scholar" (1837) in the context of Lincoln's Springfield address, delivered three months earlier, it becomes evident that for Emerson too the death of the founding generation and the transformation of the American experiment from an active process into a passive inheritance was a key reference point. But where Lincoln's focus on politics and law resulted in a call for conservative preservation, Emerson demanded a continuation of the very process of the Revolution's self-invention. "Washington and Jefferson . . . shocked their contemporaries with their daring wisdom," he wrote in his journal in 1841. "Have you not something which would have shocked them?" Addressing Harvard undergraduates, he heralded the end of America's "day of dependence, our long apprenticeship" and the coming of a new literature "that will revive and lead in a new age," but only by an embrace of "the active soul," a heroic refusal to be pinned down by any inherited institutions and instead a resolve to welcome "the pure efflux of the Deity" in acts of new inspiration. "The aim of the true teacher," as he reminds himself in his journal, "[is] to teach the doctrine of perpetual revelation."

Though Emerson has long been recognized as a central figure in the rise of a distinctive American literature, the extent to which his ideas derive from the contingencies of the nation's distinctive self-constituting has been insufficiently appreciated. Yet his unceasing promotion of American creativity relied upon the assumptions of what could be called a Constitutional poetics. A national literature, no more than a nation, had never before been the product of conscious invention, and both necessitated a claim of authority that would somehow override the sheer arbitrariness of the naked fact of simply setting out. Whether the nature of such a claim is best understood as deistic, or as romantically self-deifying, or as some more particularly American form of innocence or arrogance, Emerson continuously preached that the way to begin in the new United States was by means of a self-assertion amounting almost to prophecy. An American was to utter the inspired word, though inspired by whom, and how, was a matter of endlessly slippery and evasive maneuvers. Here is a central passage from Emerson's "Self-Reliance," where he pauses to voice a challenge to the source of his own exalted authority: "On my saying 'What have I to do with the sacredness of traditions, if I live wholly from within?' my friend suggested,—'But these impulses may be from below, not from above.' I replied, 'They do not seem to me to be such; but if I am the Devil's child, I will live then from the Devil.' No law can be sacred to me but that of my nature." This is not Satanic pride but Yankee wit. It is an evasive response to an impossible question, akin to the way the founders signed the Constitution. The form of a secular revelation, like any deep paradox, is not susceptible to logical analysis. If it is secular it cannot be revealed, and if it is revealed it cannot be secular; and yet it makes a claim to both.

Emerson's lectures and essays were recognized at once as the odd hybrid of secular sermons. Though he abandoned the pulpit for which he had been educated, and thenceforth spoke as a secular citizen, his every utterance conjured a religious aura, often as not addressing concerns traditionally within the religious realm. Indeed, Emerson's very method of composition reflected the Constitution's paradox of secular revelation. He did not compose a work so much as assemble it, culling the moments of inspiration he had recorded in his daily journal and cobbling them together, sentences from years apart following one another throughout, making for an emphatically saltatory style. In a characteristically bemused acknowledgment, he noted of his own literary method: "I had found when I finished my new essay that it was a very good house, only the architect had unfortunately omitted the stairs."

In his championing of a new American literary culture, an elitist egalitarianism in which every man is free to turn his back on tradition and become his own prophet, Emerson predicted a great new American poet would arise to sing of this new dispensation. As if in answer to this call came the small self-published volume *Leaves of Grass* by an anonymous author pictured in the frontispiece as a common workingman. Walt Whitman described himself as at a simmer, brought to a boil by Emerson, and indeed the Sage of Concord, though of a vastly different temperament and culture, recognized the obscure New Yorker's genius from the first. In composing his "new Bible" Whitman turned his back not merely on the inherited furniture of English poetry but, by abandoning all meter, on the fundamental assumptions of its very poetics. What, after all, had Emerson urged but that an American be "free even to the definition of freedom, 'without any hindrance that does not arise out of his own constitution?'"

Whitman, no less than Emerson, habitually invoked the traditional terms of religious authority, God and the soul, all the while affirming a shamelessly secular perspective: "I call to mankind, Be not curious about God,/For I who am curious about each am not curious about God," to which he immediately adds, "No array of terms can say how much I am at peace about God and about death." Self-consciously outrageous in his mixing of these contrary perspectives—"The scent of these arm-pits aroma finer than prayer"—Whitman was so bold as to claim a virtual conquest of death—"And as to you, death, and you bitter hug of mortality . . . it is idle to try to alarm me." Where Emerson refused to parse the source of his own authority, accepting paradox and scorning "foolish consistency" as "the hobgoblin of little minds," Whitman went him one better: "Do I contradict myself?" he asks, "Very well then I contradict myself, / (I am large, I contain multitudes.)" And just as Emerson teaches his "perpetual revelation" to all, the altogether exceptional Whitman asserts an untiring allegiance to the common and the democratic:

> Do you take it I would astonish?
> Does the daylight astonish? does the early redstart twittering through the woods?
> Do I astonish more than they?
> . . . .
>
> What is a man anyhow? what am I? what are you?
>
> All I mark as my own you shall offset it with your own,
> Else it were time lost listening to me.

Like an Emerson *in extremis*, Whitman was possessed by a kind of America-madness, all but identifying himself with the diversity of the Union of the States without ever relinquishing the most unyielding individuality, singing "Song of Myself" as "one of the roughs, a kosmos . . . no more modest than immodest." Indeed in the preface to *Leaves of Grass* he went so far as to insist that the invention of "We the People" is itself the greatest song, that "the United States themselves are essentially the greatest poem."

The classic American writers who followed Emerson and Whitman continued to resonate to this ambition. Emily Dickinson's and Herman Melville's startlingly original versions of their respective genres, for instance, can both be understood as attempts at answering this same inner demand. Nor did the impulse exhaust itself in antebellum America. Consider Wallace Stevens, a century later, and his "supreme fiction": "The final belief is to believe in a fiction, which you know to be a fiction, there being nothing else. The exquisite truth is to know that it is a fiction and that you believe in it willingly." What is such a "final fiction" but yet another secular revelation, one more reassertion of the nation's founding act of imagination? Madison's *Notes* assure us that the Constitution is a made-up thing, and yet such knowledge has never inhibited the nation from believing in it. It has been the burden, and the originality, of at least one central strain of American literary tradition to suffer this ever-new ambition of finding poetic forms that will participate in the nation's founding paradox.

Bibliography: Hannah Arendt, *On Revolution* (New York, 1963). James Madison, *Notes of Debates in the Federal Convention of 1787 Reported by James Madison* (1840; New York, 1987). Mitchell Meltzer, *Secular Revelations: The United States Constitution and Classic American Literature* (Cambridge, MA, 2005). John M. Murrin, "A Roof without Walls: The Dilemma of American National Identity," in *Beyond Confederation: Origins of the Constitution and American National Identity*, ed. Richard Beeman, Stephen Botein, and Edward C. Carter II (Chapel Hill, NC, 1987). Jack N. Rakove, *Original Meanings: Politics and Ideas in the Making of the Constitution* (New York, 1996).

MITCHELL MELTZER

1787–1790
John Adams defends the new Constitution

DISCOURSES ON DAVILA

"Democracy is Lovelace, and the people are Clarissa." So wrote John Adams in defending the new United States Constitution, debated and ratified in 1787 and 1788. The critics of the Constitution—in America known as the anti-Federalists, and in France a group that included many of the leading *philosophes*—charged that the new republic had no need of all the mechanisms of checks and balances and that democracy, requiring unrestrained freedom, would perish under any system of political controls. In response, Adams cited Samuel Richardson's famous novel *Clarissa* to demonstrate why democracy may be its own enemy—why, as he put it, "the artful villain will pursue the innocent young girl to her ruin and death." The existence of democracy is no guarantee that it will not be seduced and betrayed by those who speak its language, only better to subvert its liberties in pursuit of power and conquest.

As the second president of the United States, John Adams succeeded George Washington and remained overshadowed by the great military hero; he was harassed even by members of his own Federalist Party, especially Alexander Hamilton, who believed that the bookish New Englander was too weak to turn back the rising opposition Republican Party, led by Thomas Jefferson.

But Americans and Europeans have yet to appreciate Adams as a thinker as well as a historical actor, a political philosopher who invoked literary figures such as Alexander Pope and Samuel Johnson to tell us the truth about human nature. One truth was the inevitability of social distinctions among the classes of society. Adams loved to quote Shakespeare's *Troilus and Cressida:* "Take but Degree away; untune that string / And hark! What discord follows!" To Shakespeare as well as to Adams, human behavior remains the same whether under a monarchy or republic, and it is driven by a restless desire for power and status that even a democracy would prove incapable of controlling. John Adams, together with Abraham Lincoln, another great student of Shakespeare, may be the only president who belongs to the annals of American literary history.

In America, Adams's critics were mainly Southerners, especially the Virginians Jefferson and John Taylor. They grew suspicious of the centralized government that the Constitution brought into being out of the thirteen colonies. Advocates of states' rights and local sovereignty, they opposed Adams and Hamilton, whose Federalist Party proposed a national banking system and looked forward to a rising commercial republic, leaving rural America behind. But it was to the French critics of the Constitution that Adams directed his thoughtful counterarguments, first in the three-volume *A Defense of the Constitutions of the United States of America* (1787–1789) and then in *Discourses on Davila* (1790). The first work is rather dense and meandering and has been little read by scholars; the latter is lucid and prescient in light of developments closer to our time.

Unlike the Virginians, the French critics had no sympathy for state sovereignty. In royalist France the influence of the aristocracy depended upon the power of the provinces in opposing the centralization of political authority. Hence French intellectuals were less concerned about the division of powers between the states and the national government than the separation of powers among the three branches of government, the executive, legislature, and judiciary, as well as the bicameral scheme consisting of a Senate and a House of Representatives presiding in different chambers. From their perspective, the future of liberty in the modern world depended not on the separation of powers but on the unification of all authority in a single national assembly. Some of their thoughts echoed Jean-Jacques Rousseau's idea of the General Will, which would draw all people together as a coherent whole enjoying a rational collective voice. But some critics of the new American government also drew upon Niccolò Machiavelli to claim that civic virtue remained the animating ideal that guarantees the survival of a republican form of government. Adams, who well knew that neither ancient republics nor Renaissance city-states had survived very long, scrutinized Machiavelli's writings to find out why they had failed, and lasted no more than "the fury of an ocean waterspout."

J. G. A. Pocock's *The Machiavellian Moment: Florentine Political Thought and the Atlantic Tradition* (1975) turned out to be the most influential work on the history of Western political philosophy in the last half of the twentieth century, and it set off students and scholars in a rush to trace classical republicanism from Athens and Aristotle to Philadelphia and the founders. Pocock treated Machiavelli and his legacy literally, as though words were the equivalent of deeds, and rhetoric almost synonymous with reality. Ironically, centuries earlier, John Adams did the opposite, and read between Machiavelli's lines, to discern the nature of the Florentine and other Italian regimes, to discover the politics of the time apart from the language conventions of the era. Does not Machiavelli contradict himself? Adams demonstrated how the philosopher lamented the existence of bloody violence and at the same time upheld the ideal of civic duty—as though power-hungry partisans put their daggers away as they dedicated themselves to the public good. Machiavelli managed the trick by attributing all that was good to virtue and all that was bad to bad luck, the curse of *fortuna*. Machiavelli may have been deceiving the Italians to persuade them that they were capable of noble, patriotic behavior, but Adams concluded that they were left defenseless in their city-states because they lacked the separation of powers and especially a strong executive, all necessary to mediate among factions and mitigate political conflict. "You must not impute the factions of our ancestors to the nature of the men," exhorted Machiavelli, "but to the iniquity of the times."

In *Thoughts on Machiavelli* (1958), the political philosopher Leo Strauss claimed that Machiavelli was the "defender of evil" in lowering politics to the level of deception and intrigue and eliminating ethics from the study of government in order to establish it on a modern scientific basis. But Adams showed how Machiavelli, in avoiding "the nature of men" and citing "the iniquity of the times," denied the idea of evil and original sin. As would Friedrich Nietzsche centuries later, Machiavelli assumed that religion unmanned the will to power and rendered Christians weak and submissive. But Adams remembered how the New England Calvinists rose up against their mother country, England, then the mightiest military empire in the world—and won!

Machiavelli recognized that liberty lay in the legitimacy of opposition, but the French critics of the American Constitution stood adamantly for unanimity and saw conflict as perpetuating the destructive rivalries that tore apart the Old World. Why, they asked, should America depend upon the separation of powers and a bicameral legislature when in the New World there was no aristocracy or monarchy, no dominance of the few and no despotism of the one? The French critics assumed that because aristocracy would be swept away in the throes of revolution, the presence of the nobility would no longer be a threat; a half-century later Karl Marx prophesied that with the elimination of private property, the presence of power would "wither away" along with the state. Both radicals and socialists identified freedom with the coming of consensus and the absence of conflict. More than two hundred years later, the assumption is often just the opposite, especially when postmodernists claim that unity and homogeneity result in conservatism and passivity while freedom and resistance depend upon conflict and opposition. Adams's thought confounds all positions. He believed that conflict had less to do with class structures than with deeper human emotions and even anxieties residing in competitive insecurities, the worry about being ignored and neglected and the yearning for recognition and distinction. "We are told that our friends in the National Assembly of France," wrote Adams, "have abolished all distinctions. But do not be deceived, my dear countrymen. Impossibilities cannot be performed. Have they leveled all fortunes and equally divided all property? Have they made all men equal and women equally elegant, wise and beautiful? . . . Have they blotted out all memories, the names, place of abode, and illustrious actions of their ancestors?" Postmodernists argue that differences and diversity must be asserted against liberal consensus and conservative order; the conservative Adams sought to demonstrate that people have a natural need to distinguish themselves from others and to be recognized as different and special. Hence liberty would depend not on community and solidarity but on conflict and adversity.

Explaining why the "machinery of government" was necessary to deal with political conflicts arising from social classes as well as religious sects, the authors of *The Federalist* reaffirmed Adams's position. Factions cannot be eliminated, James Madison insisted: they are to liberty what air is to fire. But Adams and the theorists of the Constitution were not to have the last word, especially in their assumption that the divisions of government represent the clashing divisions of society. The correction would be made when Alexis de Tocqueville visited America in the 1830s and was astonished to discover that in the American Revolution all classes fought on the same side. He refuted the theory of "mixed government" espoused by Adams by demonstrating that if America really had classes antagonistic to one another, the American Republic would have followed that of the French and collapsed at the first outburst of conflict. The wisest book on this subject is Louis Hartz's *The Liberal Tradition in America* (1955), where he argues that Adams's conclusions were right only because his premises were wrong: the structure of government worked only because the social conditions the framers expected never materialized, as all Americans turned out to be committed to the same values of property and opportunity. Only within some kind of common consensus is conflict possible as people compete for the same objectives. Diversity and difference presuppose the deeper strife of similar desires.

Adams may have erred in his conflict theory of liberty, but he was prescient in showing how any understanding of politics must address the nature of society as a stage or spectacle. In *Discourses on Davila,* Adams drew upon Adam Smith's *A Theory of Moral Sentiments* (1759) to demonstrate why men and women are not so much Aristotle's "political animal" as society's performers, behaving almost as actors commanding, in his words, "the eyes of the spectators" through "the language of signs." Humankind has a need to "emulate" those above in seeking approbation and recognition. Although eighteenth-century French thinkers may have criticized Adams, he presaged their twentieth-century counterparts, such as René Girard, Pierre Bourdieu, and Gilles Deleuze, arguing that the drive for status and distinction is as ineluctable as the reality of power and the ubiquity of desire.

Unlike Jefferson, Adams did not see human beings as autonomous and self-reliant individuals; he saw them as hopelessly dependent and needy. In *Davila* he described the desire to be recognized by others as an essence as pitiable as it was ridiculous.

> To be wholly overlooked, and to know it, are intolerable. Instances of this are not uncommon. When a wretch could no longer attract the attention of man, woman, or child, he must be respectable in the eyes of his dog. "Who will love me then?" was the pathetic reply of one, who starved himself to feed his mastiff. In this *who will love me then* is the key to the human heart; to the history of human life and the manners; and to the rise and fall of empires.

In addition to anticipating the social implications of politics, Adams was the only theoretician of the Constitution who foresaw that the presidency would become the country's most important political institution. Others distrusted the executive office as a residue of monarchism that threatened to return to undermine the Republic. Hamilton, it is true, called for "energy in the executive," but he looked to the "rich, well-born, and able" to guide government, whereas Adams remained skeptical of the elites at the top as well as the masses at the bottom. His severest criticism of Machiavelli is that the Renaissance political philosopher failed to see the primacy of the executive as essential to mediating and controlling intrigue and strife in the Florentine assembly. Rome had its tribunes, but seldom could they rise above factional squabble, and those who wrote about the decline and fall of Rome confused the causes for the effect. "The Romans charged the ruin of their commonwealth to luxury," observed Adams; "they might have charged it to the want of a balance in their constitution." In arguing for a strong executive, Adams went against many of the currents of American political culture, especially a Jeffersonian distrust of centralized power and a more contemporary sentiment that has resonated to Ronald Reagan's exhortation about government being not the solution to our problems but the very problem itself.

Adams may be classified as partaking of a "counter-Enlightenment" in warning that popular sovereignty without checks risks turning democracy into the very problem itself: what Tocqueville called the tyranny of the majority. The radical sixties'-generation cry for "all power to the people" Adams had heard centuries earlier from Thomas Paine. Such shibboleths, he recognized, create the illusion that power will disappear as it becomes democratically collectivized, when in reality power expresses itself singularly, not in the deliberation of the many but in the determination of the few. In *On Revolution* (1963), Hannah Arendt admired Adams's keen grasp of the nature of political power that required constitutional checks, even though she sided with Jefferson and "participatory democracy" at the local level. Adams believed that educated elites must serve in the Senate, or else they would prey upon and "devour" the intellectually inferior members of the House. With his sense of sin, he saw talent as a temptation as much as a gift, and he dreaded aristocracy as much as democracy. When Adams's critics told him that people could be trusted with their own affairs because their love of freedom was so great, Adams replied that lions also love their freedom and feel no need to be governed. He liked to quote Shakespeare: "Power into will, will into appetite / And appetite an universal wolf." Only government, and not the innocent people preyed upon by Lovelace, can deal with "the fever whereof all power is sick."

John Adams died at the age of ninety-one, on the same day that Thomas Jefferson passed away, July 4, 1826. Although they had been bitter rivals in their early presidencies, they came to enjoy a warm affection for one another in their twilight years. Adams's last letter to Jefferson reads: "I look back with rapture to those golden days when Virginia and Massachusetts lived and acted together like a band of brothers and I hope it will not be long before they may say *redeunt Saturnia regna*" — the golden age is returning.

Bibliography: John Adams, *The Portable John Adams,* ed. John Patrick Diggins (New York, 2004). John Patrick Diggins, *John Adams* (New York, 2003). Joseph J. Ellis, *The Passionate Sage: The Character and Legacy of John Adams* (New York, 1994). Zoltan Haraszti, *John Adams and the Prophets of Progress* (Cambridge MA, 1952). Arthur O. Lovejoy, *Reflections on Human Nature* (Baltimore, 1961). Page Smith, *John Adams* (New York, 1976). C. Bradley Thompson, *John Adams and the Spirit of Liberty* (Lawrence, KS, 1998).

JOHN DIGGINS

1791

Philip Freneau takes a job translating French documents at the State Department

THE *NATIONAL GAZETTE*

Philip Freneau's sense of timing was impeccably bad. In January 1800 the rest of the nation was swooning in sentimental transport at the death of George

Washington. In sermons, prints, on souvenir pitchers and other memorials, the old general was anointed Father of His Country and pictured as a divine figure lifted into heaven by choirs of angels. Freneau, the erstwhile "poet of the Revolution," took this moment to renew an old complaint against the Washington cult. In his "STANZAS Occasioned by certain absurd . . . panegyrics and encomiums on the character of the late Gen. Washington," Freneau reminded readers that Washington was a mere mortal, and as fallible as anyone. To deify the leader of a republic "as *abba father*" sickened him. "He was no god, ye flattering knaves," the poet asked. "What temples have been rent in twain?"

Sounding the only non-hosanna in memory of George Washington was just one of Freneau's many unwise career moves. The scion of failed but ever hopeful Huguenot merchants, Philip Freneau was sent to Princeton for a temporary stay among the colonies' rising elite. His fellow students included James Madison and Aaron Burr. In college, Freneau discovered the joys of aping fashionable English poetry and produced, with future novelist Hugh Henry Brackenridge, "The Rising Glory of America" (1771). This was an early example of the American Revolution's most prominent literary genre, the windy nation-building epic, in which allegorical characters were shown visions of the continent's history and future by other allegorical characters. "Rising Glory" was also one of the very first literary expressions of the incipient republic's imperial ambitions, looking forward to the day "when Britain's sons shall spread / Dominion to the north and south and west / Far from th' Atlantic to Pacific shores."

During the Revolution, Freneau published many barrages of patriotic verse, while washing out as a lawyer and a schoolteacher and finally settling on the unsettled life of a mariner. He spent most of the war years in the Caribbean, learning navigation with one Captain Hanson, a plantation owner on the Danish island of Santa Cruz (St. Croix). Having avoided most of the fighting, Freneau returned to the United States in 1778. Eventually he signed on with the Philadelphia privateer *Aurora* in 1780, only to have the vessel swiftly captured by the British and its crew consigned to prison hulks anchored in the East River. In the six weeks he was held as a prisoner of war, Freneau conceived a deep antipathy for the British Empire and its bloodthirsty, hierarchical system. In a widely read poem about the experience, "The British Prison Ship," he imparted the dire view that the British were a "selfish race" of "infernal miscreants." Their goal was to "Subject, destroy, absorb, and conquer all, / As if the power that form'd us did condemn / All other nations to be slaves to them," Freneau versified. "Death has no charms, except in British eyes."

Critics have differed over whether Freneau was a "poet of social commitment" or just a "good hater," but it is certain that he was better at generating intense emotional responses than delicate aesthetic effects. Thus his most lasting contributions came in the areas of politics and journalism rather than literature. Not that Freneau's political career was carried on any more steadily than his other activities. His editorship of the Philadelphia *Freeman's Journal* just after the Revolution lasted only a year and a half before the criticism of other editors made command of a coastal trading vessel seem a better option. A few years at sea did temporary wonders for Freneau's literary reputation, and set up his big political opportunity. A successful edition of his revolutionary poetry came out in 1786, and two years later *The Miscellaneous Works of Mr. Philip Freneau* attracted heavy advance subscriptions and notices declaring him "the Pindar of the United States."

Thus the "Captain" Freneau who came ashore in 1790 was a celebrated, but still impoverished, writer. Having moved to New York, where he worked for the *Daily Advertiser* and hoped for a government job—the city was then the capital of the United States—Freneau fell into a dark mood as he witnessed the new Congress convene. The United States should have been in the vanguard of universal enlightenment, but as Congress enacted Alexander Hamilton's system of government finance, explicitly based on British models, Freneau saw an uglier, meaner spirit abroad in the land. Crowds of people descended on the seat of government, scrambling to influence and profit from its policies: "Four hours a day each rank alike,/They that can walk or crawl/Leave children, business, shop, and wife,/And steer for Congress Hall."

Like his old friend Representative James Madison and his future employer, Secretary of State Thomas Jefferson, the poet preferred to blame political malefactors for the corruption he saw, rather than the American people themselves. "It would seem as if some demon, unfriendly to human happiness, had whispered in the ears of the first Congress," Freneau would write later. One of the demon's most insidious tricks was the exaltation of President Washington's person in imitation of the British and French monarchies, with birthday tributes, a magnificent coach and mansion, and little access beyond official "levees" at which the guests were forbidden the democratic gesture of shaking the president's hand.

The larger issues for Freneau were the inequalities of wealth and the corruption of democratic government that came with the heavy financial speculation and rapid, government-subsidized economic development envisioned by Hamilton. With some justice, Freneau and Jefferson and many others suspected Hamilton's congressional supporters of having "a deep stake in the game" and using their inside knowledge to speculate in government securities themselves. Freneau's satire "Modern Explanations of a Few Terms Commonly Misunderstood" mocked the emergence of wealth as the sole measure of status or merit: "*Genius*—Money-catching . . . *Great men*—Excellent judges of horse-flesh and horse-tricks . . . *Patriotism*—Speechifying in C——ss at six dollars per day, and clearing 20 or 40,000 per annum by sleight of hand."

Emerging opposition leaders Madison and Jefferson soon gave Freneau his chance in the political forefront. Philadelphia became the new capital at the end of 1790; friends of Madison arranged with the printer Francis Childs to establish a new newspaper there, aimed at a national circulation. This would become the *National Gazette*. Meanwhile Jefferson offered Freneau a position in his office, translating French documents that the Francophile Jefferson had no need to have translated. The salary was modest, but the position "gives so little to do as not to interfere," Jefferson averred mildly, "with any other calling the person may chuse."

That calling was nothing less grandiose than saving a "constitution" they be-

lieved to be "galloping fast into monarchy." Madison and Jefferson never actually
controlled Freneau, but he came to play a crucial role in their plans. While opposition to Hamilton's policies was coalescing in Congress, and Jefferson was arguing against them within the cabinet, the Republicans (as they came to call themselves) faced a severe problem in marshaling the political forces necessary to
change those policies. It was almost universally agreed among the elites of the
founding generation that party divisions were extremely dangerous in a republic,
likely to end in civil war, foreign intervention, or both. Unable to publicly oppose
the Washington administration while serving in it, Jefferson needed some sort of
surrogate.

Jefferson's great political panacea, which he and many others believed had
been crucial to bringing the thirteen colonies together before the Revolution,
was newspapers. He and Madison were sure that Freneau's "genius" was "so superior to that of his competitors" that he would find the "ground as good as unoc-
cupied." Before Freneau came to Philadelphia, the only would-be national newspaper was entrepreneur John Fenno's *Gazette of the United States*. Modeling his
journal on the *London Gazette,* Fenno sycophantically praised all the government's
personnel and actions while dismissively cuffing at its critics. Increasingly, he also
opened its pages to various antidemocratic writers, including Vice President John
Adams.

While almost never mentioning Washington or Jefferson's names outside of
official documents, Freneau's *National Gazette* succeeded in forming the skeleton of what became the world's first opposition political party, and the eventual
means of redirecting the policies and basic constitutional approach of the new
government. Freneau's complaints about the corrupt, pseudo-aristocratic political culture that had developed at the seat of government were put into the same
pages as Madison and Jefferson's policy critiques and documents that reflected a
less Anglo-centric view of world affairs than was allowed into the *Gazette of the
United States*. Like-minded subscribers were recruited around the country. Then
the movement that these ideas and people formed together was given a name,
Republican (in the long run, Democratic-Republican), a term first used in connection with Jefferson and his followers in Freneau's April 1792 essay "Sentiments
of a Republican." In an era and a country where parties were agglomerations of
opinion rather than membership organizations, the *National Gazette*—and the
thousands of partisan newspapers that followed in its footsteps—defined the
terms of party affiliation for its readers.

Party building was not primarily accomplished through systematic political
philosophy or literary elegance. Madison's well-reasoned essays for the *National
Gazette* stopped after a time. It was Freneau's histrionic satire and doggerel verse
that emotionally framed the party struggle in Philadelphia as a desperately compelling one for every American, a battle "between the general mass of the people,
attached to their republican government and republican interests, and the chosen band devoted to monarchy and mammon."

Above all, Freneau confronted the elective quasi-monarchy toward which the presidency almost immediately tended. He railed against the overpowering influence of "great names," like George Washington, "over the human mind." Once the officer and the office were thoroughly conflated, popular esteem toward the great personage made criticism of the government seem churlish and near treasonous. Freneau insisted on the right to criticize government and whoever was running it, even churlishly if necessary. One of the basic questions facing early American political culture was the legitimacy of political discussion "out of doors," that is, outside the halls of government. For Washington and most of his Federalist supporters, democracy ended once the votes were in, and continuing debate, especially among ordinary people, amounted to social disorder. Freneau upheld not only the aggressive discussion of public affairs but the right of even socially and economically marginal people to engage in it.

Freneau never actually accused Washington of trying to make himself a king, however much sport he had with the "monarchical prettinesses" that surrounded the first president. His most cutting observations were usually couched in satires written in the character of some would-be aristocrat or imagined Indian. Yet even these oblique criticisms were too much for the men in power. So Freneau received the high honor of inspiring the first recorded presidential tantrum on the subject of biased press coverage. Jefferson recorded the scene:

> The Presidt. was much inflamed, got into one of those passions when he cannot command himself. Ran on much on the personal abuse which had been bestowed on him . . . That he had rather be on his farm than to be made *emperor of the world* and yet that they were charging him with wanting to be a king. That that *rascal Freneau* sent him 3. of his papers every day, as if he thought he would become the distributor of his papers, that he could see in this nothing but an impudent design to insult him.

Effective as the *National Gazette* was, Treasury Secretary Hamilton proved more than a match for his opponents in close bureaucratic quarters, and pulled President Washington even closer by exposing the origins of the paper. Neither Jefferson nor Freneau lasted long after that. The editor flamed back at Hamilton for many months, bogging himself down in personal disputation and alienating some of his own readers. The *National Gazette* folded in October 1793, and Freneau fled to rural New Jersey. Jefferson stoutly defended the paper to Washington but shaded the truth about its founding and left the cabinet at the end of the same year.

As the 1790s wore on, the party Freneau and Jefferson had helped found, and the role of newspapers in it, would expand and flourish. Legions of other Democratic-Republican editors would emerge, inspiring and beating back the Alien and Sedition Acts. With their help Thomas Jefferson would return to the capital as vice president, in Philadelphia, and then president, the first to take office in Washington, D.C. Newspaper-centered parties became the norm for nineteenth-century democracy. Yet Philip Freneau would not be among the beneficiaries. A few other short-lived newspapers came and went, and occasional contributions to the press continued, but in later years the editor of the first major party newspaper would rededicate himself to the poetry that time, somewhat justly, would quickly go about forgetting.

Bibliography: Emory Elliott, *Revolutionary Writers: Literature and Authority in the New Republic, 1725–1810* (New York, 1982). Lewis Leary, *That Rascal Freneau: A Study in Literary Failure* (New Brunswick, NJ, 1941). Philip M. Marsh, ed., *The Prose of Philip Freneau* (New Brunswick, NJ, 1955). Jeffrey L. Pasley, *"The Tyranny of Printers": Newspaper Politics in the Early American Republic* (Charlottesville, VA, 2001). Fred Lewis Pattee, ed., *The Poems of Philip Freneau, Poet of the American Revolution* (Princeton, NJ, 1902–1907).

JEFFREY L. PASLEY

1796

A departing president calls upon Americans to take their bonds of union as "sacred ties"

WASHINGTON'S FAREWELL ADDRESS

The retirement was in the grandest traditions of George Washington's career. More than a decade earlier, as the War of Independence drew to a close, it was said that Washington could have made himself king of the young nation. But he had retired to his farm instead. "If he does that," King George III reportedly said, "he will be the greatest man in the world." And so he was considered: a modern-day Cincinnatus who gave up his sword to return to his plow. But his republican virtue was not merely a personal quality; it shaped the political institutions and traditions of the new nation.

Some years after the close of the war, when a group of Americans gathered in Philadelphia to forge a new constitution, Washington sat among them. Though he kept mostly silent in the debates, his presence was keenly felt. Pierce Butler of South Carolina later observed that the strong executive powers granted by the Constitution would not have been so extensive "had not many of the members cast their eyes toward General Washington as President; and shaped their Ideas of the Powers to be given to a President, by their opinions of his Virtue." And they were not mistaken. As with his generalship during the Revolution—cast as a personal sacrifice, when he ostentatiously refused any compensation for his service—Washington acceded to the presidency denying any personal ambition. Indeed, if his correspondence is to be credited, retirement was never far from Washington's mind, and it might not be an exaggeration to say he had an eye on his farewell from the moment he took office.

Washington hoped to retire at the end of his first term, in 1792, and spent some time contemplating "the *mode* and *time*" for an announcement. But at the insistence of his friends and advisers, who united in urging him to stay in office, he remained through a second term. This time, stung by the criticism he had received during that divisive period, believing he would not live to see another term through, and determined not to die clinging to power, Washington was resolved. And so he announced his final retirement from public life in his Farewell Address of 1796, a work that stands as one of the most important public documents in American history.

Though it is generally called "Washington's Farewell Address," the text's authorship is more complicated. In fact, it emerged from several pens, of which the first and most important was Washington's. When he retired as commander in chief of the army in 1783, Washington had addressed the nation in the form of an open letter emphasizing the necessity of "an indissoluble Union of the States under one Federal Head," and the importance of overcoming "local prejudices and policies." Both the format of that 1783 farewell—a publicly circulated text—and its theme of national unity were reprised in the 1796 address.

If the 1783 circular stands as a first draft of Washington's Farewell Address, a second draft had since been composed. When contemplating retirement in 1792, Washington had sent James Madison a letter summarizing the points he wished to make. Madison, with his felicitous style, turned the outline into a draft address, which he returned a month later along with suggestions on its publication. When Washington decided to stand for a second term he set Madison's draft aside for later use.

The third and fourth pens were those of Alexander Hamilton and John Jay. When Washington once again turned his thoughts to retirement in 1796, he sent Hamilton a new outline, quoting extensively from Madison's earlier version—and adding more heated warnings against partisanship and foreign intrigue. Hamilton boiled the text down to its most essential elements. Using Washington's instructions to develop a new draft, he and John Jay "proceeded deliberately to discuss and consider . . . paragraph by paragraph, until the whole met with our mutual approbation."

The text was perfected over the course of subsequent months, as drafts passed back and forth between Washington in Philadelphia and Hamilton and Jay in New York. Jointly written by Madison and Hamilton, with important contributions from John Jay, backed with all of Washington's prestige, the Farewell Address might well be seen as the last—and certainly the most influential—Federalist Paper.

The central theme of the Farewell Address was the importance of Union. "The Unity of Government which constitutes you one people," it declared, "is a main Pillar in the Edifice of your real independence, the support of your tranquility at home; your peace abroad; of your safety; of your prosperity; of that very Liberty which you so highly prize." Without unity, there could be no liberty: "Your union ought to be considered as a main prop of your liberty . . . the love of the one ought to endear to you the preservation of the other." It urged audiences "to think and speak" of the Union as "the Palladium of your political safety and prosperity." The bonds of Union were more than political; they were "sacred ties," and the address's central message was stark: should the Union collapse, so would Americans' freedom, peace, safety, and prosperity.

What threatened this sacred Union? The specter of geographical division was the first and perhaps most important danger. "In contemplating the causes which may disturb our Union," read the address, "it occurs as a matter of serious concern, that any ground should have been furnished for characterizing parties by *Geographical* discriminations—*Northern* and *Southern*—*Atlantic* and *Western*." The essential problem here was the same as that addressed in Madison's Federalist Papers, especially numbers 10 and 14: standard political theory of the age held that only small republics could survive and that large republics inevitably collapsed. The address would have none of this: "Is there a doubt, whether a common government can embrace so large a sphere? Let experience solve it. To listen to mere speculation in such a case were criminal." The text urged its audience to consider the benefits of unity and stressed that all sections, East and West, North and South, were bound in ties of affection as well as commerce, "directed by an indissoluble community of Interest as *one Nation*."

The second national danger was that of faction, or party spirit. The Farewell Address was downright Shakespearean on the subject:

> It serves always to distract the Public Councils and enfeeble the Public Administration. It agitates the Community with ill founded Jealousies and false alarms, kindles the animosity of one part against another, foments occasionally riot & insurrection. It opens the door to foreign influence & corruption, which find a facilitated access to the government itself through the channels of party passions.

Hark, what discord would follow. Next would come anarchy, which would lead in turn to "a more formal and permanent despotism . . . and sooner or later . . . [to] the ruins of Public Liberty." Faction was a universal wolf "of fatal tendency." Thus, the Farewell Address warned "in the most solemn manner against the baneful effects of the Spirit of Party," and urged Americans to equate partisanship with disloyalty. Historians and political scientists commonly turn to Madison's great Federalist Number 10 when considering the problem of faction in the late eighteenth-century United States—but in the nineteenth century Washington's Farewell Address was far more widely read than any Federalist essay, and far more influential in framing the problem of faction for American audiences. Reprinted in pamphlets and newspapers, read by children in school and adults on Washington's Birthday, the Farewell Address would inculcate a powerful and enduring suspicion of partisanship among generations of Americans.

The third, longest, and most original section of the Farewell Address concerned foreign affairs. Shortly after Washington's inauguration, revolution had broken out in France, unleashing a fifteen-year period of Europe-wide warfare and international turmoil that deeply marked U.S. politics. As European geopolitics pitted British and French superpowers against each other in the 1790s, so American politics split between the pro-British Federalists and the pro-French Republicans. Political parties fought bitterly over matters including John Jay's Treaty of 1794 between the United States and Britain and the public controversy surrounding French ambassador Edmond Charles Genet, who sought to undermine Washington's foreign policy. Washington's response to the international and domestic turmoil was to straddle both divisions, guiding his country toward the same neutrality in the international sphere that he personally aimed for in domestic politics. Thus, his address warned Americans against "a passionate attachment of one nation for another." Concerned about foreign governments' meddling in the domestic politics of the United States, it denounced "the insidious wiles of foreign influence . . . one of the most baneful foes of republican government." The address advocated a new kind of foreign policy—"It is our true policy to steer clear of permanent alliances with any portion of the foreign world"—counseling a more instrumental approach to diplomacy. "It is folly in one nation," read the address, "to look for disinterested favors from another." Instead, it argued for a mutually beneficial "commercial policy" of free trade with all nations.

The Farewell Address was a sensation. Never given as an oration, it made its way to the public through the elaborate network of printers doing so much to bind the young nation together. First published in Philadelphia, it was soon reprinted by nearly every newspaper in the nation and republished in both pamphlet and broadside form. Over the course of the next century, the text would be reprinted in newspapers on patriotic occasions, excerpted in almanacs and schoolbooks circulating in the millions of copies, and read aloud at home and in schools and at public events: diffused, in short, on a scale unknown for most canonical political works. Cast as an unmediated personal appeal from Washington directly to his countrymen, it would be hard to exaggerate the impact of a text delivered with all the paternal authority of a man many considered their political father, and addressed in the most familiar terms to "you."

Washington's Farewell Address would leave an enduring legacy in American political culture, of which the first and most important was its message of national unity. Over the course of the nineteenth century—and most often at times of political crisis—Americans would quote from or reprint the text to promote the cause of union and rekindle Americans' devotion to their nation. This tendency reached its culmination in January 1862, during the Civil War, when Congress provided that "the Farewell Address of Washington be read aloud on the morning of that day [Washington's Birthday] in one or the other of the Houses of Congress." The Farewell Address seems to have somewhat declined in popularity after the Civil War, once the nation had passed its greatest test of its national unity, although at the end of the nineteenth century the Senate established the reading of the address as an annual event on Washington's Birthday.

The second important legacy was the lingering antipartisan sentiment the address promoted. Although formal political parties emerged during Washington's second term in office and still remain with us today, a suspicion of partisan*ship* long persisted. Even when, by the 1840s, political parties came to be accepted as legitimate elements of the political system, many Americans continued to believe—in the classical republican tradition that underlay this aspect of Washington's thought—that true national feeling required the sublimation of partisan sentiment. Although political scientists and historians generally interpret political parties as stabilizing forces—through their capacity to bring dissent into the political system—the term "partisanship" continues, even to this day, to carry negative connotations: something we might call the Washingtonian tradition in American politics.

But it was in the domain of foreign affairs that Washington's Farewell Address would prove most influential. Its warning against "permanent alliances"—the term "foreign entanglements," often wrongly attributed to the Farewell Address, was in fact coined by Jefferson in his first inaugural address—would serve as a pillar of the isolationist tradition in U.S. political culture. That tradition would uphold the resistance to America's imperial adventures in the Philippines and Cuba at the turn of the twentieth century, would remain powerful through the debates surrounding the League of Nations in 1919, would continue through the 1930s with the United States' reluctance to enter World War II, and would break only with Pearl Harbor in 1941. When the United States joined the North Atlantic Treaty Organization in 1949, that was its first "permanent alliance" since the Treaty of Amity and Commerce signed with France in 1778. Although frequent U.S. interventionism during the cold war era—a period when Washington's Farewell Address fell into near obscurity—led many to see isolationist sentiment as anachronistic, it remains to be seen whether that tradition will reemerge in the twenty-first century.

Retiring presidents ever since Washington have continued to give farewell addresses, but only a few—like Dwight D. Eisenhower's, with its warning against the "military-industrial complex"—have held much public interest, and none would prove as influential as Washington's. In the final account, the reason for its uniqueness may lie less with the address than with the farewell. If it is true, as Pierce Butler said, that the Constitution's robust executive powers were possible only because Americans were willing to gamble on Washington's virtue, his farewell was the winning payoff. The precedent that presidents serve for two terms and no longer would continue to be followed for more than 150 years—a hidden constitutional clause, one might call it, added by Washington in 1796 and rendered manifest by the Twenty-second Amendment in 1951—exercising the most decisive limit on the powers of the executive. At a time when the scope of executive power has reemerged as a controversial question, it may be that Washington's Farewell Address offers lessons more relevant than we might expect from a largely forgotten text.

Bibliography: Samuel Flagg Bemis, "Washington's Farewell Address: A Foreign Policy of Independence," *American Historical Review* 39 (January 1934): 250–268. Joseph Charles, *The Origins of the American Party System: Three Essays* (Williamsburg, VA, 1956). Robert A. Ferguson, *The American Enlightenment, 1750–1820* (Cambridge, MA, 1997). François Furstenberg, *In the Name of the Father: Washington's Legacy, Slavery, and the Making of a Nation* (New York, 2006). Felix Gilbert, *To the Farewell Address: Ideas of Early American Foreign Policy* (Princeton, NJ, 1961). Victor Hugo Paltsits, ed., *Washington's Farewell Address, in Facsimile, with Transliterations of all the Drafts of Washington, Madison, & Hamilton, Together with Their Correspondence and Other Supporting Documents* (New York, 1935).

FRANÇOIS FURSTENBERG

1798

Congress passes its version of the Indian captivity narrative

MARY ROWLANDSON AND THE ALIEN AND SEDITION ACTS

Signed into law by John Adams and only incompletely repealed four years later under Thomas Jefferson, the Alien and Sedition Acts lengthened the time required to become a naturalized citizen of the United States, legalized the deportation of any citizen of a country with whom the United States was at war, criminalized "combination," or an assembly of persons "with intent to oppose any measure or measures of the government of the United States," and defined as "libelous" the publication of "false, scandalous, and malicious writing or writings against the government of the United States."

The Acts were passed under Adams's presidency to prevent the spread of revolutionary ideas from France that might undermine the Federalists in the next election. Vice President Thomas Jefferson denounced the laws as unconstitutional. Joining the debate in 1799, the state of Kentucky passed a version of the Acts that called itself a "protest" and countered the federal laws point for point. Did the Alien and Sedition Acts protect the freedom of U.S. citizens, or did they encroach on the authority reserved both for states and for individual citizens? By formalizing this opposition, the Alien and Sedition Acts transformed two warring concepts of national government into a nation of warring concepts. Enjoying peak popularity during the same period, American captivity narratives—accounts of whites taken and kept by Indians—not only reproduced this argument in narrative form, but also introduced a third and equally important position in the debate, marking this as a formative moment in American cultural history.

The conventional genealogy of the American captivity narrative bears an uncanny resemblance to the now discredited historical argument that has the nation going from Puritan settlements in New England to a secular culture of artisans, merchants, planters, and slaves. Having settled along the Atlantic seaboard, these enlightened people are credited with bringing the United States out of theological absolutism and into a contractual government that promoted assimilation. While there is much to recommend this movement from prohibition to assimilation and a unified national culture, one has to ignore the history of American publishing in order to make literature mirror this account. For one thing, Mary Rowlandson's story of heathen captivity and Christian salvation and redemption in the seventeenth-century wilderness, first published in 1682, reached far more readers a full century later; more than twenty editions appeared in the last two decades of the eighteenth century alone. Indeed, the evidence indicates that publication of the Puritan captivity narrative peaked exactly when secular—often semisalacious—captivity versions were also in vogue. Of the 155 different Indian captivity narratives published between 1682 and 1800, 115 appeared between 1780 and 1800, the same period when Rowlandson's narrative was in greatest demand.

A further complication: British readers in North America were certainly familiar with a long tradition of accounts of captives taken by pirates on the high seas and imprisoned in North Africa. It was only at the end of the eighteenth century, when both variations of Indian captivity narrative were attracting so many readers, that American readers developed an appetite for these Barbary captivity narratives as well. Between 1785 and 1810 as many as a hundred first-person accounts of capture and imprisonment at the hands of Barbary pirates appeared in print. Captain James Riley's *Sufferings in Africa* (1817) went through no fewer than twenty printings. Before appearing as a book, however, Riley's story was widely reported as a news event, and afterward the book was widely reviewed and anthologized. As a result, hundreds of thousands of American readers became familiar with the basics of the narrative. Only modestly successful by comparison, Royall Tyler's *The Algerine Captive* (1797) is perhaps the best-known novelistic appropriation of the Barbary tale. This third kind of narrative endorses neither the theological absolutism of Puritan narratives nor the assimilationism of secular narratives but argues instead for a very different concept of the social body. When we fold in the Barbary narratives, the traditional literary genealogy collapses. Rather than see the one coming after as if to cancel out the other, it is more accurate to think of the Puritan and secular versions of the captivity narrative as mutually dependent forms. In engaging each other in an argument over the definition of freedom, the kind of authority that would guarantee it, and the citizen-subject each government presupposed, these narratives occupied the same two positions defined by the controversy over the Alien and Sedition Acts.

In all varieties of the captivity narrative, privation inversely defines the form of government that would eliminate it. Mary Rowlandson's account asserts the absolute difference between the Native American and British forms of government in terms of lack and plentitude. Rowlandson sees the lush natural landscape as void of all meaning and value unless it bears some signs of Englishness. Even cattle droppings will do: "I saw a place where English cattle had been," she recalls; "That was comfort to me, such as it was: quickly after that we came to an English path which so took with me, that I thought I could have freely lain down and died." Englishness and Christianity are indistinguishable at all such moments, when Rowlandson insists that she would rather be dead with her soul intact than merely alive but less than pure in spirit. To ward off any suspicion that survival might have compromised her Christian identity, she goes to great lengths to turn such physical privation into proof of her refusal to assimilate. She claims, for example, never to have lost her disgust for the unclean food she ate when near starvation. As for the integrity of her womanhood, she is not compromised in the least. Alone and in the company of both Indians and other captives, "sleeping all sorts together," she insists, "not one of them offered the least abuse of unchastity to me in word or action." To the degree that her faith endures through enormous hardships, Rowlandson's privation testifies, as the title to the first American edition declares, to *The Sovereignty and Goodness of God*.

Attributed to Abraham Panther, the six-page "A Surprising Account of the

Discovery of a Lady Who Was Taken by the Indians" (1787) demonstrates how the secular or assimilationist narrative revised the Puritan narrative and, in doing so, appeared to uphold an entirely different form of government. Reprinted over twenty times, Panther's narrative features a heroine who disobeys her father and elopes with a lover. Panther compromises his heroine's sexual purity in this way, however, only to reclaim it by having her defend herself against a giant who murders her lover and tries to force himself upon her. By means of the ritual decapitation and elaborate burial of her captor, Panther's "Lady" appropriates the father's prerogative in defense of her own chastity. The slaying of the giant is consequently less important for the physical violence it seems to share with Indian practices than as the means of transferring sovereignty from such a transcendent authority as God, father, or husband to the individual subject.

Men are usually the ones to translate otherwise primitive behaviors into signs of a specifically American culture—the freeborn African American and evangelist John Marrant, for example, dons his captors' Indian clothing and later goes unrecognized by his own family. Such accounts of captivity place less emphasis on what the protagonists refuse to do—they are hardly concerned with staying pure—than on their personal sense of honor and how to meet that standard. It should come as no surprise, then, if their improvisational talent should run roughshod over the very prohibitions associated with Puritan captivity narratives. The brutal murder of her would-be rapist by Panther's heroine amounts to an appropriation of male authority that would seem to define her as the very antithesis of Mary Rowlandson. The point of the narrative, however, is not to exonerate a woman for adapting to Indian ways, but, on the contrary, to prove that she could take on the father's authority by performing a rather elaborate cultural ritual. Publication of narratives endorsing self-sovereignty coincided with the many republications in the late eighteenth century of Mary Rowlandson's narrative and so suggests that both narrative forms addressed a readership in agreement on everything except whether authority should be centralized or dispersed.

These two narratives forms authorized contrary models of government. Where one narrative imagines a nation that congeals as it excludes forms of difference, the other imagines a nation that has assimilated various peoples—though indeed not everyone—under a government able to incorporate cultural differences. When the Barbary narrative enters the argument, it refigures the entire field of debate in terms of an opposition between models of nationalism, of federal, state, local, or even individual authority, similar to those in contention in the Alien and Sedition Acts, and a cosmopolitan model of people and goods in circulation that exposes the artificiality of national boundaries. Barbary narratives rarely involve the kind of soul searching found in Puritan narratives or the personal struggles that testify to self-command in narratives of life on the frontier. Barbary narratives raise an entirely different set of questions: What enables bodies and commodities to circulate around the Atlantic? What is the role of government in facilitating this circulation? At what point does government intervene to guarantee the circulation of people and goods? Can any government regulate the equitable distribution of goods and guarantee the safety of all individuals?

These questions force us to abandon contractual models of government designed to deal with an aggregate of individuals and to imagine instead a government capable of managing a heterogeneous population. Such a political model requires a subject who understands himself, as Barbary captives do, as indistinguishable from a group that interacts, combines, and recombines with other groups in a dynamic flow. Accordingly, Barbary captivity narratives describe events in quantitative terms—the number of pirates as opposed to American sailors, the number of captives taken as opposed to the number ransomed, the price of the ransom, and the number that remained enslaved. These narratives are concerned with the physical condition of such groups—how many slaves grew ill and perished at sea, how many recovered, which captives received food or were allowed to roam the city, and which were thrown into unspeakably foul dungeons. Barbary narratives imply that governments are good to the degree that they enable the free circulation of both goods and people. Arguably expressing a commercial ethic that equates freedom with the freedom of exchange, these narratives assume that people, being human, cannot be objects of exchange, and they make this point by putting their citizen protagonists in the intolerable position of slaves.

Tyler's *The Algerine Captive* starts off in the territory of Indian captivity narratives, with an account of internal differences between peoples and regions along the eastern seaboard, differences that make it as difficult for the migratory protagonist, Dr. Underhill, at first leaving New England for the South, to make an honest living as to court a woman: "Every attempt at familiarity, in a young stranger, habituated to the social, but respectful intercourse, customary in the northern states, excited alarm in Southerners." Although he does not exactly consider himself quite the captive while within the United States, Underhill is repeatedly alienated from his countrymen by his regional identity. This is not a matter of prohibition or prescription so much as the interplay of populations. When out of desperation he signs on as a ship's surgeon, Underhill's account begins to read remarkably like the journals of John D. Foss recounting his captivity in Algiers, which were published in 1797, in that both speak as part of a population and an object of international exchange. As Underhill puts it in the opening to volume two, "The wretched are all of one family; and ever regard each other as brethren." The Atlantic world indeed differentiates only between those who "own" themselves and stand to gain from the exchange and those who are captives and thus objects of exchange. From an international perspective, the captive on a British ship belongs in the same category as a slave laboring in Algiers, and the man who lords it over his household is not all that different from an Algerine in a similar position of power. In a world composed of national and ethnic populations, individual experience ceases to matter except as the means of accounting for the experience of a group and how it fares in its encounters with other groups.

The first two concepts of government—one upholding central authority, the other dispersing authority to regions, groups, and ultimately individuals—presuppose subjects capable of entering into a contractual relationship with the state. The third form of government presupposes a population whose body is simply too extensive, mobile, and mutable to be governed through the mind, one individual at a time. Rather than think in terms of the contractual obligation of citizens to a sovereign or to the collective body of citizens, the Barbary captivity narrative requires its readers to consider what a government owes its populations in the way of security, or their freedom to circulate. The discrepancy between this concept and those based on seventeenth- and eighteenth-century forms of contractualism did not fade with the waning of demand for captivity narratives.

A novel like Harriet Beecher Stowe's *Uncle Tom's Cabin* imaginatively attempts to close the logical gap between actual and potential citizens of the United States and their wives and children, and the human population required to sustain a national economy. The Barbary narrative tradition is at work in Stowe's reversal of the roles of American captive and African captor. Where in Tyler's novel captivity achieved its peculiar affect by demoting Underhill to the status of a slave, forcing him to rethink his identity within a vast differential system of human populations, in Stowe's novel the role of captive elevates the slave. Like those who end up in the unspeakably foul bagnos of Algiers, people who end up on Simon Legree's swampy plantation expose the failure of a national government to protect its population. During the mid-nineteenth century, a narrative form like that organizing accounts of Barbary captivity refashioned the American novel. It did so by bringing the problem of population from the background into the foreground of the novel so that it could openly challenge the liberal fantasy of building a nation one individual at a time.

Bibliography: Nancy Armstrong and Leonard Tennenhouse, *The Imaginary Puritan* (Berkeley, 1992). Paul Baepler, *White Slave, African Masters: An Anthology of Barbary Captivity Narratives* (Chicago, 1999). Katherine Zabelle Derounian-Stodola, *Women's Indian Captivity Narratives* (New York, 1998). Gordon M. Sayre, *American Captivity Narratives* (New York, 2000). Royall Tyler, *The Algerine Captive; or, The Life and Adventures of Doctor Updike Underhill* (New York, 2002).

NANCY ARMSTRONG

1798

Charles Brockden Brown publishes *Wieland; or, The Transformation*

AMERICAN GOTHIC

"Before the beginning, there is Brown," says Paul Auster in *Ghosts*. Of course he may have in mind only the telluric color that gives birth to all the others, but because of the capital letter perhaps, one cannot help feeling the spectral presence of the (almost) first American novelist: Charles Brockden Brown. In a bout of feverish energy between 1798 and 1801, Brown published four groundbreaking romances, three less interesting ones, a host of unsigned stories, and countless articles, pamphlets, and essays, thus winning himself the title of pioneer voice of America.

Although his gothic novels are seldom read today, one certainly recognizes the shadow of Theodore Wieland, Brown's murderous maniac, when a father pursues his offspring with an axe in Stephen King's *The Shining*. One unmistakably thinks of Edgar Huntly, Brown's wild sleepwalker, when confronted with the psychotic splitting and character doubling at work in James Ellroy's *Silent Terror*. But one should perhaps understand the importance of Brown less in terms of possible direct borrowings than an overwhelmingly dark inspiration. How could one resist the sulfurous charms of breathtaking plots that powerfully intertwine incest, murder, madness, and even homoeroticism and necrophilia?

Wieland; or, The Transformation (1798), for example, starts off alluringly with Clara Wieland stating how her ordeals have almost deprived her of the power to recapture them and produce an organized narrative: "The storm that tore up our happiness, and changed into dreariness and desert the blooming scene of our existence, is lulled into grim repose; but not until the victim was transfixed and mangled; till every obstacle was dissipated by its rage; till every remnant of good was wrested from our grasp and exterminated."

She then moves on to recall the strange circumstances of her father's death when she and Theodore, her brother, were but children. Having gone to pray in his private temple, he was suddenly surrounded with a cloud of fire that scorched him to cinders. Brother and sister grew up constantly interrogating the mystery: God might have sentenced their father to spontaneous combustion (which in the late eighteenth century was still believed scientifically plausible), or was it merely an attack by unknown aggressors? It's no wonder that, some twenty years later, Theodore, understandably upset by various occurrences of a voice apparently coming from Heaven, should fall prey to madness and a murderous mania, killing his wife and children in obedience to a divine command that he is the only one to hear. The origin of the voices is never clearly established: are they God's orders, hallucinations, or the snare set by a ventriloquist whose almost supernatural talent enables him to imitate any speech and to cast his voice in all directions?

Truth matters less than psychological verisimilitude. The narrator's fear is shown to alter her perspective to the point of auditory anamorphosis, as she both literally and metaphorically errs in the dark:

> My ears were still open to any sound of mysterious import that should occur. I thought I heard a step in the entry. My purpose was suspended, and I cast an eager glance at my chamber door, which was open. No one appeared, unless the shadow which I discerned upon the floor was the outline of a man . . . My teeth chattered, and a wild confusion took place of my momentary calm . . . What horrid apparition was preparing to blast my sight?

It is into the universal ground of childish and irrational fear that Brown is digging. The display of horror goes way beyond easy sensationalism. Brown thus powerfully distills a streak of gloom in the country of the Enlightenment, much darker in its implications than those in contemporary English or German productions.

Having dreamed as a teenager of writing America's first post-Revolutionary epic poem, Brown was haunted by the idea of endowing his country with a litera-

ture of its own. Given the commercial success of English gothic novels in Philadelphia at the end of the eighteenth century, it is not surprising that, seeking ways
of circumventing an inherited Puritan distaste for mere entertainment, Brown
should have thought of terror as a suitable means to win himself an audience. His
first and best-known novel, *Wieland,* which places its heroine in the middle of
perils that owed much to the English school of terror, was set in America and testified early to Brown's desire to find indigenous sources of dread. In the preface to
Edgar Huntly; or, Memoirs of a Sleepwalker (1799), he trumpets his departure from—
and amused contempt for—contemporary Old World practice in fiction and his
quest for originality:

> It is the purpose of this work to profit by some of those sources [peculiar to our-
> selves, Americans]; to exhibit a series of adventures, growing out of the condition
> of our country . . . One merit the writer may at least claim; that of calling forth the
> passions and engaging the sympathy of the readers, by means hitherto unemployed
> by preceding authors. Puerile superstitions and exploded manners; Gothic castles
> and chimeras, are the materials usually employed to this end. The incidents of In-
> dian hostility, and the perils of the Western wilderness, are far more suitable; and,
> for a native of America to overlook these, would admit of no apology.

Under Brown's somewhat sophomoric boasting tone, the seriousness of the
issue readily appears. How can one break ground and start building a national literature? In spite of the emergency of its pressing difficulties—basically imagining
a way to survive predictable English resentfulness and understandable Indian
diffidence—the young nation constantly testified to the imperative need to find
for itself a creative voice. Was it enough, while using the same language as the
Mother Country's authors, to set a plot in local surroundings to produce a literature so essentially different that it would be recognized as "American"?

At first sight, Brown seems to think, "Yes. It is enough." However, a given language informs a text down to its very essence, and in order to sound different, an
American writer had to find a new *tessitura,* an originality that went way beyond
settings and themes.

Brown tried—and one might think that he failed. In spite of a renewal of criti-
cal academic interest since the 1960s, he remains largely viewed as the naïve fol-
lower of recognized English gothic recipes whose immature attempts influenced
Poe, Melville, and Hawthorne, not to mention James, Faulkner, and O'Connor.
Brown's "power of blackness" was thus reduced to a ghostly foreshadowing of future and more sophisticated fiction. Hawthorne himself, in his story "The Hall of
Fantasy" (1842), had struck the note by placing Brown on a pedestal, along with
Cervantes, Shakespeare, Milton, Fielding, Richardson, and Scott—but in "an ob-
scure and shadowy niche."

Brown, with a degree of consciousness difficult to achieve, translated into his
fiction both personal and national difficulties, leading to the expression of an
epistemological crisis that goes far beyond the naïve, thrilling techniques entailed
by the gothic label. Should one actually believe in a Calvinistic cloud of fire coming down to punish a sinner? In divine commands demanding human sacrifices?

In demonic powers magically transporting characters from one place to another? In human resurrection from the dead? As suggested earlier, what appear to be supernatural and wonderful occurrences can *also* be understood as errors of perception, mental illusions that bring us into contact with our latent and potential lunacy. English gothic writing had hitherto produced fiction that either conveyed its readers away from reality into a distant world of the terror-inducing supernatural, or presented them with apparently ghastly and spectral events, explained away before the end as mere trappings. In contrast, the close-at-hand universe Brown takes us into is based on a reality that constantly threatens, through its never-solved mysteries, to bring its protagonist to destruction. In *Edgar Huntly,* for example, we are made to share the narrator's anguish when he wakes up in total darkness, in an obviously unknown place, after he had peacefully gone to sleep in his bed:

> My return to sensation and to consciousness took place in no such tranquil scene. I emerged from oblivion by degrees so slow and so faint, that their succession cannot be marked . . . I perceived that my posture was supine, and that I lay upon my back. I attempted to open my eyes . . . The exertion which I made cost me a pang more acute than any which I ever experienced. My eyes, however, were opened; but the darkness that environed me was as intense as before.

Having set himself the task of discovering the murderer of his best friend, following the (false) tracks of an Irish somnambulist who leads him through the rugged space of unconquered territories, Edgar will finally emerge as a very likely culprit, although he will remain blind to this possibility. Brown will thus have created the first detective novel, and a considerably sophisticated one.

Delving into the core of what he called "a double mental existence," torn between an affable, daily engagement in the optimistic process of the birth of a nation, and the torture of painful nocturnal fiction writing, Brown did move away from "puerile superstitions and Gothic . . . chimeras," the better to express the most intimate realities of the human psyche. Doesn't Clara Wieland—understandably shocked when her psychotic brother, a model of serenity and wisdom, obeys the "divine command" to murder his wife and children—discover a streak of madness barely less potent in herself? Isn't the refined and arrogant Edgar Huntly eventually forced to realize his own somnambulistic affection and repressed ferocity after having self-righteously tried to save Clithero, an Irishman he represented to himself as the only sleepwalking maniac he knew? Both novels—but it is also true of Brown's other two books, *Ormond; or, The Secret Witness* (1799) and *Arthur Mervyn; or, Memoirs of the Year 1793* (1799–1800)—thus blur the distinctions between savage and civilized, sane and mad. In *Edgar Huntly,* the author stages an elaborate representation of what Freud was a hundred years later to theorize as the Unconscious: the protagonist finds a reflection of himself in the sleepwalking European *and* in the "wild" Native American. He thus comes to realize, if only partially, that an entire part of himself had so far remained "unknown to himself." The readers, prisoners of Edgar's perspective, had believed that Clithero was the only somnambulist, the one referred to in the subtitle: they are now made to realize that the main narrator is totally unreliable and, one step further, that they may be unwittingly walking in their sleep too. As Leslie Fiedler, reading Brown's implications to the core, perfectly summarized: *"We are all sleep-walkers!"* By regenerating the figure of the villain through placing him *inside* the virtuous hero, and by creating a fictional universe where madness fluctuates in a lethal stream of unconsciousness, Brown designed a disquieting metaphor for the workings of the human psyche.

Such destabilization finds its poetic equivalence in the depiction of the unconquered territories that Edgar visits while awake and revisits in his sleep, places that he both knows and ignores, in a typically uncanny way: "The desert tract called Norwalk . . . my curiosity had formerly induced me to traverse in various directions. It was in the highest degree, rugged, picturesque and wild. This vale, though I had never before viewed it by the glimpses of the moon, suggested the belief that I had visited it before."

The movement toward utter disorientation reaches its apex when, in the already quoted excerpt, the protagonist wakes up in the middle of the night, enveloped in complete obscurity and surrounded with craggy rocks. It will take him another 130 pages and many adventures—which include primitive crawling in the dark, fighting against a panther and drinking its blood, meeting with half-asleep Indians and killing them in proclaimed self-defense—to understand how his sleepwalking steps had led him to fall into a cave in the heart of the wilderness, and to start realizing that he is perhaps less "civilized" than he had thought. The blurring of ready-made categories and simplistic oppositions thus informs Brown's literary attempts.

It did take time, but Brown's work is now appraised for what it is—and no longer only for the influence that it exerted. Literary history has come to acknowledge how Brown's most decisive innovations lay in the realm of formal experimentation, going farther, as he did, than any of his predecessors in the creation of unreliable narrators and fallacious accounts as the mainsprings of his fiction. What knowledge can characters share if their very understanding is that they have not achieved (cannot achieve) any? What truth can we, readers of the novel and of the world, ever reach?

Brown's novels combine a fascination for psychological reactions to extreme situations and, less evidently, a streak of suspicion toward fiction that may well constitute the hallmark of the most ambitious American literature. Metafictional before the word was coined, Brown's work draws attention to its own process of creation and to the illusion that *dares* require a "willing suspension of disbelief." Countless are the references to the very process of writing the text that constitutes the novel we read, to forged letters *(Ormond, Arthur Mervyn)*, to the danger of immersing oneself in fiction *(Carwin, The Biloquist)*. The "double-tongued" deceiver in *Wieland*—that is, the ventriloquist, "the *author* of evil"—whose power of imitation brings about the fateful confusion is also a representation of the writer, similarly blurring the distinction between fiction and reality. Doubling, somnambulism, schizophrenia, near-death experiences, and also plain deception, disguise, and dissimulation, are but echoes of Brown's awareness of the splitting of the human mind and of the artist's—and even, perhaps, America's—simultaneous engagement in and alienation from the world.

Bibliography: Marc Amfreville, *Charles Brockden Brown: La part du doute* (Paris, 2000). Alan Axelrod, *Charles Brockden Brown* (Austin, TX, 1983). Charles Brockden Brown, *The Novels and Related Works by C. B. Brown,* Bicentennial Edition, ed. S. Krause and S. W. Reid, 6 vols. (Kent, OH, 1977–1987). Bill Christopherson, *The Apparition in the Glass* (Athens, GA, 1993). David Lee Clark, *Charles Brockden Brown: Pioneer Voice of America* (Durham, NC, 1952). Leslie Fiedler, *Love and Death in the American Novel* (New York, 1966). David Punter, "Early American Gothic," in *The Literature of Terror: A History of Gothic Fictions from 1765 to the Present Day,* vol. 1 (London, 1996). Stephen Watts, *The Romance of Real Life: Charles Brockden Brown and the Origins of American Culture* (Baltimore, 1994).

MARC AMFREVILLE

1801, March 4

After a bitterly partisan election, the new president asserts "We are all republicans: we are all federalists"

JEFFERSON'S FIRST INAUGURAL ADDRESS

Two centuries after it was delivered, what is most remarkable about Jefferson's First Inaugural Address is how well it was received. The election of 1800 had aroused great anxiety on the part of both of the nascent political parties, the Federalists—the party of the incumbent, John Adams—and the Republicans—the party of the challenger, Thomas Jefferson. For several years, each party had feared the takeover of the government by force. Federalists had enacted the Alien and Sedition Acts to prevent the overthrow of the government by the French and their supposed American allies. That such fears were irrational did not make them any less real. As the election approached, each party saw in its opponent a potential Napoleon. "The enemies of our Constitution are preparing a fearful operation," Jefferson worried. He imagined "our Bonaparte"—Alexander Hamilton—"surrounded by his comrades in arms," stepping in "to give us political salvation in his way." Hamilton thought that if Jefferson won the election, the result might be a "REVOLUTION after the manner of BONAPARTE." When the election was thrown into the House of Representatives after both Jefferson and his running mate Aaron Burr received the same number of votes in the Electoral College, the anxiety only increased. The Federalists decided that Jefferson was the lesser of two evils, and on the thirty-sixth ballot, on February 17, they allowed him to be elected. That left him barely two weeks to write his Inaugural Address.

Jefferson prepared three drafts of the address. The first was a rough draft. The second was a revised version, still with many crossings-out and corrections, that he gave to Philip Freneau, the editor of the *National Intelligencer,* early on the morning of the inauguration so that he could have copies ready to distribute immediately after Jefferson had delivered the address. The third draft, written on several smaller sheets of paper that could be folded and carried into the Senate chamber, where Jefferson would deliver the address, was filled with abbreviations and short, indented lines, making it look like an outline. This was the script from which Jefferson would speak.

Jefferson need not have taken so much care in preparing his script: he spoke so inaudibly that almost no one in the audience of more than a thousand (about 150 of whom were women) could hear him. Jefferson was a notoriously poor public speaker. In a large group, his voice typically "sank into his throat" and became "guttural and inarticulate," if he spoke at all. His posture was awkward, somehow stiff and exceedingly loose at the same time.

Yet the time Jefferson spent revising his first draft was time well spent. The alterations were of two sorts. Some effected stylistic improvements, for example changing "thousandth generation" to "thousandth & thousandth generation" and replacing a couple of clotted sentences at the end of the second paragraph with language that was more poetic.

Other changes made the address more conciliatory by moderating terms that might have seemed provocative or arrogant. Violating the rights of the minority became "oppression" rather than "tyranny." In a phrase about relations with other nations, Jefferson changed the categorical "alliance with none" to the more qualified "entangling alliances with none." A self-deprecatory sentence in the penultimate paragraph became even more conciliatory when Jefferson compared himself unfavorably with a singular Revolutionary War hero, George Washington, instead of a host of unnamed heroes. In this way Jefferson not only invoked the revolutionary heritage but paid homage to the late president as well. In 1797, he had scandalized the nation when a private letter to the Italian Philip Mazzei that was published in a flawed translation appeared to disparage Washington as an "apostate" and one of the "Samsons in the field & Solomons in the council . . . who have had their heads shorn by the harlot England." Now, by changing a few nouns and pronouns, Jefferson hoped finally to be able to undo some of the damage the Mazzei letter had caused.

Jefferson's attempts at conciliation worked. Not surprisingly, his supporters were effusive in their praise. The address was "incomparable," "fully of wisdom," "eloquent and dignified," "the best I had ever met with," "I cannot read [it] . . . without great tears of admiration & joy." Significantly, many of Jefferson's supporters applauded his efforts to pacify the opposition, and they reported to him that those efforts were succeeding.

Federalists who feared that the third president of the United States was a dangerous visionary were pleasantly surprised by Jefferson's Inaugural Address. John Marshall, the chief justice of the Supreme Court and one of Jefferson's most implacable political foes, complained to a friend just before swearing Jefferson in that "the democrats are divided into speculative theorists & absolute terrorists." After hearing the address, however, he found it "in the general well judg^d & conciliatory." Other Federalists agreed. The speech was "Mild Conciliatory and Philosophic." It had "a wonderful lullaby effect." It was a "benevolent, conciliatory, yet manly address." Henry Knox, a Federalist who had been Washington's secretary of war, praised Jefferson for his efforts at conciliation. "The just manner in which you appreciate the motives of the two parties . . . and the strong incitements you display for cementing more closely our union . . . evince conspicuously . . . your intelligence patriotism and magnanimity."

Given the political tumult of the preceding several years, such a reaction was extraordinary. Moreover, when we read Jefferson's First Inaugural Address today, though we may notice the efforts at conciliation—most famously in the line "We are all republicans: we are all federalists"—we cannot help being struck by the vigorous assertion of liberal principles. Jefferson's critics called these ideas "visionary" with good reason. Stripped of the elegant and conciliatory language in which Jefferson encased them, many of them may seem visionary still: equal justice for all, regardless of religion or political principles; protection of the right of election; supremacy of civil over military authority; the wide diffusion of information, unchecked by government intervention; freedom of the press; habeas corpus; trial by jury; peace, commerce, and friendship with all nations; a government that protects people from injuring one another but otherwise leaves them alone. So important were the corollary principles of majority rule and protection of the rights of the minority that Jefferson mentioned them twice. So also with religious and political tolerance. These are all core liberal values, which Jefferson and subsequent liberals have set forth as timeless.

It should be noted that Jefferson included other principles that he considered timeless but may now seem more particular to his time: preference for the militia rather than a standing army; the support of state governments as the best protectors of liberty; a commitment to the federal union. The important point, however, is that almost no one who heard or read Jefferson's address distinguished among the array of principles that he set out or picked and chose among them. Like Jefferson, most people were willing to consider them as he presented them— "the creed of our political faith, the text of civic instruction, the touchstone by which to try the services of those we trust"—and at worst as somewhat visionary, but not particularly threatening. Hamilton read Jefferson's address as a reassurance that "the new President will not lend himself to dangerous innovations."

It was the way in which Jefferson presented his principles that commanded assent. In fact, rather than speaking of the substance of Jefferson's address, almost everyone commented upon the style. It was called "philosophic" without reference to the elements of the philosophy it reflected; it was praised as an "admirable Compendium of Republican Principles," as if the compendium were more important than the particular principles themselves. We do not conventionally think of Jefferson as a modern politician, one who could craft a message that obscured the content of his policies. Yet in his Inaugural Address he was able to gain widespread assent, even from political adversaries, by crafting it in a way that made it seem conciliatory.

Jefferson's capacity to please friend and foe alike, to transform a moment in American history that had seemed fraught with peril into one of celebration, is a testament to his skills as a writer and thinker both. It bears noting that, as Margaret Bayard Smith, one of those who heard Jefferson deliver his address, observed, "The changes of administration, which in every government and in every age have most generally been epochs of confusion, villainy and bloodshed, in this our happy country take place without any species of distraction, or disorder." Even discounting Smith's tendency to depict contemporary events in dramatic terms, Americans understood that the peaceful transfer of power in a republican government was almost a novelty in world history. Jefferson set out to conciliate so that his presidency and the nation itself would succeed—although in this his predecessor gave him no assistance. John Adams departed Washington at 4:00 a.m. on the day of the inauguration so that he would not have to witness it, and he saddled Jefferson with a number of Federalist judges—the so-called midnight appointments—who would ensure that one branch of the government, at least, remained under Federalist control.

Shortly after his election, Jefferson had told a supporter that he hoped to "once more get social intercourse restored to its pristine harmony," and he was gratified subsequently to learn from Henry Knox that his address was "considered as holding out a ground for conciliation and union." He told Knox that the response to his speech confirmed his belief "that the great body of those called Federalists were real Republicans as well as federalists." He also believed that his true opponents—he called them "Monarchists"—were only a small minority, and that if only the truth were presented to them, the people could be trusted to make the right choices.

The challenge Jefferson gave himself was to find a basis for reconciling Federalists and Republicans, and for doing it on Republican terrain. He found it in history, both the past and the imagined future. Would the experiment in republican government survive? "Let history answer this question."

Jefferson told his fellow Americans that they were united by a shared history, one that diverged sharply from that of the Old World and pointed to a glorious future, if only Americans would remain faithful to their principles. He called forth that future in the second sentence of the address: "A rising nation, spread over a wide and fruitful land, traversing all the seas with the rich productions of their industry, engaged in commerce with nations who feel power and forget right, advancing rapidly to destinies beyond the reach of mortal eye." Even before the sentence was finished, he set up the contrast with the Old World "nations who feel power and forget right." This was a contrast between us and them.

Twice more Jefferson returned to the contrast between a "chosen country"— "the world's best hope"—and an Old World characterized by "exterminating havoc" and "degradations." Each time, he widened the distance between the two. In the second paragraph, Jefferson remarked that Americans had already "banished from our land that religious intolerance under which mankind so long bled," although they had not yet fully abolished "political intolerance," which was just as "wicked" and "capable of . . . bitter and bloody persecutions." Yet such intolerance was quite literally foreign. "During the throes and convulsions of the ancient world, during the agonising spasms of infuriated man, seeking through blood and slaughter his long lost liberty, it was not wonderful that the agitation of the billows should reach even this distant and peaceful shore." Americans could escape this bloody history by realizing that they were a single people with a different destiny. It was at this point in the address that Jefferson uttered his famous words, "We are all republicans: we are all federalists," leaving the terms uncapitalized, to indicate that he meant not the rival parties but principles that every American shared. Jefferson summoned the American people—"fellow citizens," "us," "we," "brethren of the same principle"—to "unite with one heart and one mind." This was Jefferson's first move in constructing an American national identity: to ask Americans to think of themselves as a single people, united by shared beliefs.

Jefferson asked too for their support so that he could "steer with safety the vessel in which we are all embarked amidst the conflicting elements of a troubled world." Completing this metaphor in the second paragraph, Jefferson brought the American ship to "this distant and peaceful shore." Here he made his second move: America has already reached its destination, and the land and the character of its people will write for Americans a separate history. "Kindly separated by nature and a wide ocean from the exterminating havoc of one quarter of the globe; too high minded to endure the degradations of the others, possessing a chosen country, with room enough for our descendants to the thousandth and thousandth generation," the American people might realize their providential destiny.

Only one thing more was necessary to make them "a happy and prosperous people," and that was "a wise and frugal government." It was only here, in the fourth paragraph, that Jefferson laid out his long list of "the essential principles of our government." And he tied them to the new American history, for they were "the bright constellation, which has gone before us and guided our steps through an age of revolution and reformation." They were not dangerous innovations— Hamilton's fear—but instead the principles that "the wisdom of our sages, and blood of our heroes" had sanctified.

In delivering his First Inaugural Address, Thomas Jefferson also delivered his people—the American people. He summoned them as a nation, united by distinctive principles and sharing a distinctive history. To be American was to agree that these principles and this history marked the new United States as a chosen country. And to dissent from these principles or depart from this history marked one as something other than fully American.

Bibliography: Noble E. Cunningham, *The Inaugural Addresses of President Thomas Jefferson, 1801 and 1805* (Columbia, MO, 2001). Robert A. Ferguson, *Reading the Early Republic* (Cambridge, MA, 2004). Jay Fliegelman, *Declaring Independence: Jefferson, Natural Language, and the Culture of Performance* (Stanford, CA, 1993). James P. Horn et al., eds., *The Revolution of 1800: Democracy, Race, and the New Republic* (Charlottesville, VA, 2002). Barbara B. Oberg et al., eds., *The Papers of Thomas Jefferson,* vol. 33 (Princeton, NJ, 2007), 134–152. Peter S. Onuf, *Jefferson's Empire: The Language of American Nationhood* (Charlottesville, VA, 2000).

JAN ELLEN LEWIS

1804, January

The former French colony of Saint-Domingue declares independence

THE MATTER OF HAITI

The Haitian Revolution established Haiti as a place of shocking firsts: first defeat of Napoleon's army, first successful slave revolt, and first black republic in the world. From the moment of its declaration of independence, Haiti's past, present, and future have been read primarily through the lens of this revolution. Called Saint-Domingue under French rule, Haiti was the most valuable of France's colonial possessions at the time of the revolution, coveted by all the imperial powers of Europe. The colony's hugely profitable sugar industry was sustained by the forced labor of 500,000 enslaved Africans. However, with a nonslave population of a mere 20,000 whites and 30,000 free persons of color, Saint-Domingue was a sociopolitical powder keg.

When conflict erupted in 1791, the revolting slaves initially aligned themselves with the Spanish, fighting against the French Empire. By 1793 they had changed their allegiance and were battling alongside the French under the leadership of the slave-turned-general Toussaint L'Ouverture—on the condition that universal freedom be established on the island. L'Ouverture succeeded in ousting the Spanish and British armies from Saint-Domingue by 1801, reinstating the island as a French colony and abolishing slavery, only to be betrayed, captured, exiled, and ultimately killed by Napoleon's forces in 1802. Napoleon's treachery and subsequent reinstitution of slavery sparked the second phase of the revolution, led now by L'Ouverture's principal lieutenant, Jean-Jacques Dessalines. It was Dessalines who ultimately defeated Napoleon's troops and proclaimed independence, massacring or expelling all whites and declaring himself governor-general for life (and later, emperor) of the newly rebaptized Ayiti. In 1806, Dessalines was assassinated, and the island was divided between the black northern kingdom ruled by Henri Christophe and a southern mulatto republic under Alexandre Pétion.

Haiti's revolution, at once a civil war, an imperial war, and a war for independence, had "the slavery question" at its center. In the slaveholding United States, which doubled in size with the acquisition of the Louisiana Territory—a direct consequence of Napoleon's disengagement from the Americas following his defeat at the hands of the Haitian army—and received more than 15,000 white, "free colored," and slave refugees, the Haitians' call for radical antislavery a mere 700 miles off the coast of Florida was especially resonant. For Jefferson's government, Haiti's battle for freedom exposed the contradictions of the American Revolution that had proclaimed the inalienable human right to liberty in the Declaration of Independence while maintaining slave labor.

American literature about Haiti reflected this conflict between humanist

ideals and racialist realities. In 1808 Mary Hassal, a white woman from Philadelphia living in Haiti during the final years of the revolution, published a collection
of letters titled *Secret History, or, The Horrors of St. Domingo*. Hassal abhors the excessive violence that pervaded revolutionary Haiti, yet throughout the book she
is unwavering in her condemnation of Napoleon's unjust reinstitution of slavery
and racist legislation on the island. Her letters document the contrast between
the pleasure-filled decadence of the French planter population and the profound
misery and debasement of the slaves in colonial Saint-Domingue. She further
draws a distinction between the greedy capitalist profiteering of U.S. commercial interests and the noble intentions underlying the blacks' struggle for liberty.
While Hassal's reactions to blacks range from sympathetic to repulsed, she suggests that their efforts to achieve freedom from servitude—even through violence—provides the most basic proof of their humanity.

In a chapter of Harriet Beecher Stowe's *Uncle Tom's Cabin,* the unjustified beating of a slave leads to a charged discussion between brothers Alfred and Augustine St. Clare. Evoking both the French Revolution and Jefferson's Declaration—
characterized by the proslavery Alfred as so much "republican talk," inconsistent
with observable reality—Stowe posits the "San Domingo Hour" as the inevitable
fate of a hypocritical society in which the degradation of men into animals is tolerated. She argues that blacks in Haiti deployed horrific violence against their
masters because the institution of slavery had broken "all human ties," and suggests that the Haitian Revolution resulted mainly from the failure of whites to
behave as Christians.

Benito Cereno, Herman Melville's 1855 novella, is decidedly ambivalent toward
slavery and violence. A tale of the brutal revolt of black slaves aboard a Spanish
sailing vessel—tellingly named the *San Dominick*—and their subsequent manipulation of their white masters, the narrative both condemns the duplicity and viciousness of the slaves and criticizes the whites' misperception that blacks passively accepted enslavement. The slaves' actions appear at once to disgust and to
impress Melville, and the drama that unfolds is described in terms of madness,
contagion, and unthinkable savagery. The discomfort that the slave revolt evokes
for Melville turns specifically on the question: How much violence is justifiable in
the face of the institution of slavery? And, further, is not such violence inevitable
when basic human rights are at stake—"might not the San Dominick, like a slumbering volcano, suddenly let loose energies hid?"

In his 1861 lecture "Toussaint L'Ouverture," Wendell Phillips, New England
lawyer, philanthropist, and president of the Anti-Slavery Society, makes an egalitarian argument through biography. Evoking Washington, Cromwell, and Napoleon, Phillips characterizes the Haitian general as equal to them if not superior in
every respect. He lauds Toussaint's extraordinary prowess on the battlefield, his
foresight, his statesmanship, and, above all, his steadfast nobility in the face of
the dishonorable actions of the so-called civilized nations. Phillips likens the Haitian Revolution to antislavery uprisings in the United States—obliquely referencing John Brown—and suggests that black violence in the interest of liberation is
justified and exemplary of human audacity. There are numerous later artistic trib-

utes to Toussaint's role as a soldier and a symbol. From poet and educator Leslie Pinckney Hill's 1928 poem *Toussaint L'Ouverture: A Dramatic History,* to playwright and *New York Times* editor William Dubois's *Haiti,* a part of the Federal Theatre Project, to Jacob Lawrence's *Toussaint L'Ouverture* paintings, a series of forty-one panels chronicling Toussaint's life and revolutionary exploits, Toussaint L'Ouverture has been positioned in American culture as the spectacular focal point of the Haitian Revolution.

At the dedication ceremonies of the Haitian Pavilion at the 1893 World's Fair in Chicago, Frederick Douglass—minister to Haiti in 1889—evoked the Haitian Revolution as the affirmation of aspiration to race-blind human dignity. The World's Fair also saw the production of the dramaturge William Edgar Easton's *Dessalines: A Dramatic Tale.* The four-act play in blank verse depicts the romantic figure of Dessalines as more swooning lover than bloodthirsty soldier. Easton's *Christophe: A Tragedy in Prose of Imperial Haiti* (1911) portrays Dessalines's successor as an equally complex and noble hero, undone by his own tragic flaws. Himself a descendant of a general in the Haitian revolutionary army, Easton writes of Haiti's revolution as the sum of the acts of its larger-than-life leaders.

Other literary evocations of Haiti in the literature of the United States appeared in response to the occupation of Haiti by U.S. Marines from 1915 to 1934. Marine captain and public relations director John Houston Craige published his military travel memoirs, among them *Black Bagdad,* in which he represents blacks as deceitful, sadistic, and irrational by nature. This chronicle in particular is replete with descriptions of cruelty and gratuitous aggression among the Haitians, and makes the argument that American intervention was necessary to maintain order in Haiti. Craige relates, for example, an anecdote about the *cacos*—a guerrilla army of Haitian peasants who in 1918 revolted against occupation forces and were suppressed by the Marines with terrific brutality—who killed and ate a white officer sympathetic to their cause. Craige reduces the rebels to ignorant cannibals and argues that America's intentions were primarily to save Haiti from what it had become in the century since independence.

William Faulkner's *Absalom, Absalom!* (1936) evokes Haiti's revolution through meaningful silence, as Faulkner inserts a blatant anachronism at the antebellum foundations of his American narrative: his main protagonist, the white Southerner Thomas Sutpen, travels to Haiti in 1823 and four years later quells a slave uprising on a French sugar plantation, a clear historical impossibility. This act of apparent heroism sets the stage for Sutpen's attainment of great wealth and power, yet leads eventually to the tragic fall of his entire family. Thus while seemingly denying Haiti's revolutionary achievement, Faulkner ultimately casts the revolution as a persistent legacy for as long as and wherever slavery continued in the Americas.

Eugene O'Neill's one-act play *The Emperor Jones* (1920) is centered on an allegorical portrayal of Haiti's self-proclaimed king, Henry Christophe. O'Neill never precisely identifies the site of the play's drama as Haiti, and his first stage directions read: "The action of the play takes place on an island in the West Indies, as yet un-self-determined by white marines. The form of native government is, for the time being, an Empire." This sets the stage for a drama that merges the outcome of the Haitian Revolution with a critique of the U.S. Marines in the political present.

In her ethnographic study *Tell My Horse,* Zora Neale Hurston is decidedly ambivalent about Haiti's revolutionary history and extols the American occupation period for bringing relative stability and prosperity to Haiti. Hurston doubts that Haiti has ever been a functioning republic, and contends that Haiti's post-occupation government amounts to an "elected monarchy" whose president is "really a king with a palace." This choice of language is particularly significant inasmuch as it subtly evokes the notoriously corrupt reign of Christophe. Moreover, Hurston's multiple references to class and color divisions of the Haitian population further allude to Haiti's 1807 mulatto-black fracturing. Not unlike Craige, Hurston condemns the ignorance, superstition, and "barbarity" of Haiti's masses, pointing to the illiteracy and political disenfranchisement of the peasant class as one of the most significant obstacles to building a true Haitian republic. Hurston views popular memory of the revolution as a hindrance to Haiti's political health, a tale of bygone glory manipulated by self-serving politicians: "The bones of L'Ouverture, Christophe and Dessalines were rattled for the poor peasants' breakfast, dinner and supper." She denounces the political elite's reliance on the revolutionary narrative as a distraction that prevents the Haitian people from doing "those things which will prove that they deserve their freedom." She compares this with the posturing of black leaders in the United States, the "tongue-and-lung" "Race Men" whose "claim to greatness [is] the ability to mount any political platform at short notice and rattle the bones of Crispus Attucks." Hurston paints Haiti's distant battle for self-determination as an event of limited value in the present moment: "What happened in 1804 did what was necessary then," she writes. "It is now another time that calls for patriotism." Similarly, Langston Hughes in *The Emperor of Haiti* (1936), a historical drama he later reworked as the libretto for William Grant Still's 1949 opera *Troubled Island,* writes of Haiti's revolution as tragically unfulfilled. Hughes focuses on Dessalines, exploring the social tensions that ultimately undermined revolutionary objectives. Hughes laments the extent to which color consciousness and class hierarchy—then as in his own time, in Haiti as in the United States—thwart Pan-African unity.

Other writers of the same period presented the Haitian Revolution as a model for black nationalist consciousness and unified Pan-African modernity. Claude McKay relies on this theme most explicitly in his 1928 novel *Home to Harlem.* He narrates the encounter between the intellectual Ray, a political exile from occupied Haiti, and the African American working man Jake. Ray enlightens Jake as to Haiti's political significance, past and present, at one point citing Wordsworth's 1802 sonnet, "To Toussaint L'Ouverture," as if to confirm the far-reaching importance of Haiti's revolutionary struggle. He suggests to Jake that Haiti's proud past and uncertain future are the heritage and responsibility of blacks everywhere. McKay uses the friendship between the two men to suggest that African American ignorance of the greater black world has meant missed opportunities for Pan-African political solidarity. Bridging differences of both class and country, Ray and Jake's relationship offers a vision of ideal black unity that would take the Haitian Revolution as its originary moment.

In *Drums at Dusk* (1939), Arna Bontemps characterizes Haiti's revolution as a divinely inspired mythic event of particular significance to the era of the New Negro. His historical novel presents an idealized image of revolutionary Haiti, a crucible of black empowerment and political promise in the modern world. Bontemps romanticizes the heroic single-mindedness and unbridled violence of Haiti's revolutionary leaders and so tacitly excuses the violence done by Haitian heads of state since the revolution. In his historical account *The Black Jacobins,* C. L. R. James, too, emphasizes that violent means were required to realize black freedom in Haiti, focusing primarily on the heroic figure of L'Ouverture and linking the Haitians' struggle to the broader anticolonial and antiracist battles being fought by people of color in the United States and throughout the world. Whether derisive, disappointed, or hopeful, writings on Haiti reflect the extent to which its revolution has had an impact on American political and literary consciousness.

Bibliography: Arna Bontemps, *Drums at Dusk* (New York, 1939). J. Michael Dash, *Haiti and the United States: National Stereotypes and the Literary Imagination* (New York, 1997). C. L. R. James, *The Black Jacobins: Toussaint L'Ouverture and the San Domingo Rebellion* (1938; 2nd ed. New York, 1963). John Houston Craige, *Black Bagdad* (New York, 1933). Mary Hassal, *Secret History, or, The Horrors of St. Domingo: In a Series of Letters, written by a Lady at Cape Français to Colonel Burr, Late Vice-President of the United States* (1808; repr. New York, 1971).

KAIAMA GLOVER

1809

Diedrich Knickerbocker constructs the Empire City

CUPOLA OF THE WORLD

Preparing a new edition of his *History of New York by Diedrich Knickerbocker* in 1848, Washington Irving had reason to feel gratified. A comic history of the Dutch colonial period, fictively authored by a curmudgeonly old bachelor-historian, Irving's fledgling book had been a surprise hit when first published in 1809, drawing admiration even abroad for its side-splitting humor. It had gone through five major U.S. editions, as well as editions in England and France. But foremost in the veteran Irving's mind was the book's phenomenal local success:

When I find, after a lapse of nearly forty years, this haphazard production of my youth still cherished among [New Yorkers]; when I find its very name become a "household word," and used to give the home stamp to every thing recommended for popular acceptation, such as Knickerbocker societies, Knickerbocker insurance companies; Knickerbocker steamboats; Knickerbocker omnibuses; Knickerbocker bread, and Knickerbocker ice, and when I find New Yorkers of Dutch de-

scent, priding themselves upon being "Genuine Knickerbockers," I please myself
with the persuasion that I have . . . opened a vein of pleasant associations and
quaint characteristics peculiar to my native place.

Irving's pride is justified. Despite early grumblings at the book's buffoonish
Dutch caricatures, Knickerbocker (who had not only "authored" the History but
was also the putative source for Irving's most famous tales, "Rip Van Winkle" and
"The Legend of Sleepy Hollow") had been heartily embraced as a patron saint for
the city; he was the very emblem of "olde" New York. However, Knickerbocker's
legacy was by no means all quaintness and gentility.

Venerable as he came to seem, the Diedrich Knickerbocker of 1809 was actually an upstart, a huckster, a hypester and prestidigitator—more a forefather to
P. T. Barnum, who a few decades later would hawk his wonders in New York, than
to Edith Wharton—and he had a monumental scheme of civic boosterism hidden up his old-fashioned sleeve: to take an as yet secondary city, in a nation with
an inferiority complex, and through the magic of hyperbolic assertion transform
it into the greatest show on earth. In other words, for all his reactionary ranting,
what Knickerbocker is really doing in the *History* is *building up* his "beloved isle of
Manna-hata."

Knickerbocker is quite up-front about his audacious designs. In his preface,
for instance, he imagines his work as "a foundation" on which others would "raise
a noble superstructure . . . until *Knickerbocker's New York* shall be equally voluminous, with *Gibbon's Rome,* or *Hume and Smollet's England.*" The clearest blueprint
for Knickerbocker's project comes in the book's second chapter, "Cosmogony, or
the Creation of World": defending absurd forays into extraneous history, philosophy, myth, and astronomy, Knickerbocker explains that he is merely "building up
my work, after the manner of the able architect who erected our theatre; beginning with the foundation, then the body, then the roof, and at last perching our
snug little island like the little cupola on the top."

This is a remarkable passage. Two hundred years after Henry Hudson spied
Manhattan Island, it heralds the birth of the Empire City. It represents nothing
less than the original manifesto of an ascendant New York worldview, an exaggerated cosmopolitan-imperial sensibility that casts the city as both amalgamation
and apex of the world, if not the universe. That Irving excised this passage from
the second edition by no means eliminated its spirit from the book; the *History* as
a whole elaborates on its model, from the opening chapters that enlist history
and lore from around the world as supporting props for Knickerbocker's starring
city, through the inflated rhetoric of the history proper, which invests the most
trivial local events with epic import. And though Irving certainly has his tongue
in Knickerbocker's cheek (the antiquarian in part plays the straight man in a parody of pretension and pedantry), the book's facetious self-mockery does nothing
to diminish its boosting effects. That the cupola passage itself winks cheekily at
the *constructedness* of the tip-top status it bestows—that it admits itself a deliberate, quixotic, aerial feat of staging—keeps Knickerbocker's boasts from being either ridiculous or insufferable, while epitomizing an everything-goes humor that
is essential to the Knickerbockerist project.

So often, and in so many ways, has Knickerbocker's tall tale of New York's cosmopolitan-imperial supremacy been repeated that traces of it can be found just about anywhere one looks in the New York scene. Start as the proverbial tourist, looking up at the buildings. This is not to say that architects were directly influenced by Knickerbocker's simile. Rather, by fixing on the cupola—a device of Roman ancestry and European kinship that already topped prominent city buildings of his day—the architecturally attuned Irving captured a worldly, imperial New York idiom that would be repeated time and again as the skyline grew, not simply in the renowned reaches of the structures, but also in their stylistic tendencies. Indeed, in the heroic age of skyscraper building, from the late nineteenth century through the early twentieth, when avant-garde Chicago towers wore flat tops, New York's tall buildings collectively staged a Beaux-Arts fantasy, a pastiche of appropriated world styles that expressed itself most of all in their caps—imitation cathedrals, pyramids, and chateaus, along with any number of cupolas. Just try to count them in, say, Moses King's *New York Views* of 1896 or, better yet, his Knickerbockeresque *Dream of New York: The Cosmopolis of the Future* of 1908, where airships from around the globe dock at these tops.

Or, since Irving's choice of a cupola implied a reciprocal spectatorial effect—it was a lookout, as well as an ornament—start at the top. Knickerbocker's model prefigures an insistent windows-on-the-world iconography—ranging from an extraordinary proliferation of bird's-eye panoramas in the mid-nineteenth century to Saul Steinberg's 1976 *New Yorker* cover, *View of the World from 9th Avenue*—which revels in the sense that New York *is* the world, or all of the world that matters.

Or start with words. "For after all," Knickerbocker claims, "cities *of themselves* . . . are nothing" without semantic support from historians and other writers. Knickerbocker's vision of New York first began to flower in the antebellum decades, when the city became the center of the world in the United States, outpacing Philadelphia as the print capital of the country. The writings radiating from this epicenter continually reinforced the cupola sensibility, especially the city's mushrooming periodical literature, from sensationalistic newspapers like the *Sun* and the *Herald,* to cultural magazines, including the *Knickerbocker; or New York Monthly Magazine.* Knickerbocker's guiding spirit becomes most evident in the introductory issues of his namesake magazine, which began publication in 1833. The editors open by calling up the apparition of their "tutelary saint" in their offices, where they promote their venture in his own centripetal terms: "the rest of the country naturally looked to this metropolis for the mart of intelligence, as well as that of business." In the first issue of the second volume, Knickerbocker's ghost is again invoked, this time as the visionary wizard of Gotham, magically producing for the astonished editors "a range of windows" that looked out over "buildings of towering magnitude." The "outlandish appearance of the inhabitants" prevent the editors from guessing "to what country they belonged," until Knickerbocker reveals that they are in "New-York, the Metropolis of the great empire of North America [in] A.D. 2833."

Although the *Knickerbocker* came to be cast as conservative, and Irving and his so-called Knickerbocker cronies figured as old fogies by the "Young Americans" who produced more bombastically nationalistic competitors like the *Democratic Review,* a Knickerbockerist agenda ran across the periodical boards. At an implicit level, as each little cosmos of collected news and literature took the city as its base, it added gravitational force to the idea promulgated by the *Knickerbocker,* that New York was the "natural" cultural clearinghouse of the world. Similarly, the expansionist rhetoric that many periodicals hotly espoused could be seen as an outgrowth of their rooting in Knickerbocker's city. ("Manifest Destiny" was a New York coinage.) Most to the point, magazines and papers, along with New York guidebooks and fictions, explicitly and vigorously fortified Knickerbocker's construction by continually showcasing New York itself, declaring it "one of the most beautiful and exciting spectacles ever looked upon," as one reporter, standing atop Trinity steeple in 1846, described the city "stretching far away in every direction."

Because New York dominated the national press, such Knickerbockerish claims colored the view of millions of Americans. They also nurtured the world-views of authors who would go on to literary fame, including the all-encompassing, infinitely aspirational "Walt Whitman, a kosmos, of Manhattan the son," as he identified himself in a later edition of "Song of Myself." Whitman did time in the antebellum newsrooms of New York and knew how to talk the half-tongue-in-cheek, ultra-boosterish talk, proclaiming, for instance, in the *Aurora* in March 1842, "Whoever does not know that our city is the great place of the western continent, the heart, the brain, the focus, the main spring, the pinnacle, the extremity, the no more beyond, of the New World . . . must have been brought up in a place where they 'didn't take the papers.'" It may seem a long way from the seemingly narrow Knickerbocker to the promiscuous poet, and Whitman outwardly dismissed the Knickerbocker *History* as "shallow burlesque"; yet the statement shows he read the book, and influences emerge—in Whitman's cosmic terminologies, his affinity for "vistas," his penchant for the name "Manna-Hatta," and, most of all, his poetic invocations of New York as cosmopolitan-imperial hub of America. Whether or not he realizes it—or admits it—Whitman is standing in Knickerbocker's cupola as he sounds his famous "yawp over the roofs of the world" in 1855.

As New York became ever taller and more heterogeneously populated through the late nineteenth century, Knickerbocker's cupola mentality only thrived, reaching an apex in the hyperactive "airmindedness" and multiculturalism of Manhattan of the 1920s. The flamboyantly over-the-top attitude of the Jazz Age city is nicely encapsulated in F. Scott Fitzgerald's 1920 story "May Day." When an elevator man informs two drunken revelers that they are already on the top floor, they simply respond, "Have another floor put on," so that they can continue their course skyward. Yet if this period represented the apotheosis of Knickerbocker's aerie, it also exposed cracks in the inflated, pasteboard model on which the New York worldview rested. Even in "May Day," headiness veers toward unsustainable dizziness, and Fitzgerald realized more fully in hindsight that there was such a thing as getting too high. In part, this was because supports might collapse, as they did with the Wall Street crash of 1929, causing the whole "flimsy structure to settle earthward," as Fitzgerald put it in a 1931 essay, "Echoes of the Jazz Age."

More ironic, though, was the "crowning error" that he recognized atop the ultimate avatar of Knickerbocker's cupola, the Empire State Building, completed in 1931: "Full of vaunting pride," Fitzgerald wrote in "My Lost City" in 1932, "the New Yorker had climbed here and seen with dismay what he had never suspected, that the city . . . *had limits* . . . And with the awful realization that New York was a city after all and not a universe, the whole shining edifice that he had reared in his imagination came crashing to the ground."

A different sense of Knickerbocker's vision grown monstrous in this period arises in a 1926 story, "He," by the horror writer H. P. Lovecraft. The story, like the 1833 *Knickerbocker* magazine, seems to directly implicate Knickerbocker as progenitor, though to much less congratulatory ends. The story's narrator, disenchanted with modern New York, goes nightly in search of the vestiges of the old city, and thus encounters a figure who promises to show him what he seeks. Dressed in "mid-Georgian costume," the antiquarian bears suspicious resemblances to Knickerbocker as described in the preface of *History of New York*. (Lovecraft's narrator twice remarks on his shoe buckles—items spotlighted in the 1809 depiction.) And he leads the narrator to a structure topped by a cupola. Once inside, the ancient man reveals a visionary power, drawing the narrator to a magic window to provide the desired glimpses into local antiquity. But when the narrator ventures to ask about the future, the old man produces what is, for the narrator, a nightmare: "I saw the heavens verminous with strange flying things, and beneath them a hellish black city of giant stone terraces with impious pyramids flung savagely to the moon . . . And swarming loathsomely on aerial galleries I saw the yellow, squint-eyed people of that city." Confronted with this "shrieking fulfillment" of his fears, the narrator feels the structure give way, and goes crashing down, followed by "something which must have been the cupola."

Although Lovecraft's rejoinder to Knickerbocker marks a racist, anti-urban extreme, lengthening shadows of vulnerability haunted the Empire City through the twentieth century, finding horrific realization in the first year of the twenty-first. Still, as we reach the two-hundredth anniversary of the *History*, its cupola-of-the-world mentality remains resiliently in place, from anthemic renditions of "New York, New York," to the Trump Towers, from the United Nations to the often fantastical plans for Ground Zero, submitted from around the globe. In 1809 Knickerbocker imagined leaping ahead "two or three hundred years" and "casting back a bird's eye view" to find himself "progenitor, prototype and precursor of them all." Was he justified? If his hand in constructing New York's worldview has been rendered nearly invisible—if, even though his name still marks New York institutions (including the too-tall basketball team), his foundational status goes largely unremembered by those in the upper stories—this is just evidence of how successful an architect he was.

Bibliography: Hans Bergmann, *God in the Street: New York Writing from the Penny Press to Melville* (Philadelphia, 1995). Van Wyck Brooks, *The World of Washington Irving* (New York, 1950). Ann Douglas, *Terrible Honesty: Mongrel Manhattan in the 1920s* (New York, 1995). Washington Irving, *A History of New York by Diedrich Knickerbocker* (1809 ed.), in *Washington Irving: History, Tales and Sketches*, ed. James W. Tuttleton (New York, 1983). Moses King, *King's Views of New York 1896–1915 and Brooklyn 1905,* ed. A. E. Santaniello (New York, 1980). Vincent Scully, *American Ar-*

chitecture and Urbanism (1966; rev. ed., New York, 1988). Edward L. Widmer, *Young America: The Flowering of Democracy in New York City* (New York, 1999).

JUDITH RICHARDSON

1819, February

Representative Tallmadge of New York proposes that slavery be gradually abolished in the new state of Missouri

THE MISSOURI CRISIS

As the U.S. House of Representatives considered a bill to admit Missouri into the Union as a slave state, an antislavery amendment put forth by New York Representative James Tallmadge had the effect of a powder keg. The ensuing debate erupted "like a firebell in the night," as Thomas Jefferson noted, and became what was known as the Missouri crisis.

For many congressmen, the fate of slavery in the new nation hinged on whether Missouri would be a free or slave state, for the twenty-third state would tip the nation's fragile balance. Henry Clay, the Speaker of the House, eventually negotiated a compromise that allowed Missouri to enter the Union as a slave state (without the abolition provision) while prohibiting the spread of slavery north of the $36°30'$ parallel (the latitude of Missouri's southern border) within the Louisiana Territory. When Congress finally passed these compromise measures in 1821, Maine also entered the Union, as a free state, keeping the count even between free and slave states. While many Northerners viewed the compromise as a victory for the South, a number of Southerners sowed seeds of future division by arguing that the provision restricting the spread of slavery conceded too much to the North and gave unwarranted power to Congress. Henry Clay emerged from the crisis as "the Great Compromiser," the man most responsible for saving the Union.

The Missouri crisis prompted works of fiction as well as political debate. In the immediate wake of the compromise, James Madison, the chief architect of the Constitution, now retired from public life, wrote an allegorical tale exploring poetic and national truths stemming from the Missouri crisis. The untitled tale, which he never published, is Madison's only known work of fiction. It is an allegory for the basic debate that would lead to civil war.

The central characters in Madison's tale are Jonathan Bull (the North) and Mary Bull (the South), both descendants of old John Bull (the personification of England). Jonathan and Mary "became well acquainted," acquired many of the same interests, and eventually married, combining "their two estates under a common superintendence." Every year or two "a new member of the family" was added. A portion of land was set aside for each child for when he or she attained adulthood, and in the meantime these lands were rapidly settled by tenants coming from the estates of Jonathan or Mary—from the North or South—or sometimes from both.

Eventually a crisis ensued. After twenty-two children had reached adulthood—corresponding to the eleven free states and eleven slave states at the time of the Missouri crisis—Jonathan became "possessed with a notion" that all future lands be settled and cultivated by tenants from his estates alone. His prejudice stemmed from "a certain African dye" that had stained Mary's left arm in her youth, making it "perfectly black and somewhat weaker than the other arm." This misfortune "arose from a ship from Africa loaded with the article which had been permitted to enter a river running through her estate"; a part of the "noxious cargo" had been dumped on her property, leaving a permanent stain on her.

Mary's stain had been well known to Jonathan when they married, but at the time he had not objected. Indeed the "fatal African dye" had "found its way" onto his body as well, spattering it with black "spots & specks." Only by "certain abrasions" had he been able to remove them, and still there were "visible remains" of the "noxious" stain. Despite his lingering blemishes, Jonathan now demanded that if the color could not be taken off Mary's black arm, then she must "either tear off the skin from the flesh or cut off the limb." "One or [the] other should be done," he demanded, "or he would sue [for] a divorce, and there should be an end of all connection between them and their Estates." "White as I am all over," he told Mary, "I can no longer consort with one marked with such a deformity as the blot on your person."

Mary was "stunned" by her spouse's tirade. Although she was "generous and placable" in temper, she "almost choked with the anger and indignation swelling in her bosom." But she regained her composure "and changed her tone to that of sober reasoning." "You know as well as I do that I am not to be blamed for the origin of the sad mishap; that I am as anxious as you [are] to get rid of it" as soon as it is "safe and feasible" to do so; and "that I have done everything I could to mitigate an evil that cannot as yet be removed," she told her husband. Moreover, his prescription for removing the evil would be disastrous. Tearing off her black skin or cutting off the unfortunate limb would lead to "a mortification or a bleeding to death." She also reminded Jonathan of how important her lands and wealth were to their marriage. Now Jonathan "had a good heart as well as [a] sound head," and he "was touched with this tender and considerate language." He retracted his demand, and their relationship returned to one of "affection and confidence."

Madison's tale reveals three major themes that over the next forty years would shape national identity. First, it reflects a tacit agreement that existed between many Northerners and Southerners from the Constitutional Convention to the Missouri crisis. The agreement stipulated that the North would not interfere with slavery in Southern states, much as Jonathan was supposed to accept Mary's "blackened arm," and the South would recognize slavery as an evil that should be discouraged, and eventually abolished whenever it was safe and feasible to do so, much as Mary was anxious to rid herself of the stain.

Second, Madison's tale illuminates the symbolic importance of race in America. The imagery of blackness underscores the widespread belief among Madison's generation that slavery was a sin. Indeed Madison called slavery America's "original sin." For many white Americans, slavery obstructed the path to the millennium. The road would be clear, the new age in sight, were it not for the presence of blacks. Such beliefs lay at the heart of the many proposals for colonizing blacks outside the United States. Hence, African Americans, the victims of slavery, became in the mind of whites "the embodiment of sin," according to David Brion Davis.

In Madison's story, sin and blacks are intertwined. After all, a "noxious" African dye had been dumped on Mary's unstained property. And abrasions were required to remove Jonathan's black spots, leaving blemishes on his skin. For most whites during Madison's era, both slavery and blacks were stains on the fabric of America's destiny.

Finally, Madison's story points to signs of a new era, a shift in the ways that national boundaries were defined. These reinterpretations of boundaries took many forms: the emergence of a national market economy; rapid westward expansion, which became the battleground of slavery; the belief that the United States was destined to control the continent; and a blurring of God's law and national law. During the Missouri crisis, the New Yorker Rufus King became the first politician to call for applying a "higher law" to slavery; any law upholding slavery was "absolutely void, because [it is] contrary to the law of nature, which is the law of God," he declared. The higher-law thesis would become a central rhetorical weapon in the writings of a later generation of black and white abolitionists.

The Missouri Compromise thus marked a moment in which Americans became increasingly unwilling to compromise with sin and accept limits, the rule of law, and traditional boundaries in their quest to realize their visions of a new age. This newfound sense of urgency manifests itself in Madison's story when Jonathan suddenly becomes intolerant of Mary's stained limb. In the historical parallel, the tacit agreement between the North and South became untenable after the Missouri Compromise. Over the course of the 1820s, Southerners affirmed their proslavery ideology, repudiated the belief that slavery was a sin, and began to envision an empire of slavery. At the same time, the North witnessed the rise of "modern" or immediate abolitionism, which distinguished itself from the earlier generation of abolitionists in its refusal to compromise with sin. Immediate abolitionists advocated an immediate end to all evil, and they saw slavery as the bolt on which all other evils hung.

In the broadest sense, the national rite of passage that occurred in 1819 reflected a move away from "gradualism" and toward "immediatism." This shift was linked to signs that the old Republic, defined by Enlightenment beliefs, was disappearing. Gradual abolitionism, inspired by Enlightenment thought, was torn between two ideals: the autonomy of the individual, which was antithetical to slavery; and a rational and clearly defined social order, which feared the chaos that would result from ending slavery too quickly.

Immediate abolition represented both a shift in strategy and a change in outlook. Immediatists, blacks and whites, advocated a total and swift transformation of society. Immediatism also reflected a shift from an Enlightenment to a romantic worldview, from a "detached, rationalistic perspective on history and progress, to a personal commitment to make no compromise with sin," according to Davis. Immediatism was an expression of inner freedom and triumph over worldly conventions: it reflected a sharp break from linear notions of progress and history, and it assumed that a new age was dawning. It was thus an appropriate doctrine for a romantic age.

No wonder, then, that Abraham Lincoln loved the Missouri Compromise. He considered Henry Clay his beau ideal of a statesman and was himself, like Clay, a great compromiser and more of an Enlightenment thinker than a romantic. After the 1854 passage of the Kansas-Nebraska Act, which repealed the Missouri Compromise and opened Northern territories to slavery, Lincoln was "aroused as he had never been before." He reentered politics in the hope of reinstating the Missouri Compromise and defeating his rival Stephen Douglas, the author of the Kansas-Nebraska Act. Now antislavery Northerners viewed the Missouri Compromise as protecting their interests.

To Lincoln, the repeal of the Missouri Compromise altered the progress and destiny of the nation. Before 1854, he believed that "slavery was in the course of ultimate extinction," which would take not "less than a hundred years at the least." But Stephen Douglas and his Kansas-Nebraska Act had derailed this vision of slow progress. Suddenly, the nation's destiny was no longer on an upward trajectory. It had peaked and was now regressing. To Lincoln and his followers, the national decline accelerated when the Supreme Court's *Dred Scott* decision of 1857 affirmed the Kansas-Nebraska Act; whereas Congress had repealed the Missouri Compromise, the Court now rendered it unconstitutional. The nation's highest tribunal, hoping to solve the sectional dispute, declared that the federal government had no authority to prohibit the spread of slavery into its territories. The Supreme Court's decision, coupled with the Kansas-Nebraska Act, led the nation into civil war.

After the war, the Missouri Compromise became a symbol for reconciling North and South and encouraging westward expansion. In 1895, Owen Wister published in *Harper's Magazine* a short story entitled "The Second Missouri Compromise." Set in Boise City, Idaho, a few years after the war, the story describes how the territorial assembly virtually reenacted the Civil War. The assemblymen were divided between a Northern governor and treasurer and secessionist Missourians who had refused to surrender after Appomattox. Once again the fight is over money, but this time the disputed wealth stems from gambling rather than slaves. With the passage of the "Second Missouri Compromise," poker debts are forgiven and the assemblymen agree on the "correct construction" of the territory's statutes and the proper way to "deal with Indians."

A "third" Missouri Compromise, as it were, occurred in 2005, during a fight between environmentalists and businessmen over the use of the Mississippi River. When a court case was transferred out of the jurisdiction of a Missouri judge sympathetic to environmentalists, and into the hands of a probusiness Minnesota judge, the *Washington Monthly* hailed the move, and the subsequent victory for businessmen, as a "Missouri Compromise" that rejected "any efforts to alter the status quo."

The original Missouri Compromise marked the end of bisectional support to end slavery gradually. In subsequent incarnations, however, it has been viewed in a much more positive light, as reflecting bipartisan pursuit of a common goal and the preservation of the status quo. What was once seen as a victory for the slave-owning South subsequently became a victory for the nation and a triumph of unhindered progress. Madison's tale was thus prophetic, for after their near divorce, Jonathan and Mary reconciled their differences and reaffirmed their affectionate and very fruitful marriage.

Bibliography: Roy P. Basler, ed., *The Collected Works of Abraham Lincoln,* vols. 2–4 (New Brunswick, NJ, 1953). David Brion Davis, *Challenging the Boundaries of Slavery* (Cambridge, MA, 2003). Robert Pierce Forbes, *The Missouri Compromise and Its Aftermath: Slavery and the Meaning of America* (Chapel Hill, NC, 2007). Bill Lambrecht, "The New Water Wars," *Washington Monthly,* May 2005. Matthew T. Mellon, *Early American Views on Negro Slavery* (Boston, 1934). *The Writings of James Madison,* vol. 9 (1819–1836), ed. Gaillard Hunt (New York, 1910). Sean Wilentz, *The Rise of American Democracy: Jefferson to Lincoln* (New York, 2005). Owen Wister, "The Second Missouri Compromise," *Harper's New Monthly Magazine* (March 1895): 534–545.

JOHN STAUFFER

1820, November 27

Audubon paints a Bald Eagle at Little Prairie, Mississippi

LANDSCAPE WITH BIRDS

Picture the scene: a flatboat traveling down the Mississippi River, past sights few people have ever seen. The winds are blowing hard, and treacherous sandbars, time and again, threaten to halt the boat's progress. The places on the shore have the kinds of names that suggest someone might have set up camp there just yesterday: Wolf Island, Little Prairie, Point Rock. One day, near Arkansas Post, someone can be seen riding a velocipede, a curious reminder that the world elsewhere is, inexorably, moving on. But otherwise time seems to have come to a standstill, a good thing for the birds that live here: flocks of geese, boat-tailed grackles, great-footed hawks, pelicans, plenty of ivory-bills, all of them untouched by the human greed diminishing their numbers elsewhere. Aboard the skiff you see a long-haired, buckskin-clad, tired-looking man in his thirties who will tell everyone, in heavily accented English, that all he wants in life is to paint, "from Nature," the birds of America, and a young man from Cincinnati who has come along as his assistant, a job description so vague that it seems to include everything from shooting possums to sometimes painting in the trees and flowers his master wants as backgrounds for his birds.

We may assume that John James Audubon and Joseph Mason—these were the names of the two travelers—did not look much better than the people they encountered during their voyage: men and women in ragged clothes, surviving on raccoon meat and muddy river water, Indian squaws who drank liquor freely and cracked the lice on their skin with bare hands. But unlike them, Audubon had a goal, and one he pursued doggedly.

The shotgun is a rough collector's tool, but when it came to procuring birds for his art, Audubon didn't hold back. On November 23, near Little Prairie, Mississippi, he killed a bird he had coveted for a long time, a "white-headed" or bald eagle, a handsome male. Although the eagle was 150 yards off, Audubon's "ball," as he noted proudly in his journal, cut straight through the bird's body. It took him four days, in unrelentingly raw weather, to paint it. The finished composition shows the eagle, its ferocious beak open, perched on the ravaged body of a bloody Canada goose. One of the bird's claws has penetrated the goose's eye (the image of violated sight is a recurrent one in Audubon's compositions).

For days, Audubon had been watching the eagles watch their prey, how they would dash from the tops of tall trees after anything that came near them: "to secure a Goose, the Male & Femelle, Dive alternatively after it and give it so little time to breath that the poor Fellow is forced in a few Minutes." Note how Audubon here already sketches out what will become the main theme of his art and writing: the tangled web of relationships between the human observer and the birds he pursues (birds that in turn are frequently in the process of pursuing, or eating, other birds), between predator and prey, victor and vanquished. In his Little Prairie watercolor, Audubon revels in the chromatic similarity between the eagle's and the goose's dark bodies, an effect enhanced by the starkly rendered landscape he depicts. The bold, horizontal strokes of the brush with which Audubon has painted the sky enhance the powerful horizontal line created by the eagle's body. The parallel diagonals formed by the bird's beak and talons underscore his absolute domination of his prey. On the eagle's taut, horizontal body every feather seems to be in place, in sharp contrast with the torn, violated, prostrate, twisted mass of feathers and blood that once was a Canada goose.

Barely a week later, Mr. Aumack, the owner of Audubon's boat, wounds and captures another bald eagle: "The Noble Fellow Looked at his Ennemies with a Contemptible Eye." When Audubon ties a string around one of the eagle's legs, the bird jumps overboard and, to Audubon's surprise, begins to swim away, dragging a fifteen-pound pole from the skiff after him as if this were nothing. Mason goes off in pursuit of the bird; meanwhile the eagle's companion, "the femelle," hovers over them, shrieking with "the *true Sorow* of the *Constant Mate*." Later that day, Audubon, too, leaves the boat to look at a nest he has seen two bald eagles build nearby, and he takes a shot at the female bird. The contrast that Audubon sets up here is one that haunts him throughout his work: surrounded by images of family life and animal fecundity, he, the human observer, is inevitably reminded of his own loneliness. Audubon claims to be "friendly Inclined" toward his recaptured eagle, but when he comes too close, the eagle sinks its powerful talons into

Audubon's flesh, "lancing" his "thum." Unafraid, Audubon's birds, in life as well as in art, refuse to accept their role as the ornithologist's prey.

Audubon's native language was French, and this shows on every page of his diary, in his erratic spelling, the wayward syntax, the unconventional choice of words. Born in Haiti in 1785 as the illegitimate son of a French sugar planter, ship's captain, and dealer in slaves and liquor, Audubon came to the United States when he was eighteen, and the French language—and, more generally, the fact of his foreignness—inflects his writing style throughout his life. Sometimes the influence is more indirect: traveling down the Mississippi, for example, he is enthralled by the "Blood Red Raising Sun" (which to my ear sounds better than if the sun were merely "rising"). At other times, the sounds of French are more directly present, and we hear Audubon talk, stretching the vowels or pausing before what in his native language would have been a silent *h:* the black man he sees catching catfish isn't "dipping" but "deeping" his large scoop net in the water, and Joseph is suffering from a "head Hacke." In one of his last messages to his collaborator John Bachman, having just returned from the West, Audubon is ecstatic about the possibility of having discovered a new porcupine. But then he checks himself: "*Nous verrons,*" he writes: only time will tell.

Audubon was as embarrassed about his lack of formal artistic training as he was about his illegitimate birth; hence his claim—made, like many others during Audubon's lifetime, to boost his public image—that he had studied with Napoleon's favorite painter, Jacques-Louis David. But he literally learned his craft in the field, comparing what he saw around him to the deficient images produced by his predecessors (though some critics have in fact seen parallels between David's glassy realism and Audubon's crisply rendered birds, his intuitive mastery of compositional space). When he painted his eagle in November 1820, Audubon was responding directly to a previous representation of America's national bird by the Scottish poet, weaver, and ornithological painter Alexander Wilson, whom he had met in 1810 in Louisville, Kentucky, where Audubon, with mixed success, was trying his hand at storekeeping. In Wilson's illustration from *American Ornithology,* the eagle is perched on a gutted fish. Everything—with the interesting exception of the terrifying claws—is made up of straight horizontal lines, even the body of the fish, which looks as if it has been dead a long time. For the background, Wilson added a stylized depiction of Niagara Falls; distantly, other eagles can be seen hovering over the mist rising from the waters. The bald eagle, Wilson writes in the accompanying description, though "noble and interesting," is unpredictable, always distant.

While Wilson's eagles seem to be forever disappearing from human view, Audubon's eagles stare him down. His watercolor shows a bird that seems more lifelike than Wilson's flat image (in his copy of Wilson's *Ornithology* Audubon corrected Wilson's figure, penciling in better, more likely positions for the eagle's neck and head). But what Audubon accomplishes as a writer is perhaps equally remarkable; who can forget the eagle lancing the hand that holds him captive? It doesn't matter that Audubon's story comes to us in the form of a never-revised journal riddled with errors. If anything, Audubon's weird English (to use Evelyn

John James Audubon, Bald Eagle *(Haliaeetus leucocephalus),* 1822. Watercolor, pastel, graphite, selective glazing, selective scraping with brown ink inscriptions

Collection of the New-York Historical Society (acc. no. 1863.17.31)

Charles Wilson, White-headed Eagle (American Bald Eagle), from John James Audubon's copy of Wilson's *American Ornithology*, corrected by Audubon

John James Audubon Museum, Audubon State Park, Henderson, Kentucky

Ch'ien's term) makes his prose more pliable, more suitable to record, decades before Thoreau's self-consciously polished *Walden,* the fragility of all human encounters with nature, the foolishness of the human desire to own what, at close range, will turn out to be more alien than comfortably familiar.

Audubon, who became an American citizen in 1806, knew that the bald eagle was the emblem of his adopted country. Was that one of the reasons he so obsessively returned to it? In 1828, while in England, Audubon redid his Little Prairie watercolor, painting an entirely new version in which he replaced the bleeding Canada goose with a catfish. He also changed the background to a vaguely alpine landscape, one that would have been more appealing to his European patrons. And this is how Robert Havell, Jr., engraved the eagle, as Plate 21 in Audubon's magnificent *The Birds of America.* In the essay on the bald eagle included in his 3,000-page series of bird essays, *Ornithological Biography* (1831–1839), Audubon conjures up a memorable scene from his 1820 trip: a majestic eagle and his mate, perched high in a tree on the banks of the Mississippi, silently survey "millions of waterfowl on whistling wings" until a trumpeter swan appears that strikes their fancy, whereupon the male glides "through the air like a falling star, and, like a flash of lightning, comes upon the timorous quarry." The swan soon surrenders, and Audubon imagines the sensuous delight the eagle feels sinking his claws into the defenseless body, as if Zeus were raping Leda all over again: "He presses down his powerful feet, and drives his sharp claws deeper than ever into the heart of the dying swan. He shrieks with delight, as he feels the last convulsions of his prey, which has now sunk under his unceasing efforts to render death as painfully felt as it can possibly be." The sinister effect of the passage is that we are almost made to feel the swan's soft flesh giving way under the pressure of the eagle's powerful body before we realize how wrong it would be to identify with such a malevolent force.

Audubon's unflattering picture of America's national bird is continued in the rest of the essay: though powerfully equipped to obtain their own food, bald eagles steal other birds' prey; they prove to be cowards when surprised and fly away, uttering unpleasant hissing sounds; their call is a disagreeable imitation of a laugh; they do not shy away from eating putrid carcasses, and they mate in a particularly offensive way, circling up and down ("a fierce, gyrating wheel," as Walt Whitman would later say), caressing each other with their ferocious beaks while making loud cackling noises.

For Audubon, here as elsewhere in his work, anthropomorphic language doesn't bring birds any closer to the world of humans. Benjamin Franklin once suggested that the turkey, though a little "vain and silly," would have made a much better choice as America's national bird, and Audubon (whose personal crest did in fact show a turkey and the motto "America My Country") likewise doesn't seem to be of the eagle's party. But his point in this essay is really a larger and, as we would say today, ecocritical one, one that in different form would have to be applied to the turkey, too: the avian world will not accommodate the human wish for easy identification. (In his essay on the turkey, Audubon in great detail describes the mating habits of male turkeys: a turkey will kill a competitor in a heartbeat but will then caress his body "with all the motions he employs in caressing the female"). In Audubon's world, birds don't care about humans and what they do. People, when they appear in Audubon's paintings or his prose, are dwarfed into insignificance in a landscape where the birds will always be more comfortable.

Almost two decades after Audubon painted his "white-headed eagle," on June 20, 1838, Audubon's British engraver Robert Havell pulled an impression of the final copper plate for *The Birds of America:* a pair of little dippers balancing precariously on cliffs above the Columbia River. One of the world's most expensive books was now complete—435 plates, superbly hand-colored aquatint engravings three feet high and more than two feet wide, made after Audubon's original watercolors. But the "Contemptible Eye" of the eagle at Little Prairie still hovers over Audubon's last work, *The Viviparous Quadrupeds of North America,* begun in 1845: radiant with hostility, rearing up in defiance, Audubon's gophers, rats, and raccoons bare their fangs at the viewer. The terrain they inhabit is often flat, bare to the point of austerity. Consider the two little ground squirrels ("leopard spermophiles") Audubon paints next to their hole, with a view of the Missouri River and the American Fur Company's Fort Union in the distance. Perversely, these rodents take the place normally reserved for the human observer in landscape paintings; their habitat, the burrow, appears to be the only appropriate one in an environment where no one has asked for humans to come and build their fortresses.

Stricken with dementia, Audubon wasn't able to complete his last book himself; half of the illustrations for *Quadrupeds* were supplied by his sons, and most of the text came from his collaborator, the Reverend John Bachman. But the raw power of Audubon's vision is still very much in evidence, as it is in the diary Audubon composed when he traveled west in 1843 to collect material for the new book. The *Missouri River Journals,* written during Audubon's last expedition to the mouth of the Yellowstone, show him and his men moving through a bleak landscape littered with the rotting bodies of buffalo: "Before many years," muses Audubon, "the Buffalo, like the great Auk, will have disappeared." However, the aging Audubon often seems as unappealing here as his quadrupeds. He watches in horror as the buffalo are being hunted down, but then he participates in the slaughter himself, firing thirteen shots at one before the wounded animal finally dies. And while he feels sorry for the mud-besmeared Native Americans he meets, he also robs the grave of an Indian chief, White Cow, twisting off his head, "under jaw and all," presumably so that he could add it to his collection of birds, skins, animal furs, and dried plants.

When Audubon is back in New York again, he has a hard time fitting into the civilized world: "Now that I am in the lap of Comfort and without the hard and continued exercise So lately my lot, I feel Somewhat lazy and disinclined even to write a long letter," he tells Bachman. He works fitfully on his *Quadrupeds,* but before he can finish it, darkness descends upon him.

"The noble mind is all in ruins," reports a shocked Bachman in 1848. It is as if, rather than relinquish—for one last time—the many sights it had seen, Audubon's brain had finally shut down upon itself. Listening to little French songs, John James Audubon—the first truly transatlantic painter of, and writer about, American nature—spent his last days oblivious to everyone and everything around him.

Bibliography: John James Audubon, *The Birds of America, from Drawings Made in the United States and Their Territories,* 7 vols. (Philadelphia, 1840–1844); *Writings and Drawings,* ed. Christoph Irmscher (New York, 1999). John James Audubon and John Bachman, *The Quadrupeds of North America,* 3 vols. (New York, 1849–1854). Evelyn Nien-ming Ch'ien, *Weird English* (Cambridge, MA, 2004). Christoph Irmscher, *The Poetics of Natural History: From John Bartram to William James* (New Brunswick, NJ, 1999). Alexander Wilson, *American Ornithology; or the Natural History of the Birds of the United States,* 9 vols. (Philadelphia, 1808–1814).

CHRISTOPH IRMSCHER

1821

Sequoyah demonstrates his syllabary to the Cherokee Council

CHARACTERS CUT IN THE TREES

The Cherokee artist and artisan Sequoyah, also known as George Guess, dramatically debuted an innovative form of communication before a group of Cherokee leaders in 1821. Returning home from his travels in Arkansas Territory, he brought letters composed in a writing system he had developed: a syllabary of eighty-six characters, each representing a particular sound in the complex Cherokee language. Standing before the council, he demonstrated the method through which ideas could be recorded on paper and transmitted between individuals, by writing down the words of one councillor and then having his daughter read them aloud before the assembly. Although Cherokees had been exposed to writing in English for some time through participation in treaties and trade, interactions with missionaries and settlers, and limited participation in English-language schools, writing in their own language was an entirely new phenomenon. It is said that Sequoyah, a man known for his artistry and inventiveness in drawing, painting, and silverwork, labored for twelve years to create his syllabary, after telling some of his relations that he thought the English system of writing was no mystery but could be easily achieved for any language, given a bit of thought and labor.

By most accounts, Sequoyah was born in the Cherokee town of Tuskegee on the Tennessee River and raised by his mother, who operated a small trading post. As a young man, Sequoyah became an accomplished silversmith and blacksmith. According to Charlie Rhodarmer of the Sequoyah Birthplace Museum, it may have been the need for an accounting system that led him to writing. It is said that he began with a pictographic system modeled on indigenous mnemonics, moved to a logographic system, and finally homed in on a syllabary, which could accommodate the many tones and phonemes of the Cherokee language. While

Sequoyah was initially ridiculed for his scholarly endeavor, the syllabary spread like wildfire among the Cherokee people once he had established its efficacy. Cherokee citizens used it for a variety of purposes, from record keeping to preserving traditional medicinal knowledge to communicating with relations living in distant places. A visitor to the Cherokee Nation in the 1820s remarked that he saw characters "painted or cut in the trees by the roadside, on fences, houses, and often on pieces of bark or board, lying about the house." The Cherokee National Council awarded Sequoyah a medal of honor in 1824, "as a token of respect & admiration for your ingenuity in the invention of the Cherokee Alphabetical Characters" and later granted him permanent financial support, what biographer Grant Foreman called the "first literary pension in American history."

Sequoyah's syllabary not only garnered popularity within the Cherokee Nation but also became an international sensation. Sequoyah was celebrated as a "native genius" and his invention as a remarkable achievement. Speaking to audiences in the North, Cherokee leaders Elias Boudinot and John Ridge held up the syllabary as evidence of the Cherokees' "advancement," fostering a strong counterargument against Removal, the U.S. government's policy of forcibly moving native tribes to territory west of the Mississippi. In his *Lectures on American Literature,* published in 1829, Samuel Knapp hailed Sequoyah as "the American Cadmus." Only seven years after Sequoyah's demonstration before the council, the Cherokee Nation launched its own newspaper, printed in English and Cherokee on a press specially commissioned by the nation. The *Cherokee Phoenix* debuted in February 1828, with a distribution that reached across the Cherokee Nation and beyond, and included a wide audience in New England. It became a crucial vehicle for information dissemination and dialogue, particularly as the controversial issue of Removal came to a head. Indeed the syllabary and the newspaper proved so influential that the paper's printing press was confiscated by the State of Georgia during the Removal crisis and used instead to publish pro-Removal propaganda. The publication of the *Cherokee Phoenix* was later resumed by the Cherokee Nation of Oklahoma, and it is widely distributed in both print and online versions today.

Sequoyah's influence extended to the political realm as well. He served in a Cherokee company with the U.S. military in the infamous Red Stick War against the Creek Nation, and shortly thereafter moved to the lower towns of the Cherokee Nation (in northern Alabama), established by the Chickamauga resistance leader Tsiyu Gansini (Dragging Canoe). Sequoyah joined the lower-town leadership in a movement to carry the towns to the Arkansas River, away from the American settlements. He participated in a controversial treaty with the U.S. government to trade lands in Alabama Territory for lands in Arkansas Territory, against the wishes of the central Cherokee government, and in 1821 escaped indictment by the National Council for this infraction, in part, perhaps, because of his contribution of the syllabary. Sequoyah emerged as a leader among the "old settlers" in the west, and when much of the Cherokee Nation was brutally forced to relocate to Indian territory (in present-day Oklahoma), he played a critical role in uniting the two groups into one Cherokee Nation, which gradually recovered from the devastation of Removal and continues to flourish. Indeed, Cherokee communities in North Carolina and Oklahoma still use the syllabary in the teaching of traditional knowledge, in the services of the Cherokee churches, and for the preservation and revitalization of the Cherokee language.

Although Sequoyah's syllabary is unique, it is not without comparison in native North America. His invention is an excellent example of the innovation displayed by Native American artists, intellectuals, and leaders, who made creative use of the materials they had at hand to help their nations adapt to the changing circumstances wrought by colonization. Indeed, as early as the seventeenth century native people began adapting writing and using new forms of communication within indigenous networks. For example, in 1675 the Jesuit Chrétien Le Clercq noticed his young Mik'maq pupils recording the Lord's Prayer using mnemonic figures drawn on birch bark. He standardized this system, and within six months it had spread throughout Mik'maq communities on the coast and in the interior. This glyphic system is still used today. In Mesoamerica, at least fifteen distinct writing systems thrived before the Spanish invasion, including the logographic-syllabic systems of the Mayan people and the codified pictorial systems of the Mixtec and Nahua peoples. Today, many indigenous writers in Mexico and Central America, such as the Mayan poet Briceida Cuevas Cob, publish literature in their indigenous language and in Spanish, and Mayan scholars are beginning to bridge the gap between traditional indigenous knowledge and archaeology in interpreting the graphic communication of their ancestors.

In 1821, the year of Sequoyah's introduction of the Cherokee syllabary, native scribes across the Great Plains recorded graphic representations on their buffalo-hide "winter counts" of a spectacular meteor that traveled across the sky, "exploding with a great noise" over "Dakota territory," enabling future generations to recall other important occurrences that corresponded with the year of this memorable event. During the same year, Mexico and Central American nations achieved independence from Spain, although the relationship between the new governments and their indigenous peoples, many of whom had participated in the revolts against Spain, proved continually contentious.

In New England and New York, the 1820s and 1830s brought a proliferation of Native American speakers and writers to the public stage. While Elias Boudinot and John Ridge visited Boston, giving speeches that relayed the Cherokees' "progress" in "civilization" and their opposition to Removal, the Pequot writer William Apess challenged New England audiences to turn their "sympathy for the red men of the Cherokee nation, who have suffered much from their white brethren" to the native people in their midst, who "wish" to be "free" as "much as the red men of Georgia." Unlike Sequoyah, Apess wrote exclusively in English, publishing works such as *An Indian's Looking-Glass for the White Man* (1833), *Indian Nullification of the Unconstitutional Laws of Massachusetts* (1835), and the *Eulogy on King Philip* (1836) largely for an Anglo-American readership, on behalf of his native "brethren." However, Apess was not an anomaly. By this time, the majority of native communities in New England had adopted and adapted to writing in English, and were composing petitions, correspondence, tribal records, public speeches, journey journals, and communal histories. In 1826 Mohican leader Hendrick Aupaumut's *Extract from an Indian History* and *Narrative of an Embassy to the Western Indians* were published posthumously by the Massachusetts Historical Society. In them he described not only the history of his own nation but also the relationships among multiple nations in the East. His *Narrative* demonstrated the complex relationship between the United Indian Nations of the Ohio Valley and the newly formed United States, and included accounts of the "outcast Cherokees," who carried an "alarming voice" of settler violence in the South to their northern relations in 1792. In 1825, Tuscarora author David Cusick published his *Sketches of Ancient History of the Six Nations,* which relayed a long history of the Haudenosaunee (Iroquois) Confederacy, arranged according to the chronology of the Haudenosaunee Great Law and the "reigns" of "Atotarho" leaders (keepers of the central council fire), and recounted events that took place in the thousands of years "before Columbus discovered the Americas." His narrative included extensive descriptions of the Six Nations' relationships with other indigenous nations east of the Mississippi, including the Cherokees, to whom they are linguistically and historically related.

A Cherokee tradition, recorded by trader Alexander Long in 1717, held that "we are told by our ancestors that when we first came on this land that the priests and beloved men were writing but not on paper as you do but on white deer skins and on the shoulder bones of buffalo for several years but . . . the writing was quite lost and could not be recovered again." Indeed, evidence of indigenous graphic representation, on animal hide, bone, clay, and stone, is prolific in the Southeast as well as along the Mississippi and the Ohio, to which its trails lead. Some believe that there is a direct link to the writing systems and cultural knowledge of Mesoamerica, which spread up the Mississippi Valley, north to the Great Lakes, west to the Great Plains, and east to Cherokee country.

Whether Sequoyah's syllabary was a completely new invention, the return of an ancient tradition, or an innovation based on a writing system that had recently arrived, it played an essential role in the emergence of Native American (and American) literary traditions. Amid a rising chorus of Native American authors, Cherokees have been among the most prolific, ranging from the humor of Will Rogers to the stormy plays of Lynn Riggs, from the poignant prose and poetry of Marilou Awiakta to the frank autobiography of Wilma Mankiller, from the playful stories of Thomas King, most of which take place far from Cherokee territory, to the historical novels of Robert Conley, which are deeply rooted in the Cherokee homeland, including his meticulously researched and empathetically imagined portrait of Sequoyah. As Daniel Justice demonstrates in *Our Fire Survives the Storm,*

> Written words have particular resonance among Cherokees, as so much of our cultural expression explicitly invokes the generative powers of language, from the syllabary and bilingual *Cherokee Phoenix* to novels, poetry, political texts, and the written sacred formulae of Cherokee medicine-makers. In spite of the five-hundred-plus-year insistence of Eurowesterners that we're dying out or fading

before the onslaught of White supremacy, our stories endure to give strength to each new generation, who add their own stories to the mix, sharing new knowledge with old.

Bibliography: Margaret Bender, *Signs of Cherokee Culture: Sequoyah's Syllabary in Eastern Cherokee Life* (Durham, NC, 2002). Gordon Brotherston, *Book of the Fourth World: Reading the Native Americas through Their Literature* (New York, 1992). Grant Foreman, *Sequoyah* (Norman, OK, 1938). Daniel Justice, *Our Fire Survives the Storm: A Cherokee Literary History* (Minneapolis, 2006). Martha J. Macri, "Maya and Other Mesoamerican Scripts," in *The World's Writing Systems,* ed. Peter T. Daniels and William Bright (New York, 1996), 172–182. William C. McLoughlin, *Cherokee Renascence in the New Republic* (Princeton, 1986). Theda Perdue, "The Sequoyah Syllabary and Cultural Revitalization," in *Perspectives on the Southeast: Linguistics, Archaeology, and Ethnohistory,* ed. Patricia B. Kwachka (Athens, GA, 1994). Russell Thornton, *The Cherokees: A Population History* (Lincoln, NB, 1990). On Plains Indians' winter counts, see *wintercounts.si.edu.*

LISA BROOKS

1821, June 30

Junius Brutus Booth brings romantic acting to America

Desperate Valor

Abandoning a stalled career on the London stage, where he had tried to challenge Edmund Kean's ascendancy as the leading tragedian in the new romantic style of acting, Junius Brutus Booth arrived in Norfolk, Virginia, on June 30, 1821. Within a week, he made his debut in Richmond in *The Iron Chest,* a dramatic adaptation of William Godwin's *Caleb Williams.* In the next thirty years, Booth remade his career and himself in the United States, performing more than 2,000 times on stages from Natchez to New Brunswick, and as far west as San Francisco, until his death in 1852.

Booth was born in London in 1796 to a lawyer devoted to the idea of republican government and its realization in the United States. Booth's name reflects this passion. Lucius Junius Brutus, ancestor of the Brutus who led the conspiracy to assassinate Caesar, started the popular uprising that drove the last king from Rome and established the republic. Between 1769 and 1772, a series of letters in a London newspaper criticizing the government of George III had been signed "Junius."

While Booth was never active in politics, his offstage life was stamped by the Jacksonian credo of egalitarianism and individualism. Unlike Kean and other English actors who visited the United States but returned to pursue careers in England, he bought land in Maryland and became a yeoman farmer in the Jacksonian mold. He raised a family of ten children there, among them Edwin Booth, the greatest American actor of Shakespeare in the post–Civil War period, and John Wilkes Booth, whose infamy as the assassin of Abraham Lincoln echoes with cruel irony the legacy of Brutus.

Junius Booth began acting in provincial theaters in England in 1817. Kean had already taken the London stage by storm in his debut as Shylock in 1814, and reigned supreme as the originator of a wholly new style of acting. Following on the era of classic acting dominated by the formal, idealizing, declamatory style of John Philip Kemble, Kean, as Joseph W. Donohue has written, illuminated the fitful inner life of his characters—their fleeting impulses, contradictions, and extremes of passion—through "abrupt transitions, unexpected pauses, lightning descents from the grand to the colloquial." In the words of Hazlitt, describing Kean's Shylock, "The character never stands still; there is no vacant pause in the action; the eye is never silent." Championed by other leading critics of the romantic era as well—Coleridge and Leigh Hunt—Kean stamped major Shakespearean roles with his explosive, fluid intensity. This focus on a character's subjective response to his world conveyed the impression that he was an individual and thus by nature unique—which in turn encouraged the audience to identify sympathetically with the character, and to see the play's meaning in terms of his fortunes and fate. In its affirmation of individual subjectivity per se, romantic acting merged with the ideals underlying the French and American revolutions, and also resonated with the egalitarianism of the Jacksonian era.

Booth had the misfortune not only to resemble Kean in appearance—both were short, strikingly handsome, and emotionally intense onstage—but also to act in a similarly "natural" style. The English theater system, following the binary lines of a zero-sum game, enabled and abetted the rivalry between the two actors. Under royal patent first issued in 1660, only two theaters in London, Drury Lane and Covent Garden, could perform spoken drama, as opposed to spectacles, musical entertainments, and pantomime. By approximately 1750 a network of provincial theaters flourished, but only an engagement at one of the London theaters could signify professional success. Not only were these theaters in constant competition but, given the romantic stress on subjective, individual experience, theater belonged to the actor, rather than to the playwright or the ensemble. Audiences passionately defended their favorites and attacked any rivals. Kean, contracted to Drury Lane, was supported by his fan club, the "Wolves," which was determined to beat off all challengers.

In 1817, Booth made his London debut at Covent Garden in the title role in *Richard III*. Recognizing him as a potential rival, Kean ensnared him into playing Iago to his own Othello at Drury Lane. The novice was paired with the star in what audience and reviewers saw as a showdown. While some critics praised Booth's performance as "creditable," or even "a fair specimen of dramatic powers," Kean won hands down. In one reviewer's words, Kean "arose on the wings of genius like an eagle above his opponent," while the influential Hazlitt pronounced Booth's Iago "a very close and spirited repetition of Mr. Kean's manner of doing that part." Though in the next few years Booth played with critical and financial success both in London and the provinces, he continued to be seen merely as Kean's imitator. In the United States, however, Booth was eventually able to escape Kean's long shadow. Of Booth's Richard, an American reviewer declared, "In the tent scene, he showed much originality; rising from the couch, he dashed to the bottom of the stage, and with an attitude and expression of countenance . . . which was neither that of Cooke, Cooper, Kean nor Wallack, he made an extraordinary, and most sensible, impression upon the audience."

When Booth arrived in Norfolk in 1821, he found a theater scene strikingly different from England's in some respects, but similar in others. Though permanent theaters and resident playing companies flourished in New York, Philadelphia, Boston, Baltimore, and in the South, none of them had London's power to make or break careers. As in England, however, the independent stock or repertory company was the norm. Actors were strictly typed according to "lines of business": leading man and leading lady for principal roles in tragedy and melodrama, juvenile or ingénue for comic roles, the heavy for villains, and so forth. Each actor knew perhaps thirty or forty roles from the standard repertoire, and could quickly learn new ones within established "lines." In a thirty-nine-week season, 40 to 130 plays might be performed, well-worn favorites being repeated season after season while interspersed with new plays, with a narrow range of Shakespeare plays forming the core. By the 1820s, however, the star system was emerging on both sides of the ocean. Actors famous for a certain range of leading roles were hired by a company manager to display their talents for a few nights or weeks, supported by the company. Audiences were drawn not only by the star's reputation but also by the fascination of seeing familiar plays and roles, especially Shakespearean ones, in multiple versions.

Stars such as Booth functioned as entrepreneurs selling their own talents independently, yet they depended on companies for engagements, a theater, and a supporting cast. They were essentially itinerant players, on the road from one engagement to the next, repeating the same roles with one company after another. Over Booth's thirty-five-year career, ten roles took up almost three-quarters of his performing life. The title role in Shakespeare's *Richard III,* which he played 579 times, accounted for 20 percent of his main-bill performances—when the play was the main attraction on a bill that might include acrobats and Spanish dancers. Next in frequency was the part of Sir Giles Overreach, the arch-villain of Philip Massinger's *A New Way to Pay Old Debts,* written in the 1620s. Of his other most often performed roles, five were Shakespearean—Lear, Hamlet, Iago, Othello, and Shylock—and three were villains in melodramas of long-standing popularity.

Like all actors after 1700, Booth performed *Richard III* as the English playwright Colley Cibber had rewritten it. Shortening the play and often substituting his language for Shakespeare's, Cibber reduced its fifty-seven characters to thirty-one, but gave Richard 40 percent of the lines, thus creating the perfect vehicle for a star. In the fall of 1821, Booth made his New York debut as Richard with great success, praised for "the desperate valor, the haggard look, the madning thrusts, the rage and fury . . . and finally the Satanic smile which played upon his lips when in the last agonies of death." Similarly, when Booth played Sir Giles Overreach, he produced electrical effects at climactic moments: as one critic wrote, "The change of the old man from rage to idiocy, the violent struggles of the maniac, & his dropping senseless into the arms of his attendants . . . all the leading passions of his nature as shown in the last scene of the play were sufficient to establish the fame of Mr. Booth as a great actor—that is, one who follows nature."

After a lucrative first year in the United States, Booth had earned enough to purchase 150 acres of woodland twenty-five miles from Baltimore, which he turned into a farm. There he spent long periods sowing, plowing, and taking his own produce to market: suddenly, after spending his entire life in the metropolis, he was a farmer. His daughter Asia describes this property as a pristine pastoral retreat:

> There are huge rocks with tiny cascades; streams and springs of delightful water gushing out in the most remote places. Natural bowers of flowering vines, and groves of tall interlacing trees, wild flowers of every shape and hue . . . abound. Away off in the great forest, where the light seldom penetrates . . . is the old well-trodden foot-path of the Algonquin Indian . . . Here in these wild forests my father made his home, far removed from the turmoil of city life, and surrounded by his growing family and faithful servants, among whom he labored with the zeal of an anxious farmer.

Sequestered on his farm between performances, Booth prohibited the killing of any animals, the eating of meat, and even the felling of trees. In the evenings, he read aloud to his family from his personal library, which included the English romantics, Milton, Locke, Shakespeare, Tasso, and Dante.

Booth's life thus straddles the contradictions of the Jacksonian era between the explosion of urban growth and industrialization enabled by the dispossession of Native Americans from their lands and the idealization of the independent farmer who stands apart from cities and factories, getting his learning and his livelihood from nature. Andrew Jackson was frequently promoted as "the American Cincinnatus" who had left his farm only to defend it, when he won the Battle of New Orleans against the British in the War of 1812 and came into national prominence. As Jackson was said to do (Booth once visited him at the Hermitage, his Tennessee home), Booth plowed, planted, and revered nature—but the theater circuits on which his earnings depended were enabled by the city, whose increasingly dense and stratified populations supplied his audiences. The railroads and steamboats that took him from one playing venue to another opened up land formerly populated by Indians to industry and an expanding market system.

Over the three decades of Booth's career, increasingly nationalistic audiences sought a mirror of distinctively American identity in the theater. Rumors of an English star's allegedly aristocratic disdain prompted riots and stopped performances, as when, on Kean's second American tour in 1825, a Boston audience refused to hear his apology and trashed the theater. In 1849, New York audiences pitted Edwin Forrest, the first American-born tragedian to win fame, against the leading English Shakespearean actor Charles Macready, which resulted in the Astor Place riots. Forrest, by commissioning romantic dramas in which he starred as a Jacksonian hero of the people, defending their ancestral ties to the land against a new corporate aristocracy, made himself an icon of the nation. Forrest and

Booth, however, were friends. Though Booth never became a citizen, he was perceived as a virtual American, and never suffered the fierce opprobrium visited on English stars.

As early as 1824, however, amid continuing professional success and the pleasures of his retired country life, Booth began to suffer bizarre episodes of mental derangement. They worsened when, in 1833, three of his children died in a cholera epidemic; a fourth died in 1836. At various times, he murderously attacked fellow actors, broke down onstage (crying, "I can't read—I am a charity boy . . . Take me to the Lunatic Hospital!"), walked from Boston to Providence in midwinter without a coat, jumped off a steamboat in a suicide attempt, and summoned a minister to perform last rites for a heap of dead pigeons. He also took to drinking heavily and failed to appear for numerous engagements. Yet between these fits of madness he continued to perform almost at the height of his powers, and audiences forgave him. One night in Boston, he was so drunk he was unable to finish Richard's opening soliloquy; at the next night's performance, a reviewer declared that Booth "fully sustained his claim to wear, unrivalled, the 'tragic crown.'"

Bibliography: Stephen M. Archer, *Junius Brutus Booth: Theatrical Prometheus* (Carbondale and Edwardsville, IL, 1992). Asia Booth Clarke, *Booth Memorials: Passages, incidents, and anecdotes in the life of Junius Brutus Booth (the elder) by his daughter* (New York, 1866). Joseph W. Donohue, *Theatre in the Age of Kean* (Totowa, NJ, 1975). Bruce McConachie, "The Theatre of Edwin Forrest and Jacksonian Hero Worship," in *When They Weren't Doing Shakespeare,* ed. Judith L. Fisher and Stephen Watt (Athens, GA, 1989). John William Ward, *Andrew Jackson: Symbol for an Age* (New York, 1971). Simon Williams, "European Actors and the Star System in the American Theatre," in *The Cambridge History of American Theatre,* ed. Don B. Wilmeth and Christopher Bigsby (Cambridge, 1998).

COPPÉLIA KAHN

1822

Henry Rowe Schoolcraft eavesdrops on Ojibwe children playing in Sault Sainte Marie, Michigan

LONGFELLOW'S *SONG OF HIAWATHA*

In the summer of 1822, while Henry Rowe Schoolcraft was the Indian agent at Sault Sainte Marie (and while he wooed Jane Johnston, the half-Irish and half-Ojibwe daughter of the band's chief), he overheard some Ojibwe children playing in the creeping dusk. He wrote:

> In the hot summer evenings, the children of the Chippewa Algonquins, along the shores of the upper lakes and in the northern latitudes, frequently assemble before their parents' lodges, and amuse themselves by little chants of various kinds, with shouts and wild dancing. Attracted by such shouts of merriment and gambols, I walked out one evening, to a green lawn skirting the edge of St. Mary's river, with the fall in full view, to get a hold of the meaning of some of these chants. The air

and the plain were literally sparkling with the phosphorescent light of the firefly. By dint of attention, repeated on one or two occasions, the following succession of words was caught. They were addressed to this insect.

The "Chant to the Fire-Fly," as the nursery rhyme would become known, reads as follows:

> Wau wau tay see!
> Wau wau tay see!
> E mow e shin
> Tshe bwau ne baun-e wee!
> Be eghaun—be eghaun-ewee!
> Wa Wau tay see!
> Wa wau tay see!
> Was sa koon ain je gun
> Was sa koon ain je gun.

Schoolcraft offered three translations, the shortest of which is:

> Fire-fly, fire-fly, light me to bed.
> Come, come, little insect of light,
> You are my candle and light me to go.

Fireflies have been appearing, reappearing, and re-reappearing in literature since long before Schoolcraft collected the little thing in 1822, and for long after. They are mentioned, for instance, in a rather poetical rumination by the Blackfeet chief Crowfoot from around the time Schoolcraft was in Sault Sainte Marie. "What is life?" he asked. "It is the flash of a firefly in the night. It is the breath of a buffalo in the wintertime. It is the little shadow which runs across the grass and loses itself in the sunset."

Crowfoot was, unbeknownst to him, echoing Shakespeare. As Hamlet's ghost departs in *Hamlet*, act 1, scene 5, he remarks: "Fare thee well at once!/The glowworm shows the matin to be near,/And 'gins to pale his ineffectual fire:/Adieu, adieu! Hamlet, remember me." Hamlet's glowworm appears several hundred years later in Nabokov's *Pale Fire*, where, as in Crowfoot's homily, fireflies connect life and afterlife. It first appears (in nomenclatural disguise as "luciola"—a corruption of Luciolinae, the palaearctic subfamily of Lampyridae, or Old World fireflies) when Kinbote (possibly the alias of an imaginary king) recounts the death of Queen Blenda, the last Queen of Zembla:

> A peasant woman with a small cake she had baked, doubtlessly the mother of the sentinel who had not yet come to relieve the unshaven dark young *nattdett* (child of night) in his dreary sentry box, sat on a spur stone watching in feminine fascination the luciola-like tapers that moved from window to window; two workmen, holding their bicycles, stood staring too at those strange lights; and a drunk with a walrus mustache kept staggering around and patting the trunks of the lindens.

The fireflies make another, later appearance in *Pale Fire*, at the moment when Kinbote gains possession of the poem "Pale Fire" while he and the poet John

Shade walk across Kinbote's front lawn: "Solemnly I weighed in my hand what I was carrying under my left armpit, and for a moment I found myself enriched with an indescribable amazement as if informed that fireflies were making decodable signals on behalf of stranded spirits, or that a bat was writing a legible tale of torture in the bruised and branded sky."

But back to Schoolcraft: The Ojibwe children's ditty, collected in print but lost to the evening of the Sault, was released into the world in 1855 in Longfellow's *The Song of Hiawatha*:

> At the door on summer evenings
> Sat the little Hiawatha;
> Heard the whispering of the pine-trees,
> Heard the lapping of the waters,
> Sounds of music, words of wonder;
> "Minne-wawa!" said the Pine-trees,
> "Mudway-aushka!" said the water.

> Saw the fire-fly, Wah-wah-taysee,
> Flitting through the dusk of evening,
> With the twinkle of its candle
> Lighting up the brakes and bushes,
> And he sang the song of children,
> Sang the song Nokomis taught him:
> "Wah-wah-taysee, little fire-fly,
> Little, flitting, white-fire insect,
> Little, dancing, white-fire creature,
> Light me with your little candle,
> Ere upon my bed I lay me,
> Ere in sleep I close my eyelids!"

The delicate Ojibwe firefly has been anthologized, translated, retranslated, re-retranslated, dissected, and reassembled at least a dozen times. To date it is the most popular Native American "poem."

Longfellow had been consumed with the desire to write an American epic since he first tried, and failed, with *Evangeline*. He thought the country needed one, desperately, after reading Elias Lönnrot's collage of Finnish folk poetry that Lönnrot strung together as the *Kalevala*. Lönnrot was a district health officer, but he had a passion, and while on business trips, beginning in 1822, he recorded Finnish folk artists singing what was still "sung poetry." He recorded the poems and their variants and published them in two volumes in 1835 and 1836. The *Kalevala* was immediately considered Finland's most important folk epic. The rest of the world, and the poets who sought to describe it, wanted the same for themselves. Poets across the globe searched for the right balance of modernity and folk-ernity that would transmit the essence of their national character.

So eager were many of these questing poets that not a few fake epics were either fabricated or discovered. This had been happening long before the *Kalevala*. The most famous fake was James MacPherson's Scottish tale, *Ossian,* published along with other "fragments" as *The Works of Ossian* in 1765. America had been struck by the same desire for an emblematic national story, and many—such as William Gilmore Simms, James Fenimore Cooper, Nathaniel Hawthorne, Charles Brockden Brown, and Longfellow—felt that the American character was shaped by two forces that American industry was busy trying to kill: the landscape and the Indians who inhabited it. Many of the myths that America told about itself in order to distinguish itself from Europe involved Indians. These myths endure: Pocahontas, the first Thanksgiving, the Boston Tea Party, the Battle of the Little Bighorn, and more recently the occupation of Wounded Knee.

But not everyone thought that Longfellow's *Hiawatha* was good, or that Indians were good subject material. The *New York Times* review of *Song of Hiawatha* (December 28, 1855) went so far as to state that Longfellow should not be commended for "embalming pleasantly enough the monstrous traditions of an uninteresting, and, one may almost say, a justly exterminated race." So much for subject matter. Parodists (and while *Hiawatha* was very popular through the last half of the nineteenth century, it has largely been eclipsed by its parodies—in a move that presages twenty-first-century instant communication, one parody appeared in the *New York Times* four days *before* the *Hiawatha* review) were more disturbed by the numbingly repetitive meter. "The madness of the hour," said a writer in the *New York Times*, "takes the metrical shape of trochees, everybody writes trochaics, talks trochaics, and thinks in trochees." The parodies themselves are often better than the original. The most famous, written by the Reverend George A. Strong in 1856, introduced American readers to the "fur-side inside":

In one hand Peek-Week, the squirrel,
in the other hand the blow-gun—
Fearful instrument, the blow-gun;
And Marcosset and Sumpunkin,
Kissed him, 'cause he killed the squirrel,
'Cause it was a rather big one.
From the squirrel-skin, Marcosset
Made some mittens for our hero,
Mittens with the fur-side inside,
With the fur-side next his fingers
So's to keep the hand warm inside;
That was why she put the fur-side—
Why she put the fur-side, inside.

Speaking of squirrels. They make a curious appearance in Nabokov's quiet masterpiece, *Pnin*. The main character, Pnin, is an exiled Russian teaching in a sleepy New England college called Waindell. Squirrels scamper throughout the text: on Waindell's grounds one squirrel demands that Pnin turn on the water fountain for him. Squirrels also scamper through Pnin's memories of a destroyed childhood. Pnin might very well be experiencing a heart attack in the first chapter of the novel, and as he faints on a park bench he remembers the wallpaper in his childhood bedroom, which depicted a squirrel holding "a nut, a pinecone?"

Pnin's adult life has also been a little disaster, his marriage to the psychoanalytically inclined Liza Wind being chief among Pnin's emotional tragedies. She perambulates only to find a new bed, bench, or chair she can transform into the analytical couch. The only good result was that her son, Victor, managed to forge a strong and loving relationship with the hapless Pnin, largely in spite of their differences. Pnin writes to Victor on the back of a postcard that depicts a squirrel: "The card belonged to an educational series depicting Our Mammals and Birds; Pnin had acquired the whole series specially for the purpose of this correspondence. Victor was glad to learn that 'squirrel' came from a Greek word which meant 'shadow-tail.'"

Squirrels end up connecting Pnin to Victor and to his past. They serve as a motif that bridges time and trauma—uniting past and present, sorrow and joy— and allow Pnin to transcend his mean realities. Nabokov found his squirrels while doing research on Pushkin's *Onegin,* research that unearthed all sorts of connections between Norse epics (such as the *Kalevala* and Snorri Sturluson's *Younger Edda*) and European (particularly English, French, and Russian) literature. It was in the *Edda* and the *Kalevala* that Nabokov discovered the Yggdrasil, a giant ash tree that connects heaven and hell. A squirrel scampers up and down the trunk of the tree delivering messages (mostly insults) between a dragon that gnaws at its roots and an eagle that perches in its highest branches. Later in *Pnin* Victor gives Pnin a punch bowl, which, in addition to strengthening their unlikely friendship, further strengthens the substructure of the novel itself.

> Margaret Thayer admired [the punch bowl] in her turn, and said that when she was a child, she imagined Cinderella's glass shoes to be exactly of that greenish blue tint; whereupon Professor Pnin remarked that, *primo,* he would like everyone to say if contents were as good as container, and, *secundo,* that Cendrillon's shoes were not made of glass but of Russian squirrel fur—*vair,* in French. It was, he said, an obvious case of the survival of the fittest among words, *verre* being more evocative than *vair* which, he submitted, came not from *varius,* variegated, but from *veveritsa,* Slavic for a certain beautiful, pale, winter-squirrel fur, having a bluish, or better say *sizïy,* columbine, shade—from *columba,* Latin for "pigeon."

Pnin has, unwittingly, connected his squirrels to a rainbow (which, in the *Edda,* is called the Bifröst, a rainbow that connects heaven and earth) and connected his past to the promise of a heaven on earth consisting of unforeseen affinities primarily between himself and Victor.

Squirrels also connect heaven and earth, but in a slightly different way, in Hemingway's "Fathers and Sons," one of the last of the Nick Adams stories that Hemingway wrote. These semiautobiographical tales take place, for the most part, in the Upper Peninsula of Michigan, where Hemingway and his family vacationed every summer. The Adams stories revolve around Nick's struggle to emerge into adulthood. They are preoccupied with parental failings ("The Doctor and the Doctor's Wife"), death and sex ("Indian Camp"), and heartbreak ("Ten Indians"). There are as many Ojibwe Indian characters in these stories as white characters, and they provide most of the action. It is through them that Nick learns the lessons of life. In "Fathers and Sons" Nick reflects on his childhood as he drives through America with his own son after his father's suicide. Principal among his memories is the sad and tender scene in which Nick loses his virginity with the Ojibwe girl Trudy, while Nick, Trudy, and Trudy's brother Billy are out in the woods hunting squirrels: "Then afterwards they sat, the three of them, listening for a black squirrel that was in the top branches where they could not see him. They were waiting for him to bark again because when he barked he would jerk his tail and Nick would shoot where he saw any movement." The irony, of course, is that squirrels (and sex) simultaneously highlight the connection and disconnection—the coming together and reminder of separation—inherent in the "sex act," or at least in the sex act for Hemingway:

> Then, later, it was a long time after and Billy was still away.
> "You think we make a baby?" Trudy folded her brown legs together happily and rubbed against him. Something inside Nick had gone a long way away.
> "I don't think so," he said.
> "Make plenty baby what the hell."
> They heard Billy shoot.

Hemingway's fictional Trudy had a real-life counterpart. Her name was Prudence Bolton, and she lived near Walloon Lake. Hemingway claimed she was the first woman he ever "pleasured," though there is no way to know if this is true: Prudence Bolton died in February 1918 after taking strychnine with her lover, Richard Castle. She was pregnant and eighteen years old. And who knows, as an Ojibwe girl of the Upper Peninsula, it is quite likely Prudence descended from the children who, once upon a time, played in the dusk of the Sault, on a green lawn by the lodges of their parents, capturing fireflies as night winged in, and singing about it, loudly, happily, and often enough so Schoolcraft could catch those fireflies with his pen and preserve them, winking, glowing, forever.

Bibliography: Ernest Hemingway, *The Complete Short Stories of Ernest Hemingway* (New York, 1998). Henry Wadsworth Longfellow, *Poems and Other Writings,* ed. J.D. McClatchy (New York, 2000). Vladimir Nabokov, *Pale Fire* (New York, 1992); *Pnin* (New York, 1985). Henry Rowe Schoolcraft, *Schoolcraft's Indian Legends: From Algic Researches, the Myth of Hiawatha, Oneóta, the Race in America, and Historical and Statistical Information Respecting the Indian Tribes of the United States,* ed. Mentor L. Williams (East Lansing, MI, 1991).

DAVID TREUER

1825, November

John Trumbull is delighted by
Thomas Cole's paintings of the American landscape

THE HUDSON RIVER SCHOOL

In the spring of 1825, twenty-four-year-old Thomas Cole arrived in New York City from Philadelphia and, working in the garret of a house his father had rented on Greenwich Street, began painting landscapes. He exhibited a number of his works at the carving and gilding shop of George Dixey, where they were seen by George Washington Bruen, a patron of the American Academy of Fine Arts. Bruen bought one or more of Cole's paintings and later provided the artist with money to visit the Hudson Highlands and the Catskills, where the recently opened Catskill Mountain House, perched at the top of a palisade with a panoramic view of the Hudson River Valley, had become a fashionable resort. In late August or early September, Cole traveled up the Hudson, accumulating a portfolio of sketches. When he returned to New York, he executed perhaps as many as five paintings. In October, Bruen helped the artist place three of the paintings at the shop of the bookseller and art dealer William A. Colman.

At Colman's, the landscapes came to the attention of Colonel John Trumbull, the United States' leading history painter, creator of the four Revolutionary War paintings in the Capitol Rotunda, and president of the American Academy. Trumbull paid twenty-five dollars for Cole's *View of Kaaterskill Falls,* a depiction of a tourist attraction near the Catskill Mountain House. Later Trumbull expressed his excitement over Cole's work to the painter and playwright William Dunlap and the artist and engraver Asher B. Durand. Dunlap purchased one of the remaining paintings at Colman's, *Lake with Dead Trees,* and almost immediately resold it at a profit to the collector Philip Hone. Durand then acquired the third painting, a *View of Fort Putnam.* Trumbull, Dunlap, and Durand soon met Cole, although whether they first encountered him together or individually is unclear. All three, especially the influential Trumbull, proved important for the young landscapist's career.

Nineteenth-century writers, beginning with Dunlap, gave the story of Cole's first months in New York a romantic twist. In their accounts the artist arrives as a youthful genius from the hinterland whose creations overwhelm the older and more experienced Trumbull. In a brief laudatory article published in the *New-York Evening Post* on November 22, 1825, Dunlap described Cole as "a young man from the interior of Pennsylvania," "untutored and unknown." He quoted Trumbull telling Colman, "What I now purchase for 25 dollars I would not part with for 25 guineas. I am delighted, and at the same time mortified. This youth has done at once, and without instruction, what I cannot do after fifty years' practice."

Subsequent versions of the story altered details while retaining much of Dunlap's original plot line. In 1848 the poet William Cullen Bryant, in his funeral oration for Cole, described Trumbull addressing the same words to both Dunlap and Durand. And in 1853, Louis Legrand Noble, in his full-length biography of the artist, invented a scenario in which the older artists meet Cole at Trumbull's studio. Cole arrives at the appointed hour, "a young man, in appearance no more than one and twenty, of slight form and medium height, soft brown hair, a face very pale, though delicately rosy from agitation, a fair fine forehead, and large light blue eyes." The young artist's agitation increases as Trumbull confronts him directly with the words, "You surprise me, at your age, to paint like this. You have already done what I, with all my years and experience, am yet unable to do."

The Cole discovery story, as it might be called, has been repeated many times since Noble published his biography, and while some facts of the tale remain un-

Thomas Cole, *Lake with Dead Trees (Catskill)*
Allen Memorial Art Museum, Oberlin College, Ohio

certain, Cole's arrival on the New York art scene was, according to the artist's contemporaries, a momentous event. "From that time," Bryant proclaimed in his oration, Cole "had a fixed reputation, and was numbered among the men of whom our country had reason to be proud." Similarly, Noble reported that more than twenty-five years after the event Durand recalled how Cole's "fame spread like fire."

After their initial meeting, Trumbull put Cole in contact with his network of collectors and patrons, including Robert Gilmor of Baltimore and Daniel Wadsworth of Hartford (later the founder of the Wadsworth Atheneum), who took it upon themselves to help sponsor Cole's career. Aristocratic gentlemen such as Trumbull, Gilmor, and Wadsworth saw themselves as connoisseurs (Wadsworth was also an amateur landscapist). Patronizing American artists was for them not only an opportunity to acquire works of art but also a form of noblesse oblige, an assumption of the patriotic responsibility of fostering the arts in the young republic. By advancing Cole's career Trumbull may also have hoped to shore up the sagging fortunes of his American Academy, which in the fall of 1825 had to contend with competition from the newly formed National Academy of Design, a breakaway institution run by its artist-members instead of by gentleman-patrons. Cole accepted an invitation to become an associate member of the new academy while maintaining friendly relations with Trumbull. He sealed his dual allegiance by showing his work at the annual exhibitions of both institutions.

The founding of the National Academy of Design signaled not only the appearance of a new generation of artists but also a shift from deferential artist-patron relations to a new set of market-driven relations in which traditional patronage played a lesser role and collectors often purchased works of art out of public exhibitions. During the 1830s and 1840s, as the influence of the old aristocratic elite declined, artists increasingly had to depend on newly wealthy merchants and financiers, such as Luman Reed, Jonathan Sturges, and Samuel Ward, who may have known little about art but were willing to be guided in their decisions about buying and commissioning paintings—a situation that Cole at times deftly exploited.

Shortly after his arrival in New York, Cole became acquainted with James Fenimore Cooper and began attending gatherings of Cooper's Lunch or Bread and Cheese Club, a meeting place for artists, writers, scientists, academics, lawyers, and merchants. In 1823 Cooper had scored an unprecedented success with his popular novel *The Pioneers*, which introduced the reading public to Natty Bumppo, Cooper's ideal frontiersman. Cooper's descriptions of the American landscape in *The Pioneers* and later novels in the Leatherstocking series paralleled Cole's painting technique, in which he set closely observed natural details—trees, rocks, mountains, clouds—within an idealized framework. Cole probably drew much of his inspiration for his early paintings of American wilderness from *The Pioneers* and from Cooper's *The Last of the Mohicans* (1826), which he took as a subject for at least five of the works he painted between 1826 and 1829.

About the same time, Cole formed a friendship with William Cullen Bryant, who also had arrived in New York in 1825 to embark on a career as a journalist and editor. Cole, who was widely read in English and (in translation) Italian and German literature and was something of a poet himself (he published two poems in *The Knickerbocker*), was familiar with Bryant's poetry. For his part, Bryant became a great admirer of Cole's art, celebrating Cole's vision of the American landscape in his sonnet, "To Cole, The Painter, Departing for Europe" (1829), in which he exhorted the artist to "keep that earlier, wilder image bright." Cole, like Bryant, saw a close relation between poetry and painting, in accord with the theory of *ut pictura poesis* ("as with painting so with poetry"), asserting that "to walk with nature as a poet is the necessary condition of a perfect artist." He and Bryant were often linked as exemplary figures in their love of American nature. After Cole's death, his patron Jonathan Sturges commissioned from Asher Durand a painting entitled *Kindred Spirits,* which Sturges presented to Bryant in gratitude for his funeral oration. Cole and Bryant had gone walking in the Catskills together, and the painting shows the two standing on a promontory in one of the Catskill cloves, with Cole using a telescope as a pointer to single out the features of the landscape while a reverential Bryant, who has removed his hat and bowed his head, contemplates the scene.

Scholars have seen Cole's precocious success in the fall of 1825 as the founding moment of the Hudson River school. And indeed Cole played a seminal role in the school's development. In the late 1830s he persuaded Durand, who had given up engraving for portraiture and genre painting, to concentrate on landscapes. In 1844, at the urging of Daniel Wadsworth, he invited the young Frederic Church to spend two years studying landscape painting with him at his home in Catskill, New York. Cole's death in 1848 at the age of forty-seven robbed the school of its father figure just as it was beginning to come into its own. His importance for the development of American landscape painting and as a model for a younger generation of artists was widely acknowledged at the time. As Bryant proclaimed in his funeral oration, Cole's untimely "departure has left a vacuity which amazes and alarms us . . . It is as if we were to look over the heavens on a starlight evening and find that one of the greater planets, Hesperus or Jupiter, had been blotted from the sky."

Such extravagant rhetoric aside, the Hudson River school owed Cole a debt for having done so much to establish the American landscape as an artistic subject in its own right. Other early American landscapists—among them Alvin Fisher, Thomas Birch, and Thomas Doughty—were already well known when Cole first appeared in New York, but their work did not elicit the same enthusiasm among artists, writers, and patrons. Cole's early success derived from his ability to dramatize American nature, to turn the representation of untouched wilderness into complex symbols that appealed to patriotic sentiment and reinforced the nascent interest among urban elites in landscape literature and landscape tourism.

Early on, Cole became expert in adapting European landscape painting conventions to the depiction of American subject matter, producing American pastorals and prospects as well as sublime prospects, such as his *Lake with Dead Trees* and *Landscape with Tree Trunks* (1828), in which a point of transcendence—a sunset, a clearing sky—offers a resolution to the fear and turmoil associated with the sublime. Cole made trips to Europe (from 1829 to 1832 and again from 1841 to

1842) and painted scenes associated with the Grand Tour, including *The Cascatelli, Tivoli, Looking toward Rome* (1832), *Aqueducts in the Campagna di Roma* (1843), and *The Arch of Nero* (1846). He also aspired to what he deemed a "higher form of landscape" and created historical and religious scenes as well as such allegories as his five-part *Course of Empire* series (1836), commissioned by Luman Reed, and his four-part *Voyage of Life* series (1840; second version, 1841–42), commissioned by Samuel Ward. *The Voyage of Life* enjoyed enormous popularity during the decade following the artist's death and, in the form of engravings, became familiar to several generations of middle-class Americans.

Reaching its high point of popularity in the 1850s and 1860s, the Hudson River school celebrated American expansion and scientific and material progress in such works as Durand's allegory *Progress (The Advance of Civilization)* (1853), Church's *Heart of the Andes* (1859), and Albert Bierstadt's *The Rocky Mountains: Landers Peak* (1863). Cole's example as an innovative painter of American scenery secured his reputation with the public and with subsequent generations of Hudson River school painters, but he shared little of his followers' optimism. A conservative antimodernist living in a time of unprecedented democratic ferment, he identified with his aristocratic patrons, who had subscribed to a version of classical republican theory in which democracy equaled demagoguery and was responsible, along with increasing affluence, for undermining republican virtue, thus leading to the downfall of republics ancient and modern—a belief the artist spelled out in the five paintings of *The Course of Empire.*

Despairing of the United States' future, Cole increasingly turned to religion. It was for him but a short step from *The Course of Empire* to *The Voyage of Life,* his popular Bunyanesque allegory in which the theme of individual salvation replaced the historical drama of the rise and fall of empires.

Bibliography: William Cullen Bryant, "On the Life of Thomas Cole," funeral oration delivered before the National Academy of Design, New York, May 4, 1848, Catskill Archive, *catskillarchive.com.* James T. Callow, *Kindred Spirits: Knickerbocker Writers and American Artists, 1807–1855* (Chapel Hill, NC, 1967). Angela Miller, *Empire of the Eye* (Ithaca, NY, 1994). Louis Legrand Noble, *The Life and Works of Thomas Cole,* ed. Elliot S. Vesell (1853; Cambridge, MA, 1964). Ellwood C. Parry III, *The Art of Thomas Cole: Ambition and Imagination* (Newark, DE, 1988). William H. Truettner and Alan Wallach, eds., *Thomas Cole: Landscape into History* (New Haven, CT, 1994).

ALAN WALLACH

1826, July 4
Jefferson and Adams die; Stephen Foster is born

SONGS OF THE REPUBLIC

"Is it the Fourth?" asks an eighty-three-year-old delirious Thomas Jefferson in the dying hours of the third, his last words before lapsing into an unconsciousness from which he won't recover. For all the ways the former president of the United

States considers himself an eminently *reasonable* man—the Age of Enlightenment's most conspicuous result, holding down whatever phantom corner might
be teased out of the trinity of Locke, Bacon, and Newton—nothing betrays Jefferson's romanticism more than this question at this moment. Urged on by his
daughters gathered around his bedside, even in his coma he's determined to see
the fiftieth anniversary of the Republic's birth, which has come to be signified by
nothing so much as his authorship of that birth's certificate. That he should die
half a century to the day since the adoption of the Declaration of Independence
speaks to that flair for drama Jefferson always has kept so private, and to a flair for
symmetry he might insist on calling science but obviously is more cosmic. There
is to be about this birthday—and this deathday—the exquisite happenstance of
a song.

On the desk near his bed, somewhere amid the bills that have gone unpaid
and driven the dying man to the verge of bankruptcy, is the most recent letter
from the only other one left. Jefferson was thirty-three when he wrote the Declaration, a philosopher-prince but the quieter junior partner of a collective led by
the colonies' greatest legal mind, John Adams, Jefferson's senior by seven years.
With the encouragement of house genius and aging bad boy Benjamin Franklin—
with whom Adams ultimately didn't get along, but then ultimately he didn't get
along with anyone but his wife—Adams drove that Continental Congress of '76
to the precipice of revolution and then over, with the decision of each state to
draft its own constitution. Almost as an afterthought it occurred to the subver-
sives to add a postscript of sorts, in case England's dim throne missed the point—
an explicit statement of independence. The volatile and occasionally charmless
Adams suggested to the still-green Jefferson that since the older man was considered "obnoxious" (Adams's own word) by many of the delegates, and since the
younger man was ten times (Adams's own math) the writer of anyone else in the
building, this business of dotting insurrection's *i*'s and crossing its *t* should fall to
the Virginian, who was in a rush to get his treason over with and return home to
his bride of a few years, in whom waited what would be a stillborn son. Jefferson
would father with more success the American idea.

Perhaps that was the beginning of the problem between the two men. When
the Declaration turned out to be more than a postscript, more than fine print,
when it became a sacred covenant for the country and Jefferson loomed as its authorial deity, his name an invocation whispered in the streets of regicidal capitals
throughout Europe, relegating the magisterial and proud Adams to runner-up in
the race of history . . . well, worse rifts are born of less. Then, in President Washington's first term, Adams suggested the chief executive should have a title along
the lines of, say, "His Majesty," and that the new republic was in need of a little
"monarchial" mojo—this from the Revolution's most incendiary firebrand short
of Tom Paine. Former kindred spirit Jefferson publicly called it "the most superlatively ridiculous thing I've ever heard." In revolution, in country-creating, in
the vice presidency and presidency, in what was left of their countrymen's hearts
that wasn't occupied by Washington, Jefferson kept following Adams and one-
upping him. Defeating Adams's bid for reelection, Jefferson won, after a daz-

zling first term, the reelection his predecessor had been denied. For years Adams stewed. As outgoing president he refused to attend his old friend's inauguration. Couldn't everyone see through that whole "man of the people" thing? Shuffling around Monticello in his bedroom slippers . . . sleeping with his slave girl, thirty years younger! Renaissance figure! Leviathan of letters and science! "He must know," Adams fumed on Jefferson's departure from the White House, "that he leaves the government infinitely worse than he found it, from his own error or ignorance. I wish his telescopes and mathematical instruments may secure his felicity."

Now on the country's fiftieth anniversary, Americans are of two minds about it. The first is that the republic has survived *fifty years,* by God! And who knew? But for bungling by the king of England in the revolt's infancy, the men whose act Americans now celebrated would have ornamented gallows from Boston to Charleston. The second is that the bloom, nonetheless, may be off the American rose, and has been since almost three decades earlier when Washington left the presidency and died precipitously after, sealing the political fate of Adams and the Federalists in the process. Improbably, now Adams's son is president. "We weren't that crazy about the old man—now we have the *son?*" Thus the beginning of what will 176 years from now become a tradition of dubious sons rising to the seats of their fathers in dubious elections. Two years before, Quincy Adams won neither the popular nor electoral vote in the presidential contest against Andrew Jackson, the most imposing American military figure since Washington and inheritor of Jefferson's populism, a surrogate for that stillborn son. But when Jackson came up short of a majority in the Electoral College, throwing the election to the House of Representatives, another would-be president, Speaker of the House Henry Clay, supported Quincy Adams and delivered to him the presidency, to the outrage of Jackson partisans. Although Clay genuinely believed Quincy Adams the lesser of the evils presented him, it didn't look right to some when the newly anointed president made Clay secretary of state. So among other things, this year the country's semicentennial has been marked by a duel between Secretary Clay and a senator accusing him of corruption. It's the most high-profile such encounter since the one that marked the Jefferson administration in which Vice President Aaron Burr shot and killed Alexander Hamilton, who—like Clay with Quincy Adams—made Jefferson president over Burr, if not altogether happily. Fifty years in, Americans can't help wondering if their country is a rat in history's wheel, reliving past dramas except in diminishing versions, each turn differentiated only by imperceptible shifts in axis, imperceptible ascents in velocity that lead nowhere faster.

Of course Americans don't know from Nowhere, not on any physical map. Americans are too obsessed with Anywhere and Everywhere, the country leaping out of its skin; on this fiftieth anniversary there are now two dozen states, and the frontier is a dream of the future. The twelve months of 1826 see the publication of James Fenimore Cooper's *The Last of the Mohicans* and the election of Davy Crockett to Congress. And the country and its growing contradictions, its adventurous spirit and dark passions, and the promise and betrayal of the American idea are embodied by no one so well as the man who exalted the endowment of liberty by

God even as slaves kept his house and worked his property, and who finally succumbs on this day just past noon. Fifty years after the Declaration of Independence, the tension between promise and betrayal remains unresolved, deferred in
a series of soul-killing compromises that alternate free states with slave, that attempt to erode the enterprise of slavery while reinforcing the institution, compromises that began with the Declaration itself, from which was jettisoned an
antislavery clause that slave-owner Jefferson himself wrote.

In the same exact hour that Jefferson dies, there is born in western Pennsylvania, beyond earshot of the Liberty Bell but within the peal of lesser bells, the last
of ten children to Eliza Foster and her husband, William, a Federalist state legisla-
tor and an admirer of the Adamses. Whatever stars are in young Stephen's future,
apparently none concerns money. By the time of his arrival his father has drunk
first the family's modest fortune and then the mortgage, on which the bank recently has foreclosed. The first great American songwriter, whose early hit "Oh!
Susanna" will drive his countrymen across a continent in pursuit of gold, Stephen
will his entire life be robbed spectacularly by song publishers, to die at the age of
thirty-seven with, to his name, thirty-eight cents. Sometimes the exquisite happenstance of songs perversely insists on getting things almost right but not exactly.

The exquisite perversity of Stephen Foster's songs is that they're steeped not
in the American South but in a vision of it. No songwriter ever has written a more
autobiographical title than does the composer of "Beautiful Dreamer." Exactly
once in his life Foster will visit the South, on a honeymoon voyage down and back
up the Mississippi. Thus are love and perhaps even sex—one never can be sure
about honeymoons—joined to an American revelation, in which case one can't be
sure about revelations either, except that this is the sort that creates "Swanee
River," "My Old Kentucky Home," "Jeannie with the Light Brown Hair." On
wafts of magnolia, the unresolved American contradiction rages in Foster's music; though they might not withstand the scrutiny of more sophisticated sensibilities two centuries later, "Old Black Joe" and "Nelly Was a Lady" try in their own
white way to come to grips with a growing understanding that the antebellum
beast of burden is a human being. Born in that auspicious peal of bells, it doesn't
seem possible Foster could have no politics. Later it will be claimed that near the
end of his life he harbored abolitionist sympathies. He will die, at the height of
the war that finally addresses Jefferson's paradox, in New York, not Richmond or
Atlanta.

At the eastern edge of Massachusetts, within sight of the sea, as the light begins to fade on this most extraordinary Fourth of July since the first, John Adams
dies. This morning he was stricken while reading, as though yanked toward the
other side by a God who believes that today, of all days, America needs an epiphany. Adams has lost consciousness at virtually the instant his old rival passes on.
Over the previous years they became friends again, the bond of revolution too
strong; these were men who forty years ago, after all, stood side by side as American ambassadors in the court of King George, who literally turned his back on
them. After the glacial first decade of the nineteenth century, the ice between the
two men broke, characteristically, with an Adams outburst to a mutual acquain-

tance: "I've always loved Jefferson and still do!" This was followed by a letter to the former foe, in response to which Jefferson, with a victor's magnanimity, acclaimed Adams "the Colossus of Independence." Moved, mollified, and seizing the redemptive moment, for nearly a decade and a half Adams wrote over a hundred letters to Jefferson, who answered with less than half that number; no matter, the paternal patriot assured the protégé who eclipsed him, "your one is worth more than my four." Not really. Jefferson always was a man to keep things close to his vest, whereas Adams barely buttoned his vest at all. Expressing a yearning to talk again personally after so long, secretly the two knew better; written correspondence allowed them to control the exchange, skirt minefields. Even when Adams wandered into what might have seemed harmless, lighthearted talk of women, Jefferson, whose slave had become his mistress of a quarter century, was circumspect. So the conversation was curious as much for what wasn't said: the man who wrote the most immortal political phrase in history—"all men are created equal"—and who as a young idealist introduced antislavery measures in the Virginia legislature now could not bring himself to even write the word "slavery." There were ways in which Adams was the prophet after all.

With the passage of these titans, who would be eulogized together in Boston four weeks later by Daniel Webster, their unyielding if tempered and affectionate argument is set to music amid American gunfire, in a volley of songs that catches the argument midair and continues it. The North and South Poles of the American Revolution, as they're called, never know Stephen Foster, of course—never hums one of his tunes. By the time Foster will grow to know of them, they're ancients consigned to history and all its specious pantheons. But Foster's melody already waits in the American night when Jefferson calls out, "Is it the Fourth?" and rides the smoke of American clashes to come when, nearly twenty-four hours later, with his own dying words, Adams answers, "Jefferson lives."

Bibliography: The Adams-Jefferson Letters: The Complete Correspondence between Thomas Jefferson and Abigail and John Adams, ed. Lester J. Cappon (Chapel Hill, NC, 1959). R. B. Bernstein, *Thomas Jefferson* (Oxford, 2003). Fawn M. Brodie, *Thomas Jefferson: An Intimate History* (New York, 1970). Joseph P. Ellis, *Founding Brothers: The Revolutionary Generation* (New York, 2000). Ken Emerson, *Doo-Dah! Stephen Foster and the Rise of American Popular Culture* (New York, 1997). David McCullough, *John Adams* (New York, 2001).

STEVE ERICKSON

1826

Natty Bumppo returns in *The Last of the Mohicans*

COOPER'S LEATHERSTOCKING TALES

James Fenimore Cooper wrote more than thirty novels and a number of travel diaries and political essays, but he became popular, and important, for his five

Leatherstocking novels. In his narratives of a wilderness character, he created a figure of freedom and a critique of official culture that after nearly two hundred years—and through the work of countless imitators and followers, from Honoré de Balzac and Eugène Sue in France to Karl May in Germany, from mid-nineteenth-century American dime novels to films of the twentieth century—has not lost its hold on American and world audiences: a critique embodied by the lone "outworldly" man who renounces civilization but generates, within the woods and within himself, the elementary virtues on which civilization supposedly rests.

Named variously Leatherstocking, Hawkeye, Pathfinder, and Deerslayer, Cooper's Natty Bumppo is rarely completely alone; outside of civilization, from the earliest period of his adult life, in *The Deerslayer* (1841), he has a companion, a Delaware Indian chief, Chingachgook, and later, in *The Last of the Mohicans* (1826), the chief's son, Uncas. Natty grew up within the Delaware tribe and knows Native American culture from the inside. Natty is present when both son and father die, Uncas as a young man, last in the lineage of tribal chiefs, and Chingachgook as an old man who cedes the world of his tribal nation to the Euro-American settlers as he burns to death in a forest fire at the end of *The Pioneers* (1823).

Cooper discovered the significance of his wilderness hero in the course of writing the first published of the five novels, *The Pioneers,* supposedly an homage to his father, a frontier land-developer who founded the town of Cooperstown, New York. When Natty enters the scene, he is an archaic figure from the original forest wilderness. He is cantankerous, homely, lives in a log hut outside the village, ceaselessly grumbles about the destructiveness of development, interrupts a Christmas Eve communal church service with his Indian companion. In the course of the novel, as Cooper warms to his character, we sympathize with Leatherstocking's views in his criticism of Judge Marmaduke Temple, founder of the village of Templeton, and the "wasty ways" of the settlers, who are proud of the "wondrous changes" taking place in the village that accompany the destruction of the natural environment.

D. H. Lawrence was one of the first to emphasize that Cooper begins his series with Natty as an old man of the forest, who dies in the third book he writes, *The Prairie* (1827), and that when Cooper returns to his wilderness themes thirteen years later to write the last two books, he depicts Natty and Chingachgook in their youth. Lawrence imposed his own myth on America: the Leatherstocking novels "go backwards from old age to golden youth. That is the true myth of America." In *The Pathfinder* (1840) and *The Deerslayer,* the two are young men in their twenties, guiding white men and rescuing white women from captivity. Natty lives within the purity of an unspoiled natural world:

> Untutored as he was in the learning of the world and simple as he ever showed himself to be in all matters touching the subtleties of conventional taste, he was a man of strong, native, poetical feeling. He loved the woods for their freshness, their sublime solitudes, their vastness, and the impress that they every where bore of the

divine hand of their creator . . . Thus constituted in a moral sense, and of a steadiness that no danger could appal, or any crisis disturb.

Natty is uncompromisingly a man of "honest heart, manly nature, and simple truth." His elementary philosophy is plain: "all is contradiction in the settlements, while all is concord in the woods."

Whereas Judge Marmaduke Temple is recognized by the community as the authority for development, since he is the owner of thousands of acres of wilderness, Cooper understands that economic authority alone is unable to establish the discipline necessary for an orderly community. The frontier society of Templeton is diverse, and Judge Temple is pitted against the moral authority of Leatherstocking, an exemplar of self-discipline who, because of the way he lives, nevertheless lacks the practical authority to direct the rising community. Natty does not support any version of social development. In 1823 Cooper spoke for the anxiety of the country itself over the legitimacy of the white man's presence and hold on the land. In his complicated rendition of the problem of rights to the land, he suggests that the natives have ownership rights. In this respect, Cooper is more open to, more attuned to, the complexities of the new nation than the Supreme Court, which that same year ruled that any native claim to the land derived from England's claim, on the grounds of an ancient European legal precedent, "rights of discovery." Thus, when the United States defeated England in the Revolutionary War, the United States claimed England's rights to the land. Cooper, however, finds a novelistic solution to the various claims to ownership of the land in the person of Oliver Effingham, whose English grandfather had received a royal patent to the land and had received land from the Delaware tribe that had also adopted Oliver. By marrying Judge Temple's daughter, Oliver gathers all possible claims to ownership—Temple's commercial right of purchase as well as the English titles and the Indian rights as original occupants and "rightful owners of the country."

While such a fictional claim might be convincing only to readers of romances, Cooper understood that the law could ultimately perform the service of holding a diverse people together. Several of his novels take as their theme the challenge of establishing both law and the institutions to support the law. In the end, Cooper celebrated the law. His readership, however, remained more interested in the dramas of Leatherstocking, the outsider who serves as the scout, pathfinder, guide, Hawkeye, Indian friend, and Indian killer, the grouch who lives on the border of the developing nation—even though, as a Christian pagan educated by the Moravian-influenced Delaware tribe, Leatherstocking holds to an elementary worldliness of value that would negate economic and urban progress. Natty's renunciation of civilization does not entail a commitment to life outside the law, although he does not want Temple or anyone else to interfere with his freedom—to kill a deer, for instance, or to live in his cabin without fear of intrusion.

Throughout the novels, Leatherstocking clearly believes in some versions of the laws—the laws of nature as the laws of God, the primitive laws of war. But Cooper places him in a wilderness that is untrammeled by European-American encroachers and imposers. This wilderness is God's creation, and there is a sense that the creation is so close to the creator that Natty's values derive from the immediacy of his relationship to nature, and from his Moravian education. Whereas *The Deerslayer* emphasizes the development of Leatherstocking's consciousness by "experience," there is always a sense that his closeness to the woods and to the native inhabitants expresses an innate purity that cannot be fully joined to the civilized world. So long as Leatherstocking stays in the woods and rejects domestic life, his experience and sense of rightness combine to uphold the ethical values that the traditions of more or less Christianized Western thinkers had promoted. When the beautiful, slightly aggressive Judith Hutter asks him if he has a "sweetheart," his reply is absolute: "She's in the forest—Judith—hanging from the boughs of the trees, in a soft rain—in the dew on the open grass—the clouds that float about in the blue heavens—the birds that sing in the woods—the sweet springs where I slake my thirst—and in all the other glorious gifts that come from God's Providence." Leatherstocking can serve as the moral exemplar for the new nation, a pathfinder toward an original rightness of the world. Such a figure, emulated in his values if not in his threateningly half-savage, antisocial behavior, might serve a rising empire as a measure, reminding a nation how to avoid betraying its stated democratic and moral intentions.

Although Cooper grew up in Cooperstown surrounded by natives, and used a Moravian missionary's account of the practices and myths of the Delaware tribes, his Indians bear little reference to any actual Native Americans, and his fictional representations have been long lasting and deleterious to Native Americans, as, no doubt, Mrs. Stowe's depictions of slaves have been for African Americans. Cooper's concept of Indians is more indebted to the traditions of Puritan demonizing, on the one hand, and Rousseauian romanticizing, on the other. There are always two groups of natives, one evil and the other benevolent. Inspired by the Enlightenment interest in primitive tribes, with the romances of Ossian and Scott's Highlanders and de Staël's German tribes, Cooper could hold up the image of the Indian as at once a moral and a cautionary mirror to civilization, an empire vanishing as another empire rises.

The idea of native tribes is crucial to Cooper's critique of the emergence of the United States of America, the name itself speaking of limitlessness and dominance because, as for European Enlightenment intellectuals, he found in the primitive values of the natives an irreducible reminder of the qualities that he thought were on the verge of being lost forever. Indians might be "savage" but they were not corrupt, unless they got too close to Europeans, making treaties with European powers, a form of intermarriage that Cooper would not allow among his characters. Cooper's fundamental belief, however, especially in *The Last of the Mohicans* and *The Deerslayer,* is that the ancient virtues of the Native Americans reside in Leatherstocking himself, the white man of the wilderness whose loyalty to the ancient virtues is designed to remind the white settlers and developers of the principles on which a republic dedicated to the preservation of human freedom is based. Hawkeye is the *translatio* of the ancient virtues to the new land. Although he cannot reconcile the conflicting issues in *The Pioneers*—in sharing his cabin with an Indian and a former British officer, conversant with both civilization and savagery—Leatherstocking reminds the nation of the foundational truth within the pretensions of civilization.

Cooper offered a dream of racial harmony in the camaraderie of Natty and Chingachgook, but always at the expense of natives who may embody virtue but have to disappear. Today, we may still give Cooper credit, the way Ralph Ellison gave credit to American novelists such as Mark Twain or William Faulkner. Their writings might be construed as having a racist tinge, but at least they acknowledged the importance of race in the story of the nation. Cooper may not have been knowledgeable in native ethnography, but he invoked natives as a critical element within the formation of the nation. He appreciated what Susan Scheckel has called the insistence of the Indian. That he represented natives to dramatize the replacement of tribal nations by modern contractual societies is a perspective that he learned from Enlightenment thinkers and novelists, who were trying to imagine new nations in the aftermath of revolutions.

Martin Thom has written that Rousseau and a host of European intellectuals recommended "a retreat to the woods" from the city during a prenationalist period—and that "America, and more specifically, America's frontier, had represented an asylum, at once beyond cities and the imagined heart of a new city. By the time this European dream of an untainted place had dissolved, a nationalist vision had taken hold." But while Cooper was undoubtedly thinking in this mode, his ambitions were far greater and his vision more radical: he links Natty's commitment to the forested wilderness, as the landscape of God's creation, to American nationalism. The narrative of building a city within the wilderness of upstate New York (*The Pioneers*) is fraught with the ambivalence of this inherited conflict between the city and the wilderness. Entailed here is the question of what kind of social model is available to establish a foundation for liberty and happiness—the ancient cities of Greece or Rome or the newly found primitive peoples of the woods? Who is the hero of the nation, Temple, the developer of the wilderness, in his new village, or Leatherstocking in the forest? What model will best serve the nation, sustain it against the fear that, as Enlightenment and romantic thinkers understood, all empires and nations will inevitably fall? Cooper tried to erase the question, and thus white guilt, by placing the burden of the decline of nations on the native tribes whose leaders accept that they are about to vanish.

Like almost all of the politicians of the United States, at least up to the time of Lincoln, Cooper's thoughts were on what Lincoln called "the unfinished work" of building a nation. He wrote at a time when writers of romances could feel that they were contributing to the work of the nation. Lawrence called Cooper the "national grouch," but novelists could enter the public sphere to think—and write—about the success or failure of the promises of the nation, whether or not it could remain a beacon to itself as well as to the world. Cooper's generation feared what it thought were the lessons of the past, that nations rose and inevitably fell, and his novels were written to remind readers of the moral ground on which the nation, as a democratic experiment, presumed to be built. As with

Thoreau later, we might ask how Cooper could have thought that an exemplary figure in the wilderness might guide a nation. When at the end of *The Prairie* Natty dies, at age ninety, on the barren Plains, he is like his native cohorts who cede their world to civilized development. But in the last two novels, Cooper reinvents his white and native heroes, perhaps in answer to a need felt by this time, when all of the fathers of the Revolution and the nation had passed away.

Critics have lamented the fact that Cooper inherited a romance form that seems inappropriate for writing about the American frontier. But what Cooper understood, for his time, was that the romance, in its sluggish bagginess, allowed him the widest latitude to encompass a great many themes and topics. Despite his actual memories of growing up in Cooperstown, his concept of the frontier derives from Scottish, English, and continental political theorists. In their treatises, and in the cultural and intellectual background of the writings of Chateaubriand, Scott, Sterne, Goldsmith, Irving, Smollett, Austen, and others, he found the literary relevance of his own personal frontier experience verified. He turned his Anglo-European models into American themes and affirmations, and achieved a cultural authority that still echoes deeply in American culture.

Bibliography: James Fenimore Cooper, *The Leatherstocking Tales,* ed. Blake Nevius, 2 vols. (New York, 1985). D. H. Lawrence, *Studies in Classic American Literature* (New York, 1923). Susan Scheckel, *The Insistence of the Indian* (Princeton, NJ, 1998). Martin Thom, *Republics, Nations and Tribes* (London, 1995).

RICHARD HUTSON

1826; 1927

Henry Wadsworth Longfellow sails to Europe; William Carlos Williams returns to America

POETRY CROSSES THE OCEAN

Henry Wadsworth Longfellow's first trip to Europe, made in 1826, may not have seemed, even to him, like the beginning of a poetic career: he meant to become fluent in French and Spanish in order to teach modern languages at Bowdoin College, where he had just earned his degree. As it turned out, Longfellow's three years abroad commenced the studies that let him become, by the end of the 1860s, by far the most famous poet in America, and among the most popular in the world. Having crossed the Continent from Madrid to Florence to Prague, Longfellow returned to Maine in 1829 fluent in French, Spanish, and Italian, conversant in German, and able to read Portuguese. From Bowdoin he published translations, instructional works, articles on continental literature, and a well-received travel memoir, *Outre-Mer* (1833). He sailed again in 1835, visiting England, Denmark, Sweden, and Switzerland; on his return he became a professor of modern languages at Harvard, where he remained—lecturing on Dante, Goethe, and Lope de Vega—for almost twenty years, until he could live comfortably off the sales of his books.

Longfellow's transatlantic voyages inaugurated what now looks like his life's work: he would bring to the English-speaking United States an appreciation for the literary styles of other languages and places, and he would establish in America their nearest appropriate equivalents, by translating poetry, by writing about it, by writing it, and by giving American places and stories the kind of treatment—technically polished but determinedly accessible, reflecting its region yet fit for polite society—that romantic nationalists in nineteenth-century Europe sought for their own terrain.

Readers today think of Longfellow's poetry—if we do think of it—as conventional, even anodyne, and so its sentiments ("Let us, then, be up and doing") often were. Otherwise it could not have fit so well the taste of his day. Yet the story of Longfellow's poetry (including his translations) is not only a story of public success; it is also a story of syncretism, of a man who made his work formally various, and made the best of it worth reading now, by importing into American English—and installing in his American places—as many techniques as he could.

Few lines seem more amicably characteristic of popular poetry in nineteenth-century America than the refrain from "My Lost Youth" (1858): "A boy's will is the wind's will, /And the thoughts of youth are long, long thoughts." That poem about the Portland of Longfellow's boyhood provided the title for Robert Frost's first book. Yet that ur-American sentence is itself a translation twice over: it is Longfellow's version of Herder's German version of a folk song from Lapland. *Evangeline* (1847), his romance of the Acadian diaspora, derived its dactylic hexameter ("This is the forest primeval; the murmuring pines and the hemlocks . . .") from Homer via the Swedish of Esias Tegnér. *The Song of Hiawatha* (1855) took its stories from the Ojibwe lore collected by Henry Rowe Schoolcraft, but took its meter from the Finnish synthetic folk-epic the *Kalevala,* whose author, Elias Lönnrot, Longfellow had met.

Longfellow also mastered that Italianate form, the sonnet, as few Americans have, making faithful versions of Michelangelo's notoriously dense sonnets, and using the form for his own most personal works (such as "The Cross of Snow," about the death by fire of his second wife). No continental literature or language, though, did more for him than Spanish. He was one of few American travelers to enter Spain in the 1820s, when it was a poor and comparatively dangerous country. He kept a diary in Spanish, and retained what one of his biographers calls a "fascination with *Hispanidad,*" both in peninsular and in New World manifestations. He translated Lope de Vega, Saint Teresa, Jorge Manrique, and Luis de Góngora, among others. His last finished poem, "The Bells of San Blas," imagines the secular and sacred messages in the winds at a Mexican port, where the chimes of a Catholic church are "a voice of the Past."

Of course, Longfellow used English models too. His most ambitious narrative project, *Tales of a Wayside Inn* (1860–1873), is a deliberately Chaucerian compilation in which friendly travelers "of different lands and speech" exchange stories in

verse: among them he places a "young Sicilian," a "Spanish Jew," a Norwegian musician, and a student "to whom all tongues and lands were known / And yet a lover
of his own." The first poem in *Tales,* "Paul Revere's Ride," remains the most famous, but the most inventive must be "The Saga of King Olaf," whose assembled
stanzas and songlike forms portray the warlike ruler who Christianized Norway.
The "Saga" pays homage not to its brutal king (who does not understand the patient "peace-cry" at the core of his own religion) but to the Scandinavian skalds
who shaped their rough history into intricate song.

We can see in *Tales,* and in the hybridized Swedish-American-Canadian *Evangeline,* and in fact throughout Longfellow's career, his sense that the American poetry he aimed to create, and did in fact create, would have to be syncretic, distinguished for its eclectic craft. "As the blood of all nations is mingling with our
own," says the schoolmaster in Longfellow's novella *Kavanagh,* "so will their
thoughts and feelings finally mingle in our literature." Longfellow also contributed to that hoped-for mingling as translator, critic, and anthologist. He produced—among many other books and essays—the enormous anthology *The Poets
and Poetry of Europe* (1845), spent some decades translating Dante's *Commedia* into
English (finished and published in 1867), and compiled the thirty-one-volume *Poems of Places* (1876–1879), with verse about locales from Newfoundland to Tasma-
nia, as if to bring all the Earth to America's shelves.

Modernist where Longfellow was traditional, agitated and purposely fragmentary where Longfellow worked hard to seem calm and clear, William Carlos Williams can easily sound like Longfellow's opposite. And yet the two poets share an
important goal: for all his "sometimes violent partisanship toward America" (as
he himself put it) Williams, too, created his distinctively American poetry in part
by looking beyond national and linguistic divisions. Williams spent "a year and a
half in Switzerland," when he was eleven and twelve, in a boarding school; Swiss
culture and French language, he remembered, "altered the whole perspective of
my life." As a young doctor in New Jersey he founded a club that would read aloud
"poems from the masters . . . in the original language in every case." Williams traveled to London, Paris, Antwerp, and Leipzig in 1909 for medical education, and
visited France and Italy in 1924, there meeting James Joyce, Ford Madox Ford,
and Valéry Larbaud, and rejoining his college classmate Ezra Pound. Returning to
Europe in 1927 to take his son to the same Swiss school he'd attended, Williams
turned that last trip into the novel *A Voyage to Pagany* (1928), whose narrator, Dr.
Evans, becomes "jealous of French painting" and imagines building a "miraculous
modern" art to answer the glory of Rome.

Williams's first innovative books of poetry and poetic prose—*Kora in Hell*
(1918), *Spring and All* (1923), *The Great American Novel* (1923)—took their stuttering rhetoric, their frequent changes of topic and perspective, and their collage
techniques from the paintings and writings of European cubists and early surrealists, especially from the Paris-based Spanish painter Juan Gris. "The French poets
have had no influence on me whatever," Williams claimed in 1932, but added, "I
have, however, been influenced by French painting and the French spirit which,

through my mother, is partly my own." Even as he called for an explosive break with older European literature, denouncing T. S. Eliot as a "subtle conformist," Williams in *Kora* acknowledged Rémy de Gourmont's "plea for a meeting of the nations," hoping to present there a newly American art.

Like Longfellow, Williams favored models of poetry as craft: the poet is someone who has become able to make, from the appropriate raw materials, a distinct object, "a small (or large) machine made of words." "Kéramos," one of Longfellow's best late productions, follows the art of "the potter at his task" (that is, by an obvious allegory, the poet) across the globe from Brittany to Japan. For Williams, the craft of poetry resembles "Fine Work with Pitch and Copper"—as he titled one poem—and the making of measured "strips" (poetic lines) with trained hand, eye, and ear. The craft of poetry, however, takes as its raw material the spoken language, which in Williams's America is a rough polyglot, "a living coral" that includes "English, a stream of Magyar, Polish," Caribbean bi- and trilingual speakers, a "Sicilian Emigrant's Song," a "Yiddishe springtime" to welcome Albert Einstein, and reminiscences from Norway in "Lofoten Islands." Williams even published poems consisting entirely of overheard speech: "Her milk don't seem to . . . / She's always hungry but . . . / She seems to *gain* all right, / I don't know" (thus the fragmentary, revealing monologue of a new father). Williams's vision of a demotic poetry for an immigrant-driven America resembles Whitman's, but in its notion of the poet's role in arranging and framing the language(s) he finds, it resembles Longfellow's as well.

Williams's near-lifelong attention to the Spanish-speaking world reflected his heritage: the son of a Francophile Puerto Rican mother and an English father whose business often took him to the Caribbean, Williams grew up speaking "Spanish and French . . . frequently" at home. Juan Ruiz's *Libro de buen amor* suggested to Williams a model for American letters, not least because it reflected the mix of traditions ("Moslem, Christian and Jew") in Moorish Spain. The first book of his own poems that Williams preserved, *The Tempers* (1913), included translations from the Spanish; subsequent volumes contained versions of Spanish folk ballads, the Spanish Civil War poet Miguel Hernández, the Puerto Rican Luis Palés Matos, and even a poem titled "Imaginary Translation from the Spanish," a kind of hymn to the republic of letters, whose twenty-four lines name Sappho, Villon, Goethe, and Li Po. The "lack of integration" between Spanish literature and "our British past," Williams argued, "gives us an opportunity" to "branch off into a new diction" for American verse.

Like Longfellow, Williams wrote again and again with "pagan wonder" about the seas that separated and connected nations. Williams depicted a mythic Caribbean for his versions of "Adam" and "Eve," a choppy Atlantic whose waves represent the tumult of capitalism in "The Yachts," and an ocean voyage in "The Descent of Winter," a verse-and-prose sequence composed during Williams's 1927 trip home. "The sea as I looked at it," Williams wrote in a contemporaneous letter, "is exactly the same sea, given the right day and weather, that Columbus, Eric the Red and the Puritans looked at. Thus it annihilates time and brings us right up beside these men in the imagination."

Sea voyages—Columbus's, or King Olaf's—could also convey conquerors bent on slaughter. "History begins for us with murder and enslavement, not with discovery," Williams wrote in *In the American Grain* (1925), an account of discoverers, *voyageurs*, early American outcasts, and public figures from the Vikings to Abraham Lincoln. Its aggressively dissonant poetic prose conjures up the United States as it looked before a national culture could regard its unity (however falsely) as a fait accompli. Longfellow, too, saw a nation not wholly assembled: his effortfully optimistic, polemical poem "The Building of the Ship" (1849) envisions the Union as a vessel under construction, requiring timber and other raw materials from "every climate, every soil."

Poets of ships and the sea, of polyglots, translation, and immigration, of an America still being put together, both Longfellow and Williams suggest that the perennial drive to create an American poetry for Americans is—when aesthetically successful, when intellectually interesting—connected to the literature and languages that come from the rest of the world. If Longfellow and Williams nonetheless stand for opposing principles, the reasons lie not with geography but with history—with their attitudes toward the past. For Longfellow, the strongest new poetry built on the old through respectful imitation, and only thus discovered or created for literature a new local character. "His 'European' culture and his native," said Henry James, "kept house together." For Williams, new writing could measure up to the best of the old (from whatever nation) only by confuting it, rejecting it, making up something new in its place: history was "a barrier which [the artist] must surmount."

"Listen, my children, and you shall hear," Longfellow wrote, and millions of children heard—of Paul Revere, Hiawatha and Minnehaha, Miles Standish, John Alden and Priscilla—in classrooms and parlors for more than a century. The man who began as a teacher of Romance languages became both an icon maker and an icon, after whom parks, schools, and even an entire neighborhood in Minneapolis were named. Inspired so often by translation, Longfellow's poetry also circulated internationally, in Europe, South America, Canada, China, and even Uganda (where Okot p'Bitek called "Hiawatha" a model). Less icon maker than iconoclast, Williams and his style proved harder to export: instead, he inspired generations of American poets, from Lorine Niedecker in Wisconsin to C. D. Wright in her "Ozark Odes," to situate regional speech in modernist forms.

Longfellow's gifts lay in assimilation and synthesis, in his sense of the sounds and rhythms of words, in English and in other tongues. The strongest objection to those gifts, in retrospect—the great difference between his projects and Whitman's—is that Longfellow undertook to make his poetry both international and American without trying to make poetry itself new. Edgar Allan Poe called Longfellow, absurdly, a plagiarist. "The reason of [Longfellow's] being overrated here," Margaret Fuller decided in 1845, "is because through his works breathes the air of other lands." No plagiarist by any literal definition, Longfellow risked becoming one of the artists Williams denounced, in capital letters, as "TRADITIONALISTS OF PLAGIARISM," who learned all they could from the past but never broke with it. While in *In the American Grain* Williams aligns himself instead with the cantankerous, restless Poe, he says of Longfellow, accurately, that he was "the apotheosis of all that had preceded him in America, to this extent, that he brought over the *most* from 'the other side'. . . Longfellow did it without genius, perhaps, but he did no more and no less than to bring the tower of the Seville Cathedral to Madison Square."

Bibliography: Charles Calhoun, *Longfellow: A Rediscovered Life* (Boston, 2004). A. Frank and C. Maas, *Transnational Longfellow* (Frankfurt, 2005). Christoph Irmscher, *Longfellow Redux* (Urbana, IL, 2006). Ivan Jaksic, *The Hispanic World and American Intellectual Life, 1820–1880* (New York, 2007). Henry Wadsworth Longfellow, *Poems and Other Writings,* ed. J. D. McClatchy (New York, 2000). Julio Marzán, *The Spanish American Roots of William Carlos Williams* (Austin, TX, 1994). William Carlos Williams, *Collected Poems,* 2 vols., ed. A. Walton Litz and Christopher MacGowan (New York, 1986–1988); *In the American Grain* (New York, 1956).

STEPHEN BURT

1827

The air is thick with rumors of a "new Religion," a "new Bible"

THE BOOK OF MORMON

By 1827 two powerful cultural forces were converging that conditioned the public reception of the most influential religious text ever produced by an American. First was the Second Great Awakening, the revisiting of the religious enthusiasm and spiritual seeking that had swept through the Puritan settlements of New England a generation before the Revolution. This time, spiritual awakening was augmented by a wider variety of denominational interest, an urgent sense of the imminence of the millennium, more uninhibited modes of expression, and an expansion of emphasis from personal renewal and regeneration to institutional reform or restoration. In other words, many seekers were looking not just for a mighty change in their own hearts, but for a dramatic change in the form that religion itself would take. As the biographer of Campbellite minister Walter Scott pointed out, spectacular manifestations of the coming dispensation were expected.

The second force was the prevalent interest in the origins of the American Indians. One popular theory connected them to the Lost Tribes of the Old Testament, the inhabitants of Israel who were carried off by the Assyrians and disappeared from history in the eighth century BC. This connection was suggested as early as the sixteenth century, by the Dominican friar Diego Duran, and saw print by 1607 in Gregorio García's *Origin of the Indians of the New World.* The first English-language publication on the subject was probably Thomas Thorowgood's *Jews in America, or, Probabilities that the Americans are of that Race* (1650), which influenced the Puritan John Eliot. In the era of the Revolution, James Adair published his influential *History of the American Indians* (London, 1775). No armchair historian, Adair lived and traded among America's southeastern tribes, and spent a substantial portion of his book arguing for their Israelite ancestry. Elias Boudinot followed suit in 1816 *(A Star in the West),* Ethan Smith in 1823 *(View of the Hebrews),* and Josiah Priest two years later *(The Wonders of Nature and Providence,* 1825). In 1825 Ethan Smith published a second edition of his 1823 *View of the Hebrews,* explaining that "the importance of the question, Where are the Ten Tribes of Israel?; the speedy sale of the first edition of the work; and the obtaining considerable additional evidence relative to the origin of the American Indians" had made another edition necessary. Smith's was but one in a long line of tracts and treatises that placed the American Indian into the history of the tribes of Israel. Many other theories were in competition, but believers and skeptics were coming to agree that Indians were descended from Jews.

Few in 1827 would have expected the questions over authentic religion and the Native American past to be answered authoritatively by one and the same miraculously appearing text. Nevertheless that is precisely the claim that was rooted in a farm boy's midnight visit to a hillside in upstate New York, on the night of the autumnal equinox of 1827. Twenty-one-year-old Joseph Smith had seven years earlier created a minor stir in his neighborhood when he claimed God and Christ had appeared to him in back of his family's farm, instructing him to remain aloof from organized religions because they were all "an abomination." Now, after a once-a-year series of visions that had begun in 1823 revolving around an ancient record of American aborigines, Joseph at last would take a step that would set him apart from dozens of contemporary ad hoc prophets and visionaries. At the same time, he set in motion events that would soon lead not just to more visionary claims but to the organization of a major Christian denomination.

Instructed by an angel named Moroni to visit a nearby hill, Joseph retrieved from there a set of gold plates, along with a set of "Interpreters" and other artifacts, and returned to his home. Over the next tempestuous twenty-one months, punctuated by harassment, poverty, relocation, and persecution, but also by the steadfast support of family and friends and the rapturous reception of numerous seekers, Joseph and a series of scribes produced the Book of Mormon. Joseph called it a translation from a thousand-year chronicle, written in "Reformed Egyptian" and spanning the millennium 600 BC to AD 400. When he at last offered it for sale to the public in March 1830, Joseph did not have the gold plates to buttress his claims that the text originated in antiquity and was transmitted by an angel, and then miraculously translated. But he had the affidavits of eleven men who claimed they had seen and, in eight cases, handled the plates. And he had the tangible product of his efforts and principal evidence for his authority as God's prophet, seer, and revelator.

The Book of Mormon may well be the most controversial text in the history of American literature. No consensus is likely to emerge on the details of its production, the authenticity of the history it narrates, or even its inherent value as sacred text or quality as religious literature. Mark Twain famously called it "chloroform in print," but even as staunch a critic of Joseph Smith as his psychobiographer Fawn Brodie realized that it had an impressive degree of coherence, learning, and imagination.

A mélange of genres, the Book of Mormon has long been colloquially referred to as "the golden bible," but comparisons with that sacred text conceal more than they reveal. Like the Bible, the Book of Mormon purports to be the word of God, delivered to his prophets, collected and transmitted to believers as a way of providing core beliefs and doctrines as well as liberal doses of history and prophecy. Unlike the Bible, the Book of Mormon is largely the product of one editorial hand. Its transmission history is relatively simple and direct: ancient American prophets wrote (or engraved) the record, which passed without intermediaries to a modern prophet, who transcribed it. Purporting to be for the most part a contemporary chronicle, recurrently situating itself relative to contemporary dates and places, it is fairly resistant to the allegorizing and mythologizing increasingly common among biblical readers and scholars. And perhaps most important, devoid as it is of most of Mormonism's distinguishing doctrines, the Book of Mormon has fundamental significance in Mormonism as a sign of Smith's prophetic authority, not as a guide to the faith or source of doctrine.

The Book of Mormon consists largely of the political, military, and religious history of the descendants of the Nephites, a people descended from one Lehi, through his son Nephi, who depart the Old World for the New six hundred years before Christ. Lehi leads a small clan to the Arabian coast, where his son Nephi builds a ship that conveys them to a site in the Western Hemisphere, taken by some Mormon scholars to be the west coast of Central America. Nephi inaugurates the record, and his one hundred pages or so are included unabridged in the final Book of Mormon. Subsequent writers (the stewardship of the plates was passed on, usually but not always, along patriarchal lines of descent) kept the plates for a thousand years after Nephi's death, but most of those writings were abridged by Mormon, a Nephite general and prophet who lived four centuries after Christ, witnessing the eradication of his people by their enemies before bequeathing the record to his son Moroni. Moroni completed the record, and buried it in the earth before he died. It was this same Moroni, Smith said, who appeared to him as a resurrected being, or angel, and led him to the depository of the plates.

The figure of Moroni therefore became the link between the ancient world described within the pages of the Book of Mormon and the contemporary circumstances surrounding its translation and publication. His purported life as a historical personage living in the Western Hemisphere in the early Christian centuries, eyewitness to the scenes of devastation and eventual apocalypse he described, together with his return to upstate New York in the 1820s as angelic messenger, burdened the Book of Mormon with inescapable claims of literal facticity. Unlike the dream-visions and writings of a Böhme or Swedenborg, the text Joseph Smith published was nearly impossible to allegorize away or consign to manageable mystical production. Its insistence on its own supernatural means of transmission, and on its historical veracity connected to ancient Native American origins, made it unique in the annals of American literature and in its twin effects of widespread derision and enthusiastic reception.

Thematically, the Book of Mormon interweaves a number of motifs in and out of its thousand years of narrated history. Some had the comfortable feel of the familiar, and convinced nineteenth-century readers of the essential Christianity of the book and its believers, appealing to them precisely on the basis of those elements of Christianity that many found to be lacking in contemporary versions. Those same elements continue to be seen by skeptics as prima facie evidence of nineteenth-century origins. Finally, some of the book's themes and values were powerfully attractive to a nationalistic ethos prevalent in the decades after the nation's founding.

First and foremost, the record purports to embody, both by its physical presence and through thematic treatment, the perseverance of revelation, in the sense of divine communication with living prophets. The first prophet in the Book of Mormon was Lehi, contemporary of Jeremiah, who fled the impending destruction of Jerusalem with his family at the express command of God. A "visionary man," Lehi recounts several visions that relate to both national destinies and personal survival. Nephi inherits the leadership of his people, records extensive visions of his own, and establishes the principle of direct, dialogic communication with God as his gift "unto all those who diligent seek him, . . . as well in times of old as in times to come." His people flourish to the extent that they believe in and respect "the spirit of revelation and the spirit of prophecy," which informs their exodus from the Old World and their affairs in the New, the conduct of their righteous wars against the dissenting "Lamanites," and the management of their "church."

Most anomalous and seemingly anachronistic is the Book of Mormon's insistence that a church was formed among Nephi's descendants that preached a familiar Christian gospel centuries before Jesus' birth in the Old World. Nephite kings, prophets, and missionaries teach a version of Christianity that anticipates nineteenth-century Restoration movements, emphasizing faith, repentance, baptism, and the gift of the Holy Ghost. A series of prophecies, beginning around 600 BC, first make note of Christ's eventual coming; subsequent visions and revelations make known his name, place of birth, and even the name of his mother. The dramatic and theological nexus of the Book of Mormon occurs four-fifths of the way through the narrative, when the risen Christ appears to a righteous throng of Nephites amid great destructions that occur at the time of his crucifixion.

Other themes that many of Smith's contemporaries found particularly resonant included a quasi-Pelagianism that denies original sin (and hence infant baptism) and celebrates the atonement of Christ as a saving gesture that made men "free forever, . . . to act for themselves and not to be acted upon." The record also emphatically affirms the Americas as Zion, a promised land, and the site of the New Jerusalem.

Much of the nineteenth-century anti-Mormonism that culminated in pogroms and expulsions of the Latter-day Saints was aggravated by the Book of Mormon, insofar as it struck many as an affront to Bible-based Christianity, was closely tied to an offensively Pentecostal parade of charismatic gifts and angelic visitations, and was the most conspicuous evidence invoked for Joseph Smith's divine calling. The experience of Missouri Mormon Charles Allen, who was tarred and feathered because he would not leave Missouri or deny the Book of Mormon, was taken by Mormons as typifying their dilemma.

In the crowded religious marketplace of the Second Awakening, Mormons considered the Book of Mormon to be the "ensign to the nations" prophesied by Isaiah, and marketed it aggressively. The initial 1830 printing of 5,000 copies did not sell well, but they were distributed effectively enough that three new printings totaling about 10,000 copies were called for during Smith's lifetime. He was killed by a mob in Carthage, Illinois, in 1844.

Believing scholars find abundant textual evidence indicative of ancient authorship, ranging from complex poetic patterns (like chiasmus), other Hebraisms, and parallels with Old World festivals and coronation assemblies, to plausible reconstructions of Lehi's exodus and a striking example of archaeological evidence that confirms a Book of Mormon place name. Nonbelievers find the detailed Christology, preoccupation with nineteenth-century theological concerns, and anachronisms (for example, horses and steel) to be insurmountable problems. Such debates have meant the book's complexity and richness as a literary and religious text are only beginning to receive serious attention. Likewise, its importance as a pivotal document of nineteenth-century cultural history has been largely ignored. Today, more than 130 million copies of the Book of Mormon have been printed, in more than one hundred languages, making it by far the most widely distributed book ever produced by an American.

Bibliography: Fawn Brodie, *No Man Knows My History: The Life of Joseph Smith,* 2nd ed. (New York, 1995). Terryl L. Givens, *By the Hand of Mormon: American Scripture That Launched a New World Religion* (Oxford, 2003). Roger G. Kennedy, *Hidden Cities: The Discovery and Loss of Ancient North American Civilization* (New York, 1994). Scot Facer Proctor and Maurine Jensen Proctor, *The Revised and Enhanced History of Joseph Smith by His Mother* (Salt Lake City, 1996). Ethan Smith, *View of the Hebrews: 1825 2nd Edition,* ed. Charles D. Tate, Jr. (Provo, UT, 1996). Dan Vogel, *Indian Origins and the Book of Mormon* (Salt Lake City, 1986).

TERRYL L. GIVENS

1828

David Walker proclaims that "the children of Africa"
will have to "take their stand among the nations of the earth"

WHITE SUPREMACY AND BLACK SOLIDARITY

David Walker, a black American, was born free in Wilmington, North Carolina, circa 1796. As a young man he traveled extensively through the South, observing the myriad injustices of the slave system, and settled for a time in Charleston, South Carolina, home of a politically active African Methodist Episcopal (A.M.E.) church that espoused racial egalitarianism. In 1822 in Charleston, Denmark Vesey's insurrectionist plot was uncovered, resulting in the severe repression of independent black churches and thus making autonomous black collective action extremely difficult. By 1825 Walker had moved to Boston, where he joined a politically engaged and organized black community. Late in 1828 he delivered an oration to one of the most prominent local black antislavery groups, the Massachusetts General Colored Association, proclaiming the efficacy of "any thing which may have the least tendency to meliorate *our* miserable condition." Although firm and proud, the speech gave little hint of what was to come from Walker: his incendiary and, soon enough, notorious *Appeal, in Four Articles, together with a Preamble, To the Coloured Citizens of the World, but in particular, and very expressly, to those of the United States of America*, published in 1829.

The *Appeal* was the most militant antislavery document that had ever been published. Article 1 describes the core features of oppression under slavery and argues that blacks have a duty to resist their oppressors, using violence if necessary. Article 2 argues that black ignorance is a key obstacle to a unified fight against racial injustice. Article 3 exposes the ways in which the white Christian ministry upholds the slave system. And Article 4 attacks the American Colonization Society's scheme to repatriate free blacks to Africa, arguing that the ulterior motive behind this plan is to remove free blacks from North America so that the blacks who remain will be more securely held in slavery.

Slave rebellions and conspiracies had occurred before the *Appeal* was published, most famously the Haitian Revolution and Vesey's plot. But while previous pamphlets had only obliquely condoned or excused insurrection, Walker's book was an open defense of such revolts. The book was distributed covertly throughout the South via a loosely associated interracial, though mostly black, communication network and ultimately found its way into the hands of slaves and their allies. When Southern officials learned of the book, the response was swift: a bounty was immediately placed on Walker's head; Georgia and South Carolina passed laws against incendiary publications (Georgia made the circulation of such documents a capital offense); North Carolina and Georgia prohibited teaching slaves to read; and a number of Southern states took action to prevent free blacks and slaves from interacting and to keep blacks from assembling at all without white supervision. Walker was well aware of the dangers involved in publishing a document such as his, noting in the text that he expected that some would act to imprison or even kill him and that he was willing to die in the effort to free his people from bondage. The *Appeal* was in its third printing in 1830 when Walker died, probably due to tuberculosis, though foul play cannot be completely ruled out.

The *Appeal* is not a formal treatise. It is a rallying cry or a manifesto, closer to a sermon than a learned disputation. Filled with indignation and laments, vitriol and sarcasm, its rhetoric suggests that it was meant to be delivered orally to an audience rather than read privately. Its primary objective was to raise consciousness and provoke action. A secondary aim was to refute Thomas Jefferson's speculations about the natural inferiority of blacks and his claim that American slavery was milder and more benevolent than the ancient slavery of Egypt, Greece, or Rome. Jefferson's *Notes on the State of Virginia* (1787), in particular its Query 14, was a key source of racist ideology, making the former president, in Walker's eyes, an enemy of blacks.

Contrary to Jefferson's assertions, Walker insisted that blacks in the United States had been treated worse than any other people in the history of the world. The American slave system was nakedly exploitative. Blacks were excluded from all positions of honor, authority, and public trust. They were denied the right to own land or to be secure in their possessions. They were prevented from acquiring even the most rudimentary education. The slave trade broke up families, separating husbands from wives, parents from children. Whites were cruel and violent toward blacks, even murdering them in cold blood. And, to add insult to injury, whites claimed that blacks were subhuman and that God had created the dark race to be the servants of whites. In view of their record, Walker proclaimed that white Christians, from antiquity to the present, were the most unjust, greedy, cruel, hypocritical, and tyrannical people on earth.

Walker was sharply critical of the role that white Christian preachers played in reinforcing the institution of slavery, by, for instance, teaching slaves that it was their duty to obey their masters or invoking the curse of the descendants of Ham. Even when blacks had become Christians, he noted, they still were not granted the same rights as whites. Moreover, the profession of the Christian faith—with its command to treat others as one would wish to be treated—by a people who kept blacks enslaved was pure hypocrisy. Whites had effectively turned the Christian gospel into an instrument for subjugating others.

Nevertheless, Walker remained a devout Christian, rooted in the evangelical egalitarianism of the A.M.E. Church. He insisted that Christ's message is universal and should be taught to all peoples across the globe regardless of race. In fact, Walker put Christian theology to liberatory ends, explaining that slavery and racial inequality were inconsistent with Scripture. Drawing on black American homiletic oratory, he spoke in the familiar voice of a prophet, even suggesting that God was literally speaking through him. He repeatedly warned whites of God's impending wrath on them for their crimes, and he often referred to blacks as God's people. He said African Americans were God's people not because they were black but because they were oppressed, and that God is a God of justice who punishes the unjust and protects the faithful. Walker foretold the coming of a black messiah who would unify and redeem the African race.

The *Appeal* was addressed explicitly to blacks. But it is clear that the book was also written for whites. It was, in part, a jeremiad that urged whites to act justly before God took his vengeance—probably in the form of a violent black insurrection or a civil war. Although Walker encouraged whites to mend their ways, he doubted that many would do so. He thought whites had been corrupted by avarice, arrogance, and racist ideology, and he spoke of them as having a "hardened heart" like the biblical pharaoh who refused to free the people of Israel. In more measured passages, Walker referred to the oppressors of black people as white slaveholders and their abettors. But at times he wrote as if *all* whites were oppressors, frequently referring to them as "devils" and "natural enemies" of blacks. But these unqualified verbal assaults were merely rhetorical. Walker saw white depravity not as an inherent trait, but as the result of correctable pride and greed. In fact, he welcomed the assistance of white abolitionists (provided they were not associated with the American Colonization Society), and it is clear that he received such assistance with the publication and circulation of his book.

Walker did not find whites alone blameworthy for black oppression; he also harshly criticized blacks, who he felt were often servile, treacherous, and cowardly and therefore complicit in their own oppression. He regarded ignorance as the principal cause of these vices. What blacks were ignorant of was not so much their group history or national culture, but God's will. In particular, they did not properly understand the divine moral law. Many failed to recognize that whites had no right to hold them in bondage or to treat them as less than equals. Among the negative consequences of such ignorance were that blacks were made more vulnerable to proslavery propaganda; that they were prone to self-hatred and servility; that disunity was easily fostered; and that some were misled into collaborating with the enemy. Educated blacks should remedy this widespread lack of moral knowledge among their people, Walker said; they had a duty to educate the young and the benighted. And one of the ways he would have them carry out this obligation was to circulate the *Appeal* among (or read it to) those ignorant of its urgent message. Walker does not appear to have been concerned that this stance was elitist or condescending or that the differences in status between free blacks and slaves would undermine the collective effort. Indeed, the *Appeal* encouraged all blacks, slave and free, to work together to end their oppression at the hands of whites. He argued that the abolition of slavery was a necessary condition for blacks anywhere to have freedom, prosperity, and dignity.

Walker held that there was an absolute duty to fight against injustice, and that oppression was no excuse for shirking it: "The man who would not fight under our Lord and Master Jesus Christ, in the glorious and heavenly cause of freedom and of God . . . ought to be kept with all of his children or family, in slavery, or in chains, to be butchered by his *cruel enemies*." Moreover, he advocated the use of political violence if whites refused to change their ways. Indeed, he pointed out that the right to revolt against an unjust regime is asserted in Jefferson's own Declaration of Independence: "But when a long train of abuses and usurpation, pursuing invariably the same object, evinces a design to reduce them under absolute despotism, it is their *right*, it is their *duty*, to throw off such government."

Rebutting the charge that blacks were inherently docile and thus unlikely to fight for their freedom, he claimed that blacks in fact had a repressed urge to kill whites that, once released, would be difficult to contain. Whites were all too willing to murder blacks to keep them in bondage—or for mere amusement—and therefore blacks must be prepared to take white lives if necessary. Blacks needed to find the courage to risk being killed rather than remain enslaved. With injunctions such as these, Walker was articulating an ethics of the oppressed: if blacks were to regain their self-respect and freedom, then they had to become a more self-reliant, educated, unified, militant, courageous, and proud people. Without these virtues, they could not gain God's full approbation and their oppressors could not be defeated.

Considering the legacy of the *Appeal,* some commentators have described it as the founding black nationalist document. There is some truth in this, but it is also misleading. The *Appeal* was antedated, by a few months, by Robert Alexander Young's lesser-known, nationalist-oriented book, *The Ethiopian Manifesto: Issued in Defence of the Black Man's Rights in the Scale of Universal Freedom* (1829). More important, to see the *Appeal* as only a black nationalist document would miss the fact that it is also a key text in a different tradition of African American political thought. Black nationalists, such as Martin Delany, Marcus Garvey, and Malcolm X, have regarded America as an incorrigible white-supremacist nation and thus have urged those of African descent to work together to build a separate black polity. But there is another tradition, sometimes called integrationist, that, while also favoring black solidarity, has insisted that such solidarity be used to transform the United States into a true democracy, where blacks and whites can live together on terms of equality and mutual respect. The canonical figures in this latter tradition include Frederick Douglass, W. E. B. Du Bois, and Martin Luther King, Jr.

Walker did not advocate black emigration to Africa or to anywhere else. Rather, he insisted that the United States was the "home" and "native land" of American blacks, and that they had as much right to remain in the country as did whites. He made no unambiguous call for black collective self-determination in North America, at least not beyond urging political solidarity based on a common oppression and a commitment to overcome it. He did claim that Egypt was the cradle of civilization and that the ancient Egyptians were black or "colored" — to rebut the charge (by Jefferson, among others) that blacks had made no great achievements, and to build a sense of pride in a group that was constantly denigrated.

The publication of the *Appeal* in itself makes clear that Walker favored open political protest. Although he defended violent rebellion and explicitly rejected tactics of accommodation, he nevertheless engaged in moral persuasion and called on whites to repent. In terms of fundamental political values, Walker was not a racial separatist. He believed racial reconciliation in America was still possible and desirable: "Treat us then like men, and we will be your friends. And there is not a doubt in my mind, but that the whole of the past will be sunk into oblivion, and we yet, under God, will become a united and happy people. The whites may say it is impossible, but remember that nothing is impossible with God." But, it should be added, Walker insisted that this reconciliation could not, and should not, occur until blacks and whites were treated as equals and the nation acknowledged its past injustices.

Bibliography: Bernard Boxill, "Two Traditions in African American Political Philosophy," *Philosophical Forum* 24 (1992–93): 119–135. Peter P. Hinks, *To Awaken My Afflicted Brethren: David Walker and the Problem of Antebellum Slave Resistance* (University Park, PA, 1997). Wilson Jeremiah Moses, *Black Messiahs and Uncle Toms: Social and Literary Manipulations of a Religious Myth,* rev. ed. (University Park, PA, 1993). Darryl Scriven, *A Dealer of Old Clothes: Philosophical Conversations with David Walker* (Lanham, MD, 2007). Sterling Stuckey, ed., *The Ideological Origins of Black*

Nationalism (Boston, 1972). David Walker, *Appeal to the Coloured Citizens of the World,* ed. Sean Wilentz (New York, 1995).

TOMMIE SHELBY

1830, May 21
Jim Crow jumps the American stage

ROGUE BLACKNESS

As late as the first quarter of the nineteenth century, the rising mass of racial feelings that Americans endured had few categorizing icons to help them test their attitudes. Othello and Sambo had risen as characters in the Renaissance Mediterranean and in Caribbean lore; North America added Dinah and Coal Black Rose. Each icon appeared where flowing populations crossed. Each figured a newly calming blackness to rouse and souse the dominating culture's anxieties. But none addressed the perplexities a substantial black presence caused in an unequal America half a hundred years after the agreement that "all men are created equal." That's when America's second cultural generation pieced together a more oppositional icon of blackness whose rogue features still endure, seeming now both natural and ever unassimilable. Can we find the threshold this rogue crossed into American notice?

On May 21, 1830, in Louisville, an itinerant white actor inserted a black character into a play based on a two-year-old short story, "The Rifle." Like the play, the culture, and the population it reckoned, this new character was tentative and transitional. The ads called him "Sambo," but he was starting to dance out and sing about a troubling trickster new to the theater, if not to the blacks beyond its threshold, whose folklore called him "Jim Crow." It would take a few years for Sambo to morph into the character he probed, whose dance he jumped. But that gradual inhabiting of the performed personality was critical. Sambo-becoming-Jim-Crow was a shift from head-scratching demurral and stuttering deference to the rude cackles of insurgence. Instead of Sambo's shuffle, Jim Crow leapt to flash the bird at antagonists black and white. This trouble would define the culture it seized.

Was the character changing? Then his story must also. And its experience changed the people connected to it. William Leggett, original author of "The Rifle," went on independently in the same years as Jim Crow's emergence to theorize a conscience for radical democracy in New York newspaper editorials, culminating in his conversion to abolition. Leggett's change matched the arc of his story as it slid to script the experience it registered. Race had not been on Leggett's mind when he wrote "The Rifle." Leggett cataloged sharpshooters in deerskin, an upright young doctor, a weeping mother, a maiden with a breaking heart. But blackness was not yet part of the story.

The white actor who pricked blackness into the tale, yanking its locale from prairie to bluegrass, was an ambitious twenty-two-year-old named Thomas D. Rice who worked comedy in Sam Drake's troupe. Rice had grown up at Catherine Market on New York's Lower East Side, where ethnic diversity was as rich then as now. During the decade after that first performance, Rice relentlessly transformed the verbal tics ("Yah! Yah!" backtalk, and puns) and embodied gestures (irrepressible leaping akimbo) of "Jim Crow" into a broadly recognized type. Playing to black and white publics magnetized by his provocations, Rice brought both this character and his fans across a threshold. Jim Crow came into the house where all could rehearse the role, realize its incessant resistance to fit, and practice their reaction. Some saw themselves, or an energy they wanted to share, in Jim Crow's volatile integration. Others saw in him a nightmare to outlaw. At its beginning, as now, this rogue blackness was a lightning rod summoning conflicting attitudes about radical inclusion, about real democracy.

To act Jim Crow was to knot together extant strands of song and sass, dance and dialect that excited and merged with those ideas of fraternity lurking in Atlantic performance traditions for more than a century. Macheath, in John Gay's 1728 *The Beggar's Opera,* and the 1820s larks of Tom and Jerry were earlier, partial instances of this spirit's surfacing. Their crossings continued as complexly as they began. By delineating intensely local figures—Jim Crow certainly seemed cisatlantic—frontier performers bootlegged in European memories of class disdain along with the African counterpush that would batten against the developing republic. Revenant codes remained radioactive beneath the rags of Jim Crow, peeping and hiding like toes from his boots. Sometimes in view, more often hiding out, they enacted rather than resolved their puzzles.

All that spring of 1830, while Sam Drake's troupe played Louisville, a new American figure steadily dawned on them. Their youngest comedian was winning cheers singing "Coal Black Rose." Rice had learned this routine back in New York's low theaters, watching George Washington Dixon sketch black courting capers in urban oyster cellars. Rose and her beaus were roisterous alternatives to Othello. These oyster gluttons differed from the Venetian general not least in that their New York blackness, seeming separate, was content, not anguished. Rather than practice Othello's attempted integration and self-cleansing suicide, Dixon suggested that those like Rose would proliferate like bugs in cellar sawdust. They would fulfill the primary, etymological function of the proletariat. They would breed apart. But when Rice started acting Jim Crow he brought them upstairs. Not self-pitying like Mungo in Bickerstaffe's *The Padlock* ("My pain is dere game . . . Me wish to de Lord me was dead"); not comically ineffectual and separate, like Rose; neither self-effacing, like Sambo, nor self-eradicating like Othello—Jim Crow's roguery persisted wilily. It was going awry, not away.

Except for its chorus ("I wheel about and turn about and do jis so, and ebery time I wheel about, I jump Jim Crow"), we cannot specify the song's lyrics in May 1830. By June, however, Rice was advertising lyrics by the black New Orleans street singer Pickiune Butler, along with versions of "Jim Crow" that took the character to the capital (to instruct Old Hickory on government), to the theater (noticing what nonsense passed as real), and home (confronting his partner, Miss Dina Crow). Just one year on, Jim Crow was sufficiently proverbial that the Richmond *Enquirer* could deploy the phrase "jump Jim Crow" to name radical political instability: "gone over to the opposition." That's what white youths acting black must have seemed three decades before Emancipation. By 1832, printed lyrics showed Jim Crow advocating freedom for blacks and supporting force to win it. Jim Crow entered, ate, and drank where and when he wanted, took a front seat in every form of public transportation, danced with and kissed whom he desired, and warned bigots not to oppose him:

> I'm for freedom,
> And for Union altogether
> Aldough I'm a black man,
> De white is call'd my broder.
> . . .
> An I caution all de white dandies
> Not to come in my way,
> For as sure as they insult me,
> Dey'll in de gutter lay.

Already, Jim Crow was stepping out of his song to shoulder Sambo aside. Already, we sense the unseatable energy that would frighten keepers of the peace and turn comfortable cohorts of every hue against Jim Crow. His politics appeared as anarchic as Leggett's radical democracy, which *its* opponents were smearing as Loco Foco and Know Nothing. Already, the blackface extravaganzas, then plays, that Rice was starting to write were nestling Jim Crow's yack and cackle, clearing room where he might wheel about. Already, Jim Crow was instigating a viable alternative to the repertoire Americans had inherited about gladiators and capers among the English squirearchy. Already, the problems bringing this mockup of rogue blackness into the house were apparent. Its quickening momentum obscured both whatever African legacy remained and the ragged people, black and white, whose smiles nurtured it. Taking on its own life, it already provided talismans of blackness that people with more power could warp to their prejudices. And they did. Already, the vernacular scripts of rogue blackness were furthering a skein of conflicted meanings for a complex alliance.

Subsequent authors who have tongued this toothache behind the American smile are often those who matter most. The first words of Frederick Douglass's first autobiography copped Jim Crow's come-on:

> Rice: "Come listen all you galls and boys / I's jist from Tuckyhoe."
> Douglass: "I was born in Tuckahoe."

Douglass, like Rice, surely knew that Tuckahoe was the birthplace of Thomas Jefferson, Mr. "Created Equal" himself.

Nathaniel Hawthorne first noted "gingerbread figures, in the shape of Jim

Crow" in Williamstown, Massachusetts, as he wrote in his journal on Independence Day, 1838. Thirteen years later, he, like the urchin Ned Higgins who shares his initials in *The House of the Seven Gables* (1851), digested Jim Crow in his fiction. Hepzibah Pyncheon's first commercial act in her penny shop is to sell Higgins a Jim Crow cookie. Then the novel returns nine more times to the youth's appetite for spiced blackness.

Jim Crow cooked blackness, but Dan Emmett and the conventional minstrel shows following in the wake of T. D. Rice standardized the product as they spread the franchise. The Jim Crow that Rice delineated was a runaway slave, surviving on the lam with backtalk and, when words failed, biting and butting. After the winter of 1842, Dan Emmett and the minstrel show coarsened those hijinks by returning to Dixie's not-forgotten old times. Rice had Jim Crow as a journeyman looking for wages. Minstrel shows had rogue slaves wishing black flies would bite Massa's horse on the south end, dumping the old man's broken neck in the ditch. The variations were mounting.

And American literature fed on that compounding diet just like Hawthorne's Higgins did. Melville's Ishmael represented his voyage on the *Pequod,* quite literally, in the display type of a minstrel theater bill. The famous shaving scene at the center of Melville's "Benito Cereno" (1855) tried to live up to the grave humor that Dan Emmett and Eph Horn had been performing on the minstrel stage for a decade and a half. This same blackface-derived shaving scene would still be reincarnate in Charles Chesnutt's "The Doll" (1912). The primary trickster in Melville's *The Confidence-Man* (1857) was Black Guinea—who caught pennies in his mouth, just as James Brown would still be doing on the streets of Macon, Georgia, at *his* career's outset a century on. Harriet Beecher Stowe exemplifies the carrying capacity of this material. She had to absorb minstrelsy's romantic racialism through social osmosis because her social position proscribed attending shows. Topsy's "summersets"—indeed, her whole position as a living conundrum for the Ophelias of America—could never have happened had it not been for Jim Crow's wheeling leaps. Black and white, all the plantation figures in *Uncle Tom's Cabin* (1851) were minstrel stereotypes—except Stowe's eponym. She claimed Tom rose from her Christian dream life. Then she folded Tom's passive aggression back onto the blackface tradition.

Tom Rice never played the minstrel stage that was, by the mid-1840s, supplanting his narrative drama with a hifalutin' interlocutor vainly struggling to curb the noise of olios and walkarounds while end men clicked bones and walloped tambourines. But Rice notably did play Uncle Tom at the end of his career. He had acted his own street version of Othello—quickening untold latencies in the old story—on the same bill with the first staged production of *Uncle Tom's Cabin.* And a few years later, when he took on the role that Stowe may unconsciously have named after him, the *New York Tribune* studded Rice's performance with stunning approval. Noting "*the deep sentiment of human brotherhood* that lies beneath the brittle transparencies of all political ties," the anonymous reviewer wrote that *Uncle Tom's Cabin* manifested "a gross, robust unreasoning sentiment of hatred to slavery in the *very ground tier of society,* that may be the germ of a tremendous so-cial explosion" (January 17, 1854).

Even after the Civil War that this review anticipated, the uncertain effect on the ground tier remains the central concern when blackface roguery rouses per-formance. The 1854 warning points to what we might call mudsill mutuality—a recognition among disaffected audiences that they share oppression unevenly and that black roguery, enacting the worst-case scenario, diagnoses their con-dition. But this is just one response. Many observers have insisted that rogue performance increases white rage at black competition for jobs and cultural at-tention, heightens whites' anxious projection of supposed black sexuality, and ridicules black difference. Uncertainty necessarily provokes vividly conflicting responses. And crowds gather for fights—as when *The Adventures of Huckleberry Finn* shows Arkansas townspeople crowding to see blackened con men act their vulgar Royal Nonesuch, "ring-streaked-and-striped, all sorts of colors, as splen-did as a rain-bow." These multihued provocations are politically risky. They dare groups, testing their power, to control them. This struggle for authority forces a rhythm of effect, a popping up and a stamping out, not yet exhausted. Hiding out in successive generations, blackface roguery does its work and awaits its comple-tion. To paraphrase Ralph Ellison, who was describing pop zoot-suiters strutting as they emerged from New York's underground in his novel *Invisible Man* (1952), this roguery comes in the house to run and dodge the forces of history rather than attempt a dominating stand.

Bibliography: Dale Cockrell, *Demons of Disorder: Early Blackface Minstrels and Their World* (Cambridge, 1997). William Leggett, "The Rifle," in *The Atlantic Souvenir: A Christmas and New Year's Offering* (Philadelphia, 1828). W. T. Lhamon, Jr., *Jump Jim Crow: Plays, Lyrics, and Street Prose of the First Atlantic Popular Culture* (Cambridge, MA, 2003); *Raising Cain: Blackface Performance from Jim Crow to Hip Hop* (Cambridge, MA, 1998). Eric Lott, *Love and Theft: Blackface Minstrelsy and the American Working Class* (New York, 1993). Sean Wilentz, "Jacksonian Abolitionist: The Conversion of William Leggett," in *The Liberal Persuasion: Arthur Schlesinger, Jr., and the Challenge of the American Past,* ed. John Patrick Diggins (Princeton, 1997).

W. T. LHAMON, JR.

1831, March 5
Chief Justice John Marshall writes Indian people into the United States

THE *CHEROKEE NATION* DECISION

This is a story about the law. For me, however, it begins elsewhere, with a cryptic little book, measuring three by five inches and covered with a crumbling leather binding. Open it to the title page—*A History of the Black Hawk War* by "An Old Resident of the Military Tract" (1832)—and you will think it a historical mem-oir, published locally at Fort Armstrong, Iowa. The Black Hawk War, which "opened up" the Mississippi Midwest to white settlement, did indeed take place in 1832. Continue reading, however, and you will find not history, but sixty-three pages of ciphered and mnemonic figures:

Indian

1   (I) g t t e a g o * w c t chief o # # t o o a t p
2   (I) # I I —-
3   (I) a a p Indians —- (II) I w a a r * —-# VI —-%
4   (II) y w s y t a p a Indians

And so it continues, through four tantalizing sections (Indian, Squaw, Warrior, and Braves). The book feels a bit like Poe, dark, desperate, and strange. Each section represents a role in the rituals of a white fraternal group that pretended, in its secret ceremonies, to be the Indian people so recently dispossessed in the war. Holding it, I *feel* the 1830s, furtive and confused, a time of dark lanterns and sinister killings, treasure hunting and magic, secret ciphers, and houses (full of dead people and greasy playing cards) floating intact on the cresting Mississippi, with plenty of sorry to go around.

A fulcrum moment, these 1830s, of precarious cultural shifts, when the generative American contradiction between *killing Indians* and *becoming them* still lay close to the surface. That contradiction, long embodied in captivity narratives, frontier folk mythologies, and performances of Indian "American" identities, erupted in the 1830s into the realm of law. The eruption came in response to the crisis of an American nation that fully believed in its imperial destiny, yet spoke of its dominations only haltingly. It structures the lives, literatures, and politics of American Indian people—and thus *all* Americans—to the present day.

One phrase—"domestic dependent nations"—reordered the world of the 1830s. Authored by John Marshall, the chief justice of the U.S. Supreme Court, the three words translated the older cultural contradictions into new law and politics. If killing the Indian had allowed settlers to claim land and proclaim independence, "becoming" the Indian had let those same settlers incorporate themselves *into* the land, and lodge the ancient memory of Indian aboriginality in American souls. The new words applied (in reverse) the same contradictory structure of logic to Indian people themselves: somehow, they could be distinct nations—and yet be simultaneously incorporated within the American body politic. As nations, they might claim to be independent—and yet they were in fact dependent on the federal government.

John Marshall named Indian people as "domestic dependent nations" in the second of three closely linked legal cases involving the Cherokees. In the first case, *Johnson v. M'Intosh* (1823), Marshall wrote an unnecessarily elaborate opinion in which he codified the "discovery doctrine." He argued that, in the wake of contact between New World and Old, title to Indian lands no longer resided with Indian people but accrued instead to the European nation claiming first discovery. Indian people could sell the "claim" to their land, but only to the discovering sovereign—or a rightful successor, in most cases (conveniently) the United States. Marshall used this "discovery" argument carelessly, to prop up the land claims of

Virginia militiamen, former comrades during the War for Independence. This set the legal terms for the second case, *Cherokee Nation v. Georgia.*

In 1828, the discovery of gold on Cherokee lands led the state of Georgia to try to eliminate the Cherokees. Earlier, Georgians had forsworn territorial claims in return for a federal promise to remove the Cherokees as soon as was practical. The passage in 1830 of the Indian Removal Act—which encouraged tribes to exchange their eastern land for territory west of the Mississippi—suggested that the time for Cherokee removal was at hand. President Andrew Jackson was more than sympathetic.

Before the violent dispossessions of Removal, however, Cherokees, Georgians, and the federal government fought over their respective sovereignties. The federal government claimed power over the individual states—which meant the continued validity of federally negotiated Indian treaties (with the Cherokees, for example). South Carolina and other states in the South claimed primacy for themselves, insisting that they could "nullify" federal laws they deemed unconstitutional. And within their state borders, Georgians confronted the Cherokee Nation, an independent society replete with a constitution, representative government, educational institutions, written language, and other appurtenances of "civilization," including chattel slavery.

Asserting its own state sovereignty, Georgia could hardly embrace the rising sovereign nation of the Cherokees. In 1828 the Georgia legislature passed an act to make Cherokee territory part of and subject to the laws of Georgia. The following year, a second act added a provision "to annul all laws and ordinances made by the Cherokee nation of Indians." In 1830 Georgia seized and sentenced to death George Tassells, a Cherokee man who had killed another Cherokee within the bounds of the Cherokee Nation—a case in which the Cherokee justice system had clear jurisdiction. After a failed appeal at the state level (Georgians used the "doctrine of discovery" to insist on their own jurisdiction), the Cherokees sought help from the U.S. Supreme Court, and John Marshall ordered a stay of execution. Georgia defied the Court (and suddenly, a dry legal narrative turns sinister: emergency sessions of the legislature, a rushed message on horseback from the governor—probably a dark lantern involved somewhere—and a hasty Christmas Eve hanging from a tree in a lonely field).

The Supreme Court said little about the legalized murder of Tassells, however, preferring to concentrate on *Cherokee Nation v. Georgia,* filed only days before by Cherokee chief John Ross in an effort to overturn Georgia's assertions of sovereignty. In the debate over the Indian Removal Act, many advocates insisted that Indian people *did* hold title to their lands—and thus national and territorial sovereignty, recognized through treaties and land purchases. The basis for this understanding, however, had been effectively undermined by the discovery doctrine. Brandishing a Supreme Court decision, Removal advocates argued that Indians had no title to their land and could be evicted at the pleasure of the United States, inheritor of the European rights of discovery.

Marshall ignored both the discovery doctrine and the defiance of Georgia (which refused to appear before the court), focusing instead on the question of jurisdiction. He framed the case around a grand historical narrative, and situated the Cherokees at a decisive turning point, one that required political recalibration. "If courts were permitted to indulge their sympathies," he wrote,

> a case better calculated to excite them can scarcely be imagined. A people once numerous, powerful, and truly independent, found by our ancestors in the quiet and uncontrolled possession of an ample domain, gradually sinking beneath our superior policy, our arts and our arms, have yielded their lands by successive treaties, each of which contains a solemn guarantee of the residue, until they retain no more of their formerly extensive territory than is deemed necessary to their comfortable subsistence. To preserve this remnant, the present application is made.

The key words—"independent," "powerful," "uncontrolled possession"—make the beginnings of his narrative clear. Indians were distinct, autonomous peoples ("nations" in a European sense). They formed alliances and negotiated treaties. The proper executive-branch office for Indian affairs was the War Department and the proper political relation was diplomacy or formal conflict. In the 1830s, however, Americans began saying out loud that after decades of conflicts, land cessions, removals, and dislocations, those relations had changed. Witness the key terms that seemed to shift the ground: "sinking beneath," "yielded their lands," "preserve this remnant."

The first rhetoric reflects a distinct form of colonial practice, characterized by warfare, treaties, a nation-to-nation relationship, and a cultural imagination that played with Indian otherness. The second calls into being a new and different kind of colonialism. Indian people were consolidated and segregated in regional spaces—the so-called Indian territory—the better to manage, reeducate, and incorporate them. This segregation enabled the development of American imperial governance based on the demographic shift from Indian to white, and the political transitions from mixed territory to white state and from Indian "nation" to Indian "tribe." The militiamen hunting down Black Hawk in 1832 engaged in exactly this process of containment. The results were clear: the states of Iowa, Illinois, and Wisconsin, the removal of many Indians from the Midwest, and a secret fraternal order with a book of coded rituals.

In this new form of colonialism, Indian nations could be viewed as something like states, though vastly inferior. The proper executive branch office for their oversight was now the Department of the Interior (the shift from the War Department was made in 1849) and the proper relationship would be that of a paternalistic guardian to its immature ward. Marshall's historical narrative—and American cultural production in general—repositioned 1830s Indians; once a foreign affairs problem, they were now a domestic issue.

And that is how it played out. The third article of the Constitution gives the Supreme Court jurisdiction over "controversies between a state or the citizens thereof, and foreign states, citizens, or subjects." Were the Cherokees a foreign state? If they were, then the Court would have jurisdiction and Marshall might indulge his sympathies and perhaps undo the damage he had caused. And yet, as foreign states, Indian nations would also be able to sign treaties with other nations, establish trade alliances with American enemies, and subject U.S. citizens to Indian laws, all acts the United States would construe as hostile. Despite any sympathies, the Court proved unwilling to see the Cherokees as a foreign nation.

So what were they? Indian tribes were distinct nations—but they existed in relation to the United States and within the borders it claimed. And so Marshall wrote: "It may well be doubted whether those tribes which reside within the acknowledged boundaries of the United States can, with strict accuracy, be denominated foreign nations. They may, more correctly, perhaps, be denominated domestic dependent nations . . . Their relation to the United States resembles that of a ward to his guardian." Lacking jurisdiction, John Marshall could not use the case to recall the unanticipated consequences of the discovery doctrine. But when the last of the three Cherokee cases came to the Court the following year, he reversed himself, ruling in *Worcester v. Georgia* that American Indian tribes were in fact sovereign nations and that they retained all sovereign rights not given up by treaty or lost in a just war. Cherokee claims to Cherokee homelands were guaranteed by those solemn federal treaties, and Georgia's claims to jurisdiction over those homelands were invalid.

It was too late. Southern courts responded to Marshall's decisions with their own cases—*Georgia v. Tassells* (1830), *Caldwell v. Alabama* (1831), and *Tennessee v. Forman* (1835)—each of which denied not only Marshall's belated assertion of tribal sovereignty but also the power of the Supreme Court itself. These Southern cases gave the doctrine of discovery new form, primarily around stark assertions of Indian racial inferiority. And, since Andrew Jackson's executive branch refused to enforce the Supreme Court's decision in *Worcester,* calling it "stillborn," it was the Southern decisions that structured Indian removal and the new colonialism of consolidation and reservation rule. They became the de facto legal precedents, even if *Worcester* theoretically dictated the rule of law.

The decision paved the way for the Trail of Tears, a forced migration to Indian territory in 1838 during which more than 4,000 Cherokees died. Similar removals and consolidations of Indians would become central to American policy over the next six decades. The federal government stopped making treaties in 1871, began reeducating Indian children in boarding schools, chopped up reservation land, and restricted tribes' religious practices. In law and politics, the paternalist language of guardians and wards was everywhere; indeed, it seemed to take precedence over "domestic dependent nations"—not to mention the idea that a tribe might have sovereignty.

These displacements existed in complex relation to the omnipresent cultural trope of the "vanishing" Indian. James Fenimore Cooper's *Last of the Mohicans* (1826) ends with noble Chingachgook alone, with no legacy or future. John Augustus Stone's *Metamora* (1829)—one of the most popular plays of the nineteenth century—finishes with tragic Indian death and a promising white future. John Mix Stanley's evocative painting *Last of the Race* (1857) shows a sad remnant of different tribes at sunset on the shores of the Pacific. And white fraternal orders in Iowa and elsewhere gathered at night, pretending to be now-departed Indians in order to perpetuate their memory.

And yet, Indian people did not vanish but began slowly reworking John Marshall's words. Some emphasized "domestic" and "dependent," focusing on American treaty obligations and using the language of "guardian" and "ward" to press the federal government for support for education, health, economic development, and other forms of assistance enshrined in treaty agreements. Others went in a different direction, skipping over "domestic" and "dependent" to argue for Indian nationhood and autonomy. In 1972, for example, following the Trail of Broken Treaties march on Washington, D.C., Indian activists demanded that all Indian people be governed by treaty relations, that the government restore a nation-to-nation relationship, ratify unapproved treaties, and establish a commission to review violations of treaty rights. Contemporary movements have pushed for Indian sovereignty, and they emphasize the word with a range of adjectives: political, legal, economic, intellectual, cultural.

When you hear about Indian casino gaming or tribal taxing authority or license plates, you are hearing—through the word "sovereignty"—the echoes of the *Cherokee Nation* decision. That decision has come full circle with the efforts of some Cherokees to dis-enroll Cherokee freedmen, the descendants of Cherokee-owned slaves guaranteed tribal citizenship under a treaty signed in 1866. The issue plays out on the grounds of Cherokee sovereignty (in the tribe's Supreme Court cases and electoral processes), nation-to-nation relations (in the Treaty of 1866), and guardianship oversight (in federal membership lists, a federal Indian blood quantum card, and a congressional effort to strip the Cherokees of federal recognition and funding). The complications of the 1830s—and sometimes their mood and tone—have continuously erupted into a series of presents.

Bibliography: Tim Alan Garrison, *The Legal Ideology of Removal: The Southern Judiciary and the Sovereignty of Native American Nations* (Athens, GA, 2002). Lindsay G. Robertson, *Conquest by Law: How the Discovery of America Dispossessed Indigenous Peoples of Their Lands* (New York, 2005). David E. Wilkins, *American Indian Sovereignty and the U.S. Supreme Court: The Masking of Justice* (Austin, TX, 1997). Robert A. Williams, *The American Indian in Western Legal Thought: The Discourses of Conquest* (New York, 1990).

PHILIP DELORIA

1832, July 10
President Jackson refuses a bill and redefines democracy

THE BANK VETO

On July 10, 1832, President Andrew Jackson sent back to Congress, with his objections, a bill to renew the charter of the Second Bank of the United States, then due to expire in 1836. As Jackson drily noted, the measure was sent to him on the Fourth of July, a day freighted with portent.

Nothing in the republic's first half century galvanized public controversy more than questions of currency and finance. As it had in George Washington's administration, the bank issue in the 1830s spurred the emergence of new political parties, Jackson's Democrats and the opposing Whigs. Jackson's veto was also a rhetorical breakthrough, sounding what became the touchstone theme of his presidency. Speaking bluntly of rich and poor, he was the first president to frontally acknowledge social fault lines among Americans. Accepting disparities of wealth and circumstance as inescapable and just, he disclaimed any idea of intervening to promote an absolute and unnatural equality. Yet Jackson also condemned the rich and powerful for manipulating government to suit their selfish interests, creating artificial inequalities that the less fortunate had a full right to protest and resist. Speaking both to Americans' love of opportunity and their craving for fairness, Jackson's veto furnished a grammar of democratic politics, strident yet malleable, that has endured and echoed ever since.

The economic environment of the early republic was framed by rapid growth amid scarcity. Americans were already by the time of the Revolution a famously enterprising people, yet their enterprise required capital far beyond their means. Credit was therefore vital but often unsound. The only legal currency, gold and silver coin, was too rare for everyday exchange. Instead, state and federal legislatures incorporated banks and authorized them to lend their own credit in the form of banknotes that served in practice, though not technically in law, as money.

The connection of banks with government was fraught with peril. Banking was poorly understood, not yet professionalized, and its practitioners sometimes wreaked disaster on their customers. Many citizens found it baffling that lawmakers could ordain credit, and thereby create wealth, by simply waving a legislative wand. Chartered business corporations were themselves a novelty that reeked of special privilege. Paper money was intrinsically suspect, and with good reason, since if issued in excess it could quickly become worthless. Even Federalist ex-president John Adams in 1813 damned chartered banking as a giant swindle, a "sacrifice of public and private Interest to a few Aristocratical Friends and Favourites."

The Second Bank whose recharter Jackson vetoed in 1832 was a reincarnation of the original Bank of the United States, created by Congress at Alexander Hamilton's urging in 1791. Modeled on the Bank of England, the First Bank was intended frankly to buttress the new government by entangling its finances with the interests of moneyed men. While serving public ends as the government's own banker, it was a profit-making institution, with private shareholders holding four-fifths of the stock and electing four-fifths of the directors—an arrangement Hamilton deemed essential to inspiring confidence in its soundness.

Although the First Bank stabilized the currency and helped retire the Revolutionary debt, opponents led by Thomas Jefferson never accepted it. In 1811 a Jeffersonian Congress killed it. But chastened by the government's flirtation with bankruptcy in the War of 1812, Congress reversed itself and in 1816 created a Second Bank, much larger than the first. Like its predecessor, the Second Bank was chartered for twenty years and was to be a mainly private entity serving public purposes. It again had a four-to-one private-to-public ratio in ownership and directorate, and its capital was expanded from $10 million to $35 million, a huge sum for the time. Empowered to establish branches and do business throughout the states, the Second Bank was the country's only financial institution of truly national reach. It would be the federal government's banker, and Congress decreed its notes legal tender and promised to create no competitor. In return, the Bank on starting up paid the government $1.5 million in cash.

The Second Bank began badly, indulging in speculation and even outright fraud that contributed to an inflationary bubble and a crash in 1819. Recriminations and investigations followed. Yet the prudent management of its second and third presidents, Langdon Cheves and Nicholas Biddle, in time repaired its condition and reputation. Within ten years the bank proved not only useful but, to many Americans, indispensable.

But not to Andrew Jackson. Jackson came to the presidency in 1828 with a deep sense of grievance against his enemies, real and imagined, in the existing political establishment—and with a conviction that the government had fallen into profligacy and corruption. Shortly after election he learned of branch officers using the Bank as what one of his followers called "an engine of political oppression." Asked to explain, Bank president Biddle affirmed the Bank's forbearance from politics—and its complete independence from executive control.

In November 1829, Biddle approached Jackson with a proposition. The Bank would assume the last of the dwindling national debt to enable its full discharge before the end of Jackson's term, an object Biddle knew was dear to the president's heart. The quid for this quo was an early recharter for the Bank, which would boost its stock and provide a windfall for shareholders. Biddle hoped to placate Jackson by showing the Bank's friendship and usefulness. Instead Jackson spied a backstairs deal fragrant of privilege and corruption, something close to a bribe. Biddle's offer sealed his hostility to the Bank. In his first message to Congress, just days later, Jackson startled everyone by raising the question of recharter and declaring himself opposed.

Jackson found in the Bank a focus for all his fears of aristocratic subversion—fears he shared with many citizens. He expected trouble from "all the sordid, & interested, who prised self interest more than the perpetuity of our liberty, & the blessings of a free republican government," he confided to James Alexander Hamilton. A renewed charter procured by the "corrupting influence" of "this monied aristocracy" would deal "the death blow to our liberty." Hamilton, a Jackson intimate and by curious happenstance a son of the late treasury secretary, had helped craft Jackson's declaration against recharter. Now, at Jackson's prompting, he prepared a detailed critique, arraying objections to the Bank under two heads. The Bank was unconstitutional, because Congress had no power to charter corporations and withdraw them from the regulatory and taxing power of the states: Jefferson's position, which the Supreme Court had rejected in *McCulloch v. Maryland* in 1819. And the Bank was dangerous to liberty, wielding a "fearful influence" over citizens and government and inviting corruption and oppression.

Jackson copied Hamilton's critique and reworked it privately for the next two years. To Congress he proposed a wholly governmental institution as a substitute—in name a bank but really an arm of the Treasury, without power to make loans, acquire property, or issue notes.

Instead, in 1832 Congress passed, by substantial although not veto-proof majorities, a bill to extend, slightly modified, the charter of the existing bank. To Jackson the bill's timing confirmed his strictures about the Bank's political meddling. Biddle had decided to press for recharter at the urging of Senator Henry Clay, Jackson's opponent in the upcoming presidential election. In effect, they dared him to veto.

Jackson did, in a message that marked the rhetorical apex of his presidency. Following Jefferson, and defying *McCulloch,* Jackson denied the Bank's constitutionality and affirmed his right to judge that question, independent of Congress or the courts. Ingeniously, and perversely, he targeted overseas stockholders for special censure. Much of the Bank's stock was in fact held abroad, especially in Britain, but the charter barred foreigners from serving as directors or voting their shares. Still, Jackson's arguments turned investment into subversion. "If we must have a bank," he warned, "it should be *purely American.*"

But the heart of the message was its attack on monopoly and privilege. Sounding those words over and over like a tocsin, Jackson assailed the Bank stockholders' exclusive access to pelf and power. Jackson's peroration conveyed both the veto's core meaning and, for later generations, its inescapable ambiguity:

> It is to be regretted that the rich and powerful too often bend the acts of government to their selfish purposes. Distinctions in society will always exist under every just government. Equality of talents, of education, or of wealth can not be produced by human institutions. In the full enjoyment of the gifts of Heaven and the fruits of superior industry, economy, and virtue, every man is equally entitled to protection by law; but when the laws undertake to add to these natural and just advantages artificial distinctions, to grant titles, gratuities, and exclusive privileges, to make the rich richer and the potent more powerful, the humble members of society—the farmers, mechanics, and laborers—who have neither the time nor the means of securing like favors to themselves, have a right to complain of the injustice of their Government. There are no necessary evils in government. Its evils exist only in its abuses. If it would confine itself to equal protection, and as Heaven does its rains, shower its favors alike on the high and the low, the rich and the poor, it would be an unqualified blessing.

No president before had said anything like this. Presidents had sometimes warned of foreign perils, or cautioned against factionalism and divisiveness among citizens presumed to be equally well disposed and meritorious. Andrew Jackson warned Americans against their government—and against each other.

Jackson's bold juxtaposing of rich and poor, high and low, read to many then and later as an announcement of class war—an anathema to some, a clarion call for others. It was, snorted Nicholas Biddle, "a manifesto of anarchy—such as Marat or Robespierre might have issued to the mob of the faubourg St Antoine."

But Jacksonians hailed the president for exposing what the *Democratic Review* in its opening declaration of principles called "artificial social distinctions which violate the natural equality of rights of the human race" and enabled those with "wealth, splendour, and power" to subjugate "the producing mass." Jackson's attack on "the rich and powerful" would echo in the Populist platform of 1892 and in William Jennings Bryan's "cross of gold" speech in 1896, in Theodore Roosevelt's assault on "malefactors of great wealth," in Franklin Roosevelt's first-inaugural denunciation of "unscrupulous money changers" in the national temple, and in every blast against Wall Street speculators. Likewise, Jackson's exaltation of "farmers, mechanics, and laborers" and his homage to the "humble members of society" live on in invocations of the common man, the little guy, and "ordinary working families." There has been, since Jackson, no more enduring and powerful idea in American politics than that government owes a special duty to those without friends in high places.

Yet Jackson's acceptance of disparities in fortune and his call for "equal protection" and minimalist government could also fuel laissez-faire economics and resistance to an overweening state. Jackson worked from the root presumption that government intervention inevitably magnified instead of mitigated natural inequalities. Hence the masthead of the *Globe,* his Washington house organ, proclaimed that "The World Is Governed Too Much." From the logic and language of the Bank Veto flowed the antigovernment diatribes of the Jacksonian editorialist and latter-day libertarian hero William Leggett. Alongside its condemnation of "artificial social distinctions," the *Democratic Review* declared flatly that "the best government is that which governs least. No human depositories can, with safety, be trusted with the power of legislation upon the general interests of society so as to operate directly or indirectly on the industry and property of the community." Rooted in the writings of Jefferson and Thomas Paine, this strain in Jacksonian thought would resound all the way to Ronald Reagan's pronouncement in his first inaugural that "government is not the solution to our problem; government is the problem." Just as some have anointed Jackson as a working-class champion and foe of capitalist dominion, others have deemed him a spokesman of enterprise, who sought to liberate the wealth-creating energies of "superior industry, economy, and virtue" from the dead hand of encrusted privilege.

Jackson bequeathed still another legacy by expanding those who mattered politically to incorporate "farmers, mechanics, and laborers." The egalitarian democracy he proclaimed was implicitly free, male, and white; it did not include women, slaves, or Indians. But words once spoken may gain a life of their own. Jackson's embrace of "the humble members of society" as deserving of equal rights would have implications he could not foresee.

The veto held up in Congress, as all knew it would. In the 1832 presidential campaign, both sides, remarkably, circulated the text of Jackson's veto message—Jacksonians to show his patriotism and egalitarianism, foes to prove his ignorance and demagoguery. Jackson trounced Clay in the election. Reading victory as a mandate to continue, Jackson next moved to disable the Bank, whose charter ran until 1836, by removing federal deposits to state banks. The removal prompted Jackson's foes to coalesce under the name of Whigs, a term denoting opponents of royal prerogative. In 1834 a Whig Senate formally censured Jackson—an action that Jacksonians, now calling themselves Democrats, promptly expunged from the record when they regained a majority. The defeated bank accepted a Pennsylvania charter and continued after 1836 as a state institution.

The demise of the Second Bank loosed American enterprise from its only central restraint. State banks went on a lending spree that built up a speculative bubble and ended, just as Jackson left office in 1837, in a sickening crash. Jackson himself came to oppose all chartered banks and banknotes, state as well as federal, and to favor a return to gold and silver "hard money"—a radical deflation that Whigs charged would throw progress back a century. In his farewell address Jackson elaborated the language of the veto, condemning bank paper and warning of an insidious "money power" and the growing control by faceless corporations over ordinary citizens' lives.

Under Democratic presidents Martin Van Buren and James K. Polk, a new independent Treasury took charge of federal finances, realizing Jackson's aim of divorcing government entirely from banks. For a time the banking network remained semi-organized and essentially directionless. The Civil War forced the first steps toward nationalizing banking and the currency, a process advanced with the creation of the Federal Reserve in 1913.

The immediate circumstances that prompted Andrew Jackson's ringing phrases have long since passed away. The questions he raised—about the connection of wealth and power, about government intercession in the affairs of the citizenry, and about the dialectic of freedom and equality—abide.

Bibliography: Ralph C. H. Catterall, *The Second Bank of the United States* (Chicago, 1902). Donald B. Cole, *The Presidency of Andrew Jackson* (Lawrence, KS, 1993). Bray Hammond, *Banks and Politics in America from the Revolution to the Civil War* (Princeton, NJ, 1957). Robert V. Remini, *Andrew Jackson and the Bank War* (New York, 1967). James D. Richardson, ed., *A Compilation of the Messages and Papers of the Presidents, 1789–1897* (Washington, DC, 1896–1899). Sean Wilentz, *The Rise of American Democracy: Jefferson to Lincoln* (New York, 2005).

DAN FELLER

1835, January
Alexis de Tocqueville deconstructs a political system

DEMOCRACY IN AMERICA

In January 1835, a lengthy work of political theory, the first of two promised tomes, was published in Paris by a young writer who had recently finished a nine-month visit to the United States. The writer was so obscure (a shy aristocrat alienated from nearly every faction in France), and the topic of such marginal interest (what respectable person cared about the United States?), that the publisher printed only 500 copies, dubious that he would sell even that many.

The result was a publishing sensation. Alexis de Tocqueville was only twenty-nine when *De la démocratie en Amérique* was issued, but it was the culminating event of his life. Soon translated into English, *Democracy in America* was instantly recognized as a classic.

Tocqueville was far from the first foreign observer to visit the United States—they had been coming in droves since the birth of the republic. Many of them found a great deal to dislike here (Frances Trollope and Charles Dickens spring to mind), and skewered American habits with glee. Of the entire flock of scribblers, not one had as little experience as Tocqueville—he had no experience at all. And yet, no account has ever probed as penetratingly into the nooks and crannies of democracy—the matrix that so many people now inhabit—without quite understanding where it begins and ends.

For all its fame, *Democracy in America* remains an elusive document. To this day it is cited by conservatives and liberals alike to justify nearly anything they wish to justify—in fact, it is a work cited so often that one's eyes begin to glaze over as soon as a sentence begins with the reassuring words, "Tocqueville said . . ." Even in his own time, Tocqueville was notoriously hard to pin down, an aristocratic democrat, a skeptical believer, a conservative liberal. It's no wonder that his book pleased so many people.

He is certainly popular on the right. A conservative think tank called the Alexis de Tocqueville Institution lobbies for the tobacco industry, publishes Newt Gingrich, and labors heroically to debunk the science behind global warming. Former president George W. Bush called him his favorite political writer. But there is nothing naturally rightist about a writer who admired grassroots democracy, criticized materialism, and thought the democratic tradition came out of New England. Most Americans believe that Tocqueville painted an unblemished portrait of the United States, but he would have ridiculed such a facile assumption. Tocqueville wasn't saying that democracy was ineffable, he was saying that it was inevitable.

Who was this man of many parts? Alexis Charles Henri Clerel de Tocqueville was born in Paris on July 29, 1805, and grew up in a château that his parents were trying to restore to its prerevolutionary glory. Reliving the ancien régime was a daily activity for the family, which had lost several members to the guillotine and identified strongly with the conservative party hoping to restore the Bourbon line. But like his great-grandfather, Malesherbes, Tocqueville was naturally drawn to positions of moderation. After some tedious studies in the law, he prepared for a career in officialdom and met Gustave de Beaumont, like him a precocious aristocrat who questioned many of the assumptions of his tribe. They drew even closer after the regime change in 1830, when Charles X fled Paris (Tocqueville witnessed his flight in person) and the new government forced Tocqueville and Beaumont to utter a public oath of support, in effect renouncing everything their families stood for. They became a party of two, unpopular with their friends and enemies alike.

It was in the dismal aftermath of these events that the plan for a trip to America originated. Specifically, Tocqueville and Beaumont proposed to the new government that they go to the United States to study its progressive penitentiaries—and by so doing, liberate themselves. The government approved, eager to get rid of them, and soon Tocqueville and Beaumont were planning a voyage to the land that embodied the democratic energies that had brought so much anxiety to Tocqueville's house. To his credit, the contradictory young man was genuinely interested, and even before leaving, he hinted of a larger ambition to write something much bigger than a report on prisons. Beaumont wrote to his father, "We are meditating great projects."

The two friends left Le Havre on April 2, 1831, and experienced a difficult passage, nearly running out of food and water. Desperate, they went ashore at Newport, Rhode Island, on May 9, where Tocqueville confided to his journal one of his first sociological observations—that America's women were "extraordinarily ugly." A steamship picked them up and took them to New York, where they went to sleep and awoke to find themselves celebrities. With considerable fanfare, the local papers announced the arrival of these exotic commissioners from abroad, and soon the news traveled up and down the seaboard. The tables had turned—instead of observing America, Tocqueville and Beaumont found themselves the object of scrutiny, held up to view like a couple of rare insect specimens. Still, their newfound fame aided their cause, and gave them entrée into all of the best salons of New York.

That helped, for America's noise was overwhelming. Nearly everyone wanted to give advice to the young Frenchmen, but they were hindered by their difficulties with English (Tocqueville complained, "It's pitiful to hear us"). Like so many foreigners, they found their destination very different from the one they expected. The two clueless aristocrats had nurtured dreams of the romantic America that Tocqueville's cousin, Chateaubriand, had made famous through maudlin novels like *Atala*—complete with misty landscapes, noble warriors, and tawny maidens in need of rescue. But the New York that spread out before them was not unimpressive. The once-tiny Dutch port now held 240,000 people, the largest city in a nation of fifteen million, including two million slaves. "We are most certainly in another world here," Tocqueville admitted to himself.

Undaunted, they set out to explore it. It is rather moving to reflect that the book that gave us the word "individualism" was written by two people, selflessly devoted to each other. Over the next 271 days, all their letters home were written with the word "we." It is not a huge distance from Tocqueville and Beaumont to Walker Evans and James Agee, Jack Kerouac and Neal Cassady, Peter Fonda and Dennis Hopper, Thelma and Louise, Borat Sagdiyev and Azamat Bagatov and all the other reporting teams who have gone out on assignment to discover America.

What a journey it must have been! They went in all directions, west, north (even to Canada), east, and finally south. They saw Shakers performing their weird jerking dances; they saw pioneers chopping down every tree in sight, and expressed amazement at the speed with which this termite-like people could devour the wilderness. Going deeper and deeper into the interior, they finally found the edge of democracy—the famous frontier—around Saginaw, Michigan. But there Tocqueville realized that the days of unspoiled nature were numbered. He was depressed by the degraded condition of the natives, and surely there was something self-reflective in his lament for the decline of this "noble" people, displaced by the roaring engines of democracy, capitalism, and all the other modern machinery that had intruded so rudely into his powdered world. Worse, the desert was not quite as empty as he had hoped—it was full of mosquitoes ("these small flies are the scourge of the American solitudes") and he lamented that insects, like Americans, also tend to associate ("each part of the body that we left uncovered instantly served as a rendez-vous").

Eventually, as these disappointments mounted, Tocqueville relinquished the forest primeval and accepted America for what it was, a bustling society of ferocious energy, more egalitarian than any on earth but also compromised by rampant humbug. In Boston, he attended a rally of two thousand people and listened to politicians demand that Poland be allowed her "freedom," or else they would do something about it (though there was barely an American army at the time). He listened to Henry Clay predict that there would soon be an African American nation carved out of the South, with its own laws. He heard an Alabama lawyer announce that everyone he knew carried a gun. On a steamboat to New Orleans, he bumped into Sam Houston and Davy Crockett. He saw a black man caned for entering the wrong section of a Maryland horse track, and another driven insane by his beatings (Beaumont would write a novel, *Marie,* to vent his outrage at America's racial hypocrisy).

On February 20, 1832, Tocqueville and Beaumont returned to France on the same boat that had brought them to America. They immediately set out to convert their experience into something readable. Beaumont once likened Tocqueville's mind to a steam engine, and after a long bout of writer's block the pistons began to fire. It was brutal work—to Beaumont, Tocqueville wrote, "I must at all costs finish this book. It and I have a duel to the death—and I must kill it or it must kill me." In his preface, he confessed, "This book was written in the grip of a kind of religious terror occasioned in the soul of its author by the sight of this irresistible revolution"—the revolution, he meant, of equality.

Yet he powered through his doubts, and allowed the things he had seen to speak for themselves. In his preface he admitted proudly, "I never gave in to the temptation to tailor facts to ideas rather than to adapt ideas to facts." Before a world that understood very little of democracy or America (in most European nations, it was forbidden to teach American history), *Democracy in America* explained the Constitution, checks and balances, inheritance laws, trial by jury, public education, and the invisible spider's web of legal and ethical beliefs that conspire to keep this delicate balancing act from falling apart.

Even more impressively, he managed to delineate these sinews with an economy of expression, teasing out the contradictions of a system that sometimes seemed built on gaseous promises to as many people as possible. Throughout, the narrative is leavened by sharp, counterintuitive sentences that Emerson would not have disavowed. Sometimes he even reveals a bit of himself. On the subject of poetry in a democracy: "I need not traverse earth and sky to discover a wondrous object woven of contrasts, of infinite greatness and littleness, of intense gloom and amazing brightness, capable at once of exciting pity, admiration, terror, contempt. I have only to look at myself."

Could Thoreau have said it better?

The book's complexities are deepened by its binary structure. How many classic works were published in two volumes, five years apart? Or written by two authors, rather than one? Of course it belongs to Tocqueville, but still, throughout the narrative, you get the feeling that he's lying in a lumpy bed in some godforsaken inn, devoured by mosquitoes, pouring his heart out to Beaumont, while traveling salesmen and con artists play cards a floor below.

Given that his visit overlapped with Nat Turner's rebellion, the founding of *The Liberator,* and the nullification crisis, it's surprising how affirmative Tocqueville could be in his veneration of the New England town meeting, the jury, and the frontier family. But this is not a starry-eyed portrait of a perfect world coming into existence. Tocqueville goes to the heart of America's defects as well as its virtues, especially in the second volume, which probes the nation's psychology as insistently as the first volume probes its laws, and finds a vague alienation underlying all the blather about progress and human betterment. In a way, the two books imitate the democratic system itself, combining certain internal checks and balances that prevent any extremes from dominating the narrative.

To be sure, it is far from a perfect book. Tocqueville has little on the political movement that was reaching its apogee at the moment of his arrival—Jacksonian democracy. Nor does he do much to cover the rise of manufacturing, cities, financial cartels, and huge corporations. That was a pressure on the system—a tyranny of the minority—that he was largely silent about. Sometimes he was flat-out wrong, as when he predicted that federal power would eventually recede as the nation expanded west. Or when he said that the United States has "no foreign interests to discuss," at a time when Texans were clamoring to carve a new state out of a Mexican province and affix it to the Union. Or when he said America contains "no rich men."

Still, the book endures. It is surely a great essay on politics, as scientific a study of an unscientific topic as it's possible to imagine. But it is also a phenomenal piece of reporting, and it recognizes that human beings do follow certain laws of behavior, even in a place with as little government as the United States of America. For centuries the French had been sending natural historians across the Atlantic to classify the phyla of the new world. Tocqueville was a worthy successor.

In 1848, he wrote a new preface to the book that spoke movingly of the "democratic revolution" coming to Europe. That year, to general amazement, his prediction came true, and the Revolutions of 1848 seemed for a moment to redeem the hopes of humanity, before turning into a series of worthless coups. It would not be the last time that Americans were disappointed by the failure of the rest of the world to reconstitute itself according to American standards.

Tocqueville ascended to the position of minister of foreign affairs in France, and wrote other books before he died in 1859, on the eve of a civil war that would have shattered his naïve assumption about democracy's aversion to conflict. But his reputation continues to grow, perpetually tied to the impetuous journey he took to America in 1831. Thanks to a diminutive Frenchman who could barely speak English, Americans have a user's manual for the ages.

Democracy in America helps especially when Americans feel unsure where the driverless vehicle of self-government is going. At dark moments it can take on a special relevance. In 1938, for example, a revival began when George Wilson Pierson's classic study of Tocqueville was published. During the cold war, readers were comforted to see that Tocqueville had explicitly predicted the rise of Russia and America as enormous counterweights. His warning against "the tyranny of the majority" has never stopped being timely. For all it has done to unfetter human potential, democracy can also be a prison of its own, demanding certain kinds of conformity and disappointing those who do not see its promises come true. It can be downright lonely, as we hear now and then from Tocqueville's successors (for example, David Riesman's *The Lonely Crowd* and Robert Putnam's *Bowling Alone*). The popularity of MySpace and Facebook suggests that American individualists still have trouble connecting with one another.

The central fact that struck Tocqueville, in the first sentence of his introduction, was America's "general equality of condition among the people." Obviously, both wealth and poverty have deepened in the United States since 1835, and democracy has been compromised by both extremes, though politicians tremble before any discussion of economic inequality, for fear that it constitutes "class warfare." That topic can be a labyrinth with no clear exit, but still, Tocqueville knew that the hard questions are the ones worth asking. If time travel were possible, what a joy it would be to send him on assignment into the Americanized version of Paris that was built in 1999 as a Las Vegas casino, complete with 221 televisions, a half-scale Eiffel Tower, a wedding chapel, a topless show ("Ooh La La"), and a restaurant called Le Burger Brasserie (its signature dish, the $777 Kobe Beef and Maine Lobster Burger, served with Dom Pérignon champagne).

He wrote, "I confess that in America I saw more than America; I sought the image of democracy itself, with its inclinations, its character, its prejudices, and its passions, in order to learn what we have to fear or to hope from its progress." More than two centuries after his birth, one still wonders a little about the final result of this experiment unleashed upon the world. For in the long run, government of the people, by the people, and for the people will be exactly as good as the people themselves. To fear or to hope—that is the question.

Bibliography: Hugh Brogan, *Alexis de Tocqueville: A Life* (New Haven, 2007). Joseph Epstein, *Alexis de Tocqueville: Democracy's Guide* (New York, 2006). George Wilson Pierson, *Tocqueville and Beaumont in America* (New York, 1938). Alexis de Tocqueville, *Democracy in America,* trans. Henry Reeve (New York, 1945, 1980).

TED WIDMER

1835

William Gilmore Simms proposes the modern romance as substitute for the ancient epic

THE YEMASSEE

The dedicatory "Advertisement" to William Gilmore Simms's *The Yemassee: A Romance of Carolina* distills contemporary discussions of the differences between the romance and the novel. Romance seeks the "boundless horizon of art" beyond the "domestic circle" of the English novel, a fictional space for the "natural romance of our country." *The Yemassee,* like James Fenimore Cooper's Leatherstocking Tales, transplants to North America the narrative premise of Walter Scott's internationally popular historical fiction: a contest between representatives of contrasting societies ending in foreordained victory for the more progressive social order with which readers identify. The inescapable conflicts, Simms claims, render the romance the modern substitute for the ancient epic. For Simms and his contemporaries, the exemplary losers in American history were the Indians, leaving, as Longfellow writes in *Hiawatha,* "a nation's legends, / . . . the ballads of a people" to be transformed into United States property along with the land. Elegies for the inevitable defeat of archaic heroism—Indians in "their undegraded condition"—temper the celebration of progress without invalidating its necessity.

Simms came to prominence as an inclusive literary nationalist whose romances registered the progress of his country, but American audiences by the late nineteenth century granted him at best a distant respect, and he is now read only by scholars. Though Simms wrote in 1856 that "to be *national* in literature, one must needs be *sectional*" as an expression of the American quality of his literary project rather than a restriction of it, his American epic finally seemed too *Southern* to leave traces in popular culture to rival those of Cooper. While Simms accepted the role of Southern spokesman reluctantly during the tense 1850s, the new American order represented and justified in his historical fiction was always the hierarchical society of the antebellum South. Whatever doubts Simms's readers had about the exemplary part he assigned to his South in the narrative of national triumph were confirmed by its destruction. By the logic of his own romances, catastrophic defeat earned historical supersession.

Simms never forgets that the Old South was built on ground cleared by Indian Removal. However, in his first real novel, *Guy Rivers: A Tale of Georgia* (1834), set during the gold rush that had recently intensified pressure to expel the Cherokee, the Indians are excluded from the action—just as they were soon to be excluded from the lands on which the story is set. Simms's fictional project thus opens with Native Americans already effectively banished. But his novels rarely unfold in the nominally Indian-free zone of secured white dominance. Instead they range temporally backward or spatially westward to restore contact with "the Indian as our ancestors knew him early, and as our people, in certain situations, may know him still," as Simms wrote in *The Yemassee*. Indians are more than worthy opponents who vanish after testing the new American societies; they are fundamental to the typology of race and status in Simms's fictional South. *The Yemassee,* published as Removal was reaching its climax, narrates the coalescence of his antebellum world with the beginning of Removal.

The actual Yamassee War of 1715–16 was not a defeat for "Indians" as such. The colony of South Carolina was mauled by several native peoples, with the Creeks its principal opponents. The triggering of "Yemassee" hostility in Simms's book by pressure to cede lands to settlers is an anachronism that reflects the southeastern United States of the 1820s and 1830s rather than the South Carolina of 1715, which was dependent on shifting alliances with Native Americans for its own survival. Simms not only portrays the war as a colonial victory but also focuses his story on the Yemassee, who suffered losses that hastened their cultural disappearance in the following decades, as an appropriate illustration of the racial doom of all Indians. *The Yemassee* projects into the past and onto the Indians white assumptions that justified Indian Removal. It insists repeatedly that even intelligent Indians recognize that their individual and collective inferiority ruins them whenever brought into contact with white men: Chief Sanutee "was sage enough at length to perceive all this, as the inevitable result of [civilization's] progressive march." Simms does allow sympathetic Yemassee characters to model responses to their plight that range from collaboration to patriotic resistance, but once they go to war, the narrative reverts to the simple lesson preached by countless fictions, as well as histories like Francis Parkman's *The Conspiracy of Pontiac* (1851): Indian alliances can never defeat white expansion.

The leader in understanding and defeating the Indians is a white frontiersman, as in so many American frontier romances. But in *The Yemassee* the "Coosaw killer" Gabriel Harrison is an identity strategically assumed by South Carolina's governor Charles Craven. Instead of incarnating lost natural freedoms tragically superseded by civilization, as Natty Bumppo does, Simms's frontiersman is subsumed into a prototype of the idealized Southern gentleman who will dominate the new society. The war allows him to prove his merit against outsiders (Indians and English pirates) and thus win recognition from skeptical fellow whites of the inherent authority he already possesses. The resentment of Harrison's most significant challenger, Hugh Grayson, erupts in speeches pitting the self-creating energies of discontent against all forms of hierarchy. He sees himself as "a slave—a dog—an accursed thing, and in the worst of bondage—I am nothing." Grayson holds that slaves are ultimately responsible for their slavery because they accept and even seek it. Sanutee has already concluded that inferior *races* "will tacitly become subjects if not bondmen" of their racial superiors. The novel endorses both Sanutee's dictum on racial suitability and Grayson's corollary stress on personal volition. References to bondage pervade its text. Forms of "slave" and "slavery" alone appear seventy-nine times, with only a few of these uses of "slavery" labeling the legal status of characters like Harrison's African American servant, Hector. The words are primarily used by nominally free characters expressing their fears of subordination to others, a usage familiar to Simms's contemporaries. Political rhetoric—particularly from the slaveholding South—played on the conviction of Melville's Captain Ahab that to accept subordination is to lose mastery of the self. The actual African slaves in *The Yemassee* are a given feature of colonial society; they do not desire and thus do not require or deserve freedom. To show the redundancy of proslavery argument, Simms devotes one brief scene to Hector's vehement refusal of Harrison's offer to free him. But the presence of African slaves in the book, as in the antebellum United States, makes concrete the dread of servility expressed by both Euro-American and Native American characters. The fear is all the more potent for its association with the loss of racial status: to accept slavery is to be black. Grayson's harangue also displays the anxiety of men in Jacksonian America, divided between slave and free, scrambling for position in a republic that encouraged every white male to dream of mastery without allowing him to achieve it. Yet civilized freedom requires inequality, so in the end Grayson accepts Harrison's superiority.

The natural freedom of the Indians, not the condition of white frontiersmen, represents the complete antithesis of slavery in *The Yemassee*. The currency of "slave" as an insult used by the Yemassee demonstrates that their scorn for bondage surpasses even that of white characters. But extended contact with white men inevitably will bring personal corruption and racial abjection. The white man's dread of slavery, expressed by Grayson, is hyperbolic and individualized—concern for the loss of a potent self. The Indian dilemma is presented as both individual and racial. Sanutee's heir apparent, Occonestoga, epitomizes their downfall: "He hunts the slaves of the English in the swamps for strong drink. He is a slave himself." Occonestoga negates his Indian self by forfeiting his will to an English product and by becoming a protector of their system of chattel slavery. African slavery is legitimate in *The Yemassee,* but to conduct or enforce it sullies Indian freedom. Slavery is the negation of an Indian existence, whether the Indian is the slave or the master. Occonestoga's counterpart, Grayson, can be reconciled to society, learning that recognition of others' (individual or class) predominance is not slavery. Occonestoga's collapse before whites' (racial) superiority *is* slavery, so he must be killed to spare him a final enslavement. In *The Yemassee,* Indians are free or they are nothing.

In conceptually pitting Indian existence against slavery, the book obscures history that lingers in the margins of the text, as in the footnote that mentions the Indian slaves promised to Carolina's Tuscarora allies. South Carolina's export trade in Indian slaves, a major source of the colony's early wealth, eventually provoked the actual series of clashes labeled the Yamassee War. *The Yemassee* ignores the Indian slave trade to protect the roles of both its English settlers and its Native Americans. Coerced land cessions familiar to 1830s readers were shabby enough, even when excused by the belief in Indian doom, but the forcible enslavement of resisting Indians would undermine the novel's naturalization of "willing" black slavery along with white moral authority. Indians' enslavement must be the metaphorical result of their internal racial collapse, not the literal aim of English commerce, employing other Indians as agents. To depict Indians as the slavers contaminates their conceptual opposition to slavery. It also threatens to elevate them into the same category as white masters, which neither Simms nor the promoters of Indian Removal wanted. As Simms wrote his novel, the wealthy, acculturated slaveholders among the Five Civilized Tribes were not being spared from compulsory relocation to the west along with their more "savage" fellows. Hugh Grayson again anticipates 1835 and Simms's own expressed opinions in suggesting that Indians be moved from proximity to white society for their own protection. If they are to represent natural freedom that knows neither master nor slave in *The Yemassee*'s racial economy, they cannot remain in what their displacement allows to become the black and white Old South. They do have a vital function in narrative: to reenact the sad necessity of their disappearance.

The Civil War buried Simms's attraction as a model for writing "*American romance*," since the South was reduced to a defeated region with peculiarities interesting as departures from national norms rather than as illustrations of national destiny. His lost antebellum fictional world supplies no idylls for postbellum writers and readers looking to escape from the pains of Southern history. While historical romance has remained a favorite genre for the exploration of slavery and race in the United States, Simms's epic romances of the establishment of a slaveholding South necessarily contained too much overt approval of slavery, and could not compete with gothic romances of tangled racial genealogies and irrepressible pasts in rendering the dread of African American slavery's consequences, felt by many even as Simms wrote.

Simms's representation of the plight of Southern Indians had an ironic literary sequel. As writers of the twentieth-century Southern Renaissance focused on a South defined by loss rather than victory, Indians were appropriated as the original victims, severed from the land by relentless modernity, prefiguring the later defeats of their conquerors. In William Faulkner's writing, Indians appear as isolated connections to the precolonial Nature we can no longer reach, before land and labor and people were commodities. Faulkner's elegiac desire for Eden is more self-aware and self-questioning but shares roots with Simms's vision. Isaac McCaslin's craving for incorruptibility shapes our view of Sam Fathers in *Go Down, Moses* (1942), but Sam's "Indian" connection to nature doesn't erase the mother that also makes him another legacy of slavery. The degradation that William Gilmore Simms feared appears in the dark comedy of Faulkner's story "Red Leaves" (1930), in which African slaves are only the most inconvenient of all the useless consumer goods that are reducing an Indian village to grotesque mimicry of white society. But Simms's racial categories are inverted or collapsed: a slave is the only figure capable of tragic nobility, and Faulkner's Indian elders seem more bemused than anguished in the face of their incipient cultural eclipse. Like white Southerners, and white Americans generally, they embrace their corruption. These Indians are disappearing not because they lack the capacities of whites, but because they are becoming indistinguishable from whites.

Bibliography: Alan Gallay, *The Indian Slave Trade: The Rise of the English Empire in the American South, 1670–1717* (New Haven, CT, 2002). John Caldwell Guilds, *Simms: A Literary Life* (Fayetteville, AR, 1992). Louis D. Rubin, Jr., *The Edge of the Swamp: A Study in the Literature and Society of the Old South* (Baton Rouge, LA, 1988). William Gilmore Simms, *The Yemassee: A Romance of Carolina 1835* (Fayetteville, AR, 1994). G. R. Thompson and Eric Carl Link, *Neutral Ground: New Traditionalism and the American Romance Controversy* (Baton Rouge, LA, 1999). Annette Trefzer, *Disturbing Indians: The Archaeology of Southern Fiction* (Tuscaloosa, AL, 2007).

JEFFREY JOHNSON

1835

William Walker journeys north to publish *The Southern Harmony*, reputedly crossing up his brother-in-law, Benjamin Franklin White, who nine years later completes *The Sacred Harp*

SHAPE-NOTE SINGING

The history of *The Sacred Harp,* an American spiritual text of legendary importance, seems to have started with a fight. Sometime in 1835, a Baptist singing master and song collector named William Walker traveled north from his home in Spartanburg, South Carolina, to New Haven, Connecticut, carrying with him a selection of what he called "Tunes, Hymns, and Anthems" as well as "a number of excellent new Songs." The music was transcribed in the popular form of shaped notes on a musical staff. According to a much later, not wholly trustworthy account, Walker had collected the melodies and lyrics with the help of his brother-in-law, Benjamin Franklin White, and then agreed to set out alone in order to get the collection published for the both of them. Yet once Walker arranged for publication, it looks as if he completely forgot about White.

Later that year, *The Southern Harmony and Musical Companion* appeared—one source says in New Haven, although the earliest extant edition was printed in Philadelphia—with Walker's name alone on the preface, which he dated "Spartanburg, S.C., September 1835." The book was an oblong hymnal of more than two hundred pages, with about half its songs credited to well-known earlier hymnodists, above all the early-eighteenth-century British Nonconformist Isaac Watts. Many of the other songs were credited to no one; still others were credited to disparate authors ranging from Walker's brother, David, to a late-sixteenth-century writer known by the initials "F. B. P." Three songs were partly credited to American Indians, and Walker claimed quite a few of the best selections for himself, including the peculiarly fatalistic, haunting, and encouraging, "Hallelujah!"

> And let this feeble body fail,
> And let it faint and die
> My soul shall quit this mournful vale,
> And soar to worlds on high.

And I'll sing hallelujah,
And you'll sing hallelujah,
And we'll all sing hallelujah,
When we arrive at home.

Walker, who said he wanted to include the best songs in his book, appropriated freely, and he feigned utter candor about it. Given the existence, he wrote, of a "great many good airs (which I could not find in any publication nor in manuscript)," he conceded that he had sometimes thought up lines of his own and called himself the song's author. In fact, he plagiarized more of the lyrics than he let on.

As soon as Ben White learned that he had been denied the credit due him for helping to compile *The Southern Harmony*—so the story goes—he ceased speaking to Walker for the rest of his life. What is certain is that in 1844, White (having since relocated to Harris County, Georgia, and having found a new collaborator, the young tunesmith E. J. King) saw his own oblong book published in Philadelphia—*The Sacred Harp,* presenting more than 250 songs, including, its title page proclaimed, "nearly one hundred pieces never before published." The two hymnals, drawing on many common sources, then battled against each other and several other collections for public favor. White and King's book eventually prevailed. Published today in two separate editions (one of which has been through seven major revisions atop three that White himself made during his lifetime; the other version has seen six revisions), *The Sacred Harp* remains the predominant hymnal for sacred-harp singing groups in large parts of the American South. The only known occasion when *The Southern Harmony* remains in regular use appears to be at an annual conclave known as the Big Singing in Benton, Kentucky, which, having been held since 1884, does give Walker's book a smaller but undeniable distinction.

The success of *The Sacred Harp* has led many writers and listeners to lump together all shape-note (or *fa-sol-la*) singing as "sacred harp" music. It has tied that singing style closely in history to the eruption of religious revivalism in the decades before the Civil War, described as the Second Great Awakening. The so-called sacred harp tradition is also known primarily as an American Southern hymnody—what the pioneering folklorist George Pullen Jackson called "white spirituals in the Southern uplands."

Each of these propositions contains some truth but is also misleading. Although *The Sacred Harp* helped greatly to spread and popularize the shape-note form, neither it nor *The Southern Harmony* was the first important collection of its kind. The songs performed by shape-note singing assemblies over the decades have included many with texts dating back to the seventeenth century and in a few cases even earlier, and with melodies as old as Gregorian chants. Far from being a distinct American regional product, shape-note music blends styles from the British Isles and the European Continent as well as from various parts of what has become the United States. Indeed, by traveling north to get *The Southern Harmony* published in 1835, William Walker in effect carried an

American sacred form closer to where it had originated more than a century before.

Although colonial New Englanders were long used to the recitation and singing of psalms, by the early eighteenth century ministers had become alarmed at the poor quality of vocalizing in church, which they blamed on a shortage of both printed music and parishioners who could read it. Following the existing model of the evening literary school, they founded singing schools for instructing large numbers of Yankee farmers and artisans in the basic elements of music. Harvard-trained clerics duly supplied the required hymnals. The first of these, John Tufts's *An Introduction to the Singing of Psalm Tunes* and Thomas Walter's *The Grounds and Rules of Musick, Explained,* appeared in Boston in 1721. Instead of using the standard note head in his scores, Tufts inserted the first letter of the easily learned syllabic mnemonic for each note in the musical scale: *fa, sol, la, fa, sol, la, mi.* Thus simplified, the music became extremely popular during the colonial period through the American Revolution, and was taught in singing schools that spread westward with the white population. The music in turn inspired numerous songbook composers from outside the ranks of the ministry, including the Boston tanner William Billings. In 1770, at age twenty-four, Billings published the first of his six major sacred song collections, *The New England Psalm Singer.* Musicologists would eventually regard him as the greatest master of choral music in early America.

In the 1790s, just as Billings's career was ending, John Connelly, a Philadelphia storekeeper, devised a new system of notation, replacing the syllables with geometric shapes: a triangle for *fa,* a circle for *sol,* a square for *la,* and a diamond for *mi.* The use of shapes in musical notation dated back at least to the Middle Ages, but Connelly's was the first system to represent the individual notes of the scale in this way. First used in a collection by William Smith and William Little, *The Easy Instructor, or A New Method of Teaching Sacred Harmony,* which appeared in Philadelphia in 1801, the shape-note system caught on immediately and became the standard for singing classes around the country. *The Easy Instructor* appeared in more than twenty editions over the next thirty years. Both *The Southern Harmony* and *The Sacred Harp* adopted its shape-note scheme, as did numerous other new songbooks.

The opening decades of the nineteenth century brought additional developments, liturgical and theological, that altered the geographical locus of *fa-sol-la* singing. In New England and the Middle Atlantic cities, a so-called better music movement, led by the Presbyterian banker, organist, educational reformer, and music instructor Lowell Mason, displaced the eighteenth-century singing school curriculum in churches and public schools with music drawn from the European classical masters, including Mozart and Haydn. Promoting serious classical music appreciation and education in the United States, the movement transformed the model of what Americans should be listening to and performing, and smothered the traditional colonial and Revolutionary-era hymnody, which it decried as vulgar, backward, and "unscientific." In place of a hard-edged but harmonically complex tune such as "Prospect," with lyrics taken from Isaac Watts — "Why should we start, or fear to die? What tim'rous worms we mortals are"—the "better music" advocates substituted more genteel fare, such as "Joy to the World," its lyrics also written by Watts yet with music by Lowell Mason and overtones of George Frideric Handel. *Fa-sol-la* singing retreated into the rural backcountry, especially the relatively remote upland South, where northeastern gentility carried little force.

Over these same decades, the rural camp-meeting evangelicalism of the Second Great Awakening, originating in the great revival at Cane Ridge, Kentucky, in 1801, reached its crest. Alongside the major evangelical churches—Baptists, Methodists, and so-called revival Presbygationalists—arose a dizzying array of new Protestant denominations, cults, and sects, in the greatest outbreak of Anglo-American religious invention since the English Puritan Revolution of the seventeenth century. The demand for new songbooks rose accordingly, not only for use at the camp meetings and in proliferating singing societies but also for private domestic worship, in the rural South as well as the more dignified, Eurocentric Northeast. The former provided the spiritual hunger and commercial market that William Walker, B. F. White, E. J. King, and other *fa-sol-la* songbook writers aimed to tap, aided by recent innovations in printing technology that made the issuing of mass editions more efficient and inexpensive than ever before. Precise numbers are impossible to determine, but Walker claimed that *The Southern Harmony* sold about 600,000 copies in its first half-century on the market. One observer noted that, in the years just preceding the Civil War, the only book more likely to be found in a Southern household other than *The Sacred Harp* was the Holy Bible.

The *fa-sol-la* compilers Walker, White, and King were driven by more than a desire to cash in. "I have endeavoured to gratify the taste of all," Walker wrote in his introduction to the first edition of his book. This meant supplying the entire array of evangelical churches "with a number of good, plain tunes" suited to the meters of their different existing hymnals, and with contrapuntal fugued compositions, at which Billings had excelled, and newer melodies picked up from hither and yon, often credited to one of the compilers. (The latter included, in a second edition of *The Southern Harmony*, "The Lone Pilgrim," its words actually composed by Elder John Ellis of Ohio in 1838 after he had visited the New Jersey tomb of Joseph Thomas, a prophet known as the White Pilgrim, who had wandered through much of the area east of the Mississippi dressed in white raiment.) Eclecticism as well as excellence dominated the selection process. "Those that are partial to ancient music, will find here some good old acquaintances," *The Southern Harmony* claimed, while "youthful companions, who are more fond of modern music" would find enough to satisfy them. Across the abundance of sects and denominations, the hymnals would spread the lessons and pleasures of musical fellowship, open to all believers just as God's grace was open to all sinners who sought it.

As its influence spread in the 1840s and 1850s, *fa-sol-la* singing remained firmly participatory rather than grandly performative. The major singing sites became gatherings known as conventions, including the Southern Musical Convention (organized in Upton County, Georgia, in 1845, with *The Sacred Harp* as its official book), and, after the Civil War, the Tallapoosa Singing Convention (organized in Haralson County, Georgia, in 1867), along with countless others located in towns from the Carolinas to Texas. Although reputed to be uniquely popular among Baptists (especially Primitive Baptists, or those who preferred to be known simply as "plain old Baptists"), the *fa-sol-la* conventions admitted of no distinctions other than the desire to sing of and to the Lord, a cappella, with the assembled faithful seated in a square, arranged section by section—trebles, altos, tenors, and basses—and with a group leader conducting from the square's center. The basic layout survives at the scores of *fa-sol-la* singing conventions still held today, chiefly in the Deep South.

Musically, the *fa-sol-la* tradition is most readily identifiable by its insistent modality, reinforced by the frequent absence of a "third" in the chordal structure and doublings that create an empty, hollow sound. Harmonies are often not in keeping with standard tonal practice, with each vocal part sounding as if it follows its own line only to converge at climactic moments. The style—with the melody carried by the tenor line rather than the soprano, and the harmony set by the bass— is typical of the early American singing-school idiom; it also retains vestiges of Renaissance polyphony. It remains the most ancient form of popular music sung in the United States.

Lyrically, the hymns, psalms, and anthems strongly reflect the Nonconformism of the early eighteenth century and after, both in their theology and their poetry. The songs chiefly concern human frailty, death, faith, and redemption. But there are many *fa-sol-la* songs that, while pursuing these themes, break out in a strange beauty all their own. Take the *Sacred Harp* psalm tune "Africa," its melody composed some time before 1770 by Billings, who lifted the lyrics from Watts in 1778 for a compilation titled *The Singing Master's Assistant*. The song has nothing explicitly to do with Africa. (Billings freely chose the names of New England towns and foreign continents as titles for his songs.) It begins with a leap of joy at the solemn oaths that have turned God's "mercy-drops" into a shower of salvation upon Sion-Hill (which in the patriot Billings's rendition often means America). Sion would dwell upon the heart of everlasting love, says the Lord, even "should nature change / And mothers monsters prove." But the final verse, carried along by Billings's majestic musical cadences, suddenly describes a painful act of human redemption, with blood gushing in a Sion that has fallen to pieces:

> Deep on the palms of both my hands
> I have engrav'd her name;
> My hands shall raise her ruin'd walls,
> And build her broken frame.

Perhaps Billings was updating Watts in order to refer to war-torn Revolutionary America, perhaps the choice of "Africa" was a deliberate reference to slavery, or perhaps the composer was simply struck by Watts's startling image. No matter: the amazing lines would resound over hills and valleys across the South for a century and a half, as they do at *fa-sol-la* singing conventions to this day.

A full accounting of sacred harp singing's effects on American literature as well as on America music has yet to be written. Only when George Pullen Jackson published the first major study of the genre in 1933 did it come to broad notice as a popular art form. Beyond Joe Dan Boyd's fine biography from 2002 of Judge Jackson, who produced *The Colored Sacred Harp* in 1934, much remains to be learned about the distinctive African American renditions of *fa-sol-la* music. The form seems to be enjoying a new lease on life, decades after the 1960s folk revival, as shape-note assemblies gather regularly in such unlikely places as Waldoboro, Maine, and Brooklyn, New York. Those with a taste for the weird revenants of American culture need only listen to Bob Dylan singing words as if he were the dead wanderer in his rendition, based on Doc Watson's, of "The Lone Pilgrim," the poignant, consoling final track on Dylan's 1993 album, *World Gone Wrong*. And the full story of how an Indian's words transcribed "almost verbatim"—"In de dark woods, no Indian nigh / Den me look Heb'n, and send up cry"—turned up as the shape-note hymn "Indian Convert, (or Nashville)" in both *The Southern Harmony* and *The Sacred Harp* begs for a novelist as well as a historian.

Bibliography: John Bealle, *Public Worship, Private Faith: Sacred Harp and American Folksong* (Athens, GA, 1997). Joe Dan Boyd, *Judge Jackson and the Colored Sacred Harp* (Tuscaloosa, AL, 1995). Buell E. Cobb, Jr., *The Sacred Harp: A Tradition and Its Music* (1978; Athens, GA, 1989). W. M. Cooper et al., eds., *The B. F. White Sacred Harp* (Troy, AL, 1949). George Pullen Jackson, *White Spirituals in the Southern Uplands: The Story of the Fa-sol-la Folk, Their Songs, Singings, and "Buckwheat Notes"* (1933; New York, 1965). William Walker, comp., *The Southern Harmony and Musical Companion,* ed. Glenn C. Wilcox (1835; Lexington, KY, 1993). *Discography: Religion Is a Fortune: Sacred Harp Singing* (County Records, 2004). *I Belong to This Band: Eighty-Five Years of Sacred Harp Recordings* (Dust-to-Digital, 2006).

SEAN WILENTZ

1836, February 23–March 6
The Alamo comes under siege

TEXAS BORDER WRITING

It is a warm October afternoon in 2007 in San Antonio, where writer Sandra Cisneros has called together the "Macarturos," Latino recipients of the MacArthur Fellowship who gather from time to time. Over lunch, a group that includes Sandra, performance artist Guillermo Gómez-Peña, labor organizer Baldemar Vásquez, and anthropologist Ruth Behar spontaneously decides to do a healing ceremony at the Alamo. I had been to the Alamo twice before, to please out-of-state visitors. Each time, I'd entered the grounds of the former mission, which the Daughters of the Republic of Texas maintain as a "Shrine to Texas Independence," with reluctance and trepidation, feeling alienated by the tone of the place. One must maintain a reverential stance while going through the building: hats off, speak in whispers. Uniformed security guards patrol the premises, while doves swoop down to eat crumbs. Each time, I was struck by the awe some visitors displayed, which I could not reconcile with my own feelings. I had been to a battlefield in Vietnam, years after the war that took my brother, and burst into uncontrollable tears. Yet here, on the ground where so many had also died, I felt nothing.

In the courtyard some forty of us—Mexican and Tejana, Cuban American and Puerto Rican, Spanish-speaking and English-speaking—find an open area and stand in a circle holding hands. We go round-robin, trying to evoke a different kind of reverence. Documentary filmmaker Ray Santisteban, camera on his shoulder, records it all. Suddenly two security guards approach and threaten to take the camera, saying only that the Alamo and its grounds are private property and no cameras are allowed. One of the guards is Anglo and speaks in an authoritarian voice; the short one, who appears to be Mexican, barely speaks at all. Soft-spoken, spiritual Baldemar's voice is resolute and defiant as he continues his prayers. I look up at the sky and imagine that its blue was the same color of a robin's egg on those fateful days of early spring in 1836. I think: surely we will get arrested. The guards grab Ray's arm, attempting to secure the camera. In a nearby performance area, some men in period costumes—coonskin caps and all—are teaching children how to throw a knife. The tourists mill around the spectacle, and no one notices our healing circle, within feet of the knife-throwing contest. Then the guards abruptly leave.

Anticlimactic as it was, the episode resonates and stays with me for weeks after the Macarturos have gone back to their respective homes all over the country. It is a complex history, a complex present. In recent years, the bronze plaque that lists the roster of heroes who died at the Alamo has been changed to include the Tejanos who were rebelling against the centralist government of Mexican president Santa Anna and died alongside the "Texians." It even includes the troops who were following Santa Anna's orders, soldiers who were transformed in the imagination of the mainstream United States into ruthless savages, the archetypal bad Mexicans of every racist fantasy in later novels, histories, and films. The cruelty associated with the crushing siege of the Alamo was used to excuse the violence, overt and covert, that was done to Mexicans and blacks in Texas afterward—a violence that persisted well into my own childhood, in the form of discriminatory educational practices and oppressive poverty in South Texas, and that endures today.

The history of that battle for independence remains alive, not just because of the reminder that the site itself offers, but because it is one more scene in an ongoing circle of violent events strung together like beads on the unending necklace of time. The struggle to control and name territory, to regulate the space in which people can live, continues. As I write, a wall is being built that will separate lands that have been in families since before 1836. At one point it will sever parts of the campus of the University of Texas at Brownsville. For me it is the border region, with its "wound that will not heal," as Gloria Anzaldúa characterized it, that most poignantly experienced that war. It is the land where I was born, where I came of age, where I choose to live, where my ancestors have lived for generations, where I feel at home, and where I will be buried.

A number of pivotal events occurred in 1836 that set in motion a major shift in the history of two nations—and in the lives of the people who lived in the border region. We don't have accounts of how the native people of what is now South Texas reacted when they first witnessed the European intruders from the south, or when Hernando de Soto arrived at the Gulf coast. But we do have letters, reports, and recollections of Tejanos that chronicle the clash and confluence of cultures that occurred when, 130 years later, English-speaking settlers swarmed into Texas. Some Tejanos joined with those foreigners—who shared neither their religion, language, nor customs—to fight for independence from Mexico; their distance from Mexico City had left them pretty much to govern themselves. But from the perspective of the Mexican nation-state, the Anglos were foreign invaders who had taken up arms, and had to be stopped. The prosperous city of San Antonio de Bexar, founded in 1691, was pivotal for Santa Anna; some 3,000 of his troops stormed the city. The confrontation at the mission-turned-garrison where the pro-independence forces had barricaded themselves lasted an ominous thirteen days. It made heroes of frontiersmen like Davy Crockett, a former Tennessee congressman, and Jim Bowie, a former smuggler and slave trader, along with a number of mercenaries.

Meanwhile, the Republic of Texas declared its independence. Even before the final defeat of the Mexican army on April 21 in the Battle of San Jacinto, Texas had approved a constitution abolishing slavery, at least in name. By the fall, it had elected a president, Sam Houston, and replaced the interim Tejano vice president, Lorenzo de Zavala, with an Anglo. (To this day no Latino has held the state's highest office.) The earlier inhabitants of the region became a colonized people under the military rule of the Texian Army, and later the notoriously brutal Texas Rangers. The contested area between the Nueces River and the Rio Grande, where the U.S. Army provoked the military action that began the War with Mexico (1846 to 1848), became for Tejanos synonymous with violence. In Laredo, the story goes, some residents disinterred their dead and crossed the river to rebury them in Mexican soil, such was their abhorrence of the *Americanos.*

Among the "Texians," however, the Alamo and the values they associated with it—honor, courage under fire—swiftly attained the status of legend. Texas is anything but homogeneous, and each of its various regions has its distinct linguistic, culinary, and ethnic makeup. But the Alamo came to stand for a greater Texan pride and self-determination that looms large in the imagination of the world. The transformation of event into myth began almost immediately after the Alamo, with Richard Penn Smith's *David Crockett's Exploits and Adventures in Texas* (1836), which immortalized Crockett as a rugged Anglo-Saxon hero and hammered in the villainy of the Mexicans, ignoring the Tejanos and Tejanas, as well as the Jews and African Americans, who also stood behind the Alamo's walls. Cheap novels like Anthony Ganilh's *Mexico versus Texas* (1838) and Augusta Evans's *Inez: A Tale of the Alamo* (1855) sensationalized the battles and simplified cultural conflicts into formulaic plots: a Catholic and a Protestant fall in love; a beautiful Texan woman is abducted by Indians and rescued.

Women writers in particular turned the Alamo drama into romance novels about civilizing the "new" space of Texas. (Even before independence, the first book in English about the region was written by a woman: Mary Austin Holley, Stephen Austin's cousin, whose 1833 book *Texas* was an epistolary narrative intended to attract outsiders.) Amelia Barr's best-selling *Remember the Alamo* (1898) exemplifies the way the battle was depicted, even decades afterward, as an event of valor and courage—as well as an opportunity for Anglo-Saxons to rescue benighted peoples. Barr's anti-Catholic sentiment is typical: "The priesthood foresaw that the triumph of the American element meant the triumph of freedom of conscience, and the abolition of their own despotism." What will become hostility in real life against Mexicans, Native Americans, and African Americans appears in the fictions of the nineteenth and early twentieth centuries, where racial slurs and a strong undercurrent of Southern nostalgia abound.

The dime novels of the nineteenth century also created the enduring myth of the cowboy, whose self-sufficiency and deep-rooted honor code made him a direct descendant of the mythic Alamo heroes. At the same time, these works offered a pejorative view of the *vaquero,* the ranch hand, who had given the cowboy so much—language, knowledge, and lore. These *vaqueros,* with the *rancheros,* or landowners, created the Texas of the celebrated cattle range, an industry that persists to this day. Many of the range-holders, however, came into possession of their cheap, empty lands by dispossessing Tejanos of lands granted to them long before. Despite the debt that cowboy culture owes to the *vaqueros,* the contemporary novelists most strongly identified with Texas, Larry McMurtry and Cormac McCarthy, still portray the Mexican inhabitants of the region with the same disdain: I eagerly picked up McMurtry's *Streets of Laredo* (1993) only to find that my ancestors—when they were portrayed at all—were not-very-honorable types who ate rats. McCarthy's border novels realistically incorporate Spanish phrases into their lyrical language, but his Mexican characters are just as shadowy and unknowable as the stock villains and priests in nineteenth-century Anglo-American fiction. (Of course, the narratives of sixteenth- and seventeenth-century explorers like Álvar Núñez Cabeza de Vaca, Pedro de Castañeda, and Fray Alonso de Benavides had inaugurated a parallel but rather different Spanish-language publishing tradition, in newspapers, periodicals, and books, that persisted after statehood and flourished again after the Mexican Revolution.)

The violence wrought upon the bodies of Tejanos, both metaphorically and literally, surfaces in the way that our traditions have been appropriated. The cultural landscape in many parts of Texas has always been Mexican, but it is a highly selective, public Mexicanness made to suit touristic expectations, not real people. The performance of the state's Mexican heritage is often confused with Spanish markers, such as flamenco dancers, in citywide celebrations like Charro Days in Brownsville. Urban San Antonio still has a mini–trail drive as it ushers longhorn cattle through its streets in preparation for the annual rodeo that takes place every winter. It also holds a two-week fiesta that commemorates the defeat of the Mexican army at San Jacinto; April 21 is a state holiday. However, most of the millions of partygoers, including many Tejanos as well as recent immigrants from Mexico and Central America, remain oblivious to what they are celebrating.

The problem is not a lack of connection to history but what popular culture has made of the events of 1836. In Hollywood films and popular fiction, as Richard Flores ably shows, the Alamo signifies resistance and courage against great odds while vilifying the Mexican and erasing the prior Tejano presence. Its message of freedom obscures the reality that Texas, in particular South Texas, is a colonized land. Well into the 1940s and '50s, Mexicans were considered white except in terms of access to public facilities: in communities like San Antonio or Cotulla, schools, restaurants, and movie theaters remained segregated, as bilingual poet Tino Villanueva elegantly describes in his book-length sequence, *Scene from the Movie GIANT* (1993). Re-creating the movie theater in his hometown of San Marcos, where he first saw that wide-screen Texas myth, Villanueva describes his loss of innocence as he realizes that Texas Mexicans are portrayed as infantilized, powerless, waiting to be saved by the great white hero: outsiders in the land that has been theirs for generations.

Despite the popularity of the John Wayne character (in the case of *Giant*, Rock Hudson) who honorably fights the good fight, Tejano and Tejana writers have debunked the myth of the Anglo colonizer as savior, as Anzaldúa does in her poem, "We Called Them Greasers." Recent historians like David Montejano and Andres Tijerina chronicle the perspective of the Tejanos and Tejanas who were stripped of their land and made targets of severe racism and efforts at cultural eradication. The lingering effects of this oppression may explain why two important historical novels written in the 1930s, *George Washington Gomez* by folklorist Américo Paredes and *Caballero* by Eve Merriam and Jovita González, were not published until much later. Set in the aftermath of the U.S.-Mexico War, these novels depict life in South Texas without shying away from representations of the violent politics and social relations that emerge late in the nineteenth century and into the twentieth. Since then, a number of accomplished writers have chronicled not just the history but the distinct regional quality of the Texas they remember, in all its specificity—the Spanish spoken in West Texas is closer to that of New Mexicans than South Texans, for example, and their way of making tamales or preference for corn versus flour tortillas varies as well. For writers like Barbara Renaud González, Benjamin Alire Saenz, and Alicia Gaspar de Alba, it is the land of West Texas—Lubbock and El Paso, respectively; for writers like Rolando Hinojosa and Oscar Casarez, it is the Rio Grande Valley; and for others it is East Texas, Houston and Texarkana, or small towns like Nixon or Gonzalez in Central Texas.

Perhaps the reason I felt no sense of sacred connection on my first visits to the Alamo is that my childhood associations with it were shaped by a pedagogical project almost impossible to resist. In elementary school we memorized and sang "Texas, Our Texas"; in seventh grade we memorized the state bird, flower, and tree. I didn't question such assignments, but my family reinforced a different lesson. I attended an *escuelita* in the early 1950s where I was taught Spanish songs and to read and write. It was the community's attempt to instill in us a pride in our heritage, which was disparaged in the public schools, where I was physically punished for speaking Spanish. My mother made sure I dressed in a *china poblana*, the traditional dress of Mexican female identity, for various celebrations; my grandmother taught me to *declamar*, a traditional poetry recitation practice popular until fairly recently. The rupture, the terrifying rending of the fabric that was life before 1836, has made me who I am, but it has also rendered many of us Texans blind to our own history. The healing circle that October afternoon taught me that the battle is not yet over.

Bibliography: Teresa Palomo Acosta and Ruthe Winegarten, *Las Tejanas: 300 Years of History* (Austin, TX, 2003). Gloria Anzaldúa, *Borderlands/La Frontera* (Berkeley, CA, 1986). Richard R. Flores, *Remembering the Alamo: Memory, Modernity, and the Master Symbol* (Austin, TX, 2002). Dagoberto Gilb, ed., *Hecho en Tejas: An Anthology of Texas Mexican Literature* (Albuquerque, NM, 2006). David Montejano, *Anglos and Mexicans in the Making of Texas, 1836–1986* (Austin, TX, 1987). Tino Villanueva, *Scene from the Movie GIANT* (Willemantic, CT, 1993).

NORMA E. CANTÚ

1836, February 28

Richard Henry Dana, Jr., reads an old newspaper describing his Harvard classmates' graduation on a day he was "walking up and down California beach with a hide upon his head"

Two Years before the Mast

From the moment he first landed in California, Richard Dana was attuned to the contrast between manual and intellectual labor. He and his shipmates struggled to navigate their small boats through choppy swells, to the derision of "a crew of dusky Sandwich Islanders, talking and hallooing in their outlandish tongue," and drenched themselves making shore. Even more dampening to their spirits was the sight of men walking down the beach hunched over like beasts of burden, heads bent to support the stiff, folded cowhide on their backs. This was the work that the scion of one of New England's first families had signed on for when he'd impulsively decided to ship out from Boston as a common sailor. "'Well, Dana,' said the second mate to me, 'this does not look much like Cambridge college, does it? This is what I call *head work.*' To tell the truth, it did not look very encouraging."

On and off for the next fourteen months, Dana would hump those hides on his own back when he was not curing them or stuffing them, with the aid of huge hooks, into the ship's hold. By the time he received the bundle of old newspapers and letters from home he was an old California hand, surf-wise, tanned, and newly conversant in the language of the "dusky Sandwich Islanders" as well as the Spanish spoken in this far-flung Mexican outpost. From San Francisco to San Diego, he observed the Californios who came to inspect the goods his ship, the *Pilgrim,* had brought from Boston: silks, hardware, spirits, leather boots fashioned in New England from the very hides the ranchers had previously exported. He watched with great interest their weddings, funerals, and *fandangos;* he rode around their abandoned missions. But these were rare moments of leisure on a voyage that opened Dana's eyes to exploitation and cruelty, culminating in the horrific flogging of two good sailors "spread-eagled" merely for asking questions of the incompetent, intemperate Captain Francis Thompson. Letters from Boston assured Dana that he was to return home with one of the *Pilgrim*'s sister ships; Captain Thompson had other ideas.

The enduring readability of Dana's memoir *Two Years before the Mast: A Personal Narrative of Life at Sea*—an instant best seller when it was published in 1840 and never out of print since—rests in no small part on the suspense of whether Dana will escape from this maritime tyranny or be undone by it. The book experienced a second life as a California guidebook packed in the chests of hopeful forty-niners. The Melville revival of the 1920s launched a third resurgence; Melville had justly admired its dramatic portrayal of rounding Cape Horn in a terrible gale. Dana's narrative today stands as a foundational document of California mythmaking, an obligatory entry in regional literary anthologies.

Two Years before the Mast both fulfills and frustrates our contemporary expectations of memoir, where voyages are often undertaken with the goal of self-transformation. After two years at Harvard, his eyesight mysteriously weakened to the point where he could no longer study, Dana settled on a curative course of life at sea. Barely nineteen, he spurned the option of playing gentleman-passenger and signed on for a voyage of eighteen months to two years on the cramped, ninety-foot brig *Pilgrim*. His eye problems cleared up immediately, and he resolved to earn the respect of his fellow sailors quartered in the forecastle, "before the mast." He learned to furl sails with the best of them, leaving his dress clothes in his trunk when going ashore in favor of the sailor's white duck trousers, blue jacket, and straw hat. As with every story of putting on another's clothes, the drama here is whether he can ever take them off again.

Like Hemingway after him, Dana was impatient to shrug off his privilege and put his hand to authentic life—the underside of work and sweat, drunkenness and pleasure—that it was the mission of his hereditary class to transcend. And like Whitman, London, and Kerouac, Dana was also impatient to tell a story from below, from direct experience, eliciting insights not findable in books: to see through the eyes of the common "Jack," as he put it, explore "human nature under new circumstances," and record "the secrets of sailors' lives and hardships." He moralizes this process of ethnographic observation: "We must come down from our heights, and leave our straight paths, for the byways and low places of life, if we would learn truths by strange contrasts." If that sounds like a line from Emerson (who had once been Dana's schoolmaster), it only underlines how carefully shaped this story of "direct experience" actually was: his original journal was lost upon Dana's return and reconstructed many months afterward. Along with the crew's yarns, adventure stories help frame his narrative. Arriving at Juan Fernández off the coast of Chile, Dana cannot help but experience it as Robinson Crusoe's island, "the most romantic spot of earth that my eyes had ever seen." A California *ranchero* reminds him of some "decayed gentleman" in a picaresque novel.

Two Years before the Mast is also a meditation on democracy and the nature of power. Captain Thompson's brutishness proves that "the conferring of absolute power is too apt to work a great change" upon otherwise upright men; Dana closes his book with a plea for legal checks on the authority of sea captains. His admiration for many of his shipmates argues against any social privilege not based on merit. Dana calls one sailor with a steel-trap memory, who can calculate navigational logs in his head, "the most remarkable man I have ever seen"; it was surely unjust that at forty he was "still a dog before the mast, at twelve dollars a month." Yet when the crew learns to their dismay that their voyage would be extended by a year or two, Dana's Everyman persona starts to crack. As the ship appointed to take him home prepares to sail, Captain Thompson casually tells Dana he must persuade another sailor to take his place on the crew. Taking a stance more appropriate to a Massachusetts town meeting than the rigid hierarchy of the ship, Dana says he "put on a bold front, and told him plainly that I had a letter in my chest informing me that he had been written to, by the owners in Boston, to bring me home." Others had been flogged for lesser insubordinations. In the end it is not this out-of-place assertion of his citizen's rights but ready cash that liberates him: he offers an English boy six months' wages, throwing in his old clothes too. The crew mutters. "The notion that I was not 'one of them,' which, by a participation in all their labor and hardships . . . had been laid asleep, was beginning to revive." No doubt.

What became of the exhortation to learn "truth by strange contrasts"? For all his enthusiasm about putting on sailor's garb, Dana seems anxious to maintain firm distinctions between his true self and his temporary one. Fears of an irreversible transformation had been brewing ever since the first landing: "Here we were, in a little vessel, with a small crew, on a half-civilized coast, at the ends of the earth, and with a prospect of remaining an indefinite period." It was bad enough for "Jack" that the voyage would be extended, "but still worse was it for me, who did not mean to be a sailor for life . . . Three or four years would make me a sailor in every respect, mind and habits, as well as body." Yet he revels in that new body's strength and prowess. He scrambles down a sheer cliff to grab a few hides lodged in a crevice, and even the hardened sailors scold, "What a d——d fool you were to risk your life for half a dozen hides!"

It is intriguingly unclear whether the transformation Dana alternately courts and fears has to do with the occupation or the place itself: "Two years more in California would have made me a sailor for the rest of my days." Dana's impressions of the landscape and people veer from enchantment to repugnance. The red tile roofs of Monterey give a "pretty effect," but the Mexican Californios seem "an idle, thriftless people." He casts aspersions on the virtue of their women, their legal system, their claims to whiteness ("From the upper class, they go down by regular shades, growing more and more dark and muddy, until you come down to the pure Indian"). The wedding of the company's agent to the daughter of a wealthy local family arouses his distaste for racial mixing—Americans who intermarried with Californios generally spoke Spanish at home and raised their children Catholic. "If the 'California fever' spares the first generation, it always attacks the second . . . In the hands of an enterprising people, what a country this might be! . . . Yet how long would a people remain so, in such a country?"

Dana, however, is hardly immune to the intoxication of a less "enterprising" way of life. He spends a summer sleeping in a hut on the beach, learning how to prepare hides, smoke pipes, and swear in Hawaiian. One of the "Kanakas," Hope, becomes his Friday, his proto-Queequeg: "I really felt a strong affection for him, and preferred him to any of my own countrymen there; and I believe there was nothing which he would not have done for me." As one of his shipmates chided him after the book's publication, Dana has excised from this scene the Indian women who used to visit the "Oahu Coffee-house"; when Dana later sneaks medicines from the ship to treat Hope's syphilis, we get the strong whiff of a story incompletely told.

But ellipses are, after all, one of the generic requirements of memoir. Nowhere is Dana's ambivalence about self-transformation more evident than in the homecoming scene, where instead of joy he experiences "a state of very nearly entire apathy." When an old schoolmate comes aboard at Boston's Long Wharf, Dana describes himself from the other man's perspective: "There came down from aloft a 'rough alley' looking fellow, with duck trowsers and red shirt, long hair, and face burnt as black as an Indian's." However, he quickly returns to a recognizable self again — so much so that he does not sit down to reconstruct his narrative for another two years, after finishing his degree and beginning his legal studies.

Dana put nose to the grindstone, building a practice in admiralty law and serving in the Massachusetts legislature, where his nickname, "the Duke of Cambridge," suggests how fully he had returned to the role of patrician. The only hint of lingering attraction to life's "low places" are the episodes in Dana's early married life, described in *The Journal of Richard Henry Dana, Jr.*, when he ventures into prostitutes' apartments, "knowing it was a vain curiosity & tending to no good," ducking out before temptation can seize him.

On the bad advice of his father, Dana had turned down his publisher's offer of a 10 percent royalty and took a flat fee of $250 for the manuscript of *Two Years before the Mast;* the book earned tens of thousands for the Harpers and spawned many pirated editions. Finally retrieving the copyright in 1869, he prepared a new edition even more mediated than the one he had reconstructed in 1840. For the original didactic postscript he substituted an account of his return journey to California in 1859, "Twenty-Four Years After." The prose is weighted down by adjectives extolling the "glorious climate," the "golden sunlight," the "gleaming white Mission." In unrecognizable, prosperous San Francisco, he is welcomed reverentially as "the veteran pioneer of all." But the steamships are ugly and lack the grace of sail. No one remembers how to prepare a hide. The Kanakas are gone. The Mexican *rancheros* no longer strike him as shady characters but as noble "pillars of the past." He sings the praises of Juan Bandini, the very man he had once mocked as a broken-down, "dissolute," "extravagant" *caballero*. It is as if he forgot to reread his own book.

"Twenty-Four Years After" would feed into a common representation of California as both defined and ruined by constant change. It transforms "California fever" into the *tristesse* of nostalgia: "The past was real. The present, all about me, was unreal, unnatural, repellant." Carey McWilliams would later diagnose this refuge-seeking in the past as a "Spanish fantasy heritage" that dissolved the social tensions of frontier California in the rosy glow of red-tile roofs, noble horsemen, and gentle padres, most influentially articulated in Helen Hunt Jackson's *Ramona* (1884). Joan Didion writes of her Sacramento pioneer family's mythmaking: "That I should have continued, deep into adult life, to think of California as I was told as a child it had been in 1868 suggests a confusion of some magnitude, but there it was." The histories written by Californios—including several generations of Bandinis—generally tell a different tale, as do novels like Maria Amparo Ruíz de Burton's *The Squatter and the Don* (1885).

In his unfogged original, Dana repeatedly represented California as the "ends of the earth." Such a description could have arisen only in a context of Manifest Destiny that saw the continental extension of the United States as an inevitable yet implicitly melancholy fact. *Two Years before the Mast* may stand as the foundational assertion of California eschatology: the place of the last chance and the end times, populated with "smart, unprincipled fellows" and "loafers." Dana cites the example of an industrious tailor who disappeared one day and returned in a cart, barefoot, half-clothed, and "cleaned out": "This is a specimen of the life of half of the Americans and English who are adrift over the whole of California." From here it is not far to the stream of drifters, losers, and lowlifes who animate the works of Nathanael West, Raymond Chandler, John Steinbeck.

Dana is the very type of the Easterner who can never apprehend the West as anything but radically other. "Head work" to him meant stiff, folded hides and escape from the demands of thinking. Didion stands in a long line of articulate Californians who have made Dana's pilgrimage in reverse—among them Frank Norris, Josiah Royce, and Gertrude Stein—yet the phrase "California intellectual" still invites puzzlement or worse, despite ample evidence of their accomplishments and those of writers who, embracing their edgy perspective, remained. This is not all Dana's doing, but it may be his unintended legacy.

Bibliography: Richard Henry Dana, Jr., *Two Years before the Mast,* ed. Thomas Philbrick (New York, 2001); *The Journal of Richard Henry Dana, Jr.,* vol. 1, ed. Robert F. Lucid (Cambridge, MA, 1968). Joan Didion, *Where I Was From* (New York, 2003).

KIRSTEN SILVA GRUESZ

1837, August 15

Ralph Waldo Emerson warns,
"The American eagle is very well . . . But beware of the American peacock"

THE AMERICAN SCHOLAR

If you ask your average intellectually inclined French citizen if he has ever read any Descartes or Pascal or Rousseau, he will almost certainly tell you that he has (and in most cases he will be telling you the truth). To be a French intellectual and to be simply unacquainted with the classics of French thought and to be happy to admit that one is thus unacquainted is to be a very unusual person indeed. There is no American philosopher ignorance of whose work could strike a measure of fear or embarrassment in the soul of an American of letters at all comparable to what it would mean for a French intellectual to have never read a word of Descartes. If you attempt to hit upon the name of an American philosopher that almost every educated American has read, you will seek in vain. Insofar as you can find a philosopher that most educated Americans have read, it will not be an American—most likely, it will be Plato or Descartes or Hume or Kant. There is nothing you could call American philosophy which plays a role in the formation of an American intellectual identity that parallels the role that French philosophy plays in French culture, or German philosophy in German culture. To be an intellectual in the United States still means, above all, to have a certain literacy in certain landmark moments in the history of *European* thought. The intellectual in America is haunted not by the fear that he might be failing to be an *American* intellectual; more often he is haunted by the fear that he might be succeeding in being just that—and hence perhaps someone a European might look upon as a philistine. Even if someone were somehow to come into the grip of the idea that becoming an intellectual in America meant, above all, learning how to become an American intellectual, there would be few American landmarks by means of which he or she could confidently navigate the way toward such an identity.

These facts are no less true today than they were when Emerson gave his famous address to the Phi Beta Kappa Society at Harvard in 1837. This means that the call that he issued on that day has still largely gone unanswered. The call was indeed an ambitious one. It asked not only for a rethinking of the three concepts that figure most centrally in the preceding paragraph—philosophy, America, and Europe—but also for a rethinking of each of the three in the light of the other two. On Emerson's ambitious conception, the establishment of a genuinely American tradition of philosophy would have to evince a significant internal relation between the concepts *philosophy* and *America.* But Emerson did not have only philosophy in mind. He was calling, more generally, for a transformation of American letters and public discourse, for the forging of a significant internal relation between yet further concepts, ones such as *thinking, culture,* and *scholarship,* on the one hand, and *independence, representative,* and *democracy,* on the other.

In his eyes, America had not yet declared its independence. Among the opening remarks in his address, Emerson declares the following hope: "Our day of dependence, our long apprenticeship to the learning of other lands, draws to a close. The millions that around us are rushing into life, cannot always be fed on the sere remains of foreign harvests . . . In this hope I accept the topic which not only usage but the nature of our association seem to prescribe to this day,—the AMERICAN SCHOLAR." The American scholar will come into existence only when America herself comes into existence by learning to think for herself, where this requires first throwing off all that is no longer living in the ossified edifice of European scholarship. But for Emerson that task starts with each of his listeners: an American is something each of us must first *become* in order for there to be anything that is America.

Emerson sees America's relation to Europe to be largely one of cultural ventriloquism combined with the cultivation of a form of dishonesty that allows its citizens to pretend otherwise: "This mendicant America, this curious, peering, itinerant, imitative America, studious of Greece and Rome, of England and Germany." Yet the last thing he wants is for us to endorse the European view of America. (Though he thinks Americans should be interested in the degree to which they have acquired a certain reputation abroad: "Let us honestly state the facts. Our America has a bad name for superficialness.") Indeed, countless remarks in his *Journals* make it clear that he thinks America has a long way to go: "The mark of American merit in painting, in sculpture, in poetry, in fiction, in eloquence, seems to be a certain grace without grandeur, in itself not new but derivative, a vase of fair outline, but empty."

Ever since Emerson's 1837 address, and often directly inspired by its words, it has been a central ambition of much American thinking and writing and art (though seldom of American philosophy) to call forth a form of culture in which American thinkers or authors or artists can eschew European models—of philosophy or authorship or art—in a manner that will enable them finally to be able to feel at home in their homeland as thinkers or authors or artists (as they imagine their European counterparts are able to feel at home in their respective cultures). The realization of such an ambition is supposed by Emerson to require a reciprocal change on the part of American thinking and writing and art and on the part of the homeland itself; and the accomplished fact of such reciprocal change is an integral part of what it means for the American scholar finally to have come into existence. But to say that American thinking and writing and art have been fueled by such an ambition is not to say that such a vision of America has ever been realized—that the American philosopher or author or artist has ever yet been able to feel himself or herself permanently or comfortably at home in America.

"We have yet had no genius in America, with tyrannous eye, which knew the value of our own incomparable materials." A common way to understand a remark of Emerson's such as this is to construe it as a plea for cultural chauvinism. No greater misunderstanding is possible. Emerson has no wish to retain the central assumption of the conception that he opposes: namely, the assumption that Europe and America between them have only one form of culture worthy of respect and admiration. The conception he opposes takes European culture to be the real article and American culture, insofar as there is something worthy of the title, necessarily to be a pale imitation thereof. The aforementioned misunderstanding of Emerson attributes to him the intention simply to turn this way of thinking inside out: to regard European culture as sick and dying and American culture as healthy and vibrant. These two views are mirror images—each feeds on and sustains the other. There was never a more penetrating critic of American triumphalism than Emerson. The following quip, for example, remains as apt a caution for our flag-waving patriots as it was for the Jacksonians at whom it was originally directed: "Your American eagle is very well. Protect it here and abroad. But beware of the American peacock." Emerson was able to sympathize with the triumphalist's thought that one of the reasons that patriotism comes less naturally to American intellectuals has to do with their tendency to identify culture and cosmopolitanism with Europe, without sympathizing in the least with their further thought that the way for America to cure itself of this unhealthy self-conception is simply through a sheer act of will, to learn to view itself as the paradigm of a healthy nation and to look upon the glories of European culture as symptoms of illness.

Emerson's rejection of any brand of American cultural chauvinism goes hand in hand with his impatience with the correlative posture of blind patriotism. It is no accident that it is a student of Emerson's, Henry David Thoreau, who comes to be the author of that famous tract *Civil Disobedience.* For it is precisely out of a fidelity to his understanding of America's pledges to itself that Emerson enjoins his readers to see that they, too, out of a sense of their devotion to America, ought to take themselves to stand honor-bound, *hic et nunc,* to resist this or that federal law—such as the Fugitive Slave Act. To be complicit in returning a runaway slave to his or her slaveholder was to participate in a form of activity that itself contravened the very foundations of our national covenant: "I think we must get rid of slavery or we must get rid of freedom . . . If you put a chain around the neck of a slave, the other end fastens itself around your own." In the two decades following his Phi Beta Kappa address, as the Northern states' willingness to accommodate Southern demands with regard to a supposed right to retain—and, if it be fugitive, reclaim—human property seemed at first to know ever fewer bounds, so too did Emerson's scorn for what passed for politics in Washington: "It seems to be settled that no act of honor or benevolence or justice is to be expected from the American government, but only this, that they will be as wicked as they dare. No man now can have any sort of success in politics without a streak of infamy crossing his name." It would be a mistake to suppose that just because Emerson harbored a dream of what she might be, his heart was never broken by the reality of what America was.

Emerson's call for the American scholar is sometimes criticized for presupposing an overly romantic conception of the cultural aspirations of the common run of his fellow citizens and an overly utopian conception of the transformative power of democratic public opinion as an engine of cultural change. One does not need to read very far into Emerson, however, to discover that there is neither anything romantic nor utopian about his view of contemporaneous American public opinion: "It is said public opinion will not bear it. *Really?* Public opinion, I am sorry to say, will bear a great deal of nonsense. There is scarce any absurdity so gross whether in religion, politics, science, or manners, which it will not bear . . . It will bear Andrew Jackson for President." (I know just how he feels.) There is certainly nothing triumphalist about Emerson's attitude toward what passes in his day for the accomplished fact of America: "This country has not fulfilled what seemed the reasonable expectation of mankind."

The following quotation, in combination with the previous ones, gives us a glimpse of the picture that Emerson has of the American landscape he is seeking to redeem: "The Jacksonianism of the country, heedless of English and of all literature—a stone cut out of the ground without hands—it may root out the hollow dilettantism of our cultivation in the coarsest way and the new-born may begin again to frame their own world with greater advantage." The landscape is therefore populated equally by those who are animated by a false sense of their own culture ("the hollow dilettantism of our cultivation") and by those who are possessed by a no less false conception of how America may become "new-born" (through the triumph of a party of "rabble-rousers"). Thus, now at the other end of the spectrum of misplaced responses to the dilemma of the absence of the American scholar, Emerson is no less wary of a tendency among even some of his thinking countrymen to attempt to overcome their inferiority complex vis-à-vis the splendor of European modes of cultivation by attempting simply to do without the higher forms of *Bildung* altogether: "It seems to me as if the high idea of Culture as the end of existence does not pervade the mind of the thinking people of our Community . . . Could this be properly taught, I think it must provoke and overmaster the young and ambitious."

A central obstacle to the emergence of such a genuinely American form of high culture is traced by Emerson—and then even more loudly diagnosed and then denounced by Thoreau—to an attachment to forms of literary and political speech emptied of their substance. Emerson writes: "Sometimes the life seems to be dying out of all literature and this enormous paper currency of Words is accepted instead." Stanley Cavell, paraphrasing the authors whose views he here helps to articulate, gives forceful expression to why, for both Emerson and Thoreau, the American reader and the American word must be awakened together:

> Everyone is saying, and anyone can hear, that this is the new world; that we are the new men; that the earth is to be born again; that the past is to be cast off like a skin; that we must learn from children to see again; that everyday is the first day of the world, that America is Eden. So how can a word get through whose burden is that we do not understand a word of all this? Or rather, that the way we understand it is insane, and we are trying again to buy and bully our way into heaven, that we have failed, that the present is a task and a discovery, not a period of America's privileged history; that we are not free, not whole, and not new, and we know this and are on a downward path of despair because of it.

Certain forms of speech seem not to require recovery because, to so many Americans, they seem to have always been present and are everywhere still present. And, indeed, Americans often still hear their fellow citizens echoing the currently fashionable—often secularized—equivalents of sentences such as these: "This is the new world"; "We are the new men"; "The earth is to be born again"; "The past is to be cast off like a skin"; "America is Eden." (The rhetoric has been modernized but the sentiment remains much the same.) Verbal formulae such as these, in Emerson's time, after several decades of repetition (and in our time, after now several centuries of repetition), are asked not to lose any of their original expressive capacity. Yet those who make confident use of them persist in living in ways that must deprive them of meaning: as the call for Americans to be new gives way to a fantasy of freezing time—to a call to disregard any needs or hopes deemed not to accord with the supposed "intentions of the founders"; as the new world, having pledged to cast off its past like an old skin, seems now, much like the old world, weighed down by layers of history. In the face of such failures on America's part to be able to mean its descriptions of itself, the task of a properly American philosophical and literary and political discourse became, already over a century and a half ago, for Emerson, that of finding a way, first, to tell Americans, such that they *are* able to hear it, that they no longer understand the forms of words they call upon to articulate the promise of America, and, second, to demonstrate that these very words, their present apparent expressive impotence notwithstanding, can still be called upon, in speaking of America, to say something we are still able to understand and believe.

Bibliography: Stanley Cavell, *Emerson's Transcendental Etudes* (Palo Alto, CA, 2003). James Conant, "Emerson as Educator," *Emerson Society Quarterly* 43 (1997). Ralph Waldo Emerson, *Essays and Lectures,* ed. Joel Porte (New York, 1983); *Emerson in His Journals,* ed. Joel Porte (Cambridge, MA, 1982). Henry David Thoreau, *Collected Essays and Poems,* ed. Elizabeth Hall Witherell (New York, 2001). Albert J. von Frank, *The Trials of Anthony Burns: Freedom and Slavery in Emerson's Boston* (Cambridge, MA, 1998).

JAMES CONANT

1838, July 15

Emerson shakes the foundations of traditional philosophy and established Christian faith

The Divinity School Address

To this day, Ralph Waldo Emerson's 1837 lecture "The American Scholar" has intrigued readers as the quintessential statement of a courageously independent departure in American culture and in the history of thinking in general; at the time, Emerson's July 15, 1838, oration, commonly called the Divinity School Address, created quite a local and regional stir in Cambridge and the Boston area as "the latest form of infidelity," as the conservative minister Andrews Norton memorably denounced Emerson's address before the graduating class of Harvard Divinity School. The Divinity School Address has stood ever since as a momentous challenge to Western Christian belief and culture. Taken together, the two speeches may be said to have shaken the foundations of traditional philosophy and of established Christian faith.

More than Emerson's acclaimed first publication, *Nature* (1836), with its still relatively traditional philosophical structure and style, the two speeches inaugurated that radical turn in Western cultures that one may define as the still-ongoing project of modernism; the tremors caused by Emerson's philosophical and theological and cultural provocations continue to be felt undiminished in modes and moods of thinking and belief, whether they be called postmodern or poststructural or posthistorical or simply contemporary.

In "The American Scholar" and in the Divinity School Address, Emerson not only begins to undermine traditional assumptions, axioms, and principles of Western cultures. For the first time and fully, he also perfects his characteristic aphoristic style—in the early German critic Paul Sakmann's apt characterization, as "the master of the single sentence"—but the aphorism, in Emerson, is not merely a stylistic device of concentration and provocation. It is an indispensable and essential aspect of the philosophical, the theological, the cultural subject matter itself.

In his *Twilight of the Idols* Friedrich Nietzsche, in so many ways Emerson's disciple and heir, spoke of the aphorism as a "form of eternity," as the single most powerful form of articulating prophetically and philosophically authoritative insights. In the *Will to Power* Nietzsche insisted that the deepest and truly inexhaustible books would always possess an "aphoristic and sudden character," would present and enact the unforeseen, the unexpectedly powerful and innovatively surprising truth, the earthshaking new departure in a single incisive statement.

"There is never a beginning, there is never an end, to the inexplicable continuity of this web of God, but always circular power returning into itself." From "The American Scholar," this aphoristic condensation of Emerson's meditations on the meaning of nature is a unique and comprehensive, a destructively critical and at the same time reconstructively innovative statement, a program for a whole new philosophical, religious, and cultural world—in short, a powerful overture of modernism. The idea of a linear history in a Christian sense, extending from creation to a final judgment, is abandoned; the philosophical concepts of origin and ultimate goals are discarded as well; reality is an ambiguous web. The aphorism does not decide whether God weaves the web or whether God is the web weaving itself; that which *is,* Being itself, is a movement that, in creating powerfully, creates itself endlessly by returning into itself, into its own resources of creativity. In one single aphoristic stroke Emerson has jeopardized traditional visions of creation, time, and history, and he has articulated in one condensed phrase the philosophically defining twin ideas of Nietzsche's later interpretation of all existence: the will to power as a basic feature of existence, and the eternal return of the same as its mode of operation, "circular power returning into itself."

"If a man is at heart just"—reads possibly the most provocative aphorism in the Divinity School Address, which so shocked the elite audience at Harvard on that hot summer day in 1838—"then in so far is he God; the safety of God, the immortality of God, the majesty of God do enter into that man with justice." The divine and the human are seen as not essentially separate but as transitional into each other: "Within and Above are synonymous" Emerson had already stated in his 1834 journal. The divine is—potentially—housed in the human, the human transcends, goes beyond itself into the totality of all meaning and dignity, into the divine. In this way, transcendence and immanence, the here and the beyond, cease to be opposites and that dualism, so constitutive for Christian religion and for metaphysical thought, collapses "if a man is at heart just." The aphorism speaks of the authentic core of human existence, of justice in a sense laboriously unfolded in many of Nietzsche's aphorisms: justice is no longer a legal or religious term; Emerson has revalued the meaning of justice to signify authentic existence, the fullness of (a human) being that finds its ground in itself and not in its reliance on a creator or other transcendent power.

If it were only a matter of clear and distinct and seemingly authoritative or dogmatic utterances, as in the case of the two aphorisms just discussed, Emerson's style would possibly still provoke some firm traditionalist believers, but it would be almost impossible to account for the fact that his aphoristic method has occasioned widely and wildly different responses from culturally and politically and religiously diverse quarters. Both the capitalist credo of Andrew Carnegie and the Christian socialism of Leo Tolstoy could and did find support and inspiration both in Emerson's seemingly unequivocal advocacy of radical libertarian individualism and in his pantheistic vision of a divinely ordained brotherhood of humanity.

Cultural nationalists like Kuno Francke—teaching at Harvard around 1900— found Emerson a proponent of Teutonic intellectual virtues, while Italian leftist intellectuals like Elio Vittorini and Cesare Pavese saw in him a powerful spokesperson for liberal cultural internationalism, a vision that has gained more of an upper hand with the impressive array of later and latter-day Emersonians, such as William James, John Dewey, Richard Rorty, and E. L. Doctorow. The fate of Emerson's reception, in short, is very similar to that of Nietzsche—read as protofascist by some philosophers, like Alfred Bäumler, and hailed, at the same time, as the very incarnation of enlightened opposition to all totalitarian thinking, as in the case of his Italian editors Giorgio Colli and Mazzino Montinari.

The reason for such a proliferation of seemingly contradictory readings appears to be the fact that, as Nietzsche maintained in *The Antichrist,* modern thinking is characterized by and valuable primarily as a method rather than a system of so-called fixed truths. This means that it is not sufficient to consider single, seemingly authoritative aphoristic statements on society or nature or God by Emerson; rather, one has to consider the place that single aphorisms occupy in the ongoing project of Emerson's thinking. "Let me remind the reader that I am only an experimenter," Emerson stated in a moment of profound reflection on his method, addressing his audience in the 1841 essay "Circles." "Do not set the least value on what I do, or the least discredit on what I do not, as if I pretended to settle any thing as true or false. I unsettle all things. No facts are to me sacred; none are profane; I simply experiment, an endless seeker with no Past at my back." The aphoristic thinker is not concerned with truths, eternal or otherwise. His experiments—and this is what "essays," Emerson's preferred longer form of writing, essentially means—are challenges of the established, the settled beliefs; they go beyond the dualistic valuations of true or false, sacred and profane, they liberate and open a space for the new in the sense of the unprecedented. True thinkers and poets are "liberating gods" ("The Poet," 1844); Nietzsche agreed when, echoing Emerson, he characterized himself as a *Versucher,* a German pun that may mean tempter, one who provokes and seduces people, or experimenter or essayist, someone who tries things out. Nietzsche also agreed because he saw the basic effect of a philosophy that went beyond traditional system building as the destruction of what went before. Nietzsche interpreted himself in this sense as an "explosive," while Emerson had certainly inspired this violent image by picturing the genuine thinker as one who causes a devastating conflagration in a great city ("Circles"), who overcomes, supersedes all established interpretations of reality, including his own preceding (aphoristic) pronouncements.

An Emersonian essay as a collection of aphorisms, then, is a literal provocation, it calls forth thinking into a forever new openness, it does not settle things as in any single final teaching, or dogma, it keeps thinking on the move by way of constant reversals of previous judgments and statements. This is why we may and must read the essay "Self-Reliance" (1841) as at the same time an unequivocal endorsement of individualism ("Nothing is at last sacred but the integrity of your own mind") and a radical challenge of subjectivism: "Why then do we prate of self-reliance? . . . To talk of reliance is a poor external way of speaking." Similarly, the 1860 essay "Fate" begins with a searching analysis of all the relentlessly determining factors of natural and human existence only to end, without canceling the preceding insights, in a celebration of freely creative, undetermined power.

One of Emerson's too rarely read and appreciated masterpieces is the 1844 "Nominalist and Realist." In a series of breathtakingly concise aphoristic paragraphs, Emerson makes a strong case for the world as a unified totality and then, with seeming nonchalance, moves on to extol its irreducible plurality in a way that would have found the approval of William James. "Nominalist and Realist," however, also provides—aphoristically—the rationale for Emerson's method as the core of his radically innovative vision that lays the ground for what we call the modern: "Nature is *one thing and the other thing,* in the same moment." Nature, reality, Being possess no substantially identical and thus nameable ground or foundation. This means that one of the pillars of two thousand years of Western philosophical logic and system building, the principle of the excluded middle, in its classical version by Aristotle, has been abandoned. Aristotle had maintained that "there is nothing between asserting and denying." Emerson, however, both asserts and denies at the same time, because "no sentence will hold the whole truth, and the only way, we can be just, is by giving ourselves the lie." This linguistic skepticism necessitates aphoristic statements, which are open to constant revision by way of correction or contradiction without, however, resulting in a dialectical system: "Life is not dialectics" ("Experience," 1844). The aphoristic skeptic therefore speaks with assurance moment by moment: "Speak what you think now in hard words and to-morrow speak in hard words again, though it contradict every thing you said to-day" ("Self-Reliance"); he loves to attack a "foolish consistency" ("Self-Reliance"), or, as Emerson's motto is more drastically phrased in the privacy of his journal: "Damn Consistency." Looking at himself from the outside, the aphoristic skeptic would have to be—paradoxically—sure that "I am always insincere" ("Nominalist and Realist"). Every authentic aphoristic statement is always true and, at the same time, questionable and, in a relentlessly temporal world, open to endless corrections and counterstatements.

Nietzsche once said of Emerson in *Twilight of the Idols* that "he simply does not know yet how old he is and how young he will yet be." This profound and perceptive remark positions Emerson, the thinker, as mediator between an imme-

morial past and an endlessly innovative future. Like his major successors in philosophical modernism, from Nietzsche to Heidegger, Emerson finds a major initial
inspiration for his thinking and his style in the aphorisms of Heraclitus. Emerson
maintains that the eighteenth- and nineteenth-century thought of Kant and
Fichte is already predicated in Heraclitus ("Literary Ethics," 1837) and that his
sayings possess something so "primary" that they precede all later distinctions
("Intellect," 1841). Heraclitus, therefore, is pre-European; he (so it seems) has no
predecessor, bases his thought on no antecedents, assumes no lasting foundations
and therefore writes as an essential modern. Nietzsche would argue, again in *Twilight of the Idols,* that Heraclitus had shown, for all times, that there is no foundational Being on which to ground any statement. The authentic later thinker will
therefore be one who does not bow to a tradition, who does not strive toward a
closed system. The true thinker will be one who is speaking with the authority of
the momentary, the present inspiration: he will be existentially and culturally and
philosophically without foundation—that is, modern. Each single aphorism of
such a thinker will be a new departure heedless of consistency. Heraclitus's aphorism eighty-one reads: "Into the same river we step and do not step; we are and
are not." This statement violates the principle of the excluded third, as does Emerson's echo of this aphorism in "Nominalist and Realist": "Nature is *one thing
and the other thing,* in the same moment." What is truly modern, then, is both the
immemorially ancient, the ungrounded, and the possibility of ceaselessly new insights, based on the fleeting moments of present inspiration. Gertrude Stein,
probably the most sophisticated of American classical modernists, deeply indebted to the Emersonian vision, characterized the modern gestures of reading
and writing reality as determined by a "continuous present," by "beginning again
and again" and "using everything" ("Composition as Explanation," 1926). Each
single authentic moment in Stein's only seemingly repetitive texts is an initial utterance of literally unprecedented authority, fully sufficient in itself, encompassing the totality, "everything" that can be experienced in one intense instance.

    Reading Emerson is difficult. Convers Francis, the most senior member of the
so-called Transcendental Club, formed in Cambridge in 1836, complained: "His
style is too fragmentary and sententious. It wants the requisite words or phrases
of connection and transition . . . I find that his beautiful things are *slippery,* and
will not stay in the mind." The aphoristic style and mode of thought, however, is
not meant to stay in the mind, to find believers and disciples. Like Nietzsche,
Emerson abhorred the idea of founding a school through his writings: "Books are
for nothing but to inspire" ("The American Scholar"). The aphoristic utterance is
designed to open the possibility of innovative thought, to allow thinking and
writing to begin again and again without the shackles of precedent: Heraclitus
began writing that way; Emerson, and Nietzsche inspired by Emerson, reenact
that eternal return of the true beginning, the unprecedented moment, as the
blueprint for the widening vistas of a genuine modernity.

    Bibliography: Lawrence Buell, *Emerson* (Cambridge, MA, 2003). Stanley Cavell, *Emerson's
Transcendental Etudes* (Palo Alto, CA, 2003). Joel Porte, *Representative Man: Ralph Waldo Emerson*

in His Time (New York, 1979). Robert D. Richardson, *Emerson: The Mind on Fire* (Berkeley, CA, 1995). David M. Robinson, *Emerson and the Conduct of Life* (Cambridge, 1993). Dieter Schulz, *Amerikanischer Transzendentalismus* (Darmstadt, 2002).

HERWIG FRIEDL

1838, September 3

A twenty-year-old slave named Frederick Bailey slips away from his master in Maryland and makes his way to the free state of New York

THE SLAVE NARRATIVE

This was Bailey's second attempt to secure his freedom. Though the details of his successful plan are of great interest to the reader, Bailey—who had changed his last name to Douglass by the time he wrote his autobiography at the age of twenty-six—withholds this information. "How I did so,—what means I adopted,—what direction I traveled, and by what means of conveyance,—I must leave unexplained," he writes.

His reticence is understandable. At the time of his writing, slavery was still legal in the United States and any disclosures might have endangered the people who had helped him. Yet it is remarkable to compare this silence with the pages of description Douglass devotes to his first escape attempt in 1835, when he and five compatriots plotted to steal a canoe and follow the North Star toward freedom. Before they could set out, they were betrayed, jailed, and, finally, separated. "I regarded this separation as the final one," Douglass wrote. "It caused me more pain than any thing else in the whole transaction."

Douglass has much to say about the possibility of escape in the company of five friends, but when in 1838 his opportunity for success depends on his willingness to go alone, he finds few words. Even his last, expanded edition of the autobiography, published decades after the end of slavery, is sparing with details. He relates that he borrowed the clothing and papers of a retired African American sailor and made his way out of slavery via train and steamboat, but the explanation calls up as many questions as it answers: Who was this sailor and how did Douglass meet him? How did Douglass know the train and ship schedules? Douglass keeps his secrets. We can feel his pragmatism, as well as some of his internal sadness at the fact that he had made his escape alone.

Douglass's aloneness makes his freedom possible; it also separates him from his fellows in body, mind, and spirit. This is a high price for Douglass to pay, though it brings rich rewards for African American literature: Douglass's assertion of his individuality through a great, risky act stands as irrefutable proof of not only his existence but also that of all African Americans.

This may seem like a self-evident concept, but at the time of Douglass's writing neither the government nor the society recognized African Americans as full-fledged human beings. African Americans counted as only three-fifths of a person in the United States Constitution, and the 1857 Supreme Court decision against runaway slave Dred Scott reaffirmed their status as chattel, not people.

To be human in America meant to possess certain rights and freedoms—equality being the most obvious one, after liberty—that very few white Americans, including abolitionists, felt comfortable extending to African Americans. It was one thing to free the slave for the spiritual betterment of both blacks and whites; it was another to do so out of recognition that blacks were the spiritual and political equals of whites. This unwillingness to see African Americans as they are—this blindness to the individuality of African Americans—is one of the tensions that make slave narratives such compelling reading today. Though their patrons and readers may not have had a vested interest in viewing the authors of slave narratives as individual human beings, the authors themselves had an extraordinary interest in presenting themselves as such. Stripped of their right to be, they were writing themselves into existence.

The conventions of the slave-narrative genre were designed to thwart such a pursuit. The pattern is generic, directing the spotlight onto slavery's systemic problems rather than the plight of the individual slave. Nearly all of the slave narratives begin with an introduction by a white abolitionist or sponsor. Said sponsor emphasizes the author's living, breathing existence and strong character. While the sponsors' opinions seem patronizing to contemporary readers, their purpose underlines again the basic problem faced by the narratives' authors: how to assert their humanity with an individual act (in this case, the act of telling their story) in a society that insisted they were not human.

There was a political component to the introductions as well. Many Southerners seeking to defend slavery claimed that the slave narratives were hoaxes. Each introduction, then, was not only an authentication of its author but also a defense of the genre and its importance to the abolitionist cause. Such introductions became even more necessary as some wildly popular slave narratives were unmasked as fakes—such as *Archy Moore,* which was written by white antislavery author Richard Hildreth and taken for authentic by some readers.

Following the introduction, the basic slave narrative proceeds chronologically from birth and culminates with freedom. The author describes his or her parentage (or, more likely, lack of parentage) and first memories of plantation life. Various scenes from the author's early life are then recollected, with an emphasis on cruelty suffered: the hunger and cold endured, the taxing nature of the plantation labor performed, the violent whippings of other slaves he or she observed. As the author enters adolescence, there is often a horrible moment when he or she is "broken in," or indoctrinated into the true awfulness of slavery. For Douglass that moment came at the age of fifteen, when he was "transformed into a brute" by an evil "nigger-breaker" by the name of Mr. Covey. Harriet Jacobs, author of *Incidents in the Life of a Slave Girl,* was sixteen when her master requested that she sleep in his room, bringing her to the shocking conclusion that because she was a slave, she would not be permitted "any pride of character."

The author notes that this wretched inversion of the classic European bildungsroman has long and lasting effects on every slave, and goes on to explain the importance of "adaptation": the idea that slaves must adapt to the overwhelming cruelty and humiliation of their circumstances in order to survive, often by engaging in behavior that may be deemed reprehensible by outsiders. What often goes unexplored at this point is the fact that the narrative's author did not adapt to the point that most other slaves do, the point that would have resulted in remaining in chains, but the narrative is clear on the fact that the author never accepts the morality of slavery. Much of the rest of the narrative is taken up with the author's growing hatred of the slavery system and his attempts to thwart it. The author describes escape attempts, and he eventually secures his freedom. The slave narratives usually end with the author's description of his life in a free state, and a fervent declaration of how happy he is to be free.

The narratives' conventions would have been familiar to their God-fearing abolitionist audience: the genre was modeled on Christian narratives, like *The Pilgrim's Progress,* that followed a soul's progress through the hell of sin to the heaven of redemption. The hell of slavery, however, created a purely American literature. In 1846, transcendentalist Theodore Parker wrote that just as the "lives of early martyrs and confessors are purely Christian," so Americans "have one series of literary productions that could be written by none but Americans, and only here; I mean the Lives of Fugitive Slaves."

For abolitionists, the utility of encouraging slave narrators to limit themselves to the restrictions of a genre was clear: the more slaves' stories conformed to a specific, wretched pattern, the easier it became to argue for repealing the entire system. For the sake of politics, it was quantity that mattered, not quality: nearly seventy first-person slave narratives were published in America and England between 1760 and 1860. Some of America's most famous slaves followed the form— Henry "Box" Brown, for instance, who mailed himself to freedom in a three-foot wooden container, and Josiah Henson, whose story of slavery in Maryland and his dramatic escape to Canada formed the basis for the character Uncle Tom in Harriet Beecher Stowe's *Uncle Tom's Cabin.*

The slave narrative is recognized as the first and perhaps most important genre of African American literature, and African Americans found its conventions useful even after the end of slavery. Once slave narratives were no longer needed as political tools, African American authors used the conventions of the genre to write about their own feelings, hardships, and challenges in freedom. The best example is still Booker T. Washington's 1901 autobiography, *Up from Slavery.* Washington's idea of a happy ending is the successful opening of his educational institution. *Up from Slavery* was almost certainly written with both a white and an African American audience in mind, and adopting the slave-narrative format helped Washington draw a parallel between freedom and the importance of self-sufficiency in a new era.

Some African American novels recall conventions of the slave-narrative genre. For example, Charles Johnson's stunningly comic *Oxherding Tale,* published in

1982, both honors and subverts the genre's clichés. Johnson's hero is a Hume-quoting, opium-taking mulatto who passes as white for a while so that he can live as a free man in a Southern town. Johnson ironically interrupts the narrative with a chapter on the slave narrative as a genre: "In point of fact, the movements in the Slave Narrative from slavery (sin) to freedom (salvation) are identical to those of the Puritan Narrative, and *both* these genuinely American forms are the offspring of that hoary confession by the first philosophical black writer: Saint Augustine. In *The Confessions* we notice (and perceive also in the Slave and Puritan Narratives) a nearly Platonic movement from ignorance to wisdom, nonbeing to being."

Johnson's aside points out what remains vital about slave narratives for a contemporary reader: the author's journey into *being,* into becoming not simply free but an individual. What makes the narratives successful in our eyes may also be what made past audiences uncomfortable. The most enlightening passages, from our perspective, are the ones wherein the author wrests control of his experiences away from the demands of the script, thereby giving us clues to his character and motivation. Why did Douglass, for instance, feel such a burning desire to escape when so many others did not? What was it that was unique about his personality? How might he become a model not only in his own time but for contemporary African Americans who feel disempowered because of discrimination and low expectations?

In most slave narratives, the answers to such questions can be found in language. Douglass's freedom begins, he explains, on the day he is able to grasp the power of literacy. After listening to his master implore his mistress not to teach Douglass how to read, since literacy would "forever unfit him to be a slave," Douglass says this: "These words sank deep into my heart, stirred up sentiments within that lay slumbering, and called into existence an entirely new train of thought. It was a new and special revelation, explaining dark and mysterious things, with which my youthful understanding had struggled, but struggled in vain. I now understood what had been to me a most perplexing difficulty—to wit, the white man's power to enslave the black man. It was a grand achievement, and I prized it highly. From that moment, I understood the pathway from slavery to freedom." This extraordinary statement makes it seem as though Douglass has freedom in the palm of his hand, simply because he comprehends the meaning of his master's sentences. Douglass also experiences freedom in the context of Christian metaphors: "It was a glorious resurrection, from the tomb of slavery, to the heaven of freedom."

The power of language, and its ability to provide freedom, follows Douglass throughout the entire narrative. He eavesdrops on white people when they are talking about slavery, and then looks up their words in a dictionary. This is how he learns the word "abolitionist"—and how he understands that there are people who are willing to help him. He gets into a conversation with two Irish immigrants who say what a pity it is that he is a slave and tell him that he should go up North, and that is how he knows where he should head when making his escape.

For his first attempt, he forges passes for himself and his five companions, so that they might appear to be moving about legally. And of course there is the autobiography itself. Its rich language is perhaps the best indicator of Douglass's freedom, for how could a man who has so mastered the tool of his enslavers be kept in chains? And how could a man with such skill as a writer—such control over his own life story—be denied his individuality, his personhood?

Other narratives may not place the primacy on language that Douglass's does, but they acknowledge its centrality in other ways. Omar Ibn Said, a Senegalese scholar who was captured and sold into American slavery, wrote a brief autobiography in 1831 that bears this out. At the very beginning of his narrative, he issues a lamentation that casts a shadow on all that is to come. "You asked me to write my life," Said writes. "I cannot write my life for I have forgotten much of my talk [language] as well as the talk of the Arabs." Said, who wrote in Arabic, his second language, was literate before his enslavement in North Carolina. He mentions details of life in Senegambia and makes two brief references to the Middle Passage. Said was a faithful Muslim, and one of his main interests was religion. This made him different from English-language slave narrators who took a Christian context for granted. Few other slave narratives, for instance, would describe life as Said saw it—in Charleston, he said, "in a Christian language, they sold me."

After Said escaped an "infidel" master, he was fortunate enough to fall into "the hands of a righteous man who fears Allah, and who loves to do good deeds and whose name is General Jim Owen." He devotes most of his remembrances to his experience practicing both Islam and the Christian faith. In its brevity, this fascinating autobiography can be frustrating: What might Said have told the reader had he felt at ease enough in one of his languages to write a book-length autobiography?

Said's and Douglass's life stories show just how important language was to the creation of African Americans in this country. Stripped of their nationality, their freedom, and their right to personhood, they depended on language to claim their place. Said remarked that without language he could not write his life, but the poignancy of slave narratives is that they extend this much further: without language, for African Americans there is no freedom, there is no life.

Bibliography: Charles L. Davis and Henry Louis Gates, Jr., ed., *The Slave's Narrative* (New York, 1985). Frederick Douglass, *Narrative of the Life of Frederick Douglass, An American Slave, Written by Himself* (Boston, 1845). Olaudah Equiano, *The Interesting Narrative of the Life of Olaudah Equiano, or Gustavus Vassa, the African Written by Himself* (London, 1789). Harriet Jacobs, *Incidents in the Life of a Slave Girl, Written by Herself,* ed. L. Maria Child (Boston, 1861). Charles Johnson, *Oxherding Tale* (Bloomington, IN, 1982). Omar Ibn Said, "The Life of Omar ben Saeed, called Morro, a Fullah Slave in Fayetteville, N.C., owned by Governor Owen, written by himself in 1831," in *The Multilingual Anthology of American Literature: A Reader of Original Texts with English Translations,* ed. Marc Shell and Werner Sollors (New York, 2000). Booker T. Washington, *Up from Slavery: An Autobiography* (Garden City, NY, 1901).

CAILLE MILLNER

1841

Edgar Allan Poe, recognizing that "modern science has resolved to
calculate upon the unforeseen," invents the detective story

"The Murders in the Rue Morgue"

There is a story about Poe: that when his mother died in December 1811 the
two-year-old Edgar remained locked, alone, in her hotel room for several days
with the undiscovered corpse. The story is false, its source unknown, but for Edgar Allan Poe—hoaxer, fabulist, gothic hyperrationalist, the unraveler of his own
intricate falsehoods—it has a truth beyond reason or proof. The sealed chamber
with a corpse within was to be the venue of his most enduring tales and of the
detective story, which, with "Murders in the Rue Morgue," he invented in the
spring of 1841.

The genre had precursors in the gothic tale, what the contemporary mystery
writer Donald Westlake defines as "a story about a girl who gets a house." The
house has, of course, a secret, constellated in secret rooms, histories, and personages, evidence of which the girl will stumble across and then, by dint of willful or
foolish curiosity, will fully discover. But while gothic fiction had its origins in England (with, among others, Horace Walpole's *The Castle of Otranto* and Mary Shelley's *Frankenstein*), it was gothic's German variant that especially influenced Poe.
In E. T. A. Hoffmann's 1819 story "Das Fräulein von Scuderi," for example, an
early prototype of Poe's detective Dupin apprehends a serial killer whose murders reenact a psychosexual trauma undergone by his mother. Poe would call his
tales "phantasy-pieces," a term he derived from Hoffmann's *Fantasiestücke.*

Yet Poe's sources were at least as popular as they were literary. Journalism,
whether in the form of sensationalist dailies or potboiling journals such as *Blackwood's Magazine,* constituted both his livelihood and his inspiration. The cutthroat marketplace of the Grub Streets of Richmond, Philadelphia, and New
York was his making as a writer, if the undoing of his stable psyche. Poe was,
by his own contemporary understanding of the term, a maniac, possessed, much
like his fictional protagonists, by manias that expressed themselves not only in
crepuscular and repulsive imaginings but also in scorn, mockery, and fraud. He
attacked prominent writers (especially Longfellow, then considered dean of
American poets) in essays and reviews with heedless aggression: "I have not the
slightest faith in Carlyle. In ten years—possibly in five—he will be remembered
only as a butt for sarcasm." And even as he produced gothic tales for the periodicals market, he satirized them in other pieces a little too bitter to be quite hilarious. In one, called "How to Write a Blackwood Article," the magazine editor-
narrator reveals that "Confessions of an Opium-Eater" was composed by "my pet

baboon, Juniper," archly foreshadowing the perpetrator of "The Murders in the Rue Morgue."

But Poe's satires traded less in slights than sleights of hand. He was a hoaxer, a bunco artist in the medium of language, most notably with the 1844 "Balloon Hoax" unwittingly printed in the *New York Sun*. Run on the front page in an "extra" edition, Poe's concocted report of a transatlantic crossing by hot-air balloon had an effect similar to that of Orson Welles's "War of the Worlds" broadcast one hundred years later. And although he relished the attention and the chance to put one over on the editors and publishers he despised, for Poe the hoax was a trick not in the sense of a comic prank but of a puzzle to be solved. He was a cryptographer—he'd run a series of newspaper columns in Richmond in 1839 on codes and code breaking—and in 1836 he'd written an extensive and meticulously detailed analysis, titled "Maelzel's Chess-Player," of a supposedly mechanical automaton/calculator that was itself a hoax, a box that artfully concealed a human chess master. At other times Poe wrote and published pseudonymous pieces designed to promote his own reputation or to tear it down, the latter affording an opportunity subsequently to play the wronged victim or to best a nonexistent enemy in literary combat.

In one of these—an unsigned review puffing his own recently published *Tales* of 1845—the bogus critic, addressing Poe, describes the stories as having been "written backwards . . . unravelling a web which you yourself have woven for the express purpose of unravelling." A Poean tale is a puzzle for the reader set by the author, as were his hoaxes and, indeed, the confidence man–trickster essays and reviews exposing his own methods. An old Richmond acquaintance of Poe's had remarked how "dissimulation and evasion became habitual to him." The protagonist of "The Tell-Tale Heart" exclaims, "With what dissimulation I went to work!"

The mystery genre that Poe invented with "The Murders in the Rue Morgue" consisted in large part of another of his customary tales with the addition of a kind of internal narrator: the detective, who tells the story in which he is a character and which he is also deconstructing by deduction—de-dissimulating—from within the sealed room of the narration, so to speak. Such a hermetic chamber is the principal locus of "The Murders in the Rue Morgue." Two bodies, those of a mother and a daughter, have been discovered (one nearly decapitated by a straight razor, the other battered and shoved up a chimney) in a fourth-floor apartment whose windows and doors were all locked from the inside. Witnesses heard screams, keening, shrieks, and words spoken in a language variously described as German, Italian, Spanish, Russian, or English, but in every case indecipherable by the witness. Despite the ruckus, no one was seen entering or leaving.

All these facts of the case are relayed in a verbatim transcription of a newspaper report, the medium of Poe's hoaxes and critical frauds: it is as though it's the newspaper account rather than the evidence that is to be interrogated and analyzed, the language puzzle of the press story rather than the crime itself that needs to be solved. And that indeed seems to be the special expertise of Poe's detective, Dupin, who's not so much an investigator as a semiotician and code breaker.

Dupin is the first ancestor of all literary detectives—the word "detective" did not, in fact, exist in English before Poe's tale—but we are still a long way from the hardboiled, existentialist dick of the mid-twentieth century. Rather, Dupin is the archetype of Conan Doyle's Sherlock Holmes and his kin, the investigator as eccentric: high-strung but affectless, manic but hyperrational, aware of everything in its smallest detail yet displaced and preoccupied, possessed of and by a sort of autistic intimacy with objects, causes, and effects rather than persons. Dupin's only friend—and, as with Holmes, the recorder of his exploits—is an admiring and bookish bachelor with whom he lives in sexless if homoerotic isolation. Dupin has undergone, we're told, "untoward events" under which "the energy of his character succumbed," and thereafter "he ceased to bestir himself in the world."

Dupin's eccentricity is "the result of an excited, or perhaps of a diseased intelligence." He has a "frigid and abstract manner," although when he is stimulated his voice rises to a shrill "treble." But his reclusiveness and disengagement with the world are not total: Dupin is "enamored of the Night for her own sake," drawn by its "*bizarrerie*." His fractured, contradictory rational/irrational nature causes the narrator to ponder "the old philosophy of the Bi-Partite Soul" and to imagine "a double Dupin—the creative and the resolvent." Sometimes it seems that Dupin and his narrator are indeed twins or, alternatively, a single organism: "Had the routine of our life at this place been known to the world, we should have been regarded as madmen . . . Our seclusion was perfect. We admitted no visitors. Indeed the locality of our retirement had been carefully kept a secret . . . and it had been many years since Dupin had ceased to know or be known in Paris. We existed within ourselves alone." The narrator admits that "into this *bizarrerie,* as into all his others I quietly fell . . . with perfect abandon." Every night, once it was fully dark, "we sallied forth into the streets, arm in arm . . . seeking amid the wild lights and shadows of the populous city, that infinity of mental excitement which quiet observation can afford." This twinning, merging, or subsuming of one personality into another is of a piece with gothic "doubling"—the hidden mad or demonic relation, the doppelgänger, the reborn spirit or revivified corpse of the dead—although the narrator hastens to assure the reader that he "is not penning any romance."

Despite that protest, we are very much in the realm of what Freud would fifty years later call the uncanny. We're first shown Dupin's gift for detection when, during one of his and the narrator's nighttime prowls, he's able to deduct exactly what the narrator is silently thinking. Dupin's chain of reasoning is described in detail, and while its logic is faultless, this mental capability isn't really credible: it seems less rational than supernatural. Later, in the course of solving the crime, Dupin not only unravels the exact details of the murders but also successfully predicts what the suspect will do in the future. More than an acute observer and logician, he is an oracle whose gift seems to derive more from his being "enamored with the Night" than from any intellectual capacity. He delivers his explication of the murders as a kind of incantation, "very much as if in a soliloquy": "I have already spoken of his abstract manner at such times. His discourse was addressed to myself; but his voice, although by no means loud, had that intonation which is commonly employed in speaking to some one at a great distance. His eyes, vacant in expression, regarded only the wall."

Dupin's rationality seems ultimately founded upon the irrational, his gifts less those of an investigator than an exorcist or necromancer. His powers are such that the solutions he uncovers are almost beside the point. He's an infallible diviner of hoaxes, an uncanny unmasker of the uncanny. At the end of the tale, Dupin condescends to listen to the prefect of police's analysis, the first instance of a still perennial tradition of portraying the official police as plodding incompetents: "Let him talk . . . let him discourse. It will ease his conscience. I am satisfied with having defeated him in his own castle." The prefect is a mere policeman; Dupin (quoting Rousseau) is a seer: "Our friend the Prefect is somewhat too cunning to be profound . . . I mean the way he has *'de nier ce qui est, et d'expliquer ce qui n'est pas.'*"

Poe wrote two more tales featuring Dupin. The first, "The Mystery of Marie Rogêt," written a year after "The Murders in the Rue Morgue," begins with an epigraph by the German romantic writer Novalis: "There are ideal series of events which run parallel with the real ones. They rarely coincide." Poe seems to be suggesting that Dupin penetrates to the genuine quiddities of the world while others muddle amid its epiphenomena. At the same time, the tale itself portrays Dupin's investigation as essentially a formal exercise, a structure whose pattern and processes matter much more than any facts or details overlaying them. The actual mystery of "The Mystery of Marie Rogêt" was, in fact, drawn from a New York newspaper and translated to Paris, and the point seems to be that both cases are unconnected enactments of the same set of events, Nietzschean recurrences whose particulars are of no special interest. Indeed, while we see Dupin in the process of solving the case, his actual solution goes unreported in the tale—the supposed meaning of the tale *qua* mystery is deferred, not to say denied. What matters is the display of Dupin's powers and his manipulation of the structural fictions of newspaper reports.

In his third Dupin tale, "The Purloined Letter," Poe invented another motif of the detective story: the missing object or clue "hidden in plain sight." Here, a potentially embarrassing billet-doux written by a member of the royal family is stolen by a scheming minister whose identity is known to the police. Although the letter obviously must be hidden in the minister's apartments, despite several exhaustive searches it cannot be found. Flummoxed, the prefect of police confesses his discomfiture to Dupin, amid clouds of pipe smoke and debate about the madness of poets (two other later motifs of the detective story). The minister's chambers are, in effect, another hermetic chamber of which the police have dismantled every element, yet the letter, in the manner of a hoaxer, eludes them. Several weeks pass. The prefect, having had no more success, returns to Dupin and Dupin hands him the letter. In the interim, Dupin himself has visited the minister's home and found the letter in an instant, sitting fully exposed in a basket hanging in plain sight on the wall.

As before, Dupin's talent is both hyperrational and supernatural: "The material world," he explains, "abounds with very strict analogies to the immaterial," and Dupin's success as a detective depends on his unique grasp of both. He is at once a poet/maniac and logician/scientist, and together these qualities make him a kind of epistemological superman. The possibility of such a being was, together with the uncanny and the gothic, the hermetic and the hoax, one of Poe's great preoccupations. After all, "modern science has resolved to *calculate upon the unforeseen,*" Poe wrote in "Marie Roget." It only followed that the poet/prophet should become a scientist.

By 1846, Poe's reputation—aided by "The Murders in the Rue Morgue"—was being felt in Paris. Charles Baudelaire, a few years shy of composing his *Les Fleurs du Mal* of 1857, found inspiration in Poe and began translating his tales and poetry into French. For Baudelaire, as Paul Valéry would remark, Poe "open[ed] up a way, teaching a very strict and deeply alluring doctrine in which a kind of mathematics and a kind of mysticism became one." Just as "The Murders in the Rue Morgue" would found the Anglo-American mystery/detective tale, so Poe's messianic pessimism would underlie the European symbolist movement.

In 1848 Poe wrote *Eureka,* a theology of what might be called dark Unitarianism, Emerson's sunniness inverted in a gothic eclipse: "If the propositions of this Discourse are tenable, the 'state of progressive collapse' is precisely that state in which alone we are warranted in considering All Things; and, with due humility, let me here confess that, for my part, I am at a loss to conceive how any other understanding of the existing condition of affairs could have made its way into the human brain." By way of redemption, Poe could envision only infinite doubling, twinning, and recurrence: "The pain of the consideration that we shall lose our individual identity ceases at once when we further reflect that the process . . . is neither more nor less than that of the absorption, by each individual intelligence, of all the other intelligences (that is, of the universe) into its own. That God may be in all, each must become God." But as for himself, he writes, "My whole nature utterly *revolts* at the idea that there is any Being in the universe superior to *myself.*" Dupin (or Nietzsche) might have said the same thing. It might, of course, have been more of Poe's characteristic overstatement—more hoaxing—or a statement of the plainest fact. In any case, when Poe died in 1849, supposedly annihilated in both mind and body, it was widely remarked that "those who had previously known him pronounced his corpse the most natural they had ever seen."

Poe left behind a sealed trunk containing his personal effects and manuscripts. It disappeared, and there was much debate as to whether it had ever been conclusively located—whether those who claimed to have found it were frauds, or whether it remained hidden, doubtless, in plain sight.

Bibliography: Kevin J. Hayes, ed., *The Cambridge Companion to Edgar Allan Poe* (Cambridge, 2002). Patrick F. Quinn, ed., *Edgar Allan Poe: Poetry and Tales* (New York, 1984). David S. Reynolds, *Beneath the American Renaissance: The Subversive Imagination in the Age of Emerson and Melville* (Cambridge, MA, 1989). Kenneth Silverman, *Edgar A. Poe: Mournful and Never-Ending Remembrance* (New York, 1991). G. R. Thompson, ed., *Edgar Allan Poe: Essays and Reviews* (New York, 1984).

ROBERT CLARK

1846, June

James Russell Lowell's *Biglow Papers* are cut from the Boston *Courier* and pasted on workshop walls all over Boston

THE U.S.-MEXICO WAR AND THE POPULAR PRESS

In June 1846 the first of James Russell Lowell's *Biglow Papers* appeared in the Boston *Courier.* Lowell's authorship was not revealed in this extract, which included a letter to the editor, attributed to one Ezekiel Biglow, and a poem supposedly composed by the letter writer's son, Hosea. Written in Yankee dialect, the poem, which was published a month after the U.S.-Mexico War began, was an effort to voice antiwar and antislavery arguments in the idiom of a white working-man. In 1859 Lowell recalled the genesis of this Yankee character: "Thinking the Mexican war, as I think it still, a national crime committed in behalf of slavery . . . and wishing to put the feeling of those who thought as I did in a way that would tell, I imagined to myself such an upcountry man as I had often seen at anti-slavery gatherings, capable of district-speech English but always instinctively falling back into the natural stronghold of his homely dialect when heated to the point of self-forgetfulness."

Lowell was provoked to write his satire after Daniel Webster's son set up a military recruiting establishment in Boston, and in his letter the elder Biglow similarly traces his son's literary efforts to his witnessing of a Boston "cruetin Sarjunt" strutting around and trying to "hook him in." In his poem, young Biglow mocks the noisy fervor of the military recruiters, who he vows will never "git ahold" of him; complains that farmers are the ones who pay for war; blames the war on the "overreachin'" of the Southern states "thet rule us"; calls war murder and mocks the "curus Christian dooty" of "cuttin' folks's throats" as well as hypocritical talk of extending "Freedom's airy"; warns that "Chaps thet make black slaves o' niggers / Want to make wite slaves o' you"; and contends that Massachusetts should be a beacon to the oppressed instead of sending soldiers off to Mexico. In other words, Lowell adopted the Yankee persona to respond to the war "in a way that would tell," by drawing on popular ideas and modes of expression and rearticulating them in ways that made a comical common sense out of their contradictions. The papers were a big hit, and although, as Lowell put it, previously he was "far from being a popular author," he found these verses "copied everywhere," "saw them pinned up in workshops," "heard them quoted, and their authorship debated." He continued to publish additional installments until 1848.

The *Biglow Papers* in their original newspaper form, however, were dramatically different from the book version that appeared in 1848. When Lowell edited the papers for publication, he adopted the persona of another Yankee character, the more refined and pedantic Reverend Horace Wilbur, Biglow's religious and literary mentor. Dense, difficult, profusely annotated, liberally peppered with Latin and Greek, and with a lengthy and pretentious introduction and index appended to the letters, this version of the *Biglow Papers* would be rough going for even highly educated readers. It is certainly difficult to imagine workingmen reading it, quoting it, or pinning it up in workshops.

Although the *Biglow Papers* is perhaps the U.S.-Mexico War text that is most familiar to scholars today, the war was a favorite subject in the popular literature of the era. Because the United States' invasion of Mexico followed the print revolution of the 1830s and 1840s and coincided with the emergence of railroad networks and the invention of the telegraph, the U.S.-Mexico War was the first war in which newspaper correspondents were widely used and the first that people could follow on a daily basis in mass-circulation newspapers. It was also the first U.S. war that immediately inspired a wide range of responses in pamphlets, stories, and cheap novels, as well as in the labor, land-reform, and antislavery press. When this popular literature is remembered at all, however, it is usually mischaracterized as an utterly jingoistic body of writing that spoke in one voice in support of the war. Biglow's description of "them editors thet's crowin'/Like a cockerel three months old . . . Don't ketch any on 'em goin'" nicely captures the dominant memory of a monolithically pro-war popular press even as it responds to a moment in which newspaper editors and journalists were attaining new prominence and power. Elite writers such as Lowell viewed newspaper speech— what he called the "stretching and swelling" of "our language" by the "newspaper reporter"—as a threat and a serious rival to the ideal American literature that they hoped to model and foster.

But although many mass-circulation newspapers championed the war, many of the reform newspapers objected to it, often in language that resonated with that of Lowell's Yankee. Labor- and land-reform papers such as the *Workingman's Advocate* and the *Voice of Industry* advised readers that the war was conjoined to slaveholding interests, that workingmen bore the brunt of war's costs, and that war threatened republican ideals by endangering liberty, corrupting the morals of a people, adding to the expense of government, and promoting the slavish obedience of the soldier. Meanwhile, antislavery papers such as the *Liberator* and the *North Star* made slavery the central issue by insisting, like young Biglow, that the war violated Christian beliefs, promised to extend slavery rather than freedom, and represented a falling away from Puritan and Revolutionary ideals. In an editorial for the *North Star,* Frederick Douglass singled out for ridicule the military recruiters who appealed to "degraded men to vindicate the honor of our Christian country." Like Lowell, he also mocked and critically dissected the newly popular concepts of racial Anglo-Saxonism and Manifest Destiny. Instead of representing an alternative to newspaper literature, then, Lowell's *Biglow Papers* incorporated the idioms and arguments of the popular reform press even as it parodied and distanced itself from the language of the new mass-circulation dailies.

Another rival to elite visions of American literature was the large body of sensational novels that emerged with the advent of the penny press, including the best-selling mysteries-of-the-city and imperial adventure novels written by George Lippard, Ned Buntline, A. J. H. Duganne, and others. These novels were serialized in newspapers and story papers and then published in multiple editions as pamphlets or cheap novels. At the time, they circulated much more widely among readers than any of the literature of the American Renaissance. Dozens of these novels were set during the U.S.-Mexico War and incorporated its history into their plots, cannibalized newspaper descriptions of battles, and restaged debates about the war. Typical titles include Lippard's *Legends of Mexico* (1847) and *'Bel of Prairie Eden* (1848) and Buntline's *The Volunteer* (1847) and *Magdalena the Beautiful Mexican Maid* (1847). In most of these novels, U.S. soldiers fall in love with Mexican women, but happy marriages are often deferred or tragically impossible. And although they all promote the ideal of patriotism, the novels take a range of positions on the war. Lippard's initial enthusiasm for what he called the crusade of the nineteenth century was transformed by the end of the war into a bleak vision of death, national degeneration, the ascendancy of the slaveocracy, and failed international romance. And although Buntline lionized U.S. military leaders, the hero of his novel *The Volunteer* regretfully characterizes the conflict as a war of invasion, and *Magdalena* ends tragically when the eponymous maid dies after discovering the corpse of her new U.S. soldier–husband (who was of mixed Spanish and Anglo-American descent) on the battlefield at Buena Vista. While Lippard's commitment to land reform shaped his changing ideas about the war, Buntline's nativist beliefs, which made him fearful of incorporating large numbers of Catholics and nonwhites into the republic, clarify the tensions in his novels. In both cases, these sensational novels reveal doubts and anxieties about the war rather than simply and unequivocally championing it.

Some of the popular U.S.-Mexico War novels feature pairings of elite soldier-heroes and lower-class Yankee vernacular characters who speak in a strong dialect and help to defeat the villains. The Yankee characters are subordinated to the elite romantic heroes in a pattern that can be traced to Royall Tyler's 1790 play *The Contrast,* which juxtaposes Colonel Manly and the yeoman Yankee Jonathan in a comic staging of hierarchy and difference. In the 1840s, Yankee characters often unsettled the boundaries of traditional hierarchies, but they continued to be closely connected to the heroes, who were often merchants' sons. Nativism was the glue that held together many such affiliations between lower-class and upper-class Americans, which helps to explain why the novels that included such pairings often also featured not only Mexican but also Irish villains, such as the Irish officer who switches sides and is promptly denounced by a Yankee in Arthur Armstrong's *The Mariner of the Mines* (c. 1848), and the Irish deserters from the U.S. Army who try to talk Connecticut Yankee Solomon Snubbins into joining them in *The Chieftain of Churubusco* (1848). (Snubbins would rather "be ground all up intew eternal smash.") The Yankee characters trumpet egalitarian ideals even as they verbally abuse or make fun of black servant characters, a convention of the genre that can also be traced to the 1790s. By the 1840s, Yankees in popular fiction typically voiced free-labor sentiments and expressed disdain for slavery, but this by no means implied that they disavowed racial hierarchies or embraced black men as brothers.

Lowell's Yankees, then, were part of a long line of vernacular characters, as Lowell recognized in 1859 when he emphasized his dislike of some of the earlier literary Yankees and his intention to show that "high and even refined sentiment may coexist with the shrewder and more comic elements of the Yankee character." Lowell's challenge was to mobilize that stock character in behalf of the antislavery and antiwar causes. But although Lowell's abolitionist allegiances were clear, his relationship to nativism was more complex. He claimed that, for him, the Yankee dialect "was native, was spoken all about me as a boy, at a time when an Irish day-laborer was as rare as an American one is now." Here his theory of Yankee speech marks the Irish as alien in ways that resonate with other kinds of Yankee literature, including U.S.-Mexico War novels. Hierarchies of class and status also saturate Lowell's earliest memories of acquiring the Yankee "mother tongue" as a boy, while listening to the talk of the men working in his father's hay fields. Despite his obvious delight in assuming the Biglow character, he feared that his imaginative transgression of class boundaries exposed him to "the danger of being carried beyond the limits of my own opinions" and to "the risk of seeming to vulgarize a deep and sacred conviction." Perhaps because of this fear, in the book version of the *Biglow Papers* Lowell responded by expanding the role of Horace Wilbur's pedantic Yankee persona and by sharply distinguishing Wilbur's voice from those of Biglow and the other lower-class Yankees.

As Smith Professor of Modern Languages at Harvard and editor of the *Atlantic Monthly* and the *North American Review*, Lowell was a significant participant in the institutions that defined American literature in the late nineteenth century by distinguishing it from other forms of popular speech and writing, such as newspapers and sensational novels. Rather than inventing something new, however, in the *Biglow Papers* Lowell made a hit precisely by drawing on and transforming such sources. His eloquent war satire resonates with the literature of the reform press, elements of the popular novels, and the protests of other New Englanders, such as Henry David Thoreau's "Resistance to Civil Government" (1849).

After the mid-nineteenth century, the war remained a significant formative context in Gold Rush literature, narratives of banditry and crime, and dime novels, but these sources were thought by the early definers of American literature to have little literary value. The war is also important in early English-language historical romances by Mexican American authors, such as Maria Amparo Ruíz de Burton's *The Squatter and the Don* (1885) and Jovita González's *Caballero* (1930s), but these were not widely available until the late twentieth century, when they were republished for use in Latino literature courses.

While distinctions between popular and classic works mark one important boundary in what was then the emerging field of American literature—and thereby shape what is remembered and forgotten about the U.S.-Mexico War—distinctions between languages are even more fundamental: until late in the twentieth century, those defining American literary history usually excluded Spanish-language sources. However, the influential Spanish-language newspaper of New Orleans, *La Patria,* described the war as an invasion and a violation of U.S. republican principles. And Ramón Alcaraz's *Apuntes para la historia de la guerra entre México y los Estados Unidos,* which was translated into English and published in New York in 1850 under the title *The Other Side,* also exposed such contradictions. Other Spanish-language responses to the war were collected during the 1870s by agents of Hubert Howe Bancroft, who solicited narratives from the defeated Californios for his massive *History of California* (1884–1890). Despite his desire to collect such evidence, Bancroft generally relegated these accounts to footnotes or disagreed with the Californios' interpretations. The *testimonio* of Mariano Guadalupe Vallejo, the most prominent of the Californios, was almost one thousand pages long, yet his Spanish-language account of the transformation of Mexican California was ultimately subordinated to and displaced by Bancroft's English-language history. But although Spanish-language accounts of the war have been marginalized within U.S. literature and history, and although the war is virtually absent from the canonical literature of the American Renaissance, the U.S.-Mexico War repeatedly returns as a ghostly presence in Chicano literature, in popular literary and movie Westerns, and in political debates about language, race, immigration, national belonging, and the future of the United States.

Bibliography: Jesse Alemán and Shelley Streeby, eds. *Empire and the Literature of Sensation: An Anthology of Nineteenth-Century Popular Fiction* (New Brunswick, NJ, 2007). Robert Johannsen, *To the Halls of the Montezumas: The Mexican War in the American Imagination* (New York, 1985). James Russell Lowell, *James Russell Lowell's The Biglow Papers, First Series: A Critical Edition,* ed. Thomas Wortham (DeKalb, IL, 1977).

SHELLEY STREEBY

1846, late July

While living at Walden Pond, Henry David Thoreau is arrested for refusing to pay his poll tax

"CIVIL DISOBEDIENCE" AND *WALDEN*

On July 4, 1845, "by accident . . . on Independence Day," Henry David Thoreau began to live "alone, in the woods, a mile from [any] neighbor," in a house he had built himself at Walden Pond, in Concord, Massachusetts. That same month in New York the *Democratic Review* proclaimed America's "manifest destiny to overspread the continent allotted by Providence for the free development of our yearly multiplying millions." The annexation of Texas by the United States provoked conflict with Mexico. In 1846 war was declared, and by 1848 the United States had gained what would become the states of California, Nevada, Colorado, Utah, New Mexico, and Arizona. Writers were stirred. In New England, James Russell Lowell wrote in his poem "The Present Crisis": "Once to every man and nation comes the moment to decide." Ralph Waldo Emerson's "Ode, Inscribed to W. H. Channing" invoked "the angry muse." Rather than think about "the culture of mankind," he said, one must

> Behold the famous states
> Harrying Mexico
> With rifle and with knife!

Thoreau's essay "Civil Disobedience," originally published in 1849 as *Resistance to Civil Government,* has proved the most memorable literary response to that war, yet Thoreau's imprisonment did not directly spring from his response to the U.S.-Mexico War. He had already for some years not been paying his taxes. He could not accept "that political organization as *my* government which is the *slave's* government also." His arrest, so far as scholars can tell, happened simply because the town constable of Concord wanted the small fee due him for collecting back taxes. (He was released after one night in jail when a relative—without Thoreau's knowledge or consent—stepped in and paid his debt.) The scenario carries immense symbolic value: a solitary, peaceable man is taken from his retreat in the woods and incarcerated in town, as society grapples him away from his attempt to engage with nature. Yet Thoreau scarcely made this drama felt, either in "Civil Disobedience" or in *Walden*. The figure of Thoreau in *Walden* is above all that of an individual, not a man interacting with others, and so too he presents himself in "Civil Disobedience."

The individual Thoreau presents is a separatist. He feels himself apart from his fellow citizens, and he marks that distance spatially. It takes him only a little bit of space to make the mark. Thoreau's business was to magnify, to exaggerate, to notice and write about details too minute or trivial for others to register. In the hum of a morning mosquito, he hears "something cosmical . . . a standing advertisement, till forbidden, of the everlasting vigor and fertility of the world." As if it were a far journey, he reports, "I have traveled a good deal in Concord." In Concord he does not find the "sincerity" that would lead people to give accounts of themselves such as they would send to their "kindred from a distant land." For if a writer has "lived sincerely," his standpoint "must have been a distant land to me." Real individuals do not agglomerate. It distresses Thoreau that "the American has dwindled into an Odd Fellow, more gregarious than self-reliant." Americans "live" supported by the "aid of the Mutual Insurance company," and what kind of life is that when all the company promises is "to bury him decently"?

Tocqueville a few years earlier noted the same rush to join voluntary organizations, and he too found it a key to American social and political life, but even his unease with democracy was not so great as Thoreau's. Unlike Edmund Burke, the

Anglo-Irish statesman who had written to warn Britain against its policies toward the rebellious colonies, and whose perspective animated Daniel Webster, Thoreau does not understand the state as a living organism enriched by tradition. His politics are Protestant. He wants to clear away anything that comes between the individual soul and its highest values. Thoreau does not value tradition, not even American constitutional traditions. Unlike Lincoln, he does not care about the Union. The state exists purely as a convenience established by human beings for their small collective purposes. The state is a tool, but it's not simple or handy, so it's a "machine." You owe it to your humanity to "let your life be a counter friction to stop the machine."

To this moment, Thoreau provides an indispensable resource for anarchist and libertarian thought. His words reach directly across time: "When . . . a whole country is unjustly overrun and conquered by a foreign army, and subjected to military law, I think it is not too soon for honest men to rebel and revolutionize. What makes this duty the more urgent is the fact, that the country so overrun is not our own, but ours is the invading army."

"Civil Disobedience" wants a "peaceable revolution." This revolutionary ambition places it in the traditions that had founded the United States, yet it stands against the government of the United States. Revolution takes place through any true action, because novelty defines action. Making something new distinguishes action from habit, routine, repetition. Thoreau always insists on earliness, the moment of awakening. The sun rises every morning, and it challenges us afresh. The risk, the heroic task of every day is truly to see it.

The revolutionary force of action is just as transformative and dangerous to the single person as it is to the state or society. It brings not peace but a sword: "Action from principle, the perception and performance of right, changes things and relations; it is essentially revolutionary, and does not consist wholly with anything which was. It not only divides states and churches, it divides families; ay, it divides the individual." To *decide* is, etymologically, to cut apart. *Individual* comes from Latin terms meaning "not divisible," the equivalent of the Greek word that gives us "atom." So it is deeply paradoxical to say that the individual has been divided. Thoreau's age did not have the knowledge of nuclear physics that we do, so this could not have been his idea, but we get some idea of the energy Thoreau finds in true moral action if we think of it as splitting the atom.

The power of awakening, that moment of sundering that begins, as it concludes, a true action, punctuates Thoreau's writings. To the doer, the force of the moment makes it unique. Thoreau asserts that, through the Fugitive Slave Act of 1850, "what I had lost was a country": "I had never respected the Government near to which I had lived, but I had foolishly thought that I might manage to live here, minding my private affairs, and forget it." Evidently he has also forgotten "Civil Disobedience." By 1846, Thoreau had found that even if you forget the state, it does not forget you. After John Brown's raid in 1859 Thoreau discovered anew the experience of being a traveler from afar, even while at home, already a fundamental fact of feeling in *Walden*. Brown's revolutionary challenge to the American slave system and the government that sustained it appalled Thoreau's fellow citizens. Thoreau found it inspiring and therefore transformative: "We dream of foreign countries, of other times and races of men, placing them at a distance in history or space; but let some significant event like the present occur in our midst, and we discover, often, this strangeness between us and our nearest neighbors. *They* are our Austrias, and Chinas, and South Sea Islands . . . The thoughtful man becomes a hermit in the thoroughfares of the market-place." Ishmael in *Moby-Dick* time and again, yet always afresh, is cured of his misanthropy, overcoming his separation to join in comradeship. For Thoreau, the sudden distancing rather than the sudden intimacy is the thrill, but in both we find repetition rather than definitive conversion.

Just a few weeks after being jailed and released in 1846, Thoreau left Walden for an excursion into real wilderness, to Mt. Katahdin in north-central Maine. He was among the earliest recorded as reaching the summit. This was by far the wildest country Thoreau ever saw. He felt its unhomeliness: "the grim, untrodden wilderness, whose tangled labyrinth of living, fallen, and decaying trees only the deer and moose, the bear and wolf, can easily penetrate." This realm of "vast, Titanic, inhuman Nature" makes possible a radically new moral encounter: "one could no longer accuse institutions and society, but must front the true source of evil."

Thoreau had recently published in the *Dial* his translation of the Greek tragedy *Prometheus Bound*. This titanic drama opens in a terrifyingly bleak mountain landscape. Figures called Strength and Force act on behalf of Zeus, "president of the immortals," to bind Prometheus, who benefited humanity by violating the ruling power. It seems a prototype for Thoreau's imprisonment. In the generation before Thoreau, the radical English poet Shelley had written *Prometheus Unbound*. Its preface links Prometheus to Satan and argues that Christianity had mistaken the benefactor for the enemy of mankind. Thoreau describes his ascent of Katahdin with language drawn from Milton's account, in *Paradise Lost*, of Satan passing through chaos. Yet in Thoreau's *The Maine Woods* the anticipated confrontation with evil does not exactly take place.

In the most powerful sequence, Thoreau confronts sheer "Matter," not humankind's "Mother Earth" (the Latin word for mother, *mater,* is cognate with the word for matter, *materia*). It is "pure Nature . . . vast and drear and inhuman . . . savage and awful." This space is the home, Thoreau feels, of "Necessity and Fate," forces like those that bound Prometheus at the opening of Aeschylus's play. As Thoreau thinks back on this encounter, he writes, "I stand in awe of my body, this matter to which I am bound has become so strange to me." Prometheus was bound to a mountain, Thoreau to his flesh. Action divides the individual, distancing a person from neighbors, but this encounter splits the "I" from its own embodiment: "I fear not spirits, ghosts, of which I am one—*that* my body might—but I fear bodies, I tremble to meet them." In the troubling chapter of *Walden* called "Higher Laws," Thoreau reflects on "this slimy, beastly life, eating and drinking" and on the incompatibility between imagination and "flesh and fat." So far as we know, Thoreau never engaged in sexual intimacy with another human being. As Thoreau continues to ponder his materiality, he asks, "What is this Titan that has possession of me? Talk of mysteries!—Think of our life in nature,—daily to be shown matter, to come in contact with it."

The passage continues to a climax. The prose almost shatters. As spirit struggles with matter, sentences break down into nouns and phrases without the verbs that mark agency, and meaningful words yield to an eruption of mere marks—dashes upon commas, italics, and exclamation points: "rocks, trees, wind on our cheeks! The *solid* earth! The *actual* world! The *common sense! Contact! Contact! Who* are we? *Where* are we?" The English romantic poet William Wordsworth, whose work may be felt at many moments throughout Thoreau's, recalled in his youth needing to "*grasp* . . . at a wall or tree" in order to recapture a sense of "reality." Here Thoreau, inversely, finds the otherness of matter not reassuring but overwhelming. In a smaller dose, this radical otherness excites Thoreau in a way he cherishes, like the "visionary dreariness" Wordsworth found in certain bleak landscapes. The "drear" character of the terrain, its vast inhumanity, echoes in a number of Thoreau's signature statements. Stormy times on Cape Cod are "sublimely dreary." In "Walking," he proclaims in his paean to wildness, "My spirits infallibly rise in proportion to the outward dreariness. Give me the ocean, the desert, or the wilderness! . . . I enter a swamp as a sacred place . . . There is the strength, the marrow of Nature."

Thoreau's "I" is what he is known for, and what he promises us. He acknowledges at the opening of *Walden* that his book may seem egotistic because it says "I" so often, unlike "most books," in which "the *I,* or first person, is omitted." Thoreau asserts that "it is, after all, always the first person speaking." This is not to praise other writers for being themselves, but rather to call us, as we write and as we live, to a responsibility we far too rarely fulfill. In "Life without Principle" he asserts that as a speaker his job is to give auditors "a strong dose of myself."

Thoreau felt the gap between himself and other people, and he offers a vivid and vivifying account of the gap between the old self and new self that arises from action truly taken, yet his "I" lacks the dramatic internal topography, the stress and thrust within, found in some writers otherwise much like him. In his sonnet "No Worst, There Is None," Gerard Manley Hopkins, a keen writer of the natural world, did not need to visit Katahdin to find a terrifying landscape:

O the mind, mind has mountains; cliffs of fall
Frightful, sheer, no-man-fathomed. Hold them cheap
May who ne'er hung there.

Emily Dickinson read in her geography books that "Volcanoes be in Sicily/And South America," but she finds them "nearer here":

A Lava step at any time
Am I inclined to climb
A crater I may contemplate
Vesuvius at home

Such a self figures also in her poem beginning, "My Life had stood—a Loaded Gun."

For a man in so many ways self-motivated, Thoreau is remarkably defined by his responsiveness. His political statements are all counterstatements. Whatever calls him out of himself provides the occasion for his writing, whether a mink or a constable, a law or a sunrise. The proof of his "I" shows in this power to respond. Thinking of John Brown, Thoreau said of writing that "the *art* of composition is as simple as the discharge of a bullet from a rifle, and its master-pieces imply an infinitely greater force behind them."

Bibliography: Stanley Cavell, *The Senses of "Walden"* (New York, 1972). F. O. Matthiessen, *American Renaissance: Art and Expression in the Age of Emerson and Whitman* (New York, 1941). Robert D. Richardson, Jr., *Henry David Thoreau: A Life of the Mind* (Berkeley, CA, 1986). Henry David Thoreau, *Collected Essays and Poems,* ed. Elizabeth Hall Witherell (New York, 2001); *A Week on the Concord and Merrimack Rivers; Walden, or, Life in the Woods; The Maine Woods; Cape Cod,* ed. Robert F. Sayre (New York, 1985).

JONATHAN ARAC

1850

Nathaniel Hawthorne confesses his desire to "kill the public"

THE SCARLET LETTER

Nathaniel Hawthorne's long-awaited and much-desired emergence from literary obscurity can be measured by the volume of requests he received from amateur writers that he give his opinion on what they had written. Most prominent European authors even today would dismiss such requests with a flick of the wrist. This democratic accessibility—culminating in university-based writing programs—strikes me as a particularly American contract. On December 26, 1849, Hawthorne wrote in apology to Lewis Mansfield, a retired businessman and occasional poet: "I have been exceedingly reprehensible in not answering your letter sooner; but the fact is I did not read the accompanying poem until last evening; for I have been much engaged on a book which I am about to publish."

That book was *The Scarlet Letter.* Hawthorne had conceived it as a long story, which he had begun in September 1849 and intended to include as one of many tales in a four-hundred-page volume titled *Old-Time Legends: Sketches, Experimental and Ideal.* As a title, *Old-Time Legends* lacks the metaphorical specificity of later works, such as *The House of the Seven Gables,* suggesting instead a crepuscular net for diffuse pieces. Fortunately for him and for us the long story took on a life of its own, requiring its calving from the planned volume.

Hawthorne's gracious response to Mansfield belied the political harassment he had suffered through the previous spring and summer and the financial stress it had caused. Whig politicians who had come into power in the 1848 elections had engineered his dismissal as the surveyor of customs in Salem, Massachusetts, a position to which he—a Democrat and friend of U.S. Attorney Franklin Pierce from their college days—had been appointed in 1846, a period of Democratic ascendancy. His salary as surveyor had been his main income. He had also lost money invested in Brook Farm, the spiritual-agrarian commune to which he had been initially attracted and by which later disillusioned. Though already a critically acclaimed author, his royalties were not sufficient to support his family.

Until his removal from office, Hawthorne had held multiple roles in uneasy balance: as an ambitious author; as a public servant whose job security depended on party fortunes; as a dutiful man of letters who, as secretary of the Salem Lyceum, arranged lectures by the likes of Emerson and Thoreau; and as a devoted husband and father. During the ugly, protracted campaign against him by the Whig tormentors he likened to "bloodhounds" and "slang-whangers," he had been forced to deploy much of his creative energy enlisting the support of influential friends. In that earlier era of partisan politics, Whigs sought his removal from office as a justified spoil of their victory. But Hawthorne did not regard himself as a mere political appointee. On March 5, 1848, he had appealed to his friend George Hillard for behind-the-scenes help: "an inoffensive man of letters— having obtained a pitiful little office on no other plea than his pitiful little literature—ought not to be left to the mercy of these thick-skulled and no-hearted ruffians . . . There are men in Boston . . . whose support and sympathy might fairly be claimed in my behalf—not on the ground that I am a very good writer, but because I gained my position, such as it is, by my literary character, and have done nothing to forfeit that tenure."

After more than a year of this enervating resistance, Hawthorne accepted the inevitability of his dismissal from office. In a June 1849 letter to Henry Wadsworth Longfellow, another close friend from Bowdoin days, he admitted to relishing vengeful fantasies: "I will surely immolate one or two of them . . . I may perhaps select a victim, and let fall one little drop of venom on his heart, that shall make him writhe before the grin of the multitude . . . This I will do, not as an act of individual vengeance, but in your behalf as well as mine, because he will have violated the sanctity of the priesthood" to which poets and writers belong. The crime committed by his boorish enemies, Hawthorne argued, was against Imagination itself, and therefore the punishment most fitting would have to be delivered through an imaginative work. "If they will pay no reverence to the imaginative power when it causes herbs of grace and sweet-scented flowers to spring up along their pathway, then they should be taught what it can do in the way of producing nettles, skunk-cabbage, deadly night-shade, wolf's bane, dogwood."

After his ouster as surveyor, he kept his promise of avenging the "priesthood," sowing words that sting and choke in "The Custom-House," an uncharacteristically autobiographical piece that he intended as prologue to the projected *Old-Time Legends*. Hawthorne had allowed himself brief autobiographical excursions in *Mosses from an Old Manse* (1846). But the reflections in "The Custom-House" are much more pointedly political. His appraisal of his and the nation's Puritan legacy is unsentimental: he writes of his first Puritan ancestor that "he was a soldier . . . both good and evil." And what was the Puritans' besetting sin? Their persecutorial zeal. "At all events, I, the present writer, as their representative, hereby take shame upon myself for their sakes, and pray that any curse incurred by them . . . may be now and henceforth removed."

On January 15, 1850, Hawthorne rushed the manuscript of "The Custom-House" and all but the final three chapters of "The Scarlet Letter" to his trusted editor, James T. Fields, instructing Fields to read the prologue before starting on the story. Writing that prologue, Hawthorne explained, had been therapeutic: "all political and official turmoil has subsided within me, so that I have not felt inclined to execute justice on any of my enemies." Detaching the story (which he had referred to initially as "The Judgment Letter") from *Old-Time Legends,* incorporating "The Custom-House" into it, and publishing the whole as a novel was Fields's canny editorial idea. Hawthorne respected Fields's suggestion, but was anxious that the tale's implacable grimness would "disgust" some readers. "Is it safe," he agonized, ". . . to stake the fate of the book entirely on this one chance? A hunter loads his gun with a bullet and several buck-shot; and, following his sagacious example, it was my purpose to conjoin the one long story with half a dozen shorter ones; so that failing to kill the public outright with my biggest and heaviest lump of lead, I might have other chances with the smaller bits."

Hawthorne's preferred genre was the "tale." He had no ambition to produce popular novels, and made disparaging remarks about the "scribbling women" who did so. But his acute awareness of the author's moral duty to readers, "to relieve the shadows of the story with . . . light," comes through in this correspondence with Fields, as does his dependence on his editor as the mediator between Imagination and Commerce. The first print run of 2,500 copies of *The Scarlet Letter* that March sold out in ten days. Hawthorne was finally able to enjoy commercial as well as critical success, and to savor the sweetness of righteous revenge.

Fields's editorial decision to conjoin the contemporary autobiographical prologue with the period tale cues the reader to limn *The Scarlet Letter* as an allegory of the failure of later generations to nurture the original utopian concept that motivated the Puritans to clear a patch of New World wilderness. *The Scarlet Letter* then becomes a metacommentary on the competing rights of the artist, the prosperous merchant, and the winning politician to invent the myth of America's founding. The embroidered letter *A* on Hester Prynne's bosom may be for Adultery when she first emerges from prison, but the narrator-surveyor's *A* is for the Ambiguity required of the consensus-phobic artist who must survive as a public servant. Hawthorne's *A* is for America, for Author, for Allegory, for Accommodation of the Alien, for Avoidance of the inconvenient.

I first read *The Scarlet Letter* in a graduate seminar in the fall of 1965 at the University of Iowa in Iowa City, where I had initially come from India for a master of fine arts degree, and where—having fallen in love without my father's permission and married an American who wrote stories of moss-picking, gar-fishing, gator-wrestling, and cross-burning in 1940s Florida, and subsequently given birth to a son—I had become a doctoral student. By my Bengali Brahmin community's standards, my marriage to a man outside the pale of the caste system constituted a grave transgressive act against Hindu *samaj* (society). I felt immediate empathy for Hester Prynne. Also, because the brief, civil wedding had converted my official status in the United States to "permanent resident alien," I found myself engaged more by *The Scarlet Letter*'s meditation on the process of transcontinental un-housement and re-housement than by the morality play of adulterous entanglement. What had *becoming American* meant to the expatriate Puritan settlers? What did *being American* of Puritan ancestry mean to Hawthorne, and nation building to his Democratic and Whig contemporaries? At what cost to idealism, and on whose victimized back is the utopian "idea" of America transformed into a thriving nation-state with imperial reach? What did my *America* of the mid-sixties, galvanized by the civil rights movement, the antiwar movement, the women's rights movement, and other cultural, spiritual, and social identity crises, offer me, an accidental immigrant? What does it mean to invent rather than inherit one's homeland?

Of the cast of significant characters in *The Scarlet Letter,* only Pearl, Hester's daughter, is a native-born American. She did not choose America as home, but she is the rightful heir to the promises and perils of its geographical and moral wilderness. She is blessed and cursed with New World vitality and, as an illegitimate child of undisclosed fathering, with ahistoricity. Unhampered by tradition, deprived of generational memory, she can seize agency. Hers is the American myth of self-fashioning. And when she inherits impressive property on two continents from Chillingworth, her mother's cuckolded husband, hers also becomes the American rags-to-riches, shame-to-acclaim fairy tale. She is heir to the wealth of America's global trade, and unlike her mother, who is trapped in the Puritan value system of colonial Massachusetts, she can, and does, turn her back on America and claim the globe as her homeland. Hester Prynne, Roger Chillingworth, and Arthur Dimmesdale, the three principals in the melodrama of adultery and its consequences, are English expatriates. They are pioneering transplants trapped in the tedious process of negotiating what aspects of a remembered culture to replicate, reject, adapt to alien circumstances.

As a transplanted Indian foreign student, I felt excluded by the nature of Hawthorne's argument that the American Dream is an exclusivist, Protestant internal dialogue. In later readings I realized that *The Scarlet Letter* reaches out to embrace a broader American society. Perhaps the very murderous rage Hawthorne felt as he was deposed from his Custom House job was what allowed him to break through into that broader embrace. Yet Hawthorne's intellectual circle was not at all insular. He engaged in discourse with transcendentalists and with American champions of the 1848 uprisings in Europe. Sea-borne trade introduced non-European sailors, visitors, slaves, artifacts, and, most important, ideas to his Salem and to Hester's Boston. Hawthorne's entry of October 30, 1847, in *The American Notebooks* ("A young woman in England poisoned by an East Indian barbed dart, which her brother had brought home as a curiosity") reveals his awareness of the unplanned consequences of English colonialism. He befriended Melville, who was introduced to him in 1850 by Fields, and may have inspired the younger writer to transform what had started as another sea yarn into the allegory that is *Moby-Dick*. But unlike Melville, who sailed alien seas and encountered unfamiliar peoples, and brought that larger world into his American allegory, Hawthorne referenced the *out there* only as it impinged on the Puritan polity.

As a reader I thrill to the lyrical intensity and dizzying pace of *The Scarlet Letter*, to its skillful replacement of melodramatic plot with a series of incrementally momentous scenes in which the principals pursue their discrete dreams of fulfillment. *The Scarlet Letter* has the figurative precision and economy of the short story, as well as the ambitious scope of the novel. In spite of his allegorical aim, in Hester, Hawthorne provides a psychologically complex portrait of the seventeenth-century dissident: a free-thinking woman making what peace she can with the demands of submission to a doctrinaire religion and gender inequality. In the early scenes of Chillingworth's discovery of Hester's adultery and alienation of spousal affection for him, Hawthorne animates even the revenge seeker with some sympathy if not empathy.

However, as a transnational American, I yearn for more hints of the intercontinental traffic that created American prosperity. Hawthorne's excision of the institution of slavery from his version of the American foundational myth is hard to justify other than in terms of his party loyalty to states' rights and his personal loyalty to Pierce, thought by many to be overly pro-Southern. Harriet Beecher Stowe would publish *Uncle Tom's Cabin* two years after *The Scarlet Letter*. While Stowe sets her sights beyond the individual slave owner to indict the entire institution, Hawthorne—much as he sympathizes with individual dissidents like Hester or Anne Hutchinson—never challenges the Puritan social system itself.

That Hawthorne was alert to the Puritans' usurpation of Indian land and decimation of Indian languages and cultures is evidenced by his brief reference to the missionary John Eliot. Eliot was celebrated in his day for his large-scale conversion of Massachusetts Indians and for setting up reservations for the converts, called "Praying Indians." Hawthorne's contemporary readers would have been cognizant of the resentment of them felt by non-Christian Indians and colonists alike, and of their eventual massacre during King Philip's War. Referencing the dying Eliot, attended to by Dimmesdale and Hester, is Hawthorne's covert critique of Puritan policy toward the Indian "first nations."

I do not share Hawthorne's ethnicity, religion, mother tongue. I do not accept Hawthorne's redemption of Hester as a desexualized woman who "had long since recognized the impossibility that any mission of divine and mysterious truth should be confided to a woman stained with sin, bowed down with shame, or even burdened with a life-long sorrow." I am disappointed that though he makes the reader recognize middle-class Puritans' special tolerance of taboo-breaking sailors who have made possible their wealth and their state's trade-dependent stability, he ignores Asia's role in the making of America: witness the fortunes amassed in India and China by the colonial New Englanders Thomas and Elihu Yale. Unlike Hawthorne's, my identity has been forged in the seams of America's cultures. Yet *The Scarlet Letter* speaks to me intimately about the continuous destruction and re-creation of our national identity. In this age of mass migrations, when the U.S. is home to millions of documented and undocumented entrants, *The Scarlet*

Letter acquires new urgency, for each of us is impelled to reimagine and redefine the American narrative.

Bibliography: C. E. Frazier Clark, Jr., ed., *The Nathaniel Hawthorne Journal* (Englewood, NJ, 1975). Nathaniel Hawthorne, *The American Notebooks* (Columbus, OH, 1975). Joel Myerson, ed., *The Selected Letters of Nathaniel Hawthorne* (Columbus, OH, 2002.

BHARATI MUKHERJEE

1850, July 19

Margaret Fuller dies in the wreck of the *Elizabeth* off the shore of Fire Island

THE END OF AMERICAN TRANSCENDENTALISM

On July 19, 1850, with Margaret Fuller's drowning in a shipwreck off Fire Island, New York, on her return from the collapsed Italian revolution, the spirit of American transcendentalism perished. So affirmed her staunchly loyal admirer Caroline Healey Dall in one of the last assessments delivered by surviving members of the nation's first major youth movement within the Yankee intelligentsia. The mixture of astuteness and idiosyncrasy in Dall's sweeping judgment thrusts us into the messy complexities of the what, who, where, when, and, above all, the so what? of American transcendentalism.

The where and the who are easiest to pin down. The transcendentalist movement began in the early 1830s in the vicinity of Boston, and the small town of Concord soon became its epicenter—"the American Weimar," Henry James called it. There lived transcendentalism's most charismatic figure, Ralph Waldo Emerson, a self-defrocked minister turned freelance man of letters, who made his home an informal salon and lured a number of the like-minded to live there or visit. Emerson meanwhile gained a much wider, ultimately transnational audience through the publication of a half-dozen volumes of essays, starting with *Nature* (1836), and three decades of public lectures given on a circuit that grew as the lyceum movement burgeoned throughout the Yankee diaspora. Long-term residents of Concord included the idealistic albeit bumblingly impractical educational reformer Bronson Alcott, like Margaret Fuller a pioneer in improvisational dialogic or "conversational" pedagogy; Emerson's protégé Henry David Thoreau, a Concord native; the prolific minor poet Ellery Channing; and, on the fringes, Nathaniel Hawthorne, a refugee from the transcendentalist commune at Brook Farm. Among notable visitors were Fuller; Elizabeth Peabody, Hawthorne's intellectually omnivorous sister-in-law, Alcott's erstwhile associate, and a progressive educator in her own right who later ran the transcendentalists' favorite Boston bookstore and lending library; the peripatetic preacher-reformer William Henry Channing, who collaborated with Emerson and another Fuller friend, James Freeman Clarke, on Fuller's two-volume *Memoirs* (1852); Emerson's own ex-mentor and frequent houseguest, his brilliantly eccentric (and emphatic) aunt, Mary Moody

Emerson; the poet-preacher Jones Very, noted for a remarkable sonnet series composed in a state of exaltation during which he felt himself to be the Second Coming of the Holy Spirit; and the elder Henry James, one of Emerson's favorite New York City hosts, whose more famous children, William the philosopher and Henry the novelist, became playmates of the young Emersons.

In the next century Concord would be canonized anew through the fame of the two younger-generation figures whose audiences soon eclipsed Emerson's: Thoreau and Louisa May Alcott. Thoreau's *Walden* (1854) became transcendentalism's greatest literary classic and a bible for modern environmentalists and advocates of voluntary simplicity, and his essay "Civil Disobedience" became its foremost political manifesto, influencing Tolstoy, Gandhi, and Martin Luther King, Jr. Although the basis of Alcott's fame—*Little Women* (1869) and its sequels–hardly types her as a transcendentalist, she, like the young Thoreau, looked on Emerson as mentor, and her oeuvre—from her first novel, *Moods,* to her end-of-life "Recollections"—is steeped in transcendentalism, though she never claimed the mantle as Thoreau did.

Concord would never have become a transcendental haven without its increasing links to metropolitan Boston and Cambridge. Even the reclusive Thoreau regularly borrowed from Harvard's library, served Harvard's celebrity scientist Louis Agassiz as specimen collector, bought the materials for his Walden cabin from an Irish immigrant laborer on the new railway linking Boston to Concord, and found the railway's tracks more of a convenience than a nuisance for wending his way to town and back. Like the American railroad, transcendentalism thrived on the domestication of imported breakthroughs. Its proximate origin was the intellectual ferment within Boston-Cambridge liberalism: Harvard's efforts to upgrade itself to a bona fide university and Unitarianism's break in the early 1800s from mainstream post-Puritan Congregationalism, prompting a next-generation push for still further disengagement from theological formalism. But these local instabilities were activated by the currents of transatlantic reform pervading the antebellum Northeast (especially the antislavery, woman's rights, and temperance movements) and by newer strains in continental thought that transcendentalism played a major part in circulating stateside.

Its nucleus of several dozen men and women spanned two generations, born roughly between 1800 and 1830. Most of the men had ties to Harvard, typically having trained there for the Unitarian ministry. Most were from old New England families, though seldom the plutocracy, and most were highly educated by antebellum standards—the women as well as the men. Fuller, for one, knew five languages.

The transcendentalists, then, were an intellectual elite—and a vanguard of cultural, if not also political, progressivism. Their interests ranged from religion to literature to experimental education to social reform on a grand scale. In religion, even those who remained lifelong ministers favored a practice in which one's spiritual development trumped obeisance to church authority and opened one to other religious traditions, Asian (Hinduism, Buddhism, Confucianism, Islam) as well as Western. Whatever their philosophic literacy, most transcendentalists favored a post-Kantian, intuitionist brand of epistemology against the dominant Lockean confinement of the sphere of human knowledge to induction from empirical experience.

Hence the label "transcendentalism" is somewhat misleading, a piece of Kantian jargon mischievously slapped on the movement by detractors as a synonym for "foreign nonsense." It was a misnomer insofar as few transcendentalists were serious philosophical reasoners, much less erudite Kantians. Those with the best philosophical credentials were Frederic Henry Hedge, eventually a professor of German at Harvard; the radical theologian and polymath Theodore Parker, transcendentalism's closest student of the German "higher criticism," which revolutionized biblical studies by reinterpreting Christianity as mythology; and George Ripley, instigator of a ten-volume series of translations of new German and French authors, who recommended the French "eclectic" popularizers of Kantianism as more suitable for practical American audiences. Ripley's verdict spoke for the tastes of most transcendentalists: more literary than philosophical or theological. By far their favorite German writer was Goethe: "The cow from which all their milk was drawn," Emerson wryly remarked. He himself found Kant and Hegel nearly unreadable but foraged through Goethe's complete works in the original. Yet "transcendentalist" was also a good fit, both in terms of its commitment to cross-fertilization of Yankee culture and international romanticism and its reputation for a discontinuous, lapidary, associative, allusive, metaphorical, sometimes willfully paradoxical and neologistic-seeming style of expression. ("It is a ridiculous demand which England and America make, that you shall speak so they can understand you," Thoreau exclaims in *Walden*.) Almost all transcendentalists could write methodical, forthright prose, and some, like the careful explainer Ripley and the pungent polemicist Parker, always did. But outsiders tended to react to the transcendentalists' more highly wrought essays and poems (their preferred genres) as middlebrow readers a century later reacted to high modernism's aesthetics of difficulty: often as perverse obfuscation; at best as an invitation to a mysteriously electrifying new challenge. The distinctive fusion of the aphoristic and the rhapsodic in Emerson's best-known writings, in early- to mid-career Thoreau and Fuller, in the most anthologized excerpts from Alcott and Very, reflect at once a principled adherence to unsystematic spirituality and philosophic intuitionism and the rhetoric of aphoristic tessellation central to the performance modes behind much transcendentalist writing: the diary (they were voluminous journalizers; Emerson called his "my savings bank"), the lecture or sermon, the improvised dialogue or monologue.

The transcendentalists sought nothing less than to change the world. Since for most the preferred medium was language, their literary legacy—Emerson's and Thoreau's, especially—was preeminent. But it was hardly their only legacy. As already noted, they were pioneering advocates of postsectarian spirituality and comparative religion, student-centered education, and post-Kantian thought. Emerson's outspoken antiformalism also helped to inspire the framers of American pragmatism, the nation's most distinctive philosophic tradition. Theodore Parker influenced the Progressive Era's social gospel movement through his trenchant sermons against slavery and about the plight of the urban poor, and his efforts to put faith into practice as the minister to Boston's largest and most heterogeneous congregation.

The transcendentalists were strongly antislavery in principle, and some, like Parker and Thomas Wentworth Higginson, the commander and memoirist of a black regiment during the Civil War, became activists who put themselves personally at risk for the cause. Transcendentalists' penchant for armchair idealism, however, and their lingering classist prejudice against abolitionists, who were seen as rabble-rousers, made for some belated converts. Emerson, for one, conspicuously lagged behind not only his disciple Thoreau but also the rest of his own family—his aunt Mary; his wife, Lidian; and his brother Charles—in speaking out against slavery, although as sectional conflict intensified in the 1850s he became a prominent abolitionist. As was true for most Yankee progressives of the day, however, the transcendentalists' efforts on behalf of disempowered blacks rarely extended to a wholehearted belief in the equality of races or socialization across the color line. John Brown became much more of a hero to them than Frederick Douglass.

All transcendentalists favored greater equality for women, at least notionally, and the movement as a whole was remarkable for the frankness and frequency of serious intellectual exchange and sociality between the sexes. Yet a lingering androcentrism that long persisted among transcendentalism's scholarly interpreters makes it unsurprising, however ironic, that it is only since the 1990s that the full importance of the women in the movement—Mary Moody and Lidian Emerson, Elizabeth and Sophia Peabody, Caroline Dall, even Margaret Fuller herself—has been established. This new understanding will surely fortify, not dislodge, the prior view of Fuller as the most influential woman transcendentalist, both as a writer and as a magnetic personal influence. Called "the American Mary Wollstonecraft," Fuller was and remains best known as the author of the nation's first significant feminist manifesto, *Woman in the Nineteenth Century* (1845), a book that was the turning point in her own evolution, as she moved from a series of Boston-based experiments in belletristic work and experimental education to the journalistic career, first in New York and then Europe, that made her transcendentalism's most cosmopolitan intellectual. Her late-life dispatches from England, France, and Italy, where she joined the Risorgimento, reveal an increasingly active player on the transatlantic stage, to an extent unmatched even by Emerson. No other transcendentalist text could have rivaled in interest Fuller's lost eyewitness account of the Italian revolution (her manuscript was another casualty of the fatal shipwreck).

Most transcendentalists, Fuller included, were reformers rather than revolutionaries, but the movement did generate some notable attempts to remake the social world. During his brief involvement with transcendentalism before he abruptly converted to Catholicism, the formidable autodidact Orestes Brownson wrote a series of trenchant papers arguing for the redistribution of wealth and power on behalf of the "laboring classes" that established him as Marxism's foremost American anticipator. Two transcendentalist groups subsequently launched ventures in utopian socialism, by far the more important being the Brook Farm commune (1841–1847), up the Charles River from Boston, which was instigated by George Ripley and his wife, Sophia, whose model school and intermittently successful experiment in communitarian living gets short shrift in Hawthorne's fictional satire *The Blithedale Romance*.

But to what extent, finally, can transcendentalism be fairly reckoned an organized movement? The participants saw themselves as a loosely networked assemblage of sympathetic but independent-thinking souls of no one persuasion. Their collective endeavors were relatively modest: a series of informal discussion groups; the two communes; a sequence of ventures in alternative education; a half-dozen magazines, the most important being the *Dial* (1840–1844), edited first by Fuller, then Emerson. More basic than this movement-versus-assemblage issue is the question of the priority transcendentalism attached to individual reform as opposed to societal reform. Emerson insisted that "souls are not saved in bundles" and that "the infinitude of the private man" was his central "doctrine." That may come as close as any one-liner to encapsulating the transcendentalist ethos—religious, philosophical, literary, social-reformist. Yet a number of Emerson's colleagues took a whole-society-first approach to reform theory: most notably Brownson, W. H. Channing, the elder Henry James, and Ripley in his communitarian phase. This difference seems less contradictory, though, if we picture the transcendentalists as preeminently a group of would-be perfectibilitarians of varied but overlapping interests, whose strong-mindedness inevitably led to dissonance over emphases and tactics, especially when negotiating the conundrum of the one versus the many at the heart of democratic theory.

Similarly predictable were the transcendentalists' discrepant recollections of the movement's achievements, duration, and staying power. Dall's assignment of its demise to 1850 makes sense insofar as the group's most memorable organized activities had taken place during the previous fifteen years, Fuller was the first among the major figures to die, and her three biographers wrote of the movement's heyday as an ephemeral moment, long since past at the time of her drowning. Yet a decade before, Emerson had already begun to speak of the movement with genial condescension, as jejune and even stillborn, whereas its literary masterpiece, *Walden,* would not be finished until several years after Fuller's death. And the full impact of Fuller's feminism, the theological radicals' postsectarian spirituality, and the social-radical edge of transcendentalist abolitionism was yet to be felt. Altogether, transcendentalism has displayed, then and since, a peculiar susceptibility to both premature burial and lingering vitality. Of the latter, the resurrection of Ronald Reagan as a latter-day Emersonian in a 2007 biography is but one example of the surprising revivals that are sure to continue, along with the pronouncements of transcendentalism's ultimate demise.

Bibliography: Lawrence Buell, *Literary Transcendentalism: Style and Vision in the American Renaissance* (Ithaca, 1973). Charles Capper and Conrad Edick Wright, *Transient and Permanent: The Transcendentalist Movement and Its Context* (Boston, 1999). Philip Gura, *American Transcendentalism: A History* (New York, 2007). Joel Myerson, ed., *Transcendentalism: A Reader* (New York, 2000). Barbara L. Packer, *The Transcendentalists* (Athens, Ga., 2007).

LAWRENCE BUELL

1850, August 5
A literary party climbs Monument Mountain

NATHANIEL HAWTHORNE AND HERMAN MELVILLE

It's a two-hour excursion up and down Monument Mountain near Stockbridge, Massachusetts—my wife and I did it in the spring of 2007, with bad knees. Given a proper walking stick and mosquito repellant, which we lacked, it's less than a rock climb but more than a stroll. When thunder and lightning broke out on our descent, the forest canopy deadened the clamor and even shielded us from the rain. The narrow Berkshires roads and the dainty, horse-and-buggy distances between villages put the modern literary tourist in a mood of intimacy with older times.

When Nathaniel Hawthorne, Herman Melville, and their friends, editors, and publishers made the same ascent in 1850, they were carrying a few bottles of champagne—as befits a bookish outing—and when the inevitable rainstorm struck, the party huddled under an outcropping of rock, smoked cigars, drank, and chatted. From that day of outdoor bonhomie grew a brief but intense friendship—some have called it a courtship—between the forty-six-year-old Hawthorne and the thirty-one-year-old Melville that changed the course of American fiction.

With the publication of *The Scarlet Letter* five months earlier, Hawthorne had finally been earning the recognition that had long eluded him. (Four years before, Edgar Allan Poe had termed him "the example, *par excellence,* in this country, of the privately-admired and publicly-unappreciated man of genius.") In contrast, Melville's three most recently published novels—*Mardi, Redburn,* and *White-Jacket,* composed at white heat for "tobacco money," as he admitted—had confused reviewers and disappointed readers.

Melville was still shackled to his debut successes, *Typee* and *Omoo,* quasi-documentaries of life among the bare-breasted women and cannibals of the South Pacific, and he despaired of ever breaking free. (To Hawthorne a few months later he wrote, "Think of it! To go down to posterity is bad enough, any way; but to go down as a 'man who lived among the cannibals'!") The writers were each at work on new "romances" that would appear within the next year and a half: Melville's tale of coming to maturity on a South Seas whaler (as yet no whale, no Ahab), and Hawthorne's uncovering of a multigenerational curse, set inside a Salem mansion.

Two other climbers with the group that day played important roles in recording the event: Evert Duyckinck, the smooth and amiable publisher of the weekly *Literary World,* a friend to all, however disparate their tastes and talents (and early publisher of both Hawthorne and Melville), and James T. Fields, partner in Ticknor, Reed, and Fields, the most important American publishing house of its day and publisher of *The Scarlet Letter.* Without Duyckinck's and Fields's letters and memoirs, we would have only Hawthorne's desultory note: "Monday, Aug 5, 1850. Rode with Fields & wife to Stockbridge, being thereto invited by Mr. Field [Mr. Dudley Field, a celebrated lawyer] of S.—in order to ascend Monument mountain. Found at Mr. F's Dr. [Oliver Wendell] Holmes, Mr. [Duyckinck] of New-York, also Messrs. Cornelius Mathews [gadfly and novelist] & Herman Melville."

Thankfully, the occasion was memorialized in Fields's *Yesterdays with Authors,* written twenty years later, by which time Hawthorne had been dead for seven years and Melville was living out his literary half-life in New York as a $1,000-a-year customs clerk and self-publishing poet.

> We scrambled to the top with great spirit, and when we arrived, Melville, I remember, bestrode a peaked rock, which ran out like a bowsprit, and pulled and hauled imaginary ropes for our delectation. Then we all assembled in a shady spot, and one of the party read to us Bryant's beautiful poem commemorating Monument Mountain. Then we lunched among the rocks, and somebody proposed Bryant's health, and "long life to the dear old poet." This was the most popular toast of the day, and it took, I remember, a considerable quantity of Heidsieck to do it justice ... Hawthorne was among the most enterprising of the merry-makers; and being in the dark much of the time, he ventured to call out lustily and pretend that certain destruction was inevitable to all of us.

Aside from Fields's memoir, two other documents attest to the deep importance of the authors' encounter. The first, part one of which was published just twelve days later, on August 17, in the *Literary World,* was "Hawthorne and His Mosses," an inexhaustibly suggestive and enraptured appreciation of Hawthorne's 1846 collection, *Mosses from an Old Manse* (part two appeared the following week). The writer posed as "a Virginian spending July in Vermont." He denied ever having met Hawthorne ("I never saw the man; and in the chances of a quiet plantation life, remote from his haunts, perhaps never shall"). The Virginia plantation dweller was, of course, Herman Melville. Why the coyness? (One is reminded of an aside in Chapter 80 of *Moby-Dick:* "The whale, like all things that are mighty, wears a false brow to the common world.") Or perhaps Melville feared that he had come on too strong and was waiting for a sign of the older author's approval before admitting authorship.

"Hawthorne and His Mosses" is a remarkable piece of free-range criticism. In it, Melville recasts his own romance-in-progress in light of his neighbor's achievement. "This Hawthorne has dropped germinous seeds into my soul. He expands and deepens down, the more I contemplate him; and further and further, shoots his strong New England roots into the hot soil in my Southern soul." Melville was a native New Yorker with New England connections; he couldn't claim ownership of a "Southern soul," except for the appealing alliteration. Those "germinous seeds" were nothing less than the discovery of Hawthorne's "blackness":

> The hither side of Hawthorne's soul, the other side—like the dark half of the physical sphere—is shrouded in a blackness, ten times black ... Whether Hawthorne has simply availed himself of this mystical blackness as a means to the wondrous

effects he makes it to produce in his lights and shades; or whether there really lurks in him, perhaps unknown to himself, a touch of Puritanic gloom,—this, I cannot altogether tell. Certain it is, however, that this great power of blackness in him derives its force from its appeals to that Calvinistic sense of Innate Depravity and Original Sin, from whose visitations, in some shape or other, no deeply thinking mind is always and wholly free. For, in certain moods, no man can weigh this world without throwing in something, somehow like Original Sin, to strike the uneven balance.

He is precisely right in citing the blackness, and, by his lights, finding Hawthorne's tales as "deep as Dante" and the differences between "Nathaniel of Salem" and "William of Avon" not immeasurable. He was reading Shakespeare concurrently with Hawthorne, and trying to hold both in balance. Hawthorne's greatness approached Shakespeare's, Melville wrote, for the simple reason that Hawthorne "is bound to carry republican progressiveness into Literature as well as into Life." He even drove the point home with humor: "Who reads a book by an Englishman that is a modern? The great mistake seems to be, that even with those Americans who look forward to the coming of a great literary genius among us, they somehow fancy he will come in the costume of Queen Elizabeth's day; be a writer of dramas founded upon old English history or the tales of Boccaccio."

Melville, through Hawthorne's tales, was discovering a way of expanding the frame of conventional storytelling by deepening and darkening it; in a word, he had discovered the power of allegory. The American short story derives from Hawthorne in the way that Russian literature crawls from under Gogol's overcoat. Think of the Black Sabbath rituals in Cheever's suburbs—masks of a gin-drowned Eden—or Raymond Carver's marital cul-de-sacs containing a hint of divinity, or Flannery O'Connor, or Bernard Malamud, among dozens. It's the subtle manipulation of allegory that lends density, foreboding, and multiple interpretations to the simple screen of narrative presentation.

Perhaps one can appreciate Melville's "Mosses" essay all the more by contrasting his approach to that of Edgar Allan Poe—always the confident theorist—who had assessed *Mosses from an Old Manse* three years earlier. Hawthorne's chaste and precise style, his antiquarian settings and allegorical inventiveness invited Poe's impatience: "He has the purest style, the finest taste, the most available scholarship, the most delicate humor, the most touching pathos, the most radiant imagination, the most consummate ingenuity; and with these varied good qualities he has done *well* as a mystic. But is there any one of these qualities which should prevent his doing doubly as well in a career of honest, upright, sensible, prehensible and comprehensible things?"

Melville, Duyckinck, and Mathews popped in on Hawthorne just two days after their climb, and they left with two bottles of champagne. Melville was invited to visit for four days in early September (at which point he confessed his "Mosses" authorship), and the two authors began a regular correspondence, punctuated with visits. Hawthorne's letters have disappeared; we have only a dozen of Melville's effusive, nakedly revealing responses.

The second document that reveals the importance of the friends' meeting that day in the Berkshires? Nothing less than *Moby-Dick* in its final incarnation. Under the influences of Shakespeare and Hawthorne, Melville found the elixir that would deliver him from literary irrelevance.

Viewed from today, Hawthorne and Melville are an unlikely pair. Melville was a mariner, a trespasser on settled forms, a crow's-nest solipsist with infinite vistas and unsounded depths. Hawthorne was more the surveyor, a careful cultivator of confined dimensions. *Moby-Dick* is a romance in the "loose, baggy monster" tradition, musical and muscular in its language, promiscuous in its similes, aggressive in its pedantry, transcendent of the classic unities. Ishmael is not even a character after the "land" chapters and his meeting with Queequeg; he becomes an embodied authorial voice, turning from naive youth to Tiresian oracle.

Melville was part of the New York ascendancy. Hawthorne inherited a declining New England dominance. Both came from old, established families. Both lost their fathers early. Both knew financial insecurity.

Hawthorne was happily married (insofar as a depressive can be happy). Sophia Hawthorne was an artist (from an extraordinary family) and contributed in every possible way to his career. He observed and reported upon the daily pleasures of parenthood and nature with tender scrutiny. In contrast, Melville was often miserable in the early years of his marriage, a domestic tyrant at war with nature and at times violent toward his wife and (especially) his sons.

Melville was radically democratic, as color-blind as any author in our canon. In a self-defensive, confessional letter to Hawthorne (perhaps responding to a mild rebuke), he wrote: "So, when you see or hear of my ruthless democracy on all sides, you may possibly feel a touch of a shrink . . . It is but nature to be shy of a mortal who boldly declares that a thief in jail is as honorable a personage as Gen. George Washington. This is ludicrous. But Truth is the silliest thing under the sun. Try to get a living by the Truth—and go to the Soup Societies." Hawthorne, from his earliest entries in the *American Journals,* was a white, Yankee, Anglo-Saxon, Protestant chauvinist. (In August 1838: "On the whole, I find myself rather more of an abolitionist in feeling than in principle.") In the 1850s, with civil war looming, he disastrously stuck with the states'-rights, slavery-defending Democratic Party of his Bowdoin friend, President Franklin Pierce, and even wrote Pierce's campaign biography. (Of course if he had shifted his political allegiance to the Whigs, he would not have been fired from his job at the Salem Custom House, and he would not have been forced by economic necessity to write *The Scarlet Letter* and *The House of the Seven Gables.*)

Melville was self-educated, prodigiously so. His life began at twenty-five, when he returned from the sea. Hawthorne was a Bowdoin grad, a prize-winning Latin essayist, friend of many to whom he would provide lifelong support. Hawthorne was a poised gentleman, a future diplomat; Melville was irascible—people felt uncomfortable in his presence.

And of course with Melville, there's always the sexual question. From the famous letter of November 17, 1851, responding to Hawthorne's presumed praise of *Moby-Dick:* "Whence come you, Hawthorne? By what right do you drink from my flagon of life? And when I put it to my lips—lo, they are yours and not mine." Or, in the same letter, "In me divine magnanimities are spontaneous and instantaneous—catch them while you can. The world goes round, and the other side comes up. So now I can't write what I felt. But I felt pantheistic then—your heart beat in my ribs and mine in yours, and both in God's." And later, more touchingly: "Ah! It's a long stage, and no inn in sight, and night coming, and the body cold. But with you for a passenger, I am content and can be happy. I shall leave the world, I feel, with more satisfaction for having come to know you. Knowing you persuades me more than the Bible of our immortality."

Much has been speculated, but nothing is known. Was Melville gay as we know it, or as Whitman lived it? Certainly not. Did he have a homoerotic orientation? Undoubtedly—just look in any of his books. Can we confidently decipher nineteenth-century male endearments? I doubt it. (He addressed Duyckinck with "My Dear" and "My Beloved" as well.) Did he make an overt or even guarded sexual approach to Hawthorne during any of those all-night, book-brandy-and-cigar sessions in 1851 and 1852? Was sexual discomfort responsible for Hawthorne's sudden decamping from the Berkshires in November 1852? (I doubt that; Hawthorne was already railing against the Berkshires—"I de-test it, de-test it, de-test it!"—and anxious to get back to Boston.) I suspect nothing was left unsaid. Melville was no self-censurer. In Hawthorne he had found father, editor, confessor, and nurturer. I suspect they discussed everything, the way that writers do, and I trust they came to a manly (as they said back then) understanding.

Melville felt he had written a "wicked" book (but felt "spotless as the lamb"). Its secret motto was "I baptize you not in the name of God . . . (but in the name of the devil)" and he felt the book had been stewed in hell-fire. This is the legacy of the "blackness" he had discovered in Hawthorne, blown up a thousand times grander than Hawthorne could imagine. But with only one side of their two-year correspondence available to us, we don't know what Hawthorne truly believed, or wrote—only that in general he approved of *Moby-Dick,* and that was more than sufficient for Melville. He just needed Hawthorne's higher permission to get the story told.

If Herman Melville had been a cabinetmaker, he would have delivered an allegory of woods—the virtues of cherry, oak, or maple; the exotic charm of teak, mahogany, or shoondari. He would have written of their origins in the rain forests and the taiga; the forest primeval and all its inhabitants, living and legendary; hardwoods, softwoods, their servitude as houses, ships, and furniture, and the craftsmen who fashion them. Whorls, grains, and knots: the faces of the God. Charcoal: the after-life. And finally, the annual wonder of the reddening and yellowing, the dying and rebirth of the deciduous forests, and the evergreens—those dumb sentinels—spared the agony and triumph of death and rebirth.

Bibliography: James T. Fields, *Yesterdays with Authors* (Boston and New York, 1882). Nathaniel Hawthorne, *American Notebooks,* ed. Sophia Hawthorne (Boston, 1868). Herman Melville, "Hawthorne and His Mosses," *Literary Review,* August 17 and 24, 1850, and Melville's letters to Nathaniel Hawthorne, in *The Portable Melville,* ed. Jay Leyda (New York, 1952). Edgar Allan Poe,

"Nathaniel Hawthorne," in *The Works of the Late Edgar Allan Poe,* ed. Rufus Wilmot Griswold, vol. 3 (New York, 1857).

CLARK BLAISE

1851
"Give it up, sub-subs!"

MOBY-DICK; OR, THE WHALE

Moby Dick; 2.30 min. Gregory Peck, Richard Basehart, Orson Welles. A mad captain enlists others in his quest to kill a white whale. (*TV Guide,* November 20, 1961)

Isn't that America, the thing itself, right there? "I, Ishmael, was one of that crew; my shouts had gone up with the rest; my oath had been welded with theirs; and stronger I shouted, and more did I hammer and clinch my oath, because of the dread in my soul. A wild, mystical, sympathetical feeling was in me; Ahab's quenchless feud seemed mine." So said Ishmael, after Ahab's appearance on the quarterdeck of the *Pequod* to charge the crew: "I'll chase him round Good Hope, and round the Horn, and round the Norway Maelstrom, and round perdition's flames before I give him up. And this is what ye have shipped for, men! to chase that white whale on both sides of land, and over all sides of earth, till he spouts black blood and rolls fin out. What say ye, men, will ye splice hands on it, now?"

"Is it that by its indefiniteness it shadows forth the heartless voids and immensities of the universe, and thus stabs us from behind with the thought of annihilation, when beholding the white depths of the milky way?" Ishmael reflects on the white whale, the sea for the moment eddying quietly up against the hull. "Or is it, that as an essence whiteness is not so much a color as the visible absence of color, and at the same time the concrete of all colors; is it for these reasons that there is such a dumb blankness, full of meaning, in a wide landscape of snows—a colorless, all-color of atheism from which we shrink?" Do we even need to hear these voices?

Ahab is always out there, with the whale ahead of him and Ishmael always along for the ride. Here he is by way of Edmund Wilson, writing in 1962 in *Patriotic Gore* on Grant: "I do not want to add to the bizarre interpretations already offered for *Moby-Dick* by suggesting that it anticipates the Civil War, but"—and then he is off, at first starting slowly ("there are moments, in reading the *Memoirs,* when one is reminded of Captain Ahab's quest"), and then carried forward as if by the force of the story itself, as if the story itself were history, Ahab in pursuit of Moby-Dick, Ulysses S. Grant in pursuit of Robert E. Lee, the first story, not the second, the real history the country has made, or has always sought. Quickly Wilson is onto Grant's pages on how the world made Lee into a mystical figure whose victories are miraculous and his escapes no less so (Grant: "The number of his forces was always lowered and that of the National forces exaggerated"), and, while not wanting to add to any bizarre interpretations, arranging the props on the stage ("We look forward to the eventual encounter as to the final scene of a drama—as we wait for the moment when Ahab, stubborn, intent and tough, crippled by his wooden leg as Grant had sometimes been by his alcoholic habits, will confront the smooth and shimmering foe, who has so far eluded all hunters"). Here again is the novelist E. L. Doctorow, in 2007, addressing a jeremiad called "The White Whale" to a joint meeting of the American Academy of Arts and Sciences and the American Philosophical Society, riding the waves of *Moby-Dick* ("It will take more than revelations of an inveterately corrupt Administration to dissolve the miasma of otherworldly weirdness hanging over this land"), then trying to find solid ground even as the ship pitches high on the sea ("Melville in *Moby-Dick* speaks of reality outracing apprehension . . . reality as too much for us to take in, as, for example, the white whale is too much for the *Pequod* and its captain. It may be that our new century is an awesomely complex white whale"), but the white whale looms up only to disappear, now a new century, now the Constitution and the great white buildings it built, now America's enemy as Doctorow sights him. For one who does not want to add to the bizarre interpretations already offered for *Moby-Dick,* it is a relief to come back down to earth, open the book itself, and read, in its first chapter, as I write in the fall of 2008, these prosaic words:

> "*Grand Contested Election for President of the United States.*
> "WHALING VOYAGE BY ONE ISHMAEL.
> "BLOODY BATTLE IN AFFGHANISTAN."

Is any of *that* even needed? Is Herman Melville needed, sitting in his house in Pittsfield, Massachusetts, writing to Nathaniel Hawthorne in November of 1851, when Melville was thirty-two, "A sense of unspeakable security is in me this moment, on account of your having understood the book," or thinking back on that day, he not only the only one left to remember it, but the only one to care, in 1891, the year he died? Is, today, the book even needed? As James Conant has written, "Certain forms of speech seem not to require recovery, because they seem to have always been with us and are everywhere still with us." The book reads the culture and the culture reads the book; thus one might open the paper on a Friday morning, scan the "Events" listings, and find this triple bill at a place called the Great American Music Hall: "Or, the Whale, the Federalists, Emily Jane White." As Ishmael mused, just before coining his trio of headlines: "And, doubtless, my going on this whaling voyage, formed part of the grand programme of Providence that was drawn up a long time ago. It came in as a sort of brief interlude and solo between more extensive performances. I take it that this part of the bill must have run something like this."

It is the most famous opening line in American literature, in the American tall tale, in the American shaggy dog story. It contains all possibilities. When, some years ago, I saw a CALL ME ISHMAEL bumper sticker on a car in Oakland, California, it didn't occur to me that it was a souvenir of someone's visit to the Melville museum in Pittsfield; I figured it was something Oaklander Ishmael Reed had had made up.

Why is it not a cliché? Because it rings a bell, because the line snaps back like a fore boom? Or because it speaks for the American as a creature of disguise and self-invention, each one an embodiment of his or her own country, fated to act out its whole drama in his or her own skin? John Smith, James van Sciver, Abe Gratz, Sergius O'Shaughnessy, Roberto Maggiore, Fritz Schneidermann—any of those could be the name Ishmael is hiding. "Call me Ishmael" means we will never know what it is.

There are many great endings in American literature, as if the country's most poetic stories incline toward the end of America, that being contained whole in the skin of a single character, as an explicit or hidden theme. These endings are always political, whatever their costuming in private dramas of love or money: no matter what passport the reader might carry, they momentarily implicate the reader as an American. As with Fitzgerald's *The Great Gatsby,* with its Dutch sailors sighting the New York coast for the first time. As with his *Tender Is the Night,* with Dick Diver somewhere in upstate New York, waiting, "like Grant in Galena." As with Philip Roth's *I Married a Communist,* with all of those its story consumed living on forever as stars, each his or her own furnace:

> Neither the ideals of their era nor the expectations of our species were determining destiny: hydrogen alone was determining destiny. There are no longer mistakes for Eve or Ira to make. There is no betrayal. There is no idealism. There are no falsehoods. There is neither conscience nor its absence. There are no mothers and daughters, no fathers and stepfathers. There are no actors. There is no class struggle. There is no discrimination or lynching or Jim Crow, nor has there ever been. There is no injustice, nor is there justice. There are no utopias.

Roth does not say, "There is no America." Somehow given the story *Moby-Dick* has already told, his cosmology of negation cannot negate that—because the ending of *Moby-Dick* trumps all other endings, and seems to have been written to do nothing less. Ahab killed by the whale, the *Pequod* smashed by it and sinking into its own vortex, pulling down every man and boat, and as the last mast is about to disappear below the surface there is "the red arm and hammer" of the harpooner Tashtego, the pure-blooded Gay Head American Indian from Martha's Vineyard: his arm "hovered backwardly uplifted in the open air, in the act of nailing the flag faster and faster to the subsiding spar. A sky hawk that tauntingly had followed the main-truck downwards from its natural home among the stars, pecking at the flag, and incommoding Tashtego there; this bird now chanced to intercept its broad fluttering wing between the hammer and the wood; and simultaneously feeling that ethereal thrill, the submerged savage beneath, in his death-gasp, kept his hammer frozen there"—a moment John Huston, filming *Moby-Dick* in 1956, did not even try to shoot. The last chapters of the book are an action movie, a nineteenth-century version of Steve McQueen's car chase in *Bullitt,* and though, as befitting the nineteenth century, when everything was slower and simpler, this chase lasts three days, the sense of action is so furious that, for that final scene, as you read the symbols don't even begin to work as such. This is actually happening. You can't believe it as you watch. You can't believe you are alive to tell the tale.

In every way, to read *Moby-Dick* is to reread it. Given the diffusion and the presence of the book and its metaphors, any time one sits down with the book, even if it is for the first time, the act carries with it a sense of return. One can forget so much of what is there, with hardly a phrase needed to bring a hundred pages back to mind in an instant. There is the way the whole first section of the book, until the *Pequod* sets sail, is a nonstop comedy, Ishmael first as Bob Hope in *Road to Utopia,* then as Abbott running an outrageous who's-on-first routine with his New Bedford–innkeeper Costello, then Ishmael's one-night stand with the tattooed Polynesian harpooner Queequeg turning into at least a two-night marriage—but not before proving, in a set of syllogisms so precise you don't even care where they're leading, that it is a Christian's duty to worship a pagan idol. There is the language, sometimes stopping the book cold in its own pages ("He looked like a man cut away from a stake," Ishmael says of Ahab when he first sees him, and what Appalachian murder ballad was that line from, or waiting for?), often so free-swinging its slang leaps more than a century without slipping a minute into obsolescence: "Give it up, sub-subs!" "Who ain't a slave? Tell me that," "Cool as an icicle." There is the thrill of keeping up with a writer who moves so fast that you pull up short to catch your breath and wonder: how does he get from a deckhand knocked around by an overlord to the "universal thump" of democratic comradeship ("all hands should rub each other's shoulder-blades") in a paragraph? The rhetoric and the ethos of Jacksonian democracy, often taken to Olympian heights, make the wind behind so many of Ishmael's musings, but still—how does Melville move Ishmael from his ardor over Ahab casting thunderbolts on the quarterdeck to an analysis of the captain and his mates that could pass for an editorial in the *Democratic Review* on the flaws of Millard Fillmore's cabinet specifically and the state of the nation generally? "Here, then," our tour guide tells us, "was this grey-headed, ungodly old man, chasing with curses a Job's whale round the world, at the head of a crew, too, chiefly made up of mongrel renegades, and castaways, and cannibals—morally enfeebled also, by the incompetence of mere unaided virtue or right-mindedness in Starbuck, the invulnerable jollity of indifference and recklessness in Stubb, and the pervading mediocrity in Flask."

Even without rereading the book, even with only a *TV Guide* sense of the tale, one is rereading the book when one chances on John Wayne's Tom Dunson in *Red River* on late-night TV, a movie made in 1948; or recalls Elvis Presley two decades later, facing an audience for the first time in years and against the blankness of that unknown hoisting a mike stand like a harpoon, thrusting it over the crowd, and shouting "Moby Dick!"; or watches a black boy, one "Woody," an early incarnation of Bob Dylan, pitched out of a boxcar by hobo thugs and into a river, only to see a right whale gliding toward him in the 2007 film *I'm Not There;* or channel-switches into the 2008 episode of *Law & Order: Criminal Intent* where the tormented police detective Bobby Goren comes face to face with the unmistakable handiwork of the escaped serial killer Nicole Wallace, once a literature professor whose specialty was Melville. She lectures in a flashback: "The descent into madness is usually preceded by obsession. What characterizes Ahab's obsession? I always fancied it was man's unrelenting pursuit of his own potency." "I'm told she's your white whale," Goren's boss says to him—just before Goren receives a card postmarked Pittsfield, Massachusetts. When, early on in the book, Captain Peleg asks Ishmael, "Want to see what whaling is, eh? Have ye yet clapped eye on Captain Ahab?" and Ishmael answers, "Who is Captain Ahab, sir?" we're surprised he hasn't heard of him; we have.

Did Melville somehow know, or hope, that his country would always seek out the mysteries that, in his big book, the book that would for the rest of his life erase his name from the memories of his fellow citizens, he took down as if they were the plainest, most obvious facts, himself the sub-sub librarian he so confidently laughed off? That famous letter from Hawthorne, the letter in which he showed Melville that he "understood the book," the letter that, unlike Melville's response to Hawthorne, does not survive—it could have been one of Poe's hoaxes, were he still around to forge it, a trick to keep the characters alive, running their histories through history yet unmade, unmaking history as they left it behind and continued on their way.

What *did* Hawthorne say? No, Melville may not have kept letters, as Hawthorne did, but one can imagine a ceremony a little more to the point than taking out the trash. "Cool as an icicle," as Ishmael says of Queequeg sitting among the other sailors in the Spouter-Inn, his harpoon at hand, "reaching over the table with it, to the imminent jeopardy of many heads, and grappling the beefsteaks towards him. But *that* was certainly very coolly done by him, and every one knows that in most people's estimation, to do anything coolly is to do it genteelly." So how cool, how genteel of you, Herman, sitting in your writing room late at night, with no one to glimpse a single word as you burned the pages! There was no better way to keep us reading; with its author more than a century dead, the book is the sea we swim in.

Bibliography: E. L. Doctorow, "The White Whale," *The Nation,* July 14, 2008. Herman Melville, *Moby-Dick; or, The Whale* (1851), ed. Charles Feidelson, Jr. (Indianapolis, 1964); "To Nathaniel Hawthorne, November 17[?], 1851," in *The Portable Melville,* ed. Jay Leyda (New York, 1952). Philip Roth, *I Married a Communist* (New York, 1998). Edmund Wilson, *Patriotic Gore: Studies in the Literature of the American Civil War* (New York, 1962).

GREIL MARCUS

1851–1852

Readers eagerly await weekly installments of Harriet Beecher Stowe's novel, serialized in the *National Era*

Uncle Tom's Cabin

When Harriet Beecher Stowe began work on what she thought of as a serialized sketch called "Uncle Tom's Cabin," her heart was in an unquenchable uproar, so stirred was she by recent events both national and personal. By the spring of 1851 when she put pen to paper, she was pretty much fuming.

In July 1849 her beloved son Charley had died of cholera. The youngest of seven, Charley was a pale, beautiful child, only eighteen months old when he died. When he became ill, Mrs. Stowe had to tend him alone, since her husband, Calvin Stowe, was away at the time, trying to decide whether to take the teaching position he'd been offered at Bowdoin College in Maine or remain at Lane Seminary in Cincinnati. Cholera progresses quickly, and Charley didn't last long. Mrs. Stowe buried her child alone. "How we can become accustomed to anything!" she exclaimed in a letter to a friend. When little Charley died, it seemed that she would have to.

"I have been the mother of seven children, the most beautiful and most loved of whom lies buried near my Cincinnati residence," she would write two years later. "It was at his dying bed and at his grave that I learnt what a poor slave mother may feel when her child is torn away from her."

Mrs. Stowe's unusual and admirable ability to transcend the limits of her own grief and imagine that someone else, of another race and station, felt the same as she, was no accident of temperament. Her father, Lyman Beecher, a Congregationalist minister who had often blasted slavery from the pulpit, insisted upon a moral and intellectual environment at home. He encouraged Harriet and her ten siblings to conduct evening debates on current political issues. Her brother Henry Ward Beecher became an outspoken reformer and abolitionist. Her sister Isabella was an early suffragist. Harriet became a teacher. The empathic Beecher siblings took on social ills as if they were personal affronts. In the end, even though she wrote under her married name and considered motherhood her primary duty, Harriet Beecher Stowe remained a daughter to the core: in all ways, a Beecher.

The year after Charley's death proved equally wrenching. That summer, as Congress debated the Compromise of 1850—within which dwelt an amendment to the infamous Fugitive Slave Act, which criminalized the harboring of fugitive slaves and required citizens to return them to their owners, thereby transforming every American into a potential slave-catcher—the abolitionist temper rose to boiling. In July, one year after Charley's death, President Zachary Taylor fell ill after eating a bowl of cherries and drinking a pitcher of milk during a Fourth of July celebration. A doctor diagnosed *cholera morbus.* Five days later, the president was dead. Although a Southerner, Taylor had opposed the Fugitive Slave Act, but the newly sworn-in Millard Fillmore of Buffalo kept his eye on politics and, playing the odds, hedged.

In response, Mrs. Stowe—a fierce abolitionist and occasional writer of essays, sketches, and feature stories for *Godey's Lady's Book*—submitted a purposefully polemical piece entitled "The Freeman's Dream" to the antislavery newsweekly the *National Era.* Her fourth published article in the *Era,* "The Freeman's Dream," which included an emotional parable describing the damnation of a farmer who refused aid to a family of fugitives, ran on August 1, 1850. In September, Millard Fillmore signed the Fugitive Slave Act, also known as the Bloodhound Bill, into law. By this time, Calvin Stowe had accepted the job at Bowdoin College and the Stowe family had moved to Brunswick, Maine, where their seventh and final child was born.

After passage of the bill, Mrs. Stowe could no longer quell her outrage. She ranted, she fulminated, she longed to "do something even the humblest in this cause." As it turned out, in February 1851, in an effort to encourage her to contribute more work to the *National Era,* its editor, Gamaliel Bailey, sent her $100 as a kind of advance against whatever she might choose to submit. Her sister Isabella, who had been writing Harriet one letter after another describing the horrors brought on by the new law—even in Boston—eventually wrote one that pushed her to action. If *she* could use a pen the way Harriet did, Isabella wrote, she would write something to make the nation "feel what an accursed thing slavery is."

Family responsibilities dominated Mrs. Stowe's life, but by the late winter of 1851 her new baby was sleeping in his own crib, giving her time to herself, at night, to put pen to paper and—eventually—to allow her imagination to transform grief and anger into a story that would rock the country and then the world.

On March 9, 1851, Harriet Beecher Stowe sent Gamaliel Bailey a note. "Up to this year," she wrote, "I have always felt that I had no particular call to meddle with this subject, and I dreaded to expose even my own mind to the full force of its exciting power." But the events of the day had emboldened her, and she now wanted to submit some sketches for his newspaper, lengthier than any of her previous pieces, probably enough to run through three or four issues. In these sketches she hoped to create a picture of slavery as she knew it existed, in order, she said, to touch the hearts of readers and instill in their minds a new and more nearly accurate portrayal of the situation than had previously been spoken of, not just by Southerners and slaveholders but—even more to the point—by the compromisers and virtual collaborators from the North. After all, Stephen Douglas of Illinois and Daniel Webster of Massachusetts had helped draft the Compromise of 1850.

Her object, she told Bailey, was "to hold up in the most lifelike and graphic manner possible Slavery, its reverses, changes and the negro character." In other words, she wanted to do as Isabella had suggested, make readers *feel* the pain and grief of injustice and oppression, as well as the boundless love of a mother for her child, and her grief when the child is taken from her, whether by death or a slave trader.

Sometimes a writer doesn't know what she's up to. Sometimes work makes its own demands. In cahoots with the work itself, the mind plays its own tricks. To calm our fears and uncertainties, it creates the notion of an attainable task ahead, easily completed. Under that illusion, we begin. And then the job asserts its demands. A short poem becomes a three-act play. A character sketch insists on stretching itself out to become a short story, a novella, sometimes even a novel. Such is almost certainly the case with Mrs. Stowe, who had already begun writing her new sketches but perhaps could not imagine herself—a woman after all, and the mother of seven—the author of a full-length novel. And so she had to trick herself into believing she could accomplish her goal in a few weeks.

Two months later, on May 8, Gamaliel Bailey ran this announcement: "Week after next we propose to commence in the *Era* the publication of a new story by Mrs. H. B. Stowe, the title of which will be "UNCLE TOM'S CHILDREN OR THE MAN THAT WAS A THING." (In 1938, African American writer Richard Wright would title his first collection of stories *Uncle Tom's Children*.) He was, Bailey wrote, alerting readers so that subscribers—especially those who were already familiar with Mrs. Stowe's work—would not "lose the beginning of it" and so that those wishing to "read the production as it may appear in successive numbers of the *Era*" might subscribe.

Along with its political stories and essays, the *National Era* regularly ran fiction and poetry, but ordinarily the genres did not cross over. Most of the literary works confirmed the conventional beliefs of the paper's readership, by focusing on home and the family. The death of children was a particularly familiar subject, most often beautiful, intelligent, rather angelic children whose death symbolized a kind of sentimental belief in the afterlife and the beauty of death as a lesson. Mrs. Stowe was to make use of these clichés, but not with the same purpose as other women writers of the day. No reader of the newsweekly could have predicted what the work would be like or how it would be received.

But Bailey must have sensed something. On June 5, 1851, he assigned most of the *Era*'s front page to the first two chapters of Mrs. Stowe's sketch. She had changed her title to *Uncle Tom's Cabin, or, Life Among the Lowly*. It began:

CHAPTER I.—In which the Reader is introduced to a Man of Humanity.

Late in the afternoon of a chilly day in February, two gentlemen were sitting alone over their wine, in a well-furnished dining parlor, in the town of P——, in Kentucky. There were no servants present, and the gentlemen, with chairs closely approaching, seemed to be discussing some subject with great earnestness.

A quiet beginning, calm, taking its time, setting up fine details, indicating a long journey ahead. In short order, one of the gentlemen is revealed to be a slave trader; the other, a strapped slaveholder who for some unspecified financial reason cannot but agree to sell to the trader two of the people he holds in bondage: the faithful, hardworking man they call "Uncle" Tom, and a baby named Harry, child of a beauteous house slave named Eliza. Thus does the story begin.

Readers were in no way prepared for what lay ahead. Mrs. Stowe had, in fact, done the unthinkable. She had, in imagination, transferred her own sensibilities as a privileged, educated white woman into the consciousness of an enslaved black person. To the consternation of many, she presented the radical notion that slaves were capable of thoughts and feelings similar to hers, and, by extension, to those of *Era* readers.

Because she meant her work to be polemical, Mrs. Stowe's narrative voice often became that of a teacher, explaining the way of the world to restless students, whom she referred to as "you." In the chapter entitled "A Mother's Struggle," concerning Eliza's decision to flee slave country with her baby, she asks her—white, obviously—readers: "If it were *your* Harry, mother, or your Willie, that were going to be torn from you by a brutal trader, tomorrow morning,—if you had seen the man, and heard that the papers were signed and delivered . . . how fast could *you* walk? How many miles could you make in those few brief hours, with the darling at your bosom . . . ?"

Her cause was clear, and she was as shameless and obvious as a country song in its pursuit.

Over the next ten months, between June 5, 1851, and April 1, 1852, some 50,000 people read the forty-one installments that composed the serialized version of *Uncle Tom's Cabin.* The *Era*'s subscription list rose from 15,000 to 19,000. Gamaliel Bailey acknowledged his gratitude by sending Mrs. Stowe an additional $200. Letters to the editor told of families who spent every week waiting for the Friday mail to deliver their copy of the paper. "Weekly," one letter testified, "as the *Era* arrives, our family, consisting of twelve individuals, is called together to listen to the reading of *Uncle Tom's Cabin.*"

While some praised Mrs. Stowe's writing ability for its "length, breadth, finish and furniture," others wondered how in the world she could presume to know the mind of the South, where she had never been. In 1853 Stowe would answer that question by publishing *A Key to Uncle Tom's Cabin,* a kind of extended endnote that connects passages about slave life either with personal narratives written by freed slaves, or her own experience with domestic servants.

Two scenes particularly engaged the reading public: Eliza crossing the Ohio River from Kentucky into Ohio by leaping almost magically from one ice floe to the next, holding her baby tight to her chest to keep him safely out of the clutches of the slave trader, and the death of the angelic and perceptive little white girl, Eva, who, after listening to tales of brutality toward slaves, tells her friend Tom, "These things sink into my heart . . . They sink into my heart."

Neighbors came together on Friday nights to cheer when Eliza leapt to the Northern side of the river, to weep when Eva died and when, late in the serialization, Tom was beaten to death while protecting the whereabouts of two slave women, desperately pleading to his master, Simon Legree, not to imperil his soul with such a sin. Hearing the story in installments increased readers' interest and intensified their outrage, as, like television viewers a century and a half later following the story of Tony and Carmela Soprano, they waited to find out what happened next. By September 1851 Harriet Beecher Stowe had signed a book contract with Jewett and Company of Boston, which would publish *Uncle Tom's Cabin* in two volumes, after the serialization had come to a close, in 1852. The book would sell so quickly that Jewett had to keep its presses running twenty-four hours a day. It was a best seller in the United States, England, Europe, and Asia, translated into more than sixty languages. In Paris, licorice sticks were called "Uncle Tom candy." After the book was shipped to Russia, translated into Yiddish to avoid the censor, Leo Tolstoy praised it as a great work of literature, "flowing from the love of God and man." (*Uncle Tom's Cabin* was also to have another life as one of the most enduring stage shows of the nineteenth century, although with its social protest replaced, especially in minstrel performances, by "coon" antics and low comedy.)

Less than ten years after publication of the final installment of *Uncle Tom's Cabin,* the nation was at war. "So this is the little lady who started this big war,"

Abraham Lincoln supposedly said when Mrs. Stowe visited the White House in 1862.

The quote comes to us by way of Mrs. Stowe's daughter—who knows whether Lincoln actually said it. Still and all, there are useful possibilities to ponder. If there had been no *National Era* and if Harriet Beecher Stowe hadn't, then, been able to conceive of a brief story written in installments, she might never have written *Uncle Tom's Cabin* at all. Maybe Lincoln had it right. Because it is the very nature of serialization to stir up our impatience and to put our nerves on edge as we wait for the next episode, perhaps people then had time to imagine what it was like to be a slave, to *feel* what enslaved people felt, in particular a mother whose child was snatched from her arms and sold away.

And as the story continued and readers waited to find out what happened next, the outrage of a nation was stirred beyond frustration and anger, into action. Say what we will in today's terms about Mrs. Stowe and her sketches. She did what she could at the time. And people paid attention.

Bibliography: Thomas Gossett, *Uncle Tom's Cabin and American Culture* (Dallas, 1985). Joan D. Hedrick, *Harriet Beecher Stowe: A Life* (New York, 1994). Harriet Beecher Stowe, *The Annotated Uncle Tom's Cabin,* ed. Henry Louis Gates and Hollis Robbins (New York, 2007).

BEVERLY LOWRY

1852

Nathaniel Hawthorne's *Blithedale Romance* reconsiders the transcendentalist living experiment at Brook Farm

A More Natural Union

"We are all a little wild here with numberless projects of social reform. Not a reading man but has a draft of a new community in his waistcoat pocket," Ralph Waldo Emerson wrote in a letter to Thomas Carlyle in 1840. His ironic boast caught the spirit of the times. Inspired by the religious revivalism of the Second Great Awakening, a belief in human perfectibility had taken root in which the Calvinist idea of the innate depravity of man was rejected. Salvation was no longer in the hands of an angry God but within the reach of anybody willing to strive for moral improvement. Reform movements proliferated, from temperance, abolition, and women's rights to prison reform and education. And reformers became more impatient: in the pursuit of moral perfection, change could not be delayed. Gradualism was replaced by immediatism, most noticeably in the struggle to abolish slavery. The new perfectionism also transformed utopianism from a venerable literary tradition into a radical reform project. Why only fantasize about the nowhere-land of Utopia instead of putting it to the test here and now? The outlines of a new society could be drawn in one bold stroke, without violent revolution and without pain.

Utopianism was a transatlantic phenomenon. Most of the concepts had been developed in Europe by utopian socialists like Henri de Saint-Simon, Charles Fourier, Robert Owen, and Étienne Cabet, but an abundance of land, a tradition of harboring religious communities, and a government less inclined to interfere made America, long associated with the idea of a new beginning, the primary scene for communal experiments in the nineteenth century. Between 1825 and the Civil War more than a hundred utopian communities were established, far more than in any other country.

Of these, Brook Farm became the most famous and most celebrated. Founded in April 1841, it was the brainchild of the transcendentalist Unitarian minister George Ripley and his wife, Sophia, who bought a 200-acre farm in West Roxbury, near Boston. In a letter to Emerson, Ripley explained his purpose: "Our objects, as you know, are to insure a more natural union between intellectual and manual labor than now exists; to combine the thinker and the worker, as far as possible, in the same individual." In a programmatic outline, the "Plan of the West Roxbury Community," Elizabeth Palmer Peabody stressed the principle of "cooperation in social matters instead of competition or balance of interests," as well as the promise of "individual self-unfolding, in the faith that the whole soul of humanity is in each man and woman." These goals should have appealed to Emerson, but he remained hesitant to accept Ripley's invitation to join. In the end he politely declined, although he stressed his strong agreement with the principles of the community. Leading transcendentalists, such as Emerson, Orestes Brownson, Theodore Parker, William Henry Channing, and Margaret Fuller, provided moral support, but none of them joined. Brook Farm was inspired by transcendentalist ideas of self-development and spiritual growth, but it never became an institution of transcendentalism.

One of the well-known writers who did join was Nathaniel Hawthorne, who—contrary to his later image as an eccentric recluse—was one of the original shareholders in Brook Farm, not necessarily out of a strong commitment to utopian ideas but because he was hoping to find a home for himself and his future wife. His letters to his fiancée provide amusing glimpses of pastoral role-playing during the early stages of Brook Farm: "After Breakfast, Mr. Ripley put a four-pronged instrument into my hands, which he gave me to understand was called a pitchfork; and . . . we all three commenced a gallant attack upon a heap of manure."

Ten years later, Hawthorne drew on his letters and notes from the five months he spent at Brook Farm to write *The Blithedale Romance* (1852). The book has long been read as Hawthorne's satirical history of Brook Farm. (Emerson considered "that disagreeable story" unworthy of Hawthorne's genius.) But although Hawthorne had soon discovered that he was not made for communal life, and although he lost some of his investment, his memories of Brook Farm were not in fact hostile, and *Blithedale* should not be read as a roman à clef or taken as a historical account. In Hawthorne's dark romance, the merry masqueraders of Brook Farm are transformed into allegorical figures in a world of masks and disguises. All of the main characters in the novel hide their true identities or their true desires, including the reformer Hollingsworth, who uses the utopian promise to gain power over others. Hawthorne had told this story about illusionary new beginnings before, but he could now link it to a contemporary setting that was at the same time sufficiently "unreal." Without ever entering the debate about the merits of its reformist goals, Hawthorne discovered Brook Farm's usefulness as material for his particular type of romance, in which the actual and the imaginary meet and the promise of a new beginning provides the point of departure for a psychological study of manipulation, guilt, and self-destruction.

Brook Farm started out as a success. Emerson later characterized it as "an agreeable place to live in" and added: "All comers, even the most fastidious, found it the pleasantest of residences." The agrarian retreat was based on neither religious faith nor a socialist master plan for the reorganization of social life. This gave it a more relaxed and less missionary dimension than other utopian communities. The free sociability of the members, numbering about 150, the scenic location, the excellent educational program, lively discussions, and many enjoyable forms of entertainment were praised by visitors. But financial difficulties continually caused problems. Instead of achieving the anticipated balance among participants from "all trades and all modes of business," "from the lowest mechanical trade . . . to the finest art," there was a predominance of educated middle-class members in search of self-development. This made for a congenial social atmosphere, but it did not help in the community's attempt to become economically self-sufficient, despite the fact that its members "worked at the humblest tasks, milking cows . . . cleaning stables, etc., while cultivated women cooked, washed, ironed, and waited on table." The farm was not self-sustaining, so at times even milk and bread had to be bought from outside. Since fewer people had joined the community than expected, its capital stock was too small and large sums had to be borrowed. The main source of income remained the community's highly regarded school, which charged nonmembers for board and tuition. Despite several attempts to economize, the financial situation grew progressively worse. When signs of member dissatisfaction increased, Ripley had to find new ways to provide his utopia with a future. In 1844, Albert Brisbane, an American disciple of Fourier, convinced Ripley to reorganize Brook Farm along Fourierist lines.

A severe economic crisis in the 1840s had created interest in the theories of Fourier, who claimed that he could determine ideal forms of social organization on the basis of scientific calculation. Through an analysis of what he called "the springs of all action and all potential outcomes," Fourier came up with the idea of creating communal settlements of 1,620 persons each, called "Phalanxes." By mixing different kinds of work, labor could be made attractive and fulfilling again; by organizing social, cultural, and sexual relationships in such a way that all passions would be able to find full expression, the potential of human beings for growth could finally be liberated from the constraints of civilization. After he listened to an explanation of Fourier's concept laid out by Brisbane, Emerson had to concede that it "was coherent and comprehensive of facts to a wonderful degree."

Arguing that the American Revolution would remain incomplete if it was not extended to a social revolution, Brisbane adjusted Fourierism to American conditions. He dropped Fourier's promise of sexual liberation and no longer insisted, as Fourier had, on the exact number of members in a Phalanx. To take away some of the amoral stigma linked with Fourier's ideas, American Fourierism redefined itself as "associationism." The year 1842 was the beginning of a successful period during which almost thirty Fourierist associations were established.

For a short time, Brook Farm became a showcase of the Fourierist movement in America. Its newly adapted name, Brook Farm Association for Industry and Education, signaled an extension toward manufacturing and made the community more attractive to skilled workers. In following Fourier's "science of industrial association," jobs were more systematically organized into specialized groups (each individual belonged to several) and greater discipline was enforced (laboring time had to be recorded in a log). With the help of its weekly newspaper, the *Harbinger,* Brook Farm established itself as an intellectual center of influence within American Fourierism. However, when the farm's almost-completed Phalanstery, Fourier's name for a communal building in which various social and cultural activities were held, was destroyed by a fire, the heavily indebted community could not compensate for the financial loss. The Brook Farm Phalanx, which had failed to establish consistently profitable new industries, disbanded the following year. The Fourierist movement never recovered either: only one Phalanx remained after 1855.

Fruitlands, a second utopian community influenced by transcendentalist ideas, was not destined to improve this record. A group of eccentric idealists, for whom Brook Farm was not sufficiently ideal, gathered in 1843 under the guidance of transcendentalist prophet and educator Bronson Alcott and English reformer Charles Lane (who provided the funding) on a ninety-acre farm near Harvard, Massachusetts. Their aim was to establish a model for self-sufficient living, reduced to basic needs, in order to allow community members to focus on spiritual development and personal growth. Alcott, often ridiculed for being an impractical enthusiast, but steadfastly defended and supported by Emerson because of his "higher genius" and "pure intellect," was by that time a member of the transcendentalist circle. He and Lane invited other reformers to join their "consociate family," understood as a union of like-minded individuals, but not many responded. Including Alcott's family, Abba Alcott and her four daughters, made famous through Louisa May Alcott's novel *Little Women,* the Fruitlands Association never exceeded twenty members and it lasted only six months.

One reason for its failure may have been the strict ascetic regime the group propagated. Fruitlands' founders followed those transcendentalists who put self-development at the center, rather than the transformation of social conditions: "The evils of life are not so much social, or political, as personal; and a personal reform only can eradicate them . . . Hence our perseverance in efforts to attain simplicity in diet, plain garments, pure bathing." All animal substances were seen as polluting the body and, through it, the soul. Thus, the dietary program at Fruitlands was uncompromising: "Neither flesh, butter, cheese, eggs, nor milk pollute our tables, nor corrupt our bodies. Neither tea, coffee, molasses, nor rice, tempts us beyond the bounds of indigenous productions. Our sole beverage is pure fountain water."

To achieve self-cultivation, Fruitlands propagated a daily schedule of healthful labor and recreation: "Our other domestic habits are in harmony with those of diet. We rise with early dawn, begin the day with cold bathing, succeeded by a music lesson, and then a chaste repast. Each one finds occupation until the meridian meal, when usually some interesting and deep-searching conversation gives rest to the body and development to the mind." This program attracted a number of eccentrics whom Louisa May Alcott characterized with biting sarcasm in her satirical recollection "Transcendental Wild Oats" (1873): "In those days," she writes, "communities were the fashion and transcendentalism raged wildly." Her account highlights the discrepancy between self-intoxicating rhetoric and comically inept practice. Self-confidently, Lane had written: "This, I think you will admit, looks like an attempt at something which will entitle transcendentalism to some respect for its practicality." However, farming efforts at Fruitlands got started too late and remained uncoordinated and at times woefully dilettantish: "Such farming probably was never seen before since Adam delved," Louisa May Alcott observed. After the experiment collapsed because of a lack of provisions for the winter and all other members had left, a deeply disappointed Bronson Alcott had to move his family back to Concord in January. A note Emerson had written after an earlier visit to Fruitlands proved prescient: "They look well in July; we will see them in December."

The record of the best-known utopian communities of the second quarter of the nineteenth century can hardly be called impressive. The many Fourierist communities of the 1840s were all gone within a decade; Brook Farm lasted from April 1841 to September 1847. Robert Owen's New Harmony community lasted for three years (1825–1828), Nashoba lasted only one more.

Nashoba, founded in 1826 by the Scottish reformer and feminist Frances Wright near the Wolf River in western Tennessee ("Nashoba" is the Chickasaw word for wolf), was conceived as an interracial model farm that would produce enough surplus to enable the community to purchase slaves from their owners and, following the then dominant model of emancipation by colonization, resettle the freed slaves outside the United States. Wright soon transformed Nashoba into a cooperative community governed by white trustees who were to act for the "benefit of the Negro race." While Wright traveled in Europe, the farm's utopian agenda was broadened to include "unconstrained and unrestrained" choice in sexual relations. In "Explanatory Notes on Nashoba," written on her return, Wright attacked the tyranny of the institution of marriage and advocated "racial amalgamation" as the only possible solution to the race problem. With these changes, however, outside supporters (scandalized by the "immorality" of the arrangements) withdrew and cohesion within the group diminished. In her *Domestic Manners of the Americans,* Frances Trollope, who had actually come to Nashoba as a new recruit in 1827, describes not only her shock at the sight of the desolate settlement but also her sense of its impending collapse. After the dissolution of the community, Wright took to Haiti, and thus to freedom, fifteen former slaves she had purchased during her experiment. Lack of economic self-sufficiency played a role in the failure of Nashoba after only four years, but more important were the centrifugal tendencies of the utopian scheme itself, which expanded from the gradual abolition of slavery to the radical emancipation of the individual from all tyrannical restraints.

The Rappites, the Shakers, the Amana colonies, and the Oneida community survived much longer than Nashoba and Brook Farm. These religious communities could derive consent from revelation, and members were often tied together by experiences of religious persecution. In contrast, maintaining consent and member participation was a continual problem for the secular utopian communities, which often seemed to assume that the superiority of their cooperative arrangements would simply be self-evident.

A successful cooperative community required coordination and a plan of daily operations—the kind of structure that did not appeal to some independent minds. Predictably, Emerson responded to Fourier's meticulous daily schedule by reaffirming transcendentalism's anti-institutional creed: "Our feeling was that Fourier had skipped no fact but one, namely life. He treats man as a plastic thing . . . but skips the faculty of life which spawns and scorns system and system-makers." In his reply to Ripley's invitation to join Brook Farm, Emerson had argued that his private existence would allow him a greater chance for self-development and personal growth than any communal arrangement. His response draws attention to a contradiction within utopianism. If the goal was an improvement of conditions for self-development and personal growth, why not pursue this goal directly instead of taking the cooperative detour?

Despite their eventual failure, those at Brook Farm did manage to realize some basic egalitarian goals. By putting their utopian ideals into practice, if only temporarily, they helped to keep them alive.

Bibliography: Louisa May Alcott, "Transcendental Wild Oats: A Chapter from an Unwritten Romance," in *Louisa May Alcott: An Intimate Anthology* (New York, 1997), 29–45. Gail Bederman, "Revisiting Nashoba," *American Literary History* 17 (2005): 438–459. Ralph Waldo Emerson, "Brook Farm," in *Representative Selections* (New York, 1934), 277–282. Richard Francis, *Transcendental Utopias: Individual and Community at Brook Farm, Fruitlands, and Walden* (Ithaca, NY, 1997). Nathaniel Hawthorne, *The Blithedale Romance,* Norton Critical Edition (New York, 1978). Charles Lane and A. Bronson Alcott, "The Consociate Family Life," in *Transcendentalism: A Reader,* ed. Joel Myerson (New York, 2000), 435–442. Elizabeth Palmer Peabody, "Plan of the West Roxbury Community," *The Brook Farm Book: A Collection of First-Hand Accounts of the Community,* ed. Joel Myerson (New York, 1987), 11–23.

WINFRIED FLUCK

1852, July 5

Frederick Douglass addresses the Rochester Ladies' Anti-Slavery Sewing Society

"WHAT TO THE SLAVE IS THE FOURTH OF JULY?"

Rochester was a thriving industrial city in upstate New York, a center of the brand-new telegraph industry that boasted, among its signs of urban sophistication, a shopping arcade on the Parisian plan and, next to it, the country's then largest auditorium, newly built Corinthian Hall, which could hold an audience of more than a thousand. Located near Lake Ontario, across from Canada, Rochester was also a center of antislavery and other reform activities as well as of spiritualism, and it was here that Frederick Douglass had made his home in 1848.

The attractive and charismatic thirty-four-year-old was a well-known figure in town, and the spiritualist medium Margaret Fox, who found Douglass "as fine looking as Ever," predicted that a public lecture by him "would set the people *Crazy*." At 10:00 a.m. on July 5, 1852, when Douglass entered Corinthian Hall, where Jenny Lind had sung and where Theodore Parker and Emerson had lectured, he found a spellbound and reform-ready audience of six to seven hundred, to whom he directed an excoriating address that was not a conventional celebration of America's independence. Having refused to speak on the Fourth of July, he asked his audience: "What, to the American slave, is your 4th of July? I answer; a day that reveals to him, more than all other days in the year, the gross injustice and cruelty to which he is the constant victim. To him, your celebration is a sham . . . There is not a nation on the earth guilty of practices, more shocking and bloody, than are the people of these United States, at this very hour."

In his powerful delivery of one of the most significant abolition speeches of the nineteenth century, Douglass uses his skills as a public orator to stimulate his sympathetic audience's thinking about the American dilemma—the contradiction between slavery and the founding principles of the nation—and their identification with the plight of the slave. In doing so, he treats the Fourth of July as a symbolic repository of national memory and retells its narrative significance so as to record his own presence and that of Southern slaves within the origins and present crises of the body politic. His core rhetorical intent is to identify and illustrate the hypocrisies and inconsistencies of the national story as a narrative of liberation and independence, and to insist on recognition of the role of race in the making of national identity.

Douglass delivered his oration at a time of growing sectional division in the United States, as the slave and free states engaged in political, legal, and media battles to determine the balance of powers between the states. The Wilmot Proviso of 1846 and the Compromise of 1850 illustrated the clear split between Northern and Southern states on the issue of slavery as they competed to define the status of new states entering the Union. The Fugitive Slave Act of 1850, which held that the federal government must support the return of runaway slaves to Southern owners, aroused fierce opposition in the North. In his oration Douglass condemns the act as "tyrannical legislation," to the effect that "slavery has been nationalized in its most horrible and revolting form. By that act, Mason & Dixon's line has been obliterated; New York has become as Virginia." The urgency of his rhetorical admonitions is driven in part by his sense of a fast-growing national emergency, and his oration is designed to articulate this emergency as a crisis that stems from the foundations of the nation.

Douglass's speech not only directly references this turbulent historical context but is also composed with an eye on the mixed registers of cultural and political affiliation at work in his contemporary United States and with sharp attention to how these are shaped by historical narratives of a young nation. He intimately understands (as many leading orators of his age did) the unifying and affective power of America's civil religion—the myths, origin stories, rituals, and public ceremonies that provided collective identification with particular values and assumptions about the United States as an exceptional nation. At the same time, he is aware that this civil religion is a sphere of abstractions, anchored but not securely bound by the Constitution and a volatile field of clashing rhetorical claims and interpretations at the current historical moment. For almost ten years Douglass had supported the position of the leading abolitionist, William Lloyd Garrison, that the Union should be dissolved and that the Constitution was a proslavery document. By the early 1850s, however, he had come to view the Constitution as an antislavery document, and his 1852 address reflects his growing belief that one must use it as a legal and moral weapon to undo slavery. Throughout his speech he decries slavery as "the great sin and shame of America," denounces the failure of political and religious leaders to act on the principles inscribed in the founding documents of the nation, and so mimics the role of a Jeremiah.

A key theme of Douglass's oration—also central to his efforts to cast his audience in the national story he retells—is the issue of distance, temporal and spatial, between actors and spectators of historical action. He asserts this at an early stage: "The fact is, ladies and gentlemen, the distance between this platform and the slave plantation, from which I escaped, is considerable—and the difficulties to be overcome in getting from the latter to the former, are by no means slight." This is a somewhat disingenuous articulation of the narrative drive and appeal of Douglass's performance as an orator and signifies some of the paradoxes and complexities barely concealed within it. The distance between the platform and the plantation measures Douglass's own personal journey, already told in some detail in *Narrative of the Life of Frederick Douglass* (first published in 1845) but also reassembled and retold in countless speeches and editorials. His voice takes some of its authority from that journey, as does the visual and aural performance of his speeches—he is evidence of which he speaks, and in his earliest days as a speaker he was little more than this, as his rhetoric was perceived to be primarily ceremonial rather than political. Having transcended the Garrisonian framing of his identity, he is yet caught within the symbolic logic of his own identity formation, constantly refashioning his story in relation to present contexts—platform and plantation are held together in a symbolic juxtaposition that signifies the relationship between past and present that underlies the oration.

Douglass manipulates narrative distance in his speech to move between inside and outside positions in relation to his audience, and claims he "shall see [the Fourth of July] . . . from the slave's point of view." He also uses it to move those in his audience into new relations with their past, at once positioning them as the secure and sovereign holders of their fathers' revolutionary gains—"The freedom gained is yours; and you, therefore, may properly celebrate this anniversary"—and chastising them for not being true to those gains and their underlying ideals—"America is false to the past"; "Americans! Your republican politics, not less than your republican religion, are flagrantly inconsistent." Douglass appropriates the role of Jeremiah to tie the stories and destinies of white and black America together, and symbolizes this coupling when he daringly describes the Fourth of July as "the very ring-bolt in the chain of your yet undeveloped destiny." He composes the relationship between past and present as one of dynamic interpretations, each shaping the other, and asserts: "We have to do with the past only as we can make it useful to the present and to the future." Douglass realizes he has the demanding task of breaking down the distance between past and present and North and South if his retelling is to engage his audience as a call for action. And so he works his rhetorical skills to manipulate the moral imagination of his audience and elicit their recognition of the human rights of black Americans.

Douglass makes use of stock rhetorical devices to secure the expectations of his audience but also uses them to dramatize his relationship to the audience in less conventional ways. In the exordium, for example, he protests his adequacy as a public speaker and then launches into a display of elaborate praise for the character and ideals of the nation's Revolutionary fathers. These are common rhetorical conventions, but even as he uses them Douglass establishes a distance between himself and his audience by insisting the Fourth of July belongs to white Americans: "It is the birthday of your National Independence, and of your political freedom"; "I am not included within the pale of this glorious anniversary! Your high independence only reveals the immeasurable distance between us." Douglass uses the second-person pronoun extensively in this early section and at the same time ironizes his own position by addressing the audience as fellow citizens. This distancing device, holding himself (and by implication black America) both within and without the nation, symbolically measures the hypocrisies of the American dilemma.

Having established this distance, Douglass then moves to collapse it in the next section of his oration, titled "The Internal Slave Trade," where he describes a slave auction in vivid detail in order to seize his listeners' imagination and shape their emotional and ethical response to the scene. Douglass was well aware of the power of rhetoric to create visual images in the mind, and equally aware that affective response to the slave as a suffering human being could be the mechanism to change minds and exhort action. He asks those in his audience to visualize the scene and reinforces the visual sensations by directing their gaze to the imaginary characters and events: "Attend the auction; see men examined like horses; see the forms of women rudely and brutally exposed to the shocking gaze of American slave-buyers. See this drove sold and separated for ever . . . Tell me citizens, WHERE, under the sun, you can witness a spectacle more fiendish and shocking." Douglass himself performs the role of witness, affirming his authority to relate such a spectacle: "I was born amid such sights and scenes." His graphic visualization of the slave auction is a strategic venture in rhetoric and representation that casts his listeners in the role of spectators and seeks to draw them into an empathetic relationship to the slaves and into accord with Douglass's argument that slavery is a destructive force within the body politic: "Oh! Be warned! Be warned! A horrible reptile is coiled up in your nation's bosom; the venomous creature is nursing at the tender breast of your youthful republic; *for the love of God, tear away,* and fling from you the hideous monster, and *let the weight of twenty millions crush and destroy it forever!"*

Dramatizing the entanglements of slavery and the "youthful republic" Douglass underlines his belief that the destinies of black and white Americans are locked together. In an 1863 address, he proclaims that "the Negro and the nation, are to rise or fall, be killed or cured, saved or lost together." This belief echoes his fresh support in the 1852 address for the Constitution as an antislavery document; based on the principles inscribed in its preamble, he affirms it "a GLORIOUS LIBERTY DOCUMENT." The affirmation is followed by his closing peroration, which attests his belief in the United States as a redeemer nation: "I do not despair of this country. There are forces in operation, which must inevitably, work the downfall of slavery . . . I, therefore, leave of where I began, with *hope.*" This conclusion is in line with the doubled nature of his address and argument throughout, as he links freedom and oppression in his rhetorical iterations of past and present visions of "independence" in the United States. This is also to say he asserts his belief in the *ongoing* emancipatory potential of the Constitution.

At the end of his text, Douglass provides a striking contemporary rationale for such hope in the global effects of technological progress: "Nations do not now stand in the same relation to each other that they did ages go. No nation can now shut itself up from the surrounding world . . . Intelligence is penetrating the darkest corners of the globe. It makes its pathway over and under the sea, as well as on the earth. Wind, steam, and lightening are its chartered agents. Oceans no longer divide but link nations together . . . Space is comparatively annihilated." This is both a timely and prophetic recognition of the ways in which compressions of time and space effected by technological progress have an impact on ethical relations between human beings once distant from each other. It is an issue already implied in Douglass's appeal to affective recognition of the horrors of slaves' lives. At the end of his talk he magnifies the issue to its growing international dimensions and echoes broader concerns of philosophers of the age, who asked if human beings could expand their moral horizons in line with the global extension of social, economic, and political relations. This was also, Douglass knew, an issue of race and human rights.

Douglass's conclusion affirms his belief that knowledge can provide an escape from "mental darkness," a symbolic journey he strongly identified with. It also anticipates the national and international roles he would take on as a statesman (including diplomatic roles in Haiti and the Dominican Republic) and his commitment to addressing universal issues of injustice and suffrage. Mindful of his image, a newspaper he published, *Frederick Douglass' Paper,* reported on July ninth: "When the speaker sat down, there was a universal burst of applause, and William C. Bloss, Esq., rose and moved a vote of thanks to Mr. Douglass, for the learned and eloquent address to which they had just listened. It was unanimously carried." Immediately after the event, seven hundred were ready to become subscribers for a printed pamphlet version of the address. Reprinted many times since then, the speech is one of Douglass's greatest legacies and remains powerfully resonant in its scrupulous identification of the contradictions between the founding ideals of the nation and the continued oppressions suffered by black Americans. It is an address that echoes across African American cultural productions through to the present day.

Bibliography: James A. Colaiaco, *Frederick Douglass and the Fourth of July* (New York, 2006). James Daley, ed., *Great Speeches by African Americans* (New York, 2006). Frederick Douglass, *My Bondage and My Freedom* (1855; New York, 2003). Catherine Ellis and Stephen Drury Smith, eds., *Say It Plain: A Century of Great African American Speeches* (New York, 2007). Roy Hill, ed., *Rhetoric of Racial Revolt* (Denver, 1964). David Howard-Pitney, *The Afro-American Jeremiads: Appeals for Justice in America* (Philadelphia, 1990). Gregory P. Lampe, *Frederick Douglass: Freedom's Voice* (East Lansing, MI, 1998). William S. McFeely, *Frederick Douglass* (New York, 1991). William Wiggins, *O Freedom! Afro-American Emancipation Celebrations* (Knoxville, TN, 1987).

LIAM KENNEDY

1854

Nathaniel Hawthorne asks his publisher, "What is the mystery of these innumerable editions of *The Lamplighter?*"

MARIA CUMMINS AND SENTIMENTAL FICTION

The year 1854 saw the publication of Thoreau's *Walden* as well as *The Lamplighter,* the first novel by Massachusetts writer Maria Susanna Cummins. The first 2,000 copies of *Walden* took four years to sell. *The Lamplighter* sold 40,000 copies in its first month of publication. This imbalance has been more than amply redressed since, with the help of now canonized but then disgruntled peers like Hawthorne, who bitterly complained to publisher William Ticknor in 1855 about "these innumerable editions of *The Lamplighter,*" and later readers following his lead, who have lamented Cummins's inability to withstand what Nina Baym calls "the melodramatic flourish." Hawthorne's upset about the economic successes of sentimental novels became a critique of the aesthetic and political failings of the genre, and the antebellum period was thus fashioned into a clash between male and female writers, high and popular culture, novels with political vision written by men in difficult financial straits and the benighted—but extremely profitable—literary productions of middle-class women. Some would say that this divide persists in our own time.

The Lamplighter, an exemplary sentimental novel, charts Gerty Flint's journey from orphan to beloved adoptee to married woman. Under the tutelage of her guardians Trueman Flint and Emily Graham, Gerty is well on her way toward becoming the ideal woman, "learn[ing] to bear even injustice, without losing your self-control," as Emily instructs her. However, despite her efforts, Gerty, like so many other sentimental heroines, is constantly losing control. She gets angry, she faints, she cries. Though not usually mentioned in the same breath as Gerty or Ellen Montgomery (heroine of Susan Warner's 1850 blockbuster, *The Wide, Wide*

World and template for Gerty), nor thought of as particularly sentimental, one might be tempted to say the same about male heroes of the same period—Ahab rails, Dimmesdale collapses, Usher trembles. Yet unlike that experienced by some male characters, the suffering of sentimental heroines seems excessive, unnecessary. Such a reading, however, is not only deeply sexist. It's also incorrect.

True, *The Lamplighter* and the many other sentimental novels of the period register in painstaking detail the alternating feelings of their protagonists. As if equipped with emotional thermometers, the novels record every smile, blush, pout, and tear in the heroine's journey from child to woman. The tears, especially, have borne the brunt of much derision. However, there is good reason for them: virtually every child, girl or boy, in these texts has lost mother, father, or both, propelling them into the wide, wide world (to borrow Warner's title). Yet these orphaned protagonists do much more than drench their pillows. Gerty becomes a teacher. She fights with and refuses to abide by the wishes of Mr. Graham when he uses his power unfairly (from her point of view) by demanding that she care for Emily, when Gerty is urgently needed elsewhere. She enters into myriad relationships that open up her initially constricted world. Gerty does not just sit in her room and cry about the fact that she doesn't have a mother or father: in a rational and judicious way, she goes about creating a world in which she can adhere to the antebellum female ideal of being a primary caregiver for others while establishing for herself the terms upon which she will distribute her affections. Not only do these sentimental novels explore the circumscription of women's lives; they demonstrate how women might go about making their worlds more satisfying despite those limitations.

Critics have had much more to say about the tears than the decision making. Jane Tompkins, whose *Sensational Designs* established the positive terms of the debate over sentimental fiction, writes that the "uncontrollable weeping" manifests "the problem of [female] powerlessness" and "shows how one copes with it hour by hour and minute by minute." Other critics have been less forgiving. Tompkins wrote in response to Ann Douglas, who maintained that these texts "produce an atmosphere of intimacy so strong as to replace historical awareness with what seems almost biological consciousness." Others have elaborated the negative terms of the argument, branding sympathy an exercise in narcissistic projection: the protagonist, in sympathizing with the suffering of others, appropriates it as her own, and the reader does the same. This is a particular problem when sympathy is supposed to be marshaled toward political action, as in the famous example of Harriet Beecher Stowe's *Uncle Tom's Cabin:* identification with the suffering other ceases at the moment of catharsis. Once slavery had ended, the contented white reader can stop worrying about racial injustice.

Yet in one popular novel after another, provoking women's feelings is presented as the first step in a process that, when working correctly, leads to actions that alleviate other people's pain. Gerty extends her sympathy toward others and improves their lives. When Mrs. Delano's sympathies are aroused in Lydia Maria Child's *The Romance of the Republic* (1867), she adopts a young mixed-race girl and rescues her from slavery. This model could be adapted to other political ends, however. The antithesis of Child's and Stowe's antislavery novels, Caroline Lee Hentz's *The Planter's Northern Bride,* begins with a preface in which Hentz listens sympathetically to the story of "a negro woman" who claims that she would have "left [her] own father and mother first" rather than leave her master and mistress. The woman's story supposedly drives her to write this novel, to caution white readers against misplacing their sympathy for slaves who (Hentz insists) are happier within the extended-family structure of the plantation than left to fend for themselves in the cold, cruel marketplace. The stakes of emotional attachment in sentimental fiction are not usually so grave, but they are almost always tied to what one will be able to accomplish in the world. The hero in Mary Hayden Green Pike's *Ida May* (1854) declares, while lamenting his unfortunate betrothal, "between us there is no sympathy of thought, and there can be no concord of action." But when sentimental protagonists cut themselves off from sympathy, as is the case in Augusta Jane Evans's *Beulah* (1859), whose main character tosses aside her guardian's love, proclaiming "his sympathy is utterly unnecessary," it is only a matter of time until they realize the depth of their isolation and return.

The point that sympathy is the ground of human relations is driven home time and again in sentimental novels whose plots depend on a community of caregivers ready and willing to raise a child not their own. The abundance of guardians, foster parents, and stepmothers reflects the historical facts of shorter life spans, lack of medicine, and a higher incidence of death in childbirth, but this cast of substitute parents also has a narrative function. Though the protagonists spend a great deal of time mourning the loss of loved ones and seeking their replacements, without that loss there would be nowhere for the narrative to go. Ellen Montgomery's road to adulthood in *The Wide, Wide World* is paved by her parents' absence. Like so many other sentimental heroines who are presented with a panoply of substitute mothers and fathers — aunts, uncles, cousins by blood or even by designation — Ellen's main decisions revolve around whose home she will occupy, whom she will choose as her new family. With the bonds of consanguinity loosened, opportunities abound, and the best choice the child can make is the family where sympathy flourishes. This is a requirement of the genre: the novels, though saddened by the biological family in shards, nevertheless make the case for the superiority of the family that is chosen.

By focusing on these suggestive articulations of kinship, readers can bridge the gap between political and aesthetic considerations of these texts, which number in the hundreds (E. D. E. N. Southworth alone wrote sixty books). Opening up the canon of sentimental fiction beyond its three most widely read examples — *Uncle Tom's Cabin, The Wide, Wide World,* and *The Lamplighter* — demonstrates that these novels are not simply reproductions of one another, although certain conventions do apply. Transparency is an overriding concern of the genre, and the narrators reject irony in favor of straightforward address. The potential for sentimental fiction to critique the very institution it seems most committed to upholding — the family — comes out in its relentless fascination with the protagonists' constantly changing first and last names. Although marriage — the allegedly stabilizing power of having a husband's last name — is the endpoint of these plots, they do not shy away from demonstrating the frailty of that institution; a reader who gives herself over to the "happy ending" of the story does so despite all warnings to the contrary. Like *The Lamplighter,* Mary Jane Holmes's *'Lena Rivers* (1856) and Southworth's *Ishmael* (1863) circle around the question of the protagonist's last name, in these novels because fathers have flown the domestic coop, leaving their children bastards. In many cases, the child must learn the identity of her father and get her rightful last name before taking on her beloved's, lest she end up marrying her brother (as occurs in Herman Melville's *Pierre* [1852], written at the height of the genre's popularity). Sentimental novels continually walk the tightrope of incest as they use the brother-sister relation to model the husband-wife relation.

The trajectory of the white female protagonist is often imagined, directly or indirectly, in relation to slavery. Hentz's *Marcus Warland* (1852) features a scene in which the hero's beloved asks her black slave to "*mulattofy* me." This in a proslavery novel that systematically destroys its mixed-race female characters because they are evidence of a white master's rape of black women. Pike's *Ida May* (1854) depicts a young white girl who is kidnapped, disguised in blackface, beaten, sold into slavery, and adopted; she then marries into her adoptive family. Ida's suffering, though intense and physically represented in a scene in which she is beaten, is temporary, unlike a slave's, and ends when she's discovered to be white. The sentimental analogy between Ida and a slave works only up to the point where the difference between her past as a slave and her present as a free person cannot be bridged.

However problematic it may be, this "as if" plot proves that domesticity is not the same as escapism. After *The Lamplighter,* Cummins later wrote a very unusual book called *El Fureidis* (1860), which takes place in Syria and has a great deal to say about the heterogeneous religious practices of what was then called the Orient. Evans's *Beulah* includes long digressions about Emerson's philosophy and Poe's short stories. It is not the case, then, that the sentimental genre perniciously tries to avoid the religious, literary, and political currents of the day. In the same year of *The Lamplighter*'s publication, Illinois senator Stephen Douglas decided it was time to repeal the Missouri Compromise of 1820. The result was the swift passage of the Kansas-Nebraska Act, which held that slavery could be legally instituted in those territories should the settlers choose. Reflecting on "bleeding Kansas" as a national disgrace, Thoreau penned "Slavery in Massachusetts," which despairingly concludes, "What I had lost was a country." Cummins did not write anything as directly engaged as this essay was with the events of 1854, but she wasn't hiding from reality either. Three years after the Kansas-Nebraska Act and Abraham Lincoln's declaration in response to it that "the great majority, south as well as north, have human sympathies" that are manifested in "their sense of the wrong of slavery," Cummins published *Mabel Vaughan* (1857). The novel proceeds according to convention, with the pious Mabel undone by fashionable New York society, after which she must be humbled by moving west. Where in the West remains unnamed, and why Mabel's father keeps looking at charts and maps every night is not fully explained until later in the novel, when we learn that he has lost his money because he speculated on railroad construction. Toward the end, the narrator abstractly refers to "a great issue [that] had arisen and a great crisis [that] was at hand—an issue between injustice and oppression on one side, and the law of right and humanity on the other." Nothing about slavery has yet been mentioned, but just as we have concluded that this sentimental novel has nothing to say about the most important issue of its time, the narrator turns to ask the reader directly: "Shall that rich soil become the ground of the task-master,—those noble woods the retreat of the fugitive?" Mabel falls in love with a very articulate, politically engaged lawyer who gives a Lincolnesque speech ending with the words, "Nebraska shall be free." Even while focusing on her heroine's inner life and the development of her sympathies, then, Cummins—like Thoreau and Lincoln—had Kansas and Nebraska, freedom and slavery, on her mind.

Bibliography: Nina Baym, *Woman's Fiction: A Guide to Novels by and about Women in America, 1820–1870,* 2nd ed. (Urbana, IL, 1993). Ann Douglas, *The Feminization of American Culture* (New York, 1977). Jane Tompkins, *Sensational Designs: The Cultural Work of American Fiction, 1790–1860* (New York, 1985). Cindy Weinstein, *Family, Kinship, and Sympathy in Nineteenth-Century American Literature* (Cambridge, 2004).

CINDY WEINSTEIN

1855

Walt Whitman uses a letter from Emerson to advertise the first edition of *Leaves of Grass*

THE BOOK OF A LIFETIME

The first edition of Walt Whitman's poetry came unheralded into a world that could hardly know what to make of it, and in that light, at the moment of publication, its first champion was as remarkable as the poet himself. No sooner had Whitman brashly sent a copy of his poems to Ralph Waldo Emerson in Massachusetts than the famed essayist replied with unexampled speed, generosity, and insight, saluting Whitman as a poet "at the beginning of a great career." As if to demonstrate that he was just another rough and tough New Yorker, an inspired natural-talent Bowery Boy, Whitman expeditiously published Emerson's private letter along with a lengthy blurb commenting on Emerson's praise and on his own splendid ambitions. Never before or since have poetry and advertising come so close together, unless we should more exactly say that Whitman's poetry was itself a marriage of verse and tabloid journalism. But Whitman was desperate for attention, for intelligent praise, and he knew he had to strike rapidly if he was to benefit from Emerson's unexpected response.

The 1855 original edition of *Leaves of Grass,* beginning with a wildly eloquent prose discourse on the equivalence of American poetry with the United States as a larger Union, presented only twelve poems, albeit including an opening chant of seemingly inordinate length. In appearance the volume was slight and elegant; it was designed and partly hand-set in type by Whitman himself. To this day many readers regard the 1,336-line "Song of Myself"—printed without any title in this first edition—as the finest of all American poems, although a few other lyrics in the volume, notably "The Sleepers," are as strong as anything Whitman ever wrote. If we trace the later revisions, cutting, and renaming of "The Sleepers" (which appeared without a title in 1855 and was subsequently called "Night Poem" and then "Sleep-Chasings" before assuming its final, preferred title in 1871), we begin to discern how Whitman ever more experimentally imagined the implications of his "Poem of Walt Whitman, an American," which was the 1856 title given to "Song of Myself." His vision and his poems live in perpetual transition from one shore to another. By common consent "Song of Myself," notwithstanding the power of "The Sleepers," remains the great suspension bridge over which all of Whitman's other poems pass on their way to ephemeral or lasting recognition, and through this massive central poem in fifty-two sections the 1855 edition of *Leaves of Grass* declaims our finest rhapsody to Emerson's ideal, self-reliance.

If modern readers center on "Song of Myself," they produce one picture of the poetry, a powerful one. Even for Whitman, "Song of Myself" was an impossible act to follow. On the other hand, if we take Whitman at his word, which is the word of history as he understood his own life in history, we discover another picture: a *Leaves of Grass* not falling off from its first edition but instead fulfilling the "Song's" self-expressive rhapsody according to a very different poetic vision, one that would require nothing less than a whole lifetime to achieve its purpose. That formal aim seems to be what Whitman wanted to achieve—the book of a lifetime, which meant a book in several editions, designed to live a life in several editions. His different editions were imagined from the beginning as falling into a continuous, endlessly worked-over process—in a letter of July 1857 he ruminates about becoming a paid lecturer, but not "until I get out the next issue of *Leaves*." That is what a newspaperman would say, and while this to-be-continued scenario may lack the drama of the big bonanza, it seems to be the plan Whitman followed, right from the start.

When we see Walt Whitman's life as virtually the story of the eight editions of his work, we may connect him almost physically with his writing—and it is in this way that his poems differ most from those of his forebears and successors. The twin biographies of Whitman and his work begin in early July 1855, not two weeks before the death of his father. Walter Whitman, senior, was an average man, it seems, yet passionate and troubled, a carpenter and a not-very-successful member of the building trade. As we know from Whitman's correspondence, to his mother and to his siblings Walt remained a loving son and brother all his days. But the family of literature gave him a wider and even at times a wilder community—the first edition of *Leaves of Grass* appeared in the same year as Longfellow's *Hiawatha*, as strange an elegiac poem as could be imagined. At midcentury such works, like Tennyson's notoriously spasmodic *Maud*, were introducing formal experiments as the only way to express an intensified obsession with death. "The Charge of the Light Brigade" revels in this ambiguous tone. The poems spoke out for life, yet brooded upon mankind's immortality.

Emerson guessed that *Leaves of Grass* must have had "a long foreground some-

where, for such a start." In fact Whitman was a poet self-taught in new techniques. He was a jack of all literary trades. Born May 23, 1819, from his teenage
years he had worked as a journeyman printer; he taught school in several Long
Island locations; politically, he was recognized for his democratic principles,
"a well known locofoco of the town"; and he quickly became an editor for New
York newspapers, culminating with a major stint of editing at the *Brooklyn Eagle.*
In 1848 he went to New Orleans with his brother Jeff. The plan was that he would
help edit the *New Orleans Crescent,* but as often occurred with Whitman, things
did not work out, and he returned home via the Mississippi and the Great Lakes.
He was not again to travel west until his 1879 journey to Colorado, although
he made other, shorter journeys in the East, to New Hampshire, Massachusetts,
and, during the long Civil War period, Washington, D.C. His cosmos, his universe, was to be an imagined space laid out in his own most peculiar visionary
place—suggesting he would write of the Dakotas, for example, without ever seeing them.

   With its completely novel free verse and its wildly associative use of suddenly discontinuous images, Whitman's *Leaves of Grass* seemed in one blow to
dismiss all standard literary precedent, making historical narratives like Longfellow's popular 1847 poem *Evangeline* seem banal. As friends and foes alike quickly
saw, Whitman's art was like nothing seen before or likely to be doubled again,
which is not to say that its influence would be narrow—indeed, the opposite is
true, for Whitman's influence on later poets has been immense, and not only in
the English-speaking world. His stylistic innovations were so radical that initially
they seemed beyond compare; however, as we examine individual paragraphs,
lines, and phrases, we recognize a persistent rhythm of anticipation, which in a
traditional way may be identified with prophetic voice. In his great elegy "SEA-
DRIFT—Out of the Cradle Endlessly Rocking," as it was called in the final edition, Whitman virtually identifies the rustling sound of waves quietly breaking
on the sand with the five-times-repeated incantation of the word "death." What
is remarkable is that his poem identifies this incantation with the impulse of all
his "random" songs, his elegy ending in mysterious suspension:

> My own songs awaked from that hour,
> And with them the key, the word up from the waves
> The word of the sweetest song and all songs,
> That strong and delicious word which, creeping to my feet,
> (Or like some old crone rocking the cradle, swathes in sweet garments, bending
>   aside,)
> The sea whisper'd me.

The most personal expression of this voice occurs in Whitman's characteristic
stance as one person, usually a friend, waiting for another, as in the last lines of
"Song of Myself."

> Failing to fetch me at first keep encouraged,
> Missing me one place search another,
> I stop somewhere waiting for you.

Everywhere the stylistic novelty of such simple speech marks the almost shocking manner of the first issue of *Leaves of Grass*. As a piece of printing it was a spare, elegant, workmanlike affair, with its title decoratively embossed on the front cover; the quarto volume measured roughly nine by twelve inches, comprising not much more than ninety pages. Its title page carried no author's name, while opposite was an engraved portrait taken from a daguerreotype, showing Whitman (without caption), dressed like a working man—maybe a carpenter—striking a pose strangely elegant, subtly effete, a covert come-on suggesting an unknown purpose. He is an 1855 Manhattan version of the singer of the biblical Song of Songs. In the text a "Walter Whitman" is indeed named, but only on the copyright page and once later in "Song of Myself." Although Whitman unobtrusively does assert what might be called his legal identity as the copyright owner, he remains the unnamed person pictured opposite the title page, whose portrait constitutes the mysterious image, or eidolon, of the maker. His anonymity proclaims something disturbing to the old order of things, an inherently democratic personal identity, as indeed line 497 in the final edition of *Leaves* has it: "Walt Whitman, a kosmos, of Manhattan the son," or more descriptively, as the 1855 edition said: "Walt Whitman, an American, one of the roughs, a kosmos."

In an original sense this maker of poems is the ultimate adornment of his city, he is its universe, he is its microcosm, and therefore his identity is transcendental while perpetually localized. His was the flourishing presence at once recognized and praised by Emerson, a man as unlike Whitman to all superficial appearances as could be imagined, but as deeply his imaginative twin as poetry could have desired. While Emerson could praise the "wit and wisdom" of the poetry, most reviewers at the time found Whitman wild, formless, salacious, dangerous to morals, or downright disgusting. Many years later, talking with his friend and companion, Horace Traubel, he said: "I was not only not popular (and am not popular yet—never will be) but I was *non grata*—I was not welcome in the world." The intense yet somehow impersonal passion of Whitman's homoerotic sexuality was never hidden, whether in "The Sleepers" or in the "Calamus" cluster of the 1860 *Leaves*. (The "Children of Adam" cluster shows that Whitman was celebrating *all* forms of sexuality; his ideal of "adhesion" operates between any and all creatures capable of expressing affection and the life force, on all levels of intimate contact, and he is finally without bias or program, though he tells us, his readers, how *he* feels.)

To claim, then, that, as it were, "Song of Myself" had to proliferate, is simply to ask what would next be added in the next edition. Almost at once Whitman was ready with many more poems, and in 1856 he included the chanting catalog, "Poem of Salutation," where line after line celebrates his own powers of seeing and hearing, to be followed by a much more important poem, later called "Crossing Brooklyn Ferry." In 1856 this great work was given the simple, elegant, traditional title, "Sun-Down Poem." Variances of title often reflect a rich variety of perceptual and cognitive powers; another new poem begins, typically, "Whoever you are, I fear you are walking the walks of dreams." New works kept tumbling out, their rushing phrases celebrating the open road, or woman's procreative power, or sexual ecstasy in polymorphous aspects, a rapture which, for himself, Whitman naively links to his being well built—"the studs and rafters are grown parts of me." The effect of the second, 1856 edition of *Leaves of Grass* is to reinforce our understanding that this is poetry that will openly say its truth, as it finds that truth, without censorship or misplaced politeness.

The 1856 edition leads on to a major expansion into the 1860 edition, which fully establishes four main directions of Whitman's poetic work: the free-form personal elegy; the variegated hymns or chants cataloging democratic themes (for example, the second, untitled chant of 1855 becomes "Poem of the Daily Work of the Workmen and Workwomen of These States," to be finally named "A Song for Occupations"); the myriad lyrics, usually much shorter, such as are found in two sections of 1860 more or less celebrating homosexual and heterosexual love ("Calamus" and "Children of Adam"); and finally the vital but virtually fragmentary miniatures that in different texts were titled "Thought" or "Thoughts."

The 1860 edition speaks for a visionary habit, noted once by a frightening character in a story ("Deutsches Requiem") by Jorge Luis Borges, that Whitman celebrates the universe in a "preliminary" manner. Generously, we should grasp that this preliminary Whitman writes the preface to democracy, with an elegiac chant that would be later titled "Starting from Paumanok" (the Indian name used to salute his native Long Island), here called "Proto-Leaf," having begun life in manuscript simply as "Premonition." This edition of *Leaves* is also epochal in its inclusion of the exquisitely fluent elegy "A Word Out of the Sea," better known under its 1871 title, "Out of the Cradle Endlessly Rocking." Let one small example stand here for an almost incalculable number of changes (large and small) Whitman would make within his poems, within titles, within later editions as to placement, to fit different clusters of other similar poems, and so on, as the poetry revealed a lifework of infinite bricolage: originally the famous opening line just quoted was much simpler, but also much less expressive—"Out of the rocked cradle."

As Whitman revises, his second and third thoughts may seem to lose the edge of first perceptions—psychologists call it the primacy effect—yet while Whitman deployed vast improvisatory powers of the first thought and the first vision, as time passed and he permitted himself his second and third thoughts, his way of living progressively through the biography of his accumulating editions sometimes led him to prefer revised or seemingly self-corrected texts. In such fashion the publication of each new edition advanced his poetic autobiography by "going public." From this perspective "A Word Out of the Sea" brings a new tone to a persistently elegiac vision, a sort of *ricordanza* (as musicians of that time might have called it), where the memory of an utterly forming moment of illumination emanates operatically from the song or aria of singers—here two birds—communing with each other. Whitman's way of freely breathing the elegy is unique and uniquely moving, like waves breaking on an ever-changing shoreline.

If the 1860 edition was a major enlargement owing to the number of new poems, several of which had been published separately in newspapers, it did not abandon its source, the dynamic of the 1855 edition. In 1861 Whitman wrote an unpublished introduction, where he calls his poems whisperings; he will continue to "form & breathe Whisperings for yourself, in heart-felt meditations fitter far than words." The "Dearest Reader" senses a mystical longing, remembering another line, "The sea whisper'd me."

The Civil War changed American dreams forever, and Whitman went to the military hospitals in Washington, where he acted mostly the part of a kindly friend, giving a helping hand, bringing small gifts to the wounded and the dying. He had often written of his mystical sense that death is the mother of all, but now he felt impelled to write poetic vignettes acutely like the battlefield photographs of Mathew Brady, and these he published in 1865 in a book titled *Drum-Taps,* to which shortly he added an "Annex," the *Sequel to Drum-Taps,* which included his great elegy on the death of President Lincoln, "When Lilacs Last in the Door-Yard Bloom'd." In 1871 he published the powerful prose polemic against political and financial corruption in the States, *Democratic Vistas,* perhaps the most telling of all Whitman's statements of his deep belief in, and his fears for, true democracy.

With such a body of work gradually building, the course was set for continuing editions of *Leaves of Grass,* in 1867, 1871 (notable for "Passage to India"), 1876, and 1881, all issued during the years when Whitman's fame was slowly forming among more independent, more adventurous readers, in the United States and abroad. Between full-scale editions there came shorter collections, or annexes, as Whitman called them, so that finally his textual history is exceedingly complex, owing to his carpentering of his texts. The metaphor of carpentry is deliberate, for Whitman followed the methods of old-time builders, who typically added to wooden structures by means of the lean-to.

For Whitman the man, during this period of the aggregating editions of *Leaves,* except in 1879 and 1880 when he traveled West and into Canada, his days were mainly limited by a growing debility that stemmed from the Civil War years, finally ending in what he called paralysis, leaving him confined for long periods to his study chair in the Camden, New Jersey, home of his last years. To the organically developing volume of his lifework he would add annexed "final" selections, mostly short poems, always extending the lean-to of the house. When the time came for his last, so-called Deathbed edition of *Leaves of Grass* (1891–92)—even in the efficient Library of America printing it comes to 625 pages—he was ready to call it quits. This edition, which includes the prose recollection "A Backward Glance o'er Travel'd Roads," is the one most often printed and known to modern readers as *Leaves of Grass,* but it still maintains its point of origin, "Song of Myself," though not until it has opened with a grand epigraphic train of "Inscriptions." An editorial note insists that Whitman preferred and recommended this edition as published, then and for any future reprints. On March 26, 1892, he died in Camden, as if holding hands with his final publication.

Judgments of the finest works in any author's canon will always differ to a certain degree, and there can be no doubt that critics are right to admire those poems embodying Whitman's version of the American Sublime, as it has been called. These tend to be poems of more than two pages in length, but a six-line lyric such as "Reconciliation," from *Drum-Taps,* is as powerful as anything he ever wrote:

> Word over all, beautiful as the sky,
> Beautiful that war and all its deeds of carnage must in time be utterly lost,
> That the hands of the sisters Death and Night incessantly softly wash again, and
>   ever again, this soil'd world;
> For my enemy is dead, a man divine as myself is dead,
> I look where he lies white-faced and still in the coffin — I draw near,
> Bend down and touch lightly with my lips the white face in the coffin.

Such later lyrics demonstrate how Whitman's gradually changing and in many ways maturing imagination fulfilled the larger vision of his accumulating life-work, which we should experience partially as a flowing issuance from start to finish. We certainly need the 1855 edition and we need the Deathbed edition. Probably we should say that we need both books, since to perceive and revel in the interim flow, we need their complementary force.

Bibliography: Susan Belasco, Ed Folsom, and Kenneth M. Price, *Leaves of Grass: The Sesquicentennial Essays* (Lincoln, NE, 2007). Angus Fletcher, *A New Theory for American Poetry: Democracy, the Environment and the Future of Imagination* (Cambridge, MA, 2004). David S. Reynolds, *Walt Whitman's America: A Cultural Biography* (New York, 1995). Walt Whitman, *Complete Poetry and Collected Prose,* ed. Justin Kaplan (New York, 1982); *Memoranda during the War: Written on the Spot in 1863–'65,* ed. Peter Coviello (New York, 2004); *Selected Poems 1855–1892: A New Edition,* ed. Gary Schmidgall (New York, 1999).

ANGUS FLETCHER

1858

Americans are excited by the drama of the Senate campaign in Illinois

The Lincoln-Douglas Debates

Staged on the Illinois prairie less than three years before the start of the Civil War, the Lincoln-Douglas debates were a political battle that transcended politics. While they had some of the earmarks of popular entertainment, the debates also converged with antebellum literature in their themes, their demands on listeners and readers, and their novelistic overtones. The dividing line between popular and literary or elite culture was not that firm in the nineteenth century, and politics impended over everything as the crisis of the Union worsened and the nation hurtled toward internecine bloodshed.

Illinois senator Stephen A. Douglas, then the most renowned politician in America, and Abraham Lincoln, who had held no political office for almost a decade, met in a verbal match of seven parts, with Douglas's Senate seat as the prize. Strict rules governed the three-hour clashes. Each debate consisted of a speech of an hour, a reply of an hour and a half, and a final rejoinder of thirty minutes. The discourse was dense and serious, and printed versions of the debates have earned a lasting place in the country's pantheon of public documents. But the immediate electoral outcome has often surprised modern readers: though Lincoln finished slightly ahead in the popular vote in Illinois, senators were still chosen by state legislatures, and Douglas was returned to Washington for a third term.

Lincoln caught the entertainment or aesthetic value of the debates when he described them, at their sixth meeting, as "the successive acts of a drama," a performance "enacted not merely in the face of audiences like this, but in the face of the nation." Huge crowds, ranging in size from 1,200 at Jonesboro to about 20,000 at Galesburg, assembled to hear the candidates. Excitement and partisanship ran high. The audiences, much like antebellum theatergoers, made their reactions known through cheers, laughter, and shouts of encouragement and derision. Both speakers had to ask for quiet. And both enlivened their exchanges with stories, jokes, conspiracy charges, personal attacks, and a bluntness that has long since departed the public forum.

The two men's utterances bristled with multiple points of connection to high and low literature. Many authors would have felt at home with accusations of conspiracy, long a staple not only of American politics but also of American fiction (and immortalized by the historian Richard Hofstadter in the phrase "the paranoid style"). The new Republican Party, founded in 1854–55 after the Kansas-Nebraska Act, revived the Revolutionary period's fear of secret British plots by conjuring a malevolent Slave Power intent on stamping out Northern liberties. In the debates, Lincoln recycled his claim (from the "House Divided" speech) that there was a high-level cabal determined to spread slavery throughout the land. But conspiracy charges were not limited to the Republican candidate: Douglas tirelessly aired his conviction that Lincoln, along with the other Illinois senator, Lyman Trumbull, had schemed to "abolitionize" the state's Whig and Democratic parties.

We are in the world of George Lippard's sensational best seller, *The Quaker City: or, The Monks of Monk Hall* (1845), with its salacious Catholic and upper-class plotters; or of Herman Melville's *Moby-Dick* (1852), in which the paranoid Captain Ahab discerns malignant agency behind the white whale's "pasteboard" mask. Significantly, Lincoln retreated from this overheated grammar of hidden but penetrable designs. Douglas, he said in the final debate, "willingly or unwillingly, purposely or without purpose," had helped to change slavery's standing in the nation, a process underwritten by the invention of the cotton gin. This admission that men are the instruments of larger forces would surface again in his great Second Inaugural, in which Lincoln, portraying North and South alike as the sport of uncontrollable events, declared, "The Almighty has His own purposes."

Conspiracy charges and reminders of the Revolutionary past dovetailed with efforts of both speakers to represent themselves as rightful heirs to the Founding Fathers. Filiopietism saturated the ideological sparring, as it did the entire culture. Douglas defended his doctrine of "popular sovereignty" by characterizing it as a supreme act of loyalty, indistinguishable from the principle of self-determination for which the Revolution was fought. Lincoln, for his part, argued that the "Little Giant" had betrayed the founders by disregarding their wish to bottle up slavery in the South and thus set it "in the course of ultimate extinction." The candidates differed sharply in their interpretations of the Declaration of Independence. Douglas contended that Jefferson's self-evident truth, "all men are created equal," applied exclusively to whites, and not, as Lincoln seemed to think, to blacks or Malays or Sandwich Islanders. While acknowledging that blacks and whites were not equal in every respect, Lincoln insisted that they shared an equal right to "life, liberty, and the pursuit of happiness." The Declaration's core maxim was an ideal toward which the polity should strive.

Disputes over the meaning and relevance of the founders' legacy were not unique to the political arena, and Lincoln's more elastic definition of the Declaration associates him with contemporaneous writers who rediscovered in Jefferson's words an egalitarian promise forsaken by their society. An implicit but obvious affinity would be with Ishmael's paean in *Moby-Dick* to the "just Spirit of Equality" that culls "selectest champions" from "the kingly commons." Frederick Douglass, whose name cropped up repeatedly in the debates, invoked the Declaration in an 1852 speech assailing American hypocrisy, "What to the Slave Is the Fourth of July?" Thoreau moved into his cabin in the woods on July Fourth, as he reports in *Walden* (1854), and Walt Whitman self-published *Leaves of Grass,* his poetic celebration of parity among men and women, blacks and whites, and rich and poor, on the same day in 1855. Lincoln himself, as president, never doubted the Declaration's significance for the war against secession and slavery. He called Congress into special session on July 4, 1861, to ratify his measures to save the Union; and at Gettysburg in 1863, he appealed not to the Constitution but to Jefferson's "proposition that all men are created equal," announced to the world "fourscore and seven years ago."

It was the Little Giant rather than Lincoln who mentioned Frederick Douglass during the campaign's debates, and he did so in a race-baiting way that both accentuated the contrast between the two candidates and tilted his own remarks in the direction of fiction. His attacks hammered on the theme of the mulatto, or miscegenation—until the Civil War a subject, ironically, more often treated by black novelists, like William Wells Brown and Harriet Wilson, than by white ones. (In fact Democratic Party strategists would coin the word "miscegenation" for the election of 1864.) From the very first debate, Douglas kept asserting that Lincoln was the ally or "brother" of the black abolitionist "FRED. DOUGLASS." At Freeport, in the northwestern part of the state, the Illinois senator added a titillating if probably spurious anecdote about the type of black-white intimacy anathema to Illinois voters. He told a story about the last time he had campaigned in that location: "I saw a carriage and a magnificent one it was, drive up and take a position on the outside of the crowd; a beautiful young lady was sitting on the box seat, whilst Fred. Douglass and her mother reclined inside, and the owner of the carriage acted as driver." This scene of the world turned upside down, socially and, by implication, sexually as well, didn't leave a lot to the imagination, and angry spectators burst into hooting and cries of, "White, white." Lincoln did not miss the subtext. "I do not understand," he protested, "that because I do not want a negro woman for a slave I must necessarily want her for a wife."

In the Douglas narrative, Lincoln did not simply socialize with blacks; his entire rhetorical performance confounded racial boundaries. His speeches were exercises in deception that changed color, as it were, to win support in different sections of the state. In the antislavery northern counties, settled by New Englanders, Lincoln's oratory assumed the "jet black" hue of his Negro siblings. In the center, his views were "the color of a decent mulatto," and in "lower Egypt," the region bordering slaveholding Missouri, they were "almost white." Douglas himself could deliver the same speech everywhere, he said, because he took no position on slavery, his only desideratum being the local majority's will. But the linguistic chameleonism of "brother Abe" masked an abolitionist agenda that would overrule local choice to impose racial equality on all communities. And it would end by mongrelizing the Republic.

Against Douglas's lurid tale of racial pollution, Lincoln offered a counternarrative of which he was at once the author and the protagonist. The Republican's story had the condensed but classic shape of a maturation drama in which the hero outgrows his callow follies and gains an understanding of his strengths. It traced Lincoln's evolution from a comic, slightly buffoonish figure to a formidable adversary with a moral focus lacking in his opponent. Pro-Douglas newspapers were unwittingly complicit in this character development, but they were responding to the reality of Lincoln's performance.

Lincoln did not get off to a strong start. His one-liners and witty sallies, in plentiful supply from the moment of the opening exchange at Ottawa, were funnier than Douglas's, but they also created the impression that he was not as serious. Nor, for the first four debates, did Lincoln always come across as an effective counterpuncher. He allowed himself to be boxed into a corner by Douglas's virulent racism and defended himself against accusations of favoring "perfect equality" with racist comments of his own. He even pretended not to grasp one of Douglas's rare displays of playfulness. In the third debate, at Jonesboro, he called the Democrat "crazy" for saying that he, Lincoln, had trembled with fright after their previous meeting and had to be carried from the platform by friends.

Lincoln's clownish image proved to be something of a leitmotif in pro-Douglas coverage of the confrontations. As originally published in 1859, the debates were drawn from partisan accounts in the Democratic and Republican press, with each man's speeches taken from the papers that supported his election. Democratic reporters initially depicted the Republican challenger as an unworthy rival to the more dignified and famous Douglas, a view that may have been abetted by Lincoln's self-denigrations. They described the Republican as joining "feebly" in laughter at his own expense, showing great agitation, "his face buried in his hands," and chewing "his nails in a rage in a back corner." There was nothing like this in the Republican coverage of Douglas.

But then Lincoln found his footing and voice, and the narrative changed. The most conspicuous difference stemmed from his discovery of what he termed "the true issue of this controversy": the moral status of slavery. This insight, present but understated in the early debates, moved to center stage in the final three. To Republicans, Lincoln said, Negro bondage was "a moral, social, and political wrong," and they desired its eventual disappearance. Democrats like Douglas, he said, professed not to care whether the institution was voted up or down, and they fully expected it to continue forever. Their studious avoidance of judgment, on a subject about which no one could fail to have an opinion, exposed the moral bankruptcy of their position. More than that, Lincoln emphasized, the Democrats' neutrality posed a threat to white liberties. What *they* hoped to see disappear was free discussion. Douglas's party wanted the entire subject of slavery "to be stilled and subdued," claiming that it would go away if only people would "quit talking about it." Lincoln had turned a dispute about the territories into a powerful symbol of ethical and democratic obtuseness. In the debate at Alton, where the abolitionist editor Elijah P. Lovejoy had been murdered in 1837, the future president capped these arraignments with an unforgettable summation of the "two principles—right and wrong" that have faced off throughout history:

> The one is the common right of humanity and the other the divine right of kings . . . It is the same spirit that says, "You work and toil and earn bread, and I'll eat it." No matter in what shape it comes, whether from the mouth of a king who seeks to bestride the people of his own nation and live by the fruit of their labor, or from one race of men as an apology for enslaving another race, it is the same tyrannical principle.

The implied comparison of slavery to colonial rule would not have been lost on antebellum voters.

As he zeroed in on the moral gravamen of the campaign, Lincoln emerged as the bolder debater. His retorts grew more pointed and acerbic, and he began to turn Douglas into a butt of raillery, warning his opponent, "I will not be the first to cry 'hold.'" He ridiculed the allegation that Republicans had been the ones to shatter the national silence on slavery. The culprit, rather, was the sitting senator's brainchild, the Kansas-Nebraska Act, which had repealed the Missouri Compromise. Lincoln ingeniously argued that by suggesting the use of unfriendly local legislation to circumvent the *Dred Scott* decision, the Democrat was effectively siding with those Northern agitators who sought to nullify the Fugitive Slave Law. "Why there is not such an Abolitionist in the nation as Douglas, after all," he exclaimed. Clearly losing ground, Douglas could produce no good answers to these arguments, and in his final speech he lamely accused Lincoln of treason for his opposition, a decade earlier, to the U.S.-Mexico War. The reversal of stature in the debates was undeniable, and the Democratic newspapers seemed to sense it. They ceased lampooning Lincoln. The mocking tableaux of the earlier coverage simply vanished.

A happy ending? Yes and no. Like many well-crafted and subtle narratives, Lincoln's version of the debates did better with readers in the long run, helping to win him the presidency two years later. In 1863 he issued his Declaration-like proclamation abolishing slavery behind Confederate lines, and his position is secure as one of the genuine heroes of American culture. But historical developments appended some ironies to this satisfying denouement. Lincoln had famously said at the Ottawa debate that "public sentiment is everything. With public sentiment, nothing can fail; without it nothing can succeed." Although popular opinion ended slavery and started the nation on the path to color-blind civil rights, it was Stephen Douglas, not the Great Emancipator, whose attitudes prevailed after the Civil War when Reconstruction faltered. A transformed "public sentiment" undid racial equality in 1876–77, ensuring the century-long triumph of Douglas's view that the Declaration applied only to whites. And another American writer, this time from the realist period, took the measure of the new-old paradigm dominated by the Douglas narrative. Mark Twain, in a piece he didn't dare publish, said that people participated in the gruesome ritual of lynching because they lacked the courage not to. They were afraid of forfeiting "public approval."

Bibliography: Allen Grossman, "The Poetics of Union in Whitman and Lincoln: An Inquiry toward the Relationship of Art and Policy," in Walter Benn Michaels and Donald E. Pease, eds., *The American Renaissance Reconsidered: Selected Papers from the English Institute, 1982–83* (Baltimore, 1985), pp. 183–208. Richard Hofstadter, *The Paranoid Style in American Politics and Other Essays* (New York, 1965). Harry V. Jaffa, *A New Birth of Freedom: Abraham Lincoln and the Coming of the Civil War* (Lanham, MD, 2000). William Lee Miller, *Lincoln's Virtues: An Ethical Biography* (New York, 2002). James Oakes, *The Radical and the Republican: Frederick Douglass, Abraham Lincoln, and the Triumph of Antislavery Politics* (New York, 2007). James Perrin Warren, *Culture of Eloquence: Oratory and Reform in Antebellum America* (University Park, PA, 1999). David Zarefsky, *Lincoln, Douglas, and Slavery: In the Crucible of Public Debate* (Chicago, 1990).

MICHAEL T. GILMORE

1859

Lewis Henry Morgan begins his ethnographic journals "to encourage a kinder feeling towards the Indian"

THE SCIENCE OF THE INDIAN

Between 1859 and 1862 the great American ethnologist Lewis Henry Morgan made four trips west to study Indians. The first two trips took him to the territories of Kansas and Nebraska, the third to Fort Garry near Lake Winnipeg, and the fourth some 2,000 miles up the Missouri River past the Yellowstone to Fort Benton. In those days there was no railroad service beyond Jefferson City, Missouri, and vast herds of buffalo, antelope, and elk still roamed the prairies. Morgan encountered people suffering from cholera and syphilis, met Gros Ventre Indians hiding from the Sioux, and wrote about seeing a scalp drying on the ground outside an informant's house. While returning from his final excursion in 1862, he received word that his two young daughters, ages seven and two, had died from scarlet fever a month earlier. Morgan estimated that his journeys had cost him over $25,000 in expenses and lost income. What came from these arduous and costly research trips, which were recorded by Morgan in a series of "Indian journals," was an important episode in the development of American thought. It was the science of the Indian.

Morgan is considered the father of modern anthropology for good reason. He almost single-handedly invented the practice of fieldwork, initiated the long-running academic study of kinship, and most notably developed a grand theory of social evolution positing history as the teleological progression of human societies through a successive series of stages, from savagery to barbarism to civilization. His work informed Marx and Engels's theory of historical materialism and was cited by Darwin in *The Descent of Man* (1871). Morgan's methods effectively put an end to the practice of "armchair ethnology," a purely theoretical enterprise common in his day, in which intellectuals would make bold, sweeping claims about distant peoples based entirely on the reading of travel narratives. While many of Morgan's specific claims regarding Indian life have been disregarded, and even more his teleological theory of human history, Morgan remains a noteworthy figure.

Lewis Henry Morgan was born in 1818 and spent most of his childhood in Aurora, New York, a white settlement in the heart of what had only recently been the geographical center of the Haudenosaunee Confederacy. After graduating from Cayuga Academy, Morgan entered Union College in 1838 and stayed for two years; he returned to Aurora to study law and was admitted to the bar in 1840. While engaged in his studies, Morgan joined a secret fraternal society called the Gordian Knot that was mostly composed of Cayuga Academy graduates, but he soon found that the fraternity's energies and membership were lagging. Under Morgan's guidance it was reconstituted as an "Indian" organization and renamed the Grand Order of Iroquois, and it grew. New chapters were established, one of which had in its ranks a young Henry Rowe Schoolcraft, the geographer and ethnologist. To learn about their namesakes at a time when Indian life was obscured by stereotype and ignorance, Morgan turned to his real Iroquois neighbors for information about how they lived, thereby establishing the practice of conducting fieldwork that would occupy him for so much of his life. In an apparent act of reciprocation, Morgan later defended the Senecas when their territory was targeted by Ogden Land Company speculators; he circulated petitions, raised awareness, even lobbied Congress, but his efforts led to only a modicum of success. Still, in 1847 the Senecas adopted Morgan into their Longhouse and named him Tayodaowaka, meaning "bridging the gap," indicating the Senecas' view of Morgan as a translator and a negotiator.

Morgan's research on the Iroquois during the 1840s was eventually published under the title *League of the Ho-dé-no-sau-nee, or Iroquois* (1851), and it was an instant classic. Written with the assistance of the great Seneca intellectual Hä-Sa-No-An'-Da (Ely Samuel Parker), Morgan's ethnology of the Six Nations was presented in three books—*Structure of the League, Spirit of the League,* and *Incident to the League*—the first describing Iroquois government; the second dealing with myth, legend, and cultural belief; and the third focused on language, material culture, and the reproduction of daily life. The main purpose of the work, as Morgan stated in opening his preface, was "to encourage a kinder feeling towards the Indian, founded upon a truer knowledge of his civil and domestic institutions, and of his capabilities for future elevation." Incidentally, these same words can be found in the preamble of the Grand Order of Iroquois constitution.

Morgan's claim that Indians had capabilities for elevation was an important remark to make at a time when the federal Indian policy of Removal—which we would now call ethnic cleansing—was giving way to genocidal recommendations. Initiated in the 1830s, Removal was premised on the notion that Indians and whites could not coexist, so Indian nations were sent packing to territories in the West. But continued westward expansion soon crowded those territories as well, creating conflict and giving ammunition to the proponents of genocide, who proclaimed Indians incapable of change and thus fated for extinction anyway. Racial scientists, such as Samuel Morton and Charles Pickering, emerged at this time to lend a veneer of academic respectability to the rhetoric of genocide, suggesting that races had different and inbred capacities for civilization, the implication being that genocide might as well be placed on a par with buffalo hunting. Against this, Morgan's work depicted Indians who were just as capable of elevating themselves as anyone else, given the right opportunities. In Book Three he proposed "two means of rescuing the Indian from his impending destiny; and these are education and Christianity." *League* was thus not only a description of Iroquois society but also a radical argument for Indian capabilities, made at a time when the idea was questionable.

After publication of *League of the Ho-dé-no-sau-nee,* Morgan set his ethnological pursuits aside to practice law in Rochester. He married his cousin Mary Elizabeth Steele and became a railroad attorney and businessman. But five years later he attended a conference of the American Association for the Advancement of Science in Albany and found himself so fascinated with new ethnological research that he decided to resume his studies immediately. The following year, 1857, Morgan presented a paper on Iroquois kinship, and the summer after that he traveled to Marquette, Michigan, to obtain a kinship model from the Ojibwes.

Kinship—the organization of social roles and property rights through lines of descent—was of vital importance to Morgan because he believed that all tribal kinship systems could one day be reconciled and used to prove the common Asiatic origins of Indians—in other words, the Bering Strait theory. The Bering Strait theory was a popular origin story premised on the idea that Native Americans' ancient ancestors crossed a great land bridge from Siberia to North America thousands of years ago. Morgan figured that kinship analyses would confirm this because Indians identified relatives differently from Europeans but similarly to putatively primitive peoples around the world. The difference was essentially linguistic, between the descriptive terms of kinship used in European languages and the classificatory concept employed by Indians, the latter being identified by its mergers of collateral and lineal relatives at certain points—for example, calling a father's sister's son "father," a mother's sister's son "brother," and so forth. After his return from Ojibwe country in 1858, Morgan decided to collect kinship "nomenclatures" and "schedules" from tribes out West, hence his four major excursions and his journals of copious notes.

The Indian journals featured crude drawings of homes, clothing, utensils, ceremonial objects, topography, flora, fauna, and more. While his main purpose was the collection of kinship data, Morgan addressed a diverse array of subjects: things he saw, people he met, practices he observed, and questions that naturally emerged. He also chronicled his opinions, musing endlessly on the future of Indians in American society and reproducing arguments he had on the subject. During his very first trip, in fact, he lectured some Kaws about the evils of whiskey, and they argued back:

> To my remonstrance against their drinking and attempt to show them that if they drank more moderately they would enjoy it more, the chief asked me through the interpreter why the white men made it if it was bad for them to drink it. I told him we could not prevent their making it, but we considered all the makers to be common loafers and had but little to do with them; that we had passed a prohibition law in our state and were trying to get rid of all ardent spirits. I then told him he was not obliged to drink it because the white man made it. He replied that he should drink it as long as he lived.

Like many in his day, Morgan believed in temperance. At the same time, he wrote that the Indians' drinking "opened their hearts and tongues and I got with readiness and ease what at another time would be hard to draw out of a Kaw." Behold the birth of ethnography.

What did Morgan see on his trips? Plenty, of course, but one recurring theme is his fascination with Indians' bodies. He often remarked on people's phenotypes and skin color and classified them tribally. But not negatively. In fact, Morgan advocated race mixing:

> I think an amalgamation with the Indians by the white race, or the absorption of the best blood of their race into our own is destined to take place, and that Kansas will be the theater of the first honest and regular experiment. Hitherto the lowest and basest whites have been the fathers of the half breeds. Now we are to see respectable white people marry the daughters of wealthy and respectable Indians and bring up their children with the advantages of education, Christianity and wealth . . . Our race, I think will be *toughened physically* by the intermixture and without any doubt will be benefited intellectually.

Indian bodies had their benefits. Indians also moved differently in time and space. During his second trip, in 1860, Morgan started chronicling the common practice among Indians of sleeping in the nude. "The Chippewas, Sauks and Foxes, Kaws, and Osages all do this," he wrote in May 1860, and to that he soon added Omahas, Shawnees, and Eskimos too. The Eskimos were an especially important discovery, he believed, because "the existence of this custom among the Eskimos and our Indians carries with it some evidence of a common origin." The following month Morgan added more than thirty additional nations to his list of peoples who slept in the nude, never judging the practice but actually admiring it.

It all seemed so natural to Morgan, and naturalism became another theme in his journals. Morgan's final expeditions in 1861 and 1862 took him to the North Woods and the Rocky Mountains, and in addition to his usual remarks regarding kinship nomenclatures and schedules—and, yes, naked sleeping—Morgan's later entries increasingly focused on animal behaviors, such as the industriousness of prairie dogs and beavers. In one of his most deadpan entries, on June 9, 1862, Morgan wrote about Crow women at Fort Union who attempted to nurse a baby beaver "until it began to bite," and remarked how easily Indians had trained beavers as pets, adding, "I must get one." There's no evidence that Morgan ever tamed a beaver, but he did publish *The American Beaver and His Works* in 1868, which Darwin later cited. While Morgan never came close to suggesting that Indians were animals, his intermingling of ethnological and zoological discourse couldn't help but reinforce extant imagery of Indians as natural people living where the line between nature and culture appeared to blur.

The Indian journals concluded on July 3, 1862, with this entry regarding the news of his daughters: "Two out of three of my children are taken. My family is destroyed. The intelligence has simply petrified me. I have not shed a tear. It is too profound for tears. Thus ends my last expedition. I go home to my stricken and mourning wife, a miserable and destroyed man."

Morgan was not quite destroyed, however. His Indian journals were the basis of works to come, including the *Systems of Consanguinity and Affinity of the Human Family* (1871), his magnum opus on kinship, and *Ancient Society, or Researches in the Lines of Human Progress from Savagery through Barbarism to Civilization* (1877), that grand narrative of human history. From a native perspective, *Ancient Society* was easily one of the more damaging texts produced in the nineteenth century. In describing cultural differences as "stages" of a social evolution, it theoretically justified unkind practices to come, like boarding schools, allotment, and other assimilation programs imposed on the Indians. Morgan's entire intellectual corpus can be read as marking the great shift in federal Indian policy from Removal to assimilation. Two years after *Ancient Society,* the Carlisle Indian Industrial School was founded on the principle, "Kill the Indian to save the man," and by century's end twenty-five such boarding schools had opened. In 1887 the Dawes Act carved up collectively held tribal lands into individual family allotments, with the stated aim of turning Indians into entrepreneurs (meanwhile breaking down the tribes' communal social structure), and by 1934 tribal landholdings had withered from 134 million acres to 48 million. Assimilation was the scientifically informed social engineering of Indian bodies out of savagery and into civilization. Morgan provided the theory. He bridged the gap.

Bibliography: Lewis Henry Morgan, *The American Beaver and His Works* (Philadelphia, 1868); *Ancient Society, or Researches in the Lines of Human Progress from Savagery through Barbarism to Civilization* (New York, 1877); *The Indian Journals, 1859–62,* ed. Leslie A. White (Ann Arbor, MI, 1959); *League of the Ho-dé-no-sau-nee, or Iroquois,* 2 vols., ed. Herbert M. Lloyd (New York, 1901); *Systems of Consanguinity and Affinity of the Human Family* (Lincoln, NE, 1997).

SCOTT RICHARD LYONS

Emily Dickinson writes to her cousins: "When did the war really begin?"

Children, Women, Queens

An extract, all that remains from a letter Emily Dickinson wrote to her young cousins Louise and Frances Norcross, later bound with manuscripts marked "Spring 1861" but written surely after November 1861, ends abruptly with the question "When did the war really begin?"

At the opening of 1861, seven Southern states had seceded from the Union; by March the secessionists had a provisional president, a flag, and a constitution; and by May four more states would complete the final assemblage that made up the Confederate States of America. As the North and South split apart, the same divisions opened along the east-west trajectory of the frontier. In January Kansas became a state, and in February, Colorado and Nevada became official U.S. territories. Addressing this period of rapid westward expansion, the newly elected Abraham Lincoln announced that the Union would not tolerate a concomitant expansion of slavery. Yet he also declared in his March inaugural address that he would not act against slaveholding in those states where it then existed. In April, South Carolinians fired on Fort Sumter and, after a prolonged bombardment, the federal fort was surrendered to them. In May, England tacitly acknowledged the secessionists by proclaiming its neutrality. Union troops routed Virginia and Georgia brigades at the Battle of Corrick's Ford in western Virginia on July 13, and a week later Confederate soldiers repulsed a Northern attack at Manassas Junction, Virginia, in what became known as the First Battle of Bull Run, the first major battle of the war.

Is this lurching start of the Civil War the frame for Dickinson's question? Whatever isolation Dickinson held to as she selected "her own society" and rejected being "public—like a frog," the Dickinson family by 1861 was well informed about the war. They received two mail deliveries a day, subscribed to three Northern newspapers, and also received *Harper's New Monthly Magazine, Scribner's Monthly,* and the *Atlantic Monthly.* By April, the 235 students of nearby Amherst College were beginning to enlist. A month later, classes at the college were suspended because of mass departures, with 78 students volunteering for the Union side and 4 students returning home to Southern states to join the Confederates. Dickinson herself had visited Washington, D.C., and Virginia in February and March of 1855, and admired especially Mount Vernon, the "Lord and Lady" who had lived there, and the "many sweet ladies and noble gentlemen" she met in the South. Her father, Edward Dickinson, a conservative Whig, had served in Congress and the Massachusetts legislature. On May 1, he moved that the selectmen of Amherst should borrow $5,000 to provide uniforms and other support to the families of Union volunteers. Meanwhile, Emily's Southern uncle, Edward's brother Samuel Fowler Dickinson, Jr., was a fierce secessionist. When drafted in

1864, her brother, Austin, would pay a young Irish immigrant $500 to take his place. Among her primary correspondents were the Whig, but pro-feminist, Samuel Bowles, editor of the *Springfield Republican,* and Thomas Wentworth Higginson, a devotee of Margaret Fuller's writings and women's rights, who, following through on his abolitionist beliefs, would late in 1862 command the first regiment made up of former slaves.

Although in her correspondence she laments the deaths of local soldiers — the Adams brothers, only sons of their widowed mother, and later Frazar Stearns, son of the Amherst College president—in her extant writings in prose and poetry Dickinson does not seem preoccupied with the war. As she wrote to Higginson on his departure to join his regiment, "War feels to me an oblique place." In a summer letter to a friend, she wrote that she "would have no winter this year—on account of the soldiers—Since I cannot weave Blankets, or Boots—I thought it best to omit the season."

Yet the years of the war are those of her greatest production of poetry, and three of her poems appeared in 1864 in a wartime fund-raising paper in Brooklyn, the *Drum Beat.* One of these, "Blazing in gold and quenching in purple," was there entitled "Sunset," and, like a number of her sunset poems of this period, it takes on martial imagery. Another, her "The sun kept stooping—stooping—low," describes how "the Tyrian" purple of the sunset

> Was crowded dense with Armies —
> So gay—so Brigadier—
> That *I* felt martial stirrings
> Who once the Cockade wore—[. . .]

In other poems, she writes "Sunrise—hast thou a flag for me?" and

> Of Bronze—and Blaze—
> The North—tonight—
> So adequate—it forms—
> So preconcerted with itself—
> So distant—to alarms—[. . .]

The poem "Through the straight pass of suffering" describes how "The martyrs even trod" and how "The needle to the North degree,/Wades so, through Polar air"; with its mention of "streaks of meteor," this work likely refers to the May 14 fall of the Canellas meteorite near Barcelona. Images of dying figures in the sky are mixed with sunset imagery again in "I'll tell you how the sun rose":

> But how he *set,* I know not!
> There seemed a purple stile
> Which little yellow boys and girls
> Were Climbing all the while —
>
> Till when they reached the other side,
> A Dominie in gray
> Put gently up the evening bars
> And led the flock away!

The "trouble" and "bleeding . . . drops of vital scarlet" in another poem, "Bound a trouble," build to the final line: "Notching the fall of the even sun!"

Just after the fall of Fort Sumter, federal soldiers were given blue uniforms, but many of these faded to gray; at the same time, New York, Maine, Vermont, and Wisconsin were dressing their soldiers in both blue and gray uniforms. Southern soldiers at first wore their own clothes, or state uniforms of gray, blue, or brown. The volunteers of the 5th Massachusetts militia were given black coats of "shoddy" that turned gray under a wash of rain. The result of this confusion of uniforms was many deaths by friendly fire. Dickinson writes in another of her myriad sunset/sunrise poems:

> A slash of Blue—
> A sweep of Gray—
> Some scarlet patches on the way—
> Compose an evening sky—
> A little purple—slipped between—
> Some Ruby Trowsers hurried on—
> A Wave of Gold—
> A Bank of Day—
> This just makes out the *Morning* Sky—

Her thinking is inseparably allegorical and literal: the relation between the evening and morning sky is also the relation between how things have begun in the East and how they will end in the West. The asymmetrical structure is emphasized by the witty center line, "A little purple—slipped between—," like a streak or stripe of color. The "Ruby Trowsers" here are likely the baggy red pants worn by the Zouave units popular in the early months of the war—before such colorful outfits proved disastrously conspicuous targets on the battlefield. Dickinson is herself the meridian in time and space between these changes as she begins with sunset and ends in sunrise. The sunset's violent verbs "slash" and "sweep" are juxtaposed to the far more tentative "slipped" and "hurried" opening of the sunrise. It is the sunrise, however, that is shown to be magnificent, with its golden "Wave" and "Bank." The poem hinges on the difference between *composing* and *making out*—the similarly bold and tentative gestures of the poet.

To locate Dickinson in the context of the commencement of the Civil War is to consider both her metaphysical and her material coordinates in time and space, and to imagine what the war looked like from her vantage point. Rejecting the rhetoric of war that later characterized rousing lyrics like those of Julia Ward Howe's 1862 "Battle Hymn of the Republic," in the 1861 letter fragment quoted above Dickinson appears to be questioning her literal place and position. Yet the sentences that occur before the question "When did the war really begin?" seem to be about another topic entirely:

> Your letters are all real, just the tangled road children walked before you, some of them to the end, and others but a little way, even as far as the fork in the road. That Mrs. Browning fainted, we need not read *Aurora Leigh* to know, when she lived with her English aunt; and George Sand, "must make no noise in her grandmother's

bedroom." Poor children! Women, now, queens, now! And one in the Eden of God. I guess they both forget that now, so who knows but we, little stars from the same night, stop twinkling at last? Take heart, little sister, twilight is but the short bridge, and the moon [morn] stands at the end. If we can only get to her! Yet, if she sees us fainting, she will put out her yellow hands.

If the "poor children" here remind us of the yellow boys and girls climbing the royal Tyrian stile of sunset who were led away by a gray "Dominie," we also might keep in mind Dickinson's deep affection for "the Yorkshire girls," particularly for the Gondal poems of Emily Brontë, with their own many sunsets, moonlit nights, snowy scenes, orphans, lords, and ladies, who find themselves alternately imprisoned and fighting battles. Even so, how did Elizabeth Barrett Browning, who had died on June 29, 1861, and so gone to "the Eden of God," and the cross-dressing French romantic novelist George Sand come to be associated with the commencement of "the war"? The answer lies not only in Dickinson's reading in general, but in the pages of the 1861 *Atlantic Monthly* in particular. In the September 1861 issue a correspondent from Florence, writing a letter dated a week after Barrett Browning's death, described how as a girl the invalid Barrett Browning was, like her heroine Aurora Leigh, "confined to her room," before she "developed into the great artist and scholar." In the November issue, we can find Julia Ward Howe's similarly reverential tribute to George Sand, accompanying Howe's summary of Sand's still-untranslated 1855 *Histoire de ma vie*. Sand, described by Howe as "a woman of royal soul," recounts being confined to her aristocratic grandmother's care in early childhood: "Her chamber, dark and perfumed, gave me the headache, and fits of spasmodic yawning. When she said to me, '*Amuse yourself quietly*,' it seemed to me as if she shut me up in a great box with her."

The *Atlantic*'s July 1861 issue presented an extensive report on "Emancipation in Russia," which noted that "pro-slavery forces in the US condemn the Russian emancipation of serfs" enacted by a March 3 Imperial Manifesto. The czar is described as being only "an instrument in the hands of Fate." In a poem written in the summer of 1860, "I met a king this afternoon," Dickinson fancifully mentions "a Czar petite," but by 1861 her references to czars are more serious and recapitulate the progression from child to woman to queen:

> I'm "wife"—I've finished that—
> That other state—
> I'm Czar—I'm "Woman" now—
> It's safer so—
>
> How odd the Girl's life looks
> Behind this soft Eclipse—[. . .]

and in "The court is far away" she writes:

> *That* Empire—is of Czars—
> As small—they say—as I—
> Grant *me*—that day—the royalty—
> To *intercede*—for *Thee*—

In her only poem mentioning either serfs or slaves, "The lamp burns sure within," Dickinson, too, connects the two kinds of bondsmen:

> The Lamp burns sure—within—
> Tho' Serfs—supply the Oil—
> It matters not the busy Wick—
> At her phosphoric toil!
>
> The Slave—forgets—to fill—
> The Lamp—burns golden—on
> Unconscious that the oil is out—
> As that the Slave—is gone.

Just a few months before reading the July *Atlantic,* Dickinson had eagerly asked her sister-in-law, Susan Gilbert Dickinson, to loan her the April issue that included the West Virginia writer Rebecca Harding Davis's documentary novella, *Life in the Iron-Mills.* There she would have read the mill owner's complaint: "I suppose there are some stray gleams of mind and soul among these wretches . . . [but] there's something wrong that no talk of '*Liberté*' or '*Egalité*' will do away. If I had the making of men, these men who do the lowest part of the world's work should be machines,—nothing more,—hands." As the novella ends, the artist and mill worker Hugh Wolfe is unjustly imprisoned in chains and finds "freedom" only by committing suicide.

A set of revolutionary and romantic motifs runs throughout these *Atlantic* pieces: a fantasy of imprisonment and liberation, both physical and intellectual, linking slaves, serfs, the working poor, and women. Howe describes how, as a convent schoolgirl, Sand and her friends would pretend they were releasing "a prisoner, or perhaps several, cut off from liberty and light; and to *deliver the victim* became the object of a hundred wild expeditions." The adult Sand imaginatively extended this mission into history, contending that the French Revolution was "one of the phases of evangelical life: a tumultuous, bloody life, terrible at certain moments, full of convulsions, of delirium, and of sobbing. It is the violent contest of the principle of equality preached by Jesus, and passing, now like a burning torch, from hand to hand, to our own days." The eulogist of Barrett Browning analogously writes that the poet, with her "still small voice" and "forehead rayed with the truth," had "scorned to take an insular view of any political question," contending "the Revolution of 1848 kindled the passion of liberty from the Alps to Sicily."

From her 1843 "The Cry of the Children" and her 1848 abolitionist poem, "Runaway Slave at Pilgrim's Point," to her 1856 prophecy of the coming punishment of American slaveholding society, "A Curse for a Nation," Barrett Browning had been a prominent poet of social causes. But from 1859 to 1861, like Margaret Fuller before her, she committed herself to the cause of Italian liberation, writing more than two dozen poems concerned with the struggle between North and South on Italian soil. In her final volume of poetry, *Poems before Congress,* Barrett Browning chastised England's inaction as she exalted Napoleon III for "helping" the Italian cause, not recognizing the realpolitik at work in the situation. Barrett

Browning was so savagely attacked by the British press, not only for *Poems before Congress* but also, earlier, because her "Curse for a Nation" was mistakenly viewed as anti-British, that she effectively became an American poet, publishing most of her work in the New York *Independent*. Among her most devoted American readers was Emily Dickinson. She described herself as transformed by Barrett Browning's exotic spell:

> I think I was enchanted
> When first a sombre Girl—
> I read that Foreign Lady—
> The Dark—felt beautiful—

A full year after Barrett Browning's death, Dickinson was still describing herself as Barrett Browning's "unmentioned Mourner" and telling Higginson she was collecting portraits of the dead poet. And Dickinson wrote two elegies for Browning: "I went to thank her" and "Her 'last Poems.'"

A figure who seems to be a composite of Sand and Barrett Browning is memorialized in this poem from the last months of 1861:

> A Mien to move a Queen—
> Half Child—Half Heroine—
> An Orleans in the eye
> That puts it's manner by
> For humbler Company
> When none are near
> Even a Tear—
> It's frequent Visitor—
>
> A Bonnet like a Duke—
> And yet a Wren's Peruke
> Were not so shy
> Of Goer by—
> And Hands—so slight,
> They would elate a sprite
> With merriment—
>
> A Voice that alters—Low
> And on the ear can go
> Like Let of Snow—
> Or shift supreme—
> As tone of Realm
> On Subjects Diadem—
> Too small—to fear—
> Too distant—to endear—
> And so Men Compromise—
> And just—revere—

A manuscript variant for the final line is "And Men—too Brigadier—." The revolution is perpetuated by other means here—by tearful child-heroines, humble company, condescending rulers, and Christian soldiers like the Maid of Orléans. The strange juxtaposition of the duke's bonnet and wren's peruke perhaps stems from Howe's account of Sand's dual genealogy—noble on her father's side, and on her mother's, descended from a "bird-fancier," who, according to the 1855 American edition of Sand's romance *Teverino,* sold wrens and canaries on the Quai des Oiseaux.

The sense that these Eastern poet-messengers, speaking in low voices that can shift to the "tone of Realm," are bringing news of the long onset of wars of emancipation is only underscored by the association of Barrett Browning with her writer-heroine Aurora Leigh and the real name of George Sand, Amantine Aurore Lucile Dupin. In 1861 Dickinson's view of war's end was hidden far beyond her westernmost horizon, but her view of when the war *really* began stretched eastward, and far beyond the confines of her room.

Bibliography: Emily Brontë, *The Complete Poems of Emily Jane Brontë,* ed. C. W. Hatfield (New York, 1941). Jack L. Capps, *Emily Dickinson's Reading* (Cambridge, MA, 1966). Emily Dickinson, *The Letters of Emily Dickinson,* ed. Thomas H. Johnson and Theodora Ward (Cambridge, MA, 1986); *The Poems of Emily Dickinson: Variorum Edition,* ed. R. W. Franklin, 3 vols. (Cambridge, MA, 1998). Jay Leyda, *The Years and Hours of Emily Dickinson,* 2 vols. (New Haven, CT, 1960). George Sand, *Teverino: A Romance by George Sand,* trans. Oliver S. Leland (New York, 1855).

SUSAN STEWART

1862, December 13

The Battle of Fredericksburg sends thousands of wounded soldiers to a hospital where Louisa May Alcott is a volunteer nurse

THE JOURNEYS OF *LITTLE WOMEN*

The power of *Little Women* (1868) resides with readers, especially girls, who find inspiration in the adventures of Jo March. Most of the novel's events take place at home, while the transformative battles of the Civil War are fought at a distance. Yet *Little Women* is a war novel. Readers with fond memories of the March household as a paradise for girls could forget that the household was ruled by women because men were away at war, reflecting the historical circumstances of more than a million households on both sides of the battle lines. Even as the home front orients the world for the novel's four sisters, Louisa May Alcott's fiction challenges the presumption that the lives of "little women" take place quietly at home, insulated from the world's events.

The sisters of the March house, now so well known—Meg, Jo, Beth, and Amy—do remember the absent men. The man of the house, the father of the four girls, has left home to provide spiritual guidance to young soldiers. The men next door include a lonely boy, Laurie; his tutor, John Brooks; and his wealthy grandfather. Brooks, the only one of an appropriate age to be a soldier, eventually leaves to fight, but only after he has established a tie to the home front through his romance with Meg. The restlessness of the sisters keeps them fidgeting between attic and parlor while their mother counsels them to have patience and to develop an inner spiritual life. Although the home contains its own battles, they always heal wounds rather than cause them.

Throughout the novel, battle as a physical matter of blood and bodies becomes subsumed under the idea of battle as a spiritual challenge. Its deeply religious underpinning appears through an emphasis on charitable giving as well as in the attention paid to John Bunyan's allegorical fable, *Pilgrim's Progress,* which each girl receives as a Christmas present from her mother in the novel's early pages. Reading this book, the girls not only internalize its allegorical struggle toward redemption but also dramatize its actions. Bunyan's vision of the journey that Christian must take to reach the gates of the Celestial City is rendered in the form of the girls' trips to the attic. Their spiritual journeys are often acted out as theatrical manifestations of the need to curb selfish impulses—Amy's vanity, for instance, but also the girls' common desire to have more money.

Indeed, the book opens with this longing: it is Christmas, and Meg complains, "It's so dreadful to be poor." Beth attempts to remind them of the wealth they have in each other; Jo's rejoinder is, "We haven't got Father." Finding them disconsolate, their mother, Marmee, converts their longing for material goods into a charitable impulse, persuading them to give away their Christmas feast to a family in need. Later, when Jo is invited to a wealthy family's home for a party, the details of her costume show another class-specific anxiety. How does one dress for a party with spoiled gloves and no resources to buy new ones?

As the sisters playact in the attic, they try on clothes that let them imagine alternate social positions, willing another life into existence. The lasting appeal of the novel consists in the way it asks what choices a girl has. Might she find purpose and happiness through service, sacrifice, and submission, like Beth? Through a happy marriage, like Meg? Or through creative work, such as Amy's art or, most noticeably, Jo's writing? The question of service becomes a problem of how to transmute domestic work into a Christian sense of mission. When delicate Beth fades away, as the girls' mother travels to Washington to find their father in an army hospital, their home becomes a chapel, like the setting of Coventry Patmore's "The Angel in the House" (1858). A more domestic version of such worship appears in Meg's newlywed cottage, the "Dove-Cote." For Jo March, however, choosing a purpose in life always leads to the attic, where she stores her manuscripts and her writing material and where she can act out the role of writer. Success as a writer, only partially realized by Jo in *Little Women* but a repeated theme in Alcott's fiction, often uncomfortably recalls the madwoman in the attic: the success that Jo first realizes with her writing for newspapers is characterized as a manic and somewhat dangerous foray into sensational melodrama.

For Alcott herself, success arrived prior to *Little Women* with the publication of a slim semi-autobiographical volume called *Hospital Sketches* (1863). This success was triggered not by a retreat into the attic but by another journey, taken by both the narrator and the author, to work with the wounded who were arriving in the hospitals of Washington, D.C., from Civil War battlefields. The mission of its narrator, a restless young woman who resembles Jo March, is explicitly to find "something to do." Like Jo, this narrator craves action. Family members encourage her to write, teach, act, marry, and, finally, nurse. All but the last suggestion receive emphatic rejections. The choice of nursing involves a nom de guerre, Nurse Periwinkle (aka Tribulation Periwinkle), and a short vivid journey into the bloody aftermath of battle—the hospital ward. Nursing becomes the path to enter fully into the world, although it's a world made chaotic beyond recognition through the repeated arrivals of young men wounded in the Battle of Fredericksburg.

In contrast, the young girls who first appear in *Little Women* are not old enough to be out in the world except through the mediating agency of their mother. In its promotion of generosity, as well as in the allusions to *Pilgrim's Progress,* the novel presents a retrospective prequel to the actions of *Hospital Sketches.* The characters in *Little Women* negotiate a more limited domestic space, yet their passionate interactions with each other also invoke ideas of class, Christian charity, and, implicitly, race.

The concept of separate spheres that appears to orient the actions of men and women in the novel is challenged by the tremendous envy displayed by the ambiguously named boy Laurie toward the world of the "little" women. Although Laurie will eventually attend college, an option not present for his friends next door, the women's world is shown here as more saturated with possibilities. The sisters have more talent, more imagination, and more skills than the men who look in on them. Their world becomes, as Lora Romero suggests in *Home Fronts,* "a society controlled by women."

The suggestion produced by the link to *Pilgrim's Progress,* that *Little Women* aims to provide instruction, becomes transformed into the entirely pedagogical world of its first sequel, *Little Men* (1871). Within *Little Women,* however, reading and teaching are repeatedly traced back to Marmee. The pedagogy of family reading that emerges here draws on Louisa May Alcott's background. Raised in the troubled utopia of Concord, Massachusetts, with the learned companionship of Ralph Waldo Emerson, Henry David Thoreau, and her father, the radical teacher Bronson Alcott, the young Alcott found that every challenge she met as a child became a lesson to be written down and studied. Such writing became her pathway to the world.

By the time Nathaniel Hawthorne famously commented on the "damned mob of scribbling women," the commercial success of women writers in the United States was assured. Yet the crowd-pleasing style of writing they often used for that success was also well known, and Alcott's own excursion into sensation fiction—a genre for which she always employed a pseudonym, A. M. Barnard, in publishing works like *A Long Fatal Love Chase* (1866)—receives a moralistic reprise in Jo's ventures.

Alcott presents a fictional account of her own rise to fame in her later novel *Jo's Boys* (1886). The woman writer in that novel suffers from a loss of privacy as her home becomes invaded by a public trying to appropriate her identity as a writer. Through the persona of an adult Jo March, Alcott begins with the familiar account of her life when, after writing *Hospital Sketches,* her publishers urged her to write a story for girls. Drawing on memories of her life with her sisters, the character Jo, like Alcott, produced, to her surprise, a best seller. The less familiar part of the account is the disruptive sacrifice of privacy. Like the fictional Jo March, Alcott became a person with extraordinary public claims on her time. Those claims, as they are represented in *Jo's Boys,* included preposterous requests to supply material that the letter writer could publish, pleas for money, and unself-conscious solicitations from petitioners who needed help with their private romantic entanglements. Her troubles are prefigured in *Little Women*'s treatment of how the economically driven choice to write sensation fiction for money might disrupt family life.

In writing *Little Women,* as the story has it, Alcott turned a deaf ear to the pleas of her enthralled readers (the two parts of the novel were published in successive years) and refused to marry Jo to Laurie. Some have proposed that the cross-gender naming tactics of the novel affected this decision as much as Alcott's desire to have her heroine experiment with labor choices, choices that suffused her later novel *Work* (1872). In any case, after Jo tries writing sensation fiction, she finds her strongest comeuppance in the moral rigor of her Teutonic reader, Professor Bhaer. His reaction to Jo's work—he burns the newspaper in which he finds her story—recalls one of the most disturbing scenes in *Little Women,* when Amy, in a fit of pique, burns Jo's irreplaceable handwritten manuscript of stories. In spite of the frustrations associated with fame, the novel remains defiant in its presentation of writing as a way to free women from domestic labor and to bring the world into the home. And in spite of the redemptive connections established between writing and pedagogy, choosing to write remains an act of defiance for women.

The ideal way to live in *Little Women* is to travel without leaving home. As the novel presents it, to leave home and enter the world is to seek a way of returning to the home. When Jo rejects Laurie, initially she does so in the name of the desire always to be at home with her sisters. For all the growing up the sisters do (with the lamentable exception of Beth), the triumph of the novel might be that readers remember them perennially as girls. Yet Alcott's ambivalence about her choices for the characters in *Little Women* appears in her sequels.

What became of this book as a blueprint for how to have a home? In *Little Men* (1871), Jo runs a school where her biological children mingle with children gathered from the streets, sponsored by the wealthy Laurie, now happily married to Amy. These children, nonetheless, learn where they fit in the class system (appreciating patronage, they do not protest that some are destined to work as farm laborers), and they learn to forgive transgressions. Such transgressions return in odd forms in *Jo's Boys,* where the little men have become big men; they indulge in stronger versions of the "larks" that permeated *Little Women.* One ends up in jail for murder, albeit a crime of passion rather than a premeditated killing. Some of the hardest crises, as in *Little Women,* are affairs of the heart. Giving up on passion to live a life with no mate remains the hardest challenge.

A fundamental exhaustion of the material from *Little Men* occurred when Alcott returned to it in *Jo's Boys,* and it shows in her digression into autobiographical material about writing. She is preoccupied with the idea that the life of a woman writer is an unpleasant existence, yet the sensation-fiction conventions from Alcott's past reappear when the character who was locked up for manslaughter has a conversion in jail. The moral lessons of *Little Men* are presented as *lessons;* that is, they come from a teacher and they can be resisted by unruly pupils. In *Jo's Boys,* life deals the lessons, and no alternative appears except death. Some of the inconvenient characters from *Little Men* are dispatched in advance of *Jo's Boys,* simplifying the cast of characters and avoiding the possible deathbed scenes that might have been compared with Beth's tearful and prolonged dying. Satisfaction, so deferred in *Little Women,* becomes in the later books the nearly heavenly reward of marriage. The matter of social mobility becomes more conventionally wedded to the choice of a mate.

Little Women—both as a novel and in its subsequent incarnations in twentieth-century movies and even the opera by Mark Adamo—continues to ask us to imagine it as a prescription for the girl's life in America, at least the life of white girls. In this prescription, the act of reading, shared by girls from the immediate post–Civil War time when just to have a home might have appeared as an act of imagination or faith, becomes a way to share a family. The faith that the book proposes seems initially to be modeled on Bunyan's male Pilgrim, who trudges through the Slough of Despond toward the Celestial City. But the journeys of *Little Women* match these spiritual crises, and not simply by elevating domestic space closer to the gates of heaven.

The novel's saturation in mundane domestic details—such as the much-punched pillows on the family's shabby couch, or the pair of gloves that must be carried to a social outing even when they cannot be worn—makes every element of a home available for conversion to new purposes, from the garden (replete with one tree that serves as a letter box and another that serves as a horse) to the parlor to the attic. Each conversion occurs through the multiple languages of female desire and the mutual awareness of the sisters, even of their shared breathing, the shared breath of poverty and longing. The daring of Jo March has drawn readers of *Little Women* for more than a century. And yet for Jo, as for the other March sisters, all journeys begin and end at home, a place of sanctuary and healing in a nation torn apart by war. Abraham Lincoln had euphoniously declared before the war began, "A house divided cannot stand." Alcott replies that, when the war is over, a home united can always heal.

Bibliography: Mark Adamo, *Little Women: Opera in Two Acts* (Chester, NY, 2001). Louisa May Alcott, *Behind a Mask: The Unknown Thrillers of Louisa May Alcott,* ed. Madeleine Stern (New York, 1997). Sarah Elbert, *A Hunger for Home: Louisa May Alcott's Place in American Culture* (New Brunswick, NJ, 1988). Lora Romero, *Home Fronts: Domesticity and Its Critics in the Antebellum United States* (Durham, NC, 1997).

SHIRLEY SAMUELS

1865, March 4

The president delivers a six-minute speech that meets with a mixed response from listeners

LINCOLN'S SECOND INAUGURAL ADDRESS

On March 4, 1865, Abraham Lincoln delivered his Second Inaugural Address before a large crowd assembled at the east face of the Capitol. He had already produced the orations for which he is most famous—the debates with Douglas that launched him as a national figure, the Cooper Union speech that won him the presidency, his majestic First Inaugural, and the incomparable Gettysburg Address. Few thought that he would rise to those sublime heights on this rainy Saturday, for how many second inaugurals do we remember? For that matter, how many first?

Yet there were indications that something special was in store for the people who braved the elements that day. The war was in its final weeks, and a grand summation was needed. Four of the longest years in American history had elapsed since his First Inaugural Address, and 623,000 citizens lay dead. Perhaps the commander in chief would claim the victory that so many Northerners were beginning to feel? Or announce his plans for the shattered Confederacy, the rogue nation he was in the act of conquering?

Typically, Lincoln did neither. In what may be the least triumphant speech ever delivered by a conqueror, the president spoke briefly and modestly about the higher reaches of what it means to be American. His oration consisted of 703 words, 505 of which were words of one syllable, neatly distributed across twenty-five sentences tucked into four paragraphs. He did not use "I," the favorite word of politicians, until late in the first paragraph, and then never after that. As one surveys the vast terrain of presidential oratory, with its tendency toward long stretches of verbosity about nothing at all, it is startling to come across this polished gem of pure meaning. In all of American expression, it would be difficult to imagine a higher ratio of thoughts per word.

A bit of meteorological good fortune set the stage as Lincoln stood to speak. At the exact moment Lincoln was introduced, the sun broke through the clouds and, in the words of a commentator, "flooded the spectacle with glory and with light." There were other positive omens—behind him, the Capitol dome was finally finished, largely because he had insisted on it, offering an actual form of closure for a people that had never completely defined their government, despite their veneration for abstract principles of democracy. Nearby, the Lincoln family Bible lay open to Isaiah 5, a selection marked by Lincoln, ever attentive to nuance ("None shall be weary nor stumble among them; none shall slumber or sleep").

But despite these auspicious settings and props, the performance left a decidedly mixed impression. Lincoln's address lasted all of six minutes. It would be difficult to draw a headline from it, for there were no particular announcements, no grandiose promises made, no claims of victory, no self-justifications of any kind. In a nutshell, Lincoln reminded his audience that the war was not yet finished, but that when it was, he would expect all Americans to act charitably toward each other. One can forgive the crowd (memorably captured by photographer Alexander Gardner) for not quite getting it. The occasion may have been nearly as blurry as Gardner's image suggests.

But of course there was a great deal more to the address than its apparent lack of news. In a larger way, it was one of the most profound utterances ever spoken by an American president, or for that matter, by any American. Ever restless to probe to the nub of things, Lincoln didn't seek to simply announce the end of the Civil War—he wanted to *understand* it. The titanic fact of the conflict was everywhere one looked—in the amputees walking around Washington; in the large number of ex-slaves now living within the protection of Northern forces (and serving with them); in the sharpshooters lining the rooftops of Washington to protect the highly visible president. John Wilkes Booth was one of the people in the audience that day, captured by the photograph but not, alas, by the Secret Service.

In his remarks, Lincoln went back into the origins of the tragedy, reminding his listeners of the situation four years earlier, when the South "would make war rather than let the nation survive" and the North "would accept war rather than let it perish." That concise formulation drew polite applause. Boldly, he then launched into a forthright discussion of slavery, which was not required by the politics of the occasion but was demanded by his innate sense of ethics. A single sentence stated the case plainly: "All knew that this interest was, somehow, the cause of the war." Many gallons of ink have been spilled since then to argue otherwise, and to suggest that the war stemmed from other causes, such as "Northern aggression," or "economic interests." Lincoln knew better. But it was his peculiar talent to restate this volatile truth in a way that calmed tempers rather than inflamed them.

The most provocative part of the speech followed next. American presidents have always paid lip service to God during their inaugurals, often designing awkward and formal phrasings to honor the "Parent of the Human Race" (Washington), the "Patron of Order" (John Adams), or the "Infinite Power" (Jefferson). But here was Lincoln, almost visibly wrestling with the subject, searching to grasp the role that God had played in bringing unspeakable tragedy to a nation that Lincoln once called, memorably, his "almost chosen people." Rarely has a president confessed in such a public way his failure to understand his destiny. Even more rarely has that failure been something to celebrate, as a comforting reminder of the humility that lies at the essence of humanity.

Lincoln's broad theological musings examined not only the means but the very ends of the government he presided over. At times, Lincoln almost seemed to be scoffing, noting that both Northerners and Southerners had prayed to the same

God, and that he had answered neither's prayers fully. But he continued with the arresting thought, seemingly straight out of the Old Testament, that God might will the conflict to continue until the mathematical moment when Americans had endured exactly the same amount of suffering that they had inflicted through centuries of slavery. In a final swerve, he ended with the New Testament thought that Americans needed to return to their simplest virtues, and treat each other with gentleness.

The crowd's response must have been disappointing to Lincoln. According to newspaper accounts, they failed to respond to applause lines and broke up listlessly when the speech was over. But one group, well represented that day, began to respond strongly enough that an alert journalist with the *New York Herald* caught it. A large number of newly freed African Americans had assembled before the Capitol, eager to understand the country they were now joining for the first time as citizens. The *Times* of London reported that "at least half the multitude were colored people." Midway through the speech they began to murmur appreciatively, engaging Lincoln in the call-and-response pattern familiar to their church, and offering a steady chorus at the end of every sentence, full of "bless the Lord" and similar encouragements. How richly that single account deepens the drama of the moment!

Frederick Douglass was there that day, and wondered why there had been "a leaden stillness about the crowd," meaning the white audience. He decided that "the address sounded more like a sermon than a state paper," which was exactly right, and may explain why half the audience loved it and the other half ignored it. Afterward, he tried to attend a reception held at the White House but was barred by two guards who did not want to admit anyone of color. Finally he found his way into the house, and ultimately into the presence of Lincoln himself. The president earnestly sought his reaction, and Douglass replied, "Mr. Lincoln, that was a sacred effort."

Many would have disagreed; Simon Cameron, an early cabinet member, complained that it was "one of the most awkwardly expressed documents I have ever read." But slowly and irresistibly its greatness became evident to those who probed its ruminations. Technology helped—the next morning, at 3:00 a.m., the telegraph wires between New York and San Francisco were connected for the first time, and Californians could ponder the inaugural as clearly as those who had been in the audience a day earlier. Many generations later, its qualities are still emerging, for the speech assumes a particular relevance at those times when our tendency to self-absorption overwhelms our better angels. It is an especially powerful antidote to the virus of religious certainty that afflicts so many self-appointed prophets to this day.

More than most speeches, it presents a text that deserves to be *read,* for its literary qualities as well as its political insights. Lincoln had an unusual writing style, stuffing bits of paper into his pockets, then weaving his thoughts together in an era when cut and paste meant exactly that. On one occasion, about a week before giving the speech, he bumped into a guest in the White House and pulled out the emerging speech ("a roll of manuscripts"). Intriguingly, he said, "Lots of wisdom in that document, I suspect. It is what will be called my second inaugural, containing about six hundred words."

To be sure, it has internal rhythms, which one almost might call poetical. Consider this fragment, rearranged as if it were verse:

fondly do we hope—
fervently do we pray—
that this mighty scourge of war
may speedily pass away.

Further, there is more political substance than first meets the eye. For example, a line that seems inconsequential near the end held immense ramifications. Lincoln urged Americans "to care for him who shall have borne the battle, and for his widow, and his orphan." That inoffensive thought implied a brave political act that Lincoln had already ventured upon, securing benefits for the widows of black soldiers killed fighting for the North—a radical act because it recognized slave marriages as legal, and implied, therefore, that African Americans were entitled to all rights available to other Americans. Furthermore, this desire to provide for widows and children contained the seed of the idea that would ultimately grow into the notion that government ought to provide for those who cannot provide for themselves, culminating in the New Deal, the Great Society, and a social contract that most societies accept without complaint (though not always our own).

The last line of all promised "a lasting peace, among ourselves, and with all nations." That too was meaningful—for a number of nations in North America and Europe were frightened by the remarkable leap in military prowess that the United States had displayed in winning the war. An American reporter in Paris wrote that the French half expected "the appearance of an American fleet of ironsides in the port of Havre, or a fleet of gunboats sailing up the Seine to take Paris." It would be some time before Americans landed at Normandy, in a very different context, but Lincoln's remarks set an important precedent for the principle of disarmament.

What lasts more than anything from the Second Inaugural is a sense of its intellectual courage. Lincoln asked hard questions of his citizens and himself. Restlessly and relentlessly, he probed the moral assumptions that undergirded his government as surely as beams supported the new dome on the Capitol. Audaciously, he questioned the complacent assumption that God was steering the ship of state —a fundamental premise that had soothed Americans from John Winthrop through the Great Awakening to the choppy seas of the founding itself. In so doing, he was swimming against a very forceful tide. Despite the fact that the founders had built a wall of separation between the state and organized religion, a powerful tradition of mysticism had infused writing about America from the time of the earliest settlement—indeed, all the way back to Columbus himself, who believed that his voyages were laying the groundwork for the return of Christ. When charged with the design of the Great Seal of the United States, Jefferson and Franklin proposed the most nakedly biblical scenes imaginable. Jefferson conceived a scene with the "Children of Israel" following "a cloud by day and a pillar of fire by night." Franklin, despite a lifetime of skepticism, countered with Moses parting the Red Sea, guided by "a Pillar of Fire in the Clouds, reaching to Moses, to express that he acts by Command of the Deity." Judging by the seal that was adopted, the founders rarely doubted that a giant eyeball was watching over them.

Lincoln did not quite deny that, but he offered an important correction, by reasserting the deeply religious truth that divine will is ultimately unknowable. Americans were a remarkable people, as he knew better than most. But their achievements were astonishing enough without their tendency to claim divine sanction for them. In an apocalyptic landscape populated with Millerites, Mormons, transcendentalists, spiritualists, violent abolitionists, and vengeful Confederates, nearly all claiming to be speaking for God while disagreeing with each other, Lincoln provided a most valuable service by bringing all of these loose atoms forcibly back to earth. He was a strange messenger to render a theological judgment, for he had famously scoffed at organized religion as a young man. But his knowledge of the Bible was profound and personal, dating back to his childhood, when it was likely the only book in his house, and his private faith had deepened appreciably throughout the epic tragedies he had endured as president.

The audience may have responded indifferently to the speech, but one imagines that Lincoln knew its significance all along, dating from the rare compliment he paid to himself, in the hearing of his White House visitor, that his manuscript contained "lots of wisdom." It offered a much-needed balm for his divided people, all the more precious for the fact that they would soon be forced to lead themselves. Forty-one days later he was killed by a member of his audience. Booth may have understood Lincoln's ambition better than most of his constituents, for he stalked Lincoln's final speeches, hanging on every word. He was also in the crowd when Lincoln delivered his last speech, at the White House following Lee's surrender, when Lincoln announced quietly that he expected to let some African Americans vote. That simple act of justice enraged Booth, propelling him to the act of injustice we all know him for.

Speeches are dangerous, exposing a leader's body as well as his or her thoughts, and they become especially so when those thoughts run counter to the inherited assumptions of self-importance that accrue naturally over time with a prosperous people. But they are essential acts of communication for a form of government that depends on consensus, understanding, and growth. Lincoln's words remain imperishable, even if he was not, for their profound insight and humility will always find new life as successive governments struggle to live up to them—or, just as often, fail to. In his six minutes, he had offered a superb clarification. Americans may be capable of titanic feats of progress, but their government of the people, for the people, and by the people is exactly that—an institution designed by human beings, flawed and mortal like all of God's creatures.

Bibliography: Harold Holzer, *Lincoln at Cooper Union: The Speech That Made Abraham Lincoln President* (New York, 2004). Ronald C. White, Jr., *Lincoln's Greatest Speech: The Second Inaugural*

(New York, 2002). Garry Wills, *Lincoln at Gettysburg: The Words That Remade America* (New York, 1992). Douglas L. Wilson, *Lincoln's Sword: The Presidency and the Power of Words* (New York, 2006).

TED WIDMER

1865

Alexander Gardner publishes his *Photographic Sketch Book of the War*

"CONDITIONS OF REPOSE"

When the Civil War ended, photographer Alexander Gardner selected and ordered one hundred photographs to document the conflict for posterity, putting a page of commentary before each. His two-volume opus, *Gardner's Photographic Sketch Book of the War,* was history in a new form. Photography had been introduced to the world in 1839, but not even the most prescient of its inventors had anticipated its use to record historical events as they unfolded.

In 1855, the English photographer Roger Fenton raised expectations for the photography of war when he exhibited his Crimean War pictures in London. The exposure times the new wet-plate process required were short for their day but nonetheless too long (usually at least several seconds) to allow photographers to depict moving bodies without blurring. Although Fenton did not photograph scenes of death or destruction, he produced a compelling representation of the war by using photography's strengths to overcome its weaknesses. He discovered how the absence of action could yield a stage for the imagination, how the literalness of photography could strengthen its metaphors, and how the camera's equalizing attention could suggest war's brutal indifference. *Valley of the Shadow of Death,* a photograph singled out for praise by reviewers, exemplifies these ingenuities. Its depiction of cannonballs strewn at the base of an otherwise empty ravine enabled viewers to imagine both the war's action and its desolation. The several cannonballs that lie atop the road running through the ravine, by occupying an elevated space of human concourse, appear especially anthropomorphic. In this and many subsequent war pictures, the photographic gaze, so alert to particulars but equally insistent on mechanically reducing them all to its monochrome scale, connotes a martial state of attentiveness and emotional withdrawal. One reviewer wrote of the picture's "terrible distinctness."

When Gardner came to work for Mathew Brady, Fenton's photographs from Crimea were almost certainly fresh in his mind. In November 1855, Fenton's publisher had issued them singly and in sets, and a month later the Glasgow *Sentinel,* a paper that Gardner had once owned, praised them in a review. At the time, Gardner was living in Glasgow and beginning to practice photography. Over the years, he had worked as a jeweler, the manager of a loan company, and a publisher, agitated for social reform, and helped to establish a cooperative agricultural community in Iowa. In 1856 he left Scotland for the United States and joined Brady in New York City.

Brady had opened a daguerreotype gallery on Broadway in the 1840s and was pursuing the establishment of another in Washington, D.C. His galleries were elaborate portrait studios adorned with photographs of prominent national figures from his private archive, a portion of which he had published under the title *The Gallery of Illustrious Americans*. In addition to the prospect of running two businesses, Brady faced the challenge of his failing eyesight, which prevented him from operating a camera, and the advent of the wet-plate process, which threatened to render the daguerreotype obsolete. He hired Gardner, an experienced businessman who had mastered the new process, to help him in New York, and later made him manager of the Washington gallery.

When war broke out in April 1861, Brady and Gardner sought to capitalize on the commercial promise of war photography, and the Union government was eager to comply. High-ranking army officials, including Quartermaster General Montgomery Meigs, saw photography as a means to improve and exalt modern logistics and strategic planning, and Abraham Lincoln, who reputedly once said, "Brady and the Cooper Institute made me President," doubtless sensed a potential to glorify the Union cause. Brady, having received a pass directly from Lincoln, assembled an experienced team of photographers and sent them into the field with cumbersome equipment and wagons for darkrooms.

In November 1861, while still working for Brady, Gardner took up duty with the Secret Service and General McClellan. He and his associates made photographic copies of maps and took pictures of bridges and other militarily important sites. The commercial promise of the war still beckoned, and in the fall of 1862, Gardner and the photographer James Gibson made photographs of battlefield corpses at Antietam—images that were immediately exhibited by Brady in New York and reproduced in *Harper's Weekly*. Reviewers described the searing effect of seeing the dead rendered with such realism. By the end of 1862, Gardner had left Brady and opened his own studio in Washington, taking some of Brady's best photographers with him, including Gibson and Timothy H. O'Sullivan. Throughout the conflict both Brady and Gardner sold stereographs and album cards of war scenes, and afterward Gardner put his leather-bound *Sketch Book* on sale.

Although writers often treat the *Sketch Book* as a summation of Gardner's wartime operations, it was a distinct project. Indeed, Gardner's remark in the preface that "the collection from which these views have been selected amounts to nearly three thousand" is misleading. The albumen prints in the *Sketch Book* are contact prints from full-plate negatives, whereas the great majority of Civil War photographs by Gardner and his associates, including the pictures of the dead at Antietam, were made in a smaller, stereoscopic format. Like many photographers, Gardner used different formats to appeal to different customers. Stereographic negatives were well suited to the popular market. Thousands of Civil War views were sold as stereograph cards for viewing in middle-class parlors, and images from stereographic negatives were also produced singly as album cards or cut down to the dimensions of cartes de visite. The larger, more expensive full-plate format was better suited for sumptuous albums or exhibition displays. The *Sketch Book*, priced at $150, equal to nearly $2,000 today, was beyond the reach of all but wealthy buyers and institutions.

As an account of the war, the *Sketch Book* is an amalgam. It is part paean to the technical and logistical superiority of the Union war effort, part tourist guide-book, part nostalgic record of vernacular culture within the Union army, part moral tale of wickedness and just deserts, and part war memorial. It answered Gardner's demands as a pragmatic businessman and ardent socialist. The consistent if often ungainly prose style of the commentary draws together an eclectic set of photographs by eleven different practitioners. Throughout the book, Gardner hews to a modern emphasis on structures, systems, and routines. Portraiture of battlefield leaders and heroes, a category of war photography that was exceedingly popular and amply represented in Gardner's collection, is almost entirely absent from the *Sketch Book*.

Gardner tailored much of the book to the interests and egos of the officials responsible for the Union army's infrastructure. He featured photographs of pontoon bridges, telegraph construction, and medical facilities, and his commentary repeatedly extols the brilliance of Union engineering and administration. Meigs, who purchased a copy of the book in 1866, probably took special delight from *Wagon Park, Brandy Station,* a picture that represents scores of wagons assembled into a neat wedge spanning the image, turning the landscape into a diagram of mass efficiency. Gardner had good reason to flatter the quartermaster general and his peers. In the 1860s the federal government was a crucial patron of photography and a potential customer for important collections of field sketches and photographic negatives.

Throughout the book, Gardner, following Fenton, sought to turn the limits of war photography to his advantage. A writer for the *Times* of London described the challenge in 1862: "The photographer who follows in the wake of modern armies must be content with conditions of repose, and with the still life which remains when the fighting is over." Whereas the term "still life" aptly describes Fenton's cannonballs, "ruin" better fits the remains that captivated Gardner. His commentary treats structures damaged or abandoned during the war as if they belong to antiquity, discussing them in the manner of a tour guide or an armchair archaeologist. Viewers of the *Sketch Book* travel imaginatively through this sacred geography from site to site.

That Gardner resorted to such models should not surprise us. Many important early photo books depicted tours of archaeological sites. Maxime Du Camp's *Egypte, nubie, palestine et syrie* (1852), John Beasley Greene's *Le Nil—monuments—paysages* (1854), Auguste Salzmann's *Jérusalem* (1856), Captain Linnaeas Tripe's *Photographic Views in Madura* (1858), Francis Frith's *Egypt and Palestine* (1858–59), and Désiré Charnay's *Cités et ruines américaines* (1862–63) are among the best known examples. Moreover, tourism in the United States was increasingly popular among the wealthy, from whose ranks Gardner sought buyers. Nonetheless, Gardner's anticipation of Civil War tourism and his understanding of the role it offered photography were remarkable.

Consider the photograph with which the book opens, a picture of a hotel in Alexandria, Virginia, bearing the name MARSHALL HOUSE in large letters over the entrance. A street sign and roads that stretch back to the left and right reinforce

Breaking camp, Brandy Station, Virginia. Negative by J. Gardner, positive by A. Gardner. From *Gardner's Photographic Sketchbook of the War*, by Alexander Gardner (Washington, D.C.: Philp & Solomons, 1866), v. 2, no. 62

the theme of travel, while the location itself, Alexandria, recalls picture books of exotic archaeology. As the caption recounts, a few days after the firing on Fort Sumter, Union troops spied a Confederate flag flying over the hotel. When a Union officer, Colonel Ellsworth, brought down the flag, he was shot and killed by the proprietor, who in turn took a fatal bullet from Ellsworth's assistant. The *Sketch Book* thus introduces the war synoptically as a house divided. Having secured this clever device, Gardner adds two curious remarks: "Relic hunters soon carried away from the hotel everything moveable, including the carpets, furniture, and window shutters, and cut away the whole of the staircase and door where Ellsworth was shot. Finally Northern men took possession of the building, and fitted it up for business, so changing the interior as to be scarcely recognizable to those who visited it in 1861." These words, in addition to emphasizing the sacredness of the site, address the tourist's need to differentiate between the authentic and the inauthentic. A concern for the carting off or obliteration of historical traces pervades Gardner's commentary. Although many passages speak to a pastoral reclamation of war-torn countryside, Gardner was interested in all forms of material erasure. The archaeological tourist and the war photographer had to work with what remained, but photography enabled both to leave with a relic while keeping the site intact.

The *Sketch Book*'s second plate, *Slave Pen, Alexandria, Va.,* depicts a building bearing a sign that reads, PRICE, BIRCH & CO., DEALERS IN SLAVES. The picture and the caption establish a sharp contrast between the free traffic of hotels and the brutal confinements of the slave trade. The open windows and doors of Marshall House set off the barred windows of the slave pen, a structure that Gardner describes as "essentially a prison." Yet here, too, the viewer of the *Sketch Book* is on the road, visiting another historic site, another ruin, getting history through encounters with monuments, labels, and capsule texts. In later captions Gardner notes the excellence of local oysters, a location where "game and fish abound," and "historic fields" near Manassas that "will forever attract the tourist to this spot." The implication is not that Gardner made a guidebook instead of a history, but rather that he recognized that modernity and photography were making history inseparable from tourism.

Gardner's fondness for the vernacular culture of camp life is perhaps the book's most overlooked feature. He describes the makeshift army huts in affectionate detail, praising the resourcefulness of the Union soldiers who constructed them. His account of army evenings is rife with nostalgic phrases about glowing hearths, warm conversation, and happy memories. The remnants of these camps, he writes, "stand as mournful monuments of forgotten joys and aspirations." While it is tempting to see these passages as palliatives for social horror, the contradictions run deeper than that. Gardner purports to have found something utopian in the practical brotherhood of military life. Years earlier, in the bylaws of the farming cooperative in Iowa, he had described its purpose as the provision of "a comfortable home for [the partners] and families where they may follow a more simple useful and rational mode of life than is found practicable in the complex and competitive state of society from which they have become anxious to retire." In the fields of Virginia and Pennsylvania, Gardner claims to have encountered the "simple useful" mode of cooperative living he had long envisioned. But that mode of life was mobilized to kill and destroy.

The most famous photographs from the *Sketch Book* are among the least typical. The book contains four commonly reproduced pictures of battlefield corpses at Gettysburg, including O'Sullivan's rightly celebrated *A Harvest of Death*. In his 1863 catalog of war views, Gardner attributes all of his studio's large-format photographs from Gettysburg to O'Sullivan, but in the *Sketch Book* he attributes two to himself. Curiously, these two have become his most controversial pictures, for they depict the same dead soldier at two different sites on the battlefield. Perhaps O'Sullivan handled the photographic apparatus and Gardner conceived of moving the corpse. In any event, Gardner's commentary makes clear that the horror of these pictures is not simply that young men died violently, but that society left its dead to rot in a field.

The issue of burial is vital to the book's moral structure. A plate entitled *A Burial Party, Cold Harbor, Va.,* depicts African Americans interring the remains of Union soldiers. The picture bafflingly juxtaposes two subjects that Civil War imagery regularly suppressed—African American soldiers and body parts of the dead—and anchors that juxtaposition in a formal dialogue between the head of a soldier sitting beside a stretcher heaped with bodily remains and the nearest skull upon it. Nowhere in the caption does Gardner mention that the soldiers shown are former slaves, and one prominent scholar has argued that the import of the picture "eludes the author of the text," while another remarks, "Gardner seems to refuse the force of his own image." Such arguments may give Gardner too little credit for balancing the pressures on his enterprise. If Gardner had wished to suppress the existence of African American soldiers, he would not have included the picture, and his description of them merely as "soldiers" collecting "the remains of their comrades" can be understood as markedly progressive. Moreover, both history and context give reasons to understand the burial as more sacred act than menial labor. Handling death and the dead was far more important to nineteenth-century Americans than it is today, and Gardner, in his caption to the picture, rebukes the rebel army and those residing by the battlefield for leaving the dead exposed.

Gardner's *Sketch Book* was intended to appeal to an elite Northern audience, but beneath its flattery of Northern ingenuity and logistics lies a complex structure. The book preserves traces of the past, but emphasizes that they are only traces of traces. It chastises those who refuse to bury the dead, while leaving the dead exposed in its images. It ventures into a new form of history that uses photographs to both preserve the past and set it at a distance. Meditating on the remains of war, it construes history as a quickly receding remoteness, available as a geographic itinerary of sights, condensed into a set of pictures and capsule texts. To a large extent, this is a history we still inhabit.

Bibliography: William Frassanito, *Gettysburg: A Journey in Time* (New York, 1975). D. Mark Katz, *Witness to an Era: The Life and Photographs of Alexander Gardner* (New York, 1991). Anthony W. Lee and Elizabeth Young, *On Alexander Gardner's Photographic Sketchbook of the Civil War* (Berkeley, 2007). Timothy Sweet, *Traces of War: Poetry, Photography, and Crisis of the Union* (Baltimore, 1990). Alan Trachtenberg, *Reading American Photographs: Images as History: Mathew Brady to Walker Evans* (New York, 1989).

ROBIN KELSEY

1869, March 4

Carl Schurz is sworn in as the first German-born senator of the United States, representing Missouri

REMINISCENCES AND *LEBENSERINNERUNGEN*

"There is Carl Schurz," wrote a correspondent of the *Missouri Democrat* with scarcely hidden admiration when the "German Senator," as he was often labeled (the qualifier "Dutch" occasionally being exchanged for "German"), first entered the Capitol. From the beginning, Schurz struck a figure of dignity and authority with his graceful clothes and manners. His characteristic dark-red beard and sharply delineated eyebrows, which would prove such a boon for cartoonists, were "of the old cavalier type." The inevitable pince-nez, which during his tenure as interior secretary would earn him the epithet Four Eyes from an Indian chief, no doubt gave him an air of Old World distinction. The *Missouri Democrat* was so impressed by this senator with the striking personality, who skillfully charmed Washington society with regular musical performances at his house, that its correspondent felt compelled to express vicarious shame for the unfortunate Senate clerk who kept mispronouncing his name as "Shirtz," thus exceedingly offending his "nice German ear."

This newspaper report hints at what is already perhaps the dominant theme in the eventful life story of Carl Schurz, who remained perched between two national cultures. While he often made clever use of the German vote to further his political ambitions, he resented his opponents' apparent unwillingness to regard him as more than merely a "Teuton." Widely praised for his excellent command of the English language and his brilliant oratorical skills, Schurz nevertheless—or precisely because of this—was branded as the "accented foreigner" in American politics. The persistence of that image was apparently directly proportional to Anglo-Americans' inability to articulate his name without anglicizing it (significantly, the screenplay of the 1954 TV movie *Escape: The Story of Carl Schurz,* which narrates his legendary getaway from the Prussian army through the sewage system of Rastatt Fortress in Baden, enlists phonetic transcriptions of the most important characters and terms of address: SHURRZ, RAH-STATT, HAIR LOYT-NAHNT).

A figurehead of the Forty-Eighters, as the exiles of the failed liberal revolutions of 1848 were called, Schurz rose to become a prominent politician in Wisconsin, a state with a significant German population. In 1860, he won over his traditionally Democratic-leaning fellow ethnics for the Republican cause, thus influencing the election in Lincoln's favor. In recompense, he was appointed envoy to Spain, where he propagated the Northern cause at the court of Queen Isabella. After the Civil War, in which he served as brigadier general, he acquired a share of the St. Louis *Westliche Post,* which he used to win support from Missouri's large German community for his Senate bid. (One of his editorial assistants was the young Hungarian immigrant Joseph Pulitzer.) Skillfully playing on the German immigrants' desire for civil service reform, which was to remain his pet subject until his death in 1906, and downplaying his earlier radical proposals about black suffrage, Schurz managed to win on the Republican ticket. It was the beginning of a remarkable career in the front line of American national politics.

Schurz himself remembers his inauguration day in the final pages of his *Reminiscences:* "I was still a young man, just forty. Little more than sixteen years had elapsed since I had landed on these shores, a homeless waif saved from the wreck of a revolutionary movement in Europe . . . And here I was now, a member of the highest law-making body of the greatest of republics." Schurz's memoir is not just a revealing political document but also an interesting literary object. Like so many other immigrant narratives, the autobiography first appeared in serialized form in the press (in this case, *McClure's Magazine*), and it was eagerly consumed by the American reader. Above all, *Reminiscences of Carl Schurz* constitutes a moving record of how an immigrant mind negotiates the often conflicting forces of ethnic loyalty and American assimilation, through its revision and extension of the familiar rags-to-riches narrative.

Among the critics who applauded the book's literary qualities was the writer William Dean Howells, who had started his career with a campaign biography of Abraham Lincoln. As editor of the *Atlantic Monthly,* author of such novels as *A Modern Instance* (1882), *The Rise of Silas Lapham* (1885), and *A Hazard of New Fortunes* (1890), and advocate of American realism, Howells became a towering literary figure in the period. He was an intimate friend of Henry James as well as Mark Twain and recognized their different geniuses early on. He ushered into print, reviewed, or otherwise encouraged many writers who, like Carl Schurz, represented the regional, ethnic, and linguistic "local color" varierties of American life, among them the African Americans Charles W. Chesnutt and Paul Laurence Dunbar, the Russian Jewish immigrant Abraham Cahan, and the chronicler of New Orleans Creole life, George Washington Cable. It therefore carried some weight that Howells found Schurz's *Reminiscences* "utterly charming and touchingly beautiful."

"I was born in a castle." The opening line of the *Reminiscences* reveals the constitutive tension undergirding the narrative by positioning the hero's exceptional personality against the widespread image of America as "a country without castles." The implicit conflict with the typical bootstrap scenario immediately draws the reader into the story, while the following sentence reassuringly holds out the promise of a possible resolution: "This, however, does not mean that I am of aristocratic ancestry." As it turns out, Schurz's maternal grandfather was a tenant-farmer who occupied part of a moated castle in Liblar (now Erftstadt), a small town in the Rhineland. Schurz's father, a local schoolteacher continually plagued by money problems, was in fact "a true peasant boy" who lived with his wife's family. This financial embarrassment as well as, perhaps, some pedantic streaks were transferred onto the eldest son, Carl (or rather Karl), who even at the height of his fame in America had to resort to his Hamburg in-laws for support.

Schurz was too much of a strategist and too good a writer not to exploit the fascination engendered in American popular culture by "One Who Dwelleth by the Castled Rhine": "and so it happened that I, their first-born, came into the world on March 2, 1829, in a castle." Just a couple of pages further on, almost in counterpoint to this feudal world of vons and non-vons with its inherited standards of pride and romantic duels (a common practice among German university students at the time), the theme of exile and wandering is introduced: "Then I heard for the first time of that immeasurable country on the other side of the ocean, its great forests, its magnificent rivers and lakes—of that young republic where the people were free, without kings, without counts, without military service, and, as was believed in Liblar, without taxes."

Adroitly, Schurz entered in his memoir elements on which he had built his political credentials, such as tariff reduction. When recounting how a youthful drinking game gone wrong inspired in him "a profound loathing for drunkenness," he not only appealed to American standards of sobriety but was indirectly pressuring German Americans into accepting American liquor laws to amend the rift caused by prohibition policy among reform groups. Schurz's balancing act between German culture and American citizenship is most revealing, however, when we consider his language learning. On first crossing the channel with his mentor and friend Gottfried Kinkel, whom he had heroically rescued from Spandau Prison in Berlin, Schurz knew but two English words, "sherry" and "beefsteak," and these ostensibly sufficed for him to survive his first cold days in the British Isles. But although he spent two more years in Britain, he never felt compelled to considerably enlarge this rather limited vocabulary. French and German were enough to get around in the exile community.

Schurz's initial failure to apply himself to the study of English, so baffling in view of his later achievements in American politics and letters, did not stem merely from practical constraints. While attending a couple of Shakespeare plays in London, Schurz experienced an almost allergic reaction to the language: "The impure vowels and the many sibilants, the hissing consonants, in fact, the whole sound and cadence of the English language, fell upon my ear so unmusically, so gratingly, that I thought it a language I would never be able to learn." Although he could have significantly extended his diplomatic network in London, his "musical ear" rebelled too strongly against English sounds. Interestingly, he experienced no comparable disaffection toward French. Before his flight to England, he had spent some time in Paris, where he quickly became enamored with that city's vibrant history, visiting various sites of the French Revolution. His admiration of French society extended toward the country's language as well. "I immediately began reading the newspapers, including the advertisements, with the help of a dictionary . . . In a few days I was already able to get along in French, at least as far as everyday matters were concerned."

Contrary to France, England struck the Rhinelander as a class-based culture where his revolutionary ideals would never catch on. It was only when he decided to try his luck in America, after a "Eureka" experience on a bench in Hyde Park—

"The fatherland was closed to me. England was a foreign country, and would always remain so. Where, then? 'To America,' I said to myself"—that Schurz finally
conquered his resistance to the language.

During the first few weeks in America, life seemed in many ways similar to
that in Europe but also strange and unintelligible. In a passage mirroring the
epiphany scene in London, Schurz describes how, filled with doubts about his future prospects in his adopted country, he sat brooding in Union Square, then a
"little park" on the outskirts of New York, until "finally I roused myself to the
thought that in order to get into sympathy with the busy life I saw around me, I
must become active in it, become *of it*—and that, the sooner the better."

Schurz's language-learning method in America was similar to that which he
had applied in Paris: "I did not use an English grammar. I do not think I ever had
one in my library. I resolutely began to read—first in my daily newspaper, which
happened to be the *Philadelphia Ledger*." In a second step, Schurz took on literature. Rather than choosing American works, though, he opted for Scott, Dickens,
Macaulay, Blackstone, and finally Shakespeare. In other words, the writings that
in England had obstructed his entry into that society, now helped him to prepare
for a political career in the United States. In America Schurz could study these
works without scruples because, perhaps, he could legitimately claim them as
part of "his" culture. Not unlike those Americans of English descent who saw
British literature produced before the seventeenth century as their joint property, advocates of German culture believed that the works of Shakespeare belonged as much to them as to the English, on account of the translations by Schle-
gel and Tieck (which Schurz had "devoured with avidity" during his school days in
Cologne). Significantly, it was only when he decided, by way of an exercise, to
translate the *Letters of Junius* into German (and then translate them back into
English for comparison with the original) that Schurz finally got "a sense of the
logic and also of the music of the [English] language."

This process of translation and retranslation would become emblematic of
Schurz's American career. When campaigning for Lincoln in Illinois, he alternately delivered speeches in German and in English. Contrary to his teacher Kinkel, whose classes in rhetoric had been "both a musical and intellectual joy" and
who had given Schurz passages from Shakespeare as rhetorical models, Lincoln's
high-pitched voice at first struck him as "not musical" and the coarse Westerner's
gesticulations appeared awkward and even comical. In the course of the debates
with Douglas, however, Schurz came to appreciate Lincoln's pointed and witty
diction, as if he was finally able to translate it into his own idiom, and thus managed to open the door to the dissonant melodiousness of American life.

The unusual, perhaps unique medium of Schurz's autobiography perfectly ex-
presses the linguistic tension between the author's mother tongue and English.
Despite his original intention to compose the entire book in English, Schurz
soon realized that he could "describe things that happened in Germany, among
Germans, and under German conditions, with greater ease, freedom, and fullness
of expression if I used the German language as a medium." Thus, he conveyed in
German his pre-immigration years up to his exile in London, but switched to
English for the narration of his American career up to his inauguration as senator

from Missouri. (As he had feared, Schurz failed to complete the manuscript before his death.) The memoir thus literally enacts the journey from one culture to another, while at the same time drawing attention to the inevitable incompleteness of this transition. Through its bilingual format, which complicates its classification as part of one or the other national literary tradition, the narrative testifies to Schurz's oxymoronic existence as a German American.

Schurz's memoir was never published the way he wrote it. From the start, he probably had both a German and an American readership in mind. While still working on the manuscript, he asked a family friend (whom he explicitly acknowledged as his "coworker") to translate the German part into English in view of publishing the entire narrative in *McClure's*. Meanwhile, his daughter was charged with the preparation of the German edition, which was commissioned for publication by Georg Reimer in Berlin. As a result, we have at our disposal two monolingualized "first" editions, the American *Reminiscences* and the German *Lebenserinnerungen*. The two versions, however, are not literal translations but display considerable divergences. Thus, the German reader misses out on several encounters Schurz had with such interesting personalities as John Greenleaf Whittier, his involvement in a fugitive slave case in Wisconsin, and the unbelievable passage where he gets lost in a snowstorm while attempting to cross the frozen Mississippi on foot during a lecture tour. The reader of the English edition, on the other hand, will read nothing about Schurz's youthful fascination with knightly dramas and the popular actor Wilhelm Kunst, nor his advice to prospective immigrants regarding the possibilities and inevitable disappointments of American life.

The discrepancies between the two editions testify to the ways Schurz's extraordinary life took part in two distinct national cultures. In a remarkable scene, Kinkel's wife tries to alert her imprisoned husband to his imminent rescue by using coded language derived from her musical studies that she hopes will remain unintelligible to the Spandau censors. In the Reimer edition, the secret wordplay based on the etymological link between the German word *Fuge* (a contrapuntal musical composition) and Latin *fuga* (flight) is immediately apparent. In the *McClure's* version, by contrast, the archaic term "fuge" is used, which now exists only as a suffix (as in "refuge") and has a different spelling and pronunciation than "fugue" (derived from French usage). Here, in other words, the double entendre does not come off well, which makes one wonder whether the story of Schurz's hazardous escape plan, which was to make him a celebrity all over Europe and in America, would ever have circulated had he not composed his memoirs the way he did, consecutively in German and English.

Bibliography: Frederic Bancroft, ed., *Speeches, Correspondence, and Intimate Letters of Carl Schurz*, 6 vols. (New York, 1913). Michael Boyden, "A New Perspective on Carl Schurz's Autobiography," *Yearbook of German-American Studies* 42 (2008). Chester V. Easum, *The Americanization of Carl Schurz* (Chicago, 1929). Carl Schurz, *Lebenserinnerungen*, 3 vols. (Berlin, 1906–1912); *The Reminiscences of Carl Schurz*, 3 vols. (New York, 1907–1908). Hans L. Trefousse, *Carl Schurz: A Biography* (New York, 1998).

MICHAEL BOYDEN

1872, November 5

Susan B. Anthony and fifteen other women cast ballots in the congressional election, leading to their indictment for illegal voting

ALL MEN AND WOMEN ARE CREATED EQUAL

On her eighty-sixth birthday, at a large event held in her honor in Washington, D.C., Susan B. Anthony made the final public remarks of her long career campaigning for woman suffrage. Looking out over a crowd of admirers in the festive room, she observed:

> This is a magnificent sight before me . . . Yet I have looked on so many such audiences, all testifying to the righteousness, the justice, and the worthiness of the cause of woman suffrage. I never saw that great woman, Mary Wollstonecraft, but I have read her eloquent and unanswerable arguments on behalf of the liberty of womankind. I have met and known most of the progressive women who came after her—Lucretia Mott, the Grimké sisters, Elizabeth Cady Stanton, Lucy Stone—a long galaxy of great women . . . I wish I could name every one—but with such women consecrating their lives . . . Failure is impossible!

The crowd roared its approval. Two days later Anthony arrived home in Rochester, New York, suffering from pneumonia and lacking the energy to climb the stairs to her bedroom. Less than a month later, on March 13, 1906, she died. To her long-time friend Anna Howard Shaw, who came to say good-bye, Anthony confided: "Just think. I have been striving for over sixty years for a little bit of justice no bigger than that, and yet I must die without obtaining it . . . It seems so cruel."

By the time of her death, all of those with whom she had begun the struggle to win the franchise were gone—including her treasured friend and coconspirator Elizabeth Cady Stanton, the chief author of the 1848 Declaration of Sentiments—surrounding her with an "awful hush." It would take another fourteen years, until passage of the Nineteenth Amendment in 1920, to gain the federal guarantee of voting rights for women in the United States: after women had gotten the vote in Australia, Denmark, Finland, Norway, the Soviet Union, Canada, Germany, Great Britain, Austria, Poland, and Czechoslovakia. In photographs from this time, Anthony's frailty is evident. Bitterly disappointed with American politics, her body language expresses an almost palpable sense of isolation, of an uncompleted mission. Forgoing a home and family of her own in favor of a brutally unrelenting schedule of travel across the country giving speeches, calling meetings, nurturing organizations, attending conventions, guiding strategy sessions, writing letters, holding private consultations, and planning public events, Anthony had focused all her energy for decades on the "one & sole point of women disfranchised." Over and over, the alliances she built had been defeated.

Even in public her confidence was shaken. Not long after Stanton's death, dryly observing that she too "shall not be able to come much longer," Anthony appeared before the 1902 Senate Select Committee on Woman Suffrage in Washington, D.C., the last one standing among a group of women who had first appeared before that committee at its formation in 1882. She complained of the length of time it had taken for the American government to change the Constitution: "We have waited; we stood aside for the Negro; we waited for the millions of immigrants; now we must wait til the Hawaiians, the Filipinos and the Puerto Ricans [are] enfranchised; then no doubt the Cubans will have their turn. For all these ignorant, alien peoples educated American-born women have been compelled to stand aside and wait! How long will this injustice, this outrage continue?"

Here "woman suffrage" narrows into "American-born" woman suffrage, and that in turn is parsed so as to insult and exclude "the Negro . . . the Hawaiians, the Filipinos, . . . the Puerto Ricans" and "no doubt the Cubans." Anthony sets particular populations of "American-born women" against other peoples in such a way as to undermine the foundational ideals of woman suffrage. In the face of such diminishment, one wonders why Anthony would have declaimed a few years later, "Failure is impossible." One might just as easily conclude that her vituperative language in itself stood as evidence of defeat.

The ideas that originally stood behind woman suffrage were sweepingly large. It was the Revolutionary cohort of 1776 who had first announced a constitutive American claim to "inalienable Rights" to "life, liberty and the pursuit of happiness." There was protest from women at the time that the Declaration of Independence excluded women, slaves, and native peoples. Abigail Adams, for example, wrote her husband, John, while he was at the framers' meeting in 1776 to remind him that women's rights were critical to the broader effort against injustice: "Do not put such unlimited power in the hands of the husbands. Remember, all men would be tyrants if they could." His response was chilling: "Depend upon it, we know better than to repeal our masculine systems." And he ridiculed her: "As to your extraordinary code of laws, I cannot but laugh."

By the middle of the nineteenth century, however, members of all the excluded groups were demanding the basic human rights and resources attached to American nationhood. Wollstonecraft, in her widely read 1792 treatise *A Vindication of the Rights of Woman,* had laid out the argument that society as a whole would benefit from the education and enfranchisement of women. Scottish-born utopian socialist Frances Wright lectured across the country in the 1820s and '30s, encouraging American women to assume equal citizenship. Abolitionists Sarah and Angelina Grimké spoke out against the complicity of the church with slavery, and African American women preached powerful jeremiads, most famous among them Maria Stewart and Isabella Baumfree, aka Sojourner Truth. Abolitionist Lydia Maria Child drew attention to the need for women to reform child-rearing practices in order to produce a population capable of meeting these challenges. Emma Willard devised a "Plan for Improving Female Education" and founded a "Female Seminary" that offered an education potentially as productive as that offered to males. The interracial Philadelphia Anti-Slavery Society supported a wide range of efforts to obtain educational and economic opportunities for African Americans.

Grievances abounded over the direction in which the United States was moving in the realm of human rights. Britain had outlawed the slave trade in 1807, and France outlawed slavery in the West Indies in 1848, while the United States maintained it in a series of compromises that were growing increasingly ominous. Abolitionists were clearly headed for a showdown with the slave power, and Quaker and evangelical women were increasingly radicalized in service to this cause. The Louisiana Purchase, the Indian Removal Act, and the U.S.-Mexico War opened vast new lands to white settlement, but the consequent social violence was immense. The Cherokee "Trail of Tears," as well as similar forced migrations of the so-called Five Civilized Tribes and others, produced a shocking toll of death and cultural upheaval. The U.S. forces who occupied Mexico referred to Mexican women as "trophies of war"; both American Indian and Mexican women who came under U.S. control lost rights—especially property rights—guaranteed under their defeated legal and political systems. A broad spectrum of struggles was simultaneously taking shape on the world stage, as well. On February 1, 1848, Karl Marx published the *Communist Manifesto*. That year also saw revolutionary movements in Italy, France, the German states, the Hapsburg Empire, Poland, Romania, and Brazil, each demanding relief from rural starvation, the degradation of life and labor in urban slums, autocratic governance, and capitalist oppression. And back home, multiple forms of domestic violence were enabled by the legal principle of coverture, which placed divorce, custody, and property rights in the hands of husbands, who were also indemnified for physical "chastisement" of wives.

It is deceptive to portray the Seneca Falls Convention of 1848, the Women's Rights Convention in Rochester that followed two weeks later, and the woman suffrage movement that ensued simply as a demand for individual rights to broaden the frame of bourgeois domesticity. Rather, those who wrote, debated, and signed the Declaration of Sentiments on July 20 were attempting to address what we would now call "gender" as an instrument of exclusion, by means of which a vital portion of the population was barred from effective opposition on matters of national and international policy. To them, the human rights record of their parents' and grandparents' generations was manifestly incomplete; the Declaration of Sentiments was nothing less than a plan to redirect the United States government. "When, in the course of human events, it becomes necessary for one portion of the family of man to assume among the people of the earth a position different from that which they have hitherto occupied," the declaration begins. "We hold these truths to be self-evident: that all men and women are created equal." The Seneca Falls framers paralleled the language of the Declaration of Independence, laying out nineteen charges against the U.S. government just as the original signers of the Declaration of Independence had listed the "Facts" of their dispute with Great Britain. They began with the denial of the franchise, from which all other issues opened out.

One hundred women and men signed the document, including the African American abolitionist leader Frederick Douglass, one of the staunchest supporters of its call for the enfranchisement of women. Its signers stressed women's access to public political life because they believed that correcting the imbalance of power between men and women was a necessary first step in addressing the nation's growing social contradictions. Stanton "could not conceive of suffrage as standing by itself, as an issue unrelated to other issues," her daughter later wrote. "For her it was inseparable from the antislavery agitation, from women's demand for entry into the field of labor, into the universities and professions."

By their act of mirroring, the signers of the Declaration of Sentiments generated a critique of the Declaration of Independence that made it impossible to read the original text in the same way ever again. The Seneca Falls Convention took aim at the Founding Fathers' ambivalence toward their own "high ideals" with the weapon Homi Bhabha describes as "the displacing gaze of the disciplined . . . that liberates marginal elements and shatters the unity of man's being through which he extends his sovereignty." Bhabha argues that when those who are belittled by such documents mimic them, it undermines the "racist stereotypes, statements, jokes and myths" that are "the effects of a disavowal that denies the differences of the other." To many of its enemies in the nineteenth century, however, this conscious mirroring invited parody in return. Currier and Ives published an ostensibly amusing vision of misrule in a 1869 lithograph entitled *The Age of Brass, or the Triumph of Women's Rights,* in which a large group of women are shown campaigning for the "Celebrated Man-Tamer, Susan Sharp Tongue"; a cigar-smoking gender-bender shares the foreground with a barely dressed strumpet, and Anthony herself shakes a fist in the face of a feminized man who has apparently been bullied into holding a baby. Other antisuffrage fliers evince more overt racism: one contorts what Anthony had written in the *Official History of Suffrage*—"Look not to Greece or Rome for heroes, nor to Jerusalem or Mecca for saints, but for all the higher virtues of heroism, let us WORSHIP the black man at our feet"—with a suggestively salacious image.

After Reconstruction ended in 1877, Jim Crow legislators rewrote the constitutions of every former Confederate state, disenfranchising black men and launching an era of domestic terrorism meant to keep black people out of politics. In the 1890s, Anthony's National American Woman Suffrage Association (NAWSA) adopted a "Southern strategy" that conceded ground to the virulent white supremacy of the period. This strategy stripped suffrage of its historical reference to revolutionary social values, redefining it as the bare act of casting a ballot. Anthony was arrested along with fifteen other women for voting in the election in 1872, for which she stood trial and was famously convicted. "It was we, the people, not we, the white male citizens, nor we, the male citizens; but we, the whole people, who formed this Union," Anthony wrote in the lecture she gave concerning her criminal conviction, but she never mentioned any black women as her allies.

In response, African American women, and some white women both North and South, only grasped the baton of social justice more firmly, striving to return to the initial promise of suffrage as having not just the vote but equal access to education, health, safety, dignity, and a living wage. "Government of the people is but partially realized so long as woman has no vote," wrote Adella Hunt Logan in a 1905 article in *Colored American Magazine*. Indeed, one can almost catch black women at the turn of the century wondering whether it was even safe to give white women the vote. When in 1894 Anthony rejected a NAWSA membership application from a black women's suffrage group, Ida B. Wells-Barnett objected: "Although she may have made gains for suffrage, she had also confirmed white women in their attitude of segregation." When in 1913 the black Alpha Suffrage Club of Chicago sent Wells-Barnett to a major NAWSA protest in Washington, D.C., its organizers told her she should march at the end of the parade with other black women rather than with the Illinois delegation. Instead Wells-Barnett waited on the side of the road, and when the delegation walked by she took her place between two white marchers.

Anthony's speech was defiant, maintaining the sound of a woman's voice in the public sphere, where it was unwelcome. But the force of what we might call Anthony's third declaration, "Failure is impossible!" is diminished by her deafening silence at the height of the lynching era, which undermined the larger claims of suffrage in order to win a narrowed franchise and exposed, in Jacques Rancière's words, "the part of those who have not part." By the turn of the twentieth century the rhetoric of the mainstream suffrage movement largely reflected the dominant patriarchal ideology of American history, failing to employ the "displacing gaze" that had characterized the radical coalitions of 1848. Yet proponents of black suffrage were also listening, and responding to the silences they could fill. This militant voice that was unwilling to fail maintained a critical continuity in American political life. Anthony's political ambition may have fallen short of the mark, but surely success did lie in amplifying the impediments in her speech.

Bibliography: Homi Bhabha, "Of Mimicry and the Man: The Ambivalence of Colonial Discourse," in *The Location of Culture* (London, 1994). Mari Jo Buhle and Paul Buhle, eds., *The Concise History of Woman Suffrage: Selections from History of Woman Suffrage,* ed. Elizabeth Cady Stanton, Susan B. Anthony, Matilda Joslyn Gage, and the National American Woman Suffrage Association (Urbana, IL, 2005). Ann Gordon et al., eds., *African American Women and the Vote, 1837–1965* (Amherst, MA, 1997). Beverly Guy-Sheftall, ed., *Words Of Fire: An Anthology of African-American Feminist Thought* (New York, 1995). Margaret A. Hogan and C. James Taylor, eds., *My Dearest Friend: Letters of Abigail and John Adams* (Cambridge, MA, 2007). Judith Wellman, *The Road to Seneca Falls: Elizabeth Cady Stanton and the First Women's Rights Convention* (Urbana, IL, 2004).

LAURA WEXLER

1875

Colonel William F. "Buffalo Bill" Cody proclaims the Winchester Rifle "the boss" for "general hunting, or Indian fighting"

MANUFACTURING TECHNOLOGY

When William Cody penned those words about the Winchester Model 1873 lever-action rifle, he was already renowned as an army scout, Indian fighter, buffalo hunter, and vaudeville performer. He would soon achieve even greater fame as the founding owner of "Buffalo Bill's Wild West," a highly popular circuslike extravaganza that toured the United States and Western Europe putting on mock cowboy and Indian fights, buffalo hunts, roundups, sharp-shooting contests, bronco busting and roping demonstrations, and the like—all intended to commemorate, romanticize, and fix firmly in the public mind the role of American West and its associated frontier values of self-reliance and rugged individualism.

Cody's show not only celebrated the role of the frontier in American history, thereby anticipating Frederick Jackson Turner's famous "frontier thesis" by nearly a decade, but it also enshrined firearms and marksmanship as an integral part of American culture. Hence, his endorsement of the Model 1873 Winchester rifle came as a great boon to the Winchester Repeating Arms Company, which promptly used it in its advertising literature. Thanks to endorsements by Buffalo Bill, the sportsman-president Theodore Roosevelt, and other well-known hunters and Indian fighters, the Winchester rifle quickly achieved iconic status. Even Native Americans preferred Winchester products, as General George Armstrong Custer learned much to his regret at the Battle of the Little Bighorn in 1876. Popular artists like Frederic Remington and Charles M. Russell added to the company's repute by depicting many of their cowboy and Indian subjects armed with Winchesters. Adding to this romantic imagery, the advent of Western movies in the early twentieth century enhanced the rifle's reputation by showing cowboy heroes as well as villains armed with Winchester rifles. The capstone came in 1950 when United Artists released a film starring James Stewart titled *Winchester '73*—joining another Hollywood film about a firearm released earlier that year, Warner Brothers' *Colt .45*, starring Randolph Scott. Not surprisingly, with all the free publicity, it didn't take long for the Winchester Company to begin marketing its product as "The Gun That Won the West." Winchester also adopted a now-famous trademark depicting a horseman riding at full gallop with a Winchester rifle slung across his saddle. In Winchester's view, its rifles and the frontier of the American West were inextricably connected.

In point of fact, however, the Winchester was not the only gun to "win the West." As settlers moved across the Great Plains after the Civil War they carried a variety of weapons with them, ranging from surplus army rifles taken home by veterans of the great conflict to exquisitely made products like the Sharps long-range buffalo gun. Most popular of all was the Colt six-shooter, a handgun manufactured in Hartford, Connecticut, that saw widespread use in the West by the U.S. Army, settlers, ranchers, and their Indian adversaries. Colt's most famous pistol, the Model 1873 single-action revolver, was appropriately dubbed the Frontier Six-Shooter and, more ironically, the Peacemaker.

Quite apart from their iconic status, three things stand out about these guns that won the West. One is that they were made in the East (in New England), not the West. Second, as products of the East, they shared a common technological heritage that extended back to the early days of the republic. And third, they provide an apt illustration of how the U.S. Army contributed to America's rapid economic growth during the early national period, serving as a catalyst of technological innovation and propelling the dynamic expansion of the young republic's national market economy. Interestingly, Buffalo Bill's lifetime spanned the same decades in which the United States experienced a fundamental shift from a craft-based agrarian economy to an urban-industrial one. By the time of his death in 1917, America had become the world's leading industrial power and the old West was rapidly disappearing. How did this "great transformation" come about? Who was responsible? And what were the larger implications of the change?

From the outset, the federal government—particularly the U.S. Army—played a key role in the development of the American firearms industry. In his 1790 "Report on Manufactures," Secretary of the Treasury Alexander Hamilton suggested the idea of establishing government-owned armories. Four years later, Congress passed and President George Washington approved legislation establishing two national armories, one on the Potomac River at Harpers Ferry, Virginia (now West Virginia); the other on the Connecticut River at Springfield, Massachusetts. Neither armory distinguished itself up through the end of the War of 1812. But at that war's end a significant policy change occurred. At a meeting hosted by Eli Whitney in New Haven, Connecticut, and attended by the superintendents of the Harpers Ferry and Springfield armories, Colonel Decius Wadsworth, the army's chief of ordnance, advanced the idea of manufacturing military muskets with uniform parts. The idea was not new. It had been tried and briefly implemented in France prior to the French Revolution, then brought to America by several French-émigré military officers, who persuaded Wadsworth and his army colleagues that the so-called Uniformity System would solve all the problems that had plagued arms manufacturing prior to and during the War of 1812. Henceforth, proponents argued, all arms made for the United States would be better built, more reliable, and more easily repaired if they broke in the field.

Implementation of the new uniformity policy was a slow, incremental process worked out over a forty-year period. Doubters repeatedly stated their misgivings about the "visionary scheme," and lapses occurred. But, gradually, progress was made. In retrospect, the Uniformity System evolved through four stages. An important benchmark occurred in 1816, when Simeon North, a government arms contractor from Middletown, Connecticut, succeeded in making the lock or firing mechanism of army horsemen's pistols with uniform parts. Another important stage was reached ten years later when John H. Hall, a private contractor working at the Harpers Ferry Armory, succeeded in making 1,000 of his patented breech-loading rifles with interchangeable parts. By 1834, Hall and North reached another significant plateau when, after considerable difficulty, they successfully (and separately) made Hall rifles at Harpers Ferry and Middletown (some 400 miles apart) with parts that would interchange. The final stage took place at the Springfield National Armory in Massachusetts, where, during the early 1840s, the government's workshops were retooled with the latest gauges and machinery to produce 20,000 to 25,000 army muskets annually with fully interchangeable parts. Springfield would demonstrate its manufacturing prowess during the Civil War when, in 1864, it reached the unprecedented production level of 276,000 rifle-muskets a year. Such manufacturing capability would not be surpassed until the Ford Motor Company introduced the mass-production assembly line for making Model T Fords in Highland Park, Michigan, in 1913.

Openness and accessibility proved to be one of the earmarks of the small-arms industry as it developed and refined the methods that became known abroad by the 1850s as "the American system of manufactures." The system consisted of a novel assemblage of wood- and metalworking machines, special gauges, precision measuring methods, and rigid inspection procedures that made interchangeability a mechanical reality. Private arms contractors, most notably Simeon North and John H. Hall, invented fundamentally new machines and tools. Yet, interestingly, neither North nor Hall collected royalties on their inventions, because Colonel Wadsworth and his successors at the Ordnance Department insisted that they had to share their inventions with the national armories free of charge if they wished to remain government contractors. In effect, intellectual property became public property under the government's innovative arms-contracting system.

As a result of the Ordnance Department's share-all policy, the national armories—particularly Springfield—became clearinghouses for disseminating the new machine technology. Beginning in the 1820s, the Ordnance Department opened both armories to the public and made technical information available for free. Private arms makers and other manufacturers seeking to learn about the latest developments in metal- and woodworking invariably visited Springfield and Harpers Ferry. There they could examine the most advanced tools and machinery, make notes and sketches, and discuss common problems with the master armorer or one of his assistants. Visitors might then arrange to replicate what they needed at nearby machine shops, which likewise had access to the armories' patterns and drawings. Such easy movement of technical information from one shop to another contrasted with more closely guarded practices in Europe and helps to explain the surge in American manufacturing during the late antebellum period.

Second-generation arms-making companies like Winchester and Colt readily drew from this rich storehouse of knowledge to recruit workers and to equip their shops with the latest machinery and gauging methods. Thanks to the emergence of a machine-tool industry in and around Springfield and up and down the Connecticut Valley, manufacturing methods that coalesced at the national armories began to spread to all sorts of machine shops and factories turning out metal products. Helping to push this change were former ordnance officers—most of them West Point graduates—who left the army and assumed managerial posts with privately owned firearms businesses, foundries, and railroads. Experienced workers were equally important. Indeed, "armory practice," as it came to be called, was usually transmitted by skilled armorers who had received their early training at one of the public or private armories and then moved on to new positions as master machinists and production supervisors at other manufacturing establishments. Countless firms, large and small, followed this pattern, thereby acquiring the latest armory know-how—and more quickly and cheaply than they could by learning it all by themselves.

More often than not, those who borrowed the new technology had to adapt it to different uses, leading to further refinements and inventions. The spillovers were many. By the 1850s, armory methods could be found in factories making sewing machines, pocket watches, padlocks, railway equipment, shoes, wagons, and hand tools. After the Civil War, armory practices made their way into the manufacture of typewriters, business machines, bicycles—even automobiles. From the beginning, the key transmitters were New England machine-tool firms closely connected with the Springfield Armory.

The rise of the American system of manufactures provides a telling example of the role of the state in early American industrial development. Government instruments such as the protective tariff also played an important part, as did individual state investments in transportation enterprises like New York's Erie Canal. The opening of the Erie Canal in 1825 greatly benefited New York's economy, making New York City the commercial capital of America. Other states followed New York's lead, though none of them profited from canal building to the extent that the Empire State did.

Less well known but equally important was the General Survey Act of 1824, a piece of federal legislation that put U.S. Army engineers to work, at government expense, surveying and constructing roads, canals, and railroads throughout the country. Between 1824 and 1828, members of the Army Corps of Engineers worked on ninety-six different projects, most of which were surveys of either state or privately owned roads and canals. The army's railroad work proved particularly important, resulting in the construction of nearly fifty privately owned railroads by the early 1840s. Among them were the Baltimore and Ohio Railroad and parts of other trunk-line railroads that started in East Coast cities and pushed westward across the Appalachian Mountains into the Ohio and Mississippi River valleys, branching out as they went along. Even after the General Survey Act ended in 1840, former West Point–trained army engineers continued to build canals and railroads throughout the United States. One of the most famous was Major George Washington Whistler, West Point class of 1819 and father of artist James McNeill Whistler. After working on the construction of numerous railroads under the General Survey Act, Whistler resigned from the army in 1834, served briefly as superintendent of the Lowell Machine Shop in Lowell, Massachusetts, and went on to build the Western Railroad across the Berkshire Mountains in Massachusetts and the St. Petersburg and Moscow Railroad in Russia, at the time the longest railroad in the world.

Like Whistler, scores of former army officers resigned their commissions, entered the business world, and played leading roles in the industrialization of antebellum America. After the Civil War their Naval Academy counterparts did the same, while others went on to establish some of the earliest departments of mechanical engineering at places like Cornell, Purdue, Illinois, Michigan State, and Stanford. These schools owed their origins to yet another piece of federal legislation, the Morrill Land Grant Act of 1862, which led to the establishment of "agricultural and mechanical" colleges throughout the United States that, over the years, produced the vast majority of engineers and scientists educated in America.

All told, the government's role as a catalyst of technological innovation and economic growth played a critical role in America's rise as an industrial power. Government involvement came at the earliest stages of development, when investors were hard to find and the level of risk too high for private capital to undertake. Samuel F. B. Morse's telegraph system provides an apt case in point. When the electric telegraph was new and untried, Morse appealed to the federal government to fund the construction of the first line between Baltimore and Washington, D.C. As soon as the telegraph demonstrated its capability for transmitting information at "lightning speed," private investors flocked to invest in the new technology and the government got out of the telegraph business. This "state in/ state out" scenario has occurred over and over again in American history, and it continues to this day. It serves as a reminder that America's vaunted private-enterprise system has always had a large dose of government involvement, especially at the early stages of development. From the American system of manufactures to the Internet, government—especially the federal government—has played a key role in building the American economy.

Bibliography: Forest G. Hill, *Roads, Rails, and Waterways: The Army Engineers and Early Transportation* (Norman, OK, 1957). David A. Hounshell, *From the American System to Mass Production* (Baltimore, 1984). Herbert G. Houze, *Winchester Repeating Arms Company: Its History and Development from 1865 to 1981* (Iola, WI, 1994). Nathan Rosenberg, *Perspectives on Technology* (New York, 1976). Merritt Roe Smith, *Harpers Ferry Armory and the New Technology* (Ithaca, NY, 1977). Merritt Roe Smith, ed., *Military Enterprise and Technological Change* (Cambridge, MA, 1985).

MERRITT ROE SMITH

1876, January 6

The Nation asserts on the U.S. Centennial that the country "has not maintained its moral and social preeminence among the nations, if people rule slavery out of the problem"

MELVILLE IN THE DARK

In 1876, as the nation celebrated its centenary, a disputed election brought Rutherford B. Hayes to the presidency, prematurely ending what had been a bold attempt to solve the problem tabled a century earlier by the nation's founders when they failed to prohibit slavery and admit blacks as full citizens into the newly formed republic. Although the Civil War and the Thirteenth Amendment had finally redressed one failure, in ending slavery, constitutional guarantees of equal protection and male suffrage had not yet secured civic equality for black Americans. As described by twentieth-century novelist Ralph Ellison, the violent overthrow of Reconstruction continued the tragic refusal to acknowledge the humanity of black Americans, thus deepening the shadow that had covered the nation since its founding. Yet for Ellison, the refusal that marred the nation's political order had not defined its literature. In the work of the nation's most profound writers, Ellison insisted, "the conception of the Negro as a symbol of Man . . . was organic." Collectively, Emerson, Thoreau, Whitman, Melville, and Twain represented a heroic commitment to moral truth and a willingness to challenge, rather than ratify, the national consensus on black inferiority.

But if the shadow of the Negro, which weighed so heavily on the Spanish captain Benito Cereno in Melville's eponymous 1855 novella, could also be said to have likewise burdened Melville's consciousness throughout his career as an author, it did not lead him unequivocally to presume that bringing the Negro into the polity would end the national tragedy. In fact, when Melville contemplated both the war and the terms of Reconstruction in his 1866 collection of poems, *Battle-Pieces and Aspects of the War,* he asked, skeptically, in a poem titled "A Meditation," "Can Africa pay back this blood/Spilt on Potomac's shore?" Throughout *Battle-Pieces* Melville questions whether the means to emancipate and uphold former slaves as political equals were not themselves a threat to the founding ideals of the nation.

But well before the war Melville's fiction had often mused upon how "good" men, which is to say, white men, would fare absent the assumption of natural degradation attaching to black skin. For a figure such as Amasa Delano, the American ship's captain in "Benito Cereno," goodness equates with a form of blindness to the possibility of humanity lying behind a black face. Delano's innocent goodness depends on seeing the relation between master and servant, as played out in the relation between the Spanish captain, Benito Cereno, and the rebellious African, Babo, as natural subservience rather than coerced submission. Then in Melville's last novel, *The Confidence-Man: His Masquerade,* which was published on April Fool's Day in 1857, we encounter in the seventh chapter, titled "A Gentleman with Gold Sleeve-Buttons," a good white man—or perhaps it is more accurate to say, a white man—whose white garment is described as "something of an emblem, as it were; an involuntary emblem, let us say, that what seemed so good about him was not all outside; no, the fine covering had a still finer lining." In making this description the chapter invokes the potential difference between seeming good and being good, only to resolve it immediately in favor of a claimed correspondence between inside and outside—for this man, to appear good is to be good. Consequently, accounting for the man's appearance might serve just as well as narrating his biography to give us a view of the character within the white cloak. Accordingly, the narrative turns immediately to the apparently more superficial matter, namely that of explaining how the man comes to appear so "spotless" aboard the "soot-streaked" deck of the riverboat *Fidèle,* which provides the settings for the novel's various episodes. The answer to this conundrum is provided quite readily by a social fact, mainly the man's reliance on "a certain negro body-servant, whose hands nature had dyed black, perhaps with the same purpose that millers wear white, this negro servant's hands did most of his master's handling for him; having to do with dirt on his account, but not to his prejudices."

With characteristic ambiguousness the novel makes it difficult to read this account of the man's goodness. Not only does the presence of the servant raise the question of how good this good man really is, but the narrator's further words, which allude to Pontius Pilate, also reveal a potential tint of hypocrisy in the man's character. The narrator observes, "This gentleman, therefore, there is reason to affirm, was one who, like the Hebrew governor, knew how to keep his hands clean, and who never in his life happened to be run suddenly against by hurrying house-painter, or sweep; in a word, one whose very good luck it was to be a very good man." Goodness may be merely good fortune or perhaps merely a function of being able to absolve oneself of responsibility. Unlike *Billy Budd*'s Captain Vere, a character through whom Melville explores at greater length the problem of moral evasion associated with Pontius Pilate, the man with gold sleeve-buttons is spared the ill fortune of having to decide the fate of another good man standing afoul of the law. Melville's good man is also spared the burden of righteousness. The narrator makes sure to distinguish the man's goodness from the righteousness of a "Wilberforce"—a telling and fortunate contrast, because for the man to be an abolitionist on the order of Bishop Wilberforce, he would have to emancipate his servant and remove the buffer between his own spotlessness and the soot. If all men were righteous, none would be good.

By historical coincidence, *The Confidence-Man* was published less than a month after the Supreme Court handed down its decision in the *Dred Scott* case. Brought by Scott, who argued that he and his family were free by virtue of the fact that his master had for a time transported them into the state of Illinois where slavery had been outlawed by Congress, this case helped propel the nation to civil war by exacerbating fears that the goal of the slave power was to make slavery the law of the land. The Court held against Scott, with Chief Justice Roger B. Taney's opinion turning on whether or not Scott was a citizen of the United States with standing to sue in a court of law. In the Court's view he wasn't: "A free negro of the African race, whose ancestors were brought to this country and sold as slaves, is not a 'citizen' within the meaning of the Constitution of the United States." In coming to this conclusion Taney bypassed recent public opinion about the status of American blacks and canvassed the history of rulings and statues he claimed had shaped the understanding of the men who framed the Constitution. His intent was to show that despite the universality of the language the founders had used in claiming rights on behalf of humanity, they did not intend their words to apply to blacks, who "had for more than a century before been regarded as beings of an inferior order, and altogether unfit to associate with the white race, either in social or political relations; and so far inferior, that they had no rights which the white man was bound to respect."

Quoting from the Declaration of Independence's assertion of the self-evident truth of human equality, Taney acknowledged that the "general words above quoted would seem to embrace the whole human family, and if they were used in a similar instrument at this day would be so understood." Nonetheless, he concluded that to believe the founders had intended them in this way would be to impugn the character of those great men. Taney wrote: "For if the language, as understood in that day, would embrace [blacks], the conduct of the distinguished men who framed the Declaration of Independence would have been utterly and flagrantly inconsistent with the principles they asserted; and instead of the sympathy of mankind, to which they so confidently appealed, they would have deserved and received universal rebuke and reprobation." But, according to Taney, there was no reason for worry because "the men who framed this declaration were great men,—high in literary acquirements, high in their sense of honor, and incapable of asserting principles inconsistent with those on which they were acting." These were men who knew what they were saying, and who meant what they said. In effect, Taney's argument pitted the character and integrity of the founders against the citizenship claims put forward by blacks. To make the founders' words universal was to make the founders themselves frauds and charlatans, and to locate deceit at the heart of national character. The honor of the most esteemed of white men depended on "common consent" that blacks constituted a degraded race. Thus blacks, like the servant to the man with gold sleeve-buttons, were by nature dyed to handle the defilement of slavery on "the account" of the founders, but not to their "prejudice."

The language of sympathy and confidence that Taney employs in his legal opinion, and the correspondence between words and conduct he assumes on the part of the founders, attest to the pertinence of *The Confidence-Man* to the social concerns of the prewar moment in which the relationship between something like national words and national character were precisely what was at issue for literary and political men alike. *The Confidence-Man*'s various figures insist on proffering character as surety for their words in a text whose narrator remarks that "in real life a consistent character is a *rara avis*." If for Taney maintaining the adequacy of the founding words to the nation required that the meaning of words "as they were understood in that day" supersede the words as they are understood "at this day," novelists enjoyed no similar recourse to certainty. Although, according to Melville's narrator in *The Confidence-Man*, "The grand points of human nature are the same to-day they were a thousand years ago," individuals themselves were changeable and so, of necessity, were the words to be used in representing them— if those words were to be truthful. The changeable aspect of the many (or perhaps few) confidence men who populate Melville's last novel represented a way of confronting the potential inadequacy of character as a fictional tool—and from this inadequacy of character, perhaps the impossibility of the novel itself.

If, as in the view of John William De Forest, who in 1868 coined the term "the Great American Novel," the end of the Civil War thrust upon American writers the task of writing fictions that would encompass the whole of American society, Melville entered the postbellum period apparently highly skeptical of the novel as a technology for "infallibly discovering the heart of man." If the delineation of appearance and behavior does not necessarily tell for character, then character becomes only an occasion for words, for "prosing," as a figure in *The Confidence-Man* puts the matter when he worries that words are being received merely as words. Likewise plot, such as plot exists, devolves into merely setting the stage for mutual monologuing, while fiction gets dressed down into a pretext for representing claims about the world or how the world ought to be.

As the nation in 1876 sought to reestablish the terms of sectional reconciliation at the expense of black civil rights in what had been declared the age of the great American novel, in an age that had yet to produce any fictions deemed worthy of the title, Melville, at least formally, left the novel and the nation behind in publishing *Clarel,* a poem of almost twenty thousand lines, set largely in the Holy Land and staged as a pilgrimage in search of metaphysical certainty. The poem did little more than ensure that Melville would remain in the obscurity that had engulfed him in the late 1850s, but in some respects his abandonment of the national stage was in appearance only. For among the various personages whose words vie against one another on the pages of *Clarel* is a former Confederate soldier by the name of Ungar, who pessimistically predicts that the future of the nation will be one of tyranny:

> One demagogue can trouble much:
> How of a hundred thousand such?
> And universal suffrage lent
> To back them with brute element
> Overwhelming?

The novelist whose work, when rediscovered in the twentieth century, lent credence to the claim that the United States had evolved a classic literature equal to the promise of the nation was also one of that nation's most melancholy critics.

Bibliography: Sacvan Bercovitch, "The Problem of Ideology in American Literary History," *Critical Inquiry* 12 (1986). Ralph Ellison, "Twentieth-Century Fiction and the Mask of Humanity," in *The Collected Essays of Ralph Ellison,* ed. John Callahan (New York, 2003). Deak Nabers, "Shadows of Law: Melville, Stowe, and the Government of Liberty," *Law, Culture, and the Humanities* 3 (2007). Herman Melville, *Battle-Pieces: The Civil War Poems of Herman Melville* (Edison, NJ, 2000); *Benito Cereno,* ed. Wyn Kelly (New York, 2006); *The Confidence-Man: His Masquerade,* ed. Harrison Hayford, Hershel Parker, and G. Thomas Tanselle (Evanston, IL, 1984).

KENNETH W. WARREN

1876, March 10

Alexander Graham Bell places the first telephone call: "Mr. Watson—come here—I want to see you!"

The Art of Telephony

On March 10, 1876, in Boston, the first telephone call transits over the wire, bringing telephony into existence. As an art form (originally the inventors referred to the "art of telephony"), as tool or technology, as spiritual conduit or amorous connector, the telephone quickly grew into a phenomenon that exceeded its strictly technological delimitations. A synecdoche of technology—at once lesser and greater than itself, ever in excess of any full comprehension of its range of meaningful motion—it became the way one connects to an absent other, stays oedipalized ("call home!"), or gets fixed by a grid according to which activities are gathered, individuals become harassed, the elderly are solicited, and the government puts the screws on a surveilled citizenry. The list of its potential encroachments is long, yet the invasive potentialities and habits of telephony cannot be unambiguously scored. There are those who welcome its invasive reach and whose survival depends on the pull of the telephonic leash. Lodged somewhere among politics, poetry, and science, between memory and hallucination, the telephone, viewed through a wide lens, necessarily touches the state, terrorism, psychoanalysis, language theory, machinic structures—matters that concern life's daily inflections. Still, its concept has preceded its technical installation and the telephone, in tandem with its many peculiar manifestations, refers us to a metaphysical domain. In this respect, one may be rightly inclined to place the telephone not so much at the origin of a recurring motif or reflection but as a *response,* as that which is itself answering a call.

When does the telephone become what it is? It presupposes the existence of another telephone, somewhere, though its atotality as apparatus, its singularity, is what we think of when we say "telephone." To become what it is, it has to be pluralized, multiplied, engaged by another line, high strung and heading for a pinpointed addressee. It is organized, if invisibly, around the philosophically invested problem of the *call*—a problem that investigates, since philosophical day one, who or what places the call that rouses or devastates us, making us wonder how to answer a call, how even to receive a nearly transcendental calling. Inhabited by new modalities of being-called, the telephone in the end, to the extent that it offers an argument on contact taboos, has texted us its own brand of antiracist demands. From day one, Bell was a hard-hitting antiracist, on the side of those who had to struggle over vote and voice.

Come here—I want to see you.

Used for diverse and often poignant purposes, the telephone can offer reprieve from an impending death sentence. Connected to everyday, nascent forms of contact or disconnectedness, it also delivers, each time it rings, the threat of a verdict or final judgment. As tool or weapon, it often serves as a kind of existential GPS.

In the mid-1840s, in Edinburgh, Melville Bell advertised in the city directory as "Professor of Elocution and the Art of Speech," eventually finding success with his famous system of alphabetics known as Visible Speech, in which he reduced to a series of printed symbols the anatomical positions that the speaking organs take in uttering sounds. Visible Speech disembodies language as it homogenizes it, encoding the disconnectedness that will come to define the technology of the telephone.

This technology was created following the commission of Melville Bell, who challenged (or commanded) two siblings to build a speaking machine. During the summer of 1846, on a visit to London, Melville Bell had heard a performance of the philosophical toy the Euphonia, Professor Faber's famous "speaking machine," which was capable of making mechanical noises at the Egyptian Hall. Upon returning home, the father of Visible Speech offered his two elder boys, Melville ("Melly") and Alexander ("Aleck") a contest: they would receive a prize if they could themselves construct a speaking automaton. The boys' invention assumed a maternal turn, which proved important for the fate of telephony. According to Bell's recording, the machine squeaked and squawked a good deal, "but it made a very passable imitation of 'Ma-ma, Ma-ma!'" This instance represents but one of many inroads to Mama in the history of the invention.

As we know, Ma Bell was partially deaf. An attempt at corrective pathology, the prosthetic voice reaches out to Mother's disability. When, for instance, the boys went to church, they were obliged to memorize the text at the services and "to repeat the substance of the sermon afterward to their mother." The earliest performances, therefore, the first discursive repetitions, were designed to fit the ear of the partially deaf mother. Many of Bell's projects, from the construction of the telephone to the splitting of nipples in his later experimentation with ewes, were designed to produce supplementary body parts to enhance the maternal corpus. The telephone belongs to a repertory of phantasmata of body parts and artificial enhancement, conceptually plugging into genetic research and engineering—something that should come as no great surprise to those who, following Marshall McLuhan or Paul Virilio, maintain a theory of organ extension or amputation with regard to the installation of technological tools. The invention of the telephone, which cannot simply be ascribed to one theme or to a restricted notion of instrumentality, foreshadows the intricacies of modern disability studies to the extent that, like other positive technologies, it originates in and supplements the so-called disabled body. All technologies respond to a perceived sensory or operative default. Thus Helen Keller poignantly dedicates her autobiography to Alexander Graham Bell.

Precisely because the telephone was itself conceived as a prosthetic organ, it was from the start installed within a concept of organ transplant, implant, or genetic remodeling in a way configured admittedly in its ghostly version by the Promethean Frankenstein monster put into motion, when she began investigating the thrall of electricity, by Mary Shelley. The telephone was conceived with a kind of Frankenstein pathos, as supplementary organ to a mother's deafness—mother or wife, actually, since Aleck's bride, Mabel Bell, also suffered from a hearing impairment. In a certain light, we can ask the same question of the Frankenstein monster as we do of the telephone. After all, both inventors—Aleck Bell and Victor Frankenstein—were invested in the simulacrum that speaks and hears; both, we might add precipitously, were elaborating works of mourning, memorializing that which is missing, in a certain way trying to make grow the technological flower from an impossible gravesite. Both inventors were motivated to reanimate a corpse, to breathe life into dead body parts. The telephone is fraught with the complications and subterranean agendas that link post-Freudian readings on mourning disorders to crypt theories and a hermeneutics of monstrosity. The unmournable loss that would be coiled into telephony involves Aleck's brother. Let us splice into this part and portion of the telephone's otobiography, for the urgency of invention grew with the need to let the dead communicate through an eternal open mic night. In a crucial way, Melly never left Aleck's side, even after he perished, even after Aleck traveled to Canada and began his experiments there and in Boston; it is therefore important to recognize the technological complicity that the brothers shared.

From the start a creature of science, representation, and magic, Aleck's brother Melville was often a "substitute for their mother at the piano. Melly had extraordinary gifts for mimicry and sleight of hand, both of which supported his taste for practical jokes." But during the summer and fall of '68, after the death of his infant son, Melly turns in earnest toward spiritualism. He begins sending his skeptical father material on spiritualism, urging him to "test the phenomena." Of equal importance for the fate of communications history, Melly cuts an irreversible deal with Alexander Graham Bell. "Melly made a solemn compact that whichever of us should die first would endeavor to contact the other if it were possible to do so." The contractual terms put the survivor of the departed other on the receiving end. Aleck had to be in a state of preparedness to receive the call. The invention originates with the dead. It's not the living one but the first to die who has to make efforts to operate reliable communications. The contract designates Aleck as receiver. Melly died on May 28, 1870. The news of this death, though no surprise to Aleck, hit him hard. Even in his old age, the look on his face would impress his grandchildren with its depth of feeling when the tragedy was mentioned. "I well remember," he wrote several years later, "how often—in the stillness of the night—I have had little séances all by myself in the half-hope, half-fear of receiving some communication . . . and honestly tried my best without any success whatever." Nonetheless the structures installed by the compact would inform his somnambular persistence by putting up lines between invisible, disembodied voices.

The whole drama of unmournable loss becomes involved in the pathos of revival, reviving the one remaining son whose task it will be to recall fraternal spirits (Bell's other brother has perished as well), to make them respond to his secret conjurings so that the hookup that he draws between father's mouth and mother's ear might be granted a place of reception for the voices of lost sons.

As memorial hall of echoes and spectral womb, as untraceable point of origin and end station for the dead, the telephone, from the start, incubated poetic fields and scientific dreams. The telephone has already in this limited example of its birthmark so complex a matrix that the question of its placement as thing, object, or machine, theoretical intuition, scientific, gynecological, or objet d'art still bears upon us. It extends the "ear of the other," as Derrida would say. Philosophically powerful, the telephone destabilizes the identity of self and other, subject and thing, it abolishes the originariness of site; it undermines the authority of the Book and constantly menaces the existence of literature. It is itself unsure of its identity as object, thing, piece of equipment, perlocutionary intensity, or artwork. Seen to provide the technical basis to this day for communications technology (credited, for instance, as the inspiration for virtual reality), the telephone has produced a new relation to literature and related discursive formations: among other features of its intrusive capacities, it has disrupted modernist notions of coherence by introducing static and nonlinear sequencing into narrative hierarchies. The telephone cannot be, nor was it ever, according to its concept, properly fitted to the narrative event of truth-telling or decisive disclosure. The telephone stakes out that thing that is not to be believed. There is something to its not-thereness, dizzying and implacable at once—it indicates a place without location from which to get elsewhere, translating into electrical carriages the immateriality of air or ether waves that convey voices. Not itself a locality, it forms the topography of an artificial organ from which an elusive other speaks. The regime of displacements and cancellations within which it functions tells us that the telephone cannot, by definition, speak truth, even if it dangles there like an earwitness. Inducing epistemological doubts around utterance and speech enactments, the telephone, dialing down intensities associated with Logos or any guarantor of truth, makes it necessary to start with the absolute priority of the other to the self, and to acknowledge the constitutive impurity that obliges a self to respond to its calling.

At the risk of repetition—his risk and ours—we can say that Alexander Graham Bell could not tolerate separation. The name of the abyssal catastrophe from which the telephone was cast out, as its monument, was Melville, after whose departure Aleck launched a massively distributed sign of disavowal. The departure of the other was a point of radical resistance to which telephonic logic remains bound. Freely translating "Lazarus, arise!" *Come here—I want to see you* imposes the demand that Alexander Graham Bell inspired on all telephonics. The inscription that Bell has made on media technology as a voice-giving force suggests the private formation constituting the suffering other within. The figure of a perished brother to which Bell returns time and again is entered into the registries of telecommunications. In the particular case of unabatable grief, the primal loss gets mirrored and multiplied. Doubled by the death in infancy of his own son, Edward, half repeated by his wife and mother who were deaf to sound, the specter of a lost brother offers individual and unique articulations of such extensive suffering that for the most part it denies itself but gets reinvested in an artificial substitute. There is an opening, a wound for holding the other, for giving voice to the other's suffering and keeping close a fugitive alterity. Ever since Alexander Graham Bell and Thomas Watson shouted out to phantoms using the prompters of electric speech, telecommunications has been negotiating uncanny contracts with a subterranean history of the departed.

Bibliography: Alexander Graham Bell, *The Mechanisms of Speech* (New York, 1916). Robert V. Bruce, *Bell: Alexander Graham Bell and the Conquest of Solitude* (New York, 1973). Catherine Mackenzie, *Alexander Graham Bell: The Man Who Contracted Space* (Boston, 1928). Mary Shelley, *Frankenstein* (1818; repr. New York, 1996).

AVITAL RONELL

1878

Charles Sanders Peirce states the principle of pragmatism

"How To Make Our Ideas Clear"

When did pragmatism, that distinctively American contribution to philosophy, arrive on the philosophical scene? Even if we ignore the heroes identified by

Charles Sanders Peirce and William James as precursors of their philosophical position, thinkers such as Berkeley, Spinoza, Kant, and John Stuart Mill, there are several answers that could be given to this question. The first time the word "pragmatism" was used in public was in 1898, when James gave a lecture at Berkeley on "Philosophical Conceptions and Practical Results," a talk that was subsequently reprinted under the title "The Pragmatic Method" in 1904. The ensuing lively debate, spurred by James's lectures on pragmatism delivered in 1906 and 1907 and published the following year, meant that pragmatism was identified as one of the philosophical possibilities in terms of which other philosophers needed to position themselves.

But we could go back to 1870, when a "Metaphysical Club" was established in Cambridge, a focus for philosophical debate involving, among others, Peirce and James, Chauncey Wright, and lawyers such as Nicholas St. John Green and Oliver Wendell Holmes. Louis Menand has traced the importance of these meetings for the intellectual life of the country and their impact on legal thinking. The experience of the Civil War created a kind of moral crisis among New England intellectuals, making them suspicious of abstract principles and leading them to question how moral views can be reflected in our practices, a concern with a strong pragmatist flavor. Whether the word "pragmatism" was ever used in meetings of the Metaphysical Club is unknown, but they had implications for legal thinking that would later be called "realism," and we know from Peirce's manuscripts from the early 1870s that the approach to logic and the theory of knowledge that he took from those debates provided the core of his own subsequent pragmatist views. In particular, Peirce acknowledged the importance of Green's contributions to the formulation of the perspectives most central to pragmatism.

And another answer we might give is 1878, when Peirce published a paper in *Popular Science Monthly* under the enticing title "How to Make Our Ideas Clear." The second in his series of six "Illustrations of the Logic of Science"—the first was another classic essay, "The Fixation of Belief"—this essay defended what Peirce was later to call the "pragmatist maxim." It had little immediate impact. When James delivered his lectures on pragmatism in 1906 and 1907, he told his listeners that he was working through "the principle of Peirce, the principle of Pragmatism," and referred to the 1878 paper that, he said, "lay unnoticed by anyone for twenty years until I publicized it before Professor Howison's philosophical union at the University of California." Indeed, Peirce himself had soon questioned whether his principle could be defended and did not return to pragmatism until after 1900. In spite of this, James was not the only pragmatist to identify "How to Make Our Ideas Clear" as the classic statement of the position. When John Dewey wrote "The Development of American Pragmatism," he began with Peirce's paper, and C. I. Lewis established his pragmatist credentials by citing it in his *Mind and the World Order* in 1929. How far these thinkers were directly influenced by the details of Peirce's paper may be unclear, but that did not prevent its having this sort of talismanic character: it is universally accepted as the classic statement of pragmatism.

The explanation for this may lie in the irony that, in spite of its title, it contains many unclarities. Peirce's principle or maxim is not presented with the kind of clarity that he prized in philosophy and that he intended the use of the principle to provide. Its fertility may depend upon the fact that different pragmatists could refine and develop it in different ways. As is well known, Peirce rarely approved of the ways in which other philosophers (including James) formulated and used "Peirce's principle," and much of his philosophical energy in the years after 1903 was devoted to making it clear and defending it in ways that would reveal what was distinctive (and superior) about his own version of pragmatism (which he began to call "pragmaticism" after 1905, using a word that he hoped would be "safe from kidnappers"). Had he made it clear to begin with, his 1878 paper might not have had the lasting impact that it did.

The original formulation is: "Consider what effects, which might conceivably have practical bearings, we conceive the object of our conception to have. Then our conception of those effects is the whole of our conception of the object." As well as being complex and inelegant, this says nothing about what is meant by the effects of an object, and it also says little about what it means for an effect to have "practical bearings." Peirce acknowledged this and when, after 1900, he tried to find a proof of the correctness of the maxim, he announced that we would be fully clear about its content only when the proof had been constructed. Sometimes he called his position a "laboratory philosophy": we can be clear about the meaning of a concept only when we know what we would have to do in order to discover "experimentally" whether it applied to something. From the beginning he used a common pragmatist idea: beliefs are habits of action, and we clarify beliefs by trying to describe the habits of action they involve. A proposition is meaningful only if accepting it could make a difference to what it was rational for us to do; and it could make such a difference only if the truth of the proposition would make a difference in what experiences we should expect if we act upon it. The truth of the proposition thus has "practical" effects. And many concepts and propositions that appear to be important and intelligible resist pragmatist clarification. For example, Peirce argues that the doctrine of transubstantiation cannot be understood when taken seriously: if the wafer has none of the observable characteristics of flesh and has all the characteristics of bread, then it makes no sense to believe that it is the flesh of Christ.

The maxim came most into its own, and provoked most controversy, when it was used to clarify such concepts as truth and reality, the applications that were most important for the series of papers to which "How to Make Our Ideas Clear" belonged. When Peirce asks what it means ("pragmatically speaking") to believe that something is true, he answers that the practical consequence of its being true, for example, that water expands on freezing, is that anyone who inquires into the matter is "fated" or "destined" to reach a stable belief that this is so. Someone could fail to reach this conclusion only if they lacked relevant evidence or made mistakes in their reasoning. The practical consequences of truth are expressed through a general law or pattern in the progress of inquiry. Peirce's work on logic attempted to explain how scientific inquiry can lead to this sort of convergence in opinion.

James's application of the pragmatist maxim to truth results in something much less systematic. True propositions are ones that it is expedient to believe ("expedient in any way at all"); they "put us into a satisfactory relation to our experience." Religious beliefs can be true if they have "a value for concrete life," and this can occur because the idea of God possesses a majesty that can "yield religious comfort to a most respectable class of minds." James appears to allow for a plurality of kinds of truth because there are different ways in which beliefs can have good consequences. Peirce clarifies truth in a search for rules that enable us to use the method of science to identify laws that govern our experiences, and the practical consequences he appeals to reflect such law-governed patterns; James, by contrast, recognizes that our beliefs are instruments that can serve a variety of purposes, and he appears to interpret "practical consequences" more liberally.

It is a consequence of this that, unlike Peirce, who treats the pragmatist maxim as a rule whose use will enable us to apply the method of science more effectively, James treats it as a metaphysical rule whose application will resolve apparently irresoluble metaphysical debates by exposing ambiguities or by showing that concepts and ideas are empty. And where Peirce hopes to demonstrate that the maxim (properly formulated) is a provable logical principle, James points to the benefits of its applications and proposes that we put it into practice more generally in the hope that its merits will be borne out in practice. The formulation that the maxim of pragmatism received in 1878 can be understood in either of these ways.

The most immediate philosophical upshot of Peirce's paper was through its effects on a philosopher who, at that time, saw himself as an enemy of pragmatism, the idealist Josiah Royce. Soon after Peirce's paper appeared, Royce published a book called *The Religious Aspect of Philosophy,* in which he argued that all human thought and reasoning should be seen as a fragment of the activity of the absolute mind. This was required, he argued, in order to make sense of the possibility of false belief. At one point, he examined an account of truth that he attributed to "Thrasymachus," and he used this to show how difficult it was to make sense of the possibility of our having erroneous opinions. This account of truth was the one that Peirce had defended in "How to Make Our Ideas Clear." Peirce recognized this, and, in his 1884 response to Royce, he developed ideas about signs that were required for the project of the 1878 paper and that forged some important concepts for the developments of his theory of signs, his "semeiotic." By the early twentieth century, the development of Royce's thought permitted Peirce to identify him as the pragmatist whose views were closest to his own. James would not have recognized the same sort of harmony between his own pragmatism and the position that Royce eventually arrived at.

The title of Peirce's paper self-consciously indicates that Peirce saw it as marking a significant step forward in logic. The logic texts that would have been familiar to Peirce's contemporaries spoke of the importance of possessing "clear" and "distinct" ideas, using a vocabulary that was taken from Descartes, Leibniz, and others. In Peirce's work, a concept is clear when we can apply it, perhaps unreflectively, to things that we encounter: we use the concept in ways that distinguish it from other concepts. For many purposes, we need an explicit formulation of the contents of concepts that we habitually use, and the "second grade of clarity" involves doing this by providing a formal definition of the concept, showing its relations to other concepts. Peirce's paper argues that this is not enough. When we seek reflective explicit clarity about a concept or hypothesis, we need something that shows us just how it is to be used in practice, something that tells us how to establish when the concept applies to something, and what follows for practice when it does. The verbal definition is useful to us only if we are already clear about the concepts that are used in the definition. The pragmatist maxim is supposed to show us how to achieve fully explicit clarity about the roles of concepts in responding to experience and planning our actions. As Peirce expressed it in his semeiotic vocabulary, it presents us with the "ultimate logical interpretant" of the concepts or hypotheses that we wish to understand.

Many readers have interpreted Peirce's pragmatist maxim as similar to the verification principle of the logical positivists, defending a scientistic viewpoint that contrasts sharply with, for example, the romanticist and idealist tendencies found in the work of transcendentalists like Emerson or in those influenced by Hegel and German idealism. When one reads further into Peirce's writings, it emerges that, although he had doubts about transcendentalism, he was no crude positivist. Logic and the special sciences, he insisted, depend upon aesthetics and ethics; his system of philosophy contained an evolutionary cosmology, a picture of the universe as becoming steadily more law-governed and rational through time. The contrasting philosophical tendencies that governed his thought are clear from an autobiographical comment passage in "The Law of the Mind," a paper from 1892 that defended "a Schelling-fashioned idealism."

> I may mention, for the benefit of those who are curious in studying mental biographies, that I was born and reared in the neighbourhood of Concord—I mean in Cambridge—at the time when Emerson, Hedge, and their friends were disseminating the ideas that they had caught from Schelling, and Schelling from Plotinus, from Boehm, or from God knows what minds stricken with the monstrous mysticism of the East. But the atmosphere of Cambridge held many an antiseptic against Concord transcendentalism; and I am not conscious of having contracted any of that virus. Nevertheless, it is probable that some cultured bacilli, some benignant form of the disease was implanted in my soul, unawares, and that now, after long incubation, it comes to the surface, modified by mathematical conceptions and by training in physical investigations.

Bibliography: Robert Brandom, "When Philosophy Paints Its Blue on Gray: Irony and the Pragmatist," *European Journal of Philosophy* (2001): 1–28. Christopher Hookway, "The Pragmatist Principle: Peirce's Formulations and Examples," *Midwest Studies in Philosophy* (2004): 119–136. Louis Menand, *The Metaphysical Club: A Story of Ideas in America* (New York, 2001). Charles S. Peirce, *The Essential Peirce,* 2 vols., ed. Nathan Houser, Christian Kloesel, and the Peirce Edition Project (Bloomington, IN, 1992 and 1998). Cornelius de Waal, *On Pragmatism* (Belmont, CA, 2005).

CHRISTOPHER HOOKWAY

1879

John Muir makes his first trip to Alaska

"The Spirit of These Rocks and Water"

John Muir lived a life of physical adventure equaled in intensity only by his passion for the beauties of nature. *"Contact! Contact! Who* are we? *where* are we?" wrote Henry David Thoreau in recounting his 1846 climb of Maine's Mount Katahdin. While Thoreau, whose transcendental vision of nature served as one of Muir's own sources of inspiration, responded with trepidation and confusion to the heights of Katahdin, Muir sought to move closer to such wild edges. This impulse to capture the meaning of human experience in relation to the larger physical universe is also one of the abiding concerns of American literature, especially the genre described as nature writing or environmental literature.

Born in Scotland in 1838, Muir immigrated to the United States with his family in 1849. He spent his adolescence on the family farm in Wisconsin, where he resisted the fundamentalist preachings of his father but absorbed the rhythms of biblical language and developed an unusual mechanical aptitude. He invented clocks and thermometers and a study desk that shuffled book after book for allotted periods of time, which won him attention at the 1860 Wisconsin State Fair and a scholarship to the University of Wisconsin. He arrived at the university the following year, just as the nation was entering the Civil War. Muir seemed strangely unaffected by the national emergency. In a letter home, he mentioned the war-time campus turmoil, but noted that "the thrushes in that fine grove don't seem to care . . . I always keep my window open so I can hear them fine."

It would be easy to describe Muir as indifferent and naive, a rural bumpkin not sophisticated enough to appreciate the social urgency of slavery and secession. Another interpretation would emphasize his attention to matters of a different order—not otherworldliness, but worldliness in a most literal sense. After Muir left the University of Wisconsin to study instead at "the University of the Wilderness," one might have expected he would not set foot in a city again, but the need to earn money led him to a carriage-factory job in Indianapolis. Nearly blinded when a steel file pierced one eye and caused sympathetic blindness in the other, Muir vowed, should his eyesight be restored, never to do such work again and to devote his life to savoring nature. Upon regaining his sight, he embarked on a "thousand-mile walk" to the Gulf of Mexico. His plan was to continue on from Florida to South America, where he was eager to see the Amazonian rain forests, but a bout of malaria steered him to California instead. Upon his arrival in San Francisco in 1868, Muir famously asked a bystander to tell him the quickest way to the mountains, and he made his way to Yosemite Valley.

Muir was a reluctant writer. He kept lyrical and detailed journals, beginning on his long walk from Indiana to Florida in 1867, and many of his important adventures thereafter were initially recorded in journals and letters. For his first published book, *The Mountains of California* (1894), he crafted those notes into sixteen literary essays. But many of his important books, from *My First Summer* to *A Thousand-Mile Walk to the Gulf,* consist of raw or lightly reworked private writings. The fact that Muir resisted the writing process, complained about the inadequacy of words to describe his wild adventures and observations, and tended to publish books and essays that amounted to shined-up versions of informal writings is more than incidental. It reflects a larger impulse in American letters to achieve a kind of raw authenticity, a minimally mediated rendering of direct experience, as is evident in the work of many subsequent American authors, including William Carlos Williams, Jack Kerouac, and their followers. Muir himself wrote in an 1872 journal entry: "I have a low opinion of books; they are but piles of stones set up to show coming travelers where other minds have been . . . One day's exposure to mountains is better than cartloads of books."

Yet Muir also wrote and rewrote multiple versions of some of his best-known wilderness narratives, just as his fundamental drive to live on the edge of experience spurred him to Alaska again and again, five different times during his life, the wild mountains of California not quite satisfying his desire for risky adventure. *Travels in Alaska,* the manuscript Muir was working on at the time of his death from pneumonia in December 1914, emerged from the journals of those trips. Muir's complex writing process can be observed by tracing the many versions of one of his most famous stories, first described in a midnight journal entry in 1871. While positioned at the edge of Yosemite Falls to observe the moonlight in the waterfall's spray, he crept out on a six-inch ledge, into the pelting water, curious to see the moonlight from a point of literal immersion in wild nature. He wrote in his journal,

> When the moonbeams again slanted past the ever-changing edge of the torrent, I took courage to make a dash for freedom and escaped, made a fire and partially warmed my benumbed limbs, then ran down home to my cabin, reached it sometime towards morning, changed my clothing, got an hour or two of sleep, and awoke sane and comfortable, some of the earthiness washed out of me and Yosemite virtue washed in, better, not worse, for my wild bath in lunar bows, spent comet-tails, ice, drizzle, and moonshine.

Later, when he recast this giddy narrative in a letter for the benefit of his friend and de facto literary agent, Jeanne Carr, he added a layer of religious ecstasy and emphasized the physical hardship of the adventure:

> As I was gazing down past the thin edge of the fall and away beneath the column to the brow of the rock, some heavy splashes of water struck me, driven hard against the wall. Suddenly I was darkened, down came a section of the outside tissue composed of spent comets. I crouched low, holding my breath, and anchored to some angular flakes of rock, took my baptism with moderately good faith . . .
>
> How little do we know of ourselves, of our profoundest attractions and repul-

sions, of our spiritual affinities! How interesting does man become considered in his relations to the spirit of this rock and water!

Catering to his reader's presumed interest in the spiritual dimension of his outdoor experience, Muir claims to have been uplifted by this Yosemite baptism and the physical connectedness to water, rock, and moonlight.

Some forty years later, when he again rewrote this narrative for inclusion in *The Yosemite* (1912), his guidebook and political tract in defense of preserving the Hetch Hetchy Valley and other areas near the national park, he deemphasized the spiritual aspect, highlighting the idea of risky physical experience as an opportunity for realizing one's place in the universe. In this version, the adventurer's mortal danger is explicitly contrasted with images of domestic comfort, to ironic effect:

> Instinctively dropping on my knees, I gripped an angle of rock, curled up like a young fern frond with my face pressed against my breast, and in this attitude submitted as best I could to my thundering bath. The heavier masses seemed to strike like cobblestones, and there was a confused noise of many waters about my ears — hissing, gurgling, clashing sounds that were not heard as music. The situation was quickly realized. How fast one's thoughts burn in such times of stress!

Here the earlier image of a transformative spiritual immersion is replaced with repeated references to the icy, cacophonous "bath" of mountain water.

It is important to remember that what the narrator narrowly escaped was a jeopardy of his own making, having perched himself five hundred feet above the valley floor on a narrow ledge beneath pelting water. The very edge — the *end* — of his own life is thrillingly palpable. It would be easy to trivialize this sort of writing as cheap, safe entertainment for armchair adventurers. But there is something deeper going on here, a tendency to seek out encounters with extreme otherness, discomfort, and disorientation that arises frequently in American environmental literature, as if such encounters somehow clarify and give meaning to human life.

Muir traveled to Alaska for the first time in May 1879 aboard the steamer *Dakota,* eager not only to study the glacial shaping of mountains but also to engage with the purifying, life-testing qualities of the wilderness. The Alaska purchase had been arranged by Secretary of State William H. Seward scarcely a decade earlier, in 1867; the region achieved territorial status in 1912 and became a state in 1959. The *Dakota* traveled through the Alexander Archipelago to Fort Wrangell, and as recalled in *Travels in Alaska,* no sooner did Muir and his missionary companions arrive at the village than Muir "determined to get to the heart" of "the fine wild country." While the missionaries stayed in the village to enlighten the local Indians, Muir wandered through the nearby forests, collecting huckleberries and longing for wilder country, taller mountains. He soon got his wish when the party traveled to the old Hudson's Bay trading post at Glenora, near the Stickeen (Stikine) Glacier. Muir and one of the missionaries, Mr. Young, set out to climb to the high point in the area, "a walk, coming and going, of fourteen or sixteen miles, and a climb through brush and boulders of seven thousand feet." The two approached the summit just as darkness fell, and Muir "was startled by a scream for help, and hurrying back, found the missionary face downward, his arms out-stretched, clutching little crumbling knobs on the brink of a gully that plunges down a thousand feet or more." He perched himself below Mr. Young, who had dislocated both arms, and gradually helped him off the mountain by starlight. The wilderness novice, Muir implies in this story, must be prepared to risk everything: it is easy for readers to imagine themselves dangling over a precipice, just like Mr. Young.

Later American environmental writers, in the tradition of Muir, have sought a language to match the richness and intensity of their experience—a language, as each is intensely aware, that comes closest to raw experience when it brings together the energy of informal writing and the writerly calculations that occur during revision. Echoing Muir's quest for direct engagement with nature and the overcoming of modern solipsism and ennui through the undiluted adrenaline charge of risking one's life, James Dickey's 1970 novel *Deliverance* is a story of desperate survival on a wild river. However excruciating the characters' experiences on their river journey, Dickey reminds readers, the slated damming of the river will have an even more profoundly devastating effect by cutting off the opportunity for such rehumanizing contact with life-and-death reality.

There are analogues to Muir's spiritualizing of nature as well: for instance, Robinson Jeffers's communing, in 1936, with a rock wall in Ventana Creek Canyon east of California's Big Sur, where he spent a night by the light of a flickering fire, watching his college-age son and his son's friend as they slept and gazing at the rock face. By the end of his poetic meditation in "Oh, Lovely Rock," the rock itself becomes animate, even childlike, inspiring Jeffers to write that he "felt its intense reality with love and wonder, this lonely rock." Three decades later, fellow Californian Gary Snyder tested the mind's capacity to perceive the reality of rock and water in his poem "Piute Creek." Alison Hawthorne Deming describes the life-enriching wanderlust that draws her to the edges of the civilized world and even over them: in *Writing the Sacred into the Real* (2001), she tells the story of a hiking companion on a knife-edged Hawaiian mountain trail who suddenly toppled headfirst over a cliff, only to be pulled back to safety by the fast-acting Deming, whose physical rescue mirrors the activist purpose of her literary art. The objective is to be fully present in this life.

There are also analogues to Muir's attraction to extremes. In *Arctic Dreams* (1986), author Barry Lopez contemplates the mystery and beauty of Arctic species and cultures, confirming his existence on a fragile planet. *Wild to the Heart* (1987) and many other works by Montana writer Rick Bass sound the familiar note of the quest to shed domesticity and reach toward ever wilder places and more authentic language. The tonal complexities of Edward Abbey's *Desert Solitaire* (1968) and the lyrical heights of Terry Tempest Williams's *Refuge* (1991) and *Desert Quartet* (1995) similarly demonstrate the expressive extremes in environmental literature. Annie Dillard, for her part, disputes the notion that such shocking and life-enriching encounters must occur in the West, in the mountains, or anywhere beyond the ordinary neighborhood; when she stares wildness in the face in her 1982 essay "Living Like Weasels," she's describing an experience that has occurred in a Virginia suburb.

The sensibilities of all these environmental visionaries and raconteurs reverberate in the private exultations of Christopher McCandless, in the story retold and revised in three different published versions by literary journalist Jon Krakauer. McCandless graduated from college in 1990 and, as Krakauer puts it, "dropped out of sight," impatient to reach Alaska, the place many Americans take to be the ultimate home of more-than-human reality. The story of McCandless, whose adventure ended with his lonely death in an abandoned school bus on the flanks of Denali in the Alaska Range, vividly echoes both the ecstatic yearning and the social misgivings of John Muir. Krakauer is aware of the parallel: chapters fourteen and fifteen of *Into the Wild* are both titled "The Stikine Ice Cap," recalling the location of Muir's 1879 adventure. Krakauer creates an emotional palimpsest, laying the story of his own youthful, solo climb of the perilous Devils Thumb—a death-defying feat that could easily have resulted in his disappearance without a trace—over the story of McCandless's fatal trek. Krakauer asserts that he was himself "stirred by the dark mystery of mortality" but insists, "I wasn't suicidal." He projects this same state of mind, as well as an idealistic devotion to knowing the mortal essence of life and experiencing the exquisite reality of nature, onto the subject of his biography. Though apparently alone at the time of his death, Christopher McCandless was actually accompanied, in spirit, by Muir, Krakauer, and many other Americans, writers and nonwriters, who have sought to reach ever further into the wild possibilities of the world.

Bibliography: Robinson Jeffers, "Oh, Lovely Rock" (1937), in *The Wild God of the World: An Anthology of Robinson Jeffers,* ed. Albert Gelpi (Stanford, CA, 2003). Jon Krakauer, *Into the Wild* (1996; New York, 2007). John Muir, *John of the Mountains: The Unpublished Journals of John Muir,* ed. Linnie Marsh Wolfe (1938; Madison, WI, 1979); *The Mountains of California* (1894; New York, 1985); *Travels in Alaska* (1915; Boston, 1979). Scott Slovic, *Seeking Awareness in American Nature Writing: Henry Thoreau, Edward Abbey, Annie Dillard, Wendell Berry, Barry Lopez* (Salt Lake City, 1992). Henry David Thoreau, *The Maine Woods* (1864; Princeton, 2004).

SCOTT SLOVIC

1881, January 24

"I should like to see a country in a state of revolution"

PORTRAIT OF A LADY

From London, where he resided, Henry James thus commented on the recent turmoil in Ireland, his grandfather's land of origin, writing to Thomas Sergeant Perry, a longtime American friend. His "big novel," *Portrait of a Lady* (1881), was then running in installments both in the English *Macmillan's Magazine* and in the

American *Atlantic Monthly*. Perry might have been a reader of the December issue of the latter magazine, where he would have found James's comment echoed by Isabel Archer, a young American woman from Albany (where James's immigrant grandfather had settled his family and risen in status), who is enjoying her first visit to Gardencourt, an old and gracious English country residence. "I should delight in seeing a revolution," Isabel remarks, much to the amusement of her uncle and host Mr. Touchett, an American from Vermont and a successful banker in England. This young lady, curious as she is to witness a revolution, also declares that she is both a liberal and a conservative, and that finally — in a revolution "well begun" — she would definitely lean toward the conservative side, the more "picturesque" of the two. As Gustave Flaubert with his Emma Bovary, Henry James could have said, "Isabel, c'est moi," not only because he was a master at drawing female psychology, but because the weight of the unresolved opposition between old and new orders looms large in his fiction. His divided loyalties to new democratic America and to old aristocratic Europe made of him an uneasy conservative with the unusual recurring wish for enlightening revolutions. Images not of the American but of the French Revolution haunt Henry James's fiction, from his early tale "Gabrielle de Bergerac" (1869) to his political novel *The Princess Casamassima* (1886), and especially in his twentieth-century major phase — *The Wings of the Dove* (1902), *The Ambassadors* (1903), *The Golden Bowl* (1904), *The American Scene* (1907), and the prefaces to the New York Edition of his works (1907–1909). These revolutionary images often return in surprising contexts: in the New York houses marked for extinction; the salons of the Waldorf-Astoria; accompanying his light *ficelles* (minor but interesting characters) in the preface to *Portrait of a Lady;* in stressing the misery of the conventional in modern suburban lives; or in ominously pointing to a destiny of death, with the revolutionary "head on a pike" dooming the heroine of *The Wings of the Dove.*

In 1881, James had been absent six years from his home country, had traveled extensively in Europe, and had elected London as his residence, preferring it to Paris, where nonetheless he had enjoyed the advantage of the literary society of Gustave Flaubert, Guy de Maupassant, Émile Zola, and Ivan Turgenev, among others. It was in Paris that he set the action of a novel *The American* (1877), to which *Portrait of a Lady* was to be a sequel: "My novel," he wrote William Dean Howells on October 24, 1876, "is to be an *Americana* — the adventures in Europe of a female Newman, who of course equally triumphs over the insolent foreigner." Indeed the rich American naïf with the resonant name of Christopher Newman, who, wishing to marry into the French aristocracy in order to better himself, is exposed to the moral horrors of nobility, had in the earlier novel shown his democratic superiority by renouncing revenge on the murderous and scheming family of his aristocratic bride-to-be. Similarly, Isabel Archer's story is driven by the contrast between a high claim to morality and the illusion of finding it where the "art of life" is most refined, in European high culture and society.

Both claim and illusion reflect, in the Jamesian world, a native American trait, the result of a culture embedded in a deep religious heritage, whose moral righteousness stands on the unbounded potential for the individual to "do good." The Emersonian magic of self-reliance and of progressive freedom of action is, however, tested abroad by James's young Americans: in the years of the ever-increasing migration toward the United States, of those poor "huddled masses" saluted by Emma Lazarus in 1886, Henry James revived the novel of manners by transporting American elites to Europe, following their adventures there in palatial abodes, within a "web of relations" that characteristically included recent and longtime expatriate Americans and European would-be or true aristocrats, but no postrevolutionary, European bourgeois, industrialist or banker. The interest, as James would call it, lies in a fictitious symmetry between natural aristocracy and aristocracy by descent, between America as a culture of values and Europe as a culture of forms. But can there be form without value, or value without form? The French Revolution, wrote Thomas Sergeant Perry in *The Evolution of the Snob* (1887), broke the unity between value and form, and nobility was replaced by a mere vogue for aristocratic ghosts still haunting the present of American millionaires. Because "*le monde s'Americanise*" (the world is Americanizing), Perry calls for a reconciliation between "worldly success" and "admiration for the dignity of life."

   "My title would (probably) be 'the portrait of a lady,'" James wrote to Howells in August 1879: after his first international success, "Daisy Miller" (1878)—which consecrated the appearance of a new type, the innocent, freedom-loving "American girl"—"dignity of life" appears to stand foremost in the projected title. Daisy Miller had died of malaria in Rome, a budding youth romantically swept away by European evil air, and by her inability to distinguish between true and fake aristocrat; Isabel Archer is to turn the cards around and show how individual value, the dignity of life, or what may appear a fetishism for it, triumphs over evil external circumstances, even if to the detriment of one's own pursuit of happiness. James's portrait of this lady is a dynamic study of the transition from a self-reliant, freedom-loving girl, flawed by excessive imagination and self-esteem, to a lady who has learned the value of acquiring a conscience, and, as a consequence, pragmatically strives to identify a dignified position for herself in a world that has made her, not without her own complicity, the victim of a base plot. Isabel Archer is James's first fully developed exercise in narrative psychology, "a Titianesque effort," he called it in "The Art of Fiction" (1884). Psychology, he had written as early as 1865, "is the observation of the moral and intellectual character . . . the scrutiny, in fiction, of motive generally" setting the guideline for his work, but he was also positioning himself polemically against the French school of realists, such as Flaubert, or naturalists such as Zola. He haughtily dispatched Flaubert's *Madame Bovary* as a "two-penny lady," and in 1880, reviewing *Nana,* complained about the omnipresence in Zola's novel of "the figure of the brutal *fille,* without a conscience or a soul, with nothing but devouring appetites and impudences." By contrast, his own young lady's "moral and intellectual character" was to prove itself exactly against others' "devouring appetites and impudences," concealed in the character of two villains, Gilbert Osmond, the man Isabel marries, and

Madame Merle, the adulterous woman who cunningly brokers the marriage, the bridegroom's former lover and the mother of his adolescent daughter, Pansy.

It is a distinctive trait in James's fiction that the analysis of moral and intellectual character is brought about not by confronting small crimes and misdemeanors but by hidden scandalous events, as if the novel of character, or of psychology, could be developed only through a hide-and-seek game within an obscure, even sensational, plot. This may suggest a cultural affinity between the American writer and his quasi contemporary Sigmund Freud, yet James's idea of moral order, of a conscious relation between self and world, does not confront hidden motivations and relies instead on what he called reticence. At a time when social evolutionism was in vogue, he believed in an innate, natural superiority of certain individuals, who happen to be Americans. These types, from Christopher Newman to Isabel Archer, or Maggie Verver in his late novel *The Golden Bowl* (1904), resist corruption by way of coming circuitously to recognize it, and may thus triumph over it, leaving open, however, the question of whether their moral delicacy would not itself be the new serpent in the garden.

James's celebrated ambiguity is the last claim to what Lionel Trilling defined as "moral realism" in an age of growing subjective relativism. At the end of *The Portrait of a Lady*, Isabel Archer returns to a miserable conjugal life, fleeing from her old-time American suitor, Caspar Goodwood, a square, modern self-made man, who, as becomes the age of budding divorce courts, had offered her a new start, in reparation for her sufferings. Isabel's moral choice prevents her from breaking away from the sacred vows of matrimony, even in the direst of circumstances, and aligns her with the heroines of earlier sentimental fictions. What makes her abruptly leave the good American, however, is a kiss, which threatens to turn her into an adulteress and him into a man who forgot himself in the snares of passion. Fear of sexuality is undoubtedly a trait James shared with his contemporaries, and, as he insisted on the "bestiality" of Zola's work and called Oscar Wilde "a beast," beastly images are often associated with the ghost of sexuality, as in his remarkable short story "The Beast in the Jungle" (1902). For Isabel, "there were certain things she could never take in. To begin with, they were hideously unclean." These unclean things reflect on women's position in the world: "Did all women have lovers? Did they all lie, and even the best have their price?" she muses, and the narrator comments that her scorn for all this "kept its freshness in a very tainted air." The air here, as in other of James's novels—*What Maisie Knew* (1897), *The Awkward Age* (1899), and most notably *The Golden Bowl*—is tainted by adultery, the preferred motif of the fiction of the period, from *Madame Bovary* to Leo Tolstoy's *Anna Karenina* (1877). Adultery challenges constituted order, stages the conflict between morality and passion, and resorts to punishing women who betray their sacred role as ethical beacons for society. To resist adultery is what lady Isabel finally does, but such noble resistance may also confirm the egotistical nature of the "beautiful soul" and its potential to devastate other people's lives.

The villains in *The Portrait of a Lady*, though, are Madame Merle and Osmond, Americans who have renounced their birthright to become snobbish imitators of

European forms. To innocent Isabel, Osmond appears as "the first gentleman in Europe," a definition lifted from William Thackeray's satirical *Book of Snobs* (1848), and Madame Merle claims to belong to the "old, old world," and to have been born "before the French Revolution," though her literal birthplace is the nineteenth-century navy yard in Brooklyn. Their villainy is rooted in their forgetting their democratic heritage, in their cherishing forms without any value, in their ambition to transform easily acquired American wealth—Isabel's inherited fortune—into the agent of status in a paradigmatic, imaginary, prerevolutionary European world of aristocracy. In 1868, reflecting on the present corruption of American society, ruined by too quick an access to wealth, liberal Edwin L. Godkin, the founder of the *Nation* and one of James's best friends, had identified in "the breaking up of old habits" the crucial interest of Carlyle's *The French Revolution*. In James's *The Bostonians* (1886) Basil Ransom, "an immense admirer of Thomas Carlyle" and a "reactionary" in politics, would like to restore the American prerevolutionary spirit of "English Royalists and cavaliers" as a bulwark against the "dissipated habits" of his time. Symmetrical opposites, liberal Godkin and the reactionary anti-emancipation Jamesian character share a nostalgia for a morally sound, law-abiding society that apparently democracy, with its legitimate insistence on equality, free will, and variety of choice, was denying. Modern democratic crisis may result in either the denial of social and political change or a desire for it: for James both may be embodied in his wish to "see a country in a state of revolution," foreseeing, as he wrote in his 1902 essay on Balzac, "the last desolation of the modern." Mr. Touchett, however, tells Isabel: "You won't have the pleasure of going gracefully to the guillotine here just now." In this phrase, added to the 1908 revised edition of the novel, Isabel's taste for any revolution is suggested by a specific reference, qualifying the French as the mother of all revolutions: anarchist Hyacinth Robinson in *The Princess Casamassima* considers it a "great legend," a "sunrise out of a sea of blood," and a "magnificent energy" that would make "platonic democracy" a possibility. The villainy of Osmond and Madame Merle is to resist what has already changed, to distance the utopia of platonic democracies that Isabel, a "Columbia dressed in stars and stripes," still wishes to represent.

Insistently James returns to confront both the legitimacy of democratic society and the unmended rift between new and old orders. As an expatriate in England, where he became a citizen in 1915, or in his travels through France and Italy, he was at home in the highest circles of society, but his elitism was matched by his Americanism, by a crusade to establish the "American" as a cosmopolitan citizen of a world geographically limited to Europe and imaginatively built upon a modern myth, that of the migrant's return. Though none of his characters wishes to retrace an individual past in the Old World, all are engaged in retracing the collective past of civilization; moreover, Europe appears as the new "Promised Land" to Isabel. The need to possess its "visitable past" is so intrinsic to James's American characters that, reviewing *Portrait of a Lady,* a bilious Margaret Oliphant attacked him for proprietary arrogance: it appears, she writes, that it was for his Americans that "Italy and France and Old England have lived their lives and had their reverses, and built their own castles and towns, and even arranged their landscapes." She has a point: James's Europe is a self-centered claustrophobic world, closed in by the desire to bridge the national amnesia brought about by migration and revolution. But in the domain of Western fiction, a New World type takes its place: not a man of the wilderness or an uneasy Puritan, but a bourgeois of a metropolitan, incorporated, imperial nation who wishes to take on the contradictions, the perils, and the glories, modern revolutions included, of an evolutionary "heir of all ages."

Bibliography: Martha Banta, *Imaging American Women: Idea and Ideals in Cultural History* (New York, 1987). Peter Brooks, *The Melodramatic Imagination: Balzac, Henry James, Melodrama, and the Mode of Excess* (New Haven, CT, 1976). Henry James, *The New York Edition of the Novels and Tales of Henry James,* 24 vols. (New York, 1907–1909); *Portrait of a Lady* (London, 1881). Thomas Sergeant Perry, *The Evolution of the Snob* (Boston, 1887).

ALIDE CAGIDEMETRIO

1884
A man and a boy go down the Mississippi

Mark Twain's Hairball

Structurally, Mark Twain's *Adventures of Huckleberry Finn,* the story of an escaped black slave named Jim and a young white boy named Huck floating down the Mississippi River on a raft, is about as solid as a New Orleans levee and, beginning with the entrance of Tom Sawyer, seems to implode, but its epic sweep is impressive, its characters, both major and minor, engaging, and the novel tells us a good deal about how nineteenth-century Americans lived—as well as what has changed and what hasn't.

The characters are given to excessive speech-making, and some of it is reminiscent of the form of tall-tale-telling prose poetry Muhammad Ali gets credit for inventing. "I'm the old original iron-jawed, brass-mounted, copper-bellied corpsemaker from the wilds of Arkansaw!" one of Twain's characters boasts. "Look at me! I'm the man they call Sudden Death and General Desolation! Sired by a hurricane, dam'ed by an earthquake, half-brother to cholera, nearly related to the small-pox on my mother's side! Look at me! I take nineteen alligators and a bar'l of whiskey for breakfast when I'm in robust health, and a bushel of rattlesnakes and a dead body when I'm ailing!" Some of Twain's characters use gab to hustle the gullible; today they would be on Madison Avenue, and then as now using advertising to attract customers to their dubious wares. Even Jim, one of the few characters in the book with anything close to integrity, has a game. He peddles a hairball removed from the innards of an ox that, he claims, can solve mysteries and predict the future—if you feed it with money. An early talking head.

The novel is Twain's hairball, a prescient book that lays down patterns of race relations in American life, just as the hairball represents the superstitious think-ing not only of Twain's time, but, when twenty-first-century presidential candi-dates appeal to millions of voters by claiming that the earth is 8,000 years old, of ours. Superstition takes many forms: when Twain wrote, Americans were as easily turned into mobs by rabble-rousers as they are today. Once it might have been characters like "the duke" and "the king," the fast-talking con artists who take over Huck and Jim's raft; in our time their place is taken by talk-show hosts as well as by those who are considered part of the nation's intellectual elite. It was the noted commentator Charles Krauthammer who created the "crack baby" scare: part of a wider effort to paint blacks as subhuman, and a hoax.

The duke and the king provide Twain with an opportunity to poke fun at the awe with which their American cousins view European royalty. But even now, net-works raise their ratings by appealing to the insatiable curiosity of Americans about the British royalty. *Vanity Fair* and other publications regularly feature royal doings for the entertainment of the upscale, white, second-generation Ameri-cans whose forebears were regarded as among the genetically damaged. In 2007, Helen Mirren received an Oscar for her portrayal of Queen Elizabeth II, and hours of television are still devoted to Princess Diana, who has been dead since 1997. The duke and the king, so successful in their impersonations that they are able to fleece wide-eyed Americans of their money, were merely there first—and they themselves are a mirror of the impersonation of royalty that was the ante-bellum South. "Col. Grangerford was a gentleman, you see," we hear of one mem-ber of the Southern fake aristocracy. "He was a gentleman all over; and so was his family. He was well-born, as the saying is"—yet his family is meting out mindless violence to its enemies, the Shepherdsons, who are, like the Grangerfords, "high-toned, and well-born, and rich and grand." In their dedication to murdering each other, both families have been nearly emptied of male members.

Both Jim and Huck are fugitives from another form of violence: domestic vio-lence. Huck escapes from his father's beatings. Jim escapes from the "rough" treatment of Mrs. Watson, a white woman who inflicts physical as well as psy-chological damage on the captive, threatening to sell him "down the river." She not only owns slaves, she participates in the breakup of the black slave family, the central issue of Harriet Beecher Stowe's 1851 *Uncle Tom's Cabin* (which borrowed so liberally from Josiah Henson's 1849 autobiography that the black nationalist and Reconstructionist Martin Delany proposed, in a letter to Frederick Doug-lass, that Stowe's publisher pay Henson five thousand dollars). Through Huck's eyes, focusing first on two white women, Twain renders these disunions in an effective though melodramatic scene: "So the next day after the funeral, along about noontime, the girls' joy got the first jolt. A couple of nigger traders come along, and the king sold them the niggers reasonable, for three-day drafts as they called it, and away they went, the two sons up the river to Memphis, and their mother down the river to New Orleans. I thought them poor girls and them nig-gers would break their hearts for grief: they cried around each other, and took on so it most made me sick to see it. The girls said they hadn't ever dreamed of see-ing the family separated or sold away from the town." Even though the white women in this scene are attached to the blacks, the blacks are still slaves under their control. Twain's descriptions and those of others show that they could wield a whip with the best of them.

Jim commits violence against one of his daughters, not realizing she is deaf—but unlike the women who cooperated with the vile institution of slavery, Jim expresses remorse. Jim might have been surprised by the ignorant comment of Michiko Kakutani, who, in a review of Toni Morrison's *Beloved* written when Kakutani was the most powerful literary critic in the United States, concluded that black men, during the slavery period, treated black women in the same manner that white men treated blacks. "Whites carelessly beat, rape and maim their slaves, sell them for a price and kill them for a lark; and in this world," she wrote, ". . . a similar violence festers between black men and women, between parents and their children." Perhaps Ms. Kakutani hasn't toured plantations where she could have observed the instruments of torture, or, as I have in Ghana and Martinique, seen the slave dungeons where rebellious men were held. Or perhaps she, who slanders black men while honoring the misogyny of Saul Bellow, is the kind of critic, one among many, who experiments on black men but has a Stockholm-syndrome relationship with white authors. Perhaps she wasn't aware that those who trafficked in blood forced black women to undergo painful medical experiments without anesthesia, or that most of the cadavers used in nineteenth-century medical experiments were those of black men. Black men didn't have the equipment to inflict the same kind of damage on black women that white slave masters, both male and female, possessed to apply to both genders of slaves. I would be remiss in not subjecting such dangerous fantasies to the most severe form of evisceration, since such propaganda influences public opinion—and indirectly public policy.

Slavery being a more valuable mid-nineteenth-century American enterprise than all others, throughout the pages of Twain's book Jim is much sought after. In fact, along with William Quantrill, the James Brothers, whose exploits have been celebrated by Hollywood in nearly a hundred years of pro-Confederate Westerns (with, at first, Jesse James portrayed by his own son, Jesse James, Jr.), murdered 180 people in Lawrence, Kansas, in 1863, for being "negro thieves." The thin glue that holds Twain's plot together is the pursuit of Jim by different characters. Jim is no fool, and has learned like other captives to outmaneuver the whites with whom he comes in contact, sometimes through flattery. At one point he salutes Huck as "de on'y white genlman dat ever kep' his promise to ole Jim." Even Huck, whose attitude toward Jim is ambivalent (in our century he would be a *Nation*-magazine progressive), has to admire his cleverness. "Jim had a wonderful level head for a nigger," Huck says. "He could most always start a good plan when you wanted one." There are other moments in the book that show the cunning blacks had to develop in a society where they could be punished or even murdered at a white person's whim. When relaying a message from Jim to Huck, a slave invites Huck to inspect a nest of moccasins.

The book is a festival of what linguists call code switching, and of identity changing, where in order to get out of a jam characters must create bogus biographies on the spot. Another thing that hasn't changed: blacks as criminal suspects.

Whether blacks are homeless or university professors, they are constantly under surveillance by department stores, banks, and the police. Under the administration of Mayor Rudolph Giuliani of New York, 35,000 black and Hispanic men in the city were stopped and frisked without cause; even the federal government admits to racial profiling. When Huck has to cover his commission of a crime, he blames it on blacks and is believed. As in Twain's time, many American whites believe that their morality is higher than that of blacks; even Huck's father, a drunk and a ne'er-do-well, accords himself higher status.

Of all the white characters in *Huckleberry Finn,* it is Huck's father who best represents white, mainstream attitudes toward blacks in our own time. Though blacks are presented in the media as intellectually slothful, with constant reference to blacks who view reading as a "white thing," the reading and math scores of Americans would lag behind those of whites in many other countries even were no Hispanics or blacks included. To be elected president in the United States, one must avoid appearing too intellectual or bookish. Huck's father punishes Huck for his learning: "Well, I'll learn her [Miss Watson] how to meddle. And look here—you drop that school, you hear? I'll learn people to bring up a boy to put on airs over his own father and let on to be better'n what he is."

Like many contemporary white Americans, Huck's father doesn't want blacks to appear to be "better'n" what they are. He complains to Huck about a black who doesn't know his place.

> Oh, yes, this is a wonderful govment, wonderful. Why, looky here. There was a free nigger there from Ohio—a mulatter, most as white as a white man. He had the whitest shirt on you ever see, too, and the shiniest hat; and there ain't man in town that's got as fine clothes as what he had; and he had a gold watch and chain, and a silver-headed cane—the awful-est gray-headed nabob in the State. And what do you think? They said he was a p'fesser in a college, and could talk all kinds of languages, and knowed everything. And that ain't the wust. They said he could VOTE when he was at home.

With this speech, Twain exposes a consciousness that still exists among many white Americans. The three blacks who were lynched in Memphis in 1892, as described by Ida B. Wells in "Lynch Law in America," were murdered by a mob not for raping white women but for being too prosperous; they were followers of Booker T. Washington. In the twenty-first century, black voters are not deterred from voting by mobs, as was the case during the Confederate restoration, but by identification laws, vote caging, and subtler methods. Biographies of Colin Powell and Ralph Ellison, who was described by Robert Penn Warren as "every white man's favorite black man," chronicle the countless humiliations they endured so that they would never forget their place—to the point where, at a cabinet meeting, George W. Bush had Powell, as the secretary of state, locked out of the room because he was a minute late, forcing him to knock on the door to gain admission. How different from Huck's Pap, who has a candor missing from today's think-tank scholars and op-ed writers, who hide behind graphs and junk science to say what the old man said in plain words.

Mark Twain caught his time and place in a manner that statistics and policy papers can never approach. Twain takes the reader into the interiors of an age; he takes us into the minds of those who inhabit an age. While movies like *Gone with the Wind* and *Birth of a Nation* give us an age through distorted and narrow lenses, a great novel permits us to enter an age and take our time and mosey about. Twain is often criticized for the supposed crudity of his portrait of Jim, but his Jim cares about his family, finds a way to survive in the wilderness, and is a sympathetic character struggling against forces that are insurmountable. By contrast, the black male characters in the work of Bellow, Tom Wolfe, Philip Roth, David Mamet, and that of a number of feminist writers, black and white, including Gloria Steinem, Barbara Smith, Susan Brownmiller, and Robin Morgan, are ignorant, bestial sexual predators exclusively, like the typical portrait of minority men in the media of the Nazi regime, a portrait that did and does make it possible for harsh social actions to be taken against them. But when, finally, Huck literally aches for Jim, missing Jim's calling him "honey," and "petting him," Twain, like Nathaniel Hawthorne and Nathanael West, takes us to the very bottom of the American psyche, where the visibility is zero. Huck cries, "I want my nigger," like the children of the suburbs who are addicted to gangster rap, like the white Southern children after the Civil War who craved their coon songs from New York. Twain exposes this bizarre hunger, this exotic yearning of those who despise blacks yet wish to imitate them. Who wish to be called "honey" by them. Who wish to be "petted" by them. Who wish to burn them, cut out their very entrails, and take them home with them. If you can't give us our nigger, they seem to say, we'll make do with Elvis. The late Rick James asked an interviewer why there was more interest in Michael Jackson's trial for child molesting than in the war in Iraq, where the American occupation was causing ethnic cleansing and the deaths of tens of thousands. The same might be said of the near-pathological fascination with the doings of O. J. Simpson. Twain knew. *I want my nigger!*

Bibliography: Mark Twain, *Adventures of Huckleberry Finn* (London and New York, 1884).

ISHMAEL REED

1884, July

The *Inland Printer* reports that "Printers do not seem to be very greatly alarmed, as no machine has yet been devised that can think"

THE LINOTYPE MACHINE

In the space of a single decade, the pages of the Chicago-based trade journal *Inland Printer* went from regarding mechanical typesetting as an improbability to regarding it as an inevitability and then as a normal condition of the trade. For compositors, skepticism gave way to worry and bemusement to hostility as big-city publishers adopted the machines to save on labor costs. One of several typesetting machines under development in the same years, the Linotype machine—

patented by Ottmar Mergenthaler in 1884—was marketed aggressively by the Mergenthaler Linotype Company of New York, a corporation led by newspaper publishers who had invested in Mergenthaler's device and then seized control of his company. Mergenthaler continued to improve his invention from his machine shop in Baltimore, while the company solidified its position through patent litigation. Linotype offered only mediocre competition for its rivals in 1891, when the American Newspaper Publishers Association sponsored a typesetting contest, but by the turn of the century two machines dominated mechanical typesetting in the United States, the improved Linotype and the Monotype.

Neither Linotype nor Monotype is rightly a typesetting machine, because neither performs the laborious task of setting individual pieces of type. The task of hand composition—as it is called—had changed little since Gutenberg's day: pieces of type were picked one by one out of wooden cases (the "upper case" and the "lower case") and arranged right to left to form a line; lines of type were justified and transferred to the printer's form. Distributing the pieces of type back into their cases was grunt work for later on, after the printing job was finished, but unlike hand distribution, hand composition had a certain cachet: it called for quickness and intelligence, a facility with language that extended to both a knack for deciphering handwritten copy and the skill of reading words and letters backward. Though wages varied greatly from place to place, typesetting was usually paid by the piece. A compositor got so many cents per thousand ems (a unit of length based on the letter m). A few of the fastest compositors—contests were staged among celebrated "swifts"—could approach 2,000 ems per hour. The Linotype Company's advertisements boasted up to 7,500 ems per hour, and contemporary observers agreed that using Linotype machines saved about half the cost of hand composition, plus additional savings on foundry type. Linotype and Monotype machines are fast because they dispense with type. Both use matrices and molten metal to cast their own slugs. With Linotype—as the name implies— a whole line of type is cast at once, while Monotype casts character by character. Author Mark Twain disparaged so-called typesetting machines that didn't really set and distribute type, but that was just sour grapes: Twain backed the insanely complicated Paige compositor—a true typesetting machine—and eventually lost his shirt.

Whether Twain did so or not, it is safe to wager that Ottmar Mergenthaler and his backers weren't thinking about literature when they pursued the Linotype. Printing and publishing was big business, but literary works cut a slender profile within the trade. Insiders recognized three relatively distinct sectors: newspaper and periodical work, "job" or contract printing, and book work. When the Bureau of the Census collected data in 1904, the value of newspapers and periodicals produced in the United States represented fully 52 percent of the total for the trade. Job printing comprised another 30 percent of the total, while books and pamphlets were worth just 11 percent (leaving 7 percent for other, sundry work, like music publishing, lithography, and the manufacture of blank books). Of the books and pamphlets produced a few years later, roughly a third fell into the category "fiction" or "literature." In short, literary books, highbrow and low, represented something like a 3 percent blip in the economic landscape of printing and publishing at the beginning of the twentieth century. So it made perfect sense that newspaper publishers ran the Linotype Company and that newspaper publishers evaluated Linotype and its competitors. For Mergenthaler et al., literature was beside the point, with two notable if nebulous exceptions: first, the extent to which literature circulated within newspapers and periodicals, and second, the extent to which *the literary* as such must have served as a source of orientation—an ideology, one might say—amid the ongoing industrialization of communication, which entailed both an explosion in the quantity of printed information and the emergence of new, nonprint media.

Mergenthaler's great inspiration, linecasting, reimagined both the economics of the printing house and the substance of the page. As many as 36,000 hand compositors lost their typesetting jobs to Linotype machines in North America, as pages were now assembled from lines, not type, and lines were themselves a malleable form, the shape-shifting output of a mechanical process that was directed by an operator seated at a keyboard. Widely adopted by newspapers, useful for some job printing and book work, linotyping was largely invisible to readers. Unlike a number of contemporary innovations in print production—the halftone method of reproducing illustrations, for example—linecasting was never obvious on the printed page: the mass reading public in this respect has an untrained eye. When Linotype production did intrude into the experience of reading, on rare occasions, it did so incoherently. "Etaoin shrdlu," whispered the morning's bowling scores. "Etaoin shrdlu," mumbled political news of the day. If Linotype operators realized that they had made a keyboard error, they could fill out the rest of the line quickly with junk, intending to discard the slug later on, and the quickest junk came from running a finger down the left-hand side of the keyboard, where the two leftmost columns were e-t-a-o-i-n and s-h-r-d-l-u. Every once in a while, a junk line went to press unnoticed and the nonsense appeared in print. Then the nonsense started to make sense, as "Etaoin Shrdlu" became a catchphrase and personification, a term for nonsense, redolent with the comic self-regard of the press corps, playing Poor Richard to the newspaper publishers' Ben Franklin.

Toward the end of his career, literary critic Hugh Kenner waxed elegiac over Etaoin Shrdlu. For Kenner, Etaoin Shrdlu was a fading emblem of modernity, a disappearing relic of the machine age that had birthed the linguistic experimentation of high modernism and had succumbed by the late twentieth century to all things arbitrary and digital. Today, Linotype and Monotype have almost disappeared, replaced by computer typesetting—again, "typesetting" is a misnomer—while offset processes have replaced relief printing. But the machine age and the digital don't tease apart quite as easily as Kenner implies. The Linotype Company's lifelong competitor in the U.S. market, the Lanston Monotype Machine Company, proves this point. (Monotype printing is better adapted than Linotype for book work and fine printing.) Monotype, first marketed in 1893, was a primitive word processing system. The Monotype keyboard device is separate from the Monotype casting machine, and "the caster," noted one enthusiast, "is an almost human machine." Operators use the keyboard to punch a paper tape, and then the perforated tape is run through the casting machine, directing its maneuvers. The keyboard and the casting machine may be in separate rooms or in different cities. The perforated paper tape may be used right away or saved for later, and it may be reused to set the same copy, even to set the same copy in a different type-face, if a different cartridge of matrices is installed in the casting machine. The introduction of an arbitrary machine code—the program on paper tape—makes Monotype an early and important lesson in the distinction between input and output, between linguistic content and bibliographic expression. The distinction gains particular force because Monotype operators work at a keyboard without a screen. Unlike Linotype operators, who can see the matrices selected as they form a line for casting, Monotype operators work blind, producing output on pa-per that can be read only by the casting machine.

Reading and writing by machine were new and complicated propositions in the late nineteenth century, conditioned in the United States by the intersection of widely shared assumptions, among them the broad inevitability of mechaniza-tion, the exceptionalism of contemporary media (in quantity and kind), and the value of literacy as distinctively human and of literature as distinctively humaniz-ing. If mechanical typesetting remained a highly specialized endeavor, part of the long and varied mystification of the printed page, then a host of other new pro-cesses and commodities offered more vernacular encounters with mysteries of a related sort. Playing a phonograph record or typing a letter, for instance, in-tervened unfamiliarly at first into the habits of reading and writing, as the pho-nograph stylus read the record grooves that had been written by sound waves, and as the typebars wrote in mechanical letterforms that looked like print. Then as now, new media offered a means to question—tacitly as well as self-consciously—what reading and writing might consist of and what the cultural work of liter-acy should be amid the dynamic contexts of ongoing social and technological change.

Bibliography: Bureau of the Census, *Census of Manufactures: 1914, Printing and Publishing* (Washington, DC, 1918). Lisa Gitelman, *Scripts, Grooves, and Writing Machines: Representing Tech-nology in the Edison Era* (Stanford, CA, 1999). Hugh Kenner, *The Mechanic Muse* (New York, 1987). Bruce Michelson, *Printer's Devil: Mark Twain and the American Publishing Revolution* (Berkeley, CA, 2006). Kenneth E. Olson, *Typography and Mechanics of the Newspaper* (New York, 1930). Walker Rumble, *The Swifts: Printers in the Age of Typesetting Races* (Charlottesville, VA, 2003).

LISA GITELMAN

1884, November

Determined to walk from Cincinnati to Los Angeles, the journalist and Harvard dropout Charles Lummis arrives in Santa Fe

THE SOUTHWEST IMAGINED

Recovering from a bout of malaria, twenty-five-year-old Charles Fletcher Lummis set out to regain his health by this feat of manly strenuosity. But his 3,500-mile "tramp across the continent" was also a good career move: waiting for him at the end of the trail was a job at the *Los Angeles Daily Times,* to which Lummis posted regular dispatches about his adventures along the way. Lummis threw himself into his newspaper work in Los Angeles, perhaps a bit too strenuously; he suffered a stroke and backtracked to New Mexico to recuperate and write. Inspired by Hispanic and Indian cultures, Lummis produced a flurry of writings about the region. His travel sketches, local-color narratives, and folktales were collected in a briskly selling trilogy, the most famous of which, *The Land of Poco Tiempo* (1893), would circulate in U.S. culture, long after Lummis himself was forgotten, as the name for a fantasy region of stark, restorative natural power.

At the center of that imagined Southwest is northern New Mexico, with its desert landscape, Pueblo and Navajo people, and Spanish missions. Lummis famously characterized it as a land of "sun, silence, and adobe . . . It is the Great American Mystery—the National Rip Van Winkle—the United States which is *not* United States. Here is the land of *poco tiempo,* a time blurred into 'Pretty Soon,'" a space in which "the opiate sun soothes to rest, the adobe is made to lean against, the hush of day-long noon would not be broken." In the "opiate sun" there is a flicker of Orientalism, which has pervaded representations of the desert Southwest from the early explorers' biblical allusions to Egypt and the Holy Land to the persistent, somewhat eroticized images of *olla* maidens or New Mexican Rebeccas. In Lummis's time this regional exoticism had two valences. On the one hand, the Indian and Hispanic inhabitants were peaceful primitives, at one with nature, crafters of beautiful objects, participants in colorful dance rituals. On the other hand, they harbored a savage side, performing "lurid" spectacles such as the Hopi Snake Dance or the Penitente crucifixions. Both versions of the primitive established the region as outside modernity: "the National Rip Van Winkle" was dreamy and unchanging, a relic of the past.

In fact, the Southwest has a long history of violent social and cultural change. The region has repeatedly been conquered by Europeans looking for something: gold, land, health, spiritual solace. The City of the Holy Faith that Lummis entered in 1884 had been established by the Spanish in 1610. The native Pueblos had endured constant attempts by Franciscan fathers to convert them; suffered through famines, disease, and forced labor; and paid heavy tributes to Crown and Church, initiating a cycle of resistance and reconquest that would continue until Mexico gained its independence in 1821. Throughout the colonial period, political alliances among the Pueblos formed and fell apart. The Apaches kept the Spanish out of the area south of Albuquerque, and the Navajos raided sheep and horses from anyone they could. Despite this turmoil, the Indian groups maintained oral traditions based on their religious systems, and a rich colonial literature in Spanish emerged—Gaspar Pérez de Villagrá's epic poem *Historia de la Nueva México* (1610), narratives of exploration, folktales, dramas, and songs—that would influence the fiction writing by their descendants that began to appear in the nineteenth century, reaching a high point in the comic novellas by the New Mexican Eusebio Chacón.

After carving out the strategically essential southwestern territories through the 1848 Treaty of Guadalupe-Hidalgo and the 1854 Gadsden Purchase, the U.S.

government sent expeditions to explore and describe its new real estate. Their dispatches indicated that the desert was of little use and its Hispanic inhabitants were incapable of making the land productive, but that these vast regions could be transformed through the proper application of military force, capital, and Protestantism. While the Pueblos were regarded as peaceful agriculturalists, and the government recognized their rights to lands granted them by the Spanish, the U.S. military set out to secure the regions of the Navajos and Apaches, who vigorously resisted. The Navajos were defeated in 1863 and barely survived a forced march north to a reservation. Geronimo's surrender in 1886 signaled that the region was now safe from "hostile" Indians. Around the same time, paradoxically, the Bureau of American Ethnology was formed to study and record native cultures before they vanished through conquest and assimilation. In the hope of understanding the early stages of human development, these "salvage" ethnologists flocked to the Pueblo peoples, particularly the Zuni and Hopi, who seemed the most culturally intact—and proceeded to remand boxcar loads of artifacts back East to museums of natural history.

Lummis arrived, then, at the moment when the cultural and economic incorporation of the region was accelerating at a decidedly modern pace; his land of poco tiempo was already heading toward anachronism. The first train arrived in Santa Fe in 1880, making the region accessible by rail from both coasts. The railroad established not only transportation and communication systems but also a web of powerful cultural agents. Over the next sixty years, the Santa Fe Railway and the Fred Harvey Company worked in tandem to promote tourism to the region. They created publications and attractions advertising an exotic land filled with friendly Indians who made beautiful weavings, baskets, pots, and jewelry (conveniently for sale trackside and at all Harvey hotels and shops) and who obligingly posed for snapshots. Spanish-Mexican culture was a side note; missions were often featured, but the primary aesthetic was Indian. The railroad hired artists and photographers to create landscapes and romanticized Indian images that were widely reproduced on postcards, train schedules, travel posters, timetables, and the famous railroad calendars. They also hired writers, including Lummis, to pen detailed guides to the region. Well into the 1930s, this promotional literature invited potential tourists to "catch archaeology alive" while "roughing it in style."

Lummis's arrival in the Southwest also coincided with the rise of the regionalist literary movement of the post–Civil War period, which was, in part, about imagining the nation through its constituent parts. Periodicals abounded with local-color sketches and travel narratives about the South, New England, and the West, and regionalists like Lummis capitalized on their role as interlocutors who could explain far-off places and people to a national audience. They wrote in an elegiac, ethnographic mode that ran counter to cowboy pamphlets and dime novels depicting the Wild West. Archaeologist Adolph Bandelier's novel *The Delight Makers* (1890) is a fictionalized account of ancient Pueblo life. Boston poet Edna Dean Proctor wrote *Song of the Ancient People* (1892), a long poem about the prehistoric inhabitants of the region. Mary Austin's *The Land of Little Rain* (1903) collected her lyrical meditations on the people and landscape of the California desert, before she headed off to Santa Fe herself.

In such accounts, the Southwest was populated by natives who already shared American values: the peaceful, adobe-dwelling Pueblos and the industrious, sheepherding Navajos. (Apaches, still too wild and deracinated, were off the regionalist radar.) In these writings, Indian characters were sometimes persecuted by whites but remained spiritually content and in harmony with the land—a vision that persists in popular culture and New Age spiritualism. The romance of Hispanic culture, on the other hand, harkened back to the colonial period, passing lightly over Mexican and indigenous elements: Lummis himself was active in the movement to preserve the Spanish missions. The mission and Spanish-revival styles in architecture, which peaked in popularity in the 1920s, linked New Mexico and Arizona to Southern California, and it is no accident that many of the key figures who shaped this aesthetic lived in both places. On his return to Los Angeles, Lummis became editor of a chamber of commerce magazine, *Land of Sunshine,* which was instrumental in propagating the vision of Southern California as a region of orange trees, scenic vistas, and room to grow. His mission-style home became a gathering place for artists and writers like Mary Austin and Sui Sin Far, one of the first Asian American writers. In his customary green corduroy suit and sombrero, with a red Navajo sash (and sometimes a pistol) at his waist, Lummis evoked a rough-and-ready Spanish don.

The spiritual and physical regeneration that Lummis highlighted in his work appears again and again in literature of the Southwest. In *What the White Race May Learn from the Indian* (1908), former Methodist minister George Wharton James argues that studying Indian arts and crafts, such as basket making, would save American culture from creeping feminization. Discovering wholeness and authenticity in the region is also a major theme in memoirs by Austin, John Collier, and Mabel Dodge Luhan; Willa Cather's protagonists in *Song of the Lark* (1915), *The Professor's House* (1925), and *Death Comes for the Archbishop* (1927) all experience some form of regeneration. In an age of increasing industrialization, urbanization, mass production, and emerging consumer culture, the region's Native Americans seemed to offer models of the simple life: rural, agrarian, and communal.

Some believed they had found in the Southwest an authentic American idiom as well. By the 1920s the cosmopolitan artists' and writers' colonies at Taos and Santa Fe were well established, hosting such visitors as Marsden Hartley, Alfred Stieglitz, Georgia O'Keeffe, and Frieda and D. H. Lawrence. During this time, the primitivist appreciation of the Southwest took a new turn. Influenced by European modernism, painters not only painted Indians but painted *like* Indians, that is, abstractly. The desert landscape took on special appeal as painters flattened it out into swaths of color and texture. Many represented Pueblo dances, emphasizing repetition, rhythm, and patterns.

Poets, too, were drawn to the forms of Indian chants and ritual dances. In her 1923 manifesto, *The American Rhythm,* Mary Austin—herself a collector of native folklore and song—predicts the rise of a new verse form from the ancient traditions of indigenous people: "Anybody could use it, as anybody always has been able to use native verse form freely . . . It would be a statement of life . . . in terms of things lived through rather than observed or studied." Amy Lowell, Alice Corbin Henderson, Witter Bynner, Vachel Lindsay, Eda Lou Walton, Max Weber, and Carl Sandburg wrote poems suggesting Indian songs in their subject matter and rhythms. By playing Indian, they could claim a pure, American authenticity. Native American voices, on the other hand, were almost never heard in the literature, unless mediated by Anglos.

By the 1920s, tourism had developed into one of the Southwest's most important industries. After World War II the exoticism of the region hardened into a "tricultural myth," as Chris Wilson puts it, in which Spanish, Indian, and Anglo lived harmoniously together, each contributing to a modern but authentic way of life. But to paraphrase Dean MacCannell in *The Tourist: A New Theory of the Leisure Class,* tourism is the opposite of revolution—and indeed the mythology of the Southwest has overlooked the continuing poverty of most Indian residents, the hard lives of Hispanic workers, and the continual battles over land and water rights. In the tourist economy, the larger, well-capitalized entities (railroads, hotels, service industries) made real money; working-class locals saw only a minuscule part of the action. Since the early 1990s, however, almost all the Pueblos have built casinos. It remains to be seen what effects casinos will have on Native American participation in the tourist economy and what, if anything, they might learn from Las Vegas, which has thrived on a kind of inverse fantasy of inauthenticity and decadence.

Another actuality missing from the tourist vision of the region was the building and testing of the atomic bomb at Los Alamos and Alamogordo, New Mexico. During the years of highest anxiety about the bomb, the region continued to be represented as lost in time; it never really entered the region's literature until the 1980s, with Edward Abbey's *Fire on the Mountain,* about a rancher defending his land from the White Sands Missile Range.

In the wake of the civil rights movements of the 1960s, Hispanic and Native American literary voices finally began to attain national audiences. Fired by the Chicano arts movement of the 1960s and '70s, Rudolfo Anaya's *Bless Me, Ultima* (1972) became a schoolroom staple, and poet-essayists like Sabine Ulibarrí, Pat Mora, Tey Diana Rebolledo, and others renewed interest in the Spanish *corridos* and *cuentos* of the region—as well as memoirs, poems, and short stories by *hispanos* like Miguel Antonio Otero, Cleofas Jaramillo, Mario Suárez, and Fray Angélico Chávez that had been quietly appearing in regional presses since the turn of the twentieth century.

Native American writers from the region often described feelings of alienation from both Anglo and Indian cultures. Widely circulated novels like Leslie Marmon Silko's *Ceremony* (1977) and *Almanac of the Dead* (1991) and N. Scott Momaday's *House Made of Dawn* (1966) established a Native American literary canon, while the work of poets like Simon Ortiz, Larry Littlebird, and Paula Gunn Allen are regularly anthologized. At the same time, some Anglo writers critically assessed their inherited tradition of representing the Land of Enchantment: Abbey took on conflicts over land use and environmental issues in novels like *Desert Solitaire* (1968) and *The Monkey Wrench Gang* (1975), and John Nichols depicted political and cultural conflicts in his comic novels *The Milagro Beanfield War* (1974) and *The Magic Journey* (1978).

Increasingly the Southwest is represented as a postcolonial region struggling with the legacies of conquest, and as a borderland, a place where cultures collide and combine. Feminist poet-critic Gloria Anzaldúa, raised on the segregated Texas border, elevated *mestizaje,* or racial mixing, to a metaphor for a new kind of consciousness: "The new *mestiza* copes by developing a tolerance for contradictions, a tolerance for ambiguity. She learns to be an Indian in Mexican culture, to be Mexican from an Anglo point of view. She learns to juggle cultures. She has a plural personality, she operates in a pluralistic mode—nothing is thrust out, the good the bad and the ugly, nothing rejected, nothing abandoned." In the idea of the borderland and the theory and practice of *mestizaje* there may be some hope that the Southwest will come to occupy a different place in the national imaginary. But there are powerful cultural and economic forces at work, with vested interests in maintaining the Southwest as the Land of Enchantment, or the national Rip Van Winkle, as Lummis put it so long ago. Whether Americans will wake up, shake off the mojo of romance, and acknowledge the region's conflicted history, the fluidity of cultural identity and authority, and the ambiguity of meaning remains to be seen.

Bibliography: Gloria Anzaldúa, *Borderlands/La Frontera: The New Mestiza* (San Francisco, 1987). Leah Dilworth, *Imagining Indians in the Southwest: Persistent Visions of a Primitive Past* (Washington, DC, 1996). Lois Palken Rudnick, *Utopian Vistas: The Mabel Dodge Luhan House and the American Counterculture* (Albuquerque, NM, 1996). Chris Wilson, *The Myth of Santa Fe: Creating a Modern Regional Tradition* (Albuquerque, NM, 1997).

LEAH DILWORTH

1885

William James grapples with Josiah Royce's *The Religious Aspect of Philosophy*

The Problem of Error

Whereas Emersonian transcendentalism and Deweyan pragmatism, each in its own manner, regarded German idealism as in need of a transfigurative moment of American appropriation prior to its serving the cultural and intellectual needs of the democratic citizenry of the New World, Josiah Royce maintained that idealism, properly understood, was *already* the mode of thinking of every authentically American citizen: "The signers of our Declaration of Independence were idealists. Idealism inspired us during our Civil War. Idealism has expressed itself in the rich differentiation of our national religious life . . . [U]sing the term 'idealism' in this confessedly untechnical sense, I say that many of our foreign judges have failed to see how largely we Americans are today a nation of idealists."

This allows Royce to turn the Emersonian argument for the need to discover within our own shores the terms of a genuinely American philosophy on its head: idealism, though it originated on European shores, is actually more native to the spirit of the New World than to that of its own historical birthplace. For Royce, this meant that if one could simply succeed in thinking through German idealism to its logical endpoint, one would arrive at the mode of thought that possessed the greatest claim to being a genuinely American philosophy.

In his own lectures, when introducing students to his own undiluted strain of idealism, Royce lapses into eulogies of Kant's transcendental deduction of the categories of understanding:

> The Kantian deduction of the categories is the portal to the dwelling of modern philosophy. Some of you, having made previous efforts to grasp Kant's meaning, may regard that portal as a pretty closely shut door—not only closed, but perhaps locked. And, in fact, the section of Kant's *Critique of Pure Reason* which I have named is notoriously the most difficult passage in a very difficult book. But I do not believe the difficulties in question to be insurmountable. In any case, if we are to consider post-Kantian idealism at all, in any of its more technical aspects, we must make our beginning here at the doorway. Otherwise, if we endeavored to avoid such an entrance to the subject, we should be obliged to view modern idealism as a passing tourist might view a king's palace.

This is, indeed, how Royce was inclined to view even his most distinguished pragmatist philosophical contemporaries—as tourists who dabble in the ideas that they have glimpsed from surveying the palace of German idealism from afar, without ever mustering the courage to properly pass through its doorway and make arduous progress into its interior.

With these lectures of Royce's, and the generation of philosophers they nourished, we find ourselves at the inception of the first serious indigenous tradition of academic philosophy in America. Royce taught his students that in order to cease being intellectual tourists in a post-Kantian philosophical world, they must master the lessons of the transcendental deduction. Showing a much deeper grasp of Kant than many of his philosophical contemporaries, American or European, here is how Royce puts the objection to which the deduction seeks to respond:

> Why might not the genuine natural world simply ignore our categories? If it did so, and experience failed to confirm our ways of conceiving things, what could we do to enforce our conceptual constructions? Present experience, in any case, is not a mere conceptual construction. Why might not the unintelligible happen? Why might not experience break away from the forms of my intellect? Why might not chaos come at any moment? That such chaos does not now occur, what is that but itself a merely empirical fact, neither a priori nor necessary?

The worry to which Royce here understands Kant to be responding is admittedly a skeptical one. But Royce appreciates that it is a new variety of skepticism. Previously philosophy had been gripped by the following Cartesian question: How can I *know* things are as my senses present them as being—is there *really* an external world? The skeptic to which Kant, in Royce's reading of him, is trying to respond in the transcendental deduction is preoccupied by a different question: How can my senses so much as *present* things as being a certain way? How can my experience so much as be intelligibly *of* an external world? The Kantian question is focused on the problem of how the senses must be so as to able to furnish testimony. The Kantian paradox lies in its coming to seem a mystery how what impinges on my senses could so much as *appear* to be revelatory of the world.

In order properly to come to terms with this Kantian worry, we need to develop a proper appreciation of Kant's central insight, which Royce formulates as follows: "What experience itself is . . . you cannot learn through experience. *That* you must learn by reflection.—The concept of experience, strange to say, is itself not an empirical concept." This, for Royce, remains the philosophical fulcrum with which he thinks any strict form of pragmatism is unable to come to terms. The contest over the question of who can with most justice lay title to the claim to speak philosophically for America, the Jamesian pragmatist or the Roycean idealist, thus comes to hinge at the pivot of the twentieth century on this question: How ought we to frame our conception of experience—in radical empiricist terms (as James would attempt) or in post-Kantian idealist terms (as Royce would urge)?

In this controversy between William James and Royce, each paints the other as the traditionalist and himself as the revolutionary. James fashions himself as seeking a conception of empiricism sufficiently thought through as to no longer be vulnerable to idealist backlash; Royce styles himself as a post-Kantian destroyer of past philosophy and portrays James as stuck in the old assumptions that the German idealists sought to expose. Descartes and the British empiricists, on Royce's reading of them, take the unity of present experience for granted and rush ahead to frame questions pertaining to the *truth* of this or that experience. Kant's genius, according to Royce, lies in his ability to slow the inquiry down, redirecting focus onto the "very conditions which make the unity of your present experience possible." Royce will emphasize the following point, left largely implicit by Kant: these are as much conditions of the possibility of judging *falsely* as they are conditions of judging truly. What thus figures initially in the Cartesian challenge as an epistemological worry about the relation between claims to *knowledge* and reality comes to look, from the vantage point of Royce's radicalized Kantian problematic, like only an instance of a more general metaphysical worry: a worry about the relation between *any* claim and reality. The question the post-Kantian philosopher must now answer is this: What does it take to have experiences that are vulnerable to the world outside us, as even *false* experiences are? The first concern is thus no longer immediately with truth, but rather with what it is to *stick your neck out in thinking*, with what Kant calls the *objective validity* of judgment.

In his introductory lecture to a course on metaphysics, Royce tries to lead his students from the early modern Cartesian epistemological worry to the genuinely modern idealist metaphysical worry through the following anecdote:

One day on a train on Cape Cod returning towards Boston, I heard by chance two little boys talking behind me, mere voices in my memory. The little one was appealing to the elder, "What is the sky?" The elder was somewhat materialistic, "There ain't no sky." He had been taught that the sky was appearance and not reality, an optical illusion; there is no solid object there as children often think. He had reached the stage where he knew the vanity of this illusion. But the younger was the deeper thinker of the two, and asked a further question which was technically metaphysical: "What is it that ain't?"

In order to help mark the direction in which we need to move if we wish to pass through this portal and into modern idealism, Royce reformulates the matter in terms of *the problem of error*. How is error so much as possible? How is it that in thinking falsely our thought nonetheless continues to remain answerable to reality? Royce's most famous presentation of this was also his earliest: it figures as the opening step in his "argument from error," developed in chapter eleven of *The Religious Aspect of Philosophy*. It caused a sensation upon publication in 1885. In this argument, Royce claims he can derive his metaphysical position from one indubitable fact: that error exists. The schema of the argument is threefold: first, to establish that that fact is indeed indubitable; second, to reveal the necessary preconditions for the possibility of error; third, to show that any coherent doctrine of empiricism (in presupposing these conditions) entails absolute idealism. The overall strategy is to show that only given the possibility (excluded by any radical form of empiricism) of a certain kind of standpoint ("an absolute standpoint") can a coherent distinction between truth and falsity be drawn.

What captured James's attention was the first step of the argument. James's review of *The Religious Aspect of Philosophy* made Royce famous and led to his later promotion, in 1892, to full professor in the Department of Philosophy at Harvard; during his three decades teaching there, beginning in 1882, T. S. Eliot, George Santayana, and W. E. B. Du Bois would number among his students. Possibly no great philosopher has ever greeted an invitation to move to another university with louder jubilations of relief: "There is no philosophy anywhere in the state of California," Royce had written James some years earlier while teaching at Berkeley. Born in 1855, Royce grew up in the remote Gold Rush settlement of Grass Valley and became homesick after moving to Cambridge (writing a history of California and then, even more surprising to his colleagues at Harvard, *The Feud of Oakfield Creek,* subtitled *A Novel of California Life*). Nevertheless, prior to moving to New England he suffered the effects of an intellectual vacuum while isolated in that God-forsaken, westernmost outpost of the academic world, the University of California.

Much of James's subsequent work would be devoted to arriving at a version of pragmatism able to accommodate the problem posed by Royce in 1885. Particularly stinging for James, who at the time was halfway through completing his mammoth attempt, in *The Principles of Psychology,* to furnish a purely psychological account of thought and consciousness, is the fact that Royce emphasizes the hopelessness of James's line of inquiry. Royce stresses that an "account of judgement as simply a mental phenomenon, having interest only to the person who experiences it and to a psychologist" involves a conception of mental activity (as "mere phenomena") unable to come to terms with the problem. Royce asks: "How can a judgement, as thus described, fairly be called false? As a mere psychological combination of ideas it is neither true nor false." The most such a psychological inquiry can hope to uncover anywhere in this vicinity is what Royce calls the "sense of dependence, whereby the judgment is accompanied, upon an object external to it." This feeling of "dependence on an object," however combined and permuted with psychological materials drawn from the same order of phenomena, can never furnish us with materials, Royce submits, out of which we can construct a viable answer to the Kantian question: How is it possible for a particular state of affairs (in the world) and a particular judgment (in my mind) to stand in such a relation that the former is able to render the latter determinately false?

"The more one thinks, the more one feels that there is a real puzzle here," James wrote:

> Turn and twist as we will, we are caught in a tight trap. Although we cannot help believing that our thoughts *do* mean realities and are true or false of them, we cannot for the life of us ascertain how they *can* mean them. If thought be one thing and reality another, by what pincers, from out of all the realities, does the thought pick out the special one it intends to know? And if the thought knows the reality falsely, the difficulty of answering the question becomes indeed extreme.

What is far more astonishing, when viewed in the light of subsequent events, is how James's review of *The Religious Aspect of Philosophy* expresses sympathy for the shape of the philosophical bolt-hole from the problem that Royce proposes: "Our author calls the question insoluble in these terms; and we are inclined to think him right, and to suspect that his idealist escape from the quandary may the best one for us all to take." This attitude proved short-lived. As James's perplexity in the puzzle deepens, so also do his dissatisfactions with Royce's idealist conclusions—and battle is joined.

Only two years later, he writes to Carl Stumpf of Royce's book in the following terms: "The second half is a new argument for monistic idealism, an argument based on the possibility of truth and error in knowledge . . . I have vainly tried to escape from it. I still suspect it of inconclusiveness, but I frankly confess that I am *unable* to overthrow it." James went back and forth for six more years, until expressing in a letter to Dickson Miller a "final" resolve to come to terms with the challenge: "With the help of God I will go at it again this semester, when I settle down to my final bout with Royce's theory, which must result in my either actively becoming a propagator thereof, or actively its enemy or destroyer." The result would be an epic debate between the two most influential American philosophers of the period, lasting for over a quarter of a century, ending only with James's death in 1910.

Fifteen years after his initial laudatory review, James would confess in a letter to Royce: "When I write, 'tis with one eye on you, and one on the page . . . I lead a parasitic life upon you, for my highest flight of ambitious ideality is to become your conqueror, and to go down into history as such . . . in one last death-grapple of an embrace." Today, unlike those of his pragmatist contemporaries (Mead, Peirce, James, and Dewey), Royce's writings are no longer much read, let alone grappled with. Yet subsequent generations of American philosophers, hardly less than James's own, continue to lead a philosophic life parasitic upon him, and their work is still widely controlled by the ideal animating James's counterattack—to formulate a coherent form of empiricism or naturalism able to do justice to the challenge so forcefully posed by Royce, and which now goes by the name of the problem of intentionality.

Bibliography: James Conant, "The James/Royce Dispute," in *The Cambridge Companion to William James,* ed. Ruth Anna Putnam (Cambridge, UK, 1997); "Varieties of Skepticism," in *Wittgenstein and Skepticism,* ed. Denis McManus (London, 2004). William James, "1885 Review of *The Religious Aspect of Philosophy,*" in *Essays, Comments, and Reviews* (Cambridge, 1987). Josiah Royce, *The Basic Writings of Josiah Royce,* ed. J. J. McDermott, 2 vols. (New York, 1969); *Lectures on Modern Idealism,* ed. J. Loewenberg (New Haven, CT, 1919); *Metaphysics: Josiah Royce's Philosophy 9 Course of 1915–1916,* ed. W. E. Hocking, R. Hocking, and F. Oppenheim (Albany, NY, 1998); *The Religious Aspect of Philosophy* (Boston, 1885).

JAMES CONANT

1885, July
Ulysses S. Grant finishes his *Memoirs*

LIMITS TO VIOLENCE

Grant wrote his memoirs in a haze of cocaine and morphine, dying of cancer. It was a violent death. He vomited and coughed up blood with such force that he hemorrhaged badly, even killing off chunks of the plum-sized malignant tumor in his throat—and thereby buying himself just a little more time.

It was time that he needed. Only with a completed book manuscript could the bankrupt ex-general rescue his wife and children from financial ruin. The country gawked in morbid fascination at his race against time during a six-month national deathwatch. He finished his work in mid-July 1885. He died a few days later. The manuscript he produced is widely regarded as a masterpiece. It was a miracle of dogged, stubborn determination, the perfect literary match to the old soldier's relentless battle tactics, his *refusal* to stop.

The prose in *Personal Memoirs of U. S. Grant* mirrors the relentlessness of the man. It is crisp, forceful, never pausing to meditate on the damage of the moment but instead moving implacably forward. In an emblematic scene from the Battle of Belmont, Grant is almost killed. "Early in this engagement my horse was shot under me, but I got another one from one of my staff and kept well up with the advance until the river was reached." The near-death moment is almost boring, recounted robotically, and it is lexically subordinated to the—for him—more interesting detail of forward movement. Just so, in his account of the Mexican-

American War, Grant describes how the splinters of bones, musket, and brains of an exploded soldier knocked down and injured a small handful of others. This potentially macabre scene is reduced to a single sentence, presented without reaction or commentary, and immediately preceded and followed by generalized accounts of advancing lines. Equally abrupt is an oft-cited vignette from the Civil War, about the capture of Jackson, Mississippi. Grant is walking through the pacified city with General Sherman. Together they come across a textile factory where the "girls" are still diligently at work, weaving tent cloth for the Confederate Army. Inconspicuous in his scruffy army blues, Grant watches; after a quiet while, he turns to Sherman decisively: "I told Sherman I thought they had done work enough." Grant is ready to move on, and he quickly disposes of both factory and anecdote. "In a few minutes cotton and factory were in a blaze." The *Memoirs* move abruptly to the next battle.

Grant contemplates the ruin of the Civil War with the studied calm of a surgeon or, perhaps, the emotional numbness of a trauma survivor. The wartime general, Grant "the butcher," was little different. He did not practice war with either chivalrous flair or wanton violence, but instead with a patient commitment to destruction. As Herman Melville once wrote, capturing the paradox of Grant's cool ferocity: "Like a loaded mortar he is still: Meekness and grimness meet in him—The silent General."

As Grant recalls in the *Memoirs,* it was after the appalling Battle of Shiloh in 1862 that he realized he would have to completely wreck the South in order to win it. By 1863, Grant was systematically directing nonlethal force against civilians, using starvation as a weapon by seizing livestock and destroying crops, and deliberately triggering refugee crises across the South by burning civilians out of their homes. Render the land, Grant commanded, "a barren waste."

One measure of the severity of Union policies can be found in the reactions of the soldiers charged with implementing them. One Union sergeant wrote with anguish about being forced to torch: "Such mourning, such lamentations, such crying and pleading for mercy. I never saw nor want to see again, some were wild, crazy, mad, some cry[ing] for help while others would throw their arms around yankee soldiers necks and implore mercy." Wrote another Pennsylvania cavalryman about "the burning business": "I do not believe in it, and the more I see of it, the more I hate the principle. It is barbarous, cruel and rough and if we are defeated on this campaign, which by the way, I am afraid will be the result, I shall assign as the reason the wanton destruction of private property and the savageness in which this campaign is conducted."

Early in the war many had argued for conciliatory policies, and especially for respectful treatment of civilians—if not for moral reasons, then for strategic ones. How could the Union subdue an army if it was supported by an entire people shrieking for vengeance? How could it hope for peace with a population unforgivably injured? But support for restraint in war diminished as body counts rose. "What would you do in my position?" Lincoln responded to one of his critics. "Would you drop the war where it is? Or would you prosecute it in future with elderstalk squirts charged with rose water?" General McClellan's demand that the "constitutional rights of all" be respected, and that Southern noncombatants be protected, was dismissed as a dangerous moral luxury. The very survival of the nation was at stake.

As the scope of destruction increased, however, so did the desire for regulation. In 1863, the U.S. government issued General Orders No. 100, Instructions for the Government of Armies of the United States in the Field, better known as the Lieber Code. The first official government codification of the laws of war in world history, it served as a precursor to the monumentally important Hague and Geneva Conventions. The Lieber Code set an outer limit to force in wartime by establishing the principle of military necessity: namely, that the means available for injuring others are not unlimited, that violence can be justified only by the pressure of real need. The code thereby embodied the essential principle of humanitarianism, the belief that there are limits to violence, even in war, even when national survival itself is at stake. "Men who take up arms against one another in public war," the code declared, "do not cease on this account to be moral beings, responsible to one another and to God."

While one of the great developments in the history of human rights and humanitarianism, the Lieber Code was also a sternly practical manual designed to accelerate rather than impede military victory. Its primary drafter, the Prussian émigré and veteran Francis Lieber, strongly advocated harsh measures in wartime. Indeed, he once wrote with passion of the Confederacy: "Drive the fiends from our soil, and let Grant be a stern uncompromising man of the sword and sword alone, until the masses in the States rise against their own fiends, and hang them or drive them out." For Grant, who argued for "complete" but not "promiscuous" destruction in war, there was no paradox to Lieber's call for maximization of injury and minimization of brutality. Ruthless wars were shorter, Grant argued, and therefore more humane. As he wrote in a letter to his wife in 1862: "These terrible battles are very good things to read about for persons who [lose] no friends but I am decidedly in favor of having as little of it as possible. The way to avoid it is to push forward as vigorously as possible." The code concurred: "Sharp wars are brief."

The Confederacy roundly denounced the Lieber Code, judging it a work of propaganda that, with the loophole of military necessity, gave the veneer of legality to vicious behavior. Confederate secretary of war James Seddon argued that "a military commander under this code may pursue a line of conduct in accordance with principles of justice, faith, and honor, or he may justify conduct correspondent with the warfare of the barbarous hordes who overran the Roman Empire." Such criticisms, while themselves acts of propaganda, had merit: the doctrine of military necessity facilitated violence as often as prohibited it. Military necessity can justify almost anything; it certainly justified Grant's hard hand of war, which included policies that would shock the conscience of today's world. The code itself declaims that military necessity admits of "all direct destruction of life," "all destruction of property," and "all withholding of sustenance or means of life from the enemy."

However, there are some things military necessity cannot justify. The Lieber

Code emphatically banned torture: "Military necessity does not admit of cruelty—that is, the infliction of suffering for the sake of suffering or for revenge, nor of maiming or wounding except in fight, nor of torture to extort confessions." The Lieber Code's prohibition of torture affirmed a more than three-hundred-year ban on torture in Anglo-American jurisprudence. In this it was legally uncontroversial. Judicial torture was never part of English common law, although in the Tudor-Stuart period the Privy Council issued torture writs as part of the king's prerogative under emergency circumstances. Such practices were, nonetheless, considered extralegal, and were effectively eliminated with the English Bill of Rights (1689). (In the United States, the torture ban remained official policy for more than a century, until the historically unprecedented cultural and political reversals of the early 2000s.)

The Civil War loomed large in the American political imagination during former president George W. Bush's post-9/11 global war on terror. U.S. news analyses looked back to General Grant's rescue of the Union as an emotionally galvanizing symbol for the possibility of rescuing the failing war in Iraq (a purported front in the war on terror), and also to Abraham Lincoln's curtailment of civil liberties and suspension of habeas corpus to find precedent for the policies of President Bush. But what's most important here in the juxtaposition of the Civil War and the war on terror, ultimately, is not the similarity in U.S. codes of conduct but the difference. During the Civil War, when the territorial survival of the nation was at stake, the United States affirmed the torture ban.

One of the reasons why the torture ban seemed so plausible to military men committed to effective destruction, and why it has been so robust and durable in the Anglo-American legal tradition, is its perceived practicality. The torture ban has been viewed as consistent not only with the dictates of humanity but also with the necessities of evidence gathering. Since the Middle Ages it has been understood that torture produces bad information. Since the U.S. occupation of Iraq it has been understood that torture simultaneously shuts down good information. As U.S. intelligence personnel working in Iraq allegedly complained, their access to the best information—tips from locals—was jeopardized because of the perception among Iraqis that U.S. forces would use torture in following up on their tips.

The astonishing willingness to officially countenance torture in this later period of U.S. history reflects an anxious uncertainty in the United States about how to regulate widespread conflict with nonstate actors (insurgents, terrorists). But it also reflects a radical change in conceptions of war and peace more generally. In the medieval natural-law tradition, peace was viewed as the natural condition of humanity; war was an exception that required ethical justification. This view was reaffirmed and codified in the Lieber Code, which declared: peace is the world's "normal condition; war is the exception. The ultimate object of all modern war is a renewed state of peace." Accordingly, Lieber insisted when discussing torture, "military necessity does not include any act of hostility which makes the return to peace unnecessarily difficult."

The countertradition, reaching back to Greece and early, expansionist Rome, viewed international relations as a permanent state of war. As Plato declared in *The Laws,* "All states by nature are fighting an undeclared war against every other state." In this tradition, as Stephen Neff summarizes, peace was an "interlude in fighting," "no more than 'a breathing time.'" George Bush's war on terror returned the United States to this ancient political vision. The doctrine of torture was an inevitable next step, for if there is no peace to return to, all is permitted.

Such was not the view of General Grant, who was dire and relentlessly effective in pursuing war but also deliberate and controlled, steadfastly oriented toward the final goal of peace. At the end, he saw how his own death might help achieve this, and it steadied him. In those last days, writing his memoirs on the porch of the mountain cottage where he would die, Grant received affectionate visitors from North and South, Union and Confederacy. Voiceless, he quietly returned greetings to the long lines of tourists who came daily to witness his dying. Among his last words were these, from the closing pages of the *Memoirs:* "I feel that we are on the eve of a new era, when there is to be great harmony between the Federal and Confederate. I cannot stay to be a living witness to the correctness of this prophecy; but I feel it within me that it is to be so. The universally kind feeling expressed for me at a time when it was supposed that each day would prove my last, seemed to me the beginning of the answer to 'Let us have peace.'"

Bibliography: Frank Freidel, *Francis Lieber, Nineteenth-Century Liberal* (Baton Rouge, LA, 1947). Ulysses Grant, *Memoirs and Selected Letters* (New York, 1990). Mark Grimsley, *The Hard Hand of War: Union Military Policy toward Southern Civilians, 1861–1865* (Cambridge, 1995). John Langbein, "The Legal History of Torture," in *Torture: A Collection,* ed. Sanford Levinson (Oxford, 2004). William S. McFeely, *Grant: A Biography* (New York, 1981). Herman Melville, "The Armies of the Wilderness," in *Battle-Pieces and Aspects of the War,* ed. Sidney Kaplan (Gainesville, FL, 1960). Stephen C. Neff, *War and the Law of Nations: A General History* (Cambridge, 2005). Edward Peters, *Torture* (New York, 1985).

JAMES DAWES

1885, October

George Washington Cable leaves Louisiana for Massachusetts

Writing New Orleans

The writer George Washington Cable left New Orleans just as the city decided to become self-consciously American, to recast itself as a progressive, modern metropolis intent on taming nature and transforming the human horrors of its past into the material of romance. The pre–Civil War New Orleans that he chronicled was a Creole island trembling continually on its gumbo mud bed, a tropical, postcolonial world where civilization was constantly tested by sexual temptation, heat, avarice, alcohol, mosquitoes, the church, and corrupt politics. In one story in his *Old Creole Days,* the new masters of the city, the Americans, appear particularly vile: "They mock the various Latins with their national inflections, and answer scowls with their laughter. Some of the more aggressive shout pretty French greetings to the women of Gascony, and one barge-man, amid peals of laughter, stands on a seat and hurls a kiss to the quadroons." We also meet "black-bearded fishermen, Sicilian fruiterers, swarthy Portuguese sailors, in little woolen caps," "trappers, smugglers, Canadian *voyageurs,* drinking and singing; and *Américains,* too—more's the shame—from the upper rivers . . . who ply the bottle, and who will get home by and by to tell how wicked Sodom is; broad-brimmed, silver-braided Mexicans, too." Everywhere, "the quadroon women in their black lace shawls" and "the turbaned black women." And we find, sprinkled voluptuously among these many-hued humans, adjectives like "brazen" and "shameful."

We are in a loud, quarrelsome, colorful, lusty city "honey-combed with gambling dens." In this pullulating glory of color and sentiment, Cable's mixed-race citizens, plantation owners, slaves, Creoles, whores, and gamblers, navigate issues of race and propriety and live out great emotional storms. Cable romanticized the city, but not in the way its image-makers wanted it to be seen by visitors to the Cotton Exposition of 1884. Slavery is a thing of the past, proclaimed the promoters: the Civil War has been fought, lost, and then won back by white businessmen. A few old-timers still speak French, Spanish, Creole, German, Italian, and Irish, but English is the language of the future. The exhibition itself, though full of many exotic wonders (including the first mariachi band to visit the United States), was about the marvels of science and engineering. Levee construction on the Mississippi, hitherto overseen entirely by local boards, began receiving federal assistance; the channel was dredged to modernize shipping; new neighborhoods were drained and built.

Despite the best efforts of Big Engineering, floods continued to frustrate water-control efforts after the Civil War, with major overflows in 1874, 1882, 1883, 1884, 1890, 1897, 1903, 1912, 1913, 1927, and 2005 (the levees held in the floods of 1886 and 1893). Cable's "Old Creole Days" would appear to be over in 1884, but as at so many other times in her motley history, late-century New Orleans was just putting on a masque and playing a role. Progress is a cosmetic in her makeup kit—and writers, in particular, know it. The powder of Progress (or Reform) has been the stuff of satire for newspaper writers from Walt Whitman and Lafcadio Hearn to current post-Katrina chroniclers like Chris Rose. Yet for these same writers and others, from Twain to Faulkner to Tennessee Williams, heartbreak also becomes New Orleans. John Kennedy Toole's *A Confederacy of Dunces* (1980) is New Orleans literature's *Don Quixote,* while Dave Brinks's four-book cycle of poems, *Caveat Onus* (2006–2007), may be her swan song.

New Orleans literature is not a linear proposition but an uncannily repetitive one. The intensity of its ability to attract and transform, repel and expel people began well before Cable and has not ended yet, despite the renewed sense of looming apocalypse. The 1884 "List of Persons Adjudged to be Insane by the Civil District Court for the Parish of Orleans" runs to over a hundred names. Among them: "John Costello, male, white, 61 years of age, native of Ireland, suffering from Hallucinations. This unfortunate old man, for the last 6 or 9 months imagines himself possessed by the voudous, and is even impertinent if one disbelieves him." Margaret McKeon, female, white, about fifty-five years old, widowed, native of Ireland, imagines herself to be an angel who fell from the heavens "in the time of the rebellion," who she says is "one hundred thousand years old." Not all the insane were born in Ireland, as there are many "colored" and other local types listed in the record. But the Irish, like the Germans, had been lured to New Orleans by the promise of plentiful jobs and quick riches, and found instead a swamp infested by mosquitoes and yellow fever, where the daily wages of an immigrant Irishman were below those of a freed slave.

In the nineteenth century, New Orleans was the second most important entry point for immigrants to the United States, after New York. Publications directed at the newcomers were thriving. A decade before the Civil War, the young Bavarian nobleman Ludwig von Reizenstein was sent by his father to New Orleans to distance him from the revolutionary troubles in Europe. The Baron arrived in the city penniless and found employment writing a serial novel, *The Mysteries of New Orleans,* for one of the city's two German-language daily newspapers. The *Louisiana Staats-Zeitung* was the bohemian paper, full of romantic, anarchist, and revolutionary matter. The Baron's novel drew protests because he described vividly sex between women, sex between men, child prostitution, and pedophilia. But the Baron was no Émile Zola, no social realist. Though he tossed his readers references to well-known scandals, street names, and locations, von Reizenstein also took them on a breathtaking fantastical trip, in which appeared a bloodsucking immortal over five hundred years old, and an evil horseman who carried the seeds of yellow fever from a mysterious plant that grew at the source of the Red River in order to hasten the apocalyptic end that New Orleans surely deserved. The dead were everywhere—and then as now, up to no good. During the Civil War the *Staats-Zeitung* was shut down for its abolitionist views, however, and the Baron gave up literature for lepidoptery. When George Washington Cable began writing, he knew the Baron only as "the butterfly man," a skinny eccentric who frequented seedy bars in the French Quarter. *The Mysteries of New Orleans* lay unknown and unread for a century and a half.

The Mississippian flow of New Orleans literature, meandering between the opposing banks of von Reizenstein's magical realism and Cable's highly colored psychological fiction, were already in place before the coming of *les Américains.* Von Reizenstein shares a lineage with early French romances based on Charles Gayarré's *Essai historique sur la Louisiane* (1846–1847), a work derived from reports, journals, and letters of early European explorers. The first Louisiana drama, *Le Père Indien* (1753), concerns the Choctaw Indians, among whom the author, Paul Le Blanc de Villeneuve, "passed seven of the happiest years of his life." He wrote it to defend the aborigines of the New World from the "false beliefs and unkind prejudices of Europe." Local literature thus begins with a defense of oppressed people. It moves on to harbor writers of African descent: Armand Lanusse assembled a literary circle called "Les Cenelles" (the Hollyberries), consisting of seventeen free persons of color like himself who had studied in France and returned to New Orleans, and published an anthology of their poetry in 1845. These writers enjoyed relative wealth and status in comparison to enslaved blacks; their in-between social position had been permitted with limitations under the Napoleonic *Code Noir* but was already under siege from the one-drop rule of the U.S. regime. The prohibition against writing anything critical about whites or slavery dictated that some of their writing be coded.

At the same time, antebellum New Orleans was becoming known as the most brutal slave market in America: the northernmost point in the traffic of slaves, rum, and sugar that began in Martinique and traversed the Caribbean, and the southernmost hell of the fearsome journey downriver. The complexities of this Creole history, and what it represented as an alternate way of life, fascinated Cable, who grew up among its ruins. But his critical stance on race did not endear him to other Louisianans, however popular his writings may have been. By 1884, Cable may have had enough of a city and a region that, instead of heading toward the emancipation he had envisioned in *'Tite Poulette* (1881), was busily consolidating the rigid racial segregation later given legal sanction by the *Plessy v. Ferguson* Supreme Court ruling. Homer Plessy, a descendant of the same class of *gens libres de couleur* who had showcased their learning in Les Cenelles, had set out to contest the practice of segregation by pointing out to the conductor of the whites-only train car he was riding that he was, despite his looks, part black.

The complexities of race, language, and culture are at the heart of some of the underread classics of New Orleans literature in this period, most notably Hearn's *Chita: A Memory of Last Island* (1888). Hearn, following in von Reizenstein's footsteps, recorded the city's charms and misdeeds in the newspapers, before shrugging the weight of New Orleans from his shoulders and moving on permanently to Japan. Like Cable, the transplanted French-speaking Kate Chopin also earned the wrath of locals with her feminist novel, *The Awakening* (1899). Debunking the city's myth of itself as tolerant and bohemian, her heroine is destroyed by the hypocrisy of white, upper-crust New Orleans—Creole and American alike. By 1921, an old guard of Southern women steeped in Confederate nostalgia stoked the old-time romance of the city at their literary salons. The best-known of them, Grace King, had conducted a public and well-publicized debate with Cable: she witnessed New Orleans writing from antebellum romantic realism through to modernism.

But the radical creative spirit, if it ran underground for a while, never entirely disappeared. With its unyielding provincialism, vivid history, and irresistible cheap rents, the French Quarter in the early twentieth century ranked with New York's Greenwich Village, the Left Bank of Paris, and old Prague as a haven for literary bohemians. The Quarter was home to the *Double Dealer,* a publication founded in 1921 to bring "modernism" to "the New South"—a notion conceived in the wake of H. L. Mencken's dismissal of Southern literature as a "Sahara of the Bozarts." The *Double Dealer* counted William Faulkner and Sherwood Anderson among its major contributors. Faulkner took up serious writing while he was living in the French Quarter, as a description in *Mosquitoes* (1927) illustrates: "The violet dusk held in soft suspension lights slow as bell strokes, Jackson Square was now a green and quiet lake in which abode lights round as jellyfish, feathering with silver mimosa and pomegranate and hibiscus beneath which lantana and cannas bled and bled. Pontalba and cathedral were cut from black paper and pasted flat on a green sky; above them taller palms were fixed in black and soundless explosions."

Roosevelt's WPA Federal Writers' Project also attracted to New Orleans the writers who would advance a renaissance in Southern letters. Many were political radicals hired to compile oral histories — the project on slave narratives collected 2,300 interviews of ex-slaves into forty-one volumes — and tourists' guides. The 1938 *New Orleans City Guide,* a work composed by many skilled hands, constitutes the best of a peculiar New Orleans literary genre: more than guidebooks, they can also be documentary histories, including such publications as the "blue books" that listed the locations, biographies, and prices for Storyville prostitutes. Highly colored books such as *Fabulous New Orleans* (1935) by Lyle Saxon and *The French Quarter* (1938) by Herbert Asbury shade from nonfiction to fiction, and well into the zone of the tour guide as they offer glimpses into a social underworld. By midcentury, then, an imaginary New Orleans was already in place — like Venice, a destination that allowed even armchair travelers to visit it without setting foot in the place. Virtual tourists like Lamartine and Hugo had already begun employing the city this way in the nineteenth century: "On the following day, the four fellow-travelers arrived at New Orleans," Jules Verne reports in *The Earth to the Moon* (1865), beginning in this quasi-fantastical location to ease the transition to the completely invented one.

The creative, no-holds-barred bohemianism of the French Quarter was always a central part of that fantasy New Orleans, but even in the later twentieth century it was still true to some degree. The *Outsider,* a literary review published by Jon and Louise "Gypsy Lou" Webb at their Loujon Press, lent stature and a label to the writings of Charles Bukowski and others. Also notable in this context is Nelson Algren's *A Walk on the Wild Side* (1956), a novel about the demimonde of Perdido Street. Zora Neale Hurston, another outsider, wrote in 1928 that "New Orleans is now and has ever been the hoodoo capital of America," and in the twentieth century the city nourished a rich African American community of writers: Tom Dent, a major figure in the Black Arts movement; poets Kalamu ya Salaam and Brenda Marie Osbey. Race in a multilayered world is the vein that keeps pulsing through to the very latest writing today, along with the relentless intrusion of magic in everyday affairs, from the vampires of Anne Rice and Poppy Z. Brite to the mystic speculations of Valerie Martin, the mysterious stories of James Nolan, the highly colored grotesques of Barry Gifford, to my own *Messiah* (1999).

New Orleans literature is a multilingual riverine production that flows between von Reizenstein's mysticism and Cable's psychology, between the Old and the New Worlds. The novels of Walker Percy sometimes straddle both shores, with *The Moviegoer* (1961) on the psychological-existentialist bank, and *The Thanatos Syndrome* (1987) on the fog-shrouded von Reizenstein side. But such distinctions are tenuous: the psychological and historical fictions of Williams, Toole, Lillian Hellman, Truman Capote, Shirley Ann Grau, Richard Ford, Robert Olen

Butler, Ellen Gilchrist, Elizabeth Dewberry, and John Biguenet make more than occasional use of the otherworldly aura of the city. New Orleans may be the most overwritten city in America, but that has not stopped its furiously thriving literary community. To its histories (decaying into thinner and thinner strains as guides), novels, poetry, and satires, post-Katrina disaster narratives will add memoirs, indictments, manifestos, and genres yet unknown.

Bibliography: Les Cenelles: A Collection of Poems by Creole Writers of the Early Nineteenth Century, trans. Regine Latortue and Gleason R. W. Adams (Boston, 1980). Joshua Clark, ed., *French Quarter Fiction: The Newest Stories of America's Oldest Bohemia* (New Orleans, 2003). Richard S. Kennedy, ed., *Literary New Orleans in the Modern World* (Baton Rouge, LA, 1998). Ludwig von Reizenstein, *The Mysteries of New Orleans,* trans. and ed. Steven Rowan (Baltimore, 2002). Jeff Weddle, *Bohemian New Orleans: The Story of the Outsider and Loujon Press* (Jackson, MS, 2007).

ANDREI CODRESCU

1888

Eadweard Muybridge visits Thomas Alva Edison's laboratory in Menlo Park

THE INTRODUCTION OF MOTION PICTURES

The story of cinema begins before itself, in an unaccountable realm of magic lanterns, shadow shows, early still photography, and dreams. Let our first item of evidence of early film be not a film, then, but a slide-show lecture, *The Attitude of Animals in Motion,* from 1881. Eadweard Muybridge, a great secret hero in the history of photography and the culture of nineteenth-century California—also a colorful American iconoclast, and an unpunished murderer—arguably inaugurated the motion picture with his series of experiments into the serial photography of running horses, begun in 1872 under the sponsorship of Leland Stanford (California's governor and the eventual founder of Stanford University). Stanford had made a bet as to whether a running horse's four legs ever simultaneously left the ground, and Muybridge set out to settle the question photographically. His peculiar and obstinate effort in setting up twenty-four cameras to be triggered in sequence resulted in an inspiring and unsettling new record of the visual experience of motion (and the magical number twenty-four remained, somehow, enshrined as the default number of frames per second in the industry to come). By 1881 Muybridge's traveling lecture, featuring his projected sequential images of horses and other animals, as well as deliberately shocking images of seminaked human animals, enjoyed an ongoing public success.

Never mind the fact that parallel to Muybridge, in Europe and America, another dozen clever men were nudging the magic lantern and the photographic slide show in the direction of some kind of public exhibition of "moving pictures." Inventor of cinema is a crown with many claimants. Those looking for uncomplicated provenances will be forced to abandon hope, for even Muybridge has his French counterpart in serial photography, the equally miraculous, though quieter, Étienne-Jules Marey. While it can be tempting to imagine these men as a group of rivals engaged in a coherent race to make *Jaws* possible, it would be as true to say the opposite. Those history now views as candidates for Father of Cinema, whether inventors, artists, entrepeneurs, or all three, were mostly trying to make different and specific things, and succeeded in making them: the Kineopticon, the Kinematoscope, the calcium-light stereopticon, the Zoopraxinoscope. From this cloud of devices and possibilities the twentieth-century film emerged.

Nearly any account, however, settles on 1888 as the crucial year. In February 1888 Muybridge performed his lecture in Orange, New Jersey, and afterward met with Thomas Alva Edison in his nearby laboratory. Edison, inventor or patent holder of the telegraph, the phonograph, the incandescent bulb, and a microphone component of what would become the telephone, was the quintessential self-made tinkerer-genius, then recently dubbed "The Wizard of Menlo Park." Edison proposed partnership with Muybridge: why shouldn't the phonograph, which reproduced human speech, be wedded to a photographic equivalent? Muybridge agreed. Silent-film purists take note: the dream of sound synchronization arrives with film itself. Edison was one of the great spongelike appropriators of the notions of others, a talent not unlike that of a great film director, a Welles or Hitchcock, say, in whom the talents of subordinate collaborators became inextricably absorbed within the products of their own genius. So, he stalled a while, then reworked the essential notions in Muybridge's apparatus until Muybridge could be safely forgotten. Thus did Edison, with a few crucial drawings in October 1888, invent the first motion picture recording device.

Edison's claim is entrenched in a story of initiative, publicity, and patents, all of which became a working reality: among his advantages were an established name, a versatile laboratory, and a clever assistant named W. K. L. Dickson. Dickson, Edison's pocket expert on photography, became the hands-on creator of the devices Edison would display in 1889, under the names Kinetograph—the recording instrument, capable of producing films of slightly more than one minute in length—and Kinetoscope—the peephole viewer, used by one spectator at a time, with which the films could be seen. He was also the designer of the Black Maria, an experimental building featuring sliding panels to provide continuous overhead sunlight that became the Edison Company's film studio, and within which Dickson's activities qualified him as probably the world's first film director. Dickson was another genius hidden behind Edison in the story, one less romantic and more secret than Muybridge.

Edison's shop produced earlier films, but *Edison Kinetoscopic Record of a Sneeze,* from 1894, featuring the nasal convulsion of one Fred Ott, an Edison employee, was the first film Edison registered for copyright at the Library of Congress. Ott's sneeze is a sort of pivot, then, when the disparate experiments and enterprises of cinema's prehistory coalesce into an official industry. From this tiny point, everything we come to know as Hollywood, as well as its rivals or antidotes, can be seen to have grown. For Edison's company was soon busy selling its viewing instruments to exhibitors, while hoarding the means of film production within its walls. In 1894 alone more than seventy-five short films were created, under Dickson's hand. Early subjects included boxing matches, trained animal stunts, prototypes of the "animal-attack" film, sexy flexing by a body builder named Eugene Sandow, and twirling, risqué performances by dancers called Carmencita and Annabelle. These subjects were more than merely resolutely secular and vernacular; they all suggest that a strong air of vaudeville and carnival sideshow pervaded the first Edison films.

The defining difference between Edison's Kinetoscope and the vast popular sensation that moviegoing was to become was the one-at-a-time viewing mechanism. The device evoked a stereopticon or peepshow, a private diversion, rather than a public theater (let alone schoolroom or church). Together with the borderline subject matter of many of the films, this mechanical tendency rooted film in the realm of gentlemen's amusements, and even voyeurism: beginning with Muybridge (and really, earlier, with photography itself), the new technology constantly promised or threatened to unveil the forbidden. While at one level dooming American film to a legacy of censorship, this also invested the dawning narrative form with a self-conscious interest in matters of spectatorship and complicity, a key and sustaining motif in films through Hitchcock's *Rear Window* and *Psycho* and David Lynch's *Blue Velvet*.

A host of showmen-entrepeneurs were eager to adapt Edison's innovation to a projection device, but his company was selling a lot of Kinetoscopes, and Edison resisted. Here, again, the tale of innovation explodes into parallel developments, and another list of terrifically evocative names: the Eidoloscope, the Phantascope, the Mutoscope, the Vitascope. The difference between these devices and those that preceded them is that this next round of inventors all had to contend, one way or another, with Edison's patents—by furtiveness, accommodation, or licensing. A measure of the gnarled tale of the development of a widely successful projection technology is suggested by the fact that W. K. L. Dickson—our secret hero again!—participated covertly in inventing the Eidoloscope while still in Edison's ranks. It would be the Vitascope that was the winner, and Edison, in his typical manner, immediately entered into a licensing partnership with its creators. Or did the Vitascope win because of Edison's Midas touch?

In any case, the door was opened to theatrical projection to a mass of people in a darkened room. In this mode of reception, the device began to restlessly unfold its potential, to exert its opportunistic sway on the consciousness of the next century. Cinema would soon enough be claimed as a new artistic medium, an equal to foundational arts like music composition or painting (however slow such a claim would be to shed its detractors—there are some around still). More, it attracted an ideology, a rhetoric, as both new mediums and technological innovations will tend to—and this was both. Film, it was claimed, or warned, would change more than the arts or sciences, it would alter the nature of consciousness. And so, as much as radio and the automobile, film threatened to embody the acceleration of modernity, in all its ominous power. In the wrong hands—Hitler's, say—film might be a weapon. For Marxist practitioners, like Dziga Vertov, it had revolutionary potential. In its dreamlike subjective force—which the shift from peephole to mass spectatorship had paradoxically only amplified—film also displayed a propensity to roil hearts, and loins. Perhaps it possessed some hotline circumnavigating the intellect, leading straight to a well of emotion, sensuality, and primal memory.

To watch the Edison films now, and those of the other production companies that joined him in the earliest phase of the film industry, is to discover a portal peering both backward and forward in cultural time. Even the most assiduous film buffs tend to begin with Charlie Chaplin, who appeared as a performer and made his first pictures as a fledgling director in 1914, or D. W. Griffith's *Birth of a Nation* a year later. But the films that preceded those are as revelatory for their familiarity as their strangeness. Almost none presents a possibility that will fail to be exfoliated in the great boom to come, nor explores an avenue that runs anywhere but straight from the common cultural trove. A 120-second costumed Punch and Judy show like *The Clown and the Alchemist* (Edison Company, 1900), with its antic clown assisted in his abuses of the sententious alchemist by the use of stop-motion special effects, forms a lucid bridge between vaudeville and a Jim Carrey movie—*The Mask,* say. And watching the Selig Polyscope Company's thirteen-minute 1910 version of *The Wizard of Oz* provides an uncanny sense of dislocation. Presenting a series of highlight moments derived from the popular stage version (adapted by L. Frank Baum, the novel's author), the Selig *Oz,* in scenes of the Tin Man's oiling, of the tale's companions skipping arm in arm down a yellow brick road, and of the Wizard's departure by balloon, seems a precognitive appropriation of gestures that would otherwise appear to wholly belong to Judy Garland and her 1939 compatriots. The viewer may be convinced that the medium's real genius was for stopping American time, and for opening an interior eye on a cultural unconscious always rehearsing the same few dreams.

Not far away lay D. W. Griffith with his (copyright-oblivious) adaptations of works by authors living and dead, including the Bible and Darwin. In its ambition as a narrative art the new medium was unashamed of its nostalgic dependence on old forms, feeling no obedience to idealistic rhetoric about its own transformative potential. (This lesson Internet idealists might have recalled when the transformative potential of their new medium forged less a postliterate virtual reality than a revival of epistolary social relations, and a culture of scrapbooks and diaries.) That's to say, of course, that narrative film looked to the written word—mostly the novel—and the stage play. Book and stage adaptations still overwhelmingly comprise the sources for contemporary films, particularly the "prestige" films the industry tends to brandish as its proof of legitimacy, and shower with awards.

It was big movies with big stars on big screens that won the nation's imagination, and quickly inspired a sympathetic body of critical writing, by James Agee, Graham Greene, Otis Ferguson, Manny Farber, and others. The descriptive excavations by these writers of the new medium's magic, as well as responses by artists in other mediums, like the poet Frank O'Hara, the visual artist Joseph Cornell, and the singer Bob Dylan, rapidly mythologized the archetypal forms these films had so rapidly etched into our cultural life. So, since the introduction of television—for some, even, since the introduction of sound—the vitality and promise in what the great movie studios made have seemed to many commentators a possibility dwindled or tamed, into inferior forms on smaller and smaller screens. Film has persistently mourned itself, a peculiarity evident, for instance, when a movie as weird, precise, and stirring as *Sunset Boulevard* (directed by Billy Wilder, 1950) partly half ratifies the complaint of its own character, Norma Desmond (played by semiretired silent-film star Gloria Swanson): "I am big. It's the pictures that got small!" But the truth of film's origins as a series of devices enabling various public and private diversions persistently lurked in the goal of widening or multiplying its screen, or in the sport of enlisting other sensory apparatuses, with gimmicks like 3-D, Sensurround, and Smell-o-Vision. And this lurking truth explodes into relevance again in the era that began with the introduction of the VCR, and persists in a presently unfolding future that includes YouTube and handheld viewing devices, with episodic serials beamed into portable telephones already commonplace. As David Thomson points out in *The Whole Equation,* Edison's Kinetoscope may just now be having its day.

Edison's own last great contribution was, perversely, in driving the industry westward, out of the grasp of his copyrights and patents. Squatting toadlike on his rights, indeed, employing a private force of roving bully-enforcers, Edison more or less accidentally routed the fugitive innovators to California, beyond his reach. So the activities that began flourishing there, at that coastal brink of American self-invention, were branded as permanently expedient and on the run, piratically bold, and driven by a geographically renewable innocence, like the nation itself.

Bibliography: Marta Braun, *Picturing Time: The Works of Étienne-Jules Marey* (Chicago, 1992). Charles Musser, *The Emergence of Cinema: The American Screen to 1907* (New York, 1990). Rebecca Solnit, *River of Shadows: Eadweard Muybridge and the Technological Wild West* (New York, 2003). David Thomson, *The Whole Equation: A History of Hollywood* (New York, 2005). *Filmography: History of Motion Pictures: Early Films by Thomas Alva Edison, 1891–98,* 2-DVD set (A2ZCDS.com, 2005); *History of Motion Pictures: Early Films by Thomas Alva Edison, 1900,* 2-DVD set (A2ZCDS.com, 2005).

JONATHAN LETHEM

1889, August 28
Mark Twain expresses delight at Daniel Beard's illustrations

A Connecticut Yankee in King Arthur's Court

The most lighthearted passages in Twain's raucous novel juxtapose the business slang of Hank Morgan, the Connecticut Yankee, with Malory's archaic Arthurian diction, or feature slapstick anachronism and adaptation: Hank shaking and thrashing because of bugs in his armor; a plumed knight bearing a gilded advertising tabard with the slogan, "Persimmon's Soap—All the Prime-Donne Use It." Contrast and burlesque are also evident in Beard's frontispiece to the original edition, depicting Hank's arrival in Camelot. Hank is wearing a loud checkered suit and derby hat, the costume of traveling salesmen, machine politicians, and other late nineteenth-century men on the rise. He is clinging to the trunk of a tree he has just climbed to evade the lance of Sir Kay, who is charging at him in "old time iron armor from head to heel." The smile on the ornamental helmet at the border of the frontispiece—Twain's smile—seems lighthearted when first encountered but more ominous by the time one has reached the novel's end. After saving himself and gaining the admiration of the king and the Arthurians, Hank attempts to modernize their "lost land." His efforts culminate in a war that decimates chivalry with Gatling guns and traps him amid the corpses. Just before *Connecticut Yankee* went to press, Twain intensified the imagery of this shockingly dark ending. The magician Merlin, gleeful about his power to enchant Hank back into the future, reels back against a live wire and is electrocuted with his mouth spread open. What was Merlin's mere "unpleasant look" in the original manuscript, Twain turned into an eerie "petrified laugh" for the novel's first American edition. This image vividly captures the objectifying humor that pervades the novel.

Other electrifying and petrifying encounters temper the progressive and solidarity-building possibilities of technology and the "effects" performed by Hank in the novel. On his first night at the Round Table, Hank finds Sir Dinadan the Humorist's jokes so unpleasantly familiar they seem petrified; Hank casually orders him killed for this later on. Even as he remakes the country in the image of his homeland and in the name of the common man—introducing everything from soap and sewing machines to civil service and tax relief—Hank rails at the ingrained—petrified—reverential attitudes and backward prejudices of the Arthurians. Meanwhile, Hank's own self-aggrandizing and glitzy stunts, like the fireworks extravaganza accompanying his restoration of a holy fountain, transfix and awe his audiences so that, their beliefs reinforced, they clamor for more magic. Toward the end of the novel, when mistaken for an escaped slave and threatened with hanging, Hank momentarily feels "petrified" in his "clinging impotence." He fends off this feeling with games and pomps (i.e., knights on bikes), lassos and revolvers and, eventually, war. Later, on a battlefield rigged with an electrified fence, each "blue spark" or "pathetic statue" Hank sees stands for a "poor fellow" who had "touched a charged wire with his sword and been elected." This strange verb mocks the feudal and divine rights of church, nobility, and king, undermines Hank's flashy attempt at government by consent, and even casts doubt on the possibility of significant, willed human endeavor. In the end, Hank follows each shot of current with another, not giving the Arthurians a chance to "recover their faculties." The result is unforgettable. "People will read [*Connecticut Yankee*] to laugh," Hamlin Garland reported gratefully in the January 10, 1890, *Boston Evening Transcript,* "and pause in their laughter to think."

Twain's fable of power was both timeless and current. Edison harnessed electricity for use in incandescent lamps in 1878, the year before Hank's journey; in 1889, the year the novel was published, there was a spate of fatal accidents in

American cities involving falling Electric Lighting Company wires, and the State of New York put electricity to use for capital punishment. In his younger days, Twain had spent a summer tinkering with fossils in his spare time and had written a comic hoax about a funnyman turned to stone from overexposure, but by the 1880s the notion of geologic deep time had started to shape his perspective on human history.

In the latter part of that decade, the pitfalls and possibilities of technology, and its comic effects, remained on Twain's mind as he turned his attention from writing *Connecticut Yankee* to compile the *Library of Humor,* a deliberately chaotic collection of writing by himself and others, and to overinvest in the Paige typesetter, a marvelous, impracticable word machine (it had more than 18,000 separate parts) that enamored him like a devilish twin. Twain referred to himself both as a Mugwump and a Sansculotte at this time; he hobnobbed with Andrew Carnegie and John Rockefeller, declared himself antitariff and prounion, and repudiated the cant and corruption in Gilded Age politics. Given all of this, it is not surprising that the text of *Connecticut Yankee,* written in spurts over several years and never systematically revised, resembles, as Henry Nash Smith observed, "a geologist's stratigraphic series." In a framing tale, Hank's story is figured as a palimpsest manuscript given to a late nineteenth-century American tourist, and the novel is a minefield of references to popular culture ("insurance-chromos"; a song called "Sweet By and Bye") and allusions to historical texts (such as W. E. H. Lecky's 1869 *History of European Morals* and Charles Ball's 1837 slave narrative). Twain's sumptuously illustrated first edition took advantage of and poked fun at the contemporary fad for medieval kitsch. Several of Beard's drawings comment on contemporary issues: an Arthurian slave driver has the face of Jay Gould, Queen Victoria is pictured as a royal hog, and Merlin looks like Tennyson.

Its dark ending and satiric look at both past and present distinguished *Connecticut Yankee* from other time- and space-travel novels written on both sides of the Atlantic. Edward Bellamy's *Looking Backward* (1887) and William Morris's *News from Nowhere* (1890), in which protagonists dream of utopian near-futures, the former centralized and industrialized and the latter quaint and craftsy, are much more straightforward in their social commentary and more culturally highbrow. In these novels, sagacious guides reveal to observer-narrators (both Tennyson devotees) the ideals of equality and fraternity. Morris and Bellamy stir up hope in the possibility of the futures they depict. In contrast, Twain's Hank ultimately fails to herald a better new world or to become one with the people. Twain does not attribute this to a moral chasm, like the one that William Dean Howells portrays in *A Traveler from Altruria* (1894). Howells's novel, written in the midst of a severe economic depression, is fixated on the contrast between an America dominated by class inequality and an Altruria run according to the golden rule. The Altrurian visitor expresses no contempt for American ways and gains many working-class followers. Twain's Hank tries to improve the Arthurians using modern means, including technology and advertising, that take advantage of their premodern mentality. While Hank shares some common ground with the Arthurians, his power struggles with Merlin, chivalry, and the church turn that ground into a field of "human muck." Hank does not travel to an alternative present or a potential future but moves into a past pervaded by slavery and the carnage of civil war. His efforts can also be read as an attempt to trump the past, reversing the imperial relationship between Britain and the United States.

Hank was thrust into the past by the crowbar of a disgruntled worker at a Colt arms factory, where he had risen to the rank of superintendent. He knows a good deal about revolvers and how to play his know-how for all it's worth. In Camelot, he gains the position of minister to the king by convincing the Arthurians (whom he also refers to as "white Indians" and "modified savages") that he controls the sun during an eclipse. Hank claims that doing so was no plagiarism of Columbus, given that his effect was not due for hundreds of years. (Contemporary reviewers of *Connecticut Yankee* noted that this eclipse device had been used similarly in H. Rider Haggard's best-selling African adventure, the 1885 *King Solomon's Mines*). After managing his eclipse effect, Hank dynamites Merlin's tower and declares that the magician's "stock was flat." Hank soon reaps large profits selling souvenirs to pilgrims, though he "stocked the business and unloaded" when St. Stylite, whose bowing body was powering production, took ill.

Hank does have Merlin's tower rebuilt. Indeed Hank embarks on what he calls a "new deal" building project that involves the construction of factories, schools, and Protestant churches and the laying of railways and telegraph and telephone lines. He plans to teach the country to demand popular sovereignty and equal justice under the law. There are moments, too, when Hank seems on the verge of transcending the cultural and communication barrier. The "pelting sing song" medieval idiom of Alisande la Carteloise (whom he nicknames Sandy and with whom he has a child) reminds him of railway announcers he heard as a boy in Connecticut. Sandy names their child "Hello-Central" in a tribute to the telephone and to a young woman Hank used to love. The irreverent weekly newspaper in Camelot, edited by Hank's sidekick, Clarence, similarly reminds Hank of his, or rather Twain's, early days in Arkansas journalism. Twain integrates clippings of newspaper columns into the layout of the novel, so that the cultural blending is visual. Here, as is fitting in a novel whose protagonist remembers future revolutions and innovations in order to repeat them in another land, Twain conflates progressive and nostalgic impulses and shows how both contribute to utopian ambitions. Twain also juxtaposes Hank's newspaper to the king's touch, showing the reverence of the Arthurians for both, though the newspaper and later printed proclamations, gratifying as they are to Hank, do not have a beneficial effect on the people.

Hank's peculiar combination of self-serving manipulation and good-intentioned reform can come off as callous. After listening to Sandy describe how dueling knights stopped fighting and swore to love each other as brethren, Hank considers them useless "jackass[es]." Hank tries to convey this truth to the Arthurians not through argument but through mockery; by turning knights into walking advertisements, Hank tries to "extinguish knighthood by making it grotesque and absurd." There is little to suggest that Arthurians get this joke, and it only serves to further objectify the knights in Hank's eyes. When Hank turns his strategy of mockery on the common people he is trying to educate, its limits are painfully obvious. Ashamed at his failure to convince a group of master mechanics that high prices diminish the value of their earnings, Hank threatens a blacksmith with the pillory for paying unlawfully high wages and his fellow tradesmen with the same for not informing on him. Hank's explanation of his trick technique sounds like a mean-spirited segment of Twain's "How to Tell a Funny Story": "I get away off yonder to one side, and work up on him gradually, so that he never suspects that I'm going to hit him at all; and by and by, all in a flash, he's flat on his back, and he can't tell for the life of him how it all happened." When taken advantage of in this way, the workers become fearful and suspicious. Hank's message — that they consider themselves spending patrons as much as feudal clients, that they demand their rights and condemn unjust law — has gotten lost.

What bothers Hank most is evidence that people are passive and do not change: that they've laughed at the same jokes for time immemorial; that they lack courage, initiative, and imagination; that they revere rank and authority, are thankful for condescension, take comfort in tradition, do not protest against their own oppression or pity the oppressed. These characteristics undermine Hank's own efforts. Hank hopes that by emptying Morgan Le Fay's dungeon, he might provoke outrage against the nobility for wrongful imprisonment. No such luck: he finds the members of a reunited family resigned to a "dumb uncomplaining acceptance." Twain juxtaposes Hank's depressed reaction to the Arthurians' delight in Sir Dinadan's petrified joke with his realization of their "hardened" acceptance of slavery. The joke is the one "about a humorous lecturer who flooded an ignorant audience with the killingest jokes for an hour and never got a laugh; and then when he was leaving, some gray simpletons wrung him gratefully by the hand and said it had been the funniest thing they had ever heard, and 'it was all they could do to keep from laughin' right out in meetin.'" This joke particularly bothers Hank because, unable to turn to his objectifying humor when faced with slavery, he suspects he cannot get his message of liberty through to the Arthurians. When, while in disguise, he and the king are sold into slavery before an indifferent "patriotic crowd" of Arthurians, Hank loses his powers of persuasion and says "there is no use stringing out the details." Twain here conveys some of the feeling of disenchantment experienced by Northern carpetbagger reformers during the retreat from Reconstruction. Like the hand-wringing of the grateful simpletons, King Arthur's belated abolitionism has a rousing effect on Hank. But the people's tendency to obey the established church leads Hank into a war with a nation adhering to an interdict.

Hank vacillates between determination and fatalism throughout the novel, but this tension is clearest at the end. As the critic Ann Douglas has noted, Hank's stunts are "painful not only to others but finally to himself." During the final battle, which makes a mockery of both revolutionary and religious rituals, Hank seems lost, unable to comprehend his responsibility. Preoccupied with the technicalities of his weaponry, he is also drawn to tour the destruction. He has trouble recognizing the dead, and understanding the meaning behind the facts. He watches as a knight reaches out to his fellow, who had just been electrocuted, and gets electrocuted in kind, "killed," as Hank reads it, "by a dead friend." When Hank determines, after the massacre, to help the wounded, he is stabbed by the first knight who appeals to him. Hank feels too wretched to write the ending. It is the cynical Clarence who describes Merlin's final bitter laugh.

In his original manuscript, Twain included an absurd calculation of casualties in terms of pounds of flesh, emphasizing the utter destruction of individuals and the "untrustworthy" custom of determining losses in battle by aggregate count. Twain's old friend Edmund Clarence Stedman disapproved of this "technical humor," so Twain left it out. Twain's "Final P.S.," which objectifies Hank with a mournful twist, is not redemptive or sentimental, but it does point to the appeal of belief and enchantment. We encounter a delirious Hank thirteen hundred years after the battle. He believes it never occurred, denies the distance between himself and the Arthurians, expresses his adoration of Sandy and their child, and, just before dying, commands the battlements manned to mark the arrival of the king. In another passage cut from Twain's manuscript, Hank is more conscious of his frailties and needs. "Yes, we are just as pitiful and shabby as we can be, we human beings, in some of our aspects," Hank says in this lost passage. "I reckon we ought to make it a rule to honor each other's superstitions. I mean, by charitable fiction of speech, of course. We never could do it in reality." The skeptical charity of the novel's last line about Hank lends lasting relevance to his death. "He was," Twain tells us, "getting up his last 'effect'; but he never finished it."

Bibliography: Harold Baetzhold, "'Well, My Book Is Written—Let It Go . . .': The Making of *A Connecticut Yankee in King Arthur's Court,*" in James Barbour and Tom Quirk, eds., *Biographies of Books: The Compositional Histories of Notable American Writings* (Columbia, MO, 1996). Ann Douglas, "Art and Advertising in *A Connecticut Yankee:* The Robber Baron Revisited," *Canadian Review of American Studies* 6 (1975): 182–195. Bruce Michelson, *Printer's Devil: Mark Twain and the American Publishing Revolution* (Berkeley, 2006). Henry Nash Smith, *Mark Twain's Fable of Progress: Political and Economic Ideas in "A Connecticut Yankee"* (New Brunswick, NJ, 1964). Mark Twain, *A Connecticut Yankee in King Arthur's Court,* ed. and with an introduction by Werner Sollors (New Milford, CT, 2003).

YAEL SCHACHER

1893

Chief Simon Pokagon addresses the Chicago World's Fair on land his father sold to the U.S. government

THE POSE THAT TRUTH MUST ASSUME

Simon Pokagon, introducing himself as the last chief of the Potawatomi, fluent in English and "the four classical European languages," wrote in the preface to his last book: "In presenting *Queen of the Woods* to the public, I realize that many of its readers will inquire why so many Indian words are used. All such will please bear in mind that the manuscript was first written in the Algonquin language, the only language spoken by me until fourteen years of age, and that in translating it into English, many parts of it seem to lose their force and euphony." Here Pokagon both tapped into a preexisting rhetorical mode common to Native American writing—a spicy mixture of cultural truth-telling and moral sermonizing—and pushed it ahead into the twentieth century, so much so that one can still taste those sentiments in much more recent works of Native American literature. This tension within the skeleton of a fiction that has been given the pose of cultural truth is also clear in the second preface to *Queen of the Woods,* written by his friend and lawyer C. H. Engle of Hartford, Michigan:

> *Queen of the Woods* is a real romance of Indian life by Chief Pokagon. Nearly all the persons mentioned in the narrative bear their real names, and were personally known to many yet living . . . Throughout the whole narrative, the careful reader will note that the author has studiously avoided . . . all such acts of seeming cruelty as might tend to increase the existing prejudice between the two races. His greatest desire in publishing the historical sketch of his life has been that the white man and the red man might be brought into closer sympathy with each other.

This is the birth of Native American literature: "real" but also a "romance"; authenticated by living persons yet choosy about which facts get included. In a contemporary version of Pokagon's life and work that appears on the Web site Pearls in Our Past, the same contradictions remain: "His father was Chief Leopold Pokagon, a man of sterling character who had been converted to Christianity by Jesuit missionaries. Until twelve years of age Simon knew only Indian ways and spoke only native Algonquin. However, he displayed such mental curiosity that Catholic priests sent him to the newly founded Notre Dame school." So he was raised by a Jesuit-educated father but "knew only Indian ways"? The real Pokagon was not a chief (and certainly not the last Potawatomi chief), nor was he fluent in "the four classic European languages"; *Queen of the Woods* was not originally written in Potawatomi. The uncomfortable pose that truth must assume in order to be heard can be seen not just in the narratives of the life of Chief Simon Pokagon but in the whole genre of Native American fiction.

Simon Pokagon was born in Indiana but his family moved to Dowagiac, Michigan, when he was still quite young. His father died when Simon was ten or twelve years old. There is some debate as to how long he attended school and where. He claims to have attended Notre Dame, though he most likely attended the Notre Dame Manual Labor School, adjacent to but unaffiliated with the university. He would not have been taught Greek or Latin or French at that school. Pokagon claims to have then attended Oberlin College and next a vocational school in Twinsburg, Ohio. It wasn't until 1890, when he was in his sixties, that Pokagon began to write. In his final decade he published *The Red Man's Rebuke, The Red Man's Greeting,* and many occasional pieces, such as "An Indian on the Problems of His Race," "Indian Superstitions and Legends," and "An Indian's Plea for Prohibition." Pokagon was so prolific that his work was published regularly after his death in 1898: "Massacre at Fort Dearborn at Chicago," "Algonquin Legends of

Paw Paw," and "The Pottawattomie Book of Genesis," among others. Many of these were political pamphlets, though a few dealt with Potawatomi beliefs. But perhaps Pokagon's most telling piece of work was his "true life" novel *O-gi-mäw-kwě mit-i-gwä-kî,* or *Queen of the Woods,* published in 1899.

The story is, like many stories about and by Native Americans, more of a pastoral tragedy than a pastoral romance. It begins when Simon (referred to as "the chief") returns home from Twinsburg, Ohio. His first instinct is to reacquaint himself with nature.

> I had an innate desire to retire into the wild woods, far from the haunts of civilization, and there enjoy myself with bow and arrow, hook and line, as I had done before going to school. Judging from my returning love of the chase, and from various conversations with educated people of the white race, I have come to the conclusion that there is a charm about hunting and fishing, planted deep in the human heart by Nature's own hand, that requires but little cultivation to lead the best educated of even the most civilized races to engage heartily in the sport.

N. Scott Momaday's breakthrough Pulitzer Prize–winning novel, *House Made of Dawn* (1968), echoes these same themes. From the first paragraph of the prologue it, too, balances native "signifying" with prose that was modern for its time: "*Dypaloh.* There was a house made of dawn. It was made of pollen and of rain, and the land was very old and everlasting. There were many colors on the hills, and the plain was bright with many different clays and sands. Red and blue and spotted horses grazed in the plain, and there was a dark wilderness on the mountains beyond. The land was still and strong. It was beautiful all around." *Dypaloh* is the Jemez word for "beginning" and is the way in which most stories in the Jemez oral tradition begin. *House Made of Dawn* does not simply, as is often claimed, hew to the oral tradition ("writing in the oral tradition" is a bit like walking in the running tradition), drawing as it does from Momaday's love of Dickinson and Melville. Momaday's prose is conscious of itself, of its own occasion. Even the adjectival clauses seem imposed on the nouns they modify: the colors are "on" the hills, not of them; the "dark wilderness" is likewise "on the mountains." Posed in the middle of the paragraph are obligatory Indian horses, but being red and blue, they do not spring from the landscape as much as they are Seussed into it. They are ideal horses, cartoon horses, that steal the color away from the blandly described "different clays and sands." The first word functions (as does the last—*qtsedaba,* the Jemez word for "end") like Pokagon's use of Potawatomi in *Queen of the Woods:* language that communicates nothing but signifies everything. Couldn't the plots of Leslie Silko's *Ceremony* and Louise Erdrich's *Love Medicine* be said to begin the same way as *House Made of Dawn* and *Queen of the Woods,* if not with the same reliance on prose pulled from the mouth of Walter Scott? Both novels begin with the main character returning after a long absence to Indian land and hearth. A reevaluation takes place. The protagonist both belongs and doesn't belong.

In *Queen of the Woods,* immediately after his return and after being reunited with his mother, Simon sees the startling vision of Lonidaw, an "Indian maid" (whose kit is not complete without an albino pet deer and the ability to paddle a canoe solo while looking *very* good). Pokagon has been shot with a dart of love. As in many pastoral romances, the two become friends first and lovers later—the trick being to grow into adulthood and to glean knowledge and pleasure with innocence intact. Eventually Simon goes back to school, then realizes he has lost the battle with love and must return to marry Lonidaw. The novel continues in its pastoral vein:

> As I would emerge from out the woods upon the open shore, I never failed to see Lonidaw's erect and slender form on a hasty run, to the get boat to bring me home. No "wob-si" (swan) ever faster swam or more elegantly appeared than she, when bending to the oars, pushing "widg wig-wastchi-man" (her birch canoe) across the swelling bosom of the lake. As she would approach me while waiting on shore, I always hailed her "Ho" (Hallo), "O-gi-mäw-kwě mit-i-gwä-kî" (queen of the woods).

They have two children, Olondaw, a boy, and Hazeleye, a girl. But this is an Indian pastoral tragedy, and as such, paradise is defiled, happiness is destroyed, and the reader is left facing the "reality" of the advance of civilization while cherishing, nostalgically, the lost past. Within ten pages of Pokagon and Lonidaw's marriage they lose both children to alcohol. The boy drowns himself in it while away at school and the girl drowns in the lake after her little canoe is capsized by two drunken fishermen. Lonidaw never recovers. She dies, too. The novel ends hammering home a moral through a rather perplexing shift in tone and genre, with a call for prohibition and the recounting of select rulings of the Supreme Court on the sale of intoxicating drinks.

The novel's claims that the prose derives from tribal storytelling (and even a tribal language) compete with the prose itself. It is very doubtful that stock Victorian phrases like "planted deep in the human heart by Nature's own hand" and "the swelling bosom of the lake" have analogues in Potawatomi oratory. If this is true, then the Potawatomi have stories that are as clichéd as many stories in English. More interesting (for *Queen of the Woods* and for its modern derivatives, such as James Welch's *Fools Crow* and Erdrich's *Tracks*) than the story's origin are its echoes: the tale is posed as coming from the past, but it is firmly situated in the realm of modern fiction. The narrator uses all of modern fiction's tricks—the ones that work (such as contrasting action) and the ones that don't (more purple prose than purple mountains' majesty).

It is clear in *Queen of the Woods* and in Simon Pokagon's own partially fictive life that both he and his work feel caught between opposing forces—the necessary and exhilarating march of civilization and the pull of a pastoral past that seems better (in terms of morality and emotivity) than the fast-approaching future. While Pokagon was being hosted at the Chicago World's Fair in 1893 (officially called the World's Columbian Exposition), Frederick Jackson Turner was delivering his famous speech arguing that the frontier was closed, and with it an era that prized individuality, democracy, and opportunity; and Franz Boas was busy organizing the "Indian Village"—an attraction at the exposition in which various Indians dressed in costume and went about "daily life" in a dioramic faux village. The past was closed but its lessons vital. Indians had been "wiped out" or "destroyed" by the "march of civilization," yet were alive enough to mimic their old ways with enough authenticity to convince spectators of their past importance.

Modern Native American fiction has carried the same tensions forward, if with, perhaps, better ability than Pokagon did. It is possible to argue that the most widely read contemporary Native American writers, such as Joy Harjo, Welch, Momaday, Silko, and Erdrich, appeal to the same gods: morality and progress, civilization and tribalosity (if that is word; certainly it is a concept). This fact of Native American fiction—its use of writerly tricks to suggest a cultural origin—is displayed in the praise that is, more often than not, used to obscure it. Speaking of *Fools Crow,* one reviewer said that "reading *Fools Crow* is like finding a lifestyle preserved for a century and reanimated for our benefit and education," and an Erdrich scholar wrote that the multiple narrators found in *Love Medicine* usually "ascribed to the magical realism of the postmodernists probably [have their] origin in Erdrich's Chippewa heritage." It's the reviewers' offhand reference to "our benefit and education" that is so telling: the twin notions of betterment and education always seem to be pulled along in the current of Native American fiction, bumping along the river bottom of criticism. So, too, do sentiments that make fluttering hand gestures at the "postmodernism" of Native American fiction only to better bear down on the Indian origins of Indian books. Taken all together these comments sidle up nicely to those made by Pokagon himself, and make the reading and interpretation of Native American fiction like a trip to a museum. It doesn't matter how crudely the diorama is put together or how obvious the lighting is. When the subject of the exhibit is as moving as cultural death and rebirth, we can learn from our own hearts.

Sadly, Pokagon himself lived out the tension—between old and new, modern dress obscured by a cultural pose, the Indian as icon—at the Chicago World's Fair. There, according to Engle,

> he was dressed in navy blue, but wore upon his head the cap and feathers that indicated his standing in his tribe. With true native dignity the old veteran stepped in front of the bell, and taking hold of the rope of red, white, and blue, which had been made especially for the occasion, he paused. There was a look of sadness in his face, showing to a close observer that the weight of years was pressed into a moment of time. Then, realizing the significance of the occasion,—"to link the present with the past,"—he tried to smile to hide his tears as he slowly and sadly tolled the knell of a departed time and wrongs forgiven.

Very little separates Pokagon's tearful death knell rung for Indian life and culture from the weeping-Indian commercials of the 1970s. As measured by sentiment and sentience, time coalesces to a point, and vanishes. By the time of the Chicago fair Pokagon was famous as the "Bard of the Red Man" and the "Redman's Longfellow." But his fame largely rested on what might very well have been the fictions he wore—his fluency in the classics, his status as "chief," his role as spokesperson—as much as on the poetry and fiction he wrote or might have written. Perhaps this is the reason for his performance of sadness as he rang the bell of liberty over the grounds that had once been his and his tribe's: his life, like his fiction, was a made thing, not a found thing. This might very well be his most lasting contribution to Native American literature. He came to resemble the genre of Native American literature that would come to ignore him and his contributions, while sharing in the same sad feast.

Bibliography: N. Scott Momaday, *House Made of Dawn* (New York, 2000). Pearls in Our Past, *hartfordmichigan.com/hartfordhistory/Potawatomi/Pokagon-Longfellow.* Simon Pokagon, *Queen of the Woods* (1899; repr., Berrien Springs, MI, 1972). Leslie Marmon Silko, *Ceremony* (New York, 2006). James Welch, *Fools Crow* (New York, 1986).

DAVID TREUER

1895

Ida B. Wells publishes a pamphlet on the deaths of 1,115 African Americans: "However revolting these lynchings, I did not omit a single one of them"

A RED RECORD

Ida B. Wells's anti-lynching pamphlet, *A Red Record: Tabulated Statistics and Alleged Causes of Lynching in the United States, 1892–1893–1894,* published in 1895, rates as one of the most influential protest publications in American literary history. Like Thomas Paine's *Common Sense* (1776) and David Walker's *Appeal* (1829), *A Red Record* touched off its own revolution in late nineteenth-century American life and society, given the pamphlet's wide-ranging political and cultural effects.

Inspired by Wells's anti-lynching lecture tours across England in the early 1890s, *A Red Record* drew international attention to the growing popularity of these mob murders in the United States. A century earlier, lynching referred to vigilante violence that involved nonlethal, corporal forms of public humiliation, such as tarring and feathering, whipping, riding a rail, and head shaving. Typically, these practices involved white men punishing one another for such crimes as supporting the British crown during the Revolutionary War or thieving cattle and horses on frontier settlements. By the mid-nineteenth century, lynching referred to extralegal forms of capital punishment that were increasingly directed against people of color and those who supported their claims to citizenship: antislavery activists faced death threats from white mobs, and Mexican nationals were killed by Anglo vigilantes seeking to defend the expansion of U.S. territory into the southwestern and western regions of the continent. After the Civil War, lynching's racial turn was complete. The already low number of white men murdered by lynch mobs declined sharply, while Mexicans and African Americans were killed at alarmingly escalated rates: according to *A Red Record,* 1,115 African Americans were illegally executed between 1882 and 1894.

Lynching's unchecked spread troubled Ida B. Wells for three reasons. First, as she argued in *A Red Record,* lynching's racial turn ratified slavery's perverse theory of capital value. As property, enslaved blacks were costly to kill. Once freed, "the vested interest of the white man in the Negro's body was lost," Wells noted, suggesting that this market shift trumped the legal protections secured for African Americans by Emancipation and during Reconstruction-era reform. Second, lynching threatened Wells's life directly. One of her closest friends was brutally murdered by a white lynch mob in Memphis, Tennessee, in 1892. For protesting the incident in the African American newsweekly she co-owned and edited, Wells became the target of a lynch mob's fury as well: white businessmen destroyed the offices of *The Free Speech,* driving Wells into exile from the South for the rest of her life.

Third, converging with the rise of tabloid or "yellow press" journalism, news coverage of lynchings in the 1890s spread biased accounts that fostered national support for the white mobs' reign of terror on black communities. To counter this trend, Wells realized, a successful protest movement would need to mobilize the court of public opinion and "control the forces which made public sentiment." Precedents existed: when the case against U.S. slavery was put to the British public by African American abolitionists, the pressure for emancipation built to heights that anti-abolition forces could not withstand. Endorsed by Frederick Douglass—the most revered strategist from that era's effort—Wells spent 1893 and 1894 in England, delivering the lectures that led to *A Red Record*'s publication in 1895.

Wells rightly declared that *A Red Record* "awakened [the public's] conscience throughout the land," because the pamphlet garnered pivotal victories for the U.S. anti-lynching movement. State legislatures across the United States passed anti-lynching statutes, including in the Deep South, where the majority of anti-black mob murders occurred. As important, *A Red Record* debunked lynching apologists' strongest defense by pinpointing the historical moment when the charge of raping white women became an "invented excuse" meant to demonize black male lynch victims. Crucially, Wells not only backed this controversial claim with statistical evidence but also deployed it in *A Red Record* to insist that the sexual relationships that led to lynching murders often involved consensual affairs between black men and white women. Unveiling such hypocrisy along with the "silent record" of white male rapes of African American girls and women, *A Red Record* helped close the era of Victorian sexual restraint in American life.

However, *A Red Record*'s narrative intricacies are just as compelling to consider. Bearing witness to lynching's violence forced Wells to experiment with her writing styles, and *A Red Record* cultivates a detached, ironic narrative point of view, treats historical sources parodically, and disrupts linear time-space through montage-style serializing structures. Consider, for instance, the opportunity that led Wells to publish the pamphlet in the first place: her lecture tours across Great Britain in 1893 and 1894. By all accounts in the English press, Wells rallied widespread public support for her anti-lynching crusade because of her cool demeanor at the lectern. *A Red Record* was composed to elicit this effect, too. However, the pamphlet's appeals to objectivity were, in fact, an elaborate ruse on Wells's part. Adopting a masculinist voice of scientific authority—she addresses the reader as a "student of sociology" throughout—Wells parodies how arbitrary gendered ideals of knowledge and authorship could be, placing her in literary stead with Gertrude Stein, H.D., and Willa Cather, more than with such African American writing peers as Frances Harper, Emma Dunham Kelley, Amelia Johnson, or Anna Julia Cooper.

A Red Record extends this conceit of the self's malleability further, distinguishing it from other 1890s works concerned with America's transition to modernity. If, in Paul Laurence Dunbar's standard English verse, Henry Adams's *Education* (1907), and Du Bois's *Souls of Black Folk* (1903), themes of self-division ward off the world's hurt (the mask, manikin, and veil act as shields when these writers describe their encounters with history's new forms), the opposite holds true for Wells in *A Red Record*. Her fabricated self not only engages with the world but she (it) also deliberately uses artifice as a positive resource for life-affirming political action.

Nothing was more crafted about *A Red Record* than the identity of the booklet itself. One of six pamphlets that Wells published between 1893 and 1920, *A Red Record* perfects her parody of male literary authority, since publishing in this medium linked Wells's anti-lynching writings to the Founding Fathers' protest for American independence. However, one shrewd insight revealed both the efficacy and the limits of the early national examples Wells's booklet invoked: lynching threatened America's liberal democracy at its core because "the absolute unreliability and recklessness of the mob in inflicting punishment for crimes done" was but Jeffersonian popular sovereignty taken to its deadly, anarchical extreme.

At the same time, Wells's turn to the pamphlet traded off the medium's bastard standing in U.S. print culture's history. Published by small, independent shops and sold cheaply through informal, local networks of trade, pamphlets catered to writers on the social margins of American life. Anyone able to muster the money for printing costs could publish booklets about anything the author felt the world needed to know. This editorial freedom—which her African American forerunners Richard Allen, Henry Highland Garnet, Maria Stewart, and Martin Delany relished in their pamphleteering careers from the 1790s to the 1850s— no doubt prompted Wells to publish within this system. By the 1890s, though, pamphleteering existed in a different literary milieu. The national reach of mass-manufactured media magazines and newspapers edged self-made booklets farther out onto the margins they occupied before the Civil War. And once corporate streamlining of production and distribution processes made hardcover volumes cheaper to buy, book publishing lowered pamphlets' value in the literary marketplace even more.

By producing *A Red Record* as a pamphlet instead of the book, news feature, or magazine article it could have been, Wells refused to commodify lynching into a topic for this system of literary trade. Instead, her audience had to seek its reading material actively, writing Wells directly for their free copy of *A Red Record*. Her call for "co-operative aid" in an era when literature was embedded in corporate profit-making structures may have seemed naive, but Wells's approach ensured *A Red Record*'s circulation among enlightened readers.

The mounting depravity that characterized lynching murders in 1890s America demanded—and received—a literary response in *A Red Record,* in two ways. As noted, Wells provided tabulated statistics charting the alleged causes and effects of lynching murders. She drew this evidence from the necrology tables published annually by the *Chicago Tribune,* "in order to be safe from the charge of exaggeration." Indexed by the alleged crime, victim's name, murder date, and locale, this body of data not only makes Wells's political analysis possible but also, by its sheer volume and page layout, gives the mass of information a visual shape that (to recall Joseph Conrad's preface to the 1898 *The Nigger of the Narcissus*) "above all, makes you see."

And yet, Wells's discussion of the data shows that statistics could distort as much as they describe, because such "hard" evidence obscures the murder victims' life histories from clear view. Recognizing that one form of knowledge—statistical thinking—threatened to displace another way of knowing—biography—Wells juxtaposed these two kinds of accounts, in order to recall the lived experience empiricism cannot measure as part of its calculations. One after another, the stories of the individual murder victims propel readers through *A Red Record,* enjoining them to remember (and to re-member) the individuals by reading Wells's collective account of their lives and deaths. As important, Wells invents new categories to classify these case studies, demonstrating how contingent knowledge constructs and empirical facts can be.

Wells's reordering of evidence creates its own false bottoms, though. There is no linear logic structuring the three chapters in which these narratives occur. Rather, they burst before us irrespective of time or place, loosening our sense of chronology. And where visual illustrations would otherwise anchor a reader's relation to the text, the lynching photographs reprinted in *A Red Record* disorient a reader thoroughly, if one thinks about these images with the care they deserve.

The line engraving of C. J. Miller's murder in Bardwell, Kentucky, illustrates an awful case. The image shocks because of the scene's brutality, as described by the written text. However, the image raises more questions than it seems to answer when contrasted with Wells's remark that "several photographs" were made as Miller's body was dismembered. Since the engraving does not show this defilement, what kind of proof does it offer?

Likewise, the photograph of an Alabama lynching occludes what it shows. Though Wells reports this image's provenance in noteworthy detail, its placement in the text bears no relation to the case she recounts. What, then, does the photograph document? Or, more generally, what claims can be made by documentary media at all? Juggling one representational mode with another and splicing them together to create a seam-conscious whole, *A Red Record* reads like a cinematic montage. *A Red Record*'s narrative experiments remind us that lynching's history was as varied and complex as it was widespread, and that analyzing it required flexibility and innovation from those who cared to understand it.

Many studies date modernity and modernism's emergence "on or around 1910," to recall Virginia Woolf's famous claim. However, before the First World War's generation-setting styles of mass violence, lynching in 1890s America ripped long, ragged holes in the fabric of history as well. Taking *A Red Record* with its surprising literary ambitions as its prelude, the tradition of anti-lynching protest literature bears witness to this history and, so, intertwines with modernism's developments more intricately than we might otherwise suspect. Thus the montage-style technique with which Wells narrates the deaths of mob victims resonates with the genre-defying structure of Jean Toomer's *Cane* (1923). Likewise, John Dos Passos's newsreel technique in *1919* (1932) sweeps up labor activist Wesley Everett's lynching into its panorama of postwar American life the way Wells ranges across the country to turn the statistical reports of mob murders into biographical narratives. From James Weldon Johnson's *The Autobiography of an Ex-Colored Man* (1912) to E. Annie Proulx's *Accordion Crimes* (1996); from William Faulkner's *Light in August* (1932) to John Edgar Wideman's *The Lynchers* (1973); from Richard Wright's *Native Son* (1940) to Toni Morrison's *Love* (2003); from Lillian Smith's *Strange Fruit* (1944) to Toni Cade Bambara's *Those Bones Are Not My Child* (1999), lynching's death threat looms as so pervasive but speech-draining, so constant but time-stopping, that to plot and narrate a story about the violence leads prose fiction to the edge of the sublime, which Wells understood at the end of the nineteenth century.

The spectacular figurations of lynching in the sonnets and blues ballads of Claude McKay ("The Lynching," 1922), Countee Cullen ("The Black Christ," 1929), Anne Spencer ("White Things," 1923), Helene Johnson ("A Southern Road," 1926), and Sterling A. Brown ("Slim Goes to War," 1932) bravely recount its brutality with the directness Wells deploys in *A Red Record*. Doing so, they extrapolate Ezra Pound's dos and don'ts for imagist poems to an understudied range of verse. Likewise, the Brechtian prosody of Langston Hughes's *Scottsboro Ltd.* (1932), or the catharsis-thwarting arc of Georgia Douglas Johnson's one-act lynching play, *A Sunday Morning in the South* (1925), blurs the lines between poetry and drama so thoroughly that the very utility of genre becomes at once an imperative and an obstacle to representing lynching's violence.

Keenly attuned to American culture's trends and tempo, Ida B. Wells knew that history's patterns of progress required literary styles supple enough to describe the twentieth-century's newness in all of its terrifying forms, but when she wrote and published *A Red Record,* she did not set out to chart a fresh path for American modernism to follow. She meant most of all to save African Americans' lives. To say this is not to argue that *A Red Record*'s literary legacy is the result of accidental genius. On the contrary, insofar as *A Red Record* effected actual political change that safeguarded the life prospects of African Americans as fully human subjects, Ida B. Wells's grammar of motives (to recall Kenneth Burke) enlivened American writing in exhilarating ways, too. Engaging the mind and heart, beauty and the grotesque, art and politics, *A Red Record* aspired to make America as modern and democratic as it could be.

Bibliography: Jacqueline Goldsby, *A Spectacular Secret: Lynching in American Life and Literature* (Chicago, 2006). Sandra Gunning, *Race, Rape, and Lynching: The Red Record of American Literature, 1890–1912* (New York, 1996). Linda O. McMurry, *To Keep the Waters Troubled: The Life of Ida B.*

Wells (New York, 1998). Patricia A. Schecter, *Ida B. Wells and American Reform, 1880–1930* (Chapel Hill, NC, 2001). Ida B. Wells, *Selected Works of Ida B. Wells-Barnett,* comp. Trudier Harris (New York, 1991).

JACQUELINE GOLDSBY

1896

Paul Laurence Dunbar's poems in black vernacular and "literary" English earn ambivalent praise from William Dean Howells

LYRICS OF LOWLY LIFE

The future highfliers Orville and Wilbur Wright were Paul Dunbar's high school friends, but the opening couplet for one of his early poems reads: "Not they who soar, but they who plod / Their rugged way, unhelped to God." Speaking against the injustice of racial lynching in the early era of Jim Crow allowed him few options in verse; the scholar Darwin Turner concludes that "prose was his voice of protest." Nonetheless, in one poem, he adopted the voice of a personified tree, "The Haunted Oak," chosen against its will to serve for the criminal ritual:

I feel the rope against my bark,
And the weight of him in my grain,
I feel in the throe of his final woe
The touch of my own last pain.

He was a literary prodigy whose father had escaped slavery to Canada along the Underground Railroad. He became a symbol for black intellectual potential just as black inferiority and second-class citizenship were being etched into law as "separate but equal" in the Supreme Court's decision in *Plessy v. Ferguson* (1896). Praised as "the first" of his kind, Paul Laurence Dunbar would wear a mantle of fame, bestowed by audience and patrons alike, that would become a garment of infamy he could not discard. Entranced by a photograph in a magazine, he would correspond with the woman who was the image's subject for several years before meeting her in person, a meeting whose painful result would be a troubled engagement and an unstable marriage.

Singled out by the august Frederick Douglass at the 1893 World's Columbian Exposition in Chicago as a young Negro artist of notable promise, praised by the poet, composer, and later diplomat James Weldon Johnson as the "first American Negro poet of real literary distinction," and venerated by Mary Church Terrell as the "poet laureate of the Negro race," Dunbar enjoyed immense popularity among black Americans. Schoolchildren memorized and recited his poems; schools across the country bore his name.

He celebrated Malindy, a slave with a singing voice so powerful "hit's sweetah dan de music / Of an edicated band; / An' hit's dearah dan de battle's / Song o' triumph in de lan"; he praised Harriet Beecher Stowe as "Prophet and priestess! At one stroke she gave / A race to freedom and herself to fame." He was a lyric poet who also wrote novels and short stories at a time when millions of black people could not read or write. He was, moreover, one of very few black writers—and the only significant poet—to represent those millions comprehensively in orthographic and oratorical renditions of a dialect they might have spoken as plantation slaves. Dunbar also perfected formal verse written in literary standard English: in Shakespearean and in Italianate sonnets, in elegies and odes, he mused on love, mourned, addressed nature, considered classical figures such as Prometheus, lauded his personal hero, Frederick Douglass, and (in a quite limited fashion) advocated for black rights and progress.

Dunbar's unusual literary prowess found national attention after centuries during which fearsome sanctions (corporal punishment, sale as chattel, and even death) prevented slaves' access to the tools of literacy—at their finest, a book (a primer, or a Bible), a slate, and chalk. Oral forms, therefore, dominated slave life. Dunbar published verse in a black vernacular after mastering its translation to the page; he also embraced the often arcane rules of traditional English prosody. Dunbar could thus write in two voices, and he brought to both of them, in his public performances, the unusual power of his own speaking voice. Those who heard Dunbar read his poems likened his voice (in Eleanor Alexander's summary) to a "perfect musical instrument" that was "deep, resonant, mellow and beautifully handled," capable of producing both "Negro" vernacular and standard white American speech. Dunbar's published writings, and his performances, thus fit the famous terms in which W. E. B. Du Bois would describe black identity: "One ever feels his twoness,—an American, a Negro; two souls, two thoughts, two unreconciled strivings; two warring ideals in one dark body, whose dogged strength alone keeps it from being torn asunder." This twoness would embody Dunbar's life and work.

With its folk wisdom, rural settings, and evocations of Southern life, Dunbar's work seemed in the 1890s to resemble writings whose political implications he might have abhorred: on the one hand, the antebellum plantation literary school, with its saccharine memories of segregation; on the other, the local-color movement, with its overtones of national reconciliation. The wounds to the national body, land, and identity sustained during the Civil War were ostensibly bound up with President Abraham Lincoln's Emancipation Proclamation and the demise of the Confederacy. But much of the master narrative of slavery—innate black inferiority and white supremacy—remained intact, eventually shored up by the supposed failure of the Reconstruction era that hastened the end of short-lived black political autonomy and the rise of reactionary forces of white control.

Dunbar would be shaped by this dynamic and unstable era. He knew only postbellum freedom, and enjoyed the remnants of the opportunities and attitudes that had been opened by Reconstruction in education and artistic patronage. Yet he experienced an artist's version of Jim Crow, with clear limits on what he could say, and clearer limits on what kind of art he could make, imposed in part by his early fame. His life and work would chronicle this time. As the forces that had demanded racial and social equality dissipated after Emancipation in the course of a single generation, blacks faced segregation, the political and economic cousins of plantation slavery (tenant farming, sharecropping, the chain gang), the rise of the Ku Klux Klan and other extralegal forces, the onslaught of lynching, and the beginning of the Great Migration, which would propel black Southerners to the North and later West, seeking work and better lives.

Born free in 1872 in Dayton, Ohio, to Joshua and Matilda Dunbar, former Kentucky slaves, a young Paul experienced the familial instability that dogged so many newly freed blacks trying to establish their own households. His father, a skilled plasterer in slavery and freedom, could find no work in the Ohio town, forcing Matilda to be sole breadwinner as a washerwoman. His parents' marriage ended in physical abuse, alcoholism, and finally divorce. But his mother also brought the riches of literature into young Paul's life. As a house slave, she heard poetry recited in her master's house. Dunbar's early home life revolved around storytelling and recitation; his education was made possible by the incomes of two older brothers, in addition to the money from Matilda's washing. Paul was the only black student at the town's Central High School, where he excelled as editor in chief of the school newspaper, president by election of both the school's literary society and the prestigious Philomathean Debating Society, and lyricist for the class song for his graduation in 1891.

Although Central High's ostensible "Boy Most Likely," Dunbar, a star in the desegregated classroom, fell to earth in the work world of Dayton. With no possibility of funding for further study, the dream of the shingle "Paul Laurence Dunbar, Attorney-at-Law" became "Dunbar, journalist." Dunbar published several poems in the *Dayton Herald* while still in high school; after he graduated, though, that same paper told him it was not yet ready to hire a black reporter. But the Callahan Building downtown was more than eager for him—with uniform and cap and four dollars per week as its elevator boy. Did he now better discern his father's plight years earlier—the racist wall his own skills as a plasterer were unable to alter? As an elevator boy, he read English lyricists and the law and wrote poems between floors. He founded *The Tattler,* a local newsletter "for black Ohio," printed by Orville and Wilbur's printing company, and went into debt to cover the costs of publishing it. A local physician subsidized the private publication of Dunbar's first collection of poetry, *Oak and Ivy* (1893); he sold copies of that himself.

Dunbar's national debut came with the 1896 publication, by the large New York firm Dodd, Mead, of *Lyrics of Lowly Life,* a compilation of *Oak and Ivy* (1893) and *Majors and Minors* (1896). With Dayton and, later, Toledo far behind, he entered the world of high-stakes white patronage, finding coin and (more often) good words. William Dean Howells, the editor of the *Atlantic Monthly* and by some measures the leading literary critic of the day, granted Dunbar the latter: Howells's introduction to *Lyrics* would give Dunbar, at first, a literary launching pad, and later (as Dunbar himself would complain) a straitjacket.

From Howells's first sentence and before reading one word of Dunbar's verse, it is not difficult to recognize the historical, cultural, racial, and aesthetic pickle in which Dunbar found himself. With the Civil War its own memory, Howells alerts what would have been an overwhelmingly white audience to his own elastic political position on race. "The world is too old now, and I find myself too much of its mood, to care for the work of a poet because he is black" or because his parents were slaves or because he worked as an elevator boy, Howells writes. He then seems to change his mind, adducing Dunbar's racial heritage as a reason to celebrate his work: on the verge of the coming century, Howells exults that the "father and mother of the first poet of his race in our language were negroes without admixture of white blood." Dunbar's value to "his race" may therefore outdo that of France's Dumas or Russia's "far better" Pushkin, since "these were both mulattoes, who might have been supposed to derive their qualities from white blood."

For Howells, Dunbar's work reveals "the first instance of an American negro who had evinced innate distinction in literature." "Paul Dunbar," Howells goes on, "was the only man of pure African blood and of American civilization to feel the negro life aesthetically and express it lyrically" and "to have represented him as he found him to be, with humor, with sympathy, and yet with what the reader must instinctively feel to be entire truthfulness." But Howells sees Dunbar's literary contribution most clearly "in nearly all the dialect pieces"; while of the poems in "literary" English, Howells writes, "some of these I thought very good, and even more than very good," but "several people might have written them." In the wake of his patron's disturbing tribute, Dunbar's most famous poem, "We Wear the Mask," sounds an echo:

> We wear the mask that grins and lies,
> It hides our cheeks and shades our eyes,—
> This debt we pay to human guile;
> With torn and bleeding hearts we smile,
> And mouth with myriad subtleties.
> Why should the world be overwise,
> In counting all our tears and sighs?
> Nay, let them only see us, while
> We wear the mask.
>
> We smile, but, O great Christ, our cries
> To thee from tortured souls arise.
> We sing, but oh the clay is vile
> Beneath our feet, and long the mile;
> But let the world dream otherwise,
> We wear the mask!

In a historical period made topsy-turvy by the overwhelming dominance of a sociopolitical debate with staggering economic consequences for the fate of black Americans, more than four million newly freed slaves and their free-born progeny, dubbed variously the "Negro Problem" or the "Negro Question," could slavery and its immediate legacy be an aesthetic subject? Could it be the stuff of art? The literary agents and publishing houses of New York and Boston certainly thought so. Plantation fiction and local-color regional stories filled the pages of venerable national magazines. When Howells as an elite patron made a plea for more poems in which Dunbar "studies the moods and traits of his race in its own accent," the entreaty would seem to point to a dearth of such black vernacular forms. To the contrary, America in 1896 remained oversaturated with the representational flotsam of the institution of plantation slavery: happy darkies, smiling masters, bountiful pastoral landscapes, benevolent mistresses, shining mammies. Slaves as movable chattel owned nothing, not their bodies nor even the speech that came out of their mouths: slaves, and their speech, became the raw material for comic, sentimental, or romantic invention in the plantation literary tradition that began at least as early as 1832, with John Pendleton Kennedy's *Swallow Barn,* and remained in high gear with Thomas Nelson Page's contributions in the 1890s, ensuring its continued life in the new century. Dunbar's contributions to this linguistic phenomenon would be cheered by some as ironic or authentic and vilified by others as playing with the fire of negative stereotypes, of debased representations.

Can a lyric poet speak in dialect? (Can there be lyrics, properly so-called, in the speech associated with "lowly life"?) Despite his famous title, Dunbar might have answered in the negative. Is the poet's voice debased by the "broken"-ness of a nonstandard form? Dunbar would likely respond in the affirmative. Dunbar's uneasy commitment to the black vernacular would nonetheless propel twentieth-century black literary culture. What is the relation of African American poetry, particularly with regard to form, since 1900, to Dunbar's work? What is the relation of later black poets to Dunbar? What would the contemporary black vernacular, from black English to hip-hop lyrics, sound like without Dunbar?

Moving from obscurity to a remarkably limiting renown, Dunbar would travel from New York to England to Washington, D.C., then return to his mother's house in Dayton in 1904; he died young, in 1906, from tuberculosis, complicated by his fame, his tragic marriage, alcoholism, and the calcifying Jim Crow world.

Bibliography: Eleanor Alexander, *Lyrics of Sunshine and Shadow: The Tragic Courtship and Marriage of Paul Laurence Dunbar and Alice Ruth Moore—A History of Love and Violence among the African American Elite* (New York, 2001). W. E. B. Du Bois, *The Souls of Black Folk* (Chicago, 1903). Paul Laurence Dunbar, *The Complete Poems of Paul Laurence Dunbar* (New York, 1913); *The Sport of the Gods* (New York, 1902). Darwin Turner, "Paul Laurence Dunbar: The Rejected Symbol," *Journal of Negro History* 52, no. 1 (1967).

JUDITH JACKSON FOSSETT

1896, September 6

Queen Lili'uokalani is released from house arrest in Honolulu

HAWAII'S STORY BY HAWAII'S QUEEN

All of American literature, from a certain Pacific Islander point of view, can be said to begin with Queen Lili'uokalani's *Hawaii's Story by Hawaii's Queen,* a memoir written from late 1896 through 1897 by the deposed Hawaiian monarch. Published in Boston in 1898 amid the imperial scramble of the *Mana Nui* (great powers), the memoir contests the overthrow of a legitimately constituted sovereign nation by an array of white-settler forces (mostly Americans from New England and California) in 1893 and activates the power of culture and poetry to circulate as countermemory. Testimony, photographs, anecdotes, diary entries, newspaper items, and treaty, narrative and lyric—all commingle into a Christian-Hawaiian appeal for justice, sentimental empathy, and international recognition from an American government engaged in extraterritorial expansion into the Caribbean, Asia, and the Pacific Ocean.

Even as Queen Lili'uokalani worked to compile her songbook *He Buke Mele Hawaii* after her imprisonment for eight months in Iolani Palace, the last Hawaiian monarch was accused of adultery, sorcery, instability, and tyranny, and lampooned in print and cartoon: "a portly, chocolate colored lady," as one journalist put it in *Leslie's Illustrated Weekly*. She was also declared (more accurately) in Boston papers "a devout and perfect Christian" lady, after she had contributed a doll to a charity show for crippled children: a Hawaiian doll, clad in a Mother Hubbard missionary gown the queen had hand sewn, "a very pretty doll, that resembled somewhat some of my people who had intermarried with the foreigners." As a *haku mele,* this "poet-maker" of more than two hundred songs, including the first Hawaiian song to be published on the U.S. mainland ("Nani nā pua" in 1869), and composer in 1866, during the reign of Kamehameha V, of the first Hawaiian national anthem ("He Mele lāhui Hawai'i"), had composed works filled with what, in one of her *mele inoa* (name chants), she called "a troubled aloha." "Aloha Oe" is not just a song of lovers parting but is coded with the pathos of separation, brokenness, longing: a hello and farewell to Hawaiian nationhood. As a model of poetic activism, Lili'uokalani's works have influenced Hawai'i-based authors from singer-activist George Helm to the novelist and playwright descendants John Dominis Holt, Victoria Kneubuhl, and Alani Apio.

In her memoir and poems, the Hawaiian queen protests national dispossession as the ill-fated consequence of what she laments as the "grand Monroe doctrine," invoked in her time against the Spanish empire as it had been in 1842 against British and French expansion into the Hawaiian Islands. On July 7, 1898, six months after *Hawaii's Story* was published, to no political avail, the United States would ratify the annexation of Hawai'i; in 1959, Hawai'i would become the fiftieth state. Lili'uokalani's 1897 diary, containing drafts of her book, would be misplaced, lost, or (most likely) confiscated. Skeptical reviewers would discredit *Hawaii's Story* as ghostwritten by the Boston journalist Julius A. Palmer; in the 1930s missionary offspring and newspaper heir Lorrin A. Thurston would make the same claim, but the charge is spurious. As a history of injustice and dispossession, the queen's memoir still haunts American memory, echoing through a federal statute, signed into law by President Bill Clinton: "To Acknowledge the 100th anniversary of the January 17, 1893, overthrow of the Kingdom of Hawai'i, and to offer an apology to Native Hawaiians on behalf of the United States for the overthrow of the Kingdom of Hawaii."

Placed under house arrest in 1895, Queen Liliʻuokalani had turned to the translation into English of the Hawaiian creation-chant, *Kumulipo,* and to composing lyrics to communicate obliquely with her people. As the queen notes in her memoir, "The ancient bards of the Hawaiian people thus gave to history their poems and chants; and the custom is no different to this day, and serves to show the great fondness and aptness of our nation to poetry and song." Writing in diaries from 1896 through 1897, the queen keeps Hawaiian selfhood and nation alive, if only as her "story" that would endure shocks of American modernity. Dispossession of native discourse is the situation the queen exposes, telling "Hawaii's story" as a plight of colonial subjection and sacrifice, in the face of Washington's "project to annex Hawaii to the American Union."

Identifying her islands with "the vineyard of Naboth's" in the land of Jezreel, and the United States with "the punishment of Ahab" from I Kings 21 (as Melville's jeremiad *Moby-Dick* had warned through its *Pequod* captain), the queen appeals to her American readership across the ethnic and national lines of an imperial cartography dividing "us" from "them," whites from blacks, heathens from converts, metropolitan powers from peripheral nations.

> Oh honest Americans, as Christians hear me for my downtrodden people! Their form of government [constitutional monarchy] is as dear to them as yours is precious to you. Quite as warmly as you love your country, so they love theirs. With all your goodly possessions, covering a territory so immense that there yet remain parts unexplored, possessing islands that, although near at hand, had to be neutral grounds in time of war, do not covet the little vineyard of Naboth's, so far from your shores, lest the punishment of Ahab fall upon you, if not in your day, in that of your children, for "be not deceived, God is not mocked."

"Is the American Republic of States to degenerate," she wrote, "and become a colonizer and a land-grabber?"

Born Lydia Kamakaʻeha, Queen Liliʻuokalani (1838–1917), sister to King David Kalākaua, had married the American merchant John Owen Dominis in 1862, and succeeded her brother to the throne in 1891 after decades of "tormented aloha" when the legitimacy of this royal lineage, as well as its tactics of native insignia and display, were subject to contestation both by native forces and foreign settlers. Lydia was well read and well traveled, and had attended Queen Victoria's Golden Jubilee in 1887, where she was warmly received, as she was later to be in the salons of Boston and corridors of Washington. Her languages of resistance to colonial history were cultural and poetic, befitting Hawaiian traditions of chant and epic tied to mana-making hierarchies and status manifestation. Post-Enlightenment assumptions of constitutionalism and biblical morality on the part of her mentors, learned at sites like the Royal School, where she studied as a youth, and at Kawaihaʻo Church, where she became choirmaster, were tinged with pathos and historical tragedy. The foreign and native came to complex integration in her poetry as well as informed her national project and neonativist mode of literary activism, which she carried on from her brother.

In the wake of Herder, Emerson, and Longfellow, Liliʻuokalani demonstrated

a genius for *Nationalliteratur;* poetry, narrative, and song became her way of preserving *ka lāhui* (Hawaiian nationhood), a spirit founded in what she called a "patriotism, which for us means the love of the very soil on which our ancestors have
lived and died." During her imprisonment, the queen called her challenge to the
extension of the United States into the Pacific her "Literary Occupation"; as the
San Francisco Chronicle had noted of forces driving this "so-called revolution,"
which had forced King Kalākaua to submit to the 1887 "Bayonet Constitution"
that the queen later sought to abrogate to her own undoing, "The government of
the Sandwich Islands appears to have passed from the hands of the king into
hands of a military oligarchy that is more domineering than Kalakaua ever was."
A "revolution" was launched "by the foreign element of the community," as the
New York Times described the event, removing "the misrule of the native line
of monarchs" and proclaiming "guarantees to the protection of life, liberty, and
property." The queen was deposed by the forces of this settler government, under
its president Sanford Dole, which appealed, over the course of five years and
scathing censure by the Blount Commission's report during the Cleveland administration, for recognition by Washington.

Protests lodged in Honolulu (signed by some 38,000 of the 40,000 Hawaiian
citizens of native ancestry) still resonate, and we need to hear these Pacific voices.
By story and poem, in document and prayer, Lili'uokalani wrote *Hawaii's Story*
not just to legitimate the statecraft of her reign but, through appeals both to international standards of justice and the moral codes American missionaries
brought to her country in 1820, to affirm and reclaim the nationhood of Hawai'i.
Translating and writing poetry became cultural feats of ethnic transaction and
native policy, and never more so than with her translation into English of the epic
creation poem *Kumulipo:* "the chant," in her words, "which was sung to Captain
Cook in one of the ancient temples of Hawaii, and chronicles the creation of the
world and of living creatures, from the shell-fish to the human race, according to
Hawaiian traditions." Her memoir, as well as her songs and poems (written in Hawaiian but with English and Spanish words at times interspersed), comprise a
counterrecord, a grievance or plea, deft with place-specific allusiveness, historical
detail, and tropological skill as befits this poet-queen whose appeals to justice and
moral sanction depended upon a republicanism coming undone in contexts of
imperial globalization.

Lili'uokalani's Hawaiian *mele* (song poem) "Ka Wiliwiliwai" (The Sprinkler) is
on the surface a ditty personifying a lawn sprinkler near Washington Place, the
1846 Greek Revival house where she lived with John Dominis before occupying the royal palace, and where, after her imprisonment, she lived for the rest of
her life:

Oh whirly-water
gentle rain shower on the move
what do you think you're up to
circling, twirling so quietly?

But the third stanza brings out the strange power of this modern convenience, disrupting harmonious relations between people, land, the heavens, and place:

> Amazing
> the way you take over: irresistible.
> Come, slow down a little—
> so I can drink!

The *Kumulipo,* published by King Kalākaua under the title of *He Pule Hoolaa Allii* in 1889, was not just a long chant giving Hawaiian "aboriginal people" the status of a national literature with a worldview and a creation epic; it affirmed the "supreme blood" claims of the Keawe-a-Heulu line as legitimate royal successors to the Kamehameha lineage. It made this family descendants of the great fifteenth-century chief Lonoikamakahiki, and helped quiet rival Hawaiian factions who refused to legitimate their claim to royal chiefly status. As Kalākaua wrote in *Legends and Myths of Hawaii,* "Certain customs, like chants and meles, are matters of inheritance, and remain exclusively in the families with which they originate."

King and then queen were not just translating a poem of ethnographic interest to the Polynesian Society or the Bureau of American Ethnology (as Nathaniel Emerson did in 1909 with *Unwritten Literature of Hawaii: The Sacred Songs of the Hula*). As brother and sister poets and mythmakers of modern culture, they were ratifying claims to nationhood by genealogical succession and poetic sanction. Discussing how Hawaiian chants "were composed of symbolic phrases *(loina)* and hidden meanings *(kaona),*" Samuel Kamakau surveys a catalog of Hawaiian poetic and song genres *(mele)* that might fill the Whitman of "Chants Democratic" with wonderment before their social range and efficacy:

> There were chants in honor of ancestors (mele kupuna), in praise of a land (mele 'aina), in praise of chiefs (mele ali'i), in praise of favorite children (mele hi'ilani), chants of gratitude (mele mahalo), chants of affection (mele aloha), chants of reviling (kuamu-amu), prayer chants (mele pule), dirges (kanikau), chants to put a person to sleep (mele hiamoe), or to awaken one (mele ho'ala), chants asking a favor (mele noi), chants refusing the request (mele 'au'a), chants calling to be admitted (mele kahea), chants given as a gift (mele haawi), chants of boasting (mele ho'oki'eki'e), prophetic chants (mele wanana), chants foretelling events (mele kilokilo), chants of criticism (mele nemanema).

Lili'uokalani compounded Christian and native beliefs into what her biographer Helena G. Allen calls a synthesis of "Christian-Kahunaism." Her path of nonviolent resistance and aloha was profound and abiding, as in this comment to her adopted daughter Lydia Aholo, revealing her "*kaona*" (hidden meanings) in a passage worthy of Saint Augustine: "To gain the kingdom of heaven is to hear what is not said, to see what cannot be seen, and to know the unknowable—that is Aloha. All things in this world are two; in heaven there is but One." *Hawaii's Story by Hawaii's Queen* and poems of countermemory like "The Sprinkler" can help anyone hear the tale of Naboth's vineyard being absorbed by the country of

King Ahab, a country that may have squandered the kingdom of heaven in its bargain for Pacific empire. It was this biblical curse that Lili'uokalani chose to capture her vision of a lost Hawaiian homeland: "Thus saith the LORD, In the place where dogs licked the blood of Naboth shall dogs lick thy blood, even thine."

Bibliography: Samuel M. Kamakau, *Ruling Chiefs of Hawaii,* rev. ed. (Honolulu, 1992). Lili'uokalani, *Hawaii's Story by Hawaii's Queen* (Boston, 1898; Honolulu, 1990); *The Kumulipo: An Hawaiian Creation Chant* (Boston, 1897); *The Queen's Songbook,* ed. Barbara Bernard Smith (Honolulu, 1999). Mary Kawena Pukui and Alfons Korn, eds., *The Echo of Our Song: Chants and Poems of the Hawaiians* (Honolulu, 1979). Noenoe K. Silva, *Aloha Betrayed: Native Hawaiian Resistance to American Colonialism* (Durham, NC, 2004).

ROB WILSON

1897, Memorial Day
"Choose life and die": Augustus Saint-Gaudens's bas-relief is unveiled on Boston Common

THE ROBERT GOULD SHAW AND 54TH REGIMENT MONUMENT

The sight must have electrified Boston: on May 28, 1863, only five months after the belated and hedged Emancipation Proclamation made it possible, the Massachusetts 54th—the North's first regiment formed from free blacks—marched down Boylston Street past cheering crowds on their way south. In command of the unit rode a white colonel, Robert Gould Shaw—"blue-eyed child of fortune"—the twenty-five-year-old son of Brahmin abolitionists. Fifty-one days later, after a suicidal bayonet charge across almost a mile of open beach against the heavily defended Confederate Battery Wagner on Morris Island in Charleston harbor, Shaw was dead and half his regiment killed, wounded, or captured. Militarily, the assault ranks among the war's most futile actions. Politically, it became one of the Union's greatest triumphs. Frederick Douglass (whose son Lewis, a sergeant major with the regiment, was wounded at Wagner) had called for "one gallant rush" that would throw open "the iron gate of our prison." In its fatal rush, the 54th—forerunner of more than a hundred black Civil War regiments—has lived on in literature and art, inspiring and incriminating, a mirror held up to the best and worst in the American national character.

The poetic response to the regiment began even before the bloodletting. On the eve of the assault, as African Americans were being tortured and killed in the New York Draft Riots, an anonymous infantryman in Company A composed the 54th's marching song:

Oh, Frémont he told them when the war it first begun,
How to save the Union and the way it should be done.

But Kentucky swore so hard and Old Abe he had his fears,
Till ev'ry hope was lost but the colored volunteers.

The soldiers of the 54th refused pay rather than accept less than their white fellow soldiers. They faced enslavement or execution if captured. And their heroic if doomed assault shifted the stakes of the war. The battle of Battery Wagner destroyed all doubt about the black citizen-soldier's willingness to die for an America that existed only in ignored ideals. With 180,000 in uniform by 1865, the "colored volunteers" did indeed save the Union.

The initial outpouring of art commemorating the 54th focused on Colonel Shaw. Verses by Emerson and James Russell Lowell deify the young patrician who died "for noble ends." Incredibly, neither poet mentions the hundreds of black soldiers who did the same. A bit of contemporary doggerel, written out of rage at the Confederates' contemptuous common burial of the Union dead at Fort Wagner, did better than the canonical men of letters:

They "buried him with his niggers!"
But the glorious souls set free
Are leading the van of the army
That fights for liberty.
Brothers in death, in glory
The same palm-branches bear;
And the crown is as bright o'er the sable brows
As over the golden hair.

Plans for a permanent monument to Shaw began at once. Joshua B. Smith, a fugitive slave and prominent caterer who had worked for the Shaws, gathered funds from Boston's black community. Plans foundered in the Boston civic committee, cycling through various neoclassical proposals for the better part of two decades, before the commission finally went to Augustus Saint-Gaudens, an Irish-born American sculptor who, by the 1880s, had helped stamp the American Renaissance with his Beaux-Arts style. Saint-Gaudens initially proposed a conventional, heroic equestrian statue. Shaw's family vetoed the grandiosity.

Then, in one of the greatest inspirations in American civic art, Saint-Gaudens conceived of a high relief depicting the colonel alongside his regiment, officer with men, white aristocrat next to foot soldiers "of a despised race," marching together down Boylston to the shared ditch of their common burial. No hollow apotheosis or nostalgic glorification of violence: just a record of that epochal muster, a march toward the long-denied goal of democratic brotherhood. The composition Saint-Gaudens imagined had little antecedent. But neither did the 54th.

The Irish immigrant worked for fourteen years, as the sculpture grew in scale and ambition. He exceeded his modest payment and began to incur private expense. He made meticulous studies from live models, sculpting his infantrymen with strikingly distinctive, expressive faces. He gradually turned an overwhelming tableau: a column of individuated men leaning into a single rhythm of joined purpose. By the day of unveiling at the foot of the State House on Boston Common, Memorial Day, 1897, a third of a century after Battery Wagner, Saint-Gaudens had captured the transforming moment in bronze.

At the dedication, William James (whose brother Garth served as adjutant in the 54th) read in the monument the war's moral conclusion: "that common people can work out their salvation well enough together if left free to try." But Booker T. Washington warned, "This monument will stand for effort, not victory complete." Sixty-five veterans of the 54th attended the ceremony. Saint-Gaudens wrote: "These old soldiers passing the very spot where they left for the war so many years before . . . the troops of bronze marching in the opposite direction . . . the young men in the bas-relief showing these veterans the hope and vigor of youth . . . It was a consecration."

Consecration was premature. Reconstruction had died two decades earlier. The year before the monument's dedication, *Plessy v. Ferguson* sounded the collapse of egalitarian ideals. At a ceremony opening a museum in Richmond's former White House of the Confederacy, the Confederate general Bradley T. Johnson had told a crowd, "The great crime of the century was the emancipation of the Negroes." In the interests of hollow national unity, the North looked away as Jim Crow, the Klan, and lynchings took hold.

However magnificent and progressive, even "The Shaw," as it was called, betrayed a Gilded Age racism. It bore the oath of the Society of Cincinnati ("He relinquishes all to serve the Republic"), a couplet from J. R. Lowell's platitudinous Shaw poem ("With heart that beat a charge he fell / foeward as fits a man"), and the names of five white officers killed in battle. But no black soldier's name appeared anywhere.

Saint-Gaudens's work immediately sparked literary response. Three years after the dedication, William Vaughn Moody's "Ode in Time of Hesitation" made him perhaps the most prominent poet of the day. The poem begins in contemplation,

> BEFORE the solemn bronze Saint Gaudens made
> To thrill the heedless passer's heart with awe . . .
> Knowing that what I hear is not unheard
> Of this boy soldier and his Negro band,
> For all their gaze is fixed so stern ahead,
> For all the fatal rhythm of their tread.
> The land they died to save from death and shame
> Trembles and waits, hearing the spring's great name
> And by her pangs these resolute ghosts are stirred.

Moody's reflection then becomes a bitter indictment of U.S. imperialism in 1900: Did the black troops of the Civil War fight and die for freedom so their country could savagely annex and enslave the Philippines? In a remarkable confrontation, two artistic works, each needing to redeem a vision of America, create a more ghostly memorial between them.

In the same year, the prominent poet Paul Laurence Dunbar (whose father, a

The Robert Gould Shaw Memorial
The Bostonian Society—Old State House Museum, Boston Streets Collections, 1855–1999

former slave, served in the Massachusetts 55th) summoned an even bleaker indictment in his sonnet "Robert Gould Shaw":

Why was it that the thunder voice of Fate
Should call thee, studious, from the classic groves,
Where calm-eyed Pallas with still footstep roves,
And charge thee seek the turmoil of the State?
What bade thee hear the voice and rise elate,
Leave home and kindred and thy spicy loaves,
To lead th' unlettered and despised droves
To manhood's home and thunder at the gate?

Far better the slow blaze of Learning's light,
The cool and quiet of her dearer fane,
Than this hot terror of a hopeless fight,
This cold endurance of the final pain,—
Since thou and those who with thee died for right
Have died, the Present teaches, but in vain!

Just what America did the *Shaw* commemorate? Over the following two decades, Charles Ives, America's first composer of international significance, assembled his great "Three Places in New England." In its first movement, "The 'St. Gaudens' in Boston Common (Col. Shaw and his Colored Regiment)," Ives layers spirituals, ragtime, and Civil War marching tunes into startling polytonal clusters: past in present, and both marching into a shared chromatic future. At the nadir of World War II, John Berryman, in the poem "Boston Common," turned the image of a homeless man sleeping "under the impressive genitals" of Shaw's bronze horse into a meditation on the heroism of the common man and a speculation on what true democracy might look like, stripped of monuments.

Half a century after *Plessy,* the monument altered again when *Brown v. Board of Education* reversed the law of the land. In 1960, shortly after four black college students integrated the Woolworth lunch counter in Greensboro, North Carolina, Robert Lowell, a descendant of both J. R. Lowell and Shaw, read his poem "For the Union Dead" at a Boston Common festival, declaring, "We've emerged from the monumental age."

Lowell's poem begins with the Society of Cincinnati oath, with one word changed: *Relinquunt* ("they relinquish") for *Relinquit* ("he relinquishes"). The speaker in the poem sees the Saint-Gaudens propped up by planks to keep it from collapsing as the Common is excavated for a giant underground parking garage. The bronze "sticks like a fishbone/in the city's throat." The heroism of then comes back to mock the degraded now.

Shaw's father wanted no monument
except the ditch,
where his son's body was thrown
and lost with his "niggers."
The ditch is nearer.

The faces of the 54th echo in "the drained faces of Negro school-children" whose violently opposed struggle for civil rights appear on the narrator's television. The narrator reels from the vertigo of history, as if Saint-Gaudens had posted forward a crucial memory to an ideal future that failed to materialize.

In the year of Lowell's poem, half a dozen of the country's worst race riots still lay ahead. Interracial marriage was illegal in twenty-two states. "For the Union Dead" is shot through with its own racial anxiety, the anxiety of a Brahmin ringing his own death knell; a white defending yet fearing imminent blackness; a historian seeking a common future while resenting the too-common present; a man who can neither preserve his undermined monuments nor succumb to shared forgetting; a realist shamed by collapsed ideals; an identity undone by the approach of the looming ditch, that common grave that dissolves all identities. And yet Lowell embraces the shared march and marvels at how his ancestor Shaw "rejoices in man's lovely,/peculiar power to choose life and die." By 1981, Saint-Gaudens's bronze was caked in soot, guano, and graffiti ("Stop abortion holocaust!"). Shaw's sword had broken off below the hilt. Torn by years of violent, unsuccessful attempts to desegregate its schools, Boston, seeking racial reconciliation, restored the monument. After much debate, the names of the soldiers who died at Battery Wagner were at last inscribed on the back of the base. The *Shaw Memorial* is now a stop on the city's Black Heritage Trail.

The refurbished relief caught the attention of Freddie Fields and Kevin Jarre, who turned Saint-Gaudens's vision into the 1989 film *Glory*. Movies are our monuments now, revising facts even as they revive historical memory. For all its historical hiccups, *Glory* is as close to popular political art as a country deeply suspicious of ideal-driven aesthetics will allow. *Glory* may suffer from the same white bias that haunts the Saint-Gaudens and the same racial uncertainty that haunts Lowell. Yet it extends the memorial's long communal meditation on what William James, at the 1897 dedication, called "the profounder meaning of the Union cause." Millions more will see Saint-Gaudens's bronze in the credits of the film than will ever see it in person. Millions who'd never have guessed that black soldiers fought in the Civil War have come to reflect on these men and their peculiar power to choose life and die.

The verdict of Appomattox is still being contested. The South is full of memorials to the Lost Cause. In 1923, the U.S. Senate even appropriated funds for a National Mammy Monument. The measure failed in the House, curtailing that particular commemoration of slavery. The year before the centennial rededication of the *Shaw Memorial* (presided over by Colin Powell, the first African American chairman of the Joint Chiefs of Staff), South Carolina's governor David Beasley launched an unsuccessful bid to remove the Confederate battle flag from the state capitol and was subsequently voted out of office. Often our monuments are a way of burying the unresolved past.

Most memorials go invisible, once their placation is done. But America has never been able to look away from the Saint-Gaudens. It still haunts the nation's arts, prompting each new generation to witness in pride and shame. It remains

visible simply by commemorating the eternal gap between America's magnificent ideals and grim reality. Its vision of equality and brotherhood still lies worlds
away. Yet the bronze men of the 54th lean forever into their future, as if the common goal of America were clearly in sight, just beyond the next corpse-filled
ditch. Saint-Gaudens's sculpture demands that we emerge from the monumental
but not from common memory, that we relinquish private ends to build the Republic, that we exercise our peculiar power to choose, that we die to our differences in order to live that still unrealized more perfect union.

Bibliography: Steven Axelrod, "Colonel Shaw in Poetry: 'For the Union Dead' and Its Precursors," *American Quarterly* 24, no. 4 (October 1972): 523–537. Martin H. Blatt, Thomas J. Brown,
and Donald Yacovone, eds., *Hope and Glory: Essays on the Legacy of the 54th Massachusetts Regiment*
(Amherst, 2001). Ludwig Lauerhass, Jr., Gregory Schwarz, and Brigid Sullivan, *The Shaw Memorial: A Celebration of an American Masterpiece* (Plainfield, NH, 1997). Michael Thurston, "Robert
Lowell's Monumental Vision: History, Form, and the Cultural Work of Postwar American
Lyric," *American Literary History* 12, nos. 1 and 2 (Spring/Summer 2000): 79–112. Stephen J. Whit-
field, "'Sacred in History and in Art': The Shaw Memorial," *The New England Quarterly* 60, no. 1
(March 1987): 3–27.

RICHARD POWERS

1898, June 22

Guantánamo Bay, Cuba: "The Red Badge of Courage Was His Wig Wag Flag"

LITERATURE AND IMPERIALISM

The headline above blazed in bold print from Joseph Pulitzer's *New York World*
to showcase Stephen Crane's dispatch from the first major battle of the Spanish-
American War. U.S. Marines landed at Guantánamo and captured a Spanish outpost, accompanied by dozens of correspondents ferried there in special ships
owned by Pulitzer and Randolph Hearst, whose sensationalist yellow press had
been whipping up fervor for America's entry into Cuba's ongoing war for independence from Spain. While President McKinley declared it a war of liberation,
the swift defeat of Spain in Cuba and in the Philippines was soon followed by U.S.
military occupation of those islands, along with Puerto Rico and Guam, giving
rise to a new era of U.S. global interventionism. The figure of the modern war correspondent as spectator, participant, and celebrity also arose in Cuba.

The *World* used the title of Crane's novel in its headline without mentioning
his name, attesting to the book's wide recognition. Just as soldiers waved wigwag
flags to signal coded information to ships offshore, the headline signaled Crane's
authority to write about war, which commonly rested on firsthand experience.
Born years after the Civil War, Crane was only twenty-three years old when
he published *The Red Badge of Courage* in 1895. Nonetheless it was immediately
lauded for its realistic depiction of the battlefield from a foot soldier's perspec-

tive. After writing the novel, Crane had a keen desire to experience war directly. In 1896 he had attempted to reach Cuba on an illegal filibustering expedition that was smuggling guns to the insurgents, but his ship, the *Commodore,* sank off the coast of Florida, leaving him stranded at sea for thirty hours. That experience left him with the material for one of his most acclaimed short stories, "The Open Boat." After a stint reporting on the Greco-Turkish War alongside his lover, Cora Taylor, one of the few women correspondents, he told Joseph Conrad that the war in Greece had shown him that *The Red Badge of Courage* was "all right." He then tried to enlist in the U.S. Army, only to be rejected for his frail health. When Crane finally arrived in Cuba, fellow celebrity journalist Richard Harding Davis reported that Crane threw himself into the theater of battle, helping unload the marines' ships, setting up encampments, carrying the wounded, waving the wig-wag flags—even placing himself in highly conspicuous positions open to Spanish fire. The *World's* reference to Crane's Civil War novel in the context of the Cuban struggle indicates a more profound connection between the two wars than the name of a well-known author.

Crane had notoriously testified in court on behalf of a New York prostitute, incurring the wrath of then police commissioner Theodore Roosevelt; he later tweaked Roosevelt by titling his dispatch on the Rough Riders "Stephen Crane's Vivid Story of San Juan Hill," stealing a bit of glory from the famous soldier-politician. Just as his first novella, *Maggie: A Girl of the Streets* (1893), depicted the descent of a poor working girl into prostitution several years before his defense of the real streetwalker, Crane's Civil War novel prefigured his Cuban war reporting. In many respects, Crane's short life imitated his art.

The vivid appeal for so many readers of *The Red Badge of Courage* lay in more than its ability to recapture the realities of the Civil War—although some veterans claimed to recognize his fictionalized battle scenes, or even to have served with him at Chancellorsville. He achieved this realism by researching old newspaper accounts, but his account of the 1860s also reflected the heightened militarism of the 1890s. "Bloodshed has encircled the globe," proclaimed the *World* in 1895. These new wars were increasingly justified as opportunities for men to replenish the primitive valor of their forefathers, thought to have been weakened by the perceived feminization and overcivilization of contemporary life. While Frederick Jackson Turner's lament for the close of the western frontier spurred the search for new frontiers abroad, many advocated what Roosevelt called the "strenuous life" of military discipline and physical prowess, and Roosevelt urged his male contemporaries to emulate the heroism of the generation that fought the Civil War.

Cuba, long coveted as a potential U.S. territory, appeared in the 1890s to offer such a test of strenuous manhood. *The Red Badge of Courage,* however, expresses ambivalence toward this revival of martial virtues by debunking the romantic expectations of the young soldiers. The central irony of the novel is that the protagonist, Henry Fleming, receives his head wound, his visible "red badge of courage," from a fleeing Union soldier after he has abandoned his regiment. The ending leaves open the question of whether Fleming does finally display true courage when he returns to combat. Crane also challenged the conventions of the historical novel. He represented the war devoid of context, with no mention of slavery, the Union, or the Confederacy. Instead, throughout the battle Fleming has a sense of performing for an audience, whether fellow soldiers, the women left behind, or even the open eyes of a corpse. Crane became known for his highly visual style, as if freezing action scenes in the frames of a photograph or with the new technology of the "moving pictures."

"Jingoism is merely the lust of the spectator," wrote J. A. Hobson, a British critic of imperialism and journalist of the Boer War. Crane's war novel and his journalism both perfected and dissected this modern quality of war as a spectator sport. For the imperial soldier in foreign terrain, enemy and ally seemed increasingly hard to distinguish. Moreover, the assessment of soldiers' deeds became dependent on the close proximity of journalists. As Crane wrote in his less-known novel *Active Service* (1899), when soldiers "go away to the fighting ground, out of the sight, out of the hearing of the world known to them and are eager to perform feats of war in this new place they feel an absolute longing for a spectator . . . The war correspondent arises, then, to become a sort of cheap telescope for the people at home."

But Crane also succeeded in transforming the correspondent's ephemeral vision into an art form that would long be emulated, by telescoping beyond the individual psyche in battle to the vast forces behind the war. Without the trappings of patriotic propaganda, he represented war as a machine grinding down individual soldiers, a metaphor for nature's arbitrary violence. The novel depicts privates abandoned and betrayed by their officers, reacting in a fury of undirected violence they couldn't have imagined from reading books or hearing the tales of veterans. Fleming drags himself along beside the delirious walking wounded and through fields of mangled corpses. Crane also introduces a theme that would predominate in late twentieth-century war literature and film: that it is the American soldier who is most in need of rescue, whether from his heartless superiors, indifferent civilians, or his own moral questioning. That view challenges the notion of war as masculine rescue fantasy, whether of Cubans in 1898, South Vietnamese in 1968, or Afghanis in 2008.

Just as he excised historical details of the Civil War from *Red Badge*, Crane stripped his initial journalistic report about the shipwreck of the *Commodore*, "Stephen Crane's Own Story," of any references to filibustering, the presence of Cubans speaking Spanish, or the moral dilemma the men in the boat faced in leaving behind a raft of fellow survivors. In "The Open Boat," the experience is stripped even further to highlight man's subjection to the powerful contingency of nature, as voiced in the memorable phrase, "Shipwrecks are apropos of nothing." Yet in Crane's fiction the repressed historical context surfaces in key moments to remind us that history does have a role in nature's contingencies. In "The Open Boat," for example, the correspondent recalls a popular verse recited in childhood about a French foreign legionnaire dying away from home in Algiers, indirectly pointing to the imperial context of the shipwreck.

In turning away from the politics of the 1860s, *The Red Badge of Courage* very much reflected the historical period in which it was written. It starts with the vision of a "negro teamster who had been dancing upon a cracker box." Crane reduces the black figure to an entertainer, divorcing his novel from the historical context of slavery at a time when national reconciliation was effected at the cost of Jim Crow segregation and the undoing of the legal gains toward racial justice attained during Reconstruction. The contemporary sources Crane consulted for his novel emphasized tales of equally heroic exploits among Blue and Gray, to pave the "road to reunion." The war against Spain, it was thought, would heal old sectional wounds as white "brothers," formerly deadly enemies, joined under one flag to subdue black and brown people fighting for independence in Cuba and the Philippines. The reunification of whites North and South at the expense of nonwhites at home and abroad provided the narrative for popular white supremacist fiction by Thomas Dixon, whose novels *The Leopard's Spots* (1903) and *The Clansman* (1905) became the basis for what is considered America's first great movie epic, *Birth of a Nation* (1915).

Crane was less interested in such overt racial nationalism than in the details of the soldiers' experience. Yet his journalism did contribute to a major shift in U.S. attitudes toward Cubans during the war. While elements of the press had clamored to support "Cuba Libre" since the late 1860s, portraying Cubans as chivalrous caballeros or damsels in distress, after the United States entered the war Cubans were increasingly depicted as stereotypically lazy blacks and mulattoes, incapable of winning their own independence. Just as Crane excised the plight of black slaves and soldiers from his Civil War narrative, in his dispatches from Cuba he increasingly deleted Cubans from the anticolonial war they had been fighting for decades, characterizing them as unworthy allies—as did other journalists, like Richard Harding Davis, who went on to pen his own popular novels about hypermasculine soldiers of fortune (a line that leads straight to the Rambo films of the 1980s). Crane wrote smugly that the Cubans themselves were "the worst thing for the cause of an independent Cuba that could possibly exist." While Jim Crow America was disenfranchising African Americans, it made similar arguments about its newly conquered Island Empire: that nonwhite peoples were incapable of self-government.

In Crane's short life he traversed the course of empire in the late 1890s: from a New York City seething with class conflict, to the receding western frontier long heralded as a safety valve for those conflicts, to Porfirio Díaz's repressive Mexico, to the declining Ottoman empire, and finally to Cuba. After the war in Cuba, he retired to Surrey, England, to convalesce, while the United States consolidated itself as a nation-state in order to emerge on the world stage as a new empire. For this purpose, stories of the Civil War served as foundational myths. In some respects Crane resisted this mythmaking by reporting on warfare as a spectacle of male vulnerability as well as prowess. Yet Crane died in 1899 and didn't live to see the consequences of what was dubbed "the splendid little war," such as the constraints imposed on Cuban independence by a constitution that mandated U.S. intervention, including a perpetual lease on Guantánamo Bay. Nor would he witness the brutal three-year antiguerrilla war that followed the annexation of the Philippines, during which American soldiers burned villages and fields, tortured Filipino fighters, massacred civilians, and herded the residents of entire provinces into concentration camps.

Other novelists were indeed vocal about these developments. Though he initially supported the fight against Spain as a war of liberation, Mark Twain was soon disillusioned by what he saw as America's European-style colonialism, and the Anti-Imperialist League made him its vice president. In Twain's well-known pamphlet *To the Person Sitting in Darkness,* which circulated again during the anti–Vietnam War movement, the benighted narrator says with mock innocence: "There must be two Americas: one that sets the captive free, and one that takes a once-captive's new freedom away from him and picks a quarrel with him with nothing to found it on; then kills him to get his land." At stake in these debates was the meaning and identity of America: could the United States continue to be a republic while ruling an imperium across the globe? In his 1899 speech "The Strenuous Life," Roosevelt answered with a rousing affirmation that annexing the Philippines was directly continuous with the course of American history. He claimed that the criticism of the anti-imperialists, whom he portrayed as sissies, "if carried out, would make it incumbent upon us to leave the Apaches of Arizona to work out their own salvation . . . Their doctrines condemn your forefathers and mine for ever having settled in these United States." He insinuates that accepting the independence of the Philippines would be tantamount to returning the continent to Native Americans. Roosevelt's agenda was buoyed by a poem dedicated to him the same year in support of Philippine annexation: "The White Man's Burden," by Rudyard Kipling. Thomas Dixon would use this phrase as the subtitle for his revisionist history of Reconstruction, arguing against the "unnaturalness" of black self-governance.

If Stephen Crane had lived longer, one might imagine him ignoring these political debates to focus on the experience of the individual U.S. soldier in the Philippines: his dislocation, cowardice, bravery, confusion, and immersion in violence. His legacy to the century he did not survive to see was not only to redefine the war novel through the perceptions of the common soldier, but also to invent the persona of the war correspondent, who straddles the boundary between spectator and actor. But he did more than outline a protagonist and a narrative strategy to be fleshed out by Ernest Hemingway, Norman Mailer, Tim O'Brien, and others. By viewing the Civil War from the vantage of the colonial wars of the 1890s, Crane also subtly undermined the distinction between "good wars" and dirtier "anti-insurrection operations." It is Crane's anticipation of the modern spectacle of war that allowed Hemingway to assert in 1942 that *The Red Badge of Courage* was the only enduring "real literature of our Civil War." Writers and readers of the twentieth-century war novel would continue to blur the line between fact and fiction, as they did when assuming Crane had based his scenes on direct experience (readers often express similar surprise—and sometimes betrayal—when they discover that O'Brien's *The Things They Carried* is a novel, not a memoir). The vaunted realism of Crane's Civil War took as much from the militarism and jingoism of the spectator wars of the 1890s as it did from the veterans of the earlier war.

Bibliography: Stephen Crane, *Reports of War,* ed. Fredson Bowers (Charlottesville, VA, 1971); *The Third Violet and Active Service,* ed. Fredson Bowers (Charlottesville, 1976). Kristin Hoganson, *Fighting for American Manhood: How Gender Politics Provoked the Spanish-American and Philippine-American Wars* (New Haven, CT, 1998). Theodore Roosevelt, *The Strenuous Life: Essays and Addresses* (New York, 1900).

AMY KAPLAN

1899; 1924

"Since I won in the lottery I've become a regular little miser," Trina McTeague admits

McTeague and *Greed*

Frank Norris, an admirer of Émile Zola, championed literary naturalism in America and put it into practice nowhere better than in *McTeague: A Story of San Francisco,* published in 1899. Literary scholars have often thought Norris a clumsy writer, but *McTeague* is a powerful, well-constructed novel that has endured. It inspired a legendary silent movie from 1924, Erich von Stroheim's *Greed.* If Norris did something new in the literature of his country, Stroheim was breaking ground in the new art of film. Originally much longer but truncated by MGM, *Greed* nonetheless stands out in film history as a classic of realism, or naturalism. This is a singular case of adaptation, neither the novel nor the film suffering by comparison with the other, the film so faithful to the novel and yet so much an original work in its own right.

Benjamin Franklin Norris, Jr., was born in Chicago in 1870 to a wealthy family that moved to San Francisco when he was fifteen. He studied painting in Paris but developed an interest in writing and returned home and attended the University of California at Berkeley. He started publishing during his college years but, like the dentist McTeague, never earned a diploma. Norris got the idea for his novel from a story in the San Francisco newspapers. In 1893 a murder took place in a kindergarten: when one Sarah Collins, a janitor, refused to give her estranged alcoholic husband any of her money, he stabbed her to death. Norris began his story in a writing course he took at Harvard as a special student.

A well-off young man looking down from the heights of Harvard at the likes of that janitor woman and her brutish husband will for some exemplify the trouble with naturalism, the social distance separating the author, and the reader, from lower-class characters, and the condescension likely to result. But for Norris the trouble with realism—as he wrote in 1902, the year of his early death, in an article on the American realist William Dean Howells—was that the "characters live across the street from us, they are 'on our block.' We know all about them . . .

We ourselves are Mr. Howells's characters, so long as we are well behaved and ordinary and *bourgeois*." By contrast, he went on,

> The naturalist takes no note of common people, common in so far as their interests, their lives, and the things that occur in them are common, are ordinary. Terrible things must happen to the characters of the naturalistic tale. They must be twisted from the ordinary, wrenched out from the quiet, uneventful round of every-day life, and flung into the throes of a vast and terrible drama that works itself out in unleashed passions, in blood, and in sudden death.

Erich Oswald Stroheim was born in 1885 in Vienna; he added the "von" to his name on his arrival in the United States in 1909. He fabricated an aristocratic background for himself; only after his death in 1957 did it come out that he was actually the son of a Jewish hatter. He may have also made up the story that in his early years of immigrant poverty he found a copy of *McTeague* in a seedy hotel room, read the book straight through in one night, and became determined to film it one day. But if Stroheim was a liar, an impostor, he told the truth as well, and in *Greed* he tells a story that carries to an extreme something he lived himself when, in anger and despair over lack of money, he beat his first wife, Margaret Knox. Perhaps it was then that he read Norris's novel.

McTeague is full of doublings, interlocked lives: McTeague and Marcus, best friends turned mortal enemies who die handcuffed together in Death Valley; Trina McTeague and the Jewish junk dealer, Zerkow, hoarders alike, beholden to a dream of riches; Trina and Zerkow's wife, Maria Macapa, two women abused by their husbands and eventually killed by them for an unreal or useless pot of gold; McTeague and Trina themselves in their compulsive mutual dependence, symbolized in *Greed* by a pair of canaries in a gilded cage, a husband and wife bound together in health and forever in sickness. And stepping outside the fiction, we might also take Norris and Stroheim, the privileged boy and the immigrant, the Anglo-Saxon supremacist and the Jew passing for an imperial nobleman, as doubles of each other.

"Norris's ambition," Alfred Kazin wrote in *On Native Grounds*, was

> to find a literary equivalent for his nation's bigness. Yet it is in *McTeague*, that story of degeneration, that he lives . . . the first great tragic portrait in America of an acquisitive society . . . McTeague's San Francisco is the underworld of that society, and the darkness of its tragedy, its pitilessness, its grotesque humor, is like the rumbling of hell. Nothing is more remarkable in the book than the detachment with which Norris saw it—a tragedy almost classic in the Greek sense of the debasement of a powerful man—and nothing gives it so much power. For McTeague himself, it is safe to say, Norris cared very little; but out of his own instinct for brute force he invested McTeague's own brutality with an imperishable significance.

How can a character for whom the author cares so little have the stature of a tragic hero? Tragedy is traditionally about the death of kings, and we must care for kings, whatever we may think of them as individuals, because what happens to them happens to a whole society. Naturalism, as Diane Stevenson has remarked, transposes tragedy from the high reaches of society to the low, making the low representative not of the ordinary course of life but of its terrible possibilities, cards that society may deal to any of its members. McTeague is a tragic hero not because he's personally exceptional but because, whatever we may think of him as an individual, something exceptional happens to him—and to Trina, as much a tragic figure as he—that could happen to anybody.

McTeague, a dentist on Polk Street in San Francisco, falls in love with Trina while treating her as a patient. She is his friend Marcus's cousin and sweetheart, but when McTeague confesses his passion for her, Marcus tearfully gives her up:

> It was a great moment; even McTeague felt the drama of it. What a fine thing was this friendship between men! The dentist treats his friend for an ulcerated tooth and refuses payment; the friend reciprocates by giving up his girl. This was nobility. Their mutual affection and esteem suddenly increased enormously. It was Damon and Pythias; it was David and Jonathan; nothing could ever estrange them. Now it was for life or death.

Here Norris assumes an ironic, slighting superiority toward his characters, who are not Damon and Pythias or David and Jonathan—who haven't even heard of them. In the corresponding scene in *Greed,* as McTeague and Marcus pour out their emotions, Stroheim cuts to a player piano in their vicinity. This is also an ironic authorial comment, detached from the characters but, unlike Norris's, staying within their experience. The player piano is a mechanistic metaphor for the emotions in the scene, for the inflation of Marcus's sentiments—yet the quite earnest McTeague is involved too. The metaphor widens and grows unsettling, chillier. It suggests that human feelings, sincere, intense though they may be, have something mechanical about them, something programmed.

When Trina, now betrothed to McTeague, wins five thousand dollars in a lottery, Marcus feels cheated and resentful, and these feelings keep running in his head like an unceasing tune on a player piano. It's the same with the other characters: they are not in command of their feelings, their feelings are in command of them. Trina doesn't surrender to McTeague because she loves him, she loves him because she surrenders to him. Such a deterministic view of human character as effect rather than cause is typical of naturalism. Determinism is a matter of degree, however. Few would dispute that to some degree we are free, to some degree determined, but we like to think we are free, and naturalism reminds us that we are determined.

They would seem an ideal couple, or at least a perfectly normal petty-bourgeois husband and wife, McTeague big and strong, Trina pretty and tidy and thrifty. Under her civilizing tutelage his manners and his mind improve. He's happy to submit to her socially; she's happy to submit to him sexually. If not on our block, these characters live close enough to it. If a tragic flaw is inseparable from a virtue, McTeague and Trina surely qualify: what their society normally upholds as virtues end up becoming their vices. McTeague's manly strength turns into brutality, Trina's wifely thriftiness turns into utter parsimony ("'I didn't use to be so stingy,' she told herself. 'Since I won in the lottery I've become a regular little miser. It's growing on me, but never mind, it's a good fault, and, anyhow, I can't help it'"), and her sexual pleasure in submission to a man, just what a patriarchal society would expect of a good woman, turns into outright masochism. Talk about the psychopathology of everyday life.

Trina's winning the lottery is the turning point in the plot of *McTeague,* the chance event that triggers inexorable necessity. Having money leads Trina to save it compulsively; like everyone at all levels of her society, no matter how much money she has, she doesn't feel she has enough. And her five thousand dollars also bring out the worst in Marcus, who out of vengeful envy informs the authorities that the dentist is practicing without a license. With a miserly wife and now the loss of his livelihood, McTeague is doubly a victim of the lottery money (as well as a victim of his society's professionalization: a competent enough dentist forced, as he says, "to quit for just a piece of paper").

Victim changes into victimizer as Jekyll into Hyde—and a sequence in *Greed* memorably dramatizes the change. Fired from a job he found after he had to give up dentistry, McTeague arrives home early, but Trina commandeers all the money he was paid and sends him right out to look for another job. In a striking deep-focus shot taken from a low angle, we see him in the foreground, going downstairs and pausing to ask her something, while behind him, at the top of the stairs, she looks much smaller yet looms powerful over him. It's going to rain, he says; could he have a nickel for carfare? "A big fellow like you 'fraid of a little walk." So he goes out, finds no job, and is thoroughly soaked in the rain. A friend sees him in the street and, to warm him up, invites him into a bar for a drink of whiskey. "It kind of disagrees with me," he demurs—his father, we recall, died of alcoholism—but the friend insists. As McTeague gulps down the whiskey, Stroheim cuts to Trina at home polishing a coin, then back to the bar as McTeague drinks another glass of whiskey, and then, after a fade indicating a passage of time, back to Trina with her hoard of money. Switching back and forth between husband and wife at this significant moment links them together in the addictions that compel each of them, her money and his whiskey. Her money, the nickel she wouldn't give him for carfare, has led to his whiskey, and his whiskey will lead to her death. He returns home full of drink and anger and almost hits her, his hand raised and clenched into a fist. "I wonder where he got the money to buy his whiskey," she asks herself after he falls asleep.

Stroheim was a master of the reverse angle. Though he did not invent it, he employed it more intensively than anyone before him, and few since have put it to such gripping use. Usually pivoting on a character's glance, the reverse angle turns to the facing area, situating us with the character inside the space of the film. When the former dentist returns home drunk and advances aggressively toward his wife, we are put in her position and see him from her point of view as if he were coming right at us, up close in our face and getting closer; and when she looks up in fear at his raised hand, we see his clenched fist from her point of view as if it were about to strike us. We alternate between the two characters in a shot/reverse shot—an interlocked pair of reverse angles—but McTeague, unlike Trina, looks right at the camera, which is thus more directly aligned with her perspective, more identified with her than with him at this moment when he threatens violence against her.

If condescension toward a lower class is the trouble with naturalism, it mostly resides in the better-educated language the author shares with the reader but not with the characters. In this respect the reverse angle gives Stroheim an advantage over Norris. A point of view expressed in words inevitably carries the mark of a class, a social position, but a visual perspective we can all share. A big angry man getting closer, a raised fist seen from below, looks the same to everybody.

Sometimes we identify more with McTeague, sometimes more with Trina— more with the meek McTeague when the domineering Trina sends him out, more with the scared Trina when the drunken McTeague returns. In *Greed* and in *McTeague* our identification is divided between husband and wife. If you think Norris sides with the man, look, for example, at the passage in which, after McTeague leaves one morning, the novel sympathetically stays with Trina all through the day: she thinks her husband has gone fishing, and she worries about him and asks the neighbors when he fails to turn up, until she comes to realize as night falls that he has robbed and abandoned her. Norris's detachment, like Stroheim's, arises not so much from the withholding of sympathy as from its division, which keeps us from taking sides and allows us to stand back and observe the terrible pattern of compulsion in which both wife and husband are caught. *McTeague* has been called a melodrama, and the same goes for *Greed,* but no one is good in this melodrama and no one is evil. It is not sympathy but moralizing that is withheld.

The novel is a bourgeois form. In the main it portrays middle-class characters for middle-class readers. The naturalist novel, however, ventures into the life of the lower classes, foreign territory to middle-class readers, more difficult for them to identify with, but not so far from them as they may think. *McTeague* depicts the petty bourgeoisie falling into an awful abyss dangerously close to familiar reality. The characters both are and are not like us; we're brought close to them, as if the details of their lives were part of our own, yet at the same time we're kept at a distance. We observe them like insects under the clinical eye of an entomologist, these characters who are what we fear we might become.

Stroheim's use of the reverse angle helps achieve a similar combination of intense closeness and entomological detachment. We freely assume the characters' points of view but shift from one to another and never remain with any one character for long. On her wedding day Trina, afraid of the hulking husband who will now possess her, says good-bye to her departing family, and we see her mother going downstairs from Trina's perspective above, then Trina from her mother's perspective below, then her father at the door downstairs from Trina and her mother's perspective above, then Trina and her mother from her father's perspective below. Even when Trina is unconscious under ether in the dentist's chair, we alternate between McTeague's and her point of view and see what she would see if her eyes were open, the dentist unable to control his desire and coming forward to kiss his defenseless patient. We are at once right in the midst of the characters and viewing them dispassionately.

This is a detachment that observes without moralizing, without passing judgment. It has no governing moral standpoint, neither that of an omniscient author nor that of a Jamesian center of consciousness. Setting *McTeague* and *Greed* side by side lets us discern more clearly the cultural moment of naturalism. The world hasn't fallen to pieces—that will occur with the fragmentation of modernism. But if the naturalistic details and perspectives come together into a whole, it is a material, circumstantial, not a moral or spiritual whole.

Bibliography: Alfred Kazin, *On Native Grounds: An Interpretation of Modern American Prose Literature* (New York, 1942). Frank Norris, *McTeague: A Story of San Francisco* (New York, 1899); "W. D. Howells," *North American Review,* December 1902. *Filmography: Greed,* directed by Erich von Stroheim (MGM, 1924); restored and reconstructed by Rick Schmidlin (Turner Classic Movies, 1999).

GILBERTO PEREZ

1900

An artist of ideas ponders the dynamo at the Paris Exposition

HENRY ADAMS

Henry Adams was a brooder. He hadn't always been one, though he long had harbored some skepticism about his countrymen's faith in progress. A historian and fourth-generation scion of a family that included two presidents, he was appalled by the corrupt politics of the Gilded Age, lamenting the decline of the republic in his reform journalism and his novel *Democracy* (1880). But that was a conventional malaise compared with what came over him later. When his wife committed suicide in 1885, Adams plunged into a profound depression that led him to a sustained and searching reexamination of his intellectual birthright— the comfortable pieties of Brahmin Boston, above all the assumption that positivist science, liberal individualism, and rational religion would lock arms and lead us into an inevitably brighter future. Eventually Adams embraced a second career as a speculative artist of ideas, producing two major works of cultural criticism: *Mont-Saint-Michel and Chartres* (1904) and *The Education of Henry Adams* (1907).

The Chicago World's Fair of 1893 marked a key moment in Adams's midlife transition. His two visits to the fair came at a crucial moment in his personal development—and (he later decided) in the development of the United States, perhaps in that of the entire world, as well. This, at the time, was not a terribly original response to the fair; many of Adams's friends were attributing huge cultural significance to it—especially the ones who were involved in planning it.

"Not Matter, But Mind; Not Things, But Men" was the official motto of the fair, repeated often by the architect Daniel Burnham, its head designer. Burnham assembled a team of architects and artists with impeccable neoclassical credentials as well as powerful ties to the patronage establishment—and no shortage of self-esteem. "Look here, old fellow," the sculptor Augustus Saint-Gaudens burst out to Burnham at a planning meeting, "do you realize that this is the greatest meeting of artists since the fifteenth century?" Saint-Gaudens, Burnham, and their colleagues and patrons all believed that they could discipline the furious, expansive energies of American capitalism with the cool ideality of neoclassical hierarchies, values, and tastes.

The fulfillment of the planners' agenda was aptly dubbed the White City. The core of it was the Court of Honor, a cluster of plaster temples assembled around a lagoon lit by hundreds of incandescent lights. The chaste buildings were crammed with the latest products developed by Westinghouse, Krupp, General Electric, and other burgeoning trusts—traveling cranes, artillery pieces, dynamos. Ultimately the fair slipped away from its organizers' intentions, revealing a central irony: the future belonged to the consolidated force of capital, and not to the flimsy neoclassical structures that temporarily housed it. Adams would come to sense this. While his fellow patricians stood on the edge of the Court of Honor, rhapsodizing about the redemptive powers of art, Adams stood inside Machinery Hall, contemplating the dynamos.

But not at first. After a two-day visit in mid-May, Adams was ecstatic about the achievements of Saint-Gaudens, Burnham, and their colleagues. "Though I have lived among the men who are doing this work, and though I thought I knew their powers as well as their limits, I never supposed they could have risen to a level so high as this," he wrote to a friend. "I supposed I knew that Chicago could do business and make money, but I was not prepared to have her turn on me on my own ground, and tell me that she would now give me a little lesson of modesty, and would teach me something that was not business but beauty." This was conventional rhapsody, but when Adams returned for a longer look in October, he began to suspect that the lesson of the Chicago World's Fair was not as simple or coherent as it had seemed. "A pure white temple, on the pure blue sea, with an Italian sky, all vast and beautiful as the world never saw it before, and in it the most astounding, confused, bewildering mass of art and industry, without a sign that there was any connection, relation, or harmony or understanding of the relations of anything anywhere," he wrote to one of his adoptive nieces, Lucy Baxter. Despite the fair's motto, Adams was moved to ponder the things themselves. While he was staring "like an owl at the dynamos and steam-engines," he admitted to his friend John Hay that "all the time I kept up a devil of a thinking."

The dynamos, he would later conclude in *The Education*, "were new, and they gave to history a new phase." They signified the resolution of the centuries-long conflict "between two forces, one simply industrial, the other capitalistic, centralizing, and mechanical." They underwrote the new dominance of the corporations whose displays crowded Machinery Hall, whose products would create the foundation of the modern military-industrial complex that "advanced" nations would soon be using to destroy each other. These impersonal developments carried personal weight for Adams. To him, the dynamo stood for "the whole mechanical consolidation of force, which ruthlessly stamped out the life of the class into which Adams was born, but created monopolies capable of controlling the new energies that Americans adored."

Adams's reverie was a blend of sense and nonsense. The class into which he had been born was not "ruthlessly stamped out" by the concentration of force in monopoly capital. On the contrary: during and after the crisis of the 1890s, established WASP elites revitalized themselves and retooled for leadership roles in the emerging managerial society. Nor did the republican tradition disappear; it continued to animate the populist vision of a "producerist democracy" in a variety of progressive and socialist movements. Adams was not an accurate guide to the political history of his own time.

Yet in fixating on the dynamo, Adams located an apt symbol for the transition from republic to empire. By transforming mechanical energy into the invisible force of electricity, and by placing that force in the service of concentrated capital, the dynamo epitomized the imperial reach of the new corporate economy. Adams recognized that the appeal of monopolies lay in their capacity to harness "the new energies that Americans adored." Which Americans actually adored those energies remained an open question, but some (including Adams) felt magnetically drawn to them. Like many of his contemporaries on both sides of the Atlantic, Adams was obsessed with force for its own sake. He found an icon to embody it in the dynamo, one that combined his distrust of modern hubris and his fascination with the engines that powered it.

In 1900, at about the same time that the Republicans' presidential ticket was running roughshod over the anti-imperialist William Jennings Bryan, Henry Adams attended another world's fair—the Paris Exposition—to contemplate the dynamos again. As he stared at them, he felt their significance deepen. However mystifying Adams found the energy unleashed by the new technology, he was convinced that whoever controlled it would control international conflicts in the future. This was the meaning of the dynamo that most appealed to the politician manqué in Adams, the man who loved plotting intrigues and serving as "stable companion to statesmen"—especially to Hay after he became Theodore Roosevelt's secretary of state. Adams loved proximity to power, and declared his consultation with Hay to be "probably . . . the moment of highest knowledge that a scholar could reach." His fascination with the power of the dynamo sometimes reached Faustian heights, as when he announced that the twentieth-century American, "the child of incalculable coal-power, chemical power, electric power, and radiating energy . . . must be a sort of God compared with any former creation of nature."

Yet for Adams, the dynamo's importance was more philosophical than political, economic, or even technological. To him it represented an end and a beginning: the shattering of the old positivist certainties—especially the certainty that the universe was measurable and predictable—and the start of a new era characterized by profound uncertainty. "The period from 1870 to 1900 is closed," Adams wrote to Hay. "I see that much in the machine-gallery of the Champ de Mars" and "sit by the hour over the great dynamos, watching them run noiselessly and smoothly as the planets, and asking them—with infinite courtesy—where in Hell they are going." The dynamos were the most palpable of many mystifying departures from the predictable, deterministic science of the nineteenth century. "The charm of the show, to me," he wrote a niece, "is that no one pretends to understand even in a remote degree, what these weird things are that they call electricity, Roentgen rays, and what not." By embodying unprecedented power, the dynamo evoked religious awe (at least in Adams)—a sense of "profound helplessness and dependence on an infinite force that is to us incomprehensible and omnipotent."

The dynamo became a "symbol of infinity" for Adams. "Before the end, one began to pray to it," he wrote in his autobiography. To him "its value lay chiefly in its occult mechanism." It epitomized all the new, invisible forces converging to kill off the old scientific certainties—forces like X-rays, which were "occult, supersensual, irrational; they were a revelation of mysterious energy like that of the Cross; they were what, in terms of medieval science, were called immediate modes of the divine substance." Yet the X-ray and the dynamo had less in common with the Cross than with each other, as well as with other modern sources of occult energy—unconscious drives, hidden selves—that could not fit easily into the positivist conception of a completely measurable universe.

Adams's quest to make sense of a post-positivist universe stamped him as a man of his time. On both sides of the Atlantic, psychologists and physicists were redefining cosmos and self, departing from static Victorian certainties, en route to no one knew where. Avant-garde artists and writers rejected those certainties, too, as part of their broader dismissal of a bourgeois culture that seemed increasingly pinched and parochial. Vitalism challenged intellectualism at every turn. An atmosphere of experiment penetrated most academic disciplines, even philosophy, as William James, Henri Bergson, Friedrich Nietzsche, and other thinkers recast truth claims in more fluid and dynamic forms.

And the fascination with force was not confined to a handful of intellectuals. A preoccupation with releasing energy from previously untapped sources (body, soul, psyche) pervaded popular culture in the early twentieth century. In *Good Housekeeping* and the *Saturday Evening Post,* self-help writers began describing "How You Can *Do* More and *Be* More!"—redefining the scarcity psychology of the nineteenth century into an abundance psychology more appropriate for the twentieth. As economists conceived an upward spiral of production and consumption powering endless economic growth, psychologists imagined a fluid, vital self pursuing a path of endless personal growth. Adams was not impressed, not willing to bend a knee before the dynamo and embrace the emerging ideal of well-managed energy.

Adams's reasons for reluctance were far too subtle and complex to be reduced to patrician diffidence. Harboring a deep ambivalence toward the life of his time, he combined a hatred of modernity and a fascination with the engines that generated its unprecedented force. But ultimately he turned from technological power toward a different sort of regenerative force.

In 1901, the year after he stood brooding over the dynamos at the Paris Exposition, Adams penned a poem that foreshadowed the great themes of his late work, *Mont-Saint-Michel and Chartres* and *The Education of Henry Adams*. His "Prayer to the Virgin of Chartres" posed the dynamo against the virgin, masculine world mastery against "the mystery of maternity." He begged the Virgin Mother's pardon for abandoning her, for joining other men in their struggle for knowledge, wealth, and power. The quest for mastery was strongest among Americans.

> Crossing the hostile sea, our greedy band
>   Saw rising hills and forests in the blue;
> Our father's kingdom in the promised land!
>   —We seized it, and dethroned the father too.
>
> And now we are the father, with our brood,
>   Ruling the Infinite, not Three but One;
> We made our world and saw that it was good;
>   Ourselves we worship, and we have no Son.

This was the ultimate consequence of praying to the dynamo—self-absorption and sterility. The worship of technological force ended in a solipsistic blind alley, a worship of ourselves. Recoiling from this bleak, disenchanted vision of modern America, Adams turned from Father to Mother.

> Waiting I feel the energy of faith
>   Not in the future science, but in you!

In his heterodox view, the Virgin embodied the force of maternal fecundity—"the greatest and most mysterious of all energies," as the childless widower called it. The male will to mastery could not acknowledge that female power, could not even bend a knee to it but only rush by, producing dynamos and steam engines. Yet somehow the machines' power could not match the Virgin's, especially in the art they inspired. Factories were not cathedrals. As Adams wrote, "All the steam in the world could not, like the Virgin, build Chartres." This was the power he would explore in his most profound work.

Adams's confrontation with the dynamos led him to reflect on the hubris at the core of the modern worship of force, and to search for alternative forms of vitality in medieval European culture. He shared the vitalist impulse of his contemporaries but gave it an antimodern edge; with this move he made manifest what was latent in James, Bergson, and Nietzsche. Adams's antimodern vitalism, animated by religious longings for regeneration, allowed him to combine a celebration of force with a critique of its modern embodiment. He became an antimodern modernist. This was not as contradictory a stance as it might at first seem: the intellectual revolution we call modernism challenged many attitudes and assumptions considered modern at the time, in particular the deterministic universe of positivist science. Despite his yearnings for the thirteenth century, Henry Adams participated in the most regenerative intellectual movement of his time—the recapturing of chance, choice, and possibility in the life of the mind.

Bibliography: Henry Adams, *The Education of Henry Adams* (1907; New York, 1983). John Kasson, *Civilizing the Machine: Technology and Republican Values in America* (New York, 1971). T. J. Jackson Lears, *No Place of Grace: Antimodernism and the Transformation of American Culture, 1880–1920* (1981; Chicago, 1994). David Nye, *American Technological Sublime* (Cambridge, MA, 1994). Miles Orvell, *The Real Thing: Imitation and Authenticity in American Culture, 1880–1940* (Chapel Hill, NC, 1989). Alan Trachtenberg, *The Incorporation of America: Culture and Society in the Gilded Age* (New York, 1982).

T. J. JACKSON LEARS

1900

L. Frank Baum publishes a new type of "wonder tale"

THE WIZARD OF OZ

In May 1900, advance copies of the Hill Company's *The Wonderful Wizard of Oz*—text by L. Frank Baum and illustrations by W. W. Denslow—began to circulate among reviewers. In the introduction, Baum declared: "The old-time fairy tale, having served for generations, may now be classed as 'historical' in the children's library; for the time has come for a series of newer 'wonder tales' in which the stereotyped genie, dwarf, and fairy are eliminated, together with all the horrible and blood-curdling incidents devised by their authors to point a fearsome moral to each tale."

The book was generally favorably reviewed upon its official publication in September, although no one saw it as anything remarkable. It sold more than 37,000 copies in the first fifteen months, which was very good indeed, but it was not Baum's best-selling title of the moment. That was *Father Goose: His Book,* published a year earlier. (When Hill Company went bankrupt in 1902, *Father Goose* was still Baum's best-selling book.) *The Wonderful Wizard of Oz* was seen as simply a good (not great), inventive, and commercially successful children's book. Baum had no idea that this book would lead to a series (it had not been conceived as having a sequel) and that he would write thirteen more Oz books before his death in 1919. Nor could he have foreseen that the series would continue with different authors, including, most recently, Baum's great-grandson, Roger S. Baum.

The Oz books are more than a long-running series that managed to outlive their creator. As a fictional location, Oz is better known than Mark Twain's St. Petersburg and Faulkner's Yoknapatawpha County. (The only fantasy place comparable in familiarity may be Disneyland.) The word "Oz" itself is as recognized in the English-speaking world today as such American brand names as Coca-Cola and Ford. Children and adults virtually everywhere around the globe are familiar with Dorothy, the Scarecrow, the Tin Woodman, the Cowardly Lion, and the Wizard. Although these characters appear in many of the sequels, it is through the first Oz book that Dorothy and her friends have become such familiar figures in the cultural imagination. Hardly any American children's book—with the possible exception of *Adventures of Huckleberry Finn*—has been as influential in its impact on American society. It spawned one of the most successful musicals in the history of Hollywood (and the most beloved American children's film ever made): the 1939 MGM classic *The Wizard of Oz,* the film that made Judy Garland a star. Lines from the movie, like "Surrender, Dorothy" and "Lions and tigers and bears, oh my!" are today instantly recognizable almost anywhere. So is the film score by lyricist E. Y. "Yip" Harburg and composer Harold Arlen: "Somewhere Over the Rainbow" can be sung note for note by many. All of this has sprung from a children's story that for many years was dismissed by schoolteachers and librarians, who thought it was poorly written. Despite (or maybe because of) its artless style, *The Wonderful Wizard of Oz* has maintained its powerful appeal.

Baum's turn-of-the-century book ushered in what Swedish sociologist Ellen Key called the Century of the Child. Notwithstanding latter-day critical interpretations, *Oz* was and is very intensely a children's book and is much more engaged with debates swirling around the nature of children's literature than with anything else. At the same time, *Oz* ushered in the American Century. It tried very hard to be an American book in its sensibility. Indeed, Baum was determined to create a children's literature made exclusively of American objects, images, and ideas. In 1901 he published a collection of tales called *American Fairy Tales,* in which every tale is set in the United States.

When Baum wrote *Oz,* he was just emerging as a successful children's author. He had written six children's books (among them, *Mother Goose in Prose* and *Adventures in Phunnyland,* retitled *A New Wonderland*). He met illustrator Denslow in 1897, and together they developed the *Father Goose* book. His relationship with Denslow was always tense, as the men had opposing temperaments, Denslow being taciturn and sullen, Baum outgoing and sunny. Their real conflict, however, arose over who invented the characters of Oz. Denslow claimed the Cowardly Lion was a cocreation and that, as a result of the stage play of 1902, the Scarecrow and the Tin Woodman were his own work because he had invented their costumes. Certainly Denslow's pictures for *The Wonderful Wizard of Oz* were a strong feature of the book. The two men parted ways in 1902.

Baum might never have considered writing for children had not his mother-in-law, Matilda Gage—a feminist, a theosophist, and a noted author in her own right (her major book, published in 1893, argued that the foundation of oppressive patriarchy was in institutionalized Christianity)—encouraged him after hearing him tell stories to his sons. Baum was by no means an inexperienced author when he began his career as a children's writer in the 1890s. At the age of twenty-three, he started *The Poultry Record,* a monthly trade journal about the breeding of fancy chickens. (He had a lifelong interest in the subject of prize poultry.) Most of it was cribbed from other journals, but he wrote editorials and jokes. In South Dakota, Baum started a newspaper in 1890 called the *Aberdeen Saturday Pioneer,* for which he wrote editorials and a column entitled "Our Landlady." He lost the paper to bankruptcy in 1891 and moved to Chicago. A few years later, in 1897, Baum started a monthly journal called *The Shop Window: A Journal of Practical Window Trimming for the Merchant and the Professional.* While running a store, Baum's Bazaar, in South Dakota, Baum had become adept at creating attractive window displays, so he chose to exploit this skill in his new publication. The idea of seducing the eye, which is so emphasized in *The Wonderful Wizard of Oz* with the emerald-colored glasses and the theatrical tricks of the Wizard, probably has its roots in Baum's work of window dressing. He gave up publishing the magazine in 1900, when his career as a children's writer began to take off.

Baum's mother-in-law advised him to try writing for children because he seemed to be a man in search of a vocation—and not having much luck finding one. Born in Chittenango, New York, on May 15, 1856, the seventh child of Cynthia and Benjamin Ward Baum, Lyman Frank Baum as a young adult tried both acting and playwriting, with the support of his father, a successful businessman. Baum even managed a chain of theaters. He was also an oil salesman—selling being something he was good at—and he sold china during his years in Chicago. Unfortunately, because he never liked being away from his wife and family very much, he did not achieve great success as a salesman, despite his ability to sell. Also, Baum suffered from poor health all his life, particularly a bad heart (the fact that he chain-smoked cigars as an adult surely did not help), and this further inclined him to be domestic. He was, by all accounts, an easygoing and likable man who truly enjoyed telling stories and making bad puns, a prominent feature of many of his books that children and adults seemed to love.

He married Maud Gage in 1882 and was quickly converted by his mother-in-law to feminism, something that he satirized in his second Oz book, *The Marvelous Land of Oz,* a far more complex work than the first. The Oz books, with their focus on heroines, are generally suffused with a sort of romantic nineteenth-century feminism. (In the highly gendered world of children's literature, they are often considered girls' books.) Baum did not discover his gift of writing for children until he entered middle age, and his first Oz book was published when he was forty-four years old. But he did not lose any ground despite his late start, and would end up writing several dozen children's books, including the Boy Fortune Hunters series (under the pseudonym Floyd Akers) and the Aunt Jane series (under the pseudonym Edith Van Dyne).

The Wonderful Wizard of Oz was published during what is called the golden age for children's literature in Britain and the United States, the period from 1865 (and the publication of Lewis Carroll's *Alice's Adventures in Wonderland*) to 1911 (the year the novel version of J. M. Barrie's *Peter Pan and Wendy* was published). Children's literature came into its own commercially and artistically during the Victorian era as a number of well-established authors of adult books began to write for children. The field was clearly dominated by the British, with writers like Robert Louis Stevenson, Rudyard Kipling, Kenneth Grahame, Edith Nesbit, and George MacDonald. One year before *Oz* was published, Scotswoman Helen Bannerman published her picture book *Little Black Sambo,* and two years after *Oz,* Englishwoman Beatrix Potter gave the world *The Tale of Peter Rabbit,* both of which would have an impact on the world of children's books nearly equivalent to that of *Oz,* with *Sambo* providing a great deal of long-lasting controversy as well.

Lewis Carroll (Charles Dodgson) is credited with liberating and elevating children's literature. He wrote the first undisputed masterpiece of children's literature, *Alice's Adventures in Wonderland,* with its wildly unpredictable characters, nonsense rhyming, and bizarre plot. It might be said that Charles Kingsley's *The Water Babies,* published two years earlier, anticipated many of *Alice's* effects, yet no one had pulled off so revolutionary a book for children with such artistic verve as Carroll did. Carroll ostentatiously poured genius into a children's book. No one before him had taken children's literature as seriously as an art form. The debate that had persisted since children's literature emerged as a genre in the eighteenth century was whether a book for such an audience should be designed to be didactic or to provide entertainment—the latter always regarded with suspicion as being both un-Christian (leading the way to sin) and frivolous (not of any practical use to a child, as it taught nothing that would help the child live as an adult). But how was one to get children to read unless the book provided some sort of entertainment? (As Mary Poppins sang in the musical version of that children's book, "A spoonful of sugar helps the medicine go down.") Carroll believed not just that writing for children should avoid moralizing but also that children's books should challenge the status quo, as *Alice* questioned the entire enterprise of children's education and the conventional moral ordering of the world. Suddenly authors were attracted to children's literature because it was lucrative (the growing number of bourgeois parents who wanted their children to master literacy and perhaps get a bit of culture made a considerable market for children's books) and because it enabled critics of society to cloak their dissent in fantasy, nonsense, and the sentimentality of childhood innocence.

Americans were not far behind the British in producing important children's books during this golden age: Mark Twain *(Adventures of Huckleberry Finn, The Adventures of Tom Sawyer, The Prince and the Pauper)*, Louisa May Alcott *(Little Men, Little Women, Jo's Boys)*, Horatio Alger *(Ragged Dick, Luck and Pluck)*, and Frances Hodgson Burnett *(The Secret Garden, Little Lord Fauntleroy)* are just a few of the famous.

Baum greatly admired *Alice's Adventures in Wonderland,* saying in an interview that "the secret of Alice's success lay in the fact that she was a real child, and any normal child could sympathize with her through her adventures." In some sense, *Oz* is a simplified knock-off of Alice; instead of going underground, Dorothy is taken through the air by a cyclone to a fantasyland where things are very different from the drab farm on which she lives. But unlike Alice, Dorothy understands Oz, with its good and evil witches and its kingdoms controlled by various leaders. Politically, Oz is much more apparent than Wonderland; Baum has drawn it up in the way children tend to understand politics and government: acts and commands stem from either virtue or greed, rather than from process, ideas, and philosophy. Also unlike Alice, Dorothy has true companions who become friends and share her adventures. *Oz* deals not only with the standard childhood anxiety about leaving home without parents or adults but also with the need for friends, for something like a peer world, both intensely important to young children, who would be attracted to the book in great measure because Dorothy's peers—the Scarecrow, the Woodman, and the Lion—are not really adults but yet not children either. In short, Baum wrote more for children than Carroll did. Both authors resisted sentimentalizing childhood, but Baum, as a bourgeois father, came to his work with a greater empathy for children as something other than artistic objects. (Carroll was infamous for photographing young girls.) Dorothy's harsh home background and gray, defeated Uncle Henry and Aunt Em are so naturalistic that readers are delightfully surprised by the contrast in Oz. The 1939 movie in fact toned down some aspects of the novel's naturalism; it portrayed home as an object of nostalgia. In the novel, home is simply what Dorothy knows. All the citizens of Oz that she meets are puzzled to learn that she wants to go back.

Baum makes clear in his introduction to *Oz* that it is a modern fairly tale different from its predecessors. His comments are part of the still lively debate about the nature and purpose of children's literature: "Modern education includes morality; therefore the modern child seeks only entertainment in its wonder-tales and gladly dispenses with all disagreeable incidents." Baum is saying that he is writing a new book for a new age and for a new child.

The fact that Baum gave Oz a geography and a regional preoccupation resembling the United States—and the humbug character of the Wizard, a P. T. Barnum–type confidence man—has led readers over the years to read the book explicitly as a story about America. Henry Littlefield broke fresh critical ground when he argued in 1964 that the book was a pro-Populist allegory about the monetary crisis of the 1890s—the fight over whether we should be on a gold, silver, or bimetal standard—and particularly about the election of 1896 that introduced Democrat William Jennings Bryan as a presidential candidate. Several other such academic pieces have been written over the years, including Gretchen Ritter's reading of *Oz* in the context of historical memory. Many of these interpretations of the book are inventive, even occasionally incisive. But there is no evidence that Baum intended his book to be read in such a way, and it is clear that he did not write the book as an allegory. The idea that children's literature must be read as some sort of encoded adult literature is an insult to both the literature and the audience, as it assumes that this is the only way that children's literature can be important. Baum would have been appalled by such prejudice.

Bibliography: Frank Joslyn Baum and Russell P. MacFall, *To Please a Child: A Biography of L. Frank Baum, Royal Historian of Oz* (Chicago, 1961). Ranjit S. Dighe, ed., *The Historian's Wizard of Oz: Reading L. Frank Baum's Classic as a Political and Monetary Allegory* (New York, 2002). Michael Patrick Hearn, ed., *The Annotated Wizard of Oz* (New York, 2000). Henry Littlefield, "The Wizard of Oz: Parable on Populism," *American Quarterly* 16, no. 1 (1964). Gretchen Ritter, "Silver Slippers and a Golden Cap: L. Frank Baum's *The Wonderful Wizard of Oz* and Historical Memory in American Politics," *Journal of American Studies* 31 (1997). Katharine M. Rogers, *L. Frank Baum, the Royal Historian of Oz: A Biography* (New York, 2002).

GERALD EARLY

1900; 1905
Carrie Meeber, meet Lily Bart

SISTER CARRIE AND THE HOUSE OF MIRTH

We first encounter each of them in a station: Theodore Dreiser's Caroline Meeber is boarding the train in Columbus City bound for Chicago. She is eighteen years old, a provincial young woman, leaving the security of her family for life in the big city. Her belongings consist of "a small trunk, a cheap imitation alligator-skin satchel, a small lunch in a paper box, and a yellow leather snap purse, containing her ticket, a scrap of paper with her sister's address in Van Buren Street, and four dollars in money." It is August 1889. Edith Wharton's Lily Bart, age twenty-nine, having missed her train to Newport, stands amidst the hustle and bustle of a September afternoon in New York's Grand Central Station. Beautiful, sophisticated, well-dressed, she "was a figure to arrest even the suburban traveller rushing to his last train." Carrie has a plan; she is directed toward a specific goal. Lily seems lost, directionless, in need of rescue. Both Carrie and Lily encounter men who will play significant roles in the futures that unfold before them. The well-dressed "masher" Drouet, a traveling salesman, introduces himself to Carrie. The lawyer Lawrence Selden, an acquaintance, rescues Lily from the heat and the crowd. As with the trains that carry them, the women move through physical landscapes but also through class locations. For the provincial country girl, arrival in the city will initiate social mobility through greater financial security and, ultimately, professional success and a loss of moral standing. Lily acquires a stronger moral purity even as she spirals downward. Along the way, Carrie makes herself while Lily is made by a society that will also destroy her.

Published in 1900 and 1905, *Sister Carrie* and *The House of Mirth* present readers with original characters, women who are both products and reflections of their times. In a contemporary text, *Women and Economics,* Charlotte Perkins Gilman might very well have been speaking of both Carrie and Lily when she wrote: "The economic status of the human female is relative to the sex-relation." Lily's future is determined by her ability or refusal to marry a wealthy man. Carrie's stability is guaranteed by her relationships with men. Even the working-class young women who circle the edges of Dreiser's novel supplement their meager wages with "treats" and "gifts" from young men. Money, its trappings and the privilege it engenders, is the driving force of each novel. Possession of it or access to it provides luxury, comfort, and stability. Its absence inaugurates a sense of panic, fear, and desperation. Neither Carrie nor Lily stands firm on a foundation guaranteed by wealth and status, but their responses to this fact are quite different. Lily is careless, constantly risking opportunities to secure her future. Carrie is driven and determined, always willing to take a step closer to her goals no matter the costs to those around her.

Consequently, though Lily is the more thoughtful and emotionally sensitive character, Carrie is tougher, more ambitious, and less naive. She is also the more groundbreaking character. Finally, in spite of the humiliation she faces, Lily remains morally upstanding; she does not sacrifice her virtue. Yet, because of the scandals with which she is associated, because her reputation is sullied by a society that is undeserving of her, her story ends with her death. As such, she is not unlike many unmarried heroines who precede her. But Carrie, who lives out of wedlock with one man and whose marriage to a second is an act of bigamy, suffers no such death or demise. In fact each "sin," rather than leading to her downfall, is instead a step closer to economic independence and greater social standing. She is not punished nor does her creator pass judgment upon her. With Lily, Wharton makes possible the creation of emotionally complex women in American fiction. With Carrie, Dreiser slams the door on Victorian morality and lays the groundwork for the New Women who would emerge decades after the publication of his novel. Through Lily, Edith Wharton provides a devastating critique of the emptiness of "society" and its destruction of a sensitive, if misguided, young woman. Dreiser sets his attention on the middle class but, more important, on both human frailties and the devastating economic and social conditions that feed upon it. Perhaps Lily's greatest tragedy is her acute awareness of the insipid emptiness of the world she inhabits. She thinks: "How dreary and trivial these people were . . . That very afternoon they had seemed full of brilliant qualities, now she saw that they were merely dull in a loud way. Under the glitter of their opportunities she saw the poverty of their achievement." And yet she can only imagine herself among them, longs for their acceptance, longs to secure her place in their world. Carrie notes the dullness only of those she leaves behind: her brother-in-law; her lover, Drouet; and her common-law husband, Hurstwood. She is incapable of seeing beneath the glitter of the fashionable ladies she admires. For the glitter is what matters most to Carrie.

Were the two of them to have met it would have occurred at Shelly's, the restaurant frequented by Lily's set and visited once by Carrie. Lily would have been there with a friend, one of the few who will continue to be seen with her. She is a society celebrity, seated center stage, and yet she is all but ostracized by members of her former clique. The bright lights of the dining room might have revealed the twitch of her lip, the beginning wrinkle at the corner of her eye. Carrie might have seen Lily but would not have shared her meal, for she would have been sitting on the sidelines, watching her surroundings with a sense of awe, longing for the life that would make her a highly recognized regular. Should they have passed, say, on the way to the powder room, it would have been Lily's passing on the way out of the room, off the stage, down the stairs.

Both Wharton and Dreiser explore capitalism, class, and gender and both turn an unrelenting critical eye on the times in which they lived. Lily and Carrie traverse the landscape of working-class young women. Lily finds herself in the working girls' clubs that sprang up as a means of providing wholesome recreation for young women following long days of piecework in factories. Carrie's coworkers are among those young women who seem less concerned with respectability than those who frequented the working girls' clubs. Lily has no education, no training, no skills. Instead she is an investment awaiting the capital of the right, eligible man. Carrie is a commodity, selling herself first to Drouet and Hurstwood and then to the male spectators who make up her appreciative audience once she becomes an actress.

Although Lily and Carrie navigate similar times and cities, the Americas they inhabit could not seem more different. Lily's world is more sophisticated and cosmopolitan, but in fact Carrie's world is larger. Lily encounters poor and working people during her downward spiral and is unable to survive among them. Carrie's world consists not only of shopgirls and factory workers but also middle-class businessmen and their wives, theater people, immigrant workers, and Negro wait-ers. Carrie's is a world populated by those who are overworked, exploited, and economically insecure, and by social strivers and climbers for whom money and the luxuries it supplies are the road to social standing. For the most part Lily's world is filled with people who have no need to climb; they are already there, at the very top of New York society. Lily's position is precarious because she has no source of independent income and, though beautiful, she does not have a wealthy husband. In *The House of Mirth,* association with the climbers is evidence of how far Lily has fallen; in *Sister Carrie* it is evidence of Carrie's success.

Both Carrie and Lily are but one step away from poverty throughout most of the novels they inhabit. Lily thinks, "No; she was not made for mean and shabby surroundings, for the squalid compromises of poverty. Her whole being dilated in an atmosphere of luxury; it was the background she required, the only climate she could breathe in." Lily fears poverty, but because she has never known it, she is unable to even imagine it or ultimately to survive it. Carrie is surrounded by the dingy, dusty atmosphere of the less fortunate, from the factory floor to her sister and brother-in-law's apartment: "She felt the drag of a lean and narrow life. The walls of the rooms were discordantly papered. The floors were covered with matting and the hall laid with a thin rag carpet. One could see that the furniture was of that poor, hurriedly patched together quality sold by the installment houses." In the midst of this, Carrie aspires to "money, looks, clothes or enjoyment." Carrie is indomitable—a woman who, like Lily, also fears poverty, perhaps more so than Lily because she has known it and is fiercely determined to never experience it again. It first drives her into the arms of men who will provide for but not legally marry her, each a stepping stone until she is able to secure her own economic independence. Lily cannot bring herself to marry for money, yet she risks her reputation by entering into dubious economic arrangements with a married man of her set. Unlike Carrie, she does not exchange sex for financial comfort; she exchanges its promise. And when she refuses to pay she is abandoned, not only by the man but by the community to which she has been no more than a lovely expendable ornament.

Edith Wharton intimately knew the world she wrote about. Born into a proper Old New York family in 1862, as a girl she summered in Newport and traveled extensively throughout Europe. Through sheer will, discipline, talent, and ambition Wharton managed to escape this world, but not without an unhappy marriage and a nervous breakdown. When Wharton turned to "fashionable New York" as a setting for a fiction, she did so with an astute and critical eye. "There it was before me, in all its flatness and futility," Wharton wrote in her autobiography. The challenge before her was how to make such a frivolous subject worthy of her ambitions as a fiction writer. "The answer was that a frivolous society can acquire dramatic significance only through what its frivolity destroys." What the fashionable New York of *The House of Mirth* destroys is Lily Bart.

Born almost a decade after Wharton, in 1871, Theodore Dreiser experienced an Indiana childhood characterized by economic instability. Throughout his life he would remain sensitive to the plight of the working class. As did Carrie Meeber, Dreiser migrated to Chicago as a young person. After a series of menial jobs, he found work as a journalist and came to know every aspect of that big, energetic city. Inspired by his observations and the story of his own sister Emma, who had run off with her married lover, Dreiser would write his first novel, *Sister Carrie*. Whereas Lily Bart is the complicated, deeply flawed, and tragic heroine in Wharton's novel, her counterpart in *Sister Carrie* is not the title character, but George Hurstwood.

By novel's end, both Lily and Hurstwood find themselves at the bottom of a steep fall from society, in small, rented single rooms in New York, where they each die by their own hand. Carrie Meeber is situated comfortably in that same city, where she sits before a fire and expresses sympathy for those lacking money or shelter in the blizzard she observes from her window. A sense of melancholy creeps over her: *There, but by the grace of God, go I.*

Lily would never see herself in the poor and working class. And this may very well be the greatest distinction between the two lovely ladies. Carrie is the realist. Lily never imagines such a fall from grace, never imagines friends and family would turn their backs on her, not because of scandalous behavior but ultimately because of her refusal to betray a dear friend in order to save herself, because of her failure to play by the petty rules of society. When she could save herself by exposing an affair between her nemesis and her beloved Lawrence Selden, she chooses instead to protect Lawrence's reputation. She stands by him. When confronted with the choice of a life in poverty with a man who has forsaken reputation and fortune for her or a life of glamorous clothing, economic independence, and celebrity, Carrie leaves Hurstwood.

Both women are objects of visual pleasure for those who observe them. When Lily takes part in a tableau vivant, she chooses to pose as a famous portrait that requires little adornment. In the performance she allows herself to shine through, and it is the exquisite nature of this aesthetic experience, an encounter with the true Lily, that casts a spell on her audience. Carrie is too self-protective to expose her "true self"; for her, the stage is the place to play a role, inhabit a character. She is a vessel, a vehicle for the expression of another's emotion. The male members of her audience respond to their fantasies of her. Those observing Lily often note that she is made. Selden says of her, "She was so evidently the victim of the civilization which had produced her, that the links of her bracelet seemed like manacles chaining her to her fate." He later observes: "she must have cost a great deal to make, that a great many dull and ugly people must, in some mysterious way, have been sacrificed to produce her." Carrie makes herself; when a lover admires another woman, Carrie learns and adopts her mannerisms: a smile here, a toss of the neck there and she is changed, transformed. This "taste for imitation" will not only assist her as she creates her identity, it will also lift her as she seeks a career on stage. Ultimately Lily is a work of art, while Carrie is an artist; her medium is herself.

The country each woman inhabits at the turn of the twentieth century is big, bold, brash, middlebrow, and moneymaking. Carrie Meeber is its questing success story; Lily Bart, its elegant victim.

Bibliography: Theodore Dreiser, *Sister Carrie* (New York, 1900). Charlotte Perkins Gilman, *Women and Economics: A Study of the Economic Relation between Men and Women as a Factor in Social*

Evolution (Boston, 1898). Hermione Lee, *Edith Wharton* (New York, 2007). Richard Lingeman, *Theodore Dreiser: An American Journey* (New York, 1990). Edith Wharton, *A Backward Glance* (New York, 1998); *The House of Mirth* (New York, 1905).

FARAH JASMINE GRIFFIN

1901

Dr. Miller's dream hospital burns in a race riot

The Marrow of Tradition

Half a century before Ralph Ellison buries the protagonist of *Invisible Man* beneath the streets of New York, a century before flames engulfing the Twin Towers illuminate a darkness inhabited by those who believe they must gouge out America's eyes to cure her blindness, Charles W. Chesnutt's novel *The Marrow of Tradition* anticipates Ellison's use of the notion of invisibility—that peculiar, treacherous illusion of transparency that plagues people of color when they conspire with the fantasy that they are unseen unless uncolored others see them. Chesnutt also predicts the same dire consequences of invisibility—cities burning, virulent racism fostered by people's blindness to one another—that Ellison dramatizes in his novel. Ellison's unnamed invisible man and Chesnutt's Dr. Miller discover that seeking the precious visibility they desire in another's eyes may lead not to liberation but to destruction, disappearance, even death. Both characters commit the unforgiving mistake of allowing themselves to fall asleep within someone else's dream, the dream that blacks and whites coexist peacefully, voluntarily, in a just, mutually beneficial arrangement. The wake-up call of riots, Ellison's staged in Harlem and Chesnutt's set in Wellington, North Carolina, expose the dream's fragility. Nightmare interludes ravage each book's colored community, and many individuals who had crossed over and mistaken the dream for a viable reality vanish as the dream vanishes, unseen, unreal, during the riots— *Is dat you, Doctuh Miller?*—awakening later as ghosts of themselves. Others never awaken (Wellington's Mammy Jane and Jerry, Harlem's Todd Clifton), murdered by the dream in which they have been sleepwalking. Yet the illusion of a racialized Peaceable Kingdom persists. Ellison's novel ends in a welter of words, its protagonist chased underground, still attempting to convince himself that the dream just might be real after all. Chesnutt's novel concludes with Dr. Miller's dream hospital burned down like the Towers, his young son murdered, a somnambulistic, robotic Miller summoned to perform his duty as a physician and save the life of a boy whose father's vision of white supremacy provoked the riot that killed Miller's son.

In 1901, emboldened perhaps by critical praise in high places earned by his previous ventures into fiction writing, Chesnutt, whose fair complexion, straight hair, Caucasian nose and lips provided what Frantz Fanon would call a white mask to hide the black skin of African ancestry, was prepared to disengage from his lucrative legal stenography business and concentrate single-mindedly on a career as a professional man of letters. But only if sales of what he described as his "Afro-American" novel enabled him to support his family in the genteel, middle-class lifestyle to which they'd become accustomed in Cleveland, Ohio. Chesnutt's gritty optimism, his belief that he could achieve commercial success in mainstream publishing and satisfy his personal standards while also challenging the reigning attitudes of a society that consigned "negroes"—white masks or not—to segregation, to second-class citizenship for a privileged few, crushing economic exploitation for the vast majority, may have been encouraged by the success of narrative strategies honed in his earlier work. *The Conjure Woman* (1899) had deployed multiple narrators engaged in covert competition for control of each story's meaning, narrators addressing (and in a sense inventing) different audiences, narrators who delivered their conflicting points of view in diverse varieties of English, from standard literary voice-over to "Negro dialect." Chesnutt was quite aware of the contradictions inherent to his precarious project. Though he continued to critique the popular convention of Negro dialect, which had been fabricated primarily by non-Negroes to imitate, demean, and cage African American voices—"There is no such thing as Negro dialect: that what we call by that name is the attempt to express, with such a degree of phonetic correctness as to suggest the sound, English pronounced as an ignorant old southern Negro would be supposed to speak it"—he integrated basically unretouched copies of that dialect into his texts.

Literature, like all mainstream cultural institutions in America at the dawn of the twentieth century, had developed distinctive means for reflecting and circulating the ideology of white supremacy that an exhausted nation had adopted at the conclusion of a long, bloody civil war to reunify itself and facilitate material prosperity. With neoclassical zeal and rigidity, American writing, high and low, manufactured conventions—character types, genres, language styles, predictable patterns of behavior, strict limitations of intellectual and moral capacity, and so on—for representing people of African descent and their relations with people of European descent, inventing and imposing through this process lasting racialized definitions of white and black in the American language. Any writer who broke the rules by questioning, resisting, or denying the reigning model of separate, human kinds arranged in a hierarchical order—white on top, black on the bottom—risked unintelligibility or exile. For the dominant majority of Americans, including those who purchased books, the threat of political, moral, and economic chaos lurked just beyond the bounds established by literature's arbitrary construction of the social order. The voice of Charles W. Chesnutt, speaking as a man of color who considered himself the equal in every sense of his readers, would sound to most American ears like the fox demanding the keys to the henhouse.

To compose *Marrow,* Chesnutt creates a narrative voice testing the limits of not being heard, not being seen, a voice approaching the ideal of racelessness, not exactly by claiming to be white, the only voice his audience would understand as not tainted by race, but by aspiring to perfect what James Joyce describes as the penultimate third mode of narrative: the dramatic—"the personality of the artist finally refines itself out of existence, impersonalizes itself so to speak . . . within or behind or beyond or above his handiwork, invisible." Managing the difficulties of this disappearing act carries Chesnutt beyond issues of technique and aesthetics to the question of survival.

If invisibility is a kind of death, are stories generated by invisible men stillborn? Chesnutt and Ellison in fiction, and Chesnutt's contemporary W. E. B. Du Bois in his essay "Of the Passing of the First-Born," record the anguish, anxiety, and helplessness of losing children, of being denied the joy linking fathers to sons. These three highly successful (colored, mulatto, mixed, black) men share the frustrating experience of watching their literary productions become invisible, that is, not seen by the dominant majority of Americans as evidence challenging the rule of Negro inferiority, but sighted as exceptions proving the rule. Their writing was treated not as an enduring legacy that could fertilize successive generations both like and unlike them, but as isolated monuments confirming their creator's difference.

The problem with pretending you are invisible, particularly if you perform the illusion convincingly, is that the wrong someone may believe you, the worst-case scenario occurring when that someone is you. Incarcerated within a racialized context, practicing the art of self-concealment, Chesnutt, like Dr. Miller, flirts with actual extinction unless he maintains—asserts—a sense of self-awareness that transcends recognition by others. Much worse than not being seen by others is becoming invisible to oneself. In one case the self suffers from being ignored, in the other case the self is extinguished as surely as madness, drugs, unconsciousness close down the self. Slavery could work you to death or make you wish you were dead or precipitate a thousand daily deaths of shame, rage, helplessness, humiliation, could even enforce what Orlando Patterson defines as "social death," but being a slave didn't necessarily kill you, nor render you literally invisible.

An individual is truly invisible only if the individual ceases seeing herself or himself. So long as a person is able to see himself, the person understands that invisibility's locus, like that of social death or hell, is other people. Other people may pretend not to see you, but that denial doesn't end your existence and cause you to disappear. Ironically, the pain of Ellison's invisible man and Chesnutt's Dr. Miller, their hyperawareness of themselves as not being seen, and all the contortions other people go through in order to pretend not to see them are proof positive of visibility. A total disappearance of Afro-American people won't require a campaign of genocide: it could occur if we forget how to imagine and sustain ourselves as more than a race (black) defined by the gaze of others (white).

The obvious intent of *Marrow* is to register and condemn the injustice of racial segregation, a monumentally complex task during an epoch when apartheid was the visible law and custom of the land, even though the nation blindly celebrated itself as a democracy. Chesnutt's weapon of choice seems to be friendly persuasion: identifying with his general readers, complimenting them by giving them credit for a moral conscience, to which he appeals. Speaking as invisible narrator, he seeks rapport by constructing a point of view compounded of values held in common with his readers, a shared perspective, safe, distanced, expansive, plenty of wiggle room. Here we stand, my friends, we good people who deplore bad things happening around us, bad things good conscience obliges us sooner or later to ameliorate, though we bear no personal responsibility for them.

Readers willing and able to follow where the deeper structures of the novel lead will discover the book's scarier, abiding significance. *Marrow* renders visible the consequences, as alive and dangerous now as a hundred years ago, of internalizing a racialized self-identity. No matter how bright his prospects, Dr. Miller is trapped in a perilous netherworld, the looming shadow of race never more than a step behind, ready to pounce and plunge him into darkness. Despite the metaphors I'm employing to describe Miller's predicament, neither I nor Chesnutt equates black with doom, white with hope. Any person (author, character, colored or not, you, me) who exists in a society like Miller's and submits to its racialized premises—whether the premises grant a degree of visibility or not—risks complicity in his or her own erasure. When he brutally punishes Dr. Miller at the novel's conclusion, Chesnutt is also repudiating himself, the author, for naively seeking liberation through invisibility. Shedding the role of the neutral, invisible narrator, Chesnutt merges with Miller. Like Shakespeare in the history plays, Chesnutt litters his stage with bodies (including his own in the ghostly guise of Miller). The carnage of postriot Wellington speaks for itself, speaks for the novel, speaks volumes about the beliefs of the author whose mediating presence we thought we were supposed to forget.

Dead men (and women) tell no tales. Or maybe they tell the truest tales. If we learn to listen. Women in *Marrow,* particularly Miller's wife, Janet, testify through journals, diaries, caches of documents they preserve and leave behind, traces of paternity they pass on in their children's colors and bodies, the violence marking their own dead bodies (Mammy Jane, Polly Ochiltree). This compendium of material evidence creates counternarratives that contest the master narrative of the plantocracy. The twentieth-century jazz musician Sun Ra offers a fanciful but not irrelevant etymology riffing on the word "Negro" as a descendant of *nicro* (black) then enjambing *dead* and *black* and *storyteller* and *magic* into the word "necromancer," a storyteller—a tune novelist Ishmael Reed also plays in his inimitable fashion.

Even before a race riot transforms Wellington into a murderous version of Bakhtin's carnival where daytime rules of society are not simply burlesqued by reversal but suffer a nocturnal sea change as the wearing of masks (black and white) unmasks the chaos underlying all human communities, *Marrow* is full of ghostly doubles and doubling, troubled spirits crisscrossing between the known and unknown. "'Ef dat's me gwine 'long in front,' mused Sandy . . . 'den who is dis behin' here? Dere ain' but one er me, an' my ha'nt would n' leave my body 'tel I wuz dead. Ef dat's me in front, den I mus' be my own ha'nt; an' whichever one of us is de ha'nt, de yuther must be dead an' don' know it.'"

Chesnutt's Southern town abounds in missing persons, mistaken identities, purloined identities, secret identities, forged identities, suppressed documents and genealogies, mimicking, masquerades, impostors, presence and absence fused inextricably in a confusing traffic of bodies that's also hazardous to everybody's health because all identities are unstable. Any body at any moment, especially a colored body, can find itself abruptly in the wrong place at the wrong time, depending on who sees it and what that person chooses to name what they think they see—friend or foe, black or white, live or ghost, criminal or citizen.

Surprisingly, to designate an entire group of people—in the case of Wellington, "black people"—as invisible does not permanently clear space nor create a deficit of appearances but crowds space with a surfeit of appearances. No social system or institution yet devised by human beings has been able to impose a discipline that totally controls individual behavior. Though a social order may stipulate certain classes (colonized natives, slaves, convicts, women, untouchables) as beneath notice, literally below the threshold of visibility, not there unless acknowledged by a privileged class, these *invisibles* will keep turning up, usually in unwelcome, unexpected, inconvenient, incriminating, compromising, threatening circumstances. The world suddenly becomes uncomfortable, too full, overrun by multiple claimants for each available slot or status. The inadequacy of a single way of seeing, of one-way seeing based on arbitrary separation of seer and seen (black and white), is revealed as a liability, can't account for a sudden surplus of humanity. A veil lifts or is lowered. Things fall apart.

Inventing ways of seeing oneself, despite or because of overwhelming evidence that one is not seen or seen only in a distorting fashion by others, remains no less an urgent project for Americans of color today than it was for Chesnutt. Given our relative invisibility until yesterday on the standard map of American literary history, the project of visibility extends to the art we produce. Neither mainstream assertions of color-blindness nor university programs in black studies have cleared enough space in the public imagination for a discussion of art free from the contradictions of American race consciousness. We still face the impasse from which Frantz Fanon recoiled when he read Jean-Paul Sartre's preface to *Black Orpheus* (1948), an anthology of francophone writing by people of color from Africa and the Caribbean. Fanon realized that Sartre was prepared to recognize and praise this collection of "black" writing if and only if the notion of black subjectivity and the art it produced were considered as a virtual reality; a useful but minor, temporary, transparent term or stage in a dialectical process. Sartre's qualified endorsement profoundly troubled Fanon because it left "black" subjectivity marginal, blank, dependent on some undefined, larger human project to reify or erase it, thereby dooming, Fanon feared, the subject's experience of blackness to wither away or to fall asleep within some other's dreamy theorizing.

How can I sing King Alpha's song in a strange land.

Bibliography: Richard Brodhead, ed., *The Journals of Charles W. Chesnutt* (Durham, NC, 1993). Charles W. Chesnutt, *Stories, Novels, and Essays* (New York, 2002). Frances Richardson Keller, *An American Crusade: The Life of Charles Waddell Chesnutt* (Provo, UT, 1978). Joseph McElrath, Jr., and Robert C. Leitz III, *To Be an Author: Letters of Charles W. Chesnutt, 1889–1905* (Princeton, NJ, 1997). Jean-Paul Sartre, *Black Orpheus,* trans. S. W. Allen (Paris, 1963).

JOHN EDGAR WIDEMAN

1901; 1903

W. E. B. Du Bois's *The Souls of Black Folk*
rebukes Booker T. Washington's *Up from Slavery*

The Problem of the Color Line

"The most distinguished Southerner since Jefferson Davis, and the one with the largest personal following." Although this lofty claim by W. E. B. Du Bois about Booker T. Washington was a prolegomenon to an attack on Washington, Du Bois recognized his adversary's striking achievements. The central one undoubtedly was Tuskegee Institute, the vocational school for blacks that Washington founded in rural Alabama (at the behest of the state but with only its modest financial support) when he was twenty-five. In his 1901 autobiography, *Up from Slavery,* Washington offers a memorable account of his life that served to illustrate his main educational, political, economic, and cultural ideas and to catalogue his top achievements. (Exactly who wrote *Up from Slavery* is not clear. In his acknowledgments, Washington thanked above all Max Bennett Thrasher, a white speechwriter and publicist employed by Tuskegee. Nevertheless, Washington scrutinized and approved the final text.)

The basic form of *Up from Slavery* connects to the deeper roots of American literature. It is, in part, a slave narrative, the key instrument of the abolitionists at least since *Narrative of the Life of Frederick Douglass, An American Slave, Written by Himself* (1845). *Up from Slavery* is also in the classic rags-to-riches vein so popular in American culture. When riches mean civic leadership, the prototype is undoubtedly Ben Franklin's *Autobiography,* which influenced *Up from Slavery.* The slave narrative was a moribund form by 1901, but Washington breathed new life into it—although he himself was only about ten years old when slavery ended (his date of birth was never firmly established). In *Up from Slavery,* then, he represents black ex-slaves as well as blacks who were born after slavery but were still caught in its coils. No brief for slavery, his autobiography nevertheless insists that the institution taught blacks invaluable skills and a similarly invaluable respect for discipline. "Notwithstanding the cruel wrongs inflicted upon us," Washington announces, "the black man got nearly as much out of slavery as the white man did."

Washington begins with a quip about slavery. Where many slave narrators had stressed the trauma of having unknown white fathers, or known white fathers who refused to acknowledge them, or the pain of not knowing for sure the date of their birth, he cracks a joke. "I suspect I must have been born somewhere," he writes, "and at some time." Slavery, he insists, had made victims of blacks and whites alike. Bitterness was thus pointless. In never acknowledging him as his son, Washington's white father "was simply another victim of the institution which the Nation unhappily had grafted upon it at that time." When Booker's mother steals a chicken to feed her hungry family, she is also "simply a victim of the system of slavery." Washington asserts that many slaves were loyal to, and even loved, their white masters. At first, he says, Emancipation Day brings delirious feelings of joy, but by nightfall, the slaves are haunted by a sense of loss and turn to their former masters for advice.

As a boy in his native Virginia, Booker (eventually he will decide to add Taliafero and Washington to that name) toils in a salt mine and then in a coal mine—perfect emblems of ignorance—before he begins to hunger for literacy. After pestering his mother for a copy of Webster's famed "blue-black" spelling book, he learns to read. He begins to go to night school. Employed in the home of the wife of a former Northern general, he catches a glimpse of gentility and humbly comes to revere it. When he hears about a school for blacks located across the state, he sets out on foot to seek admission there. At Hampton Institute, led by the charismatic young Hawaiian-born veteran of the Civil War General Samuel C. Armstrong ("the noblest, rarest human being that it has ever been my privilege to meet"), young Washington wins a place. There he absorbs the lessons that will guide him through the rest of his life. At Hampton, book learning is matched by training in crafts as well as rules and practices reflecting Armstrong's military background. Students also learn that strong moral values are essential to the growth of their race. Personal hygiene is stressed, something typically ignored in slavery.

Up from Slavery, while glossing over major failures in post–Civil War America, supports the picture of Reconstruction as a time when often undeserving blacks and greedy white Northerners—carpetbaggers—unfairly exploited the defeated white South. The book also ignores the bloody campaign waged by Southern whites to regain power. In Washington's view, blacks who dwell on past injustices invite social and economic paralysis. To dismiss history, he suggests, is to invite freedom. As a result, he does not mention *Plessy v. Ferguson,* the decision in favor of "separate but equal" accommodations for blacks that the U.S. Supreme Court handed down in 1896, only five years before *Up from Slavery* appeared. That decision, and others like it, emboldened segregationists and dismayed most blacks; but Washington accepts segregation as the price of black progress in the South.

In *Up from Slavery,* Washington faces at Tuskegee a succession of challenges and dangers, mainly involving money, which he overcomes by sticking to his key faith in the power of hard work, pragmatism, and the natural goodness of Americans, especially whites. Tuskegee grows into a campus of enviable proportions. Its leader preaches that acquiring manual skills rather than learning the liberal arts will lead to black progress. "One of the saddest things" he ever saw, Washington writes, was an ambitious but misguided black youth wearing greasy clothing, "filth all around him, and weeds in the yard and garden, engaged in studying French grammar." Taught carpentry, brick making, plumbing, and masonry, students at Tuskegee construct all of its major buildings themselves. The school comes to symbolize the benign future awaiting hardworking blacks who accept willingly the doctrine of white supremacy. As his school prospers, Washington's prestige rises. Business tycoons, such as Andrew Carnegie, Collis Huntington,

and John D. Rockefeller, and even presidents of the United States, hail it as a superb model for modern mass education.

Although Washington supported some clandestine efforts on behalf of civil
rights for blacks, his autobiography urges blacks to pursue a strategic program of
diplomacy and compromise. In his most famous speech, delivered at the Cotton
States and International Exposition in Atlanta in 1895 (*Up from Slavery* reprints
the address), he praises the traditional way of life in the South. Voluntary black
subordination, he hopes, will lead to economic growth for whites and—to a lesser
extent, to be sure—for blacks. "In all things that are purely social," he declares,
"we can be as separate as the fingers, yet one as the hand in all things essential to
mutual progress." Blacks should eventually possess the same civil rights as whites,
but they must wait patiently until they deserve those rights. "Progress in the enjoyment of all the privileges that will come to us," Washington says, "must be the
result of severe and constant struggle rather than of artificial forcing."

Washington's autobiography offers example after example of how faith in human nature, pluck, and hard work can overcome almost all difficulties, including
white racism. His public honors and awards accumulate. Traveling in Europe, he
is triumphantly received; Harvard awards the ex-slave an honorary degree. These
are indisputable signs, he argues, of racial progress. At the end of the book, citizens of Richmond, Virginia, where, as a pauper, he had slept under a sidewalk
during his epic boyhood walk to Hampton, honor him with a reception. This reversal of fortune is both a splendid token of his personal success and an absolute vindication of his cheery gospel of hard work, humility, optimism, and compromise.

To W. E. B. Du Bois, Washington's gospel was heresy. When Du Bois published
some of his "fugitive pieces" plus new essays in the book *The Souls of Black Folk*
(1903), its third chapter, "Of Mr. Booker T. Washington and Others," was a detailed attack on Washington. The result was to break educated black Americans
into two camps. Opposing the most powerful black American was, probably, the
most learned. Born and reared in Great Barrington, Massachusetts, and schooled
at Fisk, Harvard, and the University of Berlin, Du Bois created in *Souls* a work inspired by his knowledge of fields that include history (his doctorate, in history,
was from Harvard); sociology (learned mainly at Berlin); education (he was a professor at Atlanta University); music, specifically the black "sorrow songs"; religion; and fiction (one chapter is a short story). In part, *Souls* is autobiographical.
It begins with a lament about the painful moment when Du Bois discovers as
a child that most whites see him as different racially and therefore inferior. "Of
the Meaning of Progress" touches on a revelatory summer he spent as a student
teacher in rural Georgia, where he lives for the first time among Southern black
folk. "Of the Passing of the First-Born," which mourns the death in Atlanta (from
dysentery) of his young son Burghardt, is bedeviled by the sort of rage impossible
to imagine in *Up from Slavery*. The short story, "Of the Coming of John," dramatizes the brutal, tragic conflicts over race and sex that persist in the South.

Implicitly, *The Souls of Black Folk* rebukes *Up from Slavery*. Its most famous passage invokes a degree of psychological subtlety foreign to the latter. "One ever feels his twoness," Du Bois declares of the average black person, "—an American, a Negro; two souls, two thoughts, two un-reconciled strivings; two warring ideals in one dark body, whose dogged strength alone keeps it from being torn asunder." In America, a "veil" separates whites from blacks, who have no genuine self-consciousness but see themselves only as whites see them. Being black, he thus suggests, involves an inherent complexity and a tragic potential. Boldly he prophesies: "The problem of the Twentieth Century is the problem of the color line." Du Bois also hints that this problem might be insoluble, given both the cruelties of European colonialism and the lurid events, from unjust court decisions to vicious lynchings, that accompanied the victory of Jim Crow in the South, where the vast majority of blacks then lived.

Where Washington favors plain language, Du Bois often takes the opposite approach. In his earlier, scholarly books, *The Suppression of the Slave-Trade to the United States* and *The Philadelphia Negro,* he uses restrained, almost austere prose; but in *The Souls of Black Folk* he sets himself free. In challenging Washington, he is analytical, precise, and polite even as he seeks to eviscerate Washington's arguments; but in charting certain stark disappointments for blacks during and after the Civil War, including the collapse of the Freedmen's Bureau and the Freedmen's Bank, he takes what is at times almost radical dramatic license. While imaginative language enlivens his ventures in sociology, it is fully released in his short story and in "Of the Passing of the First-Born," which involves an unprecedented torrent of fury, bitterness, and despair. Groundbreaking essays on black American religion and the spirituals combine astute analysis with striking lyricism. An artist as well as a social scientist, Du Bois deeply believes in his innate right to cosmopolitan culture, despite Jim Crow. "I sit with Shakespeare and he winces not," he muses. "Across the color line I move arm in arm with Balzac and Dumas . . . I summon Aristotle and Aurelius and what soul I will, and they come all graciously with no scorn nor condescension. So wed with Truth I live above the Veil."

In 1910, a frustrated Du Bois would give up tenure at Atlanta University and move to New York to help launch the National Association for the Advancement of Colored People (NAACP) as founding editor of its crusading magazine, the *Crisis.* He would retain that position until 1934. Washington diligently served his school to the end of his life in 1915, at which point Tuskegee began to wane in quality and prestige. Du Bois's ideas about blacks' "double consciousness" and "twin souls" would influence black literature for decades to come, from James Weldon Johnson's *The Autobiography of an Ex-Colored Man* (1912) to Ralph Ellison's *Invisible Man* (1952) and beyond. *The Souls of Black Folk* supports the judgment of the NAACP in 1934, when it declared of Du Bois that "he created, what never existed before, a Negro intelligentsia, and many who have not read a word of his writings are his spiritual disciples and descendants." He died in 1963—reviled by some people as a communist who had abandoned his U.S. citizenship, but mourned by many more as probably the most astute and militant of major African American intellectuals.

Bibliography: W. E. B. Du Bois, *The Souls of Black Folk* (Chicago, 1903). Louis R. Harlan, *Booker T. Washington: The Making of a Black Leader, 1856–1901* (Urbana, IL, 1972); *Booker T. Washington: The Wizard of Tuskegee, 1901–1915* (Urbana, IL, 1983). David Levering Lewis, *W. E. B. Du Bois: Biography of a Race* (New York, 1993); *W. E. B. Du Bois: The Fight for Equality and the American Century* (New York, 2000). Booker T. Washington, *Up from Slavery: An Autobiography* (New York, 1901).

ARNOLD RAMPERSAD

1903, May 5

Emma Lazarus's "New Colossus" is affixed to the Statue of Liberty

"The Real American Has Not Yet Arrived"

. . . Here at our sea-washed, sunset gates shall stand
A mighty woman with a torch, whose flame
Is the imprisoned lightning, and her name
Mother of Exiles. From her beacon-hand
Glows world-wide welcome; her mild eyes command
The air-bridged harbor that twin cities frame.
"Keep, ancient lands, your storied pomp!" cries she
With silent lips. "Give me your tired, your poor,
Your huddled masses yearning to breathe free,
The wretched refuse of your teeming shore,
Send these, the homeless, tempest-tossed to me,
I lift my lamp beside the golden door!"

"Liberty! A hundred Fourths of July broke loose yesterday to exalt her name," declared the *New York Times* in October 1886 of the unveiling of Bartholdi's mammoth statue *Liberty Enlightening the World*. "The whistles blew, the guns boomed, the bands played, the drums rolled, and the throngs on the island and on the river shouted one thundering paean of acclamation" as the face of the Liberty was revealed, "commend[ing] to mankind," in President Grover Cleveland's words, "a government resting upon popular will." More than sixteen years later, on May 5, 1903, a second, far more modest unveiling took place on the same site, as a bronze tablet with the words of Emma Lazarus's poem "New Colossus" was affixed to the statue's pedestal. Written in 1883 to help raise funds for the construction of the pedestal, the poem was placed there as a tribute to its deceased author by her friends. But the sonnet would transform the statue from a symbol of republicanism shining outward to the world into a "Mother of Exiles" drawing in "huddled masses yearning to breathe free."

The Statue of Liberty's silent invitation never went unchallenged. The massive influx of diverse foreigners, more than twenty million of whom arrived between 1880 and 1924, provoked intense anxiety among native-born Americans. "O Liberty, white Goddess! Is it well/To leave the gates unguarded?" asked Thomas Bailey Aldrich in his 1895 poem "Unguarded Gates." "Through them presses a wild motley throng," he warned. Describing an America increasingly incomprehensible to itself, where "in street and alley . . . strange tongues are loud, / Accents of menace alien to our air," Aldrich pressed the statue into the role of border guard for white, Anglo-Saxon America, rather than nurturing mother to its alien newcomers.

Even Lazarus's mother figure wavered in her embrace. To Lazarus, the immigrant is both oppressed dreamer "yearning to breathe free" and loathsome "wretched refuse" cast off from other lands. Her ambivalence reflects the nation's contradictory sentiments toward immigration as well as Lazarus's own complex relationship to Americanness and foreignness. A fourth-generation American of Sephardic Jewish heritage, who lived in Union Square, summered in Newport, corresponded with Emerson and Henry James, and published in the *Century*, Lazarus was a member of America's economic, social, and cultural elite. But she was also a Jew in Christian America. In 1882, when news reached her of attacks against Jews in czarist Russia, she felt compelled to take up their cause, working to ameliorate the conditions of the refugees. But despite deep concern about their plight, she, like many established Jewish Americans, feared a deluge into her America of Jews so different from herself. To rescue them while averting the threat they posed to her position, Lazarus sought to redirect them to Texas or Palestine. She further insisted that they be taught the "godliness of cleanliness, the dignity of womanhood, the delights of reason, the moral necessity of a broader humanity." Secularization and the embrace of bourgeois values were prerequisite to acceptance.

The content of Lazarus's poem reflects this ambivalence toward foreigners, while its structure suggests the conditions for their integration. Welcome is issued to the "tempest-tossed" in precisely rhymed lines, the "golden door" opened within the tightly controlled boundaries of the Italian sonnet form. At the same time that Lazarus wrote this poem, she was experimenting with blank verse. But here, high-European conventional forms dominate, maintaining order even as America breaks with the ways of ancient lands and welcomes their refuse. The threat of the wretched is contained by the preservation of tradition. It is absorbed by the sonnet just as many hoped the new immigrants could be absorbed into the nation without altering its character. But this could happen only if they radically altered themselves.

"The mighty tide of immigration to our shores has brought in its train much of good and much of evil; and whether the good or the evil shall predominate depends mainly on whether these newcomers do or do not throw themselves heartily into our national life, cease to be Europeans, and become Americans like the rest of us," Theodore Roosevelt declared in 1894 in "True Americanism." Responding to mass immigration from eastern and southern Europe, and all but denying immigration from elsewhere, Roosevelt expressed the dominant attitude toward foreigners in the Progressive Era, suggested in part by Lazarus's sonnet: Europeans are welcome so long as they erase all prior national, political, and cultural identities and "learn to talk and think and be United States."

Immigrants of the period were keenly aware of the need to remake themselves. In narratives autobiographical and fictional, they publicly attested to their
transformation. "I was born, I have lived, and I have been made over. Is it not
time to write my life's story? . . . I am just as much out of the way as if I were dead,
for I am absolutely other than the person whose story I have to tell," asserts Mary
Antin at the opening of her autobiography, *The Promised Land* (1912). The Russian
Jewish girl she once was gives way to the American, and Antin proudly announces
her passing. The reformer and Danish immigrant Jacob Riis employs similar imagery to describe his transformation in the final scene of *The Making of an American* (1901), dedicated to Theodore Roosevelt. "I have just told the story of the
making of an American. There remains to tell how I found that he was finished at
last." Riis recounts how the sight of the American flag from his sickbed in Denmark cured him from illness. "I knew then that it was my flag . . . that I also had
become an American in truth. And I thanked God, and, like unto the man sick of
palsy, arose from my bed and went home healed." His resurrection, like Antin's
rebirth, is achieved and necessitated by America.

These testimonies and many like them reveal the immigrants' compulsion to
attest to their conversion into Americans; the popularity of such accounts among
American readers signals the nation's need to be reassured of its integrity despite
the influx of foreigners. "There is no such thing as a hyphenated American who is
a good American," Theodore Roosevelt later insisted, and these narratives promised the disappearance of the hyphen, while arguing, against Aldrich and growing
numbers of nativists, that keeping the golden door open would not harm America. "You take our refuse, our lowest classes and in a generation you make Americans of them!" proclaimed an astounded Hungarian minister to his former coun-
tryman, Edward Steiner. It was to prove to themselves and the nation that this
could and would be done that Steiner and others wrote.

But the sense of being "alien refuse" until properly recast was often traumatic
for those who disassociated themselves from their former lives and identities.
"Three years had intervened since he had first set foot on American soil, and the
thought of ever having been a Yekl would bring to Jake's lips a smile of patronising
commiseration with his former self," suggests the narrator of Abraham Cahan's
1896 novel *Yekl*. Jake pities and mocks his eastern European self, refusing to integrate it into who he is now. "Once I live in America, . . . I want to know that I live
in America. *Dot'sh a' kin' a man I am!*" he insists, though never secure in his manhood or his Americanness. The hero of Cahan's later novel, *The Rise of David
Levinsky* (1917), discovers too late that his financial triumph in the United States
"is coupled with a brooding sense of emptiness and insignificance." "My past
and my present do not comport well," he reflects. "David, the poor lad swinging over a Talmud volume at the Preacher's Synagogue, seems to have more in
common with my inner identity than David Levinsky, the well-known cloak-
manufacturer." But his inner and outer identities cannot merge or coexist under
the pressure of Americanization.

Try as they might to erase all other identities, many Americanization narratives reveal individuals haunted by a past they try desperately to put behind them. "I want to forget—sometimes I long to forget . . . It is painful to be consciously of two worlds," admits Mary Antin. But despite American expectations and her own desire to have it otherwise, she remains of two worlds, struggling like the familiar Ancient Mariner to erase her past through the telling in order to transform into a "true American."

Not all would hope to be altered by and for America. Though Lazarus describes them as "homeless" and yearning for the freedoms of the United States, many émigrés came reluctantly, and many more remained closely tied to their homeland. They experienced life in the United States as exiles from promised lands abroad. Perhaps Lazarus realized this dislocation, as she called the statue "Mother of Exiles," but whether from Europe, Africa, or Asia, her foster children insisted on looking homeward. In Sui Sin Far's story "The Wisdom of the New" (1912), for example, Far describes a young Chinese wife, Pau Lin, who joins her husband in America. Standing over their sleeping son whose queue has just been shorn by his father, she declares: "Sooner would I, O heart of my heart, that the light of thine eyes were . . . quenched, than that thou shouldst be contaminated by the wisdom of the new." She takes her son's life rather than see it lost to America. At the same time, however, readers are reminded that her racially marked boy could never have become fully American. As one friend comments, "Is it not what we teach these Chinese boys—to become Americans? And yet, they are Chinese, and must, in a sense remain so." Not all are fully welcome and not all wish to belong, the story reveals.

Even many purported Americanization narratives suggest the retention of cultural and nostalgic bonds to the "old home" and reveal the construction of new transnational political and economic ties. Jacob Riis, for instance, may have discovered himself an "American in truth" and worked tirelessly to reform conditions in the United States, but at the same time he openly proclaimed his love for Denmark and his continued allegiance to the Danish crown. "Happy he who has a flag to love. Twice blest he who has two, and such two," he declares in *The Making of an American*. Perhaps it was because Riis was comfortably white, northern European, and Protestant that he could speak so openly of his dual-nationalism. Yet many other immigrants felt the same, expressing their continued ties, if not in English-language books, then in the organizations and native-language publications they founded in the United States and through the letters and money they sent back home to support personal and political causes.

Rather than altering themselves for America, some would work to remake America in their own image. The Dutch immigrant Edward Bok, who edited the *Ladies' Home Journal* for three decades, uses his foreignness as a privileged point from which to critique America. He claims that the foreigner can see "distinct lacks" in the United States that native-born Americans cannot perceive, and he insists that "there are thousands of American-born who need Americanization just as much as do the foreign born." Bok defines Americanization as the process through which all Americans, wherever they were born, improve themselves and their country by living up to its ideals. Other immigrant writers would take American ideals and realities much more harshly to task: "Everything . . . that had happened to me since I had come to America, had proved most disappointing. America, 'the land of the free and the home of the brave'—what a farce it now seemed to me!" declared Emma Goldman. She called for anarchism, others for socialism, to radically revise America's aims and self-definition.

The idea of the melting pot, popularized by the British playwright Israel Zangwill through his 1908 drama of that name, captured the national imagination by promising a different means of change. As the Russian Jewish immigrant hero of the play, David Quixano, declares: "The real American has not yet arrived. He is only in the crucible, I tell you—he will be the fusion of all races, the coming superman." By defining the real American as a race not yet arrived, Quixano makes space for all to join in creating the new American via sex that transgresses racial and ethnic borders. Overseeing this process is the Statue of Liberty. It stands as the backdrop to the final act of the play, its torch "a lonely, guiding star." Gazing upon it, David proclaims: "There she lies, the great Melting-Pot—listen! Can't you hear the roaring and the bubbling? . . . Ah, what a stirring and a seething! Celt and Latin, Slav and Teuton, Greek and Syrian,—black and yellow . . . Here they shall unite." "Peace, peace, to all ye unborn millions, fated to fill this giant continent—the God of our children give you Peace," the play ends. Gendered as female, the melting pot turns into the Statue of Liberty, who mothers not exiles but their children. Without pasts in other lands, without loyalties to other peoples, these children will merge together to create America. Whereas Lazarus's "New Colossus" contains threat and change to the nation through its sonnet form even as it silently proffers worldwide welcome, Zangwill's statue invites transformation and relishes the possibility of an unknown future.

It was fear of precisely this unknown future that would lead to the slamming of the "sunset gates" to foreigners in 1924. Yet the narratives of the prior period would continue to push the nation to confront the impact of immigration in ways that would ultimately reshape American culture, identity, and literature. Yearning freedom seekers and wretched refuse; homeless, tempest-tossed and exiles—the contradictory perceptions and experiences of the émigrés captured in Lazarus's poem reveal the persistent complexities of immigration, Americanization, and national and self definition, preserving them in bronze, literally just below the surface of Lady Liberty.

Bibliography: Edward Bok, *The Americanization of Edward Bok: The Autobiography of a Dutch Boy Fifty Years After* (1920; New York, 1924). Sui Sin Far, *Mrs. Spring Fragrance and Other Writings* (Urbana, IL, 1993). Emma Goldman, *Living My Life* (New York, 1970). Matthew Frye Jacobson, *Special Sorrows* (Cambridge, 1995). Theodore Roosevelt, *The Works of Theodore Roosevelt: National Edition* (New York, 1926). Esther Schor, *Emma Lazarus* (New York, 2006). Werner Sollors, "Americans All" (New York, 1997), published electronically, *www.nyupress.org/americansall.*

AVIVA TAUBENFELD

1903

W. C. Handy hears a new kind of music

The Invention of the Blues

In 1903, W. C. Handy was dozing in the depot in Tutwiler, Mississippi, waiting for a train that was nine hours late. He was awakened by a ragged black man playing "the weirdest music I had ever heard," fretting his guitar with a knife to produce an eerie, sliding wail, and singing about "goin' where the Southern cross the Dog"—that is, he was describing his impending trip to Moorhead, Mississippi, where the tracks of the Southern Railway cross those of the Yazoo line, also known as the Yellow Dog.

Handy, born in 1873 in Florence, Alabama, had by that time been a professional musician for six years, playing in minstrel shows and in a band sponsored by a branch of the Knights of Pythias. He was acquainted with a considerable range of the music of the black South—indeed, by his own admission, many of the songs published under his name over the years were adaptations of tunes he had heard in the field. One such, for example, was "East St. Louis Blues," which he attributed to "shabby guitarists" he had heard in St. Louis in 1892. Despite its name—presumably applied later—and a certain general resemblance to the blues, the song does not actually adhere to the twelve-bar form. The unprecedented song Handy heard in the depot in Tutwiler, on the other hand, probably did. The form may not have been what Handy found most startling in the song—the bottleneck slide, perhaps imported from Hawaii to complement local styles around the same time, might well have been new to him—but he had surely not heard it before.

Once heard, the blues is not readily forgotten. The twelve-bar form, with its three-line verse, its AAB rhyme scheme, and its line length of five stressed syllables, is a formula that, like the heroic couplet or the limerick, imprints itself upon the brain and sets off a kind of melody whether or not it is actually sung or accompanied by musical instruments. It is irreducible.

> Hitch up my pony, saddle up my black mare
> Hitch up my pony, saddle up my black mare
> I'm gonna find a rider, baby, in the world somewhere.
>   —Charley Patton, "Pony Blues"

> I hate to see the evening sun go down
> I hate to see the evening sun go down
> It makes me think I'm on my last go-round.
>   —W. C. Handy, "St. Louis Blues"

I got stones in my passway and my road seem dark as night
I got stones in my passway and my road seem dark as night
I have pains in my heart. They have taken my appetite.
    —Robert Johnson, "Stones in My Passway"

With its two-line reiteration followed by a lapidary summation line, the form could almost have been consciously designed to frame a view of the world that is fatalistic, expecting the worst, armored against fresh injury—yet by the same token indestructible, eternally renewable. Its compact shell, enclosing volumes, holding volatile emotions to a ground, was well suited to the guardedness and self-containment of African Americans in the Jim Crow era. It is equally ideal for songs of endurance, of suffering, of deflected aspiration, and of deeply concealed resistance.

So often depicted as having seamlessly evolved from field hollers and beyond that from West African griot songs, the blues was actually a sudden and radical turn in African American music. That is not to say that it materialized in a vacuum. Numerous strains of black folk music were current in the nineteenth century, from hollers and ring chants to ballads and breakdowns, each leaving some mark on the blues, in lyrics or instrumentation, and many were carried on in the twentieth century alongside the blues, by the same musicians. And although the term "blues" came to be applied to any minor-key lament—in the 1920s and '30s, to almost any kind of song—the true blues songs are those that hew to the twelve-bar structure. While the sentiments, chord progressions, and vocal and instrumental styles that came to distinguish the blues were all lying at hand in the black musical culture of the South, the form itself is just too specific not to have had a very particular origin. All we know of this origin is the result of a process of elimination.

In 1902, Ma Rainey was working a tent show in Missouri when "a girl from town" turned up to sing a "strange and poignant" song that galvanized the audience. When asked what kind of song it was, she said, "It's the blues." The earliest published description of what appears to be blues dates from 1903, the year of W. C. Handy's epiphany: an account in the *Journal of American Folk-Lore* by the Harvard archaeologist Charles Peabody, who transcribed songs sung by laborers he employed on an excavation in Coahoma County, Mississippi, in 1901. The folklorist Howard Odum published field collections of songs sung by black country people in Georgia and Mississippi between 1905 and 1908, and these include quite a few that qualify as blues.

The invention of the blues occurred, we might posit, between 1895 and 1900. This places the blues among the early manifestations of modernism—between the automobile and the airplane, and not long after the movies, radio transmission, and cylinder recordings—but also in an inaccessible backstreet of history, so that we don't know who or when or how or why, just that the invention occurred. Whoever first made up a blues assembled a number of elements at large in the black musical culture of the time, from the flatted intervals to the instrumental

accompaniment to bits and pieces of lyrics, and put them together in a way that
was not only new, but immediately reproducible as a form. It had the flexibility to
yield to various kinds of originality, but the strength to remain itself in the process. The blues is at once a musical category as capacious as jazz or rock and roll,
and a form as circumscribed as the tango or the samba. The former aspect may
suggest a gradual evolution over time and by many hands, but the latter pins it
down to a particular occurrence. As Samuel Charters, whose *The Country Blues*
(1959) was the first book on the subject, later wrote: "It is always important to
emphasize . . . that there was no sociological or historical reason for the blues
verse to take the form it did. Someone sang the first blues." Of this inventor's
identity we possess not a hint, and we likewise have no idea whether the blues was
initially rural or urban, or in what Southern state it originated. No recording of a
genuine blues was made until Mamie Smith's "Crazy Blues" was waxed in 1920,
and by then the music had spread to every hamlet in the South (and extensive recorded documentation had been made of, say, the polka). By the time it occurred
to anyone to ask the question, the trail was cold.

There are many reasons why it was so. The question took so long to occur for
a variety of reasons, from the understandable to the shameful. Certain old popular songs—even ones with a known origin—have so infiltrated the collective unconscious that it may seem as if they were never actually composed, but rather
that they mysteriously *appeared,* the way jokes and proverbs can seem as if they
have fallen from the sky. But there are also songs whose creation took place in the
darkness of poverty and segregation and illiteracy, especially in the time before
recordings, and whose authorship is attributed to "Trad." by default. This is so
much the case with black music before 1920 that the exceptions are startling. The
early history of jazz may be better documented than that of the blues or its analogues, but it is no less surprising to come upon such definite and exact statements of origin as Sterling Brown's assertion that the elemental "Shimmy She
Wobble" was written by Professor Spencer Williams to celebrate the entertainments of Lulu White's bordello in New Orleans, or E. Simms Campbell's claim
that "Ta Ra Ra Boom Dee-ay" was composed in Babe Connors's house in 1894.

And then, too, the early blues musicians were not only often illiterate, they
were also mobile, and unpredictable in their traveling patterns. And they were
often disreputable, the places where they played unsavory—jazz may have
emerged from the brothels of New Orleans, but its brasses and pianos lent it the
kind of institutional gravity that mere guitarists could not achieve. The blues was
fleeting, transient, if not actually furtive. Blues musicians were also fiercely competitive, and loath to acknowledge influence. The very success of the invention
must also have militated against anyone's knowing who was responsible. Even if a
front-porch guitarist was responsible, rather than an itinerant songster, it is easy
to imagine that within twenty-four hours a dozen people had taken up the style, a
hundred inside of a week, a thousand in the first month. By then only ten people
would have remembered who came up with it, and nine of them weren't talking.

The first researchers with an interest in the origins of the blues, who were
folklorists used to dealing with traditions that were sometimes untraceably an-

cient, did not especially concern themselves with authorship. Could the blues even truly be considered folk music? Folklorists simply assumed that it was, and proceeded with their researches accordingly. For John and Alan Lomax, for example, the blues was primarily a collective expression, with a core of African music that had been bent and shaped by the pain of slavery, of peonage, of prison, of Jim Crow—an account that is not untrue, but has obvious limitations. As Charters wrote, "It is always difficult to resist the temptation to continue to look for social influences instead of the individual performer behind the development of the blues." If the blues materialized so recently, suddenly, and specifically, it seems at best sentimental to attribute it broadly to The People.

All attempts to make categorical statements regarding the blues wind up sounding reductive. It is important to consider both the richness of the blues songs that have come down to us, and the haphazard nature of their means of transmission. For all the brilliance of the early blues as they exist on record, an unknown quantity of performers and songs at least equally brilliant were never recorded, and even their rumor has not survived. Most writers on the blues, beginning with Charters, have, for example, simply assumed that the blues was born in the Mississippi Delta. But this deduction is based on little more than the fact that an unusually high number of exceptional performers came from there. There is no proof the blues began within this circumference, no matter how rich the musical soil. Anecdotal evidence suggests that the blues had a rural origin, since whenever blues songs were heard, early on, in cities like New Orleans or Memphis or St. Louis, they always seemed to have been imported there by country people. On the other hand, Stephen Calt and Gayle Deane Wardlow, biographers of the radical Delta blues innovator Charley Patton, interviewed scores of Delta old-timers in the 1960s and were unable to find any who recalled hearing the blues before 1910. The blues might still have originated there, or its birthplace might have been New Orleans, where it would have been only one of a number of competing marvels.

Urban blues, in the 1920s known more accurately as vaudeville blues, were the form to be recorded, and they were most frequently sung by urbane and knowing women, most of them young. The received idea that these blues were somehow slicker and less authentic than the rural sort merely reflects a provincial bias. It is also true that the Delta is rivaled for fecundity in the earliest times that we know of by East Texas and western Louisiana. Could the blues have begun in two places at once? Blind Lemon Jefferson, arguably the most influential blues guitarist of the 1920s, was Texan, as was the man who sang on the corner opposite his on Deep Ellum in Dallas, the scary, rasp-voiced gospel bluesman Blind Willie Johnson. For that matter, a distinct chapter in the history of the transmission of the blues would concern sawmills and turpentine camps throughout the forests of the Deep South, settlements featuring barrelhouses, whose upright pianos engendered a particular style of keyboard blues that led directly to boogie-woogie. But the story always seems to come back to Mississippi. There is no denying that, from sometime after 1910 to the late '40s, the northwest quadrant of that state saw an astonishing conjunction of original talents amid surroundings that are at best unprepossessing. A wayside like Drew or Robinsonville begins to sound like Paris in the same period.

All we have concerning the birth of the blues are guesses regarding dates and places, and bits of assorted data that may or may not be meaningful, such as a partial list of musicians who are known to have played blues in the Mississippi Delta circa 1910 but did not survive into the recording era: Henry Sloan, D. Irvin, Mott Willis, Cap Holmes, Jake Martin, Jack Hicks, Ike Zinneman. But it is more apparent than ever that the question of where and when and how the blues began is of far more than academic interest. The blues was not a reaction or a spontaneous utterance or a cry of anguish in the night, and it did not arise from the great mass of the people like a collective sigh. It was a deliberate decision arrived at by a particular artist through a process of experimentation, using materials at hand from a variety of sources. It was taken up by others and expanded to encompass anguish as well as defiance, humor, lust, cruelty, heartbreak, awe, sarcasm, fury, regret, bemusement, mischief, delirium, and even triumph. It grew to be the expression of a people, but not before it had become as diverse and complicated as that people. It, too, ranges beyond the monochrome of its name.

Bibliography: Stephen Calt and Gayle Dean Wardlow, *King of the Delta Blues: The Life and Music of Charlie Patton* (Newton, NJ, 1988). Samuel Charters, *The Country Blues* (New York, 1959). Lawrence Cohn, ed., *Nothing but the Blues: The Music and the Musicians* (New York, 1993). W. C. Handy, *Father of the Blues* (New York, 1942). Alan Lomax, *The Land Where Blues Began* (New York, 1993). Robert Palmer, *Deep Blues* (New York, 1991).

LUC SANTE

1903

Gertrude Stein moves to Paris, and neither is ever the same again

ONE SEES WHAT ONE SEES

In the old days, American painters emigrated to Paris, not American writers. James McNeill Whistler found in Paris a culture willing to contemplate contrarian painting, almost eager for outrage; in fact Whistler exhibited at the 1863 Salon des Refusés along with Manet. An anglophone writer had less incentive to take part in French culture. Why then did Gertrude Stein decide in 1903 to settle in Paris? One reason was that she wanted to live in a place where no babbling in English would interfere with her private meditations on the English language: "But do you never read french, I . . . asked her. No . . . I have liked all these years . . . to be surrounded by people who know no english . . . I like living with so very many people and being all alone with english and myself." Another reason was that in Paris there was a there there.

The *there* was for Stein, as it had been for Whistler, a culture of the visual arts. Stein and her brother Leo became two of the most determined, thorough, and incisive collectors of contemporary painting, and they soon got to know an obscure painter from Spain, Pablo Picasso, who became, apart from Stein's companion, Alice B. Toklas, the closest friend of Gertrude Stein's life. Picasso did not like to exhibit, so those who wished to see his paintings were well advised to visit 27, rue de Fleurus, the home of Stein and Toklas, in which every vertical surface was being crammed with pictures by Matisse, Cézanne, Picasso, and other now-canonical masters. If the Stein salon became a valuable source of intellectual ferment, it was partly because of the extraordinary acuity of the hostess, and partly because *entrée* was the only ticket to Paris's best museum of modernist art.

Stein believed that painting and literature were distinct, and disapproved strongly when Picasso began to write poems—"the egoism of a painter is not at all the egoism of a writer"—but nevertheless she and Picasso evolved together in remarkable ways. During 1905 and 1906 Picasso had Stein endure eighty or ninety sittings for a portrait; in the end he painted out the face and remade it as a stark blank staring thing, confrontational in a way that anticipated the famous African masks in *Les demoiselles d'Avignon* of 1907. Stein's face, then, along with certain figures from Africa and ancient Iberia, became part of the visual complex that helped Picasso achieve the cubist revolution. But Stein had already transformed her own art with the help of an African (or African American) mask, Melanctha, in *Three Lives,* written in 1905:

> I wrote a negro story called Melanctha. In that there was a constant recurring and beginning there was a marked direction in the direction of being in the present although naturally I had been accustomed to past present and future, and why, because the composition forming around me was a prolonged present . . . I created then a prolonged present naturally I knew nothing of a continuous present but it came naturally to me to make one.

Stein was to be much attracted to cubism's all-overness, its way of treating every square inch of the canvas as equally significant—"Cézanne conceived the idea that in composition one thing was as important as another thing. Each part is as important as the whole, and that impressed me enormously." If Stein applauded the ways in which the cubists, following Cézanne, cut up the sky and the foreground with complete impartiality, it may have been because "Melanctha" was, in this sense, a cubist story before cubism existed.

As she wrote *Three Lives,* Stein kept her desk positioned in front of Cézanne's portrait of his wife, and a certain Cézannesque quality can be felt. The textual foreground and the textual background are minimally distinguished:

> Jeff Campbell had always all his life loved to be with people, and he had loved all his life always to be thinking, but he was still only a great boy, was Jeff Campbell, and he had never before had any of this funny kind of feeling . . .
> "I know you are a good man, Jeff. I always know that, no matter how much you can hurt me." "I sure don't see how you can think so, Melanctha, if you certainly did think I was trying so hard just to hurt you." "Hush, you are only a great big boy, Jeff Campbell, and you don't know anything yet about real hurting."

The narrator's stream of nobody's-consciousness-in-particular anticipates the language of the dialogue that hasn't occurred yet ("a great boy"); the Negro vernacular hovers oddly close to Stein-speak ("if you certainly did think"), as if the speech patterns of simple people were a part of figuration of the most advanced modernism. The cultivation of the "continuous present" is also a form of all-overness: instead of a graduated field in which sensation deepens into memory, Stein presents an equably lit verbal surface in which neither recollection nor hope disrupts the steady insistence on immediate feeling. The characters simply roll down the slightly inclined plane of their lives.

Stein disliked Picasso's use of African masks: she called them a "crutch," and regarded them as a diversion from his true path. If the character of a poor black woman provided Stein with something she found useful, it was not because of any respect for African American culture. As she wrote after meeting Paul Robeson, "negroes were not suffering from persecution, they were suffering from nothing-ness. She always contends that the african is not primitive, he has a very ancient but a very narrow culture and there it remains. Consequently nothing does or can happen." The character of Melanctha gave Stein an empty expanse, a free space that offered no resistance to any text she might wish to write on it. Stein later was to define a successful play as a play in which "nothing was happening . . . after all Hamlet Shakespeare's most interesting play has really nothing happening except that they live and die." A nothing character was from Stein's point of view irresistible.

If Picasso and Stein came to Africa independently, and with different inten-tions, the case of *Tender Buttons* shows Stein in the act of learning lessons from Picasso. Stein thought that Picasso's genius lay in his faculty for seeing what was *there*, the object unencumbered with the normal contexts of things—not the ob-ject as we know it ought to be:

> Really most of the time one sees only a feature of a person with whom one is, the other features are covered by a hat, by the light, by clothes for sport and everybody is accustomed to complete the whole entirely from their knowledge, but Picasso when he saw an eye, the other one did not exist for him . . . one sees what one sees, and the rest is a reconstruction from memory and painters have nothing to do with reconstruction.

When Picasso failed, says Stein, it was because "interpretations destroyed his own vision." The painter's gaze should be at once intelligent and radically mind-less, without preconception, without interpretation.

To realize this goal in the domain of literature, Stein abandoned her old style and tried to write what she called "still life": "she had been interested only in the insides of people, their character and what went on inside them, it was dur-ing that summer that she first felt a desire to express the rhythm of the visible world." The result was *Tender Buttons* (1913; 1914), a book that offers objects that possess none of the usual consolations of objectivity. Here is one of the poems:

A DOG

> A little monkey goes like a donkey that means to say that means to say that more sighs last goes. Leave with it. A little monkey goes like a donkey.

Pablo Picasso, *Gertrude Stein* (1906). Oil on canvas

In the last year of her life, 1946, Stein tried to tell an interviewer what she meant by "A Dog": "'A little monkey goes like a donkey . . .' That was an effort to illustrate the movement of a donkey going up a hill, you can see it plainly. 'A little monkey goes like a donkey.' An effort to make the movement of the donkey, and so the picture hangs complete." It is, then, a text not meant to be read but to be felt as a rhythm, partly a rhythm of walking (a patient plod?), partly a collage-rhythm of congruence among components: just as, in Picasso, the outline of half a guitar might mimic the curve of a woman's body cut from an advertisement and pasted to the canvas, so the rhymes, the stutters, the losses of momentum, try to mimic— what? Stein told Virgil Thomson that *Tender Buttons* was "'an effort to describe something without naming it,' which is what the cubist painters were doing with still life." The poem tries for an object-status equal in dignity with the object it describes, but in the absence of a name the object behind the poem remains a riddle, as certain cubist paintings remain riddles.

Stein's influence on French literature was marginal. Except for Georges Hugnet there were few French writers among her intimates, and her distaste for surrealism, for every dreamy, semiconscious, unalert artistic style, made her exclude many of the most vibrant writers from her circle—"The surrealists still see things as everyone sees them, they complicate them in a different way but the vision is that of every one else." But her influence on English literature was strong. When Hemingway was a young expatriate, writing the stories that became *In Our Time,* she worked closely with him. Alice B. Toklas called him a "rotten pupil," but he nevertheless learned much from Stein:

> I'd come back and sit down beside him and he'd pull a rope out of his pocket and start skipping rope out in the sun with the sweat pouring off his face and him skipping rope out in the white dust with the rope going cloppetty, cloppetty, clop, clop, clop, and the sun hotter, and him working harder up and down a patch of the road.

This sentence is so alliterative and so paratactic, its sentence construction so full of subordinate clauses, that it could be rearranged into Old Germanic verse:

> I'd come back   and sit down beside him
> and he'd pull a rope   out of his pocket
> and start skipping rope   out in the sun
> with the sweat pouring off his face   and him skipping rope
> out in the white dust   with the rope going
> cloppety, cloppety   clop, clop, clop,
> and the sun hotter   and him working harder
> up and down   a patch of the road.

This is less a description of a man skipping rope than a verbal incarnation of a man skipping rope. The sentence shapes itself intimately to the jumpy, first accelerating, then tiring rhythm of the exercise.

Where did Hemingway learn this trick of experimenting with the plasticity of parataxis to create peculiar sentence rhythms? Not from reading Old Germanic, but from close attention to Stein's prose. In 1924 Hemingway persuaded

Ford Madox Ford to serialize part of Stein's immense novel *The Making of Americans,* an almost inconceivably paratactic work: "Sometime then there will be every kind of a history of every one who ever can or is or was or will be living. Sometime then there will be a history of every one from their beginning to their ending. Sometime then there will be a history of all of them, of every kind of them, of every one." In a lecture Stein read this passage and commented, "In *The Making of Americans* . . . my sentences grew longer and longer, my imaginary dependent clauses were constantly being dropped out, I struggled with relations between they them and then." Hemingway was to make a career out of eliminating dependent clauses.

Stein looks like an easy writer to parody, but her canny trickiness tends to exceed that of her parodists; Hemingway was one of the few writers who could successfully spoof her: "They did not try very often on the boat cause Mrs. Elliot was quite sick. She was sick and when she was sick she was sick as Southern women are sick. That is women from the Southern part of the United States. Like all Southern women Mrs. Elliot disintegrated very quickly under sea sickness." Hemingway beautifully captures Stein's vertigos of simplicity.

The story of Stein and Hemingway is well known, but her influence extends to many odd places. Edith Sitwell's *Façade* poems have something of the hypervirtuosic childlikeness of Stein's work; Sitwell herself said that the end of Stein's *Accents in Alsace* inspired her "Jodelling Song":

> We bear velvet cream,
> Green and babyish
> Small leaves seem; each stream
> Horses' tails that swish.

According to Sitwell, "The poems in *Façade* are abstract poems—that is, they are patterns in sound. They are . . . virtuoso exercises in technique of extreme difficulty, in the same sense as that in which certain studies by Liszt are studies in transcendental technique in music." Yeats commented on another *Façade* poem, "Ass-Face": "When you listen to this poem, you should become two people, one a sage . . . one a child listening to a poem as irrational as a 'Sing a Song of Sixpence.'" To be child and sage is also good advice for reading Stein.

Perhaps most unexpected of all is Stein's influence on Samuel Beckett. In 1937 Beckett cited what he called Stein's "logographs," and approved of the ways in which Stein had made her "speech tissue" *(Sprachgewebe)* "porous." Maniacal porosity is a feature of some of Beckett's prose, as in *Watt:*

> it was not rare to find, on the Sunday, the tallboy on its feet by the fire, and the dressing-table on its head by the bed, and the night-stool on its face by the door, and the washhand-stand on its back by the window; and on the Monday, the tallboy on its back by the bed, and the dressing-table on its face by the door, and the washhand-stand on its feet by the fire

Indeed the text is composed with such a wide weave that it will hold nothing at all—a sieve that's all hole.

Borges wrote that every great writer creates a body of precursors, and I will end with a glimpse backward, at Stein's retrospective influence, so to speak. There is a peculiar piece by Jonathan Swift called *A Compleat Collection of Genteel and Ingenious Conversation* (1738), full of passages such as this:

> *Neverout.* Miss, what spells b double uzzard?
> *Miss.* Buzzard in your teeth, Mr. Neverout.
> *Lady Smart.* Now you are up, Mr. Neverout, will you do me the favour to do me the kindness to take off the tea-kettle?
> *Lord Sparkish.* I wonder what makes these bells ring.

If Gertrude Stein had never been born, this would seem a freakish and incomprehensible text. It still seems freakish and incomprehensible, but as an anticipation of Stein it is made familiar, assimilated into a canon that she caused to exist.

Bibliography: Samuel Beckett, *Watt* (New York: 1953.) Edward Burns, ed., *Gertrude Stein on Picasso* (New York, 1970). Ulla Dydo, ed., *A Stein Reader* (Evanston, IL, 1993). Robert Haas, ed., *A Primer for the Gradual Understanding of Gertrude Stein* (Los Angeles, 1971). Ernest Hemingway, *In Our Time* (Paris and London, 1924). Gertrude Stein, *Selected Writings of Gertrude Stein,* ed. Carl Van Vechten (New York, 1946).

DANIEL ALBRIGHT

1904, August 30

After twenty years abroad, Henry James arrives on the *Kaiser Wilhelm II* at Hoboken, New Jersey

The American Scene

"What you say of the Eggs (!!!), of the Vocalisation, of the Shocks in general, and of everything else, is utterly beside the mark—it being absolutely *for* all that class of phenomena, and every other class, that I nurse my infatuation. I want to see them, I want to see everything, I want to See the Country." So an exasperated Henry James on May 24, 1903, demolished his brother William's warning of three weeks earlier, that he might want to rethink his plans to visit the country of his birth. "Many features of our national life," William had cautioned, would inspire his brother with "physical loathing"—among them the "*incredibly* loathsome" "vocalization of our countrymen" and the way, in hotels and dining cars, his "fellow beings" eat their "boiled eggs." Having just had his sixtieth birthday, Henry feels the acute need, before it is too late, to make some "general renovation of one's too monotonised grab-bag" and have "one little ewe-lamb of possible exotic experience." And "time, absence and change," he insists, have come to make his native land "almost as romantic" as Europe used to be. To his "poetry of motion" he will join "the prose of *production,*" which is James's way of saying that the trip might be financially shrewd, for he plans to give a number of lectures while in the States and to publish his collected impressions as a book.

The letters exchanged around Henry's imminent voyage to America provide insights for appreciating what his 1904 repatriation reaped—the book *The American Scene* (1907). Appreciation by and large eluded *The American Scene* for decades. James's book fortunately has survived its caricature as the anxious report of a reactionary aesthete and odious social snob in flight from the twentieth century. It has come to be regarded as one of a small handful of essential works about the United States, a book marked by prophetic insight. That insight is distilled into its climactic question: "Who and what is an alien, when it comes to that, in a country peopled from the first" by migrations? This jab at the a priori assumption of Anglo-American supremacy as the sacred ground of American self-identity puts *The American Scene* in company with a work it actually mentions in passing and that William James had recommended to his brother, *The Souls of Black Folk* (1903); its author, W. E. B. Du Bois, had been William's student at Harvard. Both books put America on notice that its vaunted ethnic purity is a precarious fiction. Yet James's challenge to the most venerable American piety proved to be a message in a bottle. Because it embraced impurity (in a manner strikingly akin to William James's *Pragmatism* of 1907), the message was too radical to have an immediate impact in a political landscape hollowed out by nativism and Jim Crow. But in time the skepticism of Du Bois and Henry James, and the pragmatism of William James, would come to nurture new ways of thinking about identity, both racial and American. Ralph Ellison and James Baldwin, both warm admirers of Henry James, are two distinguished heirs of this turn-of-the-century constellation.

In a remark that would prove prescient, William conceded in a 1907 letter to Henry that *The American Scene* was, "in its peculiar way," "supremely great." But he hastened to add his regrets about what he called its perverse method: "'Say it *out* for God's sake . . . and have done with it,'" he imagines nineteen out of twenty readers saying when confronted with its "complication and innuendo and associative reference on the enormous scale." The peculiarities of *The American Scene* are indeed flagrant, its method "unheard of," as a baffled William fumed. But Henry's willful risk and defiance—I "stand naked and unashamed" on my impressions, I will "go to the stake for them," he declares in his preface—makes possible his disorienting but unflinching discovery: that "human Anglo-Saxondom"—and its "American extension"—is currently undergoing a "profane overhauling" as it "suffer[s] the indignity of change."

America in 1904 is nearing the high tide of immigration that will crest three years later when a million Europeans arrive on her shores. Rather than briskly saying it out, as William implored, rather than imposing neat categorical judgments and conclusions, distancing acts of intellectual assessment, Henry James engages viscerally with this new fact of "profane overhauling" and does so from inside its very engine, Ellis Island. When he visits the gateway for the "alien" entry to the United States, "the terrible little Ellis Island," James witnesses the immigrant's "affirmed claim," his "quantity and quality" and "settled possession"; it is the one "fixed element . . . not to be dodged" and reduces James, the native, to "*un*settled possession." Injecting a touch of Gothic melodrama, he confesses he feels shaken "to the depths of his being," for he has "seen a ghost in his supposedly safe old house."

James's eleven months of travel take him up and down the East Coast, from New Jersey and New York, New Hampshire, Philadelphia, Washington, and Boston to Virginia, South Carolina, and Florida (he also made it out to Chicago, Seattle, and San Francisco and planned to write up those impressions in a second volume that never materialized). His avid curiosity puts him in contact with a variety of people, ethnicities, classes, institutions, and locales. To this array of experiences James reacts variously, expressing contempt, condescension, exhilaration, fear, respect, pleasure, and nostalgia. Instead of circumspectly opting for a single stance, he insists on displaying the whole gamut of his responses, for only the intricate texture of multiplicity honors the "one all positive appearance" that the United States exhibits—"the growth of immeasurable muchness," the "mere looming mass of the *more,* the more and more to come." Refraining from an irritable striving after conclusions, James makes receptivity, rather than attitudinizing, the catalyst for his book's relish for risk and respect for the indeterminate.

The American Scene is a calculated act of affiliation with the new century and its possibilities. James bears uneasy witness to the transition from a Victorian culture of hierarchy and homogeneity to an urban modernity of "hotch-potch," "overflow," and unsettlement. This is not to say that James is a self-conscious modernist intellectual who, like Randolph Bourne of the younger "generation of 1910," heralds a "trans-national" America. In surprising ways, James is close to this project, but his engagement with urban modernity is not without profound, freely confessed ambivalence and even sharp unease. He salutes New York's Lower East Side cafés as "tiny temples" of immigrant intellectual vitality, but they are also, to his ears, "torture rooms of the living idiom." Yet even in his "piteous gasp" he refuses to condemn "the accent of the very ultimate future" as being bereft of unsuspected beauty. James may be mired in the nativist prejudices of his class, but he is unique in submitting them to the tonic shock of total immersion. His genius for revision flowers in the years following publication of *The American Scene*. Between 1907 and 1909 he would complete the unprecedented task of revising most of his life's work in fiction for the twenty-four-volume New York Edition that Scribner's would publish, complete with eighteen prefaces recounting his acts of alteration. The same suppleness presides in *The American Scene,* enabling him to disrupt congealed responses and dependency on reified assumptions.

This flexibility marks his distinction in the largely nativist patrician world in which he lived. Lacking deeply felt class loyalties, James in his own genteel way was an outlaw, drawn to places—the Lower East Side, Central Park, the Bowery— full of the "dangerous classes," the patricians' code for the ethnic hordes they loathed. *The American Scene* makes unmistakable James's difference from his friend Henry Adams, who barricaded himself behind anti-Semitism and medievalism, and from other friends, such as E. L. Godkin and Charles Eliot Norton, whose antimodernism hastened their retreat from urban America's multiethnic democratic culture. What James said of the consummately serene Norton—that he possessed an "absolute ease of mind about one's point of view"—is precisely the opposite of James's own attitude of "reckless" curiosity, through which he savors the bewilderment of "strain and stress." He is awed and appalled by the American hotel, especially the lobby of the Waldorf-Astoria; he notes the vapidities of wealth, be they reflected in the elephantine mansions of Newport or the way New Jersey villas eliminate the precious luxury of privacy; he laments the fond Confederate fantasies of segregation that still paralyze Richmond and Charleston four decades after the war.

Rather than remaining aloof in static contemplation, James actively solicits and corporeally experiences shock as the imprint of the material pressure of change. Indeed, on the first page of *The American Scene,* James, upon landing in Hoboken, is assaulted by "instant vibrations" of "curiosity" prompted "at every turn, in sights, sounds, smells, even in the chaos of confusion and change." This experience, of being charged with the primal, childlike avidity of insatiable curiosity, will remain with James throughout his journey. And during his flanerie in his birthplace, "inexpressibly intimate" New York—discussion of which occupies nearly a third of the book—the "instant vibrations" reach a pitch of excitement stimulated by a "past recalled from very far back." The stylistic triumph of *The American Scene* is James's discovery of a form of cultural analysis that does not simply report on but mimes the unsettling fact of American exorbitance; the dissonant rhythms of his radical curiosity feed on shocks, contingencies, and the transitory attractions of urban minutiae. In Central Park, for instance, he finds himself in the midst of a "polyglot Hebraic crowd of pedestrians" whose polished teeth and shoes draw his admiration; later at a Bowery theater he ponders the socioeconomic implications of the "cult of candy" and the dental work it requires. *The American Scene*'s pleasure in "multiplication" and "overflow" is at one with James's famous "major phase" of fiction, in which—in *The Golden Bowl,* for instance, published during his American travels, and in *The Ambassadors,* released the year before his trip—intelligibility of character and action is pushed to its limits.

By the end of *The Ambassadors,* the suave and heartless Chad Newsome is going into a new profession—"advertising scientifically worked." He will become one of the "master-spirits of management" that James so vividly evokes in *The American Scene* as the "hotel-spirit," the "ubiquitous American force" that is part of the "great assimilative organism" of a leveling democracy. The gospel of homogeneity it preaches is the true blight on the American scene; in its nativist form, this force of social control speeds "the conversion of the alien" and the shedding of ethnic qualities. The "conversion" to a flat, coerced identity dismays James, for he recognizes the alien not as a stranger but as the quintessential American: "Which is the American . . . which is *not* the alien, over a large part of the country at least, and where does one put a finger on the dividing line" between alien and native?

This pivotal question is one that James does not simply pose but *lives* over the course of his eleven months of travel. The question frames precisely the unsettling challenge that everywhere confronts him—the precariousness of his, or anyone's, claim to a genuine American identity. Reflecting on the "majesty" of the "great 'ethnic' question" and its place in the "cauldron of the 'American' character" (placing scare quotes around *American* to mark its provisionality), James imagines a skeptic asking: "'What meaning, in the presence of such impressions, can continue to attach to such a term as the 'American' character?—what type, as the result of such a prodigious amalgamation, such a hotch-potch of racial ingredients, is to be conceived as shaping itself?'" The questions are new, virtually unprecedented, certainly when posed by a white American, and their implications are not easy to accept: the "challenge to speculation, fed thus by a thousand sources," is close to "irritating," James notes, and he takes comfort in the "impossibility" of answering them. But there is no turning back. As he acknowledges on Ellis Island: "We, not they, must make the surrender and accept the orientation."

James read *The Souls of Black Folk* after William told him, "I am sending you a decidedly moving book by a mulatto ex-student of mine, Du Bois." One reason Du Bois revered his Harvard professor was that James's pragmatism, along with Franz Boas's anthropology, was skeptical of the authority of origin, essence, and identity and could serve as a tool to oppose the theory and practice of white supremacy. Addressing white America near the end of his book, Du Bois asks: "Your country? How came it yours? Before the Pilgrims landed we were here. Here we have brought our three gifts and mingled them with yours . . . Actively we have woven ourselves with the very warp and woof of this nation—we fought their battles, shared their sorrow, mingled our blood with theirs." Du Bois's pinpoint pressure on the possessive pronoun *your* begins to loosen white America's stranglehold on an American history it would prefer to bury. He alerts white America that it does not have the choice to reject black America; their blood is already mingled. In their challenges to nativism and to racial segregation, Henry James and Du Bois both portray American identity as never anything but miscegenated.

Hence there is a Du Boisian and Jamesian resonance in James Baldwin's own abiding belief that "whether I like it or not, or whether you like it or not, we are bound together forever. We are part of each other." Baldwin read *The American Scene* late in life, long after James's expatriation and also after his own novelistic reflections on the "complex fate" of being American had already shaped him. And when Ralph Ellison, like Henry James, puts scare quotes around "our 'Americanness'" in his great essay "The Little Man at Chehaw Station," he does so for similar reasons—to convey the inferential rather than a priori status of this term of identity, for "in relationship to the cultural whole, we are, all of us, white or black, native-born or immigrant—members of minority groups." In emphasizing the "motley mixtures" that constitute the United States and defy reduction to pure identity, Ellison is speaking from within the Jamesian/Du Boisian constellation. If *The Souls of Black Folk* arguably helped create a new climate in its day, embodied by the 1910 founding of the interracial National Association for the Advancement of Colored People with Du Bois as a director, *The American Scene,* an improbable ally, would prove a resource of similar visionary insight for later generations.

Bibliography: James Baldwin, *The Price of the Ticket: Collected Non-Fiction, 1948–1985* (New York, 1985). Randolph Bourne, "Trans-National America," *Atlantic Monthly* 118 (July 1916). W. E. B. Du Bois, *Writings* (New York, 1986). Ralph Ellison, *The Collected Essays* (New York, 1995). Henry James, *The American Scene* (1907; New York, 1994); *Letters,* ed. Leon Edel, 4 vols. (Cambridge, MA, 1974–1984). William James, *Correspondence,* vol. 3: *William and Henry 1897–1910,* ed. I. Skrupskelis and E. Berkeley (Charlottesville, VA, 1994).

ROSS POSNOCK

1905, October 15
Little Nemo sets off for Slumberland

THE COMIC STRIP WAKES UP

A clown outfitted in a top hat and tails enters a young boy's bedroom and, acting on orders from King Morpheus, summons the child to an audience with his royal highness in the faraway kingdom of Slumberland. With his absurdly oversized top hat in hand, the messenger bows deeply toward the boy, who is called Nemo, and intones, "Slumberland is a long way off through many miles of weird scenes," a declaration that sets the stage for the episodes that follow. As in a dream, the sequence of events becomes increasingly strange and disorienting. At one moment Nemo is pitched forward on his bed, excitedly listening as the green-faced clown, whose appearance is formal and preposterous in equal measure, presents him with a piebald pony named Somnus. The next scene finds Nemo in the same position; however, the bed he was sitting upon has been replaced by the horse. The viewer encounters the scene eye level with the mattress, as though deliberately positioned to view the episode from the vantage point of a child. In the following frames the bland colors of the boy's bedroom give way to a candy-colored sky that changes from orange to green to blue to red, and before long a bleary-eyed, unkempt Nemo, clad only in a nightshirt, is careening through deep, dark space, surrounded by stars and planets. Each leap and gallop of the horse is carefully detailed. The messenger's preview becomes reality as Nemo finds himself racing against a menagerie that includes a monkey riding a green kangaroo, a rabbit atop a pig, and a frog astride a red dog, in a tableau reminiscent of a carousel ride gone haywire.

So begins an epic adventure, relayed from 1905 to 1911 through a series of sequential panels each Sunday in the *New York Herald*'s comic supplement. The perpetually tousle-haired boy is transported weekly to locations near and far on an endless quest. His bed becomes the launching pad for his imagination, catapulting the young protagonist from fields of giant mushrooms to Martian cities. At times the bed itself becomes a vehicle, flying Nemo to the moon, or growing legs and marching out the door of his suburban home. Beyond the stark black-and-white grids of the newspaper page lay the possibility of other worlds; the riotous color and fantastic scenes of the Sunday supplement served to disrupt the or-

dered reality of the preceding pages, just as the bright lights and fanciful buildings of Coney Island provided a counterpoint to the business and industry embodied by Manhattan's skyline.

New York City at the turn of the twentieth century was a metropolis teeming
with novel and spectacular visual experiences. City dwellers navigated a new social landscape: advances in the speed of public transportation, combined with
overcrowded streets, transformed notions of both time and space. The stresses of
modern life led people to seek comfort in new forms of leisure, from the amusement parks to department stores and nickelodeons. Among the most popular diversions were the daily newspapers, whose eye-catching headlines, graphic illustrations, and rectilinear columns mirrored both the chaos and the order of New
York's urban fabric. The weekly comics in the newspapers' Sunday supplements
supplied both light entertainment and an opportunity for readers to grapple with
the new experiences of modernity.

American newspaper comics emerged as a distinctive cultural phenomenon in
1895 with the appearance of R. F. Outcault's *Hogan's Alley,* featuring the Yellow
Kid. *Hogan's Alley* was not the first; earlier comic panels and caricatures, widespread in Europe, were presented in broadsheets, comic albums, pictorial papers,
and satirical journals. American newspaper comics were distinguished by their
use of color and recurring characters, which enhanced their popular appeal. Comics proliferated throughout the nation as newspaper barons competed with each
other for readers and printing processes were refined, resulting in eye-popping
color supplements in most major city newspapers. The comic strip's portability
and ephemerality were ideally suited to the early twentieth-century urban American. Despite—or perhaps due to—their accessibility, comic strips were devalued
by cultural elites from their inception. Resisting neat categorization, they represent a delicate marriage of words and pictures, as well as art and commerce.

Born in the Midwest, Winsor McCay began his formal career as a cartoonist in New York less than ten years after the debut of *Hogan's Alley.* His work was
soon singled out for its skillful draftsmanship and intricate detail, McCay's eye
for color, and his imaginative architectural forms. At a moment when cartoonists
were afforded the full space of a newspaper broadsheet, McCay was attentive to
the design of the whole page, constructing narrative and visual symmetries that
unified the comic's panels. His graceful lines and use of flat areas of color are reminiscent of art nouveau design. *Little Nemo's* richly embellished titles recall the
exuberance of circus posters, deploying bold, eye-catching lettering and decorative flourishes in order to capture the attention of distracted readers. McCay embraced the basic elements of the comic-strip form while drawing upon a range
of high and low cultural sources, simultaneously enlarging and reconfiguring the
narrative possibilities of comic art.

The first installment of McCay's epic fantasy, *Little Nemo in Slumberland,* features many essential components that distinguish the artist's work from those of
his contemporaries and illuminate the rich creative potential of the medium. The
comic's header presents a panoramic view of the kingdom of Slumberland, split
into three panels by two red columns that also function to frame the title panel.

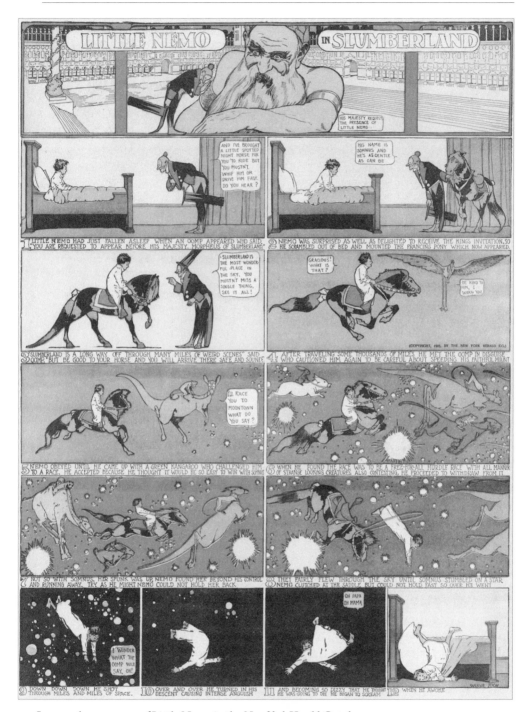

Inaugural appearance of Little Nemo in the *New York Herald*, October 15, 1905

Sunday Press Books

By extending a single scene across three panels the artist created an expansive view of the landscape, showcasing his detailed architectural tableaux. The title panel is conceived as a window frame, upon which the king's messenger stands as he is ordered to bring Nemo to Slumberland. King Morpheus's arm rests on the ledge, extending into the viewer's space and suggesting that the panel is a window onto another world. The larger-than-life presence of Morpheus looms over the events that unfold below, positioning the king at the story's threshold, mediating between the audience and the narrative space of the comic strip. As evident in this first episode, the artist was attentive to balance and symmetry; for example, the title lettering appears in two horizontal ovals on either side of the king's head, crossing the two red columns, which in turn line up neatly with the negative space dividing the panels in the bottom row.

Narration occurs at three levels. The story unfolds visually, through spoken dialogue, and in text panels below each image. The text panels are a conceit borrowed from children's storybooks. In later *Little Nemo* strips McCay would abandon them, relying solely on image and dialogue to advance the plot. Their early appearance here suggests he was still experimenting with comics and unsure of their capacity to carry a narrative.

McCay's use of line is never frenetic; the effect is that of stilled motion, as in a series of stop-motion photos or movie frames, rather than the looser, more dynamic drawing of George Herriman, the inventive artist behind *Krazy Kat,* whose pages vibrate with energy. The singular horse in motion on the gridded page recalls Eadweard Muybridge's sequential photographs of animal locomotion. However, McCay's eye for whimsy, evident in the shifting background colors and fantastic animals, evokes Muybridge's experiments as seen through a kaleidoscope. McCay had a fondness for optical toys and devices; he described finding inspiration for his designs in his children's flip books and his own stereograph collection. Inspired by new modes of visual experience, he also drew upon the work of earlier artists, including late nineteenth-century cartoonist A. B. Frost, whose comics depicting figures in motion appeared in *Harper's* and *Life* magazines.

A tenuous divide separates fantasy and terror in Slumberland, and the thrilling ride turns dangerous when Nemo loses control of his horse. The horse trips on a star and sends Nemo hurtling through space, falling through his reins like a diver heading into a pool. The final row of images includes four panels, while the previous rows contained two each. The four shorter panels indicate the increased speed at which Nemo is tumbling out of control. His bodily posture becomes increasingly awkward, the night sky grows more ominous, and Nemo cries out for his parents, thus successfully rousing himself from slumber. The final panel shows Nemo secure at home in his bedroom, half out of bed in midtumble with legs akimbo. This finale would be repeated each week throughout the entire run of the series, punctuating the comic strip and reassuring audiences that the previous panels were mere dreamscapes. Despite the terrors Nemo experiences in his dreams, he appears sad and wistful upon waking to reality. The dream world is dizzying and confusing, yet he still longs to return.

McCay varied the heights and widths of panels in Slumberland. This technique adds both visual interest and a temporal element, while calling to mind the disorienting landscapes of dreams, in which notions of time and place shift constantly. McCay was aware that prior to reading each panel in sequential order, viewers encounter the comic strip in its entirety; consequently, he was concerned with how the page design functioned as an overall image. Like film, comics are concerned with events unfolding in time. However, reading comics and watching films are very different visual experiences. Whereas a director controls how and when a cinematic narrative develops, a comic-strip artist has less power over the reader's temporal experience. The whole page is available to the viewer, who is in command of how quickly the story develops. McCay was interested in demonstrating how the comic strip can allow us to rethink our understanding of time by slowing down the action of a galloping horse or a buzzing mosquito. He imagined the possibilities that comic strips and animation had for revealing a world unavailable in photos or on film.

Another example of McCay's formal innovations occurs in his comic *Little Sammy Sneeze,* a six-panel set that follows a small boy whose potent sneezes leave a trail of mayhem in his wake. On September 24, 1905, three weeks before the debut of *Little Nemo,* McCay employed this single-joke premise as a means of exploding comic-strip conventions. The comic focuses on Sammy's dull face in close-up just as a sneeze erupts, calling to mind the Kinetoscope film of a man sneezing produced by Thomas Edison's studio in 1894. Sammy sneezes with his entire body; his utterances grow larger and more emphatic in each frame, interjecting an element of sound onto the page. When the sneeze finally explodes from his mouth it succeeds in breaking the frame of the panel into pieces resembling shards of glass. After the panel is shattered Sammy seems able to see his audience, his blank gaze meeting ours. As in the title panel of the first *Little Nemo* episode, the panels of *Sammy Sneeze* are conceived as a glass frame. The frame establishes the viewer's relationship to the world within its borders; by destroying the frame McCay deconstructs the traditional relationship between viewer and subject. Such experiments reveal the artist's propensity for interrogating the structural language of the comic strip; they also reveal the potential for mass cultural art forms to disclose the means of their construction.

A darker, more absurdist mode of humor is apparent in McCay's *Dreams of the Rarebit Fiend,* conceived as a series of adult nightmares brought on by overindulging in Welsh rarebit. On one occasion the comic strip is rendered from the perspective of a man being buried alive. Invoking a scene out of Edgar Allan Poe, the poor man must watch helplessly as onlookers berate him and dirt is hurled upon his grave. Such perspectival devices place the viewer in the position of the man in the coffin, demonstrating again McCay's preoccupation with the audience's relationship to the scene depicted.

McCay's protagonists are rarely defined by strong personalities. Nemo, from the Latin meaning "no one," is a passive actor in his dreams. Sammy is defined only by his sneezes. The rarebit dreamers are entirely anonymous. It is possible to conclude that the artist's strengths lay in spectacular draftsmanship rather than character development—but the total absence of personality is so deliberate as to suggest that McCay conceived of his protagonists as blank canvases on which the viewer could project his or her own desires and anxieties.

While fantasy is often assumed to be an escapist medium, Winsor McCay used the iconography of popular urban entertainment to bring his visions to life. Doing so allowed him to illustrate both the lures and potential snares of this new fantasyland of mass culture. While Slumberland is an intoxicating locale, it is not a utopia. McCay was finely tuned to the pleasures and pitfalls of twentieth-century capitalism, a system on which his livelihood depended. By pointing to the dark, dangerous side of dreaming, McCay revealed the slippery intersection of fantasy and commerce. He underscored the tension between dreams and the reality of the displaced urban subject; his anonymous protagonists embodied the ideal consumer: passive, yielding, and never satisfied. McCay's use of the comic art medium was highly self-reflexive and ambivalent. He produced a dreamland shaped by the visual language of modern urban experience.

A young boy performs acrobatics through space, tumbling with an apparent lack of control and calling out to those beacons of safety and home, "oh papa, oh mama." The scene ends where it began, in a child's bedroom. Nemo awakens to find he has fallen halfway out of bed and is tangled up in sheets. Slumberland has vanished; only Nemo's face, his wide oval mouth and raised eyebrows, give a hint of his nocturnal adventures. It is a world of magic and color and wonder; tantalizing and terrifying and ultimately out of our reach.

Bibliography: Scott Bukatman, *Matters of Gravity: Special Effects and Supermen in the 20th Century* (Durham, NC, 2003). John Canemaker, *Winsor McCay: His Life and Art* (New York, 1987). Ian Gordon, *Comic Strips and Consumer Culture, 1890–1945* (Washington, DC, 1998). Scott McCloud, *Understanding Comics* (New York, 1994).

KERRY ROEDER

1906, April 9

William J. Seymour, an African American preacher, and seven others fall to the floor in a humble mission in Los Angeles and begin speaking in tongues

THE AZUSA STREET REVIVAL

A crowd gathered, and one more strange thing happened: one of the seven, a woman with no musical training, is said to have started playing a standup piano with great accomplishment, and singing in what was taken to be Hebrew. In Los Angeles at the beginning of the twentieth century, an outbreak of speaking in tongues turned very quickly into a national phenomenon, and then a global one. At the Azusa Street revival in Los Angeles in 1906, the Pentecostal faith discovered its voice.

At the center of the revival was William Seymour, a Louisiana-born son of freed slaves. He was a short, stocky man, blind in one eye. For a religious movement that frequently thrived on charismatic personalities, Seymour was strikingly subdued. Arthur Osterberg, who became a leader at Seymour's mission, described him as "meek and plain spoken and no orator. He might preach for three-quarters of an hour with no more emotionalism than that there post."

In 1905 Seymour had encountered a Methodist healer named Charles Fox Parham. The itinerant Parham had joined the Holiness movement, an offshoot of Methodism that believes in the blessing known as sanctification. Originally the moment when the Holy Spirit made its presence felt, sanctification became understood as a flooding of holy power that leads to an immense sensation of spiritual cleansing, purity, and light. Sanctification became an article of faith among a fringe within Protestantism during the nineteenth century; it also became known as the "second blessing."

In Topeka, Kansas, in 1900, one of Parham's students experienced "the gift of tongues" on the last day of the year, allegedly speaking in Chinese. Parham's Apostolic Faith movement heralded the account of the Day of Pentecost described in the New Testament, in Acts of the Apostles 2, in which the followers of Jesus were filled with the Holy Ghost and "began to speak with other tongues, as the Spirit gave them utterance." They made a leap: since this had happened at the first Holy Ghost baptism, tongues should accompany all true iterations of the baptismal experience. As religious scholar Grant Wacker has described it,

> For the Kansas zealots the answer presented itself with the force of an epiphany: speaking in tongues *always* accompanied Holy Ghost baptism, first as an audible sign of the Holy Ghost's presence, second as a tool for evangelism. This claim, unique in the history of Christianity, defined a relatively rare, relatively difficult physical activity or skill as a nonnegotiable hallmark of a fully developed Christian life. Not incidentally, it also defined believers who did not speak in tongues as second-class Christians. By definition they had not received the coveted baptism experience.

By 1905 Parham was teaching in Houston, Texas, where Seymour encountered him. Seymour only had one foot in Parham's school; as a black man, he was denied full admittance to Parham's segregated classroom, though Parham permitted him to sit in the hallway and listen through a door left cracked open.

Speaking in tongues, or glossolalia, has existed throughout history—Montanists, Anabaptists, Quakers, Shakers, Molokan Spirit Jumpers, early Mormons, and nineteenth-century small-town spiritualists all upon occasion broke out in languages not their own. At an 1801 camp meeting that signaled the start of the Second Great Awakening, glossolalia erupted spontaneously. Tongues tended to be a fringe phenomenon for such groups, but the Topeka movement centralized the experience. Still, in Parham's congregations, it was more prayed for than felt. It was not until Seymour had left Parham's tutelage and traveled west that it would become fully alive in the world.

On February 22, 1906, Seymour came to Los Angeles at the invitation of a black Holiness congregation. Though he was a mild, somewhat fumbling man, he quickly stirred up trouble. Seymour's beliefs turned out to be too radical for a

church that was itself far outside the mainstream—its members' belief in sanctification had already gotten the group thrown out of their Baptist church before
Seymour arrived. His unorthodox teachings—his belief that in order to receive
the Holy Ghost's blessing one first needed to speak in tongues—in turn got Seymour evicted from his house on Bonnie Brae Street in a black neighborhood on
the edge of downtown. A revolution was afoot, though, and worse things than
evictions happen in revolutions. Seymour slogged on, adrift and without a ticket
home, taking shelter in another home on Bonnie Brae Street.

On Azusa Street, he opened a church without a name. Seymour simply took
along those who had come to the meetings on Bonnie Brae, those who had
brought down the divine fire, as the baptism is called, and started preaching.
What followed came to be known as the Azusa Street revival: for three and a half
years, round the clock, an experience that was the distillation of something purely
democratic, or maybe purely anarchic, transpired. Nobody knew what would
happen next, except that the divine fire kept falling, and people spoke in tongues
they had never known before. It was said folks spontaneously broke into ancient
tongues, as well as Bohemian, Kree, Chinese. Azusa Street launched the Pentecostal movement; within three years, word of the revival had circled the globe.

Today Pentecostalism is part of the establishment, from former attorney general John Ashcroft on down. Many think of televangelists, of Oral Roberts and
Jim and Tammy and, perhaps, rebel-girl Sister Aimee Semple McPherson. But before any of those folks, at its birth on Azusa Street, Pentecostalism was a poor
people's movement. The building Seymour used had formerly housed the first African Methodist Episcopal Church in Los Angeles, and then a tombstone shop,
and then a stable. The door and windows were broken, the rooms full of trash.
Seymour and associates cleaned the place up and scattered sawdust about, then
placed planks across nail kegs for seating. The walls of the Azusa Street building
were lined with tin mailboxes, in which visitors could place donations. Upstairs
was a small tarrying room, with rows of canes and crutches that had been tossed
off by the healed, along with pipes left by cured smokers.

There were no prayer books, no collections, no programs or prepared sermons. Spontaneity ruled. Services happened whenever they happened: it could
be 5:00 a.m. or 5:00 in the evening. Participants convulsed when the spirit hit,
and others held on while strange words flowed. Laypeople as well as clergy could
take the stand and deliver a sermon. Power was being radically decentralized,
scattered among the seats like the sawdust. One eyewitness described the scene:
"Prayer and worship were everywhere. The altar area was filled with seekers; some
kneeling; others were prone on the floor; some were speaking in tongues. Everyone was doing something, all seemingly were lost in God."

Glenn A. Cook was working as a newspaperman and part-time preacher in
1906. He visited Seymour's mission, and the intimacy of the place—where strangers touched strangers and noise lifted the roof—seemed "heretical" to him. A little later, he revisited, this time seeking to cast off "pre-conceived ideas," he wrote.
The force that shot through him he compared to "electric needles." He became
"limp as a piece of cloth." For five weeks he experienced the same Holy Ghost

power, a feeling that left him "sweet and clean," as in a "washing machine." He woke up one Saturday morning, his arms reaching heavenward, and felt "shaken violently by a great power." It was as if his head had been removed and a "large pipe" had been fitted upon his neck: energy coursed into him. Acknowledging there were no words for what was happening, Cook wrote that it all felt like the "action of a pump under terrific pressure, filling me with oil." This feeling first engorged his toes, then moved up until he sensed he might explode. He felt his spirit departing, wafting through the air while his body became "hard and metallic like iron." Thirty hours later, he said, "I began to stutter and then out came a distinct language which I could hardly restrain. I talked and laughed with joy far into the night."

A new spirit with sweeping social, even political overtones was surfacing. One change was, the mission was unusually open to women, who were free to testify. They too received Holy Ghost baptism, and they healed others and witnessed. Second, since only the individual could trigger the experience of glossolalia, not the clergy, the individual's relationship with God was direct and total—church structure and ritual were largely beside the point.

Who were the folks in the pews? They were overwhelmingly laborers, domestics, the poor, newcomers to the West who had not been assimilated into the Los Angeles's social fabric. In this vortex they found a home.

The local authorities took note, and lashed back. A 1906 article in the *Los Angeles Times* declared:

> Breathing strange utterances and mouthing a creed which it would seem no sane mortal could understand, the newest religious sect has started in Los Angeles. Meetings are held in a tumble-down shack on Azusa Street . . . devotees of the weird doctrine practice the most fanatical rites, preach the wildest theories and work themselves into a state of mad excitement in their peculiar zeal. Colored people and a sprinkling of whites compose the congregation, and night is made hideous in the neighborhood by the howlings of the worshippers who spend hours swaying forth and back in a nerve-racking attitude of prayer and supplication.

Church members were arrested for preaching on downtown streets, put on chain gangs, and in hospitals for the insane. "We are charged," one arrestee said with palpable pride, "with using boisterous language, [and making] unusual noise." The Los Angeles Police Department tried to shut the mission down; the child welfare office sought to close it because children were running around day and night; the health department cited it too.

A raw democracy was apparent in the mission. And at this mission founded and maintained by blacks (and, some scholars have emphasized, African American *women*), a radical racial harmony prevailed for a time. Seymour ministered to a congregation that included blacks and whites, Mexicans, Russians, and an increasing number of others from around the world. Racial distinctions were explicitly put aside: "The color line," wrote one white participant, "was washed away in the blood." "In the beginning, color meant nothing to us," another member wrote. "There were no blacks and no whites . . . It was God's Spirit welding us together, and that is a kind of unity that you can't define." "Everybody was just the same," explained another; "it did not matter if you were black, white, green, or grizzly."

Gaston Barnabas Cashwell, a blond-haired evangelist from Dunn, North Carolina, came to witness Seymour's integrated service. If the mixing of races wasn't shocking enough to him, having a young black man put his hand on Cashwell's head and pray for him to be baptized certainly was. The Southern gentleman said the experience caused "chills to go down my spine"—not the experience of the Second Blessing, that is, but that of being handled so familiarly by a Negro. He recoiled, but having traveled so far and being reluctant to leave, Cashwell lingered and—feeling emboldened—eventually asked black congregants to lay their hands on his head in order for him to be filled. Cashwell began speaking in German. A believer now filled with the fire, he took Azusa Street back to North Carolina and attempted to minister to integrated congregations there.

Azusa Street looked like integration in action. But to fully understand what was happening there, and to understand Pentecostalism's success and incredible spread around the world, it is necessary to weigh how the revival made contact with East African religion—and how it broke faith with Protestantism. Because in this alley of downtown Los Angeles there flourished—accidentally, clandestinely—a sense of divinity brought over in slave ships.

The accounts by whites at Azusa Street form a parable of what could happen when Europe unguardedly merged with Africa in the new country. Consider the recollection of Florence Crawford. On her first visit to the mission, Crawford felt nothing for a while, described a frustrating sense of boredom. "I went in and sat down," she wrote. "They sang a little, but that didn't seem to touch my heart. They went down in prayer; but that didn't move me at all. Pretty soon they got up, and they sang again. Finally a big black man got up on his feet and said, 'Hallelujah!' It just went into my soul. He waited a minute and again he said, 'Hallelujah!' I said, 'God, I have heard the voice from Heaven. I have heard it at last.' You say, 'Is there anything in a Hallelujah?' Yes, there is a lot in it when it has the Spirit back of it."

A lot changed in just a few short years. The mission sorted out along racial lines, and old enmities reasserted themselves. Early visitors to Azusa Street went on to form numerous branches of modern Pentecostalism. The Church of God in Christ, perhaps the largest black church in America today, traces its roots back to Azusa; today there are, by one estimate, some ten million Pentecostals in the United States, and one in four Christians on earth is said to be Pentecostal, by one unlikely estimate. No one knows the true number.

Bibliography: Larry Martin, ed., *Holy Ghost Revival on Azusa Street: The True Believers: Eye Witness Accounts of the Revival That Shook the World* (Joplin, MO, 1997). R. J. Smith, *The Great Black Way: L.A. in the 1940s and the Lost African American Renaissance* (New York, 2006). Vinson Synan, *The Holiness-Pentecostal Tradition: Charismatic Movements in the Twentieth Century* (Grand Rapids, MI, 1997). Grant Wacker, *Heaven Below: Early Pentecostals and American Culture* (Cambridge, MA, 2001).

RJ SMITH

1906, April 18, 5:14 a.m.

Jack London tells his wife, "I'll never write a word about it. What use trying?"

THE SAN FRANCISCO EARTHQUAKE

In March of 1906, Jack London was finishing *Before Adam,* the serialized tale of an ancestral band of semihumans living in a primeval California forest. The narrator recalls his previous life as a member of the Folk, a clan threatened by the primitive and brutish "Tree People" and also by an evolutionarily advanced group of "Fire People" who are destined to conquer and destroy them.

In June, London began another time-travel fable, this one set in the future. *The Iron Heel* culminates in an apocalyptic class war in which Chicago becomes a wasteland of death and destruction. Like the Folk in the earlier story, London's protagonists (a group of revolutionary socialists) are crushed between two powers: in this case, capitalist oligarchs and "the people of the abyss"—the masses of ordinary "slaves," whom London describes as "the refuse and scum of life." This triangulated evolutionary schema was a favorite London theme, and expressed not only a social Darwinist perspective fairly common among intellectuals of his era but London's own identification with an imagined figure—a superman—who possesses both the animal strength of the lower orders and the superior intelligence of an advanced "specimen." In both works, London's male hero and his female companion find themselves nearly alone as they witness the destruction of their community and their world.

In April, London and his wife experienced a real version of this scene as they walked through the burning ruins of San Francisco. "That night," Charmian London wrote, "proved our closest to realizing a dream that came now and again to Jack in sleep, that he and I were in at the finish of all things—standing or moving hand in hand through chaos to its brink, looking upon the rest of mankind in the process of dissolution."

Jack and Charmian were living fifty miles north of San Francisco in the small town of Glen Ellen when "at a quarter past five came the earthquake." They ran outside to a barn they rented at a nearby ranch, rounded up the horses that were "quivering and skittish," and rode to the construction site at their Beauty Ranch several miles away to find the walls of their half-built barn cracked and splintered. A "lurid tower" of smoke was already visible from fires burning in the distance, and within hours the Londons boarded a train headed south to see the damage that had been inflicted on Jack's birthplace. As most folks were fleeing the city for areas north and east, the Londons ferried into San Francisco and spent the night exploring what indeed looked like "the end of the world."

Though Charmian says that London had no intention of writing about the earthquake ("I'll never write a word about it. What use trying? One could only string big words together, and curse the futility of them"), he eventually agreed to send a 2,500-word eyewitness report to *Collier's Magazine.* In 1906, London was the most famous and successful writer in America—the first American to become a millionaire from his writing, though he was always struggling financially. At twenty-five cents a word, London's earthquake essay was compensated at the most lucrative rate he was ever to earn.

London may have been right about the futility of words to represent the immensity of the disaster: nonetheless, millions of words were written. One of the most noteworthy pieces was written by William James, who was teaching at Stanford that spring. James reported that his own immediate emotion when the earthquake hit was not fear but "pure delight and welcome"; he went on to theorize that people experience "mental pathos and anguish" from a distance, but at the "scene of the action" often respond as he had, with "healthy animal insensibility and heartiness."

Magazines, pamphlets, and quickie books flooded the nation. Fabricated accounts of horrific deaths, the desecration of corpses, race riots, looting, and whole communities disappearing into the sea were part of the outpouring of words that the historian Philip Fradkin claims still constitutes a record for a single disaster. An equally inaccurate counternarrative, portraying San Francisco as "imperishable," "undaunted," a picture of orderliness and cooperation, appeared almost instantly. The San Francisco business class, particularly the owners of Southern Pacific Railroad, organized a "campaign of cultural disinformation" to downplay the danger of earthquakes and deny the extent of the disaster.

London was one of the first to say that the death toll from the quake and fire would never be known. The best estimates now indicate that between 3,000 and 5,000 people were killed. That number is significantly fewer than the 8,000 to 10,000 people who died six years earlier when a hurricane and flood devastated Galveston, Texas. But for a number of reasons, the San Francisco quake and firestorm came to define for Americans the modern picture of apocalypse. Panoramas at the 1904 St. Louis World's Fair looked backward, envisioning Galveston as a biblical disaster; the images of San Francisco after the fire look forward to Dresden or Hiroshima. If the Old Testament world had drowned for its sins, the modern industrial world would end in bombs and firestorms, smoke and rubble, looting, vigilantism, and refugees.

It makes sense that the San Francisco quake would become the model of modern disaster. Galveston had a population of 42,000. San Francisco was a big city—in London's words, "an imperial city"—and the event left more than half of its population of 400,000 homeless. Property damage from the quake and firestorm amounted to between 1.3 percent and 1.8 percent of the nation's gross domestic product, proportionally higher than any other natural disaster in American history, and created an international economic aftershock that contributed to the Panic of 1907 and a 40 percent drop in U.S. industrial output.

When Jerry Falwell and Pat Robertson linked the terrorist attacks of September 11, 2001, with God's wrath at the immorality of a liberalism identified with San Francisco, they were echoing a theme voiced in 1906: San Francisco, awash in sex and sin, secularism and hubris, had called down God's punishment. But most San Franciscans, then as now, rejected the notion of a biblical curse—as one advertisement asked, "If, as some say, God spanked the town for being over-frisky, why did he knock the churches down and save Hotaling's Whiskey?" Instead of inspiring religious reform, the trauma of 1906 intensified the view that modernity is a maelstrom of social, political, and technological upheaval, an accelerating spectacle of change.

"San Francisco is gone . . . All the cunning adjustments of a twentieth century city . . . all the shrewd contrivances and safeguards of man had been thrown out of gear by thirty seconds' twitching of the earth-crust." So wrote London in *Collier's* a month after the earthquake; unlike William James, London did not find many "hearty" San Franciscans walking the streets. "While the whole city crashed and roared into ruin," London wrote, people were "quiet." The fire "advanced" and "raged" as it outflanked firefighters, "surged up from behind" and "surrounded" its victims—but people "crept" quietly down streets or stood "watching calmly." "I saw not one woman who wept, not one man who was excited, not one person who was in the slightest degree panic stricken." London's earthquake essay was not his best writing, but it remains interesting today because it deployed a number of themes that can be traced throughout London's work: the struggle between energy and entropy, the disconnection of movement from human volition, and the interpenetration of bodies and machines that, for London, define the modern world. The violent motion of the earth had, in an instant, brought to a stop the seemingly perpetual movement of modern urban life, exposing the powerlessness of even the most "shrewd and cunning" advancements of the twentieth century to control and harness speed, to regulate the natural world with science or modern planning. Among the most memorable images from 1906 are photographs of people, in up-to-date suits and hats and dress coats, standing like frozen statues—calm, motionless, waiting as the devastation advances toward them.

Even as writers like London looked for words to describe how a whole city "crashed and roared into ruin," postcards, photographs, and films created a visual history that constructed the iconography of a modern urban disaster that still dominates the popular imagination. Jack and Charmian themselves took a number of stunning photographs: a view from the ferry as it approached the burning city, the wreckage along Market Street, and the skeleton of City Hall. They were not alone: the San Francisco quake, Fradkin writes, "attracted the single greatest use of cameras and film since their invention." *Sunset Magazine,* part of the commercial empire of Southern Pacific, attempted to frame the image of San Francisco after the quake with a gorgeous cover by the celebrated illustrator Maynard Dixon that showed a beautiful young woman with flowing hair rising out of ruins, arms encircling a new and glorious city—but the most popular images depicted spectacular devastation. Thousands of amateurs and professionals rushed in, seeking to record dramatic vistas of broken buildings, dead animals, mounds of rubble, and blackened ruins.

The disaster inspired a mini–gold rush for those eager to capitalize on the visual drama of the ruins. Still breathtaking are the panoramic shots taken from hot-air balloons that document the extent of the damage across the city, creating a visual topography of destruction that "the world would not see again," as one writer put it, "until the atomic bombing of Hiroshima in 1945."

The centennial anniversary of the 1906 quake and fire was the occasion for the republication of hundreds of photographic and film images, and it is surprising to see how familiar they look. It is as if we have seen them many times before. And we have.

In the movie *San Francisco,* made in 1936, Mary Blake (Jeanette MacDonald) and Blackie Norton (Clark Gable) lead a group of survivors to the crest of a hill to look down on the city just as the last fire is extinguished. The people spontaneously burst into song. As "The Battle Hymn of the Republic" slides into "San Francisco, Open Your Golden Gate," the city below is transformed from an utter ruin to the present-day (1936) metropolis. The actual earthquake came in two jolts and lasted a little less than a minute. The film's montage of buildings crashing, water lines bursting, and people being buried in showers of bricks, jumping out of crumbling skyscrapers, or falling into huge fissures lasts several minutes. In the following scenes, San Francisco becomes a virtual war zone: a spectacle of flames, explosions, rubble, and death.

In the film, the earthquake that ruptured the earth annihilates the sinful San Francisco, but it mends the class rift between the Barbary Coast saloon owner and the wholesome daughter of a minister. It also mends relations with God. In the end, the quake brings Blackie to his knees in prayer, watched by an exceedingly satisfied priest (Spencer Tracy). But film endings are often beside the point. However obsessively the film gestures to hope and spiritual renewal in its last three minutes, it cannot erase the images of destruction it evoked.

The utility of catastrophe for romantic reconciliation is a plot device that long predates the film, but it serves to focus the issue: the cultural transmission of the earthquake and firestorm makes visible the historically specific terms of modern disasters. Born in 1906, and reenergized in 1911 when the *Titanic* went down, modern disaster narratives register anxiety about technological progress, human agency, and the nature of modernity itself. Pompeii was buried because the gods were angry. But what if the gods don't care one way or the other, or simply do not exist?

The city was a "waste of smoking ruins. Here and there, through the smoke, creeping warily under the shadows of tottering walls emerged occasional men and women. It was like the meeting of the handful of survivors after the day of the end of the world." This vision from London's essay could have been the script for the final scene of *The Day After,* the 1983 TV movie that imagined the immediate aftermath of a nuclear war. We see Dr. Russell Oakes (Jason Robards) creeping through the skeletal remains of Kansas City: an ashen landscape of rubble and twisted wreckage. Supposedly based on photographs of Japanese cities devastated by atomic bombs, the scene looked strangely anachronistic, more like the aftermath of 1906 than the possible outcome of a late twentieth-century nuclear war—a fact acknowledged in the film's final scroll, reminding us that a contemporary atomic catastrophe would likely be far more complete than anything shown on the screen. But it was not entirely inappropriate for a 1980s apocalyptic fantasy to quote images of urban disaster from nearly a hundred years before. Seven months before the San Francisco quake, Albert Einstein published a paper on special relativity that would open a chasm between the past and the future, producing a scientific tremor of vast magnitude. Humans may not have the power to control the rupture of the earth's crust, but they would split the atom, uniting the destructive power of nature with modern technology, rendering the apocalyptic scenarios of naturalist writers like London terrifyingly prescient.

Four days after the quake, a *San Francisco Examiner* editorial announced that in spite of the "catastrophe that descended upon San Francisco without warning," conditions were "marvelous." Indeed, the city would not only be rebuilt but "would be known as the most beautiful and attractive city in the wonderland of California." My favorite centennial book about the disaster, *A Crack in the Edge of the World,* by Simon Winchester, ends with wonder, not at the undeniable beauty of San Francisco, not at the power of nature, but at the hubris of people who continue to live so unthinkingly, so nonchalantly, in places like the Bay Area.

When the one-hundredth anniversary of the San Francisco earthquake was observed in 2006, seismic retrofitting companies in the Bay Area reported an upswing in demand for their services, and some folks, like me, were inspired to check the condition of earthquake-preparedness kits that had been buried in closets for decades.

But even with the frequent reminders that come to us in the form of minor tremors every few weeks, Bay Area residents seem little worried about the fact that another Big One is due any time now. Sometimes we shrug fatalistically: "Whatever happens, happens." Sometimes we are comforted by elaborate color-coded geological maps promising that our own house sits atop an orangish-yellow zone instead of a red one. Sometimes we get a thrill out of our shared nonchalance, as if our addresses make us slightly more like action heroes than those who live in safe and stable areas. Mostly, I think, we deal with living in the Bay Area in much the same way that folks living in Japan, or in the shadow of Mount Etna, or in the path of Gulf Coast hurricanes, or in the great South Asian monsoon belt deal with knowledge of the catastrophic inevitable: with a combination of low-level anxiety and concentrated denial.

Bibliography: Leonard Cassuto and Jeanne Reesman, ed., *Rereading Jack London* (Stanford, CA, 1996). Philip Fradkin, *The Great Earthquake and Firestorms of 1906* (Berkeley, 2005). Gladys Hansen and Emmet Condon, *Denial of Disaster* (San Francisco, 1989). Charmian London, *The Book of Jack London* (New York, 1921). Jack London, "The Story of an Eye-Witness," *Collier's* 37 (May 5, 1906). Kerry Odell and Mark Weidenmier, "Real Shock, Monetary Aftershock: The San Francisco Earthquake and the Panic of 1907," Claremont Working Papers in Economics, 2001. Simon Winchester, *A Crack in the Edge of the World* (New York, 2005).

KATHLEEN MORAN

1911

The biggest hit Tin Pan Alley had ever seen

"Alexander's Ragtime Band"

When "Alexander's Ragtime Band" became a hit in 1911, it established Irving Berlin as America's premiere songwriter and made ragtime part of mainstream popular music. Both Berlin and ragtime had arrived on the American scene at the same time. In 1893, the family of Moses and Leah Baline emigrated from Russia and settled into the poverty of New York's Lower East Side. Moses, who had been a cantor in Russia, had to work as a housepainter to support his family, and all the children pitched in, including five-year-old Israel, who delivered telegrams, sold newspapers, and worked in a sweatshop sewing buttons. When Moses Baline died in 1901, "Izzy" struck out on his own and lived on the streets of the Bowery as a busker, singing popular songs of the day in hopes that passersby would throw a few coins his way.

He found a steady job as a singing waiter in the Pelham Café in Chinatown. A combination opium den, brothel, and saloon, the Pelham was a rough place, but cherubic Izzy Baline charmed customers with his rendition of current sentimental ballads, especially with his risqué parodies of their lyrics. There he would have known the new style of music called ragtime, or "noodles," as it was played by such gifted black pianists as Luckey Roberts. The roots of ragtime are obscure, but it seems to have originated in the brothels of New Orleans as a swinging piano style inspired by African American imitations of European classical parlor-piano music and the steady oom-pah beat of American brass bands. It combined a syncopated melody with a strict duple-time accompaniment, the left hand thumping out a steady two-beat accompaniment while the right hand came in slightly before or after the beat to give the melody a sprightly flourish.

As ragtime spread northward up the Mississippi in the 1880s, composers such as Scott Joplin of Missouri crafted stately piano compositions structured on classical themes and variations. Ragtime came to the attention of the general public at the 1893 Chicago World's Fair (officially called "The World's Columbian Exposition" to mark the four-hundredth anniversary of the voyage of Columbus), which attracted twenty-seven million visitors. The novel musical style was quickly appropriated by Tin Pan Alley, a nickname given to the area around Broadway and 28th Street in New York where many sheet-music publishing firms had their offices at the turn of the century. Unlike older music publishers around the country which specialized in church hymnals and music instruction books, publishing an occasional song once it had become popular, the new publishers sold only popular songs and believed a song could be *made* popular through plugging—which could range from bribing a vaudeville star to use your company's song in her act to sending singing pluggers out to street corners, Coney Island, Bowery saloons—anywhere there was a crowd—to demonstrate your firm's latest wares. Their success was dramatically demonstrated in 1892 when a Tin Pan Alley song, "After the Ball" by Charles K. Harris, sold one million copies of sheet music. By contrast, Stephen Foster would have considered sheet-music sales of 75,000 copies of one of his songs—after it had been popularized through minstrel shows—a huge success.

In the hands of Tin Pan Alley's publishers, ragtime became the basis of "coon songs," rhythmic songs that caricatured African Americans in the minstrel show tradition. But where minstrel show blackface performers longed for antebellum days in the likes of "The Old Folks at Home" and "Carry Me Back to Old Virginny," coon songs portrayed blacks as belligerent lawbreakers or sexually aggressive lovers. In "Mister Johnson, Turn Me Loose," for example, the singer pleads with "Mr. Johnson" (a slang term for the police), "Don't take me to the calaboose." In "You've Been a Good Old Wagon But You Done Broke Down" the singer laments that his "wagon"—his woman—has lost her sexual drive. Demeaning as such songs were, they injected a new musical energy and colloquial wit into popular song, which had been dominated by genteel, lachrymose waltzes such as "The Letter That Never Came" and "A Bird in a Gilded Cage." Thus a coon song could contain such forthright statements as "All I want is lovin'—I don't want your money": a declaration that would be unthinkable in a sentimental ballad portraying white lovers.

In the early twentieth century, coon songs were joined by songs about ethnic groups—Italians, Germans, Jews—that had entered America in large numbers in the closing decades of the nineteenth century. These songs also parodied ethnic stereotypes, and it was with such numbers that Israel Baline made the transition from singing waiter to songwriter. In 1907, when the owner of the Pelham Café learned that a singing waiter and piano player at a rival saloon had written a hit song, "My Mariucci Take a Steamboat," he ordered Baline and pianist Nick Nicholson to write a hit of their own. What they came up with, in 1907, was "Marie from Sunny Italy." Berlin claimed that it was a printer's error that listed his name on the sheet as "I. Berlin," but he adopted the name "Irving Berlin" from then on.

While he had started out as a lyricist, Berlin soon began composing music as well. He had taught himself to play on the Pelham Café piano, but he could only play in the key of F-sharp, which consists largely of black keys. Eventually he would purchase a transposing piano, which allowed one to play in a single key and then, with the flip of a lever, hear how a melody sounded in other keys. Armed with what he called his "Buick," Berlin could play his melodies for a musical "secretary," who, since Berlin could not read music, would take them down in musical notation. Soon Berlin was producing hit songs, such as "Dorando," about an Italian Olympic runner who loses the marathon because the night before the race he eats "da Irish beef-a-stew" instead of "da spaghetti," and "Sadie Salome Go Home," about a Jewish girl who dances the scandalous Dance of the Seven Veils, to her boyfriend Mose's consternation.

In these same years, Berlin wrote ragtime coon songs, such as "Wild Cherries Rag" (1909) where "looney coons" and "spooney coons" are aroused by ragtime music. In "Alexander and His Clarinet" (1910), Berlin draws upon the comedy of an African American sporting such a grandiose name as "Alexander" and the phallic implications of a clarinet that he plays "with vim" and "like sin" until his girlfriend beseeches him to stay because "I love your clarinet." Such songs were censured by upholders of traditional morality, who saw ragtime at the center of a cultural upheaval brought on by immigration, industrialization, and urbanization. The New York City Committee of Fourteen's *Report on the Social Evil* for 1910, for example, warned that "youth is gravitating toward the city, away from home, religious and personal ideals, breaking the moorings of the past." The report blamed much of this decay on "those ungoverned, unlicensed, unregulated amusement resorts [such as] movies, vaudeville, ragtime, and cabarets." As Lewis Erenberg speculates, the fear of ragtime "suggests that many urbanites feared the rising tide of immigrant and black-inspired culture at a time when their own culture was in the midst of change."

Irving Berlin's greatest ragtime song would transform the public image of the music. He was shaving; "A melody came to me right out of the air," he recalled, yet he thought little of it. He made a memo about a song called "Alexander" and set it aside. Later, as he was going over his notes in his publishing-house office, he found the memo, recalled the strain of notes, and completed the melody. "I wrote the whole thing in eighteen minutes," he claimed, "surrounded on all sides by roaring pianos and roaring vaudeville actors."

"Alexander's Ragtime Band" was introduced in vaudeville. Vaudeville had replaced the nineteenth-century minstrel show and its ensemble performances with variety shows that emphasized one individual act after another—singers, dancers, but also acrobats and animal acts—all of which needed music and, hence, the wares of Tin Pan Alley. By the early twentieth century, vaudeville spanned the country with a circuit of more than a thousand theaters. When coon-shouter Emma Carus (who always opened her blackface act by saying, "I'm not pretty but I'm good to my folks") belted out "Alexander's Ragtime Band" in Chicago's American Music Hall, it became a sensation.

Soon vaudeville managers were besieged, with every act on the bill, from singers to acrobats to dog shows, wanting to use "Alexander's Ragtime Band." One manager had to instruct four of the five acts on his bill to "cut that band song out." By the end of the year, "Alexander's Ragtime Band" had sold a million copies of sheet music, then another million in 1912 as it spread across Europe. It was the biggest hit Tin Pan Alley had ever seen.

"Alexander's Ragtime Band" redefined the nature of American popular songs. Most nineteenth-century songs were strophic, consisting of verses that outlined a narrative ("In a cavern, in a canyon, excavating for a mine, lived a miner . . .") punctuated by brief eight-bar refrains ("Oh, my darlin', oh, my darlin', oh, my darlin' Clementine . . ."). With "Alexander's Ragtime Band," Berlin established a song pattern that would dominate popular music for the next fifty years. Although he began with a verse ("Oh, my honey, oh, my honey, better hurry and let's meander . . ."), it was very brief and, rather than relating a narrative, simply introduced the refrain, or, as it came to be called, the chorus. Initially Berlin had written a second verse but omitted it from the sheet music to place more emphasis on the chorus. And the chorus was thirty-two bars long, double or even quadruple the length of refrains in older songs. Those thirty-two bars are divided into four eight-bar sections in which an initial A melody is heard for eight bars, then a B melody is introduced for the next eight bars, then the A melody is repeated with some variation, then a new C melody completes the final eight bars. Such a thirty-two bar chorus—usually in an AABA pattern but also ABAB, ABAC, and occasionally, as in Berlin's "Always" (1925), ABCD—would become the standard form for popular songs.

Although there is little true ragtime syncopation in "Alexander's Ragtime Band," Berlin manages to use musical accents to distort verbal ones in a kind of "ragging" of music *against* words, distorting the normal accent of "*na*tural," for example, into "natur*al*" to make it rhyme with "call" in "They can play a bugle *call* like you never heard before / So natur*al* that you want to go to war." In the same phrase he subtly rhymes the first two syllables of "natural" ("nat-u") with "that you." At another point, in a line from the fourth eight-bar section of the chorus, "And if you care to hear the Swanee River played in ragtime," he places the seemingly unimportant word "in" on an octave interval that gives it a ragged emphasis.

The staggering popularity of "Alexander's Ragtime Band" made ragtime ingratiating, not threatening. "'Come on and hear! Come on and hear!'" Berlin said, "were an *invitation* to 'come,' to join in, and 'hear' the singer and his song. And that idea of *inviting* every receptive auditor within shouting distance became a part of the happy ruction . . . [and] was the secret of the song's tremendous success." The figure of Alexander himself, while derived from the coon song tradition, purveys not a disconcertingly new music but the traditional "Swanee River" in a modern form, bridging, rather than breaking from, America's past. Instead of railing against ragtime as a culprit in the collapse of American mores, newspaper headlines could affectionately ask, "Has It Got You Going Too?"

The song's success inspired Tin Pan Alley songwriters to emulate its sprightly rhythm and vernacular lyrics for a wide range of songs, and "ragtime" soon became a term that characterized all popular music with a rhythmic lilt. As the composer Harry Von Tilzer explained, "'Ragtime' is not a type of song; it is a type of song-treatment; in fact, it is the distinctive American treatment of song in general. It reflects the spirit of the American people, their extraordinary activity, restlessness, initiative, joyousness and capacity for work, and for play . . . so long as America remains the land of the brave and the free and the busy, particularly the busy, so long shall we have 'ragtime.'"

Just as "Alexander's Ragtime Band" made ragtime synonymous with American popular music, the song liberated Berlin from the coon song tradition. "None of Berlin's ragtime songs published after 1911 has an unequivocally black protagonist," notes Charles Hamm, "none uses 'black' dialect in the lyrics . . . they had moved away from the spirit of the 'coon' song." While occasionally Berlin might write a song such as "When the Midnight Choo-Choo Leaves for Alabam'" (1912) that seems to portray a black character longing to return to the South, he could write a similar song, such as "I Want to Go Back to Michigan (Down on the Farm)" (1914), where a clearly white character longs to leave the big city for his pastoral childhood home.

"Alexander's Ragtime Band" helped Berlin move up from Tin Pan Alley to Broadway. With the exception of productions of the militantly American figure of George M. Cohan, the Broadway musical was dominated by such Viennese operettas as *The Merry Widow* or American imitations, such as Victor Herbert's *Naughty Marietta*. As World War I loomed in Europe, however, Broadway impresario Charles Dillingham extended an invitation to Berlin to write a musical based on ragtime, and Berlin shifted his customary emphasis on writing hit after hit to producing an integrated score for *Watch Your Step*. The show was successful and produced a hit, "Play a Simple Melody," which counterpointed one singer's longing for an old-fashioned melody "like my mother sang to me" with another singer's demand for the new: "play me some rag." The success of the show helped the Broadway musical move to more American subjects and to base its score on the kind of song represented by "Alexander's Ragtime Band." For the next fifty years that song formula dominated the Broadway musical; it was adopted by Hollywood in 1927 when the advent of sound made possible the movie musical, and served as the bedrock of jazz improvisation.

Through those various venues, hundreds of tunes like "Alexander's Ragtime Band" have done what popular songs are not supposed to do—stayed popular. Beginning with "Alexander's Ragtime Band," songs by Berlin, the Gershwins, Rodgers and Hart, Cole Porter, and others sound as fresh today as when they were first heard. Indeed, interpreted by generations of singers, from Bessie Smith and Al Jolson, through Crosby and Sinatra, down to Linda Ronstadt and Rod Stewart, they are the closest thing America has to a lasting body of classical song.

It is remarkable that most Americans—as well as millions around the world—can sing along when they hear a song from 1911 whose chorus beckons, "Come on and hear."

Bibliography: Laurence Bergreen, *As Thousands Cheer: The Life of Irving Berlin* (New York, 1990). Edward A. Berlin, *Reflections and Research on Ragtime* (New York, 1987). Lewis A. Erenberg, *Steppin' Out: New York Nightlife and the Transformation of American Culture, 1890–1930* (Chicago, 1984). Philip Furia, *Irving Berlin: A Life in Song* (New York, 1998). Charles Hamm, *Irving Berlin: Songs from the Melting Pot: The Formative Years, 1907–1914* (New York, 1997).

PHILIP FURIA

1912, April 15

Titanic sinks; Eugene O'Neill attempts suicide and becomes a playwright

LIFEBOATS CUT ADRIFT

Just before midnight on April 14, 1912, RMS *Titanic*, the largest passenger steamship in the world, epitome of naval architecture, bourgeois affluence, luxury, speed, and technological achievement, struck an iceberg. Less than three hours later, on April 15, it sank, taking nearly 1,500 people with it. Built in a Belfast shipyard and destined for New York City, the *Titanic* was intended to dominate the transatlantic shipping trade, and its sinking has come to symbolize the end of the long nineteenth century, of an ideology of progress and middle-class optimism; it stands as a precursor of deeper disillusionment in the decades to come. Less than a year earlier, able-bodied seaman E. G. O'Neill shipped as one of the deck crew on the luxury liner SS *Philadelphia* from Southampton, England, to

New York, the itinerary the *Titanic* was to have followed nine months later. On reaching port in lower Manhattan, O'Neill returned to his recent haunt, Jimmy the Priest's saloon, across from Washington Market and doors from the river (later site of the World Trade Center), an old red-brick building with a flophouse for seamen, gamblers, and other down-and-outers above the bar. In January of 1912, the wastrel Eugene O'Neill, overcome by feelings of self-loathing, considered jumping into the harbor off the Battery but, deterred by icy waters, chose instead a method of suicide that evoked his mother's morphine addiction. He took an overdose of Veronal tablets, stretched out on a straw mattress, and waited to die.

O'Neill would come to regard 1912 as the year in which he became a playwright, and he returned to it repeatedly in his greatest plays. Both *The Iceman Cometh* (completed 1939, published 1946) and *Long Day's Journey into Night* (1941, 1956) are set in 1912—the former, which concludes with a suicide, is set in a flophouse. That year O'Neill also fell ill with tuberculosis, as Edmund does in *Long Day's Journey*, and in the quasi-spiritual, guilt-ridden language of the lapsed Catholic he later told an interviewer: "I just drifted along till I was twenty-four and then I got a jolt and sat up and took notice. Retribution overtook me and I went down with T.B. It gave me time to think about myself and what I was doing . . . I got busy writing one act plays." Most of those plays end in murder, suicide, or insanity, and most are set on or refer to the sea. *Warnings* (1913) is set on a sinking ship, *Fog* (1913) and *Thirst* (1913) in lifeboats cut adrift from wrecked steamers.

The motif of sinking to the depths pervades O'Neill's work, and he returned frequently to the sea, with its potent symbolisms of psychological depth, tidal rhythms yet inherent formlessness, impersonal destructiveness, and a deterministic force greater than that of any individual. In O'Neill the sea has a moral dimension, as the barge captain Chris Christopherson implies in *Anna Christie* (1921; another play that draws on experiences in 1912 at Jimmy the Priest's) in his refrain, "dat old davil, sea," and it can be a site of resurrection or washing clean. Orin, the Orestes figure in *Mourning Becomes Electra* (1929, 1931), despairs: "The only love I can know now is the love of guilt for guilt which breeds guilt—until you get so deep at the bottom of hell there is no lower you can sink and you rest there in peace." But like the innocent yet falsely imprisoned seaman Edmond Dantès whom O'Neill's father, the actor James O'Neill, had embodied in *The Count of Monte Cristo*, O'Neill would ultimately emerge from the depths to claim the world as his.

Saved from suicide by friends including Jimmy Byth, whom O'Neill depicted as the pipe-dreamer "Jimmy Tomorrow" in *The Iceman Cometh*, O'Neill joined his father's vaudeville tour in a cut-down version of *Monte Cristo* as a courier and jailer. In mid-April 1912, the family—Eugene, James, O'Neill's mother, Ella, supposedly fresh from a cure for her addiction, and his brother, Jamie—were back at their house in New London, Connecticut, the site of *Long Day's Journey*. If his suicide attempt had succeeded, the virtually unknown future playwright, who was born in 1888, would have concluded a life symmetrically poised between the nineteenth and twentieth centuries. He went on to become America's and, for a time, the world's preeminent playwright, earning a Nobel Prize in 1936, a figure for the dark uncertainties, the brutal honesty, and disillusionment of American modernism. But, in a vital sense, O'Neill always remained poised between the nineteenth and twentieth centuries. Growing up, he heard men reminiscence about the Civil War, a historical moment that he evokes vividly in *Mourning Becomes Electra,* just as *Desire under the Elms* (1924) re-creates America in 1850 at the time of the California Gold Rush. His father's brand of melodramatic theater and its romantic motifs, stock character types, emotional excesses, and verbal hyperbole often found their way into O'Neill's mature work, as the figures of O'Neill's own past did in plays ranging from *Ah, Wilderness!* (1933), the one comedy in his otherwise relentlessly tragic oeuvre, to the bleak *Long Day's Journey.*

As his own career began in 1912, the acting career of his father, which shaped his life and dominated his imagination, effectively ended. Like the *Titanic,* James O'Neill began in Ireland, but in spite of great early hopes, as the character of James Tyrone says in *Long Day's Journey into Night,* he became so associated with one role that "it ruined me with its promise of an easy fortune." In 1912 James O'Neill had played the Count of Monte Cristo for the last time, shooting a silent film of the play with the Famous Players Film Company. Intimately familiar with American theater since the late nineteenth century, Eugene O'Neill made comments throughout his life that reveal both his excitement at witnessing avant-garde realistic productions in his youth and a highly self-conscious reaction against his father's romantic melodrama. As he later saw it, it was the 1911 American tour of Dublin's Abbey Players that brought the possibilities of dramatic realism home to him. In 1923 he said, "As a boy I saw so much of the old, ranting artificial romantic stage stuff that I always had a sort of contempt for the theatre. It was seeing the Irish players for the first time that gave me a glimpse of my opportunity."

But revolt can be as profound a tribute as praise. O'Neill's search for a dramatic structure more flexible, open-ended, or, in his sights, realistic than the rigidly prescriptive, linear, and climax-driven plots of five-act melodrama did not eschew melodramatic effects but sought ways of representing both the emotional heights of characters and their psychological depths. This antitheatrical theatricality took a remarkable variety of forms, including the stylized use of masks, first in *The Emperor Jones* (1920) and *The Hairy Ape* (1921) and later in *Lazarus Laughed* (1927), which shows the influence of the biblical dramas his father had played (Christus in *The Passion,* 1887, and both the patriarch Jacob and Pharaoh in *Joseph and His Brethren* in 1913) and of Wilde's *Salomé. The Great God Brown* (1925), a work heavily indebted to Wilde's *Picture of Dorian Gray,* also used masks extensively, but in that play acting is explicitly associated with lying, as the prostitute Cybil instructs the Dionysian Dion: "Stop acting. I hate ham fats." *Long Day's Journey* perhaps most precisely and schematically expresses O'Neill's ambivalence about the nineteenth-century theater, as embodied by the old actor James Tyrone. In O'Neill's work, to act is to lie, whereas the dramatic art that he cultivated would be emphatically literary, if also highly theatrical in its way, as he insisted that the Provincetown Players also be called The Playwrights' Theatre. The combination of O'Neill's animus against actors and his recognition that the text must be performed is also evident in the extraordinary detail and extent of his written instructions about specific characters in the plays.

O'Neill's deepest literary debts, however, were not to Americans (with the possible exception of Melville) but to nineteenth-century European authors who had become radically critical of bourgeois affluence and complacency, as epitomized by fin de siècle decadence, aestheticism, and Pre-Raphaelite poetry. These authors, a selection of whom can be found on Edmund Tyrone's bookshelf in *Long Day's Journey* (Schopenhauer, Ibsen, Shaw, Strindberg, Swinburne, Rossetti, Wilde), also returned continually to the theme of plumbing the depths—especially O'Neill's foremost influences, Nietzsche, Wilde, and, above all, Strindberg, whose death in May 1912 may seem to have channeled the spirit of the intensely autobiographical playwright across the cold Atlantic. Like Strindberg, O'Neill would experiment with a variety of dramaturgical styles, ranging from naturalism to expressionism, focusing on mutually destructive yet tragically indestructible family bonds, and finding his métier not in a large commercial theater, despite his later Broadway successes, but in the new international movement of anticommercial Little Theatres. O'Neill would find his venue four years later in Provincetown with George Cram "Jig" Cook, Susan Glaspell, Robert Edmond Jones, John Reed, Louise Bryant, and others who had migrated from Greenwich Village. In the summer of 1916, the Provincetown Players staged O'Neill's first major work, the one-act play *Bound East for Cardiff,* about the dying sailor Yank, at the Wharf Theatre. As Glaspell later described it, "There was fog, just as the script demanded, fog bell in the harbor. The tide was in, and it washed under us and around, spraying through the holes in the floor giving us the rhythm and flavor of the sea."

Influenced by the classicism of Cook and of his favorite author, Nietzsche, O'Neill found inspiration for his art in the two art deities of the Greeks, Dionysus and Apollo, figures for intoxication and illusion, whose relationship Nietzsche described as a tremendous opposition in origin and aims. Nietzsche's *Birth of Tragedy* presents a theory of drama as knowledge, as self-confrontation, not self-transcendence or self-deception. But Nietzsche also argues that the culmination of knowledge as such, unrelieved by salutary illusion, is suicidal despair, and this problem is at the center of O'Neill's experiments in characterization and his attempts to dramatize depth psychology. The single most important development in dramatic characterization during the twenties was the combination of realistic methods with the burgeoning interest in Freudian personality theory. Freud's 1909 lectures at Clark University in Massachusetts led to the translation that year of his *Selected Papers on Hysteria* and the American publication of the lectures in 1910, followed by *Three Contributions to the Theory of Sex* in 1910, *The Interpretation of Dreams* in 1913, and *The Psychopathology of Everyday Life* in 1914. These works had a radical effect on the conception of character available to American playwrights. O'Neill's plays through this period, including *The Emperor Jones, The Great God Brown, Desire under the Elms, Strange Interlude,* and *Mourning Becomes Electra,* unsparingly probed unconscious sources of guilt, trauma, the Oedipus complex, and self-delusion. Each of these plays developed new modes of dramatizing the unconscious. But to represent the new conception of character as personality and to remain within the limits of realistic drama, O'Neill, like many of his contemporaries who were also alcoholics, turned in his late realistic plays, *The Iceman Cometh, Long Day's Journey into Night,* and a *Moon for the Misbegotten* (1943, 1952), to the simple device of self-revelation under the influence of drink.

Like Glaspell's *Suppressed Desires,* O'Neill's *Iceman Cometh* manifests a reassessment of Freud—or of popular misinterpretations—that reflected the broader doubts about Freudian methods that were beginning to be expressed in psychoanalytic circles by Jung, Rank, and Ferenczi, among others, in the 1930s. Hickey, the cunning salesman, has much in common with Sigmund Freud. "Here's the point to get," he says at the end of act two. "I swear I'd never act like I have if I wasn't absolutely sure it will be worth it to you in the end, after you're rid of the damned guilt that makes you lie to yourselves you're something you're not, and the remorse that nags at you and makes you hide behind lousy pipe dreams about tomorrow." His program of salvation is similar to that of psychoanalysis. He invites the derelicts to reexamine their illusions and to get rid of them by coming to terms with the reality principle. His analysis and plan for treatment, he imagines, will make them happy. But, of course, it doesn't. After their abortive attempts to resume their former occupations, they stumble back to Harry Hope's saloon, demoralized and defeated. They can't endure life without illusions, and Hickey deprives them of the will to live. The notion that man can be happy in this world, as Hickey suggests, is itself an illusion. O'Neill's play sets out to discredit any coherent system of thought as anything more than a pipe dream. In 1939, as he was writing this play, his friend Waldo Frank, who was to intercede with O'Neill on behalf of his estranged daughter Oona a few years later, published a novel called *The Bridegroom Cometh,* in which the heroine gives herself to a series of bridegrooms, both spiritual (Christ, Freud, Marx) and material (a husband and several lovers). She discovers ultimately that only Marx satisfies her need for love, and in the end she finds fulfillment through identification with the masses. O'Neill never supposed that a political or sociological nostrum could cure the diseases of the soul. His bridegroom, death, denies any similar kind of dogmatism.

O'Neill wrote the first draft of *The Iceman Cometh* in 1939, the year the world fell apart as Poland was invaded and Britain and France declared war on Germany. By 1946, when the play was finally produced, O'Neill's reputation had sunk. The critic Mary McCarthy referred to him as a "tone-deaf musician" whose "graceless works can find no reason for stopping, but go on and on, like elephants pacing in a zoo." In 1952, a year before O'Neill's death, the publication of his last play, *A Moon for the Misbegotten,* went largely unnoticed. But in 1956 a thirty-one-year-old Panamanian director named José Quintero revived *The Iceman Cometh* at an off-Broadway theater, with a young actor named Jason Robards as Hickey. The play was a hit. Later in that year it led to Quintero's direction of the premiere of *Long Day's Journey into Night,* which became an even greater success, bringing O'Neill, posthumously, his fourth Pulitzer Prize. Born Catholic like O'Neill, Quintero revived *A Moon for the Misbegotten* in 1973 with the Resurrection Company, to great acclaim again, solidifying O'Neill's reputation as America's foremost playwright.

O'Neill's dramas have benefited greatly from the work of directors, actors, and designers. As works of literature alone his plays can seem inarticulate, formless, both exhausting and inexhaustible, but sinking to the depths has been a precondition of their resurrection in their production history as well as in their very content. It is perhaps not mere coincidence that the site of O'Neill's suicide attempt was the location of the terrorist attack on September 11, 2001. As Nietzsche wrote in O'Neill's favorite book, *Thus Spoke Zarathustra,* "Like the sun I love life and all deep seas. And this is what perceptive knowledge means to me: all that is deep shall rise up to my heights." In this deep sense O'Neill was the playwright of the sea.

Bibliography: Ann Douglas, *Terrible Honesty: Mongrel Manhattan in the 1920s* (New York, 1995). Arthur Gelb and Barbara Gelb, *O'Neill* (New York, 1960). Mary McCarthy, "Eugene O'Neill: Dry Ice," in *Mary McCarthy's Theatre Chronicles, 1937–1962* (New York, 1963), 81–88. Louis Sheaffer, *O'Neill: Son and Playwright* (Boston, 1968).

ALAN ACKERMAN

1912

Willa Cather resigns as managing editor of *McClure's*

The Lure of Impossible Things

In Willa Cather's 1915 novel *The Song of the Lark,* the young heroine Thea Kronberg tells her friend Dr. Archie that she plans to "get something big" out of life. The doctor encourages her, telling her that if it's money she wants, she can make it, provided that she "cares more about that than anything else." Thea replies impatiently: "'But I don't. That's only one thing. Anyway, I couldn't if I did.' She pulled her dress lower at the neck as if she were suffocating. 'I only want impossible things,' she said roughly. 'The other things don't interest me.'" The story of a small-town girl with towering ambition who achieves spectacular artistic success, *The Song of the Lark* has often been read as an example of fiction as wish fulfillment. Thea is tormented for many years by her desire for "impossible things," but in the end she achieves them; her unwillingness to compromise with the ordinary and the everyday leads to her final apotheosis as "Kronberg," world-famous opera diva.

These things can happen. Cather's own rise from the relative obscurity of her childhood in Red Cloud, Nebraska, is a case in point. Growing up, Cather was burdened with exceptional talent and exceptional hunger. Like Thea Kronberg, she ultimately found a stage large enough to accommodate her outsized desires, but things might have turned out very differently. Thea herself realizes the danger posed by her situation. In the same conversation with Dr. Archie, she tells him that it is "easy to fail" and offers him the following warning: "If I fail, you'd better forget about me, for I'll be one of the worst women that ever lived. I'll be an awful woman!"

When she wrote *The Song of the Lark,* Cather had achieved moderate success as a writer: she had published a book of poems and a collection of short stories; her first two novels, *Alexander's Bridge* (1912) and *O Pioneers!* (1913), had been well received. Great critical and popular successes such as *My Ántonia* (1918), *One of Ours* (1922), and *The Professor's House* (1925) were still to come. Although Cather's career as a fiction writer was still taking off, she already had another successful career as a journalist behind her. Cather's meteoric rise in the world of magazines and newspapers began in her junior year at the University of Nebraska, when she began publishing anonymous reviews and articles to cover her room and board. Over the next few years she wrote hundreds of thousands of words, often turning out as many as four theater and book reviews a week. Cather's prominence as a reviewer yielded a job offer as the editor of *Home Monthly* magazine in Pittsburgh; Cather accepted and began work at twenty-two. During the next decade, she took several more editorial jobs, continued publishing reviews, articles, and the occasional short story, and taught high school. In 1906, S. S. McClure persuaded her to move to New York and become associate editor (she would soon be promoted to managing editor) of the highly regarded and popular muckraking magazine *McClure's*. The journal, founded in 1893, had risen to prominence with the publication of the investigative reporting of Ida Tarbell, Ray Stannard Baker, and Lincoln Steffens as well as fiction by Robert Louis Stevenson, Jack London, and Rudyard Kipling. A shake-up in the staff had created an opening for Cather, who, still in her early thirties, suddenly became one of the most important and powerful female journalists in America.

While Cather was undoubtedly proud of her achievement and of the opportunities it brought her, she was ambivalent from the start about the profession of journalism and her place in it. The demand to produce material on deadline meant that Cather had less time to work on her fiction, but she was even more concerned that writing on demand and for the market would unfit her for the great things—the impossible things—she still wanted. In what is perhaps Cather's definitive aesthetic statement, "The Novel Démeublé" (1922), she defines great writing through an explicit contrast with a form of writing she knew quite well. "If the novel is a form of imaginative art, it cannot be at the same time a vivid and brilliant form of journalism. Out of the teeming, gleaming stream of the present it must select the eternal material of art." Cather's mature style is remarkable precisely for her mastery of this principle of selection, but it's important to remember how familiar she was with the vivid art of journalism. Cather's assertion that the novelist "must learn to write, and then . . . must unlearn it" might be understood to refer to her own apprenticeship in the magazines.

While on assignment for *McClure's* in Boston, Cather met Sarah Orne Jewett, whose *Country of the Pointed Firs* she admired and whose face she remembered from an Authors card game she played when she was a child. Although Cather only knew Jewett for sixteen months—they met in February 1908 and Jewett died unexpectedly in June 1909, while Cather was in London—the older woman made a deep impression on her. Jewett was both a friend and a mentor, and the advice that she gave Cather changed the course of her life. In a letter she wrote after reading a few of Cather's recent stories, Jewett warned:

> If you don't keep and guard and mature your force, and above all, have time and quiet to perfect your work, you will be writing things not much better than you did five years ago. This you are anxiously saying to yourself! but I am wondering how to get at the right conditions. I want you to be surer of your backgrounds,—you have your Nebraska life,—a child's Virginia, and now an intimate knowledge of what we are pleased to call the "Bohemia" of newspaper and magazine-office life. These are uncommon equipment, but you don't see them yet quite enough from the outside . . . You must find a quiet place near the best companions . . . your vivid, exciting companionship in the office must not be your audience, you must find your own quiet centre of life, and write from that to the world that holds offices, and all society, and all Bohemia; the city, the country—in short, you must write to the human heart.

With a remarkable homing instinct, Jewett put her finger on Cather's own ambivalence. Cather was caught up in the world of the office and at the same time she longed to escape—her ambition still drew her to "impossible things" and to the dream of writing "to the human heart."

In urging Cather to become "surer of her backgrounds," Jewett swayed the younger woman away from the urbane realism that she admired in Henry James and toward the mythic regionalism of her great later works. In a 1922 preface to *Alexander's Bridge,* Cather regrets the shallowness and artifice of her first novel, which was set in Boston and London. She recalls Jewett's early advice to her: "Of course, one day you will write about your own country. In the meantime, get all you can. One must know the world so well before one can know the parish." Cather spent many years getting to know the world by covering it for major regional and national news outlets; in addition to *McClure's* and *Home Monthly,* she also wrote for the *Lincoln Courier,* the *Nebraska State Journal,* the *Pittsburgh Leader,* the *New York Sun,* and *Ladies' Home Journal.* However, it was only by turning to the parish—to the Great Plains—that she was to achieve the universal appeal that would transform her into a great American writer.

Jewett's appeal to find a "quiet center of life" resonated more deeply yet for Cather, who, on first meeting Jewett, had been taken with the air of calm privacy that she cultivated. In her essay "148 Charles Street," Cather describes first meeting Jewett with her longtime companion, Annie Fields, the widow of the publisher James T. Fields. Cather observes that their house is filled with the spirits of the great writers and artists who visited there, and dwells on the "great change in her life" that this contact with the past brought about. She writes, "The unique charm of Mrs. Fields' house was not that it was a place where one could hear about the past, but that it was a place where the past lived on—where it was protected and cherished, had sanctuary from the noisy push of the present . . . The ugliness of the world, all possibility of wrenches and jars and wounding contacts, seemed securely shut out. It was indeed the peace of the past, where the tawdry and cheap have been eliminated and the enduring things have taken their proper, happy place."

The sedate life shared by Jewett and Fields offered a stark contrast to Cather's experiences toiling in "bohemia." While Cather is known for her portrayals of Bohemian immigrants in her novels (particularly in *My Ántonia*), in her early journalism she was concerned with a different kind of bohemianism; she considered the lives and mores of struggling artists living in urban enclaves, as popularized by Puccini in his opera *La Bohème*. In an 1896 review of a theatrical adaptation of the source text for the opera, Henri Murger's *Scènes de la vie de Bohème* (1848), Cather reflects on the dangers of bohemia, which she calls the "kingdom of failure." Murger himself spent his youth as "a hack," she writes, someone who "could do good work" but "had to live and to do that he edited a fashion paper and a hatter's magazine." According to Cather, "For a young man [Bohemia] may be a temporary abiding place whose skies are not altogether hopeless . . . But an old man who is still hanging about the outskirts of Bohemia is a symbol of the most pitiful failure on earth."

As Cather reflects further on bohemia, it becomes clear that the danger it poses is not merely a matter of penury or artistic failure. Rather, the more significant danger posed by bohemianism is its attitude of revolt. She writes,

In essence, Bohemianism is a rebellion against all organized powers, and that in itself is a defeat, for victory is with the organized powers of the universe. A man begins by defying the accepted standards of art; if he is a great man, he will stop there, and if he is a very great man he will revolutionize art. If he is a weak man and can accomplish nothing by his objections generally he goes further and defies the accepted standards of social government . . . He may even go further and defy the accepted ethical standards without utter destruction for sometimes the wicked do prosper. But if he goes so far, he never stops there. He takes the last inevitable step and defies nature; then he goes out like a candle in a whiff of wind. He does not even leave a smoke, a name, a memory. He attains absolute annihilation and the cycle of Bohemianism is completed.

Just such a drama of "absolute annihilation" had been enacted the year before in Oscar Wilde's trial and imprisonment for acts of "gross indecency." Cather, reflecting on Wilde's fate in the *Lincoln Courier*, comments that "there is absolutely no spot on earth where this man can live": he has "gone out" like a candle in the wind. Cather's discussions of bohemianism are not only concerned with European wickedness; they also shed light on her own present-tense struggles with "the organized powers of the universe."

Cather wrote her review of the Murger adaptation the year she moved to Pittsburgh. She described the city as "divided into two parts," Presbyteria and Bohemia, adding that the former was "much the larger and the more influential kingdom of the two." It was in her first year in her new city that she migrated out of Bohemia, abandoning the social nonconformity and rebellion that had, as she wrote to a friend, "queered her" in Nebraska. As a high school student, Cather cut quite a figure in Red Cloud: she wore her hair in a buzz cut, dressed in boys' clothes, and signed her name William Cather, M.D. In college, she dressed and acted more like a girl, but still stuck out with her intense crushes on her female friends. Cather had never wholly embraced social nonconformity: in a passionate and forlorn letter to fellow undergraduate Louise Pound, Cather said she thought it unfair that relations between women were seen as unnatural, but conceded that that was indeed how things stood. After moving to Pittsburgh, she changed course, dressing in more feminine clothes, attending women's literary clubs, and even dating some young men; rather than associating dramatic, remarkable behavior with artistic innovation, Cather increasingly came to see it as a distraction from the serious work of the artist.

Cather's intimate knowledge of bohemia helps to make sense of her keen desire for artistic success. Attention to Cather's early exposures—the "jars and wounding contacts" that she suffered as a young person making her way in the world—can help to explain her rise in the world of the office as well as her eagerness to get out of it. In Red Cloud and Lincoln, Cather had a brief brush with newly public forms of homosexual identity and did not like it; she understood Wilde's life as a cautionary tale and ultimately sought to avoid the glare of publicity. When she met Jewett in 1908, the older woman's quiet domestic life with Mrs. Fields—a classic example of a nineteenth-century romantic friendship—offered an appealing alternative. The same year that Cather was finally able to take Jewett's advice and resign from her position at *McClure's*, she also moved in with Edith Lewis, who remained her steady companion until she died.

Nineteen-twelve was also the year that Cather took her first trip to the American Southwest. Cather wrote that it was only while she was there traveling with her brother Douglass that she was able to "recover from the conventional editorial point of view." Through this exploration of a distant "background"—particularly the Indian cliff dwellings of Arizona's Walnut Canyon—Cather became surer of her own. This reach back into "the peace of the past" was crucial for Cather. In the end, she was able to transform herself into a great modernist author by turning away from the modern. Not only did she reject the iconoclasm or rebellion that we generally associate with modernist aesthetics, she also rejected several key institutions of modernity: the press, the metropolis, and modern homosexual identity. The glittering promises of the modern world were touched, for Cather, by the hint of failure: a hungry Thea standing behind the magnificent figure of "Kronberg." Cather lived out the heady dreams of an impossible youth—and then she left them behind.

Bibliography: Willa Cather, *The Song of the Lark,* ed. Sherrill Harbison (1915; New York, 1999); *Stories, Poems, and Other Writings,* ed. Sharon O'Brien (New York, 1992); *The World and the Parish: Willa Cather's Articles and Reviews, 1893–1902,* ed. William M. Curtin (Lincoln, NE, 1970). M. Catherine Downs, *Becoming Modern: Willa Cather's Journalism* (Selinsgrove, PA, 1999). Sarah Orne Jewett, *Letters of Sarah Orne Jewett,* ed. Annie Fields (Boston, 1911). Marilee Lindemann, *Willa Cather: Queering America* (New York, 1999). Sharon O'Brien, *Willa Cather: The Emerging Voice* (Cambridge, MA, 1987).

HEATHER LOVE

1912

Raised by apes, a British lord takes the world stage

Tarzan Begins His Reign

At the age of sixty-four, the pulp writer Edgar Rice Burroughs finally realized a long-standing dream when on July 29, 1939, the *Saturday Evening Post* published an article entitled "How to Become a Great Writer." Burroughs, who had been a professional author since 1911, had longed to make the pages of the magazine as a sign of his arrival as a bankable writer of legitimate literary merit. Every piece he had submitted to its editors throughout his career was rejected. But that did not prevent the *Saturday Evening Post* from publishing this essay *about* him. So he made the pages of the *Post* at last. And it was not hyperbole, by any means, calling him a great writer. Alva Johnston, who wrote the article, used these criteria for selecting the person he felt was America's greatest living writer: "1. The size of the writer's public. 2. His success in establishing a character in the consciousness of the world. 3. The possibility of being read by posterity." In 1939, Edgar Rice Burroughs was the most obvious and, even allowing for the one-book author Margaret Mitchell, arguably the only possible choice, at least among writers in the English-speaking world.

Burroughs had, by this time, sold millions of books in many languages across the globe. He had established one of the most famous characters in the history of not only American literature but of any literature in the world. His character had become an archetype. And Burroughs had an excellent chance, on the basis of this one character, of being read and remembered for many years after his death. The character was Tarzan, Lord of the Jungle, whose appeal had been instantaneous and spectacular, comparable to the impact of a character like Sherlock Holmes, who came earlier, or Harry Potter, who was to come later. It was safely within the realm of possibility at the time to think that every man, woman, and child in the United States had read a Tarzan story or novel, seen one of the feature films, read the newspaper comic strip, or heard the radio program. It was also safely within the realm of possibility that virtually everyone on the planet had heard of the character.

Appearing in the *Post* was an instant of crossover for Burroughs from the world of the pulps. The *Post* article was his major moment of bourgeois recognition, of Main Street respectability, of leaving the literary slums for the modest grandeur of the suburbs of middlebrow taste. Burroughs could think of himself as a writer on a par with Zane Grey, who was regularly featured in magazines like the *Post,* and who so successfully transcended his pulp origins. And Burroughs could think of his famous character as being nearly equal in stature to Huckleberry Finn or Robin Hood or even Hercules or Beowulf, rather than, say, Nick Carter or The Spider.

In that same year, *Tarzan Finds a Son,* the fourth in the series of MGM–Johnny Weissmuller Tarzan films, was released to good box office and decent reviews. Although there were clear differences between the celluloid version of the character and the one found in Burroughs's books (Burroughs was never happy with any Tarzan movie made while he was alive, including *The New Adventures of Tarzan,* 1935, the one he produced himself), Weissmuller's depiction of the character was the most compelling and, of the Tarzan movies made before and since he played the role, the most memorable. (Eleven Tarzan movies had been made before Weissmuller came on the scene.) Weissmuller, a former champion Olympic swimmer, was indelibly identified with the part in the way Sean Connery is forever identified with James Bond or Warner Oland with Charlie Chan or Raymond Burr with Perry Mason. Many famous literary characters from the pulps, from Zorro to Doc Savage, still live with us today, but few of those characters—indeed, few literary characters from any source—have so thoroughly penetrated popular culture as Tarzan: beyond the novels, the movies from the silent era until the end of the twentieth century, the radio series, and the comics, he has been the subject of several animated features, a Broadway musical, at least one live-action television series, a hit Top-40 novelty tune (Ray Stevens's 1969 "Gitarzan and His Jungle Band"), at least two pornographic movies, and countless knockoffs, from Ka-Zar to George of the Jungle, from Ka'anga to Wambi the Jungle Boy.

It was not simply the power of the character that made this fame possible—although that power is no small part of the character's success—but the energy and ingenuity of his creator. Burroughs worked hard to make his character universally known and licensed, a brand, an imprint on the modern consciousness. "If you write one story, it may be bad; if you write a hundred, you have the odds in your favor," Burroughs said to aspiring writers. The odds were definitely in Burroughs's favor. He wrote like a machine. He wrote until he hated writing, hated his characters, especially Tarzan, wrote himself into bad health, wrote himself dry and still continued to write when his imagination was all used up. This doggedness was of course for money. Burroughs was a spender who lived beyond his means. But this doggedness, this compulsion, was not about money at all. It was about a man who wanted to be remembered as a writer. The frenzied writing was about a man who had nothing better to do with his time, who didn't know how to do anything else nearly as well or that brought him nearly as much personal satisfaction. He instinctively understood the law of competition in a capitalist society: you beat the opposition by outworking all that is arrayed against you. That opposition, of course, included indifference both from without and within.

Tarzan of the Apes appeared in its entirety in the October 1912 issue of *All-Story* magazine. Burroughs had already achieved publishing success earlier in 1912 when *All-Story* serially ran his first story, "A Princess of Mars," which featured a character who was to be a staple of Burroughs's science fiction, John Carter, who never achieved the same level of fame as Tarzan but nonetheless became a noted hero of the genre. With these successes, Burroughs did not look back and devoted himself entirely to writing to earn a living for the rest of his life.

He did not enter the lists of professional creative writers through either a natural attraction to letters or a classical or literary education. Burroughs was not an intellectual, nor of any sort of bohemian, self-consciously artistic temperament. He may have put it well when, some years after his first success, he wrote about what led him to writing: "I had a wife and two babies, a combination which does not work well without money." But few people do anything solely or purely for money.

Burroughs was born in Chicago on September 1, 1875, about as far away from the planet Mars or the African jungle as one can imagine; he died in Encino, California, next door to the town of Tarzana, on March 19, 1950. He was the fifth son of George Tyler and Mary Burroughs. His parents were well-off and Burroughs grew up in a household that included two Irish maids and a cook. Academically, he was an indifferent student and dropped out of a few different schools before he was sent to live for a time with his older brothers in Idaho, where he learned to ride horses and enjoy the outdoor life. (His interest in the outdoor life and physical culture—he found it difficult to cope with aging, for instance—clearly were psychological elements that lay behind a character like Tarzan, a supremely robust physical specimen, a child of nature and the outdoors, who, over twenty novels, never grew old.)

Burroughs eventually graduated from Michigan Military Academy, where he met Charles King, a career soldier, commandant at the school, and writer of adventure romances of the G. A. Henty sort. A friendship developed that lasted for years; King may have first planted the seed, by example, not only for Burroughs to think of becoming a writer but of the particular kind of writer Burroughs became. Burroughs failed to get into West Point and in 1896 enlisted in the army, only to leave the military for reasons of homesickness and poor health after just ten months. He returned to Idaho to make a go of ranching and prospecting with his brothers. He married Emma Hulbert in January 1900, a marriage that, producing three children and ending in divorce, endured long but not happily, as Emma suffered from depression and alcoholism. As he searched for his métier during his young manhood, Burroughs tried work running a store, and as a depot policeman, a supervisor of stenographers, a salesman. His unhappiness with these jobs, which often did not pay enough to support his family, led him to try his hand at writing the kind of stories he liked to read. He was a fan of such popular books of the era as Anthony Hope's *The Prisoner of Zenda* (1894), and he did write comic verse to entertain nephews and nieces, so he was not without an inclination as a writer and some bent toward at least pop literary material. That he was published at all as a pulp writer was not very surprising. Others have tried their hand at pulp writing with at least as little promise as Burroughs and found their way into print. But the size of Burroughs's success could not have been predicted at all.

Tarzan of the Apes, the story of Lord Greystoke, the son of British nobility whose parents are tragically killed and who is being raised by apes in sub-Saharan Africa (or by simian creatures who, in the fevered and exaggerated world of pulp fiction, are a reasonable facsimile of apes), clearly drew from the myth of Romulus and Remus, who were suckled by a she-wolf. There had been novels set in Africa before Tarzan, the most famous of which were those by H. Rider Haggard, particularly *King Solomon's Mines* (1885), which was far more authentic in its depiction of native Africans than any of Burroughs's books. Haggard had actually lived in South Africa for several years and grew to know some of the indigenous peoples there; Burroughs never set foot in Africa. But his first Tarzan novel was very much in the exotic adventure mode of Haggard's. For a boy's survival story, Burroughs clearly drew from R. M. Ballantyne's *The Coral Island* (1857), and, for gorillas and Africa, he drew from Ballantyne's *The Gorilla Hunters: A Tale of the Wilds of Africa* (1861). Burroughs was inspired by his betters, particularly Kipling and Howard Pyle, as well as Stevenson. But the primordial power of Tarzan's rising in the hierarchy of ape cultural politics, teaching himself to read, and, in a sense, fashioning his own sense of humanity, are beyond any particular sources, and these scenes, improbable as they are, convey a sense of myth almost as deep as any Greek or Norse tale or any fairy tale. Like Hans Christian Andersen's children's stories, Burroughs came up with something that seemed so natural as a narrative that it evokes a sense of timelessness. No subsequent Tarzan novel comes close to capturing the wondrous archetypical artistry and sense of originality of the first, although as boys' adventure books, some of the later Tarzans were fine exemplars of the genre.

The virulent racism that infects Tarzan and nearly all of Burroughs's fiction is a reflection of his temperament and his time. Burroughs grew up with an enormous pride in his Virginia ancestry of cavaliers and Anglo-Saxon blood; a belief in the divinity of "white" blood was reinforced by the racism of an era where the guiding ideology was social Darwinism, a faith in the competition between the races: a competition, as the whites saw it, that the whites, because of their superior blood, would win. During the years of Burroughs's youth, he saw racial segregation become increasingly and more strenuously enforced in the United States, and he also saw the United States, as a result of its success in the Spanish-American War of 1898, become an imperial presence in the "darker" world.

The racism that Burroughs expressed was quite similar in many respects to that of Thomas Dixon, the popular Southern novelist whose most successful novels about Reconstruction and Bourbon Redemption—D. W. Griffith's 1915 film *Birth of a Nation* was an adaptation of Dixon's 1905 novel *The Clansman*—appeared shortly before *Tarzan;* Burroughs would almost certainly have read Dixon, not only because of Dixon's popularity, but because Dixon wrote the pulp romances that appealed to Burroughs. He probably also read Dixon as he read many commercially successful writers of the time: to find out what made their work popular. It should also be noted that when Burroughs wrote *Tarzan of the Apes* in 1911 and 1912, Jack Johnson was in the midst of his reign as the first black heavyweight champion of the world, at a time when boxing was a far more popular and important sport than it is today. Johnson had famously beaten Tommy Burns in 1908 to win the title, and notoriously defeated retired champion Jim Jeffries on July 4, 1910, a victory that resulted in the worst outbreak of national racial violence this country was to see until the assassination of Martin Luther King in 1968. The idea of creating a white lord of the apes who is able physically not only to beat the apes but also African warriors is not without its political significance when one considers Johnson. Johnson was also hated by whites for his public love affairs with and marriages to white women. In *Tarzan of the Apes* and subsequent novels, Tarzan protects Jane from being raped by an ape and all manner of lesser breeds of masculinity. In Burroughs's science fiction novels, the white women, or the women who pass as the equivalent of white women, must be protected against all manner of alien rapists; in the world of pulp fiction, the sexual allure of white women is universal and trans-species.

Burroughs's work contains both the arrogance and the insecurity of white masculinity of his time—but unlike Dixon and other racist writers of the period, Burroughs in many respects managed to transcend its shabby politics and racial neuroses, creating a paradigm of adventure literature, literature about the relationship between people and nature, their own and that of the world outside of themselves. *Tarzan of the Apes* is in its way a profoundly important tale that is both prelapsarian fantasy in its conceit and Emersonian fable in its reach. The Tarzan story of man in a state of nature leads to a kingdom no less powerful than that of Milton's *Paradise Lost*, Thoreau's *Walden*, or Kipling's *Jungle Book. Tarzan* so sublimely captured in mythic terms the racist and naturalist assumptions and preoccupations of the culture from which it came that it left behind an eternal, inescapable narrative inscribed for better and for worse on the minds and hearts of us all.

Bibliography: Edgar Rice Burroughs, *Tarzan of the Apes* (Chicago, 1914). John F. Kasson, *Houdini, Tarzan, and the Perfect Man: The White Male Body and the Challenge of Modernity in America* (New York, 2001). Irwin Pogues, *Edgar Rice Burroughs: The Man Who Created Tarzan* (Provo, UT, 1975). John Taliaferro, *Tarzan Forever: The Life of Edgar Rice Burroughs, Creator of Tarzan* (New York, 1999).

GERALD EARLY

1913

The Armory Show, the Paterson Strike Pageant, and *Poetry* magazine bring an artistic revolution to the public

A MODERNIST MOMENT

In 1913 a spirit of revolution sought to remove the scaffolding of nineteenth-century art and present new forms for a new era. Modernism would no longer be a private matter within avant-garde circles. In Paris, the dissonances and primitive rhythms of Stravinsky's *Rite of Spring* provoked riots. In New York that February and March, the blockbuster International Exhibition of Modern Art, known as the Armory Show for its location in the Sixty-ninth Regiment Armory at Twenty-sixth Street, shunted aside the Beaux-Arts tradition with a myriad display of native and imported innovations in painting and sculpture. In June, thousands were drawn to Madison Square Garden for a dramatic pageant advertising the struggle of striking textile workers in Paterson, New Jersey. And in Chicago the newly established *Poetry: A Magazine of Verse* committed itself to "the new beauty." All of these enterprises of 1913 shared a rhetorical project: to bring broad public attention and support to the revolutionary spirit of the times.

Not surprisingly, these ventures were fraught with controversy, and their lasting influence is hard to measure. In order to imagine the literary impact of these broadcasts of new beauty, we might choose as our surrogate the aspiring poet Marianne Moore, a recent graduate of Bryn Mawr College, living with her mother in Carlisle, Pennsylvania, far from the hub of the avant-garde. Her scrapbooks for 1913 abound with clippings that suggest her vicarious excitement. The Armory Show seems especially to have caught her attention. Among her clippings one finds "Post-Impressionism Arrived" (*Letters and Arts,* March 1), "The Greatest Exhibition of Insurgent Art Ever Held" (*Current Opinion,* March 1), "Bedlam in Art" (*Current Opinion,* April 5), "Mr. Roosevelt and the Cubists" (*Current Opinion,* April 5). (Theodore Roosevelt had written a satiric "Layman's Guide to the Exhibition of Modern Art.") Moore would become one of the major poets of American modernism, but in 1913 she was looking for a style and an artistic community and savored all the cultural controversy she was reading about.

The innovative photographer Alfred Stieglitz had long been showing works of European and American modernism at 291 Fifth Avenue—Moore had marked down the address in her notebook of 1909 and would finally visit the gallery in 1915—but the Armory Show of 1913 announced modernism to America on a broader and much more public scale. The Armory's eighteen galleries of painting and sculpture represented more than 300 artists, about half of them American, including samplings of the Stieglitz group (John Marin, Marsden Hartley, Oscar Bluemner, Abraham Walkowitz, Charles Sheeler). The show aimed to educate the public in the history of modern painting from the symbolists to the cubists and synchronists. Cézanne, Van Gogh, and Gauguin were especially prominent, but so was the realist "Ashcan school," which brought the ordinary life of New York slums to the high art of painting. The principal organizers of the show, painters Walter Kuhn and Arthur B. Davies, took their own inspiration from fauvist traditions already out of fashion in Europe. But they had spent time in Gertrude Stein's Paris salon, and wished to produce for the American Association of Painters and Sculptors a show to rival the exhibitions of Europe. While the American paintings and sculptures were mostly separated out from European works, the cross-fertilizations were clear as one moved among the galleries—Rodin's direct carving, Kandinsky's spiritualism, the fauvists' primitive intensity, the violence of German expressionism, were all on display. The crowds rushed to what the popular media called the "Hall of Horrors," where they could see Duchamp's *Nude Descending a Staircase* and Picasso's *Head of a Woman.* The critic Kenyon Cox wrote that the "real meaning of this Cubist movement is nothing else than the total destruction of the art of painting." But for others, like the poet William Carlos Williams, the new art offered liberation from the arid, stately norms of American culture. "I do remember," Williams wrote in his *Autobiography,* "how I laughed out loud when I first saw it [Duchamp's *Nude Descending a Staircase No. 2*], happily, with relief." Works by Henri Matisse, Henri Rousseau, and others captured the modernist fascination with the irrational, the primitive, and the erotic energies underlying civilization. Among the many American women artists exhibited in the show was Margarite Zorach, whose Edenic landscapes would later inspire Marianne Moore to long for "the days of prismatic color" before the refinements of civilization set in.

Another rite was performed in New York a little later that spring. The Paterson Strike Pageant harnessed an ancient form of theatrical spectacle for modern social and political change. Many of the figures drawn to the artistic avant-garde in New York (the heiress and salon host Mabel Dodge, the journalist Hutchins Hapgood, the novelist, critic, and later Harlem Renaissance spokesman Carl Van Vechten, and especially the novelist and dramatist John Reed) were also caught up in radical social causes and participated in planning the pageant. The show was designed to win support for the workers' strike, led by the International Workers of the World (known as the IWW, or the Wobblies), at the Paterson Silk Mills. (The industrial and cultural history of the city would become the focus of Williams's American epic, *Paterson,* decades later.) John Reed worked with charismatic strike organizers William "Big Bill" Haywood, Elizabeth Gurley Flynn (called by Theodore Dreiser "the Joan of Arc of the labor movement"), and the labor activist Carlo Tresca to bring 1,200 (out of 50,000) silk workers to Madison Square Garden, where they dramatized their plight and the larger class struggle. A 200-foot backdrop by John Sloan (Ashcan artist and cofounder with Reed of *The Masses*) depicted the Paterson mills. The show drew an audience of 15,000 to the Garden, a monument of Progressive Era architecture bedecked for the evening in IWW red lights and banners. The program was broken into episodes narrating the progress of the strike: "The Mills Alive—The Workers Dead," "The Workers Alive—The Mills Dead." Other episodes included the death of Vincenzo Modestino, who was killed in the strike skirmishes, the evacuation of the children, and the meeting with labor leaders that led to the decision to strike. The pageant highlighted the multiethnic character of the workers, mixing socialist rallying songs with old-world ballads of the Italians, Germans, Irish, and Polish immigrants.

Some reviewers saw the performance as a utopian moment bringing together artist, worker, and audience in a united experience that crossed barriers of race, class, and gender. But it also caused considerable discord between the labor movement and the avant-garde elite. The expense of the hall and the printed program resulted in a net loss rather than financial support for the strikers, who ultimately went back to work on the mill owners' terms. While the aesthetic ambition of the spectacle was admired, the incitement to a radical cause met with severe criticism in the mainstream media, such as the *New York Times,* which dismissed the pageant as reckless provocation: "Under the direction of a destructive organization opposed in spirit and antagonistic in action to all the forces which have upbuilded this republic, a series of pictures in action were shown with the design of stimulating mad passion against law and order and promulgating a gospel of discontent." For the moment, middle-class, government-sponsored Progressive Era reforms would prevail. The radical John Reed, exhausted by the quarrels ensuing from the pageant, set off for Villa Cunonia in Florence with the bohemian heiress Mabel Dodge, and the IWW began to decline as a force in the American labor movement.

Chicago by 1913 was having its own renaissance, and civic and business leaders were joining the artistic community to ensure that New York was not the only cultural haven in America. The art of poetry could never rival the visual and dramatic arts in their ability to capture public attention, but poet and journalist Harriet Monroe felt, nevertheless, that poetry was essential to the healthy imaginative life of culture and deserved its own special venue. While Monroe moved in upper-class circles, she was not an heiress like Mabel Dodge; in middle age she supported herself as a journalist. Nor was she bohemian or avant-garde. Her greatest success as a poet was her "Columbian Ode," read at the dedication of the World's Columbian Exposition in 1892. Her review of the Armory Show in the *Chicago Tribune* called Matisse's pictures "the most hideous monstrosities ever perpetrated in the name of long-suffering art." But she was concerned about the weakness of American poetry at the turn of the century and succeeded in soliciting the help of various civic-minded friends and associates (many members of Chicago's Little Room arts club) in launching a new magazine. Having secured subscription pledges, she sent out a circular asking for the best verse. "We promise to refuse nothing because it is too good, whatever be the nature of its excellence. We shall read with special interest poems of modern significance, but the most classic subject will not be declined if it reaches a high standard of quality." From the outset, Monroe's reach was international. Among her first contributors were not only the Americans William Rose Benét and Amy Lowell, but also Alfred Noyes, William Butler Yeats, and Rabindranath Tagore—and, most significantly for the future of *Poetry: A Magazine of Verse,* the expatriate Ezra Pound.

The inaugural issue of *Poetry* in October 1912 was hardly a harbinger of the modernist verse it would later publish. The issue opened with Arthur Davison Ficke's "Poetry," a double sonnet describing the art as a "little isle amidst bleak seas," a "refuge from the stormy days," and a "sea-gate, trembling with the blast . . . [of] a whelming tide." Monroe would echo Ficke's lines in her "motives for the magazine" printed at its end: "We hope to offer our subscribers a place of refuge, a green isle in the sea, where Beauty may plant her gardens, and Truth, austere revealer of joy and sorrow, of hidden delights and despairs, may follow her brave quest unafraid." Such inflated, abstract rhetoric was the bane of younger poets looking for beauty in "small, dry things," a language of intuition that would, in the words of English poet-philosopher T. E. Hulme, "hand over sensations bodily." Perhaps Marianne Moore, who would later publish many of her works in *Poetry,* read Ficke's song of poetic retreat and disliked it. Her own "Poetry" (1919) eschews his "silver haze" and "tidings of the deep" in favor of "elephants pushing, a wild horse taking a roll." Far from being a "refuge," her poetry would mix with the everyday world and would "not discriminate against business documents and schoolbooks."

But Moore would have found much to like in *Poetry*'s numbers of 1913. While Monroe was still publishing conventional work, such as Joyce Kilmer's "Trees" ("I think that I shall never see / A thing as lovely as a tree"), she was also taking advice from Ezra Pound, who had installed himself as the magazine's London editor. Under the collective title "Contemporaneia" he published quintessential imagist work, including "In a Station of the Metro." Through Pound's interventions the magazine would introduce imagists such as H.D., William Carlos Williams, and Richard Aldington. Pound's regular prose in *Poetry* laid out the necessity for and terms of new lyric values. Not everyone was pleased with his commentaries; many, like John Reed (whose poems occasionally appeared in the magazine), found them elitist and unfair to poetry outside the modernist aesthetic. But it was in *Poetry*'s May 1913 issue that Pound published the first important review of Robert Frost's *A Boy's Will*, taking American editors to task for ignoring Frost's talents: "The man has the good sense to speak naturally and to paint the thing, the thing as he sees it. And to do this is a very different matter from gunning about for the circumplectious polysyllable."

Monroe promulgated an "open door" policy that would acknowledge exceptional talent wherever she found it. But Pound's criteria were more severe. His "A Few Don'ts by an Imagiste" was originally intended as a form letter for rejections, but published in *Poetry*, it took on the force of a manifesto. It is to Monroe's credit that she neither ceded her authority over the magazine to Pound, nor closed her mind to his ideas. On the contrary, his imprint can be recognized in her own tribute, "The New Beauty," published in the April 1913 issue. Her cultural reach is striking as she writes of Tagore: "Today it is not a poet of Anglo-Saxon race but a Hindoo with divinatory power in English, who has the keenest vision of the new beauty, and the richest modern message." To "make it new," she acknowledged, meant going back to the roots of the lyric: "Poets should pay less attention to old forms which have been worn thin by five centuries of English song. They should return rather to first principles, feel as if poetry were new, and they the first to forge rhythmic chains for the English language." Pound's creed was indifferent, even disdainful to the public. He wrote in "Tenzone," the opening poem of the April 1913 issue: "I beg you, my friendly critics, / Do not set about to procure me an audience." Monroe, by contrast, was generous and encouraging. She saw the education and elevation of an audience for poetry as her primary task. One can recognize this motive in her selections, which welcome readers with traditional tastes while introducing them to modern styles, and in her prose, which justifies to the wary the strange new beauty on which she was shedding light. Every issue began with the quotation from Whitman that first launched her project: "To have great poets there must be great audiences too."

Bibliography: Milton Brown, *American Painting from the Armory Show to the Depression* (Princeton, NJ, 1955). Martin Green, *New York 1913: The Armory Show and the Paterson Strike Pageant* (New York, 1988). 1913 Armory Show: First International Exhibition of Modern Art in America (New York, 1913), *xroads.virginia.edu.* Joseph Parisi and Stephen Young, eds., *Dear Editor: A History of Poetry in Letters—The First Fifty Years, 1912–1962* (New York, 2002). The Paterson Strike Pageant

Program, *historymatters.gmu.edu*. Jean-Michel Rabate, *1913: The Cradle of Modernism* (London, 2007). Ellen Williams, *Harriet Monroe and the Poetry Renaissance: The First Ten Years of Poetry* (Champaign-Urbana, IL, 1977).

BONNIE COSTELLO

1915

D. W. Griffith's *Birth of a Nation* is released

THE EMERGENCE OF NARRATIVE CINEMA

In 1915, in the first book-length consideration of film aesthetics, *The Art of the Moving Picture,* Vachel Lindsay, populist poet and ga-ga movie fan, was writing at a moment, very soon concluded, when all cinematic roads remained open, when American film in particular had not fully settled into what would soon become its ruling conventions, star acting and genre narratives. Lindsay spoke kindly about what he called "The Intimate Motion Picture," which he said was "the world's great new medium for studying . . . the half-relaxed or gently restrained moods of human creatures. It gives us also our idiosyncrasies. It is gossip in extremis." Nicely put. But a trifle faint-hearted in comparison to his then widely shared enthusiasm for panorama and spectacle—for epic filmmaking, especially movies that dealt in noble sentiments played out in exotic historical settings, rich in the possibilities for splendor in all its manifestations.

No one was more enthused about these possibilities than D. W. Griffith, who, in the year Lindsay wrote, premiered his epochal, distasteful, and wildly successful *The Birth of a Nation*—a soaring account of the birth, that is, of "the Invisible Empire," the Ku Klux Klan, all pitched to the rescue of Southern white womanhood from hordes of bestial black freedmen—and began shooting its follow-up flop, *Intolerance.*

Griffith was a failed poet, playwright, and actor when he began directing at the Biograph Studios in 1908; he was forty years old when *Birth* went into release. The newspapers and the public almost immediately began noticing that his many Biograph productions (he directed virtually all of the studio's output, often completing two one-reel films per week) were different from those turned out by his rivals—more aspiring in their subject matter, more sophisticated technically. The movie trade papers began to identify Griffith as the author of these smart little films, and so he began, at last, to have a prospering, coherent, and, briefly, an almost competition-free career. In the teens of the twentieth century he became America's only great (or, indeed, readily identifiable) director.

In his later years, when he stumbled into failure almost as profound as his earlier success, Griffith was sometimes heard to mourn the fact that he had been unable to patent what he regarded as his signal invention, the close-up—never mind that others had used the device before him. In fact, the close-up was only a part of what he did, during the Biograph years, to lend greater fluidity to the process of screen storytelling.

He freed the movies from the proscenium arch, the habit of plunking the camera down in what amounted to the best seat in the house to watch dramas unfold as if they were plays—all wide shots, all characters always in view, entrances and exits all carefully noted by an eye unblinking in its concentration on a single scene. By selecting this player or that to stress the importance of their actions—or reactions—Griffith literally directed the audience's attention to their emotions, enlisting his customers' visceral responses to whatever situation he was examining. As he had no resort to the dialogue that did a similar job of shifting emphases on stage, this was a matter of incalculable importance to the development of the movies' unique narrative manner. The audience's response to Griffith's innovations was more instinctive than intellectual; these movies just felt good to them, better than those provided by the competition. "Even we children sensed that Biograph pictures were 'different,'" the critic Edward Wagenknecht wrote many years later.

There were literary aspirations. In his first two Biograph years, Griffith made one-reel adaptations of Jack London's *The Call of the Wild,* Tennyson's "Enoch Arden," *The Taming of the Shrew,* Tolstoy's *Resurrection,* and Browning's *Pippa Passes.*

But there was another strand to Griffith's sensibility, and in 1909 he directed an adaptation of quite a different sort, *A Corner in Wheat,* an unacknowledged knock-off of a Frank Norris story, and this gave vent to his populism. It is possibly his first truly great film, the story of a plutocrat who attempts to corner the grain market and ends up buried alive under a cascade of wheat. The film is realistic, distinctly unpoetic in tone, and typical of Griffith's best vein, which stressed the contemporary urban anecdote, often with a strong class bias—he was very sympathetic to the struggles of poorer classes, of which he had long been a member, and grimly antipathetic to their exploiters. Between these two poles—the realistic and the poetically spectacular—the rest of his career was uneasily, eventually disastrously, suspended.

For the moment, despite the interest of the popular press in the movies' cultural aspirations, the most important work Griffith was doing was less in the realm of story selection than in storytelling. The former was relatively easy for him; he was well versed in the popular fiction, drama, and poetry of the nineteenth century, and he had noticed, especially in the first two genres, what he would call their "switchback" construction—two or more parallel stories related simultaneously by cutting back and forth between them. In his first "Enoch Arden" adaptation—made during his initial six months at Biograph—he risked parallel shots (of the shipwrecked Arden yearning for home, of Arden's wife imagining him lost on a desert island) and was chastised for them by management. "How can you tell a story humping about like that?" his wife remembered him being told. "The people won't know what it's about." "Well, doesn't Dickens write that way?" "Yes, that's Dickens; that's novel writing; that's different." "Oh, not so much, these are picture stories; not so different."

What Griffith instinctively realized was that movies could cut from one subplot to another, one scene or shot to another, in the wink of a camera's eye, without resort to all the painful, time-consuming scene shifting of the theatrical melodrama. Or, to put it another way, he saw that the movies were, in essence, an optical medium. The film historian George Pratt speaks of Griffith's "bold juggling with and breakneck pacing of film editing in 1912 and 1913—his use of motion continually intercepted, and continually resumed" and mentions the simultaneous appearance of his work and the beginnings of European and American modernism—Joyce, Picasso, Stravinsky, Gertrude Stein.

There is an important distinction to be made. Griffith's was an essentially Victorian spirit, and he was placing his innovations in the service of melodramatic forms already being displaced in the avant-garde by newer narrative inventions. Neither he nor his public at first noticed this inconvenience. Everyone's attention was particularly focused on the rise of feature-length films as Griffith prepared to leave Biograph in 1913.

Biograph remained focused on one-reel films, convinced that longer movies were no more than a passing fad. Griffith knew otherwise. He had seen the success of Sarah Bernhardt's lavish four-reel *Queen Elizabeth* in 1912 and the Italian spectacle *Quo Vadis?* a year later. He had attempted to answer with his own biblical spectacle, *Judith of Bethulia,* which Biograph had rather grudgingly released. The film is, to modern eyes, a slightly ludicrous enterprise, but there is no doubting that Griffith's usual structure worked as well at four reels as it had at one. No one, addled by narrative confusion, ran screaming from the theater.

What addled Griffith, however, was the equation he made between historical panorama and the progress of movies as an art form. For him it was clear that film had a unique capacity to re-create bygone eras in their true splendor. Vast temples, surging crowds, dancing girls, pet leopards—the only limit on placing the vast panoply of the past before the public was the budget. It could indeed be argued that this facility was of the new medium's essence; no other expressive form came close to its ability to render with thrilling and realistic immediacy the pomp and pageantry, the cruelty and decadence, of life in ancient Carthage or Pompeii or Babylon.

Perhaps, though, we should say that this was only one of its essences—the other being the camera's capacity to be "the painter of the passing moment," to borrow a phrase from Baudelaire, capturing the flicker of joy or yearning, of alarm or triumph, in a modest, contemporary setting, in a story of less than vaulting imagistic ambition. Griffith never completely abandoned this vein, and by far the best of the four narratives contained in *Intolerance* is the so-called modern story, "The Mother and the Law," about a man falsely accused of murder and rescued from execution at the last moment by his determined wife. Some later examples of this manner *(A Romance of Happy Valley, True Heart Susie, Isn't Life Wonderful)* remain among Griffith's most attractive and unpretentious works. Still, there can be no question that he was seduced by spectacle. After *The Birth of a Nation* and *Intolerance* (which was heavily, directly influenced, in its Babylonian story, by Giovanni Pastrone's great 1915 epic, *Cabiria,* with a scenario by the Italian poet Gabriele D'Annunzio), he essentially staked his career on "big" pictures (as he called them)—*Hearts of the World, Orphans of the Storm, America.* We may suppose that he imagined high poetic possibilities in the epic film—many more D'Annunzios scribbling away at their screenplays—and admit that there was nothing wrong with that idea in theory.

But that neglected the potential for bombast in the epic form, the way the telling human gesture was lost in the general hubbub. Without denying that spectacle was of the cinematic essence, it is also hard to deny, as we study the subsequent history of the movies, how often the epic has disappointed us, how often its grand gestures have been empty ones. As early as 1924 the critic Gilbert Seldes wrote that Griffith's work was now "merely lavish," that "something in Mr. Griffith has been corrupted and died." Seldes acknowledged that there were wonderful things in *The Birth of a Nation* despite its ugly racist theme (its love story, its depictions of family life, its battle scenes) and he admired *Intolerance*'s modern story. But he saw that a lack of feeling in the grander aspects of Griffith's later films diminished them. As he considered the work of Griffith's rivals, particularly in American film, he made the same argument: everyone's crosscutting achieved new levels of sophistication in the last decade of silent film production, yet he felt that there was something empty in the spectacles being flung across the world's screens.

Seldes was largely correct. There were plenty of intimately scaled movies in the 1920s; they surely constituted the majority of films. But the desire to overawe the public with "casts of thousands," whether with *Robin Hood* or *The Ten Commandments,* was the chief desire of the most aspiring filmmakers. It was where the prestige was—and, often enough, the biggest bucks. In this era, Griffith's films began to look creaky, "old-fashioned" to some critics—largely because of the sentimental stories they told, but also because others were beginning to surpass him in technique.

Looking back on this era from 1944, Sergei Eisenstein, who succeeded Griffith as the critical community's most admired director, was generous in his appraisal of the American's contributions. But he felt—rightly—that Griffith remained trapped in parallel construction (which Eisenstein interestingly saw as class driven, the privileged exploiting the underprivileged until a last-reel resolution, generally triumphant, for the latter). The "montage trope" as the Russian called it, the juxtaposition of disparate shots creating resonances, metaphors, larger than the sum of their parts, eluded Griffith. So did meaningful engagement with the contemporary world.

Eisenstein's argument (in *Film Form*) is woozy and hard to follow, and it is not the whole truth, either. Eisenstein's cinema was much more abstract than Griffith's. Yes, his montage tropes could be thrilling (see, for example, his classic Odessa Steps sequence in the 1925 *Battleship Potemkin*), but he generally neglects character—men and women the audience can care about—in favor of mass heroics and mass tragedies, and putting historical incident in the service of Soviet propaganda. Eisenstein's films—unlike many of Griffith's, corny as they often are —are not easily watchable any longer, except for the odd excerpt. In those days, there was still a drive within the motion picture mainstream to discover ways of telling stories through images, by means unique to the movies, without excessive resort to antique melodramatic conventions. Eisenstein, like Griffith, was at once vaguely appreciative of the landmark films of the later silent era and impervious to them—to Robert Wiene's surrealistically tinged *Cabinet of Dr. Caligari*, the monumental expressionism of Fritz Lang's *Metropolis,* the delicate blend of expressionist and realist elements in King Vidor's still underrated *The Crowd,* or F. W. Murnau's *Sunrise,* to name but a few signposts on the road not taken by the movies in general in this period.

The coming of sound, that greatest of technological innovations, cut off aesthetic innovation in silent picture narration just as it reached its high point in the late 1920s. And it was often deeply resented by theoreticians like Rudolf Arnheim, whose argument, crudely put, was based on the fact that art is defined by its limits—paintings can't move, music can't create images, and so on. Silence was the defect in film that drove its visual poetics to ever-greater heights. We might observe that speechlessness was not an inherent defect in the movies, like stasis in painting; it was merely a technological imperfection, bound eventually to be overcome. But never mind—when sound arrived, it quite naturally drove movies in an opposite direction, away from visual metaphor, toward tough-guy literary sources, toward a harsher realism.

It must be admitted that the first talking pictures were often uninteresting in comparison to the films of the High Silent Era. But not for long. They quickly developed a wit, and a savage urban immediacy (see, in particular, the 1930 to 1934 Warner Bros. pictures of the pre-Code era), from which a new film aesthetic could be derived—or an old one revitalized, since many of these small urban dramas (many ran only a bit more than an hour) had about them the rough presence (and proletarian sympathies) of Griffith's little Biograph dramas. And we should mark this as well: the sound movie remained wedded, if not in sentiment, then in structure, to the Griffith manner. To this day, we still very largely tell our screen stories through crosscutting between parallel melodramatic elements. Other Griffith techniques—the use of the close-up for emotional punctuation, the shot and reverse-shot construction of scenes, the alternation of panoramic shots with more intimate ones, particularly in the epic—continue to function as the cinema's most basic grammar. You need only look at any action film, playing today at a theater near you, to see how Griffith's influence abides. However sophisticated their special effects or the staging of their sexual encounters, love will eventually conquer all and the picture will climax with some kind of ride to the rescue, just as *The Birth of a Nation* did.

Late in his life, Griffith came to know Jean Renoir, then living out his World War II exile in Beverly Hills. "He had the naïveté of the authentic great man," Renoir said. It is possible that Griffith's major achievement was permanently to impose that naïveté on the medium he did so much to shape in its formative years.

Bibliography: Rudolf Arnheim, *Film as Art* (Berkeley, CA, 1957). Sergei Eisenstein, *Film Form* (New York, 1949). Mrs. D. W. Griffith (Linda Arvidson), *When the Movies Were Young* (New York,

1925). Vachel Lindsay, *The Art of the Motion Picture* (New York, 1924). Richard Schickel, *D. W. Griffith: An American Life* (New York, 1984). Gilbert Seldes, *The Seven Lively Arts* (New York, 1924).

RICHARD SCHICKEL

1915
Robert Frost leaves England for America

A LOVER'S QUARREL WITH THE WORLD

After two years in England, Robert Frost set sail for the United States with his family of six, tenuous prospects, and a little furnace of bitterness in his heart that probably could have powered the ship on which he traveled. It was 1915. The bitterness stemmed partly from the fact that Frost was forty-one years old and feeling frustrated in his career, and thus the recent appearance of his first two books (*A Boy's Will* and *North of Boston*) in England, and the news that Henry Holt would reprint one hundred and fifty copies of one of those books (*North of Boston*) in America, eased that sting somewhat. But only somewhat. It's tempting but not quite accurate to say that Frost was born into a time that was at odds with his temperament. With his old-fashioned forms and rural subjects, his emphasis on clarity and unity, and his deliberate courting of a popular audience, he seems the odd man out among the modernists. But as some of them noted (Ezra Pound early on, T. S. Eliot much later), Frost's poems bear the unmistakable mark of someone who was fully living the particular tensions of his time. "I had a lover's quarrel with the world," he wrote late in his life, gentling, as he had learned to do, the conflicting intensities that biographers and critics have been trying to untangle ever since, the weirdly buoyant bitterness at the heart of this man who was likely the greatest American poet of the twentieth century.

"American" is an interesting and tricky adjective with regard to Frost. It always has been. He'd hardly stepped off that boat from England when he discovered in a New York newsstand a review of his work in the *New Republic* by Amy Lowell in which she praised him for just this quality, his American-ness. She was referring to the New England landscapes in his poems, all the metaphorical forests and moral maple trees, all the lean country folk with their charming indigence and iambic wisdom. This wasn't—isn't—a false perception, for Frost's poems are indeed rooted in a real place and time, even as they tend to glamorize local color and stereotypical folksiness. It would take several decades for the critical pendulum to shift, when Randall Jarrell, Lionel Trilling, and others began "discovering" the dark undertow of Frost's poems and making *that* their most salient—even most American—quality. These readings were more sophisticated than Lowell's, but they tended to be—and still tend to be, for it's this vision of Frost that has dominated critical analysis since his death—reductive in another way, emphasizing the isolation in the poems over their ties to the earth, the terror over the rapture.

These conflicting intensities, this lover's quarrel that seems so much more consuming than that—it is a kind of spiritual vertigo, really—may be what is most American about Frost. One of the great ironies of American literature is that in a country in which, some new survey always seems to say, 95 percent of the people don't simply believe in a personal God but can count the whiskers on his chin, so much of our best work should be so consistently fraught with anxious unbelief, galvanizing absence, spiritual terror. From Herman Melville to Cormac McCarthy, from Emily Dickinson through Wallace Stevens and Sylvia Plath, one can trace a spiritual energy that is both passion and plight, a metaphysical compulsion as fervid as it is unfixed. But this is perhaps not so surprising, since if one American impulse is toward a kind of spiritual vertigo, an equally strong one is the impulse to disguise this feeling with optimistic personae and evangelical enthusiasm. So much of American literature is about buried intensities because so much of American life is a mask.

Frost furthered both, the buried intensities and the blithe surface, the mystery and the mask. The huckster who created the role of the traveling bard, the cunning careerist who was not above setting fire to some papers during a rival's reading, the middlebrow philosopher in love with his own feinting phrases ("I had a lover's quarrel with the world," for instance)—this identity wasn't foisted on Frost but actively, assiduously cultivated. He was the closest thing to a national poet that America had in the twentieth century, partly because he perfected a kind of entrepreneurial narcissism that has long thrived in this country, and partly—mostly—because he employed a style of such clear, untroubled surfaces that readers hardly noticed the obscure trouble into which a poem might suddenly plummet:

> One of my wishes is that those dark trees,
> So old and firm they scarcely show the breeze,
> Were not, as 'twere, the merest mask of gloom,
> But stretched away unto the edge of doom.
>
> I should not be withheld but that some day
> Into their vastness I should steal away,
> Fearless of ever finding open land,
> Or highway where the slow wheel pours the sand.
>
> I do not see why I should e'er turn back,
> Or those should not set forth upon my track
> To overtake me, who should miss me here
> And long to know if still I held them dear.
>
> They would not find me changed from him they knew—
> Only more sure of all I thought was true.

This is the first poem in Frost's first book, and you can be sure that its placement was no accident: it can be read as a kind of key to all of Frost's best work. Two separate but related tensions are strongly asserted: between the will of the poet and the doom of unbeing, first of all, and also between community or society and the integrity of the individual self. It's not at all clear that these tensions oppose each other. This poem that plummets toward doom is, after all, called "Into My Own," and what seems a straightforward withdrawal from social life turns out to be not only some ultimate engagement with it (stanza three) but also some heightened, unearthly consciousness in which the poet is *more* sure of the ties that bound him to the earth in the first place. "Into My Own" is the first example of what will become a signature effect of Frost's: meanings that are so simultaneous and multifaceted that to choose any single one is terribly reductive, even if, *especially* if, Frost himself points the way. In the original British publication of *A Boy's Will,* Frost included a cloying, defensive gloss to "Into My Own," as he did for all of the poems: "The youth is persuaded that he will be rather more than less himself for having forsworn the world." It's a typical Frostian gesture, to undercut artistic intensity with irony, to utterly engage existence while mocking the effort. By the time *A Boy's Will* appeared in the United States in 1916 the glosses were gone. Frost had discovered—partly, no doubt, from reviewers such as Amy Lowell—that his camouflage of convention was working just fine.

Nothing is harder to recognize than radical originality manifesting itself in a common style. (Nothing is harder to imitate either, which is one reason, perhaps *the* reason, why Frost's influence on subsequent American poetry has been significantly less than that of T. S. Eliot, Wallace Stevens, or William Carlos Williams.) It's worth noting, for instance, how relentlessly (almost defiantly, given the time in which it was written) plain the language is in "Into My Own"; how predictable the rhymes are; how readily Frost will resort to an archaism ("'twere," "e'er") to preserve the regular meter; how jauntily and matter-of-factly the poem fills out the form of a sonnet. All of this is the very antithesis of poetic modernism, and it's no wonder that Frost was long labeled, is still often labeled, an antimodernist. He seems to sing as unselfconsciously as Tennyson, and anyone accustomed to the rough, disruptive stylistic effects of modern poetry can glide right over the unmistakably modern consciousness that Frost's smooth surfaces conceal.

Frost's originality lies precisely in this revealing, concealing kind of poetry. There is a direct connection between the lyrical fluency of "Into My Own"—or of poems such as "The Most of It," "To Earthward," "The Sound of Trees," "Bereft," "Tree at My Window," "Desert Places," "The Oven Bird," "The Wind and the Rain"—and the spiritual vertigo I have mentioned. To be a great lyric poet requires the cultivation of a consciousness that is neither active nor passive but some fusing of both: a kind of honed vulnerability. (To be a great narrative poet— and Frost was this as well—requires different skills altogether, and often a *refusal* of lyric release.) What one remains vulnerable to is, on the most basic level, one's medium, language: some cadence or rhythm, something in the pure *sound* of words sets something in the poet's soul wonderfully, dangerously adrift. The wonder is in the deep connection between word and world, the way the anxieties of composition and the anxieties of existence can be coextensive, so that a poem that finds its true form can bring about what Frost famously called "a momentary stay against confusion." The danger is in the confusion, which even in the best poems (especially in these, in fact) is not eradicated or lessened but momentarily withstood, charmed, *stayed.* This vulnerability is no easy thing to sustain, which is why most poetry of this particular sort of lyric intensity is written by younger poets, or by older poets who have learned to brace themselves and their gift against some strong belief.

Belief in what, though? The only other American modernists who had ears as finely tuned as Frost's were T. S. Eliot and Wallace Stevens. Both men wrote masterpieces of lyrical intuition, and both men looked backward for a belief against which to brace themselves in the chaos and confusion out of which those works emerged. For Eliot the answer was religion, specifically the Church of England. Stevens turned to a modernized version of British romanticism and the power of the individual imagination. Frost, so apparently conservative, is different. It is quite possible to read through his collected poems, his letters and notebooks, and all sorts of critical and biographical material and still not be able to say clearly what exactly it was he believed in. Belief of some sort there most definitely is, though:

> Where my imaginary line
> Bends square in woods, an iron spine
> And pile of real rocks have been founded.
> And off this corner in the wild,
> Where these are driven in and piled,
> One tree, by being deeply wounded,
> Has been impressed as Witness Tree
> And made commit to memory
> My proof of being not unbounded.
> Thus truth's established and borne out,
> Though circumstanced with dark and doubt—
> Though by a world of doubt surrounded.

This little—and little-known—poem, "Beech," was written some thirty years after "Into My Own" and leads off the same late book, *A Witness Tree,* in which Frost writes of having "a lover's quarrel with the world." Much has changed. The self that in the earlier poem was projected into and upon wildness and doom is now chastened, bounded. (Or, to be more accurate, "not unbounded," a double negative that mischievously preserves a hint of its opposite meaning.) The confident, youthful way in which the speaker of "Into My Own" assumed not only his own strength and will but also that his being was coextensive with being itself, his end some sort of mysterious personal fruition rather than annihilation—all that is now "circumstanced with dark and doubt" and "by a world of doubt surrounded." It's very tempting to see this as a journey from innocence to experience—or, in more specifically American terms, from a kind of soft-focus transcendentalism to a hard-edged pragmatism—except for that lingering sense of futility when, outside of the poems and their mesmerizing music, you try to explain to yourself what exactly that transcendence consists of in the earlier poem or what, in "Beech," the "truth" that seems so solidly, painfully realized might be.

This mutual elusiveness is, finally, what binds these poems. I said earlier that "Into My Own" could be read as a key to all of Frost's work; actually, you need this latter key as well, though there is no ultimate truth into which these keys open. "Into My Own" feels like pure verb in search of a self to be its noun; "Beech" is all noun at the end of a verb that remains unspoken—and unspeakable. Each poem preserves the obscurity that impelled it, though each poem moves with such ease and apparent clarity that you hardly feel these huge occlusions the sound has somehow pulled you past. There is a siren quality to such music, in that it leads you into an ultimate existential crisis for which it has no ultimate answers. Very modern, this. The great power and mystery of Frost's lyric poetry is the way it leaves you feeling neither stymied nor despairing by this crisis, but enlarged, in- tensified, even elated. The song that leads you close to the shoals is, it turns out, the song that steers you by them.

Of course, there are more shoals than poems, more confusion than the songs that seem, briefly, to contain and control it. This is particularly true for mod- ern poets and their inheritors. With this in mind, the buffoonery and bluster of Frost's public persona become, perhaps, a bit more explicable, as do all the cutesy, folksy poems that seem to have been written solely in the service of this persona. He knew in his bones the dangers and elations of pure sound, and even late in his life (until his last two books) he found a way to keep his poetic instincts both honed and vulnerable. Outside of the poems, though, he needed something to hold on to, so he puffed up a hollow, public self that had no doubts about exis- tence, flaunted reactionary opinions, and ate adulation like a circus dog. A lover's quarrel with the world? In truth, it was more like a war, though one that, in twenty or so of the purest lyrics this country has ever produced, a contemporary reader can experience as the most miraculous, mysterious, and all-too-momentary sort of peace.

Bibliography: Robert Frost, *Collected Poems, Prose, and Plays,* ed. Richard Poirier and Mark Richardson (New York, 1995); *Selected Letters of Robert Frost,* ed. Lawrance Thompson (New York, 1964). William H. Pritchard, *Robert Frost: A Literary Life Reconsidered* (New York, 1984). Law- rance Thompson, *Robert Frost: The Early Years, 1874–1915* (New York, 1966); *Robert Frost: The Years of Triumph, 1915–1938* (New York, 1970). Lawrance Thompson and R. H. Winnick, *Robert Frost: The Later Years, 1938–1963* (New York, 1976).

CHRISTIAN WIMAN

1917

Albert C. Barnes writes to John Dewey requesting
permission to attend his Columbia seminar

THE PHILOSOPHER AND THE MILLIONAIRE

Even the closest intimates of John Dewey and Albert C. Barnes found it diffi- cult to understand how two individuals so radically different in their personalities and temperaments could enjoy such a close and long-lasting friendship—one that endured until Barnes's death in 1951. When they met in 1917, Dewey was America's most influential and beloved philosopher. He was modest, self-effacing, and friendly; democratic to the very core of his being. Barnes was cantankerous, pugnacious, unforgiving, gruff, autocratic, and subject to fits of rage. He hated phonies and snobs (which included Philadelphia society, art critics, and most academics); he refused to allow them to see his collection. Despite his professed commitment to democracy, Barnes was intolerant of those who disagreed with him and tried ruthlessly to destroy their reputations. In 1952, shortly after Dewey's death, Sidney Hook, one of his closest colleagues, wrote: "Dewey's goodness was so genuine, constant, and sustained, even under provocation, that I sometimes found it somewhat oppressive. It was almost a relief that I discovered one shortcoming in him. That was his indulgent friendship with Albert C. Barnes."

Barnes, trained as a doctor and a scientist, became an extremely shrewd businessman. He did not invent Argyrol, a silver nitrate antiseptic (although he claimed that he did), but at the beginning of the twentieth century he cleverly promoted it so that it became the standard antiseptic and cure-all used throughout the world. Argyrol made him millions and provided him with the leisure and opportunity to amass the most impressive private collection in America of impressionist and postimpressionist paintings, including dozens of the best paintings of Renoir, Degas, Seurat, Cezanne, Picasso, Matisse, Modigliani, Soutine, and many others. After their initial meeting Dewey was a frequent guest of Barnes at his home in Merion, Pennsylvania. Barnes delighted in sharing his pictures with Dewey, and invited Dewey (at Barnes's expense) to join him on visits to art museums throughout Europe, where Barnes lectured Dewey on the art of painting. (When Dewey retired from teaching at Columbia, Barnes also generously supplemented his retirement income.) Barnes introduced Dewey to a number of artists, including Matisse, who was commissioned to paint a mural for the Barnes Foundation. Until Dewey met Barnes, he had scarcely dealt with the topic of the fine arts and aesthetics, but under Barnes's tutelage, Dewey learned more about art and increasingly came to realize that art and aesthetics stood at the very center of his philosophic vision.

The significance and consequences of John Dewey's reflections on art and the aesthetic became fully explicit when he published *Art as Experience* (1934), his most original, imaginative, and neglected book. He dedicated it "To Albert C. Barnes in Gratitude," and wrote in his preface: "I have had the benefit of conversations with [Barnes] through a period of years, many of which occurred in the presence of the unrivalled collection of pictures he has assembled. The influence of these conversations, together with that of his books, has been a chief factor in shaping my own thinking about the philosophy of esthetics."

If one is looking for a single book that epitomizes Dewey's philosophic outlook, there is no better source than *Art as Experience*. The opening chapters present one of the clearest statements of what Dewey means by experience. Dewey, who was deeply influenced by Darwin (*The Origin of Species* was published in 1859, the year of Dewey's birth), tells us that experience always involves a dynamic interaction between a living creature and its environing conditions. Experience involves undergoing and doing; receptivity and activity. But experience is frequently inchoate and diffuse. In contrast to this continuous stream of experience, we can isolate what Dewey labels "an experience," which has its own rhythm, tensions, and history: "For life is no uniform uninterrupted march or flow. It is a thing of histories, each with its own plot, its own inception and movement toward its close, each having its own particular rhythmic movement; each with its own unrepeated quality pervading it throughout."

To grasp what Dewey means, think of some of the ways in which we commonly speak of significant experiences—the experience of a memorable performance of *King Lear*, the experience of solving a difficult scientific problem, the experience of surviving a death camp, the experience of an enduring friendship or a personal tragedy such as the death of a child. Such experiences have a temporal and spatial spread; they change and develop; they contain moments of tension and fulfillment; they encompass many diverse events. Yet this way of thinking about experience (which accords with one of our primary common-sense ways of speaking about experience) departs radically from the ways in which many traditional philosophers characterize experience. Much of modern philosophy has been exclusively concerned (even obsessed) with the epistemological significance of experience—how experience serves (or does not serve) as the foundation of knowledge. Yet many of our most cherished experiences are not primarily knowledge affairs, even though a great deal of knowledge may be required in order to *have* an experience. Furthermore, there is nothing intrinsically subjective or private about our experiences. They do not consist exclusively of sense data or feelings that are somehow locked up in our minds. If we speak of *an* experience as exciting, sublime, distressing, or tragic, it is the situation or experience that has these characteristics—not just our feelings.

But, we may ask, what is it that gives these experiences their distinctive unity; what enables us to distinguish these heightened experiences from the flow of experience? Dewey focuses on the pervasive quality of these experiences—a unique concrete quality that unites the diverse elements that constitute an experience. While we use words and concepts such as "aesthetic," "practical," and "intellectual" to characterize these directly experienced qualities, what we are naming is concrete and singular. These pervasive qualities are the source of the unity of an experience and guide its development. Thus, for example, when a scientist seeks to solve a complex problem, she may entertain many different hypotheses and carry out a variety of experiments, but she has a background sense of a pervasive unifying quality of the situation that helps to guide her inquiry. Dewey's distinctive understanding of the pervasive qualities that unite and guide the development of experiences provides an initial clue to what he means by "aesthetic"—an adjective that singles out the unique emotional quality of an experience that possesses "internal integration and fulfillment reached through ordered and organized movement."

There are important consequences of this way of thinking of "an experience" and its distinctive aesthetic quality. Dewey shows how art and aesthetics are grounded in, and continuous with, our everyday living. Art and aesthetics intensify and epitomize what ordinary people experience in their everyday lives. Typically we apply the term "art" to call attention to the activity of creating works of art, and "aesthetic" to the enjoyment of the meanings embodied in a work of art, but Dewey argues that although we can distinguish production from enjoyment, the two cannot be separated. These are comparable to the phases of activity and receptivity that are characteristic of every experience. Dewey reminds us how much of what we take to be art today originally played a role in the everyday practical and religious lives of ordinary people. He is sharply critical of that tradition that seeks to isolate art and the aesthetic from the rest of our experience.

The adjective "aesthetic" does not name a special *type* of experience but rather a quality or feature that can be present in *any* experience. It is the feature of consummation and fulfillment, where the diverse elements and funded (that is, required) meanings of an experience achieve integration. The experiences of thinking about or solving a problem, or the practical activity of achieving a difficult goal, may each have its own distinctive aesthetic quality. Writes Dewey: "The enemies of the aesthetic are neither the practical nor the intellectual. They are the humdrum; slackness of loose ends; submission to convention in practice and intellectual procedure. Rigid abstinence, coerced submission, tightness on the one side and dissipation, incoherence and aimless indulgence on the other, are deviations in opposite directions from the unity of an experience."

We can begin to see the political significance of this approach to the aesthetic quality of experience. Much of our modern life alternates between the extremes of aimless indulgence and coerced submission. In a manner that is reminiscent of early Marx, Dewey calls for a democratic transformation of society in which *all* experience will be enriched by enjoyed meanings, will become humane and integrated—more artistic and aesthetic.

But how are we to understand the title of Dewey's book, *Art as Experience?* In what sense is art "experience"? We touch here a theme that is fundamental for Dewey's entire philosophic outlook. Throughout his career Dewey criticized what he took to be dichotomies that plague so much of philosophy—rigid dichotomies between mind and body, the mental and the physical, the merely subjective and the truly objective. These dichotomies foster a misleading conception of the "spectator theory of knowledge." We are not passive spectators of the world; we are *actively* involved in experimenting, inquiring, imagining, and making. The work of art is *not* to be identified or confused with a physical object or the product of art. Art is a quality of *doing.* "The *product* of art—temple, painting, statue, poem—is not the *work* of art. The work takes place when a human being cooperates with the product so that the outcome is an experience that is enjoyed because of its liberating and ordered properties." A work of art is a medium that is expressive; it contains a source of emotional meanings, which are appropriated and enjoyed by the aesthetically sensitive perceiver. The work of art *works;* it is essentially dynamic: "The work of art is complete only as it works in the experience of others than the one who created it."

Consequently, a work of art is re-created every time that it is aesthetically experienced. This aesthetic perception is not passive; *receptivity is not passivity.* "To perceive, a beholder must *create* his own experience . . . [W]ith the perceiver, as with the artist, there must be an ordering of the elements of the whole that is in form, although not in details, the same as the process of organization the creator of the work consciously experienced. Without an act of recreation the object is not perceived as a work of art." Perceiving a work of art involves *work.* "The hasty sightseer no more has an aesthetic vision of Saint Sophia or the Cathedral of Rouen than the motorist traveling at sixty miles an hour *sees* the flitting landscape. One must move about, within and without, and through repeated visits let the structure gradually yield itself to him in various lights and in connection with changing moods."

But still, we may ask, how does Dewey's appreciation of art as experience and the aesthetic enjoyment of the meanings of art relate to the rest of his philosophy? When Dewey tells us that art is a quality of doing and what is done, he is not simply referring to the fine arts, for this is a characteristic of everything that we take to be an art. One of Dewey's lifelong preoccupations was to show that all inquiry (including scientific inquiry) is an *art*—a mode of practice that involves experimentation and imagination. Just as the Greeks thought of *poiesis* as the form of making that includes making a house, a statue, a poem, or a tragedy, Dewey stresses the continuity that breaks down rigid dichotomies between crafts and fine arts. He thought that the scientific revolution taught us that knowing or inquiry is also an art. Although Dewey stresses the continuity of the arts and how they are all forms of experience, he is sensitive to differences. Throughout *Art as Experience,* he carefully distinguishes the scientific art of inquiry from the fine arts. They complement each other. The primary objective of the fine arts is not to add to our knowledge of the world but rather to achieve a sense of disclosure and heightened intelligibility of the world. He argues that we must be sensitive to the different modes of *thinking* that we find in works of art and in scientific inquiry.

> The odd notion that an artist does not think and a scientific inquirer does nothing else is the result of converting a difference of tempo and emphasis into a difference of kind. The thinker has his esthetic moment when his ideas cease to be mere ideas and become corporate meanings of objects. The artist has his problems and thinks as he works. But his thought is more immediately embodied in the object . . . The artist does his thinking in the very qualitative media he works in.

Dewey defends the creative role that art can play in transforming society. "Works of art are the only media of complete and unhindered communication between man and man that occur in a world full of gulfs and walls that limit community of experience." He endorses Shelley's claim that poets have always been the moral prophets of humanity because they epitomize the creative imagination that challenges the status quo. This imaginative critical function of art is essential for Dewey's vision of creative democracy. Dewey was a visionary, but he was a visionary of the here and now—of the reforms required to come closer to a creative democracy where all share and all participate. "All art is a process of making the world a different place in which to live, and involves a phase of protest and of compensatory response." As a social critic, he consistently criticized the ways in which laissez-faire capitalism and old-fashioned individualism distorted the democratic potential of human experience. His curious friendship with Barnes (a champion of laissez-faire capitalism and old-fashioned individualism) helped Dewey to articulate a vibrant vision of a democratic society in which imagination is cultivated and all experience and all *making* become more artistic and enriched with world-disclosing meanings.

Bibliography: Thomas M. Alexander, *John Dewey's Theory of Art, Experience, and Nature: The Horizons of Feeling* (Albany, NY, 1987). Richard J. Bernstein, *John Dewey* (New York, 1966). John Dewey, *Experience and Nature,* in *John Dewey: The Later Works, 1925–1953,* vol. 1: *1925,* ed. Jo Ann Boydston, Patricia Baysinger, and Barbara Levine (Carbondale, IL, 1981); *Art as Experience,* in *John Dewey: The Later Works, 1925–1953,* vol. 10: *1934,* ed. Jo Ann Boydston and Harriet Furst Simon (Carbondale, IL, 1987). Howard Greenfeld, *The Devil and Dr. Barnes: Portrait of an Art Collector* (New York, 1987).

RICHARD J. BERNSTEIN

1920, August 10

Mamie Smith becomes the first black woman to make a phonograph record

A New Voice of the Blues

You might get her confused with Bessie Smith or Clara Smith or even Ma Rainey—legendary blues women who would easily and rapidly outshine her in the 1920s—but it is Mamie Smith who holds the distinction of being the first black vocalist to record the blues. Her "Crazy Blues," a song written by New York songwriter Perry Bradford, set off a cultural phenomenon, creating a demand that, within the New York City black community alone, resulted in a reported 75,000 copies being distributed to Harlem record shops within four weeks of its release.

Most often thought of by blues historians as significant for having broken social barriers for black musicians, "Crazy Blues" is, however, rarely hailed as a so-called authentic blues record. Because of Smith's background as a vaudeville chanteuse (she appeared in 1899 in the enormously popular all-black traveling theater company Smart Set), she is largely viewed as having lacked the kind of gritty vocal chops that would eventually characterize the genre. If anything, some have argued, "Crazy Blues" earns its name from the volatile historical context in which it emerged rather than as a result of Smith's ferocious singing ability. Released in the wake of the Red Summer race riots of 1919, its tale of woeful heartache and inconsolable grief transposes haunting memories of lynch mobs and Southern disenfranchisement into generic love gone wrong. It is to some the first (coded) blues protest song recorded by an African American.

Further, "Crazy Blues" is a recording that holds in abeyance potent contradictions. It's a song that showcases floridly realized vaudevillian racial mimicry as well as a lyrical iteration of black social resistance poetics, and either side of the coin finds these sounds emanating from the unlikely figure of a black, female, New York City cabaret singer. In this regard, we might consider whether "Crazy Blues" remains a document of a black female performer watching the white coon shouter (as she was called) Sophie Tucker—who was herself watching and working to master the aesthetics of performing black women who populated her personal world as well as the public labor force that surrounded her. More still, what if we think of the ways that "Crazy Blues" draws from black vaudeville and looks forward to black crossover theater and ultimately the complicated racial skein of rock-and-roll culture itself?

Mamie Smith's style was unmistakably vaudeville, meaning that her voice resonated with the translations and mutations of racial musical caricature found in turn-of-the-century stage shows. Black vaudeville productions gradually sought to replace a white-imagined blackface minstrel dialectic with black-authored musical expressiveness that shifted its emphasis away from folk vernacular and toward nascent jazz stylings. Alongside black female stage contemporaries such as choreographer, singer, and actress Aida Overton-Walker, who famously assumed one of her husband's musical roles in drag after his untimely passing, Smith emerged out of a performing tradition of black female entertainers who were actively rewriting blackface forms. These were women intent on carving out a space for themselves in a line of work first dominated by white men donning burnt-cork makeup in the nineteenth century and later appropriated by black male theater entrepreneurs such as Bert Williams and George Walker, who saw a point of entry to disrupt and disassemble caricature from the inside out. "Crazy Blues" holds this history in its grooves.

Just as well, in the traces of its supposedly racially inauthentic vaudeville sound it holds the history of the oft-overlooked connections and complex collaborations between white and black female entertainers in the making of a recorded blues culture. The cultural historian Jayna Brown boldly rescues this lost history of "love and theft" between black women who danced, sang, composed music, and played instruments in the early twentieth century and white women performers, such as Eva Tanguay, Fanny Brice, Mae West, and especially "the last of the red hot mamas," Sophie Tucker, who were inspired by, sometimes threatened by, and deeply desirous of their art. "All of these women," Brown argues, "learned their dances, including the shimmy, from watching Clara Smith and other black women performers on the TOBA [Theater Owner's Booking Association] circuit through Chicago." But it was Tucker who, more than any of these other figures, straddled the most overt divide between minstrel culture and the recorded blues phenomenon. Striking it popular as perhaps the most famous white female performer who worked in full cork makeup and wig, Tucker moved swiftly from appearing in the Ziegfeld Follies in 1909 to recording successful renditions of blues compositions in the subsequent decade. Long before Elvis made off with Willie Mae Thornton's "Hound Dog" thunder, it was great white female hope Tucker who became the first person to record a million-selling blues record, in 1917.

Tucker was no doubt watching black women like blues and cabaret singer Al-

berta Hunter on the TOBA, and black women—perhaps even Mamie Smith—
were watching her, in private as well as public spaces. Brown makes note, for instance, of how black dancing ingenue Ida Forsyne's role in service as Tucker's
maid from 1922 to 1924, as well as her role as Tucker's backup dancer, reinforced
the cross-cultural social and professional exchanges between these women in the
context of theater. Forsyne provides a link as well, albeit a later one, between the
Jewish coon shouter and the "Crazy Blues" celebrity: she bounced from Tucker's
chorus to Smith's in 1924 before moving on to accompany Bessie Smith—"the
empress of the blues"—in 1927.

While the power differential in these sorts of arrangements between white
performing women and the maids and dancers who worked for them cannot be
denied, and while the benefits of racial mimicry would seem to fall squarely and
most advantageously on the side of the white female blackface entertainer who
exploits the cultural currency and supposed open availability of blackness as a
product to be bought and sold, we might nonetheless stretch our understanding
of these dynamics to consider how indicative they are of a black women's blues
era that is itself a period of racial and cultural diversity and mimicry. What if
we were to rethink and reconnect Smith's "Crazy Blues" to traditions less often
linked to the aesthetic practices of blues culture? What if we were to reconsider black women's blues performances through contemporary representations
of black femininity? Through those elements that black female artists borrowed
from black men, white men, and white women? Through encounters between the
traveling black big-tent performances and those of the white vaudeville stage?
Taking these intersecting histories into consideration may tell us much more
about Smith's recording as well as the social and cultural complexities of black
women's blues performances and their legacies.

Legend has it that it was dumb luck that Mamie Smith even got the gig that would
transform American popular music culture. In early 1920, Sophie Tucker was said
to have gotten the initial tap from Okeh Records to record a pair of songs by
black composer Perry Bradford. Having tackled W. C. Handy's "St. Louis Blues"
to great success and having closely studied the emotionally expressive vocalities
and rhythmic cadences of her contemporary Alberta Hunter, Tucker was a sure-
bet entertainer whose strong sales promised healthy returns for recording companies that were reluctant to back the blues, let alone back African American
blues artists, in an industry that was still young and in an American culture shaped
by Jim Crow racial segregation. Better to hire a white female entertainer well
versed in mimicking and interpreting the sexual assertiveness and vernacular
orality of Hunter and others than to invest in black female singers.

The story goes that Okeh had booked Tucker for a session to record "That
Thing Called Love" and "You Can't Keep a Good Man Down" when she became
ill. Bradford convinced the label to allow Mamie Smith to perform his tunes, and
on February 14, 1920, backed by a white studio band, Smith went to work. Maybe.
It is now believed that Bradford and Smith had arranged the collaboration on
their own and that Tucker was never involved. It was the second time that the

songwriter, pianist, and vaudeville and minstrel performer Bradford had worked in the studio with Smith, and it was the second time that Smith had given "That Thing Called Love" a go. In 1918 Bradford had tried unsuccessfully to get Victor records to distribute a version of the song that he and Smith had recorded on the label that year. A sloping, vaudeville number, "That Thing Called Love," and the equally ragtime-inflected "You Can't Keep a Good Man Down," were hardly what one might consider classic blues songs (for one, the compositions lacked the robust swagger and grit that would, in part, come to define the genre), but the disk with these two numbers, released by Okeh in July 1920, proved to be an enormous hit—especially in the black community, as more and more residents began purchasing record players on installment plans. To hear a black voice emanating from that new technology proved a particular thrill, an affirmation of black modernity as potent as the invention of jazz itself at the turn of the century. The climate was thus set both for Smith's blues recording debut on August 10, 1920, and its enthusiastic reception by black consumers from Harlem to Philadelphia to Chicago.

The era of recording "crossovers" was officially ushered in by Smith and Bradford's determination to cut a "black" voice singing "black" cultural music and to disseminate that record widely. With an estimated one million copies of "Crazy Blues" sold in one year, their plan paid off. But more broadly, their record contributed to a climate of racial crossover that was finally evolving bilaterally. Whereas traditional minstrelsy and early blues compositions featured white musicians and performers "slipping on blackness," the 1920s began with classical black thespian Charles Gilpin winning accolades for taking on white playwright Eugene O'Neill's vision of a "black" heart of darkness in *The Emperor Jones,* followed a year later by the Broadway success of the all-black musical *Shuffle Along.* "Crazy Blues" was, then, just one of several moments when black voices—on stage and in music—emerged at the center of popular culture even as segregation persisted.

But what are we to make of a record made by a black female entertainer better known in her own time for her theatrical talents than for her blues credentials? If anything, "Crazy Blues" documents a wild experiment: Smith's voice did, indeed, resonate with the swaggering lilt of Tucker's saucy singing, itself a reflection of Hunter's notable, early blues stylings. Backed on the record by the Jazz Hounds, a band of black musicians led by trumpeter Johnny Dunn, Smith wailed out a lament that would thematically typify the existential struggles of a musical genre on the verge of mass-market popularity: "I can't sleep at night / I can't eat a bite / 'Cause the man I love / He don't treat me right." Smith's threnody is a song cast in big, enveloping loss as wide as "the deep blue sea." It is a song that registers the plaintive wail of the standard blues heroine whose sense of abandonment leads her to the depths of suicidal despair. Yet sonically it bears the traces of Bert Williams's turn-of-the-century black vaudeville musical poetry in songs such as the classic "Nobody," which finds Williams expressing his sense of social "nobody-ness." Like Williams's signature song, Smith's vocals on "Crazy Blues" weave back and forth around wailing brass. The wind instruments in fact would make her number far more akin to the sound of early jazz than to the acoustic juke-joint blues born out of Southern culture, but Bradford had seemingly planned all along to spoon-feed this new music to the masses. With traces of black minstrelsy and vaudeville, as well as white coon-shouter contrivances and early jazz instrumentation, "Crazy Blues" was the quintessential generic and cultural mash-up track of its age.

It was also a rebel yell like none other that had been heard before on a phonograph. As the blues historian Adam Gussow has noted, it's the final stanza of the song—often shortened or excised completely from future sheet music and recordings—that shifts from convention into distinctive social disturbance: Smith sings that she's going to "get myself a gun . . . and shoot myself a cop / I ain't had nothing but bad news / Now I've got the crazy blues," a move that showcases songwriter Perry Bradford's radical blues articulation of the "black bad man/outlaw" figure willing to seize upon "black violence as a way of resisting white violence and unsettling a repressive social order" in the North as well as the South (as Gussow put it).

Where does the black female vocalist fit in in this equation? If we go along with the reading that Mamie Smith was merely ventriloquizing Bradford's black male militancy, then we have a rare instance of a black female performer articulating armed agency—the likes of which hadn't been seen in black popular culture since Pauline Hopkins brought her own gun-toting heroine to the stage in the 1879 musical *Peculiar Sam,* and the likes of which hadn't been heard broadly in black communities since Ida B. Wells called for the right to bear arms in her radical anti-lynching journalism.

Part Stagolee "bad man" turned "bad woman," part signifying Sophie Tucker song stylist, and part black female performer iterating resonant black women's blues themes *on* record for the first time, it seems Smith drew from her own vaudeville versatility to create a wicked amalgam of voices and gestures in song, a compressed shellac edition of often-overlooked interracial musical women's thievery and creative adoration of one another that frames this "crazy" narrative of white repression and black revolt. Smith's moment in the blues spotlight (and it was, it seems, just a moment) is a key one to keep in mind, because it forces us to reconsider the ways that classic blues women have been scripted—if they've been referred to at all in the rock-and-roll canon—as earthy, authentic "mamas" capable of saucy double entendres, but rarely as masquerading performers who slid into complex modes of racial mimicry.

Smith's recording should challenge us to rethink our narratives of racial appropriation and to reassess our understandings of (crazy) loves and thefts, and her "madwoman" declarations live on in the howling incantations of new millennial women like English alternative-rock rebel PJ Harvey and R & B glam goddess Beyoncé, both of whom remain "crazy in love."

Bibliography: Jayna Brown, *Babylon Girls: Race Mimicry, Black Chorus Line Dances and the Modern Body* (Durham, NC, 2008). Adam Gussow, "'Shoot Myself a Cop': Mamie Smith's 'Crazy Blues' as Social Text," *Callaloo* 25, no. 1 (Winter 2002): 8–44. *Discography:* Elvis Presley, "Hound

Dog" (RCA, 1956). Mamie Smith, "Crazy Blues" (Okeh, 1920); "That Thing Called Love" (Okeh, 1920); "You Can't Keep a Good Man Down" (Okeh, 1920). Willie Mae "Big Mama" Thornton, "Hound Dog" (Peacock, 1952). Sophie Tucker, "St. Louis Blues" (1917). Bert Williams, "Nobody" (Columbia, 1906).

DAPHNE A. BROOKS

1921
Jean Toomer travels to Sparta, Georgia

CANE

In 1921 Jean Toomer is twenty-seven years old and has not yet written his masterpiece, *Cane,* which will appear in 1923 and, some say, inaugurate the Harlem Renaissance. He has directed much energy toward thinking about race, gender, and the limitations and possibilities of the body. He has not yet begun his innovative experimental writing, the sound and tone poems and visionary epics like "Blue Meridian," but he has written a literal trunkful of poetry and prose, all of which he considers unsuccessful. He is pushing at the possibilities of genre and lyric language but has not yet burst open the English language as he does in those later poems, which are written in a Toomer-invented kind of Esperanto. His work strives to suggest that we exist beyond language and its parochial limitations, beyond nation, and even beyond the body.

The next year, 1922, James Weldon Johnson will publish *The Book of American Negro Poetry,* the landmark anthology of poetry that asserts "the world does not know that a people is great until that people produces great literature and art." Toomer is asked to contribute but chooses not to appear in the volume, inaugurating a central theme in his career of standing and being placed at times squarely within an African American community, tradition, and mission, but also resisting being classified as a Negro writer.

Unlike many young men of his generation, Toomer has missed serving in the First World War because of bad eyes "and a hernia gotten in a basketball game." His work experiences are inconsistent but funnel into his writing; after working for ten days in a New Jersey shipyard, he writes to the poet Georgia Douglas Johnson, "Now I know their life, so I've quit. I'll have more time to write." In early 1921 he is not gainfully employed but is reading Dostoyevsky, Tolstoy, Flaubert, Freud, Buddhist philosophy, writings on occultism and theosophy, and the Bible "as if it were a new book." He attends Georgia Douglas Johnson's famous Saturday night literary salons, which over the 1920s will draw writers such as Langston Hughes, Alain Locke, Angelina Weld Grimké, and Alice Dunbar Nelson. In fact, Toomer is said to have suggested the salons to Johnson. He has acquired, in his own words, "the reputation of being a very queer fellow."

In 1921 Toomer has not yet encountered the Greco-Armenian mystic George

Ivanovich Gurdjieff, whose teachings will govern much of his life. He has attended half a dozen colleges without graduating, studying agriculture, "of all things," at the University of Wisconsin and physical education at the American College for Physical Training in Chicago. He is living, by his account, a rather miserable life in an apartment in Washington, D.C., tending to his declining grandparents and two uncles. His mother, Nina Pinchback, has died, and his shady father, Nathan Toomer, abandoned him and his mother soon after young Toomer's birth; thus these grandparents are essentially parents to him. This is the year that Toomer renames and reinvents himself, as he would again and again, trimming his first three names, Nathan Eugene Pinchback, to simply one, Jean, short for Eugene but also after one of his literary heroes, Victor Hugo's character Jean Valjean. He names himself away from the legacy of both his father, Nathan, and his grandfather, P. B. S. Pinchback.

Pinchback was the first African American governor of a U.S. state (Louisiana) and was also elected to the United States Senate and House of Representatives, though those elections were contested. He was by all accounts an outsized figure who had lived grandly in Louisiana and Washington. But he had suffered a reversal of fortunes—thus the cramped Washington apartment—and in these years of decline the cronies and political folks who once populated his life and sought his counsel were nowhere to be found. No more brownstone home with double parlor; no more grand fetes; no more King of the Hill.

Washington, D.C., in the early 1920s was a well-established, class-conscious Negro metropolis, the seat of much power and vested community. Earlier in the century Toomer had lived there with his grandparents in a world that he described as "an aristocracy . . . midway between the white and Negro world." He graduated from the M Street high school, which by 1921 was called Dunbar High School and where the nation's first black PhDs were among the faculty teaching an intensive academic program. There was no finer black school, no greater educational opportunity. But Washington also stifled many free-minded souls: think of Langston Hughes, who left the service of the great historian Carter G. Woodson's Association for the Study of Negro Life and History, where he was endlessly filing index cards in the office, who—to the disapproval of some of Washington's Negro elite—chose to wash dishes and wait tables to earn his keep rather than alphabetize lists for Woodson's project "Free African Americans for Free Negro Owners of Slaves in the United States in 1830." The sculptor Elizabeth Catlett—like Toomer, a Dunbar graduate—would leave Washington a few years later, citing the need to break free of the stultification of the city's black high society. Duke Ellington was born in the city in 1893, studied piano with Marietta Clinkscales and noted Dunbar teacher Henry Grant, and composed tunes such as "Soda Fountain Rag" in his hometown. But by 1923 he had left for the musical possibilities of Gotham.

Whether it was Washington, his family situation, youthful angst, or some combination of all, of 1921 Toomer writes, "I felt I would die or murder someone if I stayed in that house another day." So when a chance opportunity arises,

Toomer jumps. His break comes serendipitously and is unlikely: out of the blue, he is asked to serve as substitute principal and teacher for a few months at Sparta Agricultural and Industrial Institute in Georgia, while the regular principal tours the North to raise funds. Toomer arranges immediately for the temporary care of his grandparents and sets off for the Deep South, which he has never seen.

In Sparta, Toomer encounters the Negro culture he fears is dying. He hears the sorrow songs for the first time and, like Du Bois before him, is deeply stirred. Something is unlocked within him when he hears that music. He feels certain that this culture and way of life will be lost, and this perception fuels his writing. He has found not only his themes but also the raison d'être of his themes. On his return home to Washington after two months, as his train lumbers northward, he begins writing what will become *Cane*.

The writing that boils up as *Cane* is gorgeous, strange, besotted, purple, over-wrought. "Her soul is like a little thrust-tailed dog that follows her, whimpering." "Carma in overalls, as strong as any man." "Becky was the white woman who had two Negro sons." "Shake your curled wool-blossoms, nigger. Open your liver-lips to the clean white spring. Stir the root-life of a withered people. Call them from their houses and teach them to dream." It is less about the landscape itself than the idea of the landscape, the idea of Negroes in the South, their mythos. The names of his characters are as indelible as the characters themselves: Karintha, Rhobert, Carma, Fern, Bona and Paul, King Barlo. As *The Souls of Black Folk* was not written by one who dwelt within the particular veil of the Negro South, so too *Cane* is written by an outsider in a culture he had never known. From Sparta he writes to Alain Locke at Howard University, "99% of the people who write and talk about the Negro hardly know his name." In Sparta, he listens for the songs of a people in some ways his own and in some utterly other, and records what he hears, sometimes beautifully, sometimes awkwardly.

The idea of an agricultural school for African Americans fulfills a Washingtonian approach to Negro education. It is a practical education for the people who, as slaves, were the true custodians of the land. Though Toomer's vision of black Southern people in *Cane* is sometimes overly romanticized, the hard work of stepping into an institution and helping people learn is not at all romantic. It is hard work and real work, not the stuff of fantasy but rather the stuff of the moment. In addition to finding his subject matter as a writer, he discovers his gifts as a teacher.

Sparta was also the site of some unfinished Toomer family business. Jean's late father's first wife, Amanda America Dickson—who died in 1893—was once known as the richest colored woman in America, and in 1899, Nathan Toomer had returned to Sparta to sue Dickson's sons and mother for the contents of her house. This happened at the same time that the senior Toomer could not set foot in Washington, D.C., because a warrant was out for his arrest in the city for non-payment of alimony and child support to Jean's mother, Nina (once again a Pinch-back, in response to her ex-husband's irresponsible exploits). The Sparta case was settled in 1901 and the senior Toomer was forced to pay court costs.

Did Jean Toomer know of his father's scoundrel's history, of the previous marriage, of his ties to Sparta? Perhaps, though Nathan Toomer abandoned his wife shortly after the birth of Jean and—except for a brief accidental meeting on a Washington street—never again saw him. Jean remained intrigued with his father his entire life, despite the fact that anything he could have gleaned from his mother and the grandparents who raised him would have likely been negative, given the ignoble ending to the marriage. Sparta is a small town, though, where histories are known; what did people think on hearing the name "Toomer," once associated with their most illustrious colored resident, and how did they subsequently regard the son?

Cane will be resurrected in the 1960s, when it suits a movement open to the political and aesthetic utility of black essentialisms. Toomer, at that point, will have crossed the color line forever, or, rather, become black in another way not delimited by race, human in a fashion not delimited by gender. Was Toomer in denial about his race, ambivalent, or nuanced? Many commentators have weighed in. His years in Washington leading up to the 1921 trip to Georgia suggest that when he was in a context of other people like himself—educated African Americans of mixed ancestry who were not themselves ambivalent but did not feel the need to continually proclaim racial identity because they were in a common community—he made sense to himself and to others. The crises came when he moved in white circles, and often in his relationships with white women his racial background became an issue. This was true on numerous occasions throughout his life. And black communities like the one where he taught in Sparta were ill-fitting as well.

Toomer's interest in the body, its malleability and ostensible perfectibility, was long-standing. He writes of lifting weights and watching his body change dramatically, masturbating compulsively, playing sports and dancing, going on milk and orange juice fasts. Once he became a disciple of Gurdjieff and a teacher of his philosophy, he was no doubt compelled by the spinning, dervish-y dance that was one manifestation of Gurdjieff's philosophy. When Toomer writes about the body, the tension between what is fixed and what can be changed, he also talks about and wonders about what his blood percentages signify. And he continually quests in his writing for a language to transcend English.

Picture Jean Toomer on the train in 1921, traveling north (perhaps in a first-class seat purchased with his principal's salary, where he would be assumed white without having to so declare himself). He is writing furiously those first words of *Cane*. He of course has no inkling that his career will be written as something of an African American literary mystery story with a hint of tragedy: He "left the race," encountered difficulty publishing, and never wrote another book as great as *Cane*. To the final point, he wrote, retrospectively: "*Cane* was a swan-song. It was a song of an end. And why no one has seen and felt that, why people have expected me to write a second and a third and a fourth book like *Cane,* is one of the queer misunderstandings of my life." Toomer died in 1967, a light-skinned American writer of African ancestry, in the middle of the Black Arts movement that resurrected the one book for which he would be remembered, a book catalyzed by a chance trip to Sparta, Georgia, in 1921, which begat a book like no other.

Bibliography: Cynthia Earl Kerman and Richard Eldridge, *The Lives of Jean Toomer: A Hunger for Wholeness* (Baton Rouge, LA, 1987). Nellie Y. McKay, *Jean Toomer, Artist: A Study of His Literary Life and Work, 1894–1936* (Chapel Hill, NC, 1984). Jean Toomer, *Cane* (New York, 1923).

ELIZABETH ALEXANDER

1922

The Waste Land appears; the author of *The Rainbow* becomes an "American writer"

T. S. Eliot and D. H. Lawrence

For T. S. Eliot, the better part of 1922 was spent finding a suitable American publisher for *The Waste Land.* In January, Eliot first offered the manuscript to Scofield Thayer's *Dial,* a periodical for which he regularly contributed "London Letters." But the *Dial* didn't publish the poem until October, and then only as a result of arduous, fraught negotiation. By mid-August, when Thayer's partner and coeditor, James Sibley Watson, intervened, promising to give *The Waste Land* the second annual Dial Award as part of its payment for publication, Eliot and Thayer were no longer on speaking terms. The problem, as Eliot told Ezra Pound, was not simply that Thayer initially said he would pay only $150 for a year's work, or that Thayer and his managing editor, Gilbert Seldes, should have been more businesslike. For Eliot, the new, monthly *Dial,* a resuscitation of the transcendentalist quarterly, reminded him of how narrow-minded, conformist, and rule-bound American intellectuals could be, especially when it came to "serious" culture. "I sometimes think," he observed in a letter to John Quinn, "that with us (Americans) the serious has to be the pedantic, and that only the pedantic and the cheap are understood: the *Saturday Evening Post,* and the *Dial* or *Atlantic Monthly.*" Although better than the *Little Review,* where the second-rate stuff was so appallingly bad, Eliot said the *Dial* suffered from being bulky and, worst of all, "exceedingly dull" and "solemn."

Eliot's flight from America vividly reveals how troubled he was by the prevalence of bad taste in the American art scene, the inability of readers to appreciate seriousness in literature that had not been sapped of all originality and humor. Viewed in this light, his "Notes on the Waste Land," which was first included in the book published in New York that December by Boni and Liveright, could well be seen as something of a practical joke, a "remarkable exposition of bogus scholarship," as Eliot once described it. Whether we consider "Notes" merely an afterthought, added to allay Horace Liveright's fears that the poem was too short, or a significant revision, Eliot's annotations present a salutary admonition those he called "seekers of sources," errant American critics who, in a quest for serious culture, mistake pedantry for sensibility. At the same time, "Notes on the Waste

Land" calls attention to Eliot's abiding concern with the dual and contradictory claims of locality and universality, individual talent and a monumental canon, and it underscores the importance of acquiring, through scholarship, what Eliot called historical sense.

Evidently, the seriousness of *The Waste Land* was such that, even as an expatriate, Eliot would do all he could to reach a more general readership in the United States instead of sticking with established protocols of avant-garde publishing. Despite his ambivalent animosity toward the *Dial* and a marketplace economy driven by "us" Americans, a major consequence of Eliot's work was to restore intercultural dialogue among the United States, Britain, and European nations divided by war. Against the personal background of an impulsive marriage that crystallized his decision to stay in London, and his grueling work in the Colonial and Foreign Department of Lloyd's Bank, where he found himself immersed in the financial dismantling of postwar Europe, Eliot struggled to gain a more distanced perspective on his own Americanness, at the same time redefining perceptions of American literature and language while helping to raise awareness about events that were rapidly unfolding abroad.

We see this, for example, in a note to "What the Thunder Said," offering a quotation from Hermann Hesse's *Blick ins Chaos*. Eliot had first read Hesse the previous fall, while convalescing at a sanitarium in Switzerland, and wrote to him in March 1922, saying, *Blick ins Chaos* "possesses a seriousness not presently found in England, and I would like to enhance its reputation." At the time, Eliot asked Hesse if he would allow a translated excerpt to be published in his review, the *Criterion;* but as it turned out, the translation appeared in the June issue of the *Dial*. It is telling, and apt, that Eliot had recommended the piece for publication, and Sydney Schiff (under the name Stephen Hudson) rendered in English the same passage Eliot himself had quoted in his note. Three months later, in his "London Letter" for the *Dial*, Eliot tried to convey to his American readers a sense of Dostoyevsky's importance, not just for Hesse and the emergence of postwar German literature, but for the development of his own modernism. Dostoyevsky had "the gift," he said, "a sign of genius in itself, for utilizing his weaknesses; so that epilepsy and hysteria cease to be the defects of an individual and become—as a fundamental weakness can, given the ability to face and study it—the entrance to a genuine and personal universe."

Putting all this into words was difficult, and Eliot would subsequently criticize his contribution as poor material that might even prove damaging to the journal as well as to himself. Nonetheless, his point confirms a cosmopolitan commitment he would never renounce. For Eliot, American literature could not make sense in a vacuum, severed from the comity of cultures composing tradition. The publication of *The Waste Land* coincided with Eliot's launching of the *Criterion*, a quarterly review, as he told Ernst Robert Curtius, whose "great aim is to raise the standard of thought and writing . . . by both international and historical comparison." Drawing on contacts he had made as foreign correspondent for *La Nouvelle Revue Française*, Eliot exercised scrupulous control over the content and format of the *Criterion*, creating an essential venue for information about emerging writers, avant-garde movements, and periodicals throughout Europe, Britain, and the Americas.

At the same time that Eliot was trying to achieve a distanced perspective on all he hated most about his American past, D. H. Lawrence was eagerly pursuing his dream of becoming an American writer. After leaving London in 1919 for Italy, then Sicily, he was invited to Taos, New Mexico, by Mabel Dodge. Lawrence would pay only three brief return visits to England during the entire last decade of his life. "As for me," he observed in a letter to Amy Lowell, "in direction I am more than half American. I always write really towards America: my listener is there." In England, Lawrence's *The Rainbow* had been banned for obscenity, *Women in Love* was rejected by publishers, and, with the rise of anti-German feeling during the war years, Lawrence and his German wife, Frieda, were evicted from their home in Cornwall. By contrast, between 1920 and 1923 an American publisher, Thomas Seltzer, published no fewer than twelve of Lawrence's books, and Robert Mountsier, an American journalist who had, from very early on, encouraged Lawrence to write *Studies in Classic American Literature,* was actively serving as Lawrence's literary agent in the United States. Disillusioned with Europe and drawn to the possibilities of the New World, Lawrence and Frieda sailed to San Francisco via Ceylon, Australia, and Tahiti, and finally reached Taos in September 1922.

In late October of that year, shortly after *The Waste Land* appeared, Lawrence wrote a series of letters to the *Dial,* asking the editors to publish "Certain Americans and an Englishman," an article he had written against the Bursum Land Bill, which threatened to deprive American Indians of their land. After concluding, in a letter to Mountsier, that Seldes had "made a fool of us," Lawrence got the essay published in the *New York Times Magazine* of December 24, ten days after the bill was debated in Congress, and the *Dial* subsequently reprinted it in two installments early the following year. The essay's style is relentlessly, and even desperately ironic, as Lawrence strives through catachretic self-mockery to establish some relationship, not just to the "Red Indians," as he calls them, but to his broader American public:

> I toddle to a corner and, like a dog when music is going on in the room, put my paws exasperatedly over my ears, and my nose to the ground, and groan softly. So doing, I try to hypnotize myself back into my old natural world, outside the circus tent . . . Try to extricate my lamb-like soul into its fleecy isolation, and then adjust myself. Adjust myself to that much-talked-of actor in the Wild West Show, the Red Indian . . . Imagine me, lamb-like and bewildered . . . trying to make head or tail of myself in my present situation.

Lawrence expresses shocked bewilderment at the destruction of cherished illusions about an "old natural world" long contemplated from afar, American nature seen through the tinted lens of myth. Significantly, he derides his own wish for lamb-like innocence, and wonders at how making head or tail of his own cultural situation, his "fleecy" whiteness, is inextricable from his adjustment to, or understanding of, the Indian. Searching for a new science of psychology was closely associated in Lawrence's mind with America, as his epilogue to *Fantasia of the Unconscious* makes clear. Insofar as he examines the relationship between Indians and the psychology of whites in the United States, in "Certain Americans and an Englishman" Lawrence builds on his findings in *Studies in Classic American Literature,* which was thoroughly revised in 1922 and published a year later. There he writes what Eliot would describe as "probably the most brilliant" of critical essays on Cooper. In it Lawrence traces Cooper's examination of the white man's contradictory feelings of hostility, dread, admiration, and nostalgia for the Indian.

Lawrence was more sanguine than Eliot about the prospect of finding an American market for his work. Still, the fiction written during his American sojourn, like his dealings with editors of the *Dial,* who regularly published his writings during the early 1920s, shows him reluctantly coming to terms with the troubling realities of American culture, realities he had for years managed to hold at bay. Ever since the First World War, when, during his darkest moments, Lawrence would fantasize with his friends about "Rananim" or "The Island," an imagined, far-off retreat, he was drawn to the myth of America as a consolatory utopia. Like Melville, whom Lawrence would sympathetically portray in *Studies* as mad with hatred of the world and looking for paradise, Lawrence yearned for this mythic frontier, even while knowing its freedoms were suspect. Despite his substantial income from and solid following in the United States, just months before arriving in Taos he would complain in a letter to Mountsier, "I'm sorry the *Dial* takes that scrap of *Aaron*—What good are 35 dollars anyway?—one cheapens oneself."

For Lawrence, Cooper's popularity as a novelist came from his capacity for wish fulfillment. Partly as a result of Lawrence's own failure to sympathize with Indians during a trip, immediately after his arrival in the States, to the Jicarilla Apache Reservation, he concluded that no reconciliation was ever possible between what he called the "spirit" of the white race and the red. In "Indians and an Englishman" and "Taos," articles that were published in the *Dial* in February and March 1923, respectively, Lawrence argues that whites can never attain a sense of connection to this lost tribal heritage.

The implications for Lawrence, struggling to define his relation to his American audience, are clear: an unbridgeable divide exists between "an Englishman" and "Certain Americans," whose culture would forever remain for him a surreal Wild West show. In a fragment from an unfinished novel written in collaboration with Mabel Dodge and begun a week after he arrived in Taos, Lawrence dramatically reveals the impact of this realization on his outlook and fictional method. Posthumously titled "The Wilful Woman," it is typical of many works of fiction written during Lawrence's American sojourn, especially "The Woman Who Rode Away," *St. Mawr,* and *The Plumed Serpent,* because in it Lawrence takes on the politics of nationhood, the consequences of colonial settlement, and the theme of leadership by blood authority. The narrative centers on Sibil, a middle-aged woman, not unlike Mabel Dodge herself, in whom the "old colonial vigor had . . .

collected" and whose response to the frontier landscape recalls Lawrence's account of Cooper in his wartime analysis of American literature. But where Lawrence in that essay stressed the malevolent, uncanny aspects of a landscape haunted by a legacy of regenerative violence, in "The Wilful Woman," as in his articles for the *Dial,* he emphasizes the tragic unreality of the American cultural scene. For Lawrence, as for Sibil, the attempt to revivify and experience firsthand an ancient precolonial culture was destined for failure: when Sibil sits in a train during the first part of her journey, she feels "it would never arrive, *could* never arrive, with her in it."

In a December 1922 essay on contemporary English prose written for *La Nouvelle Revue Française,* Eliot singled out Lawrence's *Aaron's Rod* for sharply qualified praise. "In the oeuvre of D. H. Lawrence," he said, "the profoundest explorations of human nature are coupled with the most uneven style I have encountered in any writer of our generation." One reason Eliot may have been attracted to *Aaron's Rod,* which Lawrence had written concurrently with the essays on American literature, is that it touches on the mysterious commingling of Indian and European cultures in the New World. Despite his qualms about Lawrence's obsession with sexual themes and the shortcomings of his technique, Eliot would some years later, in *The Idea of a Christian Society,* praise his interest in precolonial religious rites in the New World as his "explanation and justification . . . and the excuse for his aberrations." Josephine Ford is the very first of Lawrence's characters claiming to have "aboriginal American in her blood"; a seductress, she possesses the "fixed gravity of a Red Indian, immovable, inscrutable" and walks, we are told, with "a striding savage suggestion . . . like some savage squaw."

Grasping the meaning of America in the final decade of his career, Lawrence could never fully relinquish his enervated European roots, always hoping to discover an invigorating, mythic frontier. "I feel," he wrote to Gilbert Seldes, "that there is a vast, unreal, intermediary thing, which will probably be in America, but which isn't there yet, at all . . . But probably it is here, in America (I don't just say U.S.A.) that the quick will keep alive and come through." And despite his parenthetical aside about the possibility of transnationalism, Lawrence continued to affirm a racialist ideal of American nationhood, the "spirit of place," in ways Eliot, during his formative coming of age as a poet, could not. In Eliot, sterility and dryness are figures of cultural isolation, not just in Europe but in the New World environment, isolation Eliot deplores in his writings on Henry Adams, Poe, and Whitman. Lawrence's spirit of place may have served him well as a necessary illusion, but for Eliot such a nationalist spirit precluded the very possibility of seriousness in American art.

Bibliography: T. S. Eliot, *The Idea of a Christian Society* (London, 1939); *The Letters of T. S. Eliot,* ed. Valerie Eliot (London, 1988–); *On Poetry and Poets* (London, 1957); *To Criticize the Critic, and Other Writings* (London, 1965). D. H. Lawrence, *Aaron's Rod* (New York, 1922); *Studies in Classic American Literature* (New York, 1923); *The Letters of D. H. Lawrence,* ed. James T. Boulton (Cambridge, 1979–2001).

ANITA PATTERSON

CHAPLINESQUE

There is no hint of surprise in his account of his own life. He knew what was going to happen. The "how" might be left to providence, but the fact of his prominence was not in doubt. He had a mother whose balance was disturbed, and he had fathers to sort through. In other words, we don't quite know who his father was, though a man named Charles Chaplin took the part until he died in 1901. The uncertainty allowed Charlie to think he might be Latin, or Russian, or Jewish, or something much more than dowdy Kennington, the workhouse and grim south London. That was the Dickens version where Charlie was the Artful Dodger—and no one remembers what became of that imp (he ended up "the merriest young grazier in all Northamptonshire" it says). Charlie believed he was infinite, Chaplinesque. He knew it, and he simply waited for events to get organized around that principle. Anyone can tell you the Dodgers went to L.A.

Case in point: when Charles Chaplin Senior died, Charlie was twelve, a kid, or even The Kid. He was known to a few hundred people in south London, those who had seen him on the music-hall stage, or bumped into him on the drab streets. Twenty years later, at *The Kid*'s opening, he was the most famous man in the world, and by then it was clear to the ordinary filmgoers and to poets alike that he was the representative of the great, inspiring poor, the mass of unknowns, that—one way or another—would determine the future of the twentieth century and the fate of the world. The Tramp would look after the Kid.

So, the poets did notice, and one New York night in October 1923—just after the premiere of *A Woman of Paris*—the writer Waldo Frank took Chaplin to dinner in the Village. Afterward, Frank led Charlie to a one-room apartment on Grove Street. They knocked on the door and "in walked Waldo Frank and a most pleasant-looking, twinkling little man in a black derby." That is Hart Crane, next day, writing to his mother, about how he met Charlie Chaplin.

They talked all night, and Chaplin saw in Crane one of his own characters (what else should we expect?): "Hart Crane was desperately poor. His father, a millionaire candy manufacturer, wanted him to enter his business and tried to discourage his poetry by cutting him off financially." And so education and industry customarily proceed, trying to keep perversity on track. Charlie thought some of Crane's poetry "shrill . . . Yet he had a gentle sweetness." He noted that Crane went from "poverty and neglect" to "drink and dissipation" and then jumped into the sea from a ship on its way from Havana to New York. But before then Crane had sent him a copy of *White Buildings,* which includes the poem "Chaplinesque." Don't expect a masterpiece in that, or even an especially obser-

vant eye for Chaplin the comic. But in a last image, invented by Crane (there is no
kitten in *The Kid,* the film Crane loved), the poet addresses the certain knowledge
that tonight and tomorrow night on the street outside our coziness something is
dying:

> The game enforces smirks; but we have seen
> The moon in lonely alleys make
> A grail of laughter of an empty ash can,
> And through all sound of gaiety and quest
> Have heard a kitten in the wilderness.

The poem is not crucial, or not as much as its title. Today we may be very familiar with such terms as Kafkaesque, Pinteresque, and Faulknerian. The academic rapine of our culture has invented so much apparently tender jargon to
make its narcotizing journey acceptable. But in the 1920s, that "-esque" suffix was
more novel, and Crane was trying to voice the incoherent urgings a poet might
feel, to say "amen" to the attempt by someone like Chaplin and this hectic new
mechanism, the machine that cut people's heads from their bodies, that told jagged stories in silence, that said, look, look at this beauty (does she know she's being studied? and if she knows is she a slut, or can she be my goddess still?).

Wondering what the world was going to do with the great mass outside, this
was a bristling moment for disaffiliated intellectuals like Crane (essentially people ready to plunge into the world, into life, missing Harvard et cetera on the
way). And just because so many of them were so very wordy, nothing beckoned
like those new immediate resources (sudden oceans) where the modernist advance into difficulty was being offset by media—movies, jazz, public sports
events—where anyone could go and feel none of the kind of barrier that even
advanced prosodists might face in the sentences of Joyce, Proust, Musil, and
Faulkner. Popular culture, it would be called, and all at once the jig was up—for
culture had never gone down better than medicine or been sexier than Margaret
Dumont.

Not very far ahead, in Preston Sturges's *Sullivan's Travels,* the hit-maker director John L. Sullivan yearns to make something earnest, obscure and gloomy,
instead of his silly comedies that make everyone laugh. So he heads off into America like an idiot, and before you can shout "banana skin!" he's in a Southern chain
gang where life is hard (shall we guess much harder than the film dares show?),
until relief and consolation come in the form of a movie show, with Charlie's
greatest American rival, Mickey Mouse. The point of it is not just be grateful for
small mercies (and screw the bigger ones to the floor), but be aware of that kind
of narrative fiction that can reach the illiterates, the subnormals, and the simply
evil animal class such as may be found on a Southern chain gang (if you include
the guards in the congregation).

One reason why this volume has essays on the movies is that from about the
end of the First World War the ghastly realization dawns that literature may not
be enough. That while the masturbatory delights of reading alone with a book in

your lap may still be available (a room of one's own), watch out—because some frantic kind of public orgy or séance is being talked about, which is sitting crammed together in the fearsome dark and keeping silent for the awe that descends with the switching of this unscrupulous dago-Jew-faggot-bastard, who is somewhere between the wealthiest tramp in the world and a screaming-queen ballet-dancer murderer (never forget the violence in Charlie). So let's not claim that Charlie Chaplin doesn't present some aesthetic problems (it's OK by me if you still prefer Keaton, Groucho, or Fields), but simply consider the purple-plained majesty of its happening, this crazed mixture of cruelty and sentimentality, and the sinister Puckish posing, the curve of cane, back, and Derby brim, the savage stamp of mustache. Jean-Paul Sartre (I'm pulling rank here) called it all "the frenzy on the wall," and poor Hart Crane, gasping for breath, rehearsing drowning, bubbles, "Chaplinesque! Champagne Charlie!" Nothing is ever going to be the same again.

Chaplin is challenged quite often in critical circles. But the fact is that from 1914 until as late as *City Lights,* in 1931, he was the movies for the key generation in their history. No one had foreseen the bittersweet marriage of comedy and sentiment, violence and pathos. Nobody was more inventive, or more in love with the ambiguity of his own screen personality. Audiences had never felt so close to someone who wasn't there—from the one-reelers through *The Gold Rush, The Circus,* and *City Lights,* Chaplin defined the ghostly intimacy of film. Now that no one is hardly ever "there" in our culture, we see what a pioneer of delight and alienation he was.

Chaplin was never a tramp in his adult life. And in the fiercely competitive Hollywood that he knew, he was alone among filmmakers in that he generally worked on a picture in the way Hart Crane might have approached a poem. Take as long as it needs. Although Chaplin was one of the founder members of United Artists (with his friends Mary Pickford and Douglas Fairbanks, and with D. W. Griffith), Chaplin never really played according to the one-for-all-and-all-for-one rules of the new setup. Chaplin preferred to be the source of money and the destiny of profit for his films, and in his heyday he thought nothing of keeping cast and crew waiting, on salary, while he thought of what to film. The industry that surrounded him had disproved and abandoned his method long ago—they said it was un-American!

How was this possible? Because the appetite for Chaplin films was so vast. In 1916, when he crossed over to Mutual from Keystone (in the days of his one- and two-reel films), the new studio agreed to pay Charlie $10,000 a week, with a signing bonus of $150,000. His 1997 biographer reckoned those amounts worked out in millennium spending money as $140,000 a week and a bonus of $3.1 million. And here's the real wow: those numbers were pretty cheesy by 2000, when a far smaller portion of the population went to the movies than had done so in 1916.

But by the late 1930s, Chaplin was no longer himself "Chaplinesque." He was one more film industry plutocrat behaving badly. I think it's clear now that Charlie kept the "-esque" on his name while silent pictures lasted, and of course in his own private world he persisted with silence longer than anyone else. *City Lights,* made as late as 1931, was entirely silent, except for his very sweet music, and it is a parable about the millionaire, the tramp, and the blind girl that depends on the archaic enclosure of silence—that's what lets you smell the blind girl's flowers. In due course, even Chaplin had to yield to sound, and then all of a sudden his dance became elephantine, because all his characters could utter was speechifying. In the same way, the man who had had a natural rapport with millions of strangers through a single gesture or glance was a terrible writer. *My Autobiography,* from 1964, is always awkward and stilted and often flat-out obnoxious. It omits entire wives, to say nothing of dalliances. Charlie came to America and to California with every intention of playing the game. He was prepared to go through every mass of huddled souls to find the pretty girls and give them a Chaplinesque turn thereafter—seldom done with feeling, they said, but full of pantomime gesture and sexual slapstick. Just like Hitler (they were on course to meet), he ate up strangers.

Hart Crane was spared this, but in the 1940s, especially, you could feel Chaplin turning harsher and less playful. He had lost a lot of his touch: *The Great Dictator* (1940) is of most interest as a trial of arms or routines between two sentimental mustaches who fear they are turning fake. It's not a very good film, and *Monsieur Verdoux* (1947) only showed how much human ugliness and loathing there was in Chaplin. So it was never a surprise that by the late '40s, though married to Oona O'Neill (his child-bride with literary class), he was hounded by reports of abusing younger women and embracing Marxists. It was nonsense, of course: he had tended to take any woman he laid his eyes on, not just the nymphs, and his airy out-loud ponderings about freedom were very much in line with libertarian fortune cookies.

He had never become an American citizen, but that was not anti-Americanism so much as a vague wish to belong to the world. He had been a taxpayer for forty years; he had generally pursued American girls; and he had done his bit to build Los Angeles. Taking vengeance on him was as stupid as anything else in the McCarthy show. But it's notable that neither the Hart Cranes nor the huddled masses really rallied to his side. Hardly anyone thought to say—as Crane had tried to—Look, at a moment, and a perilous moment, he was America for the world, and he was the idea of a silly comic holding people together.

It's still not clear that Chaplin had to go. Whatever the warnings, it was rather more that he elected to go himself, and as he left had his reentry visa annulled. More or less, Chaplin had coincided with the second half of the great wave of immigration into America. (Part One of that story was Christmas, Part Two Kafka.) Almost entirely, he had appealed to the hushed faces that found English a strange language. As if to show how lost he was, he went to Switzerland where he raised a mighty family, wrote his awful book and made *The Countess from Hong Kong,* his worst film, and a very American stand-off in that it came down to two bitter geniuses — Chaplin and Brando — staring at each other in mounting bewilderment.

There was a final moment. Depending on your point of view, it was very touching, or it was emotionally hideous: since this was 1972, it was likely both in riot. The Academy (which had only given Chaplin one award, for *The Circus* in 1927–28) determined to offer the white-haired man from Vevey an honorary award. You could rationalize it how you liked: it was an apology, a gesture of forgiveness, or a knock-out occasion for the sentimental television audience. Chaplin agreed to attend. He and Oona landed in New York and there was a party there — Charlie met Johnny Carson: he'd never heard of him or seen him.

In Los Angeles, at the Dorothy Chandler Pavilion, the Academy made a radical concession. As a rule, Best Picture is the climax of the evening. This year it was *The French Connection,* and if you looked hard perhaps there was a distant rhyme scheme between Popeye Doyle strutting in his porkpie hat and Charlie in his cane and bowler. If only *The French Connection* had had that charm.

There was a program of clips, the lights came up, and there was Chaplin in the greatest ovation the Academy has ever known. The president of the Academy, Daniel Taradash, gave him an Oscar "for the incalculable effect he has had in making motion pictures the art form of the century." Well, that was going some, wasn't it? Whoever said that motion pictures were as minor as an art form? If you had been alive for *The Kid* you'd know that they were a sensation, like electric light, and just as ambiguous.

There was a ball later — like a fairy-tale country, America has a taste for balls. Charlie met Jackie Coogan again, the kid from *The Kid,* that beautiful child who sits there at the table and watches Charlie like a wise child, the street urchin who has a rock to throw and tosses it in the air under a policeman's nose. Coogan, fat and hairless at fifty-seven, was unrecognizable. And people noted that Charlie didn't always remember people — not in the way they remembered him. He was interested in strangers, like performers and dictators. But he knew it was Groucho Marx loping across the room, like a wolf with a hernia, and he put his arm round Julius Henry Marx and whispered, "Stay warm, Groucho, you're next."

Groucho Marx died August 19, 1977.

Charles Chaplin died Christmas Day 1977.

There is a story told by atheists. Knowing he didn't really have the power, and beginning to be persuaded that he didn't really exist, God looked down on a troubled Earth and said, "I'll deal them three cards, three wild cards, and they'll never know where they came from."

"That's cheating," said Gabriel.

"My game," said God, "and it looks like it's going to be a rough hundred years. I'm worried about the culture, so I'll give them three bright souls, three angels, what shall we call them?"

"Saints?" suggested Gabriel.

"I like that," said God, though he made it clear that they didn't have to behave like saints. And they were Charlie, Groucho, and Satch. You don't really believe they just did it themselves, do you?

"People," said God, "they forget how good I could be when I was God-like."

Bibliography: Charles Chaplin, *My Autobiography* (New York, 1964). Hart Crane, *White Buildings* (New York, 1926). Kenneth S. Lynn, *Charlie Chaplin and His Times* (New York, 1997). John Unterecker, *Voyager: A Life of Hart Crane* (New York, 1969).

DAVID THOMSON

1924

F. O. Matthiessen meets Russell Cheney on the ocean liner *Paris,* and American literary history emerges from Skull and Bones

A JUDGMENT OF ART

F. O. Matthiessen was the legendary Harvard professor who, with the appearance of *American Renaissance: Art and Expression in the Age of Emerson and Whitman* —in 1941, that tense, signal year—all but invented American literary history. Enthroning his Gang of Five—Emerson, Thoreau, Hawthorne, Melville, and Whitman—at the crux of American literary achievement, Matthiessen was rescuing a national literature from genteel celebrants of Longfellow, Bryant, Whittier, Holmes, and Lowell. He concentrated the significance of these writers simultaneously in art—"masterpieces . . . their fusions of form and content . . . in accordance with the enduring requirements for great art"—and politics: "The normal way for an American to begin to gain . . . mastery," he wrote, discussing Emerson's recollections of the sculptor Horatio Greenough, "is by the fullest acceptance of the possibilities of democracy."

Later Americanists typically track masterpieces and democracy as opposites, as the contrarieties of a contradiction demanding exposure or resolution, but the shift would have meant nothing to Matthiessen: he insistently focused amplitude. "In proposing an ever widening range of interests for the ideal critic, I have moved from his central responsibility to the text before him out to an awareness of some of the world-wide struggles of our age," he said in his 1949 lecture "The Responsibilities of the Critic." "We must come back to where we started, to the critic's primary function. He must judge the work of art as work of art. But knowing form and content to be inseparable, he will recognize his duty to both. Judgment of art is unavoidably both an aesthetic and a social act, and the critic's sense of social responsibility gives him a deeper thirst for meaning."

Amplitude, if not inevitably contradiction, radiates from Matthiessen's own complex personal history like a biographical version of "What's Wrong with This Picture?" His four single-author critical volumes, for instance, span Sarah Orne Jewett, T. S. Eliot, Henry James, and Theodore Dreiser. Born on the West Coast, in Pasadena, in 1902, he was raised mostly in middle America, outside La Salle, Illinois, at the home of his millionaire grandfather, and graduated from Eastern universities, Yale (BA 1923) and Harvard (MA 1926, PhD 1931). On board the ocean liner *Paris* in 1924 he met Russell Cheney, a painter his elder by some twenty years, and they lived together until Cheney's death in 1945, as often as possible in Kittery Point, Maine. After studying at Oxford as a Rhodes Scholar, Matthiessen taught at Yale, then Harvard, serving as chairman of the tutors in History and Literature. Although he famously repeated he was not a Marxist but a Christian, Matthiessen tilted toward socialism from his first reading of R. H. Tawney's *The Acquisitive Society* as a Yale undergraduate. "Tawney's ideas about equality," he recounted in *From the Heart of Europe* (1948), "have remained more living for me than anything else, except Shakespeare, that I read at college." He briefly joined the Socialist Party during the 1930s, helped found the radical Harvard Teachers Union in 1935, and gave a seconding speech for Henry Wallace at the 1948 Progressive Party convention in Philadelphia. As late as "The Responsibilities of the Critic," Matthiessen argued that "despite all the excesses and exaggerated claims of the Marxists of the thirties, I still believe that the principles of Marxism—so much under fire now—can have an immense value in helping us to see and comprehend our literature. No educated American can afford to be ignorant of them, or to be delinquent in realizing that there is much common ground between these principles and any healthily dynamic America." Less persuasively, or honorably, *From the Heart of Europe,* his account of a summer and fall teaching American literature to European students at the Salzburg Seminar, all but excuses the February 1948 Communist seizure of power in Czechoslovakia and, two weeks later, the suicide—or murder—of Foreign Minister Jan Masaryk.

Although in *American Renaissance* Matthiessen created something like an authorized version of our national literary culture, his leftist activism and sexuality obviously pitched him against official America—or, as he could hardly have helped imagine, vice versa. When he threw himself from the twelfth-floor window of Boston's Hotel Manger on April 1, 1950, some recognized a bitter parody of Masaryk's defenestration. "When Professor Matthiessen died," his friend Barrows Dunham suggested, "the cold war made its first martyr among scholars." Others, along various political axes, caught different repressive strains: the closet, or homophobia. But Matthiessen resists full reassignment into outsider or underground America. For all his celebration of "the people," "the community," and "living speech" in *American Renaissance,* he shunned the American demotic. In *From the Heart of Europe* he is repulsed by French enthusiasm for James M. Cain and his noirish confreres: "The grouping together, particularly in Paris, of Hemingway and Faulkner with Caldwell and O'Hara and even Cain, is a . . . more sinister sign of the intellectuals' present state of ill health." And before he killed himself, Matthiessen carefully left—as Robert Lowell wrote—"his Yale *Skull and Bones* pin on the dresser," beside his keys, glasses, and a note. Cheney also was a loyal member of this secret society that reaches far into American establishments in government, intelligence, and business, and Matthiessen's earliest declaration of his homosexuality apparently occurred during the sexual-history rituals of the

566	A JUDGMENT OF ART	1924

Skull and Bones initiation. The touching collection of Matthiessen and Cheney's private correspondence, *Rat & the Devil,* opens, in fact, with the Devil (Matthiessen) announcing his "complete harmony" with Rat (Cheney) in a letter to another Bonesman.

But inside *American Renaissance,* in the words of Reeve, the narrator of Mark Merlis's 1994 novel *American Studies*—along with May Sarton's 1955 *Faithful Are the Wounds,* one of at least two fascinating historical fictions based on the critic —Matthiessen "made a little country of his own." Once one of the golden boys gathered around Professor "T. F. Slater," Reeve recalls "that famous seminar of his, that he first had the audacity to call 'American Studies'":

> Nowadays that means dissertations on "Gilligan's Island." But that wasn't what Tom meant at all. He never meant to study America, the whole shebang, in all its imbecile complexity . . .
>
> He had made a little country of his own. In those first few years during and after the second war, America was what we talked about in Tom's overheated seminar room. Every week someone came into the room with a chance notion or an off reading destined to become holy writ for the generation that came after. As Jefferson thought it would take a millennium to settle the continent, so we thought it would take forever just to cut a few paths through the forest primeval of nineteenth-century letters. Now it's used up, all of it, from Massachusetts Bay to Calaveras County.

Reeve remarks of *The Invincible City,* as *American Renaissance* is recast here, "Oh, it was all stunningly new, forty years ago . . . You have to make yourself remember that he thought it was a book about the revolution." In Sarton's novel, the Matthiessen figure, Edward Cavan, author of "the American giants book," prompts the literary antagonism of even his savviest Harvard colleague because of his "emphasis on . . . the periphery of literature—economics, history, all that could be rolled up in the term 'cultural historian.'" Sarton never indicates that Cavan might be gay—though the word "queer" is curiously ubiquitous, a recurrent synonym for "strange" and "surprising," as in, "It's so queer you never noticed that house," or "The queer thing is that we none of us really know Edward, do we?" But as T. F. Slater tells Reeve, in the course of a monologue on *The Invincible City,* his theme is not so much culture as sex—and love:

> "Emerson, Hawthorne, Melville, all of them except Whitman. Idealists slashing away at the beauty they can't hold on to, wanting it dead or transcendent, anything but material, there in front of them but out of their reach. Emerson, do you really read Emerson? Always trying to get inside people and failing and then saying you're not an angel, you're a penis, no wonder I couldn't get inside you."
>
> I couldn't recall this in Emerson. He was clutching my knee almost fiercely. "What I'm after, what the book is about, is the revolution built on love and not bloodletting. A world where I can watch a Billy Budd walk away and not want to obliterate him because I just can't get inside his skin."
>
> He let go of my knee, sat back, and murmured the lines from Whitman that gave him his title:

I dream'd in a dream I saw a city invincible to the attacks
of the whole of the rest of the earth,
I dream'd that was the new city of Friends.

Man in the Open Air, Matthiessen's original title for *American Renaissance,* derived from a different Whitman passage ("We have the man indoors and under
artificial relations . . . but never before have we had man in the open air"), and
the whole vast enterprise shapes a scholarly valentine to Cheney, for it was the
painter who introduced his companion to American literature, particularly to
Whitman, who earns the closing spot in the book. Trained in the English Renaissance, Matthiessen wrote a thesis on Elizabethan translation, but as he retraced
his initial travels with Cheney for *From the Heart of Europe,* "Whitman was my first
big experience, particularly *The Children of Adam* and *Calamus* poems, which
helped me begin to trust the body."

American Renaissance wasn't the first American literary history—chronicles of
national letters date at least to Moses Coit Tyler (incidentally also Skull and
Bones) and his two-volume *History of American Literature during the Colonial Time,
1607–1765* (1878). Into the twentieth century a farrago of historians, critics, and
writers intensively projected fresh maps of American poetry and fiction—from
Irving Babbitt, Van Wyck Brooks, and Norman Foerster through D. H. Law-
rence's *Studies in Classic American Literature* (1923), William Carlos Williams's *In the
American Grain* (1925), Thomas Beer's *The Mauve Decade* (1926), and Constance
Rourke's *American Humor: A Study of the National Character* (1931). Even for its moment, as a coruscating history of ideas and corrosive prose, Perry Miller's *The
New England Mind: The Seventeenth Century* (1939) now looks more audacious than
American Renaissance, and left less that came before it standing. But *American Re-
naissance,* as Sacvan Bercovitch once put it, "reset the terms for the study of Amer-
ican literary history."

Matthiessen realized his influence through an original mix of New Critical
close readings—the still-virtuoso set pieces on the "I went to the woods" episode
from *Walden,* "The Pacific" chapter of *Moby-Dick,* or the fall from the mast at the
close of *White-Jacket*—and, traversing the luminous years 1850 through 1855, zealously plotted correspondences and contrasts along the fault lines of idealism and
tragedy, the individual and society, "organic form" and "a sense of actuality." If
there is a ghost inside *American Renaissance,* it is T. S. Eliot, notably for his notion
of literary tradition registered in "Tradition and the Individual Talent" and "Andrew Marvell," which Matthiessen paraphrased as the "presentness of the past is
what Eliot has meant by tradition." Eliot sanctioned him to read Emerson, Thoreau, Hawthorne, Melville, and Whitman through the telescope of Joyce, Pound,
Mann, or Eliot himself, as contemporaries, and as modernists. The "very absence
of a living native tradition," Matthiessen argued, allowed American artists "to arrive at fundamental discoveries in advance of current European practice." Thus
Eliot also sanctioned him to read "my five writers" through the magnifying glass
of the English Renaissance, particularly Shakespeare, Marvell, Sir Thomas

Browne, Donne, Herbert, and Milton, and as classical. Both strains surge through Matthiessen's poised opening:

> The starting point for this book was my realization of how great a number of our past masterpieces were produced in one extraordinarily concentrated moment of expression. It may not seem precisely accurate to refer to our mid-nineteenth century as a re-birth; but that was how the writers themselves judged it. Not as a *re-birth* of values that had existed previously in America, but as America's way of producing a renaissance, by coming to its first maturity and affirming its rightful heritage in the whole expanse of art and culture.

Part Popular Front nationalism, part collage, *American Renaissance* shades a vast, tangled, serpentine conversation among the dead and the living. The vexation, though, is Matthiessen's magisterial poise—his mulishness on sounding so above his writers as to talk another tongue. D. H. Lawrence also appreciated that the American nineteenth century anticipated the European vanguard, but this is how he put it: "The furthest frenzies of French modernism or futurism have not yet reached the pitch of extreme consciousness that Poe, Melville, Hawthorne, Whitman reached. The European moderns are all *trying* to be extreme. The great Americans I mention just were it. Which is why the world has funked them, and funks them today."

Thomas Beer, similarly, shadowed Emerson as though reporting from inside a nineteenth-century echo chamber:

> They laid Jesse James in his grave and Dante Gabriel Rossetti died immediately. Then Charles Darwin was deplored and then, on April 27, 1882, Louisa May Alcott ... made a lyre of yellow jonquils for Ralph Waldo Emerson's preposterous funeral and somehow steered Bronson Alcott through the dreary business until he stood beside the coffin in the damp cemetery and mechanically drawled out the lines of a dire poem.

Eschewing argument, analysis, often advocacy, Beer and Lawrence practiced criticism as improvisation, parody, seduction, fantasy, memoir, mimicry, insult— as literature. Constance Rourke, like Matthiessen, situated American novelists and poets as traditional—yet a tradition of storytellers and tricksters she retold through jokes, legends, and tall tales.

In May Sarton's *Faithful Are the Wounds,* Edward Craven jumps under a subway train in despair over Czechoslovakia, hounded by the left and the right. In Mark Merlis's *American Studies* T. F. Slater shoots himself after the president of Harvard threatens to ruin one of his students, another former golden boy, if Slater won't cooperate with a committee investigating foreign influences on education.

Russell Cheney was dead almost five years when Matthiessen left behind his suicide note at the Hotel Manger. "I have taken this room in order to do what I have to do & I am exhausted," he wrote. "I have been subject to so many severe depressions during the past few years that I can no longer believe that I can continue to be of use to my profession and my friends & How much the state of the world has to do with my state of mind I do not know."

Bibliography: F. O. Matthiessen, *American Renaissance: Art and Expression in the Age of Emerson and Whitman* (New York, 1941); *From the Heart of Europe* (New York, 1948). Mark Merlis, *American Studies* (New York, 1994). May Sarton, *Faithful Are the Wounds* (New York, 1955). *Rat & the Devil: Journal Letters of F. O. Matthiessen and Russell Cheney,* ed. Louis Hyde (Hamden, CT, 1978).

ROBERT POLITO

1924, May 26
President Coolidge signs the Johnson-Reed Act, halting mass immigration to the United States

AMERICANS ALL

The Johnson-Reed Act was the culmination of a long campaign to designate certain ethnic groups foreign to the United States. It reduced immigrant admissions to 2 percent of the population of each nationality already present in the United States, as enumerated in the 1890 U.S. Census. This drastically curtailed immigration from countries in southern and eastern Europe, whose nationals, many of them Catholic and Jewish, were considered by nativists to be inferior to the northern and western Europeans who had immigrated earlier. The act excluded all aliens who were ineligible for citizenship, which shut out almost all Asians—there were exceptions for merchants and their families, clergy, and students—because by 1924 U.S. courts had ruled that Chinese, Japanese, and Indian immigrants were not white and therefore could not naturalize. Among its unintended consequences was the proliferation of "paper sons," immigrants claiming to be the China-born children of American citizens of Chinese ancestry in order to enter the country. Last but not least, the Johnson-Reed Act called for the development of a system of immigration quotas proportionate to the allegedly discrete European national origins of the contemporary American population. To calculate national origins, intermarriages between people of different European nationalities were disaggregated and intermarriages between Europeans and African Americans or Native Americans were ignored. Indeed nonwhites—including those of African and Asian ancestry born in the United States and therefore citizens—were not considered part of the American population.

Though the act and the national-origins system, partly in deference to agricultural interests, put no numerical limitation on immigration from independent countries in the Western Hemisphere and from American colonies, the advent of the U.S. Border Patrol criminalized migrant workers of Mexican descent in the Southwest and broadened antimiscegenation statutes targeted at workers from the Philippines. Scapegoating and repatriation campaigns during the 1930s did not distinguish between undocumented Mexican immigrants, legal Mexican immigrants, and their American-born children. The Johnson-Reed Act required consular visas for all immigrants, and during the Depression, American consuls in Europe strictly enforced the bar against those "likely to become a public charge" for lack of money and work, with the result that refugees remained shut out and quotas unfilled.

In the 1920s and 1930s, then, U.S. immigration law and its enforcement essentialized ethnicity, whitened nationality, and emphasized territoriality in a way that denied the possibility of cultural mixing, the very presence of certain inhabitants, and the need for border crossing. More specifically, it prompted the incorporation of "older" immigrants, the invention of a "back door" importable-and-disposable status for migrant laborers, and the rendering of Asians racially alien even if native born.

By cutting off new arrivals and marginalizing or alienating certain residents, immigration policy fostered reinforcing and competing tendencies toward diasporic nationalism, assimilation, and protest in U.S. immigrant communities. In the 1920s, restrictive laws were coupled with "Americanization" programs—run by employers, public schools, and settlement, ethnic, and welfare organizations —that emphasized the adoption of English, domestic science, and civics. Some ethnic writers broke into the mainstream with "Anglo" help: the Italian-American writer Frances Winwar (born Vinciguerra) changed her name to secure publication of her first book in 1927; Thomas Wolfe brought *The Grass Roof* (1931), by Korean American writer Younghill Kang, to Scribner's. Within immigrant communities, however, non-English periodicals remained popular, functioning as agents of transnationalism, as vehicles of advice and acculturation, and as forums for demanding better treatment. Many of these periodicals featured serialized fiction in which the issue of language maintenance itself was a theme (a good example is Daniel Venegas's *Las aventuras de Don Chipote,* serialized in the Los Angeles periodical *El heraldo de Mexico* in 1928). References to American capitalism and materialism, mechanization at the workplace, mass-produced consumer goods, and urban amusements pervade ethnic literature of the interwar period, typically placed in contrast to traditional ethnic values and customs and attesting to deepening rifts between first- and second-generation immigrants. The inadequacy of welfare programs for migrants from Mexico and Puerto Rico loomed large in the writings of the 1930s; Americo Meana's satirical "Oracion al Home Relief," published in Brooklyn's *El Curioso,* is a good example.

Some immigrant groups, especially the Chinese and the Japanese (restricted from voting and in their ability to own or lease farmland and bring over spouses), Mexicans (who kept up a postrevolutionary nationalism and traveled across the border for work), and Armenians and Jews (concerned with the welfare of their stateless kin abroad), maintained family, economic, organizational, or political ties to their native lands. In the 1930s, immigrants and their descendants were involved in the projects of the Works Progress Administration, labor unions, and Popular Front organizations that promoted a spirit of "Americans All" and international proletarian unity. The rise of fascism and the Sino-Japanese war had galvanizing effects on ethnic communities and made visible their attachments to America and to their native countries. The Bracero program, a contract-labor arrangement between the U.S. and Mexican governments that brought Mexican agricultural workers north to labor in American fields, elicited mixed reactions from Mexican Americans.

By the 1940s, ethnic writing had found a prominent place in literary journals, though mainstream publishers were interested in novels featuring conventional Mexican American and Asian American types. World War II prompted the repeal of Asian-exclusion laws and a mood of pluralist nationalism based on American diversity, though Japanese Americans were flagrantly excluded from this official embrace.

The formalization of immigration status into what historian Mae Ngai calls a regime of quotas and papers divorced it from meaningful experience. This disjuncture, along with many others, is palpable in ethnic literature exploring relationships between inner and outer worlds, realities and aspirations. Legislative history and state policies notwithstanding, ethnic literature proliferated in the second quarter of the twentieth century.

In the post–World War I period, varieties of estrangement distinguish colonial and assimilated ethnic characters. In the Jamaican-born writer Claude McKay's *Home to Harlem* (1928), Ray, an intellectual in exile from U.S.-occupied Haiti, believes "races and nations . . . poisoned the air of life," feels like a misfit, and longs to lose himself in "some savage culture in the jungles of Africa." Also in 1928, the German-born writer Ludwig Lewisohn published a bildungsroman about the discontent of a successful psychologist who longs to express his ancestral "Jewish heart," or, as the novel's title refers to it, "the island within." In contrast, Carlos Bulosan, in his semiautobiographical novel *America Is in the Heart* (1946), describes the Depression-era struggle of a migrant Filipino worker to overcome "the narrowing island of despair" born of racism, exploitation, and degradation by asserting, in good Popular Front form and as the title proclaims, that a better America is to be found "in the heart." Bulosan's account reflects the idealistic nationalism of the World War II years but his protagonist is insecure: he is poor and ill, his efforts at worker organizing and education are tentative, and his ideal America is always deferred. Bulosan's depiction, with its insistence on his protagonist's incessant flight and hunger for humanity, seems indebted to Richard Wright.

In both Lewisohn's and Bulosan's narratives, white, Protestant women—symbols of modernity—help to define American identity. Lewisohn's protagonist feels that his wife, a writer, is too frigid and ambitious; her negative example pushes him to serve as a commissioner investigating the persecution of Jews in Romania. Bulosan's protagonist both demonizes and idealizes white women, with whom he never sexually engages. In the dance hall and the labor movement these women degrade and manipulate. In contrast, maternal teachers he encounters give him books that inspire him to write about his ideals. Both Lewisohn and Bulosan opt for self-reflexive protagonists and narrators that interrupt the action with interpretive and historical commentary. This heightens the feeling that their stories are most concerned with representing subjective alienation from the past (family) and the present (social life).

For some Depression-era writers, modernism captured this psychological predicament and figured it as a clash of languages and a locus of creative adaptation. The repose suggested in the title of Henry Roth's *Call It Sleep* (1934) comes only after an extended depiction of discovery and fear in the life of its young protagonist, David, who is caught between modern New York City and the distant world of his immigrant parents. At the end of the novel, after provoking the wrath of his father by denying his paternity, David shocks himself on the rail of the Eighth Street trolley, has a vision of light, and returns to a home more reassuring than before. To capture this "strangest triumph, strangest acquiescence," Roth cuts between the elevated language of David's interior monologue, vulgar and accented outside street talk, and echoes of important images associated with his family and faith.

Another work that links generational reconciliation and aesthetic accession is Américo Paredes's bilingual poem "Guitarreros" (1935). The poem starts with a quotation from a *corrido* about a young cowboy who challenges his father's order that he stop fighting and then, before facing death as a result of his disobedience, requests that he be buried in earth where he could be broken by livestock. The poem then describes the performance of the guitar players:

> Black against twisted black
> The old mesquite
> Rears up against the stars
> Branch bridle hanging,
> While the bull comes down from the mountain
> Driven along by your fingers,
> Twenty nimble stallions prancing up and down the *redil* of guitars.
>
> One leaning on the trunk, one facing—
> Now the song:
> Not cleanly flanked, not pacing,
> But in a stubborn yielding that unshapes
> And shapes itself again,
> Hard-mouthed, zigzagged, thrusting,
> Thrown not sung,
> One to the other.

The poem ends with the observation of an old man that this was the way it was in the old days, presumably the old days of ranches and livestock now displaced by Anglo-owned commercial farms. At a time when, as Paredes writes in a more famous poem of the same year, the Texas-Mexican "no gotta voice, all he got is the han'/To work like the burro; he no gotta lan,'" a reshaped song—or at least a modernist poem rendering it—could be both a heroic refuge and a creative assertion.

A combination of memorialization and manly protest is evident, too, in Pietro di Donato's *Christ in Concrete* (1937). In the first, wrenching chapter, an Italian American bricklayer, Geremio, is buried alive in a construction site accident. By the novel's end, the title has shifted from referring to Geremio's martyrdom to his son's disillusionment; Donato depicts both in stream-of-consciousness passages that move from the first to the third person. His prose also shows how workers' nicknames (based on physical features and translated literally from the Italian) make them indistinguishable from cogs in the wheel of "Job," at their construction site: "Snoutnose steamed through ragged mustache whip-lashing sand into mixer Ashes-ass dragged under four-by-twelve beam Lean clawed wall knots jumping in jaws masonry crumbled dust billowed thundered choked."

"Never," Donato writes of the old worker called Lean, "did he bear his toil with the rhythm of song."

In contrast, H. T. Tsiang ends his novel *And China Has Hands* (1937) with a song of interracial solidarity:

All the workers in the cafeteria paraded
The workers in the other cafeterias joined:
The white, the yellow, and the black,
The ones between yellow and black,
The ones between yellow and white,
And the ones between white and black.
They were marching on, singing their song:
The song of the white,
The song of the yellow,
The song of the black,
The song of the ones who were neither yellow nor white,
The song of the ones who were neither yellow nor black,
The song of the ones who were neither black nor white,
And the song that knows nothing of white, yellow, or black.

This solidarity is echoed in the romantic love of Tsiang's protagonists, a "paper son" laundryman and a half-black, half-Chinese girl from the American South, who had finally given up their stereotyped views of each other along with their timid vanities about their places in America. Also on the workers' picket line is Tsiang himself, an author of experimental and proletarian fiction condemned by American critics who feel "his chief literary influence is the decadent Gertrude Stein," and kicked out of the cafeteria by its Chinese owners when he tries to peddle his self-published books inside.

Like other ethnic fiction, the novels of Donato and Tsiang provide readers with a sense of inter- and intraethnic dynamics and the relationship between the ethnic community and the state. An uncaring priest, a kind Italian midwife, Irish and Jewish tenement dwellers, a callous policeman, and a dismissive welfare officer are some of the people Geremio's son encounters when not on the job. In Tsiang's account, American salesmen and prostitutes have their Chinese counterparts; white health inspectors and Chinese loan sharks are "fakers" and speak pidgin. Laws do not protect Chinese immigrants but bleed them dry and turn them against each other. The one thing that unites many in Chinatown, including the different secret societies, or tongs, is the war with Japan. Especially by the late 1930s and 1940s, antifascism helped define the ethnic and gender identities of characters in fiction created by writers as diverse as Jerre Mangione, Irwin Shaw, and Laura Hobson.

Japanese American identities were simultaneously scrutinized, reduced, and misread during the World War II policy of internment. This is the theme of Hisaye Yamamoto's 1950 short story "The Legend of Miss Sasagawara," whose protagonist remains "tantalizingly obscure." We learn of Miss Sasagawara, a thirty-nine-year-old former ballet dancer, from rumors that even Kiku, the gossipy and conventional nisei narrator, is wary of. Everyone in Block 33 of the Arizona internment camp thinks Miss Sasagawara is aloof and crazy because she seems at times wary and at times desiring of attention, characteristics that are accepted as dignified and normal in male characters, like her meditative father, a Buddhist priest, and the excited ambulance driver given leave to escort her to a sanitarium outside the camp. Kiku attributes Miss Sasagawara's behavior to the loss of a lover or son, but she later discovers an alternate explanation, one of father-daughter conflict, revealed in a poem that Miss Sasagwara published. The poem is about a man who found freedom in circumstances of imprisonment by engaging in meditation—to an extreme that ignored and tormented his companion. Yamamoto does not give us Miss Sasagawara's actual poem, itself a legend, but only Kiku's gloss. As in so much ethnic literature, family drama, a writer-protagonist, and the community dynamics surrounding them give the reader a sense of the humanity of the characters. Yamamoto's story also conveys the distance of literature from official accounts.

The historian John Higham noted that the termination of mass European immigration in the 1920s led to the memorialization of the immigrant experience in America in a way that encouraged both assimilation and, later, agitation to repeal the national-origins system. The recovery of poems written by Chinese immigrants detained on Angel Island in San Francisco Bay helped turn the island into a site of memory; translating the poems has led to different interpretations of the immigrant experience. The same poem, for example, has been translated in one way that emphasizes a desire for revenge and independence—"Detained in this wooden house for several tens of days . . . I can only await the word so that I can snap Zu's whip"—and in another way that emphasizes feelings of exile and nostalgia—"Several scores of days detained in this wood house . . . He can only wait for the word to whip his horse on a homeward journey."

Bibliography: Carlos Bulosan, *America Is in the Heart* (Seattle, 1977). Pietro Di Donato, *Christ in Concrete* (New York, 1939). John Higham, *Send These to Me: Jews and Other Immigrants in Urban America* (New York, 1975). Ludwig Lewisohn, *The Island Within* (Philadelphia, 1968). Claude McKay, *Home to Harlem* (New York, 1928). Mae Ngai, *Impossible Subjects* (Princeton, NJ, 2004). Américo Paredes, *Between Two Worlds* (Houston, 1991). Henry Roth, *Call It Sleep* (New York, 1991). Marc Shell and Werner Sollors, eds., *The Multilingual Anthology of American Literature* (New York, 2000). H. T. Tsiang, *And China Has Hands* (New York, 2003). Hisaye Yamamoto, *Seventeen Syllables and Other Stories* (New York, 1988).

YAEL SCHACHER

1925

"Americans, while occasionally willing to be serfs, have always been obstinate about being peasantry"

THE GREAT GATSBY

In 1919, when F. Scott Fitzgerald's betrothed, Zelda Sayre, broke off their engagement because his financial prospects in advertising seemed dim, he quit his job and turned to the literary arts to make his fortune—not typically a smart career move for someone wanting to line his pockets. Fortunately for Fitzgerald, it was the beginning of the Jazz Age, an era of previously inconceivable wealth and opportunity in the United States, and Fitzgerald was a very talented writer. So the next year, as America fox-trotted into the riches of the Roaring Twenties, Scribner's decided to publish Fitzgerald's first novel, *This Side of Paradise,* which brought him fame and money. Fitzgerald married Zelda a week after the book came out. As other successful books and writing projects followed, including *The Beautiful and Damned* in 1922 and *The Great Gatsby* three years later, Fitzgerald came to earn far more during his twenties as a literary celebrity than the average American of his time. At a time when Ford Motor Company paid its assembly-line workers $1,300 a year, Fitzgerald's annual income averaged $25,000. He and Zelda led a very glamorous life, living abroad in various European cities where Gertrude Stein and Ernest Hemingway were their artistic expatriate peers. Back in the United States, the beautiful young couple lived at affluent addresses, tooled around in a Rolls Royce, and kept three servants.

As a young student I was fascinated by details such as these, much as Jay Gatsby was drawn to the glowing green light of possibility, across the way. No one I knew made money by telling stories. There were no classroom visits from novelists, poets, or playwrights for Career Day at Narbonne High School in Harbor City. I did, however, have an English teacher, Mr. Wimbish, who loved to gab during AP English. From him I learned MGM paid *Gatsby*'s author $1,000 a week in 1937, in accordance with Fitzgerald's own cheeky assessment of Hollywood's pay rate:

> Junior writers $300.
> Minor poets — $500. a week.
> Broken novelists - $850.-$1000.
> One play dramatists - $1500.
> Sucks - $2000. —Wits - $2500.

And for the first time in my life the thought occurred: *Writing can make money.* Hmm . . .

So as we studied Fitzgerald's classic American novel about a fabulously wealthy self-made millionaire and the price he pays for love, *Gatsby* introduced me to a glamorous portrait of Jazz Age decadence, as well as the artful quality of its author's writing. Among some of the most iconic moments in the swift, compelling prose is this intoxicating description of one of Gatsby's infamous parties:

> The orchestra has arrived, no thin five-piece affair but a whole pitful of oboes and trombones and saxophones and viols and cornets and piccolos, and low and high drums. The last swimmers have come in from the beach and are dressing up-stairs; the cars from New York are parked five deep in the drive, and already the halls and salons and verandas are gaudy with primary colors, and hair shorn in strange new ways, and shawls beyond the dreams of Castile. The bar is in full swing, and floating rounds of cocktails permeate the garden outside, until the air is alive with chatter and laughter, and casual innuendo and introductions forgotten on the spot, and enthusiastic meetings between women who never knew each other's names.

The lights grow brighter as the earth lurches away from the sun, and now the orchestra is playing yellow cocktail music, and the opera of voices pitches a key higher. Laughter is easier minute by minute, spilled with prodigality, tipped out at a cheerful word. The groups change more swiftly, swell with new arrivals, dissolve and form in the same breath; already there are wanderers, confident girls who weave here and there among the stouter and more stable, become for a sharp, joyous moment the center of a group, and then, excited with triumph, glide on through the sea-change of faces and voices and color under the constantly chang-ing light.

Or this inventive boyhood schedule of Gatsby's, clearly rendering the protago-nist's disciplined determination from very early on:

Rise from bed	6.00	A.M.
Dumbbell exercise and wall-scaling	6.15 — 6.30	"
Study electricity, etc.	7.15 — 8.15	"
Work	8.30 — 4.30	P.M.
Baseball and sports	4.30 — 5.00	"
Practice elocution, poise and how to attain it	5.00 — 6.00	"
Study needed inventions		"

GENERAL RESOLVES

No wasting time at Shafters or [a name, indecipherable]
No more smokeing or chewing.
Bath every other day
Read one improving book or magazine per week
Save $5.00 [crossed out] $3.00 per week
Be better to parents

I was impressed that Fitzgerald could "unfold the shining secrets that only Midas and Morgan and Maecenas knew" with such literary craft. Thematically, there was also something resonant to me in the novel about the nouveau riche being economic immigrants to the upper class.

Though Jay Gatsby is rich, he is far from royal. And for that reason he, along with the rest of the less pedigreed West Egg community, is tolerated by the blue-blood East Egg residents, like foreign labor when it can be of service. When a snobby riding party deigns to stop on Gatsby's porch, he scurries to fetch drinks while his friend Nick Carraway, the narrating voice of the book, is taken aback that Gatsby caters to the three riders "as though they cared!" Of the trio, Nick notices that one "didn't enter into the conversation, but lounged back haughtily in his chair; the woman said nothing either." The third horseman is Gatsby's rival, Tom Buchanan, who doesn't even recall that they have met before. Gatsby's pala-tial mansion is little more than a roadside rest stop for their equestrian outing. They extend an insincere dinner invitation to Gatsby, which he guilelessly ac-cepts, but the arrogant threesome disappears before Gatsby can join them. Even privileged princess Daisy Buchanan, Gatsby's love interest and wife of Tom, is "appalled by West Egg, this unprecedented 'place' that Broadway had begotten upon a Long Island fishing village — appalled by its raw vigor that chafed under the old euphemisms and by the too obtrusive fate that herded its inhabitants along a short-cut from nothing to nothing. She saw something awful."

These reactions to Gatsby and his freshly flush ilk, that they're uncouth, mirror the ill will directed at foreigners by the novel's ruling class. When Tom passionately rails against the possible "rise of the colored empires," warning, "It's up to us, who are the dominant race, to watch out or these other races will have control of things," this equally captures his disdainful attitude toward the encroaching population of "crazy fish" newly rich. The distinction in the book between Tom's East Egg and Gatsby's West Egg community is also geographically analogous to the American regions associated with old money (East) and new opportunity (West). Likewise in those days, the majority of immigrants had left statelier, old countries of Europe to the east and come to the gleaming new land of possibility in the west. Here, however, despite their hard work and efforts to improve themselves, they were still seen as threatening interlopers and were treated with suspicion and animosity—sentiments that I myself was familiar with.

I first read *Gatsby* in Southern California, in the early 1990s, around the same time Proposition 187 called out the immigration problems of modern California. This so-called citizen initiative loomed over our social landscape, like the billboard of Doctor T. J. Eckleburg, and sought to deny illegal aliens social services, health care, and public education. And though neither my parents, who are naturalized U.S. citizens, nor I myself (born in the American South) were targeted by the proposed law, we nonetheless felt lumped in because of our ethnic appearance, and swept up by the campaign to "Save Our State." "What's your nationality?" folks often asked.

"American."

"No, where were you *born?*"

"Texas . . ."

It was clearly not they answer they wanted, a denial that served as a constant reminder to my family of how others were, paraphrasing Nick Carraway, "unutterably aware of our identity with this country." We were self-conscious about being viewed as outsiders similar to the ones unwelcomed by our fellow citizens. In 1994, Prop. 187 passed with a 58.8 percent majority vote. That we were, ultimately, a nation of immigrants was a fact lost on the masses.

During Fitzgerald's Jazz Age (a phrase he coined himself), an especially prominent example of hostility toward alien newcomers was the Massachusetts case of Nicola Sacco and Bartolomeo Vanzetti. In 1927, these two Italian-immigrant working-class men were convicted of and given the death penalty for an armed robbery and murder that it was very likely they did not commit. Though neither had a previous criminal record, their ethnic background and radical activism drew much prejudice during the trial. Even presiding judge Webster Thayer made it notoriously apparent that he was against them for having associated with Italian anarchists. He even counseled the jury against Vanzetti, saying, "This man, although he may not have actually committed the crime attributed to him, is nevertheless culpable because he is the enemy of our existing institutions."

Thayer's unlawful disregard for the truth is similar to that of the public toward the factual circumstances surrounding Gatsby's death. "Most of those [newspaper] reports were a nightmare," Nick says: "—grotesque, circumstantial, and untrue." Though Gatsby is actually innocent of Myrtle Wilson's murder, it is a useful hook upon which to hang him for his other social transgressions; more than the bootlegging, Gatsby is guilty of trying to steal Tom's wife. So, when Myrtle's distraught husband kills Gatsby based on information Tom has given, Tom rationalizes that (like Sacco and Vanzetti) Gatsby got what was coming to him anyway. When not being discriminated against for being foreigners, Sacco and Vanzetti were condemned for being radical militants who supported anarchist bombing and other violence as a means of political agitation. That they must answer for their offenses one way or another was evident in comments such as the infamous exclamation of the jury foreman during the trial: "Damn them, they ought to hang them anyway!" Gatsby's folly was to presume that he could spend his way into the Buchanans' America, when in actuality they would never accept him.

These themes of exclusion and excess in *Gatsby* are also evident in Fitzgerald's own life. Though he may have been handsomely paid, Fitzgerald spent his money faster than he was able to earn it, claiming that he and Zelda needed at least $35,000 a year to maintain their high-flying lifestyle. The two were also debauched in their drinking. Though alcohol sales were illegal from 1920 to 1933, Prohibition, for the Fitzgeralds, was more a joke than a law. One of their saucy house rules requested visitors "not to break down doors in search of liquor, even when authorized to do so by the host and hostess." Ultimately, such reckless living took its toll on the couple, just as the Roaring Twenties' overexuberant stock speculation did on America. In 1930, as the nation sank into the Great Depression, Zelda also suffered the first of several mental breakdowns. Eventually diagnosed with schizophrenia, she would be in and out of hospitals the rest of her life. Fitzgerald, meanwhile, had his own "crack-up," which he wrote about in an essay by the same name for *Esquire* magazine in 1936. In it, he frankly discussed his inordinate drinking, exorbitant debt, and alienation from his wife and child.

Yet perhaps what isolates Fitzgerald most, as an individual of his era, is his artistic achievement. During a time when others made their fortunes as industrialists or through investments, here was a young man audacious enough to throw over his steady corporate job in advertising to make it big as a writer. And he succeeded! Prominent and well paid for selling his written thoughts, he was as much a self-made man as Gatsby, who "sprang from his Platonic conception of himself." Fitzgerald was the ultimate upstart newcomer—an immigrant, of sorts, to the world of letters.

As a young student, I was definitely aware of how unusual it was for a novelist to do what Fitzgerald did. I certainly didn't imagine that being a writer was a fast track to riches. And yet, the fact that success like his was possible—at an age not far from my own—whispered to my teenage mind, the way aspiring immigrants in the old country must have absorbed stories about America as the land of opportunity. *Really? You can live like that?*

Apparently, yes. Yes, you could.

In my adult life, after several years of dabbling in other less-fulfilling careers, I gradually came to realize that I wanted to be a writer and began pursuing that ambition in earnest. Then the United States was attacked by foreign terrorists on 9/11. In the subsequent political climate, which harbored wariness and suspicion of alien immigrants, I wondered aloud to my parents how many of their fellow foreign-born Americans regretted coming to the United States. Knowing what they knew now, would they have chosen differently? In response, my father pointed out how all over ethnic communities like our Little Saigon in Orange County, American flags were being flown. When I cynically speculated that they were probably displayed to discourage anti-immigrant vandals, my father pointed out that many of his friends were thankful for things they had in America that they likely couldn't have had back in Vietnam: luxury cars, five-bedroom houses, children who were doctors, lawyers, or otherwise commanding six-figure salaries. Okay, I conceded. He had a point. But I still wondered. Though they've earned graduate degrees from leading American universities, my parents drive an old Honda and live near an oil refinery, in a neighborhood with drive-by shootings. The air quality there is just about the worst in Los Angeles County and local gangs frequently tag my parents' garage door, using it as a bulletin board to broadcast death threats to rival gangs. As for me, the only child, I am neither doctor nor lawyer and am certainly not making a six-figure salary. So what were my parents grateful for?

"For you," my father said, "for the opportunities you have here, to live and be and do your art."

Today, *The Great Gatsby* is read in high schools and colleges across the nation. Half a million copies are sold every year. Its popularity among academics and students, as well as the general public, is a testimony to the resonance of the book's themes along with the quality and accessibility of its author's written craft. But what resonates for me most is not the glamorous Jazz Age wealth Fitzgerald chronicled so well. It is the very fact that he so boldly made a living as an artist by pursuing his heart's desire. That accomplishment is a beacon. It is my green light of possibility.

At the final sentencing of Sacco and Vanzetti, Vanzetti made the following statement: "My conviction is that I have suffered for things that I am guilty of. I am suffering because I am a radical and indeed I am a radical. I am suffering because I am an Italian, and indeed I am an Italian . . . If you could execute me two times, and if I could be reborn two other times, I would live again to do what I have done already." One imagines that, if given the chance, F. Scott Fitzgerald would have done the same. Despite the family they left behind and the hardships they have had living in America, I now know that if my immigrant parents were given the choice, they too would do it all over again. Because in doing so they, like Fitzgerald, allow me to live my dream.

Bibliography: Matthew Joseph Bruccoli, ed., *Some Sort of Epic Grandeur: The Life of F. Scott Fitzgerald,* rev. ed. (Columbia, SC, 2002). F. Scott Fitzgerald, *The Great Gatsby* (New York, 1925). Bruce Watson, *Sacco and Vanzetti: The Men, the Murders, and the Judgment of Mankind* (New York, 2007).

LAN TRAN

1925, June

Nation's Business, the journal of the U.S. Chamber of Commerce, declares the
word "Babbitt" "common coin in everyday conversation"

SINCLAIR LEWIS

Sinclair Lewis, who described his only virtue as an "almost reckless hatred of hypocrisy" and "bunk," stood at the head of a generation of satirists that ridiculed the foibles of adolescent post–World War I America. Including novelists Don Marquis and William Woodward, humorists Ring Lardner and Dorothy Parker, African American authors George S. Schuyler, Wallace Thurman, and Rudolph Fisher, and the dean of American letters in this period, editor H. L. Mencken, this group of writers constituted a golden age of serious literary mockery in the tradition of Mark Twain and Ambrose Bierce. In addition to biting humor, these debunkers held in common a list of typical targets, all of which served their general assault on American moralism, sentimentalism, and cultural backwardness. These included the provincialism of small-town America, the vapidity of popular culture, the blindness of unreflective patriotism, the narrow pettiness of fundamentalist crusaders, and the hypocrisy of American racism.

The debunkers represented only one wing of a more general intellectual and cultural rebellion in the United States that began in the decade or so before World War I and continued until the Depression. Although this movement involved many intellectual positions, the cultural norms of the Victorian period, especially assumptions concerning the oneness of modernity and progress, constituted its general target. Whether they were modernists who experimented with artistic form, pluralists who opposed Anglo-conformity, socialists who questioned the invisible hand, or antipuritans who challenged sexual repression, the rebels of the 1920s carried out a many-sided assault on values that they found constricting under new circumstances. Because it marked so forcefully the element of barbarity at the heart of modernity, World War I provided momentum for the skeptical spirit of these thinkers, as did postwar government repression of the left and the ascendancy for the first time of the city over the small town as the dominant locus of American life.

Looked at from the standpoint of his status as a leading debunker, Lewis's writing career reads like a systematic attempt to attack the favorite targets of this group with a kind of obsessive thoroughness, one after the other. After several unsuccessful novels generally written in the more serious vein of American realism between 1912 and 1919, which included *Our Mr. Wrenn* (1914) and *The Job* (1917), Lewis produced *Main Street* (1920), his first satire and his first commercial success. An attack on American small-town provincialism, it inspired controversy as it sold thousands of copies both to Americans who regarded themselves as the superiors of small-town hayseeds and to the Main Streeters themselves, who presumably wondered what the other half had to say of them. Lewis followed *Main Street* quickly with *Babbitt* (1922), a send-up of the small-town businessman; *Arrowsmith* (1925), which targeted science and the medical profession; *Elmer Gantry* (1927), an unforgettable spoof of American fundamentalism; and *Dodsworth* (1929), which laughed at the shortcomings of the small-town upper class. After turning down the 1926 Pulitzer Prize, in part to avoid association with its attempt to promote "the wholesome atmosphere of American life, and the highest standard of American manhood," in 1930 Lewis became, following his richest decade of work, the first American to win, and accept, the Nobel Prize for Literature. Subsequently, Lewis continued writing along the same lines but to much less effect, producing most notably *It Can't Happen Here* (1935), on American fascism, and *Kingsblood Royal* (1947), his only work focusing directly on the American race problem.

Of the many compliments that Lewis received during his long career, the best may have come from his adversaries. In the first of several articles published over several months targeting his satire *Babbitt,* the journal of the United States Chamber of Commerce, *Nation's Business,* attempted to reverse what it could not erase. Admitting Lewis's achievement as one of the few writers ever to invent a character whose name took on independent meaning as a common noun, it pragmatically encouraged readers to embrace the negative stereotype implicit in the name "Babbitt." In a style reminiscent of unfairly labeled racial and ethnic groups, *Nation's Business* exhorted its audience to show pride and to remember the achievements of the greatest and mightiest Babbitts, such as the inventor and philanthropist George Eastman, who gave lavishly to the city of Rochester. "Dare to be a Babbitt!" it proclaimed defiantly. Recalling the qualities of good Rotarians, who "live orderly lives, and save money, and go to church, and play golf, and send their children to school," *Nation's Business* asked of Lewis's main character, the Zenith realtor George F. Babbitt: "Was Babbitt so evil a thing? Should we despise him for his pride in his real estate business . . . [or] his simple joy in the conveniences of his life and his home?" "Would not the world be better off," it asked, "with more Babbitts and fewer of those who cry 'Babbitt'?" One month later, an article in the same journal by Harper Leech (a name that Lewis himself could not have improved on) entitled "Babbitt Pays for Babbitt-Baiting" proclaimed in more aggressive terms the basic aims of the *Nation's Business* counterattack on Lewis. According to Leech, "Babbitt-baiters," the name he chose for Lewis and his followers, could only survive because productive and clean-living capitalists supported them. Yet despite their many group accomplishments, these Babbitts thought of themselves only in individual terms. Even worse, they accepted the word of so-called intellectuals without question. To Leech's consternation, this made the decent and hardworking easy prey for Lewis's charge of willful blindness. And like fools, Leech admonished, the insecure Babbitts allowed this unfair charge to go virtually unopposed.

A satirist could not hope for a better response from the heart of the enemy camp. Staggering from Lewis's jabs, *Nation's Business* could only answer him by adopting his rhetoric. A product of the best name-calling pen in the history of American literature, the word "Babbitt" had become a handy common weapon for anyone wishing to attack the element of faddishness endemic to American business in the 1920s. Could a go-go atmosphere of giddiness and greed seriously pass itself off as modest clean living? Many had asked this question before, but Lewis crystallized the thought into a single word that neatly associated the businessman with conformity, mediocrity, banality, and other common American democratic flaws. Notably, Lewis achieved his effect by setting aside the style of the typical left attack, which depicted the business class as rapacious and dangerous but also technically creative and efficacious. Unwilling to allow his opponent the concession inherent in the term "evil," Lewis attempted to laugh him out of school. Thus, rather than a nefarious exploiter, he painted the businessman unforgettably as a confused and somewhat lovable bungler: George F. Babbitt, the man in the middle—a middle-aged, middle-class, middle man in a midsized city in middle America—who held as sacred doctrine the average beliefs of the typical member of the American herd.

Distinguished only by his exemplary lack of distinction, Babbitt holds fast to the common American belief in progress; in worldly success as the automatic reward of virtue; in the class structure as an exact reflection of talent; in the deferral of satisfaction as the key to a happy life; in government as the servant of business; and in the benevolent businessman as the caretaker of community. A glad-handing realtor and a slave to reputation, he is a Republican, a family man, a Presbyterian, a member of the Booster Club, the Athletic Club, the Rotary Club, the chamber of commerce, the Elks, the Good Citizen's League, and all other associations of "good, jolly, kidding, laughing, sweating, upstanding, lend-a-handing Royal Good Fellows." Nevertheless, good influences from good fellows often led him astray. More a pragmatist than a moralist, "he advocated, though he did not practise, the prohibition of alcohol; he praised, though he did not obey, the laws against motor-speeding; . . . he followed the custom of his clan and cheated only as it was sanctified by precedent." Babbitt's conformity even in dishonesty shines through most prominently in the oily and manipulative ads he writes for his real estate firm, one of which asks quite humorously:

> DO YOU RESPECT YOUR LOVED ONES?
> When the last sad rites of bereavement are over, do you
> know for certain that you have done your best for the
> Departed? You haven't unless they lie in the Cemetery Beautiful
> LINDEN LANE
> the only strictly up-to-date burial place in or near
> Zenith, where exquisitely gardened plots look from daisy-
> dotted hill-slopes across the smiling fields of Dorchester.

One imagines that Babbitt himself would like to choose the modern Linden Lane as his own final resting place. In the context of his living death as a modern, striving American, such a wish would seem most appropriate. Yet for the first half of the novel, Babbitt does not fully realize, indeed cannot face, his problem. A dead man walking, he can only wonder at the vague sense of fatigue that accompanies his every gesture. He yearns for escape, but does not know why. Symbolically, Babbitt spends his nights on a sleeping porch as a spiritually dispossessed escapee from the domestic space, dreaming of a young, slim, white-skinned fairy princess who negates everything that he serves in his waking life, including his loyal but sexually uninspiring wife. Rather than a home, his house resembles a theme park backdrop for his role as a man of progress. Like his kitchen, his "royal bathroom of porcelain and glazed tile" stands out in this regard, exemplifying the excessive desire to clean up what must remain associated with dirt. "The towel-rack was a rod of clear glass set in nickel. The tub was long enough for a Prussian Guard, and above the set bowl was a sensational exhibit of tooth-brush holder, shaving-brush holder, soap-dish, sponge-dish, and medicine cabinet, so glittering and so ingenious that they resembled an electrical instrument-board." As a man who took pride in a baronial bathroom, Babbitt relished the time that he spent there, where he could revert to the carefree days of childhood while shaving in the bathtub. There, immersed in soothing warm water, he appeared "as a plump, smooth, pink, baldish, podgy Goodman, robbed of the importance of spectacles, squatting in breast-high water, scraping his lather-smeared cheeks with a safety-razor like a tiny lawn-mower, and with melancholy dignity clawing through the water to recover a slippery and active piece of soap." Of course, the soap in this scene symbolizes Babbitt's soul, which the very act of cleaning places further out of grasp.

As one might glean from the handful of passages cited so far, most of the satire in *Babbitt* resides in its masterful description of seemingly unimportant detail, which the first third of the novel, an account of a single day in the life of an utterly ordinary realtor, accomplishes to the near exclusion of significant action. We wake up with Babbitt, look through his house, get dressed with him, listen to family small talk, chuckle over his efforts to start the car, watch him deal with the other bunglers at work, follow him through the preparations for a dinner party, and so on. All of this reflects well the utterly banal consciousness of the main character as it provides room for Lewis's weaving of satire with the characteristics of the realistic novel.

The rest of the plot appears equally prosaic, but for different reasons. The whole matter centers on an affair, which Babbitt falls into with clocklike predictability. Exhausted but dimly aware of the reasons why, he attempts a reinvigorating trip to Maine with his best friend, Paul Riesling, the melancholy victim of a domineering wife named Zilla. After the vacation, Babbitt achieves minor fame as an orator at real estate conventions and in local Zenith politics, but has his world turned around when Paul shoots his wife and goes to jail. Now consciously doubtful concerning the ultimate meaning of his own life, and conveniently freed by his wife's extended visit to her sick sister, Babbitt strikes up an affair with Tanis Judique, a tantalizing bohemian possessing every characteristic that his wife lacks. After a temporary immersion in the Zenith version of bohemia, which proves just as inbred and petty as his native circle of "good fellows," Babbitt quits the affair. Disgust at a strike by Zenith workers helps him to recoup his capitalist identity, and guilt over his wife's falling ill returns him to the family fold, beaten but augmented by his trip through the gauntlet. Freed from his former fears, he supports his son's choice to skip college, join the working class, and elope with the flapper next door. In other words, essentially finished with his own life, he invests in the next generation. Now more self-aware than ever before, Babbitt says to his son: "I've never done a single thing I've wanted in my whole life . . . But I do get a kind of sneaking pleasure out of the fact that you knew what you wanted to do and did it . . . Go ahead, old man! The world is yours!" At this moment, Babbitt finds his misplaced manhood. The novel ends with him and his son arm in arm, a picture of virile fraternity, going to face bravely the disapproving women of the family.

Notwithstanding its bracing invocation of authenticity, this conclusion might seem a little less than appetizing to contemporary readers. The heartwarming image of the resurrected protagonist joined with his son depends directly on an opposition to the qualities and preferences of women, who presumably suffer from the bane of conformity even more than men. Although Babbitt's newfound masculinity stands against the bare-chested and womanizing versions of manhood that he wishfully entertains at the beginning of the novel, it improves on these only incrementally. And even more than the specific content of Lewis's moral, the very descent into moralism itself may well spoil *Babbitt* for some readers. On this score, the author's fun-poking toward his main character might reveal a sense of moral superiority not so different from that of the Rotarians he despised. In writing *Babbitt,* Lewis implicitly claimed a superior, perhaps even intimate knowledge of the small-minded American. In doing so, he leaves us to wonder whether it really does take one to know one. Do we really achieve distance from Babbittry by laughing along with Lewis? Or does his classic novel succeed more in rendering fascinating an aspect of American identity that remains powerful because we cannot wash it away? Does *Babbitt* truly undermine the values of its main character? Or by naming them so well and marking them so indelibly, does it preserve them by imbuing them with an odd and unavoidable attraction?

Bibliography: Sinclair Lewis, *Babbitt* (New York, 1922). Richard Lingeman, *Sinclair Lewis: Rebel from Main Street* (New York, 2002). Edward A. Martin, *H. L. Mencken and the Debunkers* (Athens, GA, 1984). Michael Seidel, *Satiric Inheritance: Rabelais to Sterne* (Princeton, NJ, 1979). Mark Schorer, *Sinclair Lewis* (Minneapolis, 1963). Gore Vidal, "The Romance of Sinclair Lewis," *New York Review of Books,* October 18, 1992, 14, 16–20.

JEFFREY FERGUSON

1925, July
"I do not think about things I don't think about"

THE SCOPES TRIAL

For a reputed "trial of the century," *State of Tennessee v. John Thomas Scopes* lacked nearly all the elements of a classic courtroom drama. Both the defense — led by Clarence Darrow — and the prosecution — whose most prominent figure was William Jennings Bryan — agreed that the defendant was guilty as charged. While substituting for the regular biology instructor at Dayton High School one day, John Scopes had unwittingly violated a statute the legislature had passed just six months earlier. It banned the teaching in public schools of "any theory that denies the story of the Divine creation of man as taught in the Bible, to teach instead that man has descended from a lower order of animals." Knowing little about the subject, the twenty-four-year-old instructor did not even take the stand in his own defense. Although convicted of the misdemeanor, he suffered in no way for his crime. In fact, Scopes, who had been hired more to coach the Dayton High football team than to teach science, basked in the renown of the case for the rest of his life.

Yet his trial, which opened on July 10, 1925, and ended on July 21, drew almost two hundred reporters from the U.S. and abroad and a national radio audience, and became a symbolic marker for a debate between the truth claims of science and of the Bible that continues to rage. As Bryan commented at the end of the eight-day event, "Here has been fought out a little case of little consequence as a case, but the world is interested because it raises an issue and that issue will some day be settled right, whether it is settled on our side or the other side."

The issue in what came to be known as "the monkey trial" was not simply whether one could reconcile the Bible with the writings of Charles Darwin. The Tennessee law also raised the question of whether a teacher in a public school was free to teach the truth as he saw it or "whether the people . . . have the right to control the educational system which they have created and which they tax themselves to support," as Bryan wrote to local supporters. Clarence Darrow agreed to head Scopes's defense only after learning that Bryan was joining the other side. Once a close ally of the politician, a three-time Democratic nominee for president, the great attorney now reviled him as a foe of intellectual liberty and a symbol of "despair and bigotry." The six-year-old American Civil Liberties Union financed the defense to protect free speech, not to pit science against Christianity. In fact, of the four lawyers who represented John Scopes, only Darrow, a proud agnostic, was willing to mock the authority of Scripture.

The spectacle of a divided nation stirred the popular imagination. H. L. Mencken—hero to skeptical modernists—regaled his big-city, Northern readers with descriptions of Bryan's "peculiar imbecilities" and "theologic bilge." Darrow later called Bryan "the idol of all Morondom." But to millions of evangelical Christians, the popularity of such figures as Mencken and Darrow, and the rise of the pluralistic urban culture that had spawned them, only increased the urgency of standing by the one text that would never fail them. In the smirking Darrow and his admirers in the press, they saw proof of Bryan's warnings about the perils of amoral education.

The climax of the seven-day trial, and its literary touchstone, was an unusual cross-examination. On July 20, Darrow called Bryan to the stand as an expert on the Bible. Bryan agreed, on the condition that he would also have a chance to grill one of the defense attorneys. That day, the proceedings took place on a lawn outside the courthouse, before as many as 3,000 spectators. The judge, John T. Raulston, feared the floor inside might collapse under the weight of all who wanted to witness the confrontation.

"You have given considerable study to the Bible, haven't you, Mr. Bryan?" "Yes, sir, I have tried to," was how it began. For the next two hours, the celebrated attorney kept his foe on edge with a cascade of short queries about the trustworthiness of Scripture: "Do you believe a whale swallowed Jonah?" "Do you believe Joshua made the sun stand still?" Do you take "the story of the flood to be a literal interpretation?" "Do you think the earth was made in six days?"

Bryan avoided giving an unqualified yes to any of Darrow's questions. The whale, he supposed, was only "a large fish" and perhaps God had not specifically directed it to ingest a man. Neither did Bryan speculate about how the Lord had suspended the laws of physics long enough to stop the rotation of the earth. And he flatly rejected the notion that each day of creation mentioned in Genesis referred to a period of twenty-four hours. Like many pious critics of Darwin, Bryan had long assumed that a biblical "day" referred to an eon of time. An exponent of common sense in worldly affairs, he could not easily abandon it when discussing the loftiest text of all.

But this attitude forced him to evade direct questions with answers that seemed merely thoughtless and dogmatic. When Darrow asked for the date of the Flood, Bryan responded that he'd "never made a calculation." The skeptic pressed on, "What do you think?" Bryan bristled, "I do not think about things I don't think about." The door to ridicule was wide open: "Q— Do you think about things you do think about? A— Well, sometimes." "Laughter in the courtyard," noted the court reporter, in the laconic custom of his trade.

The next morning, the judge ordered Bryan's testimony expunged from the official record. It could, he argued, "shed no light upon any issues that will be pending before the higher courts." This spared Bryan further embarrassment, but it also prevented him from cross-examining any defense attorney. Then Darrow made sure that the last meaningful words uttered in the trial would be his. He quickly asked the judge to instruct the jury to bring in a guilty verdict, making any closing arguments unnecessary. After huddling briefly in the hall, the twelve stalwarts of Rhea County, Tennessee, did their duty. Judge Raulston fined Scopes $100, which Mencken's paper, the *Baltimore Evening Sun,* immediately agreed to pay.

Bryan's clumsy performance embarrassed his anti-Darwinist supporters and probably helped defeat their attempts to pass laws in other states similar to the one Scopes had violated. Of course, millions of Americans continued to believe in Genesis rather than *The Origin of Species,* but they were increasingly thrown on the defensive in a nation whose citizens viewed scientists as value-free wizards whose magic resulted in better products, faster transportation, and longer life spans. Moreover, by the 1920s American culture was shaped as much by white Catholics, Jews, and African Americans in big cities as by people in towns like Dayton, Tennessee, seat of a rural county in which nearly every resident was white and Protestant. In this environment, the strict separation between church and state that the ACLU championed seemed the only rational solution to the divisive hectoring of "fundamentalists" who defended Bryan.

Thus, for about half a century after the Scopes trial, most writers echoed Darrow's arguments. In 1931, the journalist Frederick Lewis Allen in *Only Yesterday,* his best-selling saga of the twenties, breezily depicted a battle between ignorant pietists and clever modernists that the latter were destined to win. The views that Bryan espoused would, he was certain, gradually fade away. Indeed, by 1955 the historian Richard Hofstadter could remark that, at least to his fellow intellectuals, "The evolution controversy seems as remote as the Homeric era."

That same year, the play *Inherit the Wind,* written by Jacob Lawrence and Robert E. Lee, opened on Broadway. A fictionalized version of the trial and the controversy that swirled around it, the production ran for more than eight hundred performances. In 1960, it was adapted into an equally successful film, starring Spencer Tracy as Henry Drummond (Darrow) and Frederic March as Matthew Harrison Brady (Bryan). To cast Tracy, one of the most adored leading men of his day, in that role guaranteed that audiences would be on Darrow's side, even if the script itself didn't lead them there.

The liberal playwrights were no more concerned than Hofstadter had been about a creationist threat to the teaching of science. They had chosen the trial as a metaphor for the repression of free thinking and First Amendment rights they associated with McCarthyism. Still, they relied on one of the defense attorneys in the Scopes trial, Arthur Garfield Hays, to convey "much of the unwritten vividness of the Dayton adventure." They also made their historical sympathies clear by portraying Brady as a grim-faced dogmatist eager to see the young defendant imprisoned. In fact, Bryan was a famously witty orator and was rather fond of Scopes (they had attended the same Illinois high school, and Bryan was the commencement speaker at the young man's graduation in 1919). He had even offered to pay the teacher's fine.

Whatever its merits as history, *Inherit the Wind* is a tautly crafted, provocative drama. Revivals of it continue to be performed around the country and on television. By the 1950s, most biblical literalists were avoiding public debates about evolution, so there was no one in the wider culture to challenge the hostility toward them expressed in the play and movie. Only at the end of *Inherit the Wind,* when Drummond "thoughtfully" balances the King James Bible in one hand and a biology text in the other were audiences reminded that the scriptwriters' main point was to defend free speech, not to impugn religious convictions.

However, conservative evangelicals did not intend to stay silent forever, and their forceful return to the public square in the late 1970s helped revive debate about creationism—and about the famous trial half a century in the past. At the time, opinion pollsters reported that about as many Americans swore by the account in Genesis as in some version of evolution. In 1986 the Supreme Court ruled against new state laws that called for biology teachers to offer "a balanced treatment" of "creation science." But in a vigorous dissent, Justice Antonin Scalia argued that "the people . . . including those who are fundamentalists, are quite entitled . . . to have whatever scientific evidence there may be against evolution presented in their schools, just as Mr. Scopes was entitled to present whatever scientific evidence there was for it."

By the early twenty-first century, the development of intelligent design theories by certain scientists who happened to be devout Christians had given foes of Darwinism a new, more sophisticated way to fight for equal time in biology classes. In 2005, a widely covered trial in Dover, Pennsylvania, turned on precisely this issue. The judge in the case ruled that intelligent design is not scientifically valid and "cannot uncouple itself from its creationist, and thus religious, antecedents." But the battle in other school districts continued.

Meanwhile, scholars and writers who are not biblical literalists began to voice a more nuanced set of views about the meaning of what occurred in Dayton in the summer of 1925. Some separated Bryan's motives for mistrusting Darwinism from his clumsy behavior at the trial during that hot week in July. The recognition that most evolutionists in the 1920s were dedicated to "improving" the human race through eugenics made Bryan seem more sympathetic, even to a secular Darwinist like Stephen Jay Gould. Gould pointed out that *A Civic Biology*, the textbook by George William Hunter that Scopes was prosecuted for using, had described two particular families that were plagued for generations by "immorality and feeble-mindedness." People like these, wrote Hunter, "are true parasites . . . if such people were lower animals, we would probably kill them off to prevent them from spreading." Alas, sighed Hunter, forced sterilization was the only legal remedy. The fact that the Nazis both preached and practiced eugenics also made Bryan's concerns seem less irrational. Darwinism, observed lawyer and author Alan Dershowitz in *America on Trial* in 2004, was often "misused . . . by racists, militarists, and nationalists to push some pretty horrible programs." In 1998, Edward J. Larson's careful history of the Scopes trial, *Summer for the Gods,* which refrains from bestowing praise or criticism on either side, won the Pulitzer Prize for History.

So, more than eighty years after it occurred, the Scopes trial thrives in American culture—as a dramatic narrative and a powerful symbolic marker in the argument between religious orthodoxy and the scientific consensus. Since we are unlikely to lose our zeal for either of these matters, the final settlement Bryan expected may never come to pass.

Bibliography: Stephen Jay Gould, "William Jennings Bryan's Last Campaign," *Nebraska History* 77 (Fall/Winter 1996): 177–183, originally published in *Natural History,* November 1987. Michael Kazin, *A Godly Hero: The Life of William Jennings Bryan* (New York, 2006). Edward J. Larson, *Summer for the Gods: The Scopes Trial and America's Continuing Debate over Science and Evolution* (Cambridge, MA, 1997). Jacob Lawrence and Robert E. Lee, *Inherit the Wind* (New York, 1955). Jeffrey Moran, *The Scopes Trial: A Brief History with Documents* (Boston, 2002).

MICHAEL KAZIN

1925, August 16

The *New York World* runs Dorothy Parker's two-line poem
"News Item": "Men seldom make passes at . . ."

GIRLS WHO WEAR GLASSES

In a 1933 story called "The Little Hours," Dorothy Parker pretended to resign herself to obscurity: "My name will never be writ large on the roster of Those

Who Do Things. I don't do anything. Not one single thing. I used to bite my nails, but I don't even do that anymore." In 1925, critical pens busily recorded names on the roster of Those Who Do Things, or at least Those Who Write Things. F. Scott Fitzgerald published *The Great Gatsby;* Ernest Hemingway, *In Our Time;* Langston Hughes, *The Weary Blues.* That same year, Parker published "News Item." This accident of historical timing juxtaposes the Great American Novel with the feminine aside. Women wits of the 1920s, such as Parker, Edna St. Vincent Millay, and Anita Loos, scribbled in the margins of literary history. In Millay's poem "The Singing-Woman from the Wood's Edge," a girl learns from her mother, a leprechaun, to rewrite the solemn messages of her father, a priest, through "some funny little saying / that would mean the opposite of all that he was praying!" Humor and irony allowed these women to voice opposition couched in a funny little saying.

The 1920s saw a boom in magazines thanks to the growth of the advertising industry, and Jazz Age insouciance offered a hospitable zeitgeist for humor magazines. During the late 1910s and 1920s many young women, and the writers among them, migrated to cities and entered the workforce. The urbanite Parker lamented that she was not technically a New York City native, since she was born in New Jersey while her family was on summer vacation. Maine-born Millay moved to Greenwich Village upon graduating from Vassar in 1917, and Loos, a Californian, relocated to New York in 1919. Loos wrote scripts for Hollywood and Broadway, and Millay published poetry and prose in *Vanity Fair.* In these popular forms and the arena of humor, women writers cleared a professional space for themselves. Parker defended this territory in "Fighting Words," inviting any kind of insult with equanimity except a literary one: "Say my verses do not scan / And I'll get me another man!"

Parker was one of the only female members of the Algonquin Round Table, the group of journalists, playwrights, and humorists who gathered and traded quips at the famous Midtown hotel. In Anita Loos's 1928 sequel to *Gentlemen Prefer Blondes,* titled *But Gentlemen Marry Brunettes,* Lorelei Lee observes (with her characteristically quirky spelling) that she "soon found out that the most literary enviroment in New York is the Algonquin Hotel, where all the literary geniuses eat their luncheon. Because every genius who eats his luncheon at the Algonquin Hotel is always writing that that is the place where all the great literary geniuses eat their luncheon." These self-promoting great literary geniuses founded the *New Yorker* in 1925, and Parker's name was on the list of editors.

Being a professional female writer meant using certain shibboleths—puns, allusion, irony, self-deprecation—to open the door to the boys-only clubhouse. In a 1931 book review, "Home Is the Sailor," Parker pretends modesty in the face of male intellectualism: "Reading, according to Bacon—and you will tell me if it isn't Bacon, won't you you big stiffs?—reading makes a full man; but to achieve the same end, I know a trick worth two of it." Pretending to defer to "big stiffs," she mocks their pedantry and flirts. Socializing with men in a professional setting was part of the job and required a worldly, urbane attitude. In a 1957 *Paris Review* interview, Parker joked about sharing a small office with her friend and fellow humorist Robert Benchley: "an inch smaller and it would have been adultery."

Such professional cohabitation was not always so sanguine. Edna St. Vincent Millay published a collection of satirical stories, *Distressing Dialogues* (1924), under the pseudonym Nancy Boyd, the name being a play on the slang phrase "Nancy boy." In the story "Two Souls with but a Single Thought," Millay as Boyd ridicules the competition between a man and his wife, professional humorists who steal each other's work. Millay mocks the ideal of cooperation between male and female humor writers: "When we were married, everybody said, 'How perfect! The wedding of the cap and the bells! The comic sock and mask!' . . . We were taken in along with everybody else. We expected to go laughing through life like a couple of hyenas." Women had broken into the field of humor writing, but full cooperation and equality remained elusive.

Through ironic lenses, female humor writers could see the discord underneath the surface of a sophistication-thirsty, consumer-obsessed American society. They looked askance at idealized female bodies in movies, magazines, and advertisements. Parker and Millay further recognized that, as they became celebrities themselves, even their own bodies were on imagined display. In an August 28, 1928, book review in the *New Yorker* ("Back to the Bookshelf"), Parker describes her recent appendectomy: "How long is *your* scar?" In a November 1922 *Vanity Fair* article, "Diary of an American Art Student in Paris," the writer Nancy Boyd (Millay herself) observes with shock the "ethereal" Millay eating sausage and sauerkraut, tweaking her own image as lyrical poet and winsome beauty.

Wit provided a platform from which these writers could summon the glamour girl, gently place the noose around her neck, and then, before she or the culture at large knew what was happening, make the bottom drop from under her. In her November 19, 1927, *New Yorker* book review, "Adam and Eve," Parker approaches the idea of the modern glamour girl with sadistic glee: "She is always cool and wise and epigrammatic. In short, the sort of woman about whom my happiest day-dreams centre. I love to lie and think of dropping a girder on her head." As this fantasy suggests, Parker uses a macabre skepticism about contemporary images of femininity to fashion her own claim to modernity and detachment.

Loos similarly celebrates her superiority, gazing sardonically at the type of blonde glamour girl—embodied in her character Lorelei Lee—over whom her male colleagues fawn. While the blonde is big, Loos is trim, a mere "ninety pounds," she notes in "The Biography of a Book." (In the 1920s, "reducing" became a national mania for women.) Loos concludes her comparison with this assessment: "We were of about the same degree of comeliness; as to our mental acumen, there was nothing to discuss; I was the smarter." The big blonde Lorelei is a symbol of excess and lack of linguistic control, while Loos is the controlled wit. Loos uses Lorelei as a narrator to show off her own epigrammatic zing. As Lorelei observes of her friend Dorothy: "My brains reminded her of a radio because you listen to it for days and days and you get discouradged and just when you are getting ready to smash it, something comes out that is a masterpiece." In this masterpiece of feigned brainlessness, Loos pays tribute to her own artistry.

Playing the seductive, self-deprecating wit provided a successful strategy for ambitious professional women. In 1929 Joan Rivière, a psychoanalyst, published the essay "Womanliness as a Masquerade" in the *International Journal of Psycho-analysis,* in which she described this strategy of deflection used by the professional and intellectual woman: "When lecturing . . . to colleagues, she chooses particularly feminine clothes. Her behaviour on these occasions is also marked by an inappropriate feature: she becomes flippant and joking . . . She has to treat the situation of displaying her masculinity to men as a 'game,' as something *not real,* as a 'joke.'" Rivière concludes that such behaviors allow professional women to mask their sadism toward their male colleagues. The strategy also disguises their controversial bid for status and professional success. Parker, Loos, and Millay cloak their aggression in comedy when they delineate reductive feminine stereotypes.

Loos uses the chirping voice of the flapper to make cultural critiques. Lorelei Lee muses about an admirer: "Gerry seems to like me more for my soul. So I really had to tell Gerry that if all the gentlemen were like he seems to be, Madame Frances' whole dress making establishment would have to go out of business. But Gerry does not like a girl to be nothing else but a doll, but he likes her to bring in her husband's slippers every evening and make him forget what he has gone through." It is a short trip from traditional feminine domesticity to modern feminine consumerism, but even those few steps, Loos hints, may be liberating. At least Lorelei can put on her own shoes (and dress), rather than delivering her husband his slippers.

While these women writers target the flaws in consumer culture, their use of wit—rather than broad slapstick or scatological humor—confirms their possession of taste. In a November 1918 *Vanity Fair* theater review, "The New Plays," Parker laments that the villain in the production failed to do away with the heroine: "Any woman who would wear that green dress and that purple hat should have been strangled." In a September 28, 1928, book review for the *New Yorker* entitled "How It Feels to Be One Hundred and Forty-Six," Parker describes shopping for the latest fashions—in the junior misses' section, with the free gift of a doll's tea set accompanying her purchase. Parker thus mocks the infantilization of the flapper ideal while still espousing the feminine role as shopper. Her judgments about fashion—what was in and what was out—overlap with the implied judgments in her irony, a rhetorical technique that distinguishes those who know to read ironically from those who fail to recognize the cues.

In her *Distressing Dialogues,* Millay (as Boyd) also focuses on fashion and cosmetics and their relationship to gender identity. In *"Madame a tort,"* an avalanche of beauty products overwhelms a female salon patron: "Eye-brighteners, wrinkle-eradicators, and freckle-removers." In "Powder, Rouge, and Lip-Stick," the husband who criticizes his wife's makeup regimen adopts it himself to look clownish: "HE *(blissfully, after a moment, turning upon her two apoplectic cheeks, a nose like a tomb-stone, and the morbid eye-sockets of a coal-heaver):* All right. I'm ready." Then he complains when she strips her face of paint: "You look like the very devil!" The chaos of these scenes flouts the serene sophistication on the *Vanity*

Fair advertising pages, which suggest only opportunity for women, not oppression.

While Millay plays with these definitions on the high wire of farce, Parker visits the freak show, adopting a macabre persona to oppose the carefree flapper. In her book reviews and poetry, Parker insists on projecting pain, boredom, illness, unattractiveness, and depression—flying in the face of the Jazz Age premium on the blithe and the upbeat and up-tempo. Henri Bergson's "Laughter: An Essay on the Theory of the Comic," published in 1900 in France and translated into English in 1911, suggested that humor was a social corrective. Laughing at the behavior of those who had not adapted would apply social pressure on them to keep up with society's norms. Thus, those who were out of step would be encouraged to catch up and "Charleston"—to translate his theory into 1920s terms. The humor of Parker and fellow *New Yorker* writers Benchley and James Thurber works in the opposite way. Their professed inability to keep pace indicates their superiority within a woefully precipitous (in their estimation) modern culture. But even as they dramatize their slowness to keep up, their wit speeds up. Though Parker's "The Little Hours" describes motionlessness—trying to fall asleep in bed at night—her monologue, whirring through literary quotations, has a zany velocity.

In another tribute to modern motion, Parker and Millay use light verse to evoke velocity, currency, lightness through rollicking rhymes (passes/glasses) and syntactic simplicity. In the content of their poetry, Parker and Millay also parody the instructional dimensions of nursery rhymes—instructions that often teach little girls how to be little girls and little boys how to be little boys. The nursery rhyme titled "A Candle" describes "Little Nanny Etticoat" who wears "a white petticoat" and shrinks as she burns. This version of femininity is prim, proper, even retiring. In "First Fig," published in *A Few Figs from Thistles,* Millay casts aside the petticoat when she views herself as a candle. Her burning candle implies sexuality, possibly nudity, and definitely pleasure. She writes: "My candle burns at both ends / It will not last the night / But ah, my foes, and oh, my friends, it gives a lovely light."

In such verse, Millay offers herself as a sexy spectacle. When Parker refers to herself, she never conjures an image of glamour. However, her self-deprecation does not short-circuit a claim to superiority. While Parker describes a miserable dance in "The Waltz," she shows off her education and intellect at her partner's expense: "Probably he grew up in the hill country and never had no larnin.'" Parker's short stories can be divided into two major types: the monologue, like "The Waltz," and the dialogue between two characters, usually a man and a woman. As in Loos's work, in Parker's dialogues the vapid, repetitive speech of modern women is used to expose cultural ironies. In "Arrangement in Black and White," a society woman meeting an African American singer coos to the party host: "I think you're simply marvelous, giving this perfectly marvelous party for him, and having him meet all these white people and all . . . I don't see why on earth it isn't perfectly all right to meet colored people. I haven't any feeling at all about it, not one single bit."

Each of Parker's monologues features some form of social embarrassment or personal discomfort: Parker is seated next to an attractive man at a dinner party and is unable to gain his attention ("The One on the Right"); her garter snaps in the middle of a party ("The Garter"); she endures a calamitous dance ("The Waltz"). Parker flouts social perfection and poise, even attractiveness, as she compares herself in "The Waltz" to a monster, "something out of the 'Fall of the House of Usher.'" By treating her embarrassment and ugliness as a cue for her verbal ingenuity, Parker allows us to believe that wit can conquer social conventions and proscriptions.

Each of these women writers extends the possibility that a lithe sentence could reflect or even supersede the lithe body in cultural importance. The romantic defeat shrugged off in "News Item" might have tricked many into believing that Parker saw the girl who wears glasses as an ugly duckling waiting to become a glamorous swan. Instead, as the rest of her work reveals, Parker asks her readers to put on the corrective lenses of humor and to observe the show of modern culture with sharper vision. Parker, Loos, and Millay report the "News Item" that the monolithic Modern Woman is a myth.

Bibliography: Nancy Boyd [Edna St. Vincent Millay], *Distressing Dialogues* (New York, 1924). Catherine Keyser, "Girls Who Wear Glasses: New York Women Magazine Writers and the Culture of Smartness," PhD diss., Harvard University, 2007. Anita Loos, *Gentlemen Prefer Blondes* and *But Gentlemen Marry Brunettes* (New York, 1998). Edna St. Vincent Millay, *A Few Figs from Thistles: Poems and Sonnets* (New York, 1922); *The Selected Poetry of Edna St. Vincent Millay,* ed. Nancy Milford (New York, 2002). Dorothy Parker, *The Portable Dorothy Parker,* ed. Marion Meade (New York, 2006). Nina Miller, *Making Love Modern: The Intimate Public Worlds of New York's Literary Women* (New York, 1999). Joan Rivière, "Womanliness as a Masquerade," in Victor Burgin, James Donald, and Cora Kaplan, eds., *Formations of Fantasy* (London, 1986), 35–44.

CATHERINE KEYSER

1926

A new literary journal announces its mission: "Burning wooden opposition"

Fire!!

Over a string of hot summer nights in 1926 a group of young novelists, poets, artists, and intellectuals crowded into a steamy New York City living room to plot a new literary journal designed to "burn up a lot of the old, dead conventional . . . ideas of the past, *épater le bourgeois.*" Determined to handle all aspects of production themselves, and thus evade any bourgeois constraints, each member of the collaborative committed to a fifty-dollar contribution, a substantial sum, which none of them had. But propelled forward by the weight of their own enthusiasm and the quality of the submissions they received, they laid out the magazine, chose good paper, deliberated over type, and, just before year's end, produced a compelling first issue, bound in dramatic red and black, that "some of the Greenwich Village bookshops . . . put on display," and that their elders "roasted" for being obscene, incomprehensible, or both. Displaying the revolutionary disdain for tradition characteristic of modern manifestos, the journal's foreword announced its contributors' intent to penetrate "far beneath the superficial items of the flesh to boil the sluggish blood." *Fire!!* was to be "a cry of conquest in the night, warning those who sleep and revitalizing those who linger in the quiet places dozing." It continues in this vein: "FIRE . . . melting steel and iron bars . . . [and] burning wooden opposition with a cackling chuckle of contempt." The journal was either criticized or, worse yet, ignored, and "in the end . . . [it] cost almost a thousand dollars, and nobody could pay the bills."

However familiar this tale of youthful aesthetic idealism may sound—young artists in their sweltering Greenwich Village studio, plotting their flight from convention—this particular story takes place in Harlem, not in New York's downtown. The young Turks in question were Wallace Thurman, Langston Hughes, Gwendolyn Bennett, Richard Bruce, Zora Neale Hurston, Aaron Douglas, and John Davis. And their points of departure, from both modernism and the Harlem Renaissance, provide a particular perspective on the decade. Their journal *Fire!!* existed only in its debut issue of a thousand copies, most of which, ironically enough, were lost in an apartment house fire, and between that and the relatively steep dollar-a-copy price that its editors charged, few people actually ever saw the magazine. This is unfortunate. The small magazine (a slim forty-eight pages) posed large challenges to many of the ideas most central, and precious, to what was then known as the "New Negro" movement. Republications of *Fire!!*—notably the one introduced by Thomas Wirth—preserve and make accessible a document of historical importance and a debate about the cultural politics of identity that are still relevant today.

The young black intellectuals who created *Fire!!* look very different as proto-modernists than as disgruntled Harlemites. And this may have motivated Alain Locke, the Harlem movement's chief aesthetic architect, to dismiss *Fire!!* as "left-wing literary modernism." Comparing the "artistic secession" of *Fire!!* with the *Little Review* and *Quill,* Locke claimed that "a good deal of it is reflected Sherwood Anderson, Sinclair Lewis, Dreiser, Joyce and Cummings." Locke's insistence on this relation is interesting, especially so in light of his own description of the New Negro as one unwilling to practice "protective mimicry," one who is "shaking off the psychology of imitation." Surely Locke could tell that his own recent collection, titled *The New Negro,* with its rehearsals of New Negro militancy and "racial expression," was much more the referent for *Fire!!* than the modernists he lists. And that *The New Negro* in no wise was being imitated by *Fire!!*

A few of the contributors to *Fire!!* did describe the magazine as an attempt to do uptown what white intellectuals were achieving downtown. "Since white folks had [little magazines]," Langston Hughes remembered, "we Negroes thought we could have one, too. But we didn't have the money." But money was not the only or even the primary issue that the editors faced. And having what the white folks had wasn't really the goal. More than any attempt to respond to—or imitate—modernism, *Fire!!* was an intensely focused response to New Negro ideas about sexuality, race, and representation, a significant reworking of the term New Negro and of its newness.

The New Negro appeared as a trope as early as the late 1880s and by 1920 had become a ubiquitous signal of opposition to any racial subordination. While some have argued that Locke's consolidation of the capacious meanings of this term, in his widely influential *The New Negro,* romanticized a figure for militant social activism, most would agree that his description of the New Negro "new psychology" as a "new spirit" of "self-respect," "self-dependence," "race-pride," and "collective effort" had considerable cultural currency. Even as it uses these associations, however, *Fire!!* resists the concept's gendered history—the New Negro was almost always a young heterosexual man—and also its implied audience, its attempt to influence white opinion or engage white viewers. *Fire!!* weds nonnormative and queer sexualities to both modernist aesthetic innovations and a very particular brand of "racialism" or "race-consciousness," to model a new New Negro-ness that challenged the prevailing idea that racial uplift could be achieved through the right combination of race, gender, sex, and class—even as *Fire!!* built on those very constructions to do so, taking for granted the reader's familiarity with them.

Even the journal's cover announces its contributors' refusal of what its editor, Wallace Thurman, called "butter side up" racial politics—or best-foot-forwardism. Aaron Douglas's arresting cover art plays with African iconography and American race mythologies through both a visually stabilized seated lion and a stylized, male, jeweled African face that comes in and out of focus, like an optical illusion, making the point that racial detection or presence is always a matter of perspective, and emphasizing, as did Countee Cullen's well-known poem "Heritage," that African foundations are ephemeral, shifting, and questionable. Reinforcing both views, but with a special wink to its implied young audience, the back-cover illustration (also by Douglas) features what at first seems to be an abstract design but, through clues on internal pages, resolves itself into the face of a monkey: the animal most often used to deride blacks as subhuman and, hence, most often avoided by New Negroes. Both of these now-you-see-us, know-you-don't illustrations take a poke at much that New Negro ideology held dear.

The foreword underscores the journal's rebellious stance by taking one of the most painful—and racially specific—images in black American history—"flesh on fire"—and reading it not as a horrific symbol of lynching but, surprisingly, reading such "fy-ah" for "searing" and "vivid" "Beauty." This is a shocking move. Deliberately so. Nothing is out of bounds.

Of the many negative stereotypes that New Negroes sought to topple, negative sexual stereotypes, "chief among them the myths of the sexually rampant male and lascivious female," were paramount. Reestablishing the sexual respectability of black Americans was considered such a vital cultural imperative that the editor of the *Illustrated Feature Section* of the Negro press warned contributors to "keep away from the erotic! Contributions must be clean and wholesome! Nothing that casts the least reflection on contemporary moral or sexual standards will be allowed." But the *Fire!!* editors were having none of it. According to Richard Nugent, "Wally [Thurman] and I thought that the magazine would get bigger sales if it was banned in Boston. So we flipped a coin to see who wrote the banned material. The only two things we could think of . . . were a story about prostitution or about homosexuality." Wallace Thurman's story, "Cordelia the Crude," is the journal's lead piece. Without condemnation it follows a sixteen-year-old "potential prostitute" through the eyes of a white narrator who, Cordelia says, "gimme ma' firs' two bucks." The story judges not her morals but his, suggesting that his intentions are largely irrelevant to his inevitably negative effect on her destiny. In the face of a sudden "vogue" for blackness that had produced both substantial white patronage and also an influx of white tourists to Harlem, this depiction of the power of white markets, capital, and values is especially damning, and it subtly references the very white patrons of *Fire!!*—Carl Van Vechten included—listed on the inside cover.

Also published in *Fire!!* was "Smoke, Lilies and Jade," by Richard Bruce (Nugent), probably the first openly gay story in the African American tradition, and a celebration of both sexual pleasure and bisexuality—"one *can* love two at the same time . . . one *can* . . . one *can* . . . one *can*." As Thomas Wirth notes, "Such an explicit, sympathetic treatment of same-sex desire was not yet acceptable to mainstream publishers . . . [This story] was unique—a forthright, uncoded invitation to the reader of any sexual orientation . . . There is none of the guilt and anguish that had previously characterized most writing about male same-sex desire."

If the most explicitly sexual pieces in *Fire!!* challenge New Negro respectability, its treatment of intraracial color prejudice exposes the divisive feelings that race solidarity can mask. Hurston's play *Color Struck,* appearing in the magazine directly after "Cordelia the Crude," breaks ranks by airing dirty laundry about intraracial prejudice. Disloyalty to the male-centered Harlem Renaissance continues in pieces such as Hurston's "Sweat," with its scathing depiction of black male oppression of black women (rather than white oppression of blacks): "Tain't no law on earth dat kin make a man be decent if it aint in 'im. There's plenty men date takes a wife lak dey do a joint uh sugar-cane. It's round, juicy an' sweet when dey gits it. But dey squeeze an' grind, squeeze an' grind an' wring tell dey wring every drop uh pleasure dat's in 'em out." And Arthur Huff Fauset's essay, "Intelligentsia," reads as an attack on leaders like Du Bois, although it is white men whom Fauset explicitly names. Such a reading is reinforced, at the very end of the magazine, when Wallace Thurman blasts "the so-called intelligentsia of Harlem" for their "inherent stupidity." Nothing is sacred.

The magazine's disloyal politics is especially interesting given how calls to loyalty were playing out across the decade, and across race lines. Skeptical modernists were challenging all forms of allegiance. But loyalty and its many synonyms were powerful on both the cultural left and right. And in the larger national discourse, loyalty remained salient as a fundamental concept for anti-immigration nativists and "One Hundred Percenters" who cast all forms of complex (or hyphenated) cultural identity as national disloyalty. In Woodrow Wilson's words, "Any man who carries a hyphen about him carries a dagger that he is ready to plunge into the vitals of this Republic." Groups like the American Legion and racists like Lothrop Stoddard took the value of loyalty as a given in advocating "Americanism" and a "cohesive instinct" against the "alien slackers" and a "cycle of ruin." Harlem Renaissance racial and cultural politics, in the main, did not join forces with modernist performative disloyalty, but advocated fierce concepts of what Alain Locke called the "admirable principle of loyalty" or "racial solidarity." In *The New Negro,* Locke had written that each African American generation "will have its creed, and that of the present is the belief in the efficacy of collective effort, in race co-operation." Indeed, notions of loyalty, for much of the Harlem Renaissance intelligentsia, seemed to solve a fundamental conflict in the movement's politics of race. Race men and women could argue that it did not so much matter *what* race was; what mattered was loyalty to *one's people:* a racial ethic. Even when this racial ethic was not explicitly evoked, it was, nonetheless, in the air. The *Fire!!* group's ethic of disloyalty thus stood out, as it extended beyond the sexual and the political and was part of their general sensibility and style. Cultural insolence was fundamental to the public personae that Nugent, Thurman, Hurston, and others crafted. (Hurston, for example, had called Alain Locke a "spiteful little snot" and nicknamed W. E. B. Du Bois "Dr. Dubious," and Thurman is often described as a natural "provocateur.") Challenging New Negro ideology meant challenging not just loyalty to *one's own* race, but challenging the idea of race altogether.

One of the most interesting pieces in the magazine, and its last inclusion, was a column called "Fire Burns: A Department of Comment," Wallace Thurman's spirited defense of Carl Van Vechten—the most well-known white patron of the Harlem Renaissance and one of the most sexually flamboyant bisexuals of the decade—then under attack for his just-published novel *Nigger Heaven.* That book had set off a firestorm of debate about representing the race. Having lauded the "wealth of novel, erotic, picturesque material" available to the artist who tackles "the squalor of Negro life, the vice of Negro life," and urged black writers to "write about this exotic material" of Harlem's streets and cabarets before "white authors . . . exploit it until not a drop of vitality remains," Van Vechten had enraged many by exploiting the material himself. W. E. B. Du Bois spoke for many of Van Vechten's detractors (and not a few of his black friends as well) when he complained that Van Vechten had been disloyal in using "cheap melodrama" to portray Harlem as just the "wildly, barbaric drunken orgy" white revelers imagined. Thurman, Hughes, and Hurston all sought to protect Van Vechten from being, as Thurman put it, "lynched" by the black establishment. Defending Van Vechten meant explicitly decrying the very idea of racial loyalty, as Hughes had, in fact, already done that summer in an article in the *Nation:* "We younger Negro artists who create now intend to express our individual dark-skinned selves without fear or shame . . . If colored people are pleased, we are glad. If they are not, their displeasure doesn't matter either." In *Fire!!* Thurman writes, "Group criticism is always ridiculous . . . Why Negroes imagine that any writer is going to write what Negroes think he ought to write about them is too ridiculous to merit consideration."

Few others during the Harlem Renaissance considered this question ridiculous. Much of Harlem took it for granted that this question—posed in the *Crisis* as "The Negro in Art: How Shall He Be Portrayed?"—was precisely the question a New Negro renaissance needed to address. Being a member of the *Fire!!* "Niggerati" meant creating a compelling aesthetic alternative to the then-dominant cultural ethos of loyalty and allegiance. For many of the *Fire!!* contributors, that project remained a lifelong goal.

Bibliography: FIRE!!, ed. Wallace Thurman (New York, 1926). Henry Louis Gates, Jr., and Gene Andrew Jarrett, *The New Negro: Readings on Race, Representation, and African American Culture, 1892–1938* (Princeton, 2007). Nathan I. Huggins, *Harlem Renaissance* (New York, 1971). Langston Hughes, *The Big Sea: An Autobiography* (New York, 1940). Carla Kaplan, "Nella Larsen's Erotics of Race," Introduction to *Passing: A Norton Critical Edition,* ed. Carla Kaplan (New York, 2007). Alain Locke, ed. *The New Negro* (New York, 1925). Thomas H. Wirth, *Richard Bruce Nugent: Gay Rebel of the Harlem Renaissance* (Durham, 2002).

CARLA KAPLAN

1926

"It is awfully easy to be hard-boiled about everything in the daytime, but at night it is another thing"

POISONVILLE

Hardboiled is a state of being, not a state that any sane tourist would want to pass through on holiday. The hardboiled condition is when a man or a woman, or an entire nation of women and men, is pressed to physical, emotional, economic, and/or intellectual limits—past, present, and for the foreseeable future; it's when the hammer is coming down and there's not a friend you can count on, not a spare second for you to reflect.

In a hardboiled world there's no black and white, no shade of gray, no innocence. In this world there are only choices between evils, and the secret, unobtainable rulebook was written by Satan himself.

For some of us this state of being is a relief. No more worrying about how to be good or whether or not to go wrong. The whole damn planet is in a bad orbit and we're just along for the ride.

Criminals populate the hardboiled world. Some of these offenders take secret oaths in felonious societies while others wear badges, army uniforms, or hold the seal of state. Some are billionaires while others don't have two nickels to rub together. But they are all cut from the same moth-eaten fabric, breathing the same air of corruption.

From our prisons to our ghettos, from our boardrooms to the Oval Office, from gangsta rap to the Patriot Act, America is a hardboiled nation. To have faith is to be a fool. To expect justice is to accept tyranny. To rally round the flag is to support the torture of human beings while reading our children the Constitution and watching sitcoms about cranky old white men and their beautiful, young, and scantily clad wives—and girlfriends.

It is essential that we understand this state of being before attempting to define the art of hardboiled fiction, before trying to see the beauty in it. It's worth a few moments to consider how low our society has come before celebrating and pontificating on the beauty of the language that holds our world the way a bright and shiny stainless-steel garbage can houses maggots and rats.

If I were asked to define hardboiled language I would simply say that it is elegant and concise language used to describe an ugly and possibly irredeemable world; that, in spite of this elegance, it is a blunt object intent upon assault and battery.

I suppose I could say more but it wouldn't add to the understanding of the language made pitch perfect by Ernest Hemingway and made so again by Dashiell Hammett. Ross Macdonald was an acolyte of Raymond Chandler as Chandler was of Hammett. Macdonald modernized the genre, showing us that it could be changed along with a changing culture. Hardboiled language, like a mutating virus, followed us out from Prohibition and fascism into the world of corporate oligarchies and the Freudian compulsion to repeat. And even though these literary masters are the primary perpetrators of the form, they give us neither the first nor the last words on the subject. Because, while this language is known for its use by fictionalists describing ugly men with awful responsibilities and beautiful people with rotted souls, it is primarily a form of communication that everyday working men and women created so that they wouldn't go mad.

Hardboiled language wasn't made up by an intellectual elite or discovered by university professors who subsequently popularized it. This tongue was torn from the mouths of the masses who came out of the aftermath of the Industrial Revolution in late nineteenth- and early twentieth-century America. It festered in speakeasies and cried out in the Black Man's jazz and, most especially, his blues. This language cuts to the bone because it is the idiom of survival, of that moment when it's all or nothing.

There is no better way to describe the ideal meaning of the hardboiled state of consciousness than to go to the practitioners of the Sweet Science, boxing.

Everything about boxing is hardboiled. The mind and body and heart must shrug off any sense of weakness or charity or compassion. It is you against him or her in that ring and victory is synonymous with survival. There are no substitutes, second chances, or celebrations for the loser. And as hard as you fight, as good as you are, one day someone is going to cut you down and leave you, and everyone else you've ever known, in a wake of broken bones afloat in a stagnant pond of bodily fluids.

I can think of three perfectly good examples in the long history of pugilism that underscore differing elements of hardboiled thinking and articulation.

There is George Foreman some years after the Rumble in the Jungle, his disastrous battle with Muhammad Ali in Kinshasa in 1974. Foreman was talking about the middle rounds of the epic fight, when he had Ali on the ropes. The powerful champion had just let loose with a thunderous body shot when Ali grinned at him and asked, "Is that all you got, George?" Reflecting back on that time Foreman remembered thinking to himself, "Yep, that's just about it."

This is hardboiled humor at its apex. It was Foreman's swan song, his defeat at the hands of a man who shouldn't have been able to beat him. But there's no lament, no sadness in his tone—only a wry grin at that inescapable moment of loss.

Some years earlier Archie Moore (in my opinion the greatest boxer of all times) found himself hard-pressed by a heavy-handed Canadian named Ivan Durell. Moore was dropped four times before he rallied and defeated the one-time fisherman. When asked how he defeated this implacable foe, Moore said, "I used my left hand, which was very educated at the time." Again, this is the soul of hardboiled language. It condenses a whole life of pain and hard knocks into a seemingly nonsensical sentence that simultaneously understates and underscores a lifelong preparation for survival.

The final boxing version of hardboiled has no words to it at all. It was a middleweight bout between monstrous Gene Fulmer and the then thirty-five-year-old Sugar Ray Robinson. This was Robinson's last attempt at the middleweight crown, which he had already held three times. Fulmer was the better man that night, the better fighter. He was bludgeoning the older Robinson, bullying him around the ring up to the fifth round. The fight was all Fulmer. He was bound to win. And then, out of nowhere it seemed, Ray came up with a picture-perfect left hook. Impossibly, Fulmer went down. He tried to beat the count but the count was, the count always is, relentless.

That left hook was as hardboiled as it gets.

In this essay, at least, boxing is not a sport but a metaphor for the hard life that each and every worker, convict, and unemployed indigent in America lives through. It knocks out your teeth and scars your brain, it ruptures your internal organs and hurts more than any other animal could tolerate. The rules are sketchy and the outcome, sooner or later, is always a beating that punctuates loss.

This is the epitome of a hardboiled existence. There's no time to talk things over. There are no time-outs. Life is a hurting business and it's you, and only you, with your life on the line.

"Protect yourself at all times," the referee intones.

Is he kidding?

This metaphorical ring is where the hardboiled writer places his characters. It is the world we inhabit. If you stand tall your opponent will knock you down. If you run he'll chase you down. If you quit you'll be relegated to poverty and contempt from your peers and loved ones. If you win you'll spend the night in the hospital—worrying about the bill.

This kind of life makes no sense from the outside. How could people live like that? How can they survive? These questions represent the fallacies that Hammett and Hemingway wanted to dispel. Their language was, is, a form of understanding how helpless we are in the face of our passions, our power, and our innate inability to do right on the grand scale of society.

Boxing represents the physical element of the hardboiled; the pressure and threat of violence we live under constantly; the hope for victory, maybe even the momentary experience of victory, ultimately ending in dashed dreams and slurred speech, yellowed newspaper clippings and new youngsters out there getting their heads bashed in for a living.

If boxing is the body (i.e., the object of violence and brutalization) of a hardboiled life, then our hallowed systems of support hold the genre's putrefied spirit. Our churches and corporations, police chiefs and elected officials, our elderly moms and pops, all carry hidden weapons while sizing us up like domesticated turkeys three weeks before Christmas.

Everyone has a secret agenda and no one will ever tell the truth unless it means a larger profit than a lie could net. The priest molests the children he's entrusted with, the city comptroller skims it off the top, the president of the United States orders a burglary, and the head of the FBI tells us that there is no Cosa Nostra.

We live in a hardboiled world, a corrupt world, a kind of global Poisonville.

"For a fat, middle-aged, hard-boiled, pig-headed guy, you've got the vaguest way of doing things I've ever heard of." —Dinah Brand to the Continental Op, in Personville, aka Poisonville, Montana, in Dashiell Hammett, *Red Harvest,* 1929.

All that has been said so far is the wrapping paper around a nondescript box that holds the truth about the hardboiled tradition in fiction. These gaudy trappings are no more than ephemera. The short pithy sentences, the blunt truths about the motivations of this man or that woman—these are little more than wisecracks mouthed by unemployed malingerers who say they're waiting for a job to come by and hit them over the head.

Inside we find the real reason for the exercise.

In the pages of any hardboiled book worth its ink is the question—Can I do right in a world gone wrong? If the victim is as guilty as the assailant, if the judge is having an affair with the defendant's wife, if the president knows that there are no weapons of mass destruction, then what can a foot soldier do?

There is no one answer to this question. People in a hardboiled world have had to improvise from the moment they were born. The writer may have a notion of what is right and make a world where the ending, if not exactly happy, is at least satisfying.

For me the most important character in the genre is Dashiell Hammett's nameless Continental Op. The five-foot-six, hundred-and-eighty-pound (not all of which is fat), scarred and single-minded detective who represents the Continental Detective Agency. This is a man who gets the job done. He keeps going until the mystery is solved and the perpetrator is either dead or behind bars.

And if the Continental Op is the epitome of the hardboiled *hero,* then the flawed novel *Red Harvest* represents the peak of his adventures. I call it a flawed novel because the hardboiled genre is an art form of its own, unwilling, unable to change its structure for another system of thinking, expression, or articulation. The Op goes from barroom to pool hall, from floozie to lawyer uncovering stench that would choke a dung beetle. His adventures are necessarily episodic and what he uncovers is always vice, dishonesty, and sleaze. It's a feminist form in that women are just as bad, and often as strong, as their male counterparts.

Red Harvest is about a town that went bad when a rich man used organized crime to break a strike and found that the crooks wouldn't leave after the job was done. The Continental Op fools the old man into hiring him and spends the next two hundred pages giving as good as he gets. At the end the crimes are solved and the town is under martial law but that has nothing to do with the story.

The Op had blood on his hands all the way up to his shoulders by the time the book was done. We were told that he was a hero. He tried telling himself the same thing. But in the end, separate from all the other existentialists, Hammett knew, and he let us know, that yes, we are all guilty whether we take sides or not, whether we follow the rules or not, whether in our hearts we want to be good—or not.

Bibliography: Raymond Chandler, *The Big Sleep* (New York, 1939). Dashiell Hammett, *Red Harvest* (New York, 1929). Ernest Hemingway, *The Sun Also Rises* (New York, 1926). Ross Macdonald (Kenneth Millar), *Blue City* (New York, 1947).

WALTER MOSLEY

1926
"Good taste does pay off"

Book-of-the-Month Club

A middle-aged businessman, out for an evening of cocktails and conviviality, sits quietly at the table while his wife and friends engage in sparkling conversation. The talk has turned to the books they have been reading—all newly published novels—but the man has nothing to say. Several weeks earlier, he had noticed an intriguing advertisement for one of the best sellers the group is discussing, and he vaguely recalls seeing another of the books in a shop window, but he had been too preoccupied with work at the time even to write down the titles. Now he is paying the price for neglecting to read anything but the latest financial reports. He feels left out, superfluous, annoyed with himself. He is sure his wife will berate him about his silence when they get home.

That tension-laden scenario was described in the first brochure promoting the Book-of-the-Month Club (BOMC), an innovative enterprise for book marketing and distribution founded by Harry Scherman and his associates in 1926. First and foremost a commercial venture, the business has been, since its inception, a cultural phenomenon as well, reflecting and entrenching the values and anxieties of its creators and audience. It has also been a quintessential expression of middlebrow literary taste—and both attacked and embraced as such. Still operating today, the BOMC has influenced such phenomena as Oprah Winfrey's enormously influential television book club.

Certain economic and social characteristics of the United States in the 1920s shaped the context for the BOMC's success. The prosperity of the period extended to the nation's publishing houses, which poured forth more than ten thousand new titles in 1929, compared with around six thousand in 1920. With a shorter workweek—down to five days—and a more widespread eight-hour day, many Americans had more leisure time to read. In addition, the number of college graduates grew between 1920 and 1930 from a half million to more than one million. Although automobiles, movies, and radio competed for the public's attention, the idea that books supplied an invaluable familiarity with the world of literature and the arts—with what Matthew Arnold had called "the best that had been thought and said in the world"—retained and even gained force. At the same time, the possession of culture in that Arnoldian sense came to seem a useful attribute for anyone eager to make a positive impression on others. Popularity and its attendant financial rewards, advice manuals of the day counseled, required the cultivation of a magnetic personality; an aura of refinement could help to endow Americans aspiring to wealth and status with the personal charm and distinctiveness required in an increasingly standardized, bureaucratized society.

The Book-of-the-Month Club emerged against this backdrop. In the foreground was a more specific perception: Harry Scherman's belief that the nation's bookstores (most of which were in sizable cities) did not meet the demand for the latest books. Scherman came to this conclusion out of long experience with both literature and advertising. In 1916, he established the Little Leather Library Corporation, which manufactured tiny volumes of classics for inclusion in boxes of Whitman's chocolates. In the early 1920s, Scherman and Maxwell Sackheim formed their own advertising agency and tried to apply what they had learned about book distribution—that there were markets outside existing retail outlets—to new projects. But Scherman realized that he could not make a profit until he devised a way to generate "repeat business": customers who followed up their first book purchase with additional ones.

Eventually, he hit upon a solution—to offer consumers newly published works by subscription, and to deliver them through the mail. The concept of selling books directly to readers had already been tried in Germany, where book societies began printing and distributing cheap editions in 1919. Furthermore, the Literary Guild, which would later become the BOMC's chief competitor, was in its planning stages as early as 1921. Scherman, Sackheim, and their partner, Robert K. Haas, however, were the first club organizers to forgo manufacturing the books they sold, to rely heavily on direct-mail promotion, and to win consumer confidence by having expert judges pick the best title each month. Moreover, almost immediately Scherman came up with his most important business idea: the so-called negative option, which required subscribers to accept the selection of the month, unless they indicated that they wanted a substitute. In the late 1920s, BOMC started allowing participants to buy as few as four books a year, as well as to choose an alternate title in advance of the shipping date. During the 1930s, it began offering members lower-cost editions that it produced itself. It also implemented the book dividend plan, based on the principle of stock dividends, which allowed customers to accrue free books.

Even the BOMC's insistence, in its first year, on a purchase every month at the full retail price plus shipping was sufficiently appealing to win it 60,000 members. (The first test mailing list was the New York Social Register, and college graduates were the predominant target market thereafter.) By 1929, membership had risen to 110,588. Except during the worst years of the Depression, the enterprise grew steadily through 1946. Clearly Scherman had been right in his estimate of demand. Yet the Book-of-the-Month Club owed its profitability, and its cultural prominence, to the particular ways in which Scherman capitalized on that demand, both through advertising and through his savvy construction of the club's Board of Judges.

Both Scherman and Sackheim were masters of a copywriting style known as the "symptom and cure" technique: advertisements that pointed out, and exacerbated, consumers' fears of their deficiencies, and then pitched a product promising relief. By the 1920s, anxiety about failure ran deep among middle-class Americans, and correspondingly pervaded the ads offering them everything from breakfast cereals to socks. Scherman and Sackheim's marketing campaign featuring the persona of the hapless businessman extended this strategy to books. "Why do you disappoint yourself in this way?" the BOMC's first ad asked consumers who had defaulted on their good intentions to read a certain book. The cure the club offered could assuage both that loss of self-mastery and several related maladies. First, its monthly automatic distribution schedule imposed order on the chaotic flow of print that overwhelmed book buyers. Second, its reliance on a body of presumably disinterested experts to identify worthwhile titles assured readers that they need not worry about purchasing an inferior product. Third, the club's reduction of culture to information—the name of its bulletin was the *Book-of-the-Month Club News*—as well as its announcements of new books in advance of their publication dates, gave subscribers both a sense of being an insider and a sure way to secure the social advantages of appearing au courant. All these aspects of the BOMC's offer undermined the assumption that being genuinely cultured entailed having a grasp of aesthetic principles, which in turn required disciplined study by readers dedicated to self-reliance and high moral character.

Yet the BOMC did more than accommodate the therapeutic needs that modern consumer culture exploited. The club's early promotional materials stressed the "service" the arrangement provided to members, who remained in charge of their decisions. Furthermore, the conceit of a club preserved the face-to-face, small-town, nineteenth-century atmosphere that the anonymity of urban, industrial America had largely replaced. The BOMC's advertising generally avoided touting bargains, positioning itself above base commercial considerations. As Scherman observed, "Good taste does pay off, without any question."

This balance between an appeal to the "culture of personality" and to the values of the genteel tradition—what one might call the middleness that made the BOMC so typically middlebrow—was especially evident in the composition of the first Board of Judges (also called the Selecting Committee), which survived intact from 1926 to 1944. Its chair, Henry Seidel Canby, seemed a holdover from an earlier age. A former Yale English professor, he had moved to New York in 1920 to edit what became the *Saturday Review of Literature*. In that role, he upheld his faith in the liberal arts and in the obligation of the critic to resist materialism, vulgarity, and specialization by educating intelligent readers to discern the best literature. Although he exhibited elements of the modern American business mentality, he was primarily a figure of the surviving genteel tradition. Similarly, Dorothy Canfield Fisher, the only woman on the board, stood for the sturdy character of the Vermonter. As a novelist and nonfiction writer, she consistently warned her audience about the loss of self-discipline and the dangers of purposeless ease. She and Canby argued for the importance of literary craft in evaluating possible BOMC choices. Yet Fisher often presented herself to her myriad fans as merely an average wife and mother, a stance that limited her ability to disseminate those ideals authoritatively. The other three original judges—Christopher Morley, Heywood Broun, and William Allen White—were less powerful than Canby and Fisher but just as essential to the club's balancing act. Morley, a writer of whimsical poetry and light fiction, was also a journalist whose persona was part country gentleman, part gossip columnist. As such, he displayed both an antipathy to the business world and a mastery of the inside information that enabled Americans to navigate the urban milieu. Broun was even more the man-about-town. Although a principled liberal in politics, as a reviewer for New York newspapers he prized entertainment and performance—staples of the culture of personality—far above inner character. (His wife read most of the potential BOMC selections for him.) Finally, White was most willing to think of himself as a hawker of wares rather than as an instructor in literature. A Kansas editor and publisher, he typified the heartland, lending the club's marketing its purest exemplar of the American small-town reader, yet he wrote Scherman that his business-like principles of selection would be most useful in helping him to win "the big dollar."

The titles the BOMC sent out in its first two decades reflected the multiple perspectives of the judges. Canby and Fisher's distaste for modernist experimentation, together with the group's awareness that the club needed to make money by maximizing readers, meant that conventional narrative fiction (Edna Ferber's *Show Boat*, Elizabeth Madox Roberts's *The Time of Man*) and solid histories (Frederick Lewis Allen's *Only Yesterday*, James Truslow Adams's *The Epic of America*) dominated the list. Missing were works by Hemingway, Dos Passos, Eliot, Joyce, Lawrence, or even John Steinbeck. Richard Wright's *Native Son*, selected in 1940, appeared in an edition that censored a scene of masturbation and removed other language the club thought subscribers would find offensive. The BOMC incurred disdain and hostility for its middlebrow choices. Contemporaries complained that the enterprise promoted "literary dictatorship" and standardization. The cultural theorist Janice Radway has traced that response to the club's exposure of the illusion that literary canons arose from an open, democratic process of inquiry and adjudication. The most famous critique appeared in Dwight Macdonald's classic essay "Masscult and Midcult" (1960), which named the Book-of-the-Month Club as a key example of "midcult": an institution that "pretends to respect the standards of High Culture while in fact it waters them down and vulgarizes them." Yet, over time, observers such as Malcolm Cowley conceded that the BOMC's record was mixed, at worst, and that at best it had (as Delmore

Schwartz wrote) widened "the audience for serious literature." Moreover, Radway has compellingly characterized the club's choices as books permitting readers immersion in a "thoroughly realized imaginary world": works that in their affective dimension offer pleasures that the ambiguity and complexity of modernist or academic writing cannot supply.

By the 1950s, the BOMC was a fixture of American publishing. In 1958, its average member was a woman in her thirties (although she may have subscribed on behalf of her husband as well). Two-thirds of the membership was married; 40 percent lived in communities of fewer than 10,000; 29 percent lived in the nation's mid-Atlantic region. The majority possessed a college degree, and a disproportionate number of members were teachers. These generalist readers, who resembled the club's earlier clientele, remained its presumed best audience at least into the 1990s. The BOMC's amalgam of literary culture as a product of information and aesthetic judgment, accessibility and crafted writing, also persisted. Club officials in the 1980s continued to choose books that lent themselves to quick description while still raising the overall level of taste. Dog books and other more commercially viable titles subsidized less salable literary fiction.

Buoyed by his success, in the postwar period Scherman branched out to found additional clubs for the distribution of recorded music and books for younger readers. By then, the Literary Guild (which went after a somewhat more downscale market than the BOMC) had already replicated the club format. In 1951, W. H. Auden, Jacques Barzun, and Lionel Trilling started the Reader's Subscription, a venture that both copied the tactics Scherman had pioneered and self-consciously sought to stake out the higher cultural ground of books for intellectuals. Later another BOMC enterprise, Quality Paperback Books, occupied the same niche. Meanwhile, changes in the publishing industry affected the club's personnel and ownership. The BOMC went public in 1947. In 1977 Time, Inc., bought it; in 1988 it became part of Time Warner. By then, the BOMC Board of Judges (which now included Clifton Fadiman, Gloria Norris, and Wilfred Sheed) had a diminished presence in the club's advertising and operations: a staff of in-house editors picked the alternate titles and weighed in on the main selections. Time Warner executives, focused on profit, further reduced the judges' power, shook up management, and in 1994 abolished the Board of Judges entirely. In 2000, the Book-of-the-Month Club, which encompassed numerous specialty clubs, merged with a subsidiary of the Bertelsmann media corporation to form Bookspan. Bertelsmann bought out Time Warner's share of Bookspan in 2007, bringing the BOMC, the Literary Guild, Quality Paperback Books, and the Reader's Subscription together under the same ownership. Although its emphasis on best sellers, its plans to reduce the number of Bookspan affiliates, and the announcement of an international initiative are marked departures from the BOMC's twentieth-century priorities, a recent advertisement for the club touted not only savings and selection but also the "expert recommendations" of a resurrected group of judges made up of "great editors" and "top authors."

Outside the world of books, Scherman's innovation gave rise to countless other "of-the-month" schemes for selling everything from fruit and bacon to neckties. In addition, facets of the book club concept have migrated to television and the Internet. Oprah Winfrey's decision in 1996 to begin offering monthly book recommendations on her daytime talk show at first took the form of a book club that had neither members nor meetings; the cachet of the club idea and the guidance she proffered, as well as the middlebrow fiction she selected, owed something to the BOMC's venerable standing. Although critical authority has shifted from the man of letters to the on-line editor and to readers themselves, the availability of book recommendations at such Web sites as Amazon.com likewise testifies to the public's ongoing anxiety about reading and leisure that the Book-of-the-Month Club so accurately gauged.

Bibliography: Janice A. Radway, *A Feeling for Books: The Book-of-the-Month Club, Literary Taste, and Middle-Class Desire* (Chapel Hill, NC, 1997). Joan Shelley Rubin, *The Making of Middlebrow Culture* (Chapel Hill, NC, 1992).

JOAN SHELLEY RUBIN

1927

Carl Sandburg compiles "a glorious anthology of the songs that men have sung in the making of America"

THE AMERICAN SONGBAG

On March 23, 1927, Carl Sandburg reviewed D. W. Griffith's *Sorrows of Satan,* a film to which he ascribed "the sense of vastness, chaos, originality and sudden interludes of unimagined beauty that makes Griffith so much akin in his present stage to Walt Whitman, the poet." Sandburg's own work was much akin to Whitman, with Whitman's "Leaves of Grass" winningly resodded and reseeded in Sandburg's "Grass":

> Pile the bodies high at Austerlitz and Waterloo.
> Shovel them under and let me work—
>   I am the grass; I cover all.

Though "Grass" had appeared as early as Sandburg's 1918 volume, *Cornhuskers,* it already displayed not only Whitman's influence but the influence of the folk song, and the broader folk tradition, which Sandburg now codified in *The American Songbag,* "a collection of 280 songs, ballads, ditties brought together from all regions of America." The capaciousness of this songbag was meant to be reminiscent of the capaciousness of Whitman, needless to say, but was also meant to imply the capaciousness of Sandburg himself, what with the echo of Sandburg's name in the very word *songbag.*

Sandburg had indeed embodied these songs, including multitudes of them in his many poetry recitals throughout the country. By the time *The American Songbag* was published, Sandburg was a poetic celebrity. Born in 1878 in Galesburg, Il-

linois, to impoverished Swedish immigrants, he was forced to go to work at the
age of eleven, taking on such menial, if eventually meaningful, jobs as cleaning up
in a barbershop, driving a milk wagon, and harvesting wheat in Kansas. After a
time as a faintly hobbyistic hobo, he served as an infantryman in the Spanish-
American War, briefly attended West Point and Lombard College in Galesburg,
then took himself off to Milwaukee, Wisconsin, where from 1910 to 1912 he
worked as a secretary to Emil Seidel, the first socialist mayor in the United States.
Sandburg next moved to Chicago, becoming a reporter at the *Chicago Daily News*
(for which he wrote that review of *Sorrows of Satan*) and taking the city as one of
his major subjects, as we may deduce from the title of his *Chicago Poems* (1916) and
its lead verse:

> Hog butcher for the World,
> Tool Maker. Stacker of Wheat,
> Player with Railroads and the Nation's Freight Handler;
> Stormy, husky, brawling,
> City of the Big Shoulders.

By 1927, Sandburg had published *Cornhuskers,* which won a Pulitzer Prize for
Poetry in 1919, *Smoke and Steel* (1920), *Slabs of the Sunburnt West* (1922), and *Selected
Poems* (1926), and was much in demand. In his prefatory notes to *The American
Songbag* he writes:

> Perhaps I should explain that for a number of years I have gone hither and yon over
> the United States meeting audiences to whom I talked about poetry and art, read
> my verses, and closed a program with a half- or quarter-hour of songs, giving verbal
> footnotes with each song. These itineraries have included now about two-thirds of
> the state universities of the country, audiences ranging from 3,000 people at the
> University of California to 30 at the Garret Club in Buffalo, New York, and organi-
> zations as diverse as the Poetry Society of South Carolina and the Knife and Fork
> Club of South Bend, Indiana. The songs I gave often reminded listeners of songs of
> a kindred character they knew entirely or in fragments; or they would refer me to
> persons who had similar ballads or ditties.

A case in point would be "The Foggy, Foggy Dew," which Sandburg "heard
first," according to his "verbal footnote," from "Arthur Sutherland and his bold
buccaneers at the Eclectic Club of Wesleyan University." However bold the buccaneers might have been, Sandburg himself was not quite bold enough to print in
The American Songbag "a middle verse" that he describes as "censored from this
version as being out of key and probably an interpolation." He must be thinking
of a verse along the lines of that collected by Cecil Sharp, among others, as:

> One night she knelt close by my side
> When I was fast asleep.
> She threw her arms about my neck
> And she began to weep.
> She wept, she cried, she tore her hair.
> Ah, me! What could I do?

So all night long I held her in my arms
Just to keep her from the foggy, foggy dew.

"The Foggy, Foggy Dew" is sometimes considered one of the few songs that survived intact its transatlantic crossing from Europe to the Appalachians, as Charles Lindbergh would survive the reverse journey in May 1927, but it does not survive intact in *The American Songbag*. This middle verse of "The Foggy, Foggy Dew" is "out of key" not in the literal sense of nonmusicality but in some imagined metaphorical sense. The phrase almost certainly derives from the opening of Ezra Pound's *Hugh Selwyn Mauberley*, a long poem published in 1920:

For three years, out of key with his time,
He strove to resuscitate the dead art
Of poetry.

Part of Sandburg's own striving on behalf of these songs, made clear in his introduction to the first edition, was his belief that "*The American Songbag* comes from the hearts and voices of thousands of men and women." One aim of the book was that it might indeed resuscitate the dead (he)art of poetry "in schools, colleges, and universities." Unfortunately, yet again, Sandburg's "verbal footnote" gives nothing of an intellectual apparatus that might have made that possible. For example, nothing is made of the fact that there's a vast hinterland of punnery on the relationship between a "fair young maid" and "morning" (*maighdean/maidin*) in the Irish tradition from which this song partly derives, so that the idea of walking through the morning/maiden dew takes on a whole other significance. The word "foggy," meanwhile, refers not so much to a "thick mist" but "rank grass," which rather compounds the erotics of "the foggy, foggy dew." Such critical commentary as Sandburg gives (that this missing verse is "probably an interpolation," say) is simply not supported. Instead, Sandburg offers a bit of gossip:

Observers as diverse as Sinclair Lewis, Sherwood Anderson, Arthur T. Vance and D. W. Griffith say this song is a great condensed novel of real life. After hearing it sung with a guitar at Schlogl's one evening in Chicago, D. W. Griffith telegraphed two days later from New York to Lloyd Lewis in Chicago, "Send verses Foggy Dew stop tune haunts me but I am not sure of words stop please do this as I am haunted by the song."

One cannot help but be drawn, at least for a moment, toward the opinion expressed by Robert Frost in his May 1922 letter to Lincoln MacVeagh: "We've been having a dose of Carl Sandburg. He's another person I find it hard to do justice to. He was possibly hours in town and he spent one of those washing his white hair and toughening his expression for his public performance. His mandolin pleased some people, his poetry a very few and his infantile talk none."

The "infantile talk" may well have included some discussion of "Blow the Man Down," a song that, in *The American Songbag*, Sandburg attributes to Robert Frost. It's heartbreaking in its way to recognize how Sandburg thinks, or presents himself as thinking in his "verbal footnote," that he and Frost are best buddies:

"Robert Frost as a boy in San Francisco learned shanties from listening to sailors and dock-wallopers along the water front. He saved these tunes and verses in his heart. A favorite with him is Blow The Man Down. It has the lurch of ships, tough sea legs, a capacity for taking punishment and rising defiant of oppression and tyranny."

One wonders if "Blow the Man Down" has any more or less of "the lurch of ships, tough sea legs" than, say, "Whisky Johnny," a second song Sandburg reports as having collected from Frost in a particularly Frostian scene: "Once when the night was wild without and the wintry winds piled snowdrifts around the traffic signals on Cottage Grove Avenue, Chicago, we sat with Robert Frost and Padraic Colum. The Gael had favored with Irish ballads of murder, robbery, passion. And Frost offered a sailorman song he learned as a boy on the wharves of San Francisco."

Given that he left San Francisco at eleven, the same age at which Sandburg embarked on his multitudinous part-time jobs, I doubt if Frost spent too many nights on the wharves, but it is certainly the case that, given his father's alcoholism, the lyric of "Whisky Johnny" must have had a particular poignancy for him:

> Whisky killed my brother Tom,
> Whisky Johnny,
> I drink whisky all day long,
> Whisky for my Johnny.
>
> Whisky made me pawn my clothes,
> Whisky Johnny,
> Whisky gave me this red nose,
> Whisky for my Johnny.

Frost and Sandburg had a lifelong rivalry over anything and everything, from which of them modeled his "messed up" hairstyle on the other to which of them should most appropriately have visited the Soviet Union. We remember Frost's meeting with Khrushchev in 1962, perhaps even Khrushchev's telegram of condolence to Lesley Frost after her father's death in 1963, but we probably don't remember that Sandburg had already visited the USSR in 1959. Sandburg's Social Democratic lineage, even his commitment to the New Deal, which would have made that visit so much more likely than Frost's, tends to have been overshadowed along with almost every other aspect of his life. Yet his influence is profound, as was already clear from the musical subtitle of Frost's 1923 volume, *New Hampshire: A Poem with Notes and Grace Notes,* which came out the very year after his cutting remarks about Sandburg in his letter to Lincoln MacVeagh:

> He is probably the most artificial and studied ruffian the world has had. Lesley says his two long poems in The New Republic and The Dial are as ridiculous as his carriage and articulation. He has developed rapidly since I saw him two years ago. I heard someone say he was the kind of writer who had everything to gain and nothing to lose by being translated into another language.

What's ironic about this, and almost certainly an explanation of his particularly vehement and venomous put-down of Sandburg, is that Frost was already attempting to translate himself, in the long title poem of *New Hampshire,* into something of a poet of the people Sandburg had already succeeded in becoming with *Chicago Poems, Cornhuskers, Smoke and Steel,* and *Slabs of the Sunburnt West.* It's a poem that delights in its own leisurely—perhaps even *lazy*—procedure:

> New Hampshire raises the Connecticut
> In a trout hatchery near Canada,
> But soon divides the river with Vermont.
> Both are delightful states for their absurdly
> Small towns—Lost Nation, Bungey, Muddy Boo,
> Poplin, Still Corners (so called not because
> The place is silent all day long, nor yet
> Because it boasts a whisky still—because
> It set out once to be a city and still
> Is only corners, crossroads in a wood).

One has the sense here that, for all its artfulness, this is the first poem in which Frost's persona is indistinguishable from one of the "folk" who had turned up in his earlier dramatic monologues. More than that, though, it's as if he has taken on something of Sandburg's slapdash method, perhaps even something of the very "infantile talk" he pointed to with such disdain. The tone may have gone some way toward securing both increasing popularity and the 1924 Pulitzer Prize for Poetry, in the receipt of which he was lagging behind Sandburg by five long years. It's hard, needless to say, to determine if Frost's hail-fellow-well-met mode is directly influenced by Sandburg or if it's merely coincidental with other developments of that very year of 1927. This was, after all, the year in which the motion picture industry saw the first talkie in *The Jazz Singer,* after which a regard for what Wordsworth described as art based on a "language near to the language of men" would, quite literally, resonate as it had not theretofore. This was also the year in which Jerome Kern and Oscar Hammerstein II's *Show Boat* opened in New York. *Show Boat* was the first musical of its kind, a musical in which the plot was advanced within the musical numbers, the first serious musical play in which music furthered the action. A case in point is Hammerstein's extraordinary lyric for "Can't Help Lovin' Dat Man":

> Fish got to swim, birds got to fly,
> I got to love one man till I die,
> Can't help lovin' dat man of mine.

The first time this was heard in the 1927 production of *Show Boat,* it was sung by a character named Julie, a mulatto. Queenie, the black cook, comments that it is odd that a light-skinned person would even know this song. We discover later in the musical that Julie is passing as white. Again, this sense of the dramatic charge of a song because of its social context may not be directly attributable to Sandburg, but it is certainly in keeping with his sense, real if rudimentary, of how and why a song might be taken as authentic. For example, in his introduction in *American Songbag* to "Go 'Way F'om Mah Window," he writes: "This negro woodchopper's song came up from Arkansas and the Ozarks to Tubman K. Hedrick, author of 'The Orientations of Hohen,' when he was a newspaperman in Memphis, Tennessee . . . Phrases of it time with ax-strokes. 'Go 'way' sinks the ax, 'f'om my window' sinks it again, and so on."

It's a short step from this song to that day in 1964 when Bob Dylan visited Carl Sandburg in his home in Flat Rock, North Carolina. Robert Frost had died the previous year, and Sandburg was the only one of the terrible twins still mussing up his hair and "toughening his expression." It was in this same year, 1964, that Dylan wrote and recorded "It Ain't Me, Babe," the first lines of which, "Go 'way from my window / Leave at your own chosen speed," we may choose to rather speedily trace directly to Carl Sandburg and *The American Songbag.*

Bibliography: Robert Frost, *The Poetry of Robert Frost,* ed. Edward Connery Lathem (New York, 1969). Carl Sandburg, *The American Songbag* (New York, 1927, 1990); *The Complete Poems of Carl Sandburg* (New York, 1970).

PAUL MULDOON

1927, May 16

Louis Brandeis redefines free speech in *Whitney v. California*

"Free to Develop Their Faculties"

Justice Louis Brandeis's concurring opinion in *Whitney v. California* is the most important essay on the purposes and boundaries of free speech in American literary history. Despite its legal and political influence, however, Brandeis's philosophical justification for free speech never developed a broad constituency in the twentieth century. Now that new technologies are challenging more conventional First Amendment models in the twenty-first century, Brandeis may yet receive the recognition he deserves as America's most visionary prophet of free expression.

Brandeis's opinion in *Whitney* completed the evolution that he and Justice Oliver Wendell Holmes, Jr., began in March 1919, when Holmes wrote opinions for the U.S. Supreme Court upholding the convictions, under the federal Espionage Act, of the socialists Charles Schenck and Eugene Debs for their criticisms of World War I. (While in prison, Debs went on to win more than a million votes as the Socialist Party's candidate for president.) "The most stringent protection of free speech would protect a man in falsely shouting fire in a theater and causing a panic," Holmes famously wrote for the Court in *Schenck v. United States.* "The question in every case is whether the words used are used in such circumstances and are of such nature as to create a clear and present danger that they will bring about the substantive evils that Congress has a right to prevent."

With the guidance of Zechariah Chafee, Jr., of Harvard Law School, Holmes converted his "clear and present danger" test from an invitation to suppress free speech into a shield for its protection. In the *Abrams v. United States* case, decided in November of 1919, in which the Court upheld the conviction—and sentences of up to twenty years—of Russian immigrants for distributing leaflets protesting the deployment of U.S. troops to Russia, Holmes wrote a memorable dissent, joined by Brandeis, that represents his own most poetic statement about the meaning of the First Amendment. "When men have realized that time has upset many fighting faiths, they may come to believe even more than they believe the very foundations of their conduct that the ultimate good desired is better reached by free trade in ideas—that the best test of truth is the power of the thought to get itself accepted in the competition of the market and that truth is the only ground upon which their wishes safely can be carried out," he wrote. For this reason, he insisted that "opinions we loathe" cannot be suppressed "unless they so imminently threaten immediate interference with the lawful and pressing purposes of the law that an immediate check is required to save the country."

Holmes's libertarian defense of free speech as the cornerstone of the marketplace of ideas was consistent with his nihilistic vision of American democracy, which he developed during the Civil War, in the Union Army, when he was wounded three times. Holmes took from his wartime experience a skepticism about abolitionism, and certitudes of any kind: he came to believe that democratic majorities had to be given virtually unlimited opportunities to crush minorities in a brutally competitive and unregulated political sphere, or else their disagreements would break out into actual violence. Although Holmes believed, with Mill, that free speech was a precondition for democratic debate, he had little of Mill's confidence that truth or wisdom or liberty would actually emerge from the "free trade in ideas." "If in the long run the beliefs expressed in the proletarian dictatorship are destined to be accepted by the dominant forces of the community, the only meaning of free speech is that they should be given their chance and have their way," he wrote in dissent in the *Gitlow v. People* case in 1927. In addition to deep skepticism about the outcome of democratic debates, Holmes also seemed to suggest in the *Gitlow* opinion that political dissent could be protected only when it was unconvincing, and could be punished whenever it was likely to produce any imminent harm, no matter how trivial.

Brandeis joined Holmes's famous dissents. But in the *Whitney* case, he specified more precisely the legal conditions under which subversive advocacy could be suppressed. At the same time, he provided a more creative and more optimistic justification for protecting free expression in a democracy. In *Whitney*, a majority of the Court upheld the conviction, under California's Criminal Syndicalism Act, of a woman who attended an organizing meeting of the California branch of the Communist Labor Party. Although it was not clear that she herself had advocated terrorism, she was convicted of "assist[ing] in organizing an association to advocate" terrorism. Concurring in the Court's decision to uphold the conviction, Brandeis refined Holmes's "clear and present danger" test in crucial ways. "Fear of serious injury cannot alone justify suppression of free speech and assembly. Men feared witches and burnt women," he wrote. "To justify suppression of free speech there must be reasonable ground to fear that serious evil will result if free speech is practiced" and that "the danger apprehended is imminent." Brandeis's insight that speech could only be restricted if it threatened harms that were both imminent and serious finally came to define the parameters of free speech in America when the Supreme Court overturned *Whitney* more than forty years later in *Brandenburg v. Ohio* in 1969. Today, it is the principal barrier in America against the prosecution of hate speech and other dignitary injuries that European courts have come to take for granted.

But Brandeis's opinion in *Whitney* did not merely refine Holmes's legal test for protecting free speech; it offered an entirely different philosophical justification for doing so, and in the process achieved a kind of constitutional poetry:

> Those who won our independence believed that the final end of the state was to make men free to develop their faculties, and that in its government the deliberative forces should prevail over the arbitrary. They valued liberty both as an end and as a means. They believed liberty to be the secret of happiness and courage to be the secret of liberty. They believed that freedom to think as you will and to speak as you think are means indispensable to the discovery and spread of political truth; that without free speech and assembly discussion would be futile; that with them, discussion affords ordinarily adequate protection against the dissemination of noxious doctrine; that the greatest menace to freedom is an inert people; that public discussion is a political duty; and that this should be a fundamental principle of the American government. They recognized the risks to which all human institutions are subject. But they knew that order cannot be secured merely through fear of punishment for its infraction; that it is hazardous to discourage thought, hope and imagination; that fear breeds repression; that repression breeds hate; that hate menaces stable government; that the path of safety lies in the opportunity to discuss freely supposed grievances and proposed remedies; and that the fitting remedy for evil counsels is good ones. Believing in the power of reason as applied through public discussion, they eschewed silence coerced by law—the argument of force in its worst form. Recognizing the occasional tyrannies of governing majorities, they amended the Constitution so that free speech and assembly should be guaranteed.

Brandeis argues that free speech is necessary both for "the discovery and spread of political truth" and for men to "develop their faculties." But his justifications for free speech are not limited to self-rule and self-fulfillment. Instead, Brandeis goes on to argue that "the deliberative forces should prevail over the arbitrary"; "that the greatest menace to freedom is an inert people"; and "that public discussion is a political duty." In this sense, he is offering a defense of free speech rooted in the classical republicanism of the Greeks and Romans rather than in nineteenth-century liberalism, one that rests on the idea that people are capable of collective virtue and that the goal of political deliberation is the common good.

One of Brandeis's favorite books was Alfred Zimmern's *The Greek Commonwealth,* which he read in the winter of 1913. Zimmern, like Brandeis, viewed Periclean Athens as a model for modern democracies, and insisted that only active and serious political participation by citizens—of the kind championed in Pericles's Funeral Oration—could safeguard democratic virtue. Brandeis's law clerk Paul Freund identified the Funeral Oration as the source of Brandeis's observation in *Whitney* that the American founders "believed liberty to be the secret of happiness and courage to be the secret of liberty." Rejecting Holmes's cynical view that majority will had to be accepted even when it was brutally misguided, Brandeis worried that governing majorities could become occasionally tyrannical. But he had faith that a virtuous, engaged citizenry could achieve a good in common that they could not know alone.

Brandeis's strenuous faith in the power of reasoned deliberation and public education is most apparent in his discussion of the need to exalt liberty over order:

> Those who won our independence by revolution were not cowards. They did not fear political change. They did not exalt order at the cost of liberty. To courageous, self-reliant men, with confidence in the power of free and fearless reasoning applied through the processes of popular government, no danger flowing from speech can be deemed clear and present, unless the incidence of the evil apprehended is so imminent that it may befall before there is opportunity for full discussion. If there be time to expose through discussion the falsehood and fallacies, to avert the evil by the processes of education, the remedy to be applied is more speech, not enforced silence. Only an emergency can justify repression.

This faith in the power of "full discussion" to cool violent impulses in the heat of passion would have been foreign to Holmes, who had contempt for democratic deliberation and loathed, as he put it, "the thick fingered clowns we call the people." But Brandeis's faith in the possibility of civil discourse to improve citizens was temperamental as much as theoretical. His mother, like Holmes's, was a committed abolitionist, but Brandeis, who was a child during the Civil War, never served in the Union Army or lost faith in the rightness of its cause. While Holmes held himself apart from politics, Brandeis devoted his life to political activism; while Holmes scorned the Progressive movement, Brandeis led it. He was a prominent activist in the Zionist movement, and persuaded the Wilson administration to become involved in the negotiations leading up to the Balfour Declaration. Franklin D. Roosevelt, viewing him as an Old Testament prophet, would come to call Brandeis "Isaiah." All this influenced his faith that an activist and compassionate state could promote the freedom that he believed to be the "secret of happiness."

Although Brandeis's doctrinal conclusions about the First Amendment were eventually embraced by the modern Supreme Court, his philosophical vision has met with strenuous resistance. The Court has repeatedly endorsed Holmes's metaphor of free trade in ideas while rejecting Brandeis's competing notion that regulations on speech may promote rather than inhibit public deliberation by equalizing the playing field. "The concept that government may restrict the speech of some elements of our society in order to enhance the relative voice of others is wholly foreign to the First Amendment," the Court wrote with a Holmesian flourish in the 1976 campaign-finance case, *Buckley v. Valeo.*

But Brandeis's hour may be yet to come. On the Roberts Court, Justice Stephen Breyer has attempted the most sustained defense of a pragmatic vision of free speech, rooted in the republicanism of the ancient Greeks and Romans, since Brandeis's opinion in *Whitney* itself. In his book *Active Liberty,* Breyer, citing not Brandeis but Benjamin Constant, argues that judges should consider the effects of their decisions in promoting not only the negative "liberty of the moderns" but also the active "liberty of the ancients." "Liberty means not only freedom from government coercion but also the freedom to participate in government itself"—in particular the freedom to participate in robust public deliberation. Like Brandeis, Breyer understands the First Amendment as "protecting more than the individual's modern freedom." In his view, constitutional protections for free speech seek to encourage "a conversation among ordinary citizens that will encourage their informed participation in the electoral process."

Whether Breyer's argument for free expression will gain any more adherents than Brandeis's original statement remains to be seen. But as new communications technologies are transforming our debates about free expression, Brandeis's vision seems more prescient than ever. The classic libertarian view of the free market of ideas was useful in an age when many free-speech battles involved an oppressive government trying to silence political dissidents or the institutional press, with the judiciary as a neutral arbiter. But the free-speech battles of the future may look very different, pitting telecom corporations against private speakers. Consider Verizon's decision, in 2007, to block text messages affirming abortion rights sent by the National Abortion Rights Action League on its mobile networks. (Under pressure, Verizon rescinded the decision but stood by its position that it can decide which messages to transmit.) As several scholars have argued, the solution to this problem of corporate censorship is in the hands of Congress and the Federal Communications Commission rather than the courts —namely, open-access rules of "net neutrality" that would require telecom operators to make their services available to all speakers on equal terms. Although judges may not be at the center of these battles, armed with a mission, rooted in Brandeis's vision of encouraging democratic participation, it's possible to imagine them influencing regulatory policy, as Brandeis surely hoped.

Whether or not Brandeis's vision of free speech ever wins a majority on the Supreme Court, it has inspired citizens for nearly a century. And despite its classical roots, it remains the freshest and most uniquely American defense of the value of free expression that this country has produced.

Bibliography: Louis D. Brandeis, *Whitney v. California,* 274 U.S. 347 (1927). Stephen Breyer, *Active Liberty: Interpreting Our Democratic Constitution* (New York, 2006). Pnina Lahav, "Holmes and Brandeis: Libertarian and Republican Justifications for Free Speech," *Journal of Law & Politics* 4 (1987–1988): 451. Philippa Strum, *Louis D. Brandeis: Justice for the People* (New York, 1984).

JEFFREY ROSEN

1928, April 8, Easter Sunday

Dilsey Gibson goes to church and hears Reverend Shegog's Resurrection sermon

THE SOUND AND THE FURY

Had he stopped writing on Easter Sunday 1928, William Faulkner would be remembered as a regional Lost Generation author who had published a returning war veteran's tale *(Soldiers' Pay)* and a bohemian artists' novel *(Mosquitoes)*. He had imitated T. S. Eliot's poetry and tried to accept the emotional importance of a war in which he had not fought and been wounded—though at times he claimed he had. It dawned on him only slowly that World War I was not his war: his story was a thick Southern family epic of intricate relationships of blood, marriage, and relentless, never-ending storytelling, reaching back to the Civil War. If Hemingway's novels were set outside the United States, Faulkner followed the model of Hardy's Wessex and set much of his fiction in an invented Yoknapatawpha County, Mississippi, with its capital, Jefferson—his own "postage stamp of human soil," shaped by the history of Indian dispossession, African slavery, Southern defeat, and racial segregation. In *Flags in the Dust,* an imaginary family history, this county is still called "Yocona," and it is a strong, though unnamed presence in *The Sound and the Fury,* the novel with which Faulkner entered a thirteen-year period of intense creativity that led to the publication of *As I Lay Dying, Light in August, Absalom, Absalom!,* and *Go Down, Moses.*

Faulkner's difficulties in getting *Flags in the Dust* published had freed him from the notion that he had to fit into some preexisting mold or needed to think of publishers: "I was thinking of books, publication, only in the reverse, in saying to myself, I wont have to worry about publishers liking or not liking this at all." In early March 1928 he knew that his new writing, "Twilight," was to become a novel. He would ultimately give it the Shakespearean title *The Sound and the Fury.* It was then that Faulkner discovered anew the "Flauberts and Dostoievskys and Conrads." In this writing experience, later compared to "a series of delayed repercussions like summer thunder," Faulkner experienced "that emotion definite and physical and yet nebulous to describe: that ecstasy, that eager and joyous faith and anticipation of surprise which the yet unmarred sheet beneath my hand held inviolate and unfailing waiting for release." The "release" marked a turning point in Faulkner's career and in the history of the novel.

The Sound and the Fury is centrally about the Brothers Compson—Benjy, Quentin, and Jason, each of whom gets to speak a monologue in which their sister, Caddy, plays an important part. When Jean-Paul Sartre analyzed *The Sound and the Fury* in 1939 he attempted to summarize the plot: "Jason and Caroline Compson have had three sons and a daughter. The daughter, Caddy, has given herself to Dalton Ames and become quickly pregnant. Forced to get hold of a husband quickly . . ." Here Sartre abandoned the précis, for he was telling another story and Faulkner did not "first conceive this orderly plot so as to shuffle it afterwards like a pack of cards; he could not tell it in any other way." The way Faulkner did tell it was not in the family-saga way with its wedding and funeral, family fortune and decline. Such events are represented in the novel—as are such dramatic moments as the siblings' reactions to the death of grandmother Damuddy, Caddy's loss of virginity, Benjy's castration, Quentin's suicide, and an intrafamilial deception undertaken by Jason and a theft committed by Caddy's daughter—but not in any easily intelligible sequence, so that it is novelistic *form* that first captures the reader's attention. *The Sound and the Fury* is told in a way Faulkner had not tried before: it radically refracts the Compson family story in four different stylistic registers.

> Through the fence, between the curling flower spaces, I could see them hitting. They were coming toward where the flag was and I went along the fence. Luster was hunting in the grass by the flower tree. They took the flag out, and they were hitting. Then they put the flag back and they went to the table, and he hit and the other hit.

Thus starts the book's first section, "April Seventh, 1928," with Benjy's flat registering of repetitious actions at the golf course that once was the Compson pasture. Restrained point of view and relentless parataxis have reminded readers of Hemingway. Benjy, the idiot, describes what he hears, sees, and smells accurately, but cannot generalize. Together the verbs "hear" and "smell" are used more than a hundred times, for such unconventional observations as "we could hear the fire and the roof," "I could hear it getting night," "I couldn't feel the gate at all, but I could smell the bright cold," or "Caddy smelled like trees and like when she says we were asleep." The abstraction "golf" appears only once, in a comment by his black attendant Luster that Benjy merely records, as he records dialogues faithfully.

The linguistic register shifts to Harvard freshman Quentin's voice in the second section, "June Second, 1910," set in Cambridge, Massachusetts:

> When the shadow of the sash appeared on the curtains it was between seven and eight oclock and then I was in time again, hearing the watch. It was Grandfather's and when Father gave it to me he said I give you the mausoleum of all hope and desire; it's rather excruciatingly apt that you will use it to gain the reducto absurdum of all human experience which can fit your individual needs no better than it fitted his or his father's. I give it to you not that you may remember time, but that you might forget it now and then for a moment and not spend all your breath trying to conquer it.

Quentin is about to commit suicide that day, before his final exams, which would have started on June 6. He loves to confabulate, to abstract from experience, and to give his own interpretation to events, but his voice disintegrates, changing from lavish sentences to unpunctuated lower-case prose-poem-like fragments. Time becomes a riddle: "Quarter to what?" Two brief sentences can prefigure death: "I was. I am not." Quentin's stream-of-consciousness speech has reminded readers of Joyce and Proust. While Benjy's key words are connected to perception, in Quentin's monologue "shadow," "remember," and "clock" appear with great frequency, as does the word "time"—all already present at the beginning. At the core of Quentin's torment is the vague "expedient" of confessing that he has committed incest. Quentin also utters some memorable aphorisms: Man is "the sum of his misfortunes. One day you'd think misfortune would get tired, but then time is your misfortune." All men are "accumulations dolls stuffed with sawdust swept up from the trash heaps where all previous dolls had been thrown away." And "a nigger is not a person so much as a form of behavior; a sort of obverse reflection of the white people he lives among."

For Benjy and Quentin there is no future; the past intrudes upon the present. "The past was not dead," Hawthorne found in "The Custom-House," as "the habit of bygone days awoke" in him. Faulkner would expand this maxim in *Requiem for a Nun* to "The past is never dead. It's not even past." The presence of the past is apparent in both monologues in numerous back-and-forth time shifts, which Faulkner had unrealistically hoped to signal with different-colored printing ink, sorely needed since about a hundred time shifts occur in the Benjy section. They are indicated by a "trigger" (nail/*uncaught, froze*/cold, or caddie/Caddy) or recognizable by the changing names of Benjy's attendants—Versh, T. P., Roskus, Luster—and in most (but not all) cases visualized by alternating roman and italic fonts.

Benjy and Quentin repeatedly return to a moment in their childhood that Faulkner identified as "perhaps the only thing in literature which would ever move me very much: Caddy climbing the pear tree to look in the window at her grandmother's funeral while Quentin and Jason and Benjy and the negroes looked up at the muddy seat of her drawers." Benjy mentions Candace nearly three hundred times, by name or nickname; Quentin invokes her about a hundred times. The sounds of "damuddy" and "muddy" and "Caddy" and "drawers" seem to merge in Quentin's incantations to her: "Do you remember the day damuddy died when you sat down in the water in your drawers," or, "Caddy do you remember how Dilsey fussed at you because your drawers were muddy." The fact that Benjy's original first name was Maury (after Mrs. Compson's brother), that Caddy's daughter is also named Quentin, and that both Mr. Compson and his middle son are named Jason contributes to the confusing presence of the past.

Time returns to its reassuring order in Jason's monologue, "April Sixth, 1928." It includes historical references, not to World War I, but to Western Union stock market reports, Coca-Cola, Prohibition, the U.S. Army in Nicaragua, and Mississippi Delta flood-control legislation. Jason emerges as a misogynous, racist, and hypocritical small-town businessman, a New South Babbitt, his style hardboiled. "Once a bitch always a bitch, what I say" is his opening sentence, and he reiterates near the end: "Like I say once a bitch always a bitch. And just let me have twenty-four hours without any dam New York jew to advise me what it's going to do. I don't want to make a killing; save that to suck in the smart gamblers with. I just want an even chance to get my money back." Jason's concern is money; in comments on Quentin's death by drowning ("I says no I never had university advantages because at Harvard they teach you how to go for a swim at night without knowing how to swim") or on Benjy's castration ("you can send Ben to the Navy I says or to the cavalry anyway, they use geldings in the cavalry") his self-pitying coldness is inhuman.

In the fourth section, "April Eighth, 1928," Faulkner surprisingly shifts to a third-person narrator. "It took me better than a month to take pen and write *The day dawned bleak and chill* before I did so." (I would like to imagine that this happened on Easter Sunday 1928.)

> The day dawned bleak and chill, a moving wall of gray light out of the northeast which, instead of dissolving into moisture, seemed to disintegrate into minute and venomous particles, like dust that, when Dilsey opened the door of the cabin and emerged, needled laterally into her flesh, precipitating not so much a moisture as a substance partaking of the quality of thin, not quite congealed oil. She wore a stiff black straw hat perched upon her turban, and a maroon velvet cape with a border of mangy and anonymous fur above a dress of purple silk, and she stood in the door for a while with her myriad and sunken face lifted to the weather, and one gaunt hand flac-soled as the belly of a fish, then she moved the cape aside and examined the bosom of her gown.

Faulkner records physical reality joyfully, in long, sprawling sentences, starting with the sympathetically drawn black family servant Dilsey and continuing with the Easter service Dilsey attends with Benjy and Luster.

> The preacher removed his arm and he began to walk back and forth before the desk, his hands clasped behind him, a meagre figure, hunched over upon itself like that of one long immured in striving with the implacable earth, "I got the recollection and the blood of the Lamb!" . . . And the congregation seemed to watch with its own eyes while the voice consumed him, until he was nothing and they were nothing and there was not even a voice but instead their hearts were speaking to one another in chanting measures beyond the need for words, so that when he came to rest against the reading desk, his monkey face lifted and his whole attitude that of a serene, tortured crucifix that transcended its shabbiness and insignificance and made it of no moment, a long moaning expulsion of breath rose from them, and a woman's single soprano: "Yes, Jesus!"

One senses the parallel between the unlikely preacher who was consumed by his voice in the Resurrection sermon and the writer who arrived at a new voice in writing *The Sound and the Fury.*

The fourth section leaves behind the individual modes of pure, timeless perception, stream of consciousness of a death-bound soul, and hardboiled cynicism to arrive at a freeing narration that conveys a sense of family life, of loyalty and caring. As Faulkner wrote: "There was Dilsey to be the future, to stand above the fallen ruins of the family like a ruined chimney, gaunt, patient and indomitable; and Benjy to be the past. He had to be an idiot so that, like Dilsey, he could be impervious to the future, though unlike her by refusing to accept it at all." Not Compson "flesh and blood" (a hollow formula often invoked), Dilsey is yet the embodiment of family.

over with, and then a furious desire not to die seized him and he struggled, hearing the old man wailing and cursing in his cracked voice.

He still struggled when they hauled him to his feet, but they held him and he ceased.

"Am I bleeding much?" he said, "The back of my head. Am I bleeding?" He was still saying that while he felt himself being propelled rapidly away, heard the old man's thin furious voice dying away behind him. "Look at my head," he said, "Wait, I—"

"Wait, hell," the man who held him said, "That damn little wasp'll kill you. Keep going. You aint hurt."

"He hit me," Jason said. "Am I bleeding?"

"Keep going," the other said. He led Jason on around the corner of the station, to the empty platform where an express truck stood, where grass grew rigidly in a plot bordered with rigid flowers and a sign in electric lights: Keep your on Mottson, the gap filled by a human eye with an electric pupil. The man released him.

"Now," he said, "You get on out of here and stay out. What were you trying to do? Commit suicide?"

"I was looking for two people," Jason said. "I just asked him where they were."

"Who you looking for?"

"It's a girl," Jason said. "And a man. He had on

388

William Faulkner, *The Sound and the Fury*, page with image of an eye

While in the first three sections the brothers rarely visualize each other—Benjy once records that Jason "had his hands in his pockets and a pencil behind his ear"—the fourth section presents the Compsons in full visual detail, examining, for example, the family resemblance between Jason and Mrs. Compson: "The one cold and shrewd, with close-thatched brown hair curled into two stubborn hooks, one on either side of his forehead like a bartender in caricature, and hazel eyes with black-ringed irises like marbles, the other cold and querulous, with perfectly white hair and eyes pouched and baffled and so dark as to appear to be all pupil or all iris." Dilsey strokes a bang over Benjy's brow, wipes "his drooling mouth upon the hem of her skirt," and he is "rapt in his sweet blue gaze." If the readers see the world of the novel first through the eyes of Benjy, the novel ends with the image of "his eyes . . . empty and blue and serene."

Faulkner's third-person narrator returns to Jason's futile quest to find his niece who has stolen his money and to get it back. In a parodic advertisement (reminiscent of Dr. T. J. Eckleburg in *The Great Gatsby*), Faulkner puts an actual eyeball on the printed page of his book.

Faulkner called *The Sound and the Fury* variously "a real sonofabitch" of a novel and "the most gallant, the most magnificent failure," but retained a particular fondness for it as his "heart's darling."

Bibliography: Joseph Blotner, *Faulkner: A Biography* (Jackson, MS, 1974). William Faulkner, *The Sound and the Fury* (1929; repr. New York, 1956); introductions to planned 1933 edition, in *Southern Review* 8 (n.s., 1972): 705–710, and *Mississippi Quarterly* 26 (Summer 1973): 410–415. Leon Howard, "The Composition of *The Sound and the Fury*," *Missouri Review* 5, no. 2 (Winter 1981–82). Michael Millgate, *The Achievement of William Faulkner* (London, 1965). For a hypertext of the novel and essays by Emily K. Izsak, James B. Meriwether, Gail M. Morrison, and Jean-Paul Sartre, see *The Sound and the Fury: A Hypertext Edition,* ed. Peter Stoicheff et al., updated March 2003, University of Saskatchewan, *www.usask.ca/english/faulkner.*

WERNER SOLLORS

1928, Summer
A radical writer visits the Soviet Union and meets Sergei Eisenstein

JOHN DOS PASSOS

In the years between his graduation from Harvard in 1916 and the publication of *The 42nd Parallel* in 1930, the first novel in the trilogy that became known as *U.S.A.,* John Dos Passos wrote, traveled, and read. His letters and diary entries from the late 1910s—years he spent in the Red Cross ambulance service in France and Italy, in the American army, and then traveling independently—chronicle his wanderings. They bristle with allusions to what he has read and with catalogs of what he is reading, with planned novels and with snatches of not-very-good poetry (sample line: "my verse is no upholstered chariot"), with postadolescent bluster, ambition, and self-doubt. Sometimes they are leavened with self-mockery: after brooding that "no good will come out of Cambridge" until Harvard's library is blown up and its president assassinated, he signs one letter, "San culottely Dos"; in another, rejoicing in his post-Armistice discharge from the army, he crows, with cheerful irony, "Libertad libertad! As Walt would have cried, tearing another button off his undershirt." This familiar, fond Whitman allusion exemplifies a current that runs through these informal writings: Dos Passos's evolving perspective on America, which seems to be sharpened by his time abroad. "I want exotic ultrathings—freedom—Home life—the right spirit," he wrote in his diary in 1918. "Search for the phrases of Americanism triumphant."

His fraught combination of feelings about America and its people—irony, earnest frustration, and affection—grew more complicated in the twenties. During these years, Dos Passos, while continuing to travel widely and beginning to publish his work, became immersed in the New York literary scene and joined the chic France-based circle of artists and writers that surrounded Sara and Gerald Murphy. (He begins "La Vie Littéraire," the fourth chapter of his autobiography, with the unmatchable line, "Looking back on it, lunching at the Plaza with Scott and Zelda in the fall of 1922 marks the beginning of an epoch"; it was an epoch during which Dos Passos was especially close to Hemingway, with whom he would eventually fall out to the point of being bashed four decades later in *A Moveable Feast*—without even the satisfaction of being named there.) During these years, Dos Passos also enhanced his bohemian bona fides by directing a small New York theater, overseeing what sound to have been excruciating modernist productions. Perhaps most significantly for his writing, though, Dos Passos became a member of the editorial board and a contributor to the *New Masses,* a left-wing journal that he hoped would become "a pulpit for native American radicalism."

It was as a correspondent to the *New Masses* and to the *Daily Worker* that Dos Passos covered the attempts, spearheaded by fellow left-wing writers, to secure another, fairer trial for Sacco and Vanzetti, the Italian-immigrant laborers accused of murdering two payroll clerks during an armed robbery in Braintree, Massachusetts. (Their real crime seems—and seemed then—to have been their anarchist convictions.) In his memoirs, composed in late middle age, Dos Passos—who by then had become disenchanted with communism to the point of supporting the McCarthy hearings—summoned his old radical indignation and frustrated idealism to describe efforts on behalf of the anarchists: "When we took up for Sacco and Vanzetti we were taking up for freedom of speech and for an evenhanded judicial system which would give the same treatment to poor men as to rich men, to greasy foreigners as to redblooded Americans." Sacco and Vanzetti were executed on August 22, 1927.

All through the fall of 1927 and the winter and spring of 1928, Dos Passos was hard at work with the operations of the theater and on the book he was starting, *The 42nd Parallel.* (His *Manhattan Transfer* had been published in 1925, the literary annus mirabilis that also saw the publication of *The Great Gatsby* and *An American Tragedy.*) But the deaths of Sacco and Vanzetti still rankled, and the fund-raising and administrative work the theater required tired him. As he later wrote in his memoir, "It occurred to me this might be a good time to visit the Soviet Union."

The Soviet Union then had a thriving and innovative theater scene, and Dos Passos hoped that in addition to seeing Soviet life firsthand, he would be able to find ideas he could take back to his New York troupe. Because finances were tight, as was to remain the case throughout his writing life, in the spring of 1928 Dos Passos made an unsuccessful effort to barter passage to Leningrad for care of a shipload of live muskrats en route. When this fell through, he made arrangements through more regular channels, and reached Leningrad via third-class steamship passage to Helsinki.

In Leningrad, Dos Passos befriended a range of citizens—a freshly urbanized Kyrgyz tribesman he met in the Hermitage, in love with the idea of freedom from arranged marriage; an American assistant to Pavlov; actors, actresses, and writers. But as he wrote his Harvard friend E. E. Cummings, "The most interesting and lively people . . . were the movie directors," especially Sergei Eisenstein, then at the height of his domestic fame. Eisenstein's *The Battleship Potemkin,* with its famous Odessa Steps sequence, still a textbook example of Soviet montage, had come out in 1925; in addition, Eisenstein wrote widely and influentially about montage as a dialectical technique, where the combined force of disconnected, juxtaposed shots became more than the sum of their individual meanings.

It was a technique that Dos Passos, who traveled throughout the Soviet Union before returning to New York at Christmastime in 1928, used to great effect when resuming work on *The 42nd Parallel*—a breakthrough that carried over into the second volume of *U.S.A., 1919,* published in 1932, and the third, *The Big Money,* published in 1936. (The three volumes were collected together as a single work in 1938.) It would be unfair to argue that Eisenstein's influence was responsible for the montage-like format of *U.S.A.;* it's more accurate to say, as Dos Passos himself does in his memoirs, that the two men's ideas were congruent: "We agreed thoroughly about the importance of montage." They were both feeling the breath of the same modernist breezes. Dos Passos's *Manhattan Transfer* adopted many of the same strategies of interleaving narratives; his journals from the time of the First World War include snatches of transcribed song. But *The 42nd Parallel* and its companion volumes represent a clear departure from his earlier work in their vaulting ambition. In them, Dos Passos set out to chronicle the whole of the U.S.A.—and, as he later wrote in the prelude to the trilogy, "mostly U.S.A. is the speech of the people."

Dos Passos uses four recurring modes to record the speech of the people: collections of headlines, news briefs, and song lyrics headed "Newsreel"; autobiographical stream-of-consciousness passages headed "The Camera Eye"; more traditionally realist narrative passages tracing their characters in installments throughout the books, headed with the names of their protagonists; and brief biographies of Great Men and Women, often heavy with irony.

For the Newsreels, Dos Passos relies on headlines, articles, and advertisements culled from individual newspapers—the *Chicago Tribune* for *The 42nd Parallel,* and the *New York World* for both *1919* and *The Big Money*—which he splices, combines with the lyrics of popular songs, and rearranges to create crazy quilts of news items of various urgency and cogency. The effect is of hearing the top-of-the-hour news while drifting in and out of sleep, or of listening to a car radio tuned between stations—news as background noise, as the half-understood background to daily life. From *The 42nd Parallel*:

BUGS DRIVE OUT BIOLOGIST
elopers bind and gag; is released by dog
EMPORER NICHOLAS II FACING REVOLT OF EMPIRE
GRANTS SUBJECTS LIBERTY
paralysis stops surgeon's knife by the stroke of a pen
the last absolute monarchy of Europe passes into history
miner of Death Valley and freak advertiser of Santa Fe Road
may die sent to bridewell for stealing plaster angel
On the banks of the Wabash far away.

Any objectivity suggested by the Camera Eye sections is illusory. The earlier passages, chronicling Dos Passos's observations from his boyhood and youth, read like pastiches of *A Portrait of the Artist as a Young Man* (and in fact when he reread that book in 1918 Dos Passos wrote in his journal, "pray God I shant start imitating it off the face of the Earth")—but pastiches in the best possible sense. Often in the second person, often with fretfully repeated refrains, these passages convey an impressionistic sense of the scenes at hand, with details leaping startlingly into focus. In "The Camera Eye (25)," from *The 42nd Parallel*, "the streetcar wheels screech grinding in a rattle of loose trucks round Harvard Square" as the narrator despairs of growing "cold with culture like a cup of tea forgotten between an incenseburner and a volume of Oscar Wilde," knowing he "hadn't the nerve/to jump up and walk outofdoors." The passages are deeply personal, but their style serves to contain the runaway autobiography that had consumed Dos Passos's earlier work; their blurriness universalizes them.

The narrative passages are in many ways the most traditional element in the three books, following, as they do, the development of characters, often from childhood; it is a mode that would not seem strange to Dickens. (And as in Dickens, the stories of vastly different characters collide and intermesh.) But it is the empathy Dos Passos brings to the characters that makes them new, American, at once types who stand for thousands like them and individuals whose suffering is shared only by the reader. Dos Passos employs a cozy third person, adopting the language, inhabiting the thoughts, of well-bred Chicago girls, or sailors, or labor organizers, or PR men. When the young stenographer Janey Williams moves out of her mother's house, "she discovered," Dos Passos writes from behind her eyes, "that just a little peroxide in the water when she washed her hair made it blonder and took away that mousey look." The dissolving innocence encapsulated in this passage—the coarseness of peroxiding hair camouflaged by the careful women's-magazine-speak of "just a little" and "that mousey look"—sums up Janey's increasing self-reliance as she begins to make her way on her own. The narrative passages in *U.S.A.* are packed with such ventriloquism. The story arcs are often bleak, tracing characters through disputes, wartime cities, failed love affairs, and unplanned pregnancies; not infrequently, they end with accidental death. But it is the immediacy and vitality of the characters' voices that renders them *people,* rather than solely the victims or perpetrators or opponents of capitalism—and it is the leviathan of capitalism that Dos Passos places at the center of their stories, and thus the American story.

Dos Passos's fourth mode in the *U.S.A.* books is prose-poetry biography, portraits of the heroes and villains, often one and the same, who made their times, and his—those who even today need only one name, Edison, Morgan, Ford, Taylor, Valentino, Wilson, Veblen, and those who need two, Joe Hill, Eugene Debs, Isadora Duncan, Bob La Follette—often sardonically titled. (William Randolph Hearst is "Poor Little Rich Boy.") As in the Camera Eye segments, in the biographies Dos Passos employs repeated phrases; here, they serve to give continuity to the stories of lives told over the space of just a few pages. As in the narrative segments, the trajectory of these lives is downward; unlike the narrative segments, the massed ironies in these interludes often serve to condemn. Ford's story, for example, leaves him in paranoid old age, collecting antique buildings to re-create the America of his youth as "the newmodel cars roared and slithered and hissed oilily past (*the new noise of the automobile*)." It is in the biographies that Dos Passos is most frank in his disgust with capitalist America.

But—true to Eisenstein's writings about montage—*U.S.A.* is more than the sum of these parts. By themselves, the Camera Eye segments would have been too navel-gazing, the biographies of the age-makers too sour, the realism of the recurring characters' stories too crushing, the Newsreels too gimmicky. Interleaved, though, each of these elements lends meaning and depth to the others. Together, they are the literary anticipation of Jasper Johns's flags or Robert Rauschenberg's transfer drawings: abstracted, thickly layered, and viscerally, fundamentally American.

For all of its magic, for all of its empathy and scope and imagination, the trilogy remains not-quite-canonical; there are plenty of well-read Americans who would be unashamed to admit they haven't read it. The question that occurs to any entranced reader of *U.S.A.* is, How is this not *huge?* What happened?

It's hard to say. Dos Passos, disenchanted with the extremism that communism bred, drifted rightward; but so too did any number of his contemporaries. In later years he was hugely prolific, and veered into self-parody; but so did any number of his contemporaries. Yet there are no Bad Dos Passos contests. It may be that *U.S.A.,* clocking in at 1,300 pages in Library of America Bible paper, is just too big for the immortality conferred by inclusion in generations of undergraduate surveys of American literature—but it is a purposeful and necessary expansiveness. As Dos Passos writes in his preface to the trilogy, "it was speech that clung to the ears, the link that tingled in the blood; U.S.A."

Bibliography: John Dos Passos, *The Best of Times: An Informal Memoir* (New York, 1966); *Travel Books and Other Writings, 1916–1941* (New York, 2003); *U.S.A.* (New York, 1938). Townshend Ludington, *John Dos Passos: A Twentieth Century Odyssey* (New York, 1980). Donald Pizer, *Dos Passos' U.S.A.: A Critical Study* (Charlottesville, VA, 1988).

PHOEBE KOSMAN

1928, November 18

Steamboat Willie opens at the Colony Theater on Broadway

The Mouse That Whistled

The Colony at 1687 Broadway was one of New York City's poshest new the-aters. Built in 1924, the movie palace operated by Hollywood's Universal Pictures had everything: a soaring interior domed like a Roman bath, murals, a deeply sculpted proscenium arch, velvet draperies, crystal chandeliers, and a Skinner or-gan with no fewer than 2,153 pipes. The splendid building itself insisted that the movies were every bit as good as any highbrow live drama. What's more, for a modest admission fee the majestic Colony stood ready to make anybody feel like a king or a queen for an afternoon, ensconced in plush luxury as the gilding spar-kled in the far recesses of the balcony, the house lights slowly dimmed, and the boom of the organ died away. The curtains parted. The movie began. This was democracy *de luxe!* This was the life! "Air conditioned" in the summer. Toasty in the winter. Sheer perfection for 15¢.

In 1928, America was booming. Mae West, appearing live just down Broadway from the Colony in *Diamond Lil,* was sexy and scandalous enough to raise polite eyebrows. She was a symbol of loosening public morals. Arrests and fines for pub-lic indecency would follow. Al Jolson was back on the silver screen in *The Singing Fool,* his second talking picture; the first sound movie, Jolson's *The Jazz Singer,* had premiered in New York City in 1927 at Warner's flagship movie house. "Talkies"! What would they think of next? Lindbergh flew across the Atlantic in 1927, too. A year later, it was aviatrix Amelia Earhart (with two male pilots). Herbert Hoover was elected president on November 6, 1928, promising "a chicken in every pot and a car in every garage." And in May, United Artists released *Steamboat Bill, Jr.,* a silent comedy starring Buster Keaton.

The lordly *New York Times* didn't like the latest Keaton picture much. A "gloomy comedy," it said. "A sorry affair." Today's critics love *Steamboat Bill, Jr.* less for riotous hilarity—it *isn't* very funny—than for Keaton's effortless physical prowess, the legacy of a childhood spent cavorting on the vaudeville stage. The pratfalls, the hat-switching routine, the stunts performed while suspended from a crane, and the heart-stopping scene in which the facade of a building topples over on the star (who escapes death by a narrow margin when an upstairs window just happens to fit around his body, with hardly an inch to spare) make for grand comedic spectacle, if not for belly laughs. Film historians tend to admire the movie—Keaton's last independent production—rather than enjoy it.

The story concerns a college boy from the East coming to see his father for the first time. Steamboat Bill, Sr., is the roughhewn captain of a run-down paddle-wheeler on the Mississippi. Junior is a Boston fop with a ukulele and a nasty little mustache. The meeting, needless to say, is not a success, until the swaggering owner of a rival boat arranges to have the old *Stonewall Jackson* condemned. Then, in the middle of a tornado, Buster Keaton decides to help his old man and, of course, saves the day. Along the way, there is a tepid romance enlivened by the antics of a surly sheriff, a moonfaced first mate, and the usual cast of local boobs. But the narrative is less important than the star's almost perpetual motion. And the song that inspired his exuberant choreography.

"Steamboat Bill"—the song, that is—is part and parcel of the pop balladry of the 1920s. Victor Records specialized in sad, twangy but strongly rhythmic numbers about condemned prisoners, railroad disasters, the sinking of the *Titanic,* and various deceased folk heroes—the kinds of songs that brought Vernon Dalhart to stardom as the first major country artist. Dalhart's "Wreck of the Old 97" was one of the first authentic country hits, selling more than six million copies in 1924. "Steamboat Bill"—the tune that inspired Keaton's movie—was another Tin Pan Alley adaptation of a traditional folk song, a variation on "Casey Jones" in which the title character is killed when the boiler bursts during a race for the speed record on the Mississippi River. *Casey Jones,* based on the ballad of the same name, was a 1927 film with an almost identical plot: a mismatched father and son finally work together to prevent further disasters along the tracks.

This tangled history of music and movies helps to explain what happened in November of 1928 when *Steamboat Willie* debuted at the Colony Theater, with its creator lurking in the back of the house tugging nervously on his mustache. *Steamboat Willie* was an animated cartoon—and not a very long one, with a running time of just under six minutes. It starred a cheeky mouse named Mickey, a mouse who wore short pants and big shoes. Legend has it that Mickey Mouse was invented by Walt Disney on a train trip between New York and Los Angeles several months earlier. Disney had just learned that the distributor of his films had seized control of Oswald the Lucky Rabbit, the Walt Disney Studio's current star. And to make matters worse, the same sneak had hired away most of Disney's animators.

Now Oswald was a fairly run-of-the-mill cartoon creature of the 1920s, of a type with Felix the Cat and other easy-to-draw animal favorites. That is, Oswald was mainly black in color with a silhouette that showed up well against the white of the movie screen. He was rubbery, too: his ability to stretch and twist various body parts at will (including his phallic ears) generated most of the laughs. Walt insisted that Oswald have a "personality," however—some inner core of character that would impel his actions. Whether he succeeded in transcending the stock cartoon gag is doubtful, but Oswald was all Disney had in the opening months of 1928. Yes, the story goes that the young animator dreamed up Mickey in desperation on the westbound New York Central Express. He called him Mortimer until Mrs. Disney objected. Too sissified, she said. And so he became Mickey, a shorthand way of saying the mouse was an outsider, a bit of a tough, a rodent of Irish descent, perhaps.

The truth is less dramatic. Mickey had been on the back burner for some time, drawn by Ub Iwerks, Walt's old Kansas City partner and current Hollywood collaborator. In fact, two silent Mickey films had already been finished. The first was *Plane Crazy,* a spoof on Charles Lindbergh's epic flight starring Mickey as a barnyard Lothario cum inventor fashioning a plane from parts of a Model T with the assistance of lesser animals (turkeys, pigs, cows, wiener dogs). The second, *The Gallopin' Gaucho,* was a parody of a 1927 hit starring the swashbuckling Douglas Fairbanks as a Latin lover/revolutionary. But the debut of *The Jazz Singer* revolutionized the motion picture business. When Al Jolson dropped to one knee and sang "My Mammy" in blackface, everything changed overnight. Movies could talk. So Mickey Mouse would talk! Well, if not talk, he would squeak (in Walt Disney's voice), give his boss the ol' razzberry, and whistle a lively chorus of "Steamboat Bill."

In short order, the remaining Disney staff put away the first two mouse movies and went back to the drawing board. The third Mickey was going to be a talkie. It had been alarming and mesmerizing enough when, in the early days of the century, drawings began to move. Now they would make noises. Now they would be almost as real as Al Jolson. But for Mickey's debut as a man-made, moving, talking creature—a likable Frankenstein, a robot, an automaton—they stuck strictly to parody. This time, the subject was Buster Keaton's musically derived *Steamboat Bill, Jr.* It had every ingredient a cartoon needed: gags and stunts, an unstoppable leading man, and a manic energy. And Mickey would bring something extra to the Buster Keaton role—optimism, sass, playfulness, a travelin' man's mild disdain for country folk, and a feisty girlfriend in the person of Minnie Mouse.

Inked by the Disney brothers' wives in a rented garage and synchronized by rank amateurs squealing and playing combs as the footage was projected on a bed sheet, *Steamboat Willie*—*Jr.*'s animated love child—was soon ready. It premiered with little fanfare in the darkened recesses of the Colony Theater, sprung on an unwitting audience there to thrill to *Gang War,* a routine police shoot-'em-up (with a hastily added sound prologue). *Willie* was anything but routine. A steamboat heads downriver, fairly dancing on the water thanks to two smokestacks puffing in time to the beat measured out on the sound track. Then, playing counterpoint to the audible spurts of steam, First Mate Mickey whistles "Steamboat Bill" and blows the brass whistles, which also become actors in the drama and players in a madcap symphony. Sound and action, sound and sight, were seamlessly made one.

The boat can tweak its own body into position at the pier, like a plump matron settling into an armchair. The stacks can raise and lower themselves at will. The humanoid whistles spot obstacles ahead and blare out a warning—all in time to the music. There had never been anything like it. Mice who whistled. Gyrating smokestacks. Mayhem as art. Machines with a mind of their own and a taste for music.

This idyll of machinery at play is interrupted by the captain, a huge, sadistic cat who stretches Mickey's torso like a piece of limp spaghetti and spits tobacco juice through a sentient front tooth that opens and closes like a rolltop desk. His meanness, a faint aura of cruelty and crudeness, spices the unfolding action like a teaspoonful of pepper. The captain's parrot hoots in derision at Mickey's virtual captivity. On the pier, Mickey takes out his anger by pinching the udder of a pitiful cow while loading her aboard. The dock is labeled "Podunk," a term of contempt for rubes and their way of life. Minnie misses the boat and is hauled aboard by Mickey with a winch that pulls up her skirt and spanks her on the fanny.

When Mickey and Minnie begin to play a madcap version of "Turkey in the Straw," the animal cargo provides many of their instruments. In one scene, usually deleted from prints of *Steamboat Willie* intended for viewing in schoolrooms, a series of unique squeals comes from a litter of nursing piglets when their tails are yanked. Mother sow is left to carry the melody on her own nipples. A goat, a cat, a goose, and a bull are variously squeezed, pulled, plucked, and whacked as well to play the old folk song in wild cacophony.

The end result is a complex parable about art, technology, modernism, history, and the American character. The sound technology is brand-new stuff, tinkered into existence, by gosh or by golly, in Disney's studio with the same drive and daring that impelled Henry Ford toward his Model T and Edison to his lightbulb. Mickey improvises with Disneyesque abandon, especially in these early films of the late 1920s. Reality is mutable under his assault. Although he often operates in the countryside (Walt Disney's childhood on a Missouri farm was part of his personal mystique), four-fingered Mickey is an urban rodent, mad for cars, planes, pert mousy flappers. In common with the doughboys of World War I (Walt served in the ambulance corps in France), Mickey has jettisoned the plodding ways of Podunk while retaining the casual cruelty of farm boys toward animals. He is Walt Disney in short pants, part Missouri boy and rural memory, part citified grownup with an unquenchable drive for success. Mickey is, then, the perfect stand-in for Disney, made in the image of the striving, up-to-the-minute American who was watching his antics in the Colony Theater in New York City in 1928.

The Mickey Mouse of 1928 is a stripped-down model, wiry and lean, an art deco mouse, the latest thing. Throughout the 1930s and '40s, he got progressively rounder and rounder, from his plump white gloves to his ball-toed yellow shoes. He got friendlier, smilier, less snippy. This later, nouveau Mickey would never torture piglets, disobey the boss, or bean a parrot with a potato and then guffaw about it. Made of puffy, comfortable arcs, he became easier to draw and easier to love as an icon of bland, unthreatening good humor. Instead of sneering or spitting, he chuckled like a kindly visiting uncle with a pocketful of candy. Mickey, alas, became a trademark, a corporate logo, offensive to absolutely no one. Claes Oldenburg, Andy Warhol, and other members of the pop art generation could "draw" the iconic Mickey in any medium, in any color, with a couple of flat circles.

For his part, Walt Disney never lost his affection for Mickey, even when the star qualities of the Mouse demanded that he operate more and more often as a kind of master of ceremonies in his own movies, leaving mayhem and spite to a new supporting cast. During World War II, for example, the irascible Donald Duck's career skyrocketed while Mickey continued to simper and giggle. But on a deeper level, Disney grasped the real significance of Mickey's debut and the overnight stardom that garnered Walt a special Oscar in 1932 just for bringing him to the screen. Mickey was Disney's reward for testing the limits of technology, for manufacturing drawings that did everything people could do, including talking, thinking, moving, and arousing real emotions in an audience. Why not take the final step in the process, turning a two-dimensional cartoon into a three-dimensional being?

Throughout the late 1940s and the early 1950s, Disney personally worked on the notion of bringing the old art of drawing into the brave new world of robotics. Filming hoofer Buddy Ebsen in front of a measured grid, Walt and his team tried to duplicate the dancer's movements in mechanical figures that performed on miniature stages powered by the motors from old movie cameras. These early test runs would lead, with the opening of Disneyland in 1955, to life-size birds and animals that performed a limited repertoire of actions, absolving the park from caring for live creatures. Unlike obstreperous actors and temperamental stars, figures operated by puffs of air triggered by sound cues never tired of repetition, never complained about wages and hours, and never went out on strike. They were, in short, perfect adjuncts to the make-believe perfection of Disneyland itself.

Some early visitors to the park found Disney's robots unsettling, in the way that labor unions of the day feared their jobs were being threatened by machines for building cars or assembling parts. Were they life forms—or grotesque caricatures of life? Others thought the robots were eerie examples of the undead, doppelgangers that posed an ultimate threat to humanity. The Disney latex-and-wire Abraham Lincoln unveiled at the 1964 World's Fair spouting a bowdlerized mixture of the presidential utterances was weirder than any pirate or bear or chattering toucan. And sinister, too, as if Walter Benjamin's warnings against the dangers of technology and the psychotic fantasy of Mickey Mouse had suddenly been proved prescient.

In one sense, the Mickey of *Steamboat Willy* is Mark Twain for the 1920s, with a dark side ultimately edited out for the sake of the kiddies. As the principal in a film that revolutionized the industry, he is also profoundly modern. But the implications of spirits sprung from machines—however benign they may seem—have yet to be explored. The legacy of the twentieth century, as embodied in Walt Disney's whistling man-made mouse, is both horrifying and wonderful to behold.

Bibliography: Walter Benjamin, *Selected Writings,* vol. 3: *1935–1938* (Cambridge, MA, 2002). Neal Gabler, *Walt Disney: The Triumph of the American Imagination* (New York, 2006). Karal Ann Marling, ed., *Designing Disney's Theme Parks: The Architecture of Reassurance* (Paris, 1997). Erwin Panofsky, in *Film: An Anthology,* ed. David Talbot (New York, 1959). *Filmography: Steamboat Willie* (Disney Cartoons, 1928).

KARAL ANN MARLING

"You're Swell!"

When did Americans begin to talk? The English always talked. Not only the sublime back-and-forth of the famously witty pairs of lovers—Beatrice and Benedick, Millamant and Mirabel, Elizabeth and Darcy; not only the compulsively brilliant and self-aware conversationalists who populate the work of Wilde and Coward; but also the spouters of language like Richard III and Othello and the verbal eruptions of so many Dickens characters who seem to exist only for the gleeful satisfaction of releasing into the world the bizarre language that defines them. When in *David Copperfield* Mrs. Gummidge mutters "I'm a lone, lorn critter," she's not just complaining, she's also flexing her unique style of expressing herself, and enjoying it. Of course America's Hester Prynne, Captain Ahab, Isabel Archer, Sister Carrie spoke weighty and thrilling things, but they're not playing with words, taking pleasure in inventing themselves through tone of voice. (Is Huck Finn the exception?)

It's tempting but lazy to emphasize the convenient connection between the birth of "talk" and the coming of sound to the movies in the mid- to late twenties. "Sound" was not just a technological innovation that happened along and dragged talk along with it. It took over movies because it responded to what was already a pressing necessity. The silents were a glory that reflected their time and satisfied a huge unsophisticated public that eagerly responded to the pathos of the Little Tramp, to Griffith's melodramas and pastoral romances and DeMille's epics of sin and repentance. No one needed to know how Chaplin and Pickford and Gish and Swanson and Valentino talked or what they sounded like—they suggested their essential qualities through look and gesture, and they did it superbly. But America's moviegoers, grown more sophisticated through our involvement in the First World War and increasing urbanization, now were eager for the sophistication of dialogue. You can sense this pressure by tracking the way intertitles in the silents grew longer and more complex as the twenties progressed: They were becoming less a necessary statement of background and situation and more a substitute for—talk. But you didn't want to *read* talk, you wanted to *hear* it.

By this time, American writers had already begun letting us know how certain people actually spoke. I'm not thinking of the naturalistic fictions of Dreiser, Stephen Crane, Frank Norris, Upton Sinclair—these showed us what life in America was like (usually grim), but they didn't particularly relish the sound of individual voices. It was humorists who led the way, in what you might call the stand-up comedy of its day—the monologues in the vernacular that for years had been appearing in popular magazines and on the vaudeville stage (think Will Rogers).

In 1916, Ring Lardner published his *You Know Me Al* (it had appeared first in the *Saturday Evening Post*), the wonderful rambling letters of a bush-league baseball pitcher to his best pal. Here was a fresh, hilarious, unmistakably American voice. It wasn't the content of the material that struck home so much as the pitch-perfect ventriloquism of a previously uncaught way of speaking: "In Florries letter she says she thinks us and the Allens could find an other flat like the 1 we had last winter and all live in it to gether in stead of going to Bedford but I have wrote to her before I started writeing this letter all ready and told her that her and I is going to Bedford and the Allens can go where they feel like and they can go and stay on a boat in Michigan lake all winter if they want to but I and Florrie is comeing to Bedford." Virginia Woolf was only one of many critics who recognized its validity and charm: "With the surest touch, the sharpest insight, [Lardner] lets Jack Keefe the baseball player cut his own outline, fill in his own depth, until the figure of the foolish, boastful, innocent athlete lives before us."

It happened again just after World War I with Edward Streeter's number-one best seller, *Dere Mabel,* made up of the hero's semi-illiterate letters from army training camp to his sweetheart, Mabel Gimp. (The World War II parallel was *See Here, Private Hargrove.*) And then again in Don Marquis's "archie and mehitabel" stories and poems from the teens and twenties in which archie, the vers-libre-writing cockroach, hymns the praises of mehitabel the wayward cat ("toujours gai, toujours gai"). And yet again, with the greatest impact of all, in Anita Loos's *Gentlemen Prefer Blondes* of 1925. Not just the adventures but the voice of Lorelei Lee spoke for a generation of flappers to a generation of flapper-fanciers. Her way with words said it all. "A girl like I" wasn't just an adorable gold digger; she was an American voice, talking her own (and our) talk. James Joyce, George Santayana, and Edith Wharton were among her hundreds of thousands of admirers.

In 1928, twenty-five years before Marilyn Monroe, an actress named Ruth Taylor gave us Lorelei in a movie—a silent movie. It's now lost, and just as well—who wants to encounter a silent Lorelei? In this case, sound missed the boat by mere minutes, leaving the way clear for Carol Channing on Broadway and Monroe in Hollywood. But by Marilyn's day, of course, the silents were forgotten, their doom certified by *Anna Christie,* for which the famous ad campaign blared, "Garbo talks."

Sound films exploded not only because the world was hungry for talk but because there was a new kind of talk to exploit. The twenties had been high-flying, sybaritic. The thirties were the Depression years—tough, gritty, sassy, populist. And sound was ready for them. The very early sound picture *Lonesome,* a man and a woman, 1929: "Nice day isn't it?" "It's sweet." "Like you." "Shut up." Backstage musicals, gangster films, shop-girl weepies may have glamorized and/or sentimentalized the post-crash realities of the down and out, but they also reflected them in spreading a new lingo, a new vocabulary. Before 1929 nobody said, "You're swell!" From 1930 on, everyone said it: it was the highest praise. The voices of a Cagney, a Blondell, a Stanwyck were new American voices talking new American talk, even if the studios were trying to iron out the rough edges. Hollywood still needed its classy Ronald Colmans to inhabit its British outposts (*A Tale of Two Cities, The Light that Failed, Lost Horizon, The Prisoner of Zenda*), but he was almost a specialty act. There was nothing British or classy about Stanwyck or Clark Gable or Joan Crawford.

The top movie talkers of the period were William Powell and Myrna Loy—the *Thin Man* series: "Pretty girl," says Nora. "Yes, she's a very nice type," says Nick. "You got types?" "Only you, darling. Lanky brunettes with wicked jaws"—and Katharine Hepburn, who may have flirted with bizarrely inappropriate roles—hillbilly in *Spitfire,* Chinese in *Dragon Seed,* Clara Schumann in *Song of Love*—but whose stock in trade was her upper-class Eastern-seaboard drawl applied to sarcastic or arrogant pronouncements: "I'm going crazy, I'm standing here on my own two hands going crazy." The Hepburn with the largest claims on us is the Hepburn bantering with Cary Grant in *Holiday, Bringing Up Baby, The Philadelphia Story;* with Ginger Rogers in *Stage Door;* with Spencer Tracy in their battle-of-the-sexes comedies. She's all talk—until she melts, in the last reel.

Then, in 1940, after the continental wit of *Trouble in Paradise* and the knock-about back-and-forth of *Twentieth Century* and Warner's gum-snapping, wise-talking *Gold Diggers,* came the ultimate talk comedy: *His Girl Friday,* Howard Hawks's version of *The Front Page,* with Rosalind Russell and Cary Grant going at each other with a barrage of rat-a-tat-tat dialogue that's clearly the basis of their inability to give each other up. With whom else could they spar at that speed and with so much gratification? *His Girl Friday* may recapitulate *The Front Page*'s complicated plot, but its real subject is romance by wisecrack—love American style.

There was another crucial element to the triumph of talk in the mid-twentieth century: radio. Before radio, where could people on farms or in small towns, with theater unavailable, hear public voices? In revival meetings? At political rallies? Millions of Americans lived in a kind of cultural isolation, however wholesome it may look in retrospect; the outside world hardly impinged, except through the written word. With the wildfire success of radio, all that changed. Now housewives on farms or small towns could listen to soap operas, music, comedy, drama, advice on everything from recipes to self-beautification. The whole family could—and most families *did*—tune in to *Amos 'n' Andy,* whose attitudes and language may seem racist today but back then expanded the consciousness of tens of millions of Americans: blacks, even if they were acted by whites, were suddenly inside everyone's kitchens and living rooms. Kids did their homework (surreptitiously) to the sound of *The Lone Ranger* and *Little Orphan Annie.* The news, *The Shadow,* the symphony, *Your Hit Parade*—sound was everywhere.

By the forties, there were also the morning radio talk shows—couples who chatted about the events of the day as well as the events of their own days. Ed and Pegeen Fitzgerald (they went on for over forty years), Tex McCrary and his wife, Jinx (that's Jinx Falkenburg), Dick Kollmar and *his* wife, Dorothy (that's Dorothy Kilgallen)—their voices and their views got people through their early morning rituals and off to work or school. A deep domestic privacy was invaded when voices like these penetrated the intimacy of the home and were welcomed in. A revolution had taken place. And another took place when FDR began broadcasting his fireside chats, personalizing the relationship between national leaders and the electorate.

These myriad voices on radio, from Kate Smith and Lowell Thomas to Walter Winchell, from *Ma Perkins* to *Our Gal Sunday,* from *One Man's Family* to *The Lux Radio Theater,* became part of American lives, listened to across the nation, beginning the process of creating a more homogeneous society. Television only finished off the leveling job that radio had begun.

Of course there had always been brilliant talk. Oscar Wilde's epigrams were famous. There were the great orations in Congress and in Parliament. There were the French salons of the seventeenth and eighteenth centuries, the formal "Conversations" held in Boston by the transcendentalist Margaret Fuller, the overpublicized quips of the Algonquin crowd.

But these were all essentially elitist, with no trickle-down to the population as a whole. If, in the nineteenth century, photography brought the actual look of things to everyone, it was the twentieth-century technologies of phonograph and radio and film that democratized talk. Yes, the century of talk began with the miracle of the telephone, which first ushered outside voices into the home. But these voices were mostly familiar ones—relatives, friends, colleagues. It was the bombardment of voices from the outside world—first through radio, eventually through sound film—that proved irresistible.

And then the glamour and freshness began to fade. Fifteen years after the takeover by sound there were still unforgettable talkers on the screen, but they tended to be mordant or even dangerous oddballs—Waldo Lydecker (Clifton Webb) in *Laura* (1944), Addison DeWitt (George Sanders) in *All About Eve* (1951). Dialogue, which had vitalized the screen in the thirties, was making way for the look of noir, for epic (back to DeMille), for a Brando, a Doris Day (she may have made *Pillow Talk,* but the talk was nothing special). By the time European art film had come into its own—the nouvelle vague, Bergman, Fellini, Antonioni—talk, the province of writers and actors, had given way to the reign of the director. Who remembers the dialogue in *L'Avventura?* Did it have any?

As I write, it's only the audio book that features the voice, and it's only the cell phone that's keeping oral communication alive. Public radio is motored by content, not by the way people talk. Right now there's only one voice that truly gets to Americans: Oprah's. When she speaks, people listen. There's also our new president. But it's too soon to know whether he's really talking to us or only a master of public speaking.

Bibliography: Ring Lardner, *You Know Me Al* (New York, 1916). Anita Loos, *Gentlemen Prefer Blondes* (New York, 1925). Gerald Nachman, *Raised on Radio* (New York, 1998).

ROBERT GOTTLIEB

1930, March

Irvin S. Cobb, speaking of the Indian actor Buffalo Child Long Lance, says, "To think we entertained a nigger!"

THE SILENT ENEMY

Rewind reel to the premiere of *The Silent Enemy* earlier that year: Irvin S. Cobb, the New York socialite and World War I reporter, had beamed when he introduced Buffalo Child Long Lance to other guests at his Park Avenue apartment. Even in evening dress, tuxedo, or double-breasted suit, the striking chief with straight black hair, chiseled features, and broad shoulders exuded something primordial and fundamental. Whether telling tales of his boyhood on the Great Plains or demonstrating Indian sign language, he seemed real, substantial, when modern life seemed frivolous. Cobb was not the only one taken with Long Lance. Everyone wanted the chief at their party. "A social lion of the season is an Indian—Buffalo Chief Long Lance, who has been invited everywhere," one gossip columnist wrote. When Cobb met him, Long Lance was nearing the height of his fame. His articles about Indian life appeared regularly in *Good Housekeeping, Cosmopolitan,* and other magazines. Cobb himself wrote the foreword to his autobiography titled, simply, *Long Lance,* which told about his boyhood among the Blood Indians on the Great Plains. And Long Lance made his acting debut in 1930, starring in *The Silent Enemy,* a film about a pre-Columbian Ojibwe tribe struggling against starvation. He even had his own running shoe, styled after a moccasin, long before Michael Jordan's time. One reporter identified his appeal thus: "He is an ideal picture Indian because he is a full-blooded one." But he was not who he said he was.

Buffalo Child Long Lance was not born on the Great Plains. He was not a chief. He was not even a Blackfoot. "Buffalo Child Long Lance" was born Sylvester Long, on December 1, 1890, in Winston-Salem, North Carolina. He grew up in a small house in a black community, the grandson of slaves. In the city directory his family was coded as black, and they were treated as black in a time of Jim Crow segregation. As a young boy, Sylvester's two-mile walk to the Depot Street School for Negroes passed through a landscape far less poetic than the plains of tall grass dancing in the wind and purple mountains that he later wrote about. And while the Longs certainly had Indian ancestors, they had no way to prove it nor any connection to them; at the age of nineteen, Sylvester was able to gain entry to the Carlisle Indian School only by use of affidavits from family acquaintances in Winston-Salem attesting to his Indian ancestry. When his family and girlfriend said good-bye to him at the train station, it was the last time all but his brothers ever saw him. It was also the last time he ever rode in a Jim Crow car.

Long Lance was only one of many impostors who posed as and were seen as authentic full-blooded Indians. Iron Eyes Cody, the "Indian with a tear in his eye" in the antipollution TV commercial of the 1970s, was revealed to be Italian in 1996. Chief Seattle's famous speech, supposedly written in 1855 and thought to be so representative of Indian consciousness, included in American Indian anthologies and quoted on posters, postcards, and calendars, was written by a white screenwriter from Texas—"the single highlight of an obscure television script on pollution produced by the Southern Baptist Convention in 1972." *The Education of Little Tree,* heralded in 1976 as the beautiful recollection of a Cherokee boyhood, was later exposed as the writing of another white man, a former speechwriter for George Wallace named Asa Earl Carter. Grey Owl, the lecturer and author who was lionized in the 1930s as the "modern Hiawatha" and tagged with headlines like "There Never Came a Redder Red Indian to Britain," was really an Englishman named Archibald Belaney. Why? Why were the most famous Indians the most invented ones?

The key, perhaps, is that their identities were wrought from art, not reality, the elements borrowed from fiction, such as Cooper's Leatherstocking Tales and Longfellow's *Hiawatha,* Wild West shows, paintings, and photography. The real Indian—the kind that could excite non-Indians and Long Lance himself—was the Indian of art, imbued with the power built into narratives of adventure, epic vanishing, and spiritual quest. The possibility of faking his Indianness existed for Long Lance only because American popular culture was already stocked with the necessary ingredients for the dish—and full of people hungry for that kind of Indian meal. His audience was not interested in "blanket Indians" struggling against the pressure to assimilate. They weren't interested in the loss of land or tribal politics or even native languages. The nuances of culture, history, and present struggle were not half as interesting as cathartic primordiality and wild difference, opened by the clash between the Indian past and the modern present and closed by Long Lance's evocation of the vanished plains. As Cobb wrote in his forward to *Long Lance,* the story "reveals the spirit of the Indian in the years that are gone and the spirit of the times the like of which will never be seen again." Cobb further marveled at Long Lance's ability to put into English thoughts and instincts that were originally framed in a native language—though Long Lance's native language was not Blackfoot. Rather, it was the language of icons. "It isn't an everyday experience," one journalist wrote, "to have for your luncheon companion a full-blooded Indian chief whose conversation brings you the breadth of the great Western plains and whose recital of Indian traditions sends your imagination mounting to dazzling sun-kissed heights." It was that kind of Indian, that power of reference that made Long Lance's identity so appealing. And it was the resonance of so many impostors' personas with stories about Indians that helped them ring true. Ironically, the freedom Long Lance and Grey Owl, Iron Eyes Cody, and so many others had to construct identities and connect themselves with imaginary Indians made them appear *more* authentic to mainstream audiences than real Indians.

The premiere of *The Silent Enemy* at the Criterion Theater on Times Square was the high point of Long Lance's career. Theatergoers came in from a cityscape defined by the newly completed art deco masterpiece, the Chrysler Building, to view a world unmarked by man. Through images of vast, deep woods, and birch-bark canoes slipping through rapids, the audience followed the story of the brave Baluk and his nemesis, the evil medicine man, as the tribe searched for migrating caribou. Instead of incandescent lights, there was firelight playing against the trees. Instead of Iroquois steelworkers, many of whom were just beginning to raise the Empire State Building in record time, audiences saw Indians pitted against the fundamental forces of nature. They saw Long Lance, who played the lead, thrust a spear into a bull moose, capture a bear cub, and ascend his own funeral pyre. It garnered rave reviews: "AMAZING!—because it's REAL!" and "REAL DANGERS! REAL INDIANS! REAL ROMANCE!" But the film, like Long Lance himself, was doomed. Because it was a silent film coming at the very end of its era—talkies were showing at other theaters near the Criterion—*The Silent Enemy* was a commercial failure.

The film had been the brainchild of William Douglas Burden, an upper-class Harvard graduate who, as a child, was often taken to the forests of Quebec, where he was introduced to "the Indians." His experiences gripped his imagination:

> I soon learned how different it is to travel in the woods with an Indian as opposed to a white man. He is silent. He speaks to you only where there is something important to say, and then does so very quietly. He is entirely aware of the forest around him—he notices the wind, the change of direction in the clouds moving over the forest. He is aware of every smell, every sound. By contrast, with a white man you feel like an intruder. You make your own world. The talk is loud and the forest is, so to speak, thrust back and much of its magic disappears.

The magic that Burden wanted to capture in his film was the same magic that New York socialites felt in Long Lance's presence. To have a magical experience of the forest, one might think of being profoundly attuned to the world beyond man, a sense of ancientness, of a reality arching back through time, of wildness and mystery, of what might better be called the sublime. The way that Indians are imagined and written makes them signals of what is real, the counterpoints to a fractured modernity.

Less than half a year before the film's premiere, the stock market had crashed. The contemporary world of the city, with its soup kitchens and newspapers, contrasted sharply with the world of the film. Perhaps, then, "authentic" refers not to historical or cultural reality but instead to psychological reality. A real Indian was the one who looked like it, the one who triggered the sensation of the sublime. A real Indian, in that sense, was Long Lance. No one in the cast received more acclaim for his realness than he. Above all the other cast members, perhaps above any famous Indian of his time, Long Lance exuded the Indianness that captured the audience of *The Silent Enemy*.

But icon is nothing without irony. For Long Lance, one drop of doubt about his Indian identity robbed his persona of its power. While Long Lance impressed partygoers with Indian sign language and even war dances, other Indians in New York City began to talk. While he had "gigs," as he called them, with Mildred

McCoy and Vivian Hart, and danced with Rudolph Valentino's wife, other Indians gossiped that Long Lance was black. Just before the release of *The Silent Enemy*, Chief Chauncey Yellow Robe, also in the movie, told producers what he had been hearing. He added that Long Lance could not speak Cherokee and that he didn't "know the sign language as well as he pretends." Fearing for the authenticity of the film—and the backlash that might result if their star were exposed—the producers confronted Long Lance. He told them that he was Blackfoot but had been taken in by the "part negro" Long family in Winston-Salem after being injured in a Wild West show. They wanted to believe his story. Ilia Tolstoy, grandson of the Russian writer and a good friend of Burden's, had joined the production for the adventure. He traveled to Winston-Salem to investigate. He found that the Longs—at least Sylvester's brothers—thought of themselves as "negro," but he was also able to get an affidavit from a prominent banker attesting that he and others recognized Sylvester's father, Joe Long, as an Indian. The producers concluded that if the story broke, "The only real harm will be done to Long Lance himself. As far as we are concerned, he is an Indian . . . what tribe he belongs to is entirely secondary."

It was an interesting conclusion. Such was the strength of Burden's desire for authenticity that he had felt unhappy when they had to resort to an airplane expedition to Alaska to film reindeer herds to augment their footage of caribou (the only difference between the two is that reindeer have been domesticated). And yet Molly Nelson, whom the filmmakers found dancing at Texas Guinan's nightclub in New York and cast as Neewa, was a Penobscot woman, Yellow Robe was Dakota, and Long Lance's tribe was "entirely secondary." Ironically, the differences between caribou and reindeer were smaller than the differences between tribes.

However troubled their notion of authenticity, Cobb and others did not equivocate. Their rejection of Long Lance was devastating. Irvin Cobb and the many others who had launched Long Lance had entertained more than a "nigger"—they had entertained something much "worse"; they had entertained a fantasy more powerful but just as fragile as the human being who pretended to Indianness.

Long Lance's career, even his very self, crumbled. His last years were desperate. He was shunned by those who had once admired him. He drank heavily and fed the cats in the dark alley behind his apartment. His letters to his closest friends reveal both guilt and a sad grandiosity. Life must have felt insubstantial. He took on great risks, learning to fly and performing dangerous plane maneuvers, as if to tease out a feeling of being alive. But the thrill of flight was not enough. On March 20, 1931, he shot himself in the head.

His impromptu death song, sung as he ascended the funeral pyre in *The Silent Enemy*, is, in retrospect, as poignant as it is hokey:

Oh, look down upon me
For thou knowest me—
    The sun, the moon, the day, the night—
Tell me if this is real,

Tell me if this is real —
   This life I have lived.
Tell me if this is real,
   This death I am dying . . .

Now I see — I understand.
No, no life is not real.
No, no, death is not real.
I shall walk on a trail of stars.
I shall walk on a—
Agh, no. Agh, no.
Death is not real.

The loss of identity obviously affected Long Lance deeply. His psychological world collapsed when confronted with doubt. In a 1991 *New York Times* essay, "'Authenticity,' or the Lesson of Little Tree," Henry Louis Gates, Jr., argues that authenticity is not something that can be detected by examining a text "blindfolded." He writes, "No human culture is inaccessible to someone who makes the effort to understand, to learn, to inhabit another world . . . What, then, of the vexed concept of authenticity? To borrow from Samuel Goldwyn's theory of sincerity, authenticity remains essential; once you can fake that, you've got it made." The lesson of Long Lance is that Indianness, in a sense, can *only* be faked, so long as the real Indian is the Indian of art. And Long Lance *did* succeed in faking authenticity. Cobb hadn't perceived some crack in the facade. Judged by the merits of the identity alone, Long Lance had fooled nearly everybody. Consciously or not, Cobb and so many others had been looking for art in life. As soon as one starts debating or wondering whether an Indian is an "authentic Indian," authenticity is lost. And if we want and expect to feel a certain way in the presence of an Indian, we make the same mistake as Cobb.

Bibliography: William Douglas Burden et al., *How the Silent Enemy Was Made,* Souvenir Edition, Paramount Pictures (c. 1930). Philip Deloria, *Playing Indian* (New Haven, CT, 1998). Daniel Francis, *The Imaginary Indian* (Vancouver, BC, 1992). Long Lance, *Long Lance* (Jackson, MS, 1995). Donald B. Smith, *Chief Buffalo Child Long Lance: The Glorious Impostor* (Calgary, Alberta, 2002).

MICAH TREUER

1930, October

Grant Wood's *American Gothic* comes in third at a Chicago Art Institute exhibit

GOING HOME FOR GOOD

In August 1930, President Herbert Hoover appointed representatives from the Federal Reserve, the Federal Farm Board, the Red Cross, banks, and the railroads to form the National Drought Relief Committee in order to at least pretend to address what Secretary of Agriculture Arthur M. Hyde called "the worst drought ever recorded in this country." Meanwhile, back in Iowa, painter Grant Wood went for a ride. At the moment Hyde's department worried that dwindling stores of feed, including hay, in Southern and Midwestern states were in "critical condition," Wood spotted an old white home in the town of Eldon and thought of painting its imaginary owners out front, with the man of the house gripping a hay fork. The pair's outdated clothes would give them a nostalgic air. Or maybe as the 1930s wore on, they would come to appear nostalgic for a time when there was actually hay around to pitch.

By October, Wood's painting, *American Gothic,* would come in third at the Art Institute of Chicago's Forty-Third Annual Exhibition of American Paintings and Sculpture. Museum boosters purchased the work for $300 for the Art Institute's permanent collection, where it remains in the company of Caillebotte and Matisse—real artists from France. A week after the exhibition's opening, Wood's hero and fellow Midwesterner, Sinclair Lewis of Minnesota, would become the first American to win the Nobel Prize in Literature. (Take that, France.) "They had labored, these solid citizens," Lewis wrote in *Babbitt.* Not a stretch to describe Wood's subjects that way too.

Wood, like Lewis (and F. Scott Fitzgerald of St. Paul and Ernest Hemingway of Oak Park), would ditch his hometown for Paris in the 1920s, where he would dab out the sort of blurry paintings of cathedrals he thought he was supposed to like. According to his friend there, the journalist William L. Shirer, one day Wood up and declared:

> I'm going home for good. And I'm going to paint those damn cows and barns and barnyards and cornfields and little red schoolhouses and all those pinched faces and the women in their aprons and the men in their overalls and store suits and the look of a field or a street in the heat of summer or when it's ten below and the snow piled six feet high. Damn it, isn't that what Sinclair Lewis has done in his writing— in *Main Street* and *Babbitt?* Damn it, you can do it in painting too!

Thus Wood gave up on painting dappled French Gothic doors and hightailed it back to Iowa to start painting his famous flat, Gothic Revival window, hung with what Lewis called "curtains of starched cheap lace" probably ordered from the same mail-order catalog as those in Gopher Prairie, the town in *Main Street.* (Insert obligatory mention of the word "regionalism" here, along with legally required passing reference to painters John Steuart Curry of Kansas and the swirling pictorial narratives of Missouri's Thomas Hart Benton.)

If Shirer's memory of Wood's Parisian outburst is to be believed, the painter made good on his pledge to depict "the women in their aprons and the men in their overalls" in *American Gothic.* There's even a "damn barn" over the man's shoulder, presumably to house a few "damn cows" he's fixing to feed with his pitchfork. Though not if the aforementioned drought of 1930 has a say.

Let's start with the apron. It's a fake. The model for the farmer's daughter in the painting is Wood's sister, Nan. She later recalled that her brother requested that she sew an apron with rickrack, a "trim that was out of style and unavailable in stores. I ripped some off Mother's old dresses, and after the painting made its debut, rickrack made a comeback."

Nan's point? This is a history painting. Three years later Wood made *Portrait of Nan*. In it, his sister lets her hair down. She wears makeup and a kicky, sleeveless polka-dot blouse. Compared to the fictional plain Jane in *American Gothic,* actual Nan verges on Veronica Lake. So that rickrack is literally a dead giveaway—that woman, and flinty women like her, according to Wood, are dead and gone so let us now praise famous whatever.

In a 1941 letter, Wood claimed he wanted the painting's daughter to be "very self-righteous, like her father." Her defiant cleanliness, however, is betrayed by a curl breaking free of her tight bun. Wood goes on to say that he "let the lock of hair escape to show that she was, after all, human."

If self-righteousness was Wood's intention, he failed. Trust the painting, not the painter. What we see here is self-doubt. All the starch in Iowa cannot stiffen the look on that woman's face. Her sidelong glance betrays something more interesting than pain—ambivalence. Mixed feelings about her lot in life is the most modern feeling a woman can have. Just ask Carrie Kennicott: "That one word—home—it terrified her."

Kennicott, Lewis's protagonist in *Main Street,* turns down her college sweetheart Stewart's marriage proposal because "I want to do something with life." He rebuts, "What's better than making a comfy home and bringing up some cute kids and knowing nice homey people?" Corny, but a fair point. This, Lewis deadpans, is the "immemorial male reply to a restless woman."

Though Carrie turns down Stewart, she eventually gives up her career as a librarian to marry a doctor from Gopher Prairie, a place that is about as lively as it sounds. Mid-marriage, she abandons him too for Washington, D.C., for a while, to live and work among the suffragettes. Eventually, she gives up and goes back to her husband and Gopher Prairie, though not without screeching, "I do not admit that dish-washing is enough to satisfy all women!" So there!

The woman in *American Gothic* might even have such a backstory, if not an actual inner life. To see her, however, requires actually looking at the painting. This is harder than it sounds. There's a lot of buildup that needs to be cleaned off. Scrape away that postcard of Ronald and Nancy Reagan in rickrack and overalls. As well as Paul Newman and his daughter on a package of Newman's Own organic cookies. Along with the couple singing backup on "Dammit Janet" in the *Rocky Horror Picture Show.* And the opening credits of *Green Acres*—go ahead and sing along while you scrub: "The Chores! The Stores!" The only thing more American than turning *American Gothic* into a sight gag is the way the deep, dark, Norwegian anguish of Edvard Munch's *The Scream* is turned into a fun backdrop for dark chocolate M&Ms. (In America, stores almost always win out over chores.)

After she saw *American Gothic,* august American-in-Paris Gertrude Stein said, "We should fear Grant Wood. Every artist and every school of artists should be afraid of him, for his devastating satire." Certain ladies of Iowa concurred. Historian Steven Biel notes, "An Iowa farmwife, irate over American Gothic, told Grant Wood, by one account, that he should have his 'head bashed in.'"

Grant Wood, *American Gothic* (1930). Oil on beaver board

Wood's upstanding, folksy couple are usually the sort of characters urbanites only care about when Truman Capote writes a pretty book about how they got gunned down. To his more rural fellow Iowans, Wood was a city slicker from Cedar Rapids. So was he making fun of farmers?

Wood claimed he didn't mean to. In that 1941 letter, the artist argues:

> The persons in the painting, as I imagined them, are small town folks, rather than farmers. Papa runs the local bank or perhaps the lumber yard. He is prominent in the church and possibly preaches occasionally. In the evening, he comes home from work, takes off his collar, slips on overalls and an old coat, and goes out to the barn to hay the cow.

In fact, the model for the man in overalls was not a farmer but Wood's dentist, Byron McKeeby. In the letter, Wood goes on to say that he "did not intend this painting as satire." He adds, "It seems to me that they are basically solid and good people. But I don't feel that one gets at this fact better by denying their faults and fanaticism."

As a D.C. suffragette tells Carrie Kennicott in *Main Street,* "Your Middlewest is double-Puritan—prairie Puritan on top of New England Puritan; bluff frontiersman on the surface, but in its heart it still has the ideal of Plymouth Rock in a sleet-storm." Wood's pair lives up to that assessment—they're a tad too churchy but they won't give up. There are worse sentiments for a painting made in the first year of the Great Depression to have.

American Gothic asks the same question of the country it asks of its prim couple staring down the viewer: is the basic, earthy goodness and potted-plants-on-the-porch cheer of the United States weakened by its preachy, confrontational zeal? Answer: yep. But that doesn't mean the painting—or the country—is all that funny.

Bibliography: Steven Biel, *American Gothic: A Life of America's Most Famous Painting* (New York, 2005). Wanda M. Corn, "The Birth of a National Icon: Grant Wood's American Gothic," in *Reading American Art,* ed. Marianne Doezema and Elizabeth Milroy (New Haven, CT, 1998). Thomas Hoving, *American Gothic: The Biography of Grant Wood's American Masterpiece* (New York, 2005). Jane C. Milosch, ed., *Grant Wood's Studio: Birthplace of American Gothic* (Cedar Rapids, IA, 2005).

SARAH VOWELL

1931, March 19
Nevada legalizes gambling

PLACE YOUR BETS

On March 19, 1931, Governor Fred Balzar of Nevada signs two measures into state law: one (returning to the old tradition of Nevada, set aside in the years 1910 to 1931) that gaming, or gambling, should be legal in the state; the other, that the residency qualification for divorce be halved from three months to six weeks.

Some in America regard this as "beyond the pale" and typical of what "they" do "out there." A Methodist conference demanded federal action. The two measures were widely interpreted as concessions to depravity—which, in time and the tidal sequence of revenge, might help qualify Nevada as a place where noxious weapons systems should be tested, and where—one day—the nation's unwelcome deposits of radioactive wastes and other toxic substances may be buried within Yucca Mountain. Yucca Mountain is in the western reach of Nevada, not far from the California border, but prevailing winds would carry any damage east. The plan for the dump site is passed, yet it faces legal objections and the wrath of Nevada. You could say it was a profound or far-reaching policy, but it is a guess too, involving complicated calculations about seepage time in various kinds of rock. The long view—say 20,000 years—may be necessary for an answer, but a lot of Americans think 20,000 years is a joke.

The acts of 1931 did seem to stop the state's decline and nullity: Nevada's population has fallen to a mere 77,407 in 1920 (in a place of over 110,000 square miles), but by 1940 it is up to 110,247. As of 2000 it is 2.6 million. It has been for thirty years the most expansive state in the union, and it is now a favorite place for decent Americans, probably divorced at some stage of their lives, almost certainly vulnerable to a wager (perhaps over this month's fight of the century at the MGM Grand), to retire and watch the sun set.

Of course, the two measures are related, and it may be easiest to see that in terms of an American novel: thus in 1931, in old but steadfast age, Mrs. Isabel Osmond travels to Reno—*the* Nevadan city still—to secure her divorce from Gilbert Osmond (decrepit and stroke-afflicted these many years in a villa outside Florence). In doing so, Mrs. Osmond—the lady once portrayed by Henry James—is owning up to the unlikelihood of marriage as a contract enriched by abiding love and fondness or as an unbreakable condition of social stability. She is attesting to the alternative construction—one that will be proved over and over by the divorce statistics of the later twentieth century—that love and marriage are gambles in which the citizen (let alone the healthy and romantic red-blooded American lover) has a right to some safety net or "escape clause." It is said that during Mrs. Osmond's six-week wait in Reno, she meets and looks with warmth on a young cowboy actor, Gary Cooper, who is in town to console a woman of his acquaintance as she waits on her divorce. But that's another story.

We do not think of Henry James as an habitué of gaming clubs. Or of gaming strategies. But be careful not to be browbeaten by that solemn gaze or James's large air of exercised judiciousness. He knew the element of risk, or hazard, in any story. *The Portrait of a Lady,* remember, ends up in the air, with Henrietta Stackpole's suspenseful, "Just you wait and see!" Are we to expect something unusual to turn up? And isn't that the way James's own mind—his narrative process—is wondering for twenty years or more as he takes longer and longer to account for the contradictory processes of rationalization or decision making in his characters? Isn't James actually a novelist who comes to a brink of inaction as he sees more and more choice confronting his own characters and confounding his own determinative authority?

Why not? James was the well-read novelist, as alert to the melodramatic assertion in Dostoyevsky that "God is dead" as to the steady disappearance of godliness or religious justice in the parsonage-laden landscape of the English novel. When Dickens looks at the chance of a foundling being reestablished as an heir, he hardly counts on the forces of law and order or religious intervention (churchmen are the missing figures in Dickens's social panorama). He is already reliant on fate, or its echo in his own busy mind—the music of plot-making. The novelist sees himself as being in charge of his own world. Nothing contributes as much to the vitality or the sense of moment in the nineteenth-century novel. So novelists leave us with degrees of hope (or nostalgic faith). Dickens does believe that fate will secure a "happy" or crowd-pleasing ending, and Dostoyevsky, the notorious atheist and chronic, self-destructive gambler, cannot shrug off his guilt-ridden feelings of betrayed duty toward sublime figures and exemplary codes. It could even be that his desperate need for ruin is a response to the panic at being deserted by God—in *The Brothers Karamazov* there is not a more resonant moment than when Father Zossima bows before Dmitri in recognition of his exceptional pain. So ask yourself whether Dostoyevsky "believes in" Zossima's power of vision—it's worth a modest bet.

In the European novel, this shift away from the religious basis allows the form to reproduce increasingly complex or unguaranteed levels of ordinary experience. Admittedly, that doubt may seem lofty in Henry James, and it is still aristocratic in Proust, but in *Ulysses* the fusion of intricate levels of experience has been made with the common man and raw sensation. Leopold and Molly Bloom may be losers in life and in their crammed Dublin, but Molly's great assertion knows there is treasure amid the wreckage. We can see such an attempt working in Faulkner, Musil, Dreiser, and even Virginia Woolf. For example, it is Mrs. Dalloway's polite insistence on being more than just a conventional London hostess—on being a sentient human being in the years after the Great War—that makes the day of her party more than a minor festival. It is a day of reckoning or balance. Bloomsday serves the same purpose, and so does the astonishing, dreamlike structure of *The Sound and the Fury*. That novel, like *Ulysses,* says that these people in this book are important not in the eyes of the world, or in their own right, but because the novelist has chosen them, and because they are pitched in ordinariness.

No American novelist of the early twentieth century had a better sense of the vulnerability of the soul to a wager between greatness and anonymity than Theodore Dreiser. Dreiser is known as a "realist," and he is sometimes attacked for his plain, repetitive style. But those common defects do not hide an immense yearning of his imagination for high American success. In his first novel, *Sister Carrie* (1900), we see the social rise of Carrie set against the fall of Hurstwood, the older man who becomes her mentor and lover. The book had publication trouble because of its sexuality and its candid treatment of adultery, but more shocking still is the tacit view of power in status and career and the physics by which improvement here must be countered by failure there. *Sister Carrie*—which is a model for the story line of the classic American film *A Star Is Born*—is way ahead of its time socially and sexually in seeing a love relationship as a kind of wager. Is it sweet to both, or will one party win? Can success be made and retained in America?

Dreiser then wrote a trilogy about a less-than-honest businessman, Frank Cooperwood—*The Financier, The Titan, The Stoic.* These books are terribly neglected now, but it should be enough to point to the pioneering use of a businessman hero to show how deeply Dreiser had perceived the stock market as simply an early, concealed form of gambling and the most dramatic means in American society (short of murder) for that key dynamic, both literary and actual: rapid social transformation. The most American thing about gambling may be the suddenness of the reinvention with which the foundling becomes a titan—it is like the chance that left a poor boardinghouse keeper with a worthless deed from a defaulting boarder that proved to be the rights to the Colorado Lode: the backstory to *Citizen Kane.*

But Dreiser's most fascinating book—and the one most clearly influenced by Dostoyevsky—is *An American Tragedy,* published in 1925 and largely written in a place called Hollywood, California. Clyde Griffiths is the victim of regular American ambition—"This youth, aside from a certain emotionalism and exotic sense of romance which characterized him, and which he took more from his father than from his mother, brought a more vivid and intelligent imagination to things, and was constantly thinking of how he might better himself, if he had a chance." He is the child of poverty—his parents run a church mission in the poor part of the city. But his family is large, and a part of it has money. George seeks that contact. He moves to another city, he gets a menial job in the family factory, and there he meets Roberta—poor, like himself, but ready to be in love. He makes her pregnant. But at the same time he meets Sondra the daughter of wealth, and falls for her. Thus the novel's remarkable dilemma—his ship is coming in, but by then he is committed to Roberta. Isn't he? This is 1925, and moral dilemma has bumped none too gently against pragmatic choice.

Clyde is going to take Roberta to a lake, to go boating. He knows that accidents can happen in such circumstances:

> Oh, dreadful thought! To think it should have come to him! And at this time of all times—while she was demanding that he go away with her.
>   Death!
>   Murder!
>   The murder of Roberta!
>   But to escape her of course—this unreasonable, unshakable, unchangeable demand of hers! Already he was quite cold, quite damp—with the mere thought of it. And now—when—when—! But he must not think of that! The death of the unborn child, too!!
>   But how could any one even think of doing any such thing with calculation—deliberately? And yet—many people were drowned like that—boys and girls—men and women—here and there—everywhere the world over in summer time. To be sure, he would not want anything like that to happen to Roberta. And especially at this time. He was not that kind of person, whatever else he was.

Of course, Clyde *is* that kind of person—and Dreiser is brilliant at catching the tone of the infernal debate or gambling premeditation in his mind. The great skill of the novel is to leave the actual death subject to the possibility of accident.

While dwelling so gloomily on murder, Clyde loses his alertness so an accident occurs. That is even more deliberately pursued in the 1951 movie of the novel—*A Place in the Sun,* with Montgomery Clift, Shelley Winters, and Elizabeth Taylor. And in the movie "George Eastman" (his new name) meets the electric chair knowing that too great a part of him wanted to kill "Roberta," accident or not. Of course, in 1951, such a ploy was required to satisfy censorship on a very successful film (a film in which every voyeur watching wants Shelley Winters tactfully dead, so that the seething fantasy close-ups of Clift and Taylor can be indulged). But here is the sharpest irony: in 1952, in the first great surge of building in Las Vegas, a new casino-hotel, The Sands, was opened. And the legend was inscribed over the door, as a promise to so many Clydes and Georges whose great break might be available inside—"A place in the sun."

Gambling is a fantasy. Every shred of reason and intelligence and statistical knowledge says, yes, you might win the big one, and you might become in a few minutes at least the great Gatsby, or Montgomery Clift, or the writer of every book you've ever cherished. So, take a hard-working, Protestant country like the U.S. of A., and somehow in a trice it becomes addicted to this long-shot orgasm, this very unlikely triumph over all odds. And so we stand over the cards or a choice at marriage with the same spurious courage, we determine to be gamblers. Rather than settle for the hardboiled noir eternity of losers (it really isn't that hard to lose every day for eighty-five years), we tell ourselves we might win and believe we are the opposite of insane. The authors of our lives. We won't get far in understanding gambling without realizing how a convulsive wave of dementia has fueled the greatest of all nations. It isn't just the way California lives on such seismic faults, or the rest of America yields to natural disasters every decade. It's not even amassing the greatest arsenal of destructive weapons, or hinging ourselves to a crash-ready economy. It isn't simply the beacon of our own immense destruction of energy of which Las Vegas is a shining example so that you can see it beneath the horizon coming across the desert. It's also the stoic determination to take the game on its terms, to "play it as it lays"—accept the cards dealt to you. Don't explain, don't complain. If God no longer exists, forget the longer view and trust that that croupier—your hit man—is keeping proper score.

I should note that gambling in Nevada began very soon after talking pictures and that giddy, wisecracking dream that we all of us could be William Powell and Myrna Loy or Fred MacMurray and Barbara Stanwyck, or Bogey and Bacall, casting insane but lovely lines of dialogue out on the water like land lines in the darkness. Gambling is advertising made interactive.

Gambling destroys lives, family situations, and in time it may corrupt an economy in ways that leave it hopelessly vulnerable—may I tell you that the first casino in Reno, the one that took most early advantage of the new law in 1931, was called the Bank? But that destruction, that funeral for reality and realism is like the proviso that says of life—oh, don't worry, it's not really life, it's just a story we are telling, as if we are Humbert Humbert endlessly debating whether and how he will deflower Dolores Haze until one night she takes him in their sleep with the rapacity and lethal efficiency of an American teenager.

If you go back to Dostoyevsky—and you should, for no writer has been more uncertain over gambling—you will find a narrative that contemplates a malign deed the way any game player must calculate: if I go R-E5 and he counters with QxR, then my knight mates him in three moves. In other words, the action in life becomes an enactment in a story or a continuous performance that makes it stealthy, clammy—recollect that Robert Louis Stevenson said that reading *Crime and Punishment* was like "having an illness." Nothing is authentic now; it's pretty or ugly, like a show.

> Raskolnikov went out in complete confusion. This confusion became more and more intense. As he went down the stairs, he even stopped short, two or three times, as though suddenly struck by some thought. When he was in the street he cried out, "Oh, God, how loathsome it all is! And can I, can I possibly . . . No, it's nonsense, it's rubbish!" he added resolutely. "And how could such an atrocious thing come into my head!"

How, indeed? Except if all ideas or possibilities of plot are lurking there, like the random upheaval of numbers in a computer. We know that metaphor now. We know they nearly tossed a coin for *Sunset Blvd.* as to whether Joe Gillis is telling the story dead, facedown in Norma Desmond's pool, or in the morgue wowing the other stiffs. Either way, it was a dead man's story.

Bibliography: Theodore Dreiser, *An American Tragedy* (New York, 1925); *Sister Carrie* (New York, 1900). Hunter S. Thompson, *Fear and Loathing in Las Vegas* (New York, 1972). *Filmography: Casino,* directed by Martin Scorsese (1995). *Hard Eight,* directed by Paul Thomas Anderson (1997). *A Place in the Sun,* directed by George Stevens (1951).

DAVID THOMSON

1932

Edmund Wilson maps the Great Depression

THE AMERICAN JITTERS

In 1932 Edmund Wilson published *The American Jitters: A Year of the Slump.* For a year he had wandered the United States as a roving reporter for the *New Republic;* now he distilled his wide-ranging view into a compact, frightening study of a nation in disorder. Wilson recorded the bewilderment of the hapless, honorable Republican senator Dwight Morrow in 1931 and the triumph of the Democrats in 1932, listened to the leaders of the Communists being interrogated by a congressional committee and interviewed Dan O'Brien, the King of the Hoboes. He marveled at the constructive and destructive powers of American technology in Detroit, where he examined the savage logic of Henry Ford's system of manufacture and labor relations, and in New York, where he explored the melancholy new Empire State Building, with its long toll of workers' deaths. In Los Angeles and San Diego, Wilson peered with fascination at the evangelists and with pity at the

Midwesterners who had come to die on the coast, which he saw as America's last, grim jumping-off place. He even walked the mean streets of Staten Island and North Jersey, where he reported on murders and suicides committed by working men who had lost their jobs and identities in the slump.

Thrilling in its range of content, *The American Jitters* is even more remarkable for the boldness and precision of its language. Wilson devised a colorful, vivid, and indecorous tongue to convey the sheer energy of the new American factory: "Twice a day the old liquefied cars are poured out through the backside of the furnace into receptacles like huge iron buckets: a hot stink, a thunderous hissing, the voiding of a molten feces of gold burned beyond gold to a white ethereal yellow, a supreme incandescence, while a spray of snow-crystal sparks explodes like tiny rockets." He captured the qualities of cities with a parody of realtor's spiel, as brash and bitter as Groucho Marx's soliloquy on stucco in a recent movie, *The Cocoanuts:* "And here we are in beautiful Beverly Hills—all flats, it is true, but what flats!—classy homes of real French flimsy-flamsy, coffee, toffee, chalky, cream, chrome and bluff." And he caught the temperaments of individuals, from policemen to politicians to shanty-dwelling countrymen, with the skill of a portraitist, a Weegee of the weekly magazine: "A. J. Muste is a lean Netherlander who resembles a country schoolmaster and stands in the posture of a preacher, his hands clasped in front of him and his head tilted back, looking down his long nose through his spectacles with an expression at once dreamy and shrewd."

Most striking of all were the many passages where he let others speak. Wilson reported, often at length, the words of autoworkers in Michigan, Wobblies on the Colorado River, and workers from the textile factories in Lawrence, Massachusetts. Their jaunty courage gave his stories a vernacular dignity that he clearly prized: "On Fridays we all wore a clean cap, and I used to get a kick out of it"; "You get a kick out of pulling off a strike—get sent to San Quentin and get a kick out of it!"; "Don't you think them folks is right?—I think everybody ought to be with 'em!—all the workin' people in the United States ought to be with 'em!"

What pulled these episodes together was not a program or a proposal. Wilson believed that the Depression had called American institutions into question, but he had not yet fixed on an answer to it, and he showed amusement, as well as respect, for the American Communists. Rather, Wilson's selection of witnesses and details made clear the implicit moral implications of his engaged journalism. Half a decade before James Agee and Walker Evans set out to capture the lives and worlds of Southern sharecroppers, a decade before their *Let Us Now Praise Famous Men* appeared, Wilson found beauty and passion in the everyday lives that the slump had derailed.

Most of those who remember Wilson now think first of the persona he adopted in his later years: that of a man of letters in the mold of Samuel Johnson, who wrote in muscular plain prose about rereading classic American and British literature and revisiting the resort hotels and Christmas pantomimes of his affluent youth—a nostalgic man of the nineteenth century, as he sometimes described himself, solidly established in his houses on the Cape and in Talcottville, in upstate New York, looking backward, and at his best when offering a new interpretation of Henry James. But the Wilson who reported in *The American Jitters* was a relatively young man of the left. To convey the endlessly shifting metropolitan and industrial world that he lived in, he crafted a modernist prose that shared elements with that of his friends Fitzgerald and Dos Passos, an energetic, even syncopated English, well matched to skyscrapers and airplanes: "Big red bee-body of the motor always outside the window, with its barb-armed behind and blunt head—springs quivering in the fierce jingle and continual beat of the rhythm—what if that thick hoop that keeps them in place flew off.—Leo Wolman's brother Sam met a man in the lavatory at the Carlton who asked him what he thought of the conference."

The Wilson who recorded the worst year of the Depression in such unchastely vivid detail had prepared for his task through much of his varied career. The son of a distinguished, eccentric lawyer, he grew up in New Jersey, bookish and dreamy. As a boy at the Hill School and a young man at Princeton, he studied classics and Romance languages with the inspiring teachers Alfred Rolfe and Christian Gauss. They taught him to love grammars and dictionaries, and to set texts into historical and moral contexts—elements of scholarly self-discipline that he would cherish even when his life was at its most rackety. They also taught him to love the sound and rhythm of poetry, making him a close student of prosody and metrics—formal qualities of texts that fascinated him throughout his life. More generally, Gauss and his other teachers—above all, the philosopher Norman Kemp Smith—exemplified a particular style of intellectual life. Deeply informed about the world and the past, they were also unfazed by crossing borders and always ready for conversation on any subject. Wilson carried this model, which he sometimes called "humanistic," into the world outside the academy, and never abandoned it.

After leaving Princeton, Wilson spent time at an army camp in training and worked briefly as a reporter at the *New York Sun*. From 1917 to 1919 he took part in the war, first in a military hospital where he saw his share of horrors and more, and then in military intelligence. Watching the victims of poison gas and piling up the corpses of those who died from influenza confirmed a skeptical tendency that had its roots, for Wilson as for many others in his generation, in the reading of Shaw and Mencken. Once released, he returned to New York and began writing as a freelance journalist. One of his pieces amused Dorothy Parker, and soon he found himself managing editor of *Vanity Fair*. He would spend the 1920s there and at the *New Republic*, working as an editor and writing as a journalist.

Through the 1920s, Wilson produced a stream of articles on theater and literature, opera and ballet. He covered a wide field, always treating the present from the standpoint of one steeped in the standards and accomplishments of the past. In one characteristic piece, published in 1927, Wilson described himself dining in a speakeasy, where he read the Roman satirist Persius in an eighteenth-century British translation, pondered the meaning of literary tradition, listened to E. E. Cummings denounce the executions of Sacco and Vanzetti—and appreciated both the "stubborn endurance" of the classical tradition and the value of Cummings's language, as powerful as it was unpolished. Like Mencken, Wilson became an advocate for recent and contemporary literature. His short, sharp critical pieces were the first, or among the first, written by an American to state, with force and exactness, what was new in the writing of Joyce, Eliot, and Hemingway. When Wilson read *In Our Time* he immediately pronounced it "strikingly original," thanks to Hemingway's ability to suggest "moral values through simple statements."

One side of Wilson's early working life went on work of this kind: producing, and helping others to produce, clear accounts of what was new in the literature, art, photography, and architecture of his time. The standards he imposed on himself and those who wrote for him as an editor transformed weekly magazine reviewing into criticism of a new kind, not academic, but often erudite and always serious—as serious an art as Mencken had practiced, but more disciplined in both form and content. This Wilson, described by Cummings as the "man in the iron necktie," praised the craftsmanship and precision of an older school of novelists and poets even as he insisted on the need to make a new literature.

But there was another Wilson as well—the Wilson whose sophistication shocked Fitzgerald, when he saw the onetime "shy little scholar of Holder Court" swinging his cane in a New York street. The first time that Wilson sat on the floor at a party with Edna St. Vincent Millay, he felt "very Bohemian." But soon he became a habitué of the bars and railroad flats of Greenwich Village. A sexual innocent in college—Wilson consulted a doctor when he had an emission of semen while reading—he soon found women as fascinating as literature. His new passion led to a series of marriages—the most famous, and stormy, was with Mary McCarthy—and a much longer series of encounters with women of every kind, from the wives of friends to prostitutes he picked up on the street. It also inspired him to work up a new form of prose—one that could treat the erotic, without illusions, as part of modern life. An endless series of descriptions of sex and the female genitalia, precise and literal, became a central feature of the mosaic-like diaries in which Wilson stored his impressions of people and books for literary reuse.

Like the great newspaper writers of Vienna and Berlin in the twenties, Joseph Roth, Gabriele Tergit, and Kurt Tucholsky, Wilson applied all his gifts of precise observation and polished description to the most modern forms of popular entertainment—such as the Tiller Girls, those highly trained dancers whose kick line mimicked the uniformity and precision of the new factories. Wilson saw immediately that Gilbert Seldes's "audacious" *Seven Lively Arts* of 1924 would have an essential part in the transformation of American attitudes to artistic life. He too knew that "the magic tune, the racy flash of characterization, the moment of mad laughter" all played central roles in the new movement in the arts that linked Chaplin and Krazy Kat to Edith Sitwell, the Dadaists, and Cocteau. He portrayed the city's streets and entertainments with loving precision in his own novel, *I Thought of Daisy,* at the end of the twenties.

The two Wilsons merged, for a moment, in *The American Jitters,* and their connection was fruitful. But it was not stable. The intellectual Wilson, with his stern face and powerful mind, could not remain satisfied with the journalist's brilliant descriptions and universal irony. He looked for solutions—and found them, for a time, laid down by Marx and Engels and realized in the new society of the Soviet Union. Wilson studied Russian, spent some adventurous and dangerous months exploring the new Soviet society, and, over time, drew up an epic history of the Marxist movement—*To the Finland Station,* which began with Giambattista Vico's declaration that men make their own history and ended with Lenin's return to Russia in 1917. Too craggy and critical to accept the Marxist verities for long, too straightforward to stay with the *New Republic* as it followed the Stalinist line, Wilson tired of both political philosophy and practical politics.

Unlike many other intellectuals whose Marxist inspiration guttered out, Wilson was not attracted to the academic study of literature. He thought the newly intricate forms of criticism that flowered in the quarterlies of his middle years as sterile as the pedantic literary histories of his youth. Gradually, he found a new role in the 1940s, as an essayist on literary history. Like Mozart's Commendatore changing in reverse, from flesh into stone, he seemed to become the marmoreal man of letters, human only in his prejudices against mystery novelists and Kafka.

Yet Wilson always remained too complex, and too conflicted, to settle into any single literary role. He scandalized the remaining censors with his satirical and erotic collection of connected stories, *Memoirs of Hecate County,* in one of which he returns to the bars and dance halls of his youth, and with his searing account of England and the Continent just after World War II, *Europe without Baedeker.* Much of his time in the 1950s went on a massive and powerful literary history of the Civil War, *Patriotic Gore*—a work that denounced the war, as Wilson also denounced World War II, as mass slaughter with no higher meaning. The book found little response at first in a nation celebrating the Civil War centenary.

Wilson in this period lost most of his interest in new literature, and sometimes allowed his Johnsonian pose to reach impossible dimensions—as when he tried to teach his old friend Nabokov Russian. Nonetheless, he continued to explore new worlds—from the Indian societies of upstate New York, Canada, and the West, to the Francophone literature of Quebec and Haiti, to the literature and culture of Russia and Hungary. In the most original of his late writings, his *New Yorker* articles of 1955 on the Dead Sea Scrolls and the book he later published from those articles, Wilson even managed to bring together for one last outing the eager explorer of little streets and literary parties and the erudite master of languages and traditions. His work both revealed a bold new society and culture taking shape and blew open a scholarly world most of whose inhabitants had refused to take interpretative risks as they wrestled with the new texts that the Judaean desert had revealed. Like his early self—and like the many writers of the 1930s and after, from John Hersey and Vincent Tubbs to John McPhee and Calvin Trillin, who would carry on the experiment of *The American Jitters* and turn nonfiction narrative reporting into a high art—Wilson always knew how, as he once explained, to "load solid matter into notices of ephemeral happenings" and slip "over on the routine of editors the deeper independent work which their over-anxious intentness on the fashions of the month or the week have conditioned them automatically to reject." His work of the early 1930s marked the beginning of a long and heroic period in American magazine writing, which is only now coming to an end.

Bibliography: Edmund Wilson, *The American Earthquake: A Documentary of the Twenties and Thirties* (New York, 1958, 1964); *The American Jitters: A Year of the Slump* (New York, 1932); *Letters on Literature and Politics, 1912–1972,* ed. Elena Wilson (New York, 1977); *The Shores of Light: A Literary Chronicle of the Twenties and Thirties* (New York, 1952); *The Thirties: From Notebooks and Diaries of the Period* (New York, 1980); *The Twenties: From Notebooks and Diaries of the Period,* ed. Leon Edel (New York, 1975).

ANTHONY GRAFTON

1932

Arthur Miller auditions to be a radio singer in the Brill Building

DEATH OF A SALESMAN

By 1932, the Depression had forced serious changes in Arthur Miller's formerly prosperous immigrant Jewish family. His father's coat business had failed, the family had to move from their lavish Central Park apartment to a small home in Brooklyn, and his brother had dropped out of college to help the family make ends meet. The sixteen-year-old Arthur decided to take matters into his own hands and follow his dream of becoming a radio star. In his memoir *Timebends,* Miller describes his early love of Hollywood and Broadway show tunes. At his first audition he sang a ballad by "his favorite," Lorenz Hart, and he remembers humming the song, "If I Had a Talking Picture of You," by Buddy DeSylva and Lew Brown (1929), until he realized, to his adolescent horror, that it was a mushy love song.

> If I had a talking picture of you,
> I would run it every time I felt blue.
> I would sit there in the gloom of my lonely little room
> And applaud each time you whispered, "I love you; love you."

Miller also recalls weekly Saturday afternoon attendance at the local vaudeville theater: "always the most anticipated day of the week, the opening acts—the mildly amazing Chinese acrobat families with their spinning plates and flying children." He remembers fondly the great performers he saw week after week: "jokers and singers like Eddie Cantor and George Burns and Al Jolson and George Jessel, the black tap dancers Buck and Bubbles and Bill 'Bojangles' Robinson, and the headline acts like Clayton, Jackson, and [Jimmy] Durante."

Arthur Miller is rarely mentioned in the same breath as Hart, Cantor, or Durante. Rather, Miller is known as one of the most important of America's "legitimate" dramatists, a master of midcentury psychological-realist drama of high moral seriousness. Despite the high-culture goals of the playwright himself and many scholars of his work, Arthur Miller's plays are part and parcel of American popular culture, and their success gains clarity when understood in an American theatrical canon that includes not only Eugene O'Neill's *Long Day's Journey into Night* and Tennessee Williams's *A Streetcar Named Desire,* but also Hammerstein and Kern's *Show Boat,* Rodgers and Hart's *Pal Joey,* and the *Ziegfeld Follies.* This comparison between the plays of Arthur Miller and the more popular Broadway styles of the 1920s, 1930s, and 1940s seems counterintuitive. Miller himself worked hard to create distance between his work and those of popular culture, arguing that *Death of a Salesman* is a classical tragedy, claiming theatrical role models—Shaw, Ibsen, Odets—who had little truck with the world of vaudeville and musical comedy, and insisting that his own work favored reality over what he disparagingly called "theatrics." In numerous essays, Miller opposed the self-conscious theatricality that characterized popular entertainment, even if Miller the teenager had once found pleasure and inspiration in it. In fact, at first glance it is easier to find evidence of a passionate *anti*-theatricality in Miller's plays than the kind of liberating self-fashioning and playful artifice that made writers like Hart or performers like Cantor so beloved by their audiences.

Arthur Miller was a prolific writer, with twenty-four plays and screenplays, four works of fiction, multiple essays, and a memoir to his name. His reputation as America's most celebrated playwright, however, stems from the success and influence of his earliest plays, *All My Sons* (1947), *The Crucible* (1953), and especially *Death of a Salesman* (1949), all of which are devoted to the unmasking of hypocrisy, artifice, and illusion. These plays condemn those who live within a world of illusion, those who lie, and especially those who lie to themselves. In each play, Miller creates dramatically rich central characters—Joe Keller, Willy Loman, Abigail Williams—whom he then critiques for the very theatricality that makes them so powerful on the stage. The better these characters perform, the more immoral they are judged to be.

This anti-theatricality appears early in *All My Sons,* when Joe Keller describes how he reestablished his position after being accused of selling defective airplane parts that led to the deaths of numerous navy pilots. With his characteristic charisma, Joe describes his homecoming:

> Listen, you do like I did and you'll be all right. The day I come home, I got out of my car;—but not in front of the house . . . on the corner . . . Everybody knew I was getting out that day; the porches were loaded. Picture it now; none of them believed I was innocent. The story was, I pulled a fast one getting myself exonerated. So I get out of my car, and I walk down the street. But very slow. And with a smile . . . Fourteen months later I had one of the best shops in the state again, a respected man again; bigger than ever.

Joe's genius is his ability as a performer. No matter what really happened, no matter how his audience has prejudged him, when he emerges from his car, he *performs* innocence. He parades past the porches, filled with spectators like the rows in a theater, and without even a word, he persuades his spellbound audience to believe him. But unlike the audience of neighbors within the play, the audience of *All My Sons* is intended to view his act with horror. Joe has been so corrupted by the values of the materialistic society in which he lives that he doesn't see performance as a lie until the very end, at which point he promptly shoots himself. Likewise, artifice brings down an entire community in *The Crucible*. Abigail Williams is a brilliant actress, but the more successful her performance, the more manipulative, selfish, and immoral she appears to be. The members of the community who are, like a submissive audience, so easily deluded by Abigail are held equally responsible for the tragic results of the witch hunt. Her lover, John Proctor, is a hero and a martyr because it is he who sees through her act, exposing the truth in conceals. *Death of a Salesman* rejects the theatricality of its title character even more categorically. Willy Loman's star turn—which takes the form of a nervous breakdown—is thoroughly crippling. Audience members are meant to pity a man so wholly deluded by theatrics, but certainly not to be deluded by theatrics themselves.

Miller came of age as a writer in a deeply anti-theatrical moment in American culture. In the wake of the Depression, World War II, the postwar House Un-American Activities Committee investigation of the entertainment industry, and persistent racial segregation, many writers were questioning the viability of American self-invention and the certitude that skill, merit, and willpower could triumph over the accidents of birth and race. This mythology, which formed a secular faith for many in the immigrant generation of Miller's parents, is closely linked with theatricality, encouraging the performance of identity as the route to personal liberation and social mobility. But by the postwar period, numerous writers like Miller were lamenting the naïveté and complicity of those who continued to believe in the power of performance. Nonetheless, even in the work of an author determined, as Miller wrote in the introduction to his *Collected Plays* (1957), "to be as untheatrical as possible," this American commitment to self-made mobility is never quite defeated. It is the resiliency of this belief that renders Miller's plays distinctively American.

The struggle over the morality and effectiveness of theatricality is most blatant in *Death of a Salesman,* a play in which the overt content is clearly anti-theatrical: the American dream of material success is presented in this play as a con, a cruel deception that destroys the common man. Willy's imaginative life, his ability to speak to people who are not there, to bring the past to life, to invent and reinvent scenes of conflict and joy on the stage, defines him not as an artistic genius (as might have been the case in a different play or at a different historical moment), but as mentally unbalanced. The realist dramaturgical style of *Death of a Salesman* also emerges from anti-theatrical impulses: the overarching goal of Miller's psychological realism is to represent, as closely as possible, a believable world that will allow audiences to forget that they are in the theater for the three hours of the play. Actors in the realist theater work hard to become, as fully as possible, their characters, avoiding the habits of performers in more self-consciously theatrical genres—exaggerating gestures, voice, or emotions, breaking character, referring self-consciously to the audience beyond the footlights. But this stylistic goal of creating a perfect illusion on the stage contradicts the depiction of Willy's dire psychological state. Audiences have delighted in this play *because* it allows them to take Willy for the kind of real person he fatally mistakes his brother Ben to be. In taking illusions for realities, Willy behaves like an audience member at a realist play, but, unlike the audience, Willy suffers tragically from his delusion. Theatrical illusion thus represents, in *Death of a Salesman,* both Willy's (and America's) moral problem and the strategy for solving that problem.

Death of a Salesman is a realist play, but Willy's performance within it contains strong echoes of other popular theater forms. Popular musical theater and vaudeville are episodic, for example, with a clear division between story and song in musicals, and rapid movement between different performance modes in vaudeville. This episodic structure is distinctly not realist: it prevents audiences from forgetting that they are in a theater and demands self-consciousness on the part of both actors and spectators. We see vestiges of this self-consciously theatrical episodic structure in *Death of a Salesman* in the constant shifting between the present and past, the real and the remembered. In a musical, when a character's emotions reach a peak and the character can no longer express those feelings in a scene, the character breaks into song. Instead of breaking into song in *Death of a Salesman,* Willy goes into a memory. As is appropriate for the star, Willy gets all of the good songs and his family serves as the supporting chorus. Memory scenes— like musical numbers—are generally introduced by instrumental music and a change in lighting. In the first memory scene, the stage directions indicate that "music insinuates itself as the leaves appear." In the introduction to the second memory scene, "music is heard as behind a scrim." In dramatizing an alternate version of the characters and events of Willy's life, Willy's memory scenes use the power of the uplifting musical number to reimagine and reinvent the self in a way consistent with the central American myth that the play purports to critique.

To "break the fourth wall"—the invisible, imagined wall that divides the stage from the audience—is to commit an unforgivable breach of the rules of dramatic realism. In popular theater of the early twentieth century, however, especially in vaudeville and musical comedy, the fourth wall was highly permeable. Audiences frequently communicated with the players on stage, applauding and demanding encores, shouting out directions to the actors, and sometimes even "stopping the show." Actors showed an awareness of the audience as well, making self-conscious asides directed at the audience, breaking character to bow after musical numbers, even taking requests from the audience. Willy Loman continually threatens the stability of the fourth wall in the memory scenes of *Death of a Salesman,* which take place on the apron downstage, outside the realist set and closest to the audience. Willy moves back and forth between the two stages—his mind and the world—continually traversing the walls that should (according to the play, at least) keep a more sane man contained. At the end of the play, Willy directly acknowledges the audience ("There's all kinds of important people in the stands"), and then drives off the stage to his death.

Willy Loman is the most overtly theatrical character in the play, continually wresting the play from its realist moorings and engaging the audience in flights of fancy reminiscent of the self-consciously theatrical forms that permeated Miller's childhood. It is Willy who always has a story, who is always performing, who manages to conjure whole scenes of the past out of thin air, complete with music, lighting, actors, and sets. Willy's despair is rooted in the fear that as a theatrical character, if he runs out of stories, he will cease to exist. "The gist of it is that I haven't got a story left in my head," he tells his sons Biff and Happy. Biff wants to "hold on to the facts," and Willy refuses. Willy simply cannot perform in the style demanded by the play. He believes in the power of a charming face, a strong voice, and a persuasive narrative; the play, apparently, views these as artifice. Willy is incapable of achieving anything tangible with his theatrical hallucinations because the play insists on undercutting their power, on making them the product of insanity rather than inspiration. In *Death of a Salesman,* the breaking of theatrical walls, the following of musical dreams, can represent only a destructive concession to the illusory myth of American freedom and opportunity.

Miller wants to banish artifice; Willy himself is profoundly artful. *Death of a Salesman* celebrates the life and mourns the death of a dreamer who fights against a system that threatens to steal his dreams, to deny him his basic freedom to create himself (even if he is deluded about how effectively he can make use of that freedom). Willy is the one character who believes that it is important to be well liked, and while that appears to get him and his sons nowhere in the world of the play, it goes a long way in the theater. The tension that tears Willy Loman apart is the same tension that makes Miller's plays so popular, and so American. This representation of the gripping struggle between artifice and authenticity characterizes Miller's lasting influence on American literature. The challenge represented by Willy Loman reappears, for example, in Saul Bellow's *Seize the Day* (1956), in which failed salesman and actor Tommy Wilhelm struggles to reconcile his theatrical "pretender soul" with his authentic "real soul." In Arthur Laurents, Stephen Sondheim, and Jule Styne's *Gypsy* (1959), the failed saleswoman, Mama Rose, like Willy, struggles with her two wayward children, and ultimately, in the midst of a nervous breakdown that also echoes Willy's, reveals herself to be the most exquisitely spectacular player of all. David Mamet's *Glengarry Glen Ross* (1984) also owes a clear debt to Miller. As with Willy, the over-the-hill salesman Shelley, although a failure in the cutthroat world of the play, resists his characterization through a stunningly theatrical performance. Tony Kushner's *Angels in America* (1993) celebrates the authenticity of those who are bravely "out of the closet." But the theatrical power of the play is created not by the self-aware Belize or the guilt-ridden Louis but rather by the morally reprehensible character of Roy Cohn, who, like Abigail Williams, uses his theatrical genius to assert his power, and in doing so ends up, in defiance of the play's explicit political intention, celebrated by the very audience that is meant to reject him. Roy Cohn refuses to submit to the vision of hard, real authenticity that the play proposes, and in doing so he, like Joe Keller in *All My Sons* and Abigail in *The Crucible,* and a host of other descendants of Willy Loman in American drama and fiction, taps into the audience's own faith in the American mythology of self-fashioning, even if (perhaps especially if) its promises prove to be illusory.

Bibliography: Arthur Miller, *All My Sons* (1947; New York, 2000); *Collected Plays* (New York, 1957); *Death of a Salesman* (1949; New York, 1998); *Timebends: A Life* (1987; New York, 1995). Brenda Murphy, *Miller: Death of a Salesman* (New York, 1995).

ANDREA MOST

1932, April or May

Diego Rivera meets Henry Ford for a private lunch at Ford's Fairlane Estate

The River Rouge Plant and Industrial Beauty

I regretted that Henry Ford was a capitalist and one of the richest men on earth. I did not feel free to praise him as long and as loudly as I wanted to, since that would put me under the suspicion of sycophancy, of flattering the rich. Otherwise, I should have attempted to write a book presenting Henry Ford as I saw him, a true poet and artist, one of the greatest in the world.

This encomium for Henry Ford appears in a chapter from Diego Rivera's 1960 autobiography, *My Art, My Life.* The chapter, "A Visit with Henry Ford," includes a whimsical reminiscence of a lunch he had with Mr. Ford in early 1932. Rivera would spend eleven months in Detroit on commission to paint the twenty-seven-panel *Detroit Industry* frescoes at the Detroit Institute of Art (DIA). He began the work by visiting a variety of Detroit's industrial plants, in particular spending one month immersed in sketching Ford's 2,000-acre River Rouge manufacturing complex, then one of the wonders of the modern world. Rivera's commission had come not from Henry Ford but from his only son, Edsel, whose image, alongside that of DIA director William Valentiner, holds pride of place at the bottom corner of the great south panel—the muralist's tribute to his patrons.

Edsel, more than any other single person, would withstand a firestorm of outrage from Detroit's financial and religious elite after the murals were unveiled in March 1933. According to critics, *Detroit Industry* was communistic, atheistic, and ugly, a deformation of the museum's charming Italian courtyard. Edsel's patronage and his public defense of Rivera's finished work contrast sharply with the following year's debacle in New York, in Rockefeller Center's RCA Building lobby. Rivera's Rockefeller contract foundered because he painted Lenin among that mural's crowded mass of people. On May 9, 1933, Rivera and his team, at work on their scaffolds, were evicted. The corporation withstood a furious protest from both sides of the Atlantic, and nine months later, in February 1934, pulverized the unfinished work with axes.

In Edsel Ford, Diego Rivera had found the perfect patron for what would become his most important work in the United States. From his understated lakeshore mansion among the city's front-line wealthy in Grosse Pointe, Edsel led the city's efforts to create centers of music and the arts worthy of Detroit's growing stature as a world-class technological center.

Henry differed from his son in almost every regard. By 1932, when he lunched with Rivera at Fairlane, his 1,300-acre estate had become quietly infamous as a fenced and guarded compound. Fairlane stood out in working-class Dearborn, miles across the city from the Grosse Pointes. Apart from a handful of cronies, Thomas Edison and Charles Lindbergh notable among them, visitors were rare. A quarter century earlier, however, a supple and charismatic Ford had led the most creative technological design team in the world. Their core achievement culminated in 1914 when three related innovations—the Model T, the moving assembly line, and the five-dollar day—fused at white heat to form the symbolic identity of "Mr. Ford." The 1908 Model T, perhaps the best match between innovative technological design and market context in U.S. history, had become so popular that demand drove the design team to build a paradigm-breaking factory at Highland Park. Albert Kahn's new wide-open, high-ceiling spaces allowed the team to arrange and rearrange the flow of inputs until, in January 1914, they began operating an integrated moving assembly line. The flow of the line achieved an incomprehensibly complex integration of on-time delivery for thousands of parts that would emerge as a working Model T. That same January, Ford shocked the entire world, his face becoming instantly recognizable from news articles around the globe, when his company announced the five-dollar day for all its workers: a reduction in work time from nine to eight hours a day and a near doubling of the daily wage.

Mr. Ford's iconic status as technological genius and friend of the working man proved durable enough over the next decades to survive harsh public reaction to Ford's increasingly disturbing behavior. By 1919 he had bought out all stockholders and assumed complete control of the corporation. In the same year, during the trial in his libel case against the *Chicago Tribune,* he characterized himself on the witness stand as, to quote the *Nation,* "a Yankee mechanic, pure and simple." The *Nation's* elegiac verdict on Ford continued: "He has achieved wealth but not greatness . . . So the unveiling of Mr. Ford has much of the pitiful about it, if not of the tragic. We would rather have had the curtain drawn, the popular ideal unshattered."

By 1920 the five-dollar-day factory had devolved into the early stages of a spy-ridden police state, even as Ford began to shift central manufacturing operations to the new River Rouge plant across town. The Rouge emerged as an extreme reworking of Highland Park's logistical flow design. Taking advantage of existing rail lines intersecting the property and the Great Lakes' freight hauling capacities, Ford built corporate control of all production inputs into a seamless on-time stream from forests and mine-mouth to specific places on the moving assembly line. More ominously, the Rouge adopted a design feature that would later become infamous in the 1937 "battle of the overpass" at Miller Road Gate 4, when Ford enforcers beat union organizers at the gate and photographs of the confrontation appeared in newspapers across America. Unlike the Highland Park plant, which opened directly onto the public streets, the much larger Rouge complex was fenced, gated, and guarded, a mirror image of Henry's estate a mile up the river. Also troubling were the virulently anti-Semitic diatribes appearing in his newspaper, the *Dearborn Independent,* which a 1927 lawsuit forced him to disavow. In 1938, Henry Ford would receive the Third Reich's Grand Cross of the German Eagle.

Such incidents notwithstanding, Ford's almost sacral popularity showed remarkable staying power in the public mind. In 1923 he was the country's favorite (unannounced) candidate for president. The Ford industrial pavilion was the runaway favorite at the Chicago Century of Progress World's Fair in 1934. Through the 1930s, 150,000 visitors toured the Rouge factory annually and nearly one million toured the pavilion known as the Rotunda (now moved from the Chicago fairgrounds and relocated just north of the Rouge). Visitors were drawn by the mesmerizing sensuality of system integration and materials handling on the assembly lines in the Ford plants. A transcendent sense of awe permeates the occasional written reflections of visitors. The engineer Otto Moog wrote around 1927: "No symphony, no *Eroica,* compares in depth, content, and power to the music that threatened and hammered away at us as we wandered through Ford's workplaces, wanderers overwhelmed by a daring expression of the human spirit."

By 1932, when Rivera came to lunch, Ford's isolation had deepened into neurotic and furtive patterns. He spent many evenings in the Fairlane estate's powerhouse, sometimes working alone in his workshop, sometimes spending time with "the boys" who ran Fairlane's mechanical systems. Other nights he roamed his nearby project, Greenfield Village.

In October 1929, Ford's museum of technology and Greenfield Village, a mock nineteenth-century town, had been dedicated, over a national radio hook-up, by President Hoover and a fragile Thomas Edison, who highlighted a glittering banquet of technological and business elites in the foyer of the still-unfinished museum. Its high-profile dedication notwithstanding, the museum and village would not open to the public until June 1933. Ford sponsored a small school in the village, but whether he perceived the children as students or as props for his nostalgic reincarnation of nineteenth-century small-town America remains in doubt. Even after the public opening in 1934, Ford haunted the village, using a variety of unobtrusive access routes to come and go by day, always remaining at the margins of groups of visitors. Greenfield Village was open to the public only during daylight hours. For the rest of his life, the aging Mr. Ford continued to reclaim his private world in solitary nocturnal wanderings. Sometimes, staff members have reported in oral reminiscences, he pocketed watches from the village's replica repair shop, leaving a luckless craftsman to discover the loss the next morning.

Capricious firings were common in the little world of the museum and Greenfield Village, as they had become in the vast world of the Ford Motor Company. Perhaps most disturbing of all, six weeks before Diego Rivera arrived in Detroit, the city's Depression-driven desperation played out in a violent confrontation at the Rouge factory, where a Communist Party–led hunger march was savagely terminated by a spray of 200 to 300 machine-gun rounds, fired into the marchers outside Gate 3 of the plant. Five days later, some 8,000 marched in the funeral for four dead protesters.

How then to understand Rivera's burst of adulation for the Henry Ford of

1932? How to understand Ford's invitation to the flamboyant Communist for lunch, and his willingness to sign off on Rivera's remarkably open access to the Rouge complex and the still-private museum and village? Ford's motives are particularly elusive. One might argue, after the manner of Anne Jardim's psychological history, that Henry Ford's neurotic proclivities and his well-documented obsession with control were masked by the vast resources he commanded as owner of an industrial empire. The Ford Motor Company's own image management played on and protected his iconic status so effectively that it remains impossible to identify the man in any published statements attributed to him. Rivera wore his passions on his sleeve, but his whimsical reminiscences thirty years after his brief encounter with Mr. Ford do more to underscore the improbable nature of their connection than to explain why it happened at all. Nonetheless, both men left tracks that reveal a deep-seated aesthetic kinship. Both recognized in the other a love for the beauty of mechanical precision and system integration. Rivera's intensity is nowhere more evident than on the great north and south panels of the DIA frescoes. Pulsing with action, ablaze in color, and densely packed with intimate humanity, the murals reveal Rivera's command of classical muralist style. The panels also reveal extraordinary visual insight into the technological constraints of the Rouge's production and assembly systems.

For all the ominous signs of Ford's obsession with control and his increasing discomfort with independent thought or action in his domains, his feel for the beauty of technological precision shows through unmistakably in these same troubling years of Ford Motor Company's dominance. The 1910 Highland Park factory was set back from the site's front on Woodward Avenue to make room along Woodward for a large but conventional executive office building and a decidedly unconventional powerhouse. The powerhouse opened directly onto Woodward Avenue, its nine enormous generators enthroned behind twenty-five-foot-high plate-glass windows that were kept, at Henry's order, impeccably clean. Five years later, when Ford's Fairlane estate took shape on the banks of the Rouge River in Dearborn, Henry attended to the design of one structure in particular, the estate's powerhouse. Modest in scale, it mirrored its giant model on Woodward Avenue in the elegance of its fixtures and its walls of glass.

The most striking evidence of Ford's feel for technological beauty is his supremely self-confident floor layout for the museum. Every machine display area—locomotives, automobiles, machine tools, steam engines, farm equipment, bathtubs—shows off the elegance of his design. Ford, who continually intervened in the museum and village installations, created a floor plan featuring a straight-line entry passage that reprised American progress in the eighteenth, nineteenth, and twentieth centuries. Visitors entered an outsized replica of Philadelphia's Independence Hall, icon of eighteenth-century American democracy. As they emerged onto the eight-acre main floor, they encountered an avenue lined with tractors driven by steam, the nineteenth century's defining technology. The tractors, in turn, framed a massive generator against the back wall, one of the original generators that had powered Highland Park in earlier days.

To miss the disturbing signs of Henry Ford's retreat into a tightly controlled and neurotic world of technological and historical fantasy is to miss the character of this troubling man. To miss, in the same time frame, the unmistakable evidence of a man whose feel for mechanical elegance remained surefooted and confident is to miss the man as well. Was Ford's neurotic desire for privacy and control contained and protected by his vast wealth and the public relations machinery of the corporation? Or, the interpretation favored here, did Ford's wealth allow him to act out, sometimes in excruciating detail, a pervasive societal ambiguity—technology as liberating progress and technology as intimidating master? The increasingly sophisticated systems shaping ordinary life in the twentieth century stimulated fantasies of power while engendering a sense of impotence. What individual could grasp the workings of—let alone control—a world of complex systems? Ordinary people might head to the palatial department stores of the period and savor displays of the good life as a break from fast-paced anxiety. Ford could build his own small world, as full of comforting fantasy as the plate-glass display windows at Macy's, Wanamaker's, or Detroit's own Hudson's.

Rivera, too, suggests an ominous side of the progress that moved him so profoundly in Rouge's technology. In his 1960 memoir he rhapsodizes about Ford's assembly line in language that lifts the Rouge into the realm of the transcendent while at the same time hinting at the power of that same progress to radically diminish individual human beings. "I thought of the millions of different men by whose combined labor and thought automobiles were produced, from the miners who dug the iron ore out of the earth to the railroad men and teamsters who brought the finished machines to the consumer, so that man, space, and time might be conquered, and ever-expanding victories be won against death."

Victories won against death, it seems, require the conquest of humanity as well as space and time. Both Ford and Rivera show the wear of technological progress, as relentless as it was beautiful.

Bibliography: Linda Downs, *The Rouge: The Image of Industry in the Art of Charles Sheeler and Diego Rivera,* exhibit catalogue (Detroit, 1978). Henry Ford, *My Life and Work,* with Samuel Crowther (Garden City, NY, 1922). Thomas P. Hughes, *American Genesis: A Century of Invention and Technological Enthusiasm* (Chicago, 1990). Anne Jardim, *The First Henry Ford: A Study in Personality and Business Leadership* (Cambridge, MA, 1970). Patrick Marnham, *Dreaming with His Eyes Open: A Life of Diego Rivera* (Berkeley, CA, 1998). Diego Rivera, *My Art, My Life: An Autobiography,* with Gladys March (New York, 1960).

JOHN M. STAUDENMAIER, S.J.

1932, Christmas
Ned Cobb remembers standing in a doorway

ALL GOD'S DANGERS

He *does* go on.

Old man Jubal Reed's daughter and old lady Adeline—used to be Adeline Milliken and after old man Jubal Reed married her, him and her had one child and she went

in the name of Maggie Reed. And this old lady Adeline Reed, who was Adeline Milliken before Jubal Reed married her, she had had other men before him. I knowed
em: old man Coot Ramsey come in contact with her enough to have four children and they all went under the Ramsey name—Roland Ramsey, Reuben Ramsey,
Waldo Ramsey, Hector Ramsey. And the last time old lady Adeline—I don't say the
first time and the last time, I say this: when I come in the knowledge of that family
by my daddy marryin in it, she had married to a man by the name of Jubal Reed. She
weren't married to old man Coot Ramsey—he just getting children by this woman
—and she went in the name of Milliken, Adeline Milliken. And my daddy married
in that family to the only child of that old lady Adeline Milliken and old man Jubal
Reed had—she went in the name of Reed, Maggie Reed. And she was half-sister
to old man Waldo Ramsey; Adeline Milliken was the mother for both of em. And I
married Waldo Ramsey's daughter. In 1906, who was this old lady Adeline Milliken's granddaughter. My daddy married Waldo Ramsey's half-sister, Maggie Reed.
And I jumped up and married Waldo Ramsey's daughter. That made Maggie Reed,
you might say, my wife's half-auntie, by Waldo bein Maggie's brother by the same
woman. Well, that drawed me in to be my stepmother's brother's son-in-law—that's
the way we mixed.

Got it?

By 1932, Nate Shaw was in the clear. The federal government had furnished
him at a low interest rate, enabling him to buy fertilizer and other staples at a
time when cotton prices had hit rock bottom. With his crop pooled at a government warehouse and his debt paid in full, Nate sold one of the four bales remaining to buy shoes and clothes for the children, and stored three in the shed.

"And that's where they was standin when I was put in the penitentiary."

Having come up short the previous year Nate had been forced to borrow forty
dollars' worth of feed corn from his landlord, Mr. Lester Watson. But when he
left his bales, worth seventy-five dollars, at the shed in the landlord's name, Watson refused to acknowledge receipt of payment.

"Mr. Watson," said Nate, "what have I ever owed you and didn't pay you?"

"He said, 'You just a fool Negro,' and he walked on off. He had it in for me. He
knew I had good stock and I was a good worker . . . He just aimed to use his power
and break me down."

The boll weevil was devastating the fields, and poor families, white and black,
were leaving for the North. Landlords and merchants had been cutting off food
advances and had reduced day wages for field work. The Sharecroppers Union
had come into the neighborhood, preceded by rumors that they were arming the
colored people. At Crane's Ford, fifteen miles to the north, a sheriff's raid on a
union meeting the previous spring had resulted in the death of one farmer and
the arrest of thirty-five others on trumped-up charges; the sheriff himself had
been shot and killed by one of his deputies.

The union, Nate had heard, was a poor man's organization. "It was goin to rise
us out these old slum conditions which that we had been undergoin since slavery
times . . . I was eager for it, eager." Warned off the union by a white man named
Sloane—"as big a skunk as ever sneaked in the woods"—Nate had found what
turned out to be "just the thing to push me into it—give me orders not to join."

Now a white man named Leonard Wilcox has begun circulating a rumor that come fall Watson is going to attach everything belonging to "his niggers" Virgil Jones and Nate Shaw, and take it himself along with the land. It was right around Christmas when Watson sent the deputy to Jones's place to attach his stock. Nate went over to find a crowd already gathered. He remonstrated with the deputy, who threatened to kill him. Meanwhile a Negro man, Cecil Pickett, entered the lot with bridles to catch the mules—"Oh, they could get some nigger to follow em to hell and back."

When the deputy returned with a carful of officers, Virgil along with other men in the house fled for the swamps. Time seemed to stop; Nate saw himself standing on Jones's front porch "with my hand in my pockets, just so. Only my finger was on the trigger of my pistol and the pistol was in my hand . . . I had on a pair of Big-8 overalls, brand new, and the pockets was deep. And I had on a white cowboy hat and my jumper . . . And a pair of Red Wing boots about knee high." When Shaw turned to enter the house, Deputy Platt shot him three times with buckshot, leaving him standing in a pool of blood. Nate commenced firing his pistol; Platt took cover behind a tree until the entire crew drove off in the car. Not three days later Virgil had been shot dead by vigilantes and "Nate Shaw"— real name, Ned Cobb—was headed for prison.

Some forty years later Ned Cobb went down to the crossroads where the spoken word meets the printed book to make, as he called it, his "report." Theodore Rosengarten, a Harvard graduate student, had come to Alabama with a tape recorder—the same make and model with which Richard Nixon had outfitted the Oval Office—when he heard that the eighty-four-year-old hero of the Sharecroppers Union was still living in what Rosengarten would call Tukabahchee County. Their collaboration produced *All God's Dangers* (1974), autobiography of pseudonymous "Nate Shaw"—pioneering document of oral history, winner of the National Book Award, Book-of-the-Month Club selection—a shocking, interminable, and relentlessly absorbing book that embodies, so far as possible for a book, a life.

Prolix, repetitive, adhesively situational, exhaustive and exhausting, Cobb's story flowed copiously onto the page, sweeping away the economy of literacy in a flood of talk. Nate leads us from his boyhood in the late nineteenth century— his father was born during Lincoln's administration—through the height of Jim Crow, the triumph of the cotton system, the Depression and war, through the civil rights movement, nearly to the moment of his own death in 1973. The name "Roosevelt" appears but once; "Martin Luther King" not at all. The First World War is mentioned only incidentally: "I didn't definitely know who it was in war in them times. And it wasn't clear to me what that war was all about."

Few faraway places really exist for Nate—though he has heard from childhood that the slaves were transported from Africa "like a drove of stock." No, the whole of his story lies in the Alabama hill country, where poor folks black and white raise cotton on patches of unevenly fertile soil under a squirearchy of landlords, merchants, bankers, lawyers, judges, sheriffs, and sheriffs' deputies: for Nate less a story of place than of the land itself, which, worked by powerful mules with names like Kizzie, Mattie, and Lu—his neighbor Will Wiley accuses Nate of worshipping his mules—is the source not only of Shaw's sustenance but of his independence, determination, his keen sense of justice, even of his happiness.

Mules, cotton fields and cotton bales, the cotton warehouse and the cotton gin, guano or "fertilize," pine forests and sawmills, but also sugarcane, wheat, corn and beans, pigs, horses, and dogs, foxes, boll weevils and cotton borers, plows, rakes, hoes, hammers and tongs, ax handles, white-oak baskets and rush-bottomed chairs, brothers, sisters, fathers and mothers, women, wives and children, friends and adversaries, a brutal high sheriff murdered by one of his own men, and a pathologically racist landowner who dies of abandonment—these icons of Southern rural folklife were Nate Shaw's daily bread. Oh yes: and the prison camps—three of them, where he spent thirteen years for defending what was rightfully his.

All God's Dangers captures a voice in which experience exfoliates through the mediations of social intercourse, particularly in language, from a wellhead of immediacy almost inconceivable to a bookish mind.

> I drove on home in the mist and rain, and by the time I got five miles from my daddy I decided I'd better get my brother Peter to help me some. I was building a barn on the old Bannister place that fall—fully intendin to leave Mr. Reeve and had traded with Mr. Lemuel Tucker to rent the old Bannister place; had to rebuild the barn to fit my stock before I moved there. So I didn't quit drivin til I got to my daddy's down on Sitimachas Creek. I pulled in there—my wagon body had tightened up, caught a lot of water in the bed and the water was runnin from the back end to the front end, from the front end to the back end, whichever way the low end of the wagon was—goin down a slant the water come up over my feet and when I went up the least grade it flowed to the back end. That brand new wagon body just swelled up and sealed itself and held water like a tub.

Nate taps in the midst of this a rill of purposefulness from which the fascination of pooled water, as if the law of gravity had just at that moment come into effect, expresses the buoyancy of ownership—that of a fresh-painted wagon he has bought with his own money. Nate has eluded the pathology of oppression—that self-protective despair that aspires to nothing, to own nothing, to achieve nothing, to dream of nothing, never to provide the oppressor with the opportunity it seems he cannot resist of taking away what you've worked for and aspired to. "He made up his mind that he weren't goin to have anything," says Nate of his brother, "and after that, why, nothin could hurt him."

Nate's feats of memory seem incredible. But storytellers do not generalize. For the storyteller, experience is always ahead, never behind; like a tourist with her camera, the storyteller creates as he goes, and lives his creation. All the garrulous old black men recounting their lives in the fields, on the river or the railroad, in the mill, the auto plant, the school building, the body shop, or on the street corner, are but putting the finishing touches on a past that narration has already rescued from the power of white racism wholly to crush the creative spirit. The storytelling imagination is always narrating, always playing out as story the scenes of its own unfolding, at any given moment anticipating some momentous outcome and charging social relations with an intensity of presence and redundancy of dialogue that are already thoroughly invented. Hence that quality—call it picturesque, somehow vivid or colorful, that produces, in traditional cultures, interesting characters, tremendous events, quaint, curious, or even uncanny incidents, as well as stories about them. Talk, talk, and talk some more: and where you might digress or omit, there's always a half-brother or wife or sister-in-law there to remind you how things fit together—because they have been listening to your tales their entire lives.

White Americans have a long history of appropriating the immense verbal resources of black folk culture, with its peculiar genius for cross-tuning the American language. Ted Rosengarten, a working-class Jew who grew up three blocks from Ebbets Field when Jackie Robinson was integrating the major leagues, inherits the idealism of the young Communists who attempted to organize Southern black tenant farmers in the 1930s as well as that of his own contemporaries who had participated in the bus boycotts and civil rights marches of the segregated South in the early sixties. This idealism is compounded of a number of ideological strains. The immigrant Jewish peddlers who ventured into the rural South late in the nineteenth century had never learned to discriminate against the black farmers with whom they traded. A generation later Jewish radicals discovered in African American culture the raw materials of social protest. In New York, Yiddish vaudevillians such as Al Jolson and Eddie Cantor, composers such as Gershwin and Berlin, found in blackface, ragtime, and jazz what Irving Howe called "a mask for Jewish expressiveness, with one woe speaking through the voice of another." These historical streams of cultural and political identification converged in the civil rights movement, where the black church, the old labor movement, and the folk song revival attempted to reap the political fruits of a cultural sea change that had begun in the middle fifties, when a rights-minded white record producer named Sam Phillips found a way to channel the vocality and the performance style of the chitlin circuit though the body of a white sharecropper's son, Elvis Presley.

But *All God's Dangers'* strongest affinities are with the slave narrative, a form perfected by Frederick Douglass in 1845. Like Ned Cobb, drawing a speaking picture of himself with cowboy hat and pistol, Douglass learned that freedom was not to be found in the capacity to tell your story, or even to take ownership of it, but rather to live as if you did. Where tale and teller come together, that is fate—the moment you can't anticipate that defines a life.

Who has the time anymore for such a book? It is not only that the old cruel America has slipped unburied into the past, or even that the civil rights movement, in spite of conspicuous successes, now seems to be almost beside the point. While the cotton system was going down, the corporate system was coming up, and with it global bondage to the commodity that even a "fool Negro" like old Nate, with his Chevy and his Ford, his two strong mules and his Oliver Goober plow, could have deplored.

Each new inundation of wealth brings a new pandemic of illth, and forms of injustice we have yet to name. But it is suggestive that a story so minutely experienced, so richly remembered, so devotedly transcribed, so cleanly harvested at the edge of righteousness, should so try the patience of readers who, so many years hence, live as if life were no longer to be experienced, endured, or even remembered, but like any irksome or odious labor, swiftly and with as little trouble as possible to be put behind them.

Bibliography: David Roediger, "When Communism Was Black," *American Quarterly* 44, no. 1 (March 1992): 123–128. Theodore Rosengarten, comp., *All God's Dangers: The Life of Nate Shaw* (1974; Chicago, 2000). Jeff Todd Titon, "The Life Story," *Journal of American Folklore* 93, no. 369 (July–Sept. 1980): 276–292.

ROBERT CANTWELL

1933
Baby Face is censored

THE HAYS CODE

The Motion Picture Production Code is part of America's history of flattering itself into believing in its own purity. In the early 1930s, as the Depression made basic living increasingly difficult, the movies were the country's great pleasure, which meant the list of potentially unwholesome influences its citizens needed to be protected from was long: flagrant drug and alcohol use, broad suggestions of homosexuality, crude language, dancing girls for whom total nudity was just a few microns of beaded tulle away. All of those things were considered objectionable by the Hays Office, the organization, led by the former U.S. postmaster general Will Hays, that instituted the Code, a set of guidelines adopted by the Motion Picture Producers and Distributors of America in 1930—although they weren't rigorously enforced until 1934. "No picture shall be produced which will lower the moral standards of those who see it," the Code stated under the heading "General Principles": "Hence the sympathy of the audience should never be thrown to the side of crime, wrongdoing, evil or sin." It was a mission that, from the mid-1930s on, Hays's leading enforcer, a devout Catholic named Joe Breen, pursued with the zeal of a witch-hunter.

But what if it's not words or seminudity or even innuendo—which can all be trimmed out frame by frame—that throw an audience to the side of crime, wrongdoing, evil, or sin? The Hays Office could protect Americans from racy scenes and off-color language. But could it protect them from a face?

Could it protect them from Barbara Stanwyck?

Stanwyck's face alone doesn't tell the whole story of the Production Code, or of the way it still affects the content of American movies today. But her dangerous expressiveness as Lily Powers in the 1933 *Baby Face*—generally cited as the first picture to make the previously toothless Hays Office bare its fangs (and its scissors)—stands to this day as a symbol of the limits of artistic repression. Sometimes our sympathy needs to drift to the side of crime, wrongdoing, evil, and sin, as a way of measuring our own humanity, or of defining its limits—or of toying with the idea of blasting those limits to bits for the sheer pleasure of watching the explosion. Stanwyck's face, and the way it so confidently radiates one woman's belief in her own worth, is a map of everything the Hays Code was unable to squelch.

When we first meet her, Stanwyck's Lily is a small-town girl who, since the age of fourteen, has been pimped out by her wretched bootlegger father. In an early scene, she observes the blazing fire in which the son of a bitch is dying. At first, her face betrays faint horror. And then, in the smudge of time that occurs between seconds, her expression hardens into something like relief: even as her own flesh and blood is being turned to ash, she's free of guilt and sadness and everything that it would make us comfortable to see her feel. Her eyes betray the sense of self-preservation she's been honing for years. But even more terrifying, and more moving, is the yielding, vulnerable quality we see in them: even these always-calculating eyes suggest the ghost of the softer, warmer person that in another world, another life, she might have been.

The idea behind the Hays Code, tacit if not explicit, was that the portrayal of our best selves could somehow protect us from our worst selves. But in *Baby Face,* Stanwyck is so emotionally naked that she doesn't work as a cautionary character, a model of everything we *shouldn't* do. Contrast that with the character played by Jean Harlow in the 1932 *Red-Headed Woman.*

Harlow plays Lil, a firecracker who breaks up her boss's marriage and becomes his wife, only to go on to seduce an even more powerful man who can give her the social standing she craves. In an early scene, she tries on a new frock and asks an unseen girlfriend, "Can you see through this dress?" When she gets the answer she wants—that it's suitably transparent—she says brightly, "I'll wear it!"

In *Baby Face,* Lily Powers goes down the same road—but first she needs to leave Erie, Pennsylvania, the steel town where she's been virtually imprisoned all her life. There are two versions of *Baby Face,* one that was released to theaters, with cuts demanded by the Hays Office—that version, even with the cuts, is raw in its own right—and an uncut version, discovered in 2004 in the vaults of the Library of Congress. In the uncut version, Lily is exhorted by a kindly older man—who tries to open her to life's possibilities by lending her books—to skip town immediately and tap her potential. He leaves no doubt as to what that potential is: "Use men—be strong, defiant!" he urges her with the fervor of an evangelist, waving Nietzsche's *The Will to Power.* "Use men! To get the things you want!" Lily listens like a dutiful schoolchild. Even though the man is essentially urging her into a life of hustling, what's more important, and irrefutably thrilling, is his reassurance that she has the means—the brains, the looks, the sex appeal—to chart her own future. He wants to see her as a victor instead of a victim. Thus Nietzsche ("Crush all sentiment," reads a highlighted quote)—whose book, in the released version, was replaced by a letter in a book without a title. And what came next was cut altogether: on a train, Lily trading sex to a brakeman for the fare to New York for herself and her best friend, a black woman played by Theresa Harris, with Lily and the man crawling onto the floor of a boxcar while Harris pointedly does not turn her head.

Red-Headed Woman is the jauntier of the two pictures, partly because Harlow is a much saucier actress. You can hear the difference between these two marvelous performers in their voices: in Red-Headed Woman, Harlow's voice, light and lilting, is never far from comedy. Her sexual power is just as vital as Stanwyck's, but it's a satiny glow dusted on with a powder puff. In Baby Face, Stanwyck's voice is low and warm, as if in direct contrast to the supposed coldness of her character—but it's a voice that carries a lifetime of troubles in its suitcase. Harlow's Lil seduces the audience; she can't help winking at us each time she reaches another rung in her relentless climb to the top—she enjoys the fact that the higher she gets, the better we can see up her skirt. There's no winking in Baby Face. Lily always goes by "Lily," never "Lil": even in the early days of being an office girl, just as she's beginning to sleep her way to the top of the Gotham Trust Company (in a single panning shot, literally floor by floor), learning how to wear her hair fashionably and fine-tuning her grammar, there's none of the laughing tease to her. Both characters are unapologetic about their aims and desires: and their desires are purely monetary, not sexual. It's a significant difference between the two movies that Lil isn't punished for her actions, nor is she required to find redemption. The cut version of Baby Face has an aggressively false, patched-on ending, in which Lily returns, with her formerly rich but now ruined husband, to live a simple, honest life in Erie. Fat chance. The uncensored Baby Face ends far more ambiguously, but it at least suggests that Lily both finds love *and* refuses to return to meanness and poverty.

Both pictures are unvarnished reflections on the idea of American can-do ingenuity: Why *not* use the tools available to you to get what you need? But Baby Face is the one that's more painful to watch, the more adamant and uncompromising vision of the lengths to which human hunger—for money, for power, or even just for survival—can drive us. Stanwyck's Lily is the face of everything we don't dare to want. She is pure *self*, which is not to be confused with selfishness. The Hays Office clearly found her unwholesome, mistaking her clarity of purpose for vulgarity. Her purity isn't the kind the Hays Office wanted to push. It's the purity of the wholly corrupt, of those who can't see anything but corruption. To make a character like that sympathetic was potentially explosive, and the Hays Office knew it.

But how much could the Hays Office do to protect audiences—full of men who felt demoralized and emasculated by being out of work; full of women who needed to think about how to put food on the table for their family, or even just for themselves—from their own raw hunger? From their own fantasies, often unwholesome in the extreme, that if only they could free themselves from their staunch moral values, they might have enough money to get by, or even enough food? Or they might even feel good again? Going to the movies in America has always been a little bit dangerous, because the most rugged and admirable American qualities are inextricably bound with their opposite extremes: healthy ambition finds its evil twin in avariciousness; an unwavering belief in monogamy can become unholy passion when the right skirt passes by; a need for exploration and discovery mutates into an obsession with bloodlust and adventure.

The Production Code sought to protect audiences from their wild, untamed selves, and it still waves its long, powerful tentacles today, chiefly through the ratings board of the Motion Picture Association of America, formed in 1968 as a way of dismantling and retooling the Production Code. When contemporary filmmakers find ingenious ways to wriggle out of the ratings board's grasp, they're part of a long, proud tradition. What's more, the challenge of pushing against authority often makes for more vital art. In the 1930s, Mae West notoriously filled her pictures with the crudest, most obvious jokes imaginable, so the subtler but more salacious ones would escape the censors' attention. In 1944, when Preston Sturges made *The Miracle of Morgan's Creek,* in which Betty Hutton plays a small-town girl who becomes pregnant after a drunken encounter with a soldier she can't even remember meeting, he knew he was setting himself up for trouble. As the film historian James Harvey explains it, the censors' objections amounted to a catalog of bizarre and petty demands. They thought a mention of "screeching tires" suggested the wasting of rubber, a violation of wartime probity; they found Hutton's character to be too disrespectful toward her policeman father, Officer Kockenlocker. ("Apparently that name got by them," Harvey remarks drily.) Sturges, Harvey recounts, fought any number of battles, but essentially the picture, in all its mad, excessive, and wryly patriotic glory, was released as he wanted it. "The Hays Office," James Agee wrote triumphantly, "has been raped in its sleep."

Filmmakers responded to the constraints of the Code by finding ways to write between the lines, and audiences had no trouble reading between them. In the years before the Code took its final shape, even the studio chiefs who were willing to conform to the standards of the Hays Office started to doubt that the American public *wanted* their morals to be safeguarded. In 1927, Universal Studios president Carl Laemmle realized that the public was rejecting "namby-pamby" movies, concluding, "Much as I hate to admit it, I am beginning to think our clean-picture policy was a mistake." In the 1941 *Yankee Doodle Dandy,* James Cagney's George M. Cohan scans a *Variety* headline (borrowed from one that in 1935 ran in real life): "Stix Nix Hix Pix." The story below this headline claimed rural audiences were rejecting the movie industry's assumption that they wouldn't be interested in pictures about sophisticated, big-city life. The Hays Office thought it could safeguard Americans from their own fantasies, but even the so-called docile country folk resisted the chokehold.

And cities *are* exciting places, filled with interesting people. The city is where Fred and Ginger live—what good would a curvy white art-deco staircase do them on a farm in Idaho? Terrible things happen in cities, too. In the 1932 *Three on a Match,* a society wife and mother abandons her safe, comfortable home—and her child—for an existence fueled by booze and coke. Then again, there's danger in paradise as well: the 1934 *Tarzan and His Mate* originally included an underwater swimming scene in which Johnny Weissmuller and the swimmer standing in for Maureen O'Sullivan, the Olympic gold medalist Josephine McKim, skim through the depths in a dream of conjugal bliss. The sequence is so lyrical, so idyllic, it could be shown in Bible-study classes to underscore how much man lost in the Fall. But when the Hays Office had a look at the obviously and completely nude Jane, this unapologetic image of sexual freedom had to go.

Perhaps Depression anxiety had so magnified the already outsize American personality that the Hays Office saw a need to return citizens to some ideal of purity: as citizens of a nation founded on bloodshed, perhaps Americans need to believe in their own spotlessness. After you've killed Indians for their land, you'd better have something to show for it: cities, towns, suburbs, farms, a few nice national parks, parking lots, Hollywood. In building greatness, or even semigreatness, human beings often want to be assured of their goodness, too. In the '30s, that translated into a desire on the part of certain individuals to make sure that movies reflected national values: Americans are principled people who honor the sanctity of marriage, eschew bad habits like drinking and drug use, and never, ever take the name of the Lord in vain.

Yet Americans continue to swear, to take drugs and drink booze, to have sex for the heck of it. The history of the Production Code is the history of government-sanctioned organizations trying to keep movies safe for all citizens, and to use these sanitized pictures as a way of defining what it means to be an American. But filmmakers, and moviegoers, have defiantly reserved the right to establish that definition for themselves. Daniel Lord and Martin Quigley, who drafted an early version of the Code, wrote, "Correct entertainment raises the whole standard of a nation." What they couldn't have known is that America's character would find its truest expression in refusing to be raised.

Bibliography: Leonard J. Leff and Jerold L. Simmons, *The Dame in the Kimono: Hollywood, Censorship, and the Production Code* (Lexington, KY, 2001). James Harvey, *Romantic Comedy in Hollywood, from Lubitsch to Sturges* (New York, 1987). Filmography: *Baby Face*, directed by Alfred E. Green (1933); *Red-Headed Woman*, directed by Jack Conway (1932); see *TCM Archives: Forbidden Hollywood Collection*, vol. 1: *Baby Face, Red-Headed Woman, Waterloo Bridge* (Warner Home Video, 2006).

STEPHANIE ZACHAREK

1933, March

"I can assure you, my friends, that it is safer to keep your money in a reopened bank than it is to keep it under the mattress"

FDR's First Fireside Chat

On a Sunday evening in March 1933, when President Franklin Delano Roosevelt addressed the nation in his first "Fireside Chat," a format he had employed as early as 1929 as governor of New York, he did not employ his patrician voice to discuss the horrendous winter that had just passed, leaving nonagricultural unemployment at nearly 33 percent. Instead, his first priority was to use this ubiquitous medium, radio—in the 1930s over 80 percent of all households owned at least one radio, with poor and working-class listeners tuning in, on average, four hours a day—to shore up faith in the nation's failing banks. If banks were ultimately made of marble, their gleaming surfaces now were a shell holding crumbling remnants of the paper wealth of a decade before. Allaying the fears of small depositors—who had only recently, with the tremendous success of Liberty Bonds during the Great War, been persuaded to rely on banks to hold their savings—was thus intimately tied to a federal promise to protect the symbol of capitalism. FDR went on to broadcast many Fireside Chats, cementing connections among new electronic technologies, mass communication, politics, and the home; his first broadcast, with a president addressing his listeners as "my friends," set the tone, linking the bank vault to the bedroom, capitalism and the state to private space.

By the time of the first Fireside Chat, more American homes had radios than hearths. Radio was heralded in the years after the 1925 RCA-NBC inauguration of national broadcasting as a means to reconnect dispersed members of working-class and ethnic families torn asunder by the need for multiple wage earners. Although most working-class families had initially resisted buying on the installment plan, first designed by Henry Ford in 1915 to enable his own workers to purchase his cars, phonographs and radios (as well as most furniture) now were often purchased on time, further linking private apparatuses of communication to those of finance. The design of the large wooden radio console mimicked a hearth, with inlaid flames emanating from its center where the speaker was located; it also resembled the art deco design of the 1933 Chrysler Building. Thus this consummately modern device gestured backward toward a nostalgic image of the isolated pioneer homestead as it nodded simultaneously to a gleaming futuristic community linked through the airwaves. Radio was marketed as a remedy for the excitation of modern street life, but Bertolt Brecht offered a skeptic's view: the medium, he said, was not "an adequate means of bringing back cosiness to the home and making the family bearable again." He called for an interactive form of radio transmission, where listeners could talk back through the medium to each other instead of attending to "His Master's Voice"—as the RCA logo and FDR's stentorian tones implied.

In the early 1920s, when radio was a localized medium, people often built their own crystal or tube sets to listen in on a variety of local ethnic, religious, and union stations. After the Radio Act of 1927 introduced the federal regulation of broadcasting, mass production of the devices—usually installed in the large console—replaced the popular-mechanics tinkering of the earlier decade. Where once boys like Ralph Ellison scoured alleys for discarded ice cream cartons to use for winding tuning coils to build their own sets, and formed alliances in the name of science and for the love of engineering, by the 1930s radios were positioned centrally within the home—and thus the family. For Ellison, the homemade radio he devised with the help of a white boy became the twentieth-century equivalent of Huck's raft, forging a cross-racial tie not through movement along the flow of a river but across the connective tissue of invisible airwaves.

By the end of the 1930s, small portable radios were so affordable that many households possessed more than one. Soon sons and daughters eager to assimilate were swooning to music and other programming distinctly different from what their parents tuned in to. Radio broadcasts opened worlds for many American writers—the iconic scene, the primal scene really, of the twentieth-century ethnic writer in America begins, as E. L. Doctorow remembers, with a young person reading a book (for Doctorow one by his namesake, Edgar Allan Poe) and listening to radio dramas. A secret society of communal listening anchors Philip Roth's 2004 novel *The Plot Against America,* which begins with a paean to Walter Winchell's biting tirade against Charles Lindbergh's embrace of Nazi Germany: "Applause erupted from across the alleyway, as though the famous newsman weren't walled off in a radio studio on the far side of the great divide that was the Hudson but were here among us and fighting mad . . . lambasting Lindbergh from a microphone atop the oilcloth covering on the kitchen table of our next-door neighbor." Radio served to link working-class Newark to sophisticated Manhattan by bringing one Weequahic apartment into another. Radio knitted together Roth's lower-middle-class Jewish community; it also connected neighborhoods to nation, and homes to world events.

Through the soothing tones of polished wealth and family pedigree, FDR's first Fireside Chat precisely signaled that despite his paralyzed body and the nation's crippled economy plenty could be done together, and done through listening closely to him. FDR was careful to shield his wheelchair from public view; news photos of FDR's Chats show him masterfully sitting behind a desk laden with microphones he controls. Addressing at once economic and psychic maladies, he turned the American home into a locus of political participation; as Susan J. Douglas has written, those "listening in" felt they were being listened to.

Citizens felt prompted to respond to FDR's brand of personal delivery—and even more so to that of First Lady Eleanor Roosevelt—by writing to them. P. F. A. of Arkansas City, Kansas, wrote Eleanor Roosevelt to let her know that her husband was connecting directly with his constituents: "In our little home in Arkansas City, my family and I were sitting around the radio, to hear and we heard you when you flew over from N.Y. and entered the great hall and when he spoke it seems as though some Moses has come to alleviated us of our sufferings. Strange to say when he was speaking to see the moisten eyes and the deep feelings of emotion that gave vent to his every word." Others felt betrayed, writing to the White House: "When Pres. Roosevelt gave his promise to drive 'The Money Changers from the Temple' listeners had great hope that at last the common people of the nation would have a hearing but so far he seems zealously to be watching over the interests of financiers and capitalists and the common people are allowed to view a mirage with wonderful promises which disappear on approach."

The intimacy of the human voice is deeply associated with what the psychoanalyst Guy Rosolato calls the "sonorous envelope," a sensation that wraps the listener in a prenatal memory of hearing the mother's voice. If radio can restore the security of the womb, it also dislocates the auditor—the sound emanates from an external box. Auditory hallucinations are far more prevalent than visual ones, and the sense of a world created by a disembodied voice is an acute aspect of dreams, as the dreamer hears himself as a divided voice. Auditory hallucinations predate broadcast radio—Socrates spoke of them—but radio seems tailor-made to make concrete the sensation of extrasomatic voices invading the psyche, especially when those voices speak from a position of power.

Paranoia about transmission devices implanted in the body and unknown voices commanding actions—obsessions with surveillance and control—are tied expressly to the rise of radio and its ubiquitous use of the voice of the leader to transcend physical presence and connect directly to the population. FDR's first Fireside Chat expressly called negative attention to mental disorders affecting the populace, which his words were designed to allay.

> Let me make it clear to you that the banks will take care of all needs except of course the hysterical demands of hoarders—and it is my belief that hoarding during the past week has become an exceedingly unfashionable pastime in every part of our nation. It needs no prophet to tell you that when the people find that they can get their money—that they can get it when they want it for all legitimate purposes—the phantom of fear will soon be laid ... I can assure you, my friends, that it is safer to keep your money in a reopened bank than it is to keep it under the mattress.

FDR contrasted homegrown anxieties with the voice of reason emanating from the solid institutions of banking and government. His use of the phantom voice to do so, to bring politics and economics into the beds and heads of America, fed into larger practices—both political and psychological.

Broadcasting was an international phenomenon, with magazines such as *Wireless World* touting new possibilities for connecting populations around the globe; radio also fed fears of mass hypnosis. The first documented case of simultaneous multiple auditory hallucinations (a 1930 case described in French medical journals in 1932) concerned a syphilitic Paraguayan man claiming to have received obscene reports from government ministers and politicians in Asunción (and occasionally Buenos Aires) by means of invisible microphones located in his bedroom. At one point in "Kaddish," a liturgy for his mad Communist mother, Naomi, Allen Ginsberg recalls her paranoia from the 1930s:

> May have heard radio gossip thru the wires in her head,
> Controlled by 3 big sticks left in her back by gangsters in amnesia,
> Thru the hospital—caused pain between her shoulders—
>   Into her head—Roosevelt should know her case, she told
> me—Afraid to kill her, now, that the government knew their
> names—traced back to Hitler.

National radio in America focused on unifying its audience through common serialized and news programs, and product advertisements. It created an oxymoron: what has been called "an intimate public arena." Thus by the 1940s, when the sociologist Paul Lazarsfeld was examining radio's influence on what Theodor Adorno and Max Horkheimer called the "authoritarian personality," he found a medium designed to foster allegiance to faceless "monopolistic" bureaucracies. But he failed to understand how the effective use of radio by outsiders—Hitler before his ascension to power, the anti-Semitic Father Coughlin of Detroit— as well as presidents could directly reach or even create a public, making politics into a "private experience." In 1942, in his dystopian novel *Clark Gifford's Body*, Kenneth Fearing imagined an indigenous protofascist takeover of America through a rebel insurgency that connected to all "government transmitters" through its base at a single local station. Published three years after Orson Welles's infamous *War of the Worlds* broadcast unleashed mass panic over a supposed invasion from Mars, and ten years after FDR took to the airwaves to allay phantoms and calm hysteria over bank failures, the novel's experimental form—with time sequences cut up and scrambled fragments from fictional diaries, trial transcripts, radio announcements, case studies, and testimonies—dovetailed with the paranoia lurking within radio's content. It tapped into the unsettling way in which radio enacted a mass transmission into private spaces, perhaps best exemplified by Welles's scarily soothing voice as the title character in the long-running radio play *The Shadow*, who "knows what evil lurks in the hearts of men."

The radio was not confined to the home; automobiles acquired radios with Paul Galvin's 1929 invention of the "Motorola," a device owners could purchase and install in their car. Within a decade, as he recalled in 1994 in *It All Adds Up*, Saul Bellow found himself "walking eastward on the Chicago Midway . . . drivers had pulled over, parking bumper to bumper, and turned on their radios to hear Roosevelt. They had rolled down their windows and opened the car doors . . . You could follow without missing a single word as you strolled by. You felt joined to these unknown drivers, men and women smoking their cigarettes in silence."

Radios, car radios and police radios, drive (so to speak) the plots of many Hollywood movies; in fact, radios are all over the movies—as the newly cherished talkie made room for voices both within and beyond the diegetic space, radios came to stand in for Hollywood itself. "Yes Hollywood will get what it deserves," Ginsberg wrote in 1961 in "Death to Van Gogh's Ear!" "Time/Seepage or nerve-gas over the radio." In Anatole Litvak and Jean Negulesco's 1940 film *City for Conquest*, radio enables the emotional link among three Lower East Siders—James Cagney as the reluctant boxer Young Samson, Arthur Kennedy as Eddie, his musician brother, and Ann Sheridan as Cagney's "girl," a professional dancer. Each has escaped the Depression slums through talents that sunder their ties. But both brother and lover reconnect with Cagney through the device of a radio broadcast—Sheridan hears of Cagney's beating at Madison Square Garden while sitting in her dressing room before a show; Cagney tunes in to his brother's triumphant debut at Carnegie Hall from his newspaper stand where he works after one too many fights. These scenes move from public spaces—the fights, the concert—to private locales, not domestic, as each is a work site, but isolated and personal— the dressing room, the kiosk—where sounds from an event meant to be heard by the masses become private discourses between those separated and estranged. Intimacy becomes possible through the transmission itself.

This homage to making it in New York taps the evocative legacy of 1930s radio as FDR's private channel into Americans' homes. During the 1950s, Jean Shepherd created a form of radio novel through his nocturnal broadcasts to New York insomniacs of stories, vignettes, and diatribes that depended on a long tradition of radio as the medium that could bridge public and private life. He took the implications of FDR's first Fireside Chat to heart: speaking through a microphone into the night to the households of America was a joint curative venture. "Let us unite in banishing fear," FDR had intoned. "We have provided the machinery to restore our financial system, and it is up to you to support and make it work. It is your problem, my friends, your problem no less than it is mine. Together we cannot fail."

By 1969 the Firesign Theatre—whose name not-so-subtly invoked FDR and melded it to counterculture astrology—was rebroadcasting and overdubbing old radio shows from the 1940s: "All Hail Marx and Lennon" declared the cover of *How Can You Be in Two Places at Once When You're Not Anywhere at All,* which ended with FDR announcing, *on the radio,* the surrender of the United States to the Axis—the Marx pictured on the album jacket, after all, was Groucho. The satirical weekly the *Onion* may have provided the last word on FDR's legacy, which depended on gentle paternal assurances for moral clarity: "In a drastic departure from the traditional 'fireside chat,'" a 1999 *Onion* column declared, "President Roosevelt held American radio listeners captive last night with a stream of lurid profanities that lasted thirty minutes with nary a break to take a breath." Decency does not permit me to quote further.

Bibliography: Bertolt Brecht, "The Radio as an Apparatus of Communication" (1932), in *Brecht on Theatre* (New York, 1964). E. L. Doctorow, "Childhood of a Writer," in *Reporting the Universe* (Cambridge, MA, 2003). Susan J. Douglas, *Listening In* (Minneapolis, 2004). Ralph Ellison, "That Same Pain, That Same Place" (1961), in *Shadow and Act* (New York, 1966). Allen Ginsberg, *Kaddish and Other Poems* (San Francisco, 1961). Jason Loviglio, *Radio's Intimate Public* (Minneapolis, 2005). Robert S. McElvaine, *Down and Out in the Great Depression: Letters from the "Forgotten Man"* (Chapel Hill, NC, 1983). Philip Roth, *The Plot Against America* (New York, 2004).

PAULA RABINOWITZ

1934, September

Robert Penn Warren picks up an elderly hitchhiker who tells him how Huey is building farm-to-market roads and toll-free bridges to help the poor farmers in Louisiana

ALL THE KING'S MEN

From the earliest days of the republic, a thematic battle in American politics has been that between the Haves and the Have-Nots. Yet from the election of President Ronald Reagan in 1980 to that of Barack Obama in 2008, the Haves

have triumphed so decisively—and compiled such durable mountains of wealth—
that it is difficult to remember that Have-Nots once held brief sway in the American South and Midwest. The Texas scholar Larry Goodwyn refers to this cluster
of decades in the late nineteenth and early twentieth centuries as "the populist
moment" in American history. Thanks to the success of the short-lived Populist
Party in organizing farmers and laborers, it appeared for a while that the United
States might eventually look more like the social democracies of Western Europe
in terms of smaller income gaps between rich and poor, access to health care and
education, and a natural *right* to a safety net of social services that could not be
withheld at the whim of a new president. The American leftist novelist John
Steinbeck won the Nobel Prize for Literature on the basis of a body of work recording the watershed battles between "the people" on one side and the corporate and agricultural oligarchs on the other. But it is a single monumental novel by
a more polished stylist, Robert Penn Warren's *All the King's Men,* that stands as a
defining fictional work on American politics—and on the potential for good and
evil in political leaders who appeal to a sense of oppression among voters stuck at
the bottom of a so-called free-market economy.

For the outlines of his story of the rise and fall of the fictional "Boss," Governor Willie Stark, Warren took inspiration from material close at hand: the career
of the old hitchhiker's real-life political messiah, Governor, later Senator, Huey P.
Long of Louisiana. He was known as "the Kingfish"; he arose as a democratic reformer, exposing the flagrant corruption of New Orleans's business-controlled
"Old Regular" political machine. Once in office, however, Long became adept in
using patronage, vote-buying, and physical threats to gain near-total control of
the state government. His supporters—and there were many—defended him by
pointing out that he used tax revenues formerly diverted to the wealthy few to
bring roads, schools, and government services to the many.

Twenty-nine-year-old Robert Penn Warren was plunged into this miasmic
world of class conflict and political intrigue in 1934 when he was hired to teach
English at Louisiana State University, aka "Huey's University," in the state capital
of Baton Rouge. After a ruthless term as governor from 1928 to 1932, Long, while
still in absolute political control of his state, was by then in the United States Senate, challenging President Franklin D. Roosevelt for leadership of the Democratic
Party. Under the catchy slogan "Every Man a King," Long was building his own
national political machine, a network of Share Our Wealth clubs that promised a
guaranteed annual wage to every family. Roosevelt, then midway in his first term,
took seriously Long's threat to use his "S.O.W." clubs to take over the national
Democratic Party—but in 1935, before Long's plan could take effect, he was assassinated by an upper-class physician whose father-in-law had been ousted from
a judgeship by the Kingfish.

In the best light, the real Huey and the fictional Willie can be viewed as
working-class heroes enacting the arc of classical tragedy. These flawed protagonists provide contact points with the tensions in Warren's own background—between the modern and the traditional, between his liberal political sympathies
and a personal sensibility rooted in conservative social tradition. These seemingly
contradictory impulses informed and enriched his fiction. He was born in 1900

in a Kentucky family on the fringes of the planter class. As a boy, he eagerly consumed the Civil War stories of a grandfather who served under Nathan Bedford Forrest, the most obdurate racist among the leading Confederate generals. At Vanderbilt University, the preferred school of Border South socialites, he made a fateful turn away from Fraternity Row, joining the Fugitives, an avant-garde literary club that was studying Eliot, Pound, and Rimbaud long before they became standard fare on American campuses. The Fugitives' literary salon in Nashville spawned the Agrarian literary movement, so named for its members' reverence for the Jeffersonian ideal of an agricultural society led by educated aristocrats. Luckily for Warren, he struggled free of the romanticized attitude toward slavery and the Confederacy that marred the work of some fellow Fugitives and the landmark Agrarian manifesto, the 1930 collection *I'll Take My Stand.* The youngest of the Fugitives, Warren contributed an essay to the book, but when he moved on to graduate study at Berkeley and Yale, and at Oxford as a Rhodes Scholar, young "Red" Warren, the freckled farm boy with a razor mind and a charmingly lazy Southern accent, also moved beyond the elitist prejudices of the Fugitives.

Virtually alone among authors of major American novels of the early twentieth century, Warren did not view scholars and critics with contempt. He found his enduring métier as a literary theorist and professor. He practiced what came to be called New Criticism, analyzing each poem, short story, or novel as a discrete piece of art that had meanings independent of the author's original intention or personal history. Along with his academic colleague Cleanth Brooks, Warren and other New Critics formed an influential movement demanding greater intellectual rigor from teachers and students of literature on American campuses. This devotion to careful scholarship was a shaping force in Warren's own poetry and novels, helping make him the only American author, as of this writing, to win the Pulitzer Prize for both poetry and fiction. Some readers have found the musings about God, Time, Knowledge, and History by Jack Burden, the narrator of *All the King's Men,* to be tedious, and have faulted Burden, and by implication his creator, as excessively self-conscious intellectual show-offs; my own view is that Warren's ability to build a teleological armature inside what looks at first glance like another redneck political melodrama is one of the chief reasons for regarding *All the King's Men* as a signal example of how to blend suspenseful storytelling with multiple layers of meaning. The literary scholar Louis Rubin, Warren's contemporary, says the novel holds a high place in the American canon chiefly because "it is one of those rare books that make their appeal both to the intellectual and to the popular reader." Better than any play or novel of its era, it also dramatizes the most enduring, most vexing moral question about American society: How does one manage a capitalist economic system—with its concentration of wealth and political influence in the hands of the few—so as to give the masses a fair share in the prosperity produced by their labor?

Warren's flawed protagonist, Willie Stark, drew his answer from the suffering of the farmers and laborers whose children went barefoot, untaught, and undernourished while the state legislature showered tax breaks, kickbacks, and no-bid contracts on industrialists and plantation owners. "Friends, red-necks, suckers and fellow hicks . . . That's what you are. And I'm one, too," he says in campaign speeches that launch his career atop a coalition of the dispossessed. "Your will is my strength. Your need is my justice."

A cynical but well-read newspaperman like Jack Burden, sent to cover the suddenly popular small-town crusader, quickly understands that there has seldom been a purer distillation of the populist creed. Burden, soon to go to work for Stark himself, informs his unhappy editors that this upstart candidate has the oratorical skills to use the "hick vote" to overturn the big-shot politicians supported by the newspaper. What draws a disenchanted aristocrat like Burden to the incurably coarse Willie Stark? It is simply the fact that despite their differences in background, education, and social status, both men have figured out the same home truth: the poor are poor and ignorant and will stay that way because the American political game in which they are pawns—while ostensibly democratic—has been fixed from the start. Starting as an idealistic political naïf, Willie evolves into an iron-fisted, amoral pragmatist who believes that the methods by which the capitalist class got its advantages—political blackmail, legislative bribery, stolen elections, crooked journalism, the violent use of paid thugs—are the only tools in American politics that really work. It is this archetypal struggle at the heart of American government—timeless and unresolved, indeed vibrantly alive in the age of Bush and Cheney, Exxon and Halliburton—that accounts for the enduring hold of *All the King's Men* on the American imagination.

Willie Stark defends his use of the commonplace tools of thievery in cosmic terms. Since the fall of Adam and Eve, he says, "Evil is all you have to work with" if you are a politician aspiring to do "good" for "the people who got pushed out of the trough." The populist demagogue who uses promises of prosperity to secure dictatorial powers has become a stock character in American fiction and movies, in part because he is an actor in a familiar melodrama whose reality can be proved by even a casual reading of political journalism and scholarly historical writing in the United States. In a 1930s America beginning to worry over the rise of Hitler and Mussolini, any American politician with a Southern drawl, grandiose rhetoric, and a feel for what Warren called Long's "cold manipulation of the calculus of power" was quickly accused of being a protofascist. Warren's was one of several novels inspired by Long's career that can be read as the triumph of a law-abiding, if flawed, establishment over a demagogic destroyer of democracy. It might be called the Close-Call School of political analysis—in which we are supposed to feel lucky that bankers, industrialists, and well-paid senators and judges have pulled the republic back from an anarchy masquerading as social justice.

Such a surface reading of *All the King's Men* leads us away from an appreciation of the fact that before a novelist can write a successful naturalistic novel, he or she must achieve an evenhanded, unbiased understanding of the social universe from which any story of enduring relevance draws its models. For a novel to leave us with a sense of both factual and moral credibility, we must grant the novelist our intellectual permission to play God, and in return, for us to regard his or her work with respect, the novelist must be an honest God. That is where Warren surpasses several other writers of his time who attempted political novels based on the populist paradigm; he brought a keen fairness to his observations of Huey Long's Louisiana and the "world of 'good families'" who despised the Kingfish.

Warren well understood the brutish, violent thievery of a Huey Long, but he also saw the moral equivalency between a populist demagogue who failed to respect democratic freedoms and an ancien régime that used legalized thievery to shower on Wall Street and Standard Oil the tax dollars that should have gone to roads, schools, and hospitals. Louisiana's upper class "hated [Long] sometimes for good reasons and sometimes for bad," Warren wrote years later in explaining the roots of his novel, "and sometimes for no reason at all, as a mere revulsion of taste; but they never seemed to reflect on what I took to be the obvious fact that if the government of the state had not previously been marked by various combinations of sloth, complacency, incompetence, corruption, and a profound lack of political imagination there never would have been a Senator Huey P. Long."

All that said, an author's flair for egalitarian socioeconomic analysis of industrial democracy does not inevitably produce convincing fiction, and there is a reason that *All the King's Men* does not sink under the weight of its political preaching. Warren was a storyteller who understood that any narrative has to be rooted in what Faulkner called the "old verities of the heart." The action of *All the King's Men* is driven by four tortured love affairs: the story-within-a-story of Cass Mastern's Civil War adultery, Jack Burden's hopelessly idealistic love for his childhood sweetheart, Anne Stanton, and Willie Stark's adulterous liaisons, first with his small pox–scarred political adviser, Sadie Burke, and later, to Jack Burden's dismay, with the comely, patrician Anne Stanton. The love affairs, in turn, fit with an inexorable logic into the existential quandary that no one escapes. As Jack Burden says, we live in an "agony of will," endlessly repeated in the unpredictable "convulsion of the world" that we set down as History. All four stories are related by Jack Burden, and some critics have questioned the relevance of the detailed account of Jack's failure to write a doctoral dissertation based on his research into Cass Mastern's cuckolding of his generous plantation-owning brother, Gilbert. But in a book so obsessed with the "burden" of personal and social history in the South, the Mastern tale underscores what Yeats called the inexorable "gyres" of experience in a world where joy is braided with pain, and good interlaced with evil. And it is worth noting in passing that only a writer as skilled as Warren in drawing believable characters and maintaining plot momentum could get away with giving his narrator and protagonist the allegorical surnames Burden and Stark.

By definition, gyres, merry-go-rounds, and, not least, the political world constructed by Warren are endlessly repetitive. This fact casts an air of mystery over the end of the novel. Willie is assassinated by Anne's brother, who is himself instantly killed by Willie's bodyguard, and Anne and Jack, united in a bruised marriage, move forward "out of history into history and the awful responsibility of Time." But forward into what daily reality? Jack Burden says that he may return to politics as the coat-holder for Hugh Miller, the prissy and ineffective attorney general who resigned rather than stand up to Willie Stark—even though Jack has discovered an ironclad analogue to the supposed cycle in which a genuine populist movement ends up producing a demagogue, a crook, or both: he knows that politics as it is generally understood is shot through with evil. Are we being asked to believe that Jack Burden, after all he has seen, believes in political redemption?

Some critics think just that—and such a judgment matches the dominant view of populist political movements among American historians and journalists. Avatars of the common man can have a corrective effect on society—and, in the end, the rabble must be curbed by an elite class with the requisite wealth, social standing, and education.

I doubt that Warren, the master ironist, swallowed whole a theory that justifies the existence of a privileged class in a society supposedly founded on equality. As a student of history and classical literature, Warren is giving the reader a fatalist wink. In his soul, Burden knows that the aristocratic Hugh Miller epitomizes another stock character in the American political melodrama—the high-minded, feckless reformer who will give a surface scrubbing to the corrupt edifice that Willie Stark, for all his failings, wanted to destroy. In the end, the Hugh Millers always seem to scurry back to their redoubts of wealth, leaving rich and poor in their assigned places. Jack Burden dares to hope for a better outcome with Miller than with Stark because it is man's fate to hope—and try yet again. My bet is that neither Stark nor Burden nor their creator Warren would be surprised that the first American presidency of the twenty-first century operated as the supreme protector and promoter of the financial interests of American corporations. And Warren the ironist would have to appreciate the Washington of George W. Bush: a capital presided over by a rich fake-populist dedicated to the protection of the ruling class from taxation, and a powerful, Stark-like vice president who, unlike Willie, was perversely dedicated to punishing the working class from which he rose.

Such a political world—anchored by colorful characters warring under a cloud of systemic injustice—provided Warren with the materials for *All the King's Men,* but one wonders if any living writer could combine his ability to work on so large a social canvas with such a sustained elegance of rhetoric. Stylistically, this novel is very much a book of its time, showing the influence of Faulkner's lush language, Hemingway's cynical eye, and an awareness of social idiom as symbol and code that can be traced through James, Dreiser, Howells, Wharton, and Fitzgerald. We can argue about the relative merits of these writers, but all produced work that honored and illuminated their nation's diversity. There is no Great American Novel; there are many great American novels; and Warren, who devoted his life to studying the literature of his country and to honing his natural lyric gifts as stylist and to blending the philosophical with the palpably dramatic, left us one of them. The question then is not whether we will have a political novel to surpass *All the King's Men,* but whether we will be lucky enough to have a new one deserving to stand beside it as an enduring document of a parlous moment in history.

Bibliography: Maurice Beebe and Leslie A. Field, eds., *All the King's Men: A Critical Handbook* (Belmont, CA, 1966). Gloria L. Cronin and Ben Siegel, eds., *Conversations with Robert Penn Warren* (Jackson, MS, 2005). Robert Penn Warren, *All the King's Men* (New York, 1946). T. Harry Williams, *Huey Long* (New York, 1969). *Filmography: All the King's Men,* directed by Robert Rossen (1949).

HOWELL RAINES

1935

"For the first time I know of, artists felt themselves part of everything else"

ARTISTS AND WRITERS MOBILIZE

Nineteen thirty-five was the midpoint in a decade of unprecedented national and international crisis. It was not only a temporal but also a cultural and historical midpoint. The years leading up to it appear markedly different from those that followed, as if the chastening effects of the early Depression had produced a more seasoned, less tentative approach to the multiple trials of economic collapse, unemployment, and collective self-doubt. The limited public investment in the arts prior to 1935 (the Public Works of Art Project and the Treasury Section) was followed by the stable interlocking public arts programs of the Works Progress Administration (WPA), which began in that year. Within Communist culture, the "proletcult" of the early 1930s, in which the world was viewed through the prism of class struggle, gave way to a more capacious collectivist vision in which revolutionary, liberal, and progressive elements were to be united against the common enemy of fascism. Proletarian realism had populated the social stage with a familiar cast of characters: idle bohemians, effete self-obsessed aesthetes like Marcel Proust, "the master masturbator of the bourgeois literature," in the words of Mike Gold, editor of the *New Masses* and loyal Communist Party member; bloated businessmen, caricatured in William Gropper's cartoonlike drawings; and heroic workers, whose class consciousness transcended the boundaries of the nation to reach toward a new internationalism, achieving triumphant expression in the bald allegories of agitprop. "Away with all lies about human nature," proclaimed Gold. "We are scientists; we know what a man thinks and feels." The American radical left of the early 1930s, Gold wrote, approached the future with "revolutionary élan" and "youthful clarity." The John Reed Clubs of these years focused artistic activism around the unproblematic language of social realism: "Art is a weapon in the class struggle" was the slogan. The left's focus was clear: the epic confrontation between bosses and workers, present and future, capitalism and socialism.

German, Italian, and Spanish expansionism—the Saar Plebiscite (1935), the Italo-Ethiopan War (1935–1936), the remilitarization of the Rhineland (1936), the rise of the Spanish Nationalists under the leadership of Franco, and the ensuing Spanish Civil War (1936–1939)—would reorient the loyalties around which the American left organized its activism, from international class warfare to the threat of fascism facing the bourgeois democracies of the West. In August 1935 the Seventh World Congress of the Communist International issued a call for its members to put aside the sectarian divisions of the Communist left, as well as to change the terms in which the world struggle would be waged, in order to make cause against a common enemy. This pivotal moment gave rise to a number of responses in the second half of the 1930s. Foremost was the broad cultural coalition known as the Popular Front—or in the United States, the People's or Democratic Front, a regionally, politically, and socially varied effort to create a domestic cultural expression of the working classes in the United States.

The American Writers Congress/League of American Writers (1935) and the American Artists' Congress, or AAC (1936–1942), emerged under a broad umbrella of opposition to "War, Fascism and Reaction, destroyers of culture." The AAC called for a reengagement of the artist with a wider public and "unity of action" with other groups dedicated to the enlargement of social, intellectual, and political freedoms. The solidarity espoused by the members of the AAC (whose numbers soared from 114 to 900 by 1939) reached across a spectrum of aesthetic practices—part of a broader call for an end to aesthetic sectarianism—and drew together artists and workers across lines of class and race. Its members rallied behind freedom of expression and argued for state support of artists. The writers' and artists' congresses embodied major shifts in the definition of artistic responsibility: away from the bohemian alienation of early modernisms to a conviction that strong creative expression was tied to social truth, a stick jammed into the machinery of falsehoods on which dictatorship thrived. "Dictatorships fear artists," announced Lewis Mumford at the first meeting of the AAC, affirming art as an agent of social and political enlightenment.

Linking the pre-1935 culture of class struggle with the post-1935 culture of the Popular Front was a shared internationalism; artists of widely different stylistic persuasions and political sympathies found themselves united in condemning isolationists, regionalists, and those who linked nation to race and place. Internationalist America closed ranks against Fortress America. Essences—racial or national—were suspect; the free growth of the individual, unencumbered by political ideologies, was held to be the sign of a healthy society. The Popular Front attempted to combine Communist collectivism with enough bourgeois individualism to attract artists and sustain core beliefs of modern Western art (self-expression, personal vision, artistic genius). Infused with a deep optimism in the face of dire events, the climate of the AAC reaffirmed individual agency against the determinisms of the social. Human needs were foremost: a lingering romanticism of faith in the primacy of creative individuality impelled the most systematic thinking of John Dewey, Mumford, and others in these years. At the same time, the freedom to pursue one's work without the responsibilities of the real world came to seem increasingly sterile for the mobilized artists of the AAC. Their sense of freedom was tied to both a collective sense of well-being and a belief in the malleability of the social sphere.

The trajectory of artistic and cultural activism in the cause of antifascism went well beyond the official venues of congresses and fronts to include acute new forms of self-consciousness about the effects of formal and aesthetic practices in the world. Under the pressure of world events, artists and writers transformed their own thinking about the relationship of creative selfhood to collective destiny. Congress members made a concerted effort to avoid divisions resulting from doctrinaire positions on the relationship of aesthetic form to political content. Yet these years also witnessed vital efforts to theorize the precise relationship of aesthetic practices—from social realism to social surrealism or superrealism, expressionism, and geometric abstraction—to social and political knowledge. What united these widely different artistic approaches was a rejection of art for art's sake, the aestheticism of the fin-de-siècle generation and its lingering aura in the rarefied art world of galleries and private collectors. What took its place was "life," the vital connection between art and the forces shaping the world beyond the studio. Painter Stuart Davis, for one, vehemently rejected naturalism, abstraction, and other forms of "pure art" born of the isolation of the artist from life. The new art, he said, would express "the dynamic and moving quality of life," and would resist the "slave psychology" of those who lacked a sense of social agency—the power to change the world. Davis followed Fernand Léger's lead in declaring that form, color, and the dynamic relationships between them were the only true realities because they were not imitative of some other reality but were only themselves. Breaking with the idea of art as a "mirror of nature," a reflection of a more basic reality, Davis viewed painting as "a direct emotional or ideological stimulus." Measuring more than twelve feet by nearly twenty-nine feet, his sweeping *Swing Landscape* (1938) embodied this vision of an art that rejected bourgeois "domestic naturalism," in his contemptuous phrase, and instead inserted itself aggressively into everyday life.

Swing Landscape was originally commissioned for a public housing project in New York City. Weaving together work motifs—buoys, ladders, rope and rigging, and lobster traps, drawing on Davis's earlier wharf paintings—into a composition of bold forms and saturated colors, playful allusions to three-dimensional space undercut by arbitrary boundaries, and jarring visual rhythms, the work was steeped in the language of spatial and temporal disjunction associated with the European avant-garde. Yet Davis believed that a primary responsibility of the artist was to enliven the audience's social world through dynamic forms and a vernacular language rooted in jazz and the built environment of the modern city. With these tools the artist would find the power to shape new social collectivities rooted in everyday experience. For Davis—a fellow traveler who embraced Marxism, though he most likely never joined the Communist Party—the material life of forms on the two-dimensional canvas represented an expression of the unmasked truth of things, of life as it was truly lived.

Life, however, was more than a term of debate in the reorientation of aesthetic values during the 1930s. It was also present in the very pressing problems artists faced during the trough years of the Depression. In 1934 Stuart Davis presented a series of nonobjective watercolors to the Baroness Hilla Rebay von Ehrenwiesen, soon to become the doyenne of the Guggenheim Museum in New York. Desperate for money—he later wrote that he would have "crawled in on my hands and knees" to get the baroness's financial support—he went so far as to change the watercolors to her specifications. A year later, the hothouse of privileged private patronage had come to seem grotesquely out of step with the compulsions of hunger, social violence, political repression, and dictatorship. For Davis and many other artists in these years, government support offered an alternative to a system of private patronage that made artists into the lapdogs of the wealthy. By 1935

Davis would be marching in the May Day parade, recalling that "it wasn't a choice. It was a necessity to be involved in what was going on . . . for the first time I know of, the artists felt themselves part of everything else, general depression, the needs of money and food." By late 1934 Davis had become editor in chief of *Art Front,* the voice of the Artists' Union, which had formed to advocate the rights of artists as workers in the new cultural programs of the federal government in the first phase of the New Deal.

Fascism's challenge to Western democracies extended to the most basic terms of social understanding. How was freedom to be understood and exercised without trampling upon collective ideals? And how could collective commitments be met while preserving the integrity of individual needs? Singer and songwriter Woody Guthrie plastered a sticker on his guitar: "This machine kills fascists." But how exactly did art exercise social agency? If art was not a luxury but a necessity, what was the responsibility of the state in supporting artists? In what ways could artists contribute to stemming the rise of social, ethnic, and political persecution throughout Europe, Asia, and the United States?

For the threat of fascism existed at home as well, in the Liberty League, lynching, racism, suppression of civil liberties, and the tentacular extension of mass media into every realm of social life (witness Barbara Morgan's striking montage *Hearst over the People,* in which the image of the newspaper magnate floats like a giant octopus over a crowded public space). If the left recognized the media as a powerful instrument for forging political awareness and for creating communal myths and sympathies, it also feared the media as an unprecedentedly powerful tool for promoting fascism through mass manipulation and seduction. When Charlie Chaplin stopped acting and directly addressed his movie audience at the end of *The Great Dictator,* he was using film—stripped of its power to mold audience response through editing, lighting, and camera angle, and reduced to its most basic forms—to advance the cause of antifascism. When Orson Welles placed his forms of directorial montage alongside the *March of Time* newsreels at the beginning of *Citizen Kane,* he revealed the plasticity of such technical innovations—their very different possibilities in framing ways of knowing the world through mass media.

The AAC eventually succumbed—in 1942—to growing internal fissures over its members' positions on the Soviet invasion of Finland in December 1939. Writers' and artists' commitment to collective action proved too fragile to withstand the collapse of faith in the Soviet Union as a utopian project. The productive interdependence of individual and social freedom appeared increasingly chimerical in the wake of the Soviet betrayal of international collective action. The Molotov-Ribbentrop Pact, signed by Germany and the Soviet Union in August 1939 (also known as the Nazi-Soviet Non-Aggression Pact), devastated the American left, linking the Soviet Union to Nazi expansionism and setting the stage for the partition of Poland and the invasion of Finland. Even before 1939, the Moscow Trials (1936–1938), against the "Old Bolsheviks" of the October Revolution, and accusations from Trotsky and his American followers that the Com-

Stuart Davis, *Swing Landscape* (1938). Oil on canvas

intern's Popular Front policy had resulted in a betrayal of the true revolution in Spain had fueled disillusionment with the ideological excesses of communism. Many on the left increasingly viewed the Popular Front as another kind of front, one hiding Stalin's self-serving machinery of propaganda and international manipulation. The stage was set for the postwar merging of communism and fascism into one all-encompassing totalitarian extremism. In 1940, in *To the Finland Station*, his study of communism as "the history of an idea," the critic Edmund Wilson declared that "Marxism is in relative eclipse"; that same year Stuart Davis withdrew from politics into formal and aesthetic insularity, announcing that "there's nothing like a good solid ivory tower for the production of art." In the coming decades of the cold war, the united cultural fronts of the 1930s would give way to a deepening alienation of creative individuals from the social matrix, and the perceived incompatability of individual freedom and ideological commitment. By 1955, this aesthetic withdrawal had become canon law: "The artist," wrote Adolph Gottlieb, "must depend upon his own resources in order to survive in a hostile environment . . . [T]he modern artist does not paint in relation to public needs or social needs—he paints only in relation to his own needs . . . art thrives not only on freedom, but on alienation as well."

The years following the demise of the AAC would witness equally major shifts in artistic energies away from the communal to the private and from the social to the personal. Until then, though, the AAC represented a vision—and a critical example for later generations—of solidarity and collectivity in the face of the massive challenge to freedom of expression and a humanely ordered society posed by the rise of fascism. And it addressed the most basic divisions between artists and their audiences, the producers and the consumers of culture, calling for a shared commitment to the fundamental requirements of a just society. Against the specter of book burnings and the utter denial of the individual imagination in the face of mass psychology, the artists of the AAC collectively pursued a new model of social life in which self-fulfillment and social commitment went hand in hand. They advocated a still unrealized multiracial democracy grounded in social justice—what Michael Denning, writing about Dos Passos and his contemporaries, termed "the Lincoln Republic."

Bibliography: Matthew Baigell and Julia Williams, eds., *Artists against War and Fascism: Papers of the American Artists' Congress* (New Brunswick, NJ, 1986). Stuart Davis, "Abstract Art Today," in Francis V. O'Connor, *Art for the Millions: Essays from the 1930s by Artists and Administrators of the WPA Federal Art Project* (Greenwich, CT, 1973). Michael Denning, *The Cultural Front: The Laboring of American Culture in the Twentieth Century* (London, 1996). Mike Gold, "Proletarian Realism," repr. in Gordon Hutner, ed., *American Literature, American Culture* (New York, 1999). Adolph Gottlieb, "Artist and Society: A Brief Case History," *College Art Journal* 14, no. 2 (Winter 1955). Andrew Hemingway, *Artists on the Left: American Artists and the Communist Movement, 1926–1956* (New Haven, CT, 2002).

ANGELA MILLER

1935

"New York, you are an Egypt! But an Egypt turned inside out":
Salvador Dalí arrives in New York carrying a two-and-a-half-meter loaf of bread

THE SKYSCRAPER

Salvador Dalí's delirious exuberance for Manhattan led him to cast the city's skyscrapers as a new kind of monument: "For [Egypt] erected pyramids of slavery to death, and you erect pyramids of democracy with the vertical organ-pipes of your skyscrapers all meeting at the point of infinity of liberty!" Dalí's view was shared by many Europeans arriving in New York during what the American cultural critic Lewis Mumford referred to as modernism's "adolescence" of the 1930s and '40s. If Americans tended to read Manhattan from the interior—the office, the department store, even the interiorized street canyons—Europeans could not help but read the city as an object, first glimpsed from an offshore steamer arriving in the port of New York. Only two years after Dalí's visit, Mumford himself questions whether modernism could even *be* monumental, because monuments were necessarily retrospective, and modernism was always directed toward the future: "The very notion of a modern monument is a contradiction in terms, he wrote; "if it is a monument, it cannot be modern, and if it is modern, it cannot be a monument." Nevertheless, several Europeans during this period saw in New York the possibility of a new kind of monumentality, one that was freed of Europe's mantle of history and could therefore best symbolize democracy and the future. Their visions of the skyscrapers of New York offered springboards for new world visions that were as political, cultural, and fictional as they were architectural.

In the same breath and with the same zeal as his Egyptian vision, Dalí also compared Manhattan's skyline to "an immense Gothic Roquefort cheese," an analogy that must be understood as only the highest of compliments, as it came from someone who famously fetishized the baguette. According to his autobiography, during Dalí's initial steamer journey to New York in 1935, he anticipated dazzling the press with a fifteen-meter loaf of bread—a project he had been dreaming up for years, which he would eventually realize in full at a happening at the Théâtre de l'Étoile in Paris in 1958. The ship's baker succeeded in fabricating a version that was two and a half meters long, fortified with a wooden armature to keep it from drooping or crumbling. When Dalí disembarked into the crowd of reporters, however, not one of them inquired after the oversize loaf. As the architect Rem Koolhaas explains in his book *Delirious New York*, "If a two-meter loaf of French bread becomes unnoticeable, it means that, in Manhattan, there is no such scale against which its intended shock waves can register." The scale of the city, and of America in general, as Claude Lévi-Strauss would write in *Tristes Tropiques* of his arrival in New York in 1941, was immeasurable: "No doubt, objectively, New York is a town, but a European sensibility perceives it according to a quite different scale, the scale of European landscapes; whereas American landscapes transport us into a far vaster system for which we have no equivalent." Later, recollecting his arrival in New York in his essay "New York in 1941," Lévi-Strauss elaborated, with an evocation that brings to mind Emmenthaler rather than Roquefort: "New York (and this is the source of its charm and its peculiar fascination) was then a city where anything seemed possible. Like the urban fabric, the social and cultural fabric was riddled with holes."

Indeed, anything seemed possible in the holes of chaos that European writers, artists, and architects tore into the firmament of New York in the early 1940s. As Lévi-Strauss recounts, he spent much time with a group of surrealists in New York, including André Breton, whom Lévi-Strauss had met on board the ship during his transatlantic crossing, Max Ernst, and Dorothea Tanning. Fleeing German-occupied France—the Vichy government had proclaimed Breton's writings to be "the very negation of the national revolution"—these Europeans remained in Manhattan, an island of refuge for work, new encounters, and famously long dinners. Lévi-Strauss, Roman Jakobson, and Henri Focillon helped found the École Libre des Hautes Études, which was affiliated with the New School and which provided a home to French expatriate academics. This expat world was a constructed environment, which—in addition to the city's scale—is why Lévi-Strauss read New York in 1941 as a landscape; like the steamships on which the Europeans crossed the ocean, Manhattan was an island, a space apart for waiting out the war that provided time for reflection and innovation.

Like Dalí, the Swiss architectural historian Sigfried Giedion, Spanish architect Josep Lluís Sert, and French artist Fernand Léger—another close-knit group of European expats in New York in the early 1940s—read a possible new monumentality into this landscape. Operating from the same assumption as Lewis Mumford, that traditional monumentality was dead, Giedion, Sert, and Léger reached an entirely different conclusion when they collaborated on a response to solicitations they had each received from the American Abstract Artists group asking them to contribute to an upcoming publication. Rather than bury monumentality like Mumford, the three friends proposed its reformulation. Adopting a manifesto format, they produced the pithy, polemical "Nine Points on Monumentality," outlining a platform for a new form of monumentality within the context of American democratic society that would take advantage of the country's immeasurable scale: "Man-made landscapes would be correlated with nature's landscapes and all elements combined in terms of the new and vast facade, sometimes extending for many miles, which has been revealed to us by the air view." While Giedion, Léger, and Sert disagreed with Mumford, like him, they celebrated *freedom:* "In such monumental layouts, architecture and city planning could attain a new freedom." But whereas Mumford's freedom was the freedom of the individual from the constraints of mechanization, Giedion, Sert, and Léger's was the freedom of expression of "the collective force—the people." For these three Europeans, in other words, the horrors of the war had instilled a desire to recover or redeem collective expression. Eschewing traditional or "false" historicist monumentality, Giedion, Sert, and Léger tried to redefine monumentality to make it forward-looking and collaborative. This new expression would be achieved through scale (community centers, landscapes, and projections would all offer large-scale monuments to a shared democratic vision), modern materials (metals, laminated woods, and lighting), and new technologies (long span trusses, suspended ceilings, and mobile elements). Their hope was that this new form of monumentality could "attain a new freedom and develop creative possibilities," as had happened in the other arts.

This projective monumentality was envisioned for an urban context that was on the brink of change. While most major domestic building was suspended due to the war during the early 1940s, this pause permitted reflection, research, and anticipation. The "Nine Points" vision of Giedion, Sert, and Léger was partially inspired by Rockefeller Center, completed in 1939, which covered twenty-two acres in Manhattan and which they saw as a model for urban projects to come. A commercial complex built, as Giedion noted, at the scale of urban infrastructure, it nevertheless offered itself as a public monument to New York, complete with skating rink, hanging gardens, restaurants, and a landscaped observation deck seventy stories above the ground. Like Dalí, Giedion believed the skyscraper was the twentieth century's version of the Egyptian monuments; writing specifically in reference to Rockefeller Center, he extolled, "The skyscraper slab form of today is as significant and expressive for our period as the monolithic obelisk of Egypt and the Gothic cathedral tower were for theirs."

For Lewis Mumford, on the other hand, it was precisely the monumental skyscrapers of Rockefeller Center that ruined what was otherwise a fairly successful complex. "All of this is effective up to a height of thirty stories," he proclaimed in his *Skyline* column in the *New Yorker,* reading the tall buildings as expressions of capitalism rather than collectivity. "Above that, the added stories only increase the burdens on the elevator system and inflate the egos of great executives." This backhanded compliment comes off as high praise after Mumford's earlier review that had critiqued the project while still under construction, where he declared that "the best time to see the Center is at night . . . [when] one can forget that the buildings will constitute a planned chaos not to be distinguished objectively from the unplanned chaos around them." While Mumford's "Skyline" column enthusiastically captured the dynamism of urban life in Manhattan, he disliked the city's increasing scale; he complained twice in his Rockefeller Center review that he could see the full height of the RCA Building only by craning his neck at a very uncomfortable angle. He focused instead on a lower-scale city, writing laudatory columns on parks, shops, courthouses, and housing—such as Clarence Stein's Hillside Homes in the Bronx—whose buildings were mostly four to six stories tall.

Mumford's anti-skyline sentiments were not unusual among Americans. Sitting in the café by the skating rink at Rockefeller Center with his date, Sally, Holden Caulfield suddenly bursts out with his hatred of the city: "Taxicabs, and Madison Avenue buses, with the drivers and all always yelling at you to get out at the rear door . . . and going up and down in elevators when you just want to go outside." Published in 1951 and set in the late 1940s, J. D. Salinger's *The Catcher in the Rye* recounts a few days in New York in the life of its sixteen-year-old protagonist. While he wanders the city, Holden's descriptions almost always focus on interior spaces rather than the city's buildings as objects. Even the brown bear at the Central Park Zoo stays inside his cave when Holden visits with his sister Phoebe. As Holden moves from dark bar to hotel room to bar to luncheonette to bar to apartment to museum, he seems to spend most of his time in taxicabs and elevators. When he does walk down the street, he feels like he is going to drop into the earth—"just go down, down, down, and nobody'd ever see me again"—at every intersection he crosses. Similarly, Arthur Miller's Willy Loman sees the city as a "trap" in *Death of a Salesman* of 1949, complaining, "There's not a breath of fresh air in the neighborhood." In literature, the city perpetually seems to pale in comparison to an idealized pastoral. Nathanael West's *Miss Lonelyhearts* of 1933 describes a "sky rubbed with a soiled eraser" and "skyscrapers menac[ing] the park," and Saul Bellow's *The Victim* (1947) offers an equally unwelcoming image of the city: "The towers on the shore rose up in huge blocks, scorched, smoky, gray, and bare white where the sun was direct upon them." The combination of the Federal Highway Act of 1956 and the Federal Housing Authority's mortgage programs that favored single-family homes ensured that Americans could escape the city's soot for the greenery of suburbia, which in turn offered an endless supply of fictional fodder to writers ranging from John Cheever to Richard Yates to Rick Moody.

As Morton and Lucia White argue in their book *The Intellectual versus the City,* Americans, including Thomas Jefferson, Ralph Waldo Emerson, Henry Adams, Henry James, William James, and Frank Lloyd Wright, have long regarded the city with suspicion. In their foreword the authors even played up the uncanny resonance of Henry Ford and Gerald Ford's anti-urban sentiments: in 1922, Henry announced that "the ultimate solution will be the abandonment of the City"; fifty-three years later, little seemed to have changed when the *New York Daily News* ran the headline, "Ford to City: Drop Dead." The extreme verticals of the American city rendered many Americans nervous, and they sought respite in the seemingly endless horizons of the continent. When Frederick Jackson Turner proclaimed the closing of that horizontal frontier in 1893, claustrophobia blanketed the nation. Henry Blake Fuller's *The Cliff-Dwellers,* published that same year, described Chicago as an artificial landscape of immense cliffs inhabited by "modern yet still primitive tribes." "Life in Chicago," Fuller wrote later in the *Atlantic Monthly,* "continues to be—too largely, too markedly—a struggle for bare decencies."

If the city provided a constant critical refrain for American writers, it offered a positive magnetic pull to expats and immigrants, who tended to see potential within the chaos, filth, and crime of the early twentieth-century American city.

Samuel H. Gottscho, photographic negative of Rockefeller Center and the RCA Building from 515 Madison Avenue (1933)

Library of Congress Prints and Photographs Division

Upton Sinclair's protagonist Jurgis Rudkis described the shocking state of the Chicago stockyards in such vivid detail that the novel *The Jungle* is credited with ushering in the 1906 Food and Drug Act. Nevertheless, when Jurgis gazes at the stockyards on the evening of his arrival, he describes a land that looks more like Oz than Hell: "All the sordid suggestions of the place were gone—in the twilight it was a vision of power. To the two who stood watching while the darkness swallowed it up, it seemed a dream of wonder, with its tale of human energy, of things being done, of employment for thousands upon thousands of men, of opportunity and freedom, of life and love and joy." Forty years later, in 1948, Sigfried Giedion also focused a fascinated gaze on the stockyards, this time documenting in *Mechanization Takes Command* yet another kind of modern monumentality— the Taylorized killing and dissection of the pigs and cattle. Simone de Beauvoir also visited the stockyards around this time, chronicling her guided tour ("it's as though we were going to visit a museum") in her memoir, *America Day by Day,* which documents her four-month odyssey across the States. Marveling at the contrast between her martini and grilled lobster dinner in downtown Chicago and the darker sides of the city that Nelson Algren had showed her, she realizes that without "N.A.'s" tour "I would have known nothing of Chicago except a stage set with lights and stone, a deceptively opulent and orderly façade. At least I had a glance behind the painted set. I saw a real city, tragic and ordinary, fascinating like all cities where men of flesh and blood live and struggle by the millions." The juxtaposition of the two cities, living side by side in any urban conglomerate, is at once surreal and all too real, offering a permanent living tableau of modernity itself.

By 1960, New York's built monumentalities included the United Nations, a collaborative modern complex on the East River; Skidmore Owings and Merrill's Lever House, with its accessible plaza in the middle of its block; Mies van der Rohe's Seagram Building, which ushered in changes to the New York zoning code by offsetting the tall tower with a large plaza in front. The seventy-story RCA Building at Rockefeller Center—which became the GE Building and tomorrow might well proclaim another corporate identity—is no longer a surprising anomaly in a city whose skyline has reached higher and higher over the decades. Koolhaas's observation that "in Manhattan there is no such scale against which . . . shock waves can register" might well explain why it is that Claes Oldenburg, the sculptor known for his oversize everyday objects, has none on display in Manhattan and why his *N.Y.C. Pretzel* is not a fifteen-meter pretzel but instead an unlimited edition of seven-inch-square laser-cut cardboard pretzels.

Bibliography: Salvador Dalí, *The Secret Life of Salvador Dalí,* trans. Haakon M. Chevalier (New York, 1942). Sigfried Giedion, *Space, Time, and Architecture: The Growth of a New Tradition* (Cambridge, MA, 1941). Claude Lévi-Strauss, *The View from Afar,* trans. Joachim Neugroschel and Phoebe Hoss (New York, 1985). Morton White and Lucia White, *The Intellectual versus the City: From Thomas Jefferson to Frank Lloyd Wright* (1962; Oxford, 1977). Robert Wojtowicz, *Sidewalk Critic: Lewis Mumford's Writings on New York* (Princeton, NJ, 2000).

SARAH WHITING

1935, June 10

Bill Wilson Meets "Doctor Bob"

ALCOHOLICS ANONYMOUS

People have been drunk since Noah survived the flood. *"And he drank of the wine, and was drunken."*

1. We admitted we were powerless over alcohol—that our lives had become unmanageable.

Consider this:

I'd been sitting comfortably in a restaurant with Rita, drinking my sixth martini and hoping the waiter would forget about the lunch order—at least long enough for me to have a couple more.[1] My glass was empty. I asked her what she would have to drink, she said Scotch and soda, I ordered two of them.[2]

"He's a swell man," she said dispassionately, "when he's sober; and when he's drinking he's all right except with women and money."[3]

I didn't say anything and McCary sat down and took out a bottle of whisky. He poured a couple of drinks.

I nodded. We drank.[4]

"How do you like your brandy, sir?"

"Any way at all," I said.

"What are your charges?"

"I get twenty-five dollars a day, plus expenses."[5]

I knew I wasn't capable of keeping the bulk of the money myself, so I gave it to a white fellow who owned the bar I frequented. He kept the money for me, but I worried him to death for it. Finally, I broke the last one hundred dollar bill the Saturday before I left. I got out of that bill one pair of shoes, and the rest of that money was blown. I took the last of it to buy my railroad ticket.[6]

For the next few years fortune threw money and applause my way. I had arrived.[7]

1. "Women Suffer Too," *Alcoholics Anonymous* (1939)
2. *The Thin Man*, Dashiell Hammett (1934)
3. "Too Many Have Lived," Hammett (1932)
4. "Black," Paul Cain (1932)
5. *The Big Sleep*, Raymond Chandler (1939)
6. "Jim's Story," *Alcoholics Anonymous*
7. "Bill's Story," *Alcoholics Anonymous*

Alcoholics Anonymous, The Big Book, published in 1939, is a collection of personal stories about the ways that working through twelve conscious steps had saved the lives of alcoholics for whom nothing else had ever helped. What is it about the tone of the testimonials to sobriety written in the 1930s that sound so much like the hardboiled writing of the same time? The prose isn't pretty, and what feels similar about the tone could be nothing more than mimicry of a commercial style, but I think that the development of the hardboiled voice brought into writing the authentic voice of spoken English at the time, the spoken English of the Depression, exhausted, cautious—and added the paradox of defiant acceptance. The Big Book sounds like noir because crime gives a writer permission to describe the bottom of society; it's at the bottom of society that the alcoholic finds himself, and it was on a day in December 1934, at the bottom of a society at the bottom of an economy, that Bill Wilson, a brilliant but defeated stock analyst, drunk for twenty years, who had ruined every opportunity offered to him, found what he would call his Higher Power:

> I still gagged badly on the notion of a Power greater than myself, but finally, just for the moment, the last vestige of my proud obstinacy was crushed . . . Suddenly the room lit up with a great white light. I was caught up into an ecstasy which there are no words to describe. Complete hopelessness and deflation at depth were almost always required to make the recipient ready. *Deflation at depth* (as William James put it in *Varieties of Religious Experience*)—yes, that was *it*. Exactly what had happened to me.

He felt clear of all temptation to drink for seven months. His fortunes had improved a little, enough for old friends to give him another chance, and then he was sent to resolve a proxy fight in Akron, Ohio. Even sober, he failed.

He's alone in the Mayflower Hotel lobby. He sees the bar, hears the laughter. He feels the attraction of boozy companionship. He walks over to the church directory. He knows that he needs to talk to another alcoholic. Bill calls the Episcopal priest to put him in touch with a local Oxford Group, a thirty-year-old Christian fellowship that Bill knew had some success with alcoholics. That call led to ten more calls that brought him to Dr. Robert Holbrook Smith, a proctologist who needed to drink to keep his hands steady for surgery and, weirdly, still had remnants of a practice.

Smith agreed to hear Bill out for fifteen minutes, in a friend's kitchen. Bill got there at five and stayed until eleven fifteen. In The Big Book, Smith, writing as "Doctor Bob," tells what happened at what became the first meeting of Alcoholics Anonymous.

"That was June 10, 1935, and that was my last drink . . . What did the man do or say that was different from what others had done or said? . . . He gave me information about the subject of alcohol which was undoubtedly helpful. Of far more importance was the fact that he was the first living human with whom I had ever talked, who knew what he was talking about in regard to alcoholism from actual experience. In other words, he talked my language."

Which was also a medical language instead of a moral language. A paradox of Alcoholics Anonymous is that without the medicalization of sin, AA could not have become a religion, which it is, a religion that may yet save the world.

   2. Came to believe that a Power greater than ourselves could restore us to sanity.

3. Made a decision to turn our will and our lives over to the care of God as we under-stood Him.

4. Made a searching and fearless moral inventory of ourselves.

Thorstein Veblen reasoned that typesetters were such famous alcoholics in the 1890s simply because they could travel easily with a job that was the same wherever they went, and, lacking any other means of satisfying "the human need for ostentation" in front of an ever-shifting company of new friends, if that's what they were, spending money freely, they bought each other drinks in bars and got each other conspicuously drunk.

Veblen's journeyman printer is the modern man, in whom the "highly orga-nized and highly impersonal industrial process of the present, deranges the ani-mistic habits of thought . . . The grounds of generalization habitually present in the workman's mind and the point of view from which he apprehends phenom-ena is an enforced cognizance of matter-of-fact sequence." The creature of mod-ern industry, "endowed with the habit of readily apprehending and relating facts in terms of causal sequence," and the modern industrial process "tends selectively to eliminate these traits of human nature from the spiritual constitution of the classes that are immediately engaged in the industrial process . . . The result, so far as concerns the workman's life of faith, is a proclivity to undevout skepti-cism."

Undevout skepticism (Sam Spade, Philip Marlowe, Humphrey Bogart) is the public stance that desperation uses to protect itself, the hopelessness born from a social envy impossible to overcome, the great unsettling curse of selfishness, about which, Wilson says, "The alcoholic is an extreme example of self-will run riot. Above everything, we alcoholics must be rid of this selfishness . . . God makes that possible."

But why *this* God, the "God as we understood Him," instead of the Jesus of resurrection, or even Christ the Scientist of Mary Baker Eddy? Alcoholism was nothing new in the world, but until June 10, 1935, no one had ever formulated a cure, although in this light, the Eighteenth Amendment was a rational response to a plague as powerful as influenza. Addiction, as the prophet Bill Wilson sensed, the most modern affliction, is the terrible emotional complement to the assem-bly line in a consumer society; spiritual slavery to the internal compulsion engine. "Things are in the saddle," wrote Emerson, "and ride mankind." Emerson again: "We live in succession, in division, in parts, in particles. Meantime within man is the soul of the whole; the wise silence; the universal beauty . . . the eternal ONE."

5. Admitted to God, to ourselves, and to another human being the exact nature of our wrongs.

6. Were entirely ready to have God remove all these defects of character.

7. Humbly asked Him to remove our shortcomings.

Not this: "I *admit* to God, and to *myself,* and to another human being the exact nature of my wrongs." An ink-stained undevout skeptic would gag on a declara-tion that sounds like the Boy Scouts oath.

The steps look forward to imagine looking backward, a variation on positive thinking. To stand with God as we understood Him, and to recite all twelve steps as already completed, means that part of recovery is the recovery of the memory of this truth, which would be impossible without an eternal relationship with that personal Higher Power, since on the first day of membership, one recalls a beginning that was always there, that never began. Emerson: "The act of seeing and the thing seen, the seer and the spectacle, the subject and the object, are one." So of course the anniversaries of sobriety are birthdays. One's birthday in AA takes place in a sacred community existing outside of temporal nature in which people suffer from a disease. The cure of the spirit for the diseases of the flesh, with the help of a God who can only be understood through experience and whose miracles can only be known through one's own witness—this is nothing if not a perfect illustration of what Harold Bloom calls the American Religion. Bill Wilson was no less a religious visionary than Joseph Smith. And he became such a figure guided by his study of William James: "Religion, therefore, as I now ask you to arbitrarily take it, shall mean for us *the feelings, acts, and experiences of individual men in their solitude, so far as they apprehend themselves to stand in relation to whatever they may consider the divine.*"

"The God of the American Religion is not a creator-God," Bloom writes, "because the American never *was* created, and so the American has at least a part of God within herself. 'Original sin and God's culpability have vanished together.'" Like Veblen, Wilson understood that addiction was the new disease, the new loneliness on the border of the industrial frontier. Against the same frightening frontier of the continent, the ruined Garden of Eden, Joseph Smith saw that the American Adam, alone in the Garden of Eden, which was America, could not only walk with Jesus but could elevate himself to be a God like the God of this cosmos, to understand that the American is eternal, just like God, in a universe of unfolding social abundance.

Bill resolved, by intuitive revelation, the conflict between that Mormon God, so white, and the Baptist God, both black and white, with whom the American could also walk in the Garden, but in the solitude of personal relationship, "alone in the Garden with Jesus," and "nobody knows the trouble I've seen, nobody knows but Jesus." Alcoholics Anonymous is the spiritual reconciliation of the civil war over the Garden, the conflict between the separate yearnings of Huck's longing for solitude in the territory ahead, away from civilization, and Jim's dream of peace, in society. Wilson completed the American religion's abandonment of the torment and passion of the tortured Christ on the cross of Catholicism, completed, one can say, the Reformation, and then erased Jesus entirely. What remained in America before AA was the empty cross, symbol of resurrection, and now, with AA, not even that. The journeyman printers have heard too much of Jesus from the Salvation Army banging outside the tavern.

Frost: "And forthwith found salvation in surrender."

To personally understand God was not intentionally ecumenical, this is not Unitarianism or Ethical Culture, a religious Esperanto, but a piece of the unfolding revelation as solid, in its way, as Joseph Smith's gold plates as shown to him by Moroni. God as we understood Him might include a vision of Jesus, or might be

Buddha, or the Shekinah, the feminine principle of the Jewish God that resides only in peaceful community, but whichever it is, whoever it is, for AA to endure, even to work, that God as we understood Him must remain the private experience of the alcoholic, or else the competing doctrines of salvation would wreck the circle of folding chairs.

The anonymity of the members, a ritual fiction, is an elevation to the eternal. So many Bills, so many Bobs. A religion with no creation myth, nothing to mistake literally, a text in plain language. A cunning structure; no dues, no tithes, no president, protected from permanent officers and the development of cults by a rotating leadership for each separate group, no other requirement for membership than the declaration of fellowship in a shared condition. The meager sacrament of cookies and coffee. The making good on the American promise that all are welcome.

This is not a new idea, but the first institution in America to make this idea real.

8. Made a list of all persons we had harmed, and became willing to make amends to them all.

9. Made direct amends to such people wherever possible, except when to do so would injure them or others.

10. Continued to take personal inventory and when we were wrong promptly admitted it.

"I feel your pain," said Bill Clinton. Well, yes, there's the rub, now we have to feel yours. Spiritual pop is the demon of America, the devil who mocks the authentic by the simple trick of abbreviation, like *Reader's Digest.* There's a tableau following every public political or religious scandal: politician or minister is caught at sin, denies, then meets with his personal Billy Graham, who publicly vouches for the sinner's confession, sinner appears before the press, with his pretty wife a few feet to the side and behind, and makes his amends. Pretty wife says the marriage is stronger than ever.

In earlier times—say, the times of Wilbur Mills—partying with whores gets a congressman tossed out of the game, but in these later days (of Latter Day Sinners), partying with whores, of either sex, can now be blessed away. Anyone familiar with AA knows that working all twelve steps can take years, like learning the violin, but the new American contrition is to those twelve steps as the autoharp to the Stradivarius. The public apology has become the equivalent of going to Colonial Williamsburg and having a photo snapped of your head in the stocks, and holding this up as evidence of punishment.

11. Sought through prayer and meditation to improve our conscious contact with God, as we understood Him, praying only for knowledge of His will for us and the power to carry that out.

12. Having had a spiritual awakening as the result of these Steps, we tried to carry this message to alcoholics, and to practice these principles in all our affairs.

With the last two steps the sober alcoholics become a Kingdom of Priests charged by God to spread holiness. The pop demon of abbreviation takes advantage of an idea that is missing from the language of step nine—"Made direct amends to such people wherever possible, except when to do so would injure them or others"—that the amends may not be accepted, and even without that acceptance, the attempt at making the amends becomes its own forgiveness, as Emerson saw it: "The Supreme Critic on the errors of the past and the present, and the only prophet of that which must be, is that great nature in which we rest; the Unity, that Over-Soul . . . that common heart."

Spiritually and practically, this may be the only way to return to the river of life without drowning in useless recrimination, the self-loathing of Veblen's invidious comparisons on the scale of moral consequence and responsibility, which makes one vulnerable again to a drink. But politically, we are forced by the apology to forgive, because the spiritual offense in a universe of eternity is never a lapse but always a relapse.

In its own practice, in its own texts, AA introduces addiction as a disease and not a sin, but then demands moral responsibility for the cure of that disease. "So our troubles, we think, are basically of our own making," writes Bill, who believed in both God and medicine. In politics, the sinners declare the problem a sickness cured, and then walk away. This is not the fault of Bill Wilson. The words have been stolen.

Where will it go? It's easy to mock the spread of support groups, but the founder of any religion is nothing if not a prophet. In 1935, Wilson recognized that addiction was a new disease, the plague of modernity. Who are Veblen's journeyman printers but the advance guard of the technicians of information processing? The most modern of men is an addict.

To put this another way, how many hours will you spend online this week? For real?

Hi. My name is ——.

Bibliography: Alcoholics Anonymous (1939; 4th ed. New York, 2001). Harold Bloom, *The American Religion* (New York, 1992). Paul Cain, "Black," *Black Mask* (May 1932). Ralph Waldo Emerson, "The Over-Soul," from *Essays: First Series* (Boston, 1841). Thorstein Veblen, *The Theory of the Leisure Class* (1899; New York, 2007).

MICHAEL TOLKIN

1935, October 10
A controversial folk opera premieres on Broadway

PORGY AND BESS

George Gershwin had a dream. He wanted the respect accorded classical composers in the 1920s and '30s and denied mere pop tunesmiths. So he wrote some semiclassical pieces, and finally worked himself up to compose an actual opera, *Porgy and Bess.* Controversy dogged it for decades, though ultimately, for some, the work faded into the past or, for others, was elevated to classic status — both as an American opera and as a repository of some of the best-known songs ever composed during the golden age of American songwriting.

At this late date, the older controversies seem a little musty, too. Critics mostly enjoyed the opera in 1935, though they fretted over whether it was a real opera or a gussied-up musical. Early on, and then later in the shifting evolution of black cultural identity, some black critics attacked its authenticity as an expression of black life and black music. But the real place of *Porgy* in our cultural history seems to be as an exemplar and an anticipation of an ongoing dialogue between high and low art.

Gershwin is perhaps the most written-about American composer, and the history of *Porgy and Bess* and the history of its reception, then and since, have been exhaustively reported, most fully in Howard Pollack's *George Gershwin: His Life and Work* (2006). But here, a brief summary: the opera is based on DuBose Heyward's novel *Porgy* (1925) and its adaptation by him and his wife, Dorothy Heyward, as a Broadway play, first performed in 1927. Both novel and play were widely popular, the novel credited in some quarters as a breakthrough in the realistic and sympathetic portrayal of blacks. The novel was published at the height of the New Negro Renaissance, during which white intellectuals and artists took a newly serious interest in the depiction of African American life. *Porgy* was preceded by another novel by a white Southerner, T. S. Stribling's *Birthright* (1922), which was widely read by African American writers, and which tried to show the Negro in ways that transcended vaudeville stereotypes. The Heywards' play was part of a group of other dramas that examined black life in nonstereotypical ways, including Ridgely Torrence's *Plays for a Negro Theater* (1916) and Eugene O'Neill's *Emperor Jones* (1920) and *All God's Chillun Got Wings* (1924).

Novel and play were rife with good intentions, not that those count for much in terms of identity politics. The Heywards were white, DuBose coming from an old Charleston family that had fallen on hard economic times but had managed to retain its social cachet (the Heywards resumed DuBose's ancestral lifestyle with the financial success of *Porgy,* novel and play). Both versions of *Porgy* tell the story of the denizens of Catfish Row, of the crippled beggar Porgy's love for the wayward Bess, torn between the values of community and the goodness of Porgy and the sexual heat of the stevedore Crown and the cocaine-peddling Sportin' Life. That diabolical charmer manages to spirit Bess off to New York, which to Porgy is about as far away as the moon, presumably for a life of debauchery and prostitution. In the play, the inspirational ending has been added, whereby Porgy calls for his goat and cart and heads off in pursuit of his woman.

The novel's third-person narration (some of it powerful, as in the hurricane scene) is rendered in standard English. But the dialogue in the novel and throughout the play is a combination of Gullah and darky stage dialect, which reads painfully today ("Dat lady ob mine is a born white-folks nigger") but may well have reflected a good-faith attempt at re-creating how people spoke back then. Over the years, performers of the opera have generally toned down the dialect (and jettisoned the word "nigger," as well, a change sanctioned after George's death by his brother, Ira).

It took Gershwin some years to clear the decks and begin work on his *Porgy* opera, but when he did so, he tackled it head on, devoting months out of his hyperactive, vastly remunerative schedule of concert tours and the composing of new musicals to research, composition, and orchestration of *Porgy and Bess.* The orchestration alone was a massive task. The libretto by DuBose Heyward, with lyrics by Heyward and Ira Gershwin, hews closely to the play, although voodoo (the "conjure woman") is downplayed in favor of Christianity. The music, aside from its show-stopping tunes, is a full-tilt through-composed opera, with considerable harmonic daring and elaborate recitatives (the bridging material between the songs or arias, in other operas sometimes spoken or, in the eighteenth century, sung parlando with harpsichord accompaniment, but by the nineteenth century usually fully scored).

Gershwin did not attempt to fully integrate his big numbers into the orchestral flow, as in Wagner's "endless melody," a catchphrase that did not always reflect Wagner's actual practice. But the *Porgy* recitatives are ingeniously constructed, often bringing back familiar melodies in counterpoint to a new theme or scene, for psychological complexity. Wagner had his leitmotifs, short phrases linked to particular characters or props (Wotan's spear, Siegfried's sword). Gershwin brought back whole tunes, as in "Bess, You Is My Woman Now" behind Porgy's determination at the end to set out for New York.

Sometimes Gershwin's very attentiveness to such mechanics seems a little self-conscious. But the sweep of the music, its passion and brio and elegant craftsmanship, along with unforgettable characters and a seemingly unstoppable sequence of indelible melodies, have justly earned *Porgy* a place in the operatic repertory as well as a steady sequence of Broadway or West End revivals. People are moved by Porgy and his anguished, life-justifying love for Bess, and Gershwin gave all the characters music worthy of them and their Catfish Row community.

The Broadway premiere of *Porgy and Bess* at the Alvin Theater on October 10, 1935—the official world premiere had been at the tryout in Boston's Colonial Theater on September 30—was by some accounts the high point of Gershwin's cruelly short life (he died of a brain tumor in 1937 at the age of thirty-eight), with delirious ovations from a starry audience and a delirious after-party for 400 at Condé Nast's apartment. Although the run lasted only 124 performances, short for a Broadway hit—attributable in part to the familiarity of the play and high ticket prices during the Depression—it was a long run for an opera.

And it marked the beginning of the score's conquest of the world, interrupted by World War II but then boosted by the State Department's cold war efforts to enhance the image of American culture abroad. Since 1935 *Porgy and Bess* has been heard cut down from the original four-hour score, a compression that began on the way from Boston to New York; its recitatives have been replaced by dialogue; its orchestration has been thinned and thickened or jettisoned altogether in favor of jazz arrangements; its vocal lines teased and twisted improvisationally. Most everywhere, perhaps at first even more abroad than at home, it has been cheered as an iconic product of American culture.

From the outset there was controversy, although according to Howard Pollack, the white press seemed little concerned with the opera's accuracy as a portrayal of black culture or with the Gershwins' Jewishness. The "is it a real opera or a pretentious musical" reactions came both from classical critics, some of whom thought Gershwin was reaching beyond his status, and Broadway critics, who claimed it for their own but resisted the operatic trappings.

The orchestral recitatives proved especially controversial. That controversy has played itself out in the various revivals, though there has been a steady favoring of the full score in opera houses (like New York's Metropolitan Opera) and in recordings. Virgil Thomson, not yet ensconced at the *Herald Tribune* but already an influential critic, attacked Gershwin and the opera as amateurish—he called it "crooked folklore and halfway opera"—but seemed to be resenting its success and attention next to his own *Four Saints in Three Acts,* libretto by Gertrude Stein, which premiered on Broadway in 1934, and which wasn't black at all in tone and content but used an all-black cast.

The question of the authenticity of *Porgy* has been more divisive. For some, the story is a warm portrayal of black life in the early twentieth century, written from the outside but still profoundly sympathetic. For others, it is an ugly excrescence, glorifying prostitution, drugs, and murder, especially but not exclusively for black intellectuals who hoped along with W. E. B. Du Bois that blacks would put aside ghetto ways and join the broader society—an anticipation of latter-day hostility against rap.

Some blacks, not least members of the various *Porgy* casts over the years, deeply admired the work—like the first Porgy, Todd Duncan, who "literally wept for what this Jew was able to express for the Negro," and Maya Angelou, who appeared in a small role in a later production, and William Warfield, another Porgy, who thought the cast and black community leaders recognized that the opera was "a celebration of our culture, not an exploitation of it."

Others dismissed it—Sidney Poitier writhed with guilt for having acted Porgy in the slick Hollywood film version, directed by Otto Preminger (1959)—although Duke Ellington's famous "debunking" of Gershwin's "lampblack Negroisms" seems to have been partly invented in the magazine *New Theatre* by Edward Morrow, a white left-wing critic himself eager to debunk the work. The black press in 1935 took a generally sympathetic view, whatever their specific reservations.

As social and racial relations changed, however, by the 1950s and '60s more critics, white and black, grew uncomfortable with *Porgy*. Winthrop Sargeant of the *New Yorker* worried that it had become "almost as dated as 'Uncle Tom's Cabin.'" Harold Schonberg of the *New York Times* was a persistent, aggressive critic of Gershwin's classical pretensions (and of Leonard Bernstein's). James Hicks in the *Baltimore Afro-American* called the opera "the most insulting, the most libelous, the most degrading act that could possibly be perpetrated against colored Americans of modern time." Harold Cruse in *The Crisis of the Negro Intel-*

lectual (1967) attacked *Porgy and Bess* as a prime example of white (and especially Jewish) exploitation of black culture. Cruse's complaints against Jews could be seen in the context of the widening gap between black and Jewish activists toward the end of the civil rights movement, though again, on racial grounds, black resistance focused more on the opera's creators being white, not on its composer and co-librettist being Jewish.

Overall, there seem to be more lingering complaints against Heyward's story and libretto than against Gershwin's music. How could it be otherwise, given the wholesale adoption of songs from *Porgy and Bess* into the repertory of black jazz musicians—including Ellington? Of the innumerable jazz versions of these songs, those of Ella Fitzgerald and Louis Armstrong and of Miles Davis (with arrangements by Gil Evans) stand out, but the music is by now ubiquitous. *Porgy* has been subsumed into the larger, more bitter argument about the inherent racism of white American society.

That said, and recognizing the opera (in whatever form) and the songs as classics, lingering doubts about *Porgy* remain. This was, after all, a first opera, with all the infelicities such efforts usually entail. Who knows, had he lived, whether Gershwin could have achieved the Mozartean fusion of classical and popular, of high and low, to which he aspired? Given his genius, the chances are good, but he wasn't quite there yet with *Porgy*.

The late 1920s into the '30s, with the advent of the microphone and amplification and the nationwide radio networks with their own symphony orchestras and famous in-house conductors (Arturo Toscanini at NBC), marked the apex of middlebrow culture. Among other, less friendly ways, that can be defined as well-meaning, often naive efforts to elevate the masses through high culture, and maybe to bend high culture in more populist directions. Sometimes, the effort foundered on the unwillingness of composers to dumb down their music, as happened in part in Berlin in the 1920s. Other composers either sought a simpler style (Weill, first with Brecht, later on Broadway) or had it forced upon them (Shostakovich's and Prokofiev's cruder capitulations to Stalin).

Porgy and Bess was hardly the first work of musical theater to devote itself to black themes (Bert Williams's and George Walker's *In Dahomey* played on Broadway in 1896, and Eubie Blake's *Shuffle Along* arrived in 1921) or to plant the flag of opera on Broadway (*Four Saints in Three Acts* beat *Porgy* by a year, and Marc Blitzstein's *The Cradle Will Rock* followed soon after, with Gian Carlo Menotti's weepers yet to come in the 1950s). Some might wish to pigeonhole *Porgy* as a journeyman's "pathetic ambition to write 'straight' music" (Mosco Carner, a Puccini expert; despite the efforts of modernist *Porgy* partisans to stress its contemporaneity by allusions to Berg's *Wozzeck,* Puccini seems to be a truer template). Yet this was also the time when Broadway did indeed aspire to transcend fluffy revues and attain a new seriousness, from Jerome Kern's *Show Boat* to Richard Rodgers's *Oklahoma!*

This dream of serious American musical theater was, then, not Gershwin's alone, and it is a dream that has never died. Kurt Weill's populism, culminating in his Broadway musicals before his own premature death in 1950, helped provoke a violent modernist reaction. For a time, music seemed split between esoteric high-modernist composers who wrote for one another and melodramatists like Menotti. Popular music was dismissed as commercial corruption, despite a lingering respect for jazz and the arch-mandarin Milton Babbitt's hobby of playing Broadway show tunes at parties.

Musical polemics have since relaxed, in a way that casts new light on *Porgy*. Gershwin's classical aspirations may seem a little naive, even pompous, in the manner of (though far superior to) English art-rockers who write piano concertos and requiem masses or even operas.

The deliberate mixing of disparate idioms still carries all sorts of risks; the postmodernist era in classical music is as full of pandering as Paul McCartney's classical works are full of empty rhetoric. Gershwin adapted the styles and verse of the black ragtime, stride, and early jazz pianists and composers he knew and admired, first to Broadway, then to opera. The Who came the other way, from rock to opera, or something rather like opera. All kinds of composers (Stephin Merritt, Elvis Costello, Jeanine Tesori, Michael John LaChiusa) have assayed serious works of musical theater that don't necessarily stray too far from the idioms in which the composers established themselves; they don't have to deny their style to strike deep. Stephen Sondheim lives on, the godfather of these hybrids.

So what is *Porgy and Bess?* It is a piece of American culture, a sympathetic (despite the inevitable distancing across racial lines), often vivid and touching, sometimes awkward and sentimental, overlong piece of operatic musical theater. It epitomizes a seemingly irrepressible dream of American composers from whatever side of whatever divide: to make a dramatic, music-driven work that speaks to real people with the most sophisticated means available. It's not perfect, but it's great.

Bibliography: Hollis Alpert, *The Life and Times of Porgy and Bess: The Story of an American Classic* (New York, 1990). Howard Pollack, *George Gershwin: His Life and Work* (Berkeley, CA, 2006). *Discography: Porgy and Bess* (MCA), reissue on CD of 1940 highlights with much of original cast.

JOHN ROCKWELL

1936

Gone with the Wind is published June 30;
Absalom, Absalom! is published October 24

MARGARET MITCHELL AND WILLIAM FAULKNER

"Tell about the South. What's it like there. What do they do there. Why do they live there. Why do they live at all," says Shreve McCannon, opening a dialogue with his Harvard roommate, Quentin Compson, that will take up the last half of William Faulkner's *Absalom, Absalom!* The notable absence of question marks here underscores the way in which these sentences register on the Southerner Quentin as part of a weary refrain he would like to escape but cannot. Shreve, on the other hand—so extreme a Northerner as to be Canadian—enjoys making fun of what Faulkner himself once called "a makebelieve region of swords and magnolias and mockingbirds which perhaps never existed anywhere" at the same time that he is intent upon understanding it, committed to getting at the truth beneath the legend. Between them, the two boys deliver up a radically revisionist version of the South. Yet no matter how passionately Quentin and Shreve demystify the South, the myth refuses to die. In the very process of telling the story of Thomas Sutpen, reshaping it in accord with both newly discovered information and the demands of their young male imaginations, Quentin and Shreve reinvigorate the idea of the South by feeding the apparently fathomless hunger for stories about it. Faulkner thus recognized, and indeed built into the very narrative structure of his novel, what his contemporary Margaret Mitchell had recently demonstrated with the explosive popularity of her novel *Gone with the Wind,* that Yankees and Southerners alike were readily seducible by an author who could "tell about the South."

Lacking the millions of readers Mitchell would command, Faulkner simply situated Quentin and Shreve as readers of the Southern past inside the covers of his novel, thereby representing an audience he knew his novel would never have. Yet despite the vast difference in their commercial success (*Absalom, Absalom!* had a first printing of 6,000 copies, whereas 1,700,000 copies of *Gone with the Wind* sold within its first year), the two writers had in common a keen skepticism toward the mythical South. Mitchell would later write to a friend,

> I have been embarrassed on many occasions by finding myself included among writers who pictured the south as a land of white-columned mansions whose wealthy owners had thousands of slaves and drank thousands of juleps. I have been surprised, too, for North Georgia certainly was no such country—if it ever existed anywhere—and I took great pains to describe North Georgia as it was. But people believe what they like to believe and the mythical Old South has too strong a hold on their imaginations to be altered by the mere reading of a 1,037 page book.

Such a claim may strike us as disingenuous, but there can be little doubt that Mitchell was sincere in her belief that she had written a book more likely to offend white Southern dowagers than Northern liberals. Before the book was officially published, Mitchell expressed concern about the misunderstandings to which the early press announcements "commending me for writing a book that put the South in its true light" were likely to lead: "I can never visit Macon after publication," she said. Once the novel actually appeared, though, it became clear enough that any disapproval would come not from Southern readers, but from a few literary critics who saw the novel as stylistically simple-minded and substantively no more than another romance of the South.

Faulkner's view of *Gone with the Wind* was relatively temperate. He remarked only that "no story takes 1,037 pages to tell." But he seems to have taken a cue from Mitchell when it came to business matters. Knowing Hollywood as he did, he could not have failed to notice the $50,000 David Selznick paid Mitchell for the movie rights to *Gone with the Wind.* As *Absalom, Absalom!* neared publication, Faulkner announced that he wanted to sell its movie rights for $100,000. Within a month he reduced his price by half. Offering the proofs for a fellow screenwriter's scrutiny, he said, "The price is $50,000. It's about miscegenation." Irony has almost conquered hope here, as Faulkner was bound to realize, finally, that his new novel would find little interest from Hollywood, much less bring the same price as Mitchell's blockbuster.

Given what Hollywood did to and with Mitchell's novel, Faulkner was probably lucky to find no buyers at any price for his. It remains important to understand, however, that Faulkner would have been glad to sell the novel to the movies; he seems to have cared little that *Sanctuary* (1931) was made into a perfectly awful film. Mitchell in fact referred to the deformations performed on that novel when she expressed her own worries about what Hollywood would do to *Gone with the Wind.* Refusing to have anything to do with the movie's production, she wrote a friend, "I grieve to hear that Tara has columns."

Mitchell may sound like she is speaking in bad faith, but she is not. The movie that appeared in 1939 heavily tilted the story of Ashley and Melanie, Scarlett and Rhett toward the nostalgic end of the spectrum, largely ignoring the constitutive ambivalence at work in the novel between the traditional legend of Southern ladies and courtiers and the reality of the capitalist entrepreneurial spirit that actually drives Scarlett, and with her the novel's plot. In the novel, Tara appears without columns, and the Wilkes plantation has no grand double staircase, as in the movie. The grand Wilkes family of the novel is widely understood to be peculiar, exceptional in its habits of marrying cousins to each other, reading foreign books, and listening to classical music. The rest of the county is populated by a variety of nonaristocratic classes, both black and white, among them smaller landowners, yeomen from the hills who show up after the war trying to make a living, and hard-headed country women such as Grandma Coulter, who instructs Scarlett on the will to survive. The social spectrum is Balzacian.

More important, Scarlett's family is a mere generation away from the scene of immigration: her father, we learn, had to run away from Ireland, having killed a man in the course of that country's rebellious activities. True, his miraculous marriage to Ellen of Savannah aligns him with the old coastal culture of the genteel class, but his eldest daughter, Scarlett, is aligned with his more rugged and adventurous roots. Venerating her sainted mother, she emulates her boisterous father. In this context it is perhaps "fittin'," to use Mammy's favorite word, to observe that the novel's opening line, "Scarlett O'Hara was not beautiful," is flatly and fulsomely contradicted by the movie's opening scene, in which Vivian Leigh "abrupts," to use a favorite term of Faulkner's, upon the screen. The entire movie is thrown off course from the novel's trajectory by the simple fact of Leigh's stunning beauty.

It has long since become impossible to read the novel without the filter of the movie. Indeed, many of *Gone with the Wind*'s first readers were preemptively engaged in advising the studio on whom to cast in each role, and many of them read the novel with Clark Gable already playing Rhett Butler in their imaginations. But if one tries honestly to reread *Gone with the Wind* outside the frame retrospectively imposed on it by the film, one sees that Mitchell's novel does issue a realistic rejoinder to the mythic South. Scarlett's career defies the basic assumptions of the Old South; she is "no lady," as Rhett instantly recognizes, and she has no scruples in her drive to beat the Yankees at their own game. Her attachment to the dream of Ashley Wilkes, the archetypal aristocratic Southerner, is finally exposed as an adolescent delusion, and she then realizes what the reader has known from early on: it has always been Rhett she loves, Rhett the defector from Wilkes's aristocracy, who has made a fortune in the war and represents the essence of virile capitalist enterprise.

But just at the moment Scarlett sees through to the truth—to what Rhett has always insisted is their common bond, the capacity to see things clearly—Rhett himself defects. He turns into Ashley: longing for "the calm dignity life can have when it's lived by gentle folks, the genial grace of days that are gone . . . the slow charm," Rhett departs for Charleston. Unable to dissuade Rhett from leaving her, Scarlett is back where she began, in love with a man she cannot have. And what does she do? She determines to get him again. And how does she plan to accomplish this? By returning to Tara. So the dream is, after all, not dead. Hope resides in the land, the plantation, and of course in "Mammy," who is out at Tara awaiting Scarlett's return. The novel sutures over its radical ambivalence about the Old South by sending its heroine on a new quest. Scarlett turns her mind to Tara, hoping that by returning to its sacred soil she will be able to get Rhett back. Like him, she reverts to the past as the sole remaining source for any possible future. It is as if Mitchell had allowed herself to indulge, for hundreds of pages, in exposing the Old South legend as a reactionary and conservative tradition sustained by people who clung to a false sense of class superiority as an excuse for their economic failures, by dimwitted men who enshrined white women as goddesses but failed to realize their possible intelligence, and by ridiculous old women who guarded the gates of respectability with a vengeance matched only by their ignorance of the degree to which that respectability depended on wealth. But then, in the end, she would have us believe that what Scarlett and Rhett have in common is no longer their critical vision but their renewed devotion to the South, reborn in Rhett's fantasies about Charleston and Scarlett's fantasies about Tara.

Given the novel's miraculous power to disrobe and then re-enshrine the South, it is not so surprising that it found millions of applauding readers. The novel enabled its readers to eat their cake and have it too: to see through the sham of the aristocratic legend but to see it miraculously revived at the same time. Thanks to Scarlett, the hypocrisies of the Old South were exposed, as when Scarlett upbraids Ashley for opposing her plan to hire prison labor: "You didn't seem to have any objection to working slaves," she tartly remarks. But also thanks to Scarlett, the deep conviction that determination, intelligence, and a heavy dose of savvy would pull the nation out of the Depression was renewed as the true story of the South. The South was, after all, not different from but the very essence of America in its individualistic ambition and determined striving.

A good part of what enabled this smoke-and-mirrors performance was the novel's utterly faithful rendition of racist stereotypes. White Americans could agree on the beneficent quality of Negroes so long as they were kept under subjection. "You must realize that they are like children and must be guarded from themselves like children," Scarlett remembers her mother saying. Although the novel's treatment of race is more complex than the movie's, incorporating, for example, a second Mammy figure in the person of Dilcey (who is part black and part Indian and therefore noble), it nevertheless adheres to well-seasoned racial clichés of the American imagination. Black critics noted the utter familiarity of such characters and remarked that the civilization called the South was by no means "gone with the wind" but persisted on its racist path.

If it was a shared racism that enabled the nation as a whole to unite around the irresistible story of Scarlett O'Hara, it was that same racism that Faulkner set out to excavate in *Absalom, Absalom!* While Mitchell enabled America to see itself in a new, revised version of the South That Rose Again, Faulkner revealed America as a united state of denial, secured by its refusal to face the racist oppression crouching at its heart. *Absalom, Absalom!* tells the story of Thomas Sutpen, a man who came from nowhere, arrived in Mississippi in the mid-1830s, and with no visible means built a plantation that would soon become the largest in sight. Sutpen embodies perhaps the most deeply embedded of all American myths, that of the self-made man. His career in itself gives the lie to the myth of the aristocratic Southern planter, and in gradually but relentlessly unveiling Sutpen's story, the novel forces Quentin Compson into confronting the South as something other than an infinite historical reiteration of Jefferson's Monticello. Sutpen, abandoning his Haitian wife and son solely because they are "black," traveled to Mississippi to start over again. When that "black" son, Charles Bon, shows up twenty-five years later in Jefferson, Mississippi, Sutpen must put him aside once again, this time because he threatens to marry Sutpen's daughter, Judith. His white son, Henry, serves as his agent in this endeavor, finally murdering his half-brother in order to save his sister from incest and, even worse, miscegenation.

What had not been faced prior to *Absalom, Absalom!* is the fact that at the source of the American Dream itself lies slavery. As the great historian Edmund Morgan was to demonstrate four decades later in *American Slavery, American Freedom* (1975), the political and economic freedom of the United States depended directly upon slave labor. But in his novel Faulkner had already addressed the social roots and consequences of this tragic history. In his long midnight conversation with Shreve, Quentin Compson is finally forced to confront the violent denial of humanity at the very source of not merely the South but the nation. Like Mitchell, Faulkner knew the South from the vantage point of the frontier, in his case an even rougher frontier than northern Georgia. But perhaps in part because of its roughness, northern Mississippi foregrounded for Faulkner the fundamental violence and inhumanity of slavery. There, whites had had only twenty-five or so years before the Civil War in which to turn frontier land into plantations, to import and rationalize slave labor. Faulkner himself had had a mammy, and he had fully ingested the whole Southern legend, but he was both chronologically and spiritually closer to the source of the horror than Mitchell. In *Absalom, Absalom!*

he confronted that source head on. Whereas Mitchell's popularity reflects how she turned her story of the South into an American romance, Faulkner's novel turned the American success story of Sutpen into a racial tragedy that few foresaw in 1936 as a national dilemma.

Bibliography: Joseph Blotner, *William Faulkner: A Biography* (New York, 1974). William Faulkner, *Absalom, Absalom!* (1936; New York, 1990); *The Sound and the Fury* (1929; New York, 1994). Margaret Mitchell, *Gone with the Wind* (New York, 1936). Darden Asbury Pyron, *Southern Daughter: The Life of Margaret Mitchell* (New York, 1991).

CAROLYN PORTER

1936, July 5

Ralph Ellison meets Langston Hughes and Alain Locke outside the Harlem YMCA, leading to a meeting with Richard Wright the following year

TWO DAYS IN HARLEM

On his second day in New York after leaving Tuskegee Institute in Alabama following his junior year, Ralph Ellison encountered Langston Hughes and Alain Locke outside the Harlem YMCA. From the distance of history, the meeting seems freighted with significance: the confluence of the past, present, and future of African American literature in the very birthplace of twentieth-century black art. The reality, however, was somewhat less romantic. Locke confided in a letter to the literary patron Charlotte Osgood Mason that he had expressly tried to avoid the garrulous Hughes on his trip to New York. For his part, Hughes seemed to thrive on making new acquaintances. The poet Sterling Brown recalls first meeting Hughes outside the same YMCA, where he found Hughes with a parrot perched atop his shoulder, chatting with passersby on 135th Street. While the June meeting with Ellison may well have proved aggravating for Locke and routine for Hughes, Ellison would remember it as a turning point in his life in letters, both for the meeting itself and for the later encounter it would help bring about.

A few months before the chance encounter in Harlem, Ellison had met Locke at Tuskegee, where Locke had been the guest of one of Ellison's teachers, the classical pianist Hazel Harrison. Locke, a professor of philosophy at Howard University, had been one of the principal architects of the Harlem Renaissance, and the editor of the groundbreaking anthology *The New Negro* (1925). While he had helped cultivate the talents of a great many young black writers of the past generation, Locke's influence on Ellison would prove more cultural than personal. "What Locke did for me . . . was to act as a guide," Ellison remarked decades later at a Harvard conference in Locke's honor. "He stood for a conscious approach to *American* culture." Even as a young man Ellison was drawn to the cultural pluralism inherent in Locke's championing of black music and folklore as prototypical American art forms.

By contrast, Hughes's impact upon Ellison was immediate and direct. At the time of their meeting, Hughes was the single most visible black writer in America, having recently published his first collection of short stories, *The Ways of White Folks* (1934), and staged a play on Broadway, *Mulatto*, which had premiered in 1935. With support from a Guggenheim Fellowship, he was forging a more radically populist voice in his poetry, in contrast to his jazz- and blues-inflected work of years past. Ellison had read and admired Hughes's poems while still in grammar school in Oklahoma City, and he recognized Hughes immediately from photographs. Hughes took an interest in the precocious twenty-three-year-old, and when their conversation ended, he entrusted Ellison with several books, including André Malraux's *Man's Fate* and *The Days of Wrath*. In the months that followed Hughes became Ellison's guide to New York's cultural scene, taking him to see his first Broadway play and accompanying him to the Apollo Theatre as often as twice a week.

Moreover, Hughes emerged as Ellison's confidant in confronting his crisis of vocation and identity. In a letter to his mother dated April 20, 1937, Ellison explained that entrusting his uncertainty to Hughes had proved both comforting and clarifying. "I suppose this has made us friends," he wrote, ". . . for which I am very glad. You see in spite of my confidence in desiring to become a musician, so many things happened in school and here that I've become a little bewildered. And the urge I feel within seems not to fade away but becomes more insistent for expression, and I have yet to discover just what form it will take."

Ellison found New York to be a dazzling and at times discombobulating mélange of opportunity and absurdity. Although the concentrated energy of the New Negro Movement had died with the Great Depression, black artists nonetheless remained active in Harlem and beyond. For someone like Ellison, who grew up in the Southwest and went to school in the South, the Northeast offered a dangerous freedom. "The change of pace between New York and Tuskegee was so sudden that I suffered a shock of transition," Ellison writes in an unpublished, undated autobiographical essay entitled "Adventures of an Unintentional New Yorker":

> My responses seemed retarded, I felt a puzzling disjuncture between myself and the scene . . . Actually, given my expectations and naivete and the acceleration in tempo it was as though I were trying to telescope into three short months all the complex psychological experiences that had been spread between the Reconstruction and the Depression, trying to adapt to all those changes in tempo and hope and despair while holding its meaning in my whirling consciousness—lest I be overwhelmed and fall into that total unfreedom which is the loss of one's identity.

Like so many black Americans migrating to the urban centers of the North, Ellison faced the challenge of defining himself as an individual and as a member of a racial group. "What was more disquieting," he continues, "I felt that beneath the teeter-totter dizziness a strange sense of being at home, and even in a way I'd never felt in Oklahoma." This sense of home was best reflected in Ellison's rapid acculturation to life in Harlem. He rode the subway and ate at integrated restaurants. He listened to sidewalk preachers and danced at the Savoy. However, Ellison refused to be bounded by Harlem alone, venturing out to discover other parts of the city. "I was not exchanging Southern segregation for Northern segregation, but seeking a wider world of opportunity," he later reflected. "And, most of all, the excitement and impersonality of a great city. I wanted room in which to discover who I was."

Ellison's arrival in New York corresponded with a profound period of self-discovery and transformation. Having discarded his long-standing aspiration to compose a classical symphony by the age of twenty-three, he was now focusing his energies chiefly on sculpture. He befriended the sculptor Richmond Barthé, with whom he stayed for a time and studied. After failing to earn enough money by the fall of 1936 to return to Tuskegee for his senior year, Ellison resolved instead to make a home for himself in New York City.

It would take a second crucial meeting in Harlem, however, for Ellison to become a writer. Again, Hughes proved instrumental. Ellison had read and admired the poetry of a young writer from Chicago named Richard Wright, finding in Wright's poems the marks of a new black fiction. As it turned out, Hughes knew Wright. "With his great generosity, and without telling me," Ellison recalls, "Hughes wrote Richard Wright that there was a young Negro something-or-the-other in New York who wanted to meet him. The next thing I knew I received a postcard—which I still have—that said, 'Dear Ralph Ellison, Langston Hughes tells me that you're interested in meeting me. I will be in New York.'" In June of 1937, at Hughes's behest, Ellison and Wright met. The two men developed a fast friendship, principally centered on discussing literature, from Malraux to Joseph Conrad, Fyodor Dostoyevsky to Henry James.

Five years Ellison's senior, Wright was never precisely Ellison's mentor, but he was certainly further along in his development as a writer, having composed his first short story, "The Voodoo of Hell's Half-Acre," in middle school. Wright had grown up poor in Natchez, Mississippi, and moved first to Memphis and then to Chicago in 1927, where he was drawn into a circle of Marxist artists and intellectuals. Wright became a member of the John Reed Club, and began his first novel, published posthumously as *Lawd, Today!* as well as several short stories and poems. Chicago, however, proved inhospitable for Wright, whose relationship with the Communist Party there cooled soon after the 1936 May Day Parade. Wright left for New York to take over the editorship of the Harlem bureau of the *Daily Worker* as well as that of the literary magazine *New Challenge*.

Soon after arriving in New York, Wright won a publishing contract by submitting four stories to *Story* magazine. "Fire and Cloud," which tells of a black preacher who leads an interracial march against the white establishment in a small Southern town, won the $500 main prize out of six hundred entries. Wright would include it, along with the other three stories, in the 1938 edition of *Uncle Tom's Children*. He spent the following year composing *Native Son* on a Guggenheim Fellowship. Upon its publication in 1940, the book became a literary sensation, emerging as the first best-selling novel by a black author and launching Wright into the literary stratosphere.

Earlier, at Wright's urging, Ellison took the tentative first steps toward becoming an author himself. Wright commissioned Ellison's first book review as well as his first short story. Ellison's review of Waters Turpin's *These Low Grounds* would be the first of over twenty reviews he would publish before *Invisible Man*, many in the leftist journal *New Masses*. His short story "Hymie's Bull," though accepted for publication at Wright's *New Challenge*, never made it out of galleys and remained unpublished when the magazine folded.

Wright's influence on Ellison's early style is readily apparent. Ellison's first attempts at fiction bear the unmistakable mark of Wright's literary naturalism inflected with Ernest Hemingway's hard boiled prose. *Slick*, Ellison's unfinished apprentice novel, begun in 1937, also shares Wright's thematic preoccupation with the socioeconomic conditions of black life. It tells the story of Slick Williams, an uneducated man who loses his job to the Depression and must find a way to support his pregnant wife. When *Direction* magazine included an excerpt from it in 1938, it would be Ellison's first published work of fiction. But Ellison never completed the novel, and the direction of his fiction abruptly changed course two years later when Ellison wrote a short story that Wright believed was too derivative of Wright's own work. Ellison never again showed Wright his work in progress.

In recent years critics have characterized Ellison and Wright's relationship as distant, no doubt in part as a consequence of Ellison's efforts to distinguish his own literary aesthetic from Wright's, and yet from the mid-1930s through the 1940s the two carried on a liberal and at times dazzling correspondence. What emerges in their letters, most of which are from Ellison to Wright, is the vital role Ellison played as Wright's go-between, intellectual sparring partner, and champion in New York literary circles, particularly after Wright began traveling to Paris in 1946. While Ellison's literary apprenticeship under Wright may have ended in 1940, their friendship certainly did not.

In a letter dated November 3, 1941, only months after the tension over Ellison's short story, and just after the publication of Wright's *12 Million Black Voices*, his populist account of the Great Migration, Ellison offered strong words of kinship.

> I often speculated as to what it was that made the difference between us and the others who shot up from the same region. Well, now . . . I think it is because this past which filters through your book has always been tender and alive and aching within us. We are the ones who had no comforting amnesia of childhood, and for whom the trauma of passing from the country to the city of destruction brought no anesthesia of unconsciousness, but left our nerves peeled and quivering. We are not the numbed, but the seething. God! It makes you want to write and write and write, or murder.

These are not the sentiments of distant friends but, as Ellison would assert elsewhere in the letter, of brothers. With a pitch of passion more characteristic of Wright, Ellison bares his emotions in a way he would rarely allow in the more restrained character of his public prose. Their respective fictions, however, would continue to grow apart in style and theme. Ellison would soon harness his murderous passion in *Invisible Man,* a novel begun in the mid-1940s that eschewed some of the more brutal elements of black experience that Wright would explore in such detail in *Native Son, The Outsider,* and in his memoir *Black Boy.*

Marked both by contrast and connection, the literary fraternity between Wright and Ellison would prove to be one of the richest in twentieth-century American literature. Their respective literary styles would define the dominant modes of black fiction for decades to come. Wright, as the expositor of Dreiserian literary naturalism, wrote fiction sensitized to the black struggle, yet often wooden in characterizations and rigid in prose style. Ellison would envision a new black literary mode, inspired by the experiments of the modernists and inflected with the rich and deep humor of the black folk tradition.

Years later, Ellison would famously distinguish between his literary ancestors and his literary relatives—those influences chosen by willed association and those based on racial affinity alone. From the summer of 1936 through the early years of his literary apprenticeship, Ellison found himself unmistakably and quite comfortably among his relatives, and in the process made an unlikely home for himself far from home.

Bibliography: Ralph Ellison, *The Collected Essays of Ralph Ellison* (New York, 1995). Langston Hughes, *I Wonder as I Wander* (New York, 1956). Lawrence Patrick Jackson, *Ralph Ellison: Emergence of Genius* (New York, 2002). Arnold Rampersad, *The Life of Langston Hughes, Volume 1: 1902–1941* (New York, 1986); *Ralph Ellison: A Biography* (New York, 2007). Hazel Rowley, *Richard Wright: The Life and Times* (New York, 2002).

ADAM BRADLEY

1936, November 23

A bar in Montana, tetraethyl in your car

Life begins

In 1932, Clare Booth wrote a memo to her boss, Condé Nast, the publisher of *Vanity Fair* and *Vogue.* The crash of 1929 had nearly ruined him; he had mortgaged his magazines to keep them alive, he was nearly $5 million in debt, but Booth had a proposition. There was a rumor that an old humor magazine called *Life* was hemorrhaging money and was up for sale. Why not buy the magazine for its name, gut it, and turn it into a photo newsweekly modeled after the French magazine *VU?* An editorial/design genius named Lucien Vogel had founded *VU* in 1928. *VU* was a sepia-toned, rotogravure weekly that routinely published the work of such master photographers as André Kertész, Brassaï, and Robert Capa (expatriate Hungarian Jews, one and all). In 1933, *VU* was the first French magazine to publish photographs of Dachau and Oranienburg concentration camps.

The images were made by Vogel's daughter, Marie Claude. In 1936, *VU* published Robert Capa's iconic image, *Loyalist Militiaman at the Moment of Death*—the photograph was made at the moment the man was struck by a bullet. News needn't be boring; news could be fashionable. The new *Life,* wrote Booth, certainly didn't need to publish *all* the news—just the most *interesting* parts of it.

Nast read Booth's memo—and he went more deeply in debt to keep his existing magazines afloat. In 1936, he was forced to close *Vanity Fair.* By then, though, Clare Booth had become Clare Booth Luce, as in Henry Luce, the cofounder of *Time,* and the creator of *Fortune.*

On her honeymoon with Luce, Booth convinced him to buy *Life* and turn it into the magazine she'd first proposed to Nast. Buying the rights to *Life*'s name cost Luce $92,000. Back in 1932, it would have cost Nast only $22,000. The watercooler joke at Time, Inc., was that a four-letter word had cost Luce more than it cost to start *Time.* Luce was so happy—so excited—when he returned from his honeymoon that he pranced into his office and, according to his staff, announced, "I'm pregnant!" He meant it: on the page facing his "Introduction to the First Issue of *Life,*" he printed a giant photograph of a newborn child, just delivered, held upside down by an obstetrician. "Life Begins" was the caption.

There was one other woman besides Clare Booth who planted the seeds of *Life* in Henry Luce's brain. She was the great American photographer Margaret Bourke-White. Bourke-White's mother, Minnie Bourke, was a freethinking Irish woman whose ancestors came to the United States in the 1860s. Bourke-White's father, Joseph White, an engineer and an inventor, was the brilliant—and agnostic—son of a family of Orthodox Polish Jews who'd immigrated to the United States in the 1850s. White was obsessed with machines—particularly the newest, fastest, most precise kinds of printing presses. His obsession inspired his daughter. She became entranced with the power and beauty of everything mechanical. She was an Italian Futurist, born and bred in America.

In 1927, Bourke-White began to photograph the industrial landscape of Cleveland. Cleveland was booming then. Bourke-White photographed its mills and blast furnaces, its railroads, ore docks, and overpasses as if they were glorious facts of nature. In 1929, Luce saw a portfolio of Bourke-White's steel mill photographs and summoned her to New York, all expenses paid. Luce knew Cleveland well, having moved *Time* to Cleveland in 1926. (His partner and alter ego, Briton Hadden, despised the place, and in 1927, while Luce was on vacation, moved *Time* back to New York.)

Luce told Bourke-White that he wanted her—needed her—to take pictures for the new business magazine he was planning. He wanted to produce a magazine as beautifully designed and luxuriously printed as any magazine in America. A *Vogue* magazine for industry. He didn't know what he'd call it—maybe *Power,* maybe *Fortune,* but it "had to have the most dramatic photographs of industry ever taken." Those words, those plans made Bourke-White feel as if she'd been handed a bottle of the finest wine. Her images filled *Fortune*'s prototype; they filled its first issue, filled many more of its issues after that. Bourke-White became

Fortune's star. *Fortune* employed wonderful writers—Archibald MacLeish, Dwight Macdonald, James Agee—but the visual language *Fortune* spoke was pure Bourke-White.

In the spring of 1936, *Fortune*'s editor, Ralph Ingersoll, invited Bourke-White to lunch at New York's 21 Club. Ingersoll had not only given Bourke-White pride of place in the magazine but he'd hired other remarkable photographers—men like Erich Salomon, the German physician who used the newest Leicas and their high-speed film to make surreptitious photographs of ambassadors, presidents, and plutocrats. In 1934 he hired Walker Evans to illustrate a *Fortune* article—two years before Evans and James Agee plunged into the *Fortune* project that became *Let Us Now Praise Famous Men.*

Ingersoll escorted Bourke-White to a back table. It was midafternoon, quiet and empty. Time to tell secrets.

"We were going to have a new magazine," Bourke-White wrote in 1963 in her memoir, *Portrait of Myself:*

> Its form was amorphous, but the direction was clear. It would tell the news in pictures, but it would go much farther than that by illuminating the background that made the news . . . As when *Fortune* was in the planning stage, now again this new unnamed magazine was waiting to be born. I could almost feel the horizon widening and [a] great rush of wind sweeping in . . . This was the kind of magazine that could . . . help interpret human situations by showing the larger world into which people fitted. It [would] show our developing, exploding, contrary world and translate it into pictures . . . The new magazine would absorb everything we photographers had to give: all the understanding . . . all the speed, the imagination, the good luck; everything we could bring to bear.

In October 1936, Luce sent Bourke-White to Montana. He thought Roosevelt was likely to be reelected. Roosevelt's Public Works Administration had just finished a huge, new, earth-filled dam on the Missouri River, at Fort Peck, 2,000 miles upstream from St. Louis. The dam's public purpose was to improve navigation and encourage trade. Its political purpose was to pump $110 million into the region and put people back to work.

Luce wanted some big, Margaret Bourke-White kinds of pictures of that particular dam. American know-how, American grandeur.

On Election Day in November, 28 million people—61 percent of all eligible voters—went to the polls. Eighteen million of them voted for Roosevelt. In the Electoral College, Roosevelt had a 528-to-8 majority over Alf Landon—a margin that hadn't been seen since James Monroe beat John Quincy Adams in 1820.

Luce voted twice—once as a citizen, and once as the editor-in-chief of *Life.*

Ingersoll carried Bourke-White's Montana photos into Luce's office. "Here's your cover," Ingersoll said. Luce knew it when he saw it. Bourke-White's photo of the New Deal's newest dam became *Life*'s first cover, dated November 23, 1936. The dam's great towers were as grand and glorious as the battlements of a castle. An American castle.

Bourke-White's cover of the Fort Peck Dam and its battlements could just have easily been the cover of *USSR in Construction:* a magnificent new dam, but on the Don or the Volga. Begun in 1930, *USSR in Construction* was an unusually well-edited, well-designed, well-written, large-format news and propaganda magazine meant for export. Maxim Gorky was on the magazine's editorial board and wrote for it; the avant-garde graphic artist and designer El Lissitzky designed it; Alexander Rodchenko, one of the finest designer/photographers of the era, contributed to it. All of these men were silenced, exiled, or liquidated during the Great Purges that began in 1934.

Life's first issue appeared only two years later—and the similarity ended as soon as readers opened the magazine and saw a hairy chimp staring at them with its mouth open: "Knock knock! Who's there? Ethyl! CAN'T BE! Why not? ETHYL STOPS KNOCK! . . . and puts life in your new car!" Yessir, folks, the new tetraethyl is good for you *and* your car!

After that came a Plymouth ad, illustrated with photos of boyfriends and girl-friends, salesmen and ladies, dads and their daughters. Everyone happy. New-car happy.

Only then did *Life* begin: the upside-down, newborn child, across from Henry Luce's introduction:

> Hundreds, perhaps thousands of people contribute their photography presence to the pages of this issue. French aristocrats, New York stockbrokers, Montana bar-keeps, gooney golfers, English judges at prayer and English ladies in the rain, ba-bies, farmers, sailors, doctors, crowds, a high school class, a one-legged man, a strip artist, a bearded Russian, the President of the U.S. and the late Sarah Bernhardt . . . and most of all . . . the little Chinese girls on page 26 . . .

Two more ads—an elegant, white-on-black drawing of a Pan American China Clipper, cruising above the clouds. Across from that: back down to earth, two men, confiding in each other about Liberty Mutual's Low Rates for Safe Drivers.

Then more ads: for Heinz onion soup, baked beans, canned olives, and ketchup, illustrated with photos of everyone at a party, smiling at the food. Across from that: a new stainless-steel mixer that could mash, grind, slice, shred, juice, sift, crack ice, and shell peas. New attachments! Easy to use!

Then one more ad: for a new Ford V-8. A handsome vehicle. Seen from above. And then!

What Margaret Bourke-White saw in Montana: Two couples and a threesome, in a bar, near the site of the dam that was on the cover. The two couples are danc-ing cheek to cheek. One of the women, dark-haired, dark-eyed, unsmiling, looks straight into the lens. A "taxi dancer." There for the money. It's the other three who let the reader know that whatever's going on, it would never have happened in a Soviet magazine: the woman is leaning back on a stool, her dusty shoes are a foot off the floor; she's cuddled, snuggled back, between the legs of a happy man; he has his arm around her, his hand on her belly. The other man is much younger; he's leaning in, his face against hers; his right arm is up and over her shoulder; his right hand locked around his left wrist; he's reached across her ribcage to her breast; he cradles it, one finger under it; his thumb on her tit. She's smiling; she's pleased. And he—he's as serious as a flag bearer in an honor guard, staring, level, into Bourke-White's lens and every reader's eyes.

An editorial formula begins that repeats itself, like a fugue with variations, through the rest of the magazine:

Turn the page, leave the bar, and suddenly you're up in the air, so high up the far horizon is level with your gaze. Down below, spread across two pages of the magazine, those pages big enough (fourteen inches high by twenty-one inches wide) to block out everything that's not directly in front of you, is the shantytown of Wheeler, Montana. The place where the people you just saw in the bar, the people who built the dam on the cover, live. From up high, Wheeler's shacks and stores look like sugar cubes scattered across hard, dusty ground. "FRANKLIN ROOSEVELT HAS A WILD WEST" is the headline.

Turn the page.

Down to earth again: street-level facades: a barbershop, a bar, a beauty salon, a pile of trash, a shoe shop/dry cleaner/printer/real estate agent. Above those street scenes: a picture of a little lady, standing in a bar, tossing back a tall one. Over her left shoulder, a campaign lithograph of Franklin Roosevelt. "A Gallant Leader." Over her right shoulder, nailed up high on the wall, a big sign, bold letters, white on black: "NO BEER SOLD TO INDIANS."

There are two more pages after that: a half-dozen photos crowded with drinkers and talkers, laid out around a big picture of a gigantic steel drum built to fit inside one of the new dam's diversion tunnels. The drum is lying on its side. It's so big it can hold all the men, all seventeen of them, who are working inside it, standing and hanging on its struts, bolting everything together.

Then the finale of the piece: Back in the bar.

A huge photo, made of two images, spliced together, laid out on a diagonal. The images look like they were made within a few seconds of each other. They've been butted together so the bar extends from the bottom corner of page left to the top corner of page right.

Couples again. Up close. Narrow glasses of beer; tall, thin-necked bottles of peppers in vinegar. At the center of the diagonal, a man in a cap, forearm on the bar, hand around a glass, turns to the lens, smiling sideways: he's missing the middle of his upper front teeth. Sitting on the bar, just up from him, is a kid, a little girl with ash blond hair cut in a bob, a pageboy bob, with her right arm around her mother's shoulders. Her mother's a waitress; she's brought her little girl to work; the kid's holding an apple that she's been eating. All that's OK. The girl's a little scrawny, the guy's missing some teeth—but it's the kid's eyes, big dark eyes, and her mouth, her pinched little mouth, that stop you, hold your glance. In the first exposure the girl's looking across and away, thinking about her apple; in the second one, the kid's noticed the camera. She stares at it—stares back at every reader who's been looking—with a look as hard and angry and glum as any kid, stuck in a bar, no matter who's been elected.

The face of that little girl finishes the magazine's first sequence of point and counterpoint. It's an editorial strategy as primal as breathing in and breathing out. First near, then far; high, then low; intimacy, then distance. First: pictures made so close you think you could hear a cough or a whisper. Then: pictures made from so high above, you think, looking down, you could be a gull or an angel.

What follows is not unexpected: celebrity divorces and marriages, gruesome deaths, cigarette and liquor ads, movie stars, radio personalities, actresses and artists, ocean liners and long-distance trains, new cars—and many more aerial photos.

Life ends as it began: a hunting party of French aristocrats mirrors the working stiffs and taxi dancers in the bar in Montana. Counts and countesses, duchesses and marquises walk the grounds of the Château de Voisins near Rambouillet. There are liveried coachmen and black-clad butlers; crowds of peasants stand about, dressed in white smocks so they won't be shot when they drive the game toward their masters.

The effect of all this is to give anyone who looks the experience of being in two places at almost the same time, of seeing all and everything, the common and the uncommon, the gifted and the fools, the blessed and the bereft. Dickens did that, didn't he? So did Balzac and Tolstoy. Whitman would have loved it. *Life* sold for a dime.

Bibliography: James Baughman, *Henry R. Luce and the Rise of American Media* (Baltimore, 2001). Margaret Bourke-White, *Portrait of Myself* (New York, 1963). John Koble, *Luce: His Life, Time, and Fortune* (Garden City, NY, 1963). Colin Westerbrook and Joel Meyerowitz, *Bystander: A History of Street Photography* (New York, 1994). Isaiah Wilner, *The Man Time Forgot* (New York, 2006).

MICHAEL LESY

1938
"Look! Up in the sky!"

ACTION COMICS INTRODUCES SUPERMAN

The first issue of *Action Comics* appeared on American newsstands in the spring of 1938. It was an anthology of forgettable adventure stories by various cartoonists—Fred Guardineer's "Zatara, Master Magician," Will Ely's "Scoop Scanlon, Five-Star Reporter," and so on—all instantly and permanently overshadowed by Superman, the first superhero, casually hoisting a car over his head on the front cover. Ever since, the superhero genre has popped up all over American narrative. Superheroes are intimately tethered to the comics medium, whose fantastic images are limited only by cartoonists' imagination, but they've also become part of movies, radio, television, and prose literature. The genre's conventions are preposterous, which is sort of the point: superheroes are walking (or flying) metaphors for the cultural concerns of their time.

In 1938, Jerry Siegel and Joe Shuster, a young writer-artist team who'd met as high school students in Cleveland, had been trying to sell their Superman concept for a few years already, envisioning it as a newspaper comic strip. Nobody bit—United Features, for instance, rejected it as "a rather immature work"—until National Periodical Publications, scraping for material for *Action Comics,* picked it up. It's remarkable how many of the formal attributes of superheroes as we still know them are established in that first installment of "Superman," cut and pasted together from Siegel and Shuster's sample strips. There's the origin story, a straightforward if improbable description of how a character became more than human. (Superman was rocketed as an infant from the doomed planet Krypton to Earth. What? How? Shush!) There's the colorful skintight costume, which makes characters more fun to look at. (Siegel and Shuster modeled Superman's on circus-strongman outfits, with a cape and a symbol on the chest; every subsequent superhero's appearance is modeled on Superman's, to one extent or another.) There's the never-ending battle between absolute virtue and absolute malignancy. (In that first story, Superman deals roughly with a murderer, a wife-beater, and finally a man who's bribing a senator to get the United States "embroiled with Europe"—a few years later, of course, Superman would be fighting Nazis.) There's the sense of something grander than ordinary political existence. (The final panels of the story involve Superman looking down on the Capitol Building from above.) And, of course, there's the cliff-hanger ending. (Superhero stories are never *complete* stories: there are always past and future tales to be told.)

Most of all, the first Superman story had potent metaphorical resonance, whether its creators realized it or not. Cultural assimilation, and specifically the place in the American mainstream of "aliens" and "ethnics," was a burning topic in the 1930s (and Siegel and Shuster came from the Eastern European Jewish-immigrant community); Superman is an alien from another planet. The idea of human perfectibility was very much in play at the time; Superman is perfect, an *Übermensch,* but he's not actually a human being. American culture was discovering a grinding friction between public and private life; Superman has a double identity—a public face of repressed modesty in the person of bespectacled milquetoast Clark Kent, and a second life of flamboyant wish fulfillment.

That first thirteen-page story isn't much as far as craft goes: the plot is an incoherent string of incidents, and the standard of drawing in most newspaper strips of the time was much higher. Still, something in the American psyche responded to it, and the Golden Age of American comics was under way. *Action Comics* sold so well that, within months, newsstands were filled with knockoffs—*Whiz Comics* with Captain Marvel, *Marvel Comics* with the Human Torch and the Sub-Mariner. Batman and Wonder Woman and Captain America and Plastic Man and the Spirit and dozens of others sprang into existence within two or three years. Virtually every important superhero character initially appeared in comic books; the ones that caught on weren't necessarily the best written or best drawn but spoke to Americans' hopes and fears.

After World War II, the superhero boom receded a bit, although it made a comeback in the mid-1950s, at the beginning of what's known as the "Silver Age" of comics. The first few Silver Age superheroes were simply revived and updated versions of characters from the first wave, like the Flash and Green Lantern. But the floodgates were opened in the early '60s by Stan Lee (born Stanley Lieber), who was then the writer and editor of virtually everything published by Marvel Comics. Conventional wisdom has it that Marvel's new wave of superheroes, beginning with the first issue of *Fantastic Four* in 1961, were distinguished by having realistic concerns and problems. In fact, what the Marvel heroes had going for them was that they were resilient *symbols* for the concerns and problems of cold-war America. (It also helped that Lee was a born huckster, that he generally ceded control of pacing and sometimes even plotting to the artists he worked with, and that those artists were terrific cartoonists and storytellers—American comics are still feeling the aftershocks of Jack Kirby's hyperdynamic distortion and Steve Ditko's fluid grotesqueries.)

Spider-Man, as Lee declared bluntly at the end of the story that introduced him, was (and still is) a vehicle for telling stories about the relationship between power and responsibility; a frail young man perpetually tormented by his super-ego, he fought the Green Goblin, a cackling fountain of unchecked id to whom human life was nothing. The Fantastic Four let Lee and Kirby spin plots out of anxieties about the space race and the nuclear family. The Hulk, an irradiated man who becomes a huge green monster when he gets angry, was the personification of nuclear terror and the rage of the impotent Everyman. Under Lee and Kirby's guidance, Captain America's enemies were variously Nazis and Communists; Iron Man, an inventor in a high-tech suit of armor, fought Communists too, but his stories were less concerned with ideology than with the threat of Chinese and Russian technology.

Throughout the Silver Age, the struggles between superheroes and their villainous enemies took on even more metaphorical weight—and in return, superhero comics, which had once been read mostly by kids, were embraced by college students. (Cover caption of *Amazing Spider-Man* #68, January 1969: "CRISIS ON CAMPUS!") In the early 1970s, Jack Kirby wrote and drew four simultaneously running, interlinked series that became known as the "Fourth World": built around a cosmology involving the "New Gods" of two eternally warring planets, unsubtly called New Genesis and Apokolips, the Fourth World stories incorporated Kirby's ideas about youth culture, escape (and escapism), and the conflict between individualism and collective action. Superman's greatest enemy was Lex Luthor: initially a power-hungry inventor (at a time when Americans worried a lot about science and technology), he was transformed in the money-mad '80s into a rapacious businessman, and at the beginning of the new millennium became president of the United States (as Americans' distrust of their government hit a new peak).

The evolution of the superhero story, though, was hampered a bit by the fact that it had become very big business. The best-known superheroes are also highly profitable franchises—the economic engines behind movies, TV shows, amusement-park rides, children's sleepwear, and so on. So the particulars of characters' lives and even their appearance can never change more than fractionally: a new hairstyle, perhaps, or a character's newspaper job upgraded to a Website gig.

For that matter, the pantheon of superheroes is virtually immutable at this point. The last great mass-culture superhero franchise took shape in the mid-1970s: Len Wein and Dave Cockrum's revival of a moribund series, *The Uncanny X-Men*. Under Wein and Cockrum, and subsequently the vividly soap-operatic direction of writer Chris Claremont and artists John Byrne and Terry Austin, *X-Men*—in which not-quite-human mutants protect the ordinary humans who revile them—became a long, ornate riff on identity politics: a mutant could stand in for whatever other you liked.

By then, the superhero genre had come to dominate the comics medium so thoroughly (at least in the United States) that, for a while, American comics that *weren't* about superheroes had to make something of a point of it. Comics are still the most prolific source of superhero stories, but they aren't the most popular source any more; for complicated economic reasons, in the 1980s, comic books became the province of specialty stores frequented by collectors, and largely disappeared from newsstands and drugstores. The wildly popular *X-Men, Batman, Superman,* and *Spider-Man* movies of recent years have been seen by many more people than would ever buy a comic book about the same characters. But those characters are firmly imprinted in the American collective consciousness: your typical American won't necessarily be able to recognize the name Jay Gatsby or Nathan Zuckerman or Harry Angstrom, but can instantly identify Bruce Wayne or Lois Lane or Peter Parker.

Beginning in the mid-1980s, there's been a persistent strain of comics whose metaphorical subtext concerns the superhero genre itself. The best, and one of the first, is Alan Moore and Dave Gibbons's *Watchmen* (first serialized in 1986 and 1987), a ferociously intricate commentary on the capes-and-powers tradition that doubles as a top-notch thriller about superheroes' existence threatening to bring about atomic Armageddon. (Moore led a wave of popular British comics writers working in what's effectively an American idiom, for American publishers and a largely American audience.) In the late '80s, *Watchmen* and Frank Miller and Klaus Janson's cranked-up, design-conscious Batman story *The Dark Knight Returns* both found success in bookstores as single volumes; the term "graphic novel" caught on to describe any perfect-bound volume of comics, to the chagrin of cartoonists outside the superhero scene, who were just starting to overcome the public perception that the comics medium was the same thing as kid-stuff genres and didn't want their work confused with genre fiction.

The movement of superhero comics toward meta–genre fiction sped up around 2000, while their visual range was broadening to encompass greater extremes of both photorealism and expressive abstraction. Kurt Busiek and Brent Anderson's *Astro City* imagines a metropolis and a world dramatically changed by the presence of godlike beings; Brian Michael Bendis and Michael Avon Oeming's *Powers* and Alan Moore, Gene Ha, and Zander Cannon's *Top Ten* are both police procedurals set in cities full of superheroes; Bendis and Michael Gaydos's *Alias* explores the superhero pantheon through the eyes of a self-loathing detective/ex-superheroine. A few writers, such as Warren Ellis in *Thunderbolts* and *The*

Authority, have used their metacomics series to express disgust with the formal conventions of superhero stories—the "pervert suits" and so forth. (Those
sorts of reactions can be entertaining, although they miss the point.) The best
superhero-related prose novel to date, Michael Chabon's Pulitzer Prize–winning
The Amazing Adventures of Kavalier & Clay (2000) concerns the creators of a
(fictional) golden age character, the Escapist, molding their personal and cultural experience into the masked-adventurer idiom. Even simpler superhero
stories in other media—the television series *Heroes,* the film *Unbreakable,* Perry
Moore's young adult novel *Hero*—riff on universally understood conventions of
the genre.

    In fact, the genre and its conventions reached a particularly unstable moment
in the first years of the twenty-first century. Something felt exhausted about
them: their inward gaze had become untenable self-obsession. Superhero comics
are generally understood to be children's entertainment, although they're mostly
read by adults; the characters' corporate owners can't afford to let them change,
but their audience demands at least the illusion of constant, dramatic evolution.
(A best-selling miniseries of 2005 and 2006 was entitled *Infinite Crisis;* its 2008
sequel was *Final Crisis.* Could there possibly be anywhere to go from there?) The
only major superhero convention that's changed much since that first issue of *Action Comics* is the tradition of the secret identity or double life, which has gradually fallen away as American private life has become more transparent.

    What the smartest superhero writers—who are often also among the best-
selling superhero writers—have returned to is the practice of using superheroes
to reify ideas and ideologies. The genre has been associated with the convention
of battles between good and evil for so long that it's become an ideal vehicle for
asking questions about public morality. Mark Millar and Steve McNiven's *Civil
War* (2006–2007), nominally concerned with a struggle between two superteams
led by Iron Man and Captain America, is a fairly blatant allegory about the Patriot Act (in which Iron Man stands in for the military-industrial complex and
Captain America represents American small-L libertarianism); Greg Pak and
John Romita, Jr.'s, *World War Hulk* (2007) elliptically addresses preemptive American aggression in the Middle East and the resulting military insurgency, in the
context of a story about the Hulk coming back from outerspace exile to smash
stuff.

    The superhero writer Grant Morrison treats comics as a populist vehicle for
turning tricky concepts into narrative in order to inspire actual social praxis.
Around 1990, he transformed the nondescript series *Doom Patrol* into an extended
exploration of body panic (the heroes' and villains' superpowers double as defor-
mities that alienate them from their bodies); a decade later, he attempted to divert the focus of the *X-Men* franchise away from its threadbare identity-politics
theme toward the question of how the meaning of humanity might be changing.
His *Seven Soldiers of Victory* project (2005–2007)—named after a series from the
1940s and drawn in seven distinct visual modes—tried to reframe the entire
genre. The origin story, it suggested, is a narrative of enlightenment, and people

become superheroes when they evolve beyond their cultural context. Another Morrison project, *All-Star Superman* (illustrated with voluptuous precision by Frank Quitely), returned to Siegel and Shuster's urtext, discarding most of the coral reef of textual apparatus that's accumulated around it over the past seventy years and trying to establish what the metaphor of the perfect man can mean in the twenty-first century. It's a little sad, but not entirely surprising, that the never-ending battle in Morrison's version of Superman is mostly the battle against the self.

Bibliography: Chris Claremont and John Byrne, *X-Men: Days of Future Past* (New York, 2004), stories originally published 1980–1981. Gerard Jones, *Men of Tomorrow: Geeks, Gangsters and the Birth of the Comic Book* (New York, 2004). Stan Lee and Steve Ditko, *The Amazing Spider-Man Omnibus*, vol. 1 (New York, 2007), single-volume anthology of 1962–1966 collaboration. Scott McCloud, *Zot!* (New York, 2008), stories originally published 1987–1991. Alan Moore and Dave Gibbons, *Watchmen* (New York, 1987). Grant Morrison and Frank Quitely, *All Star Superman*, vol. 1 (New York, 2007).

DOUGLAS WOLK

1938, May
"I'm getting ahead of my story"

JELLY ROLL MORTON

At the outset, in May 1938, Alan Lomax did not expect much from his interview with Jelly Roll Morton. As assistant in charge of the Archive of Folk Song at the Library of Congress, Lomax focused on collecting endangered music: field hollers, hillbilly ballads, the old-time songs of marginal peoples that commercial recording was fast drowning out. So he was intrigued but skeptical when friends told him about Morton, a jazz composer who had generated a string of hit records before his fortunes turned sour in the Depression. For the previous eighteen months he had been running a bar above a hamburger joint in the black district of Washington, playing piano, mixing drinks, when necessary tossing out drunks. Lomax had never been a jazz fan. But friends described Morton as a great source of old melodies, so Lomax arranged to bring him together with a disk recorder in the library's Coolidge Auditorium. Morton turned up for the session on May 23 sporting gold rings, a hundred-dollar suit, and a diamond-studded incisor, unfurling his satin-lined jacket over the back of the piano, like a bullfighter wielding his cape.

At Lomax's suggestion, Morton opened the interview by singing "Alabama Bound." Lomax had first heard the song in 1933 from a black convict named Bowlegs, whom he and his father, the folklorist John Lomax, had recorded at Parchman Prison Farm in Mississippi. Bowlegs' rendition had been slow and mournful, a lament for a vanished lover that was full of the penitentiary's pain and privation, but Morton played a jaunty, sardonic version that he claimed to have written in a

Gulf Coast honky-tonk in 1904. Here the singer, not the lover, was the one who was leaving, and even the abandoned woman did not sound that bothered:

> She said "Don't you leave me here,
> Don't leave me here,
> But sweet papa, if you must go,
> Leave a dime for beer."

Between verses Morton recalled his days as an entertainer in the low-down dives from Biloxi to Mobile, composing songs, playing piano, and shooting pool when he spotted an easy mark. "I never will forget, after I beat some guys playing pool, if it wasn't for one of my piano-playing friends, you'd never heard this record because the guy was gonna knife me right in the back, I'm telling you. He said that I only used the piano for a decoy, which he was right." He played softly while reminiscing, and his speaking voice itself became music, guttural and melodic by turns.

For Lomax, all this was dizzying. One simple request for a traditional tune and Morton was spinning a picaresque novel, full of the laughter of prostitutes, the click of pool cues, and the rattle of loaded dice. "He had a knife right on me. And, of course, he had it in his mind that I was kind of nice-looking. Imagine that, huh? Of course, he wasn't such a good-looking fellow hisself. He had some awful, rubber-looking lips, I'm telling you." His tale called up a subterranean world unlike anything Lomax had ever set out to document. So when Morton concluded by saying, with patrician grandeur, "Is there any other information you would like to ask?" Lomax excused himself and rushed to his office for a boxful of blank disks and a bottle of whiskey. "Jelly Roll," Lomax resumed, setting the recording machine whirling once more, "tell us about yourself."

Over the next three weeks, Jelly Roll did. Returning daily to the Coolidge Auditorium, Morton spoke and sang of his life's adventures, recounting his childhood (he was born Ferdinand Lemothe, the son of Louisiana Creoles), his musical training, and his apprenticeship as a pianist, composer, and pool shark in the dives and brothels of New Orleans. Lomax sat at his feet, maintaining eye contact, while reaching behind him to manipulate two disk recorders. As one disk neared its four-and-a-half-minute capacity, he set the other turntable spinning, so that Morton could perform virtually without interruption. Though initially he prompted Morton with questions, that soon proved unnecessary. Morton had a clear sense of the shape of his narrative ("I'm getting ahead of my story," he remarked periodically), an unerring feel for the tale he wanted to tell.

Propelling that tale was a sense of grievance. In a decade when jazz had become big business, Morton believed that he had been defrauded. Three years earlier Benny Goodman had recorded Morton's "King Porter Stomp," and though it had become "the outstanding favorite of every great hot band throughout the world" (as Morton put it minutes after the interview began), the composer himself received little credit and no recompense. All around him he saw jazz being misrepresented, its history stolen and falsified, its pioneers tossed on the rubbish heap. Anodyne white entertainers like Goodman were winning acclaim for black innovations, and even when the press managed to credit black artists, too often it got the wrong ones. Two months earlier Morton had turned on the radio and heard the popular composer W. C. Handy labeled the "originator of jazz," and that had provoked him to unleash a furious letter to the press. "This very minute, you have confronting the world all kinds of Kings, Czars, Dukes, Princes and Originators of Swing (*swing* is just another name for *jazz*) and they know that the titles are deceiving," he wrote. "I would like to put a lie tester on many of these make-believe stalwarts of originality." In Lomax's disk recorder, he found a different sort of authenticating mechanism. It gave him the chance to establish the facts of jazz's origins, to set the record straight.

Setting the record straight meant describing where "the birth of jazz originated," and that took him to Storyville. Morton called up a cast of characters from New Orleans's turn-of-the-century Tenderloin that no jazz critic had ever bothered unearthing. He told Lomax about Tony Jackson, a sissy-man and one of the greatest pianists who ever lived, and Buddy Bolden, the blowingest man since Gabriel, who blew his brains out through his trumpet and ended up in the crazy house. He remembered the Broadway Swells, the gang of toughs he marched with in the Mardi Gras parades. They were musicians who lived off the earnings of fifth-rate whores, and he had been bewitched by their red flannel undershirts and cork-soled shoes with gambler designs on the toes, and the moseying walk they called "shooting the agate," their hands at their sides, their index fingers extended, moving in a slow, deliberate strut. In time he learned to walk that way too, and at the piano at Hilma Burt's mansion he wore a Stetson hat ("I thought I would die unless I had a hat with the emblem in it named Stetson"), a peacock-blue coat, and eighteen-dollar striped trousers that fit tight as a sausage. "I was Sweet Papa Jelly Roll with the stovepipes in my hips," he recalled, "and all the women in town was dying to turn my damper down."

Lomax soon realized that this was an interview like no other. It was not just the ribald folk history of jazz that simmered within Morton's stories; nor was it his novel reflections on the "Spanish tinge," the cosmopolitan mélange of New World rhythms that shaped early jazz technique. Above all, the interview's magic lay in elements no transcription could capture. Lomax watched Morton thrust himself physically into the music, his foot like a metronome tapping the beat, his hand slapping the piano bench to mimic the sound of cards hitting the table. He heard the stentorian tones of Morton's voice, part preacher, part medicine-show huckster, a rich, languid baritone that looped and slid, stretching one-syllable words into two. He saw how Morton seemed to light up as he faced the phonograph day after day, a one-time jazz has-been who had found a new purpose. And he marveled at the music that the microphone seemed to elicit: the Creole street cries; the obscene whorehouse melodies; and, most haunting of all, the formless, nameless chord progressions that he played as he spoke, changing from major to minor to augment the mood of his tale. "We hadn't agreed on that at all," Lomax recalled years later. "It came out of nowhere, the fact that he decided to do that."

Morton turned the recounting of his life story into an aural event, and for Lomax it was a revelation. Since the age of eighteen, when he first went song collecting with his father, he had been operating phonographic devices, but though he knew how to assemble them and take them apart, Morton showed him their potential for generating a radically innovative cultural form. The years preceding the Morton interview had seen intensifying interest in autobiographical testimony, both among social scientists (particularly those linked to the University of Chicago and Yale's Institute of Human Relations) and, more recently, within the Federal Writers' Project. Researchers gathered the life stories of the unlettered: Polish immigrants, mill workers, gamblers, and (a project initiated in part by Lomax's father) African Americans born as slaves. Yet all these reminiscences had been collected with pen and paper, a fact owed only in part to the expense and awkwardness of sound technology. The psychoanalyst and anthropologist John Dollard, positing "criteria for the life history" in 1935, maintained that "for obvious reasons" written life histories were preferable to oral ones. Transforming oral testimony into a written document was a first step toward untangling its hidden meanings, which could best be accomplished by a trained observer, the interviewer, who ordered and made sense of the subject's words.

In the recorded life story, Lomax sensed something more democratic and more revealing. "The needle writes on the disc with tireless accuracy the subtle inflections, the melodies, the pauses that comprise the emotional meaning of speech, spoken and sung," he reflected after the Morton interviews were finished in June. "Between songs, sometimes between stanzas, the singers annotate their own song . . . They are not confused by having to stop and wait for the pedestrian pen of the folklorist: they are able to forget themselves in their songs and to underline what they wish to underline." Watching Morton come alive at the microphone convinced him that in an age when mass communications were overpowering marginal voices, the recording machine could empower those who spoke into it by enabling them to document their own story. Unlike an interviewer with pen and paper, the machine was a disinterested listener; it took down the frankest reflections without embarrassment, even as it captured vocal gestures that a written transcription could not convey. Faced with a microphone, subjects felt validated, lost their reserve, and dipped into unconscious material. The Morton sessions, he recalled years later, were "exactly like an analytic interview, only without a couch"; embedded in the folk songs Morton called up were "the stuff [of which] dreams are made."

In years to come the recording machine would transform the process of collecting life stories, though not exactly as Lomax envisioned. World War II brought the invention of magnetic tape and, shortly thereafter, portable tape recorders. Suddenly what Lomax had to contrive so arduously, recording extended stretches of speech, became easy, almost routine. By 1948 that technological facility helped launch a new field that Columbia University scholar Allan Nevins dubbed "oral history." Yet this oral history documented "significant Americans": politicians who had relied on telephones, had not kept diaries, and whose key decisions lacked a paper trail. The recorded interview was a tool for establishing the missing facts. Once the tapes were transcribed, they were erased and reused, "much to the horror of psychologists," oral historian Louis Starr remarked rather blithely, "with their interests in speech slips."

Today's oral historians are more attuned to speech slips, and they take greater care to preserve their recordings. The voices they attend to have also changed. Since the 1970s, oral history in the United States has revived the Depression-era populist quest to recover the lives of nonelite peoples, the everyday struggles on the social margins that political historians had long ignored. Many oral historians echo Lomax's commitment to a documentary practice that empowers the people it chronicles. Yet most would dismiss Lomax's faith in sound recording, in the machine's objectivity, as simply naive. Subjects, they insist, never "forget themselves" as they are speaking and are invariably influenced by the interviewer's presence. Looking back on the Morton sessions, some have raised questions about Lomax's methods, asking whether the extraordinary obscenity of some recollections ("I fucked her till her pussy stunk" was one remembered lyric) was fueled by conscious or unconscious prompting, and by the glass on the piano that Lomax kept filling ("This whiskey is lovely," Morton repeatedly exclaims).

Still, one might ask whether even today's oral historians have quite encompassed what Lomax was after. "That hot May afternoon in the Library of Congress a new way of writing history began," he argued in 1950. For all their methodological sophistication, oral historians remain largely committed to a history that needs to be read, while Lomax imagined one written in sound, "history with music cues, the music evoking recollection and poignant feeling." The past, Lomax suggested, can sometimes not be reduced to mere words. With that vision—of what might be called aural history—most historians have yet to catch up.

Bibliography: John Dollard, *Criteria for the Life History* (New Haven, CT, 1935). Jerrold Hirsch, *Portrait of America: A Cultural History of the Federal Writers' Project* (Chapel Hill, NC, 2003). Alan Lomax, *The Folk Songs of North America* (Garden City, NY, 1960); *Mister Jelly Roll: The Fortunes of Jelly Roll Morton, New Orleans Creole and "Inventor of Jazz"* (1950; Berkeley, CA, 2001). *Discography: Jelly Roll Morton: The Complete Library of Congress Recordings by Alan Lomax* (Rounder, 2005).

MARYBETH HAMILTON

1939
Billie Holiday records "Strange Fruit"

LADY DAY

Billie Holiday's greatest achievement was the unfolding of a distinctive and dramatically alluring style. She was born in Philadelphia in 1915, grew up in Baltimore, and died in New York City in 1959—born into poverty, she grew up subjected to rape and juvenile detention and prostitution (one might call many of the singer's business arrangements with manager-boyfriends a form of prostitution), and she died under house arrest and police guard in the hospital, where she was being treated for liver failure. One cannot pin down, in her life, a single specific history-making moment of action in the way we can, say, a declaration of war or a vote of Congress.

Hers was an art of understatement: a mode of creation that Zora Neale Hurston called "dynamic suggestion" and "compelling insinuation." Space, timing, and the shaping of words were definitive. Holiday's first studio recordings, made in 1933 when she was eighteen, and her appearance with Duke Ellington's band in the short film *Symphony in Black,* made two years later, already reveal a storyteller's voice, with a graininess that gave it a been-there-and-gone authority. Her voice itself was thin, her pitch sometimes uncertain, her range narrow—and then narrower and lower with the years. She was one of the only great black American singers of the twentieth century who did not emerge from the Baptist church (Holiday's family was Catholic); her voice did not evoke the gospel setting. And yet sometimes her song "God Bless the Child" is sung in a black church setting. "The blues to me," she told a TV interviewer, "is like being very sad, very sick, *going to church,* being very happy." Listening to these words, one can perhaps find one moment, not beyond but focusing others, when Holiday reached a verge, when she made her own event.

Holiday first recorded the anti-lynching song "Strange Fruit" in 1939; she performed it for the rest of her life. The story of the song is now well known: it was composed by Abel Meeropol, a member of the Communist Party who wrote under the name Lewis Allan and taught for many years at DeWitt Clinton High School in the Bronx (Meeropol and his wife adopted the two young sons of Julius and Ethel Rosenberg after their parents' execution in 1953 for treason). After seeing Holiday at Café Society, one of the only integrated nightclubs in Manhattan, Meeropol offered her the song, and her presentation of the piece there caused a sensation and a scandal. Seeking to record the song, Holiday was refused by her label, Columbia, and even by her producer, John Hammond, himself once a jazz critic for the *New Masses;* it was the small label Commodore that was willing to risk such a forthrightly political song. The words Meeropol wrote and Holiday sang have become part of American literature.

> Southern trees bear a strange fruit
> Blood on the leaves and blood at the root
> Black bodies swinging in the southern breeze
> Strange fruit hanging from the poplar trees
>
> Pastoral scene of the gallant South
> The bulging eyes and the twisted mouth
> Scent of magnolia sweet and fresh
> Then the sudden smell of burning flesh
>
> Here is a fruit for the crows to pluck
> For the wind to gather, for the wind to suck
> For the sun to rot, for the tree to drop
> Here is a strange and bitter crop

Although the song was Meeropol's and was not, as Holiday often claimed, written especially for her, as art—as American speech—Holiday came to own "Strange Fruit," and she made plain her displeasure when others presumed to sing it. Comparisons of the original sheet music with Holiday's various recordings make clear that she painstakingly disassembled and then rebuilt the song in her own style—just as she routinely undid and redid songs from Broadway or Tin Pan Alley. For the first recording of "Strange Fruit," Holiday compressed the song's melody and slowed its pace to increase its searing power. Recordings from the 1940s and '50s show that, increasingly, she intensified the drama of the weighted language by extending the silences between phrases—spaces for the audience to take in the meaning, to reflect. A television clip of a performance in the mid-1950s shows, too, how she twists and extends the vowel sounds of certain words ("drop," "crop") until they become a mournful, accusatory wail. She cuts short the final, full-throated cry of "crop"; she does so with a suddenness that leaves her audience no room for sentimentality or self-pity, but instead confronts it with a void of si-lence—before the nervous applause—that is almost unbearably charged.

Holiday was an improvising jazz artist who recomposed or co-composed not only "Strange Fruit" but everything she sang. The pianist Teddy Wilson reported that, contrary to all stories, she rehearsed at length with him for their landmark recording dates in the mid- to late-1930s, running over the melodies of new songs until she could begin to shape them to her own purposes. Wilson presented Holi-day as an improvising soloist whose statements of the melody made up each work's central solo invention—and Holiday's inventions made up one event after another. Consider her two recordings of "These Foolish Things," from 1936 and 1952. In the later recording, her once-buoyant and youthful voice has become dark and oracular: the foolish things have become at once more foolish than ever, foolish beyond description, as well as more mightily alluring: beautiful but tragi-cally lost forever. Close to the meaning of the blues.

Despite the title of her autobiography, *Lady Sings the Blues,* Holiday was not primarily a blues singer, but she could take songs that were not framed in the blues form per se and charge them with the spirit of the blues. Sometimes this had to do with the technical ability to flatten certain notes or to swing the music in the train-travel/dance-beat manner associated with the blues. ("Billie could swing you into bad health," said Carmen McRae.) But most significant of all was her ability to make a Broadway song, or a cabaret torch song, yield a complexity of meaning that elevated it beyond its original setting, and made it part of a nar-rative of love, trouble, confrontation, and triumph. Ralph Ellison's 1945 essay "Richard Wright's Blues" is pertinent:

> The blues is an impulse to keep the painful details and episodes of a brutal experi-ence alive in one's aching consciousness, to finger its jagged grain, and to transcend it, not by the consolation of philosophy but by squeezing from it a near tragic, near comic lyricism. As a form, the blues is an autobiographical chronicle of personal catastrophe expressed lyrically . . . they at once express both the agony of life and

the possibility of conquering it through sheer toughness of spirit. They fall short of tragedy only in that they provide no solution, offer no scapegoat but the self.

Ellison ends by noting that imperatives for social action are implied in Wright's work, and, by extension, in the blues. "Nowhere in America today is there social or political action based upon the solid realities of Negro life depicted in *Black Boy;* perhaps that is why, with its refusal to offer solutions, it is like the blues."

The subject of the blues, wrote James Baldwin in 1964 in "The Uses of the Blues," is that as a human being you are born to suffer. But the blues also record the life of a black American: "I am talking about what happens to you if, having barely escaped suicide, or death, or madness, or yourself, you watch your children growing up and no matter what you do, no matter what you do, you are powerless, you are really powerless against the forces of the world that are out to tell your child that he has no right to be alive." This was one of the stories Holiday told.

She herself became a story; save John Coltrane, no jazz musician appears as often in the pages of American writing as Billie Holiday. Frank O'Hara's poem "The Day Lady Died" records in stark language the shock of learning, via a newspaper's bald headline, that Holiday was gone. Langston Hughes's "Song for Billie" speaks of the power of her music to purge feelings of despair, and yet there is no satisfactory resolution:

> What can purge my heart
> But the song
> Of the sadness?
> What can purge my heart
> Of the sadness
> Of the song?

"Nothing was more perfect than what she was," Amiri Baraka wrote in his prose poem "Dark Lady of the Sonnets." "Nor more willing to fail . . . Sometimes you are afraid to listen to this lady."

There are striking appearances by Holiday in *The Autobiography of Malcolm X* and Maya Angelou's *Heart of a Woman.* Malcolm uses his friendship with Holiday in the mid-1940s, as she teeters on the brink of decline into serious drug addiction, to indicate how, once, as the hustler Detroit Red, he was part of the world of Lady Day, the queen of the night herself. Malcolm presents her not only as a marker of his own decline—against which he would measure his rise, once he is saved, through Islam—but also as a singer in an ancient Greek chorus, calling out to the lost. Onstage at a club on 52nd Street, Holiday spots Malcolm walking in: "Her white gown glittered under the spotlight, her face had that coppery, Indian-ish look, and her hair was in that trademark ponytail. For her next number she did the one she knew I always liked so: 'You Don't Know What Love Is'—'until you face each dawn with sleepless eyes . . . until you've lost a love you hate to lose.'" Holiday had unearthed a blues message in the middle of the ballad, and as James Baldwin would write, it warned of a society spun out of control: of helplessness, misery, and hunger. Malcolm goes on to present the tragedy of Holiday's own circumstances and early death to suggest a larger historical drama of race and nation: "She's dead; dope and heartbreak stopped that heart as big as a barn and that sound and style that no one successfully copies. Lady Day sang with the soul of Negroes from the centuries of sorrow and oppression. What a shame that proud, fine, black woman never lived where the true greatness of the black race was appreciated!"

Maya Angelou presents Holiday just months before the end, an unsteady old lady (forty-four years old), picking her way across the room in Angelou's home in Los Angeles. She surprises Angelou (and the reader) by spending so much time with Guy, Angelou's twelve-year-old son, to whom she sings an a cappella lullaby each night—but one incident Angelou offers is a parable about the artist as an oracle, telling more of the truth than her listeners are quite ready to take in. When Guy asks Holiday to define the words "pastoral scene" in "Strange Fruit," which she sings to him on her last night in the house, the answer she gives him is frightening:

> Billie looked up slowly and studied Guy for a second. Her face became cruel, and when she spoke her voice was scornful. "It means when the crackers are killing the niggers. It means when they take a little nigger like you and snatch off his nuts and shove them down his goddam throat. That's what it means."
> The thrust of rage repelled Guy and stunned me.
> Billie continued, "That's what they do. That's a goddam pastoral scene."

This is one voice in which Billie Holiday, who sang in many voices, sang the blues.

Bibliography: Maya Angelou, *The Heart of a Woman* (New York, 1981). James Baldwin, "The Uses of the Blues," *Playboy,* January 1964. Ralph Ellison, "Richard Wright's Blues" (1945), in Ellison, *Living with Music: Ralph Ellison's Jazz Writings,* ed. Robert O'Meally (New York, 2001). Malcolm X, *The Autobiography of Malcolm X,* with the assistance of Alex Haley (New York, 1965). David Margolick and Hilton Als, *Strange Fruit: The Biography of a Song* (New York, 2001).

ROBERT O'MEALLY

1939; 1981

Ralph Ellison rehears the "Sweet-the-Monkey" tale in a Harlem bar and starts brooding over the metaphors of "not being seen" and "making hisself invisible"; a Czech translation of *Invisible Man* is published in Prague

UP FROM INVISIBILITY

"I am an invisible man. No, I am not a spook like those who haunted Edgar Allan Poe; nor am I one of your Hollywood movie ectoplasms." Ralph Ellison's novel *Invisible Man* is not an autobiographical account, and yet when asked, by the curious plebes at West Point after his lecture there in 1969, whether any of the scenes had happened to him, the writer admitted that they all had—in his head. As is common in a bildungsroman, the book presents the life story of the narrator in self-contained episodes that are part of his, and also the author's, process of growing up and maturing. In an interview with John O'Brien, Ellison put it succinctly in an almost Shakespearean mode: "Consciousness is all!" And indeed, it is the learning mind (and repeatedly hurt soul) that we follow, being driven through successive lessons of experience that we perceive with amazement, both in the life of the writer-to-be and in the happenings related by the first-person narrator of the novel. The book was published to critical acclaim and crowned with a National Book Award in 1952.

It was in 1945 in Waitsfield, Vermont, where Ellison was recuperating after service in the Merchant Marine during the Second World War, that "a rather wild notion" dawned upon him that he himself was "an invisible man." Having been born into humble circumstances in Oklahoma City in 1914 (or perhaps 1913, as Arnold Rampersad suggests), he survived an existence of "poverty and shame" in a practically fatherless Negro family (though it was his father who named him, after Ralph Waldo Emerson) in a racially segregated environment. In his youth he enjoyed a time of ambitious dreaming at Tuskegee Institute, where he studied mostly music and sculpture, but in 1935 he decided to leave Tuskegee for New York, which, with a very few breaks, became his home for the rest of his life. Lessons of all kinds were gradually transformed into awareness, understanding, reason, even wisdom—and finally into art. This is what we get, step by step, in the novel: an ambitious young Negro's contest with the hostile realities of life, first in the rural South and later in New York, and specifically in Harlem; a personal story that at the same time presents a panoramic review of African American history from the period of Reconstruction to the urban riots in the 1940s—or, more precisely, that offers a useful and badly needed retelling of *American* history of that period from the point of view of its initially forced and unwilling participant.

When recalling, in a lecture in 1983, how it felt "becoming a writer," Ellison saw his own beginnings as something of a magic turn—"The secret [that] lies in that old frontier experience, that spirit of adventure, that willingness to test ourselves against that which seems impossible." Having been "transformed" by his previous existential trials and by his intellectual reflections, he was launched as a writer who, on "the lower frequencies," along with his nameless and invisible narrator, may have been speaking for quite a few individuals and a number of citizens of the world.

Although Ellison was not willing to identify the Brotherhood of his novel with the American Communist Party, he would not and could not prevent his readers from doing so. Party censors in my country, Czechoslovakia, obviously had no difficulty seeing themselves represented (and ridiculed) in the political demeanor of the leftist organization that became so visible and quite appealing in the United States, and in Harlem in particular, during the Great Depression of the 1930s. And so our effort to have the Czech translation of the novel published was unsuccessful for years, and it remains a mystery why, in 1981, the ban was finally removed; we suspected that someone in the publishing house must have succeeded in presenting the book as a protest piece against American racism and capitalist exploitation, as had proved to be the case with other publications by or about African Americans, such as James Baldwin's *Go Tell It on the Mountain. Invisible Man* appealed to me for the reason it did to Saul Bellow: "Mr. Ellison has not adopted a minority tone. If he had done so, he would have failed to establish true middle-of-consciousness for everyone." Needless to say, the majority of Czechoslovak readers were in harmony with Ellison's narrator who, after a short period of cooperation, came to see that the objectives of the Brotherhood were not primarily focused on the interests of the people (black or white) but merely on gaining political power. It took a while before the Invisible Man could see through the game in which "the committee does the thinking" for which "he is not hired" and "the men in the street" are not to be asked what they think but *told* what to think and do. The narrator manages to liberate himself from the Brotherhood's demagogic vision of the world and its history when he is able again to look at "a crowd" and see "the set faces of individual men and women." The emphasis on the *scientific* nature of the Brotherhood ideology was, in countries behind the Iron Curtain where scientific communism was being taught at school, evocative of a widely spread political joke: If indeed Marxism-Leninism is a science, why was it not tested first on rats?

Ellison's novel is certainly a search for identity—a true identity, which means that one does not accept what others tell one to be, or not to be; one tries to see and realize one's own identity and role in society. The novel teems with allusions to invisibility, blindness, and revelation, poor or impaired vision, images of light and dark. Take the description of the statue of the Negro college's Founder, modeled on Booker T. Washington:

> It's so long ago and far away that here in my invisibility I wonder if it happened at all. Then in my mind's eye I see the bronze statue of the College Founder, the cold Father symbol, his hands outstretched in the breathtaking gesture of lifting a veil that flutters in hard, metallic folds above the face of a kneeling slave; and I am standing puzzled, unable to decide whether the veil is really being lifted, or lowered more firmly in place; whether I am witnessing a revelation or a more efficient blinding.

In the beginning the Invisible Man himself lacks social and human visibility, not just in the world around him, above all the white world, but even for himself. And so for a long time he cherishes his seemingly distant dream: "When I discover who I am, I'll be free." He gradually succeeds in his pursuit to be more than "a disembodied voice," and having spent some time literally underground, hibernating while retelling and thus learning to understand his life story, he may be coming close to his goal. And he may be getting ready to reemerge, on the surface again, "for even an invisible man has a socially responsible role to play." He has mastered his role of narrator, he has proved his creative potential as a writer, as an artist. "I wanted freedom, not destruction," we hear him say. The narrator, like the author himself, would not join the blueprints for destruction and violence, such as the revolutionary class struggle of the Brotherhood or the pretentious tribal uprising of Ras the Destroyer, modeled after Marcus Garvey's Back-to-Africa movement. Together author and narrator have produced a book, a novel in which "the interests of art and democracy converge," which was exactly the objective that Ellison as a creator had dreamed of, and that in composing and completing *Invisible Man* he also achieved.

It is not difficult to understand why young intellectuals (and not just black intellectuals) grasped the opportunities that various leftist organizations, including the Communist Party, offered in their journals and magazines to individuals otherwise invisible. Richard Wright, Langston Hughes, and Ralph Ellison were all either members of the party or fellow travelers. All three had expectations of art and literature that were clearly different from what the Soviet ideal of socialist realism demanded. Ellison maintained that he "never wrote the official type of fiction." And he later insisted: "I wrote what might be called propaganda—having to do with the Negro struggle—but my fiction was always trying to do something else." And yet, as Rampersad had to admit in his biography, "Ralph would remain something of a Stalinist for years to come," including the rather surprising support he gave to the isolationist policy line after World War II broke out in Europe. When I met with Ellison in 1969 he must have entirely wiped from his memory his earlier loyalties to the Communist reading of international affairs, as I could not and did not doubt his sincerity when he told me in detail of his deep sympathy for and feeling of solidarity with my country, not only in 1968, when the Soviets brutally quelled the Prague Spring movement, but also in 1939, when it was attacked and occupied by Hitler. Suspicions voiced by some leftist journalists that Ellison in later years intentionally suppressed information on his entanglement with the Communist Party because of the cold war sound too speculative—he simply changed his perspective on the world, including America.

In 1939 Ellison participated quite happily in the Federal Writers' Project. The job saved him from starvation and homelessness, and he had time and the opportunity to occupy himself with documents about the Negro past and present, and to discover, or rediscover, his own people's cultural lore. It was then that he heard Leo Gurley's "Sweet-the-Monkey," the tale of "a bad fellow who cut out a heart from a black cat, climbed backwards up a tree, and cursed God"—thus acquiring a capacity to do anything. Even to disappear into invisibility. A figure of a trickster that helped to sustain black people in their trying lives, just as the animal hero Brer Rabbit was capable of turning the tables on his enemies. Within the pages of his novel Ellison brings in the mythical folk character Peter Wheatstraw, "the Devil's only son-in-law," who tells the still-confused Invisible Man: "All it takes to get along in this here man's town is a little shit, grit, and mother's wit." Who advises him not to be ashamed of being a Southern boy but, on the contrary, just to "git with it." A modern trickster, indeed a confidence man, appears in the novel in the character of B. P. Rineheart, who, in masquerade, rules the chaos of Harlem.

Ellison employed his research into folktales, songs, proverbs, jokes, and verbal games, as well as the blues and jazz, for the courage and wisdom that was stored in those stories and forms. Negro culture, from slavery to modern times, was for him the final proof of the people's humanity—and it was an indelible part of the national culture, of the American experience. As he was not ready to reduce Negro folklore and culture in general to an expression of "alienation and agony," and to read the history and tradition as a story of victimization only, in the era of the civil rights movement he was even dismissed by some of the louder and more radical voices as an Uncle Tom. But what Ellison asked of America was that it come to terms with the "ideals which were so fatefully put down on paper" and which he wanted "to see made manifest," as he told Robert Penn Warren in their memorable interview from 1965. His demand was "to socialize the cost" of both the suffering and the invisibility of black Americans and of the poetry that was made out of their historical plight by, for one, Louis Armstrong—and also by Ralph Ellison himself.

Invisible Man is rich in the scope of reality absorbed and described; it is multilayered in presentation and interpretation; it is not just informed by modernist techniques but contributed greatly to their development. It is a *blues novel* not just because of the quotes in the text of the book but because the forms and the improvising spirit of the blues, and of jazz, have been allowed to shape the narrative, and because the tragic and the comic have been seriously merged into a stream of fiction that is able to live within the expressive potentials of realism and naturalism as well as symbolism and surrealism. The gallery of characters from the novel proved unforgettable not just for the narrator but for his readers as well—from the young man's slave grandfather, the poverty-stricken incestuous sharecropper Trueblood, and the treacherous college president, Dr. Bledsoe, to the Harlem motherly matron Mary, from the one-eyed Brotherhood leader, Brother Jack, to Brother Tod Clifton, who "plunged out of history" into Sambo-ism and nonexistence, and many more.

It was March 29, 1970, my last day in the United States before I returned home, when I had the pleasure and privilege to spend the evening with Ralph and Fanny Ellison in their apartment on Riverside Drive. We spoke of literature, culture, and freedom, of other black writers, which the host obviously found a topic of limited interest. Late in the evening, close to midnight, I was about to leave when Ralph insisted that he would accompany me to the bus station. I could not resist. Without any warning, and certainly without any initiative from my side, Ellison started complaining that people bothered him with questions about his new novel and started telling me of the fire in his cottage in which the manuscript of his work in progress had perished. As I had heard the story before, I dared to interrupt him with the remark that, as his first novel already "tells it all," even if it remained the only one he would ever write and publish, the job had been done and the landmark task had been fulfilled. "Thank you. An interesting thought," he retorted, and a mild smile lingered on his face—until he, quite unnecessarily, reprimanded his dog, Tucka, to behave himself. I have recalled this moment many times in the years that followed, as when, sadly, I had to write an obituary for the author of the still overshadowing and allusive *Invisible Man* for a Czech literary journal in 1994.

Bibliography: Ralph Ellison, *The Collected Essays of Ralph Ellison,* ed. John F. Callahan (New York, 1995); *Invisible Man* (New York, 1952); John Hersey, ed., *Ralph Ellison: A Collection of Critical Essays* (Englewood Cliffs, NJ, 1974). John O'Brien, ed., *Interviews with Black Writers* (New York, 1973). Arnold Rampersad, *Ralph Ellison: A Biography* (New York, 2007). Robert Penn Warren, *Who Speaks for the Negro?* (New York, 1965).

JOSEF JAŘAB

1940

Thomas Hart Benton illustrates John Steinbeck's *The Grapes of Wrath*

"No Way Like the American Way"

The publication of *The Grapes of Wrath* on April 14, 1939, sparked a bidding war among Hollywood's top studios. Even before the novel was officially out, it had seen three advance printings and prerelease sales of 42,000 copies. John Steinbeck had warned Viking Press that he didn't think his new book (his sixth novel) would do very well, and it was not picked up by any of the era's influential book clubs. Yet by early May, Steinbeck's story of the Joads, a family of sharecroppers who migrate from the Oklahoma dust bowl to the promised land of California, was the best-selling book in the nation, with some 11,000 copies—$2.75 each, featuring a dust jacket designed by well-known children's book illustrator Elmer Stanley Hader—streaming each week out of American stores. Shortly after it was published, Twentieth Century–Fox producer Darryl F. Zanuck snapped up the film rights for $75,000 and immediately started casting.

Skeptics predicted that a film version of *The Grapes of Wrath* would never be made, and that Zanuck had been forced to buy the rights in order to shelve what was both the most popular and most controversial book of the day. Banned in Bakersfield, California, where much of the second half of the book takes place, *Grapes* was also banned in Kansas City, Missouri, and Buffalo, New York, and was ordered burned in St. Louis. It was blasted as a "filthy manuscript" by Oklahoma congressman Lyle Boren, who assured his fellow representatives "that the painting Steinbeck made in his book is a lie, a black, infernal creation of a twisted, distorted mind." It was denounced as "obscene sensationalism" by the Associated Farmers of Kern County, California, the agribusiness firm that controlled the Central Valley region where hundreds of thousands of desperate job-seeking migrants flocked in the late 1930s. California's Chamber of Commerce condemned the book and potential film, and Twentieth Century–Fox was threatened with a boycott by various corporate and media concerns.

Zanuck capitalized on the controversy surrounding *The Grapes of Wrath* by appealing to issues of popularity, verisimilitude, freedom of expression, and creative courage. The film's trailer, for example, highlighted the book's best-selling status and "great stirring story," and cast Zanuck as Hollywood's version of Tom Paine:

Sweeping across the country comes one of the great literary achievements of our time. A human, revealing, great stirring story that instantly becomes the most discussed novel of modern literature: *The Grapes of Wrath* . . . Everyone, everywhere joins in the discussion of its vital problems. Speculation and rumor are rife to the effect that no producer will venture to film this great dramatic masterpiece of human heart. Darryl F. Zanuck, production head of 20th Century–Fox Studios, emphatically announces that *The Grapes of Wrath* will be made! All of the resources of this vast studio are marshaled for the production.

Fox resources included hiring John Ford to direct, Henry Fonda to star, and Thomas Hart Benton, perhaps the best-known American artist of the Great Depression, to publicize the controversial movie with a series of specially commissioned lithographs.

Benton was embroiled in his own controversies in the late 1930s, most of them centering on his pictures of female nudes. The first, painted in 1937 on assignment for *Life* magazine, was *Hollywood,* a boisterous ensemble of studio sets, industry employees, and scantily clad blonde starlets that Benton described as "sex, melodrama, and machinery." *Susanna and the Elders* (1938) and *Persephone* (1938–39) were equally salacious, both featuring sexually charged nudes in girlie-magazine poses—one a Rita Hayworth look-alike, the other sporting glossy red fingernails—being lusted after by horny farmers. Both were exhibited in New York at a major retrospective of Benton's work, and both received a good deal of media attention, especially after Benton told reporters that, in his opinion, America's art museums were "graveyards" and pictures like his best belonged in "barrooms and saloons." In February 1939, the director of St. Louis's City Art Museum announced plans to ban *Susanna* from an exhibition of contemporary Midwestern art because it was "too nude"; when he failed to make good on his threat, *Life* reported that "crowds flocked to see it." This was exactly what Darryl Zanuck hoped for with *The Grapes of Wrath:* a controversial film that millions would flock to see. Pairing regionalist artist Benton with the project was ideal.

In 1934, *Time* had coined the phrase "regional art" in its cover story on Benton, thus paying homage to a modern American art style in vogue since the late 1920s. Rooted in the familiar scenes and stereotypical subjects of everyday life, Benton's regionalism was bold and dynamic, an energetic art based on his intimate encounters with "the American environment and its people," he related in his 1937 autobiography, *An Artist in America.* Arguing against national homogeneity, Benton was drawn to diverse local and regional cultures and peoples that he felt defined all America; his regionalism was local in scope but national in perspective. During the 1930s, it was especially attuned to New Deal political culture; as Benton explained in a 1951 essay, regionalism was "very largely affirmative of the social explorations of American society and resultant democratic impulses on which President Roosevelt's New Deal was based."

It was also explicitly public: from his first major regionalist project, *American Historical Epic* (1919–1926), to 1930s murals including *America Today* (1930–31), at the New School for Social Research in New York, and *A Social History of the State of Missouri* (1936), in the state capitol building in Jefferson City, Benton was deeply committed to creating a "people's art," a popular American aesthetic that embodied "the peoples' behaviors, their *action*" as "the primary reality of American life." While he dabbled in radical politics for a time, even providing the illustrations for Leo Huberman's Marxist history of the United States, *We, the People,* in 1932, Benton's politics were more liberal than leftist. Like his fellow regionalists Grant Wood and John Steuart Curry, Benton turned to familiar, typecast images to ensure maximum public accessibility; like Steinbeck, he dotted his paintings with bawdy sexual references and occasional racist asides that would have been recognized by contemporary audiences.

Benton promoted regionalism on multiple levels. He was the key figure in Associated American Artists (AAA), a New York art gallery established in 1934 by public relations expert Reeves Lewenthal to market regionalist and American-scene art. Limited edition, hand-signed prints were sold in department stores and through mail-order advertising in popular magazines, for just five dollars each: an "unbelievably low price," one ad announced, "as the first step in this Association's purpose to stimulate greater interest in the work of contemporary American art." Sales boomed—70,000 prints were sold in two years—and AAA soon became a leading culture broker for American art, arranging numerous commercial commissions for its stable of artists. In 1937, *Life* hired Benton as a roving reporter; assignments included sketching striking autoworkers in Flint, Michigan, and picturing the movie industry in California (which produced *Hollywood*). Benton also painted pictures on commission for the American Tobacco Company that were used in an advertising campaign for Lucky Strike cigarettes. In 1939, he produced six prints for Fox's *Grapes of Wrath* campaign: five portraits of the movie's main characters and a sixth lithograph titled *Departure of the Joads.* The prints were heavily promoted by Fox, which urged its exhibitors to "make full use of this extraordinary art" in newspaper ads, theater lobby displays, and souvenir programs. As the studio's publicity office noted: "The nation is excited about works of art. The Benton art provides you with an exceptional, timely opportunity to ride the crest of this art-appreciation wave, and make it work for your playdate of *The Grapes of Wrath*." The film's premiere, at New York's Rialto Theatre, featured a twenty-four-foot enlargement of Benton's scene of the Joad family packing up to leave Oklahoma.

Benton's pictures were adapted from drawings he had made in the 1920s, when he crisscrossed America gathering visual details and local anecdotes for his regionalist art. As he put it in the opening sentences of "Going Places," the third chapter of his autobiography, "We Americans are restless. We cannot stay put. Our history is mainly one of migrations." During one trip through Oklahoma and Texas in 1928, he noted a surge of "western wanderers" with "bedding and baggage loaded on to an old Model T car, whole families . . . chugging along the road throwing dust into the wide staring faces of the sunflowers lining the way." Those images formed the basis for Twentieth Century–Fox's commission, although Benton altered his original drawings of Oklahoma migrants after he saw stills of the movie's main actors that were released along with the film's promotional trailer in the fall of 1939. Benton's *Ma Joad* thus looks like Jane Darwell, who won an Oscar for her role as the family matriarch, and his *Tom Joad* is a dead ringer for Henry Fonda. Basically celebrity head shots, Benton's images are a far remove from the miserable scenes captured by Horace Bristol, a staff photographer for *Life* who toured various California migrant workers' camps with John Steinbeck in March 1938.

Steinbeck had been writing about the workers' lives since April 1936, when the *San Francisco News* commissioned him to do a series of articles on the deplorable conditions facing California's migrant farm workers. These were published by the *News* later that year, accompanied by documentary photographs, such as Dorothea Lange's iconic *Migrant Mother* (1936), an image shot in Nipomo, California, that depicts thirty-two-year-old Florence Thompson and three of her seven children seated under a makeshift tent. Bristol had it in mind that he and Steinbeck would produce an expanded photo-essay on the economic plight of dust bowl migrants who had hoped for better conditions in California, only to encounter "starvation under the orange trees" (the title of Steinbeck's epilogue to the *News* articles, included in the 1938 collection *Harvest Gypsies*). But Steinbeck decided to write a novel that simultaneously dramatized the heartbreaking journey of a dispossessed farm family and addressed the larger issue of American migrant labor; if *The Grapes of Wrath* fits within the genre of social realism, it is also a work of fiction, a story about an American family.

Much of the controversy over the book centered on this dualism, with critics like the Associated Farmers accusing Steinbeck of fictional fabrication and others championing its documentary sensibility. *Grapes* is central to what William Stott terms the 1930s' "documentary imagination," whereby photographs, films, post office murals, and books were marshaled to illustrate the harsh realities of the Great Depression, emphasize the dignity, self-worth, and resilience of the American people, and rationalize the need for New Deal reforms. Steinbeck's novel, Zanuck's movie, and Benton's prints similarly addressed issues of social injustice and found solutions in the strength of the family and the solidarity of the nation. As Ma Joad declares in the movie's last scene, "Rich fellas come up an' they die, an' their kids ain't no good, an' they die out. But we keep a-comin'. We're the people that live. They can't wipe us out." Yet Steinbeck and Benton also subscribed to what Henry Nash Smith called the "myth of the garden," the romantic notion that the American West was essentially an agricultural paradise, meant to be owned and worked by independent American producers.

Themes of folk unity and optimistic survival, partnered with disquieting sketches of yeoman farmers and migrant labor, dominate Benton's second set of illustrations for *The Grapes of Wrath*, produced in 1940 for the Limited Editions Club (LEC). Founded in 1929 by George Macy, LEC published artist-commissioned and signed books in small runs (1,500 copies) for its member subscribers. Benton had illustrated well-received editions of *Huck Finn* and *Tom Sawyer* for the club in 1937, and after Macy saw the prints he had made for Twentieth Century–Fox, he persuaded him to expand the series. Benton made sixty-seven two-color lithographs for the LEC's two-volume set (which was reprinted and mass-produced in a single, more affordable volume by The Heritage Press): thirty as chapter headings, others as full-page illustrations, and a few as end papers.

Thomas Hart Benton, illustration from John Steinbeck, *The Grapes of Wrath*
(New York: The Heritage Press, 1940)

Again relying on drawings he had made during his travels in the 1920s, Benton's impressions of the American scene easily matched Steinbeck's similarly fluid ramblings and empathetic characterizations. Benton's sketch of the Joad family picking cotton, a full-page illustration for one of the book's last chapters, is a wrenching portrait of desperate, backbreaking labor. Centering on rows of pickers bent low over their work, trailing long sacks of cotton and worried about being defeated by the gray storm clouds looming in the picture's background, Benton's tense and agitated draftsmanship is the visual partner to Steinbeck's blatant revelation of the hardships of contemporary migrant life, and yet the human insistence on staying the course.

Both men were astute observers of American popular culture: Steinbeck's description of a Route 66 diner, its "walls decorated with posters, bathing girls, blondes with big breasts and slender hips and waxen faces, in white bathing suits, and holding a bottle of Coca-Cola and smiling" reads like a description of one of Benton's 1930s murals or his controversial girlie pictures. Both recognized the dominance of visual culture in twentieth-century America: that while millions went hungry during the Great Depression, more than 85 million Americans (out of a population of 125 million) went to the movies each week; that while consumer buying plummeted, advertising steadily increased, especially in the form of print media and outdoor signage. In 1937, the National Association of Manufacturers commissioned 60,000 outdoor billboards, prominently placed on highways and busy intersections, featuring pictures of smiling families and the upbeat, patriotic slogan "There's no way like the American Way." Benton's illustrations for *The Grapes of Wrath*, like much of his 1930s regionalist art, wrestled with the tensions implicit in that national promise: simultaneously celebrating and critiquing the American scene in anticipation of something better.

Bibliography: Thomas Hart Benton, "American Regionalism: A Personal History of the Movement" (1951), in *An American in Art: A Professional and Technical Autobiography* (Lawrence, KS, 1969); *An Artist in America,* 4th rev. ed. (Columbia, MO, 1983). Erika Doss, *Benton, Pollock, and the Politics of Modernism: From Regionalism to Abstract Expressionism* (Chicago, 1991). Warren French, *Filmguide to* The Grapes of Wrath (Bloomington, IN, 1973). John Steinbeck, *The Grapes of Wrath,* with lithographs by Thomas Hart Benton (New York, 1940). William Stott, *Documentary Expression and Thirties America* (New York, 1973).

ERIKA DOSS

1940–1944

"It is one of the tragedies of this life that the men who are most in need of beating up are always enormous." — Preston Sturges

SEVEN MOVIES IN FOUR YEARS

Of all the stupid vanities in a business that specializes in stupid vanities, the possessory credit might take the cake. That credit is the one that appears at the top of a film saying, "a film by ——," the blank then implausibly being filled by the name of a single person, the director.

Let's not get into how many other people—starting, of course, with the writer but continuing in essential ways through the cast, cinematographer, editor, and composer—create and influence the quality of a film. (Try to imagine the original choice of Ronald Reagan instead of Humphrey Bogart in *Casablanca* or Mae West as Norma Desmond in *Sunset Boulevard* to know how dependent a film's tone is on the contributions of all its elements.)

The possessory credit is silly for all kinds of reasons, not the least of which is that it's redundant: we'll see who it's by when we get to the other credits. But if anyone deserves this credit, it would have to be someone who has created a world in which the speech and actions and people, in which the tone and pacing and tenor of events are as obviously the creation of one artist as a passage of Twain's is obviously Twain's and not Charlotte Brontë's, as a Renoir is never confused with a Picasso.

It is safe to say that no one ever mistook a film by Preston Sturges for a film by anyone else. This is not something you can say of most directors, including many fine ones: George Cukor, William Wyler, John Huston. While one might plausibly expect that it was George Cukor who directed *Roman Holiday* instead of William Wyler, one could never imagine anyone but Sturges behind any of the manic yet buttery pictures that bear his name.

His was a world like no other world in the movies. Though the goings-on often border on the unreal, the world it most resembles is the real one—like our world, his is ungentrified and full of contradiction. The characters in a Sturges film are slickers and hicks, frantic, contemplative, melancholy, literate, subintelligent, vain, self-doubting, sentimental, cynical, hushed, and shouting. A hallmark of most artists is the consistency of their world—one thinks of the delicacy in René Clair's work, the droll, giddy understatement of Lubitsch, the painfully broad and clamorous tone of a Jerry Lewis movie. But Sturges's world seems the product of a man suffering from multiple personality disorder. (Sturges used to dictate his scripts aloud to a secretary as he wrote them, and when he did so, he played all the parts.) I can think of no other artist who keeps the delicate and the explosive so close together.

This collision of tones perhaps took its cue from his life. He was born in Chicago at the end of the nineteenth century. Not quite three years later, his mother, Mary, unhappy in her marriage, divorced her husband and moved to Paris with Preston. On her first day there she met the celebrated dancer Isadora Duncan—they became fast friends. Though Sturges would have complicated feelings of jealousy about his mother's close friendship with Duncan, he owed Duncan's family an enormous debt. On that first day in Paris, Sturges, always susceptible to respiratory trouble, had pneumonia with a temperature no doctor seemed able to cure. Isadora Duncan's mother arrived with a bottle of champagne out of which she fed him lifesaving spoonfuls until he was restored. Champagne and Pneumonia—it could be the title of a Sturges movie. It also suggests the conflicting elements at work in his films.

He did not come to Hollywood the way people come to Hollywood today, fresh out of film school, eager to replicate shots they like from other movies they saw in class. He'd been a stage manager, a wartime aviator, a songwriter, and the manager of his mother's cosmetics concern, where he invented a highly success-ful kissproof lipstick. ("Kissproof" also sounds like a Sturges title.) He'd written a Broadway hit, *Strictly Dishonorable,* followed by three flops. By the time he came to Hollywood in the 1930s, he'd lived a lot and seen a lot, and he had a pretty strong sense of himself.

He was quickly making a thousand dollars a week as a writer for Universal. One of his films, *The Power and the Glory,* had a structure and subject that were admiringly reproduced a few years later by Orson Welles in *Citizen Kane.* (If you have to have your ideas reworked, *Citizen Kane* is the place.) It may have been his success in business, or his age, or the sense given to him by his mother that you must dream big, but in 1940 he got himself a job directing his own script, be-coming the first credited writer/director of the talking age. He did this with ei-ther the common sense of a businessman, or the desperation of a writer: he sold Paramount his script of *The Vagrant* for ten dollars with the stipulation that he direct it.

The film became *The Great McGinty,* a more positive title than *The Vagrant,* until you see the movie and learn the irony of it. It launched his remarkable run of seven pictures in four years: *Christmas in July, The Lady Eve, Sullivan's Travels, The Palm Beach Story, The Miracle of Morgan's Creek,* and *Hail the Conquering Hero.* (There was a flop in there, too, something called *The Great Moment,* a movie about the discovery of anesthesia, which sounds like the kind of serious picture Sullivan wants to make in *Sullivan's Travels.*)

These are the touchstones of the Sturges reputation, and if you watch them close together, as I did recently, you may be struck by something I'd never noticed when I saw the pictures in isolation over the years. His films, with all their ex-cesses (possibly because of their excesses), may offer a truer idea of American life than the films of any other director of his time. Each of the seven films stands as an insouciant rebuke to the mythic America of John Ford, the inspirational America of Frank Capra, or the safe and cozy America as pushed through MGM's popular Andy Hardy series. If those films were a warm hug to their audience, the Sturges pictures are a jab in the ribs, a sexy joke whispered in church—a wink, a kiss, and a hiccup. His vision of America seems right because his pictures of life in this country are a lot like life in this country: messy, noisy, sometimes crazy, some-times sweet.

This portrait of America is indirect and probably unconscious. I don't think for a second he sat down and thought, "What can I say about my country?" While he does examine issues that are at the heart of what it means to be an American—ambition, money, heroism, morality—he treats them with a nimble wit and a po-et's gift for slang that offers American English at its most beguiling.

Not only is his dialogue spoken, as Henry Higgins says so nicely in *My Fair Lady,* with the speed of summer lightning but, under his direction, the actors weave in and out of each other's lines with such fluid ease that the spoken word achieves the euphonious quality of the sung. *His Girl Friday* is often cited as the nonpareil of this sort of rapid overtalking, and there's no question that it is expertly done. But the speed of *His Girl Friday* is dictated by the events of the story, a hyper newspaper comedy. In Sturges's world, it seems merely to be a reflection of the way people are: husbands interrupt their wives, children talk over their parents, secretaries sass their bosses, and every working person—cab driver, bartender, tailor, switchboard operator—has an opinion and they're going to tell you what it is. Because the Sturges films are not sentimental about America, free speech is dealt with as it is in real American life: people ignore it, make fun of it, talk over it, and then get back to trying to make a buck.

Though he had been a playwright, Sturges's scripts have none of the speechy muster of the theater. He could be epigrammatic: "Nothing in this world is permanent, except Roosevelt," says Mary Astor in *The Palm Beach Story*. Later in the movie, her brother, played with endearing delicacy by Rudy Vallee, ruefully states a fact known to all meek men: "It is one of the tragedies of this life that the men who are most in need of beating up are always enormous." Like all good comic writing, it is a line that not only amuses but reveals. Vallee does this earlier in the film with a line that is a perfect parody of gentlemanly good manners. Claudette Colbert, in a hurried ascent to her upper berth, accidentally steps on Vallee's face, smashing his pince-nez into bits. When she jumps down to help, he seeks to minimize her embarrassment by saying in a genially unperturbed tone, "Just pick off any little pieces you see!"

Perhaps the most persuasively American quality of Sturges's movies, what makes it impossible to confuse his movies with movies from any other source, is his use of people. His leads were often played by stars who would fit in any number of movies: Henry Fonda, Claudette Colbert, Barbara Stanwyck, Joel McCrea. But he created an extraordinary stock company of supporting players who proved what is so often said but little shown about America: it is a country of immigrants. His stories are filled not merely with Hollywood's idea of ethnic characters—the black cook and the English butler—but with people from every corner of Europe, including Jews who do the unheard-of thing and sound like Jews. The range of accents in his films sound like the dining room at the UN. Without ever directly preaching the glories of American values, about which Sturges had a fair amount of cynicism, the fact that Jews and Germans, English and Irish, Russians and Italians all inhabited the same screen, bantering, flirting, sniping, or swiping at each other, said something about America that beat the message of any war-bond rally.

He hardly presents America as a haven from greed, a shining city on a hill, or a chorus of dissonant voices that find harmony when singing as one. America is shown for what we know it to be: a carnival of bull and glory, with riches or a broken neck possible around any corner. Virtue is punished *(The Great McGinty)* as often as it is rewarded *(Hail the Conquering Hero),* and a passionate belief in one's ideas *(Christmas in July)* doesn't help as much as blind good luck.

Amazingly, he presented this satiric idea of an imperfect America at what may have been the peak of the nation's patriotism. Other movies of the time made buffoonish Germans, Italians, or Japanese the butt of their jokes. (Chaplin may have managed it best in *The Great Dictator* with the deft portrayals of Hitler and Mussolini, but even that movie can't resist a push for the betterment of humanity with a mood-killing speech of inspiration at the end, made all the worse by Chaplin's odd, debutante's voice. Chaplin's films are the opposite of Sturges's: perfectly executed physicality followed by dialogue you wish you could turn off.) But at a time when the free world was under the gravest assault and America stood apart as a saving hope, Sturges made fun of the major American institutions of the day: the press, politics, and the military. American audiences, no doubt grateful to a filmmaker who knew that laughing at their country did not preclude loving it, lapped the films up.

Was the popularity of this counterthinking an astute read of the national mood or, like many a Sturges plot turn, just a bit of sunny luck? Whatever it was, after his four-year reign of triumph, his fortunes took a turn for the worse.

Chafing under studio restraints, he left Paramount—and whatever combination of alchemy, chance, and talent existed there to make those years so fruitful, the next sixteen would be a terrible series of setbacks and humiliations for him. When his public fell off and the critics lost their enthusiasm for him, his confidence was shaken. Self-doubt is fatal to a style like his, where the success of the work is tied to an ability to sustain a tone—often so much trickier than sustaining a plot.

And sustaining a tone was difficult for him even at the top of his game. It must be said that even the seven wonders of the Sturges canon have their problems and the problems can always be traced to a break in tone. Not one of these movies is a perfect picture, the way *The Shop around the Corner* is perfect, or *The Wizard of Oz* or *Psycho* or *Zelig* or *The Godfather* is perfect. Each of those films clears its throat and sings its song and what comes out always sounds right. There is never a moment when you pull back, tilt your head, and wonder, "What was that?"

But there is always that moment in a Sturges movie. It comes when the champagne of his dialogue is poisoned by the pneumonia of his slapstick. Sometimes this is the result of poor execution or an unconvincing motivation (Joel McCrea and Veronica Lake and then the butlers falling into the pool in *Sullivan's Travels*). Sometimes it comes from the heavy-handed way Sturges frames and shoots these sequences, often at odds with his otherwise flowing and graceful photography (Rex Harrison preparing to murder his wife at the end of *Unfaithfully Yours*). Sometimes it comes from a sense that the slapstick isn't true: there are times when someone falls too fast, as if the film is speeded up (Henry Fonda going over the couch in *The Lady Eve*). Sturges's slapstick lacks the loopy inevitability of Lucy getting drunk on Vitameatavegamin or the hypnotizingly hilarious boxing match in *City Lights*.

Again: *he made seven films in four years.* Perhaps the race to get them done explains the sometimes jarring tonal shifts. One wonders if, had he spent a little more time on each film, they might have achieved a more balanced and integrated tone. Yet who knows if it wasn't the rush to make them that infused the films with their appealing pep and lack of pretension? God knows, I'd rather see *The Lady Eve* twice than Vincent Minnelli's labored *The Pirate* once.

Sturges was an American original, which is a dangerous thing to be. While America itself is an original idea, and while America claims always to value the individual voice over the roar of the mob, what America likes best is something that can be reproduced the maximum amount of times for as many people as cheaply as possible with as little interference as possible from its creator. American culture is a commercial culture above all else and nothing threatens it more than an individual who is irreplaceable.

And so he was replaced. In less than a decade, he went from being the third highest-paid individual in the United States to a state of near bankruptcy. In 1952, when he was having a hard time of it, Betty Hutton, from whom he got the performance of her career in *Miracle of Morgan's Creek* and who became a star because of it, wouldn't appear in what was to be his new film, "Look, Ma, I'm Dancin'," unless her husband, a choreographer, directed it. (Paramount refused and the film died.) Sturges looked for creative and financial independence and found what many find when they look for those things: a very dark hole.

But he did not give up. He worked on plays and television ideas and new film scripts. He married for the fourth time and had two more boys to go with his son from another marriage. It looked like his luck was going to change. But in a jarring breach of tone that matched the ones from his films, just as things seemed to be turning around, he had a heart attack, alone in his room at the Algonquin Hotel. Doctors tried to revive him with a shot of adrenaline but they could not.

They should have tried champagne.

Bibliography: James Harvey, *Romantic Comedy in Hollywood: From Lubitsch to Sturges* (New York, 1998). Diane Jacobs, *Christmas in July: The Life and Art of Preston Sturges* (Berkeley, CA, 1992). Pauline Kael, *5001 Nights at the Movies*, rev. ed. (New York, 1991). *Preston Sturges by Preston Sturges,* adapted and edited by Sandy Sturges (New York, 1990). David Thomson, *The New Biographical Dictionary of Film* (New York, 2002).

DOUGLAS McGRATH

1941

Leslie Fiedler becomes an assistant professor of English at Montana State University

AN INSOLENT STYLE

"Myth" is not only a key word in Fiedler's critical lexicon but also describes his own self-mythologizing as the enfant terrible of American letters, the Good Bad Boy who abandoned "sivilization," like Huck Finn before him, to venture out into the West relatively free from the influence of the WASP-ish world of Ivy League English departments. Leslie Fiedler's move to Montana in 1941 to take a position as assistant professor of English at Montana State University in Missoula became legendary, contributing to the persona that Fiedler cultivated as the guru of the sixties' counterculture. He was to describe the move as an exodus, an abandonment of the East and all that it signifies: namely, a bourgeois investment in high literature, replete with its elitist and anti-Semitic overtones. Reflecting on the sixties, Daniel Schwarz, an emeritus professor at Cornell, recollects that "every Jewish graduate student knew the fairy tale of Leslie Fiedler: exiled in Missoula, Montana, where he wrote and taught before returning to the East to SUNY Buffalo." In *Harper's* in 1982, Hugh Kenner described Fiedler's move to Montana in less flattering terms: "In '41, straitjacketed in his new doctorate, the burly Fiedler was bundled by implacable Fate into the train that would haul him off kicking and fuming to the academic Gulag in Montana." (Three years later, Fiedler would get his own back by saying that Kenner had a *goyisher kopf* [a goy's head] for his "queasy-making sympathy" for Ezra Pound's anti-Semitism.)

Regardless of whether Fiedler arrived in Montana as a Jewish romantic turning his back on the literary establishment or as a frustrated academic, kicking and fuming, Montana played a crucial role in Fiedler's development as a critic. The same year that Fiedler moved West, John Crowe Ransom published *The New Criticism,* a book that gave the movement its name, with the first chapter dedicated exclusively to I. A. Richards and his "scientific" mode of reading literature. Fiedler's intersection with New Criticism was not only temporal but also spatial, in that I. A. Richards and his wife had a lifelong devotion to Montana and helped to map Glacier National Park, an apt hobby for a critic dedicated to the cognitive mapping of poetic form. Fiedler's relation to Montana, however, differs greatly from that of Richards, a difference that is emblematic of their respective critical approaches: myth-criticism versus New Criticism. I. A. Richards was concerned with taming Montana by making it decipherable, rational, and navigable, while Fiedler would define the "true Montanan" as "an Eternal Stranger in a land that will, must, remain eternally strange to all white ex-Europeans."

Fiedler insists that Montana is an invention of European romanticism, where the myth of the Noble Woodsman sits uncomfortably alongside the myth of the Noble Savage, as a European projection that Montanans have internalized. Montana is for Fiedler a gothic landscape, whose white inhabitants are haunted by the guilt of indigenous genocide, with living Indians confined to "open-air ghettoes" and excluded from social life in the larger community. For such sentiments, Fiedler was made an honorary member of the Blackfoot nation.

Fiedler's close reading of Montana as a text with a context contrasts dramatically with I. A. Richards's adage: "It is never what a poem *says* that matters, but what it *is*." In contrast to New Criticism's world of organic harmony, where the poem is a self-contained entity inscribed within a Christian vision of aesthetic transcendence, Fiedler's world is characterized by conflict, change, and irreconcilable contradictions that invite affective responses such as melancholy and rage. "I long for the raised voice," Fiedler once said of literary criticism, "the howl of rage or love," and "the newest criticism . . . must be comical, irreverent, vulgar."

Toward the end of his life, Fiedler told his biographer Mark Winchell: "I spent the first half of my career trying to break down the barriers between academic disciplines and the second half trying to tear down the walls between elite and popular culture." Although Fiedler presents these concerns as two distinct stages in his career, they are in fact inextricably linked, bound together by his desire for opening up categories of any kind, whether they be the literary canon, Jewishness, or the West. The key to this desire was Fiedler's consistent commitment to his audience, which he defined throughout his career as the "general reader," or "the all-but-forgotten 'Gentle' Reader." Fiedler, like F. O. Matthiessen before him, directed his work to the general reader in order to address "that cleavage between mass civilization and minority culture," to quote Fiedler quoting Matthiessen, who in turn was quoting F. R. Leavis. For Fiedler, the ideal vehicle for bridging this "essential split of our culture" was not the monograph, with its detailed analysis, but the "irresponsible, noncommercial book review," a genre that "discourages the framing of elaborate vocabularies, and encourages a tone committed to communication and sociability."

In 1950, Fiedler proudly declared in the pages of the *Kenyon Review,* a journal closely associated with New Criticism, that he was "an amateur critic" who, in the spirit of Whitman, addressed his words toward "everyone." "The true language of criticism," Fiedler argued, "is the language of conversation—the voice of the dilettante at home." The critic is a cultural mediator, a communicator connecting the poet with the general reader. In an "age of declining sociability and the widespread failure of love," the clarity of the critic takes on a moral resonance, which is the desire to connect with others. Comprehensibility does not compromise the critical endeavor but instead regenerates criticism by forcing the critic to speculate, to make generalizations and evaluations without hiding behind exhaustive close readings that are exercises in timidity and mediocrity. For Fiedler, the professionalization of literary criticism reflects the growing alienation of postwar America.

The one critic who surpassed Matthiessen, according to Fiedler, in his ability to communicate effectively and powerfully to the general reader was D. H. Lawrence, whose *Studies in Classic American Literature* (1923) was described by Fiedler in *The Art of the Essay* as "one of the most striking and unhackneyed books ever written on our life and literature." His estimation of Lawrence's *Studies* remained constant until the very end of his life. In an unpublished fragment that was to be the start of an introduction to a new edition of *Studies,* dictated on January 23, 2003, a week before his death at the age of eighty-five, Fiedler described Lawrence's neglected book as "the best critical work ever written by anyone, even Americans." Only Matthiessen, he added, "has come close." In the original preface to *Love and Death in the American Novel* (1960), a book that boosted D. H. Lawrence's cultural capital within the academy, Fiedler described the significance of Lawrence's study in coming "closest to the truth" of recognizing the "duplicity and outrageousness" of American letters, with a voice that is at once "idiosyncratic, personal" as well as conversational, exhibiting a "true style" that "is never safe, choosing always to court extravagance."

Fiedler's description of Lawrence's style could also describe his own, most notably in *Love and Death,* which is Fiedler's most important critical contribution, though not his best-selling book (that distinction would go to his 1978 book *Freaks*). In 1960, Irving Kristol defended *Love and Death* against the onslaught of criticism that accused the book of being unoriginal, hackneyed, and bizarre (an impossible combination, Kristol muses) by acknowledging the book's debt to D. H. Lawrence: "*Love and Death* perhaps could not have been written, and certainly would not be as good as it is, if Lawrence had not previously produced his book; but it represents an improvement on the original." Kristol speculated that what made Fiedler so controversial was his insolent style, with its grand gesture, bold postures, and exaggerations. Within the U.S. academy, literary criticism, Kristol claimed, "is a recognized profession, like medicine, or law, or tax accounting; and any critic who is too aggressively self-assertive, who thumbs his nose at the formalities . . . is regarded as a traitor to his class."

Attacks against *Love and Death* came from outside the academy as well. A week before *Love and Death* was published, Robert Bly's magazine *The Sixties* described Fiedler as an "old fogey" and included "satires and insults" against him. Fiedler's own tendency toward self-promotion, as Benjamin DeMott wrote in *Commentary* in 1960, made him vulnerable to such ad hominem attacks, and one sees evidence of this tendency on the back jacket of the first edition, which has a "Glamour Photograph of the author featuring an edge of a Kerouacian plaid shirt, a black tormented brow, and some agonized lower molars—the sort of picture you expect to find on an as-told-to book by a junkie." This tendency toward "self-dramatization" was unfortunate, DeMott notes, because it blinded intelligent readers to the seriousness of *Love and Death*, which was "far from an outrage," but "one of the very few important assessments of our culture to appear since . . . Matthiessen's *American Renaissance*."

Part of the notoriety surrounding the publication of *Love and Death* came from Fiedler's article "Come Back to the Raft Ag'in, Huck Honey!" which appeared in *Partisan Review* in 1948 and was Fiedler's first published foray into American letters (he was trained at Wisconsin as a scholar of seventeenth-century English poetry). In this article, whose germ comes from D. H. Lawrence's observation of the "linked mythos of escape and immaculate male love" in American literature, Fiedler argues that the central American archetype is the "buddy-buddiness" of the white young man and the black man (or racialized other) who escape Aunt Polly's "sivilizing" to create a dream world on the raft in *Huckleberry Finn*, or in Queequeg's bed with Ishmael in *Moby-Dick*, or with Natty Bumppo and Chingachgook, sitting "night after night over their campfire in the purest domestic bliss" in James Fenimore Cooper's Leatherstocking Tales. Where European novels focus on adult heterosexual passion, American literature consists of boys' books, of an interracial homosocial fantasy of "love without passion," where a boy can be a boy and find acceptance "at the breast he has most utterly offended." By arguing that American literature consists primarily of a fantasy of white male redemption that must repress guilt and racial disparity, as well as its own homoerotic desires, Fiedler was the first American literary critic to place race and "queer" sexuality at the center of American literature.

In *Love and Death* Fiedler explores further the convergence of race, sexuality, and masculinity in order to claim that American literature is a "literature of horror for boys"; it is a "gothic fiction, nonrealistic and negative, sadist and melodramatic—a literature of darkness and the grotesque in a land of light and affirmation." Fiedler's emphasis on the gothic challenged the canonical cold war narrative of American literature epitomized in Robert Spiller's *Literary History of the United States* (1948). In his review of this work in *American Quarterly* (1949), Fiedler lambasted the volume for imposing on American fiction the religion of liberalism with its happy-ending, rags-to-riches narrative, where American literature "is not only virile, democratic, and humanitarian," but even "on the whole optimistic." Despair and melancholy are considered "un-American." A persistent theme and arguably Fiedler's most significant contribution to literary history was his use of canonical literature to show the fault lines of the mythology of American innocence by arguing that despair and melancholy are as American as apple pie.

Fiedler, however, did not simply champion despair over cheerfulness, but instead showed how the dialectic of violence and innocence—the two forces that make Huck Finn—are indicative of the very contradictions of the nation, where the gothic, with its emphasis on death and destruction, undercuts the prevailing myth of sentimental virtue and benevolence. Like the landscape of Montana, literature, for Fiedler, represents the national unconscious, the repressed desires, guilt, and obsessions that circulate just below the surface of a sentimentalism that rejects tragedy and believes in the goodness and reasonableness of life. Sentimentalism, in good Protestant fashion, can explain away mysteries, rationalize evil. The result is a national literature that represents tragedy in rational and optimistic terms, where gothic phantoms are really just jokes and the headless horseman is, after all, only a hoax. But these happy endings are not entirely convincing. Fiedler acknowledged at the end of *Love and Death* that happy endings may also be amusing shams, "blasphemous jokes on the unwary reader."

One of the ironies of Fiedler's career was that he spent much of his life demystifying national legends and mythologies only to have *Love and Death* itself become legendary. For many readers, *Love and Death* represents the entirety of Fiedler's career, despite the fact that he went on to write more than twenty books in the thirty-eight years after its publication. These later works, including *What Was Literature* and *Tyranny of the Normal,* have been largely neglected, at the cost of ignoring the extent to which Fiedler was a dynamic thinker who revised major aspects of the earlier work.

Nearly twenty years after *Love and Death* first appeared, Fiedler gave a series of lectures for the Canadian Broadcasting Corporation (published as *The Inadvertent Epic*), which challenged the male-centered canon in *Love and Death.* By this time Harriet Beecher Stowe's *Uncle Tom's Cabin* was as central to American literature as Twain's *Huckleberry Finn.* In *What Was Literature* (1982), Fiedler admitted his error: if Twain is "a literary father to us all, Hattie Stowe is our mother—however long some of us may in our macho pride have denigrated and denied her." Stowe's novel centers on the Myth of the Utopian Household, and Tom is the "Blessed Male Mother [in blackface and drag] of a virgin Female Christ." In 1960, Fiedler had no critical vocabulary with which to defend *Uncle Tom's Cabin* as a classic, since by the standards of high literature it was a failure. But in the intervening two decades, he began a process of self-interrogation and *Uncle Tom's Cabin* became the standard by which to rethink his aesthetic criteria, a self-interrogation that demarcates the second stage of his career, when he turned to popular culture as a way to demystify the sanctified realm of literature.

Though Granville Hicks would describe Fiedler at the time of *Love and Death* as "a wild man of American literary criticism," Fiedler's later career, when he challenged critics to go beyond literature to include a "post-Gutenberg" culture of the visual, such as television and movies, would be his more radical intervention. At a 1979 lecture at Harvard's English Institute entitled "Literature as an Institution," Fiedler powerfully explored the dangerous consequences of questioning the role of literature: "Any challenge to the literary *status quo,* therefore, threatens not just individual teachers, but departments of English as a whole; indeed, the very departmental structure of the university, along with the assumptions about professionalism, specialization and scholarship upon which it is based"; the function of English departments, and of freshman composition in particular, is the "instant bourgeois WASPification of all new Americans." Fiedler fought this "WASPification" in his later work by bringing his analytical skills to the cultural forms that most people watch and read, namely, such examples of popular culture as Alex Haley's *Roots, Star Trek,* comic books, biotechnology, and the cult of slimness. Fiedler described himself as the "last Jew," but he was also perhaps the last romantic, holding onto a notion of the vulgar as a way to thumb his nose at the genteel mores of "Anglo-Saxon polite culture" and to champion instead its outsiders—the nonconformists, the eccentrics, the freaks.

Bibliography: Benjamin DeMott, "The Negative American," in *Hells & Benefits: A Report on American Minds, Matters, and Possibilities* (New York, 1962). Leslie Fiedler, *The Inadvertent Epic: From* Uncle Tom's Cabin *to* Roots (Toronto, 1979); "Literature as an Institution: The View from 1980," in *English Literature: Opening Up the Canon,* ed. Leslie Fiedler and Houston Baker (Baltimore, 1981); *Love and Death in the American Novel,* rev. ed. (New York, 1966). Irving Kristol, "A Traitor to His Class?" *Kenyon Review* 2 (Summer 1960): 505–509. Daniel R. Schwarz, "Eating Kosher Ivy: Jews as Literary Intellectuals," *Shofar: An Interdisciplinary Journal of Jewish Studies* 21, no. 3 (2003): 16–28. Mark Royden Winchell, *"Too Good to Be True": The Life and Work of Leslie Fiedler* (Columbia, MO, 2002).

CARRIE TIRADO BRAMEN

1941

"Mankiewicz's contribution? It was enormous"— Orson Welles

THE SCREENPLAY AS GENRE

Citizen Kane is routinely chosen in polls as the greatest film ever made, but at the Academy Awards ceremony in February 1942, whenever the name of Orson Welles was read, many in the Biltmore Hotel audience booed. The only Oscar won by *Kane,* out of nine nominations, was for its screenplay, for which Welles shared credit (in second position) with Herman J. Mankiewicz. A veteran Hollywood hand known equally for his acerbic wit and his often-incapacitating drinking problem, Mankiewicz, for all his barbs and misbehavior, was more acceptable in Hollywood than the twenty-six-year-old Welles, who had also produced, directed, and starred in that politically and aesthetically audacious film. Like many screenwriters in that era, Mankiewicz was a former newspaperman who regarded the movie business with a contempt he hardly bothered to hide. In 1925, he sent fellow newsman Ben Hecht a telegram that has become a classic statement of writerly disdain for Hollywood: "WILL YOU ACCEPT THREE HUNDRED PER WEEK TO WORK FOR PARAMOUNT PICTURES. ALL EXPENSES PAID. THE THREE HUNDRED IS PEANUTS. MILLIONS ARE TO BE GRABBED OUT HERE AND YOUR ONLY COMPETITION IS IDIOTS. DON'T LET THIS GET AROUND." Insulting to the power structure though he may have been, Mankiewicz was still only a screenwriter and therefore harmless without an enabler. Welles, on the other hand, was a radical wunderkind who challenged many of the town's conventions and taboos, a far deeper threat, especially when he managed to win (just once) final cut from a Hollywood studio.

By the time Mankiewicz worked on *Kane,* he was little in demand professionally and then only for the kind of hackwork that consumed much of his screenwriting career and drove him to bouts of despair. Welles could see beyond "Mank's" largely mediocre list of credits. The young director valued not only Mankiewicz's bounteous wit and screenwriting savvy but also his insights into the newspaper world and the lurid life of publisher William Randolph Hearst, the unacknowledged but obvious model for Charles Foster Kane. Welles set up Mankiewicz at a desert retreat in Victorville, sans bottles but in the creative company of John Houseman, Welles's former Mercury Theatre partner, who was functioning as a combined nursemaid and uncredited writing collaborator. Together they labored on two sprawling drafts of what was then being called *American.* What happened over the next few months, as the script kept evolving and went into production, would become the most celebrated test case for the question of film authorship and the auteur theory.

Inspired by the *politique des auteurs* (policy of authors) propagated by the young critics of the French film magazine *Cahiers du Cinéma* in the 1950s, the auteur theory, as it was dubbed by New York critic Andrew Sarris in the early '60s, argues that directors are the primary creative force in the art of filmmaking. In its original incarnation, the *politique* was partly formulated to account for cases of directors who did not write their scripts (such as Howard Hawks or Raoul Walsh) but still managed to impose their personal visions on diverse material. That key nuance has often been lost in translation. Today the auteur theory is widely used to celebrate directors as a marketing tool or as shorthand for directorial authorship in the news media and therefore accepted by audiences, generally at the expense of screenwriters. In academic circles, auteurism is in disrepute, at least theoretically, because the field of film studies bows to Roland Barthes and his "Death of the Author" theory. But in practice, most academic film teaching and film writing is organized, with unconscious irony, around the work of directors.

Few directors have stirred the imagination of film aficionados more than Welles, who seemed to epitomize the romantic notion of the auteur as a one-man show. However facile and reductive that notion may be, it became the governing myth of what was called the New Hollywood, the doctrine invoked in the late 1960s to help overthrow the already tottering studio system by enabling the artists to take over from the "suits." Although that revolution would be short-lived, its threat to the cultural status quo was significant, and film critic Pauline Kael lobbed an unexpected grenade at the auteur theory in 1971 by challenging the authorship of its most sacred text. She claimed in a two-part *New Yorker* essay, "Raising Kane," that Welles had little to do with the screenplay of *Kane,* that he had tried to steal sole credit from Mankiewicz, and that the film, by implication, belonged more to Mankiewicz than to its director. Welles's work on the script, she contended, was limited to making "suggestions" to Mankiewicz, and then "a few changes on the set." Relying on the word of Mankiewicz's secretary rather than inspecting all seven complete drafts of the script in the RKO files, Kael wrote that "Welles didn't write (or dictate) one line of the shooting script of *Citizen Kane.*" Kael even disparaged critics who consider *Kane* a profound work of art. Instead she pugnaciously claimed that it was "a shallow work, a *shallow* masterpiece," more a monument to a tradition of wisecracking Hollywood craftsmanship than to the artistic vision of an outsider with such decidedly avant-garde instincts that he soon became anathema in the industry. For Kael, whose vigorous championing of popular art often went hand in hand with a mockery of what she considered highbrow pretension, the controversy over the screenplay of *Kane* was a way to reclaim a cinematic landmark, *the* cinematic landmark, from the growing hordes of youthful intellectuals who were determined to turn the movies into an academic discipline.

Kael lost that culture war resoundingly, but she had more success in winning the immediate battle over *Citizen Kane.* Welles was already a suspect figure to many in the American media and the filmgoing public because his checkered directing career after *Kane,* which led him through many peregrinations as an independent filmmaker *avant la lettre,* had become virtually invisible by 1971, eclipsed by the predominance of what Welles scholar Jonathan Rosenbaum calls "the media-industrial complex." It was not until Robert L. Carringer obtained access to the RKO script files and carefully studied the complex development of the *Kane* screenplay drafts that the issue of writing credit was definitively resolved.

In a 1978 article in *Critical Inquiry,* Carringer concluded that Kael had seriously misrepresented the evidence for her case by ignoring the way Welles's rewriting transformed Mankiewicz's early drafts:

> Herman Mankiewicz's principal contribution to the *Citizen Kane* script was made in the early stages at Victorville. The Victorville scripts elaborated the plot logic and laid down the overall story contours, established the main characters, and provided numerous scenes and lines that would eventually appear in one form or another in the film . . . Work [had] scarcely begun on the most glaring problem in the material, making *Kane* into an authentic dramatic portrait.

. . . In the eight weeks between the time the Victorville material passed into Welles's hands and the final draft was completed, the *Citizen Kane* script was transformed, principally by him, from a solid basis for a story into an authentic plan for a masterpiece.

Carringer's research established that Welles's many contributions to conceiving, shaping, and styling the screenplay justified his joint writing credit with Mankiewicz.

It would take assiduous research comparable to Carringer's, with full access to script files, to determine the fair allotment of credit between the writer(s) and the director for most films. And given the collaborative and often chaotic nature of the filmmaking process, aren't films usually made in ways that render assignment of their authorship to single creators difficult if not impossible? What does it mean to be the "author" of a film, anyway? And where does the humble screenwriter, so often ignored and sneeringly dismissed (Jack L. Warner famously called screenwriters "schmucks with Underwoods"), fit into this picture? Even if collaborative credit can be judiciously established, the philosophical question remains as to whether the screenwriter can be an "author" in any meaningful way, if the screenplay is not the final product but only an intermediate stage in the production of a motion picture.

Some who would elevate the position of the screenwriter would ask the question, are screenplays literature? But perhaps a more germane question is, are screenplays writing? That may sound disrespectful to an artistic craft that is more responsible for the quality (or lack of it) of many motion pictures than the average filmgoer, or even the sophisticated film aficionado, realizes. But it is a question that goes to the heart of the craft itself and the function of the screenplay in the complicated process of filmmaking.

Admitting that writers make enormous contributions to films should not detract from the contributions of directors unless the two functions are conflated, a frequent critical fallacy. A classical Hollywood director cited by both Kael and Welles as epitomizing the smoothly creative functioning of the studio system at its best was Howard Hawks. When I asked Hawks in the 1970s why most of his movies "look very fresh and modern today," he replied, "Most of them were well written. That's why they last." Hawks ruminated on what makes a good screenplay, offering a gnomic, paradoxical observation that has been troubling me ever since. He said, "If it reads good, it won't play good."

Many successful screenwriters are masters at writing the kind of snappy dialogue and colorful, chatty description that passes for first-rate screenwriting because it makes a script seem to play well on paper. But that kind of writing can mysteriously fall flat when a director tries to transfer it to the screen. Hawks was suggesting that a screenplay with prosaic scene description and dialogue, a script that seems flat or sketchy, could make a better film than a script that is more enjoyable to read. The kind of script to which Hawks was referring avoids self-conscious flash to fill the more modest function of serving as a blueprint for a motion picture. As screenwriter William Goldman puts it, "SCREENPLAYS

ARE STRUCTURE. Yes, nifty dialog helps one hell of a lot; sure, it's nice if you can bring your characters to life. But you can have terrific characters spouting just swell talk to each other, and if the structure is unsound, forget it."

Citizen Kane is not an obvious example to prove Hawks's case, because it does "read good"—but as such it provides a stringent test of his theory. It has an intricate and breathtakingly elegant structure, with flashbacks that provide contrasting viewpoints on the central character, sparkling dialogue, and evocative scene descriptions. Almost as thrilling as watching the opening sequence gradually reveal Kane's mansion in the Florida fog on the night of his death is the experience of reading the description of what the camera should be doing as it takes us through "THE LITERALLY INCREDIBLE DOMAIN OF CHARLES FOSTER KANE": "CAMERA TRAVELS up what is now shown to be a gateway of gigantic proportions and HOLDS on the top of it—a huge initial 'K' showing darker and darker against the dawn sky. Through this and beyond we see the fairy-tale mountaintop of Xanadu, the great castle a silhouette at its summit, the little window a distant accent in the darkness... Angkor Wat, the night the last King died."

But someone had to bring this alive on screen. Close comparison of the script and the film shows how much the artistic personality of *Kane* depends on the texture of its mise-en-scène. Welles orchestrated the rhythms of the slow progress toward that window (always seen eerily positioned in the same spot in the frame), the expressionistic depth and richness of the compositions, and the coup de théâtre when the light in the window is suddenly extinguished, helping usher us into the hushed bedchamber of the now-dead tycoon. Welles worked on the creation of this sequence first with Mankiewicz and then with such other collaborators as cinematographer Gregg Toland, art director Perry Ferguson, visual effects creator Linwood G. Dunn, composer Bernard Herrmann, and editor Robert Wise. Together they made it one of the movies' most memorable openings.

If the finished film can truly be called "Orson Welles's *Citizen Kane*," it is because he provided the overall vision that guided the work of his collaborators. Their creative teamwork, as in the making of any good movie, could also be described as multiple authorship. The "writing" that Welles (and company) did with the camera and his other directorial tools was, in effect, the final draft of the screenplay he had helped conceive and write with Mankiewicz. Welles especially acknowledged the depth of Toland's contributions to the film's baroque texture, lighting style, and compositions by sharing the final screen credit card with his cinematographer. So, in an irony often overlooked, *Citizen Kane*, the ultimate auteurist film, has two key screen credit cards shared by its auteur with his collaborators—perhaps not entirely willingly in the case of one card but enthusiastically in the other. Such shared credit is entirely fitting for a collaborative medium of which the hybrid craft of screenwriting is a crucial part but not a pure art form existing for its own sake.

Bibliography: Robert L. Carringer, "The Scripts of *Citizen Kane*," *Critical Inquiry* 5 (1978), in *Orson Welles's "Citizen Kane": A Casebook*, ed. James Naremore (Oxford, 2004). Pauline Kael, "Raising Kane," *New Yorker*, February 20 and 27, 1971, in Kael, *The "Citizen Kane" Book* (Boston,

1971), includes the shooting script by Herman J. Mankiewicz and Orson Welles (July 16, 1940) and RKO cutting continuity of the film (February 21, 1941). Joseph McBride, *Hawks on Hawks* (Berkeley, CA, 1982); *Orson Welles* (1972), rev. and expanded ed. (New York, 1996). Orson Welles and Peter Bogdanovich, *This Is Orson Welles,* ed. Jonathan Rosenbaum (New York, 1992).

JOSEPH McBRIDE

1941

"The peoples of the world are rapidly being scrambled!"

The Word "Multicultural"

The South African Bruce Campbell, who comes from an American family that "had time to become adapted to the new world of transport and communication," is a cosmopolitan and multilingual character about whom all kinds of rumors circulate: he was supposed to have been a high priest in native tribes and an intimate friend of the anarchist Prince Kropotkin. In Berlin he meets and adopts an equally cosmopolitan figure, sixteen-year-old Lancelot Tenorton, or Lance, who as an infant lost his English parents in Prussia and was adopted by a German man who raised him as Fritz Rossner. Campbell brings him back to England, after which Lance "was *both* German *and* an Englishman!"—which makes for conflicting allegiances during World War I.

Serving with the British in the wartime Balkans, Lance collects folk music and engages in social science experiments devised to show how ethnic tensions can be reduced. Using the name Rossner he also marries, in the Old-Bulgarian Orthodox rite, the beautiful Communist sympathizer Eleonora (Campbell's niece, whom Lance had met in Berlin). Preserving his legality through "all the exigencies of his bi-national career" proves to be difficult in the war, and when he leaves the trenches he is arrested by Bulgarian soldiers and handed over to the British, who try him for desertion and giving aid to the enemy. Major Campbell (who is with the British army after South Africa has entered the war) defends Lance in the court-martial proceedings.

At some point, Lance is fiddling around with his guitar, sounding, in the appropriate manner of world music, a characteristically heterogeneous medley: "Slow chord-progressions whispered about the room; disembodied, as though from nowhere: Siamese temple bells—Campbell recognized them distinctly—a Moorish love song; a Kentucky hillbilly love song; an English madrigal; and the slow progression of 'at-the-table music' from the Bulgarian village." Campbell addresses Eleonora with a programmatic message:

> You've lived for twenty-four years, but you don't yet know things that other people know at ten: They know that men in all climes and all times live by the narrow little things they know. They organize their societies by individual interest and family feeling and national patriotism and class solidarity and religious faith. This must be

so and cannot be otherwise. Their contact has been with one language, one faith, and one nation. They are unicultural.

That is not true for people like Campbell, Eleonora, and Lance.

But we, being children of the great age of transportation and communication, have contacts with *many* languages, *many* faiths, and *many* nations. We are *multi*cultural.

Campbell stresses the similarities between multiculturalists and uniculturalists:

Multicultural people . . . are just like unicultural people. They develop faith and loyalty and patriotism too: faith in science, loyalty to world organization, and patriotism for mankind. We develop it whether we realize it or not. And we develop it in different forms: some of us develop it as religion; others . . . as a political creed; others . . . as art; and others . . . even as nationalism.

Campbell views the transformation from unicultural to multicultural thinking like a stage in an ongoing natural evolution, so that the pioneering multicultural people resemble the "first animals to live on land, their fins . . . only half evolved into feet, their air-bladders only half into lungs."

So we and all multicultural people who crawl shakily out of the national narrows into the open world have no more than a half-evolved world feeling and world knowledge. We see things relatively instead of as absolutes. We think multiordinally instead of in fixed patterns. We find ourselves at odds with strong, sure unicultural people. Yet we feel sure that our vision is much truer than the vision of provincial people. We see their mistakes. We try to save us and them from themselves, and lead everyone into a higher, and we hope, happier way of life. But the more absolute their view, the more they struggle against the power of human evolution; the more they misunderstand us, suspect us, accuse and crucify us.

This new multicultural creed is also the defense Campbell pursues in the court-martial proceedings in which Lance faces the death penalty. In court, Campbell proclaims (in italics), *"The peoples of the world are rapidly being scrambled!"* And he reminds the judges that the defendant Lance "is mixed, not only biologically, but also culturally and legally." He continues: "He speaks, reads, and writes six languages well and several others fluently. He knows the customs and beliefs of all these peoples, their prejudices and their mutual misunderstandings. And while legally a German as well as a British subject no one really knows to which of all the countries in Europe his parents owed allegiance."

Campbell explains Lance's experiments as a much-needed attempt to find out more about the nature of ethnic tensions. Describing the answers given by nationalists and "raceists," on the one hand, and those offered by the Communists and internationalists, on the other, he asks the court which of the two theories is right, and adds: "Or is some *other* view, some combination or revision of both the best guide to human progress?" Lance's act was part of a scientific quest to determine the answer to this important question. It might look like desertion, he declares, but it was nothing but "disobedience on behalf of humanity and at the risk of his life." Unimpressed by that defense, the prosecutor simply requests that "this double deserter, traitor, conspirator, mutineer, and murderer be shot!"

All of this really does take place in a rather improbable-sounding novel, *Lance: A Novel about Multicultural Men,* published in 1941 to a handful of more or less positive reviews. Largely set in and around Plovdiv and Tsarevo in Bulgaria, not far from the Rodopi Mountains and the border with Greece and Turkey, *Lance* ends before the court-martial concludes its proceedings. Things look bad for Lance at the end of the novel, but a secret note that Campbell writes to Eleonora informs her that the trial will be dragged on and on until the end of the war, at which time "all military sentences will be annulled by general amnesty."

If the *Oxford English Dictionary* is right, it was this book that introduced the term "multicultural" in 1941. *Lance* employs the word abundantly—even the initial quote about Campbell's family, that it "had time to become adapted to the new world of transport and communication," is preceded by the phrase "unlike multicultural people." By the novel's end one is thus thoroughly familiar with the word and the concepts it embodies for Campbell and Lance and Eleonora. Yet none of the novel's readers in 1941 could probably have imagined the popularity that the word would achieve in the United States and the English-speaking world starting in the mid-1980s. By May 2008 more than 1,400 publications had used the word in their title.

The book's author, Edward F. Haskell, the son of Swiss-American missionaries, was born in Plovdiv and grew up in the United States, Turkey, Greece, Bulgaria, and Switzerland, before attending Oberlin, Columbia, and Harvard and becoming an activist aiding political prisoners and an investigator of political trials. As the dust jacket tells the reader, Haskell's varied schooling forced him "either to become a chameleon, changing his world-view with every change of country—a process at which he never had much success—or else to develop a world-view that fitted everywhere, a multicultural view." Hence Haskell regarded his novel "not only as the statement of a problem, but also its partial theoretical solution." The University of Chicago created for him an "Inter-Divisional Committee for Unified Science." Apparently, Haskell never finished his PhD but lectured widely on methods to bridge disciplinary boundaries in modern universities. Living near Columbia University and working on his never-published magnum opus, "Full Circle: The Moral Force of Unified Science," he succumbed to a stroke in New York in 1986.

Whereas Eleonora follows, for a long time, the lure of Communist Russia as "the only country that's going forward," the novel casts the United States as the country where the absolutisms of the Old World are destined to vanish and where multicultural people will find their true homeland and flourish. It is telling that Eleonora's little brother, also named Bruce, asks Lance in a poorly spelled letter to come to America after the war, for "America is the best country in the whole world. There are many kinds of people in America, not just one kind like Germany. Enybody who is an Englishman and a German can live in America."

The novel is hopeful that the social sciences would offer answers to the pressing questions it raises on an abstract yet plastic level. Campbell stresses that "it is a social scientist's task to investigate the powerful laws of human behavior with regard to nationality and race and class, and to do so precisely in time of war as well as peace," and explains that the desired effect of Lance's acts "is not the victory of one nation over another, as is implied in the charges, *but the general decrease of conflict.*" Lance was testing the hypotheses advanced by the antiwar sociologist and anti–social Darwinist Jacques Novicow in *War and Its Alleged Benefits,* published in 1911, that "no grim fatality obliges us to massacre one another eternally like wild beasts," and that the "Darwinian law in no wise prevents the whole of humanity in joining a federation in which peace will reign." In the envisioned proto–League of Nations structure, struggle would, of course, continue, but in the form of "economic competition, lawyers' briefs, judges' sentences, votes, lectures, books—in short by spoken and written propaganda"—and not in the form of warfare. In Novicow's view, "Antagonism will always exist, but as soon as men stop butchering one another solidarity among them will be established."

According to Haskell's Campbell, social scientists who worked on questions of ethnonational violence and came to similar conclusions on the basis of history had only general and inexact data that "have not led to efficient social engineering"—and here the novel adopts the term that was popularized by William Howe Tolman, most famously in his 1909 study, *Social Engineering.* Campbell proclaims: "Exact, detailed observations have to be compiled by trained field observers if social science is to become as useful as the other sciences." In addition, then, to undertaking peace studies by examining the conduct of the ordinary combatants who were at a great remove from the rulers who had instituted the conflict, Lance also studied the question of why "racially and ethnically dissimilar men—such as the Irish and Bulgarian soldiers in the trenches—transform their conflict to higher, more peaceful forms, while the more racially similar Irish and English soldiers at the camp transformed their conflict to lower, more warlike forms." The answer Lance finds in his experiments and observations is that the Irish and the English, unlike the Irish and Bulgarians, have "a *negative* grouping" since they have been put in conflict with each other for centuries. Lance's law is that "very violent conflicts arise between peoples who are different enough to misunderstand and dislike each other's customs and beliefs, yet similar enough to be able to understand each other's languages."

Its explicitly stated faith in the power of social engineering makes *Lance* a characteristic product of its era. The novel also bears the signs of the time when the dominant model for many countries in their policies and cultural fantasies was assimilation of ethnic minorities and immigrants. *Lance* questions this model. Instead of portraying a marginal person's progress into a given host society by an adoption or intermarriage plot, Haskell complicates both of these popular plotlines. He represents Lance's (double) adoption as a reversible process through which a new identity is added while the old one is not erased; marrying Eleonora does not symbolize Lance's assimilation to any particular society, for their marriage only strengthens both partners' cosmopolitanism. By choosing World War I in Bulgaria as a setting, Haskell called attention to the limits of an assimilationist paradigm that was bound to fail in many areas where (as in the Balkans) ethnic groups "complemented each other *negatively*" and that would, from a global perspective, do little to advance world peace. Haskell's "multicultural men" were thus represented as harbingers of a new, social-science-based world order in which war would be averted and racial and ethnic conflicts channeled into "higher, more peaceful forms." This scenario was imagined as a possibility precisely because the faith in social sciences was seen as universal—even as Haskell stressed the absence of old absolutes and praised the new way of looking at the world "relatively" in Major Campbell's many speeches.

Yet that new way of seeing is at risk in the world as it exists in the novel's own time. The most active representative of the most inclusive multicultural world order is in danger not merely of being excluded by nation-states but of being executed for treason by the representatives of the old order. The context of World War II, in which the book was published, gave more urgency to the issues of "uniculturalism" that the book castigates in the time frame within which it is set: Haskell thus emphasizes uniculturalism's racist ideological underpinnings derived from Joseph-Arthur de Gobineau to Houston Stewart Chamberlain that had only gained momentum with the rise of fascism. The *New York Times* wrote in its review of *Lance:* "At a moment when the German juggernaut menaces the continuation of culture and civilization, no problem novel could be more engrossing than one which, like Mr. Haskell's, presents a social scientist's reflections and speculations on the theme of social conflict." While Haskell's position is clearly anti-"raceist," it is striking, at least in hindsight, that although differences of language, customs, religion, and class are repeatedly invoked, the novel evinces little interest in racial difference and does not at all engage with the issue of antiblack racism in the United States or in Campbell's native South Africa.

The proliferation of the term "multicultural" two-thirds of a century after it was launched is a semantic success story. Yet *Lance,* the strange novel that started it all, parts of which read like a mix of Hitchcock's film *The Lady Vanishes* and social-scientific positivism, may also be considered a now-forgotten starting point for the conceptual history of multiculturalism, for Haskell clearly develops the need for a combined postnational and postethnic perspective in a world of scrambled peoples. As a novel of ideas, conversations, and speeches (the *New Yorker* called it a "tractarian novel"), *Lance* creates a sense of urgency for a multicultural future.

Bibliography: Drake de Kay, "Days of Wrath," *New York Times Book Review* (July 27, 1941), 7, 16. Edward Haskell, *Lance: A Novel about Multicultural Men* (New York, 1941). Jacques Novicow, *War and Its Alleged Benefits* (New York, 1911). William Howe Tolman, *Social Engineering: A Record of Things Done by American Industrialists Employing Upwards of One and One-Half Million of People* (New York, 1909), preface by Andrew Carnegie.

WERNER SOLLORS

1943

"Windemere is still the clearest part of my life, I guess,
and I suppose that is why I never go back there"

HEMINGWAY'S PARADISE, HEMINGWAY'S PROSE

By 1943, just three years after the enormous success of *For Whom the Bell Tolls,* Ernest Hemingway was already an iconic figure, as much a captive of his public image as he was its creator. The war in Europe was not his war, despite his slightly comic, albeit officially sanctioned efforts to turn his fishing boat, the *Pilar,* into a submarine destroyer for hunting German U-boats off the coast of Cuba. His third wife, Martha Gellhorn, was taken more seriously as a war correspondent than the forty-four-year-old novelist could hope to be until he got back to Europe. She would soon leave him. While thanking his sister Ursula for her birthday greetings that year, he said he remembered "the smell of cedars" in the northern forest, but he knew he couldn't return to the idyllic place in his memory.

"Windemere," with all its connections to the romantic poets and their English Lake District, was the name of the family cottage on Walloon Lake in northern Michigan. Dr. Clarence Hemingway bought the land in 1899, the same year his first son was born in Oak Park, Illinois, a suburb of Chicago. Every summer the mother and children would leave Oak Park as soon as school was out, head north by steamer to Harbor Springs, Michigan, then take a train to the village of Walloon Lake, where a boat would run them the several miles down the lake to their cottage. The family would stay as long as they could before heading back to their suburban life and the confines of school and winter. Hemingway spent every summer of his childhood at Walloon Lake, learning to hunt and fish, first from his father and then from the children of the local native people who still lived in "Indian camps" around the lakes, usually working as barkpeelers for the logging businesses or as day laborers for the new group of upper-middle-class "summer people" who, like the Hemingways, were beginning to buy up the land. Although that northern landscape had been devastated by loggers in the previous generation and by the fires that had burned through the slash left behind, for Hemingway it became an Edenic image, wild and free from parental or institutional control, that would recur in his work throughout his writing life. It was there that he learned to be confident in the natural world, where he learned the specific names for plants and animals, and where he learned about the relationships between them. After being severely wounded while serving as an ambulance driver attached to the Italian army during World War I, Hemingway returned to northern Michigan to recover, and he was married there to his first wife, Hadley Richardson, in 1921. He left shortly after and never returned, most likely because of ongoing disagreements with his mother and his uncomfortable relationship with his increasingly fragile father. It is also likely that he didn't want the altered environment to sully his childhood memory of the place that became central to his first stories.

He wrote most of those early stories about the northern forest while living in Paris; they would become part of the collection *In Our Time,* as published in 1925. While working on them, Hemingway developed the prose style that he would use for the rest of his life, a style that would be much parodied, yet would remake the expectations for English prose for the rest of that century. The declarative directness of the sentences Hemingway was using was certainly influenced by his early stints as a journalist and by his childhood education in the importance of the specifics of nature, but his real discovery came from combining the partial examples of several major modernist figures into a style that a general audience was now ready to accept. From Sherwood Anderson he learned the power of a simple unadorned sentence. Gertrude Stein provided the example of repetition and parallel construction, although, unlike Stein, Hemingway would never push those techniques toward pure sound and away from their connections to character and narrative. From Ezra Pound he learned a larger sense of the music words could make, received a lesson in the rigor of the written arts, and internalized Pound's dictum that "the natural object is always the adequate symbol." From Ford Madox Ford—for whom the young Hemingway worked at the *Transatlantic Review,* a small literary journal then published in Paris—he absorbed the Flaubertian demand for *le mot juste,* the almost mystical belief that the perfect word could be found for any particular situation.

Hemingway learned these lessons from writers who may have been more inventive, more experimental than he was, but the measure of his success as a stylist is found in the way he combined their ideas. "Indian Camp" is one of the earliest stories of *In Our Time,* and its author was only in his own early twenties when he wrote it, but the prose already bears the clear imprint of the lessons Hemingway had learned from his more avant-garde mentors and is also very clearly Hemingway's prose, a style that would remain recognizable through all of the subsequent books, even though many of his later sentences would accumulate more clauses around the core of action: "The two boats started off in the dark. Nick heard the oarlocks of the other boat quite a way ahead of them in the mist. The Indians rowed with quick choppy strokes. Nick lay back with his father's arm around him. It was cold on the water. The Indian who was rowing them was working very hard, but the other boat moved further ahead in the mist all the time." This straightforward exposition was often combined with flat, clipped dialogue. Although there was nothing natural about the speech of Hemingway's characters, it became the standard for dialogue in much of the literary fiction and the popular noir fiction written in the following decades, from which it was translated into film and then back into the general culture. Hemingway's written speech became American speech—at least for a while and among a significant part of the population.

Hemingway also borrowed his effective narrative technique from earlier, more experimental writers. In the short stories of Sherwood Anderson and James Joyce, he found an indirect narration, where much of the surrounding narrative information and certainly all of the authorial comment on the story was left to the reader's imagination. In *Death in the Afternoon,* his first attempt to apply the techniques he had mastered in his fiction to a book of nonfiction, he described this approach, his "iceberg theory" of composition: "If a writer of prose knows enough about what he is writing about he may omit things that he knows and the reader, if the writer is writing truly enough, will have a feeling of those things as strongly as though the writer had stated them. The dignity of movement of an ice-berg is due to only one-eighth of it being above water."

But all of this work developing a style and an attitude toward fiction would have made Hemingway simply another figure circling through the bohemian culture of post–World War I Montparnasse if he had not found subjects that were both appropriate to his style and that touched a resonant cultural chord. His first important novel, *The Sun Also Rises,* published in 1926, brought style and subject together in a way that reached out to a larger reading public and gave the first indication that its author might be able to write the touchstone books of his age.

In a move that feels like a signature even though it may not be, Hemingway began *The Sun Also Rises* with two epigraphs, a long one from the Bible that explained the title, and one taken from conversation with Gertrude Stein: "You are all a lost generation." She was referring to the generation of American writers who had survived World War I and who chose to stay in Europe to take advantage of the favorable exchange rates on the dollar. In *The Sun Also Rises* the war is barely mentioned, although the main character was wounded and is impotent because of that. The characters move through Paris, then take a trip to Spain to witness the bullfights that would become part of the Hemingway myth. Along the way they stop and fish in the streams of northern Spain in a scene that echoes the earlier stories Hemingway placed near his childhood summer home. Although the generation as seen in the novel is certainly lost—psychologically and spiritually—most of its members recognize a dignity in action, a courage in the face of meaninglessness, that would become the most pointed theme of Hemingway's work, and the one that would continue to intrigue his contemporaries, even if later generations might occasionally find it tedious.

When Hemingway published *A Farewell to Arms* in 1929, he completed the combination of style and subject that would occupy him for the rest of his life. In addition to the defining hunting and fishing tales that reflected his summers in northern Michigan, and the explorations of lost characters trying to find meaning within particular codes of conduct, Hemingway now became an author who would write centrally about war. Although *A Farewell to Arms* is a love story—and one that seems a bit too sentimental for some tastes—its most vivid writing is in battle scenes that take place in northern Italy. By perfecting his ability to describe men at war, Hemingway broke out of the group of writers associated only with the 1920s and prepared himself for much of his later work.

A Farewell to Arms was Hemingway's first best seller and brought him into the fairly new circle of cultural celebrities, those people whose private lives and adventures were written about by the popular press and who became known and discussed by an audience that was not likely to read their work with serious engagement. Although Hemingway did not pander to this type of journalism, and even though he was often impossible to find for interviews, he tried to control his image in the public eye. The outdoorsman, adventurer, and hard-drinking macho warrior independent of all outside influence made much better press than the careful craftsman who worked hard to learn his trade from his older contemporaries. In many ways, Hemingway became his public self.

For much of the rest of his life, until his suicide in 1961, Hemingway tried to find a balance between the work he felt compelled to do and the public's perception of him. His exquisite novella *The Old Man and the Sea,* published in 1952, brought together his old theme of man's defining and ultimately tragic encounter with the natural world and the stylistic clarity he had learned in writing those early stories. It may have been the last important publication during his lifetime, and its popularity contributed to his selection as winner of the Nobel Prize for Literature in 1954.

During the last decade of his life, Hemingway was increasingly debilitated by a growing depression and the effects of alcohol abuse. The depression seems to have come, at least in part, from a congenital predisposition to the disease; Hemingway's father had committed suicide in 1928 and a couple of his siblings would fight similar battles. But through all of this, Hemingway continued to write, often quite vigorously, although he was not able to bring most of this work to a conclusion that satisfied him. Nonetheless, his posthumous publications have changed our perceptions of him.

Some of these books, like *True at First Light,* his structurally loose and flabby account of an African safari, published as late as 1998, deserve the criticism they received. But others of the posthumously published books are among his most interesting. *A Moveable Feast,* his memoir of his early years in Paris, is one of the best books we have about a writer's discovery of his craft. Parts of the novel *Islands in the Stream* contain some of his clearest writing on art and war. In *The Garden of Eden* he was able to write about an ambivalent sexuality that completely alters our sense of the aggressive masculinity that often defined and limited an understanding of his work. And even as late as the 1950s, sick and famous and sick of being famous, he still returned to his childhood memories of northern Michigan. He still felt compelled to recover his own lost Eden. His unfinished long story "The Last Good Country" first appeared in 1972 in *The Nick Adams Stories,* the effort to pull all the work about Hemingway's youthful alter ego together into a chronology that followed the life of the character. All of the plot elements in "The Last Good Country" are left unresolved, but there are moments of wonderful writing in it. Nick and his youngest sister run away from home because government officials are looking for the boy to prosecute him for poaching. The children head off across fields and through areas recently logged. After climbing through the almost impenetrable logging slash, they enter a stand of white pine. "This is all the virgin timber left around here," Nick tells his sister. They continue:

> "But I always feel strange [here]. Like the way I ought to feel in church."
>   "Nickie, where we're going to live isn't as solemn as this, is it?"
>   "No. Don't you worry. There it's cheerful. You must enjoy this, Littless. This is good for you. This is the way forests were in the olden days. This is about the last good country there is left. Nobody gets in here ever."

By the time he wrote this, Ernest Hemingway knew that the old forests were gone forever. Sickened by the excesses of his success and close to death, he forced himself to remember his early education in the northern forest. He was still able to recall and re-create a fragment of his vanished paradise.

Bibliography: Ernest Hemingway, *Death in the Afternoon* (New York, 1932); *A Farewell to Arms* (New York, 1929); *In Our Time* (New York, 1925); *Selected Letters, 1917–1961,* ed. Carlos Baker (New York, 1981); *The Sun Also Rises* (New York, 1926).

KEITH TAYLOR

1944

"The right to rest, recreation, and adventure"

THE SECOND BILL OF RIGHTS

On January 11, 1944, America's war against fascism was going well. Ultimate victory was no longer in serious doubt. The real question was the nature of the peace. At noon, America's optimistic, aging, self-assured, wheelchair-bound president, Franklin Delano Roosevelt, delivered the text of his State of the Union address to Congress. Because he was ill with a cold, Roosevelt did not make the customary trip to Capitol Hill to appear in person. Instead he spoke to the nation via radio—the first and only time a State of the Union address was also a Fireside Chat. Millions of Americans assembled by their radios that night to hear what Roosevelt had to say.

His speech wasn't elegant. It was messy, sprawling, unruly, a bit of a pastiche, and not at all literary. It was the opposite of Lincoln's tight, poetic Gettysburg Address. But because of what it said, it has a strong claim to ranking among the most important speeches of the twentieth century.

Roosevelt began pointedly, by emphasizing that the war was a shared endeavor in which the United States was simply one participant: "This Nation in the past two years has become an active partner in the world's greatest war against human slavery." As a result of that partnership, the war was in the process of being won. "But I do not think that any of us Americans can be content with mere survival." Hence "the one supreme objective for the future"—the objective for all nations—was captured "in one word: Security." Roosevelt argued that the term "means not only physical security which provides safety from attacks by aggressors," but includes as well "economic security, social security, moral security." Roosevelt insisted that "essential to peace is a decent standard of living for all individual men and women and children in all nations. Freedom from fear is eternally linked with freedom from want."

Moving directly to domestic affairs, Roosevelt emphasized the need to bring "security" of all kinds to America's citizens. He argued for a "realistic tax law—which will tax all unreasonable profits, both individual and corporate, and reduce the ultimate cost of the war to our sons and daughters." He stressed that the nation "cannot be content, no matter how high that general standard of living may be, if some fraction of our people—whether it be one-third or one-fifth or one-tenth—is ill-fed, ill-clothed, ill-housed, and insecure."

At this point the speech became much more ambitious. Roosevelt looked back, and not entirely approvingly, to the framing of the Constitution. At its inception, the nation had grown "under the protection of certain inalienable political rights—among them the right of free speech, free press, free worship, trial by jury, freedom from unreasonable searches and seizures." But over time, these rights had proved inadequate. Unlike the Constitution's framers, he said, "we have come to a clear realization of the fact that true individual freedom cannot exist without economic security and independence . . . In our day these economic truths have become accepted as self-evident. We have accepted, so to speak, a second Bill of Rights under which a new basis of security and prosperity can be established for all—regardless of station, race, or creed."

Then he listed the relevant rights:

> *The right to a useful and remunerative job in the industries or shops or farms or mines of the Nation;*
> *The right to earn enough to provide adequate food and clothing and recreation;*
> *The right of every farmer to raise and sell his products at a return which will give him and his family a decent living;*
> *The right of every businessman, large and small, to trade in an atmosphere of freedom from unfair competition and domination by monopolies at home or abroad;*
> *The right of every family to a decent home;*
> *The right to adequate medical care and the opportunity to achieve and enjoy good health;*
> *The right to adequate protection from the economic fears of old age, sickness, accident, and unemployment;*
> *The right to a good education.*

Having cataloged the eight rights, Roosevelt immediately recalled the "one word" that captured the overriding objective for the future. He argued that these "rights spell security"—and hence that the recognition of the Second Bill of Rights was continuous with the war effort. "After this war is won," he said, "we must be prepared to move forward, in the implementation of these rights." There was a close connection between this implementation and the coming international order. "America's own rightful place in the world depends in large part upon how fully these and similar rights have been carried into practice for our citizens. For unless there is security here at home there cannot be lasting peace in the world." He emphasized "the great dangers of 'rightist reaction' in this Nation." And he concluded that government should promote security instead of paying heed "to the whining demands of selfish pressure groups who seek to feather their nests while young Americans are dying."

What made the Second Bill of Rights possible? Much of the answer lies in a simple idea, one pervasive in American culture in Roosevelt's time: *No one really opposes government intervention.* Markets and wealth depend on government. Without government creating and protecting property rights, property itself cannot exist. Even the people who most loudly denounce government interference depend on it every day. Their own rights do not come from minimizing government but are a product of government. Political scientist Lester Ward vividly captured the point: "Those who denounce state intervention are the ones who most frequently and successfully invoke it. The cry of laissez faire mainly goes up from the ones who, if really 'let alone,' would instantly lose their wealth-absorbing power."

From the beginning, Roosevelt's White House understood all this quite well. In accepting the Democratic nomination in 1932, Roosevelt insisted that we "must lay hold of the fact that economic laws are not made by nature. They are made by human beings." Or consider Roosevelt's Commonwealth Club Address in the same year, where he emphasized "that the exercise of . . . property rights might so interfere with the rights of the individual that the government, without whose assistance the property rights could not exist, must intervene, not to destroy individualism but to protect it." The key point here is that without government's active assistance, property rights could not exist at all.

In this light it seemed implausible to contend that government should simply "stay out of the way" or "let people fend for themselves." Against the backdrop of the Great Depression, and the threat from fascism, Roosevelt was entirely prepared to insist that government should "protect individualism" not only by protecting property rights but also by ensuring decent opportunities and minimal security for all. The ultimate result was his proposal for the Second Bill of Rights.

The basic idea first emerged in a meeting in August 1939. With the New Deal on hold and the fascist threat looming, Fredric Delano, Roosevelt's uncle and head of his National Resources Planning Board (NRPB), suggested the idea of expanding the Bill of Rights from the political to the social arena, to enumerate educational opportunity, health and medical care, decent shelter, the right to work, and economic security. Delano elaborated on that idea in a memorandum written for the president in the summer of 1940. On June 29, 1941, an Economic Bill of Rights was specifically proposed to Roosevelt by NRPB advisers in Hyde Park; Roosevelt approved of the idea and asked for a revision. Their list, released to Congress in March 1943, took the following form:

1. The right to work, usefully and creatively through the productive years;
2. The right to fair play, adequate to command the necessities and amenities of life in exchange for work, ideas, thrift, and other socially valuable service;

3. The right to adequate food, clothing, shelter, and medical care;
4. The right to security, with freedom from fear of old age, want, dependency, sickness, unemployment, and accident;
5. The right to live in a system of free enterprise, free from compulsory labor, irresponsible state power, arbitrary public authority, and unregulated monopolies;
6. The right to come and go, to speak or to be silent, free from the spyings of secret political police;
7. The right to equality before the law, with equal access to justice in fact;
8. The right to education, for work, for citizenship, and for personal growth and happiness; and
9. The right to rest, recreation, and adventure, the opportunity to enjoy life and take part in advancing civilization.

The NRPB proposed a number of steps to protect these rights, including a national health and education program, a broadened system of social security, strengthened protections against monopoly, and a permanent policy for large-scale public works.

The governing ideas played a role in later correspondence in 1943. Chester Bowles, director of the Office of Price Administration, sent the White House a memorandum discussing a Second Bill of Rights and urging that Roosevelt "reannounce his liberal program and his determination to push it as soon as the exigencies of war permitted." During discussions of the annual message for 1943, White House officials showed the Bowles memorandum and Delano's catalog of rights to Roosevelt, who insisted that the topic should be covered in his message. Hence the Second Bill of Rights speech was born.

Roosevelt died within fifteen months of delivering that speech, and he was unable to take serious steps toward implementing the Second Bill. But his proposal, not well known within the United States, has had a significant influence internationally. It played a major role in the Universal Declaration of Human Rights, finalized in 1948 under the leadership of Eleanor Roosevelt and publicly endorsed by American officials at the time. By virtue of its effect on the Universal Declaration, the Second Bill of Rights has influenced dozens of constitutions throughout the world.

In the 1950s and 1960s, the U.S. Supreme Court embarked on a process of giving constitutional recognition to some of the rights that Roosevelt listed. The idea that the Constitution might protect social and economic rights can be traced to an obscure Supreme Court decision in 1941—revealingly, the very same year as Roosevelt's "four freedoms" speech. California had enacted a law banning people from bringing indigents into the state. In *Edwards v. California,* the Court ruled that the ban violated the commerce clause. States are not entitled to regulate interstate commerce, and if a state prohibited people from transporting the poor from one state to another, it was effectively regulating such commerce. Justice Robert Jackson, a close adviser to Roosevelt and his former attorney general, went much further, with an emphasis on the idea of citizenship: "'Indigence' in itself is neither a source of rights nor a basis for denying them. The mere state of being without funds is a neutral fact—constitutionally an irrelevance, like race, creed, or color . . . Property can have no more dangerous, even if unwitting, enemy than one who would make its possession a pretext for unequal or exclusive civil rights."

This passage, and especially Jackson's last sentence, could be understood to have far-reaching implications. In a short period from 1957 through 1969, the Court explored several of these issues, and it reacted sympathetically to people's complaints. In some of them, the Court went so far as to hold that the government must subsidize poor people in certain domains. In several cases, the Court ruled that criminal defendants have a right to a lawyer at taxpayer expense. Building on "the right to protect your rights," the Court struck down poll taxes. In other cases, the Court went further still. In its 1970 decision in *Goldberg v. Kelly,* the Court issued an especially dramatic ruling. There it concluded that welfare benefits count as a kind of "new property," entitled to the protection of the Constitution's due process clause. Under the due process clause, the government must provide a hearing before it removes people from the rolls. In *Goldberg,* the Court emphasized the "brutal need" of those who depended on welfare benefits. The Court wrote: "Welfare, by meeting the basic demands of subsistence, can help bring within the reach of the poor the same opportunities that are available to others to participate meaningfully in the life of the community. [Public] assistance, then, is not mere charity, but a means to 'promote the general Welfare, and secure the Blessings of Liberty to ourselves and our Posterity.'"

By the late 1960s, respected constitutional thinkers thought that the Court was on the verge of recognizing a *right to be free from desperate conditions*—a right that captures many of the rights that Roosevelt attempted to catalog. But all this was undone as a result of the election of President Richard Nixon in 1968. President Nixon promptly appointed four justices—Warren Burger, William Rehnquist, Lewis Powell, and Harry Blackmun—who showed no interest in the Second Bill of Rights. In a series of decisions, the new justices, joined by one or two others, rejected the claim that the existing Constitution protects the rights that Roosevelt championed.

Bibliography: Mary Ann Glendon, *A World Made New: Eleanor Roosevelt and the Universal Declaration of Human Rights* (New York, 2002). Doris Kearns Goodwin, *No Ordinary Time: Franklin and Eleanor Roosevelt: The Home Front in World War II* (New York, 1995). William E. Leuchtenberg, *Franklin D. Roosevelt and the New Deal* (New York, 1963). Cass R. Sunstein, *The Second Bill of Rights: FDR's Unfinished Revolution and Why We Need It More Than Ever* (New York, 2006).

CASS R. SUNSTEIN

1945, February
Charlie Parker and Dizzy Gillespie record together for the first time

BEBOP

When Dizzy Gillespie and Charlie "Yardbird" Parker went into the recording studio in New York on February 28, 1945, the new musical style known as bebop, rebop, or modern had yet to be given a consistent name. The opening of "Groovin' High"—the first tune recorded on the session—had embedded in its phrase ending the scat syllables that ultimately baptized the new sound: "ba doo-dle-ah bay da *be bop.*" The historic collaboration between Gillespie and Parker radiated a musical empathy articulated in fast, energetic, curlicued melodies played in unison with the most breathtaking precision. So magical was their ability to feel melodies together that Gillespie at times couldn't hear his own trumpet: "Sometimes I couldn't tell whether I was playing or not because the notes were so close together."

The 1945 recordings of Bird and Dizzy were the fruit of a partnership simmered in the Earl Hines and Billy Eckstine bands in 1943 and 1944. Hines recruited Gillespie to the band by telling him that Parker had already agreed to join, and then ran the same ruse on Parker in reverse. At the time, the Hines band was riding the success of "Jelly, Jelly," a hit for the group sung by the suave and handsome Billy Eckstine (Mr. B). Gillespie, who was born in Cheraw, South Carolina, in 1917, had been living in Philadelphia and commuting regularly to New York jam sessions after the mercurial Lucky Millinder fired him in November 1942, without apparent cause. Parker, whose bread-and-butter gig for the previous four years had been Jay McShann's orchestra, was playing in the house band at Monroe's Uptown House with Max Roach—splitting a kitty that on a good night amounted to six dollars. Parker's notorious heroin-induced unreliability had finally driven McShann to the breaking point.

By February 1943, Parker and Gillespie were working regularly with the Earl Hines band, Parker playing tenor sax rather than his customary alto because Hines had needed a replacement for Budd Johnson. During the eight months they spent in the Hines band, Parker and Gillespie forged a musical relationship that reached its high-water mark in the 1945 recordings. They played together frequently after concerts, jamming in hotel rooms, practicing from difficult instrumental exercise books, and, most important, developing new ideas that were expressed in improvisation and new compositions. Parker, who was born in Kansas City, Kansas, in 1920, seemed less interested in the Earl Hines book than in playing with Gillespie; stories abound about his missing gigs and nodding out on stage despite Hines's levying frequent fines. Billy Eckstine recalled that Bird "was the only man I knew who could sleep with his jaws poke out to look like he was playing." After missing several performances, Parker told his bandmates that he would sleep overnight in the Paradise Theatre in Detroit to be sure he made the next afternoon's show. The performance came and went, no Parker. "This is the gospel truth," Eckstine remembered, "we played the whole show, the curtains closed, and we're coming off the band cart, when all of a sudden we hear a noise. We look under the stand and here comes Bird out from underneath. He had been there asleep through the entire show!"

Parker's photographic musical memory and prodigious musical talent nevertheless amazed Earl Hines. Bird played each show from memory, seldom needing more than one run-through to commit an arrangement to memory, and was a dazzling soloist whose reputation had become widespread in New York during Jay McShann's residency at the Savoy Ballroom. Parker composed many tunes while a member of the Hines band, although, in the end, it was often Gillespie who committed them to paper. Parker didn't have the patience to do it himself and was known to arrive at Gillespie's home in the middle of the night, horn in hand, desperate to get Dizzy to notate a newly conceived composition before it escaped him. Gillespie's knowledge of harmony and composition, abilities on piano as well as trumpet, and willingness to share his musical erudition with others led him to play a role as a teacher and mentor to many of the aspiring musicians of the new movement. Pianist Billy Taylor noted, "Of all the people who were taking part in this bebop revolution, Dizzy was the one who really intellectualized it."

Gillespie's self-assessment was that his major contribution to bebop was in harmony and rhythm and that Parker's was in phrasing. "The enunciation of the notes, I think, belonged to Parker, because the way he'd get from one note to another . . . that was just perfect for me." Gillespie viewed his own phrasing as stemming from the older style of trumpeter Roy Eldridge and tipped his hat to Parker: "Charlie Parker definitely set the standard for phrasing our music, the enunciation of notes."

When Billy Eckstine left the Hines band in August 1943, Parker and Gillespie left along with nine others and went their separate ways. They were reunited the following spring in Eckstine's band, joined by several former Hines alumni, including Sarah Vaughan. Gillespie served as musical director, and the group quickly earned a reputation as inspired and innovative. Drummer Art Blakey recalled the group as a "twenty-four-hours-a-day riot of music-making," with camaraderie second to none. Although they had to play free concerts for army bases (many in the South) to qualify for a ration card—without it there would have been no gas for the band bus—the humiliations of Jim Crow travel did not dampen their musical spirits. Nevertheless, Gillespie had bigger ambitions, and in late 1944 he left the Eckstine band to establish himself as a bandleader on 52nd Street.

In the 1940s, New York's 52nd Street between Fifth Avenue and Seventh Avenue was home to a plethora of clubs booking jazz from every era: Jimmy Ryan's, the Downbeat, the Three Deuces, the Onyx, the Yacht, and the Famous Door. A jazz connoisseur could wander from club to club and style to style in the course of a single evening. Stars of New Orleans jazz like Sidney Bechet or Louis Armstrong might be found at Jimmy Ryan's; swing era luminaries such as Lester Young, Sid Catlett, and Billie Holiday at the Downbeat; and the pathfinders of bebop like Dizzy, Bird, and Oscar Pettiford at the Onyx. The clubs were small and so lacking in amenities that people in the entertainment world sometimes referred to them as toilets.

The two long blocks of the Street also served as a racial amphitheater, allowing white aficionados of jazz to hear for the first time the revolutionary modern sounds of the new musical movement, which since 1940 had been brewing uptown in Harlem at venues like Minton's and Monroe's Uptown House. Drummer Kenny Clarke noted that the music was not called bebop until after it moved downtown: "We called ourselves modern." For the African American leaders of bebop, a desire to create a music so complex, challenging, and innovative that white musicians couldn't copy it, as they had done during the swing era, was the motivation behind a discipline and musical engagement that Clarke described as "the most intelligent phase of our music."

The symbolic significance of this musical revolution cannot be overstated. The technical virtuosity of the music, the intellectual engagement of the musicians, and the adamant refusal of African American performers to accept the role of entertainer shouted emphatically to the world that the days of the minstrel mask were over. In the context of World War II, when African Americans began voicing their desire for a "Double V"—victory abroad and victory at home against racial injustice—Dizzy Gillespie and Charlie Parker ultimately took their place as heroes in the African American imagination, along with A. Philip Randolph, Joe Louis, and Paul Robeson. Gillespie made the connection between music and politics this way:

> Within the society, we did the same thing we did with the music. First we learned the proper way and then we improvised on that. It seemed the natural thing to do because the style or mode of life among black folks went the same way as the direction of the music . . . we didn't go out and make speeches or say, "Let's play eight bars of protest." We just played our music and let it go at that. The music proclaimed our identity; it made every statement we truly wanted to make.

Gillespie and Parker's recordings in 1945 announced the arrival of this musical sea change. Although Bird and Diz were not the only architects of bebop—Thelonious Monk, Kenny Clarke, Max Roach, Bud Powell, and Mary Lou Williams were there too—their extraordinary collaboration between 1943 and 1945 made them the central icons of the new era.

The commercial recordings they made offer the listener only a glimpse at what bebop on the Street sounded like when the Gillespie and Parker quintet took the stage for four consecutive months at the Three Deuces, beginning in March 1945. The rhythm section consisted of bassist Curley Russell, pianist Al Haig, and drummer Stan Levey; Gillespie encouraged them to interact with the front line, a notable departure from swing era rhythm sections (which generally included a guitar as well). Later in the engagement Max Roach, who had been on the road with Benny Carter (and had recommended Levey in his place) rejoined the group and was recorded in a concert with the group at Town Hall on June 22. The recording session on February 28 did not make use of the new rhythm section, but, at the insistence of Guild Records, employed a swing rhythm section with Cozy Cole on drums, Slam Stewart on bass, Remo Palmieri on guitar, and Clyde Hart on piano.

Two of the compositions from that session—"Groovin' High" and "Dizzy Atmosphere"—feature signature introductions that create a musical sensation somewhat like stepping on the gas while having the other foot on the brake pedal: tautly expectant and ready to go. This effect resulted from creative use of rhythm section devices like pedal points in the bass, stop time, or using drums alone. The beginning of the main tune or head in each case releases the brakes, and the band peels out like a speeding Porsche. Indeed, the 1945 recordings of Bird and Diz include two of the most famous and unsurpassed introductions in all of jazz, those to "Shaw'nuff" and "Koko."

Introductions such as these were audacious, even reckless, since no jazz soloist wanted to improvise with less energy than had been established during the
composition. In "Dizzy Atmosphere," Parker launches confidently into long
strings of partially swallowed eighth notes that always seem to end with a singable
melodic flourish. In the second eight, Bird phrases in a way that later astounded
Miles Davis—turning around the time when the phrase begins, but resolving
back rhythmically before reaching the bridge with no apparent point of correction. Moments like this are what Dizzy means by Parker's gift for enunciating the
notes. Gillespie's trumpet solo is equally flamboyant, even one-upping Parker in
his final eight with an extended staircase of descending triplets reminiscent of
the instrumental exercise books that he and Parker had used to practice.

As usual, Parker's inability to show up at the Three Deuces on time caused
harrowing moments, yet the musical telepathy between Gillespie and Bird was
honed and polished night after night with such intensity that the world of jazz
would never be the same. As Gillespie concluded in his autobiography: "The
height of perfection of our music occurred in the Three Deuces with Charlie
Parker."

The recording session from May 11, 1945, with four-fifths of the Three Deuces
Band (Sid Catlett replaced Stan Levey on drums), reveals the group's growth since
the beginning of the engagement in ensemble execution as well as soloing. The
daredevil arrangement of "Salt Peanuts," with its startling interludes, vocal refrain, and start and stop rhythm-section acrobatics, reveals the attention to composition and ensemble cohesiveness at the heart of this modern music. On
"Shaw'nuff" both Parker and Gillespie deliver solos that are technically spectacular—Parker cascading through the bridge of the rhythm changes like a kayak
through a rapids and Gillespie proclaiming the glory of the flatted fifth in the
opening motto at the same point in his chorus.

The studio recordings of February and May are revelatory. But it wasn't until
Parker and Gillespie's live recording at Town Hall on June 22, 1945—discovered
by Robert Sunenblick in 2004—that we catch a glimpse of this historic group at
its peak. Max Roach plays drums for most of the evening (Sid Catlett plays on
two numbers) and the performances of "Bebop," "A Night in Tunisia," "Groovin'
High," "Salt Peanuts," and "Hot House" are twice the length of the studio recordings. Don Byas on tenor stands in for a tardy Parker as the concert begins, but
after Gillespie has blown a blistering three choruses on "Bebop," Parker enters
the fray. After five choruses, Bird ends his solo with a fragment that subsequently
becomes part of "Donna Lee," a composition later credited to Miles Davis. The
tempos are faster than the studio recordings and the solos longer, likely closer to
the sound heard by the club rats on 52nd Street.

When the Three Deuces gig ended in early July 1945, Gillespie took his big
band—the Hepsations—on tour without Charlie Parker. Bird began leading his
own group and recruited the nineteen-year-old Miles Davis to the trumpet chair.
A historic recording session, the first Parker had undertaken under his own leadership, took place on November 26, 1945, with a band that included Sadik Hakim
along with Davis, Gillespie, Russell, and Roach. Of the six tunes recorded, Davis
played on only three, "Billie's Bounce," "Now's the Time," and "Thriving on a

Riff." In comparison to Gillespie, Davis (who recalls wanting to quit the band every night because he didn't think he was ready) sounded tentative and technically subpar, but his understated presence seems to have allowed Parker greater musical and psychic space. Gillespie played piano for the group on all compositions except for "Thriving on a Riff." On "Koko," the undisputed masterpiece of the session, Gillespie performed on both trumpet and piano because Miles Davis didn't know Bird's remarkable introduction. Based on the chord progression to "Cherokee," "Koko" is a lightning-quick romp through the progression, bookended by a nervous introduction that also serves as the coda. Irregular in phrasing and meter (impossible to learn from the impoverished notations in later fake books), Parker and Gillespie are as tight as they had been through the previous year. Roach followed Parker's extended improvisation with a solo of his own, as Gillespie ran back to his trumpet in time for one last clairvoyant encounter with Parker.

In early 1946, Parker headed west to Los Angeles with Gillespie's group for an engagement at Billy Berg's. The well-known tragedy of Parker's next year began when he sold his return plane ticket for drugs in early February and remained in California. The Parker and Gillespie duo recorded again in a live performance at Carnegie Hall in September 1947, but did not see the inside of a studio together until the Metronome All-Stars recorded in 1949. Their 1945 recordings provide a trace of their prodigious collaboration, which was "caught up in events which made that time exceptionally and uniquely then"—and, as Ralph Ellison so eloquently observed, brought "a momentous modulation into a new key of musical sensibility; in brief, a revolution in culture."

Bibliography: Robert Bregman et al. *The Charlie Parker Discography* (New York, 1993). Miles Davis with Quincy Troupe, *Miles: The Autobiography* (New York, 1989). Ralph Ellison, *Shadow and Act* (New York, 1964). Dizzy Gillespie and Al Fraser, *To Be or Not to Bop: Memoirs of Dizzy Gillespie* (New York, 1985). Brian Priestley, *Chasin' the Bird: The Life and Legacy of Charlie Parker* (New York, 2006). Robert Reisner, *Bird: The Legend of Charlie Parker* (New York, 1962). Alyn Shipton, *Groovin' High: The Life of Dizzy Gillespie* (New York, 1999). *Discography:* Dizzy Gillespie, *Groovin' High* (Savoy), recorded February 28 and May 11, 1945. Dizzy Gillespie and Charlie Parker, *Town Hall, New York City, June 22, 1945* (Uptown). Charlie Parker, *The Charlie Parker Story* (Savoy), recorded November 26, 1945.

INGRID MONSON

1945, April 11
"Any gum, chum?" American troops liberate the Nazi concentration camp Mittelbau-Dora

THOMAS PYNCHON AND MODERN WAR

Many more people died manufacturing the V-2 rocket than were killed by it: an estimated 20,000 workers did, from exhaustion, starvation, physical and mental torture, and from summary executions. From August 1943 until April 1945, thousands of Nazi prisoners were forced to assemble V-1 "flying bombs" and V-2 rockets (known also as A-4 rockets), the first ballistic missiles ever created. They worked in an elaborate underground complex of factories, storage depots, facilities, and prison camps known as Mittelwerk (Central Works), located near Nordhausen in the Harz Mountains. The complex was an impressive technical achievement, the epitome of production and efficiency in the building of highly advanced new weapons, but it also came to represent the nadir of European civilization. As one witness observed, everything within the factory complex was "ruthlessly executed with utter disregard for humanitarian considerations." Indeed, some of the most shocking concentration camp photographs from World War II were taken by U.S. troops as they entered Mittelbau-Dora, the Nazi concentration camp that provided workers for the rocket factory. By April of 1945, the prisoners had produced 13,000 V-1 and V-2 rockets, many of which had been used to bomb London.

The technological advancement and barbarity that culminated in Mittelwerk takes center stage in Thomas Pynchon's 1973 postmodern epic, *Gravity's Rainbow*, which focuses on the design, production, and dispatch of V-2 rockets. Shaped by extensive knowledge of science and engineering as well as military and political history and their relation to colonialism and racism, the novel elaborates in intricate detail modern war's enslavement and sacrifice of humanity in the service of mass death and destruction. Starting with the German blitzing of London, the novel spans multiple places and times, ending in Los Angeles with the image of Weissmann, a Nazi archvillain known as Captain Blicero, meaning "white death," incarnated in Richard Nixon. The association is at once dead serious and humorous. If the novel suggests that Europe declined because it came to have an obscene obsession with controlling death by creating it in mass quantities, it also critiques how, in replacing Europe in world dominance, the United States played into the same culture of death. The dropping of the atomic bomb on Hiroshima is only the most obvious example. Upon discovering Mittelwerk, the United States captured as many German engineers, V-2 rockets, and spare parts as possible and used them to create a space program that would become crucial during the cold war. In fact, Wernher von Braun, the German rocket scientist responsible for the design and realization of the V-2 who surrendered to the Americans at Peenemünde, came to be known as the father of the American space program. America colluded with Europe because, according to Pynchon, at its core is the Puritan belief in the Elect (the chosen) and the Preterite (those passed over, not elected to salvation by God), a belief the country has realized through its own practices of genocide, enslavement, colonialism, and everyday racism. But there have always been those who have imagined a different America. Thus, the American serviceman Tyrone Slothrop, one of the novel's central characters, recalls a Puritan ancestor who "argued holiness" for the Preterite, "without whom there would be no elect," but who was chased out of Boston for heresy. "Could he have been the fork in the road America never took," Slothrop muses, "the singular point she jumped the wrong way from?"

So much darkness, death, and destruction—and yet reading any Pynchon novel is fun. The characters often break out into silly songs and get tangled in wild sexual practices. Pynchon relishes satire, parody, and a dark, sometimes bizarre but more often raucous, even goofy humor. Thus in *Gravity's Rainbow* we face death's violent love dance with life through a prose by turns technical, funny, poetic, obscene, and disorienting. The novel suggests a web of connections between multinational corporate cartels (composed of corporations like Bayer, Holland's Shell, England's Imperial Chemical Industries, and Germany's IG Farben, all dealers in plastics, dyes, synthetic fibers, drugs, rubber) and powerful governments in their efforts to create, and profit from, war. But while the novel thus suggests, in what some see as a supreme expression of paranoia, that They (the capitalized pronoun Pynchon playfully uses to designate megalomaniacs) have individuals under control, making them come to worship death, the novel also provides shimmering glimpses into a life force that persists.

Pynchon's novels, with the exception perhaps of the slim but still complex *The Crying of Lot 49* (1966), are encyclopedic in scope, including not only erudite historical, literary, and scientific references but also a dazzling knotting of myth, mysticism, and irreverent popular-culture references. In *Gravity's Rainbow,* Americans singing invented "Rocket limericks," "German Storm Trooper style," about deadly serious subjects, set the tone:

> There once was a thing called a V-2,
> To pilot which you did not need to—
> You just pushed a button,
> And it would leave nuttin'
> But stiffs and big holes and debris, too.

Laughing at death and human self-destruction is no small feat. Yet Pynchon achieves it with gusto. He deftly intertwines the poetry of Rainer Maria Rilke and Emily Dickinson with cocaine and hashish fantasies, hallucinations (often drug induced), abreactions (traumatic memories), analepses (memories about distant places and people narrated through the consciousness of individual characters), near-religious visions, pop songs from the 1930s and '40s, references to European and American film, American slang, and at least a dozen other phenomena.

Gravity's Rainbow is nearly eight hundred pages long and includes over four hundred characters. Yet one of the happy results of Pynchon's style is that it produces a powerful kind of tragicomedy that has also found eloquent expression in the work of writers such as Ishmael Reed, Don DeLillo, Suzan-Lori Parks, and David Foster Wallace. Like his modernist antecedents, Pynchon produces tension between calamity and farce, the solemn and the ridiculous, such that each highlights the other through opposition. But the tensions in Pynchon are multiplied and augmented, sometimes to unbearable levels, by the sheer number of cultural references embedded in his sentences, the degree of opposition between the modes he invokes, and the context within which he sets the tensions. The episode focusing on Mittelwerk is rendered from the perspective of Slothrop, who, descending into the complex, has a sense that "there is no more history, no time-traveling capsule to find your way back to," only a sense of "lateness" and "absence" in the "new Uncertainty" of a "Post-A4 humanity." Slothrop's is an elegantly concise expression of our postmodern condition in which, given the many instances of modern mass death and destruction, Enlightenment beliefs in progress and universal concepts of truth, beauty, and the good have become questionable. In this context, the tension Pynchon creates between the many styles and sources he employs has a startling effect. The first two lines of the Mittelwerk episode are: "It's a Sunday-funniest dawn, very blue sky with gaudy pink clouds in it. Mud across the cobblestones is so slick it reflects light, so that you walk not the streets but these long streaky cuts of raw meat, hock of werewolf, gammon of Beast." The metaphor in the first line is disturbing as the opening of a scene representing horror, but it serves to emphasize the fact of representation: what we are about to enter is a fiction about an all-too-real catastrophe that the fiction cannot represent. The second sentence, however, leaves no doubt regarding the episode's subject.

There are many other instances in which Pynchon pulls taut the tension between the surreal and the humorous and the painfully real and the utterly dark. When Slothrop walks the liberated but chaotic zones of continental Europe in the immediate aftermath of the war, he sees "a big chromo of Stalin" that he "could swear is a girl he used to date at Harvard, the mustache and hair only incidental as makeup, *damn* if that isn't what's her name." The humorous misrecognition comes about because he is exhausted, hungry, and high on hashish, but this condition also makes him think that he sees "enormous loaves of bread dough left to rise under clean white clouds—boy, is everybody hungry . . . wow! *Raw dough!*" The loaves, he then realizes, are "human bodies, dug from today's rubble." But the confusion "was more than an optical mistake," the narrator tells us, for as Slothrop sees the bodies rising, he thinks that the bodies "are transubstantiated" and wonders, "who knows, with summer over and hungry winter coming down, what we'll be feeding on for Xmas?" Even in an expansive novel such as *Gravity's Rainbow,* the adjective "raw" in the opening lines of the Mittelwerk episode resonates powerfully here but with a crucial difference. In the first instance Slothrop has a sense of walking over the rawness of death and evil ("gammon of Beast"). But having descended to Mittelwerk, having then left it to roam Europe in the ashes of war, he now imagines the possibility of *feasting* on that rawness.

For a novel so steeped in World War II, *Gravity's Rainbow* has few allusions to Hitler and, despite the centrality of Mittelwerk, few pages devoted to the Holocaust. Still, Hitler's genocide is everywhere. Feeding a fire with the hair of a doll he finds in an abandoned estate, Slothrop soon learns that the "doll's hair was human," that it belonged, as a little child tells him, to "a Russian Jewess." "The smell of it burning," the narrator notes, "is horrible." Slothrop is thus never simply a witness to the machinations of death but strangely contaminated by and even complicit with it. The Holocaust is also placed in the context of early German experiments in genocide in South West Africa. Pynchon thus circumvents the overdetermined historical trauma of the Holocaust by turning to less well-known histories that knot into and thus indirectly highlight that trauma.

At other times Pynchon takes more risqué approaches to stage death's reign in World War II Europe, turning to explicit scenes of sadomasochistic sex. One such scene involves the triple agent Katje, in her incarnation as the dominatrix Domina Nocturna, and an elderly man who worships her as the bride of death. In explicit detail, we learn how he submits to her, engaging in coprophilia to please her. In the large canvas that is *Gravity's Rainbow*, this scene shares billing with zany, comic escapades, fleeting but precious moments of tenderness and love, lengthy excursions into statistics, Pavlovian psychology, rocket science, and more. Hence a "terrible secret," the fact that Slothrop may have been sexually conditioned as an infant, finds expression in a song:

(lead tenor):	'Twas the penis he thought was his own—
	Just a big playful boy of a bone . . .
	With a stout purple head,
	Sticking up from the bed,
	Where the girlies all played Telephone—
(bass):	Te-le-phone . . .
(inner voices):	But They came through the hole in the night,
(bass):	And They sweet-talked it clear out of sight—
(inner voices):	Out of sight . . .
(tenor):	Now he sighs all alone,
	With a heartbroken moan,
	For the pe-nis, he thought-was, his owwwwn!
(inner voices):	Was, his, own!

The song, lighthearted as it is, nonetheless comments on the political context of the late 1960s and early 1970s in which Pynchon wrote his novel. It suggests that They can reach into the most private parts of the self and manipulate them, as in Buffalo Springfield's 1967 song "For What It's Worth," with its famous line, "Paranoia strikes deep / Into your life it will creep." *Gravity's Rainbow* is as much about World War II as it is about American disillusionment and the penchant for conspiracy theories in the wake of the Vietnam War, the Watergate scandal, and the persecution of minority and student groups by government agencies like the FBI.

The rapid and drastic shifting between characters, time and space frames, and styles in *Gravity's Rainbow* can be disorienting, even maddening. Deftly manipulating dramatic irony, Pynchon takes readers into a world where, unlike the various characters and narrative voices, they seem to know about events that occurred long ago. But at the same time, he plunges them into a complex and ever expanding structure inside which they must constantly question what they know. Perhaps for this reason the quieter, more straightforward moments in Pynchon gain a power they would not have in another context. In London, during the Blitz, Slothrop finds "a child, alive, a little girl, half-suffocated under a Morrison shelter." Holding "her small hand, gone purple with the cold," Slothrop watches as she opens her eyes and utters her first words: "Any gum, chum?" The child here echoes the question that British children would shout to American soldiers and a detail about life during the war included in many a memoir. Despite the fact that

Slothrop cannot provide the goods, she kisses Slothrop's hand and, before she is taken away on a stretcher, smiles "very faintly." At this point, writes Pynchon, Slothrop "knew that's what he'd been waiting for, wow, a Shirley Temple smile, as if this exactly cancelled all they'd found her down in the middle of." Pynchon describes the London of the scene as "a big desolate icebox," a "stale-smelling" city with "no surprises inside ever again." But the child surprises Slothrop both by beating death and by being able to give him a Shirley Temple smile in the aftermath. In a novel that does not simply represent but reenacts the almost numbing complexity and violence of a world produced by modern war, such moments become precious and devoid of the saccharine quality they would have on their own.

With its focus on how governments and corporations invade and modify the human body through information and surveillance technology, *Gravity's Rainbow* is considered a precursor to cyberpunk fiction, which focuses on marginalized characters living in dystopic futures where daily life is impacted by rapid technological change. It is thus fitting that Zak Smith, an artist associated with cyberpunk aesthetics, has produced what is perhaps the most delightful tribute to the novel, *Pictures of What Happens on Each Page of Thomas Pynchon's Novel Gravity's Rainbow,* a collection of 760 drawings that attempt to illustrate, in one way or another, every page of the book. Originally an installation exhibited at New York's 2004 Whitney Biennial, then published as a book, it occupies eleven rows and more than eleven meters of wall space and is in the collection of the Walker Art Center in Minneapolis.

Bibliography: Roy Fedden, *The Fedden Mission to Germany June 1945: Final Report* (London, 1945), 1–98. Thomas Pynchon, *Gravity's Rainbow* (New York, 1973). Zak Smith, *Pictures of What Happens on Each Page of Thomas Pynchon's Novel Gravity's Rainbow* (New York, 2006).

GLENDA CARPIO

1945, August 6, 10:45 a.m.
Nobody apologized. Nobody atoned.

THE ATOM BOMB

"I knew what I was doing," Harry Truman scowled. "I have no regrets and under the same circumstances I would do it again." Anyone would have done the same. His secretary of war, Henry Stimson, explained in 1947 that if *you* had been hoisted, trussed, and screwed into place as president of the United States in the spring of 1945, you too would have ordered the atomic attacks on Hiroshima and Nagasaki.

The men who rejoiced in the A-bomb in August 1945—Truman, Churchill, Stimson, LeMay, Groves, Oppenheimer—never lamented the parts they played.

And even if they had wanted to, it would have been impossible to thwart the co-lossal drive to use the bomb in combat. The momentum was irresistible. *Nobody* could have prevented the strike on Hiroshima. Nobody wanted to.

What everyone wanted to do was end the war. Americans were cranky. Hitler had committed suicide; the Allied Occupation Forces in Germany were prepar-ing for war crimes trials; most of the troops were unbelted and resting. General Maxwell Taylor vainly tried to revive the red-hot lust for vengeance in his men. "We've licked the best that Hitler had in France and Holland and Germany!" he bellowed. "Now where do we want to go?" "Home!" they roared.

By June 1945, the Japanese empire was extinct. Its army was shattered. Its navy and air force had been blown to smithereens. Its industries were gone. The Amer-ican navy had boxed up the home islands and was now starving the nation by bomb and blockade. The U.S. Army Air Force had wiped out its principal cities and was now picking off every last town. A half million Japanese had perished; five million more had bolted into the countryside. The warlords knew they were doomed but wouldn't knuckle under. It was baffling.

"The Japs are savages, ruthless, merciless and fanatic," Truman scrawled the day he ordered the bombing of Hiroshima. "When you have to deal with a beast, you have to treat him as a beast," he snapped at a Christian petitioner two weeks later. It was useless to probe their motives. "Japanese sanity cannot be measured by American standards of logic," observed the former American ambassador to Japan.

Everyone agreed the enemy was brutal and unfathomable; everyone swelled with malice. "Japan should be bombed so that the country could not begin to re-cuperate for 50 years!" erupted the head of Navy Civil Affairs. "It was a question of which race was to survive." "We should kill them before they kill us!" Since the Japanese were "savages," flared Roosevelt's chief of staff, Admiral William Leahy, "all previously accepted rules of warfare must be abandoned." "Kill Japs! Kill Japs! Kill more Japs!" screamed a billboard Admiral Halsey erected to greet his sailors stepping onshore. "You will help to kill the yellow bastards if you do your job well!" "I *know* the Japanese people," hissed the commissioner of war manpower in April 1945. The only way to deal with them was "extermination. *In toto.*"

There was a chance the atom bomb might deliver the coup de grâce. Surely the Japanese could "recognize the folly of a fight to the finish," the secretary of war concluded in early July. But in order to "extract a genuine surrender from the Emperor and his military advisers, they must be administered a tremendous shock." If the A-bomb could knock them silly, they might fall to their knees and everyone could go home.

"We have used it against those who attacked us without warning at Pearl Har-bor," Truman announced on August 9, 1945, "against those who have starved and beaten and executed American prisoners of war . . . We have used it in order to shorten the agony of war, in order to save the lives of thousands and thousands of young Americans." Forever after, the president would be pressed—*hounded*—to justify his decision. "We were destroying factories that were making more munitions," he informed the students of Columbia University in 1959. It was a military maneuver, it saved lives, there was nothing more to it. "You write just like the usual egghead," he snarled in a draft of a letter to a historian.

> The facts are before you but you'd like to garble them. The instruction of July 25th, 1945 was final. It was made by the Commander in Chief after Japan refused to surrender. Churchill, Stimson, Patterson, Eisenhower and all the rest agreed that it had to be done. It was. It ended the Jap War. That was the objective. Now if you can think of any other, "if, as, and when" egghead contemplations, bring them out. You get the same answer—to end the Jap War and save 1/4 of a million of our youngsters and that many Japs from death and twice that many on each side from being maimed for life. It is a great thing that you or any other contemplator "after the fact" didn't have to make the decision. Our boys would all be dead.

"I certainly regret the necessity of wiping out whole populations because of the pigheadedness of [their] leaders," Truman primly declared the day Nagasaki was bombed, "and I am not going to do it unless it is absolutely necessary." He needn't have been so squeamish. Nobody else was. Since the Great War, airpower enthusiasts had insisted that slamming enemy cities with as much concentrated violence as an air force could muster was ultimately merciful. If unsparing slaughter could yield a decisive victory, fewer people would die than if war had otherwise been prolonged by inconclusive combat. Little more than twenty years later, the U.S. Army Air Force would adopt mass destruction as its catechism. "With the proper degree of understanding," the commanding general of the Army Air Force instructed his senior staff in 1943, "the bomber becomes the most humane of all weapons." Moreover, bombing cities was strategically defensible. Since the residents in the enemy's cities manufactured the enemy's arms, they were integral to the enemy's war-making powers. America's armed forces could now, permissibly, snuff out enemy civilians. The general's deputy commander shrugged, "It made a lot of sense to kill skilled workers by burning whole areas. The man who builds a weapon is as responsible for its use as the man who carries it into battle." In fact, volunteered an Army Air Force spokesman, "the *entire population* of Japan is a proper military target. Making all-out war saves American lives . . . For us, there are no civilians in Japan."

"Anything which will achieve the desired results should be employed," explained the man who supervised the annihilation of Japan's cities in the last months of the war. "We knew we were going to kill a lot of women and kids when we burned [Tokyo]," General Curtis LeMay calmly remarked. "The enemy's potential for war had to be erased. Just as simple as that." In ferocious oaths and tirades, Americans thundered: *ANYTHING GOES!* An author in *Harper's Magazine* begged the armed forces to set every square inch of Japan ablaze. "It seems brutal to be talking about burning homes," he allowed, "but we are engaged in a life-and-death struggle for national survival, and we are therefore justified in taking any action that will save the lives of American soldiers and sailors." Nearly everyone agreed.

Indeed, it was the "rain and reign of flame," LeMay reflected with satisfaction, "which demoralized Japanese industry, shattered the military heart, and whipped the populace into a state where they could—and would—accept the idea of surrender." Since the beginning of the war the Army Air Force had looked for opportunities to prove the merits of airpower. Igniting the emperor's cities would do very well; Japanese paper-and-plywood dwellings were notoriously combustible. Army engineers helpfully bundled dozens of canisters of jellied gasoline into thin housings. On impact, the cylinders would squirt out their contents in 100-foot-long plumes, *then* detonate. On the night of March 9–10, 1945, LeMay's bombers scattered them across the breadth of Tokyo. In less than an hour, firestorms swallowed up the city. The canals boiled, the pavement melted, pedestrians sizzled like sprats. By the next morning, 120,000 people had been burned, choked, crushed, or trampled to death. Even a week later, thousands desperately shoehorned themselves into railcars leaving Tokyo. Those who remained could be seen forlornly poking through brittle twists of rubble for family remains.

The day after the emperor surrendered, a reporter in the *New York Times* paid homage to the Tokyo raid: "It marked the first all-out effort to burn down a great city and destroy its people." No one could say whether the folks back home would cry out in horror, whether fire would fortify the enemy's resolve to hold out to the bitter end. "But we won both gambles!" he cheered. Enemy cities were blotted out and Americans seemed not to mind. In fact, they said very little. LeMay would always be indignant. "Everybody bemoans the fact that we dropped the atomic bomb and killed a lot of people at Hiroshima and Nagasaki. *That* I guess is immoral," he fumed. "But nobody says anything about the incendiary attacks on every industrial city in Japan. The first attack on Tokyo killed more people than the atomic bomb did. Apparently *that* was all right." Those who did notice welcomed firebombing with malignant gaiety. It was a "dream come true," pealed the editors of *Time*. At long last, the Army Air Force could "loose avalanches of fire bombs" on the enemy, and demonstrate once and for all that "Japanese cities will burn like autumn leaves."

Nobody in Congress really liked Senator Truman. He was a boor, mirthless and thin-skinned. He had been a failure as a farmer, the son of a failed farmer, a bankrupted clothing salesman, he never finished law school, and he owed his career to the ballot-stuffing pols of the Kansas City Pendergast machine. In the 1944 election he was the worst kind of compromise candidate, a mousy *fourth* choice for vice president.

On January 20, 1945, he was sworn into office. Two days later, FDR sailed away for the Big Three conference in Yalta leaving Truman behind to mope and fidget. He hadn't been briefed on *anything*. He hadn't been asked to *do* anything. It would all come to him, surely, when the president returned. But when Roosevelt disembarked after nearly a month at Yalta, he was alarmingly gray-faced and quavering. He paid a few calls and was then whisked off to the "Little White House" in Georgia for a rest, whereupon he promptly expired. Truman was stunned, petrified. After idolizing FDR for years, how would Americans feel about *him?* Would the armed forces respect him? Would Churchill? Would Stalin? Roosevelt had spent weeks in their company; Truman knew nothing whatsoever about his plans. He groaned, "I was not familiar with any of these things!"

Soon after Truman was sworn into office as president, Secretary Stimson and the keeper of the army's most cherished secret, General Leslie Groves, revealed the facts about the atomic bomb program. Overawed and cowed, Truman unhesitatingly approved its continuation. The new president's decision, Groves noted with a touch of smugness, "was noninterference." Stepping in at the tail-end of the war, he wouldn't dare to reverse plans set in motion by the four-times elected Roosevelt—a man, Truman muttered pettishly, "the country practically *worshipped*."

When they began to finalize operational details, Truman's advisers agreed that the first use of the bomb had to be "sufficiently spectacular for the importance of the weapon to be internationally recognized." Its terrible power could best be appreciated if it engulfed a city unmarred by fire. Since atmospheric currents blew across the Japanese archipelago, if the target was not the center of a city, there was a chance that the bomb might stray into the countryside. It was therefore decided that the aiming point would be, officially, "a vital war plant employing a large number of workers and closely surrounded by workers' houses." This was a deception for the record. There were no vital war plants in the center of Hiroshima city. Ancient men and women, students, mothers, and children fabricated simple components of war materiel in tiny home workshops. The advisers knew it and Truman knew it. (Several years later, he admitted that the atom bomb had been aimed at ordinary people. Explaining his reasons for signing orders to strike Hiroshima and Nagasaki to his memoir ghostwriters, Truman remarked, "The destruction of manufacturing plants is war on civilians . . . In [modern] war, civilians were military assets.")

His advisers wanted the bomb "to make a profound psychological impression on as many inhabitants as possible." "The visual effects," the physicist Robert Oppenheimer promised them, "would be tremendous." It *was* spellbinding. The first test of the bomb in New Mexico hurled Grove's deputy into a state of rapture. Its brilliance, General Farrell gasped, was "magnificent, beautiful, stupendous . . . golden, purple, violet, gray and blue." It lit up the mountains "with a clarity and beauty that cannot be described but must be seen to be imagined. It was that beauty . . . poets dream about . . . Words are inadequate . . . It had to be witnessed to be realized."

Actually, it was hard to see in Hiroshima. Smoke enveloped everything except the spots where the wind coiled flames into whirlpools. Wind was nearly all you could hear. Nearly everyone left alive was dumbstruck. Staggering away from the center of town, one could make out yelps or mewling filtering out from the rubble. "Please help me!" "It's so hot!" "Water!" But everyone was too weak to lift up house beams. Skeins of fire ringed every standing thing. The world was mobbed with charred bodies, tumid faces like balloons, ribbons of skin dangling like pennants from the arms of walking or crawling mutes, flapping from their hands like rubber gloves, like potato parings. Corpses huddled inside wells, corpses clogged the river. A tarry pricking rain fell into their mouths, rain whose drops couldn't be washed away. These tremendous visual effects couldn't be shaped into words. People wheezed and stumbled away from the fires. "This is the way war really looks," they murmured hoarsely once they were safe. "This is the way war really looks. The whole world is dying."

Americans relieved themselves of pent-up energies by crowing wantonly. The bomb was everywhere celebrated, everywhere smothered in platitudes. The bomb was proof of Anglo-Saxon virtuosity, "the crowning demonstration of Allied technical, scientific and material superiority over the enemy." It ended the war, it was a lifesaver, a peacemaker. The *Atlanta Constitution* expressed the remorseless satisfaction of many: "If it were not for the treachery of Pearl Harbor, the horrible cruelties of the Death March, the stories told by the starved, filth-encrusted, dazed American prisoners coming out of Japanese prison camps, we might feel sorrow for the Japanese who felt the atomic bomb." Relatively few grieved—for America as well as Japan. "Let us not combine cruelty with hypocrisy," chided *Catholic World,* "and attempt to justify wholesale slaughter with a lie."

Once installed, the Allied Occupation Authorities in Berlin set out to expose the German people to the atrocities committed in the concentration camps known to everyone by name and place. The nation's moral and political rehabilitation would take root only if preceded by the masses' recognition of their *collective* responsibility for the Third Reich's crimes. People living close to the camps hadn't lifted a finger to minister to the wretches filing out of the enclosures. Even after the atrocity education campaign was well under way, most Germans recoiled from the former inmates. The military governors commanded them to offer food and lodging. By Radio Luxembourg, Occupation-controlled newspapers, posters, and pamphlets, the Occupation Authorities prodded the German people through the gas chambers and crematoria, and forced them to fix their eyes on the hills and gullies of corpses. They inducted men and women into work gangs to bury the dead. "No one was honorable," shuddered the *New York Times* queasily in January 1946. "No one was clean. No one was merciful . . . The smear of guilt lies over multitudes who under normal conditions might have been decent human beings. No court can punish all of them."

But what about Americans? objected Christians, pacifists, and some humanists. From the first report of the Hiroshima strike and throughout the successive months of the war crimes tribunals in Germany and Japan, they persisted in asking why our vanquished enemies were *uniquely* obliged to look at the victims of their atrocities. Shouldn't Americans also confront their responsibility for agonies delivered in their name? "It would be equally salutary," mused a Christian author, "to send groups of representative Americans to blasted Hiroshima. There, as at Buchenwald, are many unburied dead." "I suppose if I had lost the war," LeMay smirked, "I would have been tried as a war criminal. Fortunately, we were on the winning side."

Bibliography: Gar Alperovitz, *The Decision to Use the Atomic Bomb and the Architecture of an American Myth* (New York, 1995). Baron J. Bernstein, "The Atomic Bombings Reconsidered," *Foreign Affairs* 74, no. 1 (1995). Giulio Douhet, *The Command of the Air* (in the Italian, 1921, 1937;

in English, 1942; repr. Washington, DC, 1983). Allen Drury, *A Senate Diary, 1943–1945* (New York, 1963). David McCullough, *Truman* (New York, 1992).

SHARON GHAMARI-TABRIZI

1946, December 5

President Harry S Truman issues Executive Order 9808, establishing the Committee on Civil Rights

INTEGRATING THE MILITARY

This epochal act, which produced *To Secure These Rights,* the committee's report, issued on October 29, 1947, ushered in the civil rights era of American history. The order and the report set the United States on a course of formally and officially renouncing the idea of a society built on a hierarchy of racial distinctions, indeed of rejecting the idea of racism as a creditable or credible intellectual concept and political theory, and of dismantling the long-standing institutional practices and customs that had supported segregation and white supremacy. In short, the start of the civil rights era in the United States effectively began the deracialization of American nationalism, redefining the country as no longer a country for whites, a "white" society, or a "white" culture. White nationalism as a political reality had been inscribed in the Constitution more than 150 years earlier through its tacit but clear support of chattel enslavement of Africans.

Truman had been moved to establish the Civil Rights Committee, in large measure, because of the brutal treatment many African Americans endured immediately following the end of the Second World War, including assaults on black men returning from service in uniform. The most infamous among these assaults, a case that deeply moved Truman, took place in February 1946: Sergeant Isaac Woodard was blinded by white policemen when he was removed from a bus in Batesburg, South Carolina, because the white bus driver did not like him or considered him uppity.

"I had as callers yesterday some members of the National Association for the Advancement of Colored People [NAACP] and they told me about an incident which happened in South Carolina where a negro Sergeant, who had been discharged from the Army just three hours, was taken off the bus and not only seriously beaten but his eyes deliberately put out, and that the Mayor of the town had bragged about committing this outrage," Truman wrote to his attorney general, Tom Clark, on September 20, 1946.

On June 29, 1947, six months after issuing the order for the Civil Rights Committee, Truman became the first president to address the NAACP, a profoundly important act of national recognition. The NAACP was the oldest civil rights organization in the world, and one of the most integrated political action groups in the United States. When the Committee on Civil Rights issued its report, four months after Truman's address to the NAACP, it recommended a permanent Fair Employment Practices Committee (something that had been established on a temporary basis by President Franklin Roosevelt when he issued Executive Order 8802 in 1941), a permanent civil rights division for the Justice Department, the establishment of the United States Commission on Civil Rights, administrative support for civil rights lawsuits in federal courts, voting rights laws, and abolition of the poll tax. The report was virtually the entire legal program or bill of particulars of what was to become the civil rights movement, and it was implemented in its entirety, over time, by subsequent administrations, prodded by the insistent political action of African Americans, supported by liberal whites.

The only institution that the committee requested be desegregated was the military. The Commission on Civil Rights probably made that choice for three reasons. A good deal of the postwar racial violence by whites against blacks was directed against black veterans, and these attacks went to the heart of black patriotism and civic duty. Black civil rights leaders had been actively working to integrate the military, in particular, since 1937, when the black newspaper publisher Robert Vann *(Pittsburgh Courier)* and the African American civil rights lawyer and World War I veteran Charles Hamilton Houston demanded that President Roosevelt issue an executive order desegregating the military. The United States had just ended a major war with a troubled (plagued by racial violence) and troublesome (inefficiently utilized and demoralized black soldiers) segregated military; the nation would probably go to war again (if not on the same scale) in the near future. Because of conscription, far more men went into the military at that time than do so now. The segregated armed services thus put at risk both battle-readiness within its ranks and social harmony even outside them. Moreover, as *To Secure These Rights* makes plain, there were some instances of troop integration toward the end of World War II: in general, African Americans had performed well in combat, and whites had endured their presence without much status discomfort. This gave both African Americans and liberal whites some evidence, limited though it was, that integration could work without too much dislocation.

Truman issued Executive Order 9981, which desegregated the United States military, on July 26, 1948. The impact of the integration of American troops was not lost on Truman when he considered the cold war: "I felt also that any other course [than integration of the military] would be inconsistent with international commitments and obligations. We could not endorse a color line at home and still expect to influence the immense masses that make up the Asian and African peoples. It was necessary to practice what we preached, and I tried to see that we did it." As difficult as it would doubtless be, integrating the rigidly hierarchical and almost all-male military promised more success than the integration of other major institutions in American life.

In 1949, after Truman's election, the producer and director Stanley Kramer made the film *Home of the Brave*, based on a play of the same name. In the play, the hero is Jewish in a company of Gentile soldiers. In the film, he is black in a company of white soldiers. This "problem" drama seemed very much to reflect the new times. "Even though I knew how unlikely such 'race mixing' would be in

World War II," Kramer later wrote, "since army integration didn't begin until after the war, I figured I might be forgiven for jumping the gun by three or four years."

Stanley Kramer was not the only Hollywood filmmaker to jump the gun by depicting an integrated military on the battlefields of World War II. Three war films released in 1943, *Bataan, Crash Dive,* and *Sahara,* depict black actors playing heroic supporting parts and bravely fighting in combat. (Amazingly, in *Crash Dive* the black messmate of a submarine goes on a commando raid.) Black soldiers had been stigmatized during World War II as unable to take the pressures of battle, as cowardly and irresponsible, as less intelligent and unable to command; they were placed in segregated service units, largely under the command of white officers. The few films made during World War II that showed blacks as brave in combat were far-sighted and clearly risked alienating the white Southern audience. These efforts may also have helped segments of the white public to accept an integrated military after the end of that war: Truman's efforts did not appear out of nowhere.

Bataan, Crash Dive, and *Sahara* may have been unusual, but they were not accidents. The black leadership, under the direction of NAACP president Walter White, had been working for better roles in Hollywood for black actors since 1939, when MGM mogul David O. Selznick hired White to serve as a consultant for *Gone with the Wind,* either to improve the depiction of blacks in the controversial film or to ameliorate their disapproval of it. White continued to meet with studio heads in subsequent years, particularly pushing the actress Lena Horne as a replacement for Hattie McDaniel. Black political pressure on Roosevelt during the 1940 election did not make him integrate the armed services, but it did result in the creation of the post of African American civilian aide in the War Department, first occupied by William Hastie and then in 1943 by his assistant, Truman Gibson. Although Gibson was not as militant as Hastie, both men advocated integration, if not for the reason of social justice, then for the sake of efficiency. A good deal of black manpower was wasted during World War II; moreover, in the early years of the war, there was racial violence in many army training camps. Gibson desegregated blood supplies and got the War Department to back the documentary film *The Negro Soldier* (1944), produced by the Hollywood legend Frank Capra. Black newspapers reported in great detail on the plight of the black serviceman; partly in response, and conscious of morale, the War Department tried to improve the condition of the black serviceman to some degree, especially in the later stages of the war. Part of this attempt was a propaganda campaign to improve the image of the black military man, so as to show to the world that the United States was a true democracy, a concern that predated the cold war. In the light of these circumstances, *Sahara, Bataan,* and *Crash Dive* reflected both the transformation of the black serviceman and the transformation of the black actor.

Kramer broke no new ground in showing a black soldier in combat and in a positive light. What was new about *Home of the Brave* was that Kramer gave the black soldier the lead; that soldier, moreover, was a complex character, not simply (like the black characters in *Sahara, Bataan,* and *Crash Dive*) a brave man. The spate of war films ushered in by *Home of the Brave* and the integration of the military signaled a new era for the black actor in Hollywood—he finally was able to perform as a powerful character in dramas that dealt openly with racism.

Between 1949 and 1962, the African American actor James Edwards had significant to major roles in five Hollywood war movies, *Home of the Brave* (1949), *Bright Victory* (1952), *The Steel Helmet* (1951), *Men in War* (1957), and *The Manchurian Candidate* (1962), more appearances in such films than any other black actor of the period. If any black actor was tied to the image of the black soldier in an integrated military, it was Edwards. Three of Edwards's five war films portrayed the Korean War (1950–1953), the first war the United States fought with integrated combat troops, and the first American so-called limited war. By contrast, Sidney Poitier, the most famous black actor to emerge from the 1950s, appeared in two war films during those years, *Red Ball Express* (1952), set during World War II, and *All the Young Men* (1960), set in Korea. The Korean War, much more obviously, opened the door for filmmakers to look at racism in American society by looking at the interaction of the races in an integrated military. That war also reflected larger changes in American society: Jackie Robinson had integrated Major League Baseball in 1947, when the Brooklyn Dodgers called him up from the minors; the African American poet Gwendolyn Brooks won the Pulitzer Prize in Poetry in 1950 for *Annie Allen;* Ralph Ellison won the National Book Award in 1953 for *Invisible Man.* Trumpeter Miles Davis invented "the Birth of the Cool" in jazz with a set of compositions that featured an almost completely white band and a white arranger. It was not simply that blacks were crossing over into the "mainstream" culture but that they were crossing over in a way that challenged earlier stereotypes. Nothing makes this clearer than the NAACP-led campaign against the television version of *Amos 'n' Andy,* which aired from 1951 to 1953. In part because of black protests about its characterizations, the show, which had run on the radio since 1928, was taken off the air.

To see how the integration of the military changed the image of the black male in American popular culture, we can also look at issue fifteen of EC Comics' *Frontline Combat,* dated January 1954. The cover features an integrated army fighting in Korea, with a prominently displayed black soldier. At the time, comic books were the most popular medium for both children and adolescents; the EC comics were so controversial that protests against them, an ensuing congressional investigation into the comics industry, and the Comics Code that resulted essentially drove EC Comics out of business. Blacks were almost never depicted on the covers of comics except as savage "jungle natives" or caricatures in humor titles. War comics, depicting actual combat, arose after World War II and became especially popular during the Korean War. *Frontline Combat's* war stories were particularly grim and realistic, based on research and interviews with veterans. Wallace Wood, who drew the cover of *Frontline Combat* number fifteen, also drew and wrote the cover story, "Perimeter," which dealt dramatically with racism in the military. EC liked to use Wood for what the company called "EC Preachies," stories in its war and horror comics that dealt with racism and anti-Semitism. Clearly, the impact of the Korean War and the racial integration of the military had filtered through to areas of popular culture where one would hardly expect to find it. This social transformation, and it can be called nothing less, has not received the attention it deserves. Since the draft was still in effect—and since so many Americans had served in World War II (some of them recalled to serve in Korea)—the military in the 1950s had a far greater cultural presence in American life than it does today; that presence partly accounts for the impact of the integration of the military.

Some Korean War films portray African Americans favorably without placing questions about race front and center: Richard Brooks's *Take the High Ground* (1953), for example, about young recruits being trained for combat, depicts an African American recruit, played by William Hairston, as a highly articulate young man who constantly quotes English poets. Sam Fuller's *The Steel Helmet* (1951), on the other hand, is all about race. Its lead, a white sergeant, grudgingly befriends a Korean boy. In one tense scene, a North Korean prisoner asks a black medic, played by James Edwards, how he can fight for a country that discriminates against him. The medic says only, in effect, "It takes time." Few viewers now will find such answers compelling. But Fuller did raise—and forcefully, too—the question of whether the black soldier had a compelling reason to fight. Many other Americans asked the same question. World War II films made during the Korean War that dealt with race, such as Mark Robson's *Bright Victory* and tough-guy Budd Boetticher's *Red Ball Express,* ultimately advocated better race relations. In the first film, a blind Southern white man is able to overcome his racism to maintain his friendship with a blind black soldier; in the second, blacks and whites overcome distrust and learn to work together. *Red Ball Express* also depicted the heroism of service units in combat, an important bit of racial propaganda, as most blacks during World War II served in such units.

The integration of the military did more to alter the American conscience, so wickedly deformed by racism, than we might realize. At the least, we can now understand James Meredith's claim in 1966 that the Vietnam War was a big advance for the black soldier because by then no one questioned his ability to fight.

Bibliography: Committee on Civil Rights, *To Secure These Rights: The Report of the President's Committee on Civil Rights* (Washington, DC, 1947); Michael Gardner, *Harry Truman and Civil Rights* (Carbondale, IL, 2002). Grant Geissman, *Foul Play! The Art and Artists of the Notorious EC Comics* (New York, 2005). Daniel Kryder, *Divided Arsenal: Race and the American State During World War II* (New York, 2000).

GERALD EARLY

1947, December 3

"Hey, there! Stella, Baby!" *A Streetcar Named Desire* premieres at the Ethel Barrymore Theater in New York

TENNESSEE WILLIAMS

Marlon Brando, carrying a "red-stained package" from the butcher and sporting blue-denim work clothes as the lordly, proletarian Stanley Kowalski, ambles insolently onstage at the opening of Tennessee Williams's *A Streetcar Named Desire*. "Bellowing" for his adoring yet tart-tongued wife, Stanley is the strutting male animal in his sexual prime. The setting is a seedy tenement in the multiracial French Quarter of New Orleans, whose picturesque verandas open to the humid air. Street sounds and sultry, insinuating jazz riffs float in and out.

The exotic location, boisterous energy, and eruptions of violence in *A Streetcar Named Desire* were a startling contrast to the tightly wound gentility of Williams's prior hit play, *The Glass Menagerie* (1944), whose fractured family is cloistered in a stuffy St. Louis flat. *Streetcar* exploded into the theater world at a time when Broadway was dominated by musical comedies and revivals. At the end of its premiere, the audience sat numb and then went wild, applauding for thirty minutes. Critical responses ranged from positive to rapturous, with dissent coming only from Wolcott Gibbs and Mary McCarthy. *Streetcar* won the Pulitzer Prize and other major awards and ran for two years in New York before touring the country. European productions won enormous acclaim, except in England, where the verdict was split.

Brando as Stanley was a volcanic force of nature. Leering, brooding, belching, mumbling, scratching himself, and smashing crockery on the floor, he exemplified a radical new style of naturalistic acting, "the Method," which Brando learned from Stella Adler and which would gain public attention through Lee Strasberg's Actors Studio in New York. Focusing on emotional truth and painful personal memory, the Method was developed in the 1930s by the leftist, ensemble-oriented Group Theater, which was following Konstantin Stanislavsky's precepts for productions of realist plays (such as Chekhov's) at the Moscow Art Theater. Brando, along with his friend Montgomery Clift, would transfer the Method into movie acting, as in the 1951 film of *Streetcar*, which was directed, like the play, by Elia Kazan. The repercussions from Brando's performance in that film are still being felt among contemporary American male actors, who often "do" Brando without being aware of it.

In its taboo-breaking style, *Streetcar* belonged to an oppositional strain in American culture that emerged following World War II. The near-universal patriotism of the war years, galvanized to defeat German and Japanese imperialism, continued in mainstream American society and media for nearly two decades. But it was countered by an underground variously represented by abstract expressionism, bebop, and the Beats, as well as existentialism imported from Paris. There was a touch of the cynical hipster in Brando's impudent delivery of Stanley's brusque, satirically deadpan lines. Brando's raw primitivism was also a jolting departure from the slickness of the prettified glamour boys of the Hollywood studio, and it prefigured the youth rebellion of the 1950s, including rock and roll—to whose iconography Brando would contribute through his role as the black-leather-clad leader of a motorcycle gang in a low-budget 1953 film, *The Wild One*.

The rude, crude Stanley Kowalski, with his iconic white T-shirt and his immigrant ethnicity, was evidently based on two men: a St. Louis factory worker of that name and a Mexican boxer, Pancho Gonzalez, who was one of Williams's butch lovers. Stanley has a tinge of "rough trade," a gay male staple—the street hustler, hot and dangerous. In *Streetcar's* rowdy scenes of men playing poker, bowling, cursing, and brawling, Williams is gazing longingly at male bonding from his distant outsider's position. (An earlier title for the play, which was partly inspired by a Van Gogh painting of a billiard hall, was *The Poker Game.*) Williams was a small, effeminate gay man (his adult height was five-feet-six) who had been called "sissy" by neighborhood boys and "Miss Nancy" by his bullying, rejecting father. Williams would immortalize his father's bumptious authoritarianism in the garrulous, overbearing Big Daddy of *Cat on a Hot Tin Roof* (1955).

The shocking frankness with which *Streetcar* treated sex—as a searingly revolutionary force—was at odds with the dawning domesticity of the postwar era and looked forward instead to the 1960s sexual revolution. Williams drew much of his philosophy of sex from D. H. Lawrence, whose wife, Frieda, he visited in Taos, New Mexico, in 1939, when he was planning to write a play about Lawrence's death. What distinguishes Williams from other American playwrights of leftist social realism, such as Arthur Miller (whose *Death of a Salesman* made a sensation in 1949), is his florid Romantic emotionalism and love of beauty, as well as his Romantic reverence for barbaric, elemental nature. Emotional expressiveness is so central to Williams that Irene Selznick, the producer of *Streetcar,* refused to produce his next play, *The Rose Tattoo,* because she said it was an "opera," not a play.

Streetcar's historical background, embodied in the fluttery, flirtatious Blanche DuBois, is the decay of the agrarian Old South and the rise of gritty, prosaic urban industrialism. All of Williams's plays, until *The Night of the Iguana* in 1961, were set in the South. (The latter play takes place in a ramshackle hotel in Mexico.) Like William Faulkner, Williams portrays the psychological landscape of Southern decadence, with its guilt, squalor, and self-destructive fantasy. But Williams has greater faith in the sheer mesmerizing power of human personality. His major women characters are flamboyant, instinctive actresses—sometimes literally so, as with the aging movie star Alexandra del Lago in *Sweet Bird of Youth* (1959).

The ultratheatrical Blanche is one of Williams's relentless, nonstop talkers. Other examples are Amanda Wingfield, the suffocatingly overprotective mother in *The Glass Menagerie,* and Violet Venable, a malign New Orleans aristocrat in the 1958 one-act play *Suddenly Last Summer.* (Violet was played by Katharine Hepburn in the stunning movie of *Suddenly Last Summer,* directed by Joseph L. Mankiewicz and released in 1959.) All these women were inspired by Williams's own overpowering mother, with her pretensions of Southern refinement and her pathologically incessant talking, which one visitor described as a "nightmare."

Blanche is a dreamer who lives by language, the medium of the playwright's art. She creates poetry and illusion through her flights of rhetoric, which transform the harsh, bare environment. Blanche is literally a conduit of Romanticism: we hear that she taught Poe, Whitman, and Hawthorne to resistant high-school students in the country. It is through words alone that she re-creates the vanished world of Southern chivalry. She cries, "I don't want realism. I want magic!" Blanche's love of imagination and artifice clashes with the humdrum routine of the practical, utilitarian world, embodied in Stanley's curt, deflating minimalism. (Williams derives great humor from the two characters' competitive conversational rhythm.) As the play proceeds, the number and speed of words begin to increase and cloud the air, signaling Blanche's hallucinatory memories and descent into madness. Blanche's aggressive talking and baroque fantasies will live again in the caustic termagant Martha in Edward Albee's play *Who's Afraid of Virginia Woolf?* (1962).

Williams said of his work, "I draw every character out of my very multiple split personality. My heroines always express the climate of my interior world at the time in which those characters were created." Elia Kazan claimed that Blanche DuBois *was* Tennessee Williams. She has his sexual hedonism, restlessness, and love of illusion, as well as his chronic alcoholism (he also abused pills). The enterprisingly nymphomaniac Blanche is Williams's champion in his self-proclaimed war against American puritanism. Williams attributed his mother's hysteria and his sister Rose's mental instability to sexual repression: "They were both victims of excessive propriety." (Rose, who was lobotomized at a state hospital in Missouri, was the model for Laura Wingfield in *The Glass Menagerie*.)

Like Blanche, Williams was uprooted from his Southern birthplace and became a refugee. He spent his first seven "idyllic" years in Mississippi before his family's traumatic move to St. Louis. He would live in sixteen different houses before he was fifteen. Williams became a compulsive traveler. Though a millionaire from the movie rights to his work, he lived in hotel rooms and would die alone in one. He said in his 1975 memoirs, "I live like a gypsy, I am a fugitive." Amid his bleak St. Louis surroundings, he developed a nostalgia for what he imagined to be the grace and elegance of the antebellum South. An enormous early influence on him in Mississippi was his family's black servant, Ozzie, who told him and his sister African American and Native American folktales.

Williams understood that the Southern claim of aristocracy, enabled by the atrocity of slavery, was built on lies. Hence in *Streetcar* the ancestral DuBois plantation, lost to creditors, is called Belle Reve—that is, "beautiful dream." But the dream was always a patchwork of illogic: the French noun *rêve* is masculine, so the estate's name should properly be "Beau Reve." Williams had already used "Belle Reve" as the title of an adolescent poem where he fantasized about living on a Missouri plantation with his parents. The name was evidently suggested by a shrine of St. Louis snobbery, the Bellerive Country Club (meaning "beautiful riverbank"), where his mother strove for social acceptance and where, as a teenager, he would slip on a diving board and knock out all of his front teeth. (He had to wear dentures for the rest of his life.) Hence Bellerive/Belle Reve was a beckoning mirage that led to failure, humiliation, and mutilation.

The archetypal Southern belle whom Blanche so desperately plays, eighty years after the Civil War, would have been instantly recognizable to audiences from Scarlett O'Hara of *Gone with the Wind,* the blockbuster film (based on Margaret Mitchell's 1936 best seller) that had been released in a tremendous burst of international publicity just eight years earlier. (Coincidentally, a British actress, Vivien Leigh, would win two Academy Awards for Best Actress for playing both

Scarlett O'Hara and Blanche DuBois.) Belle Reve is partly Tara, the family planta-tion for which Scarlett fights tax collectors and carpetbaggers. But it is also (as Williams attested) the cherry orchard in Chekhov's 1904 play of that name, a pre-cious patrimony that is mortgaged and seized by vulgarians.

A residue of Williams's transsexual self-projection into the archly predatory Blanche is perhaps discernible in her seductive exchange with the newsboy, to-ward whom she directs such blatant come-ons as "You make my mouth water." Williams said that Blanche, soliciting the startled newsboy, has *become* Allan, her young gay husband, whom she shamed into suicide. *A Streetcar Named Desire* was unusually forthright about homosexuality at a time when the subject was bowdlerized or demonized by Hollywood movies. Homosexuality was explicitly forbidden under the Motion Picture Production Code: *These Three,* for example, a 1936 film based on Lillian Hellman's hit play, *The Children's Hour,* substituted a heterosexual triangle for the central plot motif of lesbianism, which was ex-punged.

Williams introduced homosexuality into *Cat on a Hot Tin Roof,* where it is the motivation for Brick's marital reticence with the hot-blooded Maggie, and into *Suddenly Last Summer,* where the backstory focuses on a promiscuous gay aesthete, Sebastian Venable, who is slaughtered and cannibalized by a pack of poor Spanish boys whom he had solicited. (The Adonis archetype invoked here is part of Wil-liams's use of Greek mythology, as in his 1957 play, *Orpheus Descending.*) Sebastian's sex tours were based on Williams's own in Mexico and Italy, where he pursued orgiastic anonymous sex and indulged what he called his "deviant satyriasis." When he got an "appetite" for blonds (a line he gives Sebastian), he would mull going north. Williams's 1950 novel, *The Roman Spring of Mrs. Stone,* fictionalized his own experiences with Italian gigolos the year after *Streetcar*'s huge success. (Mrs. Stone, his female proxy, would be played onscreen once again by Vivien Leigh in the 1961 movie.)

Williams was a bold pioneer for sexual candor: *Baby Doll,* for example, a lurid 1956 film based on his screenplay and directed by Elia Kazan, was condemned by the Catholic Legion of Decency. Yet Williams was denounced by gay activists af-ter the gay liberation movement awoke following the 1969 Stonewall Rebellion. He was accused of always linking homosexuality to guilt, self-punishment, degen-eracy, and death—themes of the closeted era in which he had written his major plays. But he himself had been courageously and even recklessly open about be-ing gay at a time when it could have proved personally and professionally costly. Though he loved New Orleans for its sexual tolerance and pleasure-seeking life-style, Williams never liked Mardi Gras and was always uncomfortable about drag queens, who he felt degraded women. With his taste for macho and even hetero-sexual men, he criticized the "swish" and "camp" style among pre-Stonewall gays.

The sex roles of *A Streetcar Named Desire,* Williams's greatest play, are cer-tainly polarized by any conventional standard. The heterosexual electricity be-tween Stanley and Stella across the gender divide is positively blinding. (Eyes re-peatedly "go blind" in the stage directions at moments of sexual arousal.) In the 1970s, after his popularity had waned with the rise of younger playwrights, Williams told a gay interviewer that he did not want to ghettoize himself: "I wish to have a broad audience because the major thrust of my writing is not sexual orientation, it's social. I'm not about to limit myself to writing about gay people." With his empathy for the suffering yet dynamic individual, Williams produced not tendentious political potboilers but works of true universality, whose passionate characters have entered world literature.

Bibliography: Jordan Y. Miller, ed., *Twentieth Century Interpretations of A Streetcar Named Desire: A Collection of Critical Essays* (Englewood Cliffs, NJ, 1971). Matthew C. Roudané, ed., *The Cambridge Companion to Tennessee Williams* (Cambridge, 1997). Donald Spoto, *The Kindness of Strangers: The Life of Tennessee Williams* (Boston, 1985). Tennessee Williams, *Memoirs* (Garden City, NY, 1975). *Filmography: A Streetcar Named Desire,* directed by Elia Kazan (1951).

CAMILLE PAGLIA

1948
"The problems of control engineering and of communication engineering were inseparable"

Norbert Wiener, *Cybernetics*

As Neil Armstrong landed on the moon in 1969, he approached to several hundred feet above the surface under automatic computer control. He peered out the window of the Lunar Module spacecraft through a graphical grid that framed his view. The computer in his cabin calculated where the spacecraft would eventually land, directing Armstrong's gaze through the window grid toward that point. But the smooth flow of the landing was interrupted by distracting computer program alarms, and the Lunar Module was also several miles off target. Armstrong turned off the computer's automatic targeting, seized his control stick, and landed the strange machine by eye and hand. Observers hailed the landing not only as a triumph of technology but also as a victory for human judgment and intuition over cold automation.

Five years after the Apollo program ended, we find a similar moment at the climax of George Lucas's film *Star Wars* (1977), as the hero Luke Skywalker pilots a space-plane in a daring attack on the Death Star. Speeding along toward the Achilles' heel of the enemy space station, Skywalker peers through a computer-generated targeting image that displays calculations of where his missiles, when fired, will eventually hit. Approaching the critical firing point, Skywalker turns off the computer display and trusts instead his own intuition and feeling, aided by the metaphysical "Force." He fires his shot without the automatic aid and succeeds in destroying the enemy (and saving civilization).

Both of these dramas elevate human skill and intuition above artificial mechanisms. The theme was not entirely new in American culture. The mythical nineteenth-century worker John Henry competed directly with a steam drill in the famous industrial folk legend, achieving victory over machine, at the cost of his life. But such industrial ballads focused on the machine's replacement of physical brawn or manual skills. Armstrong's and Skywalker's feats enacted a newer twentieth-century version of the anxiety: challenges to human beings from electronics and computers. These challenges stood alongside age-old visions of golems and automata, from Čapek's R.U.R. to Arthur C. Clarke's HAL. After World War II, industrial dramas of mechanization became anxieties of automation, threats to bodies became threats to minds, threats to blue-collar jobs became threats to white-collar professional identities.

We can identify one moment in this change in Norbert Wiener's 1948 book, *Cybernetics: Or Control and Communication in the Animal and the Machine.* Wiener, a mathematics professor at MIT, argued that "the problems of control engineering and of communications engineering were inseparable," and posited the message as the fundamental component of feedback loops, both within machines and between machines and people. Following the implications of these ideas led him to reframe a host of phenomena as information-processing activities. Wiener described how human and social behavior resembled dynamic mechanisms, with similar types of feedback loops, oscillations, and potential instabilities. He theorized an analogy between the emerging digital computer and the human nervous system. He coined the term "cybernetics" from the Greek word for "steersman," for the new science of feedback, human behavior, and information.

Wiener writes expansively, with the apparent humility of a man who sees his own mind at the center of the world. He frames his huge, ambitious agenda within the humble inquiries of a professor. Phrases like "then it occurred to me," or "it became apparent to us" move the narrative along, unfolding his complicated vision of the unities of biological, technical, and social worlds. Some of the chapters are deeply mathematical (largely repeating his statistical work from during the war), although the book's major conclusions require no such machinations. *Cybernetics* elaborates a vision of humans and machines not only for engineers and systems theorists but also for social scientists, political philosophers, and even literary critics. After a series of high-profile interdisciplinary conferences, cybernetics became a popular discourse of science, technology, and society, and Wiener, a bespectacled commentator on social implications of technology, went from the atomic bomb to industrial automation.

Wiener had been urged by anthropologists Gregory Bateson and Margaret Mead to pursue the implications of his ideas with great energy, but he hesitated because he lacked a base of social statistics for analysis. Nevertheless, Wiener followed his provocative, somewhat inscrutable first book with a more popular rendition, *The Human Use of Human Beings* (1950). This one became a best seller for its expansion on the social speculations in the original work. Here he repeated the big idea: the ties that bind are fundamentally messages and speech, whether within an organism, among organisms, between organism and machine, or among actors in social systems. Wiener elevated his thinking on control and communication to a moral philosophy of technology, and enjoyed an enthusiastic response.

The ambitious program had bloody origins. Wiener had done important work in mathematics before World War II, and during the war he had been involved in one of the era's great secret technical projects, figuring out how to shoot aircraft out of the sky with computer-controlled guns. He was assigned the problem of prediction: given a certain amount of tracking data on an attacking aircraft, how well could one estimate its future position? Wiener studied statistical approaches to calculating the amount of "lead" for an anti-aircraft gun to fire ahead of its target (the projectile could take nearly a minute to reach the target's altitude from the ground, during which time the plane could move several miles). Neil Armstrong's computer ran the same problem to predict his landing spot, and Luke Skywalker's display showed the same estimated paths of his missiles. But unlike their inert targets, Wiener's gun was shooting at an airplane controlled by an intelligent, unpredictable person. Wiener could, of course, come to certain conclusions—given a certain speed and maneuverability, the future position of the aircraft must be confined to certain areas near its past positions. But over time such regions grew infinitely large.

Ultimately, solving the problem depended on gauging the future intent of the pilot of the attacking aircraft, a problem not addressable with technical apparatus, although Wiener was attracted to its philosophical dimensions. Wiener's statistical analyses of anti-aircraft prediction had little immediate application to the war but did establish some fundamental ideas for later computation of signals. It also led him to work with physiologists and medical doctors to look at the general problem of human interaction with machines, along with its philosophical implications. A 1943 paper, "Behavior, Purpose, and Teleology," written with physiologist Arturo Rosenblueth and Wiener's engineering assistant, Julian Bigelow, identified automatic feedback controls with the "behavioristic approach" to organisms and classified the behavior of a system according to the level of prediction it exhibited. Wiener identified the prediction of moving one's hand to grasp a coffee cup, for example, with that of the anti-aircraft gun. The paper took military concepts of machine control and began to reframe them in a civilian mode, concentrating on the links between human and natural systems. Historian Peter Galison argues that Wiener, by elevating his artillery prediction circuits to the "symbol for the new age of man," enshrined an oppositional military metaphor in the civilian science of cybernetics. Cold war models of human-machine interaction, writes Galison, were based on "the ontology of the enemy." Indeed for Wiener, firing a gun at another person was a form of communication, a bullet the most elemental message.

At various times people referred to cybernetics as the science of feedback control, the science of systems, the very idea that the world was a system of flows connecting "black boxes" that could be rationally modeled and analyzed. Wiener himself believed that cybernetics, by including human capabilities in technical analysis, could impart a new kind of humanism to technical systems. Yet while generating great enthusiasm, both within the academy and without, cybernetics led to no commonly recognized discipline. Few universities in North America, for example, have departments of cybernetics, whereas many have departments of computer science (a hybrid discipline that emerged only in the late 1960s). Cybernetics did catch on behind the Iron Curtain. In the Soviet Union, though initially shunned as bourgeois science propaganda, after Stalin's death cybernetics became the ultimate unifying socialist science (many Soviet-era universities still have departments of cybernetics).

Wiener's own invocation of the steersman draws our attention to the long history of human-machine relationships that preceded him, brought into greater intimacy and mixture in the twentieth century. The photographs taken by Étienne-Jules Marey captured the body as a mechanism. The time and motion studies of Frederick Winslow Taylor and his disciples deployed that mechanism in the name of industrial efficiency. World War I brought fighter aircraft that put the body at the core of a flying machine gun, and the prosthetics of the war's amputees found disturbing, enervating echoes in Dada's machine-people. Charles Lindbergh wrote a book called *We* to describe his famous flight as a partnership of human and machine. Wiener himself wrote at the close of a war when radar blips began to represent the enemy in abstract form, and when the motions of armies could be decoded with a few clicks of a wheel on an Enigma machine.

Wiener, then, seems a critical link between the modern, mechanical machine world and the fluid, postwar world of information and networks. Indeed Wiener and his disciples tend to credit him with everything from the invention of feedback and homeostasis to the conceptualization of the digital computer. But other events in the *Cybernetics* year of 1948 indicate the rush of broader currents. In addition to the announcement of the invention of the transistor, that year also saw the publication of the Radiation Laboratory series of textbooks, based on wartime radar innovations, that codified and distributed to the world new techniques that would underlie postwar applications of automation, computers, and television. Also in that year Claude Shannon of the Bell Telephone Laboratories published his "Mathematical Theory of Communication," a less ambitious and more technical work than Wiener's (but equally profound) that calculated the basic information capacity of generalized communications "channels," and articulated a theory of codes that reframed all communications as a symbolic exchange. Shannon crystallized a half century of thinking at the telephone company about how sounds, images, and text could be extracted from humans for coding as numbers and transmission through channels, the conceptual foundations of today's networks, where computer screens attached to digital networks bristle with equivalent forms of "content."

Along with information theory, digital computing, systems engineering, and systems theory, cybernetics popularized the idea of a world populated by messages. Numerous other sciences heard the call and followed enthusiastically along. Biologists quickly took up the charge and began seeing the core of life as a code and speaking in language borrowed from cybernetics and information theory. From Lacan to Lyotard we find intellectuals eagerly adopting cybernetic language as a new, post–machine-age metaphor for everything from the unconscious mind to global social networks. NASA scientists coined the word "cyborg" in 1960 for the hybrid machine/animals that would populate spacecraft. Psychologist J. C. R. Licklider articulated a theory of "man-computer symbiosis" in which machines would aid people in the real-time work of thinking. Licklider's vision inspired a research program and a community of scientists that eventually led to the Internet. During the cold war, computerized command and control systems generated a vision (à la *Dr. Strangelove*) in which the end of the world would be directed, in real time, by men in a data-processing center. Jimi Hendrix even brought cybernetics into the counterculture with his feedback-drenched guitar performance of "The Star Spangled Banner" at Woodstock in 1969. When cultural critic Donna Haraway appropriated the term thirty years after Wiener's book in her *Cyborg Manifesto,* and when William Gibson coined the term "cyberspace" in 1982, each was invoking Wiener's legacy.

Neil Armstrong and Luke Skywalker alluded to a long tradition of American helmsmen, from sea captains and riverboat pilots to locomotive engineers and race car drivers. Yet the real and fictional spacefarers presented a cybernetic image to succeed them: their vision structured by instruments, their hands on a stick, their actions aided and mediated by computers. Ultimately, cybernetics provided a kind of figure—an image of a human connected into a machine, a picture of society as a network of communications channels, and an icon of anxiety about human identity in an age of apparently thinking machines.

Bibliography: Slava Gerovitch, *From Newspeak to Cyberspeak: A History of Soviet Cybernetics* (Cambridge, MA, 2002). William Gibson, *Neuromancer* (New York, 1984). Donna J. Haraway, *Simians, Cyborgs, and Women: The Reinvention of Nature* (New York, 1991). David Mindell, *Between Human and Machine: Feedback, Control, and Computing before Cybernetics* (Baltimore, 2002). Norbert Wiener, *Cybernetics: Or, Control and Communication in the Animal and the Machine* (Cambridge, MA, 1948); *The Human Use of Human Beings: Cybernetics and Society* (Boston, 1950).

DAVID A. MINDELL

1948
"I got a scheme!"

THE ADVENTURES OF AUGIE MARCH

When in 2005, the year he died, I decided to offer a seminar on the works of Saul Bellow, I expected students to favor *The Adventures of Augie March*—a young person's book if there ever was one. Augie is a high-spirited guide to modern times, his speech a gushing geyser, a cerebral, literary form of jazz. Though Bellow had drawn earlier critical notice with short stories and two novels, *Dangling Man* (1944) and *The Victim* (1947), this was his breakthrough book, winning him his first National Book Award.

Bellow began writing *Augie* in 1948, while on a Guggenheim Fellowship in Paris, and as he later described to Philip Roth, the idea came to him in the form of a boy from his Chicago neighborhood, who had lived on Augusta Street (hence, Augie). "I had the triumphant feeling that this is what I had been born for. I . . .

began immediately to write in a spirit of reunion with the kid who had shouted, 'I got a scheme!'" The work poured out of him:

> In the next two years I seldom looked into Fowler's *Modern English Usage*. The book had taken off, writing itself very rapidly; I was coming to be strangely independent of place. Chicago itself had grown exotic to me. A descendant of Russian-Jewish immigrants, I was writing about Chicago in odd corners of Paris and, afterward, in Austria, Italy, Long Island, and New Jersey. To speak of rootless or rooted persons is all very well, but I felt that the cultural vocabulary of the university crowd should be avoided . . . What I learned in Europe was how deeply involved I was with the U.S.A.

Among the intellectual crowd that Bellow hung out with back in America, someone had quipped that *Partisan Review* had a special typewriter key for the word "alienation." A member of that company, Lionel Trilling, coined the term "adversary culture" to describe the oppositional relation of their modernist cohort to its society. But in Europe Bellow found the confidence to speak of and for America in the voice of an adolescent very nearly like himself. The book's opening became iconic.

> I am an American, Chicago born—Chicago, that somber city—and go about things as I have taught myself, free-style, and will make the record in my own way: first to knock, first admitted; sometimes an innocent knock, sometimes a not so innocent. But a man's character is his fate, says Heraclitus, and in the end there isn't any way to disguise the nature of the knocks by acoustical work on the door or gloving the knuckles.

Here was Walt Whitman's song of himself transposed into the grit of Carl Sandburg's "Chicago," "Fierce as a dog with tongue lapping for action, cunning as a savage pitted against the wilderness, . . . / Under the terrible burden of destiny laughing as a young man laughs, / Laughing even as an ignorant fighter laughs who has never lost a battle." Bellow embraced the plenitude of Middle America with exuberance (a term the critics kept invoking), quite unlike New England's legacy of civic containment. His was an urban, Northern counterpart to Huckleberry Finn, that earlier uncoverer of American society along the Mississippi. Mark Twain had prefaced Huck's *Adventures* with assurance that he was the master of American English, that the book's various dialects were based on the author's "personal familiarity with these several forms of speech." Augie likewise flaunted his speech—"free-style" and slightly Jewish-inflected—as the key to his and his author's literary authority. The timing for such a project was perfect: by the 1950s, children of immigrants like Augie were entering the American mainstream as equals rather than members of tolerated minorities.

Augie is in some respects the familiar story of a young man in difficult straits who tries to learn about the world and how he fits into it. Semi-orphaned by an absentee father who has deserted a woman with three sons—the youngest, Georgie, retarded, and the eldest, Simon, determined to prosper—Augie has family enough to give him emotional sustenance, but not enough to prevent his self-rule. His adventures run the gamut from union organizing and riding the rails to salesmanship among the horsey set and being torpedoed during the Second World War. The adventures my students most appreciated were Augie's quests for love, chivalric in their impulse but often selfish in outcome. When his brother Simon urges him to follow his example in marrying a rich man's daughter, Augie demurs, "I didn't mount the step of power. I could have done so from love, but not to get to the objective." Augie's romantic disappointments never stop him from chancing love anew. Indeed, his impulsive marriage in the final chapters suggests that his discoveries in that sphere have not yet come to an end.

"People have been adoptive toward me, as if I were really an orphan," says Augie about his many benefactors, but adoption by the reader is what the novel truly seeks. Bellow knew that an overarticulate Jewboy had not until then been America's literary idol and, possibly in an effort to charm, he plays up some of the comic aspects of Augie's development. In parody of a Hemingway hero, Augie joins an American heiress on a scheme to train eagles in Mexico. First he studies the bird in the zoo, "the pressed-down head, the killing eye, the deep life of its feathers. Oy! . . . there seemed nothing a bird like this might want." That Yiddish *krekhts,* or sigh, between the sentences admits that the birder lacks the killer instincts of the bird. Once the training begins, "I really felt dazed in all my nerves when I saw with what we would have to deal, and dark before the eyes." This last phrase— *finster in di oygn*—straight from the Yiddish, highlights Augie's Jewishness at the very point that he strives to satisfy expectations of American masculinity. Bellow once called "characteristically Jewish" stories in which "laughter and trembling are so curiously mingled that it is not easy to determine the relations of the two." *Augie* takes American literature a giant step in this direction.

In fact, the literary work *Augie* most closely resembles in spirit is *Motl, Peysi the Cantor's Son* by the Yiddish humorist Sholem Aleichem, the author whom Bellow's father best liked reading to the family aloud. Motl's ironic refrain, "I am lucky, I'm an orphan," heralds his unexpected liberation from paternal authority—and from the guilt of having to defy it—when his sickly father dies in the opening chapter. Motl recounts how his family uprooted itself from a small town in punitive Russia and made its way across Europe to New York's welcoming Lower East Side, finding merriment in situations where the adults encounter only trouble and grief. Loss and anxiety are his weird but psychologically reasonable stimuli for creative independence. Augie's fatherless state grants him the same guiltless freedom that Motl experiences in his encounter with the world. "All the influences were lined up waiting for me. I was born, and there they were to form me, which is why I tell you more of them than of myself."

Yet Saul Bellow was not that fatherless child, he was not Augie. As it happens, having grown up in Montreal, I was well positioned to know that Saul Bellow was a native and often returned there to visit his family. He moved to Chicago as a boy of nine and there was raised under strict paternal discipline. The figure of Augie may have offered Bellow the freedom his imagination required in writing the great American novel, but his own character (his fate, according to Heraclitus) was more filial than Augie's and more heavily burdened with responsibility. *Augie March* turned out to be merely a prelude to Bellow's literary manhood.

Thus, after the several-year interval that habitually separated one major Bellow work from the next, came *Seize the Day* (1956), almost like an act of penance. This small masterpiece of compression, lacerated by guilt to the degree that *Augie* contrived to be innocent, confronted the limits of the American dream rather than its boundless possibilities. It is as though Augie had come up against his darker alternative in Tommy Wilhelm, né "Wilkie" Adler, a middle-aged charmer whose luck is running out. A pattern of water imagery presses home the theme of a man drowning in a sea of troubles. Wilkie has a couple of failed careers, a failed marriage, and two sons whom he takes to baseball games—the boyish all-American pastime. The book is situated in a recognizable corner of Manhattan, but reaches beyond its immediate subject in a way that suggests a religious text.

In the piebald spirit of laughter and trembling that Bellow calls "characteristically Jewish," *Seize the Day* yokes two opposite literary traditions of the Western world, Horace's *carpe diem* with its embrace of the precious moment, and Judaism's Yom Kippur insistence on baring the soul before an eternal, omniscient, and all-judging God. In the spirit of the former, forty-four-year-old Tommy Wilhelm is lured by a masterful con man into playing the commodities market with his last dollars; in the spirit of the Day of Atonement that is almost upon us in the book, Wilkie experiences a reckoning with his irascible father and with the string of mistakes that seem to constitute his adult life. Here is how his day begins: "After breakfast, out, out, out to attend to business. The getting out had in itself become the chief business. But he had realized that he could not keep this up much longer, and today he was afraid. He was aware that his routine was about to break up and he sensed that a huge trouble long presaged but formless was due. Before evening, he'd know."

Compare Wilhelm's mood as he sets forth with the liturgy of the Day of Atonement:

> Open for us the gate of prayer,
> Even at the closing of the gate,
> Even now that the day has declined.
> When the day declines into sunset,
> O let us enter into thy gates.
> O God, we implore thee, forgive us!
> Pardon and spare us, grant us mercy;
> Clear us and suppress iniquity.

"Oh, God," Wilhelm prays in his own language, "Let me out of my trouble. Let me out of my thoughts, and let me do something better with myself. For all the time I have wasted I am very sorry. Let me out of this clutch and into a different life. For I am all balled up. Have mercy." One could read this as the desacralized religion of secular America, or the spontaneous expression of modern spiritual life. And though I've here highlighted the Jewish resonance of the novel, Wilhelm himself is far more familiar with Shakespeare, Milton, Keats, and Tennyson, whose elegiac verses in Lieder and Lovett's 1938 anthology *British Poetry and Prose,* committed to memory as a schoolboy, he keeps recalling as touchstones of his contrition. This novel restricts itself to "a single day" with the same intensity that Tolstoy's *The Death of Ivan Ilych* confronts the singular challenge of mortality, warning against excesses of the American dream that some mistake for a promise of eternal youth.

I was right to anticipate that students would appreciate *The Adventures of Augie March,* but like Bellow, they never looked back as they grew into works of greater maturity. In *Seize the Day* Bellow found a way of mediating between first- and third-person narrative by sharing the protagonist's point of view while allowing commentary on what went on around him. While some critics objected that this kept his heroes too repetitively close to their author, the author turned out to be a man of many parts. *Henderson the Rain King* (1959) demonstrated why Bellow resisted the hyphenated label, American-*Jewish* writer. Here he pitched his imagination into the body and soul of an oversize WASP who undertakes a mythic journey to an imaginary Africa. Bellow confounded stereotypes of Jewish humor by turning this faux-African adventure into his funniest book. (It was the one he preferred reading to audiences aloud.) The most extraordinary feature of Bellow's writing was the way it developed dialectically from book to book.

The Nobel Prize he received in 1976 was less momentous to Bellow than the verdict of the local rabbi who came after the publication of *Augie,* reviews in hand, to tell Bellow's father, "Now you can be proud of your *muzinik* [youngest son]." Yet Bellow also felt he had to answer—if not to atone—for the book. For example, Augie in Paris after the Second World War is oblivious to what had just transpired on the Continent: "Well, perhaps I had a meeting with a person who used to be in Dachau and did some business with him in dental supplies from Germany. That took an hour or two. After which I may have gone to the cold halls of the Louvre and visited in the Dutch School, or noticed how the Seine smelled like medicine, or went into a café and wrote a letter, and so passed the day." That passing reference to the Nazi concentration camp near Munich is the book's only allusion to what came to be known as the Holocaust, details of which were already widely available by the time Bellow was writing this novel. To have taken any greater note of Hitler's war against the Jews in that novel would have changed the entire balance of its American project. That insouciance is part of Augie's charm.

This lapse the older and wiser Bellow regretted, not just personally, as one may regret a moral lapse, but as an American phenomenon. By the 1960s, Augie's buoyancy seemed to have been transformed into an American culture of youth that let it all hang out, testing the boundaries of individual license in sex, politics, education, and criminality, Trilling's "adversary culture" writ large. For the most part, Bellow as author stayed close to his protagonists in age and experience. His greatest deviation from that practice came in *Mr. Sammler's Planet* (1970), which adopts an aging Holocaust survivor's point of view in surveying the contemporary American scene. Disturbed by the collapse of civilizing standards, Bellow imports the moral authority of a European Jew to make the case for conscience and elemental decency. Sammler's impotence resembles that of the novelist, who can do no more than pronounce his judgments on a world he is powerless to change.

In this vein, I wish I had been able to share with Bellow the comment of the student who told me that *Mr. Sammler's Planet* had "turned her into an adult." She said she had come to college intending to change the world. "Mr. Sammler taught me that I could also change it for the worse!" This might have been how Bellow himself reflected on some of Augie's—and America's—adolescence. *Augie's* greatest bounty may have turned out to be the lifelong creative revisionism that it released.

Bibliography: James Atlas, *Bellow: A Biography* (New York, 2000). Saul Bellow, *It All Adds Up: From the Dim Past to the Uncertain Future* (New York, 1994); *Novels 1944–1953 (Dangling Man; The Victim; The Adventures of Augie March)*, ed. James Wood (New York, 2003); *Novels 1956–1964 (Seize the Day; Henderson the Rain King; Herzog)*, ed. James Wood (New York, 2007). John Jacob Clayton, *Saul Bellow: In Defense of Man* (Bloomington, IN, 1979). "Philip Roth's Compendium," *New Yorker,* April 15, 2005.

RUTH WISSE

1949–1950
Miles Davis goes into the studio with Gil Evans

"The Birth of the Cool"

The cool aesthetic existed, in spirit if not in name, long before the advent of cool jazz. Some commentators have tried, perhaps with more enthusiasm than actual evidence, to trace back this style and attitude to Aristotle's *Nicomachean Ethics.* The sixteenth-century courtier Baldassare Castiglione may be an even more likely source of inspiration for later practitioners of the cool. Castiglione advocated a mode of personal expression that he described as *sprezzatura*—which, he explained, represented the art of doing difficult things with an appearance of ease and relaxation. "Avoid affectation in every way possible," Castiglione advised. "Conceal all art and make whatever is done or said appear to be without effort and almost without any thought about it."

But other possible antecedents for cool can be traced. Indeed, almost every culture makes room for at least some relaxed and understated behavior patterns, if only to provide a much-needed counterweight to the hot, impulsive currents of social life. In West Africa, for example, the style of interaction promoted by the belief systems of the Yoruba and Ibo emphasized restraint and conciliatory practices as well as a graceful demeanor. Perhaps this African tradition of cool underpins the later African American aesthetic. Yet the unique circumstances of the African diaspora in the New World, whose survival often depended on low-key, nonconfrontational methods of dealing with hostile forces, may have made cool an inevitable cultural choice for many black Americans.

Of course, the term "cool" itself, in its modern incarnation, is a more recent development. In almost every language, words referring to temperature are used to describe emotional states. As such, cool—like cold and frigid—is not an obvious term of praise. But an 1825 reference in *Spy,* the satirical English magazine, to a young Etonian as "right cool" points to new shades of meanings, conveying a positive image of saucy impudence and daring. This usage was slow to make its way into African American discourse. When Cab Calloway published his *Hepster's Dictionary* in 1938, he did not include "cool." *Dan Burley's Original Handbook of Harlem Jive,* from 1944, ignores the term in its lexicon (although it does appear in passing elsewhere in the volume). Many jazz musicians of the era have attested that, around this same period, saxophonist Lester Young was the first to use the term cool with its modern connotation of hipness. Young's usage was initially seen as a peculiar eccentricity rather than as a new, generally accepted meaning.

Over the next decade, cool would emerge as a jazz movement, an attitude, even a way of life. The leader of this seismic shift in popular culture and the American consciousness would be a previously unheralded trumpeter, Miles Davis, a Juilliard dropout from East St. Louis who would emerge as the most influential jazz musician of his generation. In the years following the midcentury mark, Davis would epitomize cool, as an aesthetic perspective as well as a whole way of being in the world.

Gil Evans's cramped basement apartment behind a Chinese laundry on 55th Street in Manhattan served as an unlikely launching pad for the musical revolution that would come to be known as cool jazz. At the close of the 1940s, a coterie of young musicians were gathering around Evans, anxious to explore new approaches to jazz composition, arranging, and improvisation. Davis would emerge as the leader of this group, and would eventually stand out as the best known of the so-called cool school. But a host of other important jazz players gravitated to this setting, including Charlie Parker, Gerry Mulligan, Lee Konitz, John Lewis, Max Roach, John Carisi, and George Russell.

Several of these players, including Davis, had been closely associated with the emerging bebop style of the 1940s, which had relied on fast tempos, intense improvisations, and an unabashed virtuosity. The cool style, in contrast, was more overtly melodic, focused on nuances and softer shadings, and typically performed at slow and medium tempos. The music was more carefully arranged, and performances drew on instruments, such as tuba and French horn, that had been largely ignored by the bebop players.

In August and September 1948, Davis brought a nine-piece band to the Royal Roost in New York, and though the engagement garnered little attention at the time, it would later be viewed as a signal event, the moment when the new sounds of the Davis-Evans-Mulligan contingent were put on public display for the first time. The following year, Davis undertook three recording sessions for the Capitol label that provided more ample documentation of the emerging cool style.

The recordings, issued in 1949 and 1950 as two-song ten-inch 78s, sold poorly at the time, although, in retrospect, they rank among the most influential performances of the era.

These sides captured a new aesthetic, a different vision of the potentialities of jazz music. Evans's chart on "Moon Dreams" evokes an ethereal, dreamlike quality that few previous jazz performances had ever approached. On "Boplicity," Davis floats over the ensemble with a solo that eschews the flash and dazzle of bebop in favor of a more chastened dialogue with the other horns. Even when the band tackled a faster tempo, as on "Move" and "Budo," the unusual instrumentation imparted a quasi-classical ambience to the proceedings.

There was no tenor saxophone in the band—a remarkable omission, given the instrument's centrality (then as now) in the jazz tradition. Instead a French horn blended in with other saxophones. The addition of John Barber on tuba freed up Mulligan's baritone sax to move into the higher register. The result was a novel sound, with few precedents in the jazz repertoire—so much so that Winthrop Sargeant, classical music critic for the *New Yorker*, called Davis the "Claude Debussy of jazz," and added that this body of work "is really not jazz . . . If Miles Davis were an established classical composer, his work would rank high among that of his contemporary colleagues."

Despite the enthusiasm of the record company executive who dubbed this music "the birth of the cool"—the name was not applied until the reissue of this music in LP format in 1957—the cool aesthetic was not wholly unknown to earlier jazz musicians. In the mid-1920s, cornetist Bix Beiderbecke and saxophonist Frankie Trumbauer refined a relaxed, ethereal style of jazz performance that offered an understated alternative to the celebrated "Hot Five" and "Hot Seven" recordings of Louis Armstrong. Yet Beiderbecke and Trumbauer would not match the influence Armstrong exerted over the next generation of improvisers. For the most part jazz would remain a hot art form, where intensity and dramatic flourishes would predominate.

Less than a year after Beiderbecke and Trumbauer released their celebrated 1927 recording of "Singin' the Blues," a teenage saxophonist named Lester Young heard the sounds of this 78 emanating from the room of a fellow musician in a Bismarck, North Dakota, hotel. Young knocked on the door to inquire about this peculiar, free-floating jazz music, and it is little exaggeration to say that his own style of playing the saxophone was permanently marked by this event. In the 1930s, Young would emerge as the most influential exponent of what would later be called cool jazz, and he developed many followers, devotees offering an alternative to the muscular sax sounds of Coleman Hawkins, who represented the dominant paradigm of the day.

Despite these precedents, cool jazz would not emerge as a widely recognized style until the 1950s, when many ensembles, typically under the influence of the Evans-Davis recordings, began experimenting with a similar tonal palette and aesthetic vision. Only one month after the final 1950 Davis-Evans session, John Lewis recorded his "Period Suite" with an octet that also featured James Moody and Ernie Royal, and even earlier, in March 1949, the Dave Brubeck Octet performed in a celebrated concert at the Marines Memorial Auditorium in San Francisco. Musicians on the West Coast seemed especially susceptible to the emerging style, and in time the work of many Los Angeles–based octets, nonets, and dectets—led by Shorty Rogers, Lennie Niehuas, Dave Pell, Marty Paich, and others—contributed to California's growing reputation as a center of cool jazz.

Other influences, in addition to the Davis-Evans sides, could be heard in this music: Stravinsky's *Octet* (1923), the compositions of Darius Milhaud (who served as teacher to Brubeck and other members of his octet), the big-band work of Claude Thornhill (where Gil Evans had served as arranger), the quirky compositions of Raymond Scott, the impressionist music of Debussy and Ravel, and the jazz efforts of Lennie Tristano and Boyd Raeburn, among others. Davis was the catalyst, but his pioneering efforts took place in an environment in which other musical minds were moving in complementary directions.

Yet in the final analysis no one did more to promote the cool agenda than the individual musicians in the Davis nonet, whose collective efforts transformed jazz during the 1950s. Pianist John Lewis would form the Modern Jazz Quartet, an ensemble that tempered the fires of bop with a double dose of chamber-music restraint, and left behind an impressive legacy of some fifty recordings made over a forty-year period. Gerry Mulligan left for the West Coast soon after the last session with Davis, where he founded an influential combo with Chet Baker, and recorded with a larger ensemble that followed in the footsteps of his work with Davis. Lee Konitz also enjoyed a successful career in the years following the 1949–50 sessions, refining a more cerebral style and recording frequently, often in company of other musicians associated (like Konitz himself) with pianist Lennie Tristano. Gunther Schuller, for his part, advocated a merging of classical and jazz idioms in a new hybrid that he called "Third Stream," a term he coined, which came to encompass a wide range of exciting musical developments during these years. Gil Evans also built on his early efforts in a series of memorable recordings, most notably his later collaborations with Miles Davis on *Miles Ahead* (1957), *Porgy and Bess* (1958), and *Sketches of Spain* (1960).

These were considerable achievements, but Davis himself remained the brightest star in the cool firmament. In the decades following his first cool recordings, Davis constantly reinvented his sound, exploring the potential of modal, fusion, and other musical perspectives, but his trumpet sound would always reveal, to some degree, his continued allegiance to the cool aesthetic he had developed in these seminal postwar recordings. Davis never overplayed, even when those around him went into overdrive, and his solos invariably reflected his mastery of tone and texture, his unparalleled ability to say less with more.

The influence of Davis and the other cool-school mavens eventually spread beyond the world of jazz into the broader currents of literary and popular culture. "For me, Miles was what *cool* meant," Amiri Baraka would later write in his autobiography. "My last year in high school I ran into Miles' 'Venus de Milo' and 'Move.' In fact all the tunes in that series of recordings he made with the big band . . . To me that was where the definition of 'high art' began."

Davis's coolness was more than a matter of music. He would sometimes walk off the stage after finishing a solo, or play the trumpet with his back to the audience. After a half century during which jazz musicians had acted, first and foremost, as entertainers, and even offstage remained members of a subservient underclass, such gestures were bound to have powerful political and social overtones.

But Davis's onstage demeanor cannot be reduced to a simple message. The fascinating aspect of this artist was the contradiction between his aloofness, his *cool*ness, and the beauty and immediacy of his music. This was a deep paradox to consider: How could the song be so deeply felt, while the musician seemed so indifferent? But the postwar culture fed on such contradictions. After all, this was the same generation that invented the antihero—another paradoxical concept of great influence. Culture and counterculture were interacting and merging in surprising new hybrids, with bohemians, beatniks, and other outsiders finding themselves celebrated as icons and heroes by the mainstream.

Cinema stars such as James Dean and Marlon Brando brought to the silver screen the same peculiar combination of dangerous aloofness and vulnerability that Davis created in jazz clubs. Jack Kerouac, Allen Ginsberg, and other writers attempted to bring the jazz aesthetic into their literary works, with various degrees of success. Indeed when Kerouac produced a manifesto on the "Essentials of Spontaneous Prose," he adopted an attitude and methodology seemingly more aligned with contemporary jazz currents than with any previous guides to literary technique. And when Norman Mailer proclaimed that "the source of Hip is the Negro," in his 1957 essay "The White Negro: Superficial Reflections on the Hipster," he encountered some hostility and ridicule, but the debate itself indicated how the jazz ethos had spread far beyond the nightclubs and into the heart of contemporary culture. "The presence of Hip as the working philosophy in the sub-worlds of American life is probably due to jazz," Mailer wrote, and its message was bound to appeal to "that post-war band of adventurers who (some consciously, some by osmosis) had absorbed the lessons of disillusionment and disgust of the twenties, the depression and the war."

Davis himself showed little interest in such matters. No one did more than Davis to shape the cool aesthetic, yet he rarely spoke about it in interviews, and by the late 1960s the trumpeter had embraced a radically new musical vision, based on a fusion of jazz and rock. Listeners who compared his recordings from 1949, 1959, and 1969 could hardly believe that the same artist had produced such disparate works. True, his trumpet playing never lost its pathos and emotional intensity, and his presence onstage remained ever dour. Almost everything else had changed.

Just as the cool aesthetic had existed before Davis, it continued to thrive after he had moved on to other things. Jazz players today still study and emulate the Davis recordings of the 1950s. His 1959 release *Kind of Blue* remains the best-selling jazz recording of all time, and his other albums from the era would dominate any list of the most popular or influential jazz music. But Davis's legacy goes beyond the music itself, and his paradoxical attitudes—prickliness mixed with vulnerability, assertiveness blended with a haughty reserve, indifference suffused with the deepest emotion—have become lasting elements in our perception of the contradictions inherent in the artistic life, and even today contribute to our understanding of the cool.

Bibliography: Miles Davis, *Miles: The Autobiography,* with Quincy Troupe (New York, 1989). Gerald Early, ed., *Miles Davis and American Culture* (St. Louis, 2001). John Leland, *Hip: The History* (New York, 2004). Lewis McAdams, *Birth of the Cool: Beat, Bebop and the American Avant-Garde* (New York, 2001). Jeff Sultanof, *Miles Davis: Birth of the Cool: Scores from the Original Parts* (Milwaukee, 2002). *Discography:* Miles Davis, *The Birth of the Cool* (Capitol, 1957).

TED GIOIA

1950, November 28
A Jackson Pollock exhibition opens at Betty Parsons Gallery in New York

"DAMNED BUSY PAINTING"

On November 28, 1950, a one-man show of paintings by Jackson Pollock opened at the Betty Parsons Gallery on 57th Street. Good photographs survive of the exhibition, and though they do not solve every problem concerning the layout—are we being shown mirror views of a single big space, or do we move from an entrance gallery (complete with ashtray) into a second room with no daylight? —several facts stand out. It looks as if Pollock visited 57th Street in advance and measured the exact height of the gallery from floor to lintel. *One: Number 31, 1950* and *Autumn Rhythm: Number 30, 1950* are both eight feet ten inches high—and so is the black-and-white *Number 32, 1950,* hung on the wall to *One's* left. They are paintings tailor-made for the space—"site-specific" would be a later way of putting it. They go from floor to ceiling (it matters that optically they seem to rise up grandly from ground level), and one has the feeling that Pollock would have liked them to swallow the whole wall had not Parsons put in a word for her ashtray and ventilation grid.

Viewers needed air. And maybe nicotine. Since 1950 the world has got used to mammoth paintings, lording it over the rooms they find themselves in; but still, half a century later, there is a distinct whiff of claustrophobia coming off the Parsons documents. In another photograph, the camera has moved in lower and closer to *Number 32,* and the gallery ceiling slams down dark as a coffin lid. Lee Krasner, Pollock's wife, seems to be trying to inject a bit of levity into the situation by having a friend's dog go up on its hind legs. But it takes more than dog tricks to divest these rooms of their gravity.

Gravity, and certainly strangeness. These are pictures meant to dictate the terms of the viewer's engagement with them, and therefore they risk being domineering; but they are not, in my opinion, pictures intended to aggress or offend. I say "in my opinion" a bit nervously, because already in 1950 opinions about just this aspect of Pollock's intentions (and effect) were fiercely divided. Was Pollock a merchant of agonies and extreme states, a dismantler of pictorial order? Many thought so. Some approvingly. Or was he the inheritor of a great tradition of large-scale, wall-size decorative painting, rooted in the experience of landscape, whose masters were Monet, Bonnard, and Matisse? Painting whose highest ambition was to cradle and soothe and surround. Remember that one of the big three pictures at Parsons was called *Autumn Rhythm,* and another, only slightly smaller —this one even more reminiscent of Monet in its color scheme—*Lavender Mist. Lavender Mist* is visible on the wall to the left of *Autumn Rhythm.* It did very well, just a few months later, as backdrop for a model wearing spring fashion in *Vogue,* and Pollock, in a letter, seemed on the whole pleased. One of Pollock's friends proposed at the time that he give the great green-and-brown *Number 31* the title *Lowering Weather.* The title the painter eventually fixed on—the simple, all-enveloping word *One*—was, I believe, deliberately bland. There was a touch of Zen in the air. "My concern is with the rhythms of nature," Pollock jotted in a notebook, "the way the ocean moves . . . the Ocean's what the expanse of the West was for me." "I have a definite feeling for the West: the vast horizontality of the land, for instance; here only the Atlantic Ocean gives you that." "There was a reviewer a while back who wrote that my pictures didn't have any beginning or any end. He didn't mean it as a compliment, but it was." Pollock hated the notion, which was already a cliché in 1950, that he was some kind of slightly highbrow Man from Laramie, whirling a lariat and thriving on lawlessness. "NO CHAOS DAMN IT" he telegrammed *Time* a few days before the Parsons show opened—it was the term "chaos" applied to his art that had set him off. "DAMNDED BUSY PAINTING AS YOU CAN SEE BY MY SHOW COMING UP NOV 28." Of course *Time* loved it. Two cusswords in as many sentences. These artists . . .

In *Time.* In *Vogue.* Does it matter? Maybe only in the sense that the episodes demonstrate how hard the culture worked, from the beginning, to fit Pollock into an interpretive frame. *Vogue* seemed to think he was a provider of backdrops, glittering and elegant. "Wallpaper" had been a convenient term of dismissal ever since Pollock had started painting big and abstract, with the picture built out of same-size, seemingly repetitive drips and throws. The new paintings—bigger and sometimes more undifferentiated than ever—took the wallpaper metaphor and literalized it. *Time,* by contrast, couldn't get away from the stories, which Pollock himself had put in circulation over the previous two years, that the new paintings were done on the ground, in a kind of ballet with sticks and cans and Duco enamel. And weren't the results—look at *Number 32* especially—disheveled and staccato, as opposed to suave and recessive? Weren't the paintings pieces of bad handwriting, or tangles of psychic barbed wire? Didn't we all, at least sometimes, feel like barking as they closed in?

In the half century since the Parsons show, enthusiasm for (and opposition to) Pollock's painting has gone on veering between the *Time* and *Vogue* alternatives. Or it has done some dialectical footwork, and argued that the best Pollocks manage to be agonized and luscious at the same time. There is something to this. Anyone standing in front of *Autumn Rhythm* or *Lavender Mist,* and forgetting the

Jackson Pollock exhibition at the Betty Parsons Gallery, November 28–December 16, 1950

slightly too glib guidance offered by the titles, will, I think, before long get to see the paintings double—double in terms of pictorial pace and structure, and double in terms of affect. *Lavender Mist* is brittle and dangerous as well as vaporous and swell.

That Pollock is capable of holding this kind of balance in a painting—and "balance" is too comfortable a word for the tense interpenetration of aspects that happens when things go best—is one clue to his paintings' staying power. But only one. There are plenty of other abstract paintings from around midcentury, done by Pollock's competitors, that strike a balance between lonely (jagged) improvisation and final sumptuous unison. Willem de Kooning comes to mind. What is ultimately at stake in the Pollocks—and what marks him off from most of his contemporaries, I feel—is the *character* of the pictorial unity he creates. For after all, what is the unity—the coming together of aspects, the sense of experience as all one thing—available to the seeing body in 1950? Surely it is different from that of a body in 1850, say, or 1925. Can a painting state, and maybe even perfect, the sense of totality belonging to a precise historical moment? And do so without fudging—without imposing unity, as some kind of template, on the random unruliness of events?

The central way in which paintings speak to such issues, I believe, is in their creation of space. It is in experiencing how *space* is offered to us in a Pollock—with what degree of density or proximity, oriented to us or beckoning us into the abyss—that viewers will go on finding themselves, for a while, back in the midtwentieth century. "The only time I heard him use the word 'landscape' in connection with his own work," said Lee Krasner, "was one morning before going to the studio, when he said, 'I saw a landscape the likes of which no human being could have seen.'" This connects with what the most serious critics at the time saw in the drip paintings—Parker Tyler, for example, writing in response to an earlier Parsons show:

> Jackson Pollock has put the . . . labyrinth at an infinite and unreachable distance, a distance beyond the stars—a non-human distance . . . If one felt vertigo before Pollock's differentiations of space, then truly one would be lost . . . But we are safely looking at it, seeing it steadily and seeing it whole, from a point outside. Only man, in his paradoxical role of the superman, can achieve such a feat of absolute contemplation: the sight of an image of space *in which he does not exist.*

The main task of a critic of Pollock, it follows, is to describe as precisely as possible what the painter's "differentiations of space" amount to. In order to do so, I shall concentrate on a painting that had been shown at Parsons earlier in 1950. It was titled *Number 1, 1949*—a big painting, almost nine feet long, though not yet scaled up to *Autumn Rhythm*'s enormity. Pollock and his dealers evidently thought it was something of a classic: no other painting of his was shown so often in the ten years following.

Just now I used the word "proximity" in talking about a space's special character (or lack of it), and that is the term that occurs first in front of *Number 1, 1949*. Space in this painting seems close to us. It has the character of something materialized, something palpable and physically present. This does not mean that interval and emptiness have simply disappeared, to be replaced by tangled solids. Still less does it mean the picture is flat. I do not even experience the space within the rectangle as full, exactly, or crowded. The thrown lines seem to inhabit—to trace out—a void. Space is not fragmented or fragmentary, but neither is it homogeneous. It's not shallow or obstructed. The mind and eye move through Pollock's latticework as through a forest of undersea weed, giving way to the eye's least touch. The filling of the surface is done lightly, almost playfully (the final whiplashes of white are sheer coloratura). This much energy and entanglement, it seems, are necessary if the present form of our apprehension of space is to materialize.

Space, to repeat, is close to us. It is not shattered or dismembered, but maybe we could say it is *perturbed*. There is something volatile about it. I guess this is a quality that the space borrows from the apparent velocity of the lines that build it up—those white whiplashes again. They are demonstrations of mastery, but also of impatience and risk. And this range of affect is reinforced by the painting's extraordinary color—its flaring, intransigent whiteness, and the way the white is abetted by aluminum silver and pink and yellow. No reproduction will capture this. The painting is incandescent, lit from within; but it does not dazzle, it is not glaring. It burns coldly, like the afterglow of a distant big bang. The pink is the trace of primordial heat.

This leads us back to 1950. January of that year was the month when President Truman ordered work to go ahead on the "superbomb," the possibility of which had been touted in the press all through the previous year. The road to Bikini was open. Part of Pollock's achievement, then—or so I believe—was to ingest the fear and fascination that accompanied this new turn in the nuclear arms race. I did say "part of," and I did say "ingest."

That is, the achievement of *Number 1, 1949*—and of the whole hanging at Parsons the following November—was not to illustrate the fear and fascination of the nuclear but *to materialize them in a specific medium*. And further to propose, perhaps ruefully (perhaps against Pollock's wishes), the *beauty* in the fear—the stillness at the heart of the fissile storm. The color, above all, is the fear and the beauty. But so is the tempo of the paint across the picture surface—accelerated, almost runaway, but held (just) under control of brain and hand.

Color; tempo; and finally, size. *Number 1, 1949*, to give its precise dimensions, is 63 inches high and 104 inches wide. *Autumn Rhythm* is 8 feet 10 inches by 17 feet 8. The smaller painting is small only as compared to what Pollock did next. It is imposing, but not grandiose. It is not triumphant or world-historical. If the Bomb is in question, then it is a Bomb miniaturized and cooled down. A model in a ballgown could stand in front of it.

The question of size—of how big or small a painting had to be in order to register the bigness and smallness of its time—is at the heart of Pollock's abstraction. *Number 1, 1949* has the question under control. One key to the painting's classic status, in my opinion, is the feeling one has in front of it that the rectangle is exactly as large as the space inside it requires it to be. Is this still true of the paintings in Parsons Gallery in November? I wonder. Let the reader look back at the photo of room one, and notice at either end of *Autumn Rhythm* two vertical stacks of four paintings on Masonite, each twenty-two inches square. In context, the paintings are atoms, nuclei—acts of fusion or condensation, setting off their neighbors' giant scatter. They function as measures of the big paintings' bigness. They suggest what bigness may mean.

Pollock's abstraction came to an end, or anyway lost its way, almost as soon as the show at Parsons was over. Pollock hit the bottle (he had been sober for the previous three years). By 1954 he was bloated and inactive. By 1956 he was dead, age forty-four, driving under the influence. The story is sordid—a woman passenger died with him in the Oldsmobile—and it is easy to have it color our sense of the previous achievement. That would be wrong. There is nothing very unusual about an artist's period of truly innovative—truly motivated—abstraction being all too brief. It comes with the territory. Abstract art stems from the conviction that in present conditions the means with which painting can figure a world—or the loss of "world" (it comes to the same thing)—are radically restricted. Color detached from reference, line as pure velocity, size as physical fact. These things can be made to speak to an age, but maybe necessarily not for long. Bigness becomes gigantism. Atoms confetti. Spring fashions take over.

Bibliography: Francis O'Connor and Eugene Thaw, eds., *Jackson Pollock: A Catalogue Raisonné of Paintings, Drawings, and Other Works* (New Haven, CT, 1978). Michael Leja, *Reframing Abstract Expressionism* (New Haven, CT, 1993). Ellen Landau, *Jackson Pollock* (New York, 1989). John O'Brian, ed., *Clement Greenberg: The Collected Essays and Criticism* (Chicago, 1986–1993). Kirk Varnedoe and Pepe Karmel, eds., *Jackson Pollock: New Approaches* (New York, 1999).

T. J. CLARK

1951

Frank O'Hara takes a job as sales clerk at MoMA

A POET AMONG PAINTERS

It was the Matisse retrospective that opened on November 14, 1951, that prompted the twenty-five-year-old poet Frank O'Hara to apply for a job selling postcards, publications, and tickets at the front desk of the Museum of Modern Art. He had settled in the city some three months earlier, and was looking for a way both to satisfy his burgeoning interest in the New York art scene and to earn enough to live on. He loved Matisse and he loved MoMA, and he needed a job that would allow him a little time to write. Duly hired, he found his duties not too arduous; friends remember him slipping out of his booth to type up poems during lulls in activity. When the poet James Schuyler dropped in for a visit he found O'Hara simultaneously selling tickets and at work on a poem, since lost but perhaps Matisse-inspired, entitled "It's the Blue!" Nestled beside the yellow pad on which he was composing was a translation of André Breton's *Young Cherry Trees Secured against Hares.*

This initial stint at the museum lasted only a few months, but four years later O'Hara took up the post of special assistant in the museum's International Program. He played a major role in organizing traveling exhibits, the most significant of which was the 1958–59 show The New American Painting, the first major exhibition of American abstract expressionism in Europe. In 1960 he was appointed assistant curator, and in 1965, the year before his untimely death, associate curator. He also published numerous reviews of museum and gallery shows in magazines such as *Art News* and *Kulchur,* and a monograph on Jackson Pollock. From almost the start of his poetic career, O'Hara's work paid handsome tribute to the inspiration he received from painters and painting. "Picasso made me tough and quick," opens "Memorial Day 1950," an early declaration of artistic intent; "Once he got his axe going everyone was upset." The poem goes on to render homage to Paul Klee, to Max Ernst, and to a series of other iconoclastic artist heroes, including the fathers of Dada (Tristan Tzara and co.), Auden, Pasternak, Rimbaud, Gertrude Stein, and Apollinaire, with whom O'Hara frequently found himself compared as a "poet among painters."

His best-known poem about painting is undoubtedly "Why I Am Not a Painter," which describes a series of visits he pays to the studio of the abstract expressionist Mike Goldberg:

> I am not a painter, I am a poet.
> Why? I think I would rather be
> a painter, but I am not. Well,
>
> For instance, Mike Goldberg
> is starting a painting. I drop in.
> "Sit down and have a drink" he
> says. I drink; we drink. I look
> up. "You have SARDINES in it."
> "Yes, it needed something there."
> "Oh." I go and the days go by
> and I drop in again. The painting
> is going on, and I go, and the days
> go by. I drop in. The painting is
> finished. "Where's SARDINES?"
> All that's left is just
> letters, "It was too much," Mike says.

Art, in other words, is as much about what gets left out as what gets put in. O'Hara proceeds to relate his own compositional procedures:

> But me? One day I am thinking of
> a color: orange. I write a line
> about orange. Pretty soon it is a
> whole page of words, not lines.
> Then another page. There should be

so much more, not of orange, of
words, of how terrible orange is
and life. Days go by. It is even in
prose, I am a real poet. My poem
is finished and I haven't mentioned
orange yet. It's twelve poems, I call
it ORANGES. And one day in a gallery
I see Mike's painting, called SARDINES.

The deftly handled antitheses of this poem reveal much about the appeal of abstraction to poets and painters of the period. As Mike Goldberg removes the literal SARDINES from his painting, replacing them with "just / letters," so O'Hara's twelve prose poems called *Oranges* (published in 1953 to accompany an exhibition at the Tibor de Nagy gallery of Grace Hartigan's *Oranges* paintings) never actually get around to mentioning the color that inspired them—except in the title. The poem is hardly an explanation of why the poet is not a painter, but rather a spoof-parable that develops, in its faux-naïf way, a sophisticated set of analogies between the artistic processes that result in O'Hara's poetry and in Goldberg's painting. In both, the figurative is replaced by a fascination with the materiality of the medium (painting is broken down into paint and poetry into words), and both artworks are represented in an ongoing relationship with time ("the days go by") that only ends when each is finished and displayed. The poem subtly enacts O'Hara's belief in the interrelatedness of the arts, but its insistence on the obvious differences between the two in fact works to preserve an idealizing sense of the mysteries of artistic vocation. On one level a witty tribute to an artistic brother-in-arms, the poem is also a defense of their shared commitment to the ideals of experiment and improvisation.

O'Hara was quintessentially an urban poet. "I love this hairy city," he declares in "To the Mountains in New York," and his work teems with the happenings of the city's streets, with the names and doings of friends, with parties and gallery openings and nights out drinking in bars and ending in the wee hours at clubs, with visits to the movies and museums and concerts and the ballet. "One need never leave the confines of New York," he asserted in the prose poem "Meditations in an Emergency," "to get all the greenery one wishes—I can't even enjoy a blade of grass unless I know there's a subway handy, or a record store or some other sign that people do not totally *regret* life." Like the New York of Walt Whitman and Hart Crane (along with William Carlos Williams, the only poets O'Hara concedes are "better than the movies"), O'Hara's metropolis is alive with erotic possibilities, and a number of poems pay explicit homage to the pleasures of cruising: in "Homosexuality" he offers an impressionistic guide to the "merits" of various latrines ("14th Street is drunken and credulous, / 53rd tries to tremble but is too at rest"), while in "Grand Central" the station itself watches with approval as a messenger's trousers are unzipped, and he is "relieved" of his "missile."

Perhaps the most striking feature of O'Hara's oeuvre is its immediacy: invited by an editor of an anthology to outline his poetic theories, he responded with a hilarious mock-manifesto, "Personism," in which he compared writing poetry to fleeing from a mugger: "You just go on your nerve. If someone's chasing you down the street with a knife you just run, you don't turn around and shout, 'Give it up! I was a track star for Minneola Prep!'" As for the technical aspects of composition, he continues, well, "that's just common sense: if you're going to buy a pair of pants you want them to be tight enough so everyone will want to go to bed with you."

His work did depend, however, on the notion, and actual existence of, a coterie of similarly minded, artistically gifted friends (some famous, some not so) who would get his jokes, enjoy his gossip, circulate his manuscripts, and respond with poems and paintings of their own, thereby keeping the whole circle of creation "humming," to use one of his strongest terms of approbation. While he doesn't openly mythologize his friends in the manner of, say, Yeats, he does induce in the reader a longing to be part of such a witty, lively, talented crowd. His poems, like those of Byron, radiate an insouciant, intoxicating certainty that he is where it's *at,* and accordingly the social occasions he commemorates exude a hipness and glamour that seem a direct result of what John Ashbery once called O'Hara's *culte de moi.* This *culte* can become addictive, and it is what enables him to present even the to-ings and fro-ings of his lunch hours in midtown Manhattan as alluring. Here he is preparing for a weekend visiting friends in East Hampton, in a poem called "The Day Lady Died":

> I go on to the bank
> and Miss Stillwagon (first name Linda I once heard)
> doesn't even look up my balance for once in her life
> and in the GOLDEN GRIFFIN I get a little Verlaine
> for Patsy with drawings by Bonnard although I do
> think of Hesiod, trans. Richmond Lattimore or
> Brendan Behan's new play or *Le Balcon* or *Les Nègres*
> of Genet, but I don't, I stick with Verlaine
> after practically going to sleep with quandariness
>
> and for Mike I just stroll into the PARK LANE
> Liquor Store and ask for a bottle of Strega and
> then I go back where I came from to 6th Avenue
> and the tobacconist in the Ziegfeld Theatre and
> casually ask for a carton of Gauloises and a carton
> of Picayunes, and a NEW YORK POST with her face on it

How many male poets of the fifties presented themselves in the act of shopping? Certainly you don't find Robert Lowell or Anthony Hecht recounting expeditions to Bloomingdale's. The poetic persona enacted here is an intriguing one: the fact that Miss Stillwagon usually looks up his bank balance suggests he is frequently overdrawn, but in his neobohemian way he is proud rather than ashamed of it. He is also proud of the finely honed, slightly camp connoisseurship that enables him to choose Verlaine over Hesiod and Brendan Behan, despite almost going to sleep with "quandariness"—itself a choice word—as the requisite gift for the sensitive Patsy (the short-story writer Patsy Southgate), while for the hard-drinking Mike Goldberg he buys alcohol. The poem names them only as Patsy and Mike—suggesting the imagined reader of the poem is likely to be a member of this set, and on first-name terms with all concerned.

"In a capitalist country," O'Hara once observed, "fun is everything." Art is presented in these stanzas as just one more purchasable commodity to be circulated and consumed among friends. Note also the overseas provenance of what he buys, or thinks about buying: Gauloises and Verlaine and Bonnard from France, Strega from Italy, Brendan Behan from Ireland, Hesiod from ancient Greece. O'Hara is rarely explicitly nationalistic, but the range of items available for purchase here suggests that New York is now the central emporium of the world, the place where one's shopper's identity can be most fully explored and developed—the place where, for those with taste, means, and friends, capitalism can be *most* fun.

The face in question on the front of the *New York Post* is that of Billie Holiday, who, O'Hara discovers, has just died. The news triggers a memory of the last time he saw her sing:

> and I am sweating a lot by now and thinking of
> leaning on the john door in the 5 SPOT
> while she whispered a song along the keyboard
> to Mal Waldron and everyone and I stopped breathing

Like "Why I Am Not a Painter," "The Day Lady Died" is a poem celebrating the performance of an artist working in a different medium, though on this occasion the dissimilarities between the two are more pointedly stressed: somewhat in the manner of, say, Wordsworth in "The Solitary Reaper," O'Hara is inclined to discover in the female singer an enviable example of immediacy and authenticity that contrasts with his own self-consciousness, his slightly theatrical anxieties about his various consumer choices.

Holiday's art, as O'Hara recalls it, induced in him a state of aesthetic ecstasy, and one the poem now re-creates as a further gift, in addition to the book and liquor, for the consumption of his friends. O'Hara last saw Holiday perform at the Five Spot a couple of years before her death; her voice was by then a ravaged whisper, and by singing at all she was breaking the law, for after an arrest for heroin use she was forbidden to appear in any venue that served alcohol. It is typical of O'Hara, who addressed so many of his poems directly to individuals such as Mike and Patsy, to present her as whispering her song, not to a paying audience, but to her accompanist, Mal Waldron. That the poem is indeed the elegy its title first intimated only becomes clear with its concluding words: the sublime suspension ("and everyone and I stopped breathing") that he shared with the other jazz aficionados is played off against the suppressed recognition that she has now literally stopped breathing forever. Witty, charming, moving, sophisticated, and above all *knowing*, "The Day Lady Died" illustrates O'Hara's power to achieve a

graceful and dramatic fusion of the performative and the spontaneous, of the poem's occasion and the poem itself.

Bibliography: Jim Elledge, ed., *Frank O'Hara: To Be True to a City* (Ann Arbor, MI, 1990). Brad
Gooch, *City Poet: The Life and Times of Frank O'Hara* (New York, 1993). Frank O'Hara, *Art Chronicles* (New York, 1975); *The Collected Poems,* ed. Donald Allen (New York, 1971; California, 1995);
Selected Poems, ed. Mark Ford (New York, 2008); *Standing Still and Walking in New York,* ed. Donald Allen (San Francisco, 1975).

MARK FORD

1951
Holden raises hell

THE CATCHER IN THE RYE

Some critics don't like it. *Catholic World* notes its "formidably excessive use of
amateur swearing and coarse language," and there seems to be some question as
to whether an alienated, hard-drinking, chain-smoking flunkie like its adolescent
protagonist, Holden Caulfield, is going to prove a good influence on the young.
Other critics, though, "chuckle and . . . even laugh aloud," and many compare
Holden to Huck Finn. Sociologist David Riesman, who has just published *The
Lonely Crowd* (1950), assigns *Catcher* to his Harvard undergrads as a case study.
Still, the overall critical reception is within the normal bounds of book publishing; Harcourt Brace, which rejected the book, does not yet have much to live
down. As for sales, well, the book has done fine in hardcover but, what with the
recent invention of the perfect binding—a book binding using glue rather than
stitching—there is now the paperback to consider. Doesn't *Catcher* seem like the
sort of book that might do well in the new format?

And so it does, going on to sell over 60 million copies. Moreover, in 1956, some
dam in critical interest seems to burst. Study after study is published; the 1950s
are dubbed "the Decade of Salinger"; contemporaneous writers complain of neglect. Holden Caulfield is compared not only to Huck Finn but to Billy Budd,
David Copperfield, Natty Bumppo, Quentin Compson, Ishmael, Peter Pan,
Hamlet, Jesus Christ, Adam, Stephen Dedalus and Leopold Bloom put together.
What critic George Steiner calls the "Salinger industry" swells fantastically, until
it sits like a large, determined bird on a bunker-like egg.

Where did this start? In a 1940 letter to a friend, a twenty-one-year-old Salinger describes his novel in progress as "autobiographical"; decades later, too, in an
interview with a high school reporter—the only interview he's ever given—Salinger says, "My boyhood was very much the same as that of the boy in the book." Of
course, there are differences. Unlike Holden, Salinger is, among other things, a
half-Jewish, half-Catholic brotherless World War II vet who attended a military

academy. He did, though, like Holden, flunk out of prep school, and he was also, like Holden, manager of his high school fencing team, in which capacity he really did, according to his daughter, Margaret, once lose the team gear en route to a meet.

More important, Salinger seems to have shared Holden's disaffection. Numerous youthful acquaintances remember him as sardonic, rant-prone, a loner. Margaret Salinger likewise traces the alienation in the book to him, though it does not reflect for her either her father's innate temperament or difficult adolescence so much as his experiences of anti-Semitism and, as an adult, war. Where Salinger fought in some of the bloodiest and most senseless campaigns of World War II and apparently suffered a nervous breakdown toward its end, shortly after which—while still in Europe—he is known to have been working on *Catcher*—it is hardly surprising that Holden's reactions should evoke not only adolescent turmoil but also the awful seesaw of a vet's return to civilian life. Holden may be a rebel without a cause, but he is not a rebel without an explanation: it is easy to read the death of his brother as a stand-in for unspeakable trauma. And witness the notable vehemence with which Holden talks about the war—declaring, for instance, "I'm sort of glad they've got the atomic bomb invented. If there's ever another war, I'm going to sit right the hell on top of it. I'll volunteer for it, I swear to God I will."

But what of Margaret Salinger's theory regarding anti-Semitism? She characterizes Salinger as sensitive about his Jewishness, with good cause: a few years before her father's arrival at the military academy, the picture of a Jewish student who had graduated second in the class was printed on a perforated page in the yearbook, so it could be torn out. We note, too, in Ian Hamilton's unofficial biography, a letter from the father of a girl to whom Salinger once proposed, describing him as "an odd fellow. He didn't mingle much with the other guests [at their Daytona Beach hotel] . . . He was—well, is he Jewish? I thought that might explain the way he acted . . . I thought he had a chip on his shoulder."

Interestingly, Salinger's sister, in an interview, while supporting the anti-Semitism thesis, focuses on his in-betweenness as well. "It wasn't nice to be part-Jewish in those days," she says. "It was no asset to be Jewish either, but at least you belonged somewhere. This way you were neither fish nor fowl." Additionally complicating the picture is the fact that Salinger seems to have grown up revered by his Irish-Catholic mother but disparaged by his Jewish father, who wanted him to enter the family food-import business. Fish and fowl, adored and criticized, Salinger was remembered by some military academy classmates as a guy whose conversation "was laced with sarcasm," but by others as "a regular guy," and by teachers as "quiet, thoughtful, always anxious to please." Strikingly, this sometimes scathing student wrote a class song so convincingly straight ("Goodbyes are said, we march ahead/Success we go to find./Our forms are gone from Valley Forge/Our hearts are left behind") it is still sung at graduation. He edited the yearbook, too, with what so completely passed as earnest conscientiousness that though it is tempting, given his active interest in acting, to view his activities as virtuoso performances of deep subterfuge, they might also be imagined to have been painfully disconcerting. Holden's description of himself as "the most terrific liar you ever saw" might well have applied to Salinger, and Salinger's own judgment of his divided nature, in this era before "situational selves," might well have involved the word that haunts his book, "phony."

A poignant part of Salinger's genius seems, in any case, to include the way that he transmutes—as he perhaps feels he must—his particular issues and injuries into a more enigmatic "autobiography" of alienation. And it can only be counted ironic that the result comes to exemplify American authenticity: like James Dean, Holden Caulfield is for many the very picture of the postwar rebel. Young, crude, misunderstood, he stands up to conformist pressures, is drawn to innocence, et cetera. Never mind that Holden is white, male, straight, sophisticated, rich, and a product of the 1940s; he personifies anguished resistance to '50s America—indeed, for many, America's truest self. Whether Salinger intended his creation to assume anything like this role—indeed, if he had any notion of the projection of a national identity as a desirable literary goal (as did his contemporary, John Updike, for example)—is unclear.

And is there not something if not phony, then at least a little wacky, about Holden's enshrinement in American culture? To some degree, academia took its cue from the culture; *Catcher*'s skyrocketing sales amid the mid-'50s "youthquake" fairly demanded explanation. Critics like George Steiner saw the book as all too fitting for the paperback market—short, easy to read, and flattering "the very ignorance and moral shallowness of his young readers." But others saw its success as a promising development, indicative of something enduringly young, defiant, and truth-loving in the American spirit. Drawing on the work of Donald Pease, critic Leerom Medovoi has described how a new cold war American canon arose around this time, in which American Renaissance works like *Moby-Dick* and *Adventures of Huckleberry Finn* were cast as a "coherent tradition that dramatized the emergence of American freedom as a literary ideal, somehow already waging its heroic struggle against a prefigured totalitarianism." He provocatively describes how *Catcher* came to join those works and how the lot of them, read as national allegories, located the very essence of Americanness in principled dissent, even as McCarthyism cast it as un-American.

No doubt other scholars, being scholars, disagree. Still, Medovoi's ideas may, in conjunction with the book's Mona Lisa–like ambiguity, help explain how *Catcher in the Rye* came to occupy what by other measures seems a strangely high place in American letters, for it strays notably from mainstream literary values. The novel is, to begin with, often precious and sentimental. What's more, while the critic Alfred Kazin is, I think, on the mark in ascribing the excitement of Salinger's stories to his "intense, his almost compulsive need to fill in each inch of his canvas, each moment of his scene," the writing in *Catcher* is nowhere near so alive with *moti mentali*. And the whole, too, is slight. Salinger, who has published only this one novel to date, once characterized himself as "a dash man and not a miler"; and indeed, though *Catcher*'s opening episodes explode with life, the whole reads like a novella that only just managed to shed its diminutive. It does not develop appreciatively through its middle, for example; Holden neither deepens nor comes to share the stage with other characters. Instead the book starts to feel narrow and maniacally one-note; reading, one wonders whether its real contribution lies in its anticipation of Christopher Lasch's *The Culture of Narcissism.* In contrast to, say, *The Great Gatsby,* this is manifestly not a book to be studied for insight into the novel form.

Unless, that is, one is interested in how a book can hit home with no evidence of its author's ever having read Henry James's "The Art of Fiction." *Catcher* demonstrates, among other things, how variously and mysteriously novels finally work, and how even sophisticated audiences tend to genuflect to art but yield to testimony. We are enthralled by voices that tell it like it is. Or, in the case of *Catcher,* that seem to. My sixteen-year-old son—who has, coincidentally, been reading *Catcher* for his tenth-grade English class even as I write—puts it this way: "You feel [with *Catcher*] like you're in on the real story," but in the end *Catcher* is a break from reality rather than a source of information about it. He likens Holden's appeal to that of Harry Potter: just as Harry speaks to children because Harry is like them, only "special" and able to do magic, Holden interests my son because Holden rebels and "gets away with it" in a way my son guesses—rightly—he would never. In short, one part of *Catcher*'s appeal lies in its purveyance of fantasy. This can have value—helping an audience reflect on the real limits of its freedom, for example—but can support solipsism, too. Alfred Kazin takes the harsh view, characterizing Salinger's audience as "the vast number who have been released by our society to think of themselves as endlessly sensitive, spiritually alone, [and] gifted, and whose suffering lies in the narrowing of their consciousness to themselves"—ranks that would no doubt include Mark David Chapman, who had a copy of *Catcher* in his pocket when he assassinated "phony" John Lennon, as well as John Hinckley who, also under Holden's influence, attempted to assassinate Ronald Reagan.

Other explanations of the book's popularity, though, must include its outrageous humor and must-read status, as well as its author's celebrity. Aggressively reclusive, Salinger's discomfort with the commodification of his work and person leads him, first, to shun all publicity—no interviews, no author bios—and then, in 1966, to cease publication. Still, despite his reported contempt for hippies and his support of the Vietnam War, he becomes, for the '60s counterculture, the consummate dropout. And though in subsequent years he is repeatedly caught in an unflattering light, he retains an aura of martyred integrity, which the recurring censorship of *Catcher* only intensifies.

Academia, too, presses on. Critic Alan Nadel, noting that the cold war blossomed in the period between 1946—when, for unknown reasons, Salinger withdrew from publication a ninety-page version of the book—and 1951, when it was published, interestingly sees in Holden not so much heroic nonconformity as a reflection of McCarthyism. Many features of the narrative—the obsession with control in its rhetorical patterns, as well as its preoccupation with duplicity and the compulsion to "name names"—bespeak, for Nadel, a psychic imprisonment in which the performance of truth-telling can never yield truth. And indeed, the insistence of phrases such as "I really mean it" and "to tell the truth" do finally

seem to signal quicksand more than terra firma. Holden at story's end is under interrogation—more isolated than independent, more defeated than defiant. "D. B.
[Holden's brother] asked me what I thought about all this stuff I just finished telling you about . . . If you want to know the truth, I don't know what I think about
it," he says, touchingly. "I don't know what I think about it": Is this the author of
the military-academy class hymn wondering about the act and value of writing?
Has Holden, the avatar of American authenticity, become an avatar of American
inauthenticity? Here Salinger's funhouse proves, once again, I think, ours.

Bibliography: Paul Alexander, *Salinger* (Los Angeles, 1999). Harold Bloom, ed., *Holden Caulfield: Modern Critical Views* (New York, 1990). Catherine Crawford, ed., *If You Really Want to Hear
about It: Writers on Salinger and His Work* (New York, 2006). Warren French, *J. D. Salinger, Revis-
ited* (Boston, 1988). Ian Hamilton, *In Search of J. D. Salinger* (New York, 1988). Joyce Maynard, *At
Home in the World* (New York, 1998). Leerom Medovoi, *Rebels* (Durham, NC, 2005). Alan Nadel,
Containment Culture: American Narratives, Postmodernism, and the Atomic Age (Durham, NC, 1995).
Margaret A. Salinger, *Dream Catcher* (New York, 2000). J. D. Salinger, *The Catcher in the Rye* (1951;
New York, 1989). Jack Salzman, ed., *New Essays on The Catcher in the Rye* (Cambridge, 1991). J. P.
Steed, ed., *The Catcher in the Rye: New Essays* (New York, 2002).

GISH JEN

1951

James Jones sets an American romance on a military base in Hawaii

FROM HERE TO ETERNITY

Nothing marks *From Here to Eternity* as a work of popular art so much as the
way it refuses to be deep. It is a profound story, an archetypal story, but its depth
is not due to the layering effect so characteristic of modernist novels. The book is
modern but not modernist. This storyteller practices a craft that caters to our
craving for home truths. That's why this story sticks to matters of life and death,
beginning with an account of the death of the hero's mother and ending with his.
The clash of civilizations is visible but only in soft focus; the things that matter most are not generals and geopolitics but the death of a mere private, whose
long and ignominious torture ends with his accidental killing in a sand trap on an
Army golf course, making the death not grand but graphic.

Again and again, we claim that at a certain moment time stood still and everything changed. Few moments in American history offer more promise to such a
chronicle than Sunday, December 7, 1941. This moment, surely, we say knowingly,
was an exception to history, a shock even to those who caused it. "Until early in
1941, the Japanese naval plan for war against the United States was for their main
fleet to give battle in the waters near the Philippines," wrote Winston Churchill;
the idea of an attack on Pearl Harbor was developed later, and the surprise attack
ruptured the flow of history. For a moment, people had a chance to see "here" and
"eternity" fall into a pattern that allowed history to be read clearly, and in 1951

James Jones seized this opportunity. The playwright and scholar Oscar W. Firkins had written in 1930 that it was a peculiarity of American cultural life that, despite all the gifted writers it had produced, America had gone "undepicted." Ambitious American writers were preoccupied with Europe and ended up turning America "into a ward or suburb of Cosmopolis." Jones, however, was able to do what writers with much greater reputations than his own failed to do.

Perhaps "greater" overstates matters: dead since 1977, Jones has no reputation to speak of. Despite, or perhaps because of, winning the National Book Award for *From Here to Eternity,* Jones disappeared into the woodwork—which is where he came from. Jones was born in Robinson, Illinois, in 1921, in the unromantic, forgotten Midwest. He was neither upper crust nor hardscrabble poor. With his family impoverished by the Depression, the poorly educated Jones enlisted in the army.

Jones took advantage of the great blast in the continuum of time that World War II made. His book—fabulously successful with readers when it appeared in 1951 and then as a film, directed by Fred Zinnemann, starring Montgomery Clift, Burt Lancaster, Deborah Kerr, and Frank Sinatra, in 1953—centers on a hero named Robert E. Lee Prewitt, his rebel yell of a name suggesting the long-past times of frontier Kentucky.

Prewitt arrives in midcentury America looking more like Davy Crockett in a coonskin cap than a modern GI. He is simple-hearted and simple-minded; he behaves with a "meekness that was exquisitely touching." He is the American who was never painted, one of the ones left "undepicted," perhaps because all men like him died at the Alamo. He's in tune with the sorrow songs of white America. He sings and plays those sweet hillbilly songs.

But he is too sensitive a soul for the modern army, and Jones's story defies its romantic yearnings. Jones's army is full of brownnoses and bullies, and it raises up as leaders a tame version of the old warrior, defanged, declawed, professionalized, in neatly ironed boxing trunks and with boxing gloves to buffer the assaults the warrior would deliver if let loose to defend his honor.

The central action of the book is motivated by a deed, a promise, right out of European fairy tales. Prewitt is a real boxer, but his mother makes him promise that if he ever hurts an opponent in a match, he'll never fight again: "Give me your hand on it, boy. It is a deathbed promise, and you'll never break it." "She was a woman of an older time set down in a later world," Jones writes. "Such promises belong in an older, simpler, less complex and more naïve, forgotten time." She does not understand her son's world, yet he abides her word after he blinds a man during a boxing match prior to the action of the novel. The upholding of that promise is the premise of the book, the setup that compels Prewitt to choose defiance over obedience. When his commander orders him to box in the Pearl Harbor base matches, he refuses.

Here, a mysterious good guy who seems in some sense to be God's fool stands up against the military, and the country it represents, and doesn't. The rise of the military as a dominant force in national life meant the end of courage, because the professionals who lead the military abhor true courageousness. Jones does not assume the military is evil. He is as straight as Prewitt is; his book catches the transformation of America straight. Sometimes pulp catches the pulse of a country best.

Prew's nemesis is Captain Dana Holmes, a phony playacting at being a strong man, fancying the nickname "Dynamite," though he does not recognize his troops' snickers. Holmes is obsessed with boxing, his office lined with photos of prizewinners. His interest in other men's boxing seems like an attempt to make up for what he lacks as a man, something we learn a lot about thanks to his wife—with whom he no longer shares physical intimacy—and his chief sergeant, Milton Warden.

Holmes is the worst kind of overlord: the one who believes he is in fact just. "Any man who fucks up gets broken—quick and hard. The Stockade is the place for fuckups until they learn to soldier," he explains. When Prew explains to Holmes that he long ago decided to stop boxing, Holmes orders all under his command to break Prewitt and, when he refuses to break, to destroy him. Prewitt had enlisted for the long haul. A buddy tells Prew, "You cant go your own way . . . Maybe back in the old days, back in the time of the pioneers, a man could do what he wanted to do. But a man cant do that now. He's got to play ball with them."

If the hero of the book is atavistic, so is its genre. Romance pits a good man against a bad man. Northrop Frye: "At its most naïve"—and this work glories in the naïveté of both the story and its hero—romance "is an endless form" (the book is 850 pages long) "in which a central character who never develops or ages goes through one adventure after another until the author collapses. We see this form in comic strips." Jones's simplicity was in line with the growing force of popular culture in America. His novels were written inside a pulp sensibility shaped by Dashiell Hammett, William Wellman, and Frank Capra; while Norman Mailer's *The Naked and the Dead,* the only rival Jones's book has as a big story emerging from the war, ended up as sawdust on the screen, Jones's novels translated into movies as easily as *Gone with the Wind.*

The conflict is clear; the only question is whether or when Prew will break and capitulate or violently react. Zinnemann's *High Noon*—which he directed one year before *From Here to Eternity*—proceeds with the same simplicity. Will Gary Cooper's marshal crumble or lash out? Is survival worth any price, including selling your soul?

The struggle between Prew, natural-born athlete and musician, and Holmes is just the sort of unfair battle that makes the blood of any decent person boil. This game is hideous, a game to the death that usually leaves both parties spiritually dead, if not dead as dogs that fought until they killed each other. "Every soldier knows," barks Holmes, "that good athletics make for good soldiering." Prew tells a buddy: "There's nothin in the ARs says a man has got to jockstrap when he doesn't want to." This army is not about rules but attitude, and Prew's got a bad one, one that gets him arrested on trumped-up charges. This man's army wants no heroes. It doesn't want martyrs, either, but in Prew they get one: a noble man.

Like Melville's Billy Budd, Prew is doing nothing wrong. When Prew is forced to defend his refusal to fight, the colonel dismisses Prew's vow to his mother as sissy talk. Holmes has no respect for tradition, for what is sacred. What is deeply troubling about this story is how well Jones understood and portrayed the fundamental dynamic of American leadership. Jones sensed the dynamic of American life across the next fifty years, a history that is still unfolding.

As Holmes's authority descends by decree of the state, Prewitt and his companions in sin are citizens of a shadow nation, the true nation. Prew's girl is the whore whose fancy name is Lenore but whose real name is Alma—*soul!*—and Karen Holmes, the wife of the captain, and her lover, Milton Warden, the captain's chief sergeant, are the true couple. They all disobey tyrannical authority, like rebels from Adam and Eve to Bartleby and Billy Budd, and they cannot merely escape. Prewitt is haunted by duty—to his mother, to the idea of being humane even deep in the trenches, to the very notion of duty. Milton and Karen embody a love that is modern, egalitarian, and true, and yet they too are constrained, by the circumstances of Karen's marriage.

Just as Warden proves himself to be the man for Karen that Dana Holmes is not, so Warden proves himself to be the good father that Prewitt never had, a sort of paternal authority that his commanding officer—who tries to be pals with his enlisted men—never could be. While Holmes pretends he's the friend of his subordinates, Warden is demanding and withholding. Yet his care for his men is heartening. A warden is someone who makes the machinery work, and Milton Warden is a soldier who wants the military to work. In Warden, Jones invests all his hopes and dreams for American society. Warden speaks as honestly to Prewitt as he does to Karen. In a scene near the end of the book, Warden confesses he's on Prewitt's side but that it hasn't been easy. If the system is to work, Jones is suggesting, it depends on its having guardians like Warden.

Death takes center stage in the second half of the book. The heroes of romances, whether American or European, tend to die badly. But what pleases in this book is the defiance. Prew never gives in. The military brass do not prevail in their plot to break him—though, outraged by the cold-blooded murder by Sergeant Fatso Judson of his friend Private Maggio, the Wop, (played so powerfully by Frank Sinatra in the movie), Prew lashes back and murders Fatso after a fight. Yes, Prew had vowed to his mother he would not fight lest he harm someone, but he had never seen a man, a friend, tortured before. Prew is blessed with the physical prowess that the leaders of the military do not have. He is an instinctive warrior of the ancient sort.

But Prew is eventually defeated, as are Karen and Warden, failing in their dream to steal away and build a new life. Prew's defeat is not simple, because he never sacrifices the integrity of his soul, and the portrayal of the love affair between Karen Holmes and Warden gives readers a portrait of a forbidden but redeeming love. In Jones's story the growth of a bureaucratic military is cancerous, but the evolution of sexual relations in America is fecund.

At first all Warden wants out of Karen's body is revenge on Holmes and a piece of ass. "That's all you really want. Isn't it? That's what you all want. All all of you ever want." Her boldness quickens him: "Warden felt a shiver of fear run down his spine. What the hell is this, Milton? 'Yes,' he said. 'That's what I really want.

But I'll take a drink too.'" A sexy woman with a soul and a brain? *Damn straight.*
She tells him to mix his own drink. She tells him he can have the drink and her,
but he's going to have to say it clearly, out loud to her face, no snickering. "You can
have it, Sergeant, but you'll have to do the work yourself." In the end, after their
bantering and their jousting, they collapse in each other's arms kissing, Warden
consoling both of them. "'There,' he said helplessly. 'There. There.' Feeling the
absurdity, the oppressive impossibility of any human being trying to communicate with and understand another's mind in a life where nothing ever was what it
seemed to be." Here there is no dominance, no subordination. Here sex and talk
are one.

D. H. Lawrence and Leslie Fiedler both claimed there was no portrayal of
deep love between a man and a woman in American literature. For them the only
love between humans in all of American literature that is simultaneously physical
and spiritual is love between men—Queequeg and Ishmael, and Huck and Jim—
but the love that Jones traces in his book proves them wrong. It was captured in
the film in the unforgettable image of Karen and Warden embracing in the surf—
that love that must have been the other great source of pleasure for those who
loved the story. It certainly is for me.

With their new practices of love, Americans found new ways of mating that
were new ways of remaking the world, and it was going to be a world in which
partners mated as equals (or close to it) as if for the first time in human history. In
the Civil War, Americans maintained their political union; in *From Here to Eternity*
and beyond, Americans proved they wanted not just to maintain but to develop
their personal, sexual unions. What was crucial was a man like Milton Warden
learning to believe that a woman like Karen Holmes was his equal partner in the
effort to build a union, an idea that lived up to the ideal of marriage enunciated by
John Milton—"meet and cheerful conversation." Henry Adams had asked in his
Education why, although man had known woman in other civilizations, "she was
unknown in America?" What is undepicted in America is not men of force, like
Ahab, but men and women joining forces, behind the back of faces as ugly with
power as Holmes's.

Later, much later in the book, near the end, the lovers remark that "loves like
theirs have suffered." Theirs will not survive this book, but it lives in this book
and in the movie, which is why they live on. In 1949, in *Male and Female: A Study of
Sexes in a Changing World,* Margaret Mead wrote, "The American marriage ideal is
one of the most conspicuous examples of our insistence on hitching our wagon
to a star." Jones's imaginative picture of the positive possibilities for men and
women, to Mead possibilities available nowhere else in the world, offered Americans a bright light to guide them and warn them against the advances of repression that, as Jones wrote, were already a gathering storm in the military, in the
nation.

Bibliography: Stanley Cavell, *Cities of Words: Pedagogical Letters on a Register of the Moral Life*
(Cambridge, MA, 2004). Oscar W. Firkins, "Undepicted America," *Yale Review* 20 (1930): 140–
150. James Jones, *From Here to Eternity* (New York, 1951). Marshall McLuhan, *The Mechanical*

Bride: Folklore of Industrial Man (New York, 1951). Margaret Mead, *Male and Female: A Study of the Sexes in a Changing World* (New York, 1949).

LINDSAY WATERS

1951
Flannery O'Connor is diagnosed with lupus

A Soft Voice

It is said that the storyteller has but two tales. In the first, a stranger comes to town, in the second, the hero embarks on a journey. In either scenario, the protagonists emerge transformed by their experiences.

Flannery O'Connor's cast of odd characters are rarely wiser for their experiences. Even though they return to a home that is no longer familiar, they resist all evidence of its transformation. The stories of their efforts to come to terms with the drastic changes in American society during the 1950s—especially the effects of World War II, the cold war, and the civil rights movement—are very funny and very sad. O'Connor's world is littered with dismantled towns, houses, families, and individuals. It was a world she knew very well.

In 1949, when Flannery O'Connor was twenty-four years old, William Faulkner won the Nobel Prize in Literature. Faulkner's work brought the drama of the American South to the world's stage. O'Connor had already published her first short story, "The Geranium," in the quarterly *Accent,* in the summer of 1946. She got her start after college when she was admitted to the Writers' Workshop at the University of Iowa. Over the course of her short life, she completed two collections of short stories and two novels. For a person with a chronic, debilitating illness, her output was prodigious. O'Connor never married, and for most of her adult life she lived with her mother on the family's dairy farm in Milledgeville, Georgia. She died of lupus in 1964.

O'Connor's work has had an impact on writers such as Joyce Carol Oates and Louise Erdrich, but her influence also extends to the filmmaker John Huston and U2's singer Bono—in large part because she engaged topics that continue to trouble us. In "The Geranium" O'Connor explored racial integration, an especially explosive issue in the 1950s. Old Dudley has moved from the South to live with his daughter in New York City. When she explains to him that the black couple next door are not servants to the white family he assumes lives there but the tenants, he explodes, "You ain't been raised that way! . . . You ain't been raised to live tight with niggers that think they're just as good as you, and you think I'd go messin' around with one er that kind!" Suddenly he realizes where he is. "He knew yankees let niggers in their front doors and sit on their sofas but he didn't know his own daughter that was raised proper would stay next door to them." The Holocaust intrudes in stories where images of "Europeans ridden in boxcars like cattle" are used to count one's own blessing for having been spared such a fate. "The Displaced Person" recounts the story of a war refugee hired on a dairy farm in the South. Mrs. Shortley, the wife of the established hired man, is not happy about his arrival with his family. She recalls a newsreel "of a small room piled high with bodies of dead naked people all in a heap." But instead of compassion, Mrs. Shortley feels menace. She has "the sudden intuition that the Gobblehooks, like rats with typhoid fleas, could have carried all those murderous ways over the water with them directly to this place."

At the end of the Second World War, the Great Depression was over and the United States had emerged as a global superpower. Thousands of young men returned from Europe in need of jobs and "normalcy." But for black soldiers, and black Americans in general, their sacrifices in service to a free Europe demanded equal rights at home. The changes in American society were dramatic and, as O'Connor's stories illustrate, most visible in the South. The United States' status put its appalling racist practices in the spotlight. (When Emmett Till, a fourteen-year-old from Chicago visiting relatives, was lynched in Mississippi in 1955, the trial that followed was closely watched by the international press, much to the embarrassment of the State Department.)

O'Connor's stories express the fearful disorientation of the postwar period. This is evident in stories featuring returning GIs: *Wise Blood*'s Hazel Motes, Rufus in "A Stroke of Good Fortune," and Parker of "Parker's Back." The characters epitomize the mania of young men, back from military service in Europe, who are disoriented, fearful, and obsessed with finding a rock-solid certainty to combat the disintegration of their world. O'Connor's best-known character, Hazel Motes (who cannot see the beam in his own eye), is driven to found "a Church of Jesus Christ without Jesus Christ." Simple apostasy does not go far enough to express Motes's outrage at the God who has failed him. "Parker's Back" conveys Parker's anxiety in the presence of his wife's unassailable faith in Christ, a faith he is unable to share. In a desperate measure to possess a permanent, indelible response to her faith, he has a large image of Christ tattooed on his back. For Parker and Motes, faith in Jesus Christ is a matter of life or death. In the Christian view, Hazel Motes and Parker are literally members of the South's lost generation.

"Everything That Rises Must Converge" illuminates the violent impact of desegregation on both black and white folks. The story was written after the 1955 Montgomery Bus Boycott and is set on a city bus. The protagonists Julian and his mother (who is not named) take up a familiar topic: Julian refuses to believe that "blood" determines character. "Knowing who you are is good for one generation only," he tells his mother. "You haven't the foggiest idea where you stand now or who you are." Looking shocked and appalled, his mother replies, "I most certainly do know who I am." But in response to her loving description of her grandfather's plantation and two hundred slaves, Julian points to the shabbiness of their current neighborhood, the impoverished life they now live. Indeed the story begins with the mother fretting over the price of a hat she'd purchased. It is an odd-looking hat, so unique the salesperson assures her that she will not see herself "coming and going." She puts it on and boards the bus.

Julian's mother observes that they have the bus to themselves, prompting another white rider's response, "For a change. I come on one the other day and they were thick as fleas—up front and all through." But then a large black woman carrying an enormous red purse gets on with a little boy. She is also wearing the hat that Julian's mother wears. The little boy leaps onto the seat next to Julian's mother, who is enchanted by his attention. Julian, seated next to the boy's mother, can feel her anger mount with each exchange between her son and his mother, who is oblivious to the boy's mother's demands that he come to her. Even after the mother snatches the boy off the seat, Julian's mother continues to play peek-a-boo. Unfortunately they all get off at the same stop. Julian knows that his mother will try to give the boy a penny. And when she calls to the child his mother knocks her down with a swift, hard punch, saying, "He don't take nobody's pennies." As he helps her up off the sidewalk Julian realizes that his mother's shock is a symptom of a deeper dementia; he sees what he already knows, that she lives in a world that no longer exists. Just as she is blind to the shabbiness of her neighborhood, she cannot see her reflection in the black mother. And yet they mirror each other: they sit facing each other, are seated next to each other's sons, and are wearing the same odd hat. The emphasis on the visual in this scene underscores Julian's mother's blindness even to a likeness as innocent as a hat.

In "Revelation," Mrs. Turpin determines a person's social class simply by looking at her shoes. In the doctor's waiting room, she notes that the well-dressed lady's shoes match her dress; Mrs. Turpin herself is wearing her patent leather pumps, and a "white trashy" mother has on "what appeared to be bedroom slippers, black straw with gold braid threaded through them—exactly what you would have expected her to have on." Mrs. Turpin's attachment to racial and class distinctions are articles of her faith ordained by Jesus Christ. If, she muses, Jesus were to tell her that she could be either "a nigger or white-trash," she would reply, "All right, make me a nigger then—but that don't mean a trashy one." She would be "a neat clean respectable Negro woman, herself but black." This Order of Things is so fundamental to her sense of self and reality that, like in a prayer before sleep, she recites the social order, naming the classes, describing and modifying each one. Yet when she comes to a contradiction (people with good blood who have become poor, the "colored" dentist who has two Lincolns and a swimming pool), it all becomes muddled, at which point "all the classes of people were moiling and roiling around in her head, and she would dream they were all crammed together in a box car, being ridden off to be put in a gas oven."

One of O'Connor's most poignant stories is "The Displaced Person." In its stranger-comes-to-town plot, the parish priest entreats the widow Mrs. McIntyre to hire a family of Polish immigrants displaced by the war. Mr. Guizac, unlike O'Connor's American men, works tirelessly to support his wife and children and to demonstrate his gratitude for, and ability to adapt to, his new American home. As he quickly masters the farm equipment, Mrs. McIntyre admits that his industriousness has saved her thousands of dollars. But Mrs. Shortley, wife of the white "trashy" family, is determined to get rid of the foreigners. She encourages Mrs. McIntyre's own suspicions about the refugees, claiming that they will quit at the earliest opportunity. The coup comes when Mrs. McIntyre finds the young Negro worker Sulk with a photo of a lovely young white girl. Sulk announces that she is Mr. Guizac's cousin and that he has asked Sulk to marry her so that she can immigrate to the United States. Mrs. McIntyre is shocked, horrified, and enraged. She tries to express to Mr. Guizac the extent of this transgression—"You would bring this poor innocent child over here and try to marry her off to a half-witted thieving black stinking nigger! What kind of monster are you!" Even as she says these words, Mr. Guizac's face takes on a monstrous appearance. When he replies, "She in camp three year . . . Momma die, pappa die . . . she wait in camp . . . she no care black . . . . She in camp three year," Mrs. McIntyre remains unmoved. Her apparently innate racism makes it impossible for her to grasp the relentless misery of Europe during and after the war. Even though she has seen newsreel evidence of mass murder throughout Europe, Mrs. McIntyre is unable to grasp it; the ravaged Continent and its displaced people have no reality for her. On this dairy farm in the rural South, the foreign reality can be understood only (if at all) from a Judeo-Christian perspective. Mrs. Shortley, prompted by a vision, announces as though in a trance, "The children of wicked nations will be butchered." Although cloaked in biblical language, it is a sentiment she has expressed before: if the Europeans have suffered, then God has punished them and they deserve no pity. So when Mrs. McIntyre witnesses Sulk and Mr. Shortley preparing to murder Mr. Guizac, she does nothing to warn him. In that instant, her eyes dart from those of Sulk to Mr. Shortley's, in an act of complicity more meaningful than a handshake. For that second, she could have saved Guizac's life, and her own soul. Mrs. McIntyre's moral failure brings an end to her livelihood and life.

During what would be her last stay in the hospital, Flannery O'Connor hid drafts of "Judgment Day" and "Parker's Back" under her pillow so that she could continue working on them. She revised "Judgment Day," but exhaustion kept her from finishing it. Still, she continued to work on "Parker's Back" in the days before her death. This story, charged with a frenetic energy, is an allegory of the desperate seeker's struggle with faith. Sarah Ruth, Parker's wife, is not the least bit attractive. What binds him to her is her rock-hard certainty: she is Faith. The characters' names (Obadiah, Elihu, Sarah, Ruth) allude to biblical stories about man's struggle with faith. Job's unjust suffering tries his faith in God, but Elihu reminds him that suffering prepares man for God's grace. Sarah laughs when God tells her she will have a child at her advanced age. And Ruth, the Moabite, embraces the God of Abraham because she reveres her mother-in-law, Naomi. In O'Connor's story, Sarah Ruth scoffs at Parker's attempt to make faith stable and tangible, a view O'Connor shared. After a decade of living with lupus, she must have felt a little like Job. In 1962 she wrote to a friend, "Even in the life of a Christian, faith rises and falls like the tides of an invisible sea. It's there even when you can't see it or feel it, if he wants it to be there." In another letter she wrote, "I think there is no suffering greater than what is caused by the doubts of those who want to believe. I know what torment this is, but I can only see it, in myself anyway, as the process by which faith is deepened." The chronic pain of lupus, coupled with the tumultuous period in which she lived, demanded faith.

Like the crippled daughters of her stories, O'Connor was a sick, fatherless only child from a one-time wealthy family. She shuttled between Georgia, Iowa, and Connecticut, between South and North, country and city, and bore witness to the cataclysmic transformation of the United States after the Second World War. In a short form, Flannery O'Connor expressed with wisdom and compassion a world and its characters made obsolete and alien in their native land. If O'Connor's stories are the swan songs of the Jim Crow South and American isolation, her soft voice never wavers or sounds a false note.

Bibliography: Mary L. Dudziak, *Cold War Civil Rights: Race and the Image of American Democracy* (Princeton, 2000). Flannery O'Connor, *The Complete Stories,* with an introduction by Robert Giroux (New York, 1971); *Flannery O'Connor: Collected Works,* ed. Sally Fitzgerald (New York, 1988).

M. LYNN WEISS

1952, April 12

Elia Kazan places an advertisement in the *New York Times*

THE BLACKLIST IN HOLLYWOOD

"Anybody who informs on people is doing something disturbing and even disgusting. It doesn't sit well on anyone's conscience. But at the time I felt a certain way, and I think it has to be judged from the perspective of 1952." So said Elia Kazan in 1971. On New Year's Day, 1952—two weeks before Kazan's first testimony before the House Committee on Un-American Activities—the *New York Times* ran this headline on page nine: "Three Camps to Jail Spies Are Planned in West." In its report the flashy word "spies" was discarded for more inclusive usage: the camps were intended for "subversive elements of the population." These camps are largely forgotten in discussions of the McCarthy Era. The camps go unmentioned in Elia Kazan's autobiography, *A Life,* and Richard Schickel's *Elia Kazan: A Biography,* though both books discuss the McCarthy period at length; Victor S. Navasky's *Naming Names,* a classic study of the period, mentions the camps three times, briefly, without elaboration. It's fruitless to speculate why commentators across the political spectrum share this particular case of historical amnesia—but if, as Kazan suggests, we are to judge his or anyone's testimony to the House Un-American Activities Committee (HUAC) "from the perspective of 1952," we need to remember that in 1952 existence of ready-and-waiting internment camps was common knowledge, especially to those considered "subversive elements of the population."

The Emergency Detention Act was first proposed by self-described liberal senators, all Democrats, as reported in the *Times* on September 6, 1950: "Bill

Would Permit Reds' Internment." "Known Communists and others liable to become subversive" would be "subject . . . to concentration camp commitments . . . [They] could be interred" (in original) by "a declaration of an internal security emergency by the President and Congress." The camps were authorized on September 24, 1950, as Title II of the McCarran "Anti-Communist Law," the Internal Security Act. A *Times* editorial the next day praised the camps as the McCarran Act's "strengthening feature." President Truman vetoed the law; the House overrode him 278 to 113, and the Senate, 57 to 26.

The *Times* periodically reported on the Emergency Detention Act during the next several years, but only in the first instance did it use the terrifying words "concentration camp." Still, its language was fearful, stating that the camps were intended for "subversive elements," "others liable to become subversive," "probable" spies, their identity determined on "secret information" with "no hearings" —vague and inclusive usage meaning that the camps were intended for anyone the government thought fit to intern, during an emergency the government was free to define and declare.

On January 13, 1952, the day before Elia Kazan's first HUAC testimony, the *Times* reported that "as many as 15,000 persons are believed ticketed for immediate seizure." That the threat was real was not in question. It had been just seven years since the release of more than 100,000 Japanese Americans from similar camps, where they had been deprived of liberty and property—without due process, and having broken no laws—for most of the Second World War. The Emergency Detention Act's camps were the backdrop for anyone having anything to do with "the Committee," as HUAC was universally referred to at the time.

Enter Elia Kazan.

Kazan had been in the Communist Party from 1934 through 1936, when working with the Group Theatre, an experimental coalition of artists that produced such radical and acclaimed plays as Clifford Odets's *Waiting for Lefty* and *Awake and Sing!* After the Second World War, Kazan, a founder of the Actors Studio, established himself as America's premier stage director with Tennessee Williams's *A Streetcar Named Desire* and Arthur Miller's *Death of a Salesman.* Among his films, *Pinky* (1947) was Hollywood's most frank portrayal to date of race prejudice; anti-Semitism was the theme of *Gentleman's Agreement,* which won the 1947 Academy Award for Best Picture; and Kazan's film version of *A Streetcar Named Desire* made a star of Marlon Brando. *Viva Zapata!*—again starring Brando—dealt sympathetically but unsparingly with the paradoxes of revolutionary movements; it would be released weeks after Kazan testified. Elia Kazan was, in short, the most prominent American artist yet subpoenaed by HUAC.

What the committee demanded in its interrogations was that a person confess his or her own radical activities and "name names," fingering anyone else taking part in such activities. Actors and directors who refused were unofficially but efficiently blacklisted from work, as were those named—and they joined the list of those "reasonably suspect" for whom the Emergency Detention Act was designed. Artists Kazan had directed were already blacklisted for being named or failing to name: John Garfield, Sam Jaffe, and Anne Revere, of *Gentleman's Agreement;* Lee J. Cobb, of *Death of a Salesman;* Zero Mostel, of *Panic in the Streets;* and Kim Hunter, of *A Streetcar Named Desire.* Kazan well knew what was at stake.

And he no doubt had followed the testimonies and fortunes of artists the committee had questioned. Actors Gary Cooper and Ronald Reagan cooperated enthusiastically. Larry Parks, briefly a star for his lead in *The Al Jolson Story,* again and again begged during his testimony not to be forced to name names; again and again he gave in and named, pitifully ashamed as he did so. Writer Ring Lardner, Jr., refused to name anyone and was forcibly removed from the stand for berating the committee. His protest earned him time in jail.

Lee J. Cobb refused for two years to appear before HUAC, and his treatment, as he described it to Victor Navasky, sketches the life of the blacklisted. Cobb was not "able to move about without being tailed . . . After a certain point it grows to implied as well as articulated threats, and people succumb. My wife did, and she was institutionalized." Finally, "pretty much worn down," Cobb went before the committee and named twenty people.

Some, like blacklisted writer Roy Huggins, gave in because they were terrified of what Huggins called "the Concentration Camp bill." Huggins told Navasky, "So there I was with the possibility of being hustled into a concentration camp while having several people completely dependent upon me. I considered the possibility of being a hero and couldn't quite make it."

When he testified on January 14, 1952, Elia Kazan determined, as he wrote in *A Life,* he would not "hide anything that concerned me, I wouldn't 'take the Fifth,' but I would not, under any pressure, name others. That would be shameful." He frankly admitted his Communist Party activities but refused to name anyone. He also told HUAC that he'd left the party after about a year and a half, disgusted and disillusioned by its methods; and that, though still decidedly liberal, he'd had nothing whatsoever to do with communism since. "I concluded," he wrote in *A Life,* "that what these fellows were conducting was a degradation ceremony, in which the act of informing was more important than the information conveyed. I didn't doubt they knew all the names they were asking for! . . . [They] were . . . scoring points for their careers because of the publicity their investigative position brought them—all at the cost of people's lives and careers. I bitterly resented them."

Resentful or not, Kazan soon had second thoughts, spurred by his wife, Molly, and his Hollywood producers, Darryl Zanuck and Bud Leighton. He told Leighton, "The men they're waiting for me to name were once good friends." Leighton replied, "I don't care how good friends they were; there is nothing else you can do now." That is, if Kazan wanted to continue to direct films. And Kazan, "when I thought about it," agreed with Molly that "it was the duty of the government to investigate the Communist movement." The consequences of his January testimony made him ask, "What the hell am I giving all this up for? To defend a secrecy I didn't think right and to defend people who'd already been named or soon would be by someone else? I said I'd hated Communists for many years and didn't feel right about giving up my career to defend them." Kazan requested a second session with the committee, and was granted it on April 10, 1952.

He named every name he remembered. He listed his artistic achievements, arguing emphatically that they weren't communist in any way. Kazan concluded his testimony contritely: "I will be glad to do anything to help—anything you consider necessary or valuable."

Then he wrote in his diary: "Miserably depressed. Can't get my mind off it. I know I've done something wrong. Still convinced I would have done something wrong if I'd done the opposite. I spend every minute making rationalizations for my act . . . Molly keeps looking at me. Why?"

People like Lee J. Cobb and Roy Huggins were later tacitly forgiven by the artistic community for cooperating with HUAC because they openly admitted that their reasons were deprivation and terror, and that they were ashamed. As for Elia Kazan—even after his death, many have yet to forgive him because he stated boldly that naming names was the right thing to do.

The day after Kazan's supposedly private testimony, the committee released its contents to the world. The day after that, on April 12, 1952, Kazan did something unprecedented. He bought space in the *New York Times* to publish "A Statement—by Elia Kazan."

Kazan tells us in *A Life* that "A Statement" was urged and written by Molly Kazan. "She locked herself in her study and I heard the typewriter, pages being ripped out impatiently, the carriage jammed back to its start position, then more typing." Kazan agreed with what she wrote and signed it. "A Statement" reads, in part:

> I believe that Communist activities confront the people of this country with an unprecedented and exceptionally tough problem. That is, how to protect ourselves from a dangerous and alien conspiracy and still keep the free, open, healthy way of life that gives us self-respect.
>
> I believe that the American people can solve this problem wisely only if they have the facts about Communism. All the facts.
>
> Now, I believe that any American who is in possession of such facts has the obligation to make them known, either to the public or to the appropriate Government agency.
>
> . . .
>
> Secrecy serves the Communists. At the other pole, it serves those who are interested in silencing liberal voices. The employment of a lot of good liberals is threatened because they have allowed themselves to become associated with or silenced by the Communists.
>
> Liberals must speak out.
>
> . . .
>
> —Elia Kazan

In the 1970s Kazan spoke of his testimony in several interviews, adamantly stating that he'd been right—and wrong. He insisted that he "hated" communism and that it would have been "insane" to give up his career for something he didn't believe in. But he also revealed a more troubled perspective, as when he told Jeff

Young in 1971, "What I really thought, looking at it in the biggest sense, was that what I did was the better of two mean alternatives . . . Maybe I did wrong, probably did. But I really didn't do it for any reason other than that I thought it was right." He insisted more than once that his HUAC testimony "has to be judged from the perspective of 1952."

In the context of 1952, then, the business of Kazan's April 10 testimony was to name names. In addition to several Communist Party functionaries of the mid-1930s—who, in the context of *that* time, had broken no laws—Kazan named eight actors and writers of the Group Theatre in his party "unit." The unit's mission was to control the Group's artistic agenda—again, a lawful activity. Kazan testified that his unit failed in its mission. But how the Soviet threat of 1952 was alleviated by exposing "all the facts" of a bohemian theater's in-fighting of two decades before, neither HUAC nor Kazan ever explained.

Given that the purpose of his second testimony was to name names, the relevance of "A Statement" rests on those he named and what they did—the named become as important as the namer. Take, for example, the actress Phoebe Brand.

When naming her Kazan said, "I was instrumental in bringing her into the Party." Recruiting a new party member was necessarily a secretive, intimate process and a significant episode in Kazan's life as a Communist—significant enough to be mentioned to the committee. Yet, though Phoebe Brand was in Kazan's unit and appeared onstage with him in the Group's most memorable productions, she goes unmentioned in *A Life*. Even when he lists Group actors who became teachers and "helped actors become artists," he ignores Brand—though she became an influential teacher. In fact, in all the Kazan literature Phoebe Brand is mentioned but three times, briefly and in passing, by his biographer—and, of course, in the HUAC transcript.

Yet when Phoebe Brand died in 2004, at the age of ninety-six, she rated obituaries in the *New York Times,* the *Boston Globe,* and the *Los Angeles Times.* In Wendy Smith's *Real Life Drama: The Group Theatre and America,* we learn that Brand's "good looks . . . garnered her several movie offers, [but she] was notably vehement in her scorn for Hollywood." One would think a committed Communist would desire the visibility and power that might come with Hollywood stardom, but Brand went to Hollywood only after the Group disbanded and her husband, Morris Carnovsky (also named by Kazan), found work there—work she still refused. The *Los Angeles Times* told how she "once helped close a Hollywood delicatessen after the owner refused to serve a black actor," organizing picket lines outside the store. In the 1960s she was a founding member of Theater in the Street, directing free plays in New York City. The *Boston Globe* reported that she taught her last class in her hospital room a week before her death.

When one looks closely at Phoebe Brand, Morris Carnovsky, and other artists named by Kazan, the eagerness of the committee to know their names and the grandiosity of Kazan's "Statement" become, in the context of 1952, almost farcical—were it not for the very real danger those named were then immediately subject to.

Swiftly blacklisted, they were also, as the *Times* phrased it, "ticketed for immediate seizure." The Emergency Detention Act was not repealed until 1971; it would never be employed, but no one could know that from the perspective of 1952. At the time, the camps were an accepted fact of life. On December 27, 1955, in a lengthy article that included photos, the paper of record reassured readers that "in the absence of evidence to the contrary and in the light of experience of American methods, the presumption must be that these camps would be humanely conducted, according to civilized rules and procedures."

Bibliography: William Baer, ed., *Elia Kazan Interviews* (Jackson MS, 2000). Cornelius P. Cotter and J. Malcolm Smith, "An American Paradox: The Emergency Detention Act of 1950," *Journal of Politics* 19, no. 1 (1957). Elia Kazan, *A Life* (New York, 1988). Victor S. Navasky, *Naming Names* (New York, 1980). Richard Schickel, *Elia Kazan: A Biography* (New York, 2005). Wendy Smith, *Real Life Drama: The Group Theatre and America, 1931–1940* (New York, 1990).

MICHAEL VENTURA

1952, June 10
C. L. R. James is detained on Ellis Island

MARINERS, RENEGADES AND CASTAWAYS

Although he was expecting the knock at the door, the Trinidadian social activist and journalist Cyril Lionel Robert James was nevertheless filled with dread on the afternoon when federal agents arrived with a warrant requiring James to accompany them to Ellis Island. There he was detained, awaiting deportation hearings, for the next six months. Various government agencies had been keeping track of James's activities since the time of his entry into the United States in 1938, when the FBI classified him as a security risk. But their harassment of him increased dramatically during the heyday of McCarthyism in the early 1950s. As warrant for his internment, the agents cited the McCarran-Walter Act of 1952, which, despite the fact that it was passed a month *after* James's citizenship examination, would nevertheless ultimately become the juridical instrument invoked by the state to justify his deportation.

Ellis Island has been consecrated in the national imagination as a quasi-magical port of entry into the New World through which strangers, exiles, and political refugees passed on their way to taking up much-sought-after new lives as U.S. citizens. Upon turning it into a deportation center, however, the Bureau of Immigration and Naturalization dramatically reclassified Ellis Island as a site populated by the socially dead. The myth of Ellis Island as a haven for the world's disenfranchised has induced forgetting of the fact that, like Angel Island in San Francisco Bay, Ellis Island was also a place of detainment, both during and after its time as an immigrant portal. Since detainment and incarceration were considered crucial if disavowed aspects of the celebrated process of immigration, Ellis Island was used as a detention center for enemies both foreign and domestic. The act of transporting James to Ellis Island brought about a drastic transformation in his official identity: from a vulnerable immigrant under the state's protection to a dangerous subversive in the state's protective custody.

James experienced his relocation on Ellis Island as a disorienting encounter with the underside of cold war society. In 1952, Ellis Island was populated by hundreds of migrants, nomads, expellees, and refugees from the shipwreck of history across the globe. Individually and collectively they confronted a legal and bureaucratic maze in which they were denied due process, refused lawyers, and subjected to a daily routine of humiliation by guards. On taking up residence within this landscape of despair, James was overwhelmed by feelings of physical as well as psychological vulnerability. Each day confronted him with a struggle to survive. James began to fear for his physical safety after officials refused to provide treatment for his stomach ulcer. When James apprised the district director of the Port of New York of his ailment, the man replied that he considered James an alien with no human rights, and that if James did not like it there he could always return to Trinidad "and drink papaya juice."

James was even more terrified at the prospect of being assassinated by the members of the International Communist Party with whom he was inducted into his new quarters:

> The Department of Immigration knew my attitude to Communists. The first thing that happened was that within an hour of my arrival, I was placed in a special room for political prisoners, the only occupants of which were five Communists. The reader of this book knows what I think of Communists. But this was more serious than my mere thoughts. Though I had expressed radical ideas, and in fact was in trouble because of that, the Communists knew me as their open and avowed enemy. I had written or translated books against them, which had been published in England and France and the United States.

James's antipathy toward communism had begun in England fifteen years earlier, when the British Communist Party failed to support revolutionary campaigns against imperial aggression in Abyssinia (now Ethiopia) and elsewhere in Africa as well as the West Indies. During his five-year stay in England, James forged friendships with George Padmore, Claude McKay, Paul Robeson, and other black intellectuals in the Pan-African movement. The members of this circle were like James in that each had became increasingly persuaded as to the pertinence of Marxist theory to their common struggle to overthrow colonial domination. But James's primary allegiance was with the struggles for political independence in the Caribbean and Africa. Thus James left England for the United States at the behest of Leon Trotsky, who had become the focus of James's opposition to Stalinism. Under the pseudonym of W. R. Johnson, James, along with Trotsky's former secretary Raya Dunayevskaya (aka Freddie Forest), and the Chinese American Grace Lee Boggs (aka R. Stone) formed what they called the Johnson-Forest tendency, also known as the Johnsonites. The Johnson-Forest tendency exemplified the ways in which a political movement could be at once revolutionary and anti-Stalinist.

In 1938, James had published *The Black Jacobins: Toussaint L'Ouverture and the*

San Domingo Revolution, a magisterial analysis of the role L'Ouverture had played in the Haitian uprising of 1791, as an effort to close the cultural and political gap between Caribbean black history and European history. The book examined the French Revolution, whose history had formerly been monopolized by the metropolitan historians, from the perspective of the resistance led by that empire's former slaves. A prolific journalist, James had once aspired to a literary career: his novel *Minty Alley* (1936) was the first novel by a black West Indian to be published in England, and he staged the story of Toussaint L'Ouverture initially as a play. But *The Black Jacobins* marked a turning point in his writing, in which the untold stories of the past were reanimated in light of pressing present-day political issues.

Once in the United States, James transferred his Trotskyite and Johnsonite beliefs to an array of new concerns: the movies, pulp fiction, television soap operas, black Marxism, the history of American civilization, and the novels of Herman Melville. His *American Civilization: The Struggle for Happiness,* written in the late 1940s, advanced the argument that various sectors of American society—the family, the political community, the civil sphere—were in crisis along a deep racial division that could be resolved only through the development of a mass revolutionary movement that would allow for the reorganization of the culture on a more egalitarian and participatory basis.

In *American Civilization,* James had interpreted Melville's work as part of the literature of the abolitionist period. But his abrupt relocation by the state led James to a dramatic change in the scale, focus, and purpose of his Melville analysis. On the afternoon that state agents took him into custody, James managed to gather up his unfinished notes on Melville. While incarcerated on Ellis Island, James worked each day on a manuscript that he published in 1953 under the title *Mariners, Renegades and Castaways: The Story of Herman Melville and the World We Live In.* Writing this book enabled James to conceive of his internment as an episode in a larger American odyssey, in which the site from which he wrote acquired fateful significance:

> Here was I just about to write suddenly projected onto an island isolated from the rest of society where American administrators and officials and American security officers controlled the destinies of perhaps a thousand men, sailors, "isolatoes," renegades, and castaways from all parts of the world. It seems now as if destiny had taken a hand to give me a unique opportunity to test my ideas of this great American writer.

In linking his experience with the Department of Justice's Immigration and Naturalization Service (INS) authorities on Ellis Island to his reading of an exemplary national classic, James fashioned a writing practice that was in one of its aspects an interpretive exercise, and in another a legal appeal. In *Mariners, Renegades and Castaways,* James fashioned these discrepant facets into a personal memoir through which he came to literary terms with the ordeal he underwent there by entering—not just analyzing—a classic literary work.

James used the iconography of *Moby-Dick* to make sense of his contemporary experience on Ellis Island, and he conceptualized that place as a material referent for the historical truth of Melville's allegory. Specifically, he turned his experience of the state's action into a correlative of the traumatizing events that the *Pequod*'s crew had been compelled to go through under the governance of Captain Ahab. James also depicted the political refugees on Ellis Island as symbolic descendants of that crew. James thereby experienced an uncanny oscillation between the catastrophe the crew underwent on the *Pequod* and his own actual political exile:

> I read Melville during the great historical events of the last seven years, and without them I would never be able to show, as I believe I have done, that his work today is alive as never before since it was written. So far, however, the contemporary references I have made have been to events on a world scale. There remains some direct estimate of the relation of this great American to present conditions in the country which produced him.

The interpretation of *Moby-Dick* that James advanced in *Mariners, Renegades and Castaways* radically challenged the understanding of Melville's work that had been proposed by American scholars during the early years of the cold war. Between 1941 and 1952, the novel was taken up by a series of distinguished American scholars that included Richard Chase, Newton Arvin, F. O. Matthiessen, and Charles Olson. Individually and collectively these scholars fostered an allegorical understanding of *Moby-Dick* that interpreted Ahab's monomania as the symbol of America's external fascist or communist enemy of the 1941–52 period, against which they defined, elaborated upon, and defended Ishmael's love of freedom. While subsequent interpreters of the novel would introduce at times ingenious variations on this theme, the essentialized opposition between Ishmael and Ahab would dominate readings of the novel in the field of American literary studies for the next fifty years.

James confirmed the prevailing understanding of Ahab as a "totalitarian type." But after arguing that the U.S. security state had put into place the very kind of totalitarian rule that it purported to oppose, he also generalized this type to include Ishmael—whom he described as "an intellectual Ahab"—as well as the members of the McCarran Committee and other administrators who participated in the systematic persecution and expulsion of political undesirables. James replaced the Ishmael-Ahab opposition with the argument that the "meanest mariners, renegades and castaways" constituted alternatives to both forms of totalitarian rule: "They are a world federation of modern industrial workers . . . They owe no allegiance to anybody or anything except the work they have to do and the relations with one another upon which that work depends . . . Their heroism consists of their everyday doing of their work."

Mariners, Renegades and Castaways revolves around an entirely hypothetical event: the collective revolt that did *not* take place aboard the *Pequod*. James proceeds to speculate that this fictionalized past event was dependent on a future actual event—the repeal of the McCarran-Walter Act—for its completion. In the book's final chapter, James represents his fellow inmates on Ellis Island as a shipwrecked crew of castaways whose collective desire to be liberated from state tyranny continues the desire for social justice of the mariners on the *Pequod*: "This is my final impression: the meanest mariners, renegades and castaways of Melville's day were objectively a new world. But they knew nothing. These know every-thing. The symbolic mariners and renegades of Melville's book were isolatoes federated by one keel, but only because they had been assembled by penetrating genius. These are federated by nothing. But they are looking for federation."

Overall *Mariners, Renegades and Castaways* communicated two asymmetrical commentaries. The symbolic exchange James effected when he turned "the story of Herman Melville" toward "the world we live in" also changed the contours of Melville's original narrative. James's final chapter, "A Natural but Necessary Con-clusion," added to his commentary on *Moby-Dick* the heroic parts that Melville had once promised the mariners, renegades, and castaways would play. In con-cluding his Melville book with accounts of the subaltern knowledge produced by the renegades on Ellis Island, James imagined a new ending for the crew of the *Pequod* in which they survive the wreck to which Melville had consigned them, and found a new political order.

Despite (or perhaps because of) his Melville book, James was ultimately de-ported in 1953. He retraced his steps first to England and then, in 1958, to his na-tive Trinidad, where he participated in the pro-independence People's National Movement Party. He finally returned to the United States in 1968, where he taught courses at the University of the District of Columbia that articulated the relationship between the domestic civil rights movement and the Pan-African decolonization movement. During his lifetime, most of James's books were pub-lished with the help of friends who distributed them privately, and the majority of his works went out of print. But as a consequence of the spectacular renewal of interest in his work at the close of the twentieth century, the Jamesian corpus is gradually being restored. Scholarly attention has not been restricted to his cricket book *Beyond a Boundary* (1963) and *The Black Jacobins*, which had already been published by reputable presses, but has been extended to include the previ-ously unpublished works *American Civilization* (1993), *Notes on Dialectics* (1981), *Facing Reality* (2005), *The Future in the Present* (1977), *At the Rendezvous of Victory* (1984), and other writings. James is now seen as a foundational theorist of the Af-rican diaspora.

Despite his lofty aspirations for a book that he hoped would "advance the un-derstanding of literature and the cause of freedom," *Mariners, Renegades and Cast-aways* never received the recognition it deserved. Perhaps because the INS had cited the volume as an example of the subversive activities for which they were deporting James, Melville scholars said little about *Mariners, Renegades and Cast-aways* when it appeared in 1953, and it has continued to be absent from nearly all bibliographies and critical studies of Melville. James sent advance copies of the book along with the request for a one-dollar contribution to his cause to promi-nent literary critics as well as to every member of the U.S. House of Representa-tives and the U.S. Senate. Of the twenty thousand copies published, all but two thousand were reclaimed by the publisher for nonpayment.

Bibliography: C. L. R. James, *C. L. R. James's Caribbean,* ed. Paget Henry and Paul Buhle (Durham, NC, 1996); *Mariners, Renegades and Castaways: The Story of Herman Melville and the World We Live In,* introduction by Donald E. Pease (Hanover, NH, 2001). Paul Buhle, *C. L. R. James: The Artist as Revolutionary* (London, 1997). Selwyn Reginald Cudjoe and William E. Cain, *C. L. R. James: His Intellectual Legacies* (Amherst, MA, 1995). Grant Farred, *Rethinking C. L. R. James* (Hoboken, NJ, 1996).

DONALD E. PEASE

1953, January 1
Hank Williams dead at 29

THE SONG IN COUNTRY MUSIC

About 5:00 a.m. on the morning of January 1, 1953, Charles Carr, a nineteen-year-old college freshman from Montgomery, Alabama, was driving Hank Williams's blue Cadillac convertible through West Virginia, on his way from Knoxville, Tennessee, to Canton, Ohio. Hank Williams was stretched out in the backseat. The porters at the Andrew Johnson Hotel in Knoxville had positioned him there the previous evening, and, appropriately enough, they had crossed the singer's hands across his chest. Williams was booked for a New Year's Day matinee later that day. They had missed the New Year's Eve gig in Charleston because of the snow, which was still thick on the ground. The air in the convertible was chilly, so Carr reached into the backseat to adjust the overcoat beneath which Williams lay. While trying to adjust the coat, Carr tried to move one of Williams's hands and found it cold to the touch. He tried to move Williams's arm, but it snapped back into place, and Charles Carr knew he had a problem.

Stopping at his first opportunity, Carr pulled into Burdette's Pure Oil Station in Oak Hill, West Virginia, and consulted with the attendant. The attendant directed him three blocks down the street to the Oak Hill Hospital. Two orderlies at the hospital emergency room entrance extracted Hank Williams from the Cadillac and carried him into the hospital by his armpits and feet. Hank Williams was pronounced dead at 7:00 a.m. by Doctor Diego Nunnari, who told Charles Carr that Mr. Williams had probably died about six hours earlier, although he couldn't be certain. Williams's body was rolled on a gurney across the street to the Tyree Funeral Home where Ivan Malinin, a Russian orderly who spoke almost no English, performed an autopsy. Malinin noted the needle tracks on Williams's arms, the bruises on various parts of his body, the welt on his forehead, and the hemorrhages in his heart and neck. He noted traces of alcohol but didn't test for drugs. The official cause of death was described as acute right ventricular dilation, which meant that his heart stopped beating at the age of twenty-nine.

At this point, like W. B. Yeats in Auden's poem, Hiram King "Hank" Williams became his admirers, and twenty years later, when I started working in Nashville as a songwriter and journalist, he was still an ever-present absence and a force to be reckoned with. His catalog of songs had transformed Acuff-Rose into a jugger-naut in the international music-publishing business; it had built the fine building in which Broadcast Music, the performance rights company, housed its offices. His international fame and the success of his songs in the pop-music marketplace had opened a Pandora's box of untold treasure, folly, and tribulation for execu-tives in the country-music record industry, who, before Hank Williams, had been happy to run their business like a plantation on the banks of the Cumberland River, based very much on the model of a Hollywood B-movie lot. A small corps of songwriters cranked out thousands of songs that were played by a small group of studio musicians on thousands of records that sold to a rather limited niche market. The profit margins were narrow but the profits were respectable and there was always the pleasure of control. The idea was to sell a lot of product to a few people. The alien, industrial idea of selling one unit of product to a whole lot of people had not yet occurred to them.

Before Hank Williams, the people who sang the songs, who drove the South-ern highways and dodged bottles in the honky-tonks, were regarded as more or less interchangeable—they were called "the talent"—as in the old Nashville plaint, "God save me from the talent." The authenticity of these performers' mu-sic was presumed to reside in the authenticity of the culture—the virtues of coun-try life and country people—and not in the performers themselves, so it was pos-sible for a performer to betray his or her purportedly authentic country roots, as Williams was accused of doing due to misbehavior, as Elvis Presley would do a few years later to much better effect. In the plantation days, however, life was simple. A member of the talent pool would venture into a recording studio once every three months or so. The producer would hand over a sheaf of lyric sheets and usher the talent into a vocal booth. Once there, the talent would sing along with a guide vocal to prerecorded music tracks, adapting his or her voice (or the melody of the song) to the key in which the song had been recorded. Three hours later, the business would have two or three new records. During these sessions, the talent might inquire of the producer, "Now, what's this the tune to?" The pro-ducer might occasionally advise the singer to watch the sibilants. Beyond that there was not much nuance. The records were mixed, mastered, pressed, and on the shelves in a matter of weeks. The selected single would be introduced on the radio via the *Grand Ole Opry* or the *Louisiana Hayride*. The talent would then set off on a sequence of mini-tours or "loops," as they came to be called.

From the 1930s until the early 1970s these mini-tours were a staple of the country music business from which no talent was exempted. Once product was on the shelves and on the radio, the talent would be sent out as a single with maybe three stage suits and a guitar for a sequence of four- or five-day loops through the mid-South. The singers would spend their daylight hours visiting ra-dio stations and daytime television shows. They would play every night in bars and auditoriums with pick-up musicians and drive on after the show. The "regular talent" drove Fords and stayed in rooming houses. The "major talent," like Hank Williams, rode in Cadillacs, hired drivers, and stayed in railroad hotels. Other-wise it was the same tough, arduous little business, servicing the same tiny, isolated markets, local radio, and jukeboxes. Backstage gangsters, the obligatory working girls, helpful doctors, and hostile policemen provided the seasoning.

Hank Williams lived this life. He died in the midst of a mini-tour, but in his wake the landscape would change. First, the country music audience was moving to the city and Williams's fierce unhappiness found resonance in the trailer parks of ex-urban America. Second, Hank Williams's songs and singing were not interchangeable with anyone else's. He was country music's first auteur. He had grown up in what Nashville musicians called the "trash gypsy" culture of the Alabama woods, with a shell-shocked father and a predatory mother, in a world without electricity, plumbing, or pavement, personally beleaguered by bottomless need, a profound sense of social inadequacy, a predisposition to drink, and a genetic intolerance for alcohol. Georgiana, Alabama, existed somewhere below the fuzzy cloud line of Southern culture and outside the cozy realm of country community. It was a place for which the traditional longing and nostalgia of country music was some kind of terrible joke, and lacking the social and educational resources to be anyone other than himself, Hank Williams was more or less doomed to being Hank Williams. The pressure and specificity of being Hank Williams, one likes to think, both toughened and sharpened his songs.

The lessons of Hank Williams's impudence and independence were learned better by Sam Phillips, Elvis Presley, and Jerry Lee Lewis in Memphis than by anyone in Nashville, where they recognized Williams's feral edge and shied away from it. When I arrived on Music Row in the early 1970s, the country music business was still a plantation, although bands of freedmen were running in the streets. Nashville record executives and producers like Billy Sherrill and Chet Atkins had predictably misconstrued the appeal of Williams's songs for pop audiences and invented something called countrypolitan music. They jettisoned the Nudie suits and crude production values for three-button jackets and vanilla musical confections set amidst string sections and swooning background vocals. For the kids out of the hills and the woods, who had never seen an elevator, Williams's success remained the stuff of dreams. If you could just do a tenth as well as Williams had, they thought, if you could just move up from destitution to poverty, rich and famous could go to hell. For the Dixie greasers who were Williams's own kinsmen, the young Icarii on their motorcycles, Williams's life only proved the Calvinism in their bones. Flem Snopes's account book must be balanced: "Every act of creativity must be followed by an equal and opposite act of wanton destruction." As one songwriter of this generation put it: God writes the song. The Devil wrecks the Lamborghini. That was the lesson they took. Heartbreak was hard money, so hearts were broken. In most cases, the talent broke their own.

The only people in Nashville who learned any positive lessons from Williams's career were the songwriters and the cowboys. The cowboys, mostly Texans like Willie Nelson and Waylon Jennings, who were less predisposed than Southerners to life as members of an underclass, soon figured out that their problems were less with the booze than with the business, so they set about gaining control of their own destinies. The songwriters, many of whom were Texans and nurtured in the culture of the laconic West, took control of country songwriting by learning the compression of Williams's craft. That craft was the primary topic of conversation among songwriters of the period. When I asked Roger Miller what it was about Williams's songwriting that touched him, he said. "Meticulous. They're meticulous and all hooked up." When I asked him what this meant, he sang me two lines from one of his songs.

> The moon is high and so am I.
> The stars are out and so will I be pretty soon.

"That's maybe a little too hooked-up," Miller said, and sang half a verse of "Me and Bobby McGee" a song by Kris Kristofferson and Fred Foster that Miller had discovered and recorded first.

> Busted flat in Baton Rouge
> Headed for the trains.
> Feeling nearly faded as my jeans.

"That's hooked up," Miller said. "I love the 'as' that picks up 'flat' and 'bat.'"

When I asked Willie Nelson, he observed that Williams was less a "songwriter" than a "song-singer" who obviously sang songs in progress over and over until they came out right. Waylon Jennings said much the same thing. When I asked him about Williams's songs, he sang lines from two or three of them and showed me how the sounding of the consonants moved from the front to the back of the mouth so the vowels were always singable — so you didn't have to stutter or swallow the words. Billy Joe Shaver, whose junior high school English teacher sent him off to the navy with books by Robert W. Service and Dylan Thomas, admired the way Williams's figurative poetry virtually disappeared into the facts of the narrative. "'Melt your cold, cold heart' . . . 'Today I saw you on the street / And my heart fell at your feet' . . . 'The silence of a falling star / Lights up a purple sky.' Like that," Shaver said. "The closest I got was 'I'm just an ol' chunk of coal / But I'm gonna be a diamond some day,' which could describe one of Hank's songs."

Harlan Howard, the most meticulous of country songwriters after Hank Williams, went into more detail. He sang the first verse of "Cold Cold Heart."

> I try so hard my dear to say
> That you're my every dream.
> Yet you're afraid each thing I do
> Is just some evil scheme
> Some mem'ry from your lonesome past
> Keeps us so far apart.
> Why can't I free your doubtful mind
> And melt your cold, cold heart

Howard then pointed out what Roger Miller meant by hooked up. He explained that these eight short lines were invisibly held together by fifteen internal *r* phonemes. There are triples in the first two lines, four pairs, and the terminal "heart" that gives the verse closure. "Nobody notices this," Howard said. "That's the idea, but once these words are put together this way, they won't come apart. One follows the other as day the night." I asked Howard for examples from his own songs. He sang me the opening lines from one of his hits:

> Pick me up on your way down
> When you're blue and all alone.
> When their glamour starts to bore you
> Come on back where you belong

Howard then said: "The way it works is, in the first couplet, you got your two *p*'s ('pick' and 'p-on')—your two *w*'s ('way' and 'when')—overlapped with two *d*'s ('down' and 'd-all')—overlapped with four *l*'s ('blue,' 'al,' 'l-a,' and 'lone') that make it close. The last couplet relaxes and hooks on 'blue'—which is an important word —so you have 'blue,' 'bore,' 'back,' and 'belong.' Notice how 'glamour' stands out because it doesn't echo. Here's an easier one." He sang:

> The key's in the mailbox.
> Come on in.

He said: "I like that one: "'k' 'in' 'm' followed by the 'k' 'm' 'in.' That closes it off."

Howard concluded this seminar on poetic closure and euphony by pointing out that none of this was as complex as it sounded. Once you learned how to do it, you couldn't not do it. "You sang it until you could," he said, and I walked away with a sense of what Hank Williams had done. Inadvertently perhaps, and certainly with the help of Fred Rose, his mentor and cowriter, who had Tin Pan Alley skills, Williams took the brutal simplicity of the country song, which, when Williams picked it up, was little more than a faux-folk trinket designed to last a half a season, and invested it with those elements of pattern that are the mother of memory, with the complex, internal music that we associate with icons of American popular music like Larry Hart, Ira Gershwin, and Cole Porter. Having borrowed his titles and language from vernacular American English, he returned them to the vernacular much burnished, hooked up, and built to last.

Speaking for myself, I have always loved the first quatrain of "Half as Much."

> If you loved me
> Half as much as I love you
> You wouldn't stay away
> Half as much as you do.

He begins the second line with "half as much as" in eighth-note intervals and ends it with quarter-note intervals, for emphasis, on "I love you." Then by extending the third line, "You wouldn't stay away," and cutting one word from the fourth, he is able to sing the whole fourth line in accelerated eighth-note intervals. "Half as much as you do." This closes the musical phrase. In Nashville, this is called a hook. For the rest of us, it's a tiny piece of domestic magic that won't come apart.

Discography: Hank Williams, *The Complete Hank Williams* (Mercury Nashville, 1998).

DAVE HICKEY

1954

"Choosing out of himself, out of everything within him"

WALLACE STEVENS'S *COLLECTED POEMS*

Robert Lowell called the era of midcentury "the tranquillized Fifties," and contemporary publishing was still waiting, one could say, for *Life Studies.* The advent of what M. L. Rosenthal called "confessional poetry" disturbed the flattened affect that Lowell was indicting. But all the while, in the pages of Wallace Stevens's 1954 *Collected Poems,* the verse was anything but tranquil, or tranquillized. *Harmonium* (1923; 1931) had been recognized as a sparkling and memorable book, diverting in its buoyant humor ("Bantams in Pine Woods") and beautiful in its bleakness ("The Snow Man"). But after *Harmonium,* Stevens, working hard as a lawyer, fell silent for a time. "Whatever else I do, I do not write poetry nowadays," he told Harriet Monroe of *Poetry* magazine, and his second book, *Ideas of Order* (1936), was thought to be less original and less experimental than *Harmonium.* It was not until 1942, when Stevens was over sixty, that his third book, *Parts of a World,* appeared; and strong interest in him did not revive until the 1947 *Transport to Summer.* Even though his lyrics found approval, Stevens's long poems, increasingly important in the later books, were dismissed by so good a critic as Randall Jarrell as ponderous and elephantine—a common response from readers who wanted more of what they had warmed to in *Harmonium.* They were wrong to think of the long poems as coming from a source different from the short ones, but it took some time for readers to assimilate the lively early Stevens to the meditative later Stevens of "Notes Toward a Supreme Fiction," "Credences of Summer," "The Auroras of Autumn," and "An Ordinary Evening in New Haven." Once the *Collected Poems* was awarded the National Book Award and the Pulitzer Prize, Stevens won some measure of fame—but it was only after his death in 1955 that there occurred the slow general appreciation of Stevens's originality, and a realization of his contribution to American modernism.

Early modernism had been defined by its expatriate adherents: Eliot, Pound, even Frost (who could find publication for his first book only by going to England). William Carlos Williams's Americanness was adopted reactively, as a gesture of repudiation of his foreign ancestry and foreign schooling. But Stevens never traveled to Europe at all, and he paid homage to Whitman ("His beard is of fire and his staff is a leaping flame"); he became a self-consciously American poet, rather than an international or cosmopolitan writer. In what follows, I will confine myself to Stevens's more fully American poems, and ask what originality he conferred on a subject also touched in a more regional way by Frost *(North of Boston)* and by Eliot ("The Dry Salvages").

In "Notes Toward a Supreme Fiction," Stevens said that poetry must be abstract, it must change, and it must give pleasure. Of these qualities, the most original in its results in Stevens's poetry was insistence on the necessary abstraction—

that is, the symbolic nature—of poetry. Because the poem, to Stevens's mind, is not mimetically transcriptive of immediate reality, it "must resist the intelligence /Almost successfully" ("Man Carrying Thing"). In the "Almost" lies Stevens's promise that every poem contains, within its sometimes bizarre appurtenances, a revelation of feeling, a conveying of passion. But in his poems about the role of poetry in America, we will often see no explicit naming of an American scene, and must read between the lines to understand his purpose.

However, that purpose is plain in Stevens's first long poem, "The Comedian as the Letter C," as he retraces the path he took from being a "European" poet to being an American one. Departing from Bordeaux, Crispin the poet makes his way to a new world—first to an American exoticism in Mexico, then to a North American domestication "in the Carolinas," where he settles down with a "prismy blonde" and begets four daughters. That was a Utopian hope, as it turned out; Stevens's marriage was unhappy, and he had not four daughters, but one. One result of his disappointment in sexuality and his awareness of the 1929 Depression was "Farewell to Florida" (the poem that opened *Ideas of Order*) in which he declared "My North is leafless and lies in a wintry slime /Both of men and clouds, a slime of men in crowds." The Depression brought Stevens (and everyone else) to a new social consciousness, and "men in crowds" became, from then on, an intrinsic part of his poetry. But before bidding farewell to the sensual South, he had written the several Florida poems in *Harmonium,* exploring his notion of a newly crude American aesthetic (versus an eighteenth-century European aesthetic of "eglantine" and "pettifogging buds") in the grotesquely fascinating "Floral Decorations for Bananas": "And deck the bananas in leaves /Plucked from the Carib trees, /Fibrous and dangling down." At the same time, Stevens was experimenting with writing two very different poems on one subject: his abandonment of Christian religious observance was phrased in cultivated "European" sonnet-like stanzas in the now-famous sequence "Sunday Morning," but it was expressed, too, in "Ploughing on Sunday," a folk song of cocky repudiation of the reverent Sabbath:

> Remus, blow your horn!
> I'm ploughing on Sunday,
> Ploughing North America.
> Blow your horn!

It is impossible to imagine Eliot or Pound (or even Frost) writing this sort of country ballad, or adopting the persona of a singing ploughman.

Stevens had not as yet settled on the style he would finally make his own—one of perfectly turned cadence or one of demotic bravado. He did not want to lose the exquisite resources of European sophistication that he had found in Shakespeare, Wordsworth, Shelley, and Keats, but at the same time he wanted the poetry of the New World to exhibit a Whitmanian democratic solidity. This struggle never entirely left Stevens's work. When he wrote the famous poem of Florida, "The Idea of Order at Key West," he counterpointed his own elaborate diction with the single simple song of the woman walking by the shore. And when he wanted to define, at the close of that poem, what poetry does for us, he turned not to a Shelleyan exaltation but to the practical usefulness of the geographer's lines of latitude and longitude, without which we could not specify our location in space: poetry "Mastered the night and portioned out the sea," leaving us with a sense of "emblazoned zones and fiery poles." In that way, poetry, by situating us among our emotions, "helps us to live our lives," as Stevens said elsewhere. But even while he was writing the incantations of "The Idea of Order," Stevens was embodying demotic speech-acts: "What They Call Red Cherry Pie" (an uncollected poem of 1934) begins, "Meyer is a bum. He eats his pie. / . . . / He says 'That's what I call red cherry pie.' / And that's his way. And that's my way as well." Defiantly disregarding the suavities of high modernism, Stevens trudges into the world of Meyer (who is not a wistful American figure like Frost's hired man, but an aesthetically resistant "bum"). Stevens rejected this strain of naturalist Americanism—but not before he had tried it out.

Stevens was troubled by the cynicism of American society: he wrote in "The American Sublime" of the "mockers, / The mickey mockers / And plated pairs" debasing American culture. Starved, he asked "What wine does one drink? / What bread does one eat?" To find that bread and wine, he composed the post-Depression sequence "The Man with the Blue Guitar," where, writing with a deliberate simplicity of diction, he took on a pastoral persona, that of "a shearsman of sorts" who has no European instrument on which to play, only a "blue guitar" that paradoxically changes the appearance of things while leaving them as they are. Realizing that he could not permanently adopt a reductive rustic persona, Stevens resumed the attitudes of an educated American, aware of European literature but eager to achieve something different.

Stevens's early enthusiasm for the founding of a new American poetry became dampened, later, by his realization of the eventual death of all cultures, including that of the United States: "Cotton Mather died when I was a boy," he says, and the mouse that swallowed Mather's steeple is now attacking the latest temporary ideology: "Go, mouse, go nibble at Lenin in his tomb" ("The Blue Buildings in the Summer Air"). Stevens's anxiety concerning the place of art in any culture in time and space appears most intensely in a long five-poem sequence, "Owl's Clover," which he excluded (probably because of its sedulously programmatic nature) from his *Collected Poems*. In it, he imagined, first, a sublime European marble statuary-group of horses leaping toward the air—then asked how such statues would fare now in the United States, in Africa, and in Russia. The incommensurability of the art of different cultures is faced squarely in the sequence—sometimes tragically, as in "The Old Woman and the Statue" (what can such a statue mean to a destitute old woman during the Depression?), sometimes reflectively ("But could the statue stand in Africa? / . . . Could marble still / Be marble after the drenching reds?"), sometimes comically (in Russia, Basilewsky has just conducted a "Concerto for Airplane and Pianoforte," and where there is such taste there is no room for genius). In the penultimate poem of "Owl's Clover," the owl of Minerva has found no permanent wisdom, and Stevens offers a dejected query: "We walk / In the park. We regret we have no nightingale. / . . . / Where shall we find more than derisive words?" In the final poem, he attempts to imagine a better future, but concludes that "Even imagination has an end, / When the statue is not a thing imagined, a stone."

Abandoning the idea of constructing a total idea of art that might lie behind its temporary cultural instantiations, Stevens sometimes sought to lodge Americanness in his poetry by referring to indigenous history, to the time of his Pennsylvania Dutch (actually, "Deutsch," German) ancestors, as in "The Bed of Old John Zeller" or "Extraordinary References," in which a mother says to her child, "My Jacomyntje!/Your great-grandfather was an Indian fighter." These are not particularly successful poems, but they are among Stevens's ceaseless experiments in how to be an American poet. He also tries to found Americanness in space, taking Mount Chocorua as a symbol of the American sublime: "In spite of [misery], the gigantic bulk of him/Grew strong, as if doubt never touched his heart" ("Chocorua to Its Neighbor"). He mentions Hartford, Connecticut, the Farmington River. Yet in spite of such historical or geographical allusions, much of Stevens's poetry of America never identifies its country of origin at all. Instead, it puts the problem of an American art abstractly, as in the poem "Somnambulisma," where Stevens imagines a desolate land that never acquired an art of its own, that never produced a restless hovering bird of the imagination, a land whose inhabitants never were granted a version of themselves through the "pervasive being" of art:

> Without this bird that never settles, without
> Its generations that follow in their universe,
> The ocean, falling and falling on the hollow shore,
>
> Would be a geography of the dead: not of that land
> To which they may have gone, but of the place in which
> They lived, in which they lacked a pervasive being.

And Stevens, not restricting himself to North America, retains a yearning to create an all-embracing Americanness of the Western hemisphere, implying a sense of self drawn from South America as well as from the United States. His figures of "Mrs. Alfred Uruguay" (who aspires to the summit of vision "Montevideo"), of the Argentine writer (in "The Novel"), of the recurrent figure of the hidalgo (in "An Ordinary Evening in New Haven" and elsewhere), of the "Pastor Caballero" (in the poem of that name), and even the unhappy guitarist Jaime ("Ha-eé-me") of "Jouga" all reflect that wish.

But I want to end by calling attention to the saddest of Stevens's meditations on the possibility of an American poetry, the 1950 piece called "The Sick Man." It is a poem wondering whether American literature can ever heal the civil and moral wounds of slavery and the Civil War—whether it can ever combine, into a single song, the music of Southern blacks and Northern whites. Because Stevens omitted "The Sick Man" from the *Collected Poems,* only recently has it attracted comment. It begins by characterizing the two musics, both nonverbal—instrumental ("drifting bands") in the South, choral ("singing without words") in the North—each by itself incomplete:

> And in a bed in one room, alone, a listener
> Waits for the unison of the music of the drifting bands
> And the dissolving chorals, waits for it and imagines

The words of winter in which these two will come together,
In the ceiling of the distant room, in which he lies,
The listener, listening to the shadows, seeing them[.]

The sick man wants to find in himself the health that would unite the two musics by adding, to the instruments and the singing, the necessary third ingredient— words. He yearns to supply what is missing: "peaceful, blissful words, well-tuned, well-sung, well-spoken." American poetry, Stevens implies, is still an ailing art of two separate cultures; a unifying language has not yet been found. And Stevens himself, the sick man, already past the biblical three score and ten, will die without having been able to attain his country's well-being, for all his Utopian effort:

He lies,
The listener, listening to the shadows, seeing them,

Choosing out of himself, out of everything within him,
Speech for the quiet, good hail of himself, good hail, good hail,
The peaceful, blissful words, well-tuned, well-sung, well-spoken.

The reproach voiced in "The Sick Man" leaves Stevens feeling "vitally deprived" ("Americana"). He takes his leave of life in "Farewell without a Guitar":

Spring's bright paradise has come to this.
Now the thousand-leaved green falls to the ground.
Farewell, my days.

The hidalgo makes a last ghostly appearance in "A Spanish storm, / A wide, still Aragonese, / In which the horse walks home without a rider, // Head down."

When Stevens gives up on making poetry American, it is because he assents to its ultimate abstraction from mimesis. In "Of Mere Being," generally thought to be his last poem, he admits that the music of poetry is not indigenous, but foreign:

A gold-feathered bird
Sings in the palm, without human meaning,
Without human feeling, a foreign song.

It is no less satisfying for its foreignness: "The bird's fire-fangled feathers dangle down." The consent to abstraction gains its emotional power from Stevens's life-long effort to make his modernist poetry abstract *and* American, formal *and* mimetic, an effort that moves us as we perceive it unfolding through "the whole of Harmonium"—the title he first proposed for what became the 1954 *Collected Poems.*

Bibliography: Peter Brazeau, *Parts of a World: Wallace Stevens Remembered: An Oral Biography* (New York, 1983). Holly Stevens, *Souvenirs and Prophecies: The Young Wallace Stevens* (New York, 1977). Wallace Stevens, *The Collected Poems of Wallace Stevens* (New York, 1954); *Collected Poetry and Prose,* ed. F. Kermode and J. Richardson (New York, 1997); *The Letters of Wallace Stevens*, ed. Holly Stevens (Berkeley, CA, 1996).

HELEN VENDLER

1955, August 11

Zora Neale Hurston denounces *Brown v. Board of Education*

"THE SELF-RESPECT OF MY PEOPLE"

In August of 1955, Zora Neale Hurston wrote to the *Orlando Sentinel,* her local newspaper, attacking one of the most important legal decisions on race relations in American history. A well-known African American novelist, folklorist, journalist, and anthropologist with a sassy, ironic voice and deep powers of observation and description, Hurston had been a star of the Harlem Renaissance. In her thirty-year writing career, she had adhered to the unofficial Harlem maxim of fighting for "civil rights by copyright." She had always written from a place in which black humanity was assumed and black culture and creativity revered. She disdained the elitism and cultural condescension of some of the New Negro movement's architects. Hurston was an educated, modern, sophisticated woman —raised in a small all-black town, she made a way out of no way, moving from the swamps of central Florida to Baltimore, Washington (securing an education at Morgan Academy and Howard University), New York City. She won scholarships and awards that enabled her to work in New Orleans, Haiti, and Honduras. So why then, after a lifetime spent documenting and demonstrating the richness of black culture, insisting on black equality in a nation where legal and social segregation of blacks and whites was taken for granted, would Hurston decry a court decision that unanimously ruled segregation in public education unconstitutional and set the stage for the civil rights movement?

As Hurston made clear in her letter to the *Orlando Sentinel* editor, "the whole matter revolves around the self-respect of my people." That Hurston had a specific and even unique view of self-respect is revealed in the question she asks next: "How much satisfaction can I get from a court order for somebody to associate with me who does not wish me near them?" From her point of view, the *Brown* decision was an insult, because it decreed that there was a fundamental, hierarchical difference between black and white education and, perhaps, culture —a difference that, in her opinion and experience, was absolutely specious. "But if there are adequate Negro schools and prepared instructors and instructions," she wrote, "then there is nothing different except the presence of white people."

What was at issue in the *Brown* decision was not racial pride as she had defined and lived it—making the utmost of what life has dealt you—but rather an issue of social and economic justice, an adherence to the principles of the Constitution. She was writing from her own experience, seeking her own judgment— and if her world narrowed at its end, causing her to think of her remarkable life as the rule, rather than the exception, that is a result, ironically, of Hurston's originality as a racial thinker and writer. From an early age, she made a commitment not to join what she called the "sobbing school of Negrohood." Instead, she saw herself among the "Negroes Without Self-Pity," as she titled a 1943 essay. In 1955, in her response to *Brown v. Board of Education,* Hurston focused on questions of character rather than those of systemic inequality, presaging later black critics of affirmative action. One of the most controversial statements ever made by an African American intellectual, Hurston's opinion in the *Sentinel* affected her legacy indelibly, as it seemed to confirm charges of conservatism leveled at her earlier by contemporaries such as Richard Wright. Hurston's work eventually fell into obscurity, until it was famously championed by Alice Walker in the 1970s.

While Hurston's politics in general took a definite right turn in her later life, her racial thinking was somewhat atypical from the start. Her upbringing in Eatonville, Florida, all the days spent on the porch of the all-black town's general store, instilled in her a sense of racial well-being, rather than a sense of deficit. A "pure Negro town—charter, mayor, council, town marshal and all," Eatonville was, for the most part, self-sufficient, independent: in her words, a "burly, boiling, hard-hitting, rugged-individualistic setting." Filled with a spirit of black pride and self-determination, Hurston did not feel "tragically colored." In fact, she did not feel herself to be "colored" at all until her mother's death, when Hurston was thirteen, forced her to leave Eatonville, and to leave behind as well her previous sense of herself as, in some ways, unraced. As she explains in "How It Feels to Be Colored Me," Hurston left Eatonville as "Zora," and arrived in Jacksonville as "a little colored girl." Although she describes this time as a moment of crisis, in the face of segregation and relentless discrimination she worked—in a way, all of her life—to regain the feeling of the "unconscious Zora of Eatonville before the Hegira." As this "cosmic Zora," Hurston managed to preserve a sense of blackness that was gloriously different from American culture as it was defined almost everywhere. Just as Eatonville indelibly shaped her childhood, Harlem and New York made their mark on her continuing evolution as an artist and a person. When she arrived in New York City in 1925, at thirty-three, she joined with the many who believed, along with James Weldon Johnson, that "nothing will do more to change the mental attitude and raise [the Negro's] status than a demonstration of intellectual parity by the Negro through the production of literature and art."

Hurston jumped right into the fray, but on her own terms. She came to New York initially to accept an award for her play *Color Struck*—walking into the awards dinner and loudly declaring her name and the name of her work, as if to say that New York was indeed "color struck"; the black and white literary establishments wanted only a certain type of blackness. Writing about the culture of the rural, working-class, creative folk she knew, rather than about urban striving Negroes, brought her recognition; as a writer she had nothing to prove and everything to share. This allowed her to carve out a niche in the literary scene and to negotiate its patronage culture.

The leading Harlem writers were backed by influential white individuals or philanthropic organizations; Hurston and Langston Hughes shared the patronage of the socialite writer and photographer Carl Van Vechten and socialite and philanthropist Charlotte Osgood Mason. Hurston was admitted to Barnard by

Annie Nathan Meyer—a trustee of the college, whom she met at the awards dinner that had brought her to New York—and this made Hurston the woman who would integrate Barnard.

Hurston's letters to Meyer record the difficulty of her Barnard experience, with laments about fellow students making fun of her accent in French, the expense of a golf outfit for physical education classes, her triumph over an affront concerning the prom (she was asked to bring a man as light-skinned as herself). She signs some of these letters to Meyer "Your most humble and obedient servant," and refers to herself as "your little pickaninny," gestures whose irony and potential humor are difficult to parse; one can read an acknowledgment of the relationship between patronage and slavery.

After Barnard, under the direction of the revered cultural anthropologist Franz Boas, Hurston became the first trained African American anthropologist, with a particular focus on "an anti-racist version of cultural relativism," a direct challenge to the evolutionary social Darwinist perspective. With Boas, Hurston confirmed what she already knew: that there was a fundamental relationship between language and culture and that the rich, metaphor-laden, humorous, and ironic speech of the people she knew was not only worthy of study but also a key to understanding consciousness in culture. Although her main patron, Charlotte Osgood Mason, known to her charges as "the Godmother," was reportedly not in favor of Hurston's desire to pursue a PhD and Hurston never completed an advanced degree, she nevertheless used her time at Barnard and Columbia (as well as Meyer's connections and Mason's money) to define her life's work. She kept her sights on advancing her own remarkable goal: to be a creative black woman, living by the labor of her own mind.

The strength of her convictions about the integrity of black culture is what led her to the denunciation of *Brown*. Those convictions only grew as Hurston's efforts to chronicle black life and remain an independent woman became more difficult as her life advanced. In her early writing career, Hurston was supported by grants from the Rosenwald and Guggenheim foundations; her best-known novel, *Their Eyes Were Watching God* (1936), was written in just seven weeks while Hurston was researching voodoo in Haiti on a Guggenheim Fellowship. Hurston's time in Haiti, which began with research in Jamaica, and also led to *Tell My Horse* (1937), an account of the folklore she collected, inspired her to complete the allegorical novel *Moses, Man of the Mountain* (1939) and gave Hurston an interesting enough national profile to warrant the publication of her autobiography, *Dust Tracks on the Road* (1942). Despite this success, by the middle 1940s Hurston was not able to support herself by her writing alone. She worked as a choreographer and taught literature and drama; she wrote for Hollywood. In the early 1950s a financial crisis forced her to take a job as a maid. During this time she also suffered a number of shocks similar to those in her early life that had redefined how she saw herself racially. One of Hurston's biographers, Carla Kaplan, points in particular to Hurston's reaction to a false accusation of moral impropriety—she was alleged to have molested a young boy—in New York City in the 1940s. The details of the case had been leaked by a black court official to the black press, which lambasted Hurston without any proof. Having been out of the country when the incident allegedly occurred, she was easily proved innocent; nevertheless she felt as if she had been betrayed by her community and refused the support of the black literary establishment. She retreated permanently to Florida and became increasingly involved in local politics, supporting conservatives, especially those who were rabidly anti-Communist. Trying to keep body and soul together, during this period Hurston relied on what she knew and what she could count on: her sense of the innate dignity and value of the lives and lessons of the people among whom she grew up.

The seeds of Hurston's 1955 pronouncement are seen clearly in a letter she wrote to the Harlem Renaissance poet Countee Cullen in 1943. Beginning with a declaration of their shared aesthetic, the letter quickly moves to a discussion of segregation in which Hurston declares that she sees the matter only in terms of a "fierce desire for human justice. The rest is up to the individual." "Personally, I have no desire for white association except where I am sought and the pleasure is mutual," she said. "That feeling grows out of my own self-respect . . . Any other viewpoint would be giving too much value to a mere white hide." Antisegregationist arguments, even at this prescient stage of the civil rights movement, tacitly assumed the superiority of a "white hide" for Hurston. She denounced such arguments as the underbelly of liberalism and railed against whites who promoted them and blacks who bought into them, rejecting any Negro who "considers himself or herself paid off and honored by it," referring to association or intermarriage with whites. That these sentiments and those who held them were a political problem for Hurston is made clear in the rest of the letter, in which she associates such people with what she earlier called the "sobbing school of Negrohood" and "the Russians" or Communists. Both groups promoted an ideal of color blindness, which Hurston calls a "wishful illusion," while actually operating within an invisible and hierarchical conception of color consciousness.

When Hurston wrote her 1955 opinion on *Brown v. Board of Education,* she anticipated that she would be misunderstood: that she would be considered one of the "'handkerchief-headed niggers' who bow low before the white man and sell out my own people out of cowardice." But, as she goes on to explain, in a rather convoluted way, it was not cowardice but a certain bravery that drove her to take the stand that so damaged her legacy. After the many statements about the sorry state of race relations and the threat of communism that she makes in the letter— that blacks follow whites blindly, as mules follow white horses, that "govt by fiat" can replace the Constitution—she ends with a defense of Negro teachers: "It is a contradiction in terms to scream race pride while at the same time spurning Negro teachers and self-association." In a letter to a friend a year later, she admitted that as a Negro, she "could not be in favor of segregation," but she was nevertheless upset "about the way that they go about ending it," implying that her primary objection to the Supreme Court decision was the way in which the Court had argued *for* racial equality by claiming and demonstrating the insufficiency of the conditions in which blacks lived and learned. For Hurston, *Brown* assumed notions of white superiority and black inferiority; "It would be against all nature," she wrote in her autobiography, in a chapter called "My People! My People!" "for the Negroes to be either at the bottom, top, or in between. It has never happened with anybody else, so why with us? . . . It is up to the individual. If you haven't got it, you can't show it. If you have got it, you can't hide it." At the risk of infamy, Hurston chose not to hide it, to defend her people, to defend herself.

Bibliography: Valerie Boyd, *Wrapped in Rainbows: The Life of Zora Neale Hurston* (New York, 2002). Zora Neale Hurston, *Dust Tracks on a Road* (1942) and "How It Feels to Be Colored Me" (1926), in Zora Neale Hurston, *Folklore, Memoirs, and Other Writings* (New York, 1995). James Weldon Johnson, ed., *The Book of American Negro Poetry* (New York, 1983). Carla Kaplan, ed., *Zora Neale Hurston: A Life in Letters* (New York, 2002). David Levering Lewis, *When Harlem Was in Vogue* (New York, 1997). Alice Walker, *In Search of Our Mother's Gardens: Womanist Prose* (San Diego, 1983).

MONICA L. MILLER

1955, September 21
Rocky Marciano knocks out Archie Moore at Yankee Stadium

THE END OF AMERICAN SPORTING LIFE

Between the Victorian era and the sixties, boxing was a regular and prominent feature of American life. Knowing something about the fights—being good with your hands, or maintaining an opinion about the welterweight division or fixed bouts or how to beat a southpaw—was a very common piece of equipment in the toolbox of American cultural competence, especially the section of it devoted to masculinity. Boxing shared with baseball the status of the sport that mattered most (with horse racing not far off the pace), and cultural paths of least resistance allowed almost anyone to know at least a little about it. Newspapers offered daily coverage by reporters who specialized in boxing, magazines from the *Police Gazette* to the *New Yorker* prided themselves on their frequent fight pieces, and magazines devoted entirely to boxing thrived. Boxing gyms, like saloons and union halls, were typical features of working-class neighborhoods across the range of ethnic and racial variety. Middle- and upper-class boys could find their own paths to the manly art; Theodore Roosevelt boxed at Harvard and FDR at Groton, for instance. Film, radio, and then television offered boxing in heaping doses. Remember Eloise, the girl in the much-loved children's book who lives at the Plaza? Remember what her nanny does on Friday evenings? She orders beer from room service, smokes, and watches the fights on NBC's *Gillette Cavalcade of Sports*. And there was plenty of opportunity to see boxing in the flesh, from numerous fight cards in modest venues featuring local tough guys to marquee events in stadiums featuring world-famous pugilists. The land reverberated with the fight world's signature cadences, banged out on speed bags and typewriters, and called out by jargon-shouting fans: "Stop waltzin' with 'im, ya bum, and hook off the jab! Over 'n under!"

In *The Sweet Science* (1956), a collection of fight pieces first published in the *New Yorker,* A. J. Liebling elegizes this golden age of American boxing, which at midcentury was beginning to end. In his introduction, Liebling notes "certain generalized conditions today, like full employment and a late school-leaving age, that militate against the development of first-rate professional boxers." As football, basketball, and other school-based team ball games rose to dominate sports culture, the structural underpinnings of boxing in the industrial neighborhood order withered away, eroded by deindustrialization, suburbanization, and other long-wave forces that transformed the inner city. The more easily identifiable villain was television, which "by putting on a free boxing show almost every night of the week," had "knocked out of business the hundreds of small-city and neighborhood boxing clubs where youngsters had a chance to learn their trade and journeymen to mature their skills." The fights were a mainstay of early television, which kept boxing in the public eye while hastening its uprooting from the social landscape.

In *The Sweet Science,* Rocky Marciano, a TV star, ushers in the new order by beating Jersey Joe Walcott, Ezzard Charles, and Archie Moore, all superb technicians in the twilight of their careers, and by brutally retiring the radio hero Joe Louis, the premier heavyweight of the golden age. Marciano makes a grand entrance by blasting the aging Brown Bomber through the ropes and into the sad endgame of his life. Liebling observes ringsiders' reactions with characteristic acuteness:

> Right after Marciano knocked Louis down the first time, Sugar Ray Robinson [the reigning middleweight champion and the greatest fighter of that, or perhaps any, era] started working his way toward the ring, as if drawn by some horrid fascination, and by the time Rocky threw the final right, Robinson's hand was on the lowest rope of the ring, as if he meant to jump in. The punch knocked Joe through the ropes and he lay on the ring apron, only one leg inside.
>
> The tall blonde was bawling, and pretty soon she began to sob. The fellow who had brought her was horrified. "Rocky didn't do anything wrong," he said. "He didn't foul him. What you booing?"
>
> The blonde said, "You're so cold. I hate you, too."

The silver age of Muhammad Ali was just over the horizon, and the fights would sustain a strong presence on broadcast television for another generation (until cable and pay-per-view demoted them to the status of niche-market attraction), but the half century of boxing's cultural ascendancy was coming to a close. Marciano's supporters, "unsavory young yokels with New England accents," cheer their man "as if he were a high-school football team," a troubling portent. High school football is the cultural polar opposite of the urban male demimonde of sporting life in which fight people had made themselves so cozily at home in the first half of the twentieth century.

"Ahab and Nemesis," the piece that culminates *The Sweet Science,* deserves a place not only on any list of the finest fight writing but on all-time pound-for-pound lists of great essays on any subject. In it, Liebling stages Marciano's defeat of Archie Moore as a resonant confrontation between force and intellect. Marciano, by now the reigning champion, embodies force. Younger than Moore, much stronger, and stylistically cruder, he's a slugger who keeps the punches coming until the other man has had enough. Waiting in his corner just before the bell, "he resembled a Great Dane who has heard the word 'bone.'" Moore, the challenger, represents intellect. A ring-wise virtuoso, erudite and elegant in his craft, he has "the kind of Faustian mind that will throw itself against the problem of perpetual motion, or of how to pick horses first, second, third, *and* fourth in every race." The rise of Marciano has inflicted on Moore "the pangs of a supreme exponent of *bel canto* who sees himself crowded out of the opera house by a guy who can only shout."

In the second round, Moore lures Marciano into a tactical trap and knocks him down with a crisp right thrown inside the arc of Marciano's left hook. "He had hit him right if ever I saw a boxer hit right, with a classic brevity and conciseness," but the referee has counted only to two when Marciano bounces to his feet, ready for more. "I do not know what took place in Mr. Moore's breast when he saw him get up. He may have felt, for the moment, like Don Giovanni when the Commendatore's statue grabbed at him—startled because he thought he had killed the guy already—or like Ahab when he saw the White Whale take down Fedallah, harpoons and all." Moore drags "his shattered faith in the unities and humanities" back to his corner at the end of the round. "As a young fighter of conventional tutelage, he must have heard his preceptors say hundreds of times, 'They will all go if you hit them right.' If a fighter did not believe that, he would be in the position of a Euclidean without faith in the hundred-and-eighty-degree triangle." Well, he "had hit a guy right, and the guy hadn't gone. But there is no geezer in Moore, any more than there was in the master of the *Pequod*." Moore fights valiantly, brilliantly, but Marciano wears him down and overwhelms him. The challenger is counted out in the ninth round "with his left arm hooked over the middle rope as he tried to rise. It was a crushing defeat for the higher faculties and a lesson in intellectual humility, but he had made a hell of a fight."

Liebling locates the primal struggle between brawling and technique at the root not only of boxing but of writing about boxing. At the beginning of "Ahab and Nemesis" he quotes from Heywood Broun, a reporter of the 1920s and 1930s who favored classically sound boxing ("There is still a kick in style, and tradition carries a nasty wallop"); later in the piece Liebling cites Pierce Egan, "the Edward Gibbon and Sir Thomas Malory of the old London prize ring," who favored brawlers: "gluttons" and "prime bottom fighters," in Egan's Regency slang. Liebling presents himself as a dissenting Brounian surrounded by an Eganite crowd, pro-Marciano and "basically anti-intellectual" in its instincts. Most of the fans at Yankee Stadium just want to see somebody get hurt, while Liebling is looking for something else: a demonstration of principle, a lesson in being human.

The slippery work of extracting nuggets of meaning from a fight is Liebling's great subject, the problem that shapes not only the themes but also the form of his writing about boxing. He mixes registers and allusive gestures up and down the highbrow-lowbrow spectrum, assembling an interpretive repertoire suited to the challenge posed by the fights. To follow the nuances of his account of the turning point in the second round, for instance, the reader needs to know something about opera, Melville, Euclid, and Aristotle's *Poetics*. At other points Liebling compares Archie Moore not only to Faust and Ahab but also to the ballerina Margot Fonteyn, the pianist Arthur Rubinstein, the statesman Winston Churchill, the director and actor Orson Welles, Camus's Sisyphus, and a Japanese print entitled "Shogun Engaged in Strategic Contemplation in the Midst of War." Ripely colloquial language punctuates and ironically offsets this checklist of high-cultural literacy. The phrase "he thought he had killed the guy already," for example, appearing between references to Don Giovanni and Ahab, serves to denature their pompousness by underscoring it, and "geezer" both ratifies and deflates the recurring comparison of Moore to Ahab. Whitey Bimstein, a trainer, noting that Marciano abandoned the right-left combination he was attempting when Moore knocked him down, says to Liebling, "He never trun it again in the fight." Insider voices like Bimstein's carry a different kind of cultural authority, the practical working knowledge of skilled craftspeople.

Each register complements and ironizes the others. Each way of understanding boxing, from the shop-floor know-how of fight people to the symbolic and interpretive approaches suggested by references to literature and art, helps the reader see a particular order of meaning in the bout and fills in the blind spots left by others. Contrasting the variety of ways of seeing becomes the point of the piece, dramatizing the process of making sense of what would appear to most readers as opaquely chaotic violence.

Liebling took pleasure in portraying himself as a character uniquely equipped to meet such challenges. A gouty fat man who was also a distinguished war correspondent, food writer, and press critic, he had formal education (he attended Dartmouth but did not graduate) but he also cultivated the Ishmaelian charm of the autodidact, always a little too eager to share his learning and a little tone-deaf when it came to distinctions between the canonical and the esoteric. He was a sound reporter, well trained at big-city newspapers, but also an idiosyncratically well-read dabbler and aesthete. He knew his way around the fine arts and classical literature, but he also knew fight people, gamblers, songwriters, grifters, and other characters who exemplified what his editors at the *New Yorker* called "low-life." With just a few confident brush strokes he can sketch a self-portrait as a typical urban intellectual of his time, a child of the middle class drawn to both the library and the street, as he does in this sentence describing the buildup to the Marciano-Moore bout: "There was no doubt that the fight had caught the public imagination, ever sensitive to a meeting between Hubris and Nemesis, as the boys on the quarterlies would say, and the bookies were laying 18–5 on Nemesis, according to the boys on the dailies, who always seem to know."

Liebling was not just an elegist, recording the passing of what had been; he also helped assemble the materials of epic, showing the way forward to writers who responded to what came next. To the New Journalists, the wave of nonfiction innovators who mapped the changing social and cultural landscape of America in the sixties, he bequeathed his novelistic voice, his gift for combining first-person experience and a reporter's rigorous pursuit of the bigger story, his high-low cultural range, his eye for the traffic between margins and mainstream, and a digressive long-form style more suited to the magazine than the newspaper.

The New Journalists had a taste for boxing, which even in decline continued to enjoy its traditional status as excellent material. The pungent talk and secret lore of fight people still drew writers, as did the wealth of sights and sounds to capture in arresting language. Gay Talese's profile of the deposed heavyweight champion Floyd Patterson was an early landmark of the genre, and Tom Wolfe reports experiencing a stylistic awakening ("*What inna namea christ is this—*") in the fall of 1962 when he read Talese's profile of Joe Louis in *Esquire*. Norman Mailer and many other writers of the period found in Muhammad Ali a quintessential subject, an outsize figure so original and poetic that he obliged writers of nonfiction to employ the techniques of fiction.

In the opening pages of *The Kandy-Kolored Tangerine-Flake Streamline Baby* (1965), Wolfe perfectly captures the betwixt-and-between state of both boxing and writing about boxing in the early sixties. He begins by disparaging the journalistic old order, attacking the "totem newspaper" as a desiccated artifact that people carry around to mark their identity rather than to read with interest. One kind of totem newspaper serves as the "symbol of the frightened chair-arm-doilie Vicks Vapo-Rub *Weltanschauung*" (think *Boston Globe*) while the other propounds a "tough-but-wholesome outlook, the Mom's Pie view of life" (think *Boston Herald*). Those who carry the second kind of totem "can go off to the bar and drink a few 'brews' and retail some cynical remarks about Zora Folley and how the fight game is these days and round it off, though, with how George Chuvalo has 'a lot of heart,' which he got, one understands, by eating mom's pie." Wolfe turns to boxing to exemplify a fading manly blue-collar culture and the moribund orders of writing associated with it, all willfully blind to what's really happening—the encroaching grooviness, the developing transformation of morals and politics and just about everything else. But one of the chapters that follows is a profile of Ali, and on almost every page Wolfe records his debt in both approach and content to fight writers and other connoisseurs of low life who came before, including the sportswriter W. C. Heinz, Liebling's *New Yorker* colleague Joseph Mitchell, and especially Liebling himself, a graceful and far-seeing stylist who wrote lasting nonfiction literature founded on solid reporting.

Bibliography: W. C. Heinz and Nathan Ward, eds., *The Book of Boxing* (Kingston, NY, 1999). A. J. Liebling, *Just Enough Liebling*, introduction by David Remnick (New York, 2004); *A Neutral Corner: Boxing Essays,* ed. Fred Warner and James Barbour (New York, 1990); *The Sweet Science* (New York, 1956). Raymond Sokolov, *Wayward Reporter: The Life of A. J. Liebling* (New York, 1980). Tom Wolfe, *The New Journalism,* with an anthology edited by Tom Wolfe and E. W. Johnson (New York, 1973).

CARLO ROTELLA

1955, October 7

Allen Ginsberg gives his first public reading of "Howl"

A Generation in Miniature

In 1955, Allen Ginsberg was twenty-nine, ambitious for fame as a writer but completely unknown. He had recently abandoned New York to follow Neal Cassady, the first intense love of his life, westward to California. That relationship failed disastrously, but Ginsberg stayed on in San Francisco and found a job as a copywriter in a small advertising-marketing firm. He discovered a community of young artists and poets whose explorations, creative, sexual, and spiritual, provided balm for the many troubles he had suffered during the previous decade. Long-standing fears that his sexual desires must always be frustrated, that he was doomed to live isolated and lonely, melted away with a series of lovers, both men and women, who desired him as he was. The poetry he was writing changed as well. When he started drafting the lines that would take shape as "Howl," he no longer wanted to craft the orderly, erudite verse that his teachers at Columbia University lauded. He wanted to write a work that captured the wild messiness of his life. He wanted to say clearly what the experience of being expelled from school, arrested, and condemned to time in a psychiatric hospital meant to him, without fear of how anybody might respond.

While working on the first versions of "Howl," Ginsberg collaborated in planning a reading by young local poets at the Six Gallery in San Francisco, a small artist cooperative set up in an abandoned auto repair shop. Ginsberg contributed the copy for the postcard announcing the evening:

> 6 Poets at 6 Gallery
> Philip Lamantia reading mss. of late John Hoffman—Mike McClure, Allen Ginsberg, Gary Snyder & Phil Whalen—all sharp new straightforward writing—remarkable collection of angels on one stage reading their poetry. No charge, small collection for wine, and postcards. Charming event.

Approximately 150 people showed up to hear the reading. Of the poets on the program, only Lamantia had ever been published. Deep into exploring the relation of drugs and consciousness, Lamantia was not ready to put his experiences with peyote or heroin on paper. Instead, he read the verse of a friend who had died from a peyote overdose. McClure, at twenty-three the youngest reader on the program, read "Point Lobos: Animism" and "For the Death of 100 Whales," two works expressing the poet's developing biological mysticism. The second poem responded with rage to a recent news report of U.S. soldiers who had slaughtered a pod of whales just for the fun of it. Although the poem started out as protest, it ended with an austere religious vision of a spiritual force linking humanity to all other life. Even if the "undersoul" was desecrated in the nation, Mc-

Clure's poem asserted that its force was ever present in flesh, in plant life, even in rocks, ready to replenish the spirits of whoever acknowledged the emptiness of life in the modern United States.

Whalen, at thirty-two the oldest person on the program as well as the most deeply knowledgeable in Buddhism, read "Plus ça change," a stark if humorous set of punning images playing on the varied connotations of the word "brooding." His contribution to the then-trendy theme of ennui stressed how fear of communication, whether verbal or physical, effectively isolated Americans from each other and trapped each person in the prison of his or her unfulfilled longings. Snyder, about to head off to Kyoto, Japan, to begin an apprenticeship at the Daitokuji Monastery, concluded the evening with "The Berry Feast," a group of poems evoking the Native American mythic figure of Coyote, the archetypal trickster whose deceptions suddenly reveal hidden cosmic truths: a sardonic role model for young contemporary poets, whose messages of a divine order immanent in all things fell on deaf ears. Given the indifference they faced, poets would have to trick Americans into paying attention.

The emotional highlight of the evening was Allen Ginsberg's reading of the first section of "Howl" (the second and third sections were still incomplete). Ginsberg was probably the next-to-last participant in the program. Never having read in public before, Ginsberg was understandably nervous, but as his litany of images cataloging the bleak state of contemporary life in the United States marched forward, his voice grew stronger and more confident. He began with the soon-to-be-famous indictment that he had seen "the best minds of my generation" driven mad and left to face the world "starving hysterical naked." The phrase referred specifically to Carl Solomon, a young intellectual in New York whom Ginsberg had met when they were both living in a psychiatric hospital. More generally "the best minds" belonged to any young man that Ginsberg knew and loved. A quick succession of cinematic images describes events in his own life and in those of his closest friends that revealed the dangerous hypocrisy of modern American life. The insistent drumbeat of the word "who" is repeated sixty-one times, initiating precise but often puzzling images such as "who walked all night with their shoes full of blood on the snowbank docks waiting for a door in the East River to open to a room full of steamheat and opium." The cascading words create a collective persona of the alienated young male, who could be any young person frustrated with the hypocrisy of the times. The narrative spine of the poem protests the cruel medical treatments that doctors devised to destroy Solomon's individuality, but the poem speaks broadly and generally of drug addiction, of poverty and self-degradation, of turning to prostitution or robbery, of traveling randomly across the United States and Mexico, of boring jobs, of the anxieties that life in a militarized, death-oriented nation induces. Ginsberg spoke in direct language of sex, a source of sorrow and frustration, but also a path to redemption that revealed the powerful force of the divine within each person.

Ginsberg's themes, as well as his critique of U.S. society, were consistent in content and spirit with the work that Whalen, McClure, and Snyder presented, but Ginsberg did not balance his rage with images of a transcendent cosmological reality nor with clever language games. All that would come later in subsequent work. The first section of "Howl" presents the author's personal descent into the inferno of contemporary America, and he used clear, direct language to describe and diagnose the catastrophe.

Against the soul-destroying forces dominating the nation, Ginsberg invoked the figure of "NC," his actual erstwhile lover Neal Cassady, eulogized as the "Adonis of Denver." NC is a divine creature in sexual union with everyone and everything he encounters. NC's voracious phallic sexuality, expressed equally in fast cars ripping between the coasts, torrents of nonstop chatter, and a view of every relationship as a chance for another orgasm, makes him pure spirit in bodily form. Society might eventually kill him, but NC will never be conquered.

Ginsberg not only confessed but celebrated his desire for NC to possess him. To be free, Ginsberg had to celebrate everything that made him different from the American norm. Yes, he was Jewish; yes, he was a socialist; yes, he was a poet. He was also a queer who desired the caresses of other men, and that made him a threat because, of all his identities, youth and sex expressed most clearly that divine force within every person—the only force powerful enough to confront social convention. His acceptance of same-sex desire as an ordinary, positive part of life made the work appear powerfully frank and particularly suspect to defenders of public morality when the poem finally reached a broader public.

At the end of the first section, the poet stands naked, as Ginsberg did literally in 1956 when, stripping off every last stitch of his clothing, he finished reading the poem to a group gathered in Los Angeles. At the Six Gallery, the audience called out to him as they might to bebop musicians who had started with a simple tune but quickly leaped into sonic explorations granting the chaotic inner movements of the soul a temporary, fragile, but excruciatingly beautiful form. The pure passion that soared from his body was as hard-edged as a solo by Charles Parker, and, in a poem that described the cry of a jazz saxophone as an angelic voice emerging from America's desire for love, it was meant to be.

Word of mouth about the reading spread quickly. The poets gathered again perhaps a half dozen times in different locations around the Bay Area to repeat the program. Lawrence Ferlinghetti contracted with Ginsberg to publish a first book, starting off with "Howl" followed by ten shorter poems. A decision in 1957 by the U.S. Customs agent at the Port of San Francisco to confiscate and destroy a set of the books printed in England drew national attention to Ginsberg's work. Ferlinghetti reprinted the book in the United States and put it on sale. The San Francisco district attorney then filed criminal charges against Ferlinghetti and his City Lights bookstore sales clerk Shigeyoshi Murao for selling obscene materials. For the prosecutor, any poem that used words like "cocksucker" or alluded to anal intercourse could not possibly contain ideas worthy of attention. A slew of expert witnesses on modern poetry disagreed, and so did Judge Clayton Horn: "Howl" was an honest expression of personal vision. Readers might not agree with Ginsberg's assessment of contemporary America, they might well find his perspective offensive, but the First Amendment protected *their* right to receive and evaluate for themselves what he had to say.

The publicity surrounding the "Howl" case helped convince a major New York publisher to issue Jack Kerouac's novel *On the Road,* on the market without a buyer for the previous six years. Standing for what was quickly named the beat generation, after a phrase of Kerouac's, writers as different as Ferlinghetti, Bob Kaufman, LeRoi Jones (later known as Amiri Baraka), and William Burroughs found readers for works that a decade earlier might have been dismissed as self-indulgent or condemned as nihilistic.

Kerouac was the best known of the beat authors, in part because he produced a new novel almost every year. In *The Dharma Bums* (1958), written quickly at the publisher's insistence to capitalize on the commercial success of *On the Road,* Kerouac set down what has long been the best-known account of the Six Gallery reading—but while acknowledging the power of Ginsberg's breakthrough, Kerouac celebrated Snyder's reading as the emotional heart of the evening. Given that Snyder's character was the hero of the novel, the assessment reflected Kerouac's critique in *The Dharma Bums* that Ginsberg was too personal, too self-obsessed, and too "whiney"—images that simply said that Ginsberg was too Jewish and too queer. Kerouac presented Snyder's dispassionate rejection of Western rationalism as more genuinely radical than Ginsberg's path of confessional redemption. In truth Snyder appealed to Kerouac as a manly, heterosexual, old-stock American from the Pacific Northwest who fit the Jeffersonian archetype of the self-sufficient, self-governing citizen.

In the mass media, stereotyped images of beats indulging their passions regardless of what others might think provided yet another opportunity to discuss whether American institutions promoted or stifled individual creativity, whether consumer society undermined personal responsibility, whether modern bureaucracy had created a mass culture that punished anyone who strayed too far from the opinions of friends, neighbors, and employers. Ginsberg's complaints in "Howl" complemented the opinions of sociologists, psychologists, historians, novelists, and journalists. When the City Lights edition hit bookstores, it joined a broad range of books that criticized American society for repressing individual creativity. Efforts by the customs inspector and the district attorney to ban the book only confirmed the power of conformity and its deadening influence over the nation.

Discussions of conformity and individualism in the mass media typically avoided the most tangible political issues of the decade: the loyalty oaths required of educators during the McCarthy purges, the resurgent movement for civil rights fought in both the courts and in the streets of Southern cities, debates over the militarization of U.S. society during the cold war and the threat of atomic warfare, the persistent high levels of poverty in the world's wealthiest country. The problems facing the nation were defined as existential rather than political—but when in 1957 the Soviet Union put a satellite in orbit around the world, a triumph that contrasted dramatically with several spectacular U.S. failures, the media term beatnik, synthesizing Kerouac's beats with *Sputnik,* the Soviet space vehicle, suggested how much media interest in the nation's bohemian enclaves was linked to fears over U.S. decline. The beatniks were objects of derision, but they emerged as the mass media challenged readers and viewers to meet the growing Soviet threat by asserting themselves more, by pursuing personal excellence, whatever that might be, and in particular by encouraging their children to think for themselves.

The political philosopher Hannah Arendt thought that concerns over conformity were evidence that two competing ideals of social organization, equally important within the history of the United States, had once again entered into conflict. As Arendt saw it, the American Revolution had been political, with new institutions expanding the possibilities for white men to compete with each other for leadership. The pursuit of personal excellence that political liberation had broadened promoted rapid economic growth but generated fears that the country was in danger of losing its moral moorings. Liberal-minded Protestant divines promoted an ideal of social harmony to counter the negative effects resulting from increased individual mobility. As a result, Arendt noted, since Tocqueville's visit to America in 1831, European observers consistently returned home puzzled by the peculiar mixture of aggressive individualism and craven conformity in American society.

The conformism that the ideal of social harmony required endured at the cost of repressing individual ambition and channeling white male aspiration into a narrower range of competitive domains. Arendt thought that mechanisms for suppression grew increasingly costly the longer the ideal prevailed. Stalinist Russia had followed the idea of social harmony to its logical extreme, creating the ideal workers' state on the corpses of the millions who did not fit its design. The American ideal, Arendt noted, was less systematic; it still rested on the lynching, murder, and imprisonment of individuals in subordinate groups who refused to accept their inferiority. For the majority, she thought conformism meant personal isolation accompanied by unusually high rates of alcoholism and depression; periodic outbursts of mass hysteria about immigration, crime, Communist infiltration, or moral impurity; and persistently high rates of violent crime. Arendt worried that the crusade against "conformity" was likely to unleash destructive and disruptive forces. "Self-realization," to use a common phrase of the 1950s, was a matter of individual definition, not subject to collective management except through coercion. The ideal of social harmony, however repressive it could be, at least required a continuing national debate over what people were willing to sacrifice for the sake of an abstract common good. She predicted that the question of how to make personal desire morally responsible would be the greatest challenge facing the next generation.

Bibliography: Hannah Arendt, *On Revolution* (New York, 1958); "The Threat of Conformism," *Commonweal* 60 (September 24, 1954): 607–610. Richard Cándida Smith, *Utopia and Dissent: Art, Poetry, and Politics in California* (Berkeley, CA, 1995). Allen Ginsberg, *Composed on the Tongue* (San Francisco, 1980). Michael McClure, *Scratching the Beat Surface* (San Francisco, 1982). Jonah Raskin, *American Scream: Allen Ginsberg's* Howl *and the Making of the Beat Generation* (Berkeley, CA, 2004). Jason Shinder, *The Poem That Changed America: "Howl" Fifty Years Later* (New York, 2006).

RICHARD CÁNDIDA SMITH

1955, December

Graham Greene names an obscure, reputedly erotic novel one of the three best books of the year

NABOKOV'S *LOLITA*

Is *Lolita* about love? Its first readers, safe to say, fervently hoped not. They would have discovered the novel in a Parisian bookstore, its two volumes bound in the pale-green covers of the Olympia Press's "Traveller's Companion" series — said travelers being seekers of pornography, for that is the companionship Olympia's green camouflage generally promised.

But Vladimir Nabokov was not aware of the Olympian stigma, if stigma it was. The Russian-born writer, who had lived in the United States since 1940, had finished his third English-language novel in 1953 (he had written nine previous novels, among other works, in Russian), and then had watched it undergo rejection at the hands of four American houses. So he was delighted when the Olympia Press publisher, Maurice Girodias, whose notoriety was unknown to Nabokov, took it on. *Lolita* was released without fanfare in Paris in September 1955, sold about five thousand copies, and was not notably reviewed.

Who knows how long this spectacular work — to my mind the greatest American novel of the twentieth century — would have languished were it not for the voracious (or maybe just lascivious) reading habits of Graham Greene, who, in the Christmas edition of the London *Sunday Times,* anointed *Lolita* one of the three best books of 1955? (The other two, both nonfiction, were *Boswell on the Grand Tour* — culled from papers written by James Boswell in the mid-eighteenth century — and *State of France,* by the Swiss writer Herbert Lüthy.)

Greene being Greene, the accolade loosed a furor. In January 1956, John Gordon, the editor of the London *Sunday Express,* used his weekly column to pronounce *Lolita* "the filthiest book I have ever read. Sheer unrestrained pornography." The British Home Office ordered the seizure of all library copies, and in December 1956, at the very moment that the distinguished publisher Gallimard was preparing a French translation, the sale of the Olympia edition was banned in France.

But this was the 1950s, when rock and roll was busy being born, and *Playboy* magazine too; when *Baby Doll* and Brigitte Bardot were in the movie theaters and *Peyton Place* in the bookstores. Western mores were straining at their constrictive membranes as rarely before, and nothing was likelier to whet the public appetite for a thing than the banning of it. By 1958, when *Lolita* was published for the first time in America, by Putnam's, its potential readership had been generously primed. The American edition met with mixed reviews but no censorship, and it quickly became a sensation, the first book since *Gone with the Wind* to sell more than a hundred thousand copies within the first three weeks of publication.

Is *Lolita,* then, about sex? Most of its initial readers would have found the answer disappointing. As Nabokov's narrator, Humbert Humbert, tells us, "These are irrelevant matters. I am not concerned with so-called 'sex' at all." Lolita pretends to be a prison confession, Humbert's swooning, poignant, hilarious, self-loathing, self-aggrandizing portrayal of the crimes that resulted in his incarceration. The proximate crime appears to be murder, but the story's principal victim will not be someone Humbert has killed. In fact, *Lolita* is the story of a very dangerous romantic liaison. A middle-aged but still-dashing European and a scholar of French literature, Humbert contrives to marry his American landlady, the pitifully pretentious Charlotte Haze, in order to be near the real object of his desire, her twelve-year-old daughter, Dolores (called "Lolita," but only by Humbert). Minutes after discovering her new husband's true nature, Charlotte dies in a freak accident, and Humbert spirits his stepdaughter away on a trip across America, preying upon her sexually, frantically avoiding detection, and eventually losing her to his mysterious, almost invisible doppelgänger, a depraved playwright named Clare Quilty. It is Quilty whom Humbert eventually seeks out and murders.

Nabokov had first hit upon the idea of a man's marrying a woman to get at her underage daughter in the 1930s, and had worked it into a paragraph in his Russian novel *The Gift* (1938). By the next year, he had expanded the notion into a rather chilling third-person novella, again in Russian, called *The Enchanter,* with which he was not particularly pleased. He set the idea aside, but in the late '40s what he described as "the throbbing" returned, and this time "the thing had grown in secret the claws and wings of a novel."

At first, though, nothing so feral is in evidence. There is a deadpan foreword by a high-minded and wholly fictional "editor" named John Ray, PhD, and then we are launched, with perhaps the most famous opening since "Stately, plump Buck Mulligan" or "For a long time, I went to bed early": "Lolita, light of my life, fire of my loins. My sin, my soul. Lo-lee-ta." But a more telling line comes a few sentences later. Abruptly, after a dithyramb introducing the idea that Lolita might have had a precursor, Humbert delivers this aside: "You can always count on a murderer for a fancy prose style."

Which isn't true, of course. In fact, one can seldom count on a murderer for a fancy prose style. We've barely begun, and already Humbert has indicated his membership in that famously slippery literary coterie, the Unreliable Narrators. Unreliable, yes, but in this case not altogether wrong. His prose style is fancy indeed, and the way he's just copped to the fact charming in its self-deprecation. He will be a good companion, if not quite the kind Olympia's target traveler had sought.

The direct way for a narrative to excavate a monster is to plunge us right into his soul, in the manner of *Richard III,* say—or the movie *There Will Be Blood.* But there is a more circuitous, and sometimes more effective, route. The storyteller may place his quarry at the center of a narrative labyrinth, like the Minotaur, and invite us to coil our way toward him alongside a surrogate, our Theseus—someone whose responses and perceptions are more likely to mirror our own than those of the creature itself. So it is that the rather colorless Ishmael conveys us toward Ahab, the dullish Clarice pulls us toward Hannibal Lecter, bland Beauty guides us toward enthralling Beast.

With his characteristic self-consciousness, Nabokov combines—and transcends—these conventional approaches. A clue to his innovation glints from a piece he wrote in 1956 to accompany a ninety-page excerpt from *Lolita* that was eventually published in the *Anchor Review,* as a sort of prelude (and legal water-tester) to the full American publication of the book. This remarkable essay, called "On a Book Entitled *Lolita*" and now generally published as an afterword to the novel, begins by describing the "initial shiver of inspiration" for *Lolita,* which was "somehow prompted by a newspaper story about an ape in the Jardin des Plantes, who, after months of coaxing by a scientist, produced the first drawing ever charcoaled by an animal: this sketch showed the bars of the poor creature's cage."

Imagine, then, our Minotaur, pacing at the heart of his labyrinth. Would not the twists and turns that enclose him become, as in the case of the ape, his entire world? (Humbert often compares himself to an ape.) And might he not believe himself to be his story's protagonist? If only, our creature would think, if only we could understand that the labyrinth traps him as insuperably as it traps his prey—and, further, that the seeming innocent who appears simply to be his victim is actually a demon, possessed of powers as frightful, in their way, as his own. Minotaur he may be, but the monsters around him, unrecognized by the reader—these are what the Minotaur feels compelled to expose, by way of explaining his own admittedly foul deeds.

"Now I wish to introduce the following idea," Humbert says. "Between the age limits of nine and fourteen there occur maidens who, to certain bewitched travelers, twice or many times older than they, reveal their true nature, which is not human, but nymphic (that is, demoniac); and these chosen creatures I propose to designate as 'nymphets.'" Nabokov himself was a celebrated lepidopterist, drawn to the discovery and naming of new butterfly species. Likewise Humbert, who seems to insist that his true motivation in telling his tale is simply to identify the previously uncategorized creature, to warn his fellow Minotaurs, "to fix once and for all the perilous magic of nymphets." Lolita, the ultimate nymphet, is, according to Humbert, a "deadly demon," her charms "inhuman" and "bewitching" and "insidious"; she is "unconscious herself of her fantastic power." She is the true monster of the story, Humbert is telling us, and he is among the few capable of navigating the maze toward her, capturing her with the only weapon at his disposal, that fancy prose style—for, as Humbert laments, "Oh, my Lolita, I have only words to play with."

But what words—and what play! Stylistically, *Lolita* may be at once the most virtuosic and the most voluptuously pleasurable American novel. Here are all the elements of a crowd-thrilling entertainment: a crackerjack story hurtling toward a pulpy splash of murder and mayhem; a detective plot replete with cliff-hangers, reversals, and hidden clues; a plethora of sex scenes, though perhaps too euphemistically drawn for some; and lotsa laughs, of every sort—parody, high and low punning, slapstick, bathroom humor, elegant wit. Yet on practically every page, the comic effects give way to stabs of genuine romantic feeling, shafts of terror and horror, description of every description, and a wide-ranging pastiche of literary forms (diaries, letters, poems, songs, even *Who's Who* entries and school class lists). The overripe tone can veer from the acutely satirical to the sublimely pastoral within a line, and Nabokov's evocation of the postwar American landscape, cultural and physical, remains one of the most dazzling expanses of travel literature ever composed. Just as Henry James, an American expatriated to Europe, had probed the intricate dance between artless Americans and artful Europeans, so Nabokov, an expatriate on the opposite shore, lays bare a sophisticated European's ravishment by Truman-era Americana—by the vulgarity of American beauty and, equally, the beauty of American vulgarity.

The author's claim, in his afterword, that Russian is his "natural idiom," sadly abandoned for what he calls "a second-rate brand of English," has bolstered the widespread assumption that, like Conrad, Nabokov came to English relatively late in life; in fact, he was reared trilingually, speaking English along with Russian and French, and could read and write English even before Russian. It is not difficult to believe him when he suggests in the afterword that *Lolita,* proclaimed by one critic to be the record of Nabokov's love affair with the romantic novel, is more accurately seen as his love letter to the English language. Its ornate curlicues disclose a richness and density that call to mind his *cher maître* James Joyce, but whereas *Ulysses* asks for—and rewards—the reader's labor, *Lolita* asks for—and rewards—the reader's play.

For *Lolita* is also a game—or, rather, a series of games, crisscrossing and overlaid one upon another like so many transparent chessboards. Apart from the endlessly variegated wordplay, the skein of allusions and cross-references, the book's larger structure is a puzzle—a labyrinth. The solution at its center turns out to be Clare Quilty, the Minotaur within the Minotaur. But not even the most alert gumshoe will crack the case on first reading. In fact, Quilty will disappoint the first-timer, looming as he does apparently without preparation, like the unpersuasive villain an amateur suspense novelist might produce at the end of a half-baked thriller. And our first-timer will be forgiven if Quilty seems to him but a phantasmal projection of Humbert's dark side—maybe not real at all.

Yet *Lolita*'s very structure demands that we traverse the labyrinth again, and subsequent readings reveal that its windings are studded with clues. Quilty peeks from every chink and bend, and what appears to be the architecture of a detective yarn is actually the architecture of Humbert's moral development. "At this or that twist of it I feel my slippery self eluding me," he says. The moral maze leads Humbert to the realization that the nymphet he has demonized is not monster but victim after all, that the "hopelessly poignant thing" is not that he has been robbed of Lolita but that he has robbed her of her childhood. Finally—almost redemptively—he discovers that he can still love her when she is "hopelessly worn at seventeen" and has shed her nymphet nature, when she is "pale and polluted, and big with another's child."

And with that recognition comes another—that it is Quilty, the living embodiment of Humbert's guilty inner Quiltiness, who lurks menacingly at the center of the web and must be destroyed. In slaying this beast within, the finally repentant Minotaur performs a kind of self-evisceration, or perhaps a self-decapitation, the severance of bull-beast from human. Humbert the Minotaur becomes his own conquering Theseus, and can finally sing his exploits and his passion in that fancy prose of his. ("I am thinking of aurochs and angels," Humbert tells us in the last sentences of the novel, as he invokes "the refuge of art" as "the only immortality you and I may share, my Lolita." Am I overselling my Theseus thesis when I point out that the auroch is the now extinct European bull that appears on the walls of Lascaux?)

But I ask again: Is *Lolita* about love?

Lionel Trilling began his famous 1958 essay about the book by declaring, "*Lolita* is about love. Perhaps I shall be better understood if I put the statement in this form: *Lolita* is not about sex, but about love." Trilling's idea was that the novelistic study of what he called "passion-love" (after Denis de Rougemont in *Love in the Western World*) was nearly impossible in an age of loosening morals. Passion-love—the love celebrated in romantic fiction—arose only outside of marriage and was, by its very nature, attended by scandal. And since adultery was no longer particularly scandalous in the maturing society in which Trilling (and Nabokov) found themselves, the requisite *frisson* had to come from somewhere else. Hence Nabokov's concentration on pedophilia, a fresh taboo broken. Writing just after the book's publication in America, Trilling was eager to place this demonstrably important work within the modernist model of progress—the forward march of Western morality and the literature that reflected it. He could not have known that that march would proceed only by stutter-steps, hobbled by the resurgent religious and political concerns of the late twentieth century.

In 1962, the director Stanley Kubrick adapted the novel to the screen (Nabokov's own script was credited but little used), and the film that resulted, starring James Mason as Humbert, Sue Lyon as Lolita, Shelley Winters as Charlotte, and an indelible, madly improvising Peter Sellers as Quilty, is full of naughty exuberance; one can practically hear the filmmakers chortling at what they could get away with. Thirty-five years later, however, the novel was adapted to the screen again (by the director Adrian Lyne and the writer whose words you are now reading), and the new film, which starred Jeremy Irons as Humbert, Dominique Swain as Lolita, Melanie Griffith as Charlotte, and Frank Langella as Quilty, met with a tide of moralistic tut-tutting. None of the major American movie studios would touch it, and its reception seemed indicative of a moral contraction such as Trilling could never have predicted. (It finally aired in America on the Showtime pay-TV network in August 1998.)

In any case, mapping the future of the love story was not Nabokov's game. Exploding its mythology once and for all was more like it. True, Humbert's adoration of Lolita shocks us by mirroring our own moments of love, and it thrills us by vivifying the ordinary and ignored elements of our lives with the sweeping brush of passion. Lolita's rank socks and her equally rank odor, her vulgar gestures and her celebrity crushes, not to mention the down on her limbs, are all lofted to a rhetorical altar at which the narrator invites us to worship along with him. But is this love or a madman's projection? Does Humbert love simple, half-pretty, half-bright Lolita, or is he consumed with the mythic nymphet he has, in his solipsism, concocted?

In the end, what *Lolita* achieves is much greater than a mere updating of de Rougemont's romantic tradition. Nabokov anatomizes love, explores all its facets, and then redefines the species. Love in *Lolita* is not the brightly appealing specimen that flits within the reach of even the most unpracticed lepidopterist. It isn't that thing we're feeling when we say "I love you," when we propose marriage, when we cuddle on the couch watching cable TV together. There is no comfort in it, no solace. It doesn't create relationships or life plans. It creates monsters. For Humbert, love is desire transfigured. It is obsession, predation. Only when it becomes one's raison d'être can one claim to be that extraordinary personage at the center of passion's labyrinth: "You have to be an artist and a madman," Humbert explains, "a creature of infinite melancholy with a bubble of hot poison in your loins and a super-voluptuous flame permanently aglow in your supple spine." Humbert is here to show us that the little pieces of that monstrousness that we may glimpse in our own yearnings and pleasures are only tiny mirror shards of the crazed rapture he experiences — "my elected paradise," as he puts it, "a paradise whose skies were the color of hell-flames — but still a paradise."

Bibliography: Harold Bloom, ed., *Vladimir Nabokov's "Lolita"* (New York, 1987). Brian Boyd, *Vladimir Nabokov: The American Years* (Princeton, NJ, 1991). Vladimir Nabokov, *The Annotated Lolita*, ed. Alfred Appel, Jr. (New York, 1970); *Lolita* (New York, 1958). Stephen Schiff, *Lolita: The Book of the Film* (New York, 1998). *Filmography: Lolita,* directed by Stanley Kubrick (1962). *Lolita,* directed by Adrian Lyne (1997).

STEPHEN SCHIFF

1956, April 16
Chuck Berry records a declaration of cultural independence

"ROLL OVER BEETHOVEN"

Rock and roll was still a novelty when Chuck Berry, a twenty-nine-year-old St. Louis musician and songwriter, recorded "Roll Over Beethoven," some two and a half minutes of musical abandon that came to epitomize the new form as few songs have. As a bit of American slang for having a good time (and a euphemism for sexual intercourse), "rock and roll" was almost as old as Edison's invention of the phonograph. But it was only in 1952 that DJ Alan Freed began broadcasting his *Moondog Rock and Roll Party* on the Cleveland radio station WJW, and only three years later, in 1955, that rock and roll emerged as the name for a new style of popular music—recordings specifically aimed at adolescents, and relying on relatively simple songs featuring a big beat.

At the outset, in the keynote recordings that first defined the new genre—"Rock Around the Clock" by Bill Haley and the Comets, "Maybellene" by Chuck Berry, and "Tutti-Frutti" by Little Richard—it was a dance music performed by small combos, generally black but sometimes white, featuring boogie-woogie piano, saxophones that growled, and a blaring electric guitar, sometimes played hard, fast, and loose, in a lilting staccato that was half hillbilly, half blues: a string-instrument style that quickly became the genre's trademark, as well as one of Chuck Berry's personal calling cards.

Charles Edward Anderson Berry was born in St. Louis on October 18, 1926. The fourth of six children, he was raised in an upwardly mobile community of hardworking families, the vast majority of them black. His father was a construction worker, his mother a former schoolteacher with a college degree. The Berrys were prosperous enough to own a radio, and young Charles grew up listening to every sort of music, from symphonies and operas to jazz and hillbilly, from Nat "King" Cole to Gene Autry. Reared on the values of education, hard work, and black bootstrapping preached by Booker T. Washington, the boy rebelled, in 1944 dropping out of high school, running away, and getting arrested for a series of petty thefts and a carjacking that got him sent to state prison.

In 1951, after serving three years of a ten-year sentence, and after several years subsequently working at odd jobs and learning how to play the guitar, Berry bought his first amplified instrument, hoping to pick up some extra cash by performing at private parties. Within a year, he was playing professionally, first in a trio of his own, and then with a combo organized by a local barrelhouse pianist named Jimmie Johnson.

Settling into a regular gig with Johnson at the Cosmopolitan Club in East St. Louis, Berry started to fool around with hillbilly material to amuse his black audience. "Some of the clubgoers started whispering, 'Who is that black hillbilly at the Cosmo?'" Berry recalled in the *Autobiography* he published in 1987: "If you ever want to see something that is far out, watch a crowd of colored folk, half high, wholeheartedly doing the hoedown barefooted."

By the spring of 1956, when Berry came to write "Roll Over Beethoven," nearly a year had passed since the "black hillbilly" had come to national attention, thanks to his debut recording, "Maybellene"—and thanks as well to Alan Freed, who in 1954 had moved his *Rock and Roll Party* to WINS in New York City, and who constantly plugged Berry's recording in return for a share of the song's profits. In the intervening months, rock and roll had entered into the American lexicon, first as a label for a musical fad; then as a kind of musical synonym for disorder and juvenile delinquency, as depicted in the film *Blackboard Jungle* (which had featured "Rock Around the Clock"); and finally as a handy phrase for the type of music made by twenty-one-year-old Elvis Presley, a white native of Memphis who was creating a sensation on tour in the South and on national network television by singing songs like "Maybellene" and "Tutti-Frutti."

Venturing east late in 1955 to appear onstage with Alan Freed in New York

City, Berry had seen for himself that his music could appeal to white teenagers as well as black club goers. He had realized that if he could produce music that was tailored to adolescent listeners rather than adults, he might make a lot of money. "Chuck Berry is a businessman," he remarked years later in a radio interview, refusing to pretend he was ever an artist: "I admire him for being a businessman. The name of the game is dollar bills."

If Mammon was one of Berry's muses, memory was another. In an effort to grab the attention of listeners half his age, he began to write lyrics based on his own recollections of being a teenager—the boredom he felt in high school, his joy when summer vacation rolled around, the jealousy he experienced at the musical accomplishments of his older sisters, Lucy and Thelma (Lucy, in fact, was the pride of the Berry family, and had briefly entertained the idea of becoming an opera singer).

In the version of "Roll Over Beethoven" that Berry recorded in 1956, Berry and his men play fast and furious. It is the first of Berry's songs to start with an extended burst of essentially solo guitar. He rips off a riff that is less a statement of melody than the sound of a fist coming down. The rest of the band then lunges into the tune. The tempo is torrid, and the words sail by in a blur: "You know, my temperature's risin'/The jukebox's blowin' a fuse/My heart's beatin' rhythm/And my soul keeps singing the blues/Roll over Beethoven and tell Tchaikovsky the news."

The singer's time has come. It's his music on the radio now—and there is no escaping its force. The drummer (Fred Below, from Muddy Waters's band) bangs out an unforgiving backbeat, the pianist Johnnie Johnson plays a chaotic boogie, and the double bassist, Willy Dixon, adds buoyancy with a hint of melodic bounce, trying to keep the music from flying apart at the seams. Berry's guitar playing is crude, his vocal vehement—he keeps leaning into his microphone and spitting out the words. All but buried in the mix is a tenor saxophonist (Leroy C. Davis, later to lead James Brown's first important band). The distant drone of the sax is the main constant in two and a half minutes of hurtling harmony.

Berry's recording staged another version of the cold-war cultural conflict between young and old that had so memorably erupted onscreen a year earlier in *Blackboard Jungle,* the first significant movie to dramatize a rock-and-roll attitude, and to feature rock and roll on the soundtrack. One target of the rebellious teenagers depicted onscreen was a collection of rare jazz recordings that a high school teacher had brought into his class, in an effort to connect with a room full of bored inner-city students. But the punks don't dig jazz. And while a pale imitation of rock and roll plays on the soundtrack, the kids lay waste to their teacher's precious collection, hurling the fragile disks against the classroom walls. It's a stunning scene of cultural desecration: roll over, Bix Beiderbecke.

Berry's own declaration of cultural independence a few months later is, by contrast with the scene in *Blackboard Jungle,* jubilant rather than destructive. It is worth quoting at length from his account of the song's genesis and meaning in his *Autobiography*—one of the most revealing books by an American popular songwriter:

"Roll Over Beethoven" was written based on the feelings I had when my sister would monopolize the piano at home during our youthful school years. In fact most of the words were aimed at Lucy instead of Maestro Ludwig van Beethoven. Thelma also took piano lessons in classical music but Lucy was the culprit that delayed rock 'n' roll music twenty years. Telling Mother in an attempt to get support for my kind of music did no good, but writing a letter and mailing it to a local DJ might have, as stated in the opening of the song . . . Out of my sometimes unbelievably imaginative mind, the rest of the self-explanatory lyrics came forth.

This passage from Berry's *Autobiography,* begun while he was serving time for tax evasion in Lompoc Federal Prison Camp in 1979 — a month after performing at the White House at the request of President Jimmy Carter—and composed without a ghost writer, captures crucial parts of Berry's genius: the mannered syntax and diction; the author's proud awareness, tinged with a bit of defensiveness, that he (no less than his sisters) is gifted; and, above all, his self-trust, his unshakable faith in the value of his personal experience as he rediscovers it in the medium of words, "raw in form, rare in feat, but real in fact." Triumphantly self-reliant, he was able—both in his memoir, and in his prime as a lyricist—to harness, and express uniquely, in a few carefully chosen words, his adolescent memories of being a misfit in what he experienced as an oppressively can-do environment.

At the same time, Berry had come of age in a border state with a variety of Jim Crow laws that were still on the books in the 1940s and 1950s. Segregation and racial discrimination were especially salient facts of life for a young black man serving prison time. That Berry's personal alienation was amplified by his keen awareness of bigotry made him an even more fitting vessel of his moment in American history. The year that "Roll Over Beethoven" became a hit was the same year that Martin Luther King, Jr., led the burgeoning black civil rights movement to its first significant victory, after a 381-day boycott of segregated buses in Montgomery, Alabama, and after the U.S. Supreme Court ruled in *Browder v. Gayle* that the state's racial segregation laws for buses were unconstitutional.

Nineteen fifty-six was also the year that Elvis Presley became the King of Rock and Roll, in part by recording a furious version of "Hound Dog," a performance as jubilantly liberated as "Roll Over Beethoven." The new sound was barely a year old, but it had already produced a telling convergence of popular musical idioms—and a large and increasingly integrated audience for performers like Presley and Berry.

"I've been asked many times how I felt," Berry writes in his memoir, recalling the first time he realized that the crowds at his live rock-and-roll shows were mainly white. "Well, I doubt that many Caucasian persons come into a situation that would cause them to know the feeling a black person experiences after being reared under old-time southern traditions and then finally being welcomed by an entirely unbiased and friendly audience, applauding without apparent regard for racial difference."

For two years, between 1956 and 1958, Chuck Berry flourished. Inspired by memories of childhood, the songs flowed freely. "Roll Over Beethoven" was followed by "School Day," by "Oh Baby Doll," by "Rock & Roll Music," by "Sweet Little Sixteen," by "Johnny B. Goode"—almost all songs that, like "Roll Over Beethoven," have endured. (One scholar recently counted 222 different recordings of "Roll Over Beethoven" produced between 1956 and 2000, in at least fifteen countries and almost as many languages.)

Yet at the same time, Berry's approach to making music had already started to show signs of condescension and carelessness. After almost two years of steady success in pitching his lyrics at kids, he began to repeat himself. On tour, from 1956 on, he cut his costs by refusing to retain either a band or a manager. He generally appeared onstage with an unrehearsed group of available musicians. His guitar was often out of tune, both onstage and in the recording studio. As time passed, he seemed more interested in dollar bills than the music he was being paid to make.

Sent to federal prison in 1962 after two trials for violating the Mann Act (his first conviction on the charge of transporting a woman across state lines for "immoral purposes" had been vacated because the presiding judge had made racist remarks), Berry served a year. He bounced back with a handful of strong new songs—and then sank into self-parody. The quality of his songwriting became so erratic that he found himself unable to cash in on his newfound popularity after the Beatles and Rolling Stones both paid him the compliment of pillaging his songbook and copying his sound. Then, in 1972, he produced his most commercially successful recording yet, a pared-down version of a salacious sing-along novelty called "My Ding-a-Ling." From there, it was all downhill.

In the arc of this career, one can find everything that is inglorious, and also glorious, about rock and roll, a cultural form that Berry helped to invent. The self-made American musicians who have followed in Berry's footsteps, from Presley to the rap musician known as Method Man, have similarly glided between the sublime and the ridiculous in their quest for "dollar bills"—and their effort to surprise young listeners out of their propriety, by creating a new sound, often without quite knowing how, or why.

More than a genre of entertainment, "Rock & Roll Music," as elaborated by Berry and his most interesting progeny, has come to represent willy-nilly a classless, color-blind, and distinctively American form of demotic cultural vitality. And by taking this new sound to heart, more than one generation of young Americans has discovered for itself (in the words of a great American poet) "the way of life is wonderful: it is by abandonment."

Bibliography: Chuck Berry, *The Autobiography* (New York, 1987). Taylor Branch, *Parting the Waters: America in the King Years, 1954–1963* (New York, 1988). Ralph Waldo Emerson, "Circles," in *Essays* (Boston, 1841). James Miller, *Flowers in the Dustbin: The Rise of Rock and Roll, 1947–1977* (New York, 1999). Bruce Pegg, *Brown Eyed Handsome Man: The Life and Hard Times of Chuck Berry* (New York, 2002). Fred Rothwell, *Long Distance Information: Chuck Berry's Recorded Legacy* (York, England, 2001). *Discography:* Chuck Berry, "Roll Over Beethoven" (Chess, 1956); *Chuck Berry: The Chess Box* (MCA, 1988).

JAMES MILLER

1957

The cat puts on a hat

DR. SEUSS

The year before *The Cat in the Hat*'s publication, Dr. Seuss wrote to his publisher, "I've got a hunch . . . (very immodest) . . . [that] we've got a possibility of making a tremendous noise in the discussion of Why Johnny Can't Read." His hunch turned out to be quite modest indeed. *The Cat in the Hat* revolutionized the reading primer. In 1958, its success launched Random House's popular Beginner Books—a series designed to teach children to read. By 1961, *The Cat in the Hat* had sold one million copies. Seuss would later call it "the book I'm proudest of because it had something to do with the death of the Dick and Jane primers."

When Dr. Seuss wrote *The Cat in the Hat,* American schools used Dick and Jane to teach reading. Eschewing phonics, these books used the whole-word method, in which each story introduces a few new words for children to memorize, and subsequent stories incrementally add more new words, gradually building the child's vocabulary. However, as Rudolf Flesch argued in his popular *Why Johnny Can't Read* (1955), some educators felt phonics would be a more effective approach. Teaching children to recognize whole words instead of the sounds that create the words is, Flesch said, teaching "English as if it were Chinese. One word after another after another after another. If we want to read materials with a vocabulary of 10,000 words, then we have to memorize 10,000 words; if we want to go to the 20,000 word range, we have to learn, one by one, 20,000 words." However, teaching reading through phonics gives a child strategies that can be applied to unfamiliar words: knowing the sounds of letters helps children sound out words they have yet to meet. Through its rhymes, *The Cat in the Hat* helped bring phonics back into the classroom. The similar sounds of "cat" and "hat," "cake" and "rake," "said" and "head" aid the novice reader's pronunciation. As Seuss later observed, "Rhyming more or less makes kids want to pronounce words correctly."

The Cat in the Hat not only taught children how to read; it taught them why. The static, bland Dick and Jane books conveyed the idea that reading must be a chore. Through its rollicking rhythms, exciting narrative, and wily protagonist, *The Cat in the Hat* showed young people that reading is fun. Reading the book, we are hardly aware that Seuss, too, restricted his vocabulary, just as William S. Gray and May Hill Arbuthnot limited theirs when writing Dick and Jane. In *The Cat in the Hat,* Seuss fashioned a masterpiece from a limited palette.

However, working within a word list almost defeated Seuss. Although he had written a dozen children's books before *The Cat in the Hat,* Seuss had been free to invent words to describe the creatures of his imagination—the sticky Oobleck, the grouchy Grickily Gractus, the tall High Gargel-orum. For this new work,

Houghton Mifflin gave him a list of 348 different words, and stipulated that he use no more than 225 (the finished book uses 236). After conceiving several ideas that required words not on the list, Seuss was about to quit. Then he noticed a sketch he had drawn of a cat in a hat. Delighted to discover that both "cat" and "hat" were on the list, Seuss made *The Cat in the Hat* the book's title.

The limits helped Seuss create more disciplined and successful poetry. As the *New York Herald Tribune*'s Margaret S. Libby noted, "Restricting his vocabulary . . . and shortening his verse has given a certain riotous and extravagant unity, a wild restraint that is pleasing." He achieved this effect through constant and meticulous revision. "He came down with a bump / From up there on the ball" began as "He came down with a PLUMP! / He fell off the ball." The new version maintains momentum with its anapestic rhythm, offers the pleasures of alliterative *b*'s in "bump" and "ball," and creates a sharp contrast between where he was ("up there") and where he is ("down"). As Seuss once said, "To produce a 60-page book, I may easily write more than 1,000 pages before I'm satisfied. The most important thing about me, I feel, is that I work like hell—write, rewrite, reject, re-reject, and polish incessantly."

Published by Houghton Mifflin (for educational markets) and Random House (trade) in March of 1957, the book made "Seuss" synonymous with American children's literature. Seuss was Theodor Seuss Geisel's middle name and his mother's maiden name. Geisel began using it as a pseudonym for his cartoons in 1925, adding the "Dr." in 1927. As Dr. Seuss, he first became famous as the advertising artist who created the phenomenally successful "Quick, Henry, the Flit!"—an ad campaign for Flit insecticide that was the "Where's the Beef?" or the "Got Milk?" of its day. When *The Cat in the Hat* was published, advertising was Seuss's primary source of income. The book's swift sales enabled Seuss to work full-time as an author for children. Later that same year, he published another of his best-known books: *How the Grinch Stole Christmas!*

Betraying their creator's roots in advertising, the Grinch and the Cat in the Hat are examples of that classic American character type, the confidence man. Like Melville's Confidence-Man and several members of Faulkner's Snopes clan, the Grinch swindles his victims—until the final few pages of the book, when he transforms from villain to hero. The Cat in the Hat, however, is morally ambiguous. Arriving with "tricks" and his Things, the Cat comes from the tradition of L. Frank Baum's Wizard of Oz and Meredith Willson's Professor Harold Hill (from *The Music Man*). The Cat's con-artistry creates possibility and excitement. Just as Hill brings joy to River City and the Wizard helps Dorothy's friends become who they want to be, the Cat teaches Sally and her brother that "it's fun to have fun / but you have to know how."

Seuss's most famous character, the Cat in the Hat is also his most adaptable. He made his debut as an anarchic force, plunging a suburban household into merry chaos, and upending assumptions about the dullness of reading primers. Three years later, he became a corporate mascot, as the logo for Random House's Beginner Books division, the profitable series that has included P. D. Eastman's *Go Dog Go!,* Stan and Jan Berenstain's *The Big Honey Hunt* (the first of the Berenstain Bears books), and Seuss's *Green Eggs and Ham.* In the fifty years since then, the Cat has come to represent both the revolutionary and the establishment, embraced by the counterculture and endorsed by public figures.

The iconoclastic side of the Cat in the Hat emerges prominently in political satire. His first such appearance is in Robert Coover's comic novella *The Cat in the Hat for President* (1968). Entering the convention stage to accept his nomination, the Cat "arrived on roller skates, holding up a cake on a rake. On, or in, the cake, sat a goat wearing a coat, an umbrella balanced on its nose." His campaign slogan is, of course, "I Can Lead It All by Myself"—a pun on "I Can Read It All by Myself," the motto that has graced *The Cat in the Hat*'s cover since 1960. The Cat, who lost Coover's fictional election, represented people's willingness to embrace a new and exciting candidate, even one who might not be suitable for the job.

In December of 1998, while Republicans pressed for the impeachment of President Bill Clinton and the president was ordering air strikes on suspected Iraqi weapons sites, Pulitzer Prize–winning cartoonist Signe Wilkinson caricatured Clinton as the Cat in the Hat, balancing on a ball, trying to juggle his many problems: "I can hold up a thong/And the dress with the stain!/I can send off a bomb/On this cool fighter plane!/I can make up a speech/While you try to impeach!/But that is not all!" On the eve of the 2004 presidential election, *Mad* magazine's Desmond Devlin and Mort Drucker depicted George W. Bush as the Cat on a ball, carelessly juggling his plans for the country and the world. Devlin wrote, "As you listen to President George W. Bush and his administration, you may notice a sort of bizarre logic emerge, a magical childlike reality in which the only rules are the ones they make up themselves." Four years earlier, following the botched presidential election of 2000, Ward Sutton's cartoon "The Cat in the Chad" found the Cat creating the butterfly ballots that confused elderly Florida retirees, many of whom accidentally voted for Pat Buchanan instead of Al Gore. As the Cat in the Chad says, "Let's have some fun!/Let's have a surprise!/Let's mix up the voting!/Let's use butterflies!" In these cartoons, the Cat emerges as a mischievous trickster of flexible political allegiance—he may represent a Democrat, a Republican, or a Florida bureaucrat. Free of party affiliation, the Cat is a dangerous clown who can stand in for a range of ideological targets.

If in these instances the Cat is a reckless joker, he appears equally often as a beloved American icon—as a national symbol, a reading teacher, and a friend to all children. The Cat in the Hat has appeared on two U.S. postage stamps (33¢ in 1999, 37¢ in 2004). Since 1997, he has served as the official symbol of the National Education Association's Read Across America Day, held annually on or near March 2 (Seuss's birthday). On that day, teachers, parents, celebrities, and other prominent people don the Cat's hat and read Dr. Seuss books to schoolchildren— readers have included the U.S. Supreme Court justice Stephen Breyer, the tennis star Serena Williams, and the 2006 Miss Universe Zuleyka Rivera. A Cat in the Hat balloon joined the Macy's Thanksgiving Day parade in 1994, but—suggestive of the Cat's unruly nature, perhaps—broke loose in 1997, injuring four spectators. (That balloon was retired before the 1998 parade.) At the center of the Dr. Seuss National Memorial in Springfield, Massachusetts, is a statue of the Cat in the

Hat, one gloved paw resting on the chair where the figure of Ted Geisel sits, the other paw touching the brim of his hat.

In the American mind, the Cat has come to represent Dr. Seuss in particular and the power of the imagination more generally. Anticipating the Cat's role as Read Across America's symbol, the New York Public Library in the summer of 1994 featured the Cat in a mural, where he served as "the ringmaster of the imagination . . . saying 42nd Street can be magical." In the early 1990s, Cat-style hats became a hot fashion accessory among creative people. In 1991, what *Entertainment Weekly* called "floppy toppers"—hats resembling the Cat's hat—had been spotted on the rapper L.L. Cool J., the rocker Lenny Kravitz, and the actresses Diane Keaton and Jamie Lee Curtis. To wear the Cat's hat is to associate oneself not just with artistic invention, but with Seuss himself. Following Seuss's death in 1991, virtually all obituaries and tributes featured the Cat in the Hat. The *New York Times*'s front-page article placed an illustration of the Cat next to a photo of Seuss. The *Seattle Times*'s Brian Basset (better known today for his comic strips *Adam* and *Red and Rover*) drew Seuss as the Cat, exiting the house on his tidying-up machine, just as he does at the end of *The Cat in the Hat.*

That the Cat should come to represent Seuss is apt because he is at least partly autobiographical. For a July 1957 *Saturday Evening Post* profile, Seuss drew a portrait of himself as the Cat in the Hat. Like the Cat, Seuss had a subversive sense of humor, wore a bow tie, and disliked following the rules. He also collected and was inspired by hats—they play a major role in his second children's book, *The 500 Hats of Bartholomew Cubbins* (1938). Michael Frith, Seuss's editor from 1967 to 1975 and collaborator on *Because a Little Bug Went Ka-Choo!* (which Geisel wrote under the name "Rosetta Stone"), recalled a visit when Seuss turned to hats for inspiration: "We were working late and groggy, accomplishing little, and Ted announced that it was time for a thinking cap. And we worked on toward dawn, refreshed by an occasional furry fez or Madagascarian yak-herder's helm, solving all problems as they came." Frith also emphasizes the strong link between author and character: "The Cat in the Hat and Ted Geisel were inseparable and the same . . . This is someone who delighted in the chaos of life, who delighted in the seeming insanity of the world around him." Tellingly, when asked whether he associated himself with any of his characters, Seuss replied, "Yes. Especially the devious ones." Yet one should be careful to suggest *too* close a connection between author and character. Although he was an avid practical joker and shared the Cat's sense of mischief, Seuss also once said, "If I were invited to a dinner party with my characters, I wouldn't show up." When a child asked if he had ever acted like any of his characters, Seuss replied, "No, because I don't want to get put in jail."

One of Seuss's most durable characters, the Cat has never been confined to children's literature alone. He did appear in other children's books—notably, *The Cat in the Hat Comes Back* (1958), *The Cat in the Hat Songbook* (1967), *The Cat's Quizzer* (1976), and *I Can Read with My Eyes Shut!* (1978). But he has also starred in the animated cartoons *The Cat in the Hat* (1971) and *The Grinch Grinches the Cat in the Hat* (1982), the TV special *In Search of Doctor Seuss* (1994), the Broadway musical *Seussical* (2000), and the spectacularly bad film *Dr. Seuss' The Cat in the Hat*

(2003). R.E.M. sings about the Cat in "The Sidewinder Sleeps Tonite" on the band's hit album *Automatic for the People* (1992). Kevin Ryan's *Dylan Hears a Who!*— one of the more fascinating bootleg albums of 2007—features seven of Seuss's books, including *The Cat in the Hat,* all performed in the style of Bob Dylan, circa *Highway 61 Revisited.* Before Dr. Seuss Enterprises requested the songs' removal, Ryan's *Dylan Hears a Who!* Web site displayed a digitally altered image of Dylan smoking a cigarette and wearing the Cat's hat.

How to explain the Cat's broad cultural appeal? Perhaps, as the political impresario Clark says in Coover's 1968 tale of the Cat's presidential campaign, "The Cat is funny. And dramatic. We have a terrible need for the extraordinary. We are weary of war, weary of the misery under our supposed prosperity, weary of dullness and routine, weary of all the old ideas, weary of all the masks we wear, the roles we play, the foolish games we sustain. The Cat cuts through all of this. We laugh. For a moment, we are free."

Bibliography: Judith Morgan and Neil Morgan, *Dr. Seuss & Mr. Geisel: A Biography* (New York, 1995). Philip Nel, *The Annotated Cat: Under the Hats of Seuss and His Cats* (New York, 2007). Philip Nel, *Dr. Seuss: American Icon* (New York, 2004).

PHILIP NEL

1959
"Nobody's perfect"

BILLY WILDER'S *SOME LIKE IT HOT*

The story goes that Billy Wilder didn't know how to write *finis* to his gender-bending farce *Some Like It Hot* (1959), so he tacked on a flip ending until he could think of something else. That's how we got the classic scene of Tony Curtis and Jack Lemmon in drag hightailing it out of town in a speedboat, Curtis in back making out with Marilyn Monroe, Lemmon up front trying (in vain) to ward off the advances of an amorous Joe E. Brown. Nothing Lemmon does can tame Brown's libido, not even whipping off his wig to reveal he's a man. "Well," Brown says, in a line that left preview audiences in hysterics and convinced Wilder he'd found his ending, "nobody's perfect."

The irony was that for the previous quarter of a century, the movies had gone to great lengths to convince us that everybody was. Ever since the Production Code—that draconian list of do's and don'ts that determined what was allowed onscreen—took effect in 1934, Hollywood had sold us a very parochial picture of perfection: one man married to one woman, blessed with children, devoted to God and country and an American way of life that never really existed beyond the back lot. Despite the plethora of divorces and scandals offscreen, Hollywood movies imposed on an entire generation a boilerplate morality that stressed domestic commitment, capitalist dedication, and sharply delineated gender roles. Any deviance from the norm was not so much denounced as its existence was categorically denied.

So when our randy friend Joe E. Brown declared that *nobody* was perfect, he was speaking, as they say, "truth to power"—though just how cognizant Wilder and fellow scriptwriter I. A. L. Diamond were of the line's undertow is debatable. Yet those two simple words acknowledge a surprisingly radical subtext lurking beneath the film's bouncy shenanigans. *Some Like It Hot* is that rare American picture where it's obvious that if only the characters could get past the barriers of gender and sexuality they might actually obtain the very things they're so frantically seeking: love, sex, happiness, riches. Tony Curtis thinks women are just for conning—until Marilyn, so dumb she's actually smart, teaches him a thing or two. Yet she herself remains unable to recognize that the man she loves is actually the "girl" next door (that is, until "she" kisses her and tells her "no guy's worth it"). And as Jack Lemmon's drag alter ego, Daphne, discovers, if security is numero uno on the list, maybe life with Joe E. Brown wouldn't be so bad.

Post-Code Hollywood films had insisted the very opposite: that only through conformity (a fadeout at the altar, a ride off into the sunset, a move to the suburbs) could true happiness be achieved. In a way, *Some Like It Hot* recalls a more sophisticated, pre-Code worldview, when Joan Crawford's ambitious shopgirls thought nothing of sleeping with gangsters to get ahead and a tuxedo-clad Marlene Dietrich kissing another woman suggested sexualities far more fluid than fixed. Of course Wilder was aware that he was taking on taboos with this picture. Even before *Some Like It Hot* was released, none other than David O. Selznick had voiced concern about the way Wilder was mixing mirth with mob hits, going so far as to say, "It's not American." (One wonders what Selznick would have thought of *The Sopranos*.) But, as quickly became apparent in a decade defined by television comedies like *Leave It to Beaver* and *Father Knows Best,* it was the director's sexual tomfoolery that was the real sedition.

By putting men in dresses Wilder had already broken one very important rule of society; what were a few more? Always fascinated by homosexual and homosocial bonds, Wilder gives us a world where "gay" doesn't exist, where choices don't result in labels. This is—clearly—not a movie about real life, but rather the funhouse version of what the movies had been passing off as reality for a generation. As a result, when the guys-as-girls get hit on, there's none of the usual homosexual panic—the sophomoric, gay-baiting humor standard in movies where men dress as women. Wilder understood that the unexpected is always funnier than the expected. So we are spared the noxious sight of Lemmon grimacing and grousing like Adam Sandler in *I Now Pronounce You Chuck and Larry*—forty-eight enlightened years later. Instead, after his date with Brown, Lemmon is downright giddy, blissfully shaking his maracas (as obvious an allusion to masturbation as there ever has been). "I'm engaged!" Lemmon exults. When Curtis asks who's the lucky girl, Lemmon replies, "I am!"

It's not that he's gay; it's that he's broken out of Hollywood's paint-by-numbers version of reality. Implicitly, *Some Like It Hot* acknowledges there are other—possibly equally valid and fulfilling—ways of living in the world. Even its title suggests that while some might like it hot, others might like it—at least lukewarm.

In this inversion of Hollywood reality, Curtis is given the role of devil's advocate. "There are laws, conventions," he argues to Lemmon. "It's just not done!" Dissuaded at last, "Daphne" is crestfallen.

All hysterically funny stuff—but serious, too. (The best comedy is always serious.) *Some Like It Hot* isn't about two guys in drag: it's about those laws and conventions Curtis rants about. And by 1959, laws and conventions were for breaking. Over the previous few years, the more daring of Hollywood's filmmakers had confronted the censors, and each time, weakened them a little bit more. Films like *Vertigo, Touch of Evil,* and *Anatomy of a Murder* challenged the old rules of law and order, hearth and home. Now Wilder was taking on the provision in the Code that seemed the most unyielding: that broadly defined category of "sex perversion."

Hollywood's relationship with homosexuality had always been schizophrenic. Gay stars—often the industry's biggest moneymakers—were forced to toe an uneasy line if they wanted to keep their career as well as some semblance of a private life. One top star, William Haines, had been shown the door at MGM in 1932 when Louis B. Mayer grew uncomfortable with all the winking innuendos about him in the press. Yet from the very beginning of the studio era, gayness had thoroughly permeated Hollywood life. There's no denying how profoundly homosexuals have shaped the movies, from a disproportionate number of actors to the tacit sovereignty they wielded over studio departments like wardrobe, set decoration, and publicity. As Wilder knew, gayness in Hollywood wasn't just the flamboyant obviousness of James Whale or the undisguised bachelorhood/spinsterhood of George Cukor/Dorothy Arzner. It was also the dark secret of such paragons of masculinity as John Ford and Spencer Tracy, and the unspoken sorority that united many of Hollywood's ladies who lunched. Indeed, Wilder's former writing partner, the eminent Charles Brackett, was a deeply conflicted homosexual who carried on a longtime affair with his daughter's husband. Such was the truth behind Hollywood's image of family values—a twist that Wilder, with his love of paradox, no doubt found terribly amusing.

In his own way, in the making of *Some Like It Hot,* Wilder was living up to Code standards, which forbade filmmakers from even acknowledging that "sex perversion" existed. That's certainly the approach he takes with the film. Perversion is nowhere to be found. No screaming Franklin Pangborns (though Dave Barry as Bienstock comes close), no fears that marriage to Brown will turn Lemmon into an actual homosexual. In this way, Wilder is able to mock the movies' circumscribed view of the perfect life, and, consequently, normalize same-sex attraction —which was, after all, pretty normal in Hollywood.

The courtship between Brown and Lemmon is actually, in terms of Hollywood romances, very traditional. They meet cute, with the millionaire Osgood Fielding III (Brown) carrying Daphne's bags and accosting "her" in an elevator. They spit, they spar, they quarrel—not so different, really, from most Tracy-Hepburn pictures. Gradually, as in all good screwball romances, Daphne melts under Osgood's persistence. We know from the start that Osgood likes women who break (or at least bend) the rules: his last wife was a contortionist who "could smoke a cigarette while holding it between her toes." When Daphne takes over the lead while dancing a tango, both seem—at last—to have found their footing.

The Production Code Administration (PCA) let Wilder get away with a lot. Double entendres abound, especially phallic ones (after all, the movie revolves around two phalli that must remain hidden at all costs). One of the girls on the train asks, "Anyone for salami?" and waves a big one around in the air. Daphne tells one of her bunkmates to "watch that corkscrew!" A joke about a one-legged jockey pops up a couple of times, and then this: Lemmon wants to get frisky with the pretty girls on the train, but Curtis is determined to keep him in his berth so he doesn't spoil their cover. "But suppose I got to go—like for a drink of water?" Lemmon asks. "Fight it," Curtis tells him. "Suppose it's an emergency?" Lemmon counters. "Then pull the emergency brake!" Curtis shouts.

But all that was nothing compared to what else the film was proffering—an underlying message of social and sexual insurrection that was not lost on those who feared hearing it the most. "Gross suggestiveness in costuming, dialogue and situations," pronounced the Catholic Legion of Decency, the organization that had championed the Code three decades earlier. In a letter to PCA chief Geoffrey Shurlock, explaining why the Legion had branded *Some Like It Hot* "Morally Objectionable In Part For All," Monsignor Thomas F. Little wrote: "The subject matter of 'transvestism' naturally leads to complications; in this film there seemed to us to be clear inferences of homosexuality and lesbianism. The dialogue was not only 'double entendre' but outright smut"—yet, in fact, Wilder's brilliance had been in making sure there were no direct homosexual inferences. What really stirred the Legion's outrage was the far more radical notion that human sexuality can only truly be measured on a sliding scale.

Some Like It Hot wasn't the first time such an insurgent idea had been floated in Hollywood. George Cukor's *Sylvia Scarlett,* made twenty-three years earlier, had likewise posited that gender and sexual desire are not fixed constructs but are instead highly idiosyncratic and mutable. Katharine Hepburn masquerading as a boy is, in fact, far more believable than Jack Lemmon as a girl. Brian Aherne finds himself irresistibly drawn to "Sylvester," Hepburn's male alter-ego, admitting to a "queer feeling" whenever he looks at "him." The Code, predictably, chopped out whole scenes of the picture, and Cukor was forced to add an ending that refuted all the gender bending of the earlier reels—which effectively sucked all the fun out of what came before. *Some Like It Hot,* made as the Code was weakening, is what Cukor and Hepburn wanted *Sylvia Scarlett* to be—daring, provocative, and oh, yes—funny.

Yet even as the Code continued to fray and filmmakers gained the freedom to deal with subjects like prostitution, promiscuity, homosexuality, and interracial sex, few dared challenge the conventional wisdom that said these things were bad. Freethinking women and homosexuals were finally back onscreen, but always with punishment for their transgressions. Marlon Brando as a repressed homosexual in John Huston's *Reflections in a Golden Eye* (1967) is confined to a cage of misery simply because in the director's worldview there were no other choices available to him. "It is morally honorable," Brando says, "for the square peg to keep scraping around in the round hole rather than to discover and use the unorthodox one that would fit."

Orthodoxy at all costs. That remained Hollywood's motto. Consider Elizabeth Taylor in *Butterfield 8* (1960). She plays Gloria Wandrous, a beautiful young woman who makes her way in the world by following her own playbook—not her mother's, not her best friend's, definitely not any man's (and in Gloria's life, there are lots of men). But of course, as we eventually discover, Gloria is unhappy with being "the slut of all time"—though in early scenes she seems to be having a grand old time of it and doesn't appear unhappy at all. That's always been the genius of Hollywood: sell the very thing you claim to abhor. Certainly the ad campaign for *Butterfield 8*—with Taylor in a sexy satin slip and a mink coat draped over her shoulder—peddled the glamour of a woman on the make. But no matter how many young girls secretly envied her, Gloria is forced to swallow some pretty stale bromides. Girls who "kick up their heels" are doomed; only the "utterly conventional" are truly beautiful. "You can't have everything in life," Gloria says, shortly before being killed in a car accident as penance for all that heel-kicking. "Be grateful for the few things you do get." Of course she'd believe this. Gloria, like everyone else, grew up with the movies.

No matter the social upheavals and sexual revolutions of the ensuing decades, Hollywood has continued to fall back on this girdled view of perfection. For every *Thelma and Louise* and *Brokeback Mountain*—films that nudged the public along in its thinking, that encouraged people to see the beauty of relationships that don't fit conventional patterns—there have been dozens of other films that insist choices in life are limited to the proscribed few. In *The Family Man* (2000), Nicolas Cage plays a big-deal broker who's magically sent into an alternate universe, waking up to discover his sexy girlfriend and sports car have been exchanged for a wife and a minivan. Horrified at first, Cage eventually comes to see the superiority of his new (read: stable, moral, mature) life over his old one (unstable, immoral, immature). Could the inverse message ever succeed in Hollywood? An actual affirmation of the much-maligned midlife crisis, wherein a guy decides he's stifled and unfulfilled with a wife and kids in the burbs and finds self-renewal in an exciting bachelor life in the city? Not a likely movie scenario—no matter how often it happens in life.

For Hollywood, perfection is still picket fences and traditional marriage, kids on bikes and men who are men, women who are women. Small-town values continue to trump big-city sophistication. Even from previews for the 2002 chick flick *Sweet Home Alabama,* it was obvious Reese Witherspoon would choose her simple Southern husband over her hotshot New York lover. And did anyone really doubt for more than a few seconds that Anne Hathaway in *The Devil Wears Prada* (2006)—after seeing what happens to supposedly unfeminine women like Meryl Streep—would trade power and plenty for a dead-end job with a dead-end boyfriend? Happens that way all the time, doesn't it? Yes. In the movies.

But nearly half a century ago Billy Wilder let the secret out of the box: Nobody's perfect. In some ways, that final line in *Some Like It Hot* is the most profound ever uttered onscreen. It gives the lie to the idea that there are no choices in life, no different ways to live. Regardless of Wilder's claim that the last line was an afterthought, it is, in fact, the only way the movie could have ended; anything less would have been a cop-out like *Sylvia Scarlett*. The implication is that Brown isn't willing to let a little thing like gender get in the way of true love. And while Lemmon doesn't exactly seem thrilled as the words "The End" appear on the screen, he seems at least resigned to his fate—and if we recall his giddy maraca dance earlier, he'll soon be back to mooning over his fiancé and anticipating life with a millionaire. "Why would a guy want to marry a guy?" Curtis had asked. "Security!" Lemmon responded. It's nice to imagine Osgood and Daphne living out their golden years on Fire Island.

"Hot jazz"—the music Curtis and Lemmon play in the film—is all about going with one's impulses, letting the music take the lead, departing from the standard tune. That, finally, is what Billy Wilder was doing with *Some Like It Hot*—veering away from a very stale old tune, one that continues to play on the soundtrack of Hollywood even as music far more interesting and unpredictable beckons from the background.

Filmography: Some Like It Hot, directed by Billy Wilder (1959).

WILLIAM J. MANN

1960

Alfred Hitchcock engineers the violent death of Hollywood classicism

Psycho

Psycho is poised at the axis of so many vectors that it's dizzying: between art and trash, between movies and television, between classicism and postmodernism, between superficial narrative and deep symptom, between traditional-humanist and new-paradigm interpretation. It is one of the premier works of one of the premier filmmakers, the focus of furious debates about the stature of its director and about what constitutes good cinema. Beginning as a sensational provocation in the movie marketplace, it metamorphosed to imperishable masterpiece of world cinema, then to poster boy for the richness of psychoanalytic theory in textual analysis, all the while maintaining its status as founder of an entire subgenre (slasher movies) and, in the end, the single most powerful model for a whole new set of aims in filmmaking. It has done all these things while existing in its own right as a deeply unusual film, falling into no prior category and no subsequent one.

In 1960, Hollywood studio filmmaking, solid as a rock since the end of World War I and so vast, complex, and maturely adapted that only a few years earlier it had seemed eternal, was showing signs of imminent mortality. Television, suburbanization, and baby-raising on a large scale were increasingly keeping people away from theaters. Anxious movie studios countered with the material hysteria of widescreen, a Technicolor newly liberated into luridness, stereophonic sound, and big subjects. Genres began to sicken or ossify, movie stars to become as garish and brittle as their surroundings. The audience, once more or less monolithic, began to atomize into subgroups: teens who liked cheap horror and sci-fi or Sandra Dee, older folks who would come out for best-seller adaptations or socially conscious subjects, the art-house crowd, children. This period of the 1950s and early 1960s was exactly the moment when Alfred Hitchcock achieved his biggest profile, most fully realized his life-project as a filmmaker. Most of his 1950s productions had been big-budget color films with major stars, movies such as *Rear Window, The Man Who Knew Too Much, Vertigo,* and *North by Northwest.* But *Psycho* departed in essential ways from that model. It was shot for less money, in black and white, by the crew of Hitchcock's TV series *Alfred Hitchcock Presents.* And it stepped deliberately across the property line dividing the orderly, reputable habitation of Hollywood classicism from the low-rent district of burgeoning sensation-cinema, with its sleazy outrages on propriety, minimal interest in character, and shambolic plot construction. Hitchcock's reward was a very big box-office success, and the imprinting of a permanent mark on the consciousness of every spectator who saw the film, whether approving or disapproving. *Psycho* scandalized many of its contemporary viewers, and it was an instantly visible signpost on the changing route of the culture—signaled in Hollywood by the crumbling of the Production Code that legislated the morality of movie subjects, and in the wider culture by the retreat of censorship during the same period (its release was sandwiched between the un-banning of *Lady Chatterley's Lover* in 1959 and of *Naked Lunch* in 1962). Instead of resisting the flattening and cheapening of the landscape being undertaken by television and youth cinema, Hitchcock, a major Hollywood filmmaker, here embraced those qualities so fiercely, and demonstrated their logic so forcefully, as to noticeably defoliate the ground still available to traditional classicism.

The significance of the film's gesture in commercially appropriating the material of nouveau sensationalism but doing so with the imperial focus and grip of a true master of the cinematic apparatus was less clear at the time than it has become in succeeding decades. *Psycho*'s immediate successors during the 1960s still inhabited the lowest rungs of budget and cultural cachet, and that remained true even through the 1970s, when a renaissance in horror/terror cinema unfolded, but one that was if anything even cheaper and still without very much apparatus mastery. But in the 1980s and '90s sensation-cinema moved upmarket so successfully and in such a completely transformed cultural context that no one even thought to complain about its lowness or its flatness anymore. Not only the slasher genre and the serial-killer story but all forms of the thriller and the crime-saturated action movie have mostly come to inhabit that paradigm, and the phenomenon has spread across the world to some of the most highly regarded examples of East Asian, Latin American, and Western European genre cinema. In this latter-day cinema, the sovereign skill of the director in spectacularly manipulating the visceral reactions of the audience is taken as not only an absolute good, but probably the highest value anyone has a right to expect from Hollywood or para-Hollywood. Hitchcock can truly be seen as the god of this belief system — Hitchcock the most virtuosic, the most self-conscious, the most abstract and ruthless of instrumentalizing commercial filmmakers, the first in chronology and the first in stature. And *Psycho* is absolutely the purest and sharpest example of these principles in his art.

Psycho's cruel, systematic destruction of Hollywood classical narrative form remains as astonishing today as it was on the film's first appearance. That form, also known as "classical realism," enshrined (among other things) a problem-setting/problem-solving structure that followed central characters through a firm, forward-moving arc from exposition to complication to resolution, in an environment where all the events occurred in a self-contained fictional world and much invisible effort was expended to prevent viewers from being reminded they were watching a film. Hitchcock's Hollywood movies existed loosely within that model, but concentrated in a proprietary way on subjecting viewers to forensic experiments in point of view and other stimulus-and-response procedures to create particular emotional reactions. This Pavlovian activity is by no means the whole story of Hitchcock's art, but it is sufficiently important that there is almost always something detached and abstract about his films — and consequently something that always speaks to an agenda very different from that of classical realism. In Hitchcock's Hollywood films before *Psycho,* the realist project survives so robustly alongside or on top of the abstractly manipulative one as to render the latter only liminally visible to most viewers most of the time. But in *Psycho,* instead of using his apparatus in the service of the conventional narrative, he turns it against that narrative, like a weapon, and the resulting film destroys all vestiges of traditional narrative comfort for the conventional spectator.

In the first half hour of *Psycho,* Hitchcock uses every tool that can produce viewer identification to force viewers into the character position of Marion Crane, played by star performer Janet Leigh (even as he is schizoidly pursuing a parallel project to voyeurize and torment her for our sadistic pleasure and his own). He achieves this not only through a shot-countershot regime of unrelenting precision and intensity, but also by employing another familiar Hitchcockian tool, namely, getting viewers almost hysterically committed to covering up and evading the consequences of some act of transgression committed by the character. In this case it is the heroine's theft of $40,000 and her flight through a series of hideously uncomfortable situations in which, in her attempts to conceal her guilt, she succeeds only in making a series of ever more self-incriminating gaffes. When she — and we — at last emerge from this excruciating gauntlet, it is to the refuge of the Bates Motel, mercifully sheltered by darkness and "off the main road." The gothically strange yet also endearingly innocent and vulnerable proprietor, Norman Bates (Anthony Perkins), engages Marion in a conversation that causes her to reflect, and then decide to undo her hopeless crime, to go back and return the money. She takes a shower that seems to be washing away all her guilt and anxiety. And then, just before the halfway point of the movie, she is suddenly murdered.

The shower scene—surely now the most famous sequence in film history—is a traumatic event in multiple registers. It is a horrifying assault on the naked and defenseless character we have been sticking to for most of the movie, and a savage attack-by-montage on the viewer, the knife frequently slashing directly at the camera. This is bad, but the worst viewer trauma of all results from the fatal injury to the body of the traditional narrative. Killing off the star halfway though the movie is so utterly unprecedented, *illegal,* that viewers experience something as close to an actual state of shock as any movie can afford. Our stunned bewilderment facilitates the film's next astounding move: within a minute, Hitchcock has us identifying with Norman as he cleans up the murder location. In our orphaned state, we attach ourselves to the first character with a project—and, as François Truffaut pointed out early on, the cleanup is as compelling as the murder. The concentrated febrile intensity of shot-countershot and small reframing camera movements precisely repeats the treatment of Marion's crime and her attempts to conceal it. So Norman comes almost immediately to take exactly Marion's place. When the car with Marion's body in its trunk stops sinking into the cloacal swamp behind the motel, viewers still feel a surge of nervous anxiety along with the perpetrator, and when it burbles obscenely and continues into the depths, they breathe a sigh of relief. What this amazing transformation of viewer identification demonstrates, what Hitchcock is pointedly demonstrating to viewers, is how shallow and self-interested our affections are, how compelled by desire and fear rather than love or ethical judgment. How can we identify with somebody trying to dispose of the dead body of our heroine? Didn't we care about Marion? Apparently not. It is the high point of all the director's many exercises devoted to the production of conviction of sin—of the viewer, and in the viewer.

But having switched us over to Norman, the movie now abandons him in turn, and moves to Marion's boyfriend, Sam, and her sister, Lila, essentially perfunctory characters who undertake a quest to discover what has become of her. The audience knows that, but Sam and Lila's investigation now becomes the viewer's project to figure out what the hell is going on, above all to penetrate the mystery of Norman's mother and the secrets of that house. This is a radically different enterprise than the one the film started out with. At the one-hour point, a new movie starts, and like the previous one it is more or less complete and self-contained, or at least far more so than the two narratives put together. In the course of it we find ourselves identifying with Norman against the investigator Arbogast, with Arbogast and later Lila against Norman as they explore the house, and finally sharing the privileged space of Norman's mad brain as we listen to the persona of his dead mother talking to itself. *Psycho*'s procession of viewpoints turns point of view itself quite forthrightly into a token to be manipulated at will for any effect, rather than the solid life-giving backbone of classical narrative. Moreover, the transformation of the film from a central-character story to a penetrate-the-mystery story, and of its characters from subjects to objects, strikes another blow at classicism. *Psycho* offers sex, crime, violence, and psychosis as content, and sensational shatterings, reversals, concealments, and revelations as form. Its project is to murder classical cinema and to offer that murder, and then the following autopsy, as a new and different kind of commercial cinema. And that new model has been taken up in the decades following: one need only look at *Blood Simple* or *Reservoir Dogs* or *The Departed* or a hundred other movies. There, coherent, holistic classical meaning is put to the sword amid a bacchic celebration of sensation and trick narrative: a kind of pagan ritual involving humanism sacrifice. *Psycho* is an eschatological movie.

What separates it from almost all of its children, however, is the utter pessimism and despair at its root. Underneath the sex, the anxiety and hysteria, the shocks, the mystery, there is another activity going on, an obscure and awful probing, like a deep, unanaesthetized forceps-probe for a bullet buried in our body. The film's violent postmodern descendants are mostly content to be playful and inventive in the burial grounds of classical optimism and unitary meaning, but at *Psycho*'s base there is an ice-cold insistence on emptiness and dread. This remains true despite all of Hitchcock's own descriptions of the film as a joke and all the sly pranks on the viewer scattered through it. It begins in the hot, arid, sterile wasteland of Phoenix, Arizona, and its surrounding deserts, a too-bright sun-baked world void of meaning and satisfaction, with human inhabitants reduced to flat figures pursuing shallow desires. That portrait of daylight society, cursory as it is, sets an awesome standard of alienation, and when the film returns to it after its sojourn into darkness and corruption, alienation is still all that's there. But first there is the progress into the night and the rain, into the darkness of the Victorian house, into the gravelike fruit cellar with its mummified corpse, and into the black swamp-pit out back that is the receptacle for all horrors. This polarity of clammy darkness, although it does offer depth, authenticity, and even a kind of real humanity, is still less acceptable than the arid, shallow polarity of light. If the daylight is sterile and lifeless, the darkness is dead, it is human death. These are the film's only choices, reproduced almost schematically at the end in the choice of final formulations offered to the viewer: between the psychiatrist's glib, soulless explaining away of everything and Norman's deep, unreachably awful and strange internal monologue, dissolving subliminally for an instant into the mother's grinning corpse-head. The movie's very last image encompasses these opposites: the car with Marion's dead body in it being dragged from the swamp into the light where its terribleness will be exposed to a full view that can offer us nothing good. And that parting touch reminds us—belatedly, reproachfully—of how completely the life of the heroine of the movie has been just blankly stopped, how all her hopes and fears and strategies and calculations were suddenly canceled in midcourse with no after-trace, in as chillingly plain a presentation of existential mortality as can be imagined.

Bibliography: Robert E. Kapsis, *Hitchcock: The Making of a Reputation* (Chicago, 1992). William Rothman, *Hitchcock: The Murderous Gaze* (Cambridge, MA, 1982). David Thomson, "Psycho and the Roller Coaster," in *Overexposures: The Crisis in American Filmmaking* (New York, 1981). Robin Wood, *Hitchcock's Films Revisited* (New York, 1989). Slavoj Žižek, *Everything You Always Wanted to Know about Lacan (But Were Afraid to Ask Hitchcock)* (London, 1992).

WILLIAM BEARD

1960, January

"The Giants were my delight, my folly, my anodyne, my intellectual stimulation"

MORE THAN A GAME

In January 1960, at the Kenilworth Hotel on Miami Beach, the owners of the National Football League spent eleven days locked in a stalemate over who would replace the late commissioner Bert Bell. Neither of the two leading candidates could gain the supermajority necessary for election, and with a full agenda of issues still to be confronted—a challenge from a rival league, a vote on expansion, an existing franchise that wanted to move, the possibility of a new television deal —a pair of owners began quietly casting about for a compromise candidate.

After the idea of nominating Green Bay's young coach Vince Lombardi for the post was summarily and angrily rejected by the Packers, the New York Giants' owner Wellington Mara looked at his old friend, Los Angeles Rams' owner Daniel F. Reeves and said, "Dan, it's got to be Pete."

So came the improbable candidacy of the bright, engaging, gray-flannel-handsome Alvin Ray "Pete" Rozelle, the thirty-three-year-old general manager of the Los Angeles Rams. Elected later that evening on the twenty-third ballot, the "child czar" was viewed by many at the time as a well-mannered lamb being led to slaughter by the very people who hired him, the wily, combative, hypercompetitive owners. They got more than they could have imagined; over the course of the next three decades, Rozelle transformed the NFL and the face of professional sports. In the process, pro football became the nation's most popular spectator sport, taking over fall Sunday afternoons and insinuating itself into the culture, both highbrow and low, with its distinctive brand—and it was nothing if not a brand—of sports entertainment.

Rozelle's arrival as commissioner came at a time when pro football was already on the rise. Regarded as a third-class sport (behind both baseball and college football) at the end of World War II, it had been growing in popularity for more than a decade, moving in lockstep with the headlong rush and bustle of postwar America. While the nation settled into the primacy of superpowerdom and the rocket-fueled explosion of consumerism, attendance at NFL games increased every year during the 1950s. Against that backdrop of disposable income and nuclear anxiety, pro football arrived at the front door and invited itself into American living rooms. By 1958, when the Baltimore Colts defeated the New York Giants in sudden-death overtime at Yankee Stadium to win their first NFL Championship—in a game watched by 45 million television viewers across the country—the sport served notice that it was a threat to the National Pastime.

Baseball, still hermetically sealed in the self-satisfaction of its accumulated lore, wouldn't notice any of this until it was far too late. While the Yankees continued their run of seemingly preordained dominance at the beginning of the

1960s, fans witnessed the opposite phenomenon in pro football, where the Green Bay Packers, representing a city of just 62,000, beat the New York Giants in consecutive title games in 1961 and 1962. One key to the league's growth was its joint television contract, which guaranteed that small-market teams like Green Bay would enjoy the same television income as teams from New York and Chicago (the visionary baseball executive Bill Veeck had offered the same idea in baseball in the early 1950s, and was denounced as a socialist for his efforts by the Brooklyn Dodgers president Walter O'Malley).

Rozelle understood how well-suited the game was to television, where it offered more tempo and action than baseball (whose leisurely pace seemed out of step with the rhythms of TV) and more variation, complexity, and—significantly—wide-open grandeur than the cramped, often drab ritual violence that boxing offered on *Friday Night Fights*. The pugilists played well on the small screen, but boxing was simply the old world transferred to the new. In pro football, in the heart of the cold war, there was the shock of the thoroughly modern, and a better and purer reflection of the national preoccupation of the moment.

Then there was *Sports Illustrated,* which in the 1960s would emerge as the quintessential middle-class magazine of postwar America. Time Inc. founder Henry Luce was hardly a sports fan, but he was remarkably patient with the magazine (which lost money in each of its first ten years). In 1956 he summoned his old friend, *Time*'s London and Paris bureau chief Andre Laguerre (he had been de Gaulle's press attaché during World War II). Laguerre, a Frenchman born in England, spent part of his childhood in San Francisco, where he fell irrevocably in love with American sports. He became the magazine's managing editor in 1960.

"I'm developing a strong hunch that pro football is our sport," Laguerre wrote in a memo to Luce in 1962. "We have grown with it, and each of us is a phenomenon of the times . . . It seems that our reader identifies himself more with this sport than with golf or fishing. College football is too diffuse and regionalized. Baseball in some quarters is considered old-fashioned or slightly non-U."

Laguerre might have added that the weekly rhythms of the sport were perfectly attuned to *SI*'s publishing schedule; its million subscribers could read about the previous weekend's games before the next ones were played, and advertisers knew well that many of them were the same upwardly mobile professionals being targeted in commercials during pro football games. In addition to making a star out of their NFL expert Tex Maule, the magazine excerpted *Paris Review* editor-in-chief George Plimpton's foray into football, in which he went through training camp with the Detroit Lions and took a few snaps at quarterback in an exhibition game, part of a participatory journalistic niche that Plimpton's friend Ernest Hemingway once described as "the dark side of the moon of Walter Mitty."

Plimpton's subsequent book, *Paper Lion,* became a best seller, but it was hardly the only pro football book in the '60s to earn a literary audience. The emerging dynasty in Green Bay had, in 1962, yielded Vince Lombardi's *Run to Daylight!* co-written with W. C. Heinz, the first and one of the best of the insider narratives that focused on the insular environment of the football team, with its regimented schedule, dense jargon, and easy camaraderie. Later in the decade, Packer guard Jerry Kramer's *Instant Replay,* cowritten with the sports journalist Dick Schaap, provided a glimpse into the mind-set of Lombardi's players, who both loathed and loved their coach.

The fan's experience was captured in 1968 by Frederick Exley in the so-called fictional memoir *A Fan's Notes,* in which Exley depicted his passion for the New York Giants as less of a re-creation than a compulsion: "*Cheering* is a paltry description. The Giants were my delight, my folly, my anodyne, my intellectual stimulation." For Exley and millions of other similarly passionate fans, pro football had become more than a game.

No one understood that better than Rozelle, whose presence proved decisive in both the swiftness and completeness of the league's ascent. He possessed nearly unerring instincts for the ways in which pro football could resonate with a large, upscale audience. He had been raised in California as a serious fan ("Sports was my life," he said of his childhood), and spent part of the '50s working at an elite public-relations firm. Shortly after taking office as NFL commissioner, he moved the league headquarters out of a cramped, two-room office in suburban Bala Cynwyd, on the outskirts of Philadelphia, and relocated to the heart of midtown Manhattan, where the league was at the epicenter of the journalism, advertising, and television industries.

Under Rozelle, the NFL marketed itself in a way no sports organization ever had, as a sophisticated passion that would both merit and reward extended scrutiny, rather than a trivial, juvenile pastime. Baseball had always been perceived as the intellectual game, but as pro football's popularity escalated across the '60s, it developed its own following, not just among the upper middle class (who paid for season tickets), but among the literary intelligentsia, who sensed something larger.

As the English writer James Lawton put it in his outsider's view of the sport, pro football "is an activity that observes many of the conventions of sport, but always the game has a meaning and a psychology that can never be contained within the parameters of the field. This, of course, can be true of other sports, but in American football the point is insistent. If all sport is a magnificent triviality, American football seems least tolerant of the limitations."

Beginning in 1963, Rozelle keenly capitalized on that ineffable appeal, launching two ventures that would carefully burnish the league's image. One was NFL Films, headed up by a former coat salesman from Philadelphia, Ed Sabol, and his brash, talented son, Steve. In their groundbreaking work, the Sabols emphasized the visual drama and poetry in the game, through loving, lingering slow-motion replays, dramatic scores that evoked German symphonies, and the stentorian tones of narrator John Facenda, "the voice of God." As Steve Sabol would cheerfully admit, "We are not journalists, but romanticists . . . Renoir would never have painted an execution. He left that to Goya."

The same year that Rozelle helped launch NFL Films, he also oversaw the formation of NFL Properties, the league's merchandising arm, whose Creative Services division was led by an urbane graphic artist named David Boss. Under Boss, the league would mythologize itself in print and posters, tumblers and thermal blankets, making the iconography of each team's helmet logo a pop design staple of the era. Through a series of handsome, literate coffee-table books like *The First Fifty Years* and the leviathan *The Pro Football Experience,* Boss argued for the merits of football on its own aesthetic terms, with writers like Ray Bradbury and James Dickey taking up the cause.

As the sport rose in popularity throughout the 1960s and '70s almost in counterpoint to the youth movement and anti-Vietnam agitation on college campuses, it began to take on a larger symbolic meaning. "Football is not only the most popular sport, it is the most intellectual one," wrote William Phillips in *Commentary* in 1969. "It is, in fact, the intellectuals' secret vice . . . Much of its popularity is due to the fact that it makes respectable the most primitive feelings about violence, patriotism, manhood."

Some claimed the game as inherently militaristic, in fact Republican (easier to peg since the galvanizing Richard Nixon was a serious fan). In 1974, Hunter S. Thompson, covering the Super Bowl for *Rolling Stone,* described his assignment as "a crazed and futile effort to somehow explain the extremely twisted nature of my relationship with God, Nixon and the National Football League: The three had long since become inseparable in my mind."

But the game's popularity transcended race, class, politics, or any other easy categorization. At a time of social unrest, football was celebrated by both liberals and conservatives for its principles of interdependence and camaraderie. "I reject the notion of football as warfare," said a character in Don DeLillo's novel *End Zone.* "Football is discipline. It's team love. It's reason plus passion."

In the 1970s, Dan Jenkins's bawdy, funny novel *Semi-Tough* became a best seller, recounting the tale of Billy Clyde Puckett, "the humminest sumbitch who ever carried a football." Reviewing the book in the *New York Times,* David Halberstam wrote, "His writing and ear recall—there is no higher compliment—Ring Lardner, though in different times and different Americas." A year later, former Cowboys wide receiver Peter Gent published *North Dallas Forty,* a grittier take on the game's dark side that portrayed the head coach of Dallas—a thinly veiled takedown of Cowboys coach Tom Landry, whom Gent had played for in his short-lived career—as a heartless martinet. (Both books were made into films; Jenkins wrote the better novel, but Gent's work yielded the better movie.)

The premiere of *Monday Night Football* on ABC in 1970 moved pro football further into the cultural mainstream, and in 1974, in his *Sports in America,* James Michener wrote of the sport's "almost symbiotic" relationship with television. It wasn't a coincidence that other sports—the World Series, the NCAA basketball national championship game, the Olympics—moved to prime time in the years following *Monday Night Football*'s successful debut.

All of the elements came together in Roy Blount, Jr.'s, 1974 *About Three Bricks Shy of a Load: A Highly Irregular Lowdown on the Year the Pittsburgh Steelers Were Su-*

per but Missed the Bowl. Blount depicted in nonfiction what Jenkins had hinted at in his novel—that besides being privileged athletes, professional football players were a rare, fascinating breed, often more educated and ruminative than athletes in other sports, and that they were shaped, if not transformed, by the game they played. Pro football players, Blount wrote,

> are made up, loosely speaking, of rickety knees, indoctrination, upward mobility, pain tolerance, public fantasies, meanness, high spirits, brightly colored uniforms, fear, techniques, love of games, Nutrament (a diet supplement used, sometimes with steroid drugs, for "bulking up"), corporate kinesthesia, God-given quickness, and heart . . . Stoned, one of them told me, "You can be hit so hard it *burns*." High on the game he had just played, one of them told me, "There was no other world outside it. There was nothing."

Rozelle was pleased with the gravitas that the game enjoyed under his watch, but his success wasn't a mere triumph of marketing. Pro football succeeded on its own terms, because it struck a resonant chord in the American psyche. In a time of increasing alienation and urban flight, when a sense of community was dissipating, it unified cities in ways that other civic enterprises could not. For the casual fan, there was action, skill, suspense, and violence. For those with a deeper interest, the game could exist on a larger canvas—as a morality play; a cultural metaphor; a crucible of values in which teamwork, sacrifice, and dedication were rewarded, while selfishness, cowardice, and sloth were harshly punished. What those who were contemptuous of sports misunderstood was not merely that a middle-class sports fan might revere football to the same degree that an inveterate theatergoer revered Shakespeare, but that he might do so for many of the same reasons.

The game's popularity continued to increase into the new century, with some surveys revealing that American sports fans preferred pro football by a three-to-one margin over baseball. Jacques Barzun may have been right: to know America it may still be necessary to know baseball. But to *understand* the world's lone superpower at the dawn of the new century, to reconcile its passion and industry, its idealism and contradictions, it is necessary to understand the National Football League and its audience. In a land increasingly divided by demographics and niche marketing, pro football is our biggest civic tent, our last genuinely mass entertainment.

Bibliography: Roy Blount, Jr., *About Three Bricks Shy of a Load: A Highly Irregular Lowdown on the Year the Pittsburgh Steelers Were Super but Missed the Bowl* (Boston, 1974). David Boss, ed., *The First Fifty Years: A Celebration of the National Football League in Its Fiftieth Season* (New York, 1969). Fred Exley, *A Fan's Notes* (New York, 1968). Peter Gent, *North Dallas Forty* (New York, 1973). Dan Jenkins, *Semi-Tough* (New York, 1972). Michael MacCambridge, *America's Game: The Epic Story of How Pro Football Captured a Nation* (New York, 2004). George Plimpton, *Paper Lion* (New York, 1966).

MICHAEL MacCAMBRIDGE

1961, January 20

"Ask what your country is doing to you"

JOHN F. KENNEDY'S INAUGURAL ADDRESS AND *CATCH-22*

In Joe Dante's 1993 comedy *Matinee,* it's 1962, and we're in a picture-perfect American living room. A little boy in a cowboy hat kills time before Sunday dinner watching Art Linkletter's quiz show *People Are Funny* when a bulletin interrupts saying President Kennedy will speak live from the White House on a matter of "the greatest national urgency." The president informs his audience that Soviet missiles are being installed in Cuba, some containing nuclear warheads capable of reaching the United States. He has the look of a man delivering a death sentence. "They're gonna bomb us?" asks the little boy. "No," says his older brother, trying to comfort him, though he plainly doesn't believe it himself. They've spent the afternoon at a shlocky Vincent Price matinee, where the older boy has delighted in his little brother's fright. There's no delight now. And then, as if on cue, comes the real chiller moment. Kennedy's face fills the screen. "We will not prematurely or unnecessarily risk the costs of worldwide nuclear war," he says, "but neither will we shrink from that risk at any time it must be faced."

Nothing diminishes the terror of that moment: what Norman Mailer, writing a few months later, called "a bright mad psychic voice which leaps to give the order that presses a button." The grim determined stature of a man carrying out the worst burden of his office crumbles when you parse those words. Harking forward six years to the U.S. Army major who justified the destruction of the Vietnamese village Ben Tre, Kennedy is saying that if necessary he'll destroy the republic in order to save it.

Kennedy's presidency has always been celebrated for its spirit of hope and youthful vigor and renewed commitment to public service. But Kennedy's words on that Sunday evening in October (or, to be precise, the words of Theodore Sorensen, who wrote many of his speeches as well as *Profiles in Courage,* for which Kennedy received the Pulitzer Prize) are the fulfillment of what he so famously promised twenty-two months earlier, on January 20, 1961, in his Inaugural Address: "Let every nation know, whether it wishes us well or ill, that we shall pay any price, bear any burden, meet any hardship, support any friend, oppose any foe, to assure the survival and success of liberty."

In that speech, Kennedy reminded his audience that his generation of Americans had been "tempered by war." Published at the end of that year, Joseph Heller's *Catch-22* suggested how. "Now the trumpet summons us again," Kennedy said, in language more apocalyptic than stirring, "to bear the burden of a long twilight struggle . . . a struggle against the common enemies of man: tyranny, poverty, disease, and war itself." "Will you join in that historic effort?" Kennedy asked. And twelve months later, Heller's hero Yossarian answered: Fuck no.

The novel's title refers to its most logical piece of nonlogic: crazy men cannot be sent on flying missions. But because only a crazy man would go on such a dangerous mission, the fact that he doesn't want to is a sign of his sanity, and therefore, he's clear to fly.

Set in Italy near the end of the Second World War, *Catch-22* is a view of hell by way of the Borscht Belt. With its dedication to shredding any vestige of common sense, the book reads like one of the cheerful demolitions of reason and logic perfected by Groucho Marx: "Well, that covers a lot of ground. Say, you cover a lot of ground yourself. You'd better beat it. I hear they're going to tear you down and put up an office building where you're standing. You can leave in a taxi. If you can't leave in a taxi, you can leave in a huff. If that's too soon, you can leave in a minute and a huff."

Catch-22 would go on to win converts (books like this don't have mere admirers) among those disgusted by the American incursion into Vietnam, and all things military in general. But to gauge the daring and the meaning of the book, we have to remember that it appeared before any of that, before the murder of Diem, the Tonkin Gulf Resolution, Vietnamization, the Tet Offensive, peace with honor. Heller's book wasn't a reaction to a war that would eventually disgust most Americans. It was a reaction to a war that most of us still think of as having been worth fighting. Heller, who was himself a bomber pilot in World War II, looked around at the good war and saw bullshit.

Or chickenshit, to be more precise. As defined by Paul Fussell in *Wartime,* a study of World War II,

> Chickenshit refers . . . to behavior that makes military life worse than it need be: petty harassment of the weak by the strong; open scrimmage for power and authority and prestige; sadism thinly disguised as necessary discipline; a constant "paying off of old scores"; and insistence on the letter rather than the spirit of ordinances. Chickenshit is so called—instead of horse- or bull- or elephant shit—because it is small-minded and ignoble and takes the trivial seriously. Chickenshit can be recognized instantly because it never has anything to do with winning the war.

The brass, or those who aspire to be brass, are the avatars of chickenshit in *Catch-22.* The ones who pay lip service to duty, or have convinced themselves that they are involved in something really fine. Surely, Yossarian would have recognized a similar officer's club coziness in the self-regarding enthusiasm of Arthur Schlesinger's description in *A Thousand Days,* his fawning account of Kennedy's presidency, of the bright young Kennedy men who descended on Washington in 1961: "One's life seemed almost to pass in review as one encountered Harvard classmates, wartime associates, faces seen after the war in ADA conventions, workers in Stevenson campaigns, academic colleagues, all united in a surge of hope and possibility." And perhaps he might have seen the ambitious mess-hall officer Milo Minderbinder, procurer of delicacies for the brass who can aid his war profiteering, taking what Milo offers as if by divine right, in Schlesinger's description of "the pleasures of power, so long untasted . . . now being happily de-voured—the chauffeur-driven limousines, the special telephones, the top secret documents." In other words, just as Heller looks at the good war and sees a con game where the grifters have fallen for their own scam, he looks at the great-est generation and sees a procession of chazzers, putzes, nudniks, nebbishes, schnooks, schnorrers, schlemiels, schlimazels, schleps, schmucks, schmoes, and schmendriks.

And so Yossarian drops out, not out of laziness, and certainly not out of any-thing as lofty as a dedication to nonconformity or pacifism. He drops out for the same reason that Fussell said men fought: not for some noble cause, but simply to save themselves.

For Yossarian, the stupidity, the sadism all come down to one moment. Re-turning from yet another bombing raid, the plane Yossarian is flying in comes un-der attack. As Heller writes the scene, the plane diving and rolling, the flak pene-trating it with little pings that sound puny next to the groaning plane, we could be watching one of the crazy vehicles in the training films the cartoonist Tex Avery made for the army. You almost expect that the plane will stop in midair and, like a winded runner, start panting. The scene reaches a pitch of hysteria—in both senses of that word—and then it goes deathly quiet. Yossarian goes to check on the young gunner Snowden who's sitting very still, muttering "I'm cold. I'm cold." And when Yossarian removes the kid's flak jacket to examine what seems like a minor wound, he watches, helpless, as Snowden's guts spill out onto the plane's floor. From there, the scene becomes the equivalent of a shot in a movie that takes an excruciatingly long time to fade out. The dialogue—Snowden whisper-ing, "I'm cold. I'm cold," and Yossarian unable to do more than murmur "There, there"—seems to be coming to us from the back of a cave. And pretty soon we start to feel cold. We're stuck in that plane with them and Heller will not let us out. He's revealed the scene bit by bit, Yossarian always trying to push it from his mind. By the time Heller gets us there, he fixes it so we'll never be able to get it out of ours. Even with the life literally fallen out of his body, Snowden will not die. That whisper of "I'm cold. I'm cold," too serene for a death rattle, becomes a bit of aural ectoplasm, something that hovers visible in front of us, even as every-thing about it speaks of death.

Heller knows that the deaths of all the Snowdens, and the memories of those deaths in the minds of the ones who survived, was the price paid for defeating Nazism and fascism. He doesn't say it wasn't worth it. But Heller's reluctance—and the reluctance of many of his contemporaries who fought—to take any credit for that defeat didn't spring from any aw-shucks Gary Cooper American modesty. It's the realization of the obscene inappropriateness of attaching a higher mean-ing to a man's guts falling out of his stomach.

Kennedy spoke for a generation tempered by war, but he conjured a romance of national service for a generation that hadn't yet been tested, a generation that, before the decade was over, would feel much closer to Heller's view.

Kennedy's Inaugural Address continues to be cited by politicians as instru-mental in leading them to dedicate their lives to service. For others it remains a key moment of their political awareness. That's why it's so surprising now to look at film of the speech and see that Kennedy's performance is so halting, so stiff. Kennedy affects the same rising and falling tone for much of his delivery, compelling polite attention more than excitement. The effect is so lulling that when he gets to the line, "Will you join in that historic effort?" the audience, missing its cue, takes a moment before realizing it is meant to respond. It's only toward the end of the speech, with the lines, "I do not shrink from this responsibility—I welcome it," that some fire seems to be lit in Kennedy. And even then the moment isn't his, as the words can't help but recall the challenge thrown down by FDR to big business in his famous 1936 campaign speech at Madison Square Garden: "They are unanimous in their hate for me—and I welcome their hatred."

The echo is so close that it must have been deliberate. But it only emphasizes how Kennedy is trying to be so many things here that the speech is a contradictory mess. A claim of kinship with the past ("We dare not forget today that we are the heirs of that first revolution") is followed in the next sentence by the proclamation of a new start in American politics ("Let the word go forth . . . that the torch has been passed to a new generation"). Trying to silence any doubts about his lack of experience, Kennedy presents himself as a fierce cold warrior ("We dare not tempt them with weakness. For only when our arms are sufficient beyond doubt can we be certain beyond doubt that they will never be employed") only to court those counting on him to carry on the liberal tradition ("But neither can two great and powerful groups of nations take comfort from our present course—both sides overburdened by the steady spread of the deadly atom, yet both racing to alter that uncertain balance of terror that stays the hand of mankind's final war").

And then there is the missile of the speech, the line cited for its spirit of citizenship, of sacrifice, of engaged patriotism: "And so, my fellow Americans: ask not what your country can do for you—ask what you can do for your country."

In 1981, in *The Kennedy Imprisonment,* Garry Wills quotes Sorensen writing approvingly, in 1965, of Kennedy's "concept of the presidency . . . the primacy of the White House within the Executive Branch and of the Executive Branch within the Federal Government, the leadership of the Federal Government within the United States and of the United States within the community of nations." It can sound remarkably like George W. Bush's concept of the presidency—the White House commanding the government, and the country commanding the world. And so the call to service stands revealed as a call to obedience, the very obedience that so many of the young people inspired by Kennedy would, in a few years, refuse.

"The famous antitheses and alliterations of John Kennedy's rhetoric sound tinny now," wrote Wills toward the end of his bitter, sometimes disgusted book. Contrasting Kennedy with Martin Luther King, Wills notes that King's sources were ancient—"the Bible, the spirituals, the hymns and folk songs." What we remember from King's syntax, which was sometimes contrived, sometimes flowing, are the simple phrases ("I have a dream") that, perhaps because of their simplicity, were able to sound all the changes wrung upon them. Kennedy's language has a clumsy grasping for eloquence ("Ask not what your country can do for you . . .") and a tone that instructs rather than elevates. It's a patrician voice, a voice in some basic way alienated from the native ease of American speech, as the effortless eloquence of the man who followed him in the White House would not be.

There's nothing alienated about Yossarian—he's the dropout as open wound. Heller flirts with sentimentality in the last pages, giving Yossarian a Humphrey Bogart moment of walking off to join the fight, and the chaplain a Paul Henreid line, telling Yossarian, "I'll stay here and persevere" (just as Henreid, at the end of *Casablanca,* tells Bogart, "This time I know we'll win"). But Heller is pulling the rug out from every heroic final shot, replacing the swelling of a Max Steiner score with something like a kazoo playing "Yankee Doodle." Yossarian isn't running to battle but away from it: "From now on I'm thinking only of me." But he wouldn't be a hero if that were entirely true. He gives up the chance to go home because the cost of his freedom would be betraying his fellow soldiers. But he doesn't do anything to save them, either. That they'll have to do for themselves. And so, instead of asking what he can do for his country, Yossarian foreshadows the question the San Francisco punk band the Avengers would pose from their stages in 1977 with "The American in Me": "Ask not what you can do for your country/Ask what your country is doing to you." The energy, the faith, and the devotion that Yossarian brings to his escape lights all who refuse to serve. It's his eternal flame.

Bibliography: Paul Fussell, *Wartime: Understanding and Behavior in the Second World War* (New York, 1989). Joseph Heller, *Catch-22* (1961; New York, 1989). John F. Kennedy, *"Let the Word Go Forth": The Speeches, Statements, and Writings of John F. Kennedy, 1947 to 1963* (New York, 1991). Arthur M. Schlesinger, Jr., *A Thousand Days: John F. Kennedy in the White House* (Boston, 1965). Garry Wills, *The Kennedy Imprisonment: A Meditation on Power* (Boston, 1981). *Discography:* Avengers, "The American in Me," *The Avengers* (White Noise EP, 1979). *Filmography: Matinee,* directed by Joe Dante (1993).

CHARLES TAYLOR

1961, July 2
Ernest Hemingway stops listening

THE AUTHOR AS ADVERTISEMENT

Ernest Hemingway gets up, puts on his favorite red robe and comes downstairs. He goes to the basement of the house to get his Boss shotgun, then comes upstairs and finds a splash of early sun in the hallway. "He slipped in two shells, lowered the gun butt carefully to the floor, leaned forward, pressed the twin barrels against his forehead just above the eyebrows, and tripped both triggers." That careful sentence is the last in Carlos Baker's *Ernest Hemingway: A Life Story,* which was published in 1969, eight years after Hemingway shot himself in his house in Ketchum, Idaho. The Blaine County coroner gave the cause of death as a "self-inflicted gunshot to the head," but Hemingway's widow, Mary Welsh Hemingway, who was sleeping upstairs and who had tended him in his last years of illness and confusion, announced that the event had been accidental, the result of a mistake as Hemingway was cleaning his shotgun. This white lie was not much honored by those who knew Hemingway, but it was not really until the publication of the memoir *Papa Hemingway,* in 1966, that A. E. Hotchner owned up to the suicide. Hotchner had been a companion to the writer in his last years, and he had witnessed his decline. Hemingway was only sixty-one when he took his life, but he suffered for the last few years from writer's block and perhaps even the onset of Alzheimer's, and from paranoia. He had believed he was being pursued and threatened by hostile authorities; he had feared that he could not write any longer. And his father, a doctor, had shot himself. (The word "and," his own great trick, was nearly out of control.)

Hotchner describes his last meeting with Hemingway, when the writer lashed out: "What does a man care about? Staying healthy. Working good. Eating and drinking with his friends. Enjoying himself in bed. I haven't any of them. Do you understand, goddamn it? None of them. And while I'm planning my good times and world-wide adventures, who will keep the Feds off my ass and how do the taxes get paid if I don't turn out the stuff that gets them paid?" He had been having shock treatment at the Mayo Clinic. He was on drugs. There was psychotherapy. But the man who had done as much as any American to identify the exhilaration of a certain experience—that of writing—was giving up on his own life.

Hemingway had not had his best reviews for over ten years. But he had had the Nobel Prize as a shark-proof trophy for his solemn fishing expeditions. In white hair and whiter beard, he was as striking looking as any of the actors who had helped film his work. He was an immense public figure—in the fond, envious, and often very muddled thinking of a Norman Mailer, "Papa" was the champion. No, *The Old Man and the Sea* was not one of the great novels of the 1950s. In any real contest, it would have had to bow to *Henderson the Rain King, The Hamlet, Invisible Man, Lolita,* and perhaps even *The Deer Park.*

Yet as Mailer came to publish *The Deer Park,* swooning from a mixture of insecurity and self-aggrandizement that may not have been too far from Hemingway's clinical condition, he thought to send a copy of the book to Papa in Cuba, as a salute and a challenge. This is what he said: "To Ernest Hemingway— because finally after all these years I am deeply curious to know what you think of this.—   But if you do not answer, or if you answer with the kind of crap you use to answer unprofessional writers, sycophants, brown-nosers etc. then fuck you, and I will never attempt to communicate with you again."

Mailer was not as taciturn as he promised. He announced in print, in 1956, that Hemingway should run for the presidency. As it turned out, that was a fair warning of Mailer's own campaigns to come and of the strange fallacy he and Hemingway shared—that a good writer must be a good man first. But it was also a measure of that larger notion of the period, that writers (as opposed to actors) might be political candidates because they knew the human heart and could reach it through words, and because they had a standing in America that conveyed intelligence and integrity. For many ardent and creative people Hemingway stood for an idealized American: someone who had manly virtues and skills; someone who had seen some other parts of the world and found them terrific; someone who had fought in Spain and been into Paris with the relieving forces; someone who had discovered a truly American way of writing. Yes, as it turned out, it was too pretty and tidy a picture. But the Hemingway of the 1930s and '40s was a kind of advertisement for American literary selfhood. And that was a formative age of advertising in which the magazines and movies were overtaking anything that might be regarded as reality.

He was a hero for those drawn to worship. A few years after the real word on Papa's suicide was in, Mailer wrote another piece, a projection—in which he tried to imagine a wounded Hemingway gambling with the suicidal act and taking the risk one step too far. It's not a comfortable piece, or one that does much credit to either author. But it says worlds about the sultry, melancholy passion of self-regarding authorship—and of course it coincides with the time when Mailer's special Madison Avenue genius had thought of the title for a revelatory but unhinged collection, *Advertisements for Myself.*

Well, the years have passed, and it's interesting to ask, where does Hemingway stand? I see in a local bookstore that just about everything is in print. But we need now to look at Hemingway in a fresh light, not as Jake Barnes but as some extra-twisted Robert Cohn—taking the characters from *The Sun Also Rises,* his first novel (a book that came out a year before talking pictures). In other words, "Hem" was a poseur, a desperate fake gambling against exposure, a mandarin, a stylist, a man who to all intents and purposes remained an inhabitant of Proust's cork-lined room but who dropped this bomb of a legend on us all—the man of action, courage, and heroic modesty. The one thing he did straight was put words together and feel their rhythm, and the only thing to be done with Papa in our schools is to have passages read aloud every day until the red-blooded idiots who want to be men get the idea that they could be writers first, or people who use the language properly. There is a tradition of fresh-water lucidity in prose that places Joan Didion as Papa's daughter. Still, she has been entirely candid about her debt and allegiance to him, and we can all benefit from the thought of Hemingway's machoism ending up as the terrain for a little old lady whose broken places do not really show—except when she breathes.

The short stories are still surprising, and in great part that's because Hemingway rejected or could not do the excessively neat, shaped short story—think of de Maupassant, Somerset Maugham, Joyce—and so he pursued fragmentation, mood, and a broken talk that seemed more lifelike, or was it just plain beautiful? Take "The Killers," the locus classicus of a kind of talk that still influences pulp fiction, good movies, and the flirtations of e-mail.

> "Well, bright boy, why don't you say something?"
> "What's it all about?"
> "Hey, Al," Max called, "bright boy wants to know what it's all about."
> "Why don't you tell him?" Al's voice came from the kitchen.
> "What do you think it's all about?"

"I don't know."

"What do you think?"

Max looked in the mirror all the time he was talking.

"I wouldn't say."

"Hey, Al, bright boy says he wouldn't say what he thinks it's all about."

You can hear the Marx Brothers in there, and Pinter, too. It's the start of an art in which typographical layout and white space contribute to the music and the menace. Yet I doubt it came from a deep acquaintance with gangsters. Indeed, it is very literary talk that only seems idiomatic, but which is founded in pause, rhythm, and breathing. That language, allied to Hemingway's lust for prospect, changing light, and nature, is the wealth of his art. But once he put that skill to the test of full-scale stories, romances, he ran the risk of bosh — the prolonged and teary way in which war gets in the way of true love for handsome people. It's not unfair to say that all the major Hemingway novels are love stories that collapse because of the intrusions of war and its damage. That Hemingway story extends from *Gone with the Wind* and *From Here to Eternity* to *The Deer Hunter* and the movies of John Ford.

So if you want a clue to where Hemingway stands, a half century after his death, follow the nonfiction. *Death in the Afternoon* is everything you could ever want a new type of book to be. It serves as a good guide to an exotic sport (at least as it existed in the 1930s), filled with good descriptions and biting stories, and very funny. For it is when Hem the aficionado finds himself sitting beside an old lady (is it Joan Didion?) at the corrida that he introduces the first note of self-parody. Nothing draws more attention to the pompous attitudes and the clinical photographese (it was a book with illustrations) than the arguments between the two over the nature of a book.

> *Old lady:* And is that all of the story? Is there not to be what we called in my youth a wow at the end?
>
> Ah, Madame, it is years since I added the wow to the end of a story. Are you sure you are unhappy if the wow is omitted?
>
> *Old lady:* Frankly, sir, I prefer the wow.
>
> Then, Madame, I will not withhold it. The last time I saw the two they were sitting on the terrace of the Café des Deux Magots, wearing well-tailored clothes, looking clean cut as ever, except that the younger of the two, the one who had said he would kill himself rather than go back in that room, had had his hair hennaed.
>
> *Old lady:* This seems to me a very feeble wow.
>
> Madame, the whole subject is feeble and too hearty a wow would overbalance it. Would you like me to relate another story?
>
> *Old lady:* Thank you, sir. But it will be enough for to-day.

The old lady has cottoned on that Hem doesn't do wows because he likes the cool balance of enigmatic talk and a kind of ironic movie tableau. And the real secret wow in Hemingway is that he was desperately emotional about his people, his stories, and himself, but he was afraid of doing wows without breaking down.

Now, I will take on trust that Hemingway had spent many late afternoons at the bullrings, and that he had talked to experts. I don't mean to say that *Death in the Afternoon* is especially right or wrong. But I knew it was a great book before I had seen a single bullfight, and if in fact Hemingway had compiled a whole manual about a sport that never was, it would be all right with me. After all, great novels are about things that didn't happen. I don't think bullfighting as Hemingway dreamed it will ever play again, but the book is as timeless, touching, and droll as any exploration of a man's hobbyhorse (and plainly the old lady is from Laurence Sterne).

The jokes in *A Farewell to Arms* and *For Whom the Bell Tolls* are very few, and their pent-up sexuality is so dreamy and horny that it tells us a lot about a man who was likely in love with love. It's very hard to read these books now without seeing them as male weepies in which the author is struggling with a hidden Quilty figure who wants to write promotional material for northern Italy, a picnic by a stream, and sleeping-bag sex. Hem was so full of desire (yet so opposed to letting it out in a wow) that he frequently trod on that essential imaginative energy in advertising or envy, the "wouldn't you like to" impulse.

There's a fascinating gesture toward the breakup of this aortic constriction, and it comes in *Across the River and into the Trees.* That book was poorly reviewed, and no one could miss the moony love affair between a Colonel Cantwell with heart failure and an Italian aristocrat as a replay of a situation in Hemingway's own life. (He was one of the first authors to have groupies and to put them in his books.) *Across the River* is often painful bathos: there were movie plans once with Gene Hackman and Julie Christie, whereas it cries out for pastiche casting—how about Woody Allen and Mariel Hemingway? For there are moments when Hemingway seems to need this to be less a book than the enshrined fantasy of "soon to be a major motion picture." Howard Hawks might have filmed it as a comedy (like his version of *To Have and Have Not*) in which Cantwell gets his big-wow heart attack while screwing the beloved in a gondola. He could gasp, "Nobody's perfect."

So *Across the River* is still a book to read: it has absurdity and lucidity in the same breath, sometimes in the same sentence. It is far better than what followed, *The Old Man and the Sea,* which, when it appeared in its entirety in *Life,* the magazine sold more than five million copies. The man whose face was on the back of that book is the public figure who loomed in Mailer's youth. The book sold in hardcover and in Book Club versions. It was a proof of Hem as literature's crusty angel and a last hope in American publishing in the age when Norman Mailer grew older but failed to see that the Great American Novel, like the Heavyweight Championship of the World, was a myth from the past.

When Mary Hemingway tried to protect her late husband's honor, she was setting in motion the process of posthumous publication, the resorting to a writer's files and archives to find things that he had declined to publish. So far as we know, *A Moveable Feast*—by far the most valuable of these later works—was begun in the late 1950s and was meant to be finished. It is a collection of memoirlike essays, cruel to many people long dead, and achingly fond of its own author. *A Moveable Feast* is the best ad for Papa and Papa-ism. It is a fine book and it may have given Paris another fifty years of romance. Without American authors and movies, that city might have the resonance of Zurich today.

There followed *Islands in the Stream* and *The Garden of Eden,* by which time it was very hard for any reader to know how straight the house of Scribner's was playing. *The Garden of Eden* appeared in 1986 with a brief publisher's note: "This novel was not in finished form at the time of the author's death . . . We have made some cuts in the manuscript and some routine copy-editing corrections. Beyond a very small number of minor interpolations for clarity and consistency, nothing has been added. In every significant respect the work is all the author's." It was a languid book in which the descriptions were congealing and the sturdy separation of the sexes was beginning to feel suspicious. Might Papa have entertained gay dreams? Was this really a novel by the man himself, or the brand-name "Hemingway" (just as James Bond novels followed Ian Fleming's death)? To which the only answer was Hem's best ending, the one for *The Sun Also Rises:* "Isn't it pretty to think so?"

Bibliography: Carlos Baker, *Ernest Hemingway: A Life Story* (New York, 1969). Ernest Hemingway, *Across the River and into the Trees* (New York, 1950); *Death in the Afternoon* (New York, 1932); *Men without Women* (New York, 1927). Norman Mailer, *The Presidential Papers* (New York, 1963).

DAVID THOMSON

1962

The common language of an almost-remembered country

Bob Dylan Writes "Song to Woody"

They lived as husband and wife, or brother and sister, or cousins, it was hard to tell, they just lived here, that's all. Chloe had her own primitive way of looking at things, always would say mad stuff that clicked in a cryptic way, told me once that I should wear eyeshadow because it keeps away the evil eye. I asked her whose evil eye and she said "Joe Blow's or Joe Schmoe's." According to her, Dracula ruled the world and he's the son of Gutenberg, the guy who invented the printing press.

Being an heir of the '40s and '50s cultures, this kind of talk was fine with me. Gutenberg could have been some guy who stepped out of a folk song, too.

Chronicles: Volume One, the formally peculiar memoir of pop singer and songwriter Bob Dylan (born Robert Allen Zimmerman, 1941), unfolds with breathtaking off-handedness; still, passages such as this contain the irreducible kernel of Dylan's vision, and of the history that made him possible. That vision is to see the actual figures of history, and the phantasms of culture, as characters in a mythical tableau that is not a different world at all, but opens onto a modern present charged with possibility—one in which myth is preserved, as real as the landlord.

He is describing acquaintances who let him flop, on Vestry Street, shortly after his 1961 arrival in New York. The chapter, like the ones around it, is a comedy on the well-wrought magazine profiles that would come to haunt the writer, for a period one of the most famous humans alive. It starts, pro forma, by gesturing at the pivotal moment it will illuminate: in this case, the composition of his first great original, "Song to Woody." Immediately, in near-parody of industrial style, the chapter leaps backward several years—so to drive forward along some narrative highway toward the ephemeral instant in which cultural history seems to divert its course, this time with the reader riding pillion.

It never happens. The chapter ends without arriving, the next chapter begins years later on. The scheme goes unexecuted, the closure left open. His judgment of the song's importance is inarguable—but in the story as it's told, "Song to Woody" never gets written. Nothing is delivered. Things fall apart; elements of the larger story fall out of order, collapse into each other.

To gather the force of this collapse within *Chronicles,* within Dylan's imagination and songbook, one must reckon the historical collapse that allows for Bob Dylan—for his artistic achievement and for his own canonization. His apotheosis is an index of perhaps the most singular fact concerning "the literary" in the post–World War II era: the accelerating collapse of high and popular art into a seemingly homogeneous sphere of "culture." And, even more threateningly, the corresponding collapse of that sphere's distance from the daily life of the marketplace, so that those two things—culture and money—seemed to occupy all available space. How one felt about this process—populist overthrow of class-bound hierarchies, or death knell for critical distance and aesthetic autonomy—likely determined how one felt about Dylan's zenith in the years 1962 to 1968, years during which pop art (capitalized and not) had not yet been digested by the museums and academies. Dylan lyrics had yet to migrate into poetry anthologies; his oeuvre had not yet been captured for academic contemplation by such later critical epics as Christopher Ricks's *Dylan's Visions of Sin.* The debate over whether pop art—much less a pop star—could lay claim to the highest forms of cultural prestige remained fiercely contested. This cultural churning was itself inextricably braided with the social revolutions of the era. The former offered new possibilities for popular art's significance; the latter offered the subjects of Dylan's ambiguous political address. These include both the brutal prehistories of contemporary social conflict, as in the excavations informing "The Ballad of Hollis Brown" and "The Lonesome Death of Hattie Carroll," a work of such serrated sharpness that it remains painful to hear; and the "protest songs" he would both disavow and reinvent, such as "Blowin' in the Wind," "Masters of War," and "A Hard Rain's A-Gonna Fall."

That Dylan (along with the Beatles) legitimized pop music as art is a commonplace; his revolutionizing of the form, well remarked. Of particular note is his intensive knowledge of American folk and popular traditions as well as their Anglo-European wellsprings, particularly the Child ballads and murder ballads (to which he returned as a prodigal in the 1990s after largely unmaking his popular fame). However, his willingness to break these forms on the wheel of his own fascinations, and to generate great effect thereby (a capacity crystallized in his iconoclastic decision to "go electric" and break with the folk revival in 1965), might be seen as itself characteristic of modernism—a modernism that, in 1962, had found little purchase in mass culture and was elsewhere growing as archaic as "The Bonnie Lass o'Fyvie" (a version of which Dylan released in that year, under the common name "Pretty Peggy-O"). Modernism too is part of Dylan's eccentric learnedness in the European tradition—particularly vers libre, surrealism, naturalism, and social realism. In one song he breezily compares a love gone wrong to "Verlaine and Rimbaud"; a passage in *Chronicles* ends, "He questions everything. His clothes catch fire on a candle. He wonders if fire is a good sign. Balzac is hilarious."

If these provide scattered points for a popular vision, Dylan is in part defined by the profligate fluidity with which he translated it into a faraway-near vernacular, the common language of an almost-remembered country. This is the place Greil Marcus calls an "invisible republic," another America squatting inside the flattening postwar social landscape. But to name Dylan as an American artist is to find in him the Scottish highlands and Paris's *la vie bohème;* to capture his contemporaneity is to notice he is made of history, and makes it in turn. "Visions of Johanna" breaks the ten-line stanza of *ballade suprême* into something more insistent, redolent of exhausted mania: *aaabbbbcC,* with the title repeated in every last line. The images conjure Downtown surrealism: "the harmonicas play the skeleton keys and the rain," and "jewels and binoculars hang from the head of the mule." A song of erotic despair, it is also apocalyptic. "Everything's been returned which was owed," he sings; it does not sound like good news.

Other aesthetic innovations are more quantifiable: in 1965, through its six minutes of sustained invention and description, "Like a Rolling Stone" revised the understanding of possible length and scope for a pop song. Though formally mercurial, Dylan perfected a lyrical complexity able to approach the syntax and rhythm of conversational speech while still, in an almost incidental manner, managing to deliver rhymes at the appropriate metrical moments. This formal technique would later take the coolly imprecise description of "flow," used often in reference to hip-hop lyricists (suggesting one route by which Dylan has come to be a common reference for rap and hip-hop artists). Dylan's substantive inventiveness surely accounts in some degree for the consistency with which early commentators found his work to be unpleasant and even ugly. One recalls Gertrude Stein's ventriloquized verdict on Picasso: "Sure, she said, as Picasso once remarked, when you make a thing, it is so complicated making it that it is bound to be ugly, but those that do it after you they don't have to worry about making it and they can make it pretty, and so everyone can like it when the others make it."

To find in Dylan a figure on the order of Picasso or Stein—sui generis, seeming to lift the entire field on his shoulders with heroic insouciance, able to create the eventual circumstances for his own reception—is not mistaken. Nonetheless, history will sing its own tune. If Dylan helped raise up pop music to meet high culture, high culture in turn descended to gather it in. This confluence, in which Dylan and his songs resonate most deeply, is particular to the postwar era. This collapse of cultural spheres is well and variously theorized elsewhere: Benjamin's "The Work of Art in the Age of Mechanical Reproduction," Adorno and Horkheimer's "The Culture Industry," and Guy Debord's *The Society of the*

Spectacle offer notable analyses. As a process, it plays out amidst the interrelated forces of an increasingly commodified art market, the historic triumph of the bourgeoisie, and the ongoing aestheticization of politics often filed under the rubric of symbol management. The critical accounts of this shift describe a world gone wrong, turned upside down, where *seem* is the finale of *be*. Dylan provides the sensual particulars of that world, without representing any single position within it. The utterly human—life and death, and any possible approach to such things—has been, must be, cast into the image-world before it can show itself. This is the resonance of his incomparable first line to "Desolation Row," in 1965: "They're selling postcards of the hanging."

This is not what the song is about. The song is not necessarily about anything, so much as it is an evocation of the world in collapse, the jumble of space and time in which anything might appear—at the price of being merely condemned to mere appearance. Modernism sends Ezra Pound and T. S. Eliot as delegates. History, myth, and literature belch forth the Phantom of the Opera, Einstein, and Cinderella, as well as that shade of the surrealist hero Sigmund Freud summoned here as "Dr. Filth." The combinations are extravagant surrealism indeed: Lautréamont's ideal, "beautiful as the chance encounter of a sewing machine and an umbrella on a dissecting table," as played with big-ticket proper names.

For all the crowds, the song is irreducibly lonesome; for all that pours forth from the Anglo-European tradition, the song's evocation is intractably American. Indeed, it suggests that Americanness is built on those crowded traditions, near-emptied of meaning and surviving as antagonistic traces, forms, modes of production that persist somewhere near the center of political and social life, even as that life vanishes beneath the flatness of the garishly picturesque. The postcard—not the hanging itself, but a small reproduction—is the song's moment of truth, its verdict on the scenes it offers. Appearance has wrestled history to the earth in what had meant to be a triumph and ended in desolation, barely sustained by desperate playfulness and chromatic sheen.

It is in some part the America, that is to say, of Jasper Johns's painting *Flag*, or perhaps his *Map*. The years that these two works bracket are significant: 1954 to 1961. Here is the crucible of the art that will loom over the second half of the century. The period begins with Joe Turner's "Shake, Rattle and Roll" and ends with Del Shannon releasing "Runaway" even as the Beatles play their first gig at the Cavern Club. Two artists appear who will keep eccentric pace with Dylan for depth of invention, singularity, and endurance: John Ashbery and Jean-Luc Godard (both of whom, like Dylan, will continue making new art through the millennium and beyond). Amidst all this, the Johns pieces seem to hold the secret of the era. Everything has collapsed into a jumble of encaustic collage, but it appears as a new flatness. Life slips away into image, finally emptied of any content but the desire for, and memory of, content. Neither the oldest nor the most recent materials can give depth to the picture; meaning isn't even on offer. The symbols that once quilted things into place have lost their ability to mean much; they can't even conjure the pleasure of seeing them smashed. This is the faraway-near with a vengeance, the totality as a big nothing.

In Dylan this is the threat; in Warhol, the promise. *Campbell's Soup Cans* debuts the same year as "Song to Woody." They are each other's opposite number: Warhol the painter of postmodern life, of a triumphantly flat new world; Dylan a prophet of that world's fugitive, invisible depths, of the myths that the world must put away to become itself. To understand this opposition (staged now almost ritualistically in films and fictions, most mysteriously in Don DeLillo's *Great Jones Street*) is to grasp in large part the dynamic of late modernism—particularly in its latest guise.

It's the nature of dynamics to preserve what they put away. The preservation of Dylan's aesthetic devices in later artists—allusive mania, genre repurposing, and self-dissimulation, to name just a few—is as much an index of Dylan's own preservation and transmutation of older traditions. This is the action of genealogy itself.

But the process that Dylan himself grasped so intimately and profoundly—the cultural collapse of which he was ambiguous cause and effect—has come to wind down, as processes must. The moment in which Dylan *as* Dylan was possible was necessarily one in which some degree of depth had been preserved, where mythic intensity had gone to ground: a sensation for which Dylan found forms and feelings, and sang back with unequaled invention. The endgame of this larger process, however, leads to a new wasteland of flatness, lacking all depth; the impossibility of imagining a new Dylan any longer is as much a measure of historical change as it is of the artist's singularity.

Bibliography: Bob Dylan, *Chronicles: Volume One* (New York, 2004). Greil Marcus, *Invisible Republic: Bob Dylan's Basement Tapes* (New York, 1997). *Discography:* Bob Dylan, *Bob Dylan* (Columbia, 1962); *The Freewheelin' Bob Dylan* (Columbia, 1963); *Highway 61 Revisited* (Columbia, 1965). *Filmography: Don't Look Back,* directed by D. A. Pennebaker (1967).

JOSHUA CLOVER

1962

John Wayne chews through the overstuffed upholstery of *The Man Who Shot Liberty Valance* with "a hipster sense of how to sit in a chair"

"WHITE ELEPHANT ART VS. TERMITE ART"

In an era flush with memorable face-offs—Cassius Clay versus Sonny Liston, Kennedy versus Khrushchev, *The People v. Lenny Bruce*—none would have more destabilizing implications for the cultural fight game than movie critic Manny Farber's 1962 essay "White Elephant Art vs. Termite Art." A fast-paced manifesto delivered as a series of short, devastating jabs, ambidextrous hooks, and rope-a-dope feints, the piece laid the groundwork for a new "termite-tapeworm-fungus-moss art" aesthetic that chewed up and spat out high- and mass-cult conventions with evenhanded impertinence. It might take the reader years to absorb the essay's intricately latticed combativeness, or to simply catch something as recondite, thrown-away, and just possibly serendipitous as that Moss Hart/mass-art pun.

Launching an all-points challenge to the played-out Eurocentric tradition of the lumbering, significance-heavy, status-seeking masterpiece (an oppressively impressive artistic behemoth trampling everything in the path of its single-minded pursuit of prestige and intellectual respectability), Farber outlined an antithetical, antimonumental view of film art keyed to stealth gestures, stoicism, hard-bitten oddballs passing themselves off as bit players, a steady buzz of "squandering-beaverish endeavor" undercutting the tall timber of Great Art, and a (Thelonious) monkish addiction to pointed silences, eccentric corners, dice-rolling audacity.

"White Elephant Art vs. Termite Art" arrived at a moment when decisive battle lines were being drawn in film culture (not to mention *Film Culture,* the tiny magazine where the piece first appeared). You know the drill: the old Hollywood studio system was bankrupt in too many ways to count; the internationalist brigades of Bergman, Antonioni, and the French Nouvelle Vague were on the march, seemingly establishing new cinematic beachheads with each successive feature. Andrew Sarris's American-cheese version of the auteur theory was inaugurating the cult of the director-as-godlike-genius, while Pauline Kael derided party-line auteurism as so much sophomoric bunkum. In the middle of this overheated which-side-are-you-on? conflict, here was an upstart who ignored the crossfire and constructed a distinctive space of his own underneath the trenches. Compared with the instant dogma of Sarris's "Notes on the Auteur Theory" (published in the same issue) or a strict polemic à la Kael's "Circles and Squares," Farber's "Termite" is itself an exemplary display of the very tendencies it advances: as much a work of ebullient art as argument, "it goes always forward eating its own boundaries, and, likely as not, leaves nothing in its path other than the signs of eager, industrious, unkempt activity."

Already middle-aged by 1962 (born only two years after *The Birth of a Nation*), Farber's day job at the time was as a carpenter/construction worker anonymously toiling among the elevator shafts of the old Columbia Broadcasting System building in New York City. In the 1940s, he'd succeeded the late Otis Ferguson as movie critic for the *New Republic* and later followed his friend James Agee as the film critic for the *Nation* through the early 1950s, then mostly freelanced for the next decade. He was also a serious painter who had run with the abstract expressionist crowd without quite being one of them. Though his writing has been called an extension of his essentially tactile-vivacious painting, the reverse is more accurate—his artworks didn't catch up with the densely bricolaged prose his compatriot Donald Phelps once described as "a crepuscular swirl of observations, images, wise-cracks, puns, and remarks, frequently uncalled-for (in the sense of unauthorized; seldom in the sense of unwarranted)" until the lucid, cryptic, scrap-happy overhead-view paintings of the late 1970s. *Birthplace: Douglas, Arizona* is one such world-in-microcosm picture, a tabletop-like image fluently strewn with childhood totems—craftily painted patterns of wooden cowboys, open books, model railroad tracks—equally suggestive of his Western roots (taciturn, drily nostalgic, a free-ranging imagination dotted with prickly tumbleweeds) and a peripatetically knowing, citified intelligence (postimpressionist razzle-dazzle, unruffled meticulousness, the swinging approach to spatial rhythms).

In this unusual intersection of interests and shifting perspectives, Farber's writing found its multihued piquancy: a visceral feeling for abstract forms mingled with working-class commitment to minutely detailed craft, a cut-up lingo that brought the conversational critical tone established by Ferguson and Agee together with elements of no-nonsense sports writing, the post-pulp detective novel (Raymond Chandler, Ross Macdonald) stripped of its seedy Boy Scout romance, and even the occasional flash of Walter Winchell (from "The Decline of the Actor": "Item: David Lean's *Lawrence of Arabia* is a masterpiece of overdesign . . ." "Item: The lack of athleticism in *Requiem for a Heavyweight* . . .").

Farber's great contribution would be this marriage of acute worm's-eye vision to staccato musicality, fashioning broadly disparate elements into a retro-modern idiom entirely his own. An American vernacular on an iconoclastic par with the early fiction of Ishmael Reed or the films of kindred imp Sam Fuller (whose punchy scripts Farber declared "might have been written by the bus driver in *The Honeymooners*"), his prose crams a tremendous amount of high-voltage information onto the tightest possible canvas. Farber's little essays on directors (Howard Hawks, Raoul Walsh, Jean-Luc Godard, Luis Buñuel, Don Siegel) are marvels of illuminating appreciation, while his shrewd interrogations of Wellesian gimmickry, fading star power, or the precarious state of cinema at any given moment in time still have a gutty immediacy decades after they were first published. For someone so committed to the ephemeral and transient aspects of an art form, Manny Farber's work holds up largely because it is so deeply involved with the rough-and-tumble fractiousness of the movie medium itself. And in part because, just as an allusive sophisticate like Godard or a ruffian like Fuller brought an eye-catching telegraphic sense of comic-strip framing and composition to film, Farber was able to pinpoint the action-painting qualities inherent in the concept of "motion pictures."

His criticism was a defiant break from the view of movies as extensions of literature: there was no connection (or concession) at all to the authoritative erudition of the Edmund Wilson school, no suave master narrative to reconcile modernity and tradition, off-the-rack moral reckonings with avant-garde antinomianism. Robert Warshow, Dwight Macdonald, and Susan Sontag all firmly upheld the upper end of that socio-aesthetic spectrum; livelier four-letter names Agee and Kael fiercely embraced popular forms while still operating halfway inside the high-toned Wilsonian framework; Sarris ploddingly built up the reputations of midlevel directors to Olympian heights or cast down those who didn't meet his Pantheon's mystifying dress code. Farber, the least hierarchical of critics (and painters), threw himself into the specific contradictions of every film, performance, and image with tremendous hand-to-hand gusto. His dedication to *writing*—as a creative process and not a recycling plant for dead-horse conceits or academic jargon—meant he might spend years working and reworking a single essay until it teemed with "exasperated alertness" (Phelps) and vitality, shooting off in as many directions as a juiced-up Preston Sturges ensemble.

"White Elephant Art vs. Termite Art" isn't the most influential piece of film criticism ever written—no critic's style has more effectively resisted being converted into brand-label orthodoxy—but it is indisputably the coolest. Its tricky, high-wire thrust instantly establishes both a tight and wide-angle frame of reference, a certain mordant, contrarian way of seeing and summing up hip clutter even while cutting through the "idea of art as an expensive hunk of well-regulated area" as so much opulent dry rot. Farber opens with a whirligig consideration of "the feckless, listless quality" of modern art, immediately shifting from broad generalization to a very surefooted and intense single-paragraph dissection of Cézanne's gilt-y, self-stifling tendencies. Then he's on to the cagey "painting tycoon" practices of Motherwell, De Kooning, Warhol, and "James Dine's slog-footed brio," exemplifying the nexus where stubborn individuality meets celebrity, overweening calculation, inflated renown, and fresh-shucked awe, oiling the way for each shiny machine-tooled masterwork rolling onto the showroom floor.

Before this half-empathetic guerrilla strike on the overstuffed art world can sink in, there's an even headier jump cut as he starts discussing, almost as an aside, the termite-art leanings of the movies. Without any kind of apologetic transition, Farber singles out odd-couple creators "Laurel and Hardy, the team of Howard Hawks and William Faulkner operating on the first half of Raymond Chandler's *The Big Sleep.*" A Portrait of the Artist as a Non-Young Termite: up to his/her neck in the rude and/or delicate particulars of physical reality, on a first-name basis with the absurd, and gnawing away at the main obstacle course of convention-cliché-uniformity with a gustatory disregard for the niceties of plot, message, conscience (good or bad), formalist grooming, polite society, upward mobility, and artistic security.

Citing the outwardly elephantine (and talk about white) John Wayne, Farber spies him moving "at the pace of a tapeworm," bemusedly munching on the cuddlesome staginess of John Ford's *The Man Who Shot Liberty Valance.* Wayne's "hoboish spirit" here operates "in bitter-amused counterpoint" to the pallid Fordist assembly of shopworn scenery, familiar business, and nostalgic tintypes, carving out an ornery niche that cuts against the rest of the picture's inflated posturing. The passage is a quick end run around expectations: astutely picking up on a veteran actor's ability to subvert his own moth-eaten persona, spotting how the old pro lays back in the weeds and makes hot up-and-comer Lee Marvin look like a bug-eyed fool.

Beyond this, there is the nonchalant sacrilege in taking John Ford's chiseled head off Mount Rushmore and poking around in the cobwebs a little. Not in any malicious kneecapping sense of cutting-him-down-to-size, but as a matter of restoring the critical perspective and lively sense of internal tensions and contradictions lost whenever an artistic figure or work is canonized. There's Farber's sheer contentious joy in mixing it up with the big boys, keeping readers on their toes and pedants on their heels, the counterintuitive-punching wise guy who gets a near-existential kick out of trying to break through the encrusted defenses of habit, groupthink, laziness, and deep-dish pretentiousness.

In 1957, Farber had written the exciting "Underground Films," which reclaimed the classic Hollywood action directors—deft jack-of-all-trades pros like

Hawks, Anthony Mann, Walsh—from years of unjust neglect. Opening a vital door for the whole auteurist project, the key difference was that Farber retained a feel for proportion, keeping their work in clearly human scale. The nifty sleight of hand of auteur criticism was to transfer the worshipful identification audiences supposedly had for screen heroes to directors, until a Ford took on the mythic, inviolate stature of an old rugged cross between John Wayne, the pope, the Wizard of Oz, and Monument Valley itself. Since no critic has been less interested in burnishing the mythic or iconic than Farber, employing ambivalence as both inexhaustible resource and method, it was inevitable his termite tack would locate its objective in the buffed hardwood reputations of the day.

British wonder boy Tony Richardson, François Truffaut at the height of his New Wave infallibility, Michelangelo Antonioni and his alienation-chic interior décor: Farber tackles each with the élan of a happy pathologist working on prime sacred cows. (Dissecting, anatomizing, cataloging, prodding, but not butchering.) "The common quality or defect which unites" these divergent types, Farber writes, "is fear, a fear of the potential life, rudeness, and outrageousness of a film." Farber's problem with white elephant art is its paralytic self-consciousness, a mode of controlling, overdetermined expression that freezes out the world, desiccating forms and behavior by the posh deployment of a "pretentiously handsome image."

Couple this with Farber's basic disregard for narrative and all but the most skeletal, virtually random plot points, and it's easy to see why some find him a maddening if not altogether incomprehensible critic. Instead of a symmetrical, thesis-tied-up-with-a-Christmas-bow approach, the finish of the "Termite Art" piece has a decidedly capricious, Pollock-scattergun quality, declaring that the era of the "heavily insured, enclosed film art" has passed (though the esteem-powered ascendancy of the hyperconscious Truffaut-Antonioni filmmaker would seem to point to the exact opposite conclusion). Noting this "chasm of inertia" and mutually assured unintelligibility in the flat distance between white elephant impulses and termite acting, he ends a piece where you'd normally expect it to begin, throwing down a reference to the then-obscure 1952 Kurosawa film *Ikiru* like a gauntlet: outwardly as "traditional as *Greed*," but in his eyes actually a secret avatar of "buglike immersion in a small area without point or aim." And then, like a graffiti wizard scrawling aphorisms over white-on-white hospital corridors, he's gone, disappearing again back into the woodwork.

From which Farber reemerged in the 1960s, running the great pool-shark streak that started with a brief stint at *Cavalier* magazine (neo-*Playboy* skin rag), before landing at *Artforum* (*Playboy* for hardcore aesthetes) circa 1967; he seemed equally at home—or out of place—at both publications. This led to the anarcho-democratic vistas of *Negative Space*, nearly thirty years of writing compressed into a burst of bracing, screwy American vernacular: the least beholden to European airs, the most like a movie you can never get to the bottom of, as kinetically sustained as Griffith's *Musketeers of Pig Alley*, rambunctious as a Chuck Jones cartoon, seductive as *The Big Sleep*, as formally gratifying as prime Godard. Maybe the most striking thing is how tenaciously he worked to break down the straightforward praise/blame dichotomy, looking askance at everything, always questioning the majority position, including the countercultural one.

In the 1970s, he began collaborating with his wife, Patricia Patterson: their work together was somewhat more muted in its criticisms and straightforward in its enthusiasms, tilting significantly in favor of the latest imported arthaus gang (Rainer Werner Fassbinder, Werner Herzog, et al.). Writing in Francis Coppola's short-lived *City* magazine, a note of promotion and protectiveness creeps into some of this work: a hesitation to be as tough on these films as on New Hollywood effusions like *Nashville,* or as the pair are in their unsparingly incisive *Film Comment* piece on *Taxi Driver,* which turned out to be the final published Farber-Patterson collaboration. Farber continued to teach film classes at the University of San Diego for a decade, but increasingly focused his creative energies on his painting. The series of metacritical paintings from the late seventies and early eighties—including the vertiginously sustained "Auteur" pictures, homages to directorial acumen from Buster Keaton and Howard Hawks to Eric Rohmer and Jean-Marie Straub and Danièle Huillet—rendered his critical assets and attitudes as ideograms. Robust and slyly delicate, these paintings are odes to the "push-pull" attraction of cinema, its lyrical, microtonal ironies, and to the artist-critic's gift for deadpan annoyance-cum-wonder: for instance in a circular painting entitled *"Keep blaming everyone."* Or alternately a sprawling oil (roughly five feet by eleven) dubbed *Have a Chew on Me:* faux folksiness undermined by a poetics of passionate ambivalence, a worktable strewn with tools, talismans, hand-scribbled notes to self ("get it finished"), elegantly rude little nudes, and an even juicier-looking miniature rib steak.

Bibliography: Manny Farber, "Nearer My Agee to Thee," *Cavalier* (December 1965), uncollected piece on 1960s film criticism; *Negative Space* (New York, 1971). Donald Phelps, *Covering Ground* (New York, 1969). *Filmography: Ikiru,* directed by Akira Kurosawa (1952). *The Man Who Shot Liberty Valance,* directed by John Ford (1962).

HOWARD HAMPTON

1963, April
Scraps of paper begin to reach Martin Luther King, Jr.

"LETTER FROM BIRMINGHAM JAIL"

Few works of public writing have embodied a social movement as powerfully in American history as Martin Luther King's "Letter from Birmingham Jail." It began along the edges of a page of a local newspaper, continued on pieces of toilet paper and anything the author's confidantes could smuggle in to help him write. Typed up by assistants and smuggled back for revisions by the author, it was finally circulated to the press, and later expanded and altered for a book intended to make good on the interest fomented by the original letter itself and, even more, the events that formed it. "Letter from Birmingham Jail" is intimately interconnected with the tactics of a social movement in a moment of crisis. It remains an enduring reply to questions about the timeliness of insubordinate protests for justice in the public sphere.

King had come to Birmingham to revive a movement that was losing the attention of the American public. The Southern Christian Leadership Conference (SCLC), born of the Montgomery Bus Boycott of 1955 and 1956, was seeking an opportunity to reinvigorate the movement, while liberal white Americans, including those in the most influential positions of the federal government, settled into a feeling that the "Negro question" would be resolved in good time—while black nationalists such as those affiliated with the Nation of Islam, including Malcolm X, ridiculed the nonviolent philosophy of King and rejected his integrationist vision of an America that might be forced though nonviolent tactics to live up to what King would call "the true meaning of its creed."

Although the letter is ostensibly addressed to a group of eight Southern white clerics (Catholic, Protestant, and Jewish) who had assumed the role of moderates on the race question, it was never sent to them or published in a local newspaper—such as the one in which the eight had themselves published a statement criticizing "outsiders" for an "untimely" call for demonstrations against segregation. The letter was sent out initially as a news release. King used the occasion of the clerics' statement discouraging local blacks from joining his demonstration to articulate the philosophy of the movement in a multipronged argument about the nature of justice, the white church's hypocritical accommodation to white supremacy, the Negro's importance to America, and the relationship of Christian faith to time and place.

In Birmingham, the SCLC leaders believed they had found the perfect location for a demonstration of their movement's meaning and power. Home, in King's description, to the most implacable segregationists in the nation, it was also the most industrialized city of the South, with economic and political ties throughout the nation. Here the demonstrators would force the white power structure to reveal its essential nature, heightening the tension between white supremacy and professed American (and religious) ideals to an unsustainable level. The goal was to expose the viciousness that, behind calls for patience and caution, silently kept watch under the daily regimen of racial injustice—to force the inherent violence of segregation into the open.

The text situates itself at multiple dimensions of time—national, international, and local, as well as religious. Dated April 16, 1963, it came into existence in what seemed to King a sacred time. He had offered himself for arrest on Good Friday (April 12 that year), the day of Christ's crucifixion, leading a small march that had been denied a permit by the local court. He was released eight days later, having written his letter in the interim, and just following what King would describe as a dark night of the soul. The letter immediately followed a return of faith; it carries a tone of high confidence tempered by Christian humility and seasoned with the righteous anger of a prophet.

The year 1963 held special significance for the civil rights movement. Nine years had passed since the 1954 Supreme Court decision in *Brown v. Board of Education,* yet schools remained overwhelmingly segregated. Independence movements in Africa and Asia were liberating vast populations of nonwhite peoples from European powers. During the Cuban missile crisis of October 1962, the United States had displayed its willingness to use nuclear war, with the possible elimination of all human life, to protect freedom. Climactically, 1963 marked the hundredth anniversary of the Emancipation Proclamation. An entire century had passed, and still the Negro was unfree. "I hope, sirs, you can understand our legitimate and unavoidable impatience," King writes, punctuating an extended litany of the forms of trauma suffered by African American families.

King likens himself to the apostle Paul, who wrote prison letters as well. Like Paul, King instructs his audience about how to square their actions with the faith he shares with them, revealing the contradictions between the conduct of the white church and Judeo-Christian beliefs. The anger that emerges occasionally is an anger bound with love. Referring to his audience as his "brothers," King seeks a union in faith by making them recognize their resemblance to the Pharisees of old.

Not only white moderates questioned the timeliness of the demonstrations in the spring of 1963. King himself attested to the "tremendous resistance" on the part of black community leaders to mass demonstrations, only days before he was arrested, and King's forces were having trouble recruiting supporters. Most black pastors, professionals, and businessmen believed the timing was wrong. They also, according to King, resented his coming in as an "outsider" and making plans for events in their city without consulting them. The brutally racist commissioner of public safety Bull Connor had just run a losing race for mayor; with a new administration about to take over, most black leaders believed that demonstrations would only strengthen the hand of their worst enemies. On April 10, the city's black newspaper, the *Birmingham World,* declared King's planned action "both wasteful and worthless." That view was also expressed by white moderates in Birmingham, major national newspapers, and the attorney general of the United States, Robert F. Kennedy. But on April 8 and 9, King had met with religious, professional, and business leaders of the black community and won their support. On the very evening of the *Birmingham World* editorial, he announced to a mass meeting that he and his movement partner, the Reverend Ralph Abernathy, would demonstrate and go to jail.

As King revised it for his book *Why We Can't Wait* (1964), in which it constitutes a chapter unto itself, the letter exists in a perennial present outside the narrative mode of address that leads up to and follows it. It is presented as an address from sacred time, an eternal now that ruptures the daily inertia of keeping time. But in its own moment, the letter accuses its ostensible addressees of a "tragic misconception of time," a belief in inevitable progress, as if things will get better in time if we just leave well enough alone. It offers an alternative sense of time, akin to Thoreau's: "We must use time creatively in the knowledge that the time is always ripe to do right."

The decision to demonstrate marked the first time that King and his group elected to violate a court order. Indeed, the main line of the civil rights struggle going back to the turn of the century had focused on passing legislation and appealing to the courts for enforcement of civil rights statutes. In Birmingham, the SCLC had dared question the authority of the local courts themselves as arbiters of justice. In the letter, King exposes the power of structural racism—how political, social, and legal institutions have been structured by white supremacy. Hence King's appeal to the higher-law argument framed by early Jews and Christians and, later, by the likes of Roger Williams, Thomas Jefferson, and Thoreau in his essay "Civil Disobedience," also written from jail. One can distinguish just from unjust civil laws, King argues, on the basis of whether they square with natural law, moral law, and divine law (the three of which seem to be always synchronized with each other). When civil law falls out of line with natural, moral, and divine law, the time has come to resist. Like Thoreau, King speaks of the need for nonconformists in an age of acquiescence to injustice. His confinement pronounces judgment on those who are free.

As devastating as the letter is to the people it addresses, it aims at a genuine dialogue, in Martin Buber's sense. While attempting to create community, it does so not by scapegoating at the crossroads but by repeatedly claiming "brotherhood" on higher ground. King distances himself from black nationalism, even as he affirms black Americans as "a people."

In its appeal to the Negro's special relationship to America, King's essay drew on a central point of the New Negro movement of the first half of the twentieth century, and echoed aspects of W. E. B. Du Bois's epochal work, *The Souls of Black Folk*. To both Du Bois and King, America would never have come to be if not for the Negro, and the Negro people were the most American of Americans as well as the most prophetic and creative force for the realization of ideals enunciated in the nation's foundational documents. "Abused and scorned though we may be," King wrote, "our destiny is tied up with America's destiny."

> Before the Pilgrims landed at Plymouth, we were here. Before the pen of Jefferson etched the majestic words of the Declaration of Independence across the pages of history, we were here. For more than two centuries our forebears labored in this country without wages; they made cotton king; they built the homes of their masters while suffering gross injustice and shameful humiliations—and yet out of a bottomless vitality they continued to thrive and develop. If the inexpressible cruelties of slavery could not stop us, the opposition we now face will surely fail. We will win our freedom because the sacred heritage of our nation and the eternal will of God are embodied in our echoing demands.

The public attention gained by the Birmingham action convinced King of the value of a demonstration in Washington, D.C.—hence his agreement to join the March on Washington for Jobs and Freedom, already planned by A. Philip Randolph, head of the Negro American Labor Council. Indeed, King's epochal address at the Lincoln Memorial on August 28, an unexpected departure from his prepared text, was an impromptu repeat of a speech he had delivered at a mass meeting in Birmingham in April.

The letter was reproduced only fragmentarily at first in national news outlets, then disseminated in full as a pamphlet by the American Friends Service Committee under the title "Tears of Love," making its way to human rights groups and government agencies. It was circulated in churches, and then, on June 12, finally printed in full in a national periodical for the first time, in *Christian Century*, a highly respected liberal Protestant journal. After that, its reputation grew rapidly. Between mid-April and June, demonstrations in Birmingham had drawn the attention of the world when Bull Connor had his fire department and police turn fire hoses and dogs on demonstrating high school students, recruited in the wake of King's imprisonment, while bystanders and network news crews looked on.

The publicity gained through Connor's actions while television cameras recorded the scene and broadcast it to the world in early May brought a new public to King's letter. The *Saturday Evening Post* published excerpts in an article about King as an "Apostle of Crisis." Not until July 30 did the white press of Birmingham even mention the letter. It began to gain greater circulation in the lead-up to the March on Washington—and then afterward, as King's reputation soared toward sainthood. Perceived as a text that had set forth the moral and intellectual justification of the civil rights movement, the letter was on its way toward canonization. It was compared to Émile Zola's public letter defending Dreyfus in 1898 and Lincoln's Gettysburg Address. A long-playing record was made of it, and television producers sought to talk King into making a docudrama about it. His friends worried that King would lose control of the copyright and encouraged the writing of *Why We Can't Wait* to showcase the letter. The version included there would become the most widely circulated, the one reprinted in anthologies today.

The year 1963 may have been the culmination of the left wing—and black—liberal faith in American ideals. When President John F. Kennedy was shot, Malcolm X announced that the chickens had come home to roost in America. King did not exactly disagree, but mourned the loss of a leader who had tentatively come to his aid at a critical time. (The president had called King's wife while the leader was in the Birmingham jail, to express concern, to inform her that the Justice Department was monitoring his treatment, and to tell her to let federal officials know if she and her husband had any complaints. Minutes later, King was allowed to call home. Within a month, Kennedy addressed the nation on television to declare racism and segregation immoral, vowing to propose a civil rights bill.) Believing he lived in a sick nation, King felt certain that he would suffer the president's fate.

Sometime between 1963 and 1968, when King was assassinated, a seismic shift occurred in American culture. In Birmingham itself, racist bombings replaced civil rights marches, culminating in the bombing of the Sixteenth Street Baptist Church on September 15, 1963, a crime for which the killers of the four young girls who died did not face justice until 2000, almost forty years later. The term "America" came to be associated with an empire, and to a growing proportion of writers, racism was of its essence, not merely an unfortunate mistake. The Black Power movement and protests against the Vietnam War made the former belief in a true, exceptional, but as-yet-unrealized America seem an ideological phantasm. Jimi Hendrix bent the national anthem into weird contortions that expressed doubt about the whole meaning of so-called Americanism. Negro gave way to Black or Afro-American, with an emphasis on the Afro. The last phase of a New Negro era was over. Perhaps the "Letter from Birmingham Jail" contains its culminating words.

After King's assassination on April 4, 1968, members of the Black Theology Project started a movement to have the letter incorporated into the Bible. The original scraps of manuscript, in the meantime, had suffered the fate of most such utterances from the umbilicus of history, the mythic locus of events around which an era comes to definition. They had been thrown away.

Bibliography: Jonathan S. Bass, *Blessed Are the Peacemakers: Martin Luther King, Jr., Eight White Religious Leaders, and the "Letter from Birmingham Jail"* (Baton Rouge, 2001). David Garrow, *Bearing the Cross: Martin Luther King, Jr., and the Southern Christian Leadership Conference* (New York, 1989). Martin Luther King, Jr. *Why We Can't Wait* (New York, 1964). Malinda Snow, "Martin Luther King's 'Letter from Birmingham Jail' as Pauline Epistle," *Quarterly Journal of Speech* 71 (1985).

GEORGE HUTCHINSON

1964
"My hand draws back"

ROBERT LOWELL, "FOR THE UNION DEAD"

In January Robert Lowell, hospitalized for his most recent mental breakdown, which began two weeks after Kennedy's assassination—"I guess it had something to do with my crack-up"—interrupted his stay at the Hartford Institute of Living to speak on Lincoln's Gettysburg Address at the Library of Congress. In July, President Johnson signed the Civil Rights Act. In August, the U.S. Congress approved the Gulf of Tonkin Resolution allowing unlimited military activity in Southeast Asia without a declaration of war. All summer, the New York World's Fair (so-called despite a boycott by the Bureau of International Expositions), dominated by Disney, IBM, and the American automobile industry, presented the Ford Mustang, Futurama, the Unisphere, and several "audio-animatronic" displays, among them a hydraulic, periodically regreased model of President Lincoln delivering speeches in an exhibit called "Great Moments with Mr. Lincoln." In the fall, Lowell published *For the Union Dead*.

"When I finished *Life Studies* I was left hanging on a question mark," Lowell wrote of the book he published in 1959. "I am still hanging there. I don't know whether it is a death-rope or a life-line." Lowell made those sentences public in the printed program for the 1960 Boston Arts Festival, where, in the Boston Common, he read the poem that would later give its title to *For the Union Dead*. Immanent, endangering, graphic, the statement's turn from retrospect to present tense still draws a gasp. We're caught up into the moment of perilous uncertainty. And the menace reaches out, when linked to the poem, to intersect—this is Lowell's pivoting achievement as he moves from *Life Studies* to his new poems—with a direct, profoundly shareable sense of private and historical vulnerability. Lethal racism, urban upheaval, federal and civil "gangsterism," the cold war terror of nuclear catastrophe ("Fall 1961": "A father's no shield / for his child")—we don't have to belong to a patrician family, don't have to have once ferociously upheld or abjured high religious vantage points from which to denounce the fallen world, don't have to have shed an armored formalism for a more open writing style to feel that Lowell has begun to express, with a mysterious blend of subjective and objective immediacy, the moments when our erratic personal and national biographies hang from the same question mark.

All lyric poems invite us to cohabit, however partially, a position behind the speaking mask. Lowell's often manically riveted and riveting early poems—virtuosic, metaphysically fueled, jackhammering their way between certain damnation and unrealized redemption—were not always easy for others to inhabit, as if from the inside, as a speaker. Even the unclenched prose or free-verse reminiscences of *Life Studies,* written in what we might call Lowell's second style, retained a charismatic glamour, in which the poet's accounts of domestic disarray, of incarceration or dementia, strained rather than severed the ligaments of an exclusive familial and literary genealogy. Not that such ligaments could or should be severed. But as Lowell, born in 1917, entered his later forties ("At forty-five / what next, what next?"), his understanding of recurrent "suffering without purgation," whether of personal breakdowns or global afflictions, his more horizontal perspective on human fallibility, his empirical rather than transcendent grip on our common fate as individuals with bodily senses and memories, as members of a racially divided, morally and physically near-suicidal nation—these all converged on a new way of "less intimately autobiographical" writing that could bring his fellow citizens closer to the center of each poem's unfolding action. As if to mark the departure of this third style, Lowell realized it had been a mistake to add "For the Union Dead" as a new final poem for the first paperback edition of *Life Studies.* Better to end with "Skunk Hour." Better to keep his new poem, assuming he was paying out a lifeline, not tightening a death rope, for his next book. Given Lowell's inveterate "plotting," the poem would not begin but rather end its own volume four years later.

"My poem . . . is about childhood memories, the evisceration of our modern cities, civil rights, nuclear warfare and more particularly Colonel Robert Shaw and his Negro regiment, the Massachusetts 54th," Lowell told his audience in Boston Common. "I brought in early personal memories because I wanted to avoid the fixed, brazen tone of the set-piece and official ode." No easy task. Lowell's drafts, many of them exploring separate elements of the eventual compound, show how difficult it was to find the condensed form, the tonal modulations, the telling sequence and cross-referencing of images, the hinges and sinews that would make the poem lock tight yet stay in motion. "The 'Union Dead' poem took all winter and I suppose is the most composed poem I've ever written."

What was new for Lowell, perhaps for American poetry after 1945, was a poem of state that could be successfully read aloud to a large and varied audience while retaining not just its intricate texture, its measured, almost Augustan sense of formal occasion, but also its detailed first-person singular inclusion of what was autobiographically near at hand, "my hand." Allen Ginsberg's "America" and "Howl" were too extravagant for Lowell, too transgressive, too volatile, to provide a statuesque cast, or to regulate the kinds of energies that Lowell now feared in himself and in his society. At the other extreme, Frost had not yet written his impersonal, generalizing "Dedication" for Kennedy's inauguration. "For the Union Dead" would have to be a ceremonious lyric of casual gravitas that could be declaimed (neither vatically nor ecstatically) without losing the intellectual density inherited from Lowell's earliest teachers, John Crowe Ransom and Allen Tate. Tate, especially, was on his mind, as the author of the 1928 "Ode to the Confederate Dead," an intransigently difficult and introverted poem.

Certainly, Lowell had spent much of the 1950s learning to fray his lines, to add more flex and less muscle to his rhythms, to bend his Christian-symbolist rhetoric toward what he called an "imagistic directness" associated with Williams and Bishop. He admired the dramatically spoken poems of Jarrell and Berryman, even the wildly inclusive vernacular of Ginsberg's "Kaddish." But with the prose memoir "91 Revere Street," and the free-verse inventions of *Life Studies,* he had gone as far out, formally and temperamentally, as he could go. By October 1959 he looked back: "I've just published a new book of poems, my first in nine years . . . for a while my old stuff seemed like something from the ancient extinct age of the reptiles, cumbersome creatures, bogged down and destroyed by their protective hide. Now the need to be more impersonal has come again, with it a need for some third style, still unfound. There are times when nothing you do seems really yours."

The originality of "For the Union Dead"—with its free verse molded into quatrains loosely associated with those of the Bay State hymnal and the Horatian ode—arises, then, from the fact that Lowell sought a more strictly shaped container, if not an urn, for feelings that remained both raw and subcutaneously desperate: "The world is very much under my skin and really seems like a murderous nightmare when one looks outward. I am sick of nations armed to the teeth." If the "need to be more impersonal" had returned, it arrived in large part from a need to address a yet wider arena of historical forces, marked as they were by an ever more ghastly panorama, an "unforgivable landscape." The accompanying need for a greater degree of formal "composition" no doubt arose from the poet's unstable groping if not for prophetic transformation ("unforgivable" rules out any salvific economy), then at least for composure in the presence of a "compass-needle" elsewhere described as "dead on terror."

War, bound to commerce and to racism, was the reverberant occasion of Lowell's poem. First titled "Colonel Shaw and the Massachusetts' 54th," the poem circles Augustus Saint-Gaudens's bronze monument to the abolitionist Bostonian Robert Shaw and the volunteers of the North's first black regiment, whom he led to their valiant if hopeless assault on Fort Wagner, South Carolina, on July 18, 1863. More than 250 men, including Shaw, were killed in the exposed charge against entrenched positions. "The first modern war?" Lowell wondered in a draft titled "One Gallant Rush." But the Civil War, and the foreshadowed slaughter of World War I, are themselves framed by the yet earlier "graveyards of the Grand Army of the Republic," and by the later, unmemorialized horrors of World War II:

> There are no statues for the last war here;
> on Boylston Street, a commercial photograph
> shows Hiroshima boiling
>
> over a Mosler Safe, the "Rock of Ages"
> that survived the blast.

Crass commercial exploitation—a kind of historical, and religious, blasphemy— creates its own blast, worse than mere forgetting.

Lowell begins with the present destruction of the very place of private and communal memory, "the heart of Boston," site both of the poem's material and of its performance.

> The old South Boston Aquarium stands
> in a Sahara of snow now. Its broken windows are boarded.
> The bronze weathervane cod has lost half its scales.
> The airy tanks are dry.
>
> Once my nose crawled like a snail on the glass;
> my hand tingled
> to burst the bubbles
> drifting from the noses of the cowed, compliant fish.
>
> My hand draws back. I often sigh still
> for the dark downward and vegetating kingdom
> of the fish and reptile. One morning last March,
> I pressed against the new barbed and galvanized
>
> fence on the Boston Common. Behind their cage,
> yellow dinosaur steamshovels were grunting
> as they cropped up tons of mush and grass
> to gouge their underworld garage.
>
> Parking spaces luxuriate like civic
> sandpiles in the heart of Boston.
> A girdle of orange, Puritan-pumpkin colored girders
> braces the tingling Statehouse,
>
> shaking over the excavations, as it faces Colonel Shaw
> and his bell-cheeked Negro infantry
> on St. Gaudens' shaking Civil War relief,
> propped by a plank splint against the garage's earthquake.

Before we can reach Shaw and his infantry, we've suffered viscerally, from nose to tingling hand to kinesthetic sighing, a temporal and spatial "evisceration" whose current earthquake has the Statehouse and the monument propped and shaking. The stratified yet veering switches of tense, of inner and outer realms, of literal or phantasmagoric prehistory and bestial modern technology, of child and adult, snow and sand, water and air, evacuation and proliferation—all jar the very foundations upon which we first come to "face" the memorial. Are these now the premises of our access to history? And where are we in relation to our own past, or to the deep past of our own species? "My hand draws back."

The "earthquake" is now. The word immediately opens a century-deep fissure to the summer of 1863: "Two months after marching through Boston,/half the regiment was dead;" it happens in one half-sentence. Thence to 1897: "at the dedication,/William James could almost hear the bronze Negroes breathe." At the level of syntax alone, there's anger as well as genius in these compressions. No time to breathe. And thence again, as if surfacing through the waters of memory, back to the present: "Their monument sticks like a fishbone/in the city's throat." No way to swallow. Hard enough to speak. The aquarium fish, the weathervane cod, and now the storied men—all down to a fishbone, halfway, if anywhere, to a parodic return as "finned cars" at the end of the poem.

Engaging the bronze, and perhaps identifying contradictions within himself, Lowell evokes Shaw's crisis and character. With the young colonel's capacity for choice, balanced by a rigid idealism, the ethical dimension presses upon the poem and enlarges the present field of vision:

> He has an angry wrenlike vigilance,
> a greyhound's gentle tautness;
> he seems to wince at pleasure,
> and suffocate for privacy.
>
> He is out of bounds now. He rejoices in man's lovely
> peculiar power to choose life and die—

A survey of attenuating markers of faith or heroism—churches, flags, statues of "the abstract Union Soldier"—leads to one more, tonally anguished, plunge into the past:

> Shaw's father wanted no monument
> except the ditch,
> where his son's body was thrown
> and lost with his "niggers."
>
> The ditch is nearer.

Ditch then, ditch now—but nearer. Surrounded by racism in the very years of forced desegregation, Lowell can't quarantine the word "niggers" to the term allegedly used by the Confederate general who had Shaw buried with his men. Notes for the poem include "I sit rivetted to my television set, and passively watch the sit-down strikes." Also the line, "Commercial optimism, the black man's prison." What was the point of the Civil War? Is it over? Has it begun again? "When I crouch to my television set,/the drained faces of Negro school-children rise like balloons." Lowell has just preceded these two lines by his reference to Hiroshima. No way now to separate the image of those faces from the drained tanks of the aquarium, the bell-cheeked infantry, the ghastly "boiling" of nuclear holocaust. For Lowell, the agonies are if not identical definitely conjoined. Lowell's speech on the Gettysburg Address ends, "Lincoln's occasional speech of a hundred years ago still rings today when our country struggles with four almost insoluble spiritual problems: how to join equality with excellence, how to join liberty to justice, how to avoid destroying or being destroyed by nuclear power, and how to complete the emancipation of the slaves."

We may have spiraled back to Lowell's earliest obsession with apocalypse, but what had once been scriptural fantasy is now historical menace. "Colonel Shaw / is riding on his bubble." After Kennedy's assassination, Lowell recalled, "One felt as if a civil war were beginning. No rational daylight law seemed to hold, and it's easy to see how Johnson rushing to his plane feared lest an atomic war might be beginning. What destructive almost abstract dynamite we are all sitting on, though all seems comfortable, safe and controlled."

> The Aquarium is gone. Everywhere,
> giant finned cars nose forward like fish;
> a savage servility
> slides by on grease.

A more "savage" summation of his society would be hard to find. Compliance has become servility. Formally the poem has turned on itself, repeating the opening words "Aquarium," "nose," and "fish," only to undermine them with absence, and with the overriding action of the cars. Even the sounds recur, particularly the alliterating *s* of the first lines of the poem. Is it only now that we hear how much of the Anglo-Saxon alliterative verse tradition Lowell has revived throughout the poem? The fatal sonic cohesiveness takes the poem, together with our sense of history, back to the origins of its own language and craft. Around this time Lowell was working on a poem, which remained unfinished, entitled "Beowulf." The ditch is near. One can almost feel the monster nosing forward, back on the prowl.

Bibliography: Patrick Cosgrave, *The Public Poetry of Robert Lowell* (London, 1975). Robert Lowell, *Collected Letters,* ed. Saskia Hamilton (New York, 2007); *Collected Poems,* ed. Frank Bidart and David Gewanter (New York, 2003); *Collected Prose,* ed. Robert Giroux (New York, 1897). Alan Williamson, *Pity the Monsters: The Political Vision of Robert Lowell* (New Haven, CT, 1975). Stephen Yenser, *Circle to Circle: The Poetry of Robert Lowell* (Berkeley, CA, 1976).

PETER SACKS

1964, October 27

Campaigning for Barry Goldwater, Ronald Reagan delivers "The Speech"

"The Last Stand on Earth"

On November 3, 1964, President Lyndon Johnson crushed Senator Barry Goldwater in the U.S. presidential election. Johnson won more than 61 percent of the popular vote, the most lopsided tally since 1824. The Republican senator managed to carry only his native Arizona and, because of his position that federal civil rights laws were a violation of states' rights, five Southern states. Respected national pundits proclaimed that the landslide tolled the death knell for American conservatism. "[Goldwater] has wrecked his party for a long time to come," James Reston wrote in the *New York Times*. Political analysts agreed that Goldwater's right-wing views were too extreme for the country to swallow. The conventional intellectual wisdom was that in the post–New Deal era, America had reached the "end of ideology," and the election only confirmed this belief. According to sociologist Daniel Bell, the collapse of liberal illusions about the Soviet Union and the rise of the welfare state had created a "rough consensus among intellectuals on social issues." It was not even clear what American conservatism was. The future of the battered Republican Party, if it had one, lay in its moderate Eisenhower wing, whose positions were not significantly different from those of Democrats.

It was one of the great misreadings in American history. American conservatism was not dead: Goldwater was not an end, but a beginning. His supposedly extreme ideas, presented in a more palatable way, were to become the dominant force in American politics. The man who was almost single-handedly responsible for this political revolution was a second-tier Hollywood star named Ronald Reagan. And the event that catapulted Reagan onto the national stage was something now known simply as The Speech.

On October 27, a week before the election, the Goldwater campaign ran a national telecast of an address called "A Time for Choosing" that Reagan made on Goldwater's behalf. If the pundits had been blessed with a crystal ball, they would have ignored Goldwater's defeat and studied every syllable of that speech, every camera angle, every facial expression. For The Speech is one of those uncanny cultural artifacts that contains within it not just words, gestures, and ideas, but a future.

Reagan had been delivering The Speech, in various versions, for years—for General Electric. The company had hired him to do an unusual double job: to host its weekly TV show, *General Electric Theater*, and to tour the country making motivational speeches to its 250,000 employees. GE was no ordinary company. It carefully cultivated its image as a bastion of free enterprise and as a loyal corporate community. It saw its mission as selling not only lightbulbs and appliances but an entire way of life—one for which Reagan himself became an advertisement. GE fitted out his Pacific Palisades home with the latest electric gadgets— and also fitted Reagan out as a spokesman for its free market, anti-union, anti-Communist, anti-welfare creed. Reagan spread GE's conservative gospel to the company's employees, and also to community groups, Rotary Clubs, and schools across the country.

It was a perfect job for Reagan. Although he had been a union leader in Hollywood, from 1947 heading the Screen Actors Guild through the most fraught years of the cold war, he was by temperament and belief a company man. His bitter fight with unionists who he was convinced were Communists, trying to take over Hollywood on orders from Moscow, had led him to fear for his life and to work as an FBI informer. So Reagan tirelessly crisscrossed the country for GE, polishing his speech, convincing workers that they were part of a big, happy family, honing antigovernment punch lines that would appeal to business leaders. After GE fired him, for reasons that remain controversial (some say it was because he had become too right-wing for the company, others that GE was afraid that Reagan would be implicated in a pending federal antitrust lawsuit against the Screen Actors Guild), giving The Speech became Reagan's sacred cause.

Watching "A Time for Choosing" now is a little like watching *Citizen Kane* for the first time. Precisely because you know the speech is a classic, it is somewhat anticlimactic. Reagan's themes, and perhaps more important, his rhetoric and performative style, have become so deeply ingrained in American political discourse that it is hard to understand what made the address such a sensation.

But if what happens is familiar, it's also strangely unnerving. Reagan opens The Speech jumping out at the bell, a boxer who wants to overwhelm his opponent. Just seconds into it and Reagan is throwing roundhouse rights, proclaiming that America's apparent prosperity is an illusion, threatened by excessive taxation and the national debt. The viewer scarcely has time to digest this dark thought when Reagan throws down the gauntlet. It isn't just America's economy that is at risk, but her soul—and her very existence. "As for the peace that we would preserve, I wonder who among us would like to approach the wife or mother whose husband or son has died in South Vietnam and ask them if they think this is a peace that should be maintained indefinitely," Reagan says. "Do they mean peace, or do they mean we just want to be left in peace?"

Only three minutes into his speech and Reagan has sanctified himself with the blood of heroic Americans and accused Democrats of appeasement. Having performed those holy rituals, he delivers the liturgical condemnation of Evil. "We are at war with the most dangerous enemy that has ever faced mankind in his long climb from the swamp to the stars," he thunders. And then, in an ingenious transition, he makes the classic right-wing move, linking together the little Satan, big government, with the Great Satan of communism. "If we lose freedom here, there is no place to escape to. This is the last stand on Earth," Reagan proclaims. And to make that last stand against mankind's most dangerous enemy, we must return to the "freedoms that were intended for us by the Founding Fathers." If we do not, we will "abandon the American revolution and confess that a little intellectual elite in a far-distant capital can plan our lives for us better than we can plan them ourselves." The welfare state is not just a subversion of rugged American individualism, it is the first step toward surrendering the City on a Hill to the Communists.

Reagan strikes a slightly less harsh note in his assault on big-government follies, but it's clear from his relentless tone that all of the sins he denounces are connected. Mocking a government redevelopment agency that declared Rice County, Kansas, a depressed area, he asserts that its inhabitants "have over $30 million on deposit in personal savings in their banks." Then comes the punch line: "When the government tells you you're depressed, lie down and be depressed."

The banner-toting audience, which the camera occasionally shows applauding, roars with laughter. Some of Reagan's anecdotes are almost identical to ones he would use sixteen years later, when as president he attacked "welfare queens" driving Cadillacs. Reagan tells the story of a married woman whose husband made $250 a month, and who decided to divorce him because welfare would pay a single mother $330 a month. "She got the idea from two women in her neighborhood who had already done that very thing."

Then Reagan returns to his overarching theme—the moral necessity of resistance to Communist evil. "There is no argument over the choice between peace and war, but there is only one guaranteed way you can have peace—and you can have it in the next second—surrender." The accusation is now explicit: the Democratic policy of accommodation is a betrayal of everything holy.

> You and I know and do not believe that life is so dear and peace so sweet as to be purchased at the price of chains and slavery. If nothing in life is worth dying for, when did this begin—just in the face of this enemy? Or should Moses have told the children of Israel to live in slavery under the pharaohs? Should Christ have refused the cross? Should the patriots at Concord Bridge have thrown down their guns and refused to fire the shot heard 'round the world?

In his conclusion, Reagan borrows rhetorical fire from two of America's greatest presidents, Franklin Delano Roosevelt—his lifelong model of a charismatic leader—and Abraham Lincoln. "You and I have a rendezvous with destiny," Reagan intones, echoing Roosevelt. And then, from Lincoln: "We will preserve for our children this, the last best hope of man on Earth, or we will sentence them to take the last step into a thousand years of darkness."

The Speech made Reagan a national political figure overnight—in fact, even before the night was finished. After the broadcast ran, Reagan recalled in his autobiography, he was "still nervous about it and, when I went to bed, I was hoping I hadn't let Barry down." Reagan was awakened about midnight by a call from a Goldwater staffer, who told him the campaign switchboard had been lit up constantly since the broadcast. Thousands of people had pledged support for Goldwater. The Speech, replayed again and again across the country, ultimately raised $8 million for Goldwater and the GOP—the equivalent of about $50 million in 2007.

Historians agree that The Speech was such a sensation because Reagan was a better communicator than Goldwater. His anecdotes were folksier, his jokes better, his delivery more informal. He was a more familiar, less threatening, and less eccentric figure than Goldwater. As Rick Perlstein relates in *Before the Storm,* his exhaustive study of Goldwater's campaign and the rise of postwar American conservatism, Goldwater came across as an angry Jeremiah, an outsider, an image that his Democratic opponents seized on and converted into a menacing caricature reminiscent of Dr. Strangelove. As Reagan noted after the election, conservatism needed the "soft sell." But to contemporary eyes, The Speech is far from genial or reassuring. Reagan speaks much faster than he did in the years that followed, or than most politicians have done since. He smiles less. He starts citing statistics just seconds into the speech, and his arguments are relentless, almost staccato. His famous charm flashes now and then, but he is mostly deadly serious. He comes across as a stern father, exuding a controlled outrage. If Reagan is the Good Cop, Goldwater's Bad Cop must have resembled a Western version of Abel Ferrara's Bad Lieutenant.

This impression is partly due to the changed conventions of political speech. Humorless pronouncements delivered by jutting-jawed white men were the cultural norm in the fifties and early to midsixties: they didn't feel authoritarian, merely authoritative. But the real reason that The Speech feels ominous is the fact that it was filmed before history canceled out the actual meaning of its words.

Reagan displays none of his storied optimism here. There's no "Morning in America," no soaring talk about making "a new beginning." Instead, he warns that America is on the verge of an apocalyptic doom. It is a bleak speech, verging on despair, that unabashedly employs the most extravagant historical and philosophical comparisons—"Should Christ have refused the cross?"—to denounce our moral weakness and warn of our imminent demise. It is one of the great role player's darkest roles.

The Speech is disturbing because it shows the paranoid, millenarian side of American conservatism, unleavened by Reagan's Main Street sunniness. But it is also disturbing because it presents that right-wing vision in its pure form, unsullied by history. The Speech predates Reagan's entry into the world of politics, with its compromises and accommodations. As president, Reagan ended up backing away from some of his most cherished ideals. He raised taxes, reached agreement with the Communists, folded his cards in the face of terrorism, increased the federal deficit, and expanded the federal government. Reagan never abandoned his rhetoric of good versus evil, but it turned out not to apply to the real world. The Speech allows us to imagine an alternative Reaganist future, in which he lives up to his words—a world where he really does bomb the Soviet Union, get rid of Social Security, and end the progressive income tax. The Speech is a kind of distillation of Reagan's Platonic right-wing essence. Like Keats's Grecian Urn, it freezes him, an immortal figure from a strange, lost part of the American id, eternally raging against communism, big government, and liberal traitors.

That future never happened, but Americans think it did. That's one reason that New Right conservatism continues to wield a disproportionate influence in American life. But the other reason has to do with the inchoate anxieties, wishes, and fears to which The Speech appealed then, and to which the dream it spoke for appeals today.

The Speech tapped into the primordial American myth: untrammeled individuality. There must be a territory for Huck Finn to light out to, a promised land where authority—or government—does not reach. In this always-beckoning frontier, all the hindrances that drag Americans down are left behind. Businessmen can run their businesses as they like, free from the plague of do-gooder bureaucrats. White people need not carry the spurious cross of racial guilt. Unruly and ungrateful minorities—pinkos and softies and degenerates and pointy-heads and uppity women—are shown their place. Above all, the profoundly destabilizing specter of relativism, of compromise, of moral ambiguity, is banished. No longer need Americans accommodate themselves to evil. A divine certainty stretches from sea to shining sea.

This is as much a metaphysical wish as it is a political platform. It is a sermon as much as a speech. And it is in the gap between those two things—the space between the dream of absolute freedom and the reality of a fallen world—that America forever stumbles.

Bibliography: Sidney Blumenthal, *The Rise of the Counter-Establishment: From Conservative Ideology to Political Power* (New York, 1986). Sidney Blumenthal and Thomas Byrne Edsall, eds., *The Reagan Legacy* (New York, 1988). Rick Perlstein, *Before the Storm: Barry Goldwater and the Unmaking of the American Consensus* (New York, 2001). Garry Wills, *Reagan's America: Innocents at Home* (New York, 1987).

GARY KAMIYA

1965, September 11

A magazine article charges that "publishers have participated in a cultural lobotomy"

THE COUNCIL ON INTERRACIAL BOOKS FOR CHILDREN

Appearing in the September 11, 1965, issue of *Saturday Review of Books,* Nancy Larrick's "The All White World of Children's Books" stirred up the world of American children's literature. A former president of the International Reading Association, Larrick had the ear of professionals in the fields of education, librarianship, and publishing. The article garnered much attention and spurred discussion, as it continues to do decades later, partly because Larrick did more than point out the obvious fact that there was very little representation, whether stereotypical or authentic, of people of African descent in American children's books. The argument that readers would have expected is that this shortcoming in the literature is harmful, insulting, and frustrating for "Negro" readers. Indeed, Larrick suggests this. But the article argues, too, that the ramifications of this all-white world of children's books were even more serious for European American people. Her contention was that racist and white-supremacist children's literature teaches a white child, part of the world's minority by virtue of his or her light skin, to believe "that he is the kingfish. There seems little chance of developing the humility so urgently needed for world cooperation, instead of world conflict."

Larrick ends the article by discussing the 1965 formation of the Council on Interracial Books for Children, an undertaking that enjoyed the sponsorship of influential librarians and other individuals, such as Benjamin Spock and Langston Hughes, who were passionate about children. Larrick quotes the powerful words of organizing member and Harlem librarian Elinor Sinnette, who characterized the result of publishing policy and practice as a "cultural lobotomy" for most Americans, black and nonblack, who end up ignorant about the actual, inclusive history of the nation.

The Council on Interracial Books for Children (CIBC) went on to make a difference in the children's book industry largely through its review journal, the *Bulletin of Interracial Children's Books*. But another way in which it had an impact was through the establishment of a contest designed to identify talented new writers of African, Asian, and Native descent. Several winners of the contest became celebrated, history-making authors, including Virginia Driving Hawk Sneve, the first Native American author to publish a work of contemporary children's fiction, and Mildred Taylor, who went on to be the second African American winner, in 1977, of the Newbery Medal, the most prestigious award for American writers of children's and young adult literature. (The first was Virginia Hamilton, in 1975.) Other contests followed that of the CIBC, but sporadically; the only one of note that survives as of this writing is the Lee and Low New Voices Award. Lee and Low Publishers, founded by a Chinese American family, has published works by more than sixty-five first-time writers and illustrators of color.

These kinds of contests are important in and of themselves. But most significant is that they are part of a larger history of a kind of activism that has always been central in the development of multicultural American children's literature, and in African American children's literature in particular. The all-white world of children's books never would have changed due only to the changing hearts of individuals. A close historical look reveals the story of organized, collective efforts that have influenced the creation of this body of literature.

What is it that defines what is, generally, referred to as "African American children's literature"? The definition has long been a subject of critical debate. The term "children's literature" refers to an audience. The term "African American" refers to a cultural background. But when the two are combined into African American children's literature the parameters become unclear and problematic. Some scholars choose to include examinations of negative stereotypes of black people in their discussions of children's literature. Others prefer to focus on what black writers and illustrators produce themselves. Some include authors and works that depict black people in authentic ways regardless of the social identity of the writer or illustrator. But this is the crux of the argument: What work and what artists count as "black"? And what difference does this question make?

As early as 1938, Augusta Baker, then librarian of the 135th Street Branch of the New York Public Library (later head of children's services for the entire New York Public Library system), compiled and edited a publication called *Books about the Negro for Children: The James Weldon Johnson Collection;* the name of this bibliography was changed in the 1970s to *The Black Experience in Children's Books*. As indicated by both titles, the bibliography included books by both black and nonblack writers and illustrators. However, Baker decided to include at the end of the bibliography a list identifying those artists who were black. This was in response to the volume of inquiries from black parents and educators who wanted that information. One explanation for this curiosity is that given the impossibility of pre-screening every book before placing it in the hands of a child, if forced to choose, black adults were more willing to take chances with books created by writers whom they perceived as sharing a history, a culture, or a worldview.

A second explanation has to do with collection development in libraries and archives. If, for example, a collection's mandate is to gather and preserve African American children's literature, decisions have to be made about what to include—more specifically, what to purchase with limited funds. So the issue becomes not just academic but economic, a concern that is so often at or near the center of otherwise social and cultural issues. During the 1970s, when the federal government made available sizable grants for the purchase of black children's books, many publishers began to produce more African American children's literature, however successfully or not, largely out of a desire to profit financially.

However few, the African American writers, illustrators, and editors were there to respond to the need—and they were organized. Most notable was a New York–based group called Black Creators for Children, formed in the early 1970s. The group was spearheaded by such passionate individuals as educator Ernest Gregg, editor Bernette Ford, and others who went on to become celebrated writers and illustrators, such as Tom Feelings, Joyce Hansen, George Ford, Walter Dean Myers, Pat Cummings, Brenda Wilkinson, and Wade and Cheryl Hudson, founders of Just Us Books, the most successful independent publisher of African American children's literature. They functioned as a networking and support group for young African Americans connected in any way to the world of children's books. Black Creators for Children sponsored events such as book parties and panel discussions. But just as important, they functioned as a think tank; collectively, they developed a document entitled *Criteria for Critical Evaluation of Books for Black Children* and articulated "Principles of Art for Black Children: A Philosophical Statement of Purpose" as well as a sophisticated set of guidelines and criteria pertaining to creating and evaluating the words and visual images that constitute black children's literature.

Black Creators for Children was not the first group to conceptualize and articulate a vision for literature for young African Americans. The *Crisis,* started in 1910 as the house organ of the NAACP and edited by W. E. B. Du Bois, published an annual children's issue. In 1920, Du Bois and Jessie Fauset went further in establishing the children's magazine *The Brownies' Book,* putting great thought into communicating the objectives of the magazine to their audience, largely the children of NAACP members. "Designed for all children, but especially for *ours,*" *The Brownies' Book* spoke clearly and directly to black children. The publication sought to entertain, but also endeavored, among other objectives, "to make [readers] familiar with the history and achievements of the Negro race" and "to make colored children realize that being 'colored' is a normal beautiful thing." In addition, its editorial policies included featuring the work of African American visual artists and putting forth what could be characterized as an African American–centered view of world events.

The push for a usable children's literature for African Americans has a longer and more persistent historical trajectory than many scholars realize: at least three writers from the Harlem Renaissance, Countee Cullen, Langston Hughes, and Arna Bontemps, wrote several children's books each; starting in 1944 Du Bois's second wife, Shirley Graham Du Bois, wrote children's biographies of such noted black figures as Paul Robeson, Frederick Douglass, George Washington Carver, Phillis Wheatley, and Booker T. Washington, as did Ellen Tarry on Toussaint L'Ouverture and Ann Petry on Harriet Tubman and Tituba, the Carib Indian slave involved in the Salem witch trials. Lorenz Graham published his pathbreaking young adult book, *South Town,* in 1958, well before the push for black writers of children's literature in the 1960s.

The objectives that were outlined so deliberately in *The Brownies' Book* remain alive. While most African American writers and illustrators of children's books want the freedom to do projects that are not "black," they also feel a special calling to tell stories that explore African American experience (as well as the African American link to African cultures). These feelings rest within the context of the publishing world, which in too many ways is still too close to being all white. Thus, there exists the double-edged sword of the dynamics of awards, most notably the Coretta Scott King Award. Officially sanctioned by the American Library Association, the award has a long history dating back to the late 1960s, embodying the sometimes tense relationship between that organization and African American librarians. The award recognizes excellence in children's books created by black writers and illustrators. The thinking on the one hand is that if the award did not exist, many of these artists would get no recognition, despite the quality of their work. A contrary argument is that so long as the award exists, some judges of the major general awards will reason, however shallowly, that African Americans have their own award and not consider works by black writers seriously. What is clear is that the Coretta Scott King Award still serves a function in bringing attention to veteran black artists, and to new artists with the more recently established John Steptoe New Talent Award. Race still matters in the world of American children's books.

And for good or ill, black creators of children's books are still, on some level, striving "to make colored children realize that being 'colored' is a normal beautiful thing." Books about appreciating the rainbow of skin colors and the range of hair textures in black communities constitute almost an entire genre. Joyce Carol Thomas's poem "Cherish Me" is one of the most moving expressions of these concerns:

> I sprang up from mother earth
> She clothed me in her own colors
> I was nourished by father sun
> He glazed the pottery of my skin
> I am beautiful by design
> The pattern of night in my hair
> The pattern of music in my rhythm
> As you would cherish a thing of beauty
> Cherish me.

All too often, those who celebrate African American children's literature have framed its importance mainly in terms of its contribution to building the self-esteem of black children. Thomas's poem is an eloquent reminder that this literature should be celebrated for its literary quality in concert with its content. And fortunately, the content continues to expand in scope and range. There are now representations in both fiction and nonfiction for children of African Americans of every class status and educational level, of various sexual orientations, from various geographical locations, and of various religious and political orientations. And black writers and illustrators are working with material that is not "black" at all when they are moved, as artists, to do so. Sometimes this is an economic decision, based on the fact that black children's books still don't realize the sales that nonblack books do. As Nancy Larrick argued back in 1965, it may be even more true today that all children, African American or not, suffer when they are not introduced to the range of books and images that, together, tell our collective story as Americans and as world citizens.

Bibliography: Rudine Sims Bishop, *Free within Ourselves: The Development of African American Children's Literature* (Westport, CT, 2007). Dianne Johnson, ed., *The Best of the Brownies' Book* (New York, 1996). Dianne Johnson and Catherine E. Lewis, eds., *African American Review* 32, no. 1 (Spring 1998), special issue on African American children's literature. Michelle Martin, *Black Gold: Milestones of African American Children's Picture Books, 1845–2002* (New York, 2004). Osayimwense Osa, ed., *The All White World of Children's Books and African American Children's Literature* (Trenton, NJ, 1995). Katherine Capshaw Smith, *Children's Literature of the Harlem Renaissance* (Bloomington, IN, 2004).

DIANNE JOHNSON

1965, October

"I do not expect to live long enough to read this book in its finished form"

THE AUTOBIOGRAPHY OF MALCOLM X

In October 1965, Grove Press, a house notorious for the artsy, risqué, and European, published the ghostwritten life story of a conservative American cleric: *The Autobiography of Malcolm X.*

Malcolm X was introduced to the American public in 1959, by *The Hate That Hate Produced,* a television-documentary exposé of a Negro sect calling itself the Nation of Islam, which practiced a Muslim lifestyle and racial separatism. The leader of this sect, Elijah Muhammad, was in his sixties, anemic, reclusive. Malcolm X, the Nation's First Minister, in his thirties, vigorous, outspoken, inevitably was perceived as hate-monger-in-chief. The media called him "the angriest Negro in America" but reveled in the ratings generated when he expressed ideas out of step with prevailing cadences.

In 1954, in *Brown v. Board of Education,* the Supreme Court declared that the separate-but-equal doctrine, the legal basis of racial segregation, had no place in public education. In an effort to extend the Court's new logic, a number of organizations that had long struggled for equal rights confederated into what became known as the civil rights movement, and adopted a strategy called nonviolent direct action, in which the denial of rights was to be dramatized through public demonstrations, such as sit-ins and marches, that were to remain peaceable even if opposed by violence. A Baptist cleric, Martin Luther King—also in his thirties, vigorous, articulate—became the soi-disant drum major of the movement.

Malcolm X was a different drummer. "Coffee is the only thing I like integrated," he said. "I don't call it violence when it's self-defense, I call it intelligence." Two decades before "sound bite" entered the vernacular, Malcolm X was hurling such short, euphonious phrases, pointed with irony and poisoned with sarcasm. "We didn't land on Plymouth Rock; it landed on us," he said. "Capitalism used to be like an eagle, but now it's more like a vulture." And as for Martin Luther King: "He got the peace prize, we got the problem."

In August 1963, when the civil rights movement culminated in the March on Washington, King, in his now-famous "I Have a Dream" speech, exhorted a quarter of a million marchers, "We must rise to the majestic heights of meeting physical force with soul force." In the crowd, Malcolm X growled, "The only people . . . who are asked to be nonviolent are black people." Asked what his strategy would be, he said, "If you want to know what I'll do, figure out what you'll do. I'll do the same thing—only more of it." By December 1963, more of it proved too much for Elijah Muhammad, who ordered Malcolm X to silence, ostensibly for calling the assassination of President John Kennedy chickens come home to roost. By March 1964 Malcolm X was exiled from the Nation of Islam. But though he now had few followers, he had many listeners, especially on the inner-city streets. Some said he was the only man in America who could start a race riot, or stop one. He said: "I don't know if I'd want to stop one." And late at night, far from microphones and madded crowds, Malcolm X was speaking in more lyrical rhythms to journeyman journalist Alex Haley.

Haley had previously interviewed him for *Playboy* magazine. That interview, published in the spring of 1963, said little about Malcolm X's life—a bare eight hundred words, infused with racist propaganda and compulsive obeisance to "the Honorable Elijah Muhammad." But that was enough to intrigue editors at Doubleday and Company, who asked Haley to "sketch the likely highlights" of an as-told-to autobiography and also to persuade Malcolm X to reveal more details of his life. Although Haley realized "how little I knew about the man," he did approach Malcolm X, and, more important, he secured the approval of Elijah Muhammad, who, once assured that the Nation of Islam would receive Malcolm's share of the proceeds, said, "Allah approves." Malcolm X demanded his own right of approval, insisting on a separate agreement between himself and Haley, stating, "Nothing can be in this book's manuscript that I didn't say, and nothing can be left out that I want in it."

Even then, the early interviews were fraught with reticence. But eventually Malcolm X told a story almost too dramatic to be true.

He told how a man-child, Malcolm Little, was born in 1925 to a jackleg Georgia Baptist preacher and a high-strung "high yaller" from Grenada; how that child was traumatized by the arson of his family home, the murder of his father, his mother's descent into madness, the dispersal of his siblings; how yet he prospered in nominally integrated rural Michigan until he encountered a white history teacher who told nigger jokes and a white English teacher who advised him to be "realistic about being a nigger" and he "began to change—inside."

And he told how he migrated to Boston and became a hustler, hipster, and purveyor who burned his hair straight with lye; how he was drawn to Harlem, the so-called Mecca of the New Negro, where he became "Detroit Red"—adulterer, panderer, numbers runner, pusher; how his own addictions made him both a wanted man and persona non grata; how he was caught, convicted, and sent to prison where he got high on everything from Nembutal to nutmeg and cursed God so vehemently murderers called him Satan.

But to him in the dungeon's darkness came the words of Elijah Muhammad, saying it was whites who were the devil race, created by a twisted scientist; Negroes were created by Allah, and were members of an elite tribe, called Shabazz. That strange mythology touched something in his soul, moving Satan not to pride, but to humility:

> The hardest test I ever faced in my life was praying . . . My comprehending, my believing the teachings of Mr. Muhammad had only required my mind's saying to me, "That's right!" or "I never thought of that." But bending knees to pray—that *act*—well, that took me a week . . . I had to force myself to bend my knees. And waves of shame and embarrassment would force me back up. For evil to bend its knees, admitting its guilt, to implore the forgiveness of God, is the hardest thing in the world . . . Again, again, I would force myself back down into the praying-to-Allah posture. When finally I was able to make myself stay down—I didn't know what to say to Allah.

Nor did he know how to say it. Although each day he wrote a letter to Elijah Muhammad, he saw himself as "pitifully unable to express" what he was feeling. And so the eighth-grade dropout became an autodidact, learning vocabulary by copying a dictionary word by word, studying history and religion into the wee hours by the light of a distant bulb, sharpening his mind and tongue in debate.

Eventually, the man who had renamed himself Malachi Shabazz was paroled. Sustained by the Nation of Islam's strict regimen, he defied recidivism statistics, stayed clean, sober, and devout, and received from Elijah himself yet another name: Malcolm X.

This past was story enough for any autobiography, but even as Malcolm X narrated it, his present added new chapters. At the beginning he'd insisted the book be dedicated to "The Honorable Elijah Muhammad, who found me . . . in the muck . . . and stood me on my feet." But even then he'd known Elijah was less than honorable, having seduced and impregnated a succession of his secretaries. Rather than denounce Elijah, Malcolm X had concocted an interpretation of Scripture that excused adultery as a fulfillment of prophecy. In December 1963, this perverted loyalty received its reward: Elijah publicly ordered Malcolm X to silence, and wondered, privately, Would no one rid him of this troublesome priest?

To Malcolm X it seemed "as though something in *nature* had failed, like the sun, or the stars . . . I was only mouthing words that really meant nothing to me . . . my mind was filled with a parade of a thousand and one different scenes from the past twelve years . . . scenes in the Muslim mosques . . . scenes with Mr. Muhammad."

But out of turmoil came a new revelation:

> I was the invited speaker at the Harvard Law School Forum. I happened to glance through a window. Abruptly, I realized that I was looking in the direction of the apartment house that was my old burglary ring's hideout . . . Scenes from my once depraved life lashed through my mind. *Living* like an animal; *thinking* like an animal! Awareness came surging up in me—how deeply the religion of Islam had reached down into the mud to lift me up, to save me from being what I inevitably would have been: a dead criminal in a grave, or, if still alive, a flint-hard, bitter, thirty-seven-year-old convict in some penitentiary, or insane asylum.

Turning away from the Nation of Islam, he dedicated himself to the essence of Islam, and he undertook the hajj, the pilgrimage to Mecca that is the duty of all true Muslims. During that eight-day ritual he experienced a conversion, which he described in epistles to his followers, which were later transcribed into *The Autobiography:* "There were tens of thousands of pilgrims of all colors . . . ," he wrote. "But we were all participating in the same ritual, displaying a spirit of unity and brotherhood that my experiences in America had led me to believe never could exist . . . You may be shocked by these words coming from me. But on this pilgrimage, what I have seen, and experienced, has forced me to re-arrange much of my thought." He signed with yet another name: El-Hajj Malik El-Shabazz.

He returned to America determined to "turn a corner," but not to go in an appeasing direction. The "angriest Negro in America" was no less angry; in announcing the formation of his own political organization, he used a phrase some heard as a threat: "by any means necessary."

He too felt threatened. "I do not expect to live long enough to read this book in its finished form," he said, concluding his narration in *The Autobiography.* His true concern, however, was not physical death but that "the white man, in his press" would "make use of me dead . . . as a convenient symbol of 'hatred.'"

On February 21, 1965, Malcolm X was assassinated. The *Saturday Evening Post,* though it had published an excerpt from the forthcoming *Autobiography,* eulogized him as "a violent and baffling young demagogue" and wondered "did he really have a major role to play?" *Time* magazine pronounced him "an unashamed demagogue" whose "gospel was hatred" and "creed was violence." Doubleday terminated the contract for his autobiography.

Enter Grove Press. And when *The Autobiography of Malcolm X* was published, enter Eliot Fremont-Smith, in the *New York Times,* calling it "an eloquent testament." And enter I. F. Stone, in the *New York Review of Books*, predicting for it "a permanent place in the literature." Enter also Truman Nelson, in the *Nation*, lauding "its dead-level honesty, its passion, its exalted purpose."

Nelson also praised Haley who, he said, provided "the great revelation" in an epilogue, written with Malcolm X's permission but independent of his control. In fact, the epilogue offered a series of revelations: that the interviews, which took place late at night, when Malcolm was usually exhausted, often seemed more like interrogations or therapy sessions; that when Haley served coffee he purposely provided only paper napkins, so he could later analyze Malcolm X's doodlings; that he kept two sets of notebooks, one for Malcolm X's thoughts, one for his own.

The epilogue, more than the narrative, revealed a faceted Malcolm X, who, certain the room was bugged, initiated interviews with, "Testing—one, two, three," who "went jubilantly lindy-hopping around, his coattail and the long legs and the big feet flying," who cried out in frustration, "We had the *best* organization the black man's ever had—*niggers* ruined it!" It revealed also a subplot, in which Malcolm X, who once called Haley "one of the white man's tools," came to trust him "twenty-five per cent," and finally said simply, "I'll trust you"—while the middle-class, ex-military Haley, whose *Playboy* interview suggested a distaste for Malcolm X, confessed, "I tried to be a dispassionate chronicler. But he was the most electric personality I have ever met."

And the epilogue told the story Malcolm X could not tell: how he "walked out onto the stage, into the applause" . . . and the gunfire; how he was carried to a hospital on a makeshift stretcher, where "surgeons cut through his chest to attempt to massage the heart"; how "the effort was abandoned at 3:30 p.m."

According to *Time* magazine he had been, "in life and in death . . . a disaster to the civil rights movement." Certainly many who'd grown impatient with nonviolence heard in his voice a cadence more compelling that King's "soul force." In June of 1966, Stokely Carmichael, a six-year veteran of the nonviolent trenches, survivor of two dozen arrests, punctured the orotund rhetoric of yet another peaceful march with the Malcolm-esque cry, "Black Power!" The civil rights movement, and its rhetoric, would never be the same.

But Malcolm X's voice was heard beyond the political arena. The day after his death, playwright LeRoi Jones, later Amiri Baraka, formed the Black Arts Repertory Theater, the crucible of a Black Arts movement that would influence two generations of black writers. Three years later, at a celebration of Malcolm X's birth, a group of musicians later known as the Last Poets fused percussive rhythm with politics- and profanity-laced lyrics into a sound that came to be called rap.

Recorded and amplified by *The Autobiography*, Malcolm X's voice spoke to black men languishing in prisons in language they could comprehend, inspiring some to their own tough, uncompromising eloquence: Eldridge Cleaver's *Soul on Ice*, Etheridge Knight's *Poems from Prison*, Bobby Seale's *Seize the Time*, George Jackson's *Soledad Brother.*

It spoke also to young blacks who, under the aegis of the Civil Rights Act of 1964, were enrolling in historically white colleges and universities in increasing numbers. Some of those students came seeking not only education but an identity different from the Negro of the past. "Colleges," wrote Joseph A. Banks in 1968, "must facilitate this identity quest by allowing and encouraging students to read works such as *A Raisin in the Sun, The Autobiography of Malcolm X.*" In 1970 *Time* magazine lamented, "Malcolm X seems likely to endure in literature . . . The book has already sold 1.2 million copies and is used in schools and colleges all over the U.S."

That use was and is problematic. Now, as then, *The Autobiography* is often presented as social science. Certainly Malcolm X's life story retains significance, but now that significance is historical; of more immediate significance is what once was prophecy. "Thicker each year in these ghettoes is the kind of teen-ager that I was, with the wrong kinds of heroes and the wrong kinds of influences," he said. "As the Christian Crusade once went East," he wrote, "the Islamic Crusade is going West."

And now, as then, when *The Autobiography* is taught as literature, it is often presented in the context of a racially isolated narrative tradition. Certainly it has elements in common with Booker T. Washington's *Up from Slavery* and Frederick Douglass's *Narrative.* But it also has elements in common with more canonical autobiographies, like *The Autobiography of Benjamin Franklin* and *The Confessions of St. Augustine.* And it has elements that make it more literary than any simple autobiography. Malcolm X's decisions to first withhold and then confess his knowledge of Elijah's sins make him a complex first-person narrator, whose reliability changes in the course of the narration. Haley's epilogue introduces a second first-person narrator who comments on the first narrator and the process of composition. These postmodern effects, frequently noted in such 1960s novels as Heller's *Catch-22,* Barth's *Lost in the Funhouse,* and Vonnegut's *Slaughterhouse-Five,* had rarely been seen in nonfiction.

Malcolm X referred to himself as a demagogue, using the term in the classic sense: a speaker for the common people. His detractors used the same term with a more modern connotation: a speaker who will use any means necessary, including fallacies and lies. But the French philosopher Michel Foucault suggests another term: *parrhesiastes,* a speaker who "uses the most direct words and forms of expression" to express "as directly as possible what he actually believes." Such a speaker, according to Foucault, plays a vital role, speaking truth to a powerful elite that does not wish to hear it, risking "death to tell the truth instead of reposing in the security of a life where the truth goes unspoken."

Malcolm X accepted the risk, because he too had a dream: "that one day, history may even say that my voice . . . disturbed the white man's smugness, and his arrogance, and his complacency." In February 1965, Malcolm X was silenced. But in October, Grove Press published *The Autobiography of Malcolm X.*

Bibliography: George Breitman, *The Last Year of Malcolm X: The Evolution of a Revolutionary* (New York, 1968); *Malcolm X Speaks: Selected Speeches and Statements* (New York, 1966). Malcolm X, *The Autobiography of Malcolm X,* with Alex Haley (New York, 1965). Bruce Perry, *Malcolm: The Life of a Man Who Changed Black America* (Barrytown, NY, 1991). *Discography:* Malcolm X, *Ballots or* Bullets as Originally Delivered by Malcolm X (First Amendment, 1964); reissued as *Grass Roots Speech: The Bullet or the Ballot* (Collectables, 2003).

DAVID BRADLEY

1968

"America needed the war . . . the good Christian Americans
needed the war or they would lose their Christ"

An American Dream and The Armies of the Night

Private: *Gaitskill first encountered Mailer at the age of fifteen when she read Kate Millett's feminist polemic* Sexual Politics. *In a special sexism-in-literature section, Millett quoted at length from Mailer's novel* An American Dream, *a luscious comic-book story of sexual love and hate that in Millett's censorious context seemed even more thrillingly dirty than it actually is. At fifteen Gaitskill had a complex streak of practicality that was both cheerful and dour, and that allowed her to retreat into her private cave to thoroughly enjoy Mailer's fantasy as presented by Millett, only to momentarily emerge full of righteous outrage at it; she saw nothing questionable about this.*

When she heard that Mailer would be appearing on The Dick Cavett Show *to discuss feminism with Gore Vidal, she watched, anticipating a full complement of outrage and enjoyment. To her surprise, she was surprised: watching Gore Vidal was like watching a snake in a suit, all piety and fine manners, standing up on its hind tail to recite against the evils of sexism. Before this fancy creature, Mailer was nearly helpless, lunging and swiping like a bear trying to fight a snake on the snake's terms. At one point he spluttered, "You know very well I'm the gentlest person here," which made the audience laugh while Cavett and guests made ironic faces—but (horribly enough) Gaitskill sensed that this was quite possibly true, even if Mailer did head-butt Vidal in the dressing room, even if, yes, he did stab his wife in the dim past of a drunken party. For a gentle person who has been stung by clever, socially armored people adept at emotional cruelty may respond with oafish brutality; it is precisely because he is gentle that he can't modulate his rage or disguise it the way a naturally cruel person can. Gaitskill watched the bear-baiting spectacle with a not unpainful sense of cognitive dissonance dawning in her, both sides of her peculiarly American schizophrenic self finally present and blinking confusedly. The only other person who had aroused such feelings in her before was Lyndon Johnson, whose ugly, profound, helplessly emotional face had made her feel like crying for reasons she could not understand.*

Public: In 1967 Norman Mailer took part in a march on the Pentagon to protest the war in Vietnam. He marched along with Robert Lowell, Dwight Macdonald, and others whom he half-humorously called "notables"; he got arrested on purpose; he wrote a book called *The Armies of the Night* (1968), which won both the Pulitzer Prize and the National Book Award.

The Armies of the Night is part memoir, part history, and, as its protagonist,

Mailer is like a tourist with a rude sense of humor, taking snapshots of his grinning, waving, royally urinating self before every possible monument. Close to the beginning of *Armies,* Mailer recounts the drunken, grandstanding speech he gave the night before the march, in which he tried to win back the audience (which, to his hot, shamed sorrow, had liked Lowell more than it had liked him) by telling them a story about trying to relieve himself in a darkened lavatory before the speech, where he missed the pot and pissed on the floor. The speech is inept, annoying, embarrassing—and yet in its evocation of ego-comedy and the commonality of bodily needs, it is also a somehow poetic introduction to a historical moment of desperate and whimsical heroism, an attempt by spoiled, life-ignorant, self-infatuated children in romantic revolutionary costume to end a war waged by experienced men of the world—men, that is, of Mailer's generation.

Mailer wrote *The Armies of the Night* in the third-person style that became his trademark, a droll comment on his public persona, which had become so big that, like Gogol's Nose, it sometimes ran around town in fancy clothes, pissing on the floor, picking fights, and seducing all who would be seduced. "I'm as full of shit as Lyndon Johnson," cried the Novelist, trying to work the crowd that night. "That's what you got right here working for you, Lyndon Johnson's little old *dwarf* alter ego." *Yes.* "In the privacy of his brain, quiet in the glare of all that sound and spotlight, Mailer thought quietly, 'My God, that is probably exactly what you are at this moment, Lyndon Johnson with all his sores, sorrows and vanity, squeezed down to five foot eight.'" *Hell yes!* "This yere dwarf alter ego has been telling you about his imbroglio with the p*ssarooney up on the top floor, and will all the reporters please note that I did not talk of defecation commonly known as sheee-it! . . . but to the contrary, speak of you-rye-nation! I pissed on the floor. Hoo-ee! Hoo-ee!"

Dream: *Gaitskill was twenty-five when she read* An American Dream *in a state of receptivity both dreamy and bruised, a receptivity that understood that life had a top layer with several layers under it, and that sometimes, one bled through the other in strange ways.* An American Dream *is not a diatribe against women or anything that logical; it is not even a realistic novel, but a fluid rendering of archetypal forces, personalized and then stuffed into the social costumes of the time. Kate Millett had, it seemed, crudely, blindly misread the book as a literal rendering, almost seeming to confuse a sexualized fantasy of murder with the real deal. Yet, Gaitskill could see how Millett had become confused.*

The novel's protagonist, a cock in a person suit named Rojack (or "Raw Jock") is a war hero, author, and TV personality, an ex-congressman who meets his wealthy Great Bitch wife ("making love she left you with no uncertain memory of having passed through a carnal transaction with a caged animal") on a double date with "Jack" Kennedy. They are separated and he hates her guts, but still he goes to see her from time to time, and on one of these times she taunts him by reminding him that she does oral-anal with other men. He slaps her, she charges him ("like a bull"), he strangles her and tosses her ass out the window. Feeling great, feeling sexy, Rojack finds and screws his wife's maid, going back and forth between pussy and ass ("I do not know why you have trouble with your wife. You are abso-

lutely a genius, Mr. Rojack"), then meets a nightclub singer (named Cherry) at the traffic pile-up caused by his wife's corpse going splat. Cherry can tell at a glance that he killed his wife, and maybe that's why it's love at first sight.

Yes, the book is driven by outsized fear of and rage at women—for Christ's sake, after the damn wife is dead and lying in her own shit, Rojack is still pissed off at her for being violent, and wishes she would come back to life so that he can smash her nose, kick her ribs in, "kill her good this time." But even more, the book is driven by a desire to ecstatically swim in the lava of essential forces flowing beneath human life, the raw unknowns of sex and death that animate the endless social masks that charm, blur, and bedevil our existence; it wants to catch the winking demon peeping out from between the masks and personalities as they cascade through each and every strange and singular human form. Its attempts to do this—especially the successful ones—are joyous, tender, alive and filled with charged motion even in the stasis of cliché. The different faces he gives to, sees in the German maid, his wife, various cops, and especially Cherry ("A clean tough decent little American boy in her look: that gave charm to her upturned nose tip-tilted . . . at the racy angle of a speedboat skipping a wave, yes that nose gave character to the little muscle in her jaw and the touch of stubbornness in her mouth") are the visions of a faceted eye that enjoys illusions, but seeks to penetrate the core beneath them.

Reality: But *The Armies of the Night* is about real people and events that don't lend themselves so easily to archetypal conversion; the shrewd, rational facet of the Novelist's mind was thus called upon, and that must've been a grounding factor. In this book, Mailer turns his piercing eye on the antiwar movement, especially Dave Dellinger's tortured strategic unification of middle-class pacifists, old-school Communists, New Left college kids, and hippies chanting to levitate the Pentagon and/or blow smoke up the country's rear. He analyzes the uniquely American wisdom of obscenity and humor, the rhetoric of Hawks and Doves, and flexes his prescient intuition in real-world terms.

The Novelist's eye is also richly turned on people, and the book fairly pops with characters: Lawyers in Mad Hatter dialogue with a Jehovahic Commissioner; cops trembling with suppressed, unknown force; National Guardsman who are scared to use their clubs yet break girls' bones with them; jailers harried by working overtime and college boy prisoners giggling as they twit them; signifying Yippie monkeys; pure good boys; manly priests; a Nazi counterdemonstrator and a Marshal with leather testicles in psychic communion. All of these are full characters, but they are also homunculi, big, small, dignified, ridiculous, jabbering, contemplative, fine- or coarse-textured bits of a whole called America, the book's greatest character, a character rendered half in the rational words of public discourse and half in the language of images and dreams:

> The love of the Mystery of Christ, however, and the love of no Mystery whatsoever, had brought the country to a state of suppressed schizophrenia so deep that the foul brutalities of the war in Vietnam were the only temporary cure possible for the condition—since the expression of brutality offers a definite if temporary re-

lief to the schizophrenic. So the average good Christian American secretly loved the war in Vietnam. It opened his emotions. He felt compassion for the hardships and the sufferings of American boys in Vietnam, even the Vietnamese orphans.

And then there is that fuggin Nose, scheming to get arrested and get out in time to make the red-eye back to New York for a glam party with wicked chicks, worrying about the state of his suit, or what the press will say about him, or ruminating obsessively on his first drink of water in prison:

> He hardly knew if he did it for the best or worst of reasons, did it because in recognizing the value of thirst he had a small panic to destroy the temptation to search such a moral adventure further, or did he do it precisely because he was now aware of the value of thirst, and so thirst by such consciousness had lost its value since the ability to suffer drought was, by this logic, valuable only if water were not available. Or did he take a drink because he wished to study his new state after satisfying thirst? He noticed only that he was a trifle sad on the first sip, and couldn't stop going to the sink for more and more water afterward, which declared the result of the experiment: between the saint and the debauchee, no middle ground seemed tenable for his appetites.

How bittersweet to read them now, the ramblings of this doughty Nose. They are precious, annoying, and narcissistic, and yet as such, they are artifacts from narcissism's golden age, when the revelation of the self, the man behind the curtain of Art, was a refreshing surprise rather than an especially dull convention. Compared to today's relentlessly small-focus self-blathering (*of which Gaitskill may herself be on occasion not unguilty!*), Mailer's self-reporting flexibly (a little *too* flexibly in the case of that heroic drink of water) changes the lens of his vision from vast to small in a way that mimics individual perception as it moves from moment to moment, and defuses some of his natural pomposity. It is also (intentionally or not) comically honest about its low motives, its need to dominate and to be loved—especially to be loved by those whom he dominates, for example, the audience of demonstrators whom he called "One big collective dead ass," jeered for not being black, and generally harangued with drunken nonsense in order to make them—force them—to like him as much as they liked Lowell.

Masturbation: *Gaitskill had seen it before, this sore, conspicuous need. In* An American Dream, *the evil wife is evil mostly because she fails to love the hero, and he is justified in killing her for it; Cherry is an angel for knowing he killed her and loving him anyway. When her previous lover—a black jazz singer insanely named "Shago"—unexpectedly comes to visit, Rojack must prove himself by beating the man until he vomits—after which beating, Shago gives it up, the validating approval only a black man can give: "Tell Cherry, her and you, I wish you luck . . . I swear. Yes, I swear. Luck, man." To which Rojack (the gentlest man there!) replies, "Thank you, Shago."*
  How embarrassing, this need to be liked in a man so free with his fists! How nakedly it appears in An American Dream. *And yet, Gaitskill sensed something more serious embedded in Mailer's maudlin quest. If* An American Dream *expresses a wish to be loved by*

those one beats and kills, it more deeply expresses a desire for union between forces that in life on earth must pit themselves against each other, sometimes to the death.

Intercourse: This impulse toward union is more fully developed in *The Armies of the Night* as a wish not only to be liked but to like; the book is full of emotional turnarounds in which Mailer will start out dismissing someone, and then will notice something about him that completely changes his mind: he is able to tell the story of the Nazi and the Marshal who subdues him because even though they both appear to loathe Mailer, Mailer is able to align himself with them through a convincing preternatural empathy. Mailer's vision of the event is itself a unifying one; as a war veteran, and a hero to a generation that, at least in 1968, largely supported the war in Vietnam, he is someone you might expect to empathize with the Marshals and jailers—and he does. You feel his compassion as he imagines how the jailers "were here to work out the long slow stages of a grim tableau—the recapitulation of that poverty-ridden rural childhood which had left them with the usual constipated mixture of stinginess and greed, blocked compassion and frustrated desires for power," and how the insouciant protesters had "left such careful slow and over-cautious work of reconstruction in a shambles," completely unaware that they had done so. And yet he is also able to connect (though not effortlessly; one feels the effort) with the "tender drug-vitiated jargon-mired children" who mounted the offensive on the Pentagon, and finally respect their rite of passage.

Mailer is able to work this way partly because the same quality that sometimes made *An American Dream* ridiculous appears as a strength in *The Armies of the Night*. The biggest problem with *An American Dream* is that it insists on taking its big, forceful metaphors and making them literal and physical. It is one thing to create a female character who is emotionally dangerous and verbally cruel; it is another to earnestly treat these qualities as if they are physical threats, and ask the reader to believe that the beleaguered hero must kill this woman made so powerful by malice that she might, while being strangled, rise up and lift his entire body off the floor. Mailer stubbornly literalizes his metaphors in essays and interviews too; he says he does not address female writers in *Cannibals and Christians* (1966) because a writer can be judged only by whether or not he is able to make the Great Bitch of literature cum like a house on fire—and women of course aren't going to be sleeping with each other!!! He is also well known for insisting at length in an interview with Paul Krassner that masturbation is equal to suicide, though millions masturbate and live.

(Gaitskill cannot help but note here that it is odd for Mailer to react so stridently to masturbation. For onanism bears the same relationship to intercourse that dreams bear to reality, and it is in the purview of the dream world, with its profound layering of symbol, archetype, and metaphor, its fluid boundaries between life and death, that his genius shines most luminously. He only sounds like a kook when he tries to make his poetic, prophetic dreams literal.)

But in *The Armies of the Night,* despite the best efforts of his Nose, Mailer does not, overall, sound like a kook. This is in part because he seems, in all sanity, to have embraced his kook status, and he repeatedly, shamelessly refers to himself as a fool. This is also because 1968 was a historic moment for kooks. It was a moment when a door opened between the worlds of dream and reality, literal and metaphor, and in the strange light that came through that door, the most sober, serious, worldwise, experienced men in power were revealed as kooks—morally wrong kooks. The forces of the preposterous, the romantically costumed, the poetic, and the mad were for once right, magnificently right about the ultimately real question of whether or not a war should be fought. And in that moment, Norman Mailer was the ideal witness, maybe even the secret general to lead those forces to moral victory in the truer-than-life dream world only he could create.

Bibliography: Norman Mailer, *An American Dream* (New York, 1965); *The Armies of the Night* (New York, 1968).

MARY GAITSKILL

1968, March

Robert Smithson publishes "A Museum of Language in the Vicinity of Art"

The Illusory Babels of Language

The definition of the arts is usually based on a *division* of the arts, typically of the visual from the verbal, or the spatial from the temporal, and the stake of this separation usually involves an ideal of purity and/or propriety. Why this decorum seems so important at different times is a complicated question (moral, even political concerns are often implicated), but one thing is clear enough: the assumed distinction of each artistic form, its supposed autonomy, is the basis of normative aesthetics throughout the modern period, from the *Laocoön* (1766) of the German Enlightenment thinker Gotthold Lessing, an argument against the classical doctrine of *ut pictura poesis* (that is, that painting and poetry partake of one another naturally), to "Towards a Newer Laocoon" (1940) by the American art critic Clement Greenberg, a polemic for abstract painting that is purely visual in its effects.

Sometimes language has appeared in visual art, especially in the early twentieth century. It was often a locus of collage, as variously practiced by the cubists, futurists, and dadaists in the 1910s and '20s, a device that tended to be disruptive in aim, pledged, with its characteristic assemblage of fragmentary words and images from newspapers, advertisements, and the like, against the seamless surface of mute painting. Language often appeared in photomontage as well, a device that, in its frequent combination of photographs and texts from similar sources, tended to be communicative in purpose, if not downright agitational, especially as exploited by such politically committed artists in the 1930s as John Heartfield in Germany and Alexander Rodchenko in the Soviet Union. Here illustrated magazines and newsreels affected avant-garde art directly, to the point where enthusiasts like László Moholy-Nagy and Walter Benjamin came to redefine literacy as the ability to understand captioned images. Nevertheless, this vanguard support for such textual practices only underscored the cultural primacy of the strictly optical in visual art—a primacy reasserted after World War II with the prestige of abstract painting in general and abstract expressionism in particular.

By the mid-1950s, young American artists like Robert Rauschenberg and Jasper Johns had emerged to challenge this hegemony of the purely visual. In the words of the critic Leo Steinberg, they proposed "other criteria" for advanced art—other, that is, than the optical model of painting mandated by Greenberg and more. Rather than accepting given paradigms of painting such as the window or the mirror or indeed the abstract surface, Rauschenberg and Johns reconceived the image as an "opaque flatbed horizontal" on which "information [textual as well as visual] may be received, printed, impressed."

In the early 1960s this opening to the word took other forms besides the collage practice elaborated by Rauschenberg and Johns. Both artists were active in the milieu of the composer John Cage, whose experiments with found sounds and altered instruments prompted followers like La Monte Young and George Brecht to propose "the event score" as an artistic model. Essentially, this score is a simple sequence of written instructions for a performance, often staged with props arranged beforehand and sometimes with vestiges left afterward, that anyone can enact. A central manifestation of the international Fluxus movement, the event score might be exemplified here by *Drip Music (Drip Event),* first presented by Brecht in 1963:

> For single or multiple performance.
>
> A source of dripping water and an empty vessel are arranged so that the water falls into the vessel.
>
> Second version: Dripping.

The simplicity of this score points to the egalitarianism of such experiments—the artist scarcely seems necessary here. At the same time everything depends on his or her authority, a paradox that would dog other radical proposals in art of the 1960s as well. In effect, this paradox was inherited with the model of "the ready-made," through which, fifty years prior, Marcel Duchamp first implied that an artist could nominate almost any thing or act as a work of art—a bicycle wheel, a bottle rack, a snow shovel. On the one hand, Duchamp insisted that his ready-mades were visually indifferent; on the other, he defended the artistic value of his notorious urinal, *Fountain* (1917), merely on the basis that "he chose it." Rauschenberg, too, practiced this kind of verbal nomination with his 1960 portrait of the Parisian dealer Iris Clert, which consisted only of a telegram stating, "This is a portrait of Iris Clert if I say it is."

With the event score, the linguistic basis of such *performative* acts was made abundantly clear, and from there it was but a short step to a *procedural* use of language. Already by the mid-1960s a few artists had begun to employ language as a way to generate the most physical of works; the "word list," key to process art, directed a set of actions on a range of materials. Perhaps the most consequential instance is *Verb List* (1967–68) by Richard Serra: in a cursive hand, Serra wrote down the many procedures that have governed his work (first in rubber, then in lead and steel) ever since: "to roll, to crease, to fold, to store, to bend, to shorten, to twist, . . . to continue." The conceptual artist Mel Bochner produced another word list as a 1966 portrait of his friend Eva Hesse, an artist also deeply involved in process and material. Yet the words used to evoke her practice are quite different from the ones chosen by Serra: verbs like "secrete," "bury," and "cloak" form a spiral around the word located at the center, "wrap."

At the same time the corollary notion—that language is also a material to be manipulated as such—was explored as well. This line of work includes such poems by the minimalist artist Carl Andre as "Leverwords" (1966), which mimics, in almost calligrammatic fashion, the additive sculptures that he produced out of simple units of wood block, brick, and metal plate:

> beam
> clay beam
> edge clay beam
> grid edge clay beam
> bond grid edge clay beam
> path bond grid edge clay beam
> . . .

Other artists treated language less as construction material than as matter subject to decay, an entropic vision of language that was most pronounced in the work of Robert Smithson. In *A Heap of Language* (1966), for example, Smithson piled up penciled terms associated with "language"; tellingly, the heap ends with "cipher" at the bottom right. If Andre presents language as transparent in meaning as well as structure, this is never the case with Smithson, who began his 1968 essay "A Museum of Language in the Vicinity of Art" in *Art International* with this Borgesian thought: "In the illusory babels of language, an artist might advance specifically to get lost, and to intoxicate himself in dizzying syntaxes, seeking odd intersections of meaning, strange corridors of history, unexpected echoes, unknown humors, or void of knowledge." Bruce Nauman is another artist obsessed with language as an intrinsically ambiguous material, but the effects of his broken allegories are by turns comical and sinister ("Run from Fear" reads one of his typical neon signs, only to switch to "Fun from Rear"). With Nauman and others like Vito Acconci, the body also became a substance to work over, often according to linguistic directives, and its status became ambiguous as well, shuttling, performatively, between brute material presence and obscure symptomatic representation.

For all the aforementioned work Johns is perhaps a more influential precedent than Rauschenberg. Especially in his early paintings with stenciled letters and words, Johns treated language not only as a found image but as an obdurate thing to manipulate. Yet even in his literal treatment of language he highlighted its ambiguous nature, for Johns also put *reading* in tension with *seeing* in ways that made each activity seem suspicious of the other, as it were, and he extended this principle to his work as a whole (one of his sketchbook notes, from 1963–64, reads: "One thing working one way/Another thing working another way/One thing working different ways *at different times*"). In addition, among American artists Johns was an early reader of Ludwig Wittgenstein, an interest taken up by conceptualists like Bochner and Joseph Kosuth; hence he was seen to prompt the philosophical analysis of language in conceptual art as well.

With conceptualism, language became dominant in advanced American art: the verbal no longer disrupted the visual so much as displaced it. Indeed, according to the critic Benjamin Buchloh, the principal ambition of conceptual art was "to replace the object of spatial and perceptual experience by linguistic definition alone (the work as analytic proposition)." Certainly this proposition became the model for the young Kosuth, who styled his early works "investigations" after Wittgenstein. A typical piece, *One and Three Chairs* (1965), consists of three versions of an everyday folding chair: the actual wooden thing surrounded by its photographic image to scale and its dictionary definition enlarged on the wall. As though this tripartite exfoliation of the readymade into object, representation, and sign were too ambiguous for Kosuth, he soon reduced his work to the dictionary definition alone, in a series of investigations subtitled "art as idea (as idea)," here in an homage to the abstract painter Ad Reinhardt, who insisted that "art is art-as-art and everything else is everything else." Kosuth was much taken by this tautology: in his view every artwork proposed its own definition of art, however implicitly, a proposition that he moved to make explicit, pure, "analytic." In his view the definition of such terms as "idea" was idea enough, and that idea was art enough, to stand alone.

This line of conceptualism seemed to dematerialize the art object in a way that put into doubt not only its physical basis but its commodity status as well. An extreme instance of the former challenge occurred in 1969 when Robert Barry staged, as an exhibition in an Amsterdam gallery, the closure of the gallery for the duration of this (non)show. "I discarded the idea that art is necessarily something to look at," Barry proclaimed. And a focused example of the latter challenge occurred in 1963 when Robert Morris, unhappy with a collector who failed to pay for his work *Litanies* (1962), announced in a new work titled *Document (Statement of Aesthetic Withdrawal)* that he had voided "all aesthetic quality and content" from the prior piece—and implicitly all financial value as well. Such moves appeared to have critical force. And yet the Kosuth tautologies can also be viewed as a reductio ad absurdum of the modernist search for self-reflexive purity; the Barry critique of the visual can also be seen as an opening to the theatrical; and the Morris piece does not cancel the art object so much as double it. Moreover, as Buchloh has argued, all three strategies might be understood to refashion the work of art on the basis of linguistic convention and/or legal contract in ways that echo "the logic of administration" that permeates managerial capitalism at large.

Rather than be snared by such binds, other artists attempted to work through them. Lawrence Weiner extended the nominative power of the artist radically: in his mind his 1968 book of "statements," which begins "One Standard Dye Marker Thrown into the Sea," counts as a series of sculptures in its own right. At the same time Weiner was skeptical of his own assumption of artistic authority here, and all his statements have come with this rider:

1. The artist may construct the work.
2. The work may be fabricated.
3. The work need not be built.

Each being equal and consistent with the intent of the artist, the decision as to condition rests with the receiver on the occasion of receivership.

Here, in a manner that Duchamp saw as implicit in his proposition of the ready-made, the control, even the completion, of the work seems to shift from the artist to the viewer-reader, from the transmitter to the receiver. The emphasis on "condition" also signals an increased awareness of the institutional determination of the artwork. This awareness became the basis of various analyses, often textual in approach, of such cultural frames of art as the gallery and the museum, as in the work of institutional critique practiced by Dan Graham, Hans Haacke, Michael Asher, and many others to this day.

Clearly, then, there is a textual turn in art of the 1960s that parallels the more celebrated version of this turn in theory and philosophy. (The well-known definition of the text offered by the French critic Roland Barthes in 1968 — "a multidimensional space in which a variety of writings, none of them original, blend and clash" — is indeed suggestive for many practices from Rauschenberg and Johns onward.) Our partial typology of this turn has included the use of language as event score, as procedural directive, as allegorical material, as analytic proposition, and as legal contract. But another use is important to note here as well, a pop use of language as cliché. Here one might think of Roy Lichtenstein, who was intrigued by the onomatopoeic terms as well as the visual devices found in war comic books (terms like Blam, Brattatat, and Pow), yet the most sustained use of found words in this vein is surely that of Ed Ruscha. His paintings of words are also ambiguous: as in a "misspelled grocery sign," his terms can appear both declarative, even obvious, and incorrect, even obscure, like so many accidental puzzles. Several of his word paintings even evoke signals, the most direct of semiotic categories, which, as commands or warnings (such as stop signs), cannot afford to be enigmatic, and yet that is how they appear in Ruscha. What are we to make, for example, of a painting in which the word "electric" glows in yellow-and-red italics on a dark blue ground in a manner that attracts as much as it alarms? Whereas the workaday world requires clarity in its signs, Ruscha offers oddity, with effects that, as with Nauman, are often humorous, sometimes seductive, and occasionally a little sinister. As Ruscha reframes his words for us, they become refreshed before our eyes, and this, too, is part of the creative explosion of language in art of the 1960s.

And yet the sinister note here might also be taken to presage a darker view of language that emerged at the end of the decade, a view of language as a *system* (pronounced in both cybernetics and structuralism) that precedes and positions the social subject, who, rather than nominate with language, is named by it ("interpellated," in the idiom of the French Marxist Louis Althusser). Indeed, Barthes went so far as to declare language "fascist," and a subsequent generation of artists, many of whom (like Mary Kelly, Barbara Kruger, and Jenny Holzer) were inspired by feminist politics and Lacanian psychoanalysis, soon emerged to challenge the linguistic positioning of the subject in the symbolic order of society at large.

Bibliography: Benjamin Buchloh, "Conceptual Art, 1962–1969: From the Aesthetics of Administration to the Critique of Institutions," *October 55* (Winter 1990). Lucy Lippard, *Six Years: The Dematerialization of the Art Object from 1966 to 1972* (New York, 1973). Peter Osborne, ed., *Conceptual Art* (London, 2002). Ed Ruscha, *Leave Any Information at the Signal,* ed. Alexandra Schwarz (Cambridge, MA, 2002). Leo Steinberg, *Other Criteria: Confrontations with Twentieth-Century Art* (London, 1972).

HAL FOSTER

1968, August 28
William F. Buckley, Jr., meets with Gore Vidal on network television

THE PLIGHT OF CONSERVATIVE LITERATURE

On August 28, 1968, with demonstrators battling police in the Chicago streets, William F. Buckley, Jr., and Gore Vidal met on the field of ideological battle, an encounter with the aura of a set-piece confrontation. They had been hired by ABC to analyze the Democratic nominating convention and to speak as political archetypes: Buckley the conservative, the architect of conservatism and the Goldwater Republican; Vidal the progressive, sometimes a radical and always an ardent Democrat; Buckley the paterfamilias of a large Catholic family and Vidal the homosexual bohemian; Vidal the writer of novels, practitioner of belles lettres, and Buckley the intellectual, journalist, and magazine editor. On television, their adversarial commentary slipped out of control and descended to ugly name calling, mirroring the tumult in Chicago and the nervous energy of the sixties zeitgeist, unhinged by serial assassinations and a war that the United States was not winning in Vietnam. If protesters and the police could not contain their political furor in 1968, then neither could these middle-aged intellectuals, dressed for television in respectable suits and ties.

Literature could be construed as the dividing line between Buckley and Vidal, even if Vidal was intimately involved in politics, running several times for office, and even if Buckley was himself a novelist and a literary intellectual.

In America, the literary world has leaned toward of the left. The world of conservatives, Buckley's world, acquired great power at the political center in the years after 1968, without generating much of a literary culture. Twentieth-century America produced no major right-wing novelist—no Dostoyevsky, no Céline, no Solzhenitsyn. America's novelists are typically uncomfortable with established political power and especially uncomfortable if that power is tied to the Republican Party. (The situation seems to be different with poets: Ezra Pound and T. S. Eliot were anything but liberals, though they were not country-club Republicans either; Robert Frost read a poem for John F. Kennedy's inauguration in 1961, Maya Angelou for Bill Clinton's in 1993, and Elizabeth Alexander for Barack Obama's in 2009.) Conservatives have no trouble championing literature, such as the canonical texts fought over in the 1980s and 1990s, literature as a tributary of Western culture, to be protected from the Marxism, the feminism, or the postmodern relativism of the English professors. The challenge, for conservatives, has been to sponsor literature as a living branch of contemporary culture. The conservative emphasis on precedent and experience, the anti-utopian cast of the conservative mind, leads conservative authors to autobiography, to a nonfiction reckoning with the dilemmas of history, politics, and the self. The literary imagination thrives on the left, where utopia has long been at home.

Some major-league American novelists have started out on the left and drifted over to the right. In the 1930s, John Dos Passos pioneered the left-wing art novel, hoping to build a cultural left and to show that cutting-edge literature and progressive politics could be one and the same. Having achieved his aim, he defected from the left in the 1940s and 1950s, becoming a political ally of Buckley's and a proud supporter of Barry Goldwater's 1964 presidential run. Dos Passos gladly contributed to *National Review,* a magazine Buckley founded in 1955 to harness the political—and to a lesser extent the literary—intelligence of conservatives. Like Dos Passos, John Steinbeck was an icon of the Popular Front, author of *The Grapes of Wrath* (1939), a monument to American radicalism in book and film; and Steinbeck, too, would move to the right after World War II, at least to the extent that he ardently supported the Vietnam War. Dos Passos and Steinbeck did not see any necessary connection between literary creativity and being on the left, but neither did they do their best work after the Red Decade. In American cultural history, they would retain an organic association with the 1930s, entering a literary limbo when they were no longer men of the left.

Without undergoing any dramatic change of heart, John Updike chafed against the antiwar mood of the late 1960s. He associated the New Left with an uncongenial elitism, an affront to his modest Pennsylvania childhood: Updike would describe his illiberal eccentricities in a chapter of his 1989 autobiography, *Self-Consciousness,* titled "On Not Being a Dove." Updike projected the conservatism of the lower-middle-class white male, of the average American who did *not* read the *New Yorker,* onto Rabbit Angstrom, the protagonist of his Rabbit series (1960–2001). Yet Updike was not writing as a conservative. He was not interested in creating a conservative body of fiction or a literary vote for the Republican Party, and conservatives did not approach Updike's fiction as an in-house product. In literary form as in politics, Dos Passos, Steinbeck, and Updike constitute no coherent tendency or school. (Joan Didion would emerge as a writer by going in the other direction, starting out on the right, at *National Review,* and drifting away from its political assumptions over time.)

If any postwar novel is both significant and conservative, it would have to be

Mr. Sammler's Planet by Saul Bellow, a widely read novel that was a hardly a foot-note to Bellow's career. Four years after finishing *Mr. Sammler's Planet,* Bellow would be awarded the Nobel Prize in Literature. In a meaningful coincidence, Bellow published his novel in 1972, the year that Irving Kristol and Gertrude Himmelfarb asked their fellow New York intellectuals to help reelect Richard Nixon, the year the neoconservative movement was both born and baptized. The conservatism of *Mr. Sammler's Planet* was various. The novel's narrative conscious-ness belongs to Arthur Sammler, a cultivated European, an elderly man, and a Ho-locaust survivor who sees parallels between the disintegration of Europe in the 1930s and the chaos of New York in the 1970s. Sammler is a civilized man con-demned to live in an uncivilized century, and through Sammler, Bellow sets out to shock the liberal or radical reader. The novel's radical characters are either scoun-drels or fools; the sexual revolution is a cover for moral anarchy; and the primitiv-ism of New York manifests itself in the self-confidence of a black pickpocket, a barbarous villain who exposes himself to Sammler in what is surely one of the strangest scenes in American literature. This is what the sixties have emanci-pated, Bellow appears to say, contrasting an ethos of bourgeois responsibility to the mess of appetite masquerading, since the sixties, as radical virtue.

For all its many-layered conservatism, Bellow's novel was more a declaration of independence from the literary guild—from the flamboyant radicalism, say, of a Norman Mailer—than a positively conservative statement, neo- or otherwise. Nixon or Reagan cannot credibly be pictured reading Saul Bellow, in contrast to the New Journalist and novelist Tom Wolfe, a Republican, who is a favorite au-thor of George W. Bush's. Bellow's novel can be read as an indictment of the left, and perhaps enjoyed as such by conservatives, but its European protagonist is no obvious hero of the American right. He has nothing to do with the American right, which is among the most underrepresented entities in American litera-ture. Bellow would do something to correct this underrepresentation by writing a short story, "Mosby's Memoirs" (1968), about Wilmoore Kendall, a conservative political theorist and a teacher of Buckley's at Yale. Bellow's last novel, *Ravelstein* (2000), is about Allan Bloom, a scholar who published *The Closing of the Ameri-can Mind* in 1987, a scandalously provocative, idiosyncratically conservative best seller, which Bellow had urged Bloom to write.

Another conservative celebrity who has inspired a literary alter ego is Whit-taker Chambers, a good friend of Buckley's and a Communist turned conserva-tive. He appears as Gifford Maxim in *The Middle of the Journey,* Lionel Trilling's 1947 novel. *The Middle of the Journey* is not well known, and its smallness, in lit-erary terms, underscores a larger point. The space between conservatism and American literature remains a space to be overcome or to be filled. The American literary imagination continues to lean left, toward Vidal and away from Buckley. The right has no equivalent to the *New Yorker,* a solidly liberal magazine that pub-lishes important fiction and poetry. *National Review* has tried to displace the po-litical influence of magazines like the *New Republic,* without trying to match the high literary standard of the *New Yorker.* The *New Criterion,* an arts-oriented magazine founded in 1982, is conservative in tone, and it specializes more in cultural criticism than in the discovery or promotion of fiction writers.

This equation between literature and politics changes somewhat when the autobiography or memoir is substituted for the novel. Not only have conservatives written distinguished memoirs; their memoirs have had substantial influence on the conservative movement. If radicals read *The Grapes of Wrath* or Dos Passos's *U.S.A.* trilogy for inspiration, generations of conservatives have come of age reading *Witness*, Whittaker Chambers's autobiography, which he published in 1952. While writing *Witness*, Chambers had the material of an extraordinary life at hand. He had been a spy for the Soviet Union in the 1930s, and in the late 1940s he participated in a high-profile court case. He accused Alger Hiss of being a Communist, and Hiss, a successful civil servant, denied the accusation. The Hiss case, as it came to be known, was a starkly personal drama, and it was a richly political drama as well, featuring the rise of Richard Nixon and, shortly after the case came to an end in 1950, the rise of Joseph McCarthy. Chambers wrote *Witness* because he wanted to persuade Americans that he had told the truth. He also wanted to bear witness as a conservative intellectual and to make his mark as a conservative writer.

Chambers's writing is novelistic. When he was a journalist at *Time* magazine in the 1940s, he wrote an article explicating *Finnegans Wake* for *Time*'s readers—an audacious experiment in mass-market literary criticism. One can read *Witness* as a kind of conservative novel. Its hero is Chambers's suffering soul, which endures a drama in several acts. Chambers is born to a faltering middle-class family, and as an adolescent he is a young man without roots, living in the modern city and succumbing eventually to its seductions, like Clyde Griffiths in Theodore Dreiser's *An American Tragedy* (1925). Chambers becomes a Communist and practices espionage in Washington, D.C.; here *Witness* takes on spy-novel or film noir qualities. A bit like Dos Passos's *U.S.A.*, *Witness* is not structured chronologically. It begins with Chambers's flight from communism and from the Communist Party, forming into a conversion narrative that echoes the Dostoyevsky of *The Devils* (1872) and *The Brothers Karamazov* (1880). Often there are shades of Augustine that fall across *Witness*, the Augustine who travels from secular/pagan falsehood to Christian truth. Built from many literary models, Chambers's story is exemplary as he tells it, a story of the twentieth century, illustrating the century's characteristic perils and the promise it might contain.

This promise is equivalent to the conservative movement, which is intrinsically good, according to Chambers, for it accords with the goodness of Christianity or simply of faith. As a reward for its goodness, the conservative movement has the resource of American republicanism and American populism, an agrarian tradition of premodern democracy that merges piety with freedom. The conservative movement is also embattled: such is the double drama of *Witness*. The courtroom drama exposes the perfidy of the liberal, who may be educated, who may belong to a social elite, who may be close to political or financial or intellectual power but who is dangerously close to treason. Alger Hiss is one example, and others are the eminent liberals—at the *New York Times,* Harvard, and the like—who defended Hiss. How can it be, Chambers asks, that Hiss and his acolytes enjoy high prestige, while Chambers, an upright conservative, is a man of the margins? In *Witness,* this local drama widens out into a geopolitical melodrama. Conservatives like Chambers may be losing the battle within American politics, and if they do lose, America (the West) will lose the cold war. For conservative enthusiasts of the book—who have included Ronald Reagan, John Wayne, and Grover Norquist—excitement lies in identification with Chambers, with his conservatism, and, most of all, with his self-styled martyrdom.

Witness has set a crucial precedent for conservative writing and for conceptualizations of the conservative career. Its mood has been woven into the conservative movement. Its form has shaped much subsequent conservative autobiography. When the New York intellectual Norman Podhoretz abandoned the left for the right, he chose to explain himself in a book-length memoir, *Breaking Ranks* (1979), describing in meticulous detail his ascent to conservatism. When David Horowitz, a member of the New Left, became a conservative, he pictured himself as a latter-day Whittaker Chambers. It was incumbent upon him to write his version of *Witness,* which he titled *Radical Son* (1997), a book that moves between a Chambers-esque polarity, between the terrifying world of communism and the life-affirming world of conservatism. Podhoretz and Horowitz, following Chambers, fashioned newly conservative voices, crying out in the liberal wilderness of American letters. A similar mood extends from Chambers through to Horowitz. The battle between left and right is superficially a battle between political parties and rival political doctrines: its essence is a battle between good and evil. The literary savor of these texts rests on the experience of evil, the radical youth, which is the foundation for political righteousness arduously achieved. One must begin as Alger Hiss to have the privilege of becoming Whittaker Chambers.

However powerful autobiographies can be, however important, they are not the same as novels. They are circumscribed by the singularity of the author's life and cannot fully exploit the liberties of the literary imagination. Novels can offer an expansive vision of society, and such visions are politically useful. Richard Wright's vision of America, conveyed through the character of Bigger Thomas in *Native Son* (1940), is a political as well as a literary vision. Wright's was a book that encouraged the civil rights movement by allowing its readers to envision American racism through eyes that are alternately white and black. There is no analogue to *Native Son* on the right. For conservatives, Ayn Rand's novels have long been cult classics. Rand's critique of welfare-state collectivism informs her vision of freedom and creativity unencumbered by false morality; but Rand's novels are schematic and rigid, and they are as radical, radically libertarian, as they are conservative. Whittaker Chambers condemned Rand for not being a Christian, in a *National Review* essay titled "Big Sister Is Watching You" (1957). Likewise, Tim LaHaye and Jerry Jenkins's Left Behind novels (1995–2007), which are certainly Christian in tone, are narrowly conservative, expressing the conservatism of an evangelical minority more than anything like a national conservatism.

The plight of the conservative novel may be embedded in conservatism itself, but in America the plight of conservatism has something to do with political history. By the 1930s, when left-wing novels were flourishing in America, the left had a long history behind it, encompassing the socialism of the nineteenth century and the French Revolution of the eighteenth century—a magisterial subject for literature, its aftereffects enough to preoccupy a Balzac or a Zola or a Proust. By 1952, when Chambers published *Witness,* the modern conservative movement was at its beginning. When Buckley founded *National Review,* his magazine could seem whimsical in its distance from power. Its editors were united in their disappointment with Eisenhower Republicans and unsure about conservatism's viability in the political spheres that mattered—in the White House, Congress, and the Supreme Court. The first real victory for Buckley's movement came in 1980, some twelve years after he collided with Gore Vidal in Chicago, when Ronald Reagan was elected. George W. Bush left the White House a mere twenty-eight years after Reagan entered it.

Autobiographies register raw experience. Novelists may need a longer historical arc and a deeper reservoir of events than modern conservatism has given them. The conservative novel may be a figment of the future.

Bibliography: Saul Bellow, *Mr. Sammler's Planet* (New York, 1972); *Mosby's Memoirs and Other Stories* (New York, 1968). Whittaker Chambers, *Ghosts on the Roof: Selected Journalism of Whittaker Chambers, 1931–1959,* ed. Terry Teachout (Washington, DC, 1989); *Witness* (New York 1952). David Horowitz, *Radical Son: A Journey through Our Times* (New York, 1997). George Nash, *The Conservative Intellectual Movement in America, Since 1945* (New York, 1979). Norman Podhoretz, *Breaking Ranks: A Political Memoir* (New York, 1979). Lionel Trilling, *The Middle of the Journey* (New York, 1947). John Updike, *Self-Consciousness* (New York, 1989). Richard Wright, *Native Son* (New York, 1940).

MICHAEL KIMMAGE

1969

"The little that we get for free"

Elizabeth Bishop, *Complete Poems*

Bishop's 1969 *Complete Poems* won the National Book Award in 1970, but the book's title proved to be inaccurate. In 1976, she brought out *Geography III,* which though characteristically short contains poems widely numbered among her best—"One Art," "In the Waiting Room," and "Crusoe in England." Another four poems intended for publication came out after her death, most notably "North Haven," her elegy for Robert Lowell. Bishop and Lowell had been lifelong friends, literary correspondents, and admirers of each other's poetry, although Bishop had reservations about Lowell's "confessionalism" and was quite unhappy with his decision to quote letters from his ex-wife, Elizabeth Hardwick, in the text of *The Dolphin.* Bishop had always been leery of the confessional mode, and she told

Lowell that—though up to this point she had made an exception for him—in general she "deplored" it and was "sick" of her students' poems about "their mothers & fathers and sex lives and so on." Nonetheless it was the mode to which her own poetry was constantly compared.

Confessional poetry, a term coined by critic M. L. Rosenthal in a review of Lowell's *Life Studies* (1959), was arguably the most visible development in American poetry during the 1960s. The usual list of confessional poets includes, along with Lowell, W. D. Snodgrass, Sylvia Plath, Anne Sexton, John Berryman, Allen Ginsberg, and James Wright. Yet the term has from the beginning been hotly contested. Rosenthal's review begins caustically, with his observation that "Lowell's poetry has been a long struggle to remove the mask, to make the speaker unequivocally himself" and "it is hard not to think of *Life Studies* as a series of personal confidences, rather shameful, that one is honor-bound not to reveal." By the end of the review, however, Rosenthal acknowledges that this first response was superficial, and that *Life Studies* is in fact a work of order and art. The same claim has been made for the deliberate artistry of the other poets called confessional. At the end of his review, Rosenthal concedes that Lowell participates in the same project as "all the most ambitious poetry" from the romantics on: "to build a great poem out of the predicament and horror of the lost Self." This is no less true of Bishop. Though early in her career she was mistaken for a minor colorist, a word-painter entranced with description, she was as autobiographical as Wordsworth or Shelley. Her poems are "chronicles of love and loss," as her friend James Merrill once called his own poems. But confessional poetry cultivates an appearance of unfilteredness that is the opposite of Bishop's mode.

Lowell said that she was "too interested for confession," his way of noting her consistent attention to what is outside the self, foreign to it and relevant to it at the same time. Her powers of observation are duly famous, but the observer of her poems is never unmoved or unimplicated in what she observes. Often the tug of the outer world is reflected in the manifold questions the speaker is led to ask, ranging from queries about the scene or object before her—"Would that be Miss Gillespie's house?" ("Poem")—to questions turned inward in epiphanic crises: "Why should I be my aunt, / or me, or anyone?" ("In the Waiting Room"). Unlike the romantic subject, Bishop's possesses only a local elevation and no transcendence, however compromised. Her autonomy—and equilibrium—are therefore fragile: she must practice a measure of deliberate self-retrenchment. John Ashbery describes this balancing act in his review of *Complete Poems* (1969): "We live in a quandary, but it is not a dualistic conflict between inner and outer reality, it is rather a question of deciding how much the outer reality is our reality, how far we can advance into it and still keep a toe-hold on the inner, private one" for we "confusedly feel ourselves to be part thing and part thought."

Bishop's "Poem" renders our near-absorption into the life of things—and the persistence of a marginal autonomy. The speaker thinks that she recognizes the scene, in a genre painting done by a great-uncle, of a hamlet in Nova Scotia—or perhaps what she "remembers" has been shaped by the painting itself: "life and the memory of it so compressed / they've turned into each other." She and her great-uncle (whom she never knew) share a unique "vision" of "this literal small backwater," real in spite of its refractions. Then, surprisingly, Bishop widens the circle of its participants to include the animals in the painting; she sees that her own and her uncle's and everyone's possession of experience is also creature-sized. The small painting becomes an emblem of that rare unhindered ease in embodiment and thought that is "the little that we get for free," the transient experience of lucid engagement, unfortunately as brief as the life of any creature:

> Life and the memory of it cramped,
> dim, on a piece of Bristol board,
> dim, but how live, how touching in detail
> —the little that we get for free,
> the little of our earthly trust. Not much.
> About the size of our abidance
> along with theirs: the munching cows,
> the iris, crisp and shivering, the water
> still standing from spring freshets,
> the yet-to-be-dismantled elms, the geese.

Bishop chooses gravity and clarity over a plainer sorrow.

It is a temptation to think that Bishop heroically refuses self-pity—in implicit contrast to the confessional poets—but that view is too simple. Rather, her poems dramatize a negotiation with self-pity. The speaker uses her powers of observation and articulation to hold off the lapse into incoherence or despair while at the same time preserving enough of what she feels to distill the truth in its sadness, beyond personal reference. The grand results of such a strategy can be found in the closing lines of "Poem," or in the chilling words that conclude "At the Fishhouses":

> It is like what we imagine knowledge to be:
> dark, salt, clear, moving, utterly free,
> drawn from the cold hard mouth
> of the world, derived from the rocky breasts
> forever, flowing and drawn, and since
> our knowledge is historical, flowing, and flown.

Both poems build up to such moments of solemn impersonality from beginnings in a specific but mundane experience—an "I" (eye) loiters among fishhouses or gazes at a minor landscape. She observes scrupulously, and her sad thought is the final product, but she fends it off for a while by continuing her observations. Finally her individual grief is lost in the grief everyone shares.

Poems like "One Art" and "Crusoe in England" enact the speaker's struggle with self-pity more explicitly. Crusoe makes a weak joke of it—"I told myself / 'Pity should begin at home.' So the more / pity I felt, the more I felt at home." In fact, it took more than this to manage his despair. We see that work in his (enforced) attention and his tenderness toward his little world, with its one kind of tree snail, "a bright violet-blue," its fifty-two miniature volcanoes, its guano, and its goats with "horizontal" pupils. In "One Art," Bishop draws the connection between attention and writing as modes of defense:

> ... It's evident
> the art of losing's not too hard to master
> though it may look like (*Write* it!) a disaster.

In both poems Bishop comments on the manner of her own poetry. Her speakers fight to make a safe haven out of observation and articulation, a narrow isthmus between the gulfs of interiority and exteriority, thought and thing. In this way, all the putatively old-fashioned elements of Bishop's precision—her ekphrastic bent, her formalism, her slow and scrupulous pace—can be understood not only as aesthetic choices but also as means of representing psychological conflict. Despite the gentle, musing tone she so often takes, she explores the high drama of resistance and self-discipline.

Bishop's biographer, Brett C. Millier, describes "Crusoe in England" as the poem in which Bishop comes closest to writing "a verse autobiography." Clearly the poem speaks to the fact of Bishop's perpetual exile; she moved restlessly from place to place when young, and finally led the only settled—perhaps the only happy—phase of her life as an expatriate in Brazil. Her Crusoe is actually twice exiled—first on the island, and then on his return to his "homeland," which has become empty and foreign to him. The knife that was his most necessary possession has subsided into an inert object—"it won't look at me at all / The living soul has dribbled away"—and the poem ends tragically, recalling the death of his only friend, his only link with the vanished world of the island, "And Friday, my dear Friday, died of measles / seventeen years ago come March." His double alienation reflects Bishop's frequent sense of unbelonging, and his melancholy homecoming echoes her own. Bishop traveled to Brazil in 1951, without plans to stay, but on her arrival she met and fell in love with the charismatic Lota de Soares. She lived with Lota, and traveled throughout Brazil, enchanted by the country, which always remained exotic to her. Lota's mental health deteriorated in the mid-1960s and she died in September 1967 of an overdose, perhaps deliberate. In 1970, Bishop permanently relocated in Cambridge, Massachusetts, where she taught writing at Harvard until her death in 1979. According to Millier, this final phase of her life had the disappointing and anticlimactic, even posthumous, quality of Crusoe's return to England: "At nearly sixty years old, she felt the radical travel and far-ranging searches for a lover or a home were behind her." Though she had begun "Crusoe in England" in 1963, it was not until 1971, after her own weary repatriation, that she was able to finish it. In the meantime, *Complete Poems* appeared, and she began her rapid rise to canonical status.

From her reticent, surrealist beginnings in *North and South*, Bishop became gradually more relaxed about using the first person and confiding her feelings to the reader. Perhaps the confessional movement influenced her to this degree. Yet whatever change took place in her poetry is subtle, by contrast with the vivid and dramatic developments in the work of her contemporaries. There is a cautiousness and guardedness in her poetry that many of them deliberately cast off. Lowell and Plath do so most obviously, but others engaged ambition and risk in their own ways. A. R. Ammons moved from the biblical severity of his early poems to the diaristic meditations and rants of *Tape for the Turn of the Year, Garbage,* and *Glare.* His passionate and richly observed descriptions of the natural world easily rival Bishop's, while the voice of his later poems—candid, urgent, wily—has an immediacy unsurpassed by any other poet of the period. (From *Garbage:* "but here now, where we make the most // of it: I settle down: I who could have used / the world share a crumb: I who wanted the sky // fall to the glint in a passing eye.") Merrill also developed in unpredictable and surprising directions. He was often grouped with Bishop among the putatively staid formalists. The *New York Times* editorialized against Yale University Library for awarding Merrill the Bollingen Prize in 1973; once again, the editors wrote, Yale had rewarded poetry that was "hermetic," "fastidious," and merely "traditional." But Merrill was hardly the timid epigone that this reproach implies. By the 1970s he had begun to publish pieces of what became *The Changing Light at Sandover* (his version of Dante's *Divine Comedy*), a wild three-part epic about receiving messages from the other world, some concerning nuclear apocalypse. (The spirit Ephraim announces over the Ouija board: "NO SOULS CAME FROM HIROSHIMA U KNOW / EARTH WORE A STRANGE NEW ZONE OF ENERGY / Caused by? SMASHED ATOMS OF THE DEAD MY DEARS.") The novelty of this work, with its eccentric science and shameless invocation of the supernatural, made Bishop squeamish; with false modesty, she told Merrill some parts were "too philosophical for my literal mind."

The poem has made other readers uneasy, and yet her departure from Merrill at this point, after so many years of poetic fellow-feeling, is telling. The limitation of her humane approach is the limitation of any empiricism: built-in constraint and rebuke to ambition. In her elegy for Lowell, Bishop gently faults him for his changeableness: "You can't derange, or re-arrange / your poems again." But his revisionary impetus was linked to his visionary zeal. With all her clarity, Bishop makes one crave a little recklessness. Yet we must grant the integrity of her aesthetic: as Merrill said, "Her whole oeuvre is on the scale of a human life; there is no oracular amplification, she doesn't go about on stilts to make her vision wider." To borrow Nick Halpern's terms, she refused the prophetic, to choose the everyday.

Bibliography: A. R. Ammons, *Garbage* (New York, 1993); *Glare* (New York, 1997); *Tape for the Turn of the Year* (Ithaca, NY, 1965). Elizabeth Bishop, *The Complete Poems, 1927–1979* (New York, 1983); *One Art: Letters,* ed. Robert Giroux (New York, 1994). Nick Halpern, *Everyday and Prophetic: The Poetry of Lowell, Ammons, Merrill and Rich* (Madison, WI, 2003). Robert Lowell, *Collected Poems* (New York, 2003). James Merrill, *The Changing Light at Sandover* (New York, 1983). Brett C. Millier, *Elizabeth Bishop: Life and the Memory of It* (Berkeley, CA, 1993). M. L. Rosenthal, "Poetry as Confession," in Steven Gould Axelrod, ed., *The Critical Response to Robert Lowell* (Westport, CT, 1999). Lloyd Schwartz and Sybil P. Estess, eds., *Elizabeth Bishop and Her Art* (Ann Arbor, MI, 1983).

LAURA QUINNEY

1969, January 11

A conference on "The Asian Experience in America—Yellow Identity" is convened by students at the University of California, Berkeley

THE FIRST ASIAN AMERICANS

There was no first Asian American, no lone witness to the beacon call of a newly inaugurated identity. Instead, there were meetings—many, many meetings. Those most underrated of late-1960s events, it was through meetings, held in community centers and classrooms, through the commingling of students and activists, young immigrants and the elderly, that the subpopulation of Asians living in the United States summoned the spirit to christen itself. For the approximately one hundred and twenty years that Asians had roamed the United States, they had been outfitted with a host of names: Orientals, Asiatics, and the "Yellow Peril," if one wanted to generalize; for those seeking something resembling national specificity, there were "Chinks," "Celestials," or "the Heathen Chinee" for the Chinese, "Japs" and "Nips" for the Japanese, and so on. Now, starting in the Bay Area and spreading outward, there emerged a new name: Asian Americans. But what did it mean? How could such a term possibly describe the diverse backgrounds and experiences of immigrants from throughout Asia, and collapse the sometimes-contentious histories that divided them?

The first wave of immigration from Asia came in the 1840s, as Chinese laborers arrived to build the transcontinental railroad. Starting in the 1870s and 1880s, the promise of work lured immigrants from Japan, Korea, and the Philippines to the sugarcane plantations of Hawaii and the farms of the West Coast. And in the early 1900s, laborers from India arrived, also in search of work. Each wave was greeted with a different shade of animosity, usually determined by the United States' relationship with the various Asian nations. For example, China—crippled by the Opium War of 1839 to 1842 and the uneven treaties that resulted—was virtually powerless in international affairs. So when disgruntled white laborers pressured the American government to stem immigration from China, the Chinese could do nothing but accept the harsh terms of the 1882 Chinese Exclusion Act, the first American immigration policy to target the citizens of a single nation.

The story of Asian immigration in the nineteenth century is a story of imposed identities. Few Chinese or Japanese laborers arrived in the United States thinking of themselves as subjects of a nation—instead they identified with their home province or prefecture. It was deep within enclaves like the Chinatowns of San Francisco and New York that these immigrants began relinquishing their status as itinerant, wandering citizens of some lost "homeland" and exploring the contours of American cultural citizenship. Some attempted to assimilate, joining

churches and civic associations. Others sought out local, community-minded organizations like the Chinese Six Companies (also known as the Chinese Consolidated Benevolent Association), an umbrella group founded in San Francisco in
1862 to promote the commercial, political, and social interests of Chinese immigrants, or the similar Japanese Association of America, formed in San Francisco
in 1908.

These experiences are recorded in the writings of the late nineteenth and
early twentieth century. In 1883, a New Yorker named Wong Chin Foo began publishing a weekly paper titled the *Chinese American (Hua Mei Xin Bao)*, believed to
be one of the first conscious attempts among Asian immigrants to claim an American identity. Around the turn of the century, sisters Edith Maude and Winnifred
Eaton began trading on their uniquely cosmopolitan background as the daughters of a British father and Chinese mother. Edith Maude adopted the pseudonym Sui Sin Far and wrote sympathetic portrayals of the Chinese American
working class; Winnifred masqueraded as a Japanese writer, Onoto Watanna, and
published a series of popular (and less socially inclined) Japanese romance novels.
But most of the writings by Asian immigrants were autobiographical in nature:
Yung Wing, the first Asian to attend and graduate from an American university,
published *My Life in China and America* in 1909. In 1925 Etsu Sugimoto published
A Daughter of the Samurai, and two notable titles appeared in 1937, Lin Yutang's *My
Country and My People* and Younghill Kang's *East Goes West.* Even novels adopted
the form of the memoir, such as Carlos Bulosan's 1946 "autobiography" *America Is
in the Heart,* which was actually a composite portrait of the experiences of Filipino
laborers in California. Among the more unusual authors to emerge was H. T.
Tsiang, who self-published a series of lively and experimental proletarian novels
in the 1930s. But most of these works were far less popular and less influential
than representations of Asian characters created by authors like Mark Twain,
Bret Harte, Frank Norris, John Steinbeck, Pearl Buck, and Earl Biggers (founder
of the Charlie Chan detective series).

These offerings rarely imagined solidarity across ethnic lines, reflecting instead the realities of scattered immigrant communities divided by national histories. For example, Jade Snow Wong's *Fifth Chinese Daughter,* first published in 1945,
was heralded as a classic tale of American assimilation. Its simple prose and by-
the-bootstraps arc suggested a Chinese American exceptionalism, echoing the
wartime sentiment in America that the Chinese represented "good immigrants"
and anticipating the "model minority" stereotype that would emerge in the 1960s
and 1970s. The State Department circulated thousands of copies abroad, as part
of a cold war initiative to export success stories of American democracy.

Up until the 1960s the impulse to rally around a shared Asian heritage had
been dulled by the tensions of homeland politics and the absence of any coherent
or uniform immigrant experience. Even within groups there were conflicts based
on when and where one entered the United States. But in the 1960s generations
of American-born Asians began experiencing the same forces catalyzing other
marginalized communities. A critical mass of young, first-generation students en-

tered American colleges and universities. They began thinking aloud about the conditions of poverty rampant in Chinatown and Manilatown. They discovered new expressions of class, racial, and gender consciousness. And they fell under the intoxicating spell of the anti–Vietnam War and civil rights movements.

One of the most striking expressions of the nascent Asian American consciousness occurred at a conference titled The Asian Experience in America— Yellow Identity, held at the University of California at Berkeley in January 1969. It drew about nine hundred students from throughout California, Oregon, and Washington. They shared a very modest ambition: to learn more about the history and destiny of Asian American culture. The day was intended to be a wide-open forum, as the very idea of the Asian American was a young one. Many believe that the term "Asian American" was first used by Yuji Ichioka, a historian who was then teaching at Berkeley. In May 1968 Ichioka convened an Asian Caucus from a coalition of local antiwar activists and Black Panthers. The caucus named itself the Berkeley Asian American Political Association (AAPA), initially claiming ten members whose sympathies ranged from "liberal to anarchistic."

The Berkeley meeting set out to unpack this new term. But after a ho-hum morning session devoted to the work of scholars and the concerns of community workers, the proceedings were hijacked by a faction of student radicals from nearby San Francisco State University—they had come to gain support for Third World Strikes, a protest movement that had begun the previous November in the hope of adding ethnic studies to the SF State curriculum. Nobody was sure what to do about this disturbance, as they refused to yield the floor. The discussion turned radical very quickly, and as L. Ling Chi Wang, a community activist reporting for a local Chinese paper observed: "From then on there was confusion and chaos."

Wang's tone was probably more ominous than he intended. But the instability of an Asian American identity—as evidenced by some students' attempts to pull the plug on their more radical peers—was seeded in the term's creation. For many, though, this air of excitement was sustenance enough. Discussions of what constituted Asian American identity rippled throughout the West Coast. The possibilities of the moment were captured in newspapers like *Gidra,* which was founded by students at the University of California, Los Angeles. In the April 1969 issue, Larry Kubota published an essay titled "Yellow Power," describing this new movement: it is "a rejection of the passive Oriental stereotype," he wrote, "and symbolizes the birth of a new Asian—one who will recognize and deal with injustices. The shout of Yellow Power, symbolic of our new direction, is reverberating in the quiet corridors of the Asian community."

Throughout the early 1970s, it seemed enthusiasm and honest intentions alone were the hallmarks of an Asian American culture still seeking its shape. The term was a placeholder; filling it with meaning would be easy. Courses on Asian American history began appearing in college curricula. In 1970 Janice Mirikitani—who would become an acclaimed author a decade later—cofounded *Aion,* the first Asian American literary magazine. The first issue of *Amerasia Journal,* an academic journal dedicated to Asian American culture, was published in 1971—it featured a contribution from Bill Lann Lee, whom President Bill Clinton would appoint assistant attorney general for civil rights in the mid-1990s. Later that year *Roots: An Asian American Reader* appeared, an impressively diverse collection of writings by students, activists, and even anti-identitarian naysayers. Sites like New York's Basement Workshop and the Bay Area's Kearney Street Workshop opened to support a burgeoning Asian American arts scene. And in 1973, a New York folk trio called A Grain of Sand released *Music for the Struggle of Asians in America*—often recognized as the first example of Asian American music. (Interestingly, the term "Asian American" never appears in their lyrics or copious liner notes.)

It was through writing that many young Asian Americans explored and debated the parameters of their new identity. In 1972 Frank Chin debuted his play *The Chickencoop Chinaman,* which tracked a young, rudderless Asian American man's vision quest through a surreal landscape of dashed expectations and discarded icons (the Lone Ranger and Tonto make a memorable cameo). Two years later Chin, Shawn Wong, Jeffrey Paul Chan, and Lawson Fusao Inada compiled the enormously influential *Aiiieeeee! An Anthology of Asian American Writers.* Its importance was twofold: beyond its primary value as the first concerted exploration of a nascent Asian American literary tradition, the anthology's haughty, combative tone offered something for future generations of writers and critics to form their opinions around. The *Aiiieeeee!* quartet chided older authors like Jade Snow Wong and Pardee Lowe, whose polite portrayals of the immigrant experience seemed unrealistic and insufficiently political. Instead they propped up forgotten figures such as Bulosan, John Okada, and Louis Chu, piecing together a tradition of Asian American writing that resisted, deconstructed, or satirized American values. As with any literary anthology, *Aiiieeeee!* was heavily scrutinized for its selections, particularly for limiting Asian American literature to writing by "Chinese-Americans, Japanese-Americans, and Filipino-Americans" and fixating on the contributions of men.

The communal sensibility that had birthed the Asian American was not free of the impulse to police: anxieties persisted over what constituted authentic Asian American writing, even as more anthologies and literary magazines appeared. In 1975 Maxine Hong Kingston published *The Woman Warrior,* a novel that found critical and commercial success despite its occasionally baffling, postmodern approach. While the book represented a breakthrough for Asian American literature, Kingston herself was not quite sold on the value of identity politics. As she wondered in its opening pages: "Chinese-Americans, when you try to understand what things in you are Chinese, how do you separate what is peculiar to childhood, to poverty, insanities, one family, your mother who marked your growing with stories, from what is Chinese? What is Chinese tradition and what is the movies?" As Kingston settled into a position as a bona fide literary celebrity, she also became a target for critics like Chin and Chan, who accused her of portraying Chinese men in an unflattering light and trading on the most exotic extremes of her cultural heritage. It was Asian American literature's first civil war, pitting a circle of men against a suddenly powerful woman, those concerned with authenticity and representation against those who saw identity as important but also saw unfixed points of departure.

Throughout the 1980s these debates grew more and more inward-focused—arguments even arose as to whether the term "Asian American" called for a hyphen or not. Despite the narrowing discussion, there was still space for a range of literary approaches. In 1982, Theresa Hak Kyung Cha published *Dictee,* a deeply experimental book built on short, dense, and seemingly unrelated passages and poems, uncaptioned photographs, and maps and diagrams. On the opposite end of the spectrum—and incurring the same gendered criticisms that had struck Kingston—was Amy Tan's *Joy Luck Club,* a sentimental family drama that became one of the most popular books of 1989.

In the 1990s Jessica Hagedorn, Lois Ann Yamanaka, Fae Myenne Ng, and Chang-Rae Lee suggested that Asian American literature could find a broad readership while still dissecting the received wisdom about a uniform Asian American experience. In the late 1990s and early years of the new century this resulted, somewhat inevitably, in a sensibility the journalist Eric Liu described in the title of his memoir: *The Accidental Asian.* Liu claims to be Asian American by circumstance but not choice, and he downplays the identity's political dimensions. While identity and cultural heritage are at the forefront of works by Gish Jen, Jhumpa Lahiri, and the graphic novelist Adrian Tomine, their coming-of-age stories are seldom animated by moments of political or social epiphany. Instead the condition of being a migrant, a cosmopolitan, an outsider, a visitor to an imaginary homeland, or a citizen of multiple cultures becomes another device at the author's disposal, as opposed to the only one.

Two strong novels in 2003 enunciated this new freedom. Monique Truong's *Book of Salt* recounts the Parisian lives of Gertrude Stein and Alice B. Toklas, but from the perspective of their Vietnamese cook. Susan Choi's *American Woman* offers a fictionalized account of Wendy Yoshimura, a wayward Japanese American girl who spent a year on the lam with kidnapped heiress Patty Hearst and witnessed her transformation into a by-all-means-necessary radical. For decades, history had been something Asian Americans shouldered. It had divided them upon entry into America, and its imprints—the stinging lows of moments like the Chinese Exclusion Act and Japanese internment during World War II; the wide-open highs of the 1960s and 1970s—lingered. By taking history apart, displacing its particulars across time and space, and putting it all back together in novel new ways, perhaps Asian American writers have chanced upon a new destiny.

Bibliography: Elaine Kim, *Asian American Literature* (Philadelphia, 1982). Maxine Hong Kingston, *The Woman Warrior* (New York, 1976). William Wei, *The Asian American Movement* (Philadelphia, 1993). K. Scott Wong and Sucheng Chan, *Claiming America* (Philadelphia, 1998). Xiao-huang Yin, *Chinese American Literature since the 1850s* (Urbana, IL, 2000).

HUA HSU

1969, November 12

Seymour Hersh breaks the story of the My Lai massacre

THE EYE OF VIETNAM

William L. Calley, Jr., 26 years old, is a mild-mannered, boyish-looking Vietnam combat veteran with the nickname "Rusty." The Army is completing an investigation of charges that he deliberately murdered at least 109 Vietnamese civilians in a search-and-destroy mission in March 1968 in a Viet Cong stronghold known as "Pinkville." (*St. Louis Post-Dispatch,* November 13, 1969)

Visibility made the American public conscious. Seymour Hersh's investigative reporting marked a turning point in the Vietnam War, and when Ronald Haeberle's graphic My Lai photos surfaced, their publication in *Life* gave full visibility to the atrocities committed by American troops. They fueled antiwar sentiment and tilted the balance of public opinion against the war.

The army had at first described My Lai as a military victory, and senior officers, including then Major Colin Powell, investigated and reported that local relations between American soldiers and the Vietnamese people were excellent. Through Dispatch News Service, Hersh reported the deliberate killing of at least 109 Vietnamese civilians. A postwar memorial at the site of the massacre lists 504 names, with ages ranging from one to eighty-two years old.

The Kennedy administration sought to eliminate a revolutionary movement in Vietnam through military technology and the concept of a "limited war" that could be controlled and managed. Secretary of Defense Robert McNamara was committed to waging technologically integrated and capital-intensive war based on a rational model. Ngo Dinh Diem, president of South Vietnam since his rigged election victory in 1955, was not oriented toward democratic principles but was intrigued by modern technology and control in governance. Visibility was crucial for the concept of "techno-war," which required a flat terrain and empty space. The local population, by clinging tenaciously to the land, provided a shield for, even if they did not sympathize with, the enemy. The jungle foliage obstructed U.S. efforts in attaining visibility, and the landscape easily hid the insurgents. Both factors, the impenetrable jungle and the inhabitants, became the target for America's destructive force.

This desire for control found a uniquely simple yet extreme mode of expression: the removal of the trees by killing the rainforest and the removal of people to places where they could be better managed. Under Diem's regime, the Strategic Hamlet Program relocated four million people in a single year. Between 1961 and 1973, the U.S. bombed the country and dispensed an enormous amount of chemicals; 60 percent of the total released was the radically toxic defoliant Agent Orange. The key goals were to clear areas for aerial surveillance and to starve the enemy—under the terms "area denial" and "food denial"—and the surrounding civilian populations as necessary.

Defoliation was immensely surreal, almost fictional. The chemical's touch was lighter than dewy evening mist. The rice plant withered but looked as if it still held the rice grain inside. Once touched, what looked like grains dissolved into inedible powder. The leaves of the manioc plants dried up; the roots rotted. Large plants with watery trunks—banana, coconut, sugarcane—would reach full growth rapidly, then the fruits and flowers emptied and the plants died. Big and sappy trees such as peach, orange, and tangerine would dry up gradually, from top to bottom. The process was traumatic for an evergreen tropical country. The earth itself was stripped naked as the plants perished. Within about six months, the previously lush ecosystem of triple-canopy jungles would be replaced by worthless weed, dubbed "American grass."

Defoliation was used to destroy the connection between the people and the land. The soil still constituted the hard surface of the earth, but life on it was gone. Crops that had been sprayed could not be salvaged. Starvation was just around the corner. The war against the green fabric of the earth and the sustaining role of nature targeted the means of life itself, and in effect, produced community deaths as well as ecological deaths in that part of the earth. In these areas, the U.S. Army succeeded in establishing what it termed a White Zone, meaning no living things allowed.

In the quest for visibility, life disappeared. The plight of the local people was invisible. The American public at home could not fully understand what their country had done ecologically because the chemical operations were conceptually new, and the magnitude of the destruction they brought to the people and the biological fabric that supported them was hard to comprehend. The destruction of bombings was easily understood, yet even so strong a term as "ecocide" could not convey the full sinister impact of defoliation: the word had a quality of concealing the effect on people because it focused on biological life itself as detached from humans. A direct consequence of defoliation, however, was the breakdown of the essential social unit of local life. When bombs and defoliation transformed the landscape into a lunar negation of human existence, villages simply disintegrated physically. Defoliation was a part of a techno-war that aimed to remove not only the rainforest but also humans, civilians, and enemy combatants alike.

Defoliation policy carried deeply rooted American environmental and racial prejudices. American frontier attitudes toward wilderness and Native Americans were intertwined. In the westward expansion of the United States, wilderness was the villain, the white pioneer the hero who relished its destruction by clearing the land, bringing light into darkness, and ordering chaos, which simultaneously meant the destruction of Indian tribes and white man's progress. The cultural and historical energies that propelled Americans' negative conception of wilderness were slow to disappear, and circulated widely in the 1960s and constituted a particular mode of seeing Vietnam. The Vietnam War was a new crusade against the wilderness, and a popular nickname for Vietnam was "Indian Country," a metaphor that reflected the perceptual dominance that actively shaped a worldview. War correspondent Michael Herr pronounced the equation: "The Puritan belief that Satan dwelt in Nature could have been born here."

Starvation tactics were not new. To defeat and displace the Iroquois, George Washington ordered the complete destruction of crops that belonged to the Six Nations, and the prevention of replanting, in the Sullivan Campaign. The buffalo was viewed as "the Indian's commissary" and therefore required extermination.

As Americans flew into the Vietnam Highland areas, GIs felt not only the immediate discomfort the jungles created, but also a cultural sense of darkness and chaos, of losing control in a wall of trees, vines, and underbrush. Worse were the thousands of insects that thrived in the humidity and preyed on the human body. It was a landscape for ambushes, where the GI experienced a strong sense of displacement. The enemy was statistically dominant yet rarely seen. The danger was not only that the forest shielded guerrillas but that it played tricks on the American soldier's mind, touching on his anxiety about power and powerlessness. The psychological impact was shattering.

In the film *Apocalypse Now* (1979), a blanket feeling of madness about this war ran through an American camp. The Vietnamese saw madness only in U.S. actions. Nguyen Duy's poems, composed amid fierce fighting, carried love for the land while bombs were obliterating his portion of the earth, where the torn landscape fostered compassion between the tortured land and her sons.

> Bombs plowed into the red earth, ruby red
> Scorching midday sun a color of a kiln fire
> That's our country, isn't it, brother?
> Despite countless pain, the sweetness still comes from within.

The appreciation of nature could serve as a bridge between Americans and Vietnamese. It resonated in many combatants' souls and, in some instances, seemed to transcend the fatal lines between two forces. Somewhere in the jungle, a young GI named Marion Lee Kempner stopped by a flower. The contemplation stirred deep thoughts about the tragic implications of the U.S. mission, and he wrote his great-aunt:

> The plant, and the hill upon which it grew, was also representative of Vietnam. It is a country of thorns and cuts, of guns and marauding, of little hope and of great failure. Yet in the midst of it all, a beautiful thought, gesture, and even person can arise among it waving bravely at the death that pours down upon it. Some day this hill will be burned by napalm, and the red flower will crackle up and die among the thorns.

Tran Mai Nam, a revolutionary writer, responded to a similar floral phenomenon:

> My eyes suddenly see a wild orchid growing on the rotten trunk of a tree next to the path. I marvel at its vigorous, supple stem and thin leaves of shining green. Long ago, when I was a child, I watched my grandfather raise an orchid exactly like this one. He had a passion for these flowers, delicate like the wings of a butterfly, which bloom once a year, give off an intoxicating perfume and last a long time.

Here in this forest, then, is where these marvelous things come from—from rotting tree trunks like this one.

The aesthetic convergence was soon channeled into opposing directions. The revolutionary extolled the vitality and beauty that emerged out of a wasteland. The American was overcome by a vision of destruction, political agony, and a strong sense of doom. His love of nature made him think about the firepower that would rain down onto the local landscape, predicting that it would ultimately be crushed by U.S. destruction. Kempner was accurate.

The ferocity of the Vietnam War was unmatched by any conflict in the century. Massive bombings and defoliation failed to deny cover for the enemy. After the trees died, the trunks and branches remained and hid the enemy. The remnants of nature that were obstructing visibility needed to be cleared. On December 21, 1964, it was estimated that about 6,000 civilians were scattered in Boi Loi Woods. A month later, more than 395 tons of bombs were dropped on the area. Thereafter, leaflets and loudspeakers instructed the survivors on exit routes. About one-third fled for resettlement in government-controlled areas. Soon another 372 tons of bombs were dropped. After intensive bombings and defoliation, the forest was ignited with drums of diesel fuel and napalm tanks. M35 incendiary clusters were dropped to induce the fire to spread. The strategy failed. A self-sustaining forest fire could not be started. Thunderstorms moved through the area and extinguished the fires. The quest for visibility vanished with the smoke, and many civilians perished.

Herbicides were popular, yet visibility attained from chemically produced defoliation was, by many accounts, an unsatisfactory combat procedure. In February 1972, the U.S. Army's Engineer Strategic Studies Group (ESSG) released a study that addressed combat implications related to defoliation and concluded: "Much of the personal experience favorable to herbicides probably derives from an accumulation of confidence in being able to see better whether or not there is anything to see." Harvard biologist Matthew Meselson looked at the data on changes in friendly-initiated actions, enemy-initiated actions, and the numbers killed on each side of the conflict. The data suggested that benefits of herbicides for the enemy were much greater than the American war managers expected. Surprisingly, herbicide missions along friendly lines of communication were associated with sharply increased numbers of enemy-initiated actions (up by 32 percent) and an increase in the number of friendly forces that were killed in action. This finding was brought out not in the overall ESSG summary but by Meselson's close reading of the ESSG data, which revealed the fundamental paradox in the American concept of visibility: seeing better also meant being seen better. Defoliation had created circumstances that made American soldiers fully visible to the enemy. Military planning for improved visibility from point A to B forgot to make allowances for improved visibility from B to A. Chemically cleared spaces supplied a reassuring field of vision for the American eye and created a psychological sense of accomplishment and safety. Yet more American lives were lost after the spraying. The intended goal of protecting American soldiers actually created a larger killing zone for American troops, when, at the ground level, GIs had to run out of the barren zone to survive.

Militarily, ecocide was self-destructive. Defoliated territory was perfect for helicopter observation by war managers and the quick marshaling of planes and artillery. In effect, the creation of White Zones destroyed civilian lives, wreaked havoc on the ecology, and was detrimental to American war efforts.

Visibility was also an exercise in bureaucratic power, making both facts and phantasms legible by means of a controlling numerical gaze into the world. In its own way, the military strategy of attrition, body counts, and "kill ratios" required a reduction of local society into quantifiable numbers, to create a form of legibility in order to facilitate surveillance. Spraying chemicals was an invisible weapon of destruction to punish the local people who had not moved. Robert McNamara had reformulated government accounts that would permit comparison by numbers and statistics, assessing the costs and benefits of programs based on body counts and tree counts—calculations that were often criticized for offering easy arithmetic answers without complex, balanced investigations.

Visibility was a two-way process and proof of the power of images to inform. When the independent investigative journalist Seymour Hersh exposed the My Lai crime and broke the military cover-up, the massacre of a large group of villagers became highly visible. The full horror of the Vietnam War had been amassed and reduced into the vivid My Lai images. If few people had understood the strong emotions provoked by U.S. crimes in Vietnam that had induced the young American Quaker Norman Morrison to burn himself to death outside the windows of the secretary of defense's office on November 11, 1965, many would understand the enormous feelings aroused when they read the report and saw the images of My Lai four years later. My Lai gave credence to widespread anecdotal evidence presented by unofficial investigations of the time, such as those of the Russell Tribunal. Horrific stories of endemic violence against Vietnamese civilians began to be taken more seriously.

The My Lai civilians had dared to remain in their native village and were slaughtered. The chilling images of the bodies of women and children sprawled bloody and broken in a ditch shocked the nation. Their images touched the hearts and minds of the American public in ways that millions of words had failed to do. The Pentagon started its secret Vietnam War Crimes Working Group Files to investigate atrocities. The number of draftees filing as conscientious objectors grew, yet the unrepentant drive was strong. President Nixon stood in direct contradiction of the standards set at Nuremberg and Tokyo when he had William Calley released from prison pending appeal. Calley later served less than three years of his life sentence. In postwar Vietnam, most refugees returned to their native soil, despite the extreme hardship of cultivation in the White Zones. Their quest for a land-based life after years of displacement and devastation testified to the local people's strong attachment to place, where nativity is eternity.

Bibliography: Thi Phuong-Lan Bui, "When the Forest Became the Enemy and the Legacy of American Herbicidal Warfare in Vietnam," PhD diss., Harvard University, 2003. Nguyen Duy,

"Red Earth–Blue Water," in *Distant Roads: Selected Poems of Nguyen Duy,* trans. and ed. Nguyen Ba Chung and Kevin Bowen (Willimantic, CT, 1999). Engineer Strategic Studies Group, U.S. Army, *Herbicides and Military Operations,* Report, 1972. Michael Herr, *Dispatches* (New York, 1978). Seymour Hersh, Dispatch News Service, November 12, 1969. Marion Lee Kempner, Letter, October 20, 1966, in *Dear America: Letters Home from Vietnam,* ed. Bernard Edelman (New York, 1985). Matthew Meselson, unpublished interpretation of data provided by the ESSG study. Tran Mai Nam, *The Narrow Strip of Land: The Story of a Journey* (Hanoi, 1969).

THI PHUONG-LAN BUI

1970

"You love what happens to the air"

MAYA ANGELOU, TONI MORRISON, ALICE WALKER

In 1970 Toni Morrison and Alice Walker published their first novels, *The Bluest Eye* and *The Third Life of Grange Copeland. I Know Why the Caged Bird Sings,* an autobiography by another unknown, Maya Angelou, climbed the best-seller list. Toni Cade edited *The Black Woman,* a volume featuring a chorus of women including fiction writers (Paule Marshall and Sherley Anne Williams), poets (Nikki Giovanni and Audre Lorde), and essayists, from jazz vocalist Abbey Lincoln to the activist Frances Beal. Beal's essay was tellingly titled "Double Jeopardy: To Be Black and Female." In the aftermath of movements for civil rights and Black Power and at the height of the women's movement, black women began to insist on naming their own experiences. They made themselves heard. Within a decade, their voices redefined African American literature. By 1993, when Morrison was awarded the Nobel Prize in Literature, she and her black female contemporaries had remade the American literary landscape.

In the 1950s Richard Wright's Bigger Thomas, James Baldwin's John Grimes, and the nameless protagonist of Ralph Ellison's *Invisible Man* were the iconic characters of black American literature. In the 1960s they were joined by the angry young men who bestrode the stage in dramas by Amiri Baraka, Larry Neal, and Douglas Turner Ward. These characters were all, in Baldwin's phrase, "going to meet the man." Female characters watched the action from the sidelines. Good women offered succor and encouragement, while bad ones got in the way. To fulfill his quest, the protagonist usually had to leave even the supportive female characters behind.

Black women changed the script. Their plots, characters, and prose introduced something new to American literature. Their protagonists were often females, who faced choices every bit as challenging as their male precursors, though their dilemmas were often more private than public. Frequently set in small towns and rural backwaters, this writing focused on conflicts between black men and women as well as between blacks and whites. And it told its stories in language that was often itself a wonder.

> They come from Mobile. Aiken. From Newport News. From Marietta. From Me-
> ridian. And the sound of these places in their mouths make you think of love.
> When you ask them where they are from, they tilt their heads and say "Mobile"
> and you think you've been kissed. They say "Aiken" and you see a white butterfly
> glance off a fence with a torn wing. They say "Nagadoches" and you want to say,
> "Yes, I will." You don't know what these towns are like, but you love what happens
> to the air when they open their lips and let the names ease out.

This passage from Morrison's *The Bluest Eye* refers to black women who have
left the small Southern towns of their birth for the cities of the industrial Midwest. Unlike the usual historical narrative of the Great Migration, in which rural
Southern blacks found opportunity in the urban North, theirs is not a narrative
of progress. Faced with racism, economic exploitation, and alienation up North,
they look back on their hometowns lovingly. The novel does not share their nostalgia for the South. Indeed, it represents Southern violence graphically. At the
same time, it asks readers to hear the beauty and power of these women's voices, a
beauty and power that inform the narrative's prose. Through the sounds of memory, the novel asks readers to imagine places they have never been and experiences they have never had. It asks them to consider black women's experiences as
interesting for their own sake; their stories are not subordinate to those of white
people or of black men.

Women's voices predominate in the novel, whose protagonist, Pecola Breedlove, is a poor black girl. Her family has internalized the racist ideology of white
society. They believe that they are ugly and unworthy of love. Pecola's mother,
Pauline, reveres the memories of a Southern home where black people protected
each other. Alienated from her neighbors in Lorain, Ohio, she seeks affirmation
in the movies, but celluloid heroines only intensify her sense of inferiority. A domestic servant, she believes that her white employers and their children are her
superiors. The novel limns the roots of the ironically named Breedloves' self-
hatred, then depicts its devastating consequences. Because she hates herself, Pauline cannot love her daughter. When Cholly, Pecola's father, attempts to express
love toward his daughter, he rapes her. Pecola is destroyed. But her friends Frieda
and Claudia (who narrates part of the novel) help readers derive meaning from
her tragedy.

Other events around 1970 signaled the arrival of what critic Hortense Spillers
calls "the community of black women writing." In the wake of the civil rights
movement and in the midst of the women's movement, Cade's *The Black Woman*
heralded an effort by black women to define for themselves what "liberation"
meant. Thirty contributors penned autobiographical essays, poems, position papers, and short stories that marked a turning inward and to each other. *Essence,*
the first mass magazine for black women, began publication in 1970. Although its
primary emphasis was fashion and lifestyle, *Essence* was a further indication that
an audience for black women's writing existed. Writers and scholars began the
recovery of black women authors whose work had long been out of print. Originally published at the height of the Harlem Renaissance, Nella Larsen's novels,
Quicksand and *Passing,* were reissued in 1971. Paperback editions of Jessie Fauset's

There Is Confusion and *Plum Bun* appeared a few years later. In 1970, Zora Neale Hurston remained, in her biographer Robert Hemenway's words, "one of the most significant unread authors in America." Hurston's *Mules and Men,* the first volume of African American folklore collected by an African American, was reprinted that year. *Their Eyes Were Watching God,* the novel originally published in 1937, would soon reach hundreds of thousands of readers. Written in a literary language distilled from vernacular speech and set in all-black communities in rural Florida, the book marked an earlier example of turning inward. It would provide a touchstone for the writing of a new generation.

I Know Why the Caged Bird Sings was the first of Maya Angelou's six autobiographical volumes. Powerfully written and deeply unsettling in its exploration of family violence, sexual oppression and abuse, and the corrosive effects of racism and poverty, it, like *The Bluest Eye* and Walker's *The Third Life of Grange Copeland,* ran counter to the then prevailing mood in popular black consciousness of righteous anger and triumphant struggle. Angelou's book partook more in that mood, but at its dramatic center, as in Morrison's novel, was the rape of a girl. In a society ordered by hierarchies of power based on class, race, and gender, no one is more powerless, hence more vulnerable, than a poor black girl. In these pages such characters anchor the critique of social life.

As Angelou writes, "If growing up is painful for the Southern Black girl, being aware of her displacement is the rust on the razor that threatens the throat." But overcoming the temptation of silence, Angelou pens an unforgettable memoir of her girlhood in Stamps, Arkansas, St. Louis, and San Francisco. She counts the costs of being doubly disenfranchised on account of race and gender. Yet interlaced with the sadness was joy, conveyed in the spiritual peace and power of her grandmother and in the élan with which her mother lived her life. The memoir is especially adept at depicting the larger-than-life figure Momma Henderson assumes at home in contrast to the low status she occupies in public. Ultimately, *I Know Why the Caged Bird Sings* is a song of triumph: the young Maya's triumph over self-hatred, the triumph of black communities that sustained themselves during segregation, and the triumph of a writer whose love and command of language are profound. She claimed both Shakespeare and Paul Laurence Dunbar as key influences. Her memoir also incorporates the vernacular voices of the churchwomen of Stamps and the hustlers of San Francisco. Relatively few autobiographies by black women had been published before Angelou wrote hers. None had delved as deeply into the writer's intimate life. In the process, the book helped break a long-standing public silence around the issue of sexual violence.

Less widely read, Alice Walker's *The Third Life of Grange Copeland* was unsparing in its depiction of economic exploitation and domestic abuse across generations of a family of black sharecroppers. Oppressed and defeated, Grange abuses his wife and neglects his son, who in turn murders his wife and ignores his children. Women in this novel do not speak with the authority of Angelou's persona. But the novel ends on a note of redemption: Grange returns to the South to raise his youngest grandchild, Ruth, whose keen intellect and spiritual strength presage a hopeful future. Walker would return to this setting and theme in several volumes of short stories, such as *In Love and Trouble: Stories of Black Women* and *You Can't Keep a Good Woman Down,* and novels, including *Meridian, The Color Purple, Possessing the Secret of Joy,* and *The Temple of My Familiar.*

In a sharp departure from their black male precursors, Walker, Morrison, and their female contemporaries did not focus on the traumatic encounters of blacks and whites across the color line. Racism remained a major concern, but for these writers the most painful consequences of racism emerged in the most intimate relationships. Making hitherto private traumas public soon proved controversial. Women writers were accused of bashing black men and, worse, of being disloyal to the race. Ntozake Shange's *For Colored Girls Who Have Considered Suicide When the Rainbow Is Enuf,* a "choreopoem" that was clearly indebted to Baraka and the Black Arts movement for its poetic technique, became the object of controversy when it was staged on Broadway in 1977. Critics focused on the image of black male characters, none of whom appeared on stage, rather than on the female characters whose stories were being told. Ugly as it was, this controversy paled in comparison with that engendered by *The Color Purple,* both the 1982 novel and the 1986 film.

Walker's novel holds open the possibility for transformation equally to men and women. But it is Celie's story. The beaten-down protagonist reclaims herself through the inspiration of the blues singer Shug Avery and through the power of her own words. In the tradition of Ma Rainey and Bessie Smith, Shug, who enters the narrative dressed to kill in red and black, in a feathered hat and snakeskin shoes, is a self-invented woman who asserts her artistic and sexual autonomy. Celie is in awe of her. Close up, though, Shug "look like she ain long for this world but dressed up for the next." As Celie perceives Shug's weaknesses and Shug becomes less a star than a sister, Celie recognizes her own strengths. Although she is a talented seamstress, Celie's primary artistic medium is words; she writes letters to God and to Nettie, her sister who becomes a missionary in Africa. But her voice is a blues voice—laconic, blunt, and poetic—that can express at once her private feelings, spiritual longings, and social critique.

Walker's 1974 essay "In Search of Our Mothers' Gardens" offers a theory of black female creativity and defines a tradition of black women's art. Walker imagines generations of black women artists, including those who released their creativity in song and the crafts of quilt making, baking, and gardening that Walker reevaluates as art. The portrait Walker draws of her mother gardening is the portrait of an artist "ordering the universe in her personal conception of Beauty." Many writers share Walker's impulse to recuperate the artistic legacy of their foremothers: Paule Marshall pays homage to the "poets in the kitchen," Barbadian immigrants whose linguistic creativity inspires her own, while Gloria Naylor endows her protagonist Mama Day, a midwife and conjure woman, with the ability to quilt, bake, and garden superlatively. In *Sula* (1974) Morrison creates the "magnificent" Eva Peace, a character whose will to order the universe in her own personal conception is both beautiful and sinister.

Sula prefigures the power of *Beloved* (1987) and *Jazz* (1992), the novels that earned Toni Morrison the highest critical accolades. It elegizes the culture and communities that sustained African Americans from the Emancipation through the civil rights movement. It remembers life in the Bottom, a black neighborhood in the hills of the fictional city of Medallion, Ohio, that has been destroyed in the name of progress before the novel begins. From the images of destruction that introduce the text, through a series of deaths by fire and water, in rituals to stave off fear and to bury the dead, to the "circles of sorrow" that close it, *Sula* is suffused with sadness. Leavening a sadness that would otherwise be all but unbearable is the novel's precise rendering of the impromptu ceremonies of everyday life, its sassy talk, and raunchy humor. Despite racism so unyielding that it seemed another force of nature, or perhaps because of it, the community's elders bonded together out of kinship and necessity. As the novel begins and ends, their legacy has been destroyed root and branch. Like the later novels, *Sula* is very much a call to remember.

The Bottom is home to Sula Peace and Nel Wright, the main characters, who, despite differences in class and personality, become fast friends and "use each other to grow on." As young black girls, they have no other models. Meeting again after a ten-year separation, Nel's "rapid soprano and Sula's dark sleepy chuckle make a duet." Yet, not unlike black Americans who, the novel suggests, only retrospectively recognized the value of the segregated communities that nurtured them for generations, Sula and Nel fail to recognize how valuable their friendship is until they have lost it. The recognition that their friendship is the most important thing in their lives comes only after Sula dies, having improvised a life that defies convention. Neither wife nor mother, Sula is a disloyal daughter and an unfaithful friend. An American original, the character achieves an exhilarating and frightening freedom.

One could cite allusions in *Sula* to novels by William Faulkner, Mark Twain, and Virginia Woolf. Significantly, Walker numbers Woolf and Flannery O'Connor, Jean Toomer and Richard Wright, as well as Hurston and Larsen among her literary models. But from the beginning of their careers Angelou, Morrison, and Walker insisted that they told new stories; they wrote the books they had wanted to read. They add what had been missing from the national story, narratives of enslaved and exploited women and stories of black workers (cooks, seamstresses, maids, and blues singers)—some of whom come from small towns with musical names. They craft literary language distilled from these vernacular voices, and they insist that the history of the nation cannot be understood without these stories.

Bibliography: Maya Angelou, *I Know Why the Caged Bird Sings* (New York, 1970). Robert E. Hemenway, *Zora Neale Hurston: A Literary Biography,* preface by Alice Walker (Urbana, IL, 1977). Toni Morrison, *The Bluest Eye* (New York, 1970); *Sula* (New York, 1974). Ntozake Shange, *For Colored Girls Who Have Considered Suicide When the Rainbow Is Enuf* (New York, 1977). Alice Walker, *The Color Purple* (New York, 1982); *The Third Life of Grange Copeland* (New York, 1970).

CHERYL A. WALL

1970; 1972

Anne Koedt publishes *The Myth of the Vaginal Orgasm;*
the movie *Deep Throat* is released

LINDA LOVELACE'S *ORDEAL*

1972: The Pill available to unmarried women in all states
March 22, 1972: The U.S. Senate adopts the Equal Rights Amendment
June 12, 1972: *Deep Throat* opens at New York's World Theater
June 17, 1972: Five burglars arrested while breaking into the Democratic National Com-
   mittee's headquarters at the Watergate hotel
January 11, 1973: First broadcast of *An American Family* on PBS
May 17, 1973: First broadcast of Watergate hearings

Linda Lovelace: January 10, 1949–April 22, 2002

Ordeal, the third of four autobiographies of *Deep Throat* porn star Linda Bore-
man (Lovelace), isn't interesting because it's a good book, a tragic one, or even an
arousing one. Published in 1980, it's interesting as an artifact of early feminism,
just like *Deep Throat* in 1972, and because, again like *Deep Throat,* it raises endless
questions about sincerity, pleasure, the public and the private, questions that
floated in the air just a year later during the Watergate hearings, questions that
still shape our culture.

Lovelace's voice is the studiously bland voice we hear every day from politicians, in the smuggest of op-eds, in the passive-aggressive niceness of airline employees. Hypocrisy has always been with us, but the mimicking of the colorless
tone of down-to-earth "good folks," of what was once called Middle America,
seems to have become prevalent after World War II. It was diagnosed in the earnest realist novels of the 1950s, and parodied in *Catch-22, Mad* magazine, and *The
Graduate* ("Plastics!").

The deliberate impersonation of a blameless dailiness might have been an artifact of television, television commercials, and the televising of political oratory.
All of this created a national speech, a national jargon, broader and more impersonal than the regional accents of radio, and it also allowed the audience to see
how facial expressions and words played with and against each other. It is much
easier to lie with your voice when your face is hidden, or to lie with your face
when you don't talk. (*Deep Throat,* like most porn films, is light on dialogue.)

When Lovelace discusses the injuries of her past, her voice has an almost autistic blankness: "My mother has always been very emotional toward me. When I
was four years old, she started beating me—first with a belt, later with the buckle
of the belt." Is that "very emotional" a reflection of Lovelace's inability or unwillingness to understand her own history? Is it a defense against the sadness that
must underlie such a memory, if true? *Ordeal* might have been a very sad book,

but intentionally or not, it is not. Or is "very emotional" a sly understatement, allowing the reader to draw the connection between Linda's abuse by her mother and her choice to stay for years with her abusive husband and Svengali, Chuck Traynor?

Consider this bit of Linda's backstory: "I don't want to pretend that I was always Miss Holy-Holy. I fell in love once or twice; I lost my virginity at age nineteen, and when I was twenty, I gave birth to an illegitimate child that my mother put out for adoption."

"An illegitimate child." She doesn't even say whether it was a boy or girl—the important thing is that it was "illegitimate." Her mother put it out for adoption? I was under the impression that the child's mother's consent is necessary, not the grandmother's. Linda has no agency here. "My only honest conversations those days were with God," she says of her initial time with Traynor, but the question of how honest she is with herself, or us, comes up throughout her book.

Discussing sex, Lovelace blends false modesty and coyness, like the tan lines on the otherwise overexposed bodies of porn stars. Chuck Traynor may well have abused her, but Lovelace had a foot in the world he lived in before they met, through her high school best friend, Betsy, a "topless dancer."

Lovelace's ghostwriter for *Ordeal,* Mike McGrady, was an Eastern establishment journalist—Yale, the army, *Newsday*—whose *Naked Came a Stranger,* a parody of a sex novel, was a best seller in 1969. A year later, he published his self-exposé: *Stranger than Naked; or, How to Write Dirty Books for Fun and Profit; A Manual.* Linda did something similar. In 1974 she published her first autobiography, *Inside Linda Lovelace,* portraying herself as a sex addict who participated willingly in the porn world. In *Ordeal* she calls *Inside Linda Lovelace* "a pack of lies" and says it was written by Chuck Traynor. *Ordeal* doesn't mention a second, 1974 autobiography, *The Intimate Diary of Linda Lovelace,* which was put together by the man who became her producer and lover after she left Traynor; he seems to have been gay, but beat her anyway at the end. Not to mention that in 1986 Linda published a fourth autobiography, *Out of Bondage,* also cowritten with Mike McGrady. The issues become murkier still when you consider that *Out of Bondage* was published by Lyle Stuart, a division of Kensington Books, while *The Intimate Diary of Linda Lovelace* was published by Pinnacle Books, also a division of Kensington.

Why would a woman who wanted to distance herself from an earlier, false autobiography choose a collaborator with McGrady's history of hoax? Did she choose McGrady precisely in order to tantalize the reader with questions about truth? Or was he the best she could find—damaged goods, like herself? Or was *Ordeal* his idea, inspired by his own history of spoof and confession? These questions are emblematic of the early 1970s, when the first hearings on a possible presidential impeachment in American history were televised, and when the first reality TV show—*An American Family*—aired.

Appearing on PBS, *An American Family,* which entered the lives of the family of Bill and Pat Loud of Santa Barbara, California, was just a twelve-hour series, but the episodes seemed endless, weighty with barely voiceable griefs that television had never shown. And the unexpected revelation that the Louds' son Lance was gay was the first appearance of an openly gay person on television.

An American Family established a social space for the revealing of what used to be private, and the same could be said, roughly, about the Watergate hearings and the mainstreaming of pornography. (The Watergate source was nicknamed "Deep Throat" after the movie—a coarse joke impossible to imagine in our more politically sensitive times.)

But the sixty-one minutes of *Deep Throat* raise even more intimate questions about what can be seen and known, questions about the location of the female orgasm. The premise of the movie—that Linda Lovelace's clitoris is located in her throat—wouldn't even have made sense until people began to worry whether or not women were achieving orgasms in intercourse. And it's amazingly au courant, given that Anne Koedt's essay *The Myth of the Vaginal Orgasm* appeared only two years earlier. The orgasm *Deep Throat* imagines is in an unusual place, but it shares with the vaginal orgasm the fact of being hidden from view.

Koedt gave no medical evidence for her belief that the clitoris rather than the vagina is the source of female sexual pleasure. In fact, Koedt seems a highly untrustworthy guide to the female anatomy, insisting that the vagina is so insensitive that "women need no anesthesia inside the vagina during surgery." Perhaps a similar belief explains the only sadistic scene in *Deep Throat,* when a man drinks through a straw from a glass inserted in Linda Lovelace's vagina. It may have been plastic, but it's hard not to imagine the effect of glass breaking.

Leap ahead to a time when it's an article of faith that women achieve orgasm *only* through clitoral stimulation, that intercourse provides gratification only to the male, and you may wonder just what is behind this dogmatism. Perhaps it's connected to the culture of public exposure of which *Ordeal* is an early manifestation: anything that cannot be seen by everyone is possibly false, certainly suspect. Some of this attitude is probably a reaction to television, which brought both the interior of the body and the ends of the earth into the American living room. There are still people who believe that Neil Armstrong's 1968 walk on the moon was a hoax, staged in a television studio; in 1983, in *Sex Tips for Girls,* Cynthia Heimel claimed that the oral sex in *Deep Throat* was done with mirrors.

Today, a movie based on the fantasy that fellatio gives women orgasms appears shamelessly exploitative. But in 1972 taking a woman's sexual fulfillment seriously was new, as recent as access to the birth control pill, which became available nationwide only by the end of that year. For the first time in history, women of childbearing age could have intercourse without fear of pregnancy. Can it be that the new permission to have intercourse had something to do with the new doubts about whether intercourse was in fact fulfilling for women? *Deep Throat* is earnest about Lovelace's pleasure, even more so than that of Lovelace's costar Harry Reems. When Lovelace reaches her moment, we see shots of the ringing of a bell, fireworks, and the liftoff of a rocket. One small step for a man, one giant leap for mankind.

Both the defenders and attackers of *Deep Throat* assumed that a woman's sexual satisfaction was important, and even shared to some degree the hippie ethos that insisted on pleasure as a political goal. The defense in the obscenity trial of *Deep Throat*—brought in New York in late 1972—claimed that the film had the value of insisting on female sexual satisfaction. But the prosecution argued that the film will "strengthen in her ignorance" any woman who thinks that the clitoral orgasm is real. Surely this is the first time an American prosecutor took a stance on where female orgasms occur. (The film was found obscene by the court; the judgment was overturned on appeal.)

Ordeal's controversial claim—the reason Lovelace says she wrote her story a second time—is that *Deep Throat* is the record of Lovelace's rape. It is again a sign of progress that this was supposed to be a shocker. Probably the consumers of stag films in the 1920s were not so concerned with whether the actresses actually enjoyed what they pretended to enjoy, and they may have even assumed that they were coerced into participation by poverty or underworld links. But *Deep Throat* was the first respectable porn film, praised by the intelligentsia, the left, and the chic. A special January-February 1973 issue of *Film Comment* was titled "Cinema Sex." One of the contributors was Brendan Gill, who extolled the new "permissiveness." "We probably wouldn't have done that special issue if it hadn't been for *Deep Throat*," Richard Corliss, the editor of the issue, said in 2005. *Deep Throat* was a movie that middle-class couples were not ashamed to be seen seeing, so the assumption of the willing participation of the actors was important, maybe for the first time in the history of the porn film.

Some of what Lovelace tells the reader in *Ordeal* is meant to be an unpleasant surprise, but on another level it's also exactly what he would have expected to hear, because it plays into an American identification of sex with violence. This has been discussed by many writers, and the insight has even filtered down to a context that makes sense for *Ordeal* and *Deep Throat:* consumer-goods marketing.

A clever French-born consultant, Clotaire Rapaille, coined the term "the culture code" for "the unconscious meaning we apply to any given thing—a car, a type of food, a relationship, even a country—via the culture in which we are raised." The code for sex in the United States is "violence," Rapaille says, and American culture is "far more comfortable with violence than with sex." *Ordeal* fits into a narrative Americans understand implicitly, in which what is allegedly sexual pleasure is really painful rape, and what is allegedly liberation is really sexual slavery.

Ordeal is smart in another way—it's an early example of a genre now more numerous, the memoir of abuse. One of the ground rules: reassure the reader that his life is better than the writer's. Nothing goes down so well as a memoir that shows that the rich, famous, beautiful, or adventurous writer's existence has actually been shot through with misery, insecurity, pain, and fear. Think being a young, sexy porn star is enviable? Think again, *Ordeal* tells us. Tina Turner's *I, Tina,* released in 1986, was another early instance.

The pleasure that *Ordeal* provides the reader isn't arousal, but self-satisfaction. D. A. Miller has explained the phenomenon as it applies to popular novels of the nineteenth century. He argues that the limitations of the inner lives of the more sympathetic characters contrast with our own "less violated inwardness." "Though they are pathetically reduced beings," Miller writes, we find Dickens's characters charming because "their fixity" gives us "our freedom." We enjoy reading about them because we feel more powerful in comparison.

Linda's life after *Ordeal* needs no embroidery to arouse pity. It was a slow spiral back to the lower-middle-class tedium of her family history, and then down from there. Linda married a construction worker, became a born-again Christian, and a mother; she endured hard times, even a stint on welfare, a liver transplant. In 1996, after twenty-two years of marriage, Linda divorced her husband, claiming that he was an alcoholic who abused her. She was cleaning offices at night by the time she died in a car accident at fifty-three. Her daughter was herself an unwed mother at seventeen.

Perhaps what would hurt Linda most, could she come back to life, is that it's almost impossible to find *Deep Throat* for rent in a video store today. The dreadful copy I bought online seems to have been pirated directly from the screen. It may be that in fifty years or so, *Deep Throat* will be a minor footnote to students of the Watergate scandal, and Linda Lovelace's name nearly lost to history. But *Deep Throat* and Lovelace's account of it in *Ordeal* continue to ripple through American culture, from daytime TV to the best-seller lists to how we say we give and take pleasure.

Bibliography: Anne Koedt, *The Myth of the Vaginal Orgasm* (London, 1970). Linda Lovelace, *Inside Linda Lovelace* (London, 1974); *Ordeal,* with Mike McGrady (Secaucus, NJ, 1980); *Out of Bondage,* with Mike McGrady (Secaucus, NJ, 1986). Linda Lovelace and Carl Wallin, *The Intimate Diary of Linda Lovelace* (New York, 1974). D. A. Miller, *The Novel and the Police* (New York, 1988). Clotaire Rapaille, *The Culture Code* (New York, 2006). *Filmography: Deep Throat,* directed by Gerard Damiano (1972).

ANN MARLOWE

1973

The Nuyorican Poets Café is born in an apartment building on the Lower East Side

LOISAIDA LITERATURE

One of the enduring cultural legacies of the civil rights movement, the Nuyorican Poets Café began as an informal gathering in Miguel Algarín's small apartment in New York City. Within two years, this vibrant group, including Pedro Pietri, Miguel Piñero, Sandra María Esteves, and others, moved into a former Irish bar and, in 1980, into the even larger venue that the café still occupies on East Third Street. The phonetic, Latinized name for the Lower East Side, "Loisaida," was memorialized in Piñero's well-known poetic tribute to the neighborhood,

with its rhythmic inflection and incantatory rhyme so important to this group
of poets:

> Just once before I die
> I want to climb up on a
> tenement sky
> to dream my lungs out till
> I cry
> then scatter my ashes thru
> the Lower East Side.

Part anthem, part manifesto, and an even larger part performative experience,
this poem attests to the socially engaged, linguistically transformative energies
that have characterized not only Nuyorican poetry, but also a great deal of U.S.
Latino and Latina writing in general over the past four decades.

The term "Nuyorican" refers to the Puerto Rican community that concentrated in Greater New York following the *Gran Migración* from the island in the
1940s and 1950s, but it is often used to refer to all those of Puerto Rican origin
who now live stateside. As the social and political projects of the Young Lords—
an activist group influenced by the Black Panther Party—took shape in the late
1960s and early 1970s, the Nuyorican movement drew in a cultural wing of writers, artists, and musicians ready to denounce the social injustice and racism that
the community faced. As such, it paralleled the Chicano movement in California,
Texas, and the Southwest, as well as the Black Arts movement. Intellectual self-
determination, an insistence on understanding the community's aesthetic on its
own terms, was central to all three projects. Algarín was an English professor at
Rutgers, a playwright and poet who taught Shakespeare even as he was defining
this newly visible Nuyorican aesthetic in scholarly terms through what he considered its three fundamental elements: the oral expression of selfhood, a discourse
of survival, and public poetry that heals the community.

Most Nuyorican writers have been more strongly influenced by the storytelling, folklore, oratory, and recitation coming from their dominantly Afro-
Caribbean heritage than by the written word. The marginal status of the first generation of these writers, most of whom had not had access to formal education,
reaffirmed the primacy of the oral tradition. Many identified oral poet Jorge
Brandon, who walked the streets of El Barrio with a shopping cart, reciting traditional Spanish *décimas* along with his own poetry, as a major influence. The beat
poets, another culturally visible model of resistance, also helped to root the primacy of orality for the Nuyoricans.

But Nuyorican poetry was far more integral to the revolutionary social movements of the time, as reflected in the many poetry performances during demonstrations, marches, and takeovers. Pietri performed his "Puerto Rican Obituary," an indictment of the community's internalization of the colonized mentality,
at the takeover of the First Spanish Methodist Church by the Young Lords in
1969. Esteves's similarly foundational poem "My name is María Christina" insisted on women's presence in the movement: "My name is María Christina / I am
a Puerto Rican woman born in el barrio." Algarín's poem "Mongo Affair" de-

nounced the emasculation of Puerto Rican working-class men displaced to the mainland:

> mongo es el borinqueño
> who's been moved
> to the inner-city jungles
> of north american cities
> mongo is the Rican who survives
> in the tar jungle of Chicago
> who cleans, weeps, crawls.

The global anticolonial struggle was happening, these writers insisted, not in distant places but in the very heart of the nation.

The frequent code switching between English and Spanish in these poems not only reflects the nonchalant daily expression of stateside Puerto Ricans but also opens up new lexical, semantic, and rhythmic possibilities: "mongo," a slang term for "weak" or "flaccid," echoes the noun "borinqueño," a term for Puerto Rican that invokes the island's Taíno name and heritage. The Spanish "es" slides into the English "is" a few lines later, not translating between the two languages so much as pushing poetry into a new space sounding beyond both linguistic and national traditions. Afro-Caribbean musical idioms are another important "language" present in Nuyorican poetry. Salsa music is integrated into poems by way of intertextual lyrics, onomatopoeia, and the overall ethos of performance as an experience of communal coming-together. Popular music is seen as medicine for healing the fragmented, dislocated community, as in this poem of Algarín's describing a performance of famed conga drummer Ray Barreto at the café:

> Barreto, Doctor of Body Motion
> you release the monster that chews
> the working man from inside out.

Nuyorican poetry often transforms both salsa music and urban rhythms into rituals of cultural self-affirmation. Tato Laviera, author of the punningly titled collection *AmeRícan,* writes,

> i saw the congas playing
> everyone walked to the tunes
> tatatatá tutututú
> tucutupacutú
> heroine sugar hands were exploiting
> the last tune before winter oblivion.

Likewise, Victor Hernández Cruz frequently spells out Afro-Caribbean rhythms:

> The conga is a telephone
> r i n g
> bomba pu ta ka ta buum
> bomba pu ta ka ta buum.

Nuyorican poetry thus exists along a historical continuum with the ancient competitions of orators, troubadours, and minstrels. Although connections to rap inevitably come to mind, given the constant give and take between African American oral traditions and Afro-Caribbean culture, performance poetry is not a novel aesthetic that emerges only at the end of the twentieth century. The spoken-word performances for which the Nuyorican Poets Café became famous, and which expanded their reach across the United States during the 1990s, have brought back to life poetry as social event, as an interactive, collective, polyphonic performance. To evade the hierarchies of written versus oral modes of literature, this poetry may be better defined as what Arlene Elder calls "orature": a term that "establishes traditional artistry as equal in complexity to literature, not as only an early step in a people's march to literacy, an accomplishment formerly mistaken as evidence of becoming 'civilized.'" Within the political and cultural framework of Nuyorican writers in the 1970s, the valorization of orature was crucial. It promised to reconnect the diasporic community through oral memory, creating a transnational flow between the island and the mainland. And it offered poets a sense of ownership over their literary production. For the first time, Puerto Ricans on the East Coast publicly reaffirmed their new, hybrid identities as whole and real, rather than as lacking the cultural markers needed to be considered fully Puerto Rican or fully "American."

The oral elements of this poetry were centrally involved in this process. Pietri's "Puerto Rican Obituary" uses anaphoric repetition, a staple mnemonic device, to make its point about the economic injustices that the community has faced as a cheap labor force in the United States:

> They worked ten days a week
> and were only paid for five.
> They worked
> they worked
> they worked
> and they died.

Algarín's second tenet of Nuyorican aesthetics, that poetry should constitute "a discourse of survival" against such a leeching of one's essential humanity, is also reflected in the attention that many writers in this movement paid to youth culture, working to ameliorate violence and gang activity by engaging young people, in particular, in spoken-word culture.

The Nuyorican Poets Café's purpose was to "reveal poetry as a living art": that is, to democratize it, bringing it to those who had historically not had access to either the U.S. literary canon or the island Puerto Rican literary corpus. Poetry was conceived of not as an aesthetic experience geared to the individual bourgeois reader, but as a question of the very survival of the masses—and thus a collective social experience. Even the corresponding prose classics of this period, Piri Thomas's autobiographical *Down These Mean Streets* (1967) and Nicholasa Mohr's *Nilda* (1974) and its successors, highlight the way the protagonists emerge from within a living social body that they never leave, not even in prison.

In this context, it was inevitable that this poetry spoke to the stark living conditions of Puerto Ricans in New York at the time, with raw metaphors and crude

imagery of concrete, steel, tar, cockroaches, weapons, and other signals of urban poverty and alienation that rebelled against dominant ideas of lyricism and
beauty. Lucky Cienfuegos wrote, in language that recalled the beats, of

> Weaving, bobbing, conniving
> piss staining lonely night street
> gutless buildings hanging loose.

But while social marginality might be actively sought out by some, it was unwillingly inherited by others: Piñero wrote sarcastically, and pointedly,

> In the beginning
> God created the ghettos & slums
> and God saw this was good.
> So God said, "Let there be more ghettos & slums"
> and there were more ghettos and slums.

Piñero's anger against the godlike power of U.S. social policy is palpable here—
and it is this very anger, expressed in the sharp critiques of capitalism and neo-
colonialism that were so common among the Nuyorican poets, that have helped
keep their work on the margins of the U.S. literary canon. So did the other elements of the aesthetic that Algarín defined: if the essence of the poetry lay in its
communal orality rather than in the privacy of the experience on the page, how
could that sensibility be reproduced? The centrality of social experience, in every
respect, to Nuyorican poetry, as well as the extensive integration of Spanish and
musical language, which required of the listener a different kind of literacy, ran
against traditional conceptions of lyric poetry and individual genius, and surely
alienated the more conservative readers.

By the 1990s, however, poetry written by minorities, youths, and the working
class and shared at poetry slams (initiated in Chicago's Green Mills Club in the
Northside) had become a new national public space for poetry, viewed and listened to by millions on cable TV. In this context, the Nuyorican Poets Café recast
its mission as more global and multicultural. In his essay "The Sidewalk of High
Art," Algarín characterizes the new poetry of the 1990s as emphasizing "tolerance and understanding between people," more "multiethnic" and more bent on
"breaking all boundaries" than its predecessor. Today's café offers diverse programming in music, hip-hop, video, visual arts, comedy, and theater as it attempts
to support "artists who have been traditionally underrepresented in the mainstream media and culture." Poetry slams increasingly integrate the opinions of
the audience in the public performance of poetry.

While some Nuyorican poets disagreed with what they considered the coop-
tation and mainstreaming of poetry in the slams, what they saw as a business and
an insignificant process of judging poets, Algarín focuses on these performances
as examples of the democratization of art. Indeed, the conflicts over maintaining
the café as a space dedicated to the expression of the Puerto Rican nationalist
version of selfhood or embracing other minority groups and voices, as Algarín has
done, reveal the tensions in this transition from cultural nationalism to a more

multicultural and even global space. These conflicts, again, mirror those in the Chicano literary community on the other side of the continent, where the emergence of a new generation of writers following the "Chicano Renaissance" of the early 1970s prompted heated debates about the fate of the activist cultural agenda.

In the wake of the vogue of multiculturalism in the 1980s and 1990s, when many writers—novelists in particular—found considerable mainstream success by offering up their culturally specific experiences to eager audiences who flattened them into a generically exotic "Latino" category, this debate has often been cast as a struggle between virtuous small publishers and the massive marketing apparatus of contemporary publishing. Pietri, for instance, has turned away from traditional publication contexts altogether, publishing his major work of the 1990s, "El Spanglish National Anthem," on his Internet site, El Puerto Rican Embassy (it begins, "En my Viejo San Juan / They raise the price of pan / So I fly to Manhattan"). However, the Nuyorican Poets Café has joined the marketplace; its bookstore sells both its own publications and mainstream titles in poetry, theater, and fiction.

On the one hand, the fact that the U.S. Puerto Rican literary corpus remains an understudied and underrepresented area in the national literary market argues for resisting the conflation of this body of work with the Latino canon that emerged later. On the other, the younger generations of poets, writers, artists, musicians, and playwrights in urban centers such as New York and Chicago embody in themselves the racial crossings and cultural hybridities that have challenged older, nation-based boundaries. Hernández Cruz's poems, which were originally categorized as Nuyorican, have been heavily influenced in recent years by the writer's personal migratory circuits from New York to California, back to rural Puerto Rico, and from there to Morocco. Hernández Cruz now writes in three languages—Spanish, English, and Arabic—and defies any particular categorization based on nation or language. The epigraph to *Red Beans* (1991), in an uncanny prophetic way, signals the uncovering of the Arab heritage (by way of Spain) that is so silenced in Puerto Rican popular culture: he juxtaposes an Arabic phrase, "Say La ilaha illa Llah and be delivered," with the Puerto Rican island folkloric singing, "Ay lo lay lah lo lay la ley lo lay lah," by Ramito, Puerto Rico's most important mountain troubadour.

Despite the changes that have transformed the café from a space of considerable social and aesthetic marginality to a well-known space that markets itself as oppositional, the venue continues to present poetry to be recited out loud and in front of a listening public or audience. Is Nuyorican poetry a literary mode in its own right, or does it "belong" to Latino literature, a category that emerged much later? Perhaps it does not matter how one answers this question. As many younger Latino and Latina writers—not only from Puerto Rico but also from El Salvador, Mexico, Cuba, Guatemala—have attested, the aesthetic of orature and the poetry of survival are still timely. They still feel a need to argue their humanity, to document and denounce the social injustice around them, and to prove their artistic rigor in an ever-evolving language.

Bibliography: Miguel Algarín and Miguel Piñero, eds., *Nuyorican Poetry: An Anthology of Puerto Rican Words and Feelings* (New York, 1975). Raphael Dalleo and Elena Machado Sáez, *The Latino/a Canon and the Emergence of Post-Sixties Literature* (New York, 2007). Arlene Elder, "Preliminaries: Folklore and Orature," *MELUS* 16, no. 1 (Spring 1989–90): 1–3. Lisa Sánchez-González, *Boricua Literature: A Literary History of the Puerto Rican Diaspora* (New York, 2001).

FRANCES R. APARICIO

1973
"I suddenly see the world / as no longer viable"

ADRIENNE RICH, *DIVING INTO THE WRECK*

Adrienne Rich's seventh book, *Diving into the Wreck,* came bursting with clouds of furious glory, its forensic precision, dazzling images, and agonized moral passion recognized by most critics as a summation of her then-current powers; discerning readers took up the book as a vital challenge. As Margaret Atwood wrote, "This is Adrienne Rich's seventh book of poems, and it is an extraordinary one. When I first heard the author read from it, I felt as though the top of my head was being attacked, sometimes with an ice pick, sometimes with a blunter instrument: a hatchet or a hammer . . . It is a book that takes risks, and it forces the reader to take them also." Atwood's remarks echo while aggressively transforming Emily Dickinson's: "If I feel physically as if the top of my head were taken off, I know that is poetry."

Diving into the Wreck stands as an exemplary work, diagnostic of its era as well as of its author's incandescent, pared middle style. Infused with a violent energy both destructive and potentially transformative, the poems typically appear as enunciations in and of an emergency, as in the opening poem, "Trying to Talk with a Man":

> we talk of people caring for each other
> in emergencies—laceration, thirst—
> but you look at me like an emergency

The ongoing war in Vietnam, the crises in race relations, the larger horizon of the atomic era all make themselves felt, but the central predicament of the book is "the tragedy of sex," the "wreck" of human relations, the intensifying strife between men and women.

Rich has had the benefit and burden of being received as a generational bellwether. Her reception has long been filtered through political and ideological grids partly established through her poems and, especially from the midseventies onward, through her prose writings on feminism, motherhood, identity, lesbianism, Jewishness, race, class, and North American insularity. Now well known as a poetic éminence grise, lesbian feminist, and left-wing cultural intellectual, in the early seventies Rich was known primarily as a poet, and a major one: *Diving into the Wreck* won the National Book Award in 1974, shared with Allen Ginsberg's *The Fall of America*—a sign that radical critique had become mainstream among U.S. literati.

Following her metrically and tonally poised first books, Rich's work from the landmark *Snapshots of a Daughter-in-Law* (1963) increasingly reflected a painful consciousness of sexed and sexual difference. *Snapshots* appeared the same year as Betty Friedan's *The Feminine Mystique,* and its title poem may be read as a major poetic investigation of that mystique and its costs. Yet as Rich later observed, she handled this material at some remove: *Snapshots* avoids the personal "I," while *Diving into the Wreck* incessantly explores it. If Rich's poems became more expansive in the sixties—more open to fragmentation, intercut voices, and techniques adopted from the Persian and Urdu ghazal as much as from Jean-Luc Godard—more striking was her deepening inquiry into the possibilities of lyric subjectivity and intersubjectivity. If the personal was political, the political personal, how would or should "I" speak in lyric?

Diving into the Wreck proposes an "I" that is alternately visionary, historical, gendered, and generalized. Unlike later experimental poets concerned to fracture or decenter the "I" along the lines of poststructural critiques of subjectivity, Rich presents an articulate, mobile "I." Like Whitman, she strolls the polis, large, containing multitudes: "walking as I've walked before / like a man, like a woman, in the city." At times she takes up a plural, explicitly gendered position ("It is strange to be so many women"), yet her collective subject often becomes the difficult "we" of men and women grappling, "talking of the danger / as if it were not ourselves." Analysis of the "wreck" requires this mobility, as sites of enunciation are tested and claimed:

> We are, I am, you are
> by cowardice or courage
> the one who find our way
> back to this scene.

One finds in the collection not so much early intimations of identity politics as a subtler exploration of the conditions for identification:

> if they ask me my identity
> what can I say but
> I am the androgyne.

Diving into the Wreck moves from the stark diagnosis of "Trying to Talk with a Man" to the mythic submersion imagined in the title poem to a final sequence devoted to the experimental education of an eighteenth-century French "savage child." Among the most anthologized of her poems, "Diving into the Wreck" exemplifies the "revisionary mythmaking" that Rich and writers like Alicia Ostriker called for. The poem explores the possible salvaging of relations between the sexes and indeed of cultural history: "I came to see the damage that was done / and the treasures that prevail." Figuring herself as masked diver, both "merman" and "mermaid," Rich invokes the androgyne myth—"I am she: I am he"—that Virginia Woolf used decades earlier in *A Room of One's Own,* and for similar reasons: to claim for women's imagination the most complex human resources, and to preserve a hard-won feminist consciousness without moving toward a fully separatist position. (Rich would later repudiate "androgyny," as well as "humanism," as falsely transcendent, prematurely universalizing concepts.)

Diving into the Wreck is poised at the intersection of the individual and the social: the poems chart that juncture, pick at it, invent it, imagining the structure of relations between people, within the self, between person and event. Though Rich had yet to immerse herself in Marx (which she did sometime around 1980), *Diving* remains her book that best incarnates Marx's insight that the individual *is* the social being, that consciousness is a social product, that (to invoke a psychoanalytic lexicon) the contents of our inner lives are in part introjections of "external" phenomena, including other people's emotions and ideas. Rich quoted George Eliot in an epigraph—"There is no private life which is not determined by a wider public life": *Diving* tracks the seepage of a historically specific, wider public life into private life and into lyric, that supposedly most private of genres.

In an unexpected fashion Rich had followed through on some implications of W. H. Auden's infamous forward to her first book, *A Change of World* (1951), which he chose for the Yale Younger Poets Prize. Often cited as one of the more obnoxiously condescending introductions of a young woman poet (in the admittedly limited annals thereof), Auden's fey yet not inaccurate commendation of Rich's "modesty" and "disclaim[ing of] any extraordinary vision" has obscured what in retrospect looks more prophetic: "Radical changes and significant novelty in artistic style can only occur when there has been a radical change in human sensibility to require them."

Diving into the Wreck is preoccupied with the radical imagining required by just such a change in human sensibility—not least the coming-to-group-consciousness of North American women via what we now call second-wave feminism. Whether Rich ever forged "significant novelty in artistic style" is doubtful (though her style shifted dramatically over the years), and indeed on this front—of linguistic and stylistic innovation—she has come in for criticism from those partial to a more obviously experimental poetics. Experiencing, and calling for, a revolution in consciousness, should the poet also require her poetry to undergo a revolution in language and form?

One would hope that at this late date any desire for a simple correspondence between apparently radical form and apparently radical content would be abjured; militant avant-gardism too readily runs aground on the shoal of its own deadening certainties, as the excesses of Language poetry in the seventies and eighties suggest. Yet Rich herself repeatedly raises the question of "the will to change," as she called her sixth book. Her development as a poet and a public person carries with it the aura of conversion (indeed of a series of conversions, since Rich "came out" first in the sixties as a political poet, and then in the mid-seventies as a lesbian poet): thus it is not surprising that some critics read her trajectory as a form of apostasy (from the orthodox faith of polished form, decorum, or putatively ideology-free lyric), while some admirers gush as self-styled fellow congregants of the true radical church. Rich is often praised for her passion for "truth," and while this may be admirable in a citizen it is not necessarily the best trait for a poet. Yet perhaps it is worth invoking a phrase from Louise Glück, whose later mordant anatomies of marital discord (as in *Meadowlands,* 1996) may owe something to Rich: Glück suggests that the poet's obligation is to transform "the actual into the true." Here *Diving into the Wreck* succeeded, offering not the prosaic actualities of a poet's life but rather the truth of her passionate acts of poetic intelligence.

The blistering immediacy of *Diving into the Wreck* arises not least from Rich's transmutation of lyric via anger, as in the sequence "The Phenomenology of Anger." In Rich's hands the emotion becomes an analytic engine, and a clarifying lens—"my visionary anger cleansing my sight." The poet becomes a potential medium for others' experience, "gazing into the anger of old women on the bus." The standard Anglo-American map of emotions may not do justice to Rich's great-hearted imagining, which recalls nothing so much as the Athenian concept of *orge* (cognate with "orgy"), closely linking anger and eros. Anger as the spirited element of the soul, not an unpleasant, aversive emotion (especially if expressed by women): this seems a productive way to approach *Diving into the Wreck,* preoccupied as it is with an anatomy of emotion, not simply polemic.

The poems insist on transvaluation, embodied in startling images—"the faithfulness I can imagine would be a weed/flowering in tar, a blue energy piercing/the massed atoms of bedrock disbelief." But before or alongside imagining, Rich demands accurate registration, which itself produces vividly elemental, estranged visions—of the poet, for example, "compromised/curled in the placenta of the real/which was to feed & which is strangling her." Moments of reverie and dream are the more sharply etched because so provisional or counterfactual, as in "The Phenomenology of Anger":

> I would have loved to live in a world
> of men and women gaily
> in collusion with green leaves, stalks,
> building mineral cities, transparent domes.

Thus the earned pathos when Rich watches her sons in a river, in "Merced,"

>   testing their part
> in a world almost archaic
> so precious by this time
> that merely to step in pure water
> or stare into clear air
> is to feel a spasm of pain.

Diving into the Wreck is a book of deeply American consciousness, alluding to Thoreau and Eldridge Cleaver as well as the My Lai massacre, oscillating between renovation and apocalypse: "I suddenly see the world/as no longer viable." Rich typically undertakes lyric autopsy, not elegy, surveying "[a] man's world. But finished./They themselves have sold it to the machines." Waking in the dark, "in a world masculinity made / unfit for women or men," she wonders "what it all might have become." All are implicated, the poet herself one of "the half-destroyed instruments" of a culture flaming out, of a mythos no longer sustainable: "The tragedy of sex / lies around us, a woodlot / the axes are sharpened for."

Rich's achievement here resonates with that of other prominent poets: her startling images and sharp formulations recalling aspects of Sylvia Plath's late poems; the commitment to a poetics of the notebook, of the diaristic, aligning with aspects of Robert Lowell's last books; her subjecting of lyric to the ascesis of intensifying political engagement, a task undertaken, albeit differently, alongside Denise Levertov, Robert Bly, Galway Kinnell, and Gwendolyn Brooks; her preoccupation with marital and heterosexual crisis pointing to what had become perhaps the great late-twentieth-century American theme.

Rich's charged inscription of a woman's life and consciousness helped to fortify other women poets looking to claim their experience for an authoritative poetry: the Irish poet Eavan Boland, for example, cites Rich as an important groundbreaker. Younger women poets like Rebecca Wolff continue to evoke Rich's example in complex acts of homage: Wolff's "Lamb, Willow: An Arch Dolefulness Has Taken Me Thus Far" in *Figment* (2004) rings an arch yet deeply indebted variation on Rich's *A Wild Patience Has Taken Me Thus Far* (1981). Here and elsewhere we find a feminist, or perhaps postfeminist, poetry that explicitly thinks back through its mothers. And Rich's work post-*Diving* paved the way as well for an efflorescence of openly homoerotic as well as variously politically engaged poetries.

Less noted than Rich's feminism, yet predictive of her future work, was the strong ecological attentiveness informing the poems of *Diving into the Wreck,* with their impulse to map, scrutinize, and, when possible, celebrate the American land- and cityscape. So too her increasing interest in extending the possibilities of dissidence and solidarity emerged in such poems as "For a Sister," addressed to the dissident Soviet writer Natalya Gorbanevskaya. Rich thus harks back to the internationalist-left commitments of poets like Muriel Rukeyser but also presages the "poetry of witness" furthered by, for example, Carolyn Forché, whose poems later testified to the brutalities of El Salvador's regime of generals. In Rich's collection, however, her energies are focused most on witnessing the complexities and agonies of her own mind: "Self-hatred: a monotone of the mind." The mind's hum is objectified, the lurches of thought and heart caught and carved in apparently immediate bursts.

Rich's work belies even as it recalls Yeats's dictum that we make out of the quarrel with others, rhetoric, but of the quarrel with ourselves, poetry: quarrels with others fuel some of the best poems of the book, whereas a few extensions of sisterly fellowship can veer perilously close to sentimentality. A discovery of new forms of solidarity may require its own image-making and emotional mapping, and if the old argument between men and women flared openly, productively, and transformatively in the sixties and early seventies, the possible bonds among women had (and have) a comparatively impoverished history of representation in lyric as well as life. After *Diving into the Wreck,* Rich explored ever more inten sively those bonds and binds, including sexual love between women; in *Diving*, she is poised, taut yet delicate, on the high wire between a totalizing critique of masculinity, and a furious intimate engagement with the pleasures and dangers of what gender theorists call heteronormativity.

The interface of erotics and politics—a great American poetic theme since Whitman—had become especially vexed as the sexual revolution and women's movement offered new possibilities for thinking, living, struggling, and speaking. For women poets, these remained deeply fraught areas. Rich's lyrics avoid a privatization of the sexual, the erotic, or the familial: *Diving into the Wreck* explores how soul-making might relate to *communitas,* how world-making might be a communal project, and whether men and women might embark on it differently, gripped by their different "nightmares." It is a book of hard-won questions, not answers; of attempts, not conclusions—its first word "trying," its last word "why."

Diving into the Wreck is beautifully, rigorously ambivalent, imagining a possible reclamation of both private and public hope through an ethic of care and attention, enacting in other poems a coruscating critique. Some books are balms, others bombs. At the midpoint of her career, Rich offered both.

Bibliography: Jane Robert Cooper, ed., *Reading Adrienne Rich: Reviews and Revisions, 1951–81* (Ann Arbor, MI, 1984). Adrienne Rich, *Adrienne Rich's Poetry and Prose: Poems, Prose, Reviews and Criticism,* ed. Barbara Charlesworth Gelpi and Albert Gelpi (1975; New York, 1993); *Blood, Bread, and Poetry: Selected Prose 1979–1985* (New York, 1986); *A Change of World* (New Haven, CT, 1951); *Diving into the Wreck: Poems 1971–1972* (New York, 1973); *The Fact of a Doorframe: Selected Poems 1950–2001* (New York, 2002); *What Is Found There: Notebooks on Poetry and Politics* (New York, 1993).

MAUREEN N. McLANE

1975

Ursa sings, and her voice can "hurt you but make you want to listen"

GAYL JONES

When Billie Holiday died on April 17, 1959, Gayl Jones, who would become the writer whose fiction most closely approximated the aesthetic values of the great singer, was nearly ten years old. At that young age, Jones was already enthralled by the power of the written word. Her grandmother wrote plays put on at church, and her mother wrote fairy stories and tales about life in rural Kentucky—works, in both cases, to be performed out loud. The power of improvised oral expression, real lived drama reported by kitchen-table yarn-spinners, was evident to the young Gayl Jones. She was not sent from the room when grownups were talking—and adult talk of the ambiguities and cruelties of love and trouble, fights and flights, sometimes of victories, stayed with her. So did the music that expertly testified to the grace of the Holy Ghost and—in the case of recordings by Billie Holiday and certain others—the ever-present power of the blues.

Born in Lexington, Kentucky, in 1949, Jones would go on to become a major, if shamefully underrecognized, writer. She would write four novels: *Corregidora* (1975), *Eva's Man* (1976), *The Healing* (1998), and *Mosquito* (1999); one collection of short stories, *White Rat* (1977); three collections of poetry: *Song for Anninho* (1981), *The Hermit-Woman* (1983), and *Xarque and Other Poems* (1985); and *Liberating Voices* (1991), a book of literary criticism. These works often take black music not only as a key reference but as a model for form. They explore the potential for a working-class black female to engage directly with—and sometimes to gain ground against—the continuing legacies of American slavery and male authority, white and black. Again and again the victories and near victories are secured by women who assert the ineluctable power of their own liberated voices—and of the communities where their values and styles of expression have been nurtured. As a set of books overflowing with the love of black language, these works are related to those of Toni Morrison and Ralph Ellison, most emphatically; but even in the company of these better-known writers, Jones's work displays towering distinctiveness, range, and force. What distinguishes *Corregidora*, her first work, is its compressed eloquence and its insistence upon the blues—and in particular upon the music of Billie Holiday—as an agency of freedom.

Jones published *Corregidora*, a decidedly unsentimental and understated work of echoing power, sixteen years after Holiday's death. (At the time, Jones was still a graduate student at Brown University, where she studied with the poet Michael Harper.) Although the novel mentions Billie Holiday's name only in passing, it explores Holiday's robust but tragic sense of life and aesthetic values with more acuity than any other literary work. The novel prefigures the works of many black women writers who would emerge in the 1970s and '80s—among them, Sherley Anne Williams, Ntozake Shange, Alice Walker, Gloria Naylor—and establish themselves as the artistic daughters and interpreters of black female singers such as Holiday. As these black women writers asserted their own voices within a literary tradition that had long silenced their truths and ignored their formal artistic innovations, they bore witness to—and played their own changes on—her legacy, and on those of the singers who came before her.

Corregidora explicitly addresses the need to bear witness to the experiences of one's foremothers while also expressing one's own. The heroine and narrator of the novel is a gifted blues singer named Ursa Corregidora, who carries the name of a nineteenth-century Brazilian slave master. He turned her great-grandmother into a prostitute and fathered both her mother and her mother before her; Ursa has grown up listening to the stories, from her great-grandmother on down. As the novel opens, in the late 1940s, Ursa has been thrown down the stairs by her husband, Mutt; her fall kills the child she is carrying and prevents her from having any more children. Yet Ursa must somehow obey her mother's, grandmother's, and great-grandmother's imperative to produce children who will sustain the "evidence" of cruelties they suffered during and after slavery. The problem cannot, given Ursa's injury, be solved in the conventional way. How, the novel asks, can this woman "bear witness" if she cannot, literally, bear *witnesses?* If she cannot "make generations?"

Jones creates an innovative form to address this question. She tells Ursa's story through difficult remembrances and in blueslike conversations that are heavy with innuendo and highly significant intervals of silence. There are images that roll with the rhythm of the blues: "I woke up," Ursa Corregidora tells the reader, "to the smell of scorched hair and fried chicken." Like a work by such an artist as Count Basie or Duke Ellington, perhaps an arrangement featuring Billie Holiday along with horns and rhythm, this is a novel in layers and pieces (some call it a "collage-novel"), with sections that "sounded almost as if she [one of the novel's many storytellers] were speaking in pieces, instead of telling one long thing."

This also is a novel that, like a poem or like a song delivered by Billie Holiday, underscores the richness of a limited lexicon by investing certain key words and phrases with multiple meanings. (No one, it has often been observed, could pronounce the words "love" or "hunger" with more meaning than Holiday did.) Phrases from the Holiday canon like "don't explain" and "I'm crazy"—along with a prolonged meditation on "Trouble in Mind," not a song Holiday recorded but that there can be no doubt she often performed—saturate the novel. Note in particular the book's repeated uses of "strained" and "strain," words that suggest so much pertaining to Ursa—not only *pained exertion* and *injury* but also *race* and *ancestral lineage, mood,* and even elements in *music.* (The earliest recorded spirituals, songs that departed from standard hymns, were called "wandering strains.")

In a strained and bluntly flirtatious conversation with Ursa, an unnamed drunken man in a piano bar makes the novel's longest direct statement about Billie Holiday. A singer himself (as he puts it, he is a "*sanger*"), he compliments Ursa, whose "in-the-alley" blues has made him think of Holiday:

> "You know the onliest other time I felt good was when I was in the Apollo Theater. That was a long time ago cause I ain't been back to New York in a long time. But the Lady was singing. Billie Holiday. She sang for two solid hours. And then when she finished, there was a full minute of silence, just silence. And then there was applauding and crying. She came out and was nervous for a full thirty-two seconds. And then she sang. And you see what they done to her, don't you?"
>
> I said, "Yes."
>
> "If you listen to those early records and then listen to that last one, you see what they done to her voice. They say she destroyed herself, but she didn't destroy herself. They destroyed her . . . It's a sin, ain't it? It's a sin and a shame."

Through this speaker, Jones deploys a notion common to descriptions of Holiday's late sound: that of the voice that expresses painful lived experience. One of Ursa's friends follows the same theme when describing Ursa's voice. She tells Ursa that after her injury, her voice has become even more moving because "it sounds like you been through something. Before it was beautiful too, but you sound like you been through more now. You know what I mean?"

After her injury, what Ursa calls her "new voice" "sounds a little strained" and "has sweat in it," as someone else puts it. "You got a hard kind of voice," says another. "You know, like callused hands. Strong and hard but gentle underneath. Strong but gentle, too. The kind of voice that can hurt you. I can't explain it. Hurt you and make you still want to listen." All of which evokes Holiday, whose voice deepened and darkened with the years. Listen to the youthful exuberance of "My Man," from 1936, and then to the version from 1957 — talk-sung in a raspy, oracular voice that could "hurt you and still make you want to listen."

Part of the answer to Ursa's problem of how to "make generations" to sustain her foremothers' memories lies in the "birth" and the procreative power of this new voice: the hard-won creation of a personal and professional identity with which to face and to articulate, to voice, a blues-haunted, wiser sense of life. Ursa has not only returned to singing with a new witness-bearing sound; she also has discovered new dimensions of artistic self-sufficiency and independence. Eventually, she is making her own gowns — not an insignificant thing in a world where a woman artist's appearance is routinely controlled by others. Ursa is writing her own songs again. Ursa has taken more and more control over her music: she is accompanying herself on piano.

Ursa's singing sustains Holiday's legacy; it also carries the legacies of Holiday's artistic forebears. Holiday herself was the artistic daughter of Bessie Smith, Louis Armstrong, and Ethel Waters — and then of the millions of black and unknown women and artists who shaped her. Holiday is also in turn the mother of untold singers after her. In the terms of Jones's novel, Holiday "made generations," literally childless though she was. Yet as Farah Griffin has argued so compellingly, these new singers have typically proclaimed their will to follow Holiday's "strain" only so far. From Abbey Lincoln to Mary J. Blige and beyond, Lady's daughters have stood in her shoes as bold, self-determined musical stylists. Yes, they'll take the lessons about timing, space, improvisation, irony, dramatic delivery, storytelling beyond words in a personal voice that rings with tradition — and perhaps most profoundly the lessons about telling even the ambiguous hurt-you-but-make-you-want-to-listen truth. But they will purge from their lives and from their art the mad, monstrous slave owners, the unreconstructed Mutts, and other killing matrices of control.

By the end of the novel, Ursa and Mutt, whose violent act paradoxically frees Ursa from the possibility of biological parenthood and forces her to consider other ways of making generations, come back together again. True to *Corregidora*'s theme and form as a blues novel, their rough-edged reunion embraces tentative solutions and ambiguities. Those who misread the novel's last scene, of fellatio, as Ursa's surrender to male desire, ignore Ursa's frank assertion: "I knew what he wanted. I wanted it too." What was the "it" that they both wanted? This, I think, is the novel's great question — the one for which, again, sentimental answers will not suffice. What they want is love, but *what is love?* Here is where the witness of Billie Holiday, particularly late Lady Day, is so important. "Billie's Blues" (written and performed by Holiday) states the double-jointed truth with naked starkness:

I love my man
I'm a liar if I say I don't
I love my man
I'm a liar if I say I don't
But I'll quit my man
I'm a liar if I say I won't

In *Corregidora,* this grown-up love realizes not only that real love changes and may end, but that at its best love involves the pleasures and pains of the whole self: body and brain, psyche and soul, history and memory. Holding Mutt's ankles, Ursa thinks, "It was like I didn't know how much was me and Mutt and how much was Great Gram and Corregidora." This was a love that brings psychological re-tracings and subterranean furies to the surface: "I could kill you," Ursa tells Mutt, twice, during this love scene. (Here one recalls that "Mut" was the name of an Egyptian deity, a mother/father figure, Freud says—and in this sense, as Ursa at once embraces and threatens Mutt, she engages the full complexity of her tra-ditions, male and female, pathologies and all.) After the climax, the lovers' quiet exchange—framed in the conversational/call-recall pattern of the blues, with its suggestion that there are no final answers and that improvising together as we go may be the best we can do—recalls the intimate dialogues of Billie Holiday and her soulmate saxophonist, Lester Young:

"I don't want a kind of woman that hurt you," he said.
"Then you don't want me."
"I don't want a kind of woman that hurt you," he said.
"Then you don't want me."
"I don't want a kind of woman that hurt you."
"Then you don't want me."
He shook me till I fell against him crying. "I don't want a kind of man that'll hurt me neither," I said.
He held me tight.

These words close the novel; they comprise a kind of a companion piece to Jones's poem "Deep Song," dedicated to B. H. (Is it for Billie Holiday, one of whose late-career hits was "Deep Song"—or is it for Bob Higgins, the difficult man—a messianic, violent figure who committed suicide in 1998—in Jones's own life?) The poem ends with these bluesy words:

He is a dark man.
Sometimes he is a good dark man.
Sometimes he is a bad dark man.

I love him.

Like *Corregidora,* "Deep Song" refuses to explain, or to explain away, this ambi-guity. It simply requires us to bear it.

It may be personal tragedy that led to Jones's silence after 1999; what she has already written has done what Billie Holiday's body of work has done. Both art-ists helped create one generation after another: people who revere the power of the black female voice and who, with our own sometimes good sometimes bad companions, are inspired to confront our own blues-haunted histories.

Bibliography: Donia Elizabeth Allen, "The Role of the Blues in Gayl Jones's *Corregidora,*" *Callaloo* 25, no. 1 (2002). Sigmund Freud, *Leonardo Da Vinci: A Study in Psychosexuality* (1916; New York, 1945). Farah Jasmine Griffin, *If You Can't Be Free, Be a Mystery: In Search of Billie Holiday* (New York, 2001). Trudier Harris, "A Spiritual Journey: Gayl Jones's 'Song for Anninho,'" *Callaloo* 5, no. 3 (October 1982). Gayl Jones, "Gayl Jones: An Interview" (interview by Michael S. Harper), *Massachusetts Review* 18, no. 4 (Winter 1977). Cynthia J. Smith, "Gayl Jones (1949–)," *African American Writers,* 2nd ed., vol. 1, ed. Valerie Smith (New York, 2001).

ROBERT O'MEALLY

1981, March 31

A "middle aged gray haired colored lady" appears on the cover of *Newsweek*

TONI MORRISON

She had not been there yesterday. She appeared overnight. As the crowd bustled through Grand Central Station that morning in mid-March 1981, some of them noticed her. There, high above their heads, she stood, a brown goddess: all-knowing, solid, and authoritative. Curiosity stopped some commuters, "Who is she?" Others knew exactly who she was. They even may have been captivated by her prose spells and the worlds she created just for them: worlds where ancestors fly, where slain baby girls return as fully grown ghost-women, and where books talk. A few others recognized her as well; they might have looked away dismissively, thinking, "Why her?" And still others rushed past without taking notice at all.

Toni Morrison's appearance on the cover of the March 31, 1981, issue of *Newsweek* and the billboard-size replica of that cover in Grand Central Station heralded her arrival in the upper echelons of the American cultural elite. Among American newsweeklies, *Newsweek* was second only to *Time* (on whose cover Morrison would appear on January 19, 1998). *Newsweek* had a reputation for in-depth coverage of racial issues.

If only Pecola Breedlove could have seen her, on a magazine cover no less. Sula Peace would have been amused at the larger-than-life photograph of the "middle aged gray haired colored lady," as Morrison had referred to herself. Although Pilate Dead couldn't read, she surely would have intuited that her creator, the former Chloe Anthony Wofford, was on the brink of something *big.* But had it really happened overnight?

On that morning a young commuter rushed to the newsstand to purchase the magazine. Had she been familiar with Morrison already she would have cherished the opportunity to know more about this woman and her enchanting prose. Looking at the cover, the young woman noted the matter-of-factness of it. In spite of its extraordinary nature (not since Zora Neale Hurston appeared on the cover of the *Saturday Review* in 1943 had a black woman writer graced the cover of any mainstream publication), Morrison stands there self-assured, certain. This is where she belongs. Her figure does not compete with other images or extraneous print. The *Newsweek* logo sits just above her head, offering an imprimatur of *significance.* The words "Black Magic" sit unobtrusively to the left of her head, and lower down, "Novelist Toni Morrison." It is her world and we are invited to enter. Or are we? In this Richard Avedon photograph, the goddess's hands are not crossed defensively at her chest or sassily on her hips. The arms are lowered, hands clasped just beneath her abdomen, thereby softening the pose. She is at once mother and schoolteacher. There is also the suggestion of something mischievous, of a secret withheld. She wears a smile that isn't quite a smile, warm but not open. And we are drawn to the eyes, big and knowing, framed by perfectly arched brow. Her head is tilted ever so slightly away from the words "Black Magic." Novelist Toni Morrison.

These were the days of Reaganomics and Nancy Reagan Red, the days of cold-warrior Secretary of State Alexander Haig and on television, J. R. Ewing. El Salvador was in the news, and those who dared to call themselves liberals wondered if they would ever return to power. How, in this most conservative of contexts, did Toni Morrison emerge as a major cultural figure? The politics of her narratives shared little with those of the Reagan right. The critique embedded within her fiction was delivered in beautiful, haunting, and melodic prose. When James Baldwin appeared on the cover of *Time* in May 1967, it was largely because of his nonfiction essays and his emergence as a public intellectual who interpreted and articulated black frustration, longing, rage, and desire for reconciliation. Morrison shares much with Baldwin, but her appearance on the cover of *Newsweek* signaled her significance first and foremost as a writer of fiction: "Novelist Toni Morrison." As with Baldwin, her writing continued to bear witness to racial injustice and the devastating power of white supremacy, but perhaps the times themselves would be open to her vision only if it appeared as "art."

The cover story was meant to coincide with the publication of *Tar Baby* (1981), Morrison's fourth novel. *Tar Baby* is positioned between her two greatest works, the virtuosic *Song of Solomon* (1977) and her most influential novel, *Beloved* (1987), for which she would win the Pulitzer Prize. In hindsight, *Tar Baby* seems like an odd choice to have landed her on the cover of a national magazine. It is the novel that differs most from those that precede and follow it. It is the only one of her novels situated in a contemporary context. (Morrison is at her best when her stories are set in the past.) It is the only one that travels outside the borders of the United States and the only one with major white characters. It is also her least appreciated work. But the *Newsweek* article was part of a wide range of media devoted to its publication. Morrison would also appear on talk shows such as *The Dick Cavett Show,* and the novel was widely reviewed.

While the publication of *Tar Baby* provided the opportunity, it is not the reason Morrison appeared on the cover. The novels that preceded *Tar Baby* were the reason that anything she wrote thereafter would warrant attention. PBS had already devoted one segment of the series *Writers in America* to her life and work. *Song of Solomon* had been picked as a Book of the Month Club main selection.

It had been almost forty years since the last time a book by a black writer had been featured by BOMC: Richard Wright's *Native Son* in 1940. *Song of Solomon* also won the National Book Critics Circle Award in 1977. Later in 1981 Morrison would be elected to the American Academy of Arts and Letters.

The *Newsweek* article, written by Jean Strouse (herself an important biographer and New York intellectual), paints a portrait of the black woman artist as a national cultural figure. Strouse, who was *Newsweek's* book editor, remembers that her own editor, Charles Michener, assigned her the profile and that he pushed the idea of the cover story through the "upper echelons" of the publication. Strouse spent nearly six weeks with Morrison, accompanying her to her son's music lessons as well as to television studios. The resulting article is one of the most in-depth and personal pieces in all coverage of Morrison. It does not focus on one novel but on Morrison's work as a whole and her influence as an editor at Random House. It is also an introduction to black women writers and a lesson in African American literary history. It provides an important pedagogical function, and unlike most essays about extraordinary individuals, this one places her in context and community without diminishing the uniqueness of her contribution. As such, it seems to spring from Morrison's own sensibilities.

While black women have been writing and publishing since our nation's beginning, the explosion of new voices in the 1970s and 1980s brought them to the attention of a broader and more varied audience. Strouse's article rightly situates Morrison as part of this movement and as one of its major architects. The essay has all of the apparatus reserved for profiles of important American figures. It is accompanied by photographs of biological family as well as literary sisters, Toni Cade Bambara and Gayl Jones (both of whom Morrison edited) and Alice Walker. In addition there is a "Morrison sampler," paragraphs of prose from her novels.

By the time of the *Newsweek* cover, Morrison had written *The Bluest Eye* (1970), the story of a young dark-skinned black girl who longs for blue eyes and the love that she is sure will follow their attainment; *Sula* (1973), about an unconventional, independent black woman who lives her life with a masculine sense of abandon, and the price she pays for doing so; *Song of Solomon;* and the new *Tar Baby,* a reflection on a post–civil rights generation "New World African woman" who, while reaping the benefits of integration, is estranged from the strength and power of her foremothers. As editor, Morrison had introduced new literary voices (Bambara, Jones, Henry Dumas, Wesley Brown, Leon Forrest) and published poets and essayists (Quincy Troupe, June Jordan, Lucille Clifton) and the autobiographies of American icons (Muhammad Ali and Angela Davis). Literary critic Cheryl Wall notes: "No other editor before Morrison or since has boasted a comparable list of African American writers. As an editor, she helped to define two decades of African American literary history."

From the opening line of *The Bluest Eye,* "Quiet as it's kept, there were no marigolds in the fall of 1941," to its devastating conclusion, this small novel announced the arrival of an extraordinary literary talent. She took the familiar phrase of black women's gossip, "Quiet as it's kept," married it to the magical, "there were no marigolds in the fall of 1941," and immediately brought the reader to her side. Of course we want to know why. The novel established much of what would characterize her later work. Her narratives presented black life as an epic struggle of a people under siege, a wandering people for whom a sense of place is only temporary: "In that place," as Morrison wrote in *Sula*, "where they tore the nightshade and black-berry patches from their roots to make room for the Medallion City Golf Course, there was once a neighborhood." Yet she wouldn't focus on interracial conflict; instead she placed her keen gaze on intraracial relationships across class, gender, and generational boundaries. Not that she let racism off the hook: white supremacy is always there, just under the surface of many of the pathologies that plague her characters. In *Sula*, as elsewhere, there are the meditations on love in its various shapes and forms. And of course, there is her language: grounded in the poetry of the black vernacular, it shares resonances of the King James Bible, Faulkner, and James Baldwin. Although he did not encourage or claim her, Morrison was also heir to Ralph Ellison. If he freed black writers from social realism by insisting that the aesthetic was too limiting for black creative expression, then Morrison would escort them into a realm sometimes associated with magical realism, even into a kind of surrealism. Still, while acknowledging the importance of Ellison, Morrison would claim a more direct literary kinship with James Baldwin. In a eulogy to Baldwin in 1987 published in the *New York Times*, Morrison wrote: "You gave me a language to dwell in, a gift so perfect it seems my own invention." For many literary souls who came of age in her wake, she did the same.

As with any great writer, the originality of Morrison's style is evident in even the smallest detail. There are Morrisonisms that reappear throughout the oeuvre: the presence of three women who share a domestic space, always on the margins, on the outskirts of town, outlaw women for whom sex is not a sin and doing what you have to do to feed self and kin is not a crime. In *The Bluest Eye*, the three whores, Marie, China, and Poland, offer the novel's protagonist, Pecola, the only love and affirmation she receives. In *Sula*, there are the Peace women, Eva, Hannah, and Sula, all of whom love male attention and sex. Then there is the bootleg household of Pilate, Reba, and Hagar in *Song of Solomon*. *Beloved* finds Sethe, her daughter, Denver, and the ghost woman-child, Beloved, all sharing the haunted 124. (In 2006 a panel of distinguished critics named *Beloved* the best American novel of the past twenty-five years.) But in the context of Morrison's novels, women are not all marginal. Dark-skinned little girls, the victims of incest, and pariah grown women sit at the center of her narratives. And just when she is heralded as *the* black woman writer who writes about *the* black female experience, she gives us *Song of Solomon* with a spoiled, privileged, middle-class black man as protagonist.

In addition to her own fiction and her work with other authors, following the publication of *The Bluest Eye* Morrison became an important social commentator and literary critic. Her byline could be seen in a number of publications, including the *New York Times*. In fact, on the pages of the *Times* she engaged in debates about black fiction, black autobiography, and the relationship between black women and mainstream feminism. While she would eschew the role of media figure, she published highly influential essays such as "The Black Woman and

Women's Lib," in which she made distinctions between the aspirations of the women's movement and those of most black American women.

By 1981, Morrison had also started work on a body of literary criticism that would teach critics how to read her own work as well as that of other black writers. Her interviews and short essays would provide a critical framework and vocabulary. Her own work generated a cottage industry of criticism and literary theory. In short, through the sheer volume and brilliance of the work, as well as her influence on other writers, she earned her status as an important literary figure; it was not a status bestowed upon her. Nor did it come overnight.

While it did not establish her status among the literati, the *Newsweek* cover was an important step in the making of Toni Morrison, American literary icon. It marked the beginning of the Morrison era, not its climax. In fact, much of her best work would follow the cover. Her words continue to seduce us, draw us in, envelop us in a magical Morrisonian world of words and images. (For many black women readers, especially, her phrases are so on target in naming the world as they know it.) Morrison's sentences are conceived with a poet's ear and constructed with a painter's eye: "A colored man floats down out of the sky blowing a saxophone, and below him, in the space between two buildings, a girl talks earnestly to a man in a straw hat." Throughout her corpus Morrison renders sound as luscious and indelible as that of the greatest blues masters.

Since her appearance on the cover of *Newsweek,* Morrison has written another five novels: *Beloved, Jazz* (1992), *Paradise* (1998), *Love* (2003), and *A Mercy* (2008). With her son, Slade, she has written a number of children's books, and she has continued to shape public discourse by introducing and editing important collections that provide intelligent analysis of such events as the Anita Hill–Clarence Thomas hearings and the O. J. Simpson verdict. And she has become a profoundly influential literary critic. Her book *Playing in the Dark: Whiteness and the Literary Imagination* (1992) energized the study of literature. The *Newsweek* cover was the beginning of the thrilling but steady march toward the Nobel Prize, which she won in 1993, establishing Morrison as a global cultural figure.

Bibliography: Toni Morrison, "James Baldwin: His Voice Remembered; Life in His Language," *New York Times,* December 20, 1987, section 7, 27. Cheryl Wall, "Toni Morrison as Editor," in *The Cambridge Companion to Toni Morrison,* ed. Justine Tally (Cambridge, 2007).

FARAH JASMINE GRIFFIN

1982

Edmund White steals the sensuous from John Milton

A Boy's Own Story

Upon its publication, *A Boy's Own Story,* Edmund White's autobiographical novel about growing up gay in the 1950s Midwest, was greeted with universal acclaim. Not only was this acclaim widespread—the gay and straight media alike embraced the book—but the praise itself focused on the work's universality. The *New York Times* made a point of saying, "This is not exclusively a homosexual boy's story. It is any boy's story, to the marvelous degree that it evokes the inchoate longing of late childhood and adolescence . . . it may be any girl's own story as well." Certainly, other important gay novels had been published in the decade before the appearance of Edmund White's autofiction, among them Larry Kramer's *Faggots,* Andrew Holleran's *Dancer from the Dance,* and White's own *Nocturnes for the King of Naples,* but none had explored so frankly the nature of childhood sexuality and desire, and none had been so warmly ushered into the literary mainstream. As *Washington Post Book World* proclaimed: "American literature is larger by one classic novel." Such was the excitement surrounding the book's arrival. Gay readers, of course, felt the momentousness of the occasion, thrilled that the novel was published by a trade press ("the august E. P. Dutton," as Robert Gluck remembers), grateful to "see our new identities in the national forum," incredulous that "this book, which treated our sex in such an offhand manner, got past the guards." But straight readers and critics joined in the celebration as well, comparing White to J. D. Salinger, apparently eager to understand coming out as another anguished aspect of coming of age.

The very qualities that made *A Boy's Own Story* potentially shocking to a general audience—its detailed, matter-of-fact depictions of gay sex, the enraptured sensuousness with which White writes about the male body—contained perhaps the secret of its broad success. To quote Adorno, as quoted by White in an essay about his beloved Nabokov, "The universality of beauty can communicate itself to the subject in no other way than in an obsession with the particular." The prose in *A Boy's Own Story* feels guided purely by this principle. In White's world, the magic of the particular is achieved through a direct and impassioned appeal to the reader's senses: when he describes the twelve-year-old houseguest with whom the narrator makes love in the opening chapter of the book, he conjures up a vision of the boy's naked torso in the darkness (a "ghost shirt" created by the lines of his suntan), his slightly acrid smell ("scallions in the rain"), the feel of the fine hair, damp with sweat, on the back of his neck ("just above the hollows the sculptor had pressed with his thumbs into the clay"). The moment is evoked with such deep attention that it becomes impossible not to swoon vicariously with the pleasure and tenderness of the encounter. White is a champion of the sensuous detail, and his work a testament to its power—its ability to vanquish any prejudice or parochialism on the part of the reader, its insistence that one enters fully into the world of the story.

When *A Boy's Own Story* was published, the sheer beauty of the language took on political meaning. White's novel asserted—jubilantly—that gay lives demanded to be written about in a serious and literary way. Moreover, it embraced without shyness or apology the erotic component of gay lives. Before this book, as White remembers, "gay writing had been either very, very fancy and nonsexual, or sexual and pornographic." White insisted that it was possible to be both. In fact, his prose makes a convincing argument that carnality is a necessary element in great writing. When speaking about craft, White uses the term "sensuous" to describe his approach rather than the neutered language favored by writing textbooks, which speak of "concrete" or "sensory" details. If John Milton coined the term "sensuous" in an attempt to avoid the sexual overtones of "sensual," then three hundred years later Edmund White has undone all his hard work; the lush, palpable quality of his writing seems animated by an intense aliveness to sexual pleasure and desire. In White's novel, literary pyrotechnics and passionate content are inextricably linked. At the time, some critics were disconcerted by the tension between the unvarnished subject matter and the dazzling finish of the prose; Alan Hollinghurst, when he reviewed the book on its publication in Britain, was decidedly uncertain in his response. But years later, after he had himself become a celebrated novelist, Hollinghurst acknowledged the crucial lesson he learned from *A Boy's Own Story*, "that there was a need to tell the truth about gay lives, and a belief that those lives deserved the full richness of literary attention."

The richness of that attention has resulted in a wealth of major novels published in the years since, represented most dramatically by the tremendous success of Michael Cunningham's *The Hours* (2000), and by the runoff for the 2004 Booker Prize between Colm Tóibín's *The Master* and Alan Hollinghurst's *The Line of Beauty*. White's once unsettling mixture of sensuality, impeccable craftsmanship, and high style is now widely employed; it has become the hallmark of a contemporary gay aesthetic whose appeal is so far-reaching as to be no longer specifically gay. Its influence can be felt not only in the literary world but also in the choreography of Mark Morris, the screen and television writing of Alan Ball, the films of Todd Haynes (especially the visually luscious *Far From Heaven*), and even in the realm of reality TV, where no aesthetic decisions can be made without the approval of the charming but exacting gay expert.

In *A Boy's Own Story*, White, the most exacting of sensualists, lavishes detail on the boys and men his narrator yearns for, but he also describes with equal fervor the experience of racing across a midnight lake in a motorboat, falling under the spell of an eccentric coquette, or whiling away a long winter afternoon with his slightly murderous sister. In these illuminated moments, White demonstrates that he is as nimble as a landscape painter, a portrait artist, and a dramatist as he is at taking the quickened pulse of sexual desire. He is an incisive social observer as well; with dispassionate and amused precision, he dissects the complicated caste system within the Midwestern upper middle class, the hodgepodge European pretensions of the boarding school he attends, and his own hazy notions about the fraternity that exists among poor people. (Though he is known as the dean of gay American writing, one could argue that White is also an important chronicler of an even more taboo subject: class.)

The novel suggests that these powers of observation are in fact a bitter gift, a skill honed out of necessity and survival, born in a primal moment of betrayal. The narrator's mother grows so exasperated with him that she asks his father, whom he adores and fears, to beat him with a strap. His father complies, and in the process becomes possessed by a terrifying rage. "The belt fell again and again, much too long and much too harshly to my mind, which had suddenly turned strangely epicurean. The solace of the condemned is scorn, especially scorn of an aesthetic stripe. In that moment the vital energies retreated out of my body into a small, hard gland of bitter objectivity, a gland that would secrete its poison through me for the rest of my life." From an early age, the narrator is forced to keep constant, exhausting surveillance over his speech, his comportment, and his enthusiasms in order to ferret out any telltale signs of sissiness. He makes an elaborate study of the popular kids at school, hopeful that with sufficient strategy and subterfuge, he will be mistaken for one of them, and accepted. His dread of homosexuality turns him into a tireless analyzer of manners and mores, just as his parents' betrayal refines his aesthetic sensibility and keen perceptions. In short, what are terrible burdens for the boy prove to be invaluable training for the writer.

A childhood spent feeling powerless and disguised makes this boy into a seemingly deformed creature—unnaturally watchful and detached, with an avidly artistic eye—but in the end he is avenged, for it is the heightened quality of his observations, his alertness to the sensuous world, his aesthete's appreciation for the beautiful image and the glittering sentence, that make Edmund White such a strong writer. In the cauldron of his inspired language a Nabokovian alchemy takes place; like his idol, White writes "phrases so joyful and highly colored that they transform tales of dimwits, freaks and madmen into ecstatic tributes to youth, glamour and the exhilaration of genius." If the raging father, the untrustworthy mother, and the repressive era turned the boy into a freak, then the freak-turned-writer emerges triumphant as the damaged boy is transformed through language into the shining youth.

Since the book's publication, perceptions of gay life have also been transformed, so it is startling to revisit the era in which the novel first appeared—1982—when it was still perfectly acceptable for a well-known radio interviewer to ask Edmund White, "How *do* homosexuals see themselves? Because obviously most of America, which is straight, views homosexuality with disgust and revulsion." The interview covers a great number of topics—including whether homosexuals are born that way, and whether White considers himself a supporter of NAMBLA (the North American Man/Boy Love Association)—but never gets around to *A Boy's Own Story,* despite the fact that this particular show is dedicated to authors discussing their work. White fields these questions with unfailing poise and equanimity and good-humored intelligence; he wears the mantle of spokesman gracefully. Implicit in his genial response is his understanding that given the scarcity of widely available books about "minority" experiences, their authors must inevitably bear the responsibility of speaking to and speaking for the entire group. Indeed, he says that he wrote *A Boy's Own Story* thinking of "a thousand gay men struggling with their sexuality reading over his shoulder," and with fiction's permission he toned down his own extreme precocity as a child in order to render his narrator more recognizable, and thus representative. The fact that his autobiographical novel was met with such overwhelming enthusiasm, and is still considered the seminal coming-out narrative, speaks to how desperately such representation was wanted. In retrospect, White has noted, "I don't think it's really the coming-out gay novel that everyone really needed, even though it was received as such. The boy is too creepy, he betrays his teacher, the only adult man with whom he's enjoyed a sexual experience, etc." But gay readers at the time didn't have the luxury of making such distinctions; it was enough that this book existed; it was enough that White declared himself a gay writer, rather than a writer who happened to be gay.

The appearance of the book at this particular moment feels even more significant, and even more poignant, when one realizes that it coincided with the beginning of the AIDS epidemic. During the same time Edmund White was preparing *A Boy's Own Story* for publication, he was gathering with other concerned men in a New York apartment to discuss alarming reports of "gay cancer." These meetings led to the creation of the Gay Men's Health Crisis, now the oldest and perhaps most important AIDS organization in the country, of which White was a founder. That a gloriously written book about gay life and sexuality should burst into the national consciousness at the very moment when so many gay lives were about to be lost seems almost too ironic to bear. White himself was diagnosed as HIV positive a few years following the novel's publication, and several of his subsequent books grapple directly with the challenges and tragedies precipitated by AIDS.

Paradoxically, the AIDS crisis has completed, on a far larger scale, the work that *A Boy's Own Story* had begun, which was to make homosexuality a much more visible, much more familiar part of American life. So familiar, in fact, that the burning issue has become whether gay literature should even be referred to as such. If White once considered himself partly responsible for that "meretricious tendency, the ghettoization of literature according to minority group status," now he finds himself ceremoniously escorted out of the ghetto and into the canon of the Modern Library series, where his novel's universal status has been cemented. The highest honor to be conferred upon a gay book—is it to be relieved of the adjective "gay"? The near-closing of the Oscar Wilde Bookshop in New York City in 2005 prompted a debate over the usefulness of gay and lesbian bookstores and even the category of gay fiction itself; David Leavitt, a prominent gay novelist, urged readers to step into a "post-gay future" where the titles from a once-segregated shelf would be democratically mixed in with those from general fiction. This vision of inclusiveness is compelling, but one also wonders if the price of inclusion might be a new sort of invisibility. Now that it's been officially anointed, will Edmund White's radical novel get washed away in the wide, muddy, turbulent river of American classics? If there's a young gay reader out there who is searching for another boy's story like his own, one hopes he will be able to find it.

Bibliography: James Campbell, "Out of the Past," *Guardian,* January 22, 2005. Mark Doten, "An Interview with Edmund White," *Bookslut,* February 2007, *www.bookslut.com.* Robert Gluck, "A Boy's Own Story," *Review of Contemporary Fiction,* 16, no. 3 (Fall 1996). David Leavitt, "Out of the Closet and Off the Shelf," *New York Times,* July 17, 2005. Christopher Lehmann-Haupt, "A Boy's Own Story," *New York Times,* December 17, 1982. Don Swaim, "Interview with Edmund

White," CBS Radio New York, January 1, 1983. Edmund White, *A Boy's Own Story,* Modern Library ed. (New York, 2002); "Edmund White Speaks with Edmund White," *Review of Contemporary Fiction* 16, no. 3 (Fall 1996); "Nabokov: Beyond Parody," "Out of the Closet, on to the Bookshelf," "The 'Paris Review' Interview," in Edmund White, *The Burning Library: Essays,* ed. David Bergman (New York, 1994).

SARAH SHUN-LIEN BYNUM

1982
Hip-hop travels the world

WILD STYLE

"So now they're making graffiti on canvases." These are the words of Zoro (Lee Quinones), the young graffiti writer and moral center of the 1982 film *Wild Style,* and they resound with resignation. A reporter is on her way uptown to write a story about the South Bronx's outlaw artists, the kids who have been sneaking into the subway yards late at night to spray-paint their names on trains. She is coming to make them all famous. Soon more people just like her will arrive, offering them vast sums of money for their stories and signatures, and all the graffiti writers and their comrades—the MCs, DJs, and B-boys and girls (later dubbed break-dancers)—will leave their crumbling neighborhood far behind. But Zoro is worried: what of the art? Where does *it* reside? Is it in their paint or in their own trespassing selves? "Graffiti ain't canvases," he scoffs, "graffiti's on the trains and on the walls." He senses that once graffiti migrates downtown, onto the pages of newspapers and magazines, into the dreams of gallery owners and art collectors, nothing will ever be the same. Zoro and his friend stand in the husk of an abandoned building and watch the painted-over trains speed by, each more colorful than the last. "You gotta go out and paint—and be called an outlaw at the same time," he declares. But of course, if you can say it, if you can say you're an outlaw, it is already too late.

When Charles Ahearn began filming *Wild Style* in 1981, he was attempting to capture a sense of restless, rootless idealism that had already passed, if it had existed at all. By 1981 hip-hop was an arts movement, no longer the neighborhood sport of Zoro and his friends; it was global, and it was money. The scene had essentially formed in the early 1970s around seminal Bronx DJs like Kool Herc and Afrika Bambaataa, who specialized in a helter-skelter, anything-goes sound that absorbed the most frenetic bits of rock, soul, funk, jazz, and disco into their mixes. Bambaataa, a former gang warlord, had named hip-hop after an African American term more commonly heard from parents—that "hippity-hop thing." By 1982 hip-hop had already made contact with the rest of the world: the Sugar Hill Gang's 1979 hit single "Rapper's Delight" had traveled the globe, graffiti writers had already crossed over to the gallery scene, and the legendary block parties—powered by pilfered juice from city lampposts—had come and gone, with the DJs and dancers graduating to the nightclubs. Ahearn had witnessed little of this firsthand, having grown up in relative comfort in upstate New York. But he still found the scene thrilling, especially as real-life versions of the Zoro character confronted the vexing question of mass appeal. On one side stood former graffiti writers turned gallery superstars like Keith Haring and Jean-Michel Basquiat; on the other stood figures like Quinones, whose dedication to the "art of the mission" was so staunch that he refused Ahearn's request to film him painting in a train yard. Most stood somewhere in between, trying to figure it all out. To document this turn in the culture, Ahearn began making a film, collaborating with Quinones and an artist and promoter named Fred "Fab 5 Freddy" Brathwaite.

Wild Style depicts the internal struggles of Ray, a sensitive and passionate young man who guards his secret alter ego as Zoro, one of the city's most fabled graffiti writers. As lesser writers find work painting murals or selling canvases to galleries, Ray is paralyzed by his refusal to sell out his craft, whatever that might mean. Perhaps the stubbornness with which he guarded his identity echoed Norman Mailer's romantic view that the New York graffiti writer bore witness to a broken system. It was a form of power that resisted *their* power: "Your name is over their name," he wrote, "your alias hangs over their scene."

In the end, Zoro's integrity is saluted. He wins back his girlfriend—a fellow graffiti writer—and paints a remarkable mural that serves as the backdrop for the film's spectacular outdoor-party finale. It is their own private utopia: nobody is collecting tickets, rival MCs and DJs work the crowd together, and everyone transcends the urban decay just out of the camera's frame, if only for a stolen moment.

Wild Style was supposed to be "authentic," so Ahearn cast the neighborhood's artists and musicians to play approximations of their true selves. As such, it is not a perfect film—far from it. The acting is stilted, the plot thin. But the young men and women of *Wild Style* rise to the conflicts of their characters in a deeply felt way. They embrace the idea of being outlaws, they are charmed by the possibility of being famous, and they know they can't have it both ways, at least not in the local economy of 1982 New York. At the time, this did not seem like something worth thinking about too deeply. Very few of the film's leads dreamed of fame beyond the five boroughs of New York, and even Ahearn imagined his ideal audience to be the film's cast and crew and their friends and family. Ahearn was merely attempting to reflect this modest little part of the world.

Ahearn named the film after "wildstyle," a new, abstract form of lettering that advanced graffiti writers had begun to experiment with. Wildstyle was a dense and beautiful new way of writing graffiti: overlapping, interweaving letters and words threatening to riot. It was utterly indecipherable to the untrained eye, and this was precisely what drew the infidels uptown: the quest for a style that, in some perverse way, denied them—a style for which they would lay out cold cash but never truly understand. The same tension drives the film. While Zoro stands apart, refusing to sever his art's umbilical attachment to the neighborhood, others welcome the cut—what's the harm, they wonder, of writing on a canvas and selling it for irrationally high sums of money? There is something they covet in the status and wealth offered by downtown galleries, even though they seem to know better. When Zoro and his comrades venture into a posh penthouse party held by a gallery owner, they play the roles expected of them, feeding the elites chummy lines about their outsider art and winking at each other from across the room.

It is in that knowing wink that hip-hop would explode. *Wild Style* ends before any of this can happen, the closing credits scrolling as the cream of the city's hip-hop scene party their new society into existence. But the success of the film itself suggested the shape of things to come. *Wild Style* gave substance to the notion that hip-hop was a cultural front, and it allowed that culture the opportunity to travel. It infected youth around New York, throughout the United States, and around the world with a new code of style. Ahearn's screening of *Wild Style* in Tokyo in 1983, for example, is often identified as the moment Japan's fierce hip-hop scene was born.

Not everyone recognized hip-hop for its transformative possibilities. Hollywood regarded the culture of break-dancing as a novel new backdrop for their coming-of-age films. In the years following *Wild Style,* audiences were treated to titles like *Flashdance* (1983), *Breakin'* (1984), and *Beat Street* (1984), dull, lifeless knockoffs that were nonetheless influential in promoting what then seemed a great, soon-to-pass fad.

But hip-hop's ascension from the hyperlocality of specific Bronx streets to galleries, record labels, radio, and television meant that it had already grown beyond the cradle-cup of New York. Hip-hop was tailor-made for a postmodern age, when skepticism—of authentic origins, of universalism, of notions of humanistic progress—reigned supreme. What few realized at the time was that hip-hop was more than merely a bundle of expressive arts. It was a new way of thinking, a survival tactic, a philosophy of freedom, a blueprint for the new world. As art, hip-hop was a novel enough intervention. But animating it was a process that threatened to destroy and rebuild the norms of culture and speech.

The most notable example of this was hip-hop's embrace of "sampling," an aesthetic that ignored nothing in its never-ending quest for raw material. Anything was fair game for appropriation; anything familiar could be remade as something strange and new. Graffiti writers riffed off corporate logos and familiar cartoon characters, while rappers adapted everything from nursery rhymes and prison poetry to political slogans and masterpieces of the Western canon. DJs and producers continued to tinker with hip-hop's sonic possibilities, moving from the abrasive, minimalist sound of the mid-1980s to the cut-and-paste collages of the late 1980s, which "sampled" the best melodies, bass lines, horn stabs, and drum patterns of existing songs. Even after the copyright lawyers showed up, DJs and producers adapted by shredding their samples into indistinguishable units to be rearranged at will. It was this resiliency, this capacity for shape-shifting with style, that allowed hip-hop to survive as both an idea and a practice.

While sampling echoed accepted artistic practices of pastiche and collage, hip-hop's late-1980s growth tapped into simmering anxieties about the nature of creativity and cultural production. What separated parody from tribute from ob-

scenity? When did borrowing become theft? And who was allowed to draw the
lines in the sand and on the stand? As hip-hop slowly began dominating the cultural conversations of the 1990s, the range of questions expanded. It forced its
listeners to think about origins—not just of the music itself, but of the historical
legacies that converged in its creation. Was hip-hop petty voyeurism or a referen-
dum on issues of race, class, and gender? Could the cultural capital of hip-hop be
converted into political power?

It had all started innocently enough for the kids in the Bronx, as a way to pass
time while the city fell apart around them. By the mid-1990s, however, hip-hop
had become a remarkably huge and all-encompassing cultural and commercial
force. It was an animating spirit in the work of such writers as Junot Díaz, Zadie
Smith, Paul Beatty, and Jonathan Lethem, and poets such as Sarah Jones and Saul
Williams. Hip-hop influenced theater and film, cartooning—Aaron McGruder's
path-breaking *Boondocks*—and graphic design. It inflected nearly every form of
expression imaginable. And it became a subject for academic study, as colleges
and universities began recognizing rap as a contribution to the American language.

Of course, just as *Wild Style* inspired a string of counterfeits, the staggering
sales of hip-hop music created problematic new possibilities of wealth. "Blackness" and urban multiculturalism became marketing tactics: hip-hop was, quite
literally, changing the face of American culture. The music became a mere
stepping-stone for bolder, more profitable pursuits, as rappers opened restaurants, started fashion lines, and became commercial pitchmen. As J., the disillusioned African American journalist in Colson Whitehead's *John Henry Days*
(2001), sighs, "Both he and the music are jaded. They grew up together and are
too old to pretend that there is anything but publicity."

J. is thirty-something, well-educated, cunningly smart, and professionally successful. Yet he is deeply cynical about the culture around him; he never seems
comfortable in his own skin. Long ago, hip-hop—"the music of his teenage
years"—meant something to him. It was an identity. He imagines what it must
have been like to be there at the very beginning, to witness the "cobbled-together
and gaffer's-taped sound system" transporting dancers far away from their grim
Bronx basketball courts. He imagines going there now and leaning on the chain-
link fence, looking in at where these parties of world-historical importance once
went down. Just as with *Wild Style*, J. wishes to return to that moment, to be privileged with the secret that will change the world.

But what does one find here, on our side of the chain-link fence? Perhaps hip-
hop's greatest contribution is the ease with which it inhabits contradiction. It is
the idea that a code interlaces the randomness of street violence, that even ad-
dicts have principles and outlaws have limits. It is a team of self-made men. It
is situational morality capable of rationalizing anything. It is an omnigenre, a
sponge capable of absorbing anything, even a poor white rapper from Detroit.

Our intellect recognizes hip-hop as artifice and performance, but it preys on
our soul's desire for authenticity, realness, heroism. It is a barbed criticism of the
powers that be and the structures that hem us in, yet it aspires to the limitless fu-

tures that that system promises us. It is Stringer Bell, the hypnotically charming gangster of the television series *The Wire* (2002–2008), sitting awkwardly in a community college classroom and trying to learn the ways of a legitimate businessman—it is simultaneously appalling and deeply inspiring.

The eruption of style that began in the Bronx in the 1970s permanently transformed the look and feel of American culture. More important, it has emboldened those who yearn to remake culture in their own image—those who strive to make a language of quotation. There is no greater symbol of hip-hop's ascension to the mainstream of cultural forms than Sean "Puff Daddy" Combs, an occasional performer and a freakishly gifted executive. In the late 1990s, Combs began staging extravagant parties in the Hamptons, New York's playground of the rich. No longer were Zoro and his friends crashing high society; Combs was now one of them, an arriviste hosting the old and the moneyed. He was new for the time, a character nobody had ever encountered before. Hip-hop—as both a culture and a business—had made him possible. Upper-crust partygoers and business associates were seduced by Combs's style, and they continued to compare him to Jay Gatsby, the doomed striver of F. Scott Fitzgerald's *The Great Gatsby.* No doubt they meant it as a compliment. But behind his sunglasses, Combs eyed a world of new possibilities: the green light, the orgiastic future that year by year awaits, the tomorrow when we will all run faster.

Bibliography: Jeff Chang, *Can't Stop Won't Stop: A History of the Hip-Hop Generation* (New York, 2005). David Toop, *Rap Attack: African Jive to New York Hip-Hop* (Boston, 1984). Colson Whitehead, *John Henry Days* (New York, 2001). *Filmography: Wild Style,* directed by Charles Ahearn (1982).

HUA HSU

1982
"The point is to see yourself reflected in the names"

MAYA LIN'S WALL

The story still seems improbable, despite its endless retelling: it was a twenty-one-year-old student, and a woman at that, who won the commission to commemorate the some 58,000 U.S. soldiers who died or went missing in the Vietnam War. What were the odds of this particular fairy tale's really coming true? Any prudent bookie would surely have said that the outlook was dim. For a start, the manifold losses inflicted by the war in question were hardly forgotten, not when both individual lives and the nation's integrity had fallen victim to the strife. Could any memorial find the means to salve such wounds? And what if those means had been dreamed up by the unknown, untried Maya Lin, a Yale College senior from Akron, Ohio? A real gamble: say 1,420 to 1.

The one was Lin, the sole member of her funerary architecture class (besides the professor) to figure among the outpouring of entrants (1,421 in all) in a competition that also drew some of the country's best designers (Frank Gehry, Steven Holl, Rodolfo Machado, Jorge Silvetti) and most august architectural firms (Skidmore, Owings and Merrill; Shepley Bulfinch Richardson and Abbott). She had no degree, no backers, no accreditation, and no experience. All that stood in her favor was the fact that the competition was open and anonymous—nothing more. Except, of course, that she was young, gifted, well educated, passionate, full of gumption, Chinese American, female, and too young to remember the war as much more than the backdrop to her childhood years. All these qualities inevitably shaped her design—how could it be otherwise?—and it is a painful irony that only when these key determinants were hidden behind a mute number—Entry 1026—did she stand the slightest chance of winning out. Her victory was unanimous, and the distinguished jury—all male, all over sixty—entirely convinced: "All who come here," they declared categorically, "can find it a place of healing."

Here, alas, is where the fairy tale starts getting grim. Lin's triumph did not mean that she and her design lived happily ever after. Instead the trials both underwent ring the changes on the themes of nation, gender, and power so amply present at the outset in the competition itself. Ogres appeared. Vitriol flowed freely. Sides were drawn left and right. On one, the likes of H. Ross Perot, the financial sponsor of the contest (and future presidential candidate); James Watt, secretary of the interior under Ronald Reagan (who temporarily stopped construction by withholding the necessary permit); and Tom Wolfe, a phrase-making conservative journalist ("a perfect piece of sculptural orthodoxy," he opined). Little wonder that the heat-seeking antifeminist Phyllis Schafly saw fit to speak out in the name of the Moral Majority. On the other, the rather less numerous defenders of the design—for example, senators Charles Matthias and John Warner, themselves Vietnam veterans and supporters from the start. Somewhere in the middle, and far from consistent in its public position, stood the group that had actually commissioned and paid for the memorial, a particularly determined (and still extant) veterans association, the Vietnam Veterans Memorial Fund (VVMF), the brainchild of the former infantry corporal Jan C. Scruggs. Scruggs was a grunt who, having enlisted at nineteen, was soon enough wounded in battle, an experience that helped to catalyze his mission to speak and act on behalf of the men with whom he served. Under his direction the VVMF collected at least $8 million dedicated to the realization of the memorial. Of this sum Lin saw $20,000 —on the great scale of things, little more than spare change.

Despite the fixed positions of the major protagonists, it won't quite do to suggest that Lin and the VVMF were opponents in the dispute, at least not in any simple way. Yet they were not precisely allies either. Each had their own battles to fight. Lin, for her part, was frequently called upon to defend the integrity of her design during the course of its realization. Not easy: not only did she consult a lawyer for guidance, but she also turned to Miss Manners (Judith Martin) for help devising a persona—a means of self-presentation—that played by the Washington rules. Good-bye cutoffs, hello business attire, or whatever else was needed to avoid being patronized by men in suits.

Meanwhile the VVMF felt real pressure from a few vocal and well-organized members of its veteran base, including at least one author of a failed design. To such opponents it did not seem to matter that Lin's design took the contest's every proviso to heart. The Wall's expanse amply provided for the inscription of the names of the U.S. dead and missing. (Here, as with so many other memorials since World War I, which catalyzed the work of Edwin Lutyens at Thiepval, such a listing was standard for commemorations of the losses of the rank and file.) Its sleek surface and recessive profile, which put its upper edge flush with the earth, gave it the necessary reflective and contemplative character. Thanks to its radical abstraction, it apparently avoided any political statement about the war. Lin's schema gave its patrons exactly what they asked for, in starkly simple terms: two somber black granite planes that climb from ground level and meet to make an enormous open chevron backed by mounded earth. At their juncture they rise ten feet high. Each wing is devoted to the seemingly endless roster of names, and each is fronted by an inclined walkway leading into and away from the chevron's crux. Visitors are meant to tarry along this pathway, and in their checkered passage to encounter graphic evidence of the war's human toll.

But this is not all. This brief description hasn't yet touched on what is most original to Lin: precisely how she decided to treat the roster of the dead. Her solution means everything for her conception of the memorial as figuring—even materializing—the war as a "segment of time." To put the matter in a nutshell: rather than alphabetically—the usual solution—the names appear chronologically, according to date of death. Some days show many more names than others; some months and years do the same. The result of this simple variation on the customary convention is a means to represent the pace and costs of the war, the days when the fighting was at its hottest, the weeks and months of lives expended in a losing campaign. And what is more, to weigh the losses oneself—to register their waxing and waning over time—is to trace and retrace one's steps back and forth along the Wall. This is because of Lin's treatment of the monument's meeting point, the juncture that is both its physical vertex and conceptual crux. There two dates appear: overhead, on the right-hand panel, 1959, the year America began to send troops to the Vietnamese jungles; on the left, at ground level, 1975, the year of the final retreat. There, in other words, the time represented in (or encompassed by) the memorial begins and ends. And this is decisive for how the Wall is seen.

Say, for example, that a viewer has approached from the south, as most do; the way inevitably leads straight to this temporal hinge. Only then does it become clear how the work is ordered, where it stops and starts. Its ending is also its beginning (and vice versa), and to register the names of the dead, even superficially, is to proceed along the remaining half of the chevron. Yet to leave the work at that point is impossible, even though the walkway comes to an end. Instead, to experience how the war reached its final chapter (to take bodily cognizance of its temporal layout), viewers cannot help but retrace their steps to the "entrance," and there start again.

The results of these decisions are enormous. In so radically divorcing the

The Vietnam Veterans Memorial, Washington, D.C.

Photograph by James P. Blair, National Geographic (Getty Images)

physical structure of the memorial from its temporally ordered conception, even while engaging the two on a rhetorical or allegorical level, Lin built into her memorial a way to visualize, even materialize, time. And the door thus stands open to the various ritualized habits and observances that viewers were quick to devise.

But this gets ahead of the story. To understand how the Wall operates as a memorial—the kinds of behaviors it both solicits and enables—depends on grasping why responses to the "black gash," so called, were so venomous. Why did they so promptly lead to a countermonument, the alternative memorial *Three Fighting Men*? Designed by the figurative sculptor Frederick Hart and inaugurated in 1984, the work stands as a wholesale corrective to the "errors" of the Wall: its abstraction, its conceptual ordering, its refusal to deploy any sort of sculpted simulacrum of the bodies of the dead. Lin makes them merely names, too many to remember, too many to count. They simply accumulate, to repeat, with the passage of time. And then there was the Wall's earthbound character: horizontal, not vertical, it offered no transcendence, no glory, no blinding glints of white.

What Hart (who called himself a humanist) bemoaned above all, however, was the self-evident absence of the sculpted male body—in other words, the lack of (masculine) figurative form. This was what cut closest to the quick. Though not a veteran, he counted himself among the soldiers' too few friends and champions, and pointedly compared his easy knowledge of their mores ("I became close friends with many vets, drank with them in the bars") with Lin's (inevitable) distance from the world of war. Little wonder that when a new design was sought by the Wall's opponents, Hart, whose own submission to the competition had placed third, was all too ready to comply. Only at the last minute was Lin spared having to witness Hart's sculpture being sited within the arms of her chevron, on axis with the crux of her work.

Thank heaven for small mercies. Though not out of sight of the Wall, *Three Fighting Men* stands apart, in its own shady grove. And while the gap between them can be covered in a matter of moments, there is no bridging of the conceptual gulf that keeps them apart.

Hart's group tries to be popular and realistic—not necessarily compatible goals. On the one hand, the men's gear is quasi-photographic. It aims at authenticity, but instead imparts a period flavor, not least because the sculptor collected and copied items that, like their owners, had seen service: one man's battered combat boots, another's worn-out hat. Yet these props fit their bronze wearers with real discomfort, because Hart had no appropriate model of popular masculinity he was able to deploy. For if popular nowadays mostly means mythologized or commodified, then the sculpture, its realism notwithstanding, amply fits the bill. Its virile soldiers are would-be Rambos, their bulging muscles more like Hollywood than life. The same with their ethnic good looks. In their utter falsity, these bodies mock war's true reality, the fact of death.

In the end what was most provocative about Maya Lin's memorial—and most disturbing to its opponents—is its willingness to dispense entirely with any evocation of the bodies of the fallen. Which is to say her conception underscores—

even replicates—a central, irrefutable fact. Death is loss. When translated into sculpture, bodily absence may register as poignant or threatening, necessary or unbearable; viewers, Hart among them, have always responded and continue to respond in all these ways. But one thing is certain: with the body and its surrogates so thoroughgoingly banished by the work's abstraction, various animating rituals have been revived or devised to take its place. When viewers visit the Wall, they often supplement its blank surfaces by leaving some relic or talisman—a letter, flowers, photographs, a piece of clothing their loved one once wore—against its slick black planes. And they may well depart with a pencil rubbing of his name. (All the names on the wall, save those of eight female nurses, are male.) This pattern of giving and taking stretches back centuries and has been found at the holiest of sites. When it happens at the Wall, however, there can be no doubt that it responds to—is catalyzed by—Lin's radical simplicity of form.

So, speaking of fairy tales, does the nation's capital really possess a place where such time-honored rituals continue against all odds? Can this be true? Well, yes and no. The Wall is still a place of pilgrimage, and will surely remain so in years to come. How long, there's no telling, though the question arises, of course. Yet, strangely enough, the memorial's popularity has not forestalled the construction of several simulacra: reproduction Walls. There are now not one, but two different half-size fiberglass replicas, one sponsored by the VVMF itself. The latter tours the country with tireless regularity, stopping at a courthouse here, an armory there, next the local park. It is this version—this peripatetic knockoff—that has been christened *The Wall That Heals*. Meanwhile, for the real stay-at-homes, the VVMF has inaugurated The Virtual Wall: go to *www.vvmf.org* and take a tour. The site exists to allow visitors to post personal memories—photos, tapes, and texts—of those who died.

Do not be too certain that these simulacra can only detract from the Wall's aura. Remember that in the eyes of the faithful, a carved crucifix can summon the Passion, and socialize it; so much the better when the single object is the center of a life-size tableau. Yet there is something that the various virtualizations of the Wall (electronic and otherwise) cannot offer, a capacity that Hart's *Three Fighting Men* also lacks. This is its highly polished surface, which, as Lin put it, allows you "to see yourself reflected in the names." It is this coming together of life and death in a single optical moment that may be what is most powerful about this memorial—this, and that seeing yourself in the names also means that the names inevitably appear in you.

Bibliography: Daniel Abramson, "Maya Lin and the 1960s: Monuments, Time Lines, and Minimalism," *Critical Inquiry* 22, no. 4 (Summer 1996). Kristin Ann Hass, *Carried to the Wall: American Memory and the Vietnam Veterans Memorial* (Berkeley, CA, 1998). Elizabeth Hess, "A Tale of Two Monuments," *Art in America* (April 1983). Karal Ann Marling and Robert Silberman, "The Statue Near the Wall: The Vietnam Veterans Memorial and the Art of Remembering," *Smithsonian Studies in American Art* 1, no. 1 (Spring 1987). Marita Sturken, *Tangled Memories: The Vietnam War, the AIDS Epidemic, and the Politics of Remembering* (Berkeley, CA, 1997).

ANNE M. WAGNER

1982, November 8

The rediscovery of *Our Nig* is reported in the *New York Times*

HARRIET WILSON

A penniless black woman scribbler is hunched over a table, writing, brooding, stealing time in order to commit a few more lines to paper. Sequestered in a poorly heated room off the kitchen, she tries to gather her thoughts and weave the fragments of memory into narrative as her hands and feet grow numb from the cold. She banishes the vision of the poor house and of her child (a ward of the state boarding with strangers), only through the strenuous effort of trying to find the right words. She doubts herself, crosses out the first sentence, and starts again, wondering whether she should use "her" or "me," all the while calculating the costs and the consequences, all the while disbelieving that anyone will be interested in her tale, but struggling to convince herself of the contrary.

Had any dared to suppose that she might exist, or anticipated that there were other women writing in the nineteenth century besides Harriet Jacobs and Frances Ellen Watkins Harper? Unnamable ancestors and unremembered, albeit remarkable, foremothers had charted a path for us, a path that they were unable to secure, largely because no one noticed or honored it, and which we were required to find again and again. How many lost lives, minor victories, and obscure works were waiting to be unearthed?

With all the hope and the hubris that accompanies every pronouncement of discovery, Henry Louis Gates, Jr., introduced *Our Nig* to the national public in 1982 and bestowed upon Toni Morrison and Alice Walker and Toni Cade Bambara and Gloria Naylor an as-yet-unheard-of literary foremother. *Our Nig; or, Sketches from the Life of a Free Black, in a Two-Story White House, North,* which by all objective measures had been a failure in its own time and had been lost to American letters for more than a century, was recast as the antecedent of triumph and possibility in our times. The promise of this literary feat: dead letters could be resuscitated and the unnoted made canonical. If this were at all true or even remotely possible, then one hundred and twenty years of literary oblivion might be less painful to bear.

How is an obscure and forgotten work transformed and remade into the precursor of literary achievement? How does a neglected and minor author acquire significance? While Gates's discovery provided black women writers with another literary forebear, it was also clear that the daughters' success had, in turn, created a place for forgotten and lost mothers. In 1981, Toni Morrison had been the first black woman to appear on the cover of *Newsweek* magazine. In 1983, Alice Walker won the Pulitzer Prize and the National Book Award for *The Color Purple.* It was a time in which it was possible to imagine black literary foremothers and, as well, to reclaim them.

 In Search of Our Mothers' Gardens: Womanist Prose (1983) contained Alice Walker's landmark essay on black female creativity, explored the historical and social forces that thwarted the black female imagination, and dared ask: "What did it mean for a black woman to be an artist in our grandmothers' time? . . . It is a question with an answer cruel enough to stop the blood." Wondering how all those mothers and grandmothers and great-great-grandmothers "who had dreamed dreams that no one knew," "moved to music not yet written," and "waited for a day when the unknown thing that was in them would be made known" had survived without creative outlets, Walker turned her attention to the quotidian and the domestic. The discovery of *Our Nig* lent literary credence to the claim made by Walker and other black feminist intellectuals and writers: black female genius hadn't sprung whole cloth from nothing; it too possessed a genealogy. And *Our Nig* was the mother's signature.

 The literary debut of *Our Nig* stripped away Harriet Wilson's veil of anonymity and placed her within the ranks of Wheatley, Douglass, and Jacobs. It is important to say that *Our Nig* had never been entirely forgotten, even if Harriet Wilson had. Published in 1859, *Our Nig* had appeared in bibliographies of Negro literature, and the rare-book dealer from whom Gates purchased the book described the author in catalog copy as the "first black woman novelist." The nagging questions that plagued Wilson's identity—who exactly was the author and could it be proven that she was a black woman?—were the ones that Gates, in part, resolved.

 What foremother could be more obscure than a *nig?* As a title, *Our Nig* brings into view the anonymous, the despised, and the exploited. The malediction announces the violence of defacement and the identity produced as its consequence. By employing it, Wilson attempted to represent a milieu outside the realm of visibility and beyond the concern of abolitionists and enlightened Northerners. The racism and exploitation that free blacks experienced in the North wasn't readily or willingly discussed in abolitionist circles. In choosing "Our Nig" as the authorial signature, Wilson tried to capture the vulnerable lives confined in this zone of opacity while remaining ensconced within it. The "narrations and sketches" rendered Wilson's life, through the protagonist Frado, as representative of the wretched, but without casting the author as an exceptional subject. The reluctance to call attention to herself as authorial subject can be attributed in large measure to the fear of reprisal from Northern whites, whose racism, as Wilson had depicted it, was no less cruel or violent than that of their Southern counterparts. The agency of writing as she envisioned it had less to do with writing her way into humanity than with securing the financial means to ensure a more than meager life. The narrative takes no obvious delight in the mastery of form; it is not a preening novel, nor is there a scene of instruction deployed to establish the girl's humanity or even a line of demarcation between Frado, the black girl, and Fido, her dog.

 In his introduction to the 1983 reissued edition of *Our Nig,* Gates speculates about the one-hundred-year oblivion into which Harriet Wilson disappeared and wonders whether this condition "resulted from the boldness of her themes"—

racism in the North, interracial sexual unions and marriage, the precariousness of freedom for blacks North and South—and "from turning to that hated epithet, 'nigger,' both for title and authorial, if pseudonymous, identity." Whether Harriet Wilson's oblivion resulted from this boldness is an open question. But one can say with certainty that *Our Nig* accurately and tragically anticipated a future that replicated the present and from which she desperately sought to escape.

Born in 1825 in Milford, New Hampshire, Harriet E. Adams Wilson was an indentured servant, an abandoned wife, and an impoverished and struggling single mother forced to place her son in a county home for the poor. Dire circumstances induced her to take up the pen and "experiment" with writing in a bid for survival. No doubt Harriet Wilson hoped, as had other black writers and storytellers before her, that recounting her past might make a difference for her future. Although the novel is autobiographical, Wilson narrated her story with minimal self-disclosure or, more aptly, cloaked by anonymity. The risk entailed in telling an unwelcome story, a tale likely to anger and alienate white abolitionists and Northern "friends of the negro," would be worth it, if it provided the financial means for Wilson's survival and that of her child. It was a gamble she didn't win.

Frado, the protagonist of *Our Nig*, was a poor black girl who was orphaned by the death of her African father, abandoned by her white mother, and indentured to a cruel mistress who brutalized her. In representing Frado's life, Wilson sought to demonstrate that slavery's shadows fell even in the North and that racism was no less cruel or life threatening in a two-story house in New Hampshire. In offering her "crude narrations" for public scrutiny, the author walked a fine line between exposing Northern racism and the hypocrisy of white abolitionism, and purposefully omitting "what would most provoke shame in our good anti-slavery friends at home."

By her own admission, *Sketches from the Life of a Free Black* was a plea for help, which, if heeded, or, at the very least, noticed, would aid Wilson in maintaining herself and her child. The author's preface states plainly that by writing the narrative she hoped to escape poverty and despair: "Deserted by kindred, disabled by failing health, I am forced to some experiment which shall aid me in maintaining myself and child without extinguishing this feeble life."

The faithful band of supporters who Wilson hoped would rally around her when the book was published failed to appear. Neither white abolitionists eager to eradicate slavery's appurtenances in the North nor colored brethren desiring to help a sister in need replied to Wilson's appeal. The narrative attracted no notice. The life of a black girl in a "Two-Story White House, North" failed to solicit the attention of a single reviewer or journalist or politician. By no fault of her own, Wilson's literary efforts were not able to sustain her "feeble life" or that of her son. If she, like other writers, hoped that her words might at the very least provide evidence that she had existed and a small safeguard against oblivion, then this expectation too was defeated.

Like so many of the exceptional and incomparable acts of the oppressed, the publication of *Our Nig* was a nonevent. The text was not heralded as the first novel written by a black woman, or as the first autobiography of a black indentured servant; nor were the character of black letters or the constituents of a national literature debated in the wake of its appearance. No one compared *Our Nig* to *The Scarlet Letter* or *The Heroic Slave* or *Clotel* or wondered how black female scribes might transform the world of letters.

It comes as no surprise that few remembered the life of an indentured black woman and an impoverished writer; phrases like "feeble life" and "ugly black dog" and "evil nig" suffice to explain it. Few acts of black women are deemed epochal or recognized as catalysts for those moments when new subjects and aspirations emerge and old identities and beliefs die. Wilson's novel troubled the divide between slavery and freedom by challenging the symbolic topography of North and South and detailing the ways in which subjection defined the experience of freedom. By so doing, she anticipated what would become conundrum, crisis, and the counterrevolution of property. Yet in the grand narrative of history, *Our Nig* found its place in the pile of ruins, in the detritus, in the waste.

The 1859 publication of *Our Nig* was momentous for few beyond the author. The indifference with which the novel was received is startling, precisely because of the accomplishments of the narrative. It is not an exaggeration to suggest that Wilson's achievement resides in representing "a portion of unimagined existence," to borrow the words of James Agee, and finding an innovative form, which weds the sentimental novel and the slave narrative. Seduction, bondage, escape, and the marriage plot were especially suited to depicting "up South" and the collusion of slavery and freedom in the republic. Wilson translated into prose the life of an unknown and created an account, a red record, which, like its protagonist, Frado, would pass from memory, disappearing into the ranks of those "swallowed by history."

Less than six months after the publication of *Our Nig,* Wilson's seven-year-old son, George, died of fever. Her hope had been defeated. Wilson was unable to save her son's life with the publication of her narrative, but in a cruel twist of fate, his death certificate rescued her from literary oblivion. At the time of its republication, the only extant proof of Harriet Wilson's identity was her son's death certificate. "The death certificate of George Mason Wilson established that 'Mrs. H. E. Wilson'—the name that appears on the copyright page of the first edition of *Our Nig* . . .—was a black woman, apparently the first to publish a novel in English."

Harriet E. Wilson did not write another book after *Our Nig.* Had she decided to abandon a path that had not been fruitful, or at the very least, that failed to produce the outcome for which she had hoped? Or had her continued poverty and itinerancy made writing too difficult? Or did she abandon writing because she had chosen a different medium of communication?

Wilson believed in the possibility of reanimating dead lives. Less than a decade after the publication of *Our Nig,* Harriet Wilson had become an important spiritual medium in Boston, praised for her talents in communing with the dead. As a spiritual medium, Wilson was able to encounter again all those whom she had loved and lost. With this in mind, perhaps we do best to understand the rediscovery of *Our Nig* as faith in the possibility of redeeming the dead and enabling the forgotten to live with us, and to live again. For what is rediscovery if not a second chance at life, or, at the very least, an opportunity to become "part of the memory of our century."

No doubt Wilson would have been surprised that, albeit belatedly and a century too late to be of any use, the narrative did outlive her.

Bibliography: Leslie Bennetts, "An 1859 Black Literary Landmark Is Uncovered," *New York Times,* November 8, 1982, C13. Alice Walker, *In Search of Our Mothers' Gardens: Womanist Prose* (New York, 1983). Harriet E. Wilson, *Our Nig; or, Sketches from the Life of a Free Black, in a Two-Story White House, North,* repr. with introduction by Henry Louis Gates, Jr. (1859; New York, 1983).

SAIDIYA V. HARTMAN

1985, April 24

Henry Roth overcomes a writer's block that had lasted half a century

CALL IT SLEEP AND SHIFTING LANDSCAPE

Henry's shuffling approached, and stopped. "What's taking you so long," he said. From underneath the bed I could see his slippers and the rubber end of his stick. "I can't get it out," I said. "It's stuck." I turned on my back, raised my knees, and pushed against the sagging underbelly of the bed. Faint dust rained on me. The big box moved a little. I tried again.

"When in doubt," he said, "swear."

"That's what I've been doing. It won't come."

"Swear again," he said.

I did, and the box moved. I turned on my stomach and crawled backward, dragging the box out with me.

Henry shuffled back to his armchair in the kitchen. I picked up the box and carried it to the round table. I set it in front of him, and sat down. He was looking through the window toward the open chain-link gate of the mobile home park. A stretch of the Sandia Crest was visible through the top branches of the eucalyptuses.

"What you waiting for," he said. "Start taking the damn stuff out."

I had asked him if he ever thought of collecting his published pieces other than *Call It Sleep.* He had looked at me, smacking his lips. He always did that when he was thinking. "Who the hell would be interested?" he said.

"Critics," I said. "People who'd like to know about you."

He looked out through the dusty windowpane. A light breeze moved the leaves of the dusty trees above the row of mobile homes. "There isn't enough to make a book," he said.

"Let's see what you have." I took a pad of yellow paper and started. First, "Broker" and "Somebody Always Grabs the Purple," the *New Yorker* stories with which at the end of the thirties Roth tried to whip up a literary career that was going nowhere. Then the two stories published in *Commentary* in 1959 and 1960. I added "Final Dwarf," then "The Surveyor." Henry was looking at me. I could see he was more amused than interested.

"Nature's First Green," I said, and wrote it down.

"That's only four pages."

"Doesn't matter," I said. "Everything."

He chuckled. "Some literary career."

Then interest prevailed over amusement. "In my freshman year at CCNY I wrote a paper for English Composition One. It was supposed to be an expository kind of paper but I did something else and called it 'Impressions of a Plumber.' I got a D in the course but the teacher had it published in the students' magazine." He laughed. "But you don't want *that*."

"Of course you do," I said.

"Well." He mused for a few moments. Then, without looking at me, he said: "*You* do the book." He smacked his lips. "There's a big box under the bed. Go get it. There may be something else. Besides a lot of dust."

This is how *Shifting Landscape: A Composite, 1925–1987,* Henry Roth's first book since *Call It Sleep,* was born. It was the twenty-fourth of April, 1985, almost exactly half a century after the novel's publication in December of 1934.

The idea was to collect all the writings, independently of their literary value, that over six decades Roth had published in various magazines, journals, dailies, and trade periodicals, some defunct, others difficult to locate. The result was a "composite" of thirty-one pieces: short stories, a chapter from the unfinished second novel, public letters, political statements, a technical article on how to raise poultry, the Nonino International Prize acceptance speech, and other occasional pieces. When it was published in 1987 by the Jewish Publication Society, the book turned out to be a literary event. It made the front page of the *New York Times Book Review,* was reviewed nationally, and prompted a TV documentary. A kind of watershed of sorts, it forced readers to reconsider *Call It Sleep* from the distance of over half a century, and to think of Henry Roth not as a "dead" writer but as one from whom further works could be expected. It paved the way to *A Star Shines over Mt. Morris Park* (1994), the first of the four volumes of *Mercy of a Rude Stream.*

For more than fifty years Roth constituted a nagging mystery in American letters. Why had the author of one of the most beautiful novels of the twentieth century stopped writing? Where had he disappeared? Was he still *alive?* For decades, it was always the same question: "You mean—he's not *dead?*" Now a new phase began. After *Shifting Landscape* established that, no, Henry Roth was still

alive, hardly any review, article, or reference to the aging writer resisted the temptation to play with the sleep/awakening dichotomy; a temptation that a few years
later was rekindled by *A Star Shines over Mt. Morris Park.* It was as though Roth
had engineered his public figure according to an astute organization of appearances and disappearances, as well as of startling contradictions: the literary *enfant
prodige* become creatively sterile; the self-taught modernist embracing the aesthetic ideology of the Proletarian Novel; the card-carrying member of the Communist Party siding with Israel against the Arabs; the supposedly "dead" writer
taking center stage with a final opus of thousands of pages; the creator of David
Schearl, one of the most moving child portraits in contemporary American literature, shockingly revealing the young man's incestuous relationships with his
younger sister and with his cousin. It was as though throughout his life Roth had
orchestrated his image according to an unnerving series of changes in perspective. Who was, indeed, Henry Roth? Why did most literary histories barely mention or totally ignore the author of *Call It Sleep?*

Roth often talked about himself as "this dead writer." He also referred to
Mercy of a Rude Stream by its acronym, MORS. Throughout his adult life, the
shadow of the dybbuk, as he called the malevolent entity that suffocated his will
to write, hung from his neck as an unshakable white albatross. Both in conversation and in his correspondence, he never ceased asking himself what had caused
his creative paralysis. The answers he found lasted him for a while, then gave way
to different hypotheses. He blamed it on his having forsworn the safe harbor of
his Jewish heritage, then on having embraced the crippling aesthetics of socialist
realism. In line with the party directives, he abjured his early dependence on
Joyce's apolitical aestheticism ("It is a pity that so many young writers from the
proletariat make no better use of their working class experience than as material
for introspective, febrile novels," wrote his anonymous reviewer in *New Masses*).
Soon, however, he found himself unable to proceed with his second, ideologically
orthodox novel based on a party organizer. So he abandoned the project, stopped
writing, and disappeared, spending decades musing upon his "death" as a writer.
Only with the publication of the tetralogy and the disclosure of his early sexual
crime has it become clear that *this* was indeed the dybbuk that obscurely punished him into silence.

What the big box standing on the kitchen table of Roth's mobile home contained, what it could reveal of his past, I had no idea. Nor had Henry, for all I
knew. In front of us sat a Pandora's box that might help me delve into the mystery
of a work of litrature seemingly born out of nowhere—the result of three years of
solitary work on the part of a young man of twenty-five with no literary culture to
speak of, no family tradition of interest in reading, no previous experience of
youthful scribbling. So I opened the damn box, as Henry said.

One of the first items to surface was the issue of *Lavender,* the student magazine, with "Impressions of a Plumber," a sketch about a youngster's day as a
plumber's assistant in the Bronx. As limited in its scope and juvenile in its diction
as the sketch is, everything in it pointed to the novel to come: the first-person
narrative, heralding the autobiographical tendency; the interaction of urban con-

text and individual experience; the laserlike precision in the treatment of the surroundings as well as of the action sequence; the concentration on everyday reality; and, surprisingly, the fact that both here and in the opening of *Call It Sleep* the narrative focuses on pipes, and on the hidden life of water that pipes provide.

Surely a coincidence, but a deeply significant one. For Henry Roth, the self-made writer who turned precision grinder, then a raiser of geese and a nurse in a psychiatric hospital, rarely had a book in his pocket—but he never failed to travel with a box of tools. As his wife, Muriel, said, "Henry believes that if the hotel lights go out, he better have with him his own screwdriver to fix them."

At the end of December 1927, Henry Roth left his family home in Harlem and moved to Greenwich Village to start a ten-year-long relationship with Eda Lou Walton, a poet and teacher at New York University twelve years his senior and the center of a brilliant coterie of artists, writers, and scholars, all keenly aware of contemporary culture and, particularly, of modernism in all its various manifestations. This was the exciting milieu into which young Roth plunged, leaving behind the confining world of his childhood and adolescence. A silent listener to the challenging discussions of new ideas going on around him, he culled from that stimulating environment all he needed for his own future as a writer; and while playing the somewhat awkward role of the young man kept by his mistress, he fast developed from an uneducated young man to a self-made and self-sufficient intellectual. He assimilated the lessons of the best minds of the time—Joyce, Eliot, Freud, Bergson—and he grafted what he had learned onto the trunk of his proletarian background and his experience as a laborer. The result was *Call It Sleep*.

Call It Sleep is the story of David Schearl, the only child of a Jewish family of immigrants in the early twentieth century, from approximately the age of four to the age of six. A short prologue shows little David's and his mother's arrival at Ellis Island and the rude welcome they receive from the father, who had left before the child's birth. The stage of the novel is set: there is David's morbid attachment to his mother, his terror of the father (a cold, violent man who suspects him of not being his own child), and a family conflict foreshadowing a troubled childhood for the boy. The narrative proper focuses on David's search for stability. First he gropes for certainties in the teachings of his rabbi, particularly in the story of Isaiah and his burning coal. Then, venturing beyond the scope of his heritage, he succumbs to the fascinating model presented by a streetwise Catholic boy. At the end, guilt-ridden and terrorized by his wrathful father, he runs from home and, attempting to synthesize his conflicting experiences, he tries to reach for God (the Father, for lack of a viable father) by means of a short circuit that he provokes by thrusting a metal ladle onto the third rail of the Eighth Street trolley tracks, which nearly destroys him.

In the seven decades from its publication, *Call It Sleep* has represented a perfect mirror of all major literary and cultural concerns in America. It has been read, successively, as a document of the Jewish American experience at the beginning of the twentieth century; as a sui generis proletarian novel; as a paradigmatic fictionalization of the Freudian theory of the Oedipal complex; as a compound of modernist, and particularly Joycean, experimentation with language; as a link between modernism and the nineteenth-century novel. Roth's David Schearl has been equated to the protagonists of the two greatest American novels introducing a child's perspective, Mark Twain's Huck Finn and Henry James's Maisie. His realistic depiction of the New York urbanscape has been associated with the Ashcan school of painting. His use of the different languages spoken in the multiethnic world of the immigrants has been seen to anticipate today's focus on the multicultural nature of America. In short, *Call It Sleep* has aroused the most diverse critical attention, ranging from the literary to the political.

And so has the writer himself. The resurfacing of the novel in the early sixties and its extraordinary international success initiated a heated debate, which is still going on, about its baffling, elusive, and controversial author. For some, the most vivid image of Roth is that of the raiser of geese in rural Maine; for others, that of the old man at his computer in the stifling mobile home in Albuquerque, New Mexico, trying to resurrect the "dead" writer. He is the static, navel-gazing writer unable—or perhaps unwilling—to overcome his dybbuk, and the elderly man rushing to join an antifascist demonstration in Florence, Italy, amid hundreds of waving red flags. He is the squalid youth who took advantage of his sister, and the writer who a few years later painted the portrait of an extraordinarily sensitive child.

Like his novel *Call It Sleep*, Henry Roth—this complex, difficult, mercurial individual—resists all attempts at reduction to order.

Bibliography: Henry Roth, *Call It Sleep* (New York, 1934); *Mercy of a Rude Stream,* vol. 1: *A Star Shines over Mt. Morris Park* (New York, 1994); *Shifting Landscape: A Composite, 1925–1987,* ed. with introduction by Mario Materassi (Philadelphia, 1987).

MARIO MATERASSI

1987
Wittman Ah Sing foresees postethnic humanity

DYSTOPIAN SURFACE, UTOPIAN DREAM

As his name might imply, Wittman Ah Sing—the trickster hero of Maxine Hong Kingston's 1987 novel *Tripmaster Monkey*—has a propensity for mystical acts of imagination. To look into the future of humankind is an urge that both Whitman and Wittman are more than likely to indulge. Yet the two visionaries differ in what they behold. The poet of "Song of Myself" sees an infinite vista of generations united by a common humanity. The hero of *Tripmaster Monkey* sees "a mutating generation" whose members barely seem human at all. In one of the novel's most memorable scenes, Wittman "trips" through a futurescape where nuclear apocalypse has transformed humanity into "a parade of freaks." Minotaurs emerge from the fusion of cattle and dairy farmers, "werecoyotes" from the fusion of Angelenos and wild dogs, monstrous dual-generational bodies from the fusion of mothers and their piggyback-riding children. Languages, too, have fused, resulting in babble through which "vowels like 'Aaaaaaah!'" confusingly resound.

Such a vision appears nightmarishly bleak. Its dystopian surface, however, belies a strangely utopian dream. The outlines of this utopia become visible when Wittman's hallucinatory trip is seen in the context of a postethnic America. Introduced by Werner Sollors in 1986, and quickly adopted by critics of multiculturalism such as David Hollinger, the term "postethnic" refers to a mindset that deemphasizes historical lineage and biological descent as factors of social and personal identity. As the prefix suggests, postethnicity grew out of the ethnic discourse of the 1970s (the decade when "ethnicity" first entered the American vernacular). Ethnic consciousness was itself a reaction to the species-consciousness that prevailed among U.S. intellectuals in the years following World War II. This pre-ethnic mindset of the 1950s tended to overlook ethnic diversity while making unself-consciously universal claims on behalf of "mankind." By contrast, the ethnic mindset focused attention on cultural particularities while regarding universal claims with active distrust. Postethnicity goes beyond the antithesis between pre-ethnic and ethnic. It is neither insensitive to cultural differences nor inherently hostile to species-wide claims. While it acknowledges that ethnic boundaries are real, it views these realities as constructed and thus amenable to acts of revision—including those that transcend ethnic borders to take humanity as their purview.

The futurescape that Wittman sees is one where the postethnic mindset has turned inside out and inflated to hyperbolic extremes. In the wake of near extinction, matters of historical and biological descent are more than simply deemphasized: they are destroyed. Now that the human "race" has fused with animal species, racial divisions of old have lost their materiality and divisive power. Now that everyone belongs to "a mutating generation," intergenerational conflicts within ethnic groups (for example, Chinese American immigrants versus their second-generation American children) no longer obtain. Now that all languages have dissolved into primal vowels like "Aaaaaaah," debates over multilingualism literally sound hollow. Now that the invention once known as ethnicity is a thing of the past, the species once known as *Homo sapiens* is truly postethnic.

Wittman's postethnic fantasy goes on to outlive the psychedelic trip, reappearing in a scene near the end of the book. This time, an interview with an employment counselor becomes the unlikely occasion for Wittman to evolve a utopian narrative culminating in a postethnic Garden of Eden. In an inspired and vividly embellished fabrication (based on a menial job he once held), Wittman recounts handling "raw R.N.A.-D.N.A. life stuff" for a science lab in California. The top-secret substance in Wittman's charge is nothing less than the essence of humanity.

"Yeah, I myself have looked inside the vault that stores the essence of life. There's a pool, a well of raw life. We poured in the new stuff. It ran in a rainbow stream. Ribbons and streamers of pure R.N.A.-D.N.A. We stirred it with a glass wand that flashed with the running snot of pure germ. You should be glad to know, in case the bombs go off, the quiddity of pure life is hidden away to start us up again, unless a bomb lands smack dab on that vault on the mound in the circle of trees."

Distilled to its purest form, humanity is fluid, translucent, and alive with hues reflecting the color-coded ribbons and streamers of genetic information. This prismatic "mucous gist" is saturated with utopian possibilities awaiting the apocalypse that will one day catalyze their activation: "When the bomb goes off," Wittman tells the employment counselor, "the radiation will cook the stuff." Emerging from the radioactive aftermath will be not the parade of freaks that Wittman earlier envisioned but rather "the prettiest little men and women avid for daylight," each one fourteen inches tall (everyone literally a minority in stature) and racially ambiguous. Such a futurescape evokes a postethnic poetics innocent of ideology. Instead of using "color" and "melting pot" as figures of speech for ethnicity and race, Wittman literalizes these figures to depict the essence of humanity as a vibrant swirl where color lines dissolve into aesthetically appealing iridescence. (Walt Whitman could actually feel at home here: "I effuse my flesh in eddies, and drift it in lacy jags.") By literalizing color in this way, and by evoking biological descent in terms of subcellular units (rather than racially typed skin, hair, or physiognomy), Wittman creates a framework wherein familiar ethnic metaphors are freed of their ideological attachments and transmogrified into oddly gorgeous forms of life.

Wittman's fantasy operates on a violent logic: in order for postethnic utopia to be achieved, there must first take place some kind of revelatory cataclysm that will eradicate existing descent relations and posit a wholly new origin from which to restart humanity. Wittman himself is aware of this paradox. As the violence of his fantasy indicates, the circumstances under which postethnicity becomes most accessible to the mind are narratives of posthumanity—narratives set in worlds where received notions about ethnicity and humanity have been cleared away. Such science-fictional settings provide an open space in which the complexities of postethnicity reveal themselves.

Although *Tripmaster Monkey* is largely non-science-fictional, its science-fictional elements make it representative of a trend in American science fiction of the late twentieth century. In the 1960s and into the 1980s, when the conditions of possibility for postethnic humanity were beginning to emerge, writers like Samuel Delany, Philip K. Dick, Octavia Butler, Isaac Asimov, and William Gibson—not to mention films like *Aliens* (1986) and *Blade Runner* (1982)—were offering science-fiction narratives of posthuman ethnicities. Of these narratives there are two major categories. The first is populated by hybrid creatures transcending the boundary between humans and extraterrestrial aliens. The second is populated by cyborgs transcending the boundary between organic and constructed forms of sentient life.

Octavia Butler's Xenogenesis trilogy (1987–1989) experiments with narratives of genetic transmission to create posthuman anatomies embodying the postethnic psyche. *Dawn, Adulthood Rites,* and *Imago* are set in the centuries following a nuclear war in which humankind has nearly annihilated itself. Earth is now inhabited not only by surviving humans (few in number, significantly diverse in nationality) but also by the extraterrestrial Oankali and by their hybrid alien-human progeny. Known as "constructs," these posthuman children are literal incarnations of postethnic subjectivity. Their bodies shape-shift in response to their physical and social environments. In the absence of other people, they risk dissolving into amorphous matter. Posthuman construct flesh—supple, porous, alive to contingencies—plays a vital part in Butler's representation of postethnic being. In particular, such posthuman textures bring to life the postethnic experience of identifying with (or without, or across, or despite) plural ethnicities and homelands.

The physiology of Butler's posthuman constructs must be understood in the context of the xenogenetic family structure. Each construct has five parents: a human father, a human mother, an Oankali mother, an Oankali father, and finally what is known as an Oankali "ooloi." Neither male nor female, the ooloi functions as the central medium of reproduction. It genetically engineers each child through a specialized bodily organ that the ooloi alone possess. Using hereditary material extracted from the bodies of its four partners, the ooloi deliberately synthesizes an offspring that will differ radically from all five parents. Each offspring, then, is a mutant by definition and by design. The result is a familial configuration shaped, paradoxically, by a shared experience of mutual alienation. At the same time, family members are inextricably linked together by a biochemical interdependency so fierce that their bodies crave one another's proximity. What the posthuman xenogenetic family configuration makes so richly available for representation is the postethnic condition of being at once deeply implicated in a multiethnic social fabric and intimately familiar with the unfamiliarity of intimacy itself in a globalizing world.

A similar postethnic sensibility can be felt in the later writings of Isaac Asimov. Both "Segregationist" (1967) and "The Bicentennial Man" (1976) depict societies where the line between constructed and organic sentient life has become a site of energetic contention. In "Segregationist," organic and constructed lives coexist not just among individual members of society but also within individual bodies. More and more humans are "metallizing" themselves, choosing to undergo medical procedures to replace original flesh with metal parts. At the same time, more and more "Metallos" are de-metallizing themselves, choosing to replace mechanical parts with flesh and blood. The story centers on a debate between two characters. One character believes that flesh and metal should be permitted to mix: the "two varieties of intelligence on Earth" (human and robot) should be allowed to "approach each other" until "we won't be able to tell the difference." The other character—a segregationist who happens also to be a Metallo—disagrees: "Isn't it logical to suppose an individual would be too proud of his structure and identity to want to dilute it with something alien?" Leaving the debate unresolved, "Segregationist" applies a posthuman scenario to postethnic questions with the forceful clarity of a parable.

In "The Bicentennial Man," the parable takes on the dimensions of a bildungsroman. Most instances of this genre narrate the protagonist's development from youth to maturity. "Bicentennial Man" narrates the life of an individual who over the course of two centuries develops from a mechanical product labeled "NDR" into a biological person named Andrew Martin. His physical evolution from posthuman robot to flesh-and-blood mortal is closely paralleled by his social evolution from manufactured property to fully accepted citizen of human society. Indeed, the story presents these two evolutionary processes as virtually indistinguishable. Andrew's lifelong campaign to be recognized legally as a human person is precisely what makes possible the medical process through which he becomes biologically human: each newly won civil right authorizes him to undergo a new surgery replacing yet another mechanical part with organic tissue. The process of Andrew's humanization is naturally completed by his death. Only after he has secured mortality (by arranging a medical procedure that will enable every cell of his body to decay) does all of humanity finally see him not as an ethnic robot but as a member of their own tribe: "It was odd how that last deed caught at the imagination of the world. All that Andrew had done before had not swayed them. But he had finally accepted even death to be human and the sacrifice was too great to be rejected."

For many people living in the late twentieth century and beyond, the issues raised in Asimov's stories are more than hypothetical. As scholars such as Donna Haraway and Katherine Hayles have noted for years, the dichotomy between "born" and "constructed" is less than fully useful as a criterion for distinguishing between human beings and humanoid artifacts. "Born" and "constructed" exist on a single continuum. Many human bodies today contain artificial components like pacemakers, retinal microchips, and psychopharmacological chemicals capable of restructuring the drug-taker's consciousness. Such bodies are partly born and partly constructed, yet surely the humans to whom these bodies belong are no less worthy of human rights than are those whose bodies are entirely organic.

If "posthuman" can refer not only to hypothetical futures but also to experiences being lived today, then what is the distinction between postethnic humanity and posthuman ethnicity? Compare David Hollinger's *Postethnic America* (1995) with Katherine Hayles's *How We Became Posthuman* (1999). Just as postethnicity (according to Hollinger) is a "perspective" that "resists the grounding of knowledge and moral values in blood and history," posthumanity (according to Hayles) is a "point of view" that regards biological embodiment as "an accident of history rather than an inevitability of life." Just as the postethnic subject favors "voluntary over involuntary affiliations," the posthuman subject favors the amenability of "informational pattern" over the intransigence of "material instantiation." Just as the postethnic "I" is actually a "we" whose "multiple identities" undergo constant "renewal and critical revision," the posthuman "I" is actually a "we" of "heterogeneous components" that "undergo continuous construction and reconstruction."

Postethnicity and posthumanity are contemporaneous discourses whose emergence reflected a turning point in American history. What changed was the importance of biology as a way of defining "I" and "we." Developments in globalization and technology (cyberspace personas, for example; fast, relatively cheap international travel) let us approach the materiality of biological descent—its relevance to the choices we make about our identities and affiliations—as a question with many more possible answers than previously imaginable. That the question of descent had never been a foregone conclusion is a fact vivid in the United States. Neither postethnic nor posthuman requires post-American as a necessary consequence. In some sense, the idea of America has always occupied the same temporality that the posthuman and the postethnic share—an anachronistic space where hybrid tenses like the future perfect seem to thrive. "How do you know who shall come from the offspring of his offspring through the centuries?" Walt Whitman asks in "I Sing the Body Electric": "Who might you find you have come from yourself, if you could trace back through the centuries?" Like Whitman himself, the idea of America is ever open to possibilities; it is large enough to contain multitudes and transcend contradictions. The future America of Whitman's vision has already encompassed the posthuman ethnicities and postethnic humanities that Wittman Ah Sing will foresee.

Bibliography: Isaac Asimov, *Robot Visions* (New York, 1991). Octavia Butler, *Lilith's Brood* (Xenogenesis trilogy) (New York, 2000). Katherine Hayles, *How We Became Posthuman: Virtual Bodies in Cybernetics, Literature, and Informatics* (Chicago, 1999). David A. Hollinger, *Postethnic America: Beyond Multiculturalism,* 10th anniversary ed. (New York, 2005). Maxine Hong Kingston, *Tripmaster Monkey: His Fake Book* (New York, 1990).

SEO-YOUNG CHU

1995

President Clinton tells the families of victims of the Oklahoma City bombing, "You have lost too much, but you have not lost everything. And you have certainly not lost America"

PHILIP ROTH, *AMERICAN PASTORAL*

"The Swede." So begins *American Pastoral.* "During the war years, when I was still a grade school boy, this was a magical name in our Newark neighborhood," for the Swede was a Jewish "boy as close to a goy as we were going to get." Nathan Zuckerman, the narrator of several other Roth novels before he makes his appearance in this one, recalls: "Of the few fair-complexioned Jewish students in our preponderantly Jewish public high school, none possessed anything remotely like the steep-jawed, insentient Viking mask of this blue-eyed blond born into our tribe as Seymour Irving Levov." By way of the Swede, an immigrant community for whom advanced degrees were the traditional source of pleasure could enter "into a fantasy about itself and about the world . . . almost like Gentiles (as they imagined Gentiles)." The Swede gave second-generation Jewish Americans a glimpse of themselves inhabiting an American pastoral of physical prowess, grace, and well-being.

Nostalgia propels this book, as the Swede's generation looks back to that heady moment when the sons and daughters of immigrants saw their own children passing into the promised land of full Americanization, and the Swede, object of veneration, exemplar of his generation's success, "lived in America the way he lived inside his own skin . . . everything that gave meaning to his accomplishments had been American." What made the Swede exemplary? To start with, his financial success manufacturing gloves, based on "a business" his "father built, a man whose own father couldn't speak English," which enables him to buy an estate dating back to the Revolutionary War in the "prettiest spot in the world," the town of Rimrock (the rim of Plymouth Rock?). This upward social mobility is clinched by his marriage to the Gentile beauty queen Dawn Dwyer, former Miss New Jersey and contestant in the Miss America pageant, whose genteel hobby is raising prize cattle. According to his brother Jerry, "She's post-Catholic, he's post-Jewish, together they're going to go out there to Old Rimrock to raise little post-toasties." Zuckerman admits that "in our idolizing the Swede and his unconscious oneness with America, I suppose there was a tinge of shame and self-rejection."

What makes *American Pastoral* shocking and controversial is that Roth takes the familiar trajectory of the multigeneration immigrant success story one disturbing generation further: Merry Levov, daughter of the Swede and Miss New Jersey, turns student radical during the Vietnam era, bombs the local post office and three other targets, resulting in four fatalities, and then, in hiding, becomes a Jain. "Three generations. All of them growing. The working. The saving. The success. Three generations in raptures over America. Three generations of becoming one with a people. And now with the fourth it had all come to nothing. The total vandalization of their world." Swede Levov cannot comprehend his daughter's actions. "Killing people? . . . Killing people was as far as you could get from all that had been given to the Levovs to do."

What accounts for Merry Levov? How and why does this daughter "transport him out of the longed-for American pastoral and into everything that is its antithesis and its enemy, into the fury, the violence, and the desperation of the counterpastoral—into the indigenous American berserk?" How is this realistic novel, with its meticulous attention to detail, also an allegory about America? Insofar as a pastoral is a retreat from history and society toward a romantic idyllic existence in nature, it has been a major strain in America's conception of itself, evident in the rhetoric of the first Virginia settlers, Thoreau's cabin in the woods, Emerson's nature as ultimate book, Twain's raft on the Mississippi, Cather's Nebraska prairie, and Fitzgerald's dark fields of the republic, to name only a few. How is it that Roth's narrator identifies *his* American pastoral as taking place

"during the war years," as nothing could be more counterpastoral than war? Perhaps because, unlike the American pastoral of Emerson or Twain that transcends
material and social goals, the American pastoral of the Jewish immigrant story is
one of upward social mobility into bourgeois suburbia, of ethnic and racial whit-
ening, and of *almost* passing as real Americans. "Swedian innocence" on the playing field during the war years serves as an icon of this Jewish American version of
the pastoral. Although fighting the Germans and the Japanese imperils the men
in their families who have been conscripted, the war also accelerates their Americanization and their subsequent surge into the professions and the suburbs
through their GI Bill–sponsored education. Like television images from Vietnam, Merry Levov shatters this suburban pastoral by reintroducing it to history
beyond America's shores, with a vengeance.

American Pastoral begins with World War II and ends with Vietnam. Since the
Second World War saw Anglo-Americans and members of ethnic groups, Jewish
Americans among them, closing ranks in what was perceived to be a just war and
a moral victory over evil enemies, the Holocaust is not mentioned anywhere in
Zuckerman's nostalgic rhetoric about growing up in a homogeneous Jewish neighborhood in the 1940s. The intense pleasure of being comfortable among Jews and
the fervent belief that each generation would surpass the previous one materially
and socially constituted a "Paradise Lost," the title of the third section of *American Pastoral.* The irony of the decade of the 1940s as a time when Jews were "Safe
at Home" in America, the title of the equally nostalgic first chapter of Roth's autobiography *The Facts,* is not lost on the author; it is underscored. Philip Roth has
been outspoken about how this discrepancy has shaped his writing: "The disparity between [the] tragic dimension of Jewish life in Europe and the actualities of
our daily lives as Jews in New Jersey was something that I had to puzzle over myself, and indeed, it was in the vast discrepancy between the two Jewish conditions
that I found the terrain for my first stories and later for *Portnoy's Complaint.*" As
early as 1959 in his debut volume, *Goodbye, Columbus,* in the story "Eli, the Fanatic," Roth satirized bourgeois Jews unwilling to shelter religious Holocaust survivors for fear of jeopardizing their recent entry into Gentile suburbia. Decades
later, in *The Plot Against America* (2004), Roth examined anti-Semitism in America's heartland and the White House, by writing an imaginary counterhistory in
which Charles Lindbergh is elected president. It is possible, therefore, to read
Merry Levov as the monstrous inevitable outcome of the Swede's, and his community's, abandoning of their religious and ethnic identity in order to pass as full
Americans. "Where was the Jew in him?" asks Zuckerman. "You couldn't find it
and yet you knew it was there." If this is an allegory of attenuated ethnic identity
and its price, what aspect of Jewishness does Roth believe has been evaded or
abandoned in this American pastoral?

An answer to this requires looking at the other war that infiltrates this book,
Vietnam. Merry's radical politics during the Vietnam War, her transformation
into a bomber, is ascribed to the return of history to the American landscape.
"History, which had made no drastic impingement on the daily life of the local
populace since the Revolutionary War, wended its way back out to these clois-

tered hills . . . broke helter-skelter into the orderly household of the Seymour Levovs and left the place in shambles. People think of history in the long term, but history, in fact, is a very sudden thing." So spanking new is the luxury of the Swede's "gentleman farmer's castle" in the New Jersey countryside that to Seymour Levov it feels "foreign." For the Emersonian imperative to shake off the past, to abjure travel, and to regard the eternal present of Nature as a guidepost to the future is indeed foreign to Jewish culture, for which the sine qua non is remembering—other landscapes, other journeys, other languages. Seymour Levov's generation's turn inward to pastoral isolation, disconnected from the past and from the world beyond America's shores, sows the seeds for Merry Levov's violent rejection of Rimrock and everything that it represents.

As if to accentuate the erasure of history as a cause of Merry's tragic fall, Roth inflicts her with a telling physical disorder—she is a stutterer. Representative of great numbers of her peers in her generation, Merry, whose cheery name marks the passage from religious Mary to commercial "Merry Christmas," is the great-granddaughter of an immigrant who knew no English, and the granddaughter and daughter of Jews whose making it in Gentile America, and whose passing as Gentiles, depended largely on their "voices," on the diction and pronunciation that would not give them away as Jews. Insofar as stammering might be the price of forgetting, this is undoubtedly echoing Psalm 137: "If I do not remember thee, Jerusalem, may my tongue cleave to the roof my mouth," the psalm that expresses the Hebrews' inability to "sing our songs in a foreign land." The absence of all references to the Holocaust, and in turn of any identification with the Jewish people, marks one form of the Levovs' forgetting. The Swede admits that "they raised a child who was neither Catholic nor Jew, who instead was first a stutterer, then a killer, then a Jain. He had tried all his life never to do the wrong thing, and that was what he had done." Like Isabel Archer in James's *Portrait of a Lady,* a novel that had a profound effect on Philip Roth, Seymour Levov wants never to harm anyone but soon discovers what James's heroine learns, that her own self-willed Emersonian ignorance of the past is exactly what will turn her into an instrument of others and will be her doom. Ironically, Merry's stammering improves in only two settings, both related to history beyond the boundaries of the United States: when she is surrounded by posters of *The Diary of Anne Frank* and when she practices speaking Spanish in training for her unsuccessful attempt to join the revolution in Cuba (under the name Mary Stoltz, meaning "proud" in Yiddish). Anne Frank as ghostly saint and as the return of repressed Jewish history come to haunt American Jews preoccupies Roth in his novels before and after *American Pastoral, The Ghost Writer* and *Exit Ghost.*

Insofar as the Swede's "unconscious oneness with America" is the product of evading history, Roth chose not to tell the story through his mind. "There had to have been consciousness and there had to have been blight," but the Swede is depicted as so comfortable in his American skin that the past no longer has a hold over him. Zuckerman cannot seem to imagine a mind so unmoored from history and so at one with a timeless American landscape as to be immune to the anxieties, uncertainties, and doubts that come with cognizance of the past. As a result, the novel becomes Zuckerman's, and America's, fantasy about two past glorious eras when viewed only within the boundaries of the United States: the moral and military victory of World War II and the golden days of Camelot in the presidency of John F. Kennedy, to whom Seymour is compared. Nostalgia for these eras, however, is blind to traumatic events outside the United States that are intertwined with them: the Holocaust and the Vietnam War.

If *American Pastoral* is Zuckerman's lens on the war in Vietnam, through Seymour Levov's romantic lens on the war years of the '40s, then it is hardly surprising that the novel was written in 1996, after the (first) Gulf War, when four years of strife in Bosnia and Serbia came to an end, The Hague opened war-crimes trials, and newly reelected President Bill Clinton decided to keep American troops in Bosnia as part of NATO's peacekeeping forces. That same year, a U.S. military base in Saudi Arabia suffered a bomb attack, and in 1997 Timothy McVeigh was convicted and sentenced to death for domestic terrorism in the 1995 Oklahoma City bombing. Debates as to whether America should intervene to end the atrocities in Bosnia invoked two opposing models for America's role in the world, World War II and the Holocaust, or Vietnam. In the final scene of the novel, the Swede imagines that his family's dinner party in a landscape of "solace, beauty and sweetness" is brutally interrupted by the return of "ex-terrorist" Merry, whose confession to the murder of four affects her grandfather so profoundly that "his heart gave up, gave out, and he died." Merry's reappearance as a return of the repressed to pastoral Rimrock rehearses the haunting question posed in this book: What is the cause of Merry's disorder? Or to rephrase it as Roth does in the last two lines: "And what is wrong with their life? What on earth is less reprehensible than the life of the Levovs?"

Perhaps what is wrong is the very quest for the American pastoral itself. Recent discussions of Philip Roth's work have tended to take sides as to whether he is a Jewish American writer or an American writer, on the assumption that the pastoral ideal, which has been used to define America for decades, is by definition opposed to the emphasis on history in Jewish civilization. *American Pastoral,* however, belies any strategy to place Roth in only one of these categories, because the evasion of history in the Emersonian idea of the pastoral assumes a monolithic view of the representation of America that does not sufficiently account for the antipastoral mode that has characterized authors such as Henry James (Roth's acknowledged major influence), as well as Hawthorne, Faulkner, and others. When the Levovs, decent hardworking children and grandchildren of immigrants, invest exclusively in the immigrant success story severed from their past and from the rest of the world, history takes its revenge. When his characters, well meaning as they may be, seek the pastoral in woodsy Rimrock and attribute Merry's stuttering (as the Swede does) to their personal family drama alone, Roth's Jewish American voice is as much the voice of James as it is the voice of the biblical psalmist. Roth makes this clear when he declares Thanksgiving, that foundational legend of Plymouth Rock predicated on national forgetting, the ultimate American pastoral. "Thanksgiving . . . a moratorium on funny foods and funny ways and religious exclusivity, a moratorium on the three-thousand-year-old nostalgia of the Jews, a moratorium on Christ and the cross and the crucifixion for Christians, when everyone in New Jersey and elsewhere can be more passive about their irrationalities than they are the rest of the year. A moratorium on all the grievances and resentments, and not only for the Dwyers and the Levovs but for everyone in America who is suspicious of everyone else. It is the American pastoral par excellence and it lasts twenty-four hours." If *American Pastoral* is a moratorium, a flight from history and moral responsibility, then Philip Roth is the chronicler of its allure, and of its devastating price.

Bibliography: Philip Roth, *American Pastoral* (New York, 1998); "Defender of the Faith" and "Eli, the Fanatic," in *Goodbye, Columbus* (New York, 1966); *The Facts: A Novelist's Autobiography* (New York, 1988); *The Ghost Writer* (New York, 1979); *The Plot Against America: A Novel* (London, 2004).

HANA WIRTH-NESHER

2001

"Comrades, be not in mourning"

TWENTY-FIRST-CENTURY FREE VERSE

Anyone who followed American poetry at the start of the twenty-first century encountered repeated complaints that nobody read it. One well-received study of poems at the twentieth century's end adopted the title *After the Death of Poetry*; poet Dana Gioia—later tapped by George W. Bush to direct the National Endowment for the Arts—titled a 1992 book *Can Poetry Matter?* No poet seemed—as Robert Lowell and, before him, Robert Frost seemed—at once prominent and professedly central, a "culture poet" in Robert von Hallberg's polemical sense, taken by many readers (rightly or wrongly) to speak for America as a whole. Mid-career poets admired within the academy—notably the so-called Language writers—did not expect broad audiences outside it, embracing instead, in verse styles and prose self-explanations, the modus operandi of earlier avant-gardes. Americans in the post of poet laureate (an annual, renewable position, though British laureates serve for life) tried to serve as publicists for poetry, but their greatest successes—such as Robert Pinsky's Favorite Poem Project *(www.favoritepoem. org)*—could feel like rear-guard actions, born in part from nostalgia for decades now ended in which memorized, recited poetry figured largely in K–12 curricula, and in other parts of American social life.

Yet other indicators suggest that American poems have plenty of readers. In 2004 U.S. colleges and universities offered 720 degree programs in creative writing (in 1975, there were just 80); almost all gave instruction both in prose fiction and in the writing of verse. *Poetry* magazine receives more than 90,000 submissions per year. Poets whose verse strikes many readers either as funny or as inspirational still sell books in remarkable numbers: Billy Collins's *Sailing Alone around the Room* went through two printings of 30,000 and 55,000 copies in 2001; Mary

Oliver's readings fill 2,500-person arenas, where her fans pay ticket resellers up to $100 per seat. When one looks past the page and the codex book, art forms that incorporate verse are flourishing: consider the rise of hip-hop, and of poetry meant for live performance, in and away from the competitions called slams.

Complaints about a decline likely reflect—and are probably right to lament—not a decline in poetry broadly defined, but a diminished attention, among Americans, to inherited techniques of meter and rhyme. Collins and Oliver write (respectively) a conversational and a breathily rapturous free verse: their kind of popularity once belonged not only to Frost (who notoriously compared free verse to tennis played without a net) but also to the ably constructed rhyming stanzas of Phyllis McGinley, and to the sonnets of Edna St. Vincent Millay. The lack of memorization, and the lack of older poetry, in K–12 education has meant that fewer students arrive at college able to pick out (for example) the iambic units that make up a line of blank verse, or the symmetries in a rhymed quatrain. The poets most agitated about the supposed decline of poetry in America are almost always writers (Gioia among them) temperamentally if not polemically committed to rhyme and meter; the ablest younger writers with such commitments (the classical scholar John Talbot; the North Dakota farmer-poet Timothy Murphy) write from self-consciously marginal, even antiquarian positions. As fewer living poets excel in inherited rhymed or metered forms, fewer younger readers see, in those forms, ways to address their own concerns. James Merrill's "Self-Portrait in Tyvek Windbreaker" (1995), one of the last major poems of his long career, turns its rhymed eight-line stanzas into a peripatetic, preemptive elegy at once for the endangered Earth ("dead forests, filthy beaches," "the oncoming bulldozer") and for the sort of poetry Merrill writes, to be preserved (like Neapolitan folk song under Mussolini) by scattered caretakers in a dark age.

And yet the decline in rhyme and meter as techniques has meant no decline in the total resourcefulness, the set of sounds and approaches to language, in recent American verse. The absence of any poet who speaks convincingly for America as a whole (a confidence perhaps always unwarranted, despite the example of Whitman) has enabled more poets to speak with confidence, and some to speak with great invention, about America in and through its parts: localities, states, demographics, ethnic and religious groups—those groups recognized by the Census Bureau (Chicanos and Chicanas, for example, in the startling poetry of Juan Felipe Herrera) and those no official survey reflects (ecology-minded Americans, for example, and those sympathetic to Buddhism, in the very different poetries of Gary Snyder and Robert Hass). Regional, ethnic, and idiosyncratic attachments have made possible, in turn, an unprecedented variety in the kinds and sounds of American free verse.

Three examples suggest the flower of the whole. C. D. Wright draws on the Ozark speech of her youth for lines—often long ones—whose frequent imperatives invoke a Whitmanian aspiration to prophecy, though her mouthfuls of consonants and folksy phrases suggest low-pressure conversation instead. That mix gives Wright's lines their distinct sound, evident in love lyrics and in ambitious, long poems about visits to prisons (*One Big Self,* 2003) or about the geography of the rural South (*Deepstep Come Shining,* 1998). Her longest lines (some incorporating overheard speech) move confidently and almost without caesurae (stops inside the line) through the high peaks and rough valleys of Arkansas talk and biblical terminology. Wright has avoided mere regional nostalgia through the intellectual efforts that the disjunctions within her poems invite, and through her attention to other parts of North America. These recent lines describe one of her many visits to Mexico:

> I have been lured by my host's pellucid face and the blue salvia
> where the rooster is buried.

> Though I have worn the medal of the old town with forlorn pleasure
> I say unto you:

> Comrades, be not in mourning for your being

> to express happiness and expel scorpions is the best job on earth.

Rae Armantrout came to prominence as one of the California Language writers, whose left-wing politics and aversion to easy decoding she still shares. (The term "Language writing"—sometimes "Language poetry" or "L=A=N=G=U=A=G=E writing"—comes from the magazine L=A=N=G=U=A=G=E, edited by Charles Bernstein and Bruce Andrews, from 1978 to 1981, in New York, though its most memorable experiments often came from Washington, D.C., or from the West Coast.) She invented, during the 1980s and 1990s, a new kind of halting, self-critical free verse, in which any line break can let the poet ask whether she still believes what she has just said. Such self-skepticism—evident in her deliberately angular, only apparently unmelodic phrasings—grows partly from Armantrout's early years in San Diego, at that time a conurbation of Navy bases, prefab houses, transplanted Midwesterners, and brand-new Anglo suburbs: after her youth there, brought up by very pious, patriotic parents, notions such as authentic voice and deep feeling seemed to her a right-wing trap.

"I became a poet," Armantrout has written, "in order to defend myself from dubious stories." Her free verse finds a cadence to fit her skepticism, as one stressed syllable follows hard on another, suspending her sense until the end of a sentence (or later), in line after pensive line. A recent poem called "Two, Three" introduces its setting (a suburban street) in a stanza made up almost entirely of stressed syllables: "Sad, fat boy in pirate hat. / Long, old, dented / copper-colored Ford." Has she really seen this tableau, or has she seen only what she—informed by class prejudice, by prior experience—expected to see? So the poem asks: perhaps "Echo persuades us / everything we say / has been said at least once before." Armantrout's corrosive skepticism, inseparable from her slow and irregular line, can find unlikely beauty only in places (in San Diego and out of it) where few other poets, few sounds, have found it before: for example, in the "evenly hovering attention" of trees above "pocked concrete":

> Long tangles of gray-
> green eucalyptus leaves

> twizzle,
> throwing sharp shadows.

If I could just signal
so variously.

Yusef Komunyakaa's verse, like Armantrout's, favors short lines and a deliberate pace: unlike Armantrout's, it owes a great deal to music, and to the African
American musical traditions that sometimes combine, or collide, in his verse.
Raised in Bogalusa, Louisiana, Komunyakaa came to poetry in the 1970s after
serving in uniform (as a reporter for a military newspaper) during the war in Vietnam: soldiers' memories of their own experience became in *Dien Cai Dau* (1988)
one of his subjects, in poems whose meditations fit the slow tempi of some Southern rural speech. Yet all his poems also draw forms and sounds from the jazz
("Miles, Monk and Coltrane") that became, he recalls, "part of my life as a continuous score" during the years in which he began to write.

In Komunyakaa's free verse the three impulses that Craig Werner identifies in
all African American (hence in all recognizably American) music—the blues impulse, to lament and to repeat; the jazz impulse, to innovate; the gospel impulse,
toward unity and action—reappear as the three aspects common to all effective
verse, metered or free: the aspect of iteration or repetition (the pattern that says,
for each poem, what counts as a line); the aspect of novelty (no line sounds just
like the one before); and the aspect of closure, or resolution (what happens when
the end of a poem feels like "the end"). We can hear the spirit of blues in Komunyakaa's poems about Vietnam: he has called Maya Lin's memorial in Washington
a "monumental and concrete" version of a blues song, and his own poem about
that memorial, "Facing It" (perhaps his best-known work), a "blues moment of
introspection." We can hear the hopeful, gospel impulse (often secularized into
sex, as in 1960s soul music) within poems about his Bogalusa years, with their
celebrations of youth and of play. We can hear the jazz impulse throughout his
work, but most obviously when he writes about musicians. Here is one of the
twenty-eight quatorzains (fourteen-line unrhymed stanzas, quasi-sonnets) that
make up "Testimony," a poem about the saxophonist Charlie Parker ("Bird"):

Bird was a pushover, a soft
touch for strings, for the low
& the high, for sonorous catgut
& the low-down plucked ecstasy
of garter belts. He loved
strings. A medley of nerve endings
ran through every earth color: sky
to loam, rainbow to backbone
strung like a harp & cello.
But he never wrung true blues
out of those strings, couldn't
weave the vibrato of syncopated
brass & ghosts
till some naked thing cried out.

"A poem doesn't have to have an overt jazz theme," Komunyakaa has written,
to learn from jazz, "but it should embrace the whole improvisational spirit of this

music," with its "emotional mystery" and its "spiritual connection . . . to the places where its forms originated." That spirit animates his prosody here. Komunyakaa avoids almost all regular pattern, giving lines asymmetrical nonce structures: line one stresses the first, fourth, and eighth of eight syllables; line two the first, third, and sixth of six; line three the third, fifth, and eighth of nine. At the same time Komunyakaa keeps the poem together, as bebop players keep their ensembles together, through momentum, through shared-yet-violated expectation (melodic shapes in bebop, line shapes here), and through the emotional unity the triple-entendres on music, sex, and clothes maintain. Parker's aesthetic facility acquires its link to emotional power, the jazz aspect of this free verse its link to blues (and to the conclusive unity Werner calls "gospel"), once Parker gives up his big band and records with a quintet: there Komunyakaa brings the poem to its end, yanking its syncopations into a three-syllable, two-stress line, then slowing down into a consonant-rich, eight-syllable, perhaps even eight-stress, close.

Walt Whitman, in frequently quoted lines, asked the Muse to "Cross out, please, those immensely overpaid accounts," to leave behind the Europe of Homer and Virgil in order to find the new poetry of America. In much less famous lines from the same poem, Whitman told Americans "not to create only, or found only / But to bring from afar what is already founded, / To give it our own identity," and "not to repel or destroy." The variety of American free verse from the beginning of the twenty-first century deserves celebration not for its supposed freedom, and surely not for the loss of older conventions, but for the contemporary poems it makes possible, whose sounds and wholes represent new ways of hearing and living with parts of these United States, including some not represented (or not often, or not ably) in verse before. Since Whitman, American poetry has excelled in lines without meter; since Dickinson and Emerson it has excelled in lines whose meter seemed broken, approximate, remade. The poets of the American 1960s and 1970s derived their most effective free verse from Whitman, from transformations and breakings wrought on the Anglo-American meters they earlier mastered, or else from the cadences of one master, William Carlos Williams, turning his acoustics to their own ends. All those poets learned how to read poems, and wrote their first poems, in a time when popular poetry arrived in rhymed and metered forms. Poets like Wright, Armantrout, and Komunyakaa, and the poets who will record the American twenty-first century, have come of age in another time: to them and their heirs, older resources may now seem alien, but new ones are clearly at hand.

Bibliography: Rae Armantrout, *Next Life* (Middletown, CT, 2006); *Veil* (Middletown, CT, 2002). Yusef Komunyakaa, *Pleasure Dome* (Middletown, CT, 2001). Aldon Nielsen, *Black Chant: Languages of African-American Postmodernism* (Cambridge, 1997). Joan Shelley Rubin, *Songs of Ourselves: The Uses of Poetry in America* (Cambridge, MA, 2007). Vernon Shetley, *After the Death of Poetry* (Durham, NC, 1993). Helen Vendler, *Soul Says: On Poets and Poetry* (Cambridge, MA, 1994). Robert von Hallberg, *American Poetry and Culture 1945–1980* (Cambridge, MA, 1985). Craig Werner, *A Change Is Gonna Come: Race, Music and the Soul of America* (Ann Arbor, MI, 2006). C. D. Wright, *Rising, Falling, Hovering* (Port Townsend, WA, 2008); *Steal Away* (Port Townsend, WA, 2005).

STEPHEN BURT

2003

Joseph Strom sets down his brother's story

RICHARD POWERS, *THE TIME OF OUR SINGING*

1992: After performing with his European Old Music ensemble in San Francisco, Jonah Strom dies of injuries suffered in the Rodney King riots in Los Angeles.

1970: David Strom dies of pancreatic cancer in New York City.

1967: In *Loving v. Virginia* the Supreme Court rules state laws criminalizing interracial marriage unconstitutional.

1965: Just after completing his first album, with his brother, Jonah Strom is almost killed in the Watts riots in Los Angeles.

1961: Jonah Strom wins a national singing competition at Duke University in Durham, North Carolina.

1955: Delia Daley dies in a house fire in New York City.

1953: Joseph Strom enters Bolyston Academy of Music in Boston.

1952: Jonah Strom enters the Boylston Academy.

1948: In *Perez v. Sharp* the California Supreme Court becomes the first state court to rule that statutes forbidding interracial marriage violate the Fourteenth Amendment.

1945: Ruth Strom is born in New York City.

1942: Joseph Strom is born in New York City.

1941: Jonah Strom is born in New York City.

1940: Delia Daley and David Strom are married in Philadelphia.

April 9, 1939: As Marian Anderson sings on the steps of the Lincoln Memorial, Delia Daley, a young black singer from Philadelphia, and David Strom, a German-Jewish émigré physicist at Columbia University, meet in the crowd.

In *The Time of Our Singing,* the 631-page novel Richard Powers published in 2003, each of these events contains every other. Just as places swirl—in the same way that, in historical time, the story begins with citizens from the first two capitals of the United States of America meeting in the third—in Powers's pages time curves. "In some empty hall, my brother is still singing," Joseph Strom begins. "His voice hasn't dampened yet. Not altogether. The rooms where he sang still hold an impression, their walls dimpled with his sound, awaiting some future phonograph capable of replaying them." Joseph Strom is back in the music building at Duke University, in 1961, on the night of his brother's "first open triumph," the night he became "America's Next Voice": "My brother sings to save the good and make the wicked take their lives. At twenty, he's already familiar with both. This is the source of his resonance, the sound that holds his audience stilled for a few stopped seconds before they can bring themselves to clap. In the soar of that voice, they hear the rift it floats over." The rift is time, opening up beneath the feet and above the heads of every character, so that any moment can be snatched away from what its putative owner might flatter himself or herself is its proper chronicle and set loose to light down in another's lifetime. "Given the courage, we live by moments of interference between past and present, moments in which time comes back into phase with itself," Roger Shattuck wrote in 1958. "It is the only meaning of history. We search the past not for other creatures but for our own lost selves." "I thought about Johnson a lot, wondering who his audience could have been," Bob Dylan wrote in 2004 of first hearing the 1930s visionary Mississippi blues singer Robert Johnson in 1961, decades after Johnson's death. "It's hard to imagine sharecroppers or plantation field hands at hop joints, relating to songs like these"—like "Stones in My Passway," "Hellhound on My Trail," "If I Had Possession Over Judgment Day." "You have to wonder if Johnson was playing for an audience only he could see, one far off in the future." Joseph Strom hears that audience in its silence as it awaits the note from the long-vanished Jonah Strom that will wake it from the dead. "If any voice could have sent a message back to warn the past and correct the unmade future, it would have been my brother's."

The Time of Our Singing opens, on that night at Duke, with two pages in perfect pitch—two complete pages where plain, barely inflected phrases somehow steal the magic of the music they are describing. The pacing; the way the reader is brought fully into a drama of which he or she has no inkling; the sense of lift and suspense; and the manner in which all great events public and private still to come in the hundreds of pages backing the first are somehow present in the way a singer drops his head toward his shoulder as he reaches for a note (that is the suspense)—all of it is so rightly balanced on its own air that when the first false note breaks you feel it as if you had dozed off to be wakened by the phone ringing. This is where the novel establishes itself, with those pages where everything is right, the book establishing its own lost utopia and insisting that it remains to be found, signaling the tragedy that in historical time has already occurred and has yet to take place, making the reader afraid to turn to the next page.

It is no small thing to write two perfect pages—two pages where the reader cannot find the seams, the artifice, the vanity of art. Richard Powers's first novel, in 1985, the dynamically playful *Three Farmers on Their Way to a Dance*—which took up the figures in the 1914 August Sander photograph and gave them lives, descendants, even a literal inheritor, and played history as if it were a deck of cards (the Roger Shattuck passage above is an epigraph there)—is all invention; the reader reads always from the distance of admiration for the author, never not aware that the author has marked the deck. In six subsequent novels Powers moved with assurance and command through ever-smaller, more airless tales, marshaling deep affinities for science, mathematics, and music into a realm of literary artfulness so refined it was very nearly solipsistic. There was no hint of what was looming: a novel in which a writer, or rather his characters, a story he set in motion but over which, one can always feel, he has surrendered control, would through the few members of a single family stake a claim to the nation itself.

As time curves in *The Time of Our Singing*, what the nation is—where it is, who it is, when it was founded, where and when and how it ends, if it does—shifts shape in instants too tiny to track, in events too great to see all at once. "Ca Ca Caliban," D. H. Lawrence chanted in 1923 as he began his *Studies in Classic Ameri-*

can Literature: "Get a new master, be a new man." The American invents itself: Jonah, Joseph, Ruth, each of them will be a new nation, if they can. That is their birthright. The same is true for David Strom and Delia Daley, separately and far more profoundly as a couple. But when the five together make a nation, in the different colors they present to the world ("the public record," Joseph Strom says, "of our family's private crime"), have they kept the nation's promise, or seceded from it? Are they cast out?

One of the people at the side of Martin Luther King, Jr., as he spoke on the steps of the Lincoln Memorial on August 28, 1963, was Marian Anderson. "My God," says David Strom, present in the crowd with Ruth. "Oh my God. It is her." Twenty-four years before, on the same spot, he and Delia Daley had come together with 75,000 others to hear the greatest voice in the land: "Something happened to her," to him, "to her country, as the contralto sang it into being." "Who?" Ruth says. "The woman who married your mother and me." A new America came into being that day in 1939; as David Strom and Delia Daley met in that new nation, all laws were abolished, all laws were made, and so a wedding took place even before they met; they themselves made that new America.

Sol Hurok, Anderson's manager, had determined to present the singer in the finest halls; in the nation's capital, that was Constitution Hall, owned by the Daughters of the American Revolution. They refused: no black person would appear on their premises. Harold L. Ickes, the secretary of the interior, arranged for Anderson to perform in front of the Lincoln Memorial instead. She began with "America." "My country, 'tis of thee," she sang. "From every mountainside."

"Maybe they could make an America more American than the one the country has for centuries lied to itself about being," Delia Daley and David Strom think, after Anderson has married them, before they are married under the laws of the old nation they went back to after the concert was over. In 1963, again under Lincoln's "symbolic shadow," Anderson steps forward, and she is singing "America" as before. But then the song is passed to King: "'My country, 'tis of thee,'" he says. "'From every mountainside'." Ruth has fallen asleep in the crowd, and her father shakes her. "You must wake up," he says. "You must hear this. This is history."

> She hears a swelling baritone, a voice she has heard before, but never like this. We also have come to this hallowed spot to remind America of the fierce urgency of now.
>
> Now: the reason why her father wakes her. But the thought nags at her between the rolling baritone thunder: her father couldn't have known the words were coming until after he shook her awake. Then she forgets, posting the question to a later her. Something happens in the crowd, some alchemy worked by the sheer force of this voice. The words bend back three full times in staggered echoes. Her father is right: history. Already she cannot separate these words from all the times she'll hear them down the years to come.

In the America the Stroms make, from which they secede, from which they are cast out, the fact that in New York or Pennsylvania in 1940 marriage between a black American and a white American is not illegal is no deliverance. Every-

where in America, the Stroms will discover—as Delia Strom is spit on in an elevator as she stands with her sons, whose light skin betrays her violation; as she is
forced to sit in the backseat of their car while her husband drives so as not to be
stopped by police; as every day brings a humiliation seemingly more ingenious,
more cruel, than any that existed the day before—their union is morally illegal.
This is the citizenship they are passing on to their children, and all those who, in
the music they make in their own home, all of them singing, they embody: the
America not of the more perfect union but of the fugitive. They are passing on a
confusion that in a great public drama mere individuals cannot turn into speech,
a confusion in which the citizen cannot explain the country to himself or herself,
where he or she cannot explain himself or herself to the country. *Brokeback Mountain,* the film critic Mick LaSalle wrote in 2006, "is saying that if you can't be yourself in America, it doesn't make sense. What other country asserts that it's everyone's right to pursue happiness?" The Fourteenth Amendment will not rescue the
Stroms from a torment, an oblivion, from which legally they are already exempt;
the Declaration of Independence is shamed by the America in which they are
forced to live, but by their failure to make the new nation they promised each
other they are shamed by the Declaration of Independence. That is the rift their
son's voice was meant to carry them, carry anyone, across.

All through the book, characters embody metaphors and symbols, act out
ideas and historical dramas, but they do not enact them; they do not act them out
in the same way that anyone else, any other character invented by anyone else,
including their own author, would, for these characters are not their author, and
it is his job to understand how they would act in a given situation, not how he
might wish them to. For his ending, in historical time, did he plan the most metaphorically outrageous of Jonah Strom's acts, or did Jonah Strom force the author
to write it out, once Jonah Strom gave the author a glimpse of who Jonah Strom
really was?

Jonah Strom is black; he is white; he is neither; he is a Jew; he is not. In Los
Angeles when the Rodney King riots break out, he is drawn in as he was in 1965
—and then, in this setting, the light-skinned man of fifty claiming citizenship in
the America of that day, comes an audacity of symbolism that at first the reader
can hardly take as anything but manipulation. But the delirium of the moment
supersedes the facts of author, plot, and reader; in the moment in history that is
being recounted, that is being made, that is being discovered, all sense of pup-
petry burns off. You feel the panic, the flood of identity, the release. On the
streets, a piece of paving stone smashes into Jonah Strom's left ear. "Kids are
pouring out of a hardware store, arms full," he tells his brother on the phone afterward, in the early morning hours of the day he dies. "One of them stops, and I
think he's going to dust me. Shoot me. He stoops and hands me this can of paint
and a handful of brushes." And then he wakes up from history: "I started walking
around, marking people. Started with myself. I thought I was the angel of the
Lord, putting a safe marker on everyone I could find. Passover. Everyone was going to be medium brown."

Just as, in scenes set in the homes of the Daleys or the Stroms, the feeling is so intimate the reader can feel like a guest of the family, with all the tensions that might include, here, as the almost unrelieved pain of the last two hundred pages of the book crashes down in a single moment of revelation, the reader can feel as if he or she has been given a window into a great historical event, that he or she is seeing what no one else who was there even noticed, or if they noticed, failed to understand, or if they understood, sealed their lips against a vision no one else would ever believe, in that moment when each was his own anarchy and there was no country, except for the one man with his brush summoning a nation in exile from thousands of years before, the nation, once, of his own family dinner table.

And then, in historical time, the novel returns to its beginning, and present like Lincoln's seated statue is everything the country ever gave to make or lose, to claim or have taken away.

Bibliography: Bob Dylan, *Chronicles, Vol. 1* (New York, 2004). Mick LaSalle, "Ask Mick La-Salle," *San Francisco Chronicle,* February 5, 2006. Richard Powers, *The Time of Our Singing* (New York, 2003). Roger Shattuck, *The Banquet Years: The Origins of the Avant-Garde in France, 1885 to World War I* (New York, 1958).

GREIL MARCUS

2005

"A great part of the city is below the level of the river during the high flood tides, which last for a few days each year, and is protected by levee or embankment"

New Orleans Is Lost in the Flood

People had seen it before. In 1937, in Faulkner's "Old Man," published in sections alternating with "Wild Palms" in the book Faulkner wanted to call *If I Forget Thee, Jerusalem,* a convict is ordered to rescue a pregnant woman who is stranded on a cypress mound the narrator calls "that earthen ark out of Genesis." The title of the story refers to the Mississippi, and the story captures the Great Mississippi Flood of 1927—a flood that was understood, in the moment, as at once commonplace and biblical, something that would simultaneously disrupt the regular comings and goings of individuals and initiate them into a ritual of history. The convict hears a sound:

> He did not know what it was because he had never heard it before and he would never be expected to hear such again since it is not given to every man to hear such at all and to none to hear it more than once in his life. And he was not alarmed now either because there was not time, for although the visibility ahead, for all its clarity, did not extend very far, yet in the next instant to the hearing he was also seeing something such as he had never seen before. This was that the sharp line where the phosphorescent water met was now about ten feet higher than it had been an instant before and that it was curled forward upon itself like a sheet of dough being

rolled out for a pudding. It reared, stooping; the crest of it swirled like the mane of a galloping horse and, phosphorescent too, fretted and flickered like fire.

The weirdness of such incongruous similes in this passage as pudding dough and horse's mane only enhances the awe-inspiring grandeur of the flood. In other passages the vast gray extent of the river flooding that makes streets invisible is described as "a single perfectly flat and motionless steel-colored sheet in which the telephone poles and the straight hedgerows which marked section lines seemed to be fixed and rigid as though set in concrete . . . It looked as though you could walk on it." As history moved on, people did walk on it, or under it. In Zora Neale Hurston's novel *Their Eyes Were Watching God* it is only a year later when the Okeechobee Hurricane walks like a man:

> Ten feet higher and far as they could see the muttering wall advanced before the braced-up waters like a road crusher on a cosmic scale. The monstropolous beast had left his bed. Two hundred miles an hour wind had loosed his chains. He seized hold of his dikes and ran forward until he met the quarters; uprooted them like grass and rushed on after his supposed-to-be conquerors, rolling the dikes, rolling the houses, rolling the people in the houses along with other timbers. The sea was walking the earth with a heavy heel.

"The wind came back with triple fury," Hurston wrote, "and put out the light for the last time. They sat in company with the others in other shanties, their eyes straining against crude walls and their souls asking if He meant to measure their puny might against His. They seemed to be staring at the dark, but their eyes were watching God." In 1974, the singer Randy Newman, who spent his early childhood in New Orleans, went back with "Louisiana 1927." He saw "President Coolidge come down in a railroad train / With a little fat man with a note-pad in his hand / President say, 'Little fat man, isn't it a shame / What the river has done / To this poor cracker's land.'" Oddly, though, the song seemed loosed from any event, a floating song, waiting as much as looking back. In the days after Katrina it was, as one commentator put it, "a song *everybody* knows." Again and again, Newman stepped forth to play it. What did it mean? Where was history, and what did it want? Tom Paine proclaimed in *Common Sense:* "We have it in our power to begin the world over again. A situation, similar to the present, hath not happened since the days of Noah until now. The birthday of a new world is at hand, and a race of men, perhaps as numerous as all Europe contains, are to receive their portion of freedom from the event of a few months." Hoping for a completely new, postdiluvial, free American beginning, Paine did not seem to think of God's pronouncement before flooding the world: "I will destroy man whom I have created from the face of the earth; both man, and beast, and the creeping thing, and the fowls of the air; for it repenteth me that I have made them." It was more the divine blessing of the chosen survivors that seemed to fit: "God blessed Noah and his sons, and said unto them, Be fruitful, and multiply, and replenish the earth." That was America, Melville insisted in *White-Jacket:* its citizens "the peculiar, chosen people" and the nation itself the "ark of the liberties of the world" on which they sailed.

Cover of 1948 Signet paperback edition of William Faulkner's *The Old Man*

But what was New Orleans? In 1909, the second edition of Baedeker's *United States with Excursions to Mexico, Cuba, Porto Rico, and Alaska* advised travelers that "passports, though not necessary in the United States, may be useful in procuring delivery of registered and poste-restante letters," and praised the country's 286,000-mile railroad grid ("more than half the total mileage of the world"), with eight great lines leading to and from the five stations in New Orleans alone, a city with "picturesque" French and Spanish street names ("the Anglicized pronunciation will sometimes puzzle a stranger"); the reader also learned that "a great part of the city is below the level of the river during the high flood tides, which last for a few days each year, and is protected by levee or embankment." That was New Orleans; but imagine now that it was any place, any great city, any small town, on which, for a moment, the attention of the nation was fixed. The place then becomes a mirror, the face of the nation itself. In the national imagination the place becomes the nation, or its negation—the face the nation faces, or the face from which the nation turns away.

Those were the circumstances as, beginning on August 29, 2005, Hurricane Katrina, and then Hurricane Rita, overwhelmed the city. Preparations made by the mayor and the governor were swept away as they pleaded for help from the national government, representatives of which either claimed that everything was under control or that they could not confirm what the world was watching on the news. Fifty-three levees were breached. Eighty percent of the city went under the water. Citizens climbed to the roofs of their houses, called for help, and were told that nothing could be done. Hundreds and hundreds of people drowned; no one knows how many. The city was left to drown. Countless Americans, from National Guard units from every state to relief organizations to solitary engineers, firefighters, medical workers, and aid workers from foreign countries, went to Louisiana to help; most of the nation decided it had seen enough, that there was nothing to be done, that there were more important things to think about.

If, for that moment, New Orleans was the nation, did the nation still exist? If it did, did it deserve to? The community would flourish if its members "make others Condicions our owne rejoyce together, mourne together, labour, and suffer together," John Winthrop told the nation as it was in the company before him in 1630; it would justly disappear if it did not. Did it?

"They passed a dead man in a sitting position on a hummock, entirely surrounded by wild animals and snakes," Hurston wrote. "Another man clung to a cypress tree on a tiny island. A tin roof of a building hung from the branches by electric wires and the wind swung it back and forth like a mighty ax. The man dared not move a step to his right lest this crushing blade split him open. He dared not step left for a large rattlesnake was stretched full length with his head in the wind."

"I saw a man rowing a boat, vigorously pulling on the oars, his back turned toward two bodies that were piled in the bow, his face set with stoic determination, as though his efforts could undo fate's worst cut," police detective Dave Robicheaux says in James Lee Burke's *Tin Roof Blowdown,* his Katrina murder mystery—but the real murder was not who shot the looter in the back or tortured the woman to death. Burke was calling down the cadences of Bob Dylan's "A Hard Rain's A-Gonna Fall," and, unlike in that song, in his pages the rain was rain before it was symbolic: "I saw a black baby hung in the branches of a tree, its tiny hands trailing in the current, its plastic diaper immaculate in the moonlight. I saw people eating from plastic packages of mustard and ketchup they had looted from a café, dividing what they had among themselves."

It was an event in which every word turned into poetry; the event was just that charged. The front page of the *New York Times,* September 2, 2005: beneath the headline DESPAIR AND LAWLESSNESS GRIP NEW ORLEANS AS THOUSANDS RE-MAIN STRANDED IN SQUALOR is a photo, stretching almost the width of the newsprint. On the right, on an overpass strewn with garbage, a woman pours water from a glass bottle into a Styrofoam container of dry dog food, trying to interest her brown and white dog, which hangs its head, as if it can no longer see, hear, taste, or smell, or no longer wants to. The image has deep gravity; you could look at it for a long time without noticing that on the left, on the water, is a body floating face down, arms outstretched, someone dressed in a white garment that covers the body from the top of the head to the knees. The woman on the overpass has either looked away or not seen it. What matters? As John Adams wrote in 1790 in *Discourses on Davila,* given the choice between feeding himself and his dog, a man will always feed his dog, because then at least someone will be left to look up to him.

And President Coolidge will always come down to take a look.

"What did you think of Lyndon Johnson?" Sheriff Helen Solieau asks Dave Robicheaux in *Tin Roof Blowdown.*

> "Before or after I got to Vietnam?"
> "When Hurricane Betsy hit New Orleans in '65, Johnson flew into town and went to a shelter full of people who had been evacuated from Algiers. It was dark inside and people were scared and didn't know what was going to happen to them. He shined a flashlight in his face and said 'My name is Lyndon Baines Johnson. I'm your goddamn president and I'm here to tell you my office and the people of the United States are behind you.' Not bad, huh?"

Do you, can you believe this story? If you do, is it because it is a story that is pointedly not about a photo opportunity, with directors and lighting technicians and makeup artists and dressers securing the site, but rather about a dark room and a man enacting the odd, violent, finger-snapping clap-of-thunder gesture of shining a flashlight into his own face, combining vanity with nakedness? Or did James Lee Burke put this story into the mouth of his hardest-to-fool character simply to let it stand as a rebuke to all the stories from Katrina that were not rumors, tall tales, folk legends?

On September 3, 2005, five days into the horror movie that was now called Hurricane Katrina, President George W. Bush arrived in New Orleans. On Air Force One, he met with the Democratic governor of Louisiana, Kathleen Blanco, and attempted to force her to turn the Louisiana National Guard over to the federal government, thus signaling that she was incapable of governing her own state; he met with New Orleans mayor Ray Nagin, U.S. Senator David Vitter, a Republican, and U.S. Senator Mary Landrieu, a Democrat. Then, in a helicopter, they toured the city. There had been no federal help for the living or the dead, but now, at the 17th Street Canal, the site of the most disastrous levee breach, the Army Corps of Engineers had begun the work. "I was so excited," Senator Landrieu later told the historian Paul Alexander, "because they were finally doing something."

The next day, Senator Landrieu again toured the city by helicopter, this time with the television correspondent George Stephanopoulos. "We still have people stranded on their roofs," she said; he had to see it. They saw it. But she felt she had to show him that there was hope; he had to see what was happening at the 17th Street Canal. "I swear as my name is Mary Landrieu I thought that what I saw with the president was still there—people working, trucks, sandbags, everything. Then I looked down and saw one little crane. It was like someone took a knife and stabbed me through my heart. I lost it."

"I could not believe that the president of the United States," Senator Landrieu remembered, in words that communicate how hard, years later, she was still trying not to believe the nakedness that she had seen with her own eyes, "had come down to the city of New Orleans and basically put up a stage prop. It was like you had gone into a studio in California and filmed a movie. They put the props up and the minute we were gone they took them down. All the dump trucks were gone. All the Coast Guard people were gone. It was an empty spot with one little crane. It was the saddest thing I have ever seen in my life. At that moment I knew what was going on and I've been a changed woman ever since."

She had seen the country, the United States of America in all its power, seen it plain, read its symbols, saw its history, her history, playing out before her eyes, past and present. She had seen the country, and saw it disappear.

Bibliography: Paul Alexander, *Machiavelli's Shadow: The Rise and Fall of Karl Rove* (New York, 2008). James Lee Burke, *Tin Roof Blowdown* (New York, 2007). William Faulkner, *The Old Man* (New York, 1948); *The Wild Palms [If I Forget Thee, Jerusalem]* (New York, 1995). Zora Neal Hurston, *Their Eyes Were Watching God* (Philadelphia, 1937). International Katrina Aid, *eccentricstar. typepad.com/international_katrina_aid*. *Discography:* Randy Newman, "Louisiana 1927," on *Good Old Boys* (Reprise, 1974); recorded with the Louisiana Philharmonic Orchestra with members of the New York Philharmonic on the anthology *Our New Orleans 2005* (Nonesuch, 2005).

GREIL MARCUS AND WERNER SOLLORS

2008, November 4

Barack Obama is elected 44th President of the United States

NOVEMBER 3, 2008

DAY OF COLLECTIVE HEART-

PALPITATIONS

HOW COULD WE DO THIS?
       WHAT HAVE WE DONE!
THIS ISN'T SAFE? OUR HOPES, OOH,
                OUR HOPES are
              Perilously High!
  What will I do if?
           What if he loses?
What was He Thinking?
     How Could he put us
        through   the
         Long National Nightmare
    of Tradition and
                   DeConstruction of
  Mercy, Magic und
            wide-eyed disbelief
All night - one night - a future
   depends on if I
      Sleep tonight. He better
 the Hell survive This
        Grace of. Grace of
          God shit.

   AAH. One more glass Please, The Red.

THE ERA OF NO BLACK PRESIDENTS IS OVER

KARA WALKER

CONTRIBUTORS

ALAN ACKERMAN · 1912, April 15 ★ English, University of Toronto

DANIEL ALBRIGHT · 1903 ★ English, Harvard University

ELIZABETH ALEXANDER · 1921 ★ Author of *American Sublime* and *Praise Song for the Day;*
African American Studies, Yale University

MARC AMFREVILLE · 1798 ★ American Literature, Paris 12 Val de Marne University

FRANCES R. APARICIO · 1972 ★ Latin American and Latino Studies, University of Illinois
at Chicago

JONATHAN ARAC · 1846, late July ★ English, University of Pittsburgh

NANCY ARMSTRONG · 1798 ★ English, Duke University

WILLIAM BEARD · 1960 ★ Film Studies, University of Alberta

RICHARD J. BERNSTEIN · 1917 ★ Philosophy, The New School

CLARK BLAISE · 1850, August 5 ★ Author of *Time Lord* and *I Had a Father*

DAVID BLIGHT · 1700 ★ History, Yale University

MICHAEL BOYDEN · 1869, March 4 ★ University College Ghent

ADAM BRADLEY · 1936, July 5 ★ English, University of Colorado, Boulder

DAVID BRADLEY · 1965, October ★ Author of *South Street* and *The Chaneysville Incident;*
Creative Writing, University of Oregon

CARRIE TIRADO BRAMEN · 1941 ★ English, State University of New York at Buffalo

DAPHNE A. BROOKS · 1920, August 10 ★ English and African American Studies, Princeton
University

LISA BROOKS · 1821 ★ History and Literature and Folklore and Mythology, Harvard
University

ALFRED L. BROPHY · 1683 ★ University of North Carolina School of Law

LAWRENCE BUELL · 1850, July 19 ★ English, Harvard University

THI PHUONG-LAN BUI · 1969, November 12 ★ International Studies, Hanoi University

STEPHEN BURT · 1826, 1927; 2001 ★ English, Harvard University

SARAH SHUN-LIEN BYNUM · 1982 ⋆ Author of *Madeleine Is Sleeping* and *Ms. Hempel Chronicles;* University of California, San Diego

ALIDE CAGIDEMETRIO · 1881, January 24 ⋆ American Studies, University of Venice

RICHARD CÁNDIDA SMITH · 1955, October 7 ⋆ History, University of California, Berkeley

NORMA E. CANTÚ · 1836, February 23–March 6 ⋆ English, University of Texas at San Antonio

ROBERT CANTWELL · 1932, Christmas ⋆ American Studies, University of North Carolina

GLENDA CARPIO · 1945, April 11 ⋆ African and African American Studies and English, Harvard University

SUSAN CASTILLO · 1692 ⋆ American Studies, King's College, London

JOYCE E. CHAPLIN · 1722 ⋆ History, Harvard University

SEO-YOUNG CHU · 1987 ⋆ English, Queens College, City University of New York

ROBERT CLARK · 1841 ⋆ Author of *In the Deep Midwinter* and *Mr. White's Confession*

T. J. CLARK · 1950, November 28 ⋆ Art History, University of California, Berkeley

JOSHUA CLOVER · 1962 ⋆ Author of *The Totality for Kids;* English, University of California, Davis

ANDREI CODRESCU · 1885, October ⋆ Author of *The Disappearance of the Outside* and *The Posthuman Dada Guide;* English and Comparative Literature, Louisiana State University

JAMES CONANT · 1837, August 31; 1885 ⋆ Philosophy, University of Chicago

BONNIE COSTELLO · 1913 ⋆ English, Boston University

LEO DAMROSCH · 1765, December 23 ⋆ English, Harvard University

JAMES DAWES · 1885, July ⋆ English, Macalester College

PHILIP DELORIA · 1831, March 5 ⋆ History, University of Michigan

JOHN DIGGINS · 1787–1790 ⋆ History, Graduate Center at the City University of New York

LEAH DILWORTH · 1884, November ⋆ English, Long Island University, Brooklyn Campus

WAI CHEE DIMOCK · 1666, July 10 ⋆ English and American Studies, Yale University

ERIKA DOSS · 1940 ⋆ American Studies, University of Notre Dame

LAURENT DUBOIS · 1673 ⋆ French and History, Duke University

GERALD EARLY · 1900; 1912; 1946, December 5 ⋆ Center for the Humanities, Washington University in St. Louis

EMORY ELLIOTT · 1670 ⋆ English, University of California, Riverside

STEVE ERICKSON · 1826, July 4 ★ Author of *Zeroville;* Critical Studies, California Institute of the Arts

DAN FELLER · 1832, July 10 ★ History, University of Tennessee

JEFFREY FERGUSON · 1925, June ★ Black Studies and American Studies, Amherst College

ANGUS FLETCHER · 1855 ★ Graduate Center at the City University of New York

WINFRIED FLUCK · 1852 ★ American Studies, Free University of Berlin

MARK FORD · 1951 ★ English, University College, London

JUDITH JACKSON FOSSETT · 1896 ★ American Studies and Ethnicity and English, University of Southern California

HAL FOSTER · 1968, March ★ Art and Archaeology, Princeton University

HERWIG FRIEDL · 1838, July 15 ★ American Studies, Heinrich Heine University, Düsseldorf

PHILIP FURIA · 1911 ★ Creative Writing, University of North Carolina at Wilmington

FRANÇOIS FURSTENBERG · 1796 ★ American Studies, University of Montreal

MARY GAITSKILL · 1968 ★ Author of *Don't Cry, Veronica,* and *Two Girls Fat and Thin*

MICHAEL GAUDIO · 1585 ★ Art History, University of Minnesota

SHARON GHAMARI-TABRIZI · 1945, August 6, 10:45 a.m. ★ Author of *The Worlds of Herman Kahn: The Intuitive Science of Thermonuclear War*

MICHAEL T. GILMORE · 1858 ★ English, Brandeis University

TED GIOIA · 1949–1950 ★ Author of *Delta Blues, Work Songs,* and *Healing Songs*

LISA GITELMAN · 1884, July ★ Media Studies, Catholic University of America

TERRYL L. GIVENS · 1827 ★ Literature and Religion and English, University of Richmond

KAIAMA GLOVER · 1804, January ★ French and Africana Studies, Barnard College, Columbia University

JACQUELINE GOLDSBY · 1895 ★ English, University of Chicago

ADAM GOODHEART · 1607 ★ C.V. Starr Center for the Study of the American Experience, Washington College

ROBERT GOTTLIEB · 1930 ★ Former Editor in Chief of Simon and Schuster, Alfred A. Knopf, and *The New Yorker,* author of *Balanchine,* editor of *Reading Jazz* and *Reading Dance*

ANTHONY GRAFTON · 1932 ★ History, Princeton University

FARAH JASMINE GRIFFIN · 1900, 1905; 1981, March 31 ★ English, Comparative Literature, and African-American Studies, Columbia University

KIRSTEN SILVA GRUESZ · 1521, August 13; 1836, February 28 ⋆ Literature, University of California, Santa Cruz

MARYBETH HAMILTON · 1938, May ⋆ American History, Birkbeck College, University of London

HOWARD HAMPTON · 1962 ⋆ Author of *Born in Flames*

SAIDIYA V. HARTMAN · 1982, November 8 ⋆ English, Comparative Literature, and Women's and Gender Studies, Columbia University

DAVE HICKEY · 1953, January 1 ⋆ Author of *Air Guitar;* English, University of Nevada, Las Vegas

CHRISTOPHER HOOKWAY · 1878 ⋆ Philosophy, University of Sheffield

HUA HSU · 1969, January 11; 1982 ⋆ English, Vassar College

GEORGE HUTCHINSON · 1963, April ⋆ English, Indiana University

RICHARD HUTSON · 1826 ⋆ English, University of California, Berkeley

CHRISTOPH IRMSCHER · 1820, November 27 ⋆ English, Indiana University

JOSEF JAŘAB · 1939, 1981 ⋆ English and American Literature, Palacký University, Olomouc, Czech Republic

GISH JEN · 1951 ⋆ Author of *Typical American* and *The Love Wife;* English, Brandeis University

DIANNE JOHNSON · 1965, September 11 ⋆ As Dinah Johnson, author of *Hair Dance!* and other books for children; English, University of South Carolina

JEFFREY JOHNSON · 1835 ⋆ English, University of Central Arkansas

COPPÉLIA KAHN · 1821, June 30 ⋆ English and Gender Studies, Brown University

GARY KAMIYA · 1964, October 27 ⋆ Writer at Large, *Salon*

AMY KAPLAN · 1898, June 22 ⋆ English, University of Pennsylvania

CARLA KAPLAN · 1926 ⋆ English, Northeastern University

MICHAEL KAZIN · 1925, July ⋆ History, Georgetown University

FRANK KELLETER · 1776 ⋆ North American Studies, University of Göttingen

ROBIN KELSEY · 1865 ⋆ History of Art and Architecture, Harvard University

LIAM KENNEDY · 1852, July 5 ⋆ American Studies, University College, Dublin

CATHERINE KEYSER · 1925, August 16 ⋆ English, University of South Carolina

MICHAEL KIMMAGE · 1968, August 28 ⋆ History, Catholic University of America

PHOEBE KOSMAN · 1928, Summer ⋆ Editorial Assistant, Harvard University Press

JASON D. LaFOUNTAIN · 1670 ⋆ Doctoral candidate in the History of Art and Architecture at Harvard University

T. J. JACKSON LEARS · 1900 ⋆ History, Rutgers University

MICHAEL LEJA · 1784, June ⋆ History of Art, University of Pennsylvania

TOBY LESTER · 1507 ⋆ Author of *The Fourth Part of the World;* contributing editor, *The Atlantic*

MICHAEL LESY · 1936, November 23 ⋆ Author of *Murder City* and *Angel's World;* Literary Journalism, Hampshire College

JONATHAN LETHEM · 1888 ⋆ Author of *Chronic City, You Don't Love Me Yet,* and *Motherless Brooklyn*

JAN ELLEN LEWIS · 1801, March 4 ⋆ History, Rutgers University

W. T. LHAMON, JR. · 1830, May 21 ⋆ American Studies, Smith College

HEATHER LOVE · 1912 ⋆ English, University of Pennsylvania

BEVERLY LOWRY · 1851 ⋆ Author of *Harriet Tubman, Imagining a Life* and *Her Dream of Dreams;* George Mason University

SCOTT RICHARD LYONS · 1859 ⋆ English, Syracuse University

MICHAEL MacCAMBRIDGE · 1960, January ⋆ Journalism, Washington University in St. Louis

WILLIAM J. MANN · 1959 ⋆ Author of *Kate* and *Men Who Love Men*

GREIL MARCUS · 1851; 2003; 2005, August 29 ⋆ Author of *Lipstick Traces, The Dustbin of History,* and *The Shape of Things to Come*

KARAL ANN MARLING · 1928, November 18 ⋆ Author of *As Seen on TV* and *The Colossus of Roads*

ANN MARLOWE · 1970, 1972 ⋆ Author of *How To Stop Time* and *The Book of Trouble*

MARIO MATERASSI · 1985, April 24 ⋆ Literature of the United States, University of Florence

JOSEPH McBRIDE · 1941 ⋆ Cinema, San Francisco State University

DOUGLAS McGRATH · 1940–1944 ⋆ Writer and director of *Infamous* and *Nicholas Nickleby*

MAUREEN N. McLANE · 1973 ⋆ Author of *Same Life* and *Balladeering, Minstrelsy, and the Making of British Romantic Poetry*

MITCHELL MELTZER · 1787 ⋆ Liberal Studies, New York University

ANGELA MILLER · 1935 ⋆ Art History and Archaeology, American Culture Studies, and Comparative Literature, Washington University in St. Louis

JAMES MILLER · 1956, April 16 ⋆ Author of *The Passion of Michel Foucault* and *Flowers in the Dustbin;* Political Science and Liberal Studies, The New School

MONICA L. MILLER · 1955, August 11 ⋆ English, Barnard College

CAILLE MILLNER · 1838, September 3 ★ Author of *The Golden Road* and coauthor of *The Promise*

DAVID A. MINDELL · 1948 ★ Science, Technology, and Society, Massachusetts Institute of Technology

INGRID MONSON · 1945, February ★ Music and African and African American Studies, Harvard University

KATHLEEN MORAN · 1906, April 18, 5:14 a.m. ★ American Studies, University of California, Berkeley

WALTER MOSLEY · 1926 ★ Author of *The Long Fall* and the Easy Rawlins detective novels

ANDREA MOST · 1932 ★ English, University of Toronto

BHARATI MUKHERJEE · 1850 ★ Author of *Holder of the World* and *Jasmine;* English, University of California, Berkeley

PAUL MULDOON · 1927 ★ Author of *Horse Latitudes* and *Moy Sand and Gravel;* Creative Writing, Princeton University

PHILIP NEL · 1957 ★ English, Kansas State University

ROBERT O'MEALLY · 1939; 1975 ★ English, Columbia University

CAMILLE PAGLIA · 1947, December 3 ★ Author of *Sexual Personae;* Humanities and Media Studies, University of the Arts, Philadelphia

JEFFREY L. PASLEY · 1791 ★ Author of *"The Tyranny of Printers";* History, University of Missouri

ANITA PATTERSON · 1922 ★ English, Boston University

DONALD E. PEASE · 1952, June 10 ★ English, Dartmouth College

GILBERTO PEREZ · 1899 ★ Film History, Sarah Lawrence College

JOHN PICKER · Late 1740s; 1814, September 13–14 ★ English, Harvard University

ROBERT POLITO · 1924 ★ Author of *Hollywood and God* and *Savage Art,* editor of *Farber on Film;* Writing Program, The New School

CAROLYN PORTER · 1936 ★ English, University of California, Berkeley

ROSS POSNOCK · 1904, August 30 ★ English and Comparative Literature, Columbia University

RICHARD POWERS · 1897, Memorial Day ★ Author of *Generosity* and *The Echo Maker;* English, University of Illinois, Urbana-Champaign

LAURA QUINNEY · 1969 ★ English, Brandeis University

PAULA RABINOWITZ · 1933, March ★ English, University of Minnesota

HOWELL RAINES · 1934, September ★ Author of *Whiskey Man* and former executive editor of *The New York Times*

ARNOLD RAMPERSAD · 1901, 1903 ★ English, Stanford University

ISHMAEL REED · 1884 ★ Author of *Mumbo Jumbo, Blues City,* and *Conjure*

JUDITH RICHARDSON · 1809 ★ English, Stanford University

JOHN ROCKWELL · 1935, October 10 ★ Author of *Outsider* and *All-American Music*

KERRY ROEDER · 1905, October 15 ★ Doctoral candidate in Art History at the University of Delaware

AVITAL RONELL · 1876, March 10 ★ German, Comparative Literature, and English, New York University

JEFFREY ROSEN · 1927, May 16 ★ George Washington University Law School

CARLO ROTELLA · 1955, September 21 ★ English, Boston College

JOAN SHELLEY RUBIN · 1926 ★ English, University of Rochester

PETER SACKS · 1964 ★ English, Harvard University

SHIRLEY SAMUELS · 1862, December 13 ★ English and American Studies, Cornell University

LUC SANTE · 1903 ★ Author of *Low Life* and *Kill All Your Darlings;* History of Photography, Bard College

YAEL SCHACHER · 1889, August 28; 1924, May 26 ★ Doctoral candidate in the History of American Civilization at Harvard University

RICHARD SCHICKEL · 1915 ★ Author of *D. W. Griffith* and *The Disney Version*

STEPHEN SCHIFF · 1955, December ★ Author of screenplays for *Lolita* (1997) and *True Crime*

TOMMIE SHELBY · 1828 ★ African and African American Studies and Philosophy, Harvard University

SCOTT SLOVIC · 1879 ★ Literature and the Environment, University of Nevada, Reno

MERRITT ROE SMITH · 1875 ★ History of Technology, Massachusetts Institute of Technology

RJ SMITH · 1906, April 9 ★ Author of *The Great Black Way*

WERNER SOLLORS · 1693–1694, March 4; 1928, April 8, Easter Sunday; 1941; 2005, August 29 ★ African and African American Studies, English, and Comparative Literature, Harvard University

JOHN M. STAUDENMAIER, S.J. · 1932, April or May ★ History, University of Detroit Mercy

JOHN STAUFFER · 1819, February ★ English and African and African American Studies, Harvard University

ILAN STAVANS · 1536, July 24 ★ Latin American and Latino Culture, Amherst College

SUSAN STEWART · 1861 ★ English, Princeton University

SHELLEY STREEBY · 1846, June ★ Literature, University of California, San Diego

CASS R. SUNSTEIN · 1944 ★ Harvard Law School, Harvard University

AVIVA TAUBENFELD · 1903, May 5 ★ Literature and Writing, State University of New York at Purchase

CHARLES TAYLOR · 1961, January 20 ★ Writer, Brooklyn

KEITH TAYLOR · 1943 ★ Author of *If the World Becomes So Bright* and *Guilty at the Rapture*

DAVID THOMSON · 1923, October; 1931, March 19; 1961, July 2 ★ Author of *The New Biographical Dictionary of Film*, *The Whole Equation*, and *Try to Tell the Story*

MICHAEL TOLKIN · 1935, June 10 ★ Author of screenplay for *The Player*; writer and director of *The New Age* and *The Rapture*

LAN TRAN · 1925 ★ Creator of the solo shows "Elevator/Sex" and "How to Unravel Your Family"

DAVID TREUER · 1822; 1893 ★ Author of *The Translation of Dr. Apelles* and *Little*; English, University of Minnesota

MICAH TREUER · 1930, March ★ Student, University of Minnesota Medical School

JOANNE VAN DER WOUDE · 1740 ★ English, Harvard University

HELEN VENDLER · 1954 ★ English, Harvard University

MICHAEL VENTURA · 1952, April 12 ★ Author of *The Death of Frank Sinatra* and *Shadow Dancing in the USA*; columnist, Austin *Chronicle*

SARAH VOWELL · 1930, October ★ Author of *The Wordy Shipmates* and *Assassination Vacation*

ANNE M. WAGNER · 1982 ★ History of Art, University of California, Berkeley

KARA WALKER · 2008, November 4 ★ Author of *After the Deluge* and *Bureau of Refugees*; artist, Visual Arts Division, Columbia University

CHERYL A. WALL · 1970 ★ English, Rutgers University

ALAN WALLACH · 1825, November ★ Art and Art History, College of William and Mary

KENNETH W. WARREN · 1876, January 6 ★ English, University of Chicago

LINDSAY WATERS · 1951 ★ Executive Editor for the Humanities, Harvard University Press

CINDY WEINSTEIN · 1854, March ★ English, California Institute of Technology

M. LYNN WEISS · 1951 ★ English and American Literature, College of William and Mary

LAURA WEXLER · 1872, November 5 ★ American Studies and Women's, Gender, and Sexuality Studies, Yale University

SARAH WHITING · 1935 ★ Princeton University School of Architecture

JOHN EDGAR WIDEMAN · 1901 ★ Author of *God's Gym* and *A Glance Away*; Africana Studies and Creative Writing, Brown University

TED WIDMER · 1643; 1835, January; 1865, March 4 ★ John Carter Brown Library at Brown
    University

SEAN WILENTZ · 1835 ★ History, Princeton University

ROB WILSON · 1896, September 6 ★ Literature, University of California, Santa Cruz

CHRISTIAN WIMAN · 1915 ★ Editor, *Poetry* magazine

ELIZABETH WINTHROP · 1630 ★ Author of *Fireworks* and *December*

HANA WIRTH-NESHER · 1995 ★ English and American Studies, Tel Aviv University

RUTH WISSE · 1948 ★ Yiddish and Comparative Literature, Harvard University

DOUGLAS WOLK · 1938 ★ Author of *Reading Comics* and *James Brown Live at the Apollo*

STEPHANIE ZACHAREK · 1933 ★ Senior writer, *Salon*

RAFIA ZAFAR · 1773, September ★ African and African American Studies and English,
    Washington University in St. Louis

INDEX

Scott, Dred, 250. *See also Dred Scott* decision
Scott, Randolph, 354
Scott, Raymond, 807
Scott, Walter, 133, 185, 187, 221
Scott, Winfield, 8, 9
Scruggs, Jan C., 1007
Seagram Building, 694
Seale, Bobby, *Seize the Time,* 936
Seattle, Chief, 637
Second Bank of the United States, 210, 211–215
Second Bill of Rights, 766–770
Second Great Awakening, 81, 192, 196, 226, 228, 292, 499
Seddon, James, 399
Seldes, Gilbert, 554, 556, 558, 652
Selig Polyscope Company, 409
Seltzer, Thomas, 556
Selznick, David O., 706–707, 788, 881
Selznick, Irene, 792
Seneca Falls Convention, 351, 352
Seneca Falls Declaration, 102
Sequoyah (George Guess), 160–162, 163–164
Serra, Richard, *Verb List,* 945
Sert, Josep Lluís, 690–691
Seuss, Dr. *See* Geisel, Theodore Seuss
Seussical the Musical, 879
Seventh World Congress of the Communist International, 683
Sewall, Samuel, 8, 43, 65; *The Selling of Joseph,* 69–74
Seward, William H., 373
Sexton, Anne, 954
Seymour, Samuel, 20
Seymour, William J., 498–500, 501
The Shadow (radio serial), 634, 676
Shakers, 217–218, 297
Shakespeare, William, 38, 117, 133, 169, 280, 281, 346, 426, 567, 617, 632, 848, 970; *Troilus and Cressida,* 113
Shange, Ntozake, 989; *For Colored Girls Who Have Considered Suicide When the Rainbow Is Enuf,* 971
Shannon, Claude, 798
Shannon, Del, "Runaway," 907
Shaver, Billy Joe, 845
Shaw, Anna Howard, 349
Shaw, G. B., 651, 655
Shaw, Irwin, 573
Shaw, Nate (Ned Cobb), 663–668
Shaw, Robert Gould, 434, 435, 438, 920, 922
Sheed, Wilfred, 606
Sheeler, Charles, 527
Shelley, Mary, 364; *Frankenstein,* 254
Shelley, Percy Bysshe, 848, 954; *Prometheus Unbound,* 266
Shepherd, Jean, 677
Sherman, W. T., 398

Sherrill, Billy, 844
"Shimmy She Wobble," 480
Shirer, William L., 641
The Shop around the Corner, 746
Shurlock, Geoffrey, 883
Shuster, Joe, 719–720, 724
Sibley, Mary, 60
Sidney, Philip, 38
Siegel, Don, 910
Siegel, Jerry, 719–720, 724
The Silent Enemy, 636, 637–638
Silko, Leslie Marmon, 419; *Almanac of the Dead,* 391; *Ceremony,* 391, 417
Simms, William Gilmore, 171; *Guy Rivers,* 221; *The Yemassee,* 221–224
Simpson, O. J., 384
Sinatra, Frank, 512, 824
Sinclair, Upton, 632; *The Jungle,* 694
The Singing Fool, 627
Sinnette, Elinor, 929
Sitwell, Edith, 652; "Ass-Face," 487; *Façade,* 487; "Jodelling Song," 487
Sixteenth Street Baptist Church, bombing of, 917
Skidmore Owings and Merrill, Lever House, 694
Skillern, Thomas, 85, 86
Slave narrative, 469
Sloan, John, 528
Sloane, Sir Hans, 18
Smith, Adam, *A Theory of Moral Sentiments,* 116
Smith, Barbara, 384
Smith, Bessie, 512, 545, 991
Smith, Clara, 545, 546
Smith, Ethan, *A View of the Hebrews,* 193
Smith, Henry Nash, 412, 740
Smith, John, 21–26; *Advertisement for Unexperienced Planters,* 26; *Generall Historie of Virginia,* 19, 25; *A Map of Virginia,* 24; *A True Relation,* 24; *The True Travels, Adventures, and Observations of Captaine John Smith,* 25
Smith, John Stafford, "Anacreon in Heaven," 87
Smith, Joseph, 8, 193, 194, 195–196, 698
Smith, Joshua B., 435
Smith, Kate, 635
Smith, Lillian, *Strange Fruit,* 424
Smith, Mamie: "Crazy Blues," 480, 545–546, 547–549; "That Thing Called Love," 548; "You Can't Keep a Good Man Down," 548
Smith, Margaret Bayard, 138–139
Smith, Norman Kemp, 651
Smith, Richard Penn, *David Crockett's Exploits and Adventures in Texas,* 232
Smith, William, *The Easy Instructor,* 227
Smith, Zadie, 1005
Smith, Zak, *Pictures of What Happens on Each Page of Thomas Pynchon's Novel Gravity's Rainbow,* 780

OVER NIGHT BOOK

This book must be returned before the first class on the following school day.
